INDIANA

ONE HUNDRED AND FIFTY YEARS OF AMERICAN DEVELOPMENT

By

CHARLES ROLL, A.M.

Assisted by an Advisory Council

82881

INDIANA BIOGRAPHY
(Gratuitously Published)

By Special Staff of Writers

ISSUED IN FIVE VOLUMES

VOLUME V

ILLUSTRATED

THE LEWIS PUBLISHING COMPANY

CHICAGO AND NEW YORK

1931

Copy 2

William Fortune

HISTORY *of* INDIANA

WILLIAM FORTUNE. Few men record extraordinary achievements in the early years of their lives. Of those who do, even fewer continue to strive for still greater things until they round out a long career of usefulness.

It was an unusual event when a group of one hundred leading citizens of Indianapolis back in 1898 presented to William Fortune, then scarcely thirty-five years of age, a loving cup in recognition of his services in promoting the general welfare of the city. In that group were such men as former President Benjamin Harrison; James Whitcomb Riley, the Hoosier poet; and Harry S. New, Thomas Taggart and John W. Kern, themselves destined to be great political leaders and all of them to represent their state in the United States Senate.

It was thus early that William Fortune was started upon a life-time of service for the public welfare. Almost thirty years later, in 1926, at a banquet in his honor, there was presented to him another appreciation, this time as "chairman of the Indianapolis Chapter, American Red Cross, on completion of ten years of notable voluntary service in the cause of humanity in time of war and peace."

Now other years have passed and still this life of service for public good continues on its beneficent course. Few men have had such long and useful careers of public service.

The tribute at this Red Cross banquet ranged from President Coolidge down to prominent friends and co-workers of Mr. Fortune in Indianapolis and Indiana, and the emphasis was upon his constructive service to the cause of humanity everywhere. There has never been a time when he has been any less faithful in his efforts toward the general welfare of Indianapolis, but in the meantime his activities have constantly broadened so that they have comprehended a much wider field than his home city and even his home state.

The latest instance of his public beneficence occurred in December, 1930, when he voluntarily contributed the full purchase price of thirty acres in Riverside Park of Indianapolis as the location of a new general hospital for World War veterans of the state to be erected by the U. S. Veterans Bureau.

This act was inspiringly described to the members of Congress by Representative Louis Ludlow in a speech on February 16, 1931, published in the Congressional Record.

"I arise in this brief interlude between serious debates," Mr. Ludlow said, "not to discuss this bill but to tell the House how one man found an opportunity in a big humanitarian way to do something worth while for the men who in their own turn of sacrifice had offered all they had that civilization might survive. More than a year ago the public-spirited officials and civic leaders of my home city, Indianapolis, promised the Veterans Bureau Board of Hospitalization that if the board would locate a World War veterans hospital in Indianapolis a suitable site would be furnished to the Government without a cent of cost. The board took them at their word. A wonderful site of thirty acres of park land in a setting of transcendent beauty was chosen. Then arose a dilemma. The city had no legal right to give away any part of the public domain but it did have a right to have park land appraised and sold at the appraised value. The Federal Government, on its part, could not erect a hospital except on land of which it owns the fee-simple title. The solution obviously was through appraisal and sale to third parties and a retransfer by those parties to the Government.

"So this beautiful and valuable site of thirty acres was appraised and a value was placed upon it, and while there was talk of soliciting contributions to buy it and much speculation was going on as to how the money would be raised, one of our citizens whose life has been a life of service and who has done many acts of benefit to the world in which he lives, modestly asked permission to buy the site and donate it to the Government. Through the generosity of this citizen—a generosity that reflects the size of his heart—the title to this tract has already passed to the Government and nowhere in America, or perhaps around the world, is there a hospital site better located or more admirably adapted to general hospitalization purposes.

"Mr. William Fortune, of Indianapolis, who made this munificent gift to the Nation, is a modest philanthropist whose unostentatious beneficences have endeared him to the citizens of our city and state. His activities are multilateral. He has been a leader in movements for the welfare of those who served in the military and naval forces of the United States. He was chosen chairman of the Indianapolis Chapter of the American Red

Cross at its inception in July, 1916, and has been its chairman ever since. He goes about constantly trying to do good and his latest act donating the hospital site has made possible the construction of that splendid institution without delay.

"James E. Watson, the senior senator from our state, who has a rare gift of expression, made articulate the sentiments of our Indiana people when he wrote to Mr. Fortune:

'I want to congratulate you upon your most generous gift of the site for the new United States veterans hospital. This is but renewed evidence of the public spirit that has characterized your conduct for a long number of years.'

'I can not conceive of a finer life to live or of a more satisfactory way to make the journey than the one you have chosen and followed so religiously. You were richly endowed by nature for this work and you have added to those natural endowments an invaluable experience that has strengthened your fitness to carry on in this favored fashion.

'If we had more people willing to sacrifice for the benefit of the public and for the improvement of living conditions generally our country would be all the better off, our private lives all the more beautifully lived, and our public affairs more harmoniously and happily conducted. I count it a privilege to know you and to number you among my friends.'

"I can not add anything to what Senator Watson has so well said, but the more I reflect on what Mr. Fortune has done in extending the blessings of the very best hospital treatment to sick and suffering soldiers the more I admire the nobility of the example he sets to other men of means whose hearts, I hope, will be similarly touched."

In a letter to Congressman Ludlow expressing appreciation for his tribute to Mr. Fortune, Judge John Barton Payne, national chairman of the American Red Cross, said: "I have been associated with Mr. Fortune since I came to the Red Cross, nearly ten years ago, and have constantly relied upon his advice and judgment with the greatest satisfaction. I have found him always constructive and helpful and it affords me the greatest pleasure to join with you in a tribute to him and his splendid generosity and patriotism."

In a brief sketch of the life of William Fortune is obvious that only the high lights of his work can be noted, and perhaps in such a way as to suggest how his activities and influences have fitted into movements involving many other public spirited men in creating new standards and new ideals for his city and state.

William Fortune is a native of Indiana, born at Boonville, Warrick County, May 27, 1863. His father, William Harrison Fortune, was born in Ohio, in 1836, and was a Union soldier in the First Indiana Cavalry. The mother of William Fortune was Mary Sinclair, daughter of Wayman and Elizabeth (Douglas) Sinclair, of Virginia and North Carolina, who purchased a large plantation in Breckenridge County, Kentucky, in 1813 and settled there a few years later. William Fortune had little formal schooling, but at the age of thirteen was given employment in the printing office of the *Boonville Standard*, and like many other men found a printing office a university of opportunities for intellectual growth and development. Before he was seventeen years of age he wrote a history of his native county, and he was handling much of the editorial work of the paper. When he was eighteen year old he accompanied Gen. James C. Veach in a tour of the Lincoln country of Southern Indiana, taking interviews from people who remembered the Lincoln family while they were living in Spencer County, and thus he helped to contribute to the great mass of "Lincolniana."

Mr. Fortune in January, 1882, began work on the *Indianapolis Journal*, then owned by John C. New and his son, Harry S. New, and two years later he succeeded Harry New as city editor, serving four years. During the Harrison presidential campaign of 1888 he acted as special representative of the *New York Tribune, Chicago Tribune, Philadelphia Press, Pittsburgh Dispatch* and *Cleveland Leader*. For a brief period he was editor and publisher of the *Indianapolis Press*. Soon afterward he was called to editorial work on the *Indianapolis News*, under John H. Holliday, the founder of that paper. This work brought him his first opportunity for influencing the advancement of his city. With the encouragement of Mr. Holliday he sought through a series of editorial articles in the *News* to overcome the ultra-conservatism that controlled the city. Under his initiative there was organized in February, 1890, the Indianapolis Commercial Club, with whose activities a new era in the development of the city was started. The charter membership of twenty-seven increased to over a thousand within a month. Mr. Fortune became the executive officer of the club as secretary, with Col. Eli Lilly as the first president. He served as secretary until 1895, as vice president until 1897, and thereafter for a term as president.

One of the first apparent needs of Indianapolis was the development of a modern system of streets. Only two blocks of the city at that time were paved. In this, as in many public improvement ideas, there was lack of understanding and this new Commercial Club felt one of its first duties was to awaken Indianapolis to the possibilities for itself through such improvements. It was not possible to take large numbers of citizens to other cities to see results for themselves, and so Mr. Fortune conceived the idea of having an exposition on street paving brought to the citizens of Indianapolis. Accordingly such an exposition, the first of its kind, was organized. It attracted wide attention, mayors and councils of many other cities coming to Indianapolis, to learn of street paving methods through this exposition.

There was immediate recognition of the fact that the then confused and inefficient form of government of the City of Indianapolis needed radical changes, if the city was to embark upon a program of physical development. The Commercial Club under its leadership went about getting such a new charter, and did get it, even against great opposition.

Another immediately apparent improvement needed for the city was elimination of railroad grade crossings. Main line railroads crossed the center of the city. The city administration proposed construction of a few viaducts. Realizing that the beginning of such a solution would commit the city to use this method thenceforward, Mr. Fortune, as secretary of the Commercial Club, made an extensive investigation and brought in a report, urging elevation of the tracks, instead of a system of viaducts for a city of level streets. At a dinner for consideration of the subject, this report was submitted, and it resulted forthwith in the creation of a Track Elevation Commission. Colonel Lilly, as president of the Commercial Club, was made its chairman, and Mr. Fortune its secretary. Four years later, at Colonel Lilly's death, Mr. Fortune was made chairman, and continued at the head of the movement for sixteen years.

Only the determination of a leader who would not be swerved from his course could have brought success to the movement. There were innumerable delays and interventions of every sort, the opposition making use of political situations, court actions, and every other method known to the era. It was not until shortly before the beginning of the World war that success of the effort was assured, and a program of downtown elevation, involving expenditure of ten million dollars, was brought under way. With success assured, there seemed no further necessity of active effort, but in 1918 a reactionary move again made itself apparent, and once again Mr. Fortune, then president of the reorganized Chamber of Commerce, was called into action. This time the intervention of the Federal Government was necessary to make certain of final success. Downtown elevation was completed in 1920, itself a monument to the tireless, determined leadership of this man.

The success of the paving exposition perhaps suggested the value of making Indianapolis a convention city. It was under Mr. Fortune's leadership that Indianapolis in 1893 entertained the reunion of the Grand Army of the Republic, the greatest and most successful encampment in the history of that organization, in the course of which more than three hundred thousand visitors were in the city. As executive director of the encampment Mr. Fortune perfected a new form of organization for more efficient and economical management, and the encampment in Indianapolis was conducted at an expense far below the amount of the fund provided. Consequently he was able to turn back a large part of the appropriations and contributions, retaining enough to establish a permanent organization for the bringing of conventions to Indianapolis. This was the first permanently organized activity

for the bringing of conventions to any American city.

From his work in Indianapolis in promoting street paving and track elevation it was only a natural development that Mr. Fortune should become a leader in the Indiana good roads movement. He was president of the first Indiana Good Roads Congress, held in 1894.

These were some of the public services emphasized by the hundred citizens who presented him with a loving cup in 1898, but then, as always, William Fortune's private business has been invested with a public interest. In connection with his advocacy of street paving he saw a field for a magazine devoted to municipal engineering problems, and in 1890 founded the *Municipal Engineering Magazine*, of which he was owner until 1912. For twelve years he was at the head of nine of the independent telephone companies in Indiana, including the New Long Distance Telephone Company and the Indianapolis Telephone Company, which were operated at rates for service, involving savings to the public estimated at more than twelve million dollars. It was under his direction that automatic service was inaugurated in Indianapolis in 1917. He was for several years president of the Inter-State Life Assurance Company, which afterwards was merged with the Federal Life Insurance Company. In 1913 he became a large stockholder, director and chairman of the finance committee of Eli Lilly & Company, continuing until 1927. Since 1920 his time and efforts have been occupied almost wholly with tasks for public benefit.

The success of the Indianapolis Commercial Club led to many similar organizations in other cities of Indiana, and Mr. Fortune subsequently brought many of them into a statewide organization known as the Indiana State Chamber of Commerce, of which for several terms he was president. In this capacity he led a successful campaign for a new form of county and township government, and in the first year after the new form of government was in operation official reports showed tax savings of over three million dollars.

In the winter of 1894 Mr. Fortune was one of a committee, the other members of whom were H. H. Hanna and Colonel Lilly, which administered a plan of relief to the unemployed so effectively that it became internationally known as the "Indianapolis Plan of Relief for Unemployed." The plan involved, fundamentally, furnishing work on useful public projects to unemployed needy men to enable them to earn the relief needed, and improvement in the machinery of relief to make sure that all were adequately and fairly provided for. It aimed to save the unemployed from pauperizing influences. Nearly forty years later, in the winter of 1930-1931, the fundamental purpose of the plan was again put into use in Indianapolis and other cities in a program of "made work" by which needy unemployed persons again were given opportunity to earn their relief.

In 1911 Mr. Fortune represented his city and state in a tour of European cities to study municipal and commercial problems under the auspices of the Boston Chamber of Commerce, and was chosen as speaker for the delegation at dinners or luncheons in London, Berlin, Paris, Vienna, Prague and several other European cities.

When the Indianapolis Chapter of the American Red Cross was organized, in 1916, Mr. Fortune was made its chairman. He has served as its chairman continuously since its organization. In the early days of American participation in the World war the Indianapolis Chapter was called into action to mobilize the city for Red Cross war service. One of the first tasks was the raising of a large sum of money for the national Red Cross war service program. Indianapolis was assigned a quota not thought possible of achievement, yet $200,000 of it was raised at a dinner, preliminary to the soliciting campaign, and the full amount was oversubscribed by nearly $200,000, with $494,000 actually raised. The chapter in its second roll call enlisted over 100,000 members in Indianapolis. During the war Mr. Fortune was at the head of all organized war activities in Indianapolis except three.

When, early in 1917, the old Commercial Club was reorganized as the Chamber of Commerce, Mr. Fortune was by unanimous vote asked to serve as its first president, which he consented to do on the condition that the Chamber would raise a fund of $50,000 devoted specifically to expanding the work of the organization. They actually raised nearly double this amount. Thus the Chamber of Commerce launched upon a broad program of activity for the advancement of the city, its foremost task at that time being the organization of Indianapolis industries for war service. Mr. Fortune was leader of public movements that during the war raised more than four million dollars for war relief and other public purposes, and is credited with leadership in raising more money by private contributions for public purposes than any other citizen in the history of Indiana.

There was growing evidence of the need of a new plan of action in the raising of war funds. Almost every week a new campaign for war funds was started. As president of the Chamber of Commerce and chairman of the Indianapolis Chapter of the Red Cross, Mr. Fortune caused a study of similar situations in other cities to be made, and from this determined that Indianapolis needed to merge its money raising activities in an orderly way. He called a meeting of leading citizens, and there submitted his recommendations. At that meeting organization of the Indianapolis War Chest was voted and Mr. Fortune was drafted as its chairman, with broad powers to determine the methods under which it should operate and to select all members of the board of directors in addition to himself. Three weeks from that night an organization of 4,000 workers had been formed and had raised as the goal a fund of $3,000,000 for the support of local charities. The Indianapolis Community Fund three years later became the successor to the War Chest.

In 1923 the Indianapolis Chamber of Commerce again called Mr. Fortune to a public task. Impressed with the necessity of attention to the cost of local government, it asked Mr. Fortune to lead a movement for reducing its cost. Under his direction the civic affairs department of the Chamber was reorganized for this purpose. In the succeeding eight years his committee has been instrumental in saving millions of dollars in taxes for the citizens of Indianapolis, and the work of the committee has been described in national publications, the Chamber of Commerce of the United States holding it up as a model for other Chambers and commercial organizations desiring local tax economies.

Mr. Fortune, in recognition of his work with the Indianapolis Chamber, was made a member of the committee on state and local taxation of the Chamber of Commerce of the United States, at a time when it was entering the movement to organize local chambers for taxation activities. He served as chairman of this committee for the year 1926, and has been a member of the committee continuously.

Through Mr. Fortune's initiative the law was enacted creating the Community Welfare Board as an executive department of Indianapolis, and Mr. Fortune has been chairman of the board since its organization in 1919.

After the close of the war many national Red Cross responsibilities were placed upon him. He was member of the committee of three which administered the fund of three million dollars for relief in the tri-state tornado disaster of Missouri, Illinois and Indiana in 1925.

In 1926 he was chairman of the National Convention of the Red Cross.

In 1927 he was the honorary national representative of the Red Cross at the American Legion convention in Paris, and in the same year was elected to life membership on the General Board of Incorporators of the American National Red Cross.

In appreciation of services rendered by him he was, in 1904, honored by edict of the Emperor of China with the decoration of the Order of the Double Dragon, with the rank of a mandarin, and emissaries were sent to him three times to try to induce him to come to China, with the offer on the third visit to provide for him a palace to be furnished in American fashion.

Mr. Fortune was elected sixteenth president of the American Peace Society, founded in 1828, oldest national organization in the peace movement, as the successor of Senator Theodore E. Burton, and served two years in that office, effecting a reorganization of the society for the purpose of making it the more effective voice of the business leaders of the country in the cause of peace. He has been

honorary vice president and a member of the board of directors of the society since that time.

He is a life member of the American Historical Association and the Indiana Historical Society, and honorary life member of the Southwestern Indiana Historical Society and a member of the Mississippi Valley Historical Society. In 1926 the Indiana Society asked him to join in the movement for a memorial to George Rogers Clark, and he became chairman of the movement and subsequently, after the creation of the George Rogers Clark Memorial Commission, he was a member of the commission and served as its president until June, 1928.

Mr. Fortune was a warm friend of James Whitcomb Riley, the friendship starting when both were on the staff of the *Indianapolis Journal*. In 1906 they made a trip through Mexico together, and in the last year of the poet's life Mr. Fortune was chairman of the executive committee in charge of the national dinner given in tribute to Riley at Indianapolis. In 1920 Mr. Fortune purchased Riley's old home on Lockerbie Street, in Indianapolis, preserving it until it could be taken over for permanent maintenance by the James Whitcomb Riley Memorial Association.

Mr. Fortune is a member of the Metropolitan Club (Washington, D. C.), Century Club (president 1892), University, Indianapolis Athletic, Contemporary and Woodstock Clubs, the Indianapolis Art Association, and an honorary director of the Boys' Club.

Mr. Fortune married, November 25, 1884, Miss May Knubbe, daughter of Frederick and Jerusha A. Knubbe, of Michigan City. She died September 28, 1898, leaving three children, Russell, Evelyn (Mrs. Frederic Clay Bartlett) and Madeline (Mrs. Bowman Elder).

It has not been possible to quote from the numerous tributes of friends and associates to Mr. Fortune's manifold activities as a public benefactor, but to conclude this brief biography it seems appropriate to quote a few of the sentences spoken by the Indiana author, Meredith Nicholson, at the time of the Red Cross dinner: "Those of you who know him as a good citizen, as a man who is always doing something of importance, who is unselfishly giving of his time, his energy and his brains to good causes, and has done it all his life, think of him as a public character, a valuable citizen. But for a minute I am going to talk of William Fortune in that day when I knew him first, away back yonder when he built his first home in Woodruff Place. It was my privilege to see the building of William Fortune's home, and what a sweet and beautiful spirit he brought to that labor! He had come up from the country and developed as a newspaper man; he worked hard and had ideas and was a valuable man to his newspaper and newspapers elsewhere that he served. And what a joy it was to know the beautiful wife, and the children that came to them in that home out there under the beeches, one of the sweetest homes it has ever been my privilege to know! And what a lovely spirit presided over that home—her unfailing sympathy, her cheer and understanding meant so much, not only to Mr. Fortune and the dear children, but to all who were privileged to know their home!"

CHARLES E. PAULEY, who died April 15, 1930, was one of Indiana's most prominent and successful business men in his chosen vocation, that of printer and publisher, having gained an enviable reputation and amassed a competence in the twenty-four years he had been located in Indianapolis. His word was accepted by his business associates in lieu of a contract and his force of character is indicated by what he accomplished. His plant was housed in the Printcraft Building, at 225 North New Jersey Street, which he built in 1922.

Mr. Pauley was born January 15, 1868, near Greenfield, Hancock County, Indiana, the son of Joseph H. and Nancy (Morris) Pauley, the latter a native of Missouri. The mother died when Charles was but two years old. His education was obtained largely in the country school known as Lemon's Corner School, about seven miles northeast of Greenfield, Indiana. He was issued a teacher's license but decided to learn the printer's trade, which continued to hold an extreme fascination for him even long after he had attained financial affluence. As a journeyman printer he set type by hand on the *Indianapolis Sentinel* and in the United States Weather Bureau printing offices in Vicksburg and New Orleans.

It was during this time that the hand compositor or typesetter faced the certainty of being supplanted by the linotype machine, a mechanical device for the production of printing surfaces. Mr. Pauley, possessing a remarkable amount of mechanical and inventive genius, at once began studying the intricacies of this device, culminating his education with matriculation at the Mergenthaler School in Brooklyn, New York. He then moved his family to Logansport, Indiana, where he took charge of the linotype machines of the *Logansport Journal*.

In May, 1906, he returned to Indianapolis and purchased one linotype machine and started in business for himself in the Union Block. The growth of his business was remarkably progressive, as evidenced by the fact that for the next eleven years he added one linotype each year until the battery consisted of twelve machines. To these he added a general printing equipment. This growth naturally necessitated a number of changes to larger quarters, the first move being to 37 South Capitol Avenue, the second to 19 North Alabama Street, and then to the Elks Building at 112 East Maryland Street, which he purchased. His last move was to the Printcraft Building, a modern, six story structure which he had erected as an ideally arranged building for printers, the *C. E. Pauley Company* occupying the entire first floor.

Mr. Pauley was married on July 27, 1888, to Gertrude Chamberlain at Greenfield, Indiana. She was the daughter of Mary M. and Samuel Chamberlain (the latter an attorney), both natives of Ohio. She died April 9, 1928.

The only surviving child is Hazel Gertrude, the wife of Edmund H. Koon. Mrs. Koon is president of *C. E. Pauley & Company*, Inc., which organization continues the business Mr. Pauley had established.

The other children, now deceased, were: Mary Ethel, who married Lee V. Merriman; Mabel Edna, who married Frank H. Meredith, and Margaret K. Pauley.

HENRY HOLLIS WEAVER is a Howard County merchant and has been in business at Greentown for over thirty years. This community respects him not only as an able business man but a citizen whose public spirit has again and again been an important element in the success of local undertakings.

Mr. Weaver was born in Hendricks County, Indiana, June 30, 1866. His father, A. C. Weaver, was born in the same county in 1844 and died in 1923. His active life was spent in farming and merchandising. A. C. Weaver married Mirian Wells, who was born at Clayton, Hendricks County, and lived to be nearly seventy-eight years of age, passing away February 5, 1919. These parents had three children. Besides Henry H. one son, Urban R., lives at Indianapolis, and Indianapolis is also the home of the daughter, Mrs. Grace Weaver Wood.

Henry Hollis Weaver was educated in the common schools of Hendricks County and largely through his own efforts gained a college training. He attended the Central Normal School at Danville and later Butler College at Indianapolis.

Mr. Weaver moved to Greentown in 1898 and has been continuously in business there as a clothing merchant. He is a Republican in politics, is a member of the Masonic fraternity and Knights of Pythias. In the fall of 1899, soon after becoming established in business at Greentown, he married Miss Effie May Henderson. She was born in Ohio.

EDWARD SHIELDS GOODRICH. The Goodrich family of Randolph County have lived there for almost a century, and have been represented by some of the earnest and substantial pioneers, by good citizens always, and one member of the family is particularly well known as a former governor of Indiana.

Mr. Edward Shields Goodrich, of Winchester, whose name is associated with many public utility and financial enterprises over the state, was born at Winchester November 3, 1868, a son of John B. and Elizabeth P. (Edger) Goodrich. His grandfather, Edmond Goodrich, was a native of Virginia and settled in Randolph County, Indiana, in 1832. He was one of the early merchants of Winchester. John B. Goodrich was born at Parkersburg, Pennsylvania, and spent most of his active life on a farm a short distance northeast of Winchester. That old homestead has always been known as the John B. Goodrich

farm. He was a very successful man and during the Civil war was employed as a special agent by Governor Morton. He died in 1872. He had also been in the mercantile business and for two terms was county clerk of Randolph County. His wife, Elizabeth P. Edger, was born in Randolph County, daughter of Edward and Jane Gray (Putnam) Edger. Her father was a native of County Tyrone, Ireland, while Jane Gray Putnam was born in Madison County, Ohio, and was a descendant of the famous Revolutionary family of Israel Putnam. Mrs. John B. Goodrich passed away December 31, 1917. During her lifetime she donated part of the old homestead farm to Winchester for park purposes. She kept her young children together during her widowhood, carefully educated them, and more than any one else provided them the inspiration for worthy lives. These children were: Ernest, who died in infancy; Percy P., of Winchester; James P., former governor of Indiana; John B., of Winchester; Edward S.; and William W., of Winchester.

Edward Shields Goodrich was educated in the grade and high schools of Winchester, and left school to clerk in a bank at Farmland, also clerked in the carpet department of the Knollenberger store for six months, after which he was back on the home farm until 1891. He then bought a half interest in a hardware store at Winchester, his brother Percy owning the other half.

Mr. Goodrich's broader business career began during the natural gas era. In 1894 he became a contractor, laying the natural gas pipe line from Union City into Delaware County, and in 1895 was the contractor for the building of the pipe line from Sweetzer to Wabash. In November, 1895, he returned to Union City, where he operated the gas plant until 1905. Following that he was manager and director and a third owner of the Woodbury Company at Parker City, which later was dismantled and moved to Winchester. Mr. Goodrich in 1900 was one of the incorporators and became secretary, treasurer and manager of the Citizens Water & Light Company, now the Citizens Heat, Light & Power Company, and was active in connection with this public utility until it was sold in 1927. He has been a stockholder of the Randolph County Bank since 1898, subsequently becoming vice president, and since the death of S. D. Coats has been president. For a number of years he and his brothers have owned the Etna Trust & Savings Company of Indianapolis and he is chairman of its board of directors. The Goodrich brothers also owned the Goodrich Grain Company of Winchester. Mr. Goodrich is a director of the Union State Bank at Redkey, and was one of the incorporators and is vice president of the Interstate Telephone & Telegraph Company.

He married in 1894 Miss Elizabeth Neff, of Winchester, daughter of Allen O. and Eliza (Foutz) Neff. They have one daughter, Florence, wife of Francis Wesley Dunn, of Marion, Indiana. Mr. and Mrs. Dunn have two chil-

Maurice R. Lohman
M.D.

dren, Wesley A. and Edward G. Mrs. Goodrich is a member of the Presbyterian Church. Mr. Goodrich for many years was treasurer of the school board of Winchester. He is a Republican, a thirty-second degree Scottish Rite Mason and Shriner, member of the Knights of Pythias, the Columbia Club of Indianapolis and the Winchester Rotary Club.

HON. MARMADUKE MCCLELLAN STOOPS has in the course of thirty or forty years accumulated a great many responsibilities, both pleasant and burdensome, honors and symbols of achievement and experience in old Pike County. To set down some of these is not for the purpose of making Mr. Stoops well known in his home community, for that would be superfluous, but to give a record that is due to a more than representative Indiana citizen.

Mr. Stoops was born at Decatur, Adams County, in Northern Indiana, January 7, 1862. His father, James Stoops, Jr., was born in Greene County, Pennsylvania, served as a lieutenant in the Union army during the Civil war and twice was elected and served as sheriff of Adams County. He married Rebecca Flagg, a native Indiana girl.

Marmaduke McClellan Stoops was working in a printing office while learning the trade when only eleven years of age. His work as a newspaper man began at Petersburg in Pike County in 1892, when he bought the *Pike County Democrat*, and for thirty-three years he published this in the interests of the Democratic party and as a wholesome news organ for the city and county.

Mr. Stoops married, September 17, 1884, Mary Alice Parry, of an old Quaker family of Richmond, Indiana. She died December 22, 1926. Having no children of their own, they found additional incentive for many lines of work bringing them in contact with child welfare, health and civic organizations. Mr. Stoops during his many years of labor for the Democratic party of Indiana served as precinct committeeman, secretary and chairman of the county Democratic central committee, was a delegate to the national convention at Baltimore in 1912, and also to the famous deadlock convention in New York in 1924, representing the First Indiana District. Mr. Stoops is president of the County Board of Charities, president of the American Red Cross Chapter, secretary of the Pike County Tuberculosis Association, president of the Pike County Historical Association. During the past year he has been a member of the Petersburg School Board, and sat in the session of 1929 in the Indiana Legislature. He has been a stockholder in many business enterprises. For twenty-five years he was superintendent of the Sunday School of the Methodist Episcopal Church at Petersburg.

Mr. Stoops is affiliated with the Knights of Pythias and Pythian Sisters, the Masonic fraternity, Independent Order of Odd Fellows, Lodge, Encampment and Rebekahs, Improved Order of Red Men, Haymakers Society, Modern Woodmen of America, is an honorary member of Conrad Post of the American Legion, member of the Petersburg Art Club, Democratic Editorial Association, Packet Publishers League, Indiana Historical Society, Southwestern Historical Society, Pike County Fish and Game Club, Petersburg Kennel Club, Pike County Fox Chasers Association, Indiana Jefferson Club, Thomas Jefferson Memorial Association, National Geographic Society, and is a member of the Old Home Club at Decatur, Indiana.

MAURICE ROSENTHAL LOHMAN, M. D. For fifteen years an active practitioner at Fort Wayne, Dr. Maurice R. Lohman has won a leading position in his profession and during his career has been identified with numerous movements connected with the health and sanitation of the city. He comes by his vocation naturally, and during his practice has had the fortune to have been associated with two of Fort Wayne's most able and distinguished physicians.

Maurice R. Lohman was born at Fort Wayne, September 15, 1889, and is a son of Joseph and Rebecca (Rosenthal) Lohman. His father, a native of Germany, was brought by his parents to the United States as a child, the family settling at Fort Wayne when he was seventeen years of age. Here he passed the remainder of his life as a business man, and died in 1927, at the age of seventy-three years. Mr. Lohman married Rebecca Rosenthal, one of seven children of the late Dr. Isaac M. Rosenthal, one of the foremost physicians and surgeons of his day, whose name is held in the fondest memory by thousands of Fort Wayne people as well as members of the profession throughout the state.

The only child of his parents, Maurice R. Lohman graduated from the Fort Wayne High School and attended the University of Pennsylvania, following which he entered the University of Michigan, from which institution he received the degree of Bachelor of Arts in 1912 and that of Doctor of Medicine in 1915. During his early career he had the assistance, instruction and encouragement of his distinguished grandfather, and when he embarked in practice it was in association with his uncle, Dr. Maurice I. Rosenthal, also one of Fort Wayne's leading medical men and chief surgeon to the St. Joseph Hospital. Doctor Lohman has attained to a high place in his calling and has the full confidence and esteem of the people. During the World War he served as medical examiner on the draft board, and also had charge of the medical work on all troop trains that entered Fort Wayne. He likewise served as city health commissioner and as a member of the city board of health during that period, was health commissioner of Allen County from 1922 until 1926, and is now deputy commissioner on the health board and a member of the staff of the St. Joseph Hospital. Doctor Lohman is a fellow of the American Medical Association, a member of the Indiana State Medical Society and the

Allen County Medical Society, and also belongs to the Masons, the Benevolent and Protective Order of Elks and the Fort Wayne Country Club. He takes an active part in all movements for the benefit and advancement of his native city and is known as a citizen of public spirit.

On October 11, 1915, Doctor Lohman was united in marriage with Miss Bernice Bippus, who was born at Huntington, Indiana, a daughter of Fred Bippus, a capitalist and the owner of the La Fontaine Hotel, one of the finest and most modern hostelries in the state. Doctor and Mrs. Lohman are the parents of three children: Robert Maurice, Joan and James Frederick.

REV. AUGUSTUS CLELAND WILMORE, of Winchester, one of the highest dignitaries in the United Brethren Church in Indiana, spent over half a century in the active ministry. For the past twenty-four years he has been a member of the Court of Appeals of the United Brethren Church of the White River Conference, this being the highest judicial body of the church.

He was born at Jackson, Ohio, June 2, 1849, son of Levi and Nancy Agnes (Golden) Wilmore. His father was born in Gallia County, Ohio, and his mother in Uniontown, Pennsylvania, and they were married April 6, 1848, and in 1849 settled near Portland, Jay County, Indiana. In August, 1860 they moved to Huntington County, near Warren. Levi Wilmore was a teacher and farmer, and died September 13, 1877, and his wife, on February 4, 1890.

Augustus Cleland Wilmore was educated in the Warren Academy, Liber College, Ridgeville College and DePauw University. From 1867 to 1877 he was engaged in work as a teacher in the public schools, spending eight years in Huntington County and two years in a high school in Wabash County. In August, 1877, he began his long service as a minister of the United Brethren Church, comprising forty-one years of duty as a pastor and nine years as superintendent of the White River Conference of Central Indiana. His many friends and fellow churchmen celebrated his golden jubilee in August, 1927. In May, 1880, he organized a summer school of theology at Honey Creek, Indiana, and that school has been kept going ever since, and from 1889 to 1929 Mr. Wilmore served as instructor of systematic theology. He resigned from the school June 6, 1929. Five general conferences of his church during the past forty years have enjoyed the wisdom of his counsel as a delegate. He was a trustee of the Indiana Central United Brethren College from 1912 to 1918, two terms, and from 1893 to 1897 was a trustee of the United Brethren Publishing House at Dayton, Ohio. He was secretary of the White River Conference from 1878 to 1886, resigning when made superintendent of the conference. From 1894 to 1920 he was president of the Conference Direction Society and since 1906 has been secretary of the

Preachers Aid Society. He wrote in his own hand the articles of incorporation of the White River Conference in 1920, and these are filed with the secretary of state at Indianapolis. He was president of the board of trustees of the conference. One of his many services to his church is the authorship of a complete history of the White River Conference, a volume of 530 pages, covering the record of the church for 115 years, from 1810 to 1925. Since 1911 he has been conference registrar.

Mr. Wilmore from 1920 to 1925 was chaplain of the Indiana Society of the Sons of the American Revolution. His membership in that body comes from the record of his great-great-grandfather, John Wilmore, who was one of General Morgan's soldiers and fought at the battle of Saratoga on September 19 and October 7, 1777, and died in 1779, before the end of the war. This old Revolutionary soldier was a native of Virginia. Mr. Wilmore is a member of Winchester Commandery of the Knights Templar Masons and the Indianapolis Consistory of the Scottish Rite.

He married, August 14, 1870, Miss Julia A. Tremmel, a native of Randolph County, Indiana, daughter of James and Mary (Wagner) Tremmel, who came from Preble County, Ohio. Mrs. Wilmore passed away March 14, 1890. On March 9, 1892, he married Minnie Alice Rice, who was born in Marion County, Indiana, November 18, 1870, daughter of Archibald C. and Frances Ellen (Schofield) Rice, her father from Frederick County, Maryland, and her mother of Clark County, Indiana. Mrs. Wilmore has been secretary of the United Brethren Conference Missionary Women's Society and in 1921-22 was regent of Winchester Chapter, Daughters of the American Revolution, and was registrar of that chapter for nineteen years.

LEE BURNS, prominent Indianapolis architect, has for a number of years been deeply interested in the program of work of the Indiana Historical Society and Society of Indiana Pioneers and is a member of the executive committees of both of these organizations. While not a professional historian, he is author of two valuable contributions to the historical literature of the state, the *National Road in Indiana* and *Life in Old Vincennes*, both of which are publications of the Indiana Historical Society.

Mr. Burns was born at Bloomfield, Indiana, April 19, 1872, son of Harrison and Mary Constance (Smydth) Burns. He was educated in the public schools of Indianapolis, in Butler College, and for a number of years was connected with the law book department and afterwards with the general publishing department of the Bobbs-Merrill Company.

Mr. Burns in 1911 founded the Burns Realty Company, for the purpose of designing and constructing the better types of residences. This soon developed into a general architectural practice. Mr. Burns is now senior member of the firm Burns & James, architects. The work of this firm has been accorded many

Henry Thornton

honors and in 1929 the firm was awarded a gold medal by the Indiana Society of Architects for the excellence of their work. Mr. Burns is an officer of the Indiana Society of Architects.

During the Spanish-American war he was a private in the One Hundred and Fifty-eighth Indiana Volunteers. Mr. Burns is a member of the board of trustees of Butler University, is a member of the Sons of the American Revolution, the George Rogers Clark Memorial Commission and other organizations. He married in 1909 Anna Ray Herzsch. They have two children, Betty Lee Burns and David Vawter Burns.

DAVID FOSTER as a man officially credited with the distinction of being the founder of Kokomo is a subject of considerable interest to Indianans in general, and particularly to the residents of the thriving center of commerce and industry in Howard County.

He was a pioneer of Indiana and was a native of Virginia, born in Albemarle County, July 20, 1808. His parents were farmers and he grew up with a liberal education and at the age of nineteen started out to make his own way in the world, having no capital but his determination and his industry. On coming to Indiana he first settled in Johnson County, where he learned the trade of cabinet making. After a short time he moved to Mooresville, where he met and on January 7, 1832, married Miss Elizabeth Grant. In 1835 another move was made, to Burlington in Carroll County. There he set up a little trading post, dealing with the Indians, and in March, 1840, moved to Ervin Township, where he also opened a trading post.

It was in the fall of 1842 that he moved to Center Township of Howard County and took possession of a cabin that had been erected by the Indian Chief MacKokomo. This cabin stood not far from the corner of Main and High streets in the present City of Kokomo. With this cabin as his home he continued his dealings with the Indians, and as long as the Indians remained a considerable part of the population of this section of Indiana he remained their trusted friend and adviser. He had a fluent command of the Indian language.

David Foster continued to reside in Kokomo until his death on November 25, 1877, at the age of sixty-nine years. He was of Quaker birth and belief, and perhaps no other sect of people got along so well in their dealings with Indians. His only secret order was the Masonic fraternity. From those who knew him some of the characteristics of this pioneer Indiana man have been preserved. He belonged to a very sturdy, honest class of business men, possessed a sly vein of humor which all enjoyed, and he abhored fashion and finery and dressed in a manner after his own taste. He was generous to a fault, giving largely to public improvements and the advancement of religion and education. Every man and woman in Howard County knew him at the

time of his death. It was then said that his good deeds would live after him, and so they have.

HENRY C. THORNTON was an Indiana citizen whose activities and personal character are worthy of every record and study. For nearly half a century his home was in Indianapolis, where he was one of the founders and president of the Thornton-Levey Company, printers and manufacturers of blank books for commercial, banking and government work.

Mr. Thornton was born at Bedford, Indiana, November 8, 1851, and his long and useful life was closed by death on December 29, 1930, when in his eightieth year. He was a son of Mr. and Mrs. George A. Thornton and he spent his early youth in Bedford, attending public school there. In 1871 he was graduated from Hanover College with the Bachelor of Arts degree. He was for many years a member of the Beta Theta Pi fraternity.

After leaving college Mr. Thornton was in the drug business at Bedford until 1875 and then established a general mercantile store in that city. In 1884 he removed to Indianapolis, where he participated in the establishment of the Thornton-Levey Company, and his energy and spirit went into that business and permeated it through the succession of years when it was building up as one of the largest concerns of its kind in the Middle West. At the time of his death Mr. Thornton was also vice president of the Bankers Trust Company, and his place on the board of that institution was filled by the election of his son, Henry C. Thornton, Jr.

A mere statement of the positions held tells little of his real work and influence. One of the eminent Masons of Indiana said that in his death "Scottish Rite Masonry in Indiana has lost one of its finest characters. He was a very lovable man and I know he is going to be greatly missed in his community and more especially among the brethren in the Valley of Indianapolis, where he labored so faithfully and efficiently for so many years."

Of all the numerous contacts he made during his life perhaps the one that meant most to him was his church. He and his wife had joined the Tabernacle Presbyterian Church on October 7, 1892. On April 4, 1898, he was elected a trustee and served continuously in that capacity for over thirty years. He became a ruling elder April 11, 1918, and was at the time of his death president of the board of trustees. His friends and family will especially appreciate what a committee of the church wrote after his death: "Generally, in proportion as men become engrossed in business, their sphere of human interest is contracted and thoughts of spiritual life too often wane. Those of us on this board who have so many times met with Mr. Thornton, know that it was not so with him. We know that he had a depth of Christian faith and an intensity of spiritual feeling such as few men possess. We know of his profound devotion to the church, his helpfulness to its pastors and his warm hearted interest in its membership."

Among other institutions that felt a deep debt of gratitude for his helpful service was the Indianapolis Home for Aged Women, of which he was a member of the board for many years.

Another quality of his life and character was noted by one of his close friends and fellow Masons, who said: "I came to marvel at his genuine spirit of youth—his understanding of men—freedom from criticism—his love of his fellow men and his belief and faith in the Divine Father. In spite of his actual years he was a young man, and such he would have been had he lived beyond a hundred years, for the spirit of youth—dignified youth—seemed to have been born in him."

The Indianapolis *Star* said editorially: "A certain characteristic crispness of expression and dignity of manner could not mask the genial comaraderie which marked the relationship with a host of friends and acquaintances. Mr. Thornton was a warm supporter of every movement involving community uplift. In all of his various contacts with Indianapolis life he was an ideal citizen."

Perhaps best of all as a brief character sketch is the following in memoriam tribute: "He was strong, serene, clear minded, and charitable in all his relations in life. He fulfilled the duties of his long life with rare dignity and becoming fidelity. As a scholar and student of affairs he was learned and discriminating in his approach and judgment. He wore his honors lightly, with becoming poise and gentleness. These he forgot entirely in his daily life with all sorts and conditions of men, for he was ever, in the truest sense, a brother to his fellow men. He also exemplified the highest type of friendship. Everyone, capable of love, loved him. He stood for the noblest type of Christian character, but in it all he exercised a far-seeing type of Christian leadership."

Mr. Thornton married at Hanover, Indiana, June 12, 1873, Miss Nancy Hines Speer. She died before his removal to Indianapolis. In 1890 he married Miss Harriet Emma Hall, who survives him and continues to reside in their old home at 1609 North Delaware Street.

AARON GRIGSBY ROGERS, of Parker City, an active physician for over half a century, was born in Stony Creek Township, Henry County, Indiana, August 18, 1849. Doctor Rogers is a son of Thornton F. and Eliza (Luellen) Rogers. His ancestors on both sides come from Virginia and were pioneers of Henry County, Indiana, where his grandparents, Aaron Grigsby and Elizabeth (Baumgardner) Rogers, settled on a farm in 1830. His maternal grandparents, David and Abigal (Jones) Luellen, came from Virginia in 1835 and settled in Prairie Township of the same county. Doctor Rogers' great-grandfather, Joseph Rogers, was shot through the left shoulder at the battle of Bunker Hill and a brother of this Revolutionary soldier, John, was killed

at the battle of Brandywine. The Rogers family has supplied soldiers to every war since America became a nation. Doctor Rogers' grandfather, Aaron G. Rogers, served as a soldier in the Indian campaigns under General Wayne and later was with William Henry Harrison at the battle of Tippecanoe. The father of Doctor Rogers was an Indiana farmer and was honored with various township and road offices.

Doctor Rogers attended school at Middletown, Indiana, and graduated from the Miami Medical College at Cincinnati. He practiced as an undergraduate at Farmland from 1878 to 1880 and then located at Parker City, where he carried on his work until 1902. For three years he practiced medicine at Terre Haute and then yielded to the pursuasions of his old friends and clients and resumed his practice at Parker City. Doctor Rogers volunteered on October 8, 1918, as a member of the United States Medical Corps and is still on the reserve list. He is a member of the Randolph County, Indiana State and American Medical Associations.

Doctor Rogers married in 1879 Mary E. Carter, a native of Wayne County, Indiana. She died in 1892, leaving a daughter, Sylvia May, who is the wife of Thomas Swan, a merchant at Muncie, Indiana. Doctor Rogers in 1897 married Nancy A. Dorsey, a native of Henry County, Indiana, and widow of Cornelius Dorsey, by whom she had two children, Arthur and Edward. In January, 1925, Doctor Rogers married Ada Taylor McProud, who was the mother of a daughter, Luta, now Mrs. Robert Meeks, of Delaware County, Indiana.

Doctor Rogers has served as a member of the school board and board of charity. He is a Republican and a member of the Masonic fraternity. Since he was a boy he has been interested in acquiring Indian relics and is a noted authority on Indian archeology. He has one of he largest private collections of such relics in Indiana.

NOAH N. SMITH. Hundreds of thousands of smokers everywhere know and recognize the merits of the "Bankable" cigar, but probably most of them are unacquainted with the career or personality of the originator and maker of this famous smoke. Most of these cigars are made in a model plant at Frankfort, Indiana, and the owner and active head of the business is Mr. Noah N. Smith.

Mr. Smith is a native of Indiana, born at Jonesboro in Grant County, February 24, 1877. His father, Mahlan Smith, was born near Warren, Huntington County, Indiana, February 22, 1847, and spent his last years with a brother in Montana, where he died in 1914. Mahlan Smith married Josephine Pulley, who was born in Grant County, August 12, 1851. She died when her son Noah was eight years of age.

Partly for that reason Noah N. Smith had a boyhood deficient in opportunities for an education but with experiences and hardships that

E L Weesner

no doubt trained and perfected his abilities and made him at home in the world, regardless of circumstances. Only for three short terms did he regularly attend a school and that was at Anderson. He was eleven years old when he first came to Frankfort, and for a time he literally lived outdoors, sleeping in brush heaps and outbuildings until finally a man permitted him to sleep in his barn, paying him fifty cents a week to take care of the horse. These and other experiences were his lot during several years when he knocked about over Howard, Grant, Madison and Delaware counties. At Anderson he was employed as a helper in the Butler Bottle Factory, at a time when glass bottle blowing was all a manual industry. At Anderson, too, he began his apprenticeship at the cigar maker's trade. This apprenticeship was finished at Muncie, with C. C. Schuffelberger.

In 1893, when he was sixteen years old, he again came to Frankfort, and while living with his brother, O. B. Smith, started a small cigar factory. He did all the work himself, made a cigar that was popular with the local trade and was able to hire a few cigar makers and eventually had a factory employing the skilled labor of nine operatives. In 1898, as a result of some trouble with the Cigar Makers Union, he was practically put out of business. Leaving Frankfort, he opened another cigar factory, at Flora, Indiana. It was at Flora that he first perfected and put on the market the now famous "Bankable" cigar. His business outgrowing his plant at Flora, he returned to Frankfort in 1910, in order to have a larger supply of labor. Here he put up a factory in which 200 persons were employed. This was outgrown in five years and in 1917 the present plant was erected, containing 32,000 feet of floor space. In normal seasons 400 workers are on the payroll of this plant. In 1922 Mr. Smith built another factory, at Lebanon, Indiana, and this factory employs 200 people. Mr. Smith is practically sole owner of this business, which in its growth and development is a notable tribute to his skill and management as a manufacturer.

Thirty years ago Mr. Smith started experimenting with a view to eliminating the seedy taste from seed tobacco. The idea was never entirely lost sight of, and, bringing his mind to the problem again and again, from the viewpoint of fresh experience, he finally solved the problem, perfecting a process which extracts the ammonia from tobacco and at the same time retains the sweet honey taste of the natural flavor. This smoke from this improved product is, to quote Mr. Smith's own words, "sweet to the very last puff." Mr. Smith votes as a Republican but has never sought the honors of public office. He and his family are members of the Christian Church and his fraternal affiliations are with the Masonic Order, Knights of Pythias, Loyal Order of Moose and B. P. O. Elks.

Mr. Smith married, October 4, 1896, Miss Lucy Maude Alexander, a resident of Frankfort. They have two children, the son, Glenn Ransom, being a child of Mrs. Smith's first marriage. Glenn Ransom is now associated with his step-father in the cigar manufacturing business at Frankfort. He married in 1926 Mary Sarhent, of Frankfort, and has a daughter, Jane.

Mr. Smith's daughter, Geraldine Frances Smith, is a very unusual young woman, highly educated, having completed the four-year course at Purdue University, graduating with high honors in 1921, and won a scholarship that gave her a period of study at Bryn Mawr College in Pennsylvania. She is now superintendent of the Gladwynne Colony at Gladwynne, Pennsylvania. She was recently married there to Mr. Lynn Seiler.

EDWIN LENOX WEESNER. The Weesner family have been residents of Grant County, Indiana, for over eighty years. It is an honored as well as an old family name, and its representatives have been numbered among the substantial people of the county, industrious farmers and business men, always doing a sustaining part in local religious, moral and educational affairs. One of the best known in the present generation is Mr. Edwin Lenox Weesner, the prominent Marion manufacturer and business man.

He was born near Marion, in Franklin Township, August 2, 1867. His birthplace was a log cabin that stood on the farm of his grandfather. His father, Elihu J. Weesner, was born near Jonesboro, Grant County, was a successful farmer, held the office of justice of the peace, and died in 1917, at the age of seventy-two. He married Margaret Osborn, who was born in Marion and who died in 1915, at the age of sixty-nine. Both are buried in the I. O. O. F. Cemetery at Marion.

Edwin Lenox Weesner attended the Franklin Township schools until graduating in 1883, then took a teachers' preparatory course in the Indiana State Normal at Terre Haute, and during 1884-85 taught a school in Monroe Township of his native county.

Mr. Weesner's business experience has connected him during the greater part of his life with the paper industry in some phase or another. His first commercial job was that of traveling salesman for Fisher Brothers, a wholesale paper house of Ft. Wayne. After seven years he left the road and at Marion joined Mr. George Osborn in founding the Osborn Paper Company. He is still financially interested in this business, though his active connection was given up some years ago. About 1910 Mr. Weesner became general manager of the Spencer Table Company, and the result of his five years of active work put this local industry on a highly satisfactory plane.

Mr. Weesner for a number of years has given most of his time to the Economy Box & Pie Plate Company, an industry which he and Mr. George C. Cole bought and of which Mr. Weesner and his family are now the sole owners. It was one of the earlier industries of Eastern Indiana manufacturing paper and strawboard specialties. It was started in 1898, with a capitalization of only $10,000. Today the company has an investment of $300,000, and during the past ten years the scope of the industry has broadened tremendously to keep pace with the demand for the paper specialty products it turns out.

Mr. Weesner's name is officially connected with a number of business corporations, not only in Marion but elsewhere in the state. He is secretary of the Osborn Paper Company, treasurer of the Midwest Paper Company, president of the Marion Mattress Company, president of the L. P. Cubberly Tobacco Company of Marion, director of the Spencer-Cardinal Furniture Company, president of the Hoosier Stove Company, and president of the Washington Theater Company of Marion. He is a director of the Consolidated Finance Company of Indianapolis and was formerly a director of the Grant Trust & Savings Company.

Mr. Weesner is affiliated with the Knights of Pythias and B. P. O. Elks, is a member of the Meshingoneshia Country Club, the Mecca Club. A Republican, he has satisfied his conscience in political matters by doing his duty as a business man and citizen. He is a member of the Presbyterian Church. His favorite pastime is travel, and his travels have taken him to many remote and interesting parts of the wide world. In traveling he has always been accompanied by his wife and two daughters. In 1912 they went to the Bermuda Islands, in February, 1925, they made a voyage to the West Indies, Panama and the Spanish Main. This was followed in January, 1926, by a more extended cruise to South America, South Africa, East Africa and the Mediterranean ports. In 1927 they went through the Panama Canal and over the Pacific to Honolulu. In 1929 their travels took them to the Holy Land and Egypt, in the course of which they visited Damascus and many other interesting places in the Holy Land. During the first five months of 1931 they made another trip around the world, taking them to Africa, India, Egypt, China, Japan, Formosa, Ceylon, Philippines, Hawaiian Islands, Panama and Cuba.

It was during one of these voyages that his daughter Margaret met Mr. Haram, then purser on the ship on which they were traveling. As a result of the romance between the young people Mr. Haram came to the United States, married Miss Weesner and became an American citizen. Besides being general manager of the Economy Box & Pie Plate Company, he is also a director of the Marion National Bank and associated with Mr. Weesner in most of his enterprises.

Mr. Weesner married in February, 1897, Miss Edna Redding Snelson. They were married at Anderson. Her father, George Andrews Snelson, was a contracting carpenter of that city. He died in 1897, at the age of sixty-five, and is buried at Anderson.

Mr. and Mrs. Weesner had four children, but their third daughter, Harriett, born in 1910, died in 1912, and the fourth child, born in 1912, died in infancy.

The older of the surviving daughters is Margaret, who was born at Marion, August 31, 1905, attended local schools and the Tudor School at Indianapolis, and then went to the University of Wisconsin. Her husband, Mr. B. L. Haram, was born in England, March 4, 1901, was educated in the University College of North Wales, and in 1917 volunteered. He was attached to the Royal Naval Transport Service between English ports and Halifax, Nova Scotia. After the war he was transferred to the mercantile service with the Royal Mail Steam Packet Company, and was in that work until he came to America.

The second daughter, Elizabeth Ann, was born at Marion January 17, 1907. After the schools of Marion she attended the Emma Willard Preparatory School at Troy, New York, was in a girls' school at Rye Beach, New Hampshire, and is now a student of home economics and journalism at the University of Wisconsin.

ELMER ULYSSES POWELL was born and reared in Howard County, and the people of that county for over forty years have appreciated and esteemed his abilities as an accomplished physician and surgeon, and his great devotion to his work. He has a host of friends all over the district around Greentown, where he has his personal headquarters.

Doctor Powell was born on a farm near Greentown, September 3, 1862. His father, Amos Powell, was born in Fayette County, Indiana, in 1844, gave all his active life to farming and died in 1908. Doctor Powell's mother was Mary Scott Powell, a native of Grant County, Indiana, who passed away in 1866. There was one other child, Cora, who is the wife of Judson Costlow, of Kirkland, Indiana.

Elmer Ulysses Powell was four years of age when his mother died. He grew up on a farm and in rural surroundings, attended school at Greentown, and at an early date resolved on a professional career. He won his M. D. degree in the Indiana Medical School at Fort Wayne in 1884 and also attended the Ohio Medical College in 1892, and has kept in touch with the profession by his membership in the medical societies and by attending conventions and clinics.

Doctor Powell first practiced at Sexton in Rush County, Indiana, but in 1892 returned to his old home community at Greentown, and there he has practiced among old friends and the newer generation of people for upwards of forty years. He owns a beautiful home in the town and has one of the best farms in the county, which is at once an investment and a hobby. Doctor Powell is a Republican in politics, a member of the Masonic fraternity and Independent Order of Odd Fellows, and is a Methodist.

He married, September 18, 1884, soon after qualifying for medical practice, Miss Minnie R. Ayers. She was born in Rush County, Indiana, in 1865, daughter of Thomas and Nancy J. Ayers, also natives of Indiana. Doctor and

Mrs. Powell had two children: Arsie Opal, deceased; and Merle, wife of Harry McGonigal, of Kokomo.

RALPH ALEXANDER LEMCKE. Lemcke is one of the most familiar names in Indianapolis, associated with the title of several of the skyscrapers of that city. It is the name of an old and distinguished family of Indiana, a family that laid the foundation of its wealth in the Ohio River steamboat industry. The name has also been a distinguished one in Indiana public affairs.

Ralph Alexander Lemcke, who represents the present generation of the family, was born at Evansville, Indiana, February 5, 1880, son of Julius and Emma (O'Riley) Lemcke. His father was a native of Hamburg, Germany, and his mother of Evansville. Julius A. Lemcke when fourteen years of age was sent to the United States, in the care of the captain of a ship, and on reaching Vanderburg County, Indiana, lived with an uncle on a farm for ten years. Later he and his brother conducted a country store. When he was twenty-five years of age he moved to Evansville, worked for a time in the bank of William H. Heilmann, became city treasurer and sheriff of Vanderburg County, was associated with David K. Mackey in the building of the Saint George Hotel, and owned a group of steamboats plying on both the Ohio and Mississippi rivers.

Julius A. Lemcke after many years of active leadership in local politics in Southern Indiana was elected to the office of state treasurer in 1886, and in the spring of the following year moved his home to Indianapolis. He served two terms, and was offered the post of treasurer of the United States by President Benjamin Harrison, but declined. He retired from all business activities in 1891 and died January 22, 1909. His wife passed away in March, 1925. Their surviving children are Katherine L. Ernos, Ralph Alexander and Mrs. Russell Fortune, who share in the extensive Lemcke estate.

Ralph Alexander Lemcke was liberally educated, spending part of his early youth abroad in Germany and Switzerland, graduated from Saint John's Military Academy, attended Lawrenceville, New Jersey, Preparatory School and Princeton University, and his first connection with practical business was in the insurance line. For several years he had charge of the Evansville Woolen Company. On returning to Indianapolis he became associated with his father, and after his father's death became a trustee of the Lemcke Estate. In recent years he has made extensive additions to the Lemcke Building at Indianapolis, also built the Lemcke Annex, now known as the Consolidated Building, these being two of Indianapolis' largest and finest office structures.

Mr. Lemcke married, January 6, 1904, Cornelia Cunningham, who was born at Evansville, daughter of George A. and Susan (Garvin) Cunningham. Her maternal grandfather, Thomas Garvin, was an Indiana commissioner to the Chicago World's Fair of 1893. Mr. and Mrs. Lemcke have three children: George A., of Indianapolis; Cornelia L. Grassi, of Florence, Italy; and Ralph A., attending the Lawrenceville Preparatory School in New Jersey. Mr. Lemcke is a member of the Episcopal Church, while his wife is a Presbyterian. He was chairman of the Republican city committee of Indianapolis in 1917, and from 1920 to 1924 was treasurer of Marion County. He was a member of the board of governors of the Board of Trade, is a Mason, belongs to the Columbia Club, is a charter member of the University Club and a life member of the Country Club.

LEVI GALE WARREN was one of the distinguished Warren family whose individual and combined resources and abilities made Terre Haute a business center of great prestige in the early days of the old National Road and the Wabash River, and also contributed to the intellectual and social activities of that community.

The Warrens were of New England stock, and the family first came to Vigo County in 1820. A half-brother of Levi G. Warren was Chauncey Warren, one of Terre Haute's early merchants. Beginning in 1839 there was in Terre Haute an important business firm known as C., L. G. & W. B. Warren, usually referred to as the Warren Brothers. The Warrens carried on business on an extensive scale and were interested in the flat boat transportation of merchandise to the South. All of the brothers were distinguished figures in the life of the city. Levi Gale Warren was not only a merchant but became widely known throughout the state for his connection with the Terre Haute branch of the State Bank of Indiana. The great Indiana financier, Hugh McCulloch, afterwards comptroller of the treasury, pronounced Levi G. Warren one of the safest, most prudent and sagacious financiers connected with the Indiana banking system.

The Warren family have been in America for three centuries. The founder of the family was John Warren, who was born in England in 1585 and came to America with the Massachusetts Bay Colony in 1630, settling at Watertown, Massachusetts, where he died in 1667. The subsequent generations were: Daniel Warren; Jonas Warren; Samuel Warren; Bernard Warren; and Levi Gale. Samuel Warren was a soldier in the American Revolution.

Levi Gale Warren was born at Adams, Jefferson County, New York, January 31, 1816, and died at Terre Haute in June, 1865. He and his brother, William B. Warren, were the children of Bernard M. and Abigail (Gale) Warren. By a previous marriage Bernard Warren was the father of three children, one of whom was Chauncey. Abigail Gale was also of old New England ancestry and was a descendant of Abraham Gale of Shrewsbury, Massachusetts, who was a soldier in the American Revolution.

Bernard M. Warren brought his family to Indiana from New York State in 1820 and made a brief stop at Morristown, a settlement on the Blue River. From there he moved to Vigo County and located in the settlement known as Markle's Mill in Otter Creek Township. Bernard M. Warren died within a month after his arrival. His widow then took her two sons, William B. and Levi Gale, back to Morristown, where she lived until her death December 3, 1845.

Levi Gale Warren came to Indiana at an early age. While he had the advantages of few schools, he possessed a rugged character and a keen sense of business, so that he was a valuable helper and associate to his brothers and other business men from an early age. He and his brother became extensively identified with the pork packing industry during the height of its fame along the Wabash Valley, and they shipped great quantities of pork products south along the rivers to New Orleans. He invested heavily in real estate, and what was known as the Warren Park Farm was one of his properties, and for years it was one of the show places of Vigo County.

However, it is proper to associate his name chiefly with the great financial institution known as the State Bank of Indiana, which was chartered about 1834 and eventually had thirteen branches, one of which was located at Terre Haute. In 1853 Levi G. Warren became president of the Terre Haute branch. At the expiration of the original charter of the bank, he was elected president to wind up the affairs of the institution. Then under the law of 1855, providing for the establishment of the Bank of the State of Indiana, he and some other stockholders organized a branch at Terre Haute and became one of the directors, continuing with the institution until it surrendered its charter as a result of the passage of the National Bank Act in 1863. He then helped organize and became the first president of the First National Bank of Terre Haute and held that office at the time of his death.

Levi G. Warren was an active Republican from the formation of the party. He was a thirty-second degree Scottish Rite Mason. C. C. Oakey, of Terre Haute wrote the following tribute of this splendid pioneer banker: "Mr. Warren was a firm, square-built, handsome man. He was never demonstrative, but exceedingly agreeable when approached. He had an unusual sense of the ludicrous, and his quiver was always supplied with darts of repartee. He was liberal, but never foolishly so. His home was a model of good cheer. He died suddenly before his energies were half wasted, but his house was in order and his large estate well disposed. His death was a public calamity."

Levi G. Warren married Martha Ellen Clark. She was born at Charles Town, Virginia, daughter of Walter and Sarah (Conway) Clark. To this marriage were born three children: Sallie W., now deceased, who was the wife of William P. Ijams, for many years a leader in the financial and social life of Terre Haute; Jesse E., deceased; and the only survivor is Miss Mary Alice Warren.

J. ARTHUR BRICE, M. D. Included among the capable, reliable and thoroughly educated members of the medical fraternity of Ripley County is Dr. J. Arthur Brice, who has been engaged in the practice of his profession at Batesville since 1924 and has built up a large and constantly increasing professional business. Prior to coming to Indiana he had varied and valuable experience as physician for several large corporations in the South, and this training, although hard and trying, has proved greatly valuable to him.

Doctor Brice was born in 1883, at Oneonta, the county seat of Blount County, Alabama, and is a son of M. W. and Gertrude (Parker) Brice. On both sides he is a descendant of old and distinguished Southern families. His paternal ancestors were early settlers of North Carolina and Virginia, whence his grandfather, William Brice, moved to Alabama about 1847. The Parkers came from Virginia, and Doctor Brice's grandfather, Rev. William T. Parker moved from that state to Alabama about 1840. M. W. Brice, the father of Doctor Brice, has for many years been extensively engaged in the dairy business in Alabama, where he is the owner of a large dairy farm.

After attending the public schools of his native community J. Arthur Brice entered the University of Alabama, from the medical department of which institution he was graduated with the degree of Doctor of Medicine with the class of 1913. He served his internship at the Hillman Hospital, Birmingham, Alabama, and commenced his medical practice with the Tennessee Coal, Iron & Railway Company, where he was the head physician in charge of the Bessemer rolling mill and five blast furnaces. He continued to act in that capacity from 1914 until 1920, when he resigned to accept a position with the Majestic Coal Company, as physician in charge at Majestic, twelve miles north of Birmingham. The men engaged in work in the mines are subject to constant danger and injuries, necessitating the prompt attention of a skilled and tireless medical man, who must be prepared to be in attendance at any minute, day or night. The life of the company physician and surgeon is by no means a pleasant or easy one, but Doctor Brice does not regret this hard and strenuous training, for it was of the most varied and comprehensive character and brought him into close touch with human nature. In 1924 he resigned his position at Majestic, and in June of that year settled permanently at Batesville, where he has since been in the enjoyment of a gratifying general practice in medicine and surgery, with offices at 201 North Main Street. He is held in high esteem by the people of his community, and for two years served in the capacity of health officer. He is a member of the Ripley County Medical Society, the Indiana State Medical

F. Harold Van Arman

Society and the American Medical Association, and is a constant student of his profession, keeping fully abreast of its developments. As a fraternalist he belongs to Jefferson Valley Lodge No. 795, A. F. and A. M., of Bessemer, Alabama; and Cameron Grotto, of Birmingham, that state. Doctor Brice is a Republican, but has not cared for public office, his only service in that direction having been as health officer. He is a wide-awake citizen, however, and a helpful and constructive participant in all public spirited movements. His religious connection is with the Methodist Episcopal Church, South.

Doctor Brice married Miss Addie Parker, of another old Southern family, a different branch from that of his mother, of Cleveland, Alabama, and to this union there have been born two children: Miss Joy, who is attending Belmont College, at Nashville, Tennessee; and George, a student in the Batesville schools.

WALTER SCOTT ARMSTRONG throughout his active life was a resident of Howard County. The people of that county respect his memory as that of a strong and fine character, a man successful in business and no less successful in his varied relationships with public affairs.

He was born in Clinton County, Ohio, February 3, 1838, and was a boy of about twelve years of age when his parents, Thomas Andrew and Sarah East (Grant) Armstrong, moved to Howard County, Indiana. His education was acquired partly in Clinton County, Ohio, also in Howard County, and he attended an academy at Pittsburgh, Pennsylvania. Mr. Armstrong had the character and the education that made him during his early manhood a successful teacher. He taught in Kokomo and Tipton. While in Tipton County he was elected county auditor. For a number of years he was a farmer there, and after returning to Kokomo, engaged in business as a hardware merchant.

He served two terms as mayor of Kokomo during the early '80s and from 1884 to 1889 was postmaster of that city. Again he became mayor for the years 1898-1902. From 1879, the year he first entered the Kokomo City Council, continuously until his death in 1908 he was one of the most active and vigilant members of that body except while engaged in the responsibilities of the other offices just named. Politically he was a Democrat and from early youth was a member of the Church of the Disciples.

Mr. Armstrong married at Tipton, Indiana, December 28, 1869, Miss Martha Ellen Winfield, daughter of William Shipley and Martha (Cochran) Winfield. Her father was a minister of the Disciples Church. Mr. and Mrs. Armstrong had five children: Walter Winfield, deceased; Horace Howard, who married Nellie Smith; Miss Jessamine Armstrong; Merle, wife of Paul Conner, an artist living at Long Beach, California; and Ralph, who is a newspaper man in New York City and married a talented literary woman, Roberta Yates.

The five grandchildren of Mr. Armstrong are: Dan, of Kokomo; Virginia, wife of John Duke, of Kokomo; Dorothy, wife of Harney Watson Stover, both of them holding teaching positions in the Penn State College; Edith, librarian of the Kokomo High School; and Margaret Conner, a girl who has won distinction as a violinist and is the wife of Robert Hall Rockwell, of Long Beach, California.

FREDERICK HAROLD VAN ORMAN, president of the Van Orman chain of Hotels, has spent most of his life at Evansville, and over the state his name is familiarly associated with politics and public affairs. Mr. Van Orman is a former lieutenant governor of Indiana.

His father, the late Fred Van Orman, who died at Evansville, was one of the first hotel men to apply to the business the modern principle of centralized management of a group or a chain of hotels, and at one time the Van Ormans operated or were actively interested in perhaps a dozen modern hotels in Indiana, Michigan, Ohio, Illinois and other states. Fred Van Orman was born at Kalamazoo, Michigan, March 17, 1860, of Holland Dutch ancestry and of Revolutionary stock. In early life he was a traveling salesman. In 1887 he took over the management of the Murdoch Hotel at Logansport, Indiana. From that he extended his management and financial control to other hotels, including a number that are very familiar to the traveling public. In 1900 he acquired the management of the St. George Hotel at Evansville and moved his headquarters to that city, from which he directed his hotel interests in seven different states. Fred Van Orman married Demaris Paddock, a native of Coldwater, Michigan, and Frederick Harold, their only child, was born at Flint, Michigan, September 26, 1884.

Frederick Harold Van Orman made his approach to business life with the best of training and early environment. He is a college man, his parents having given him liberal advantages. He attended the Evansville High School, graduated from the Phillips Exeter Academy of New Hampshire in 1904, and this was followed by four years in Harvard University, where he took his A. B. degree in 1908. Immediately after leaving college he joined his father in the hotel business. He was manager of the old St. George Hotel at Evansville until the building was torn down in 1915. He then supervised the construction of the Hotel McCurdy, which was opened in 1917 and of which he continued as manager until 1926, since which year he has been president of the Van Orman chain of Hotels. This system now comprises three modern, European, fireproof hotels, the Hotel Shawnee, at Springfield, Ohio, Hotel McCurdy, at Evansville, and the Hotel Orlando, at Decatur, Illinois.

Mr. Van Orman for a number of years has been a recognized leader in the Republican party of Indiana. In 1920 he was elected to the State Senate from Vanderburgh County, serving four years, and in 1924 was elected lieutenant governor of the state. He is a former president of the Evansville Rotary Club, a director of the Evansville Chamber of Commerce, and in 1922 was elected president of the Hotel Men's Benefit Association of the United States and Canada, the largest and oldest hotel men's association in America. He is at present a director of the American Hotel Association. He is a past potentate of Hadi Temple of the Mystic Shrine and a past exalted ruler of the B. P. O. Elks, both of Evansville.

Mr. Van Orman married, September 26, 1913, Miss Susie Beeler, daughter of Dr. Jerome and Florence (Barrett) Beeler. Her father was a distinguished physician and surgeon at Evansville. Mr. and Mrs. Van Orman have three sons: F. Harold, Jr., born November 27, 1916; Jerome Beeler, born March 20, 1918, and William Henry, born February 19, 1922. Mr. and Mrs. Van Orman are members of the Episcopal Church.

The bare recital of the outline of Mr. Van Orman's activities such as limited space allows, hardly gives a true picture of the ceaseless energy that dominates his daily work nor the genial spirit with which he greets all with whom he come in contact regardless of the pressure of his work. To quote another commentary on this point: "Mr. Van Orman's personality is injected into his every activity, which includes his business, public appearance as a speaker and entertainer, and politics." In fact, this spirit permeates his relations with his 800 employees as well as with the general public. To watch him work at his desk for even an hour is an inspiration to the casual observer.

BENJAMIN W. COOPER, M. D., who passed away April 18, 1931, had been established in the successful general practice of his profession at Connersville during a period of about fifteen years, and his ability and prestige distinctly marked him as one of the representative physicians and surgeons of Fayette County.

Doctor Cooper was born in Hendricks County, Indiana, September 1, 1874, a son of Rev. Shelby Tipton Cooper and Marthy E. (Rynerson) Cooper, both likewise natives of that county. Lewis Cooper, grandfather of the Doctor, was a native of North Carolina and became a pioneer settler in Hendricks County, Indiana, where he acquired an entire section of land and developed a productive farm, the remainder of his life having there been passed. Though Rev. Shelby T. Cooper became a clergyman of the Methodist Episcopal Church and gave earnest and effective service in the ministry, the greater part of his active life was given to farm industry. He died in Hendricks County in the year 1903, and his widow passed away in 1924, at the venerable age of eighty-four years.

In his native county the public school discipline of Dr. Benjamin W. Cooper included that of the high school at Cartersburg, and his education was thereafter advanced by his attending the Indiana State Normal School at Danville. In the medical department of the University of Louisville, Kentucky, he was graduated as a member of the class of 1907, and after thus receiving his degree of Doctor of Medicine he initiated the active practice of his profession in the City of Muncie, Indiana, whence he soon removed to Henry County, where he continued his professional activities seven years, he having then removed to Connersville, judicial center of Fayette County, where he continued in practice and where his pronounced success stood in evidence of his technical skill and his personal popularity. He maintained his office at 1820½ Virginia Avenue and the pleasant family home is at 2131 Iowa Avenue. The Doctor had membership in the Fayette County Medical Society, the Indiana State Medical Society and the American Medical Association. He was a Republican in political alignment and he gave eight years of loyal service as coroner of Fayette County. He was affiliated with the Masonic fraternity and the Knights of Pythias, and he held membership in the Methodist Episcopal Church, as does also his widow.

The year 1908 was marked by the marriage of Doctor Cooper to Miss Jennie Pierson, who likewise was born and reared in Hendricks County, and who is a daughter of Charles and Margaret Pierson. Helen, elder of the two children of Doctor and Mrs. Cooper, is the wife of Merle Luckett, of Connersville, and Everett here remains at the family home.

C. EARNEST ROGERS has been well known as a business man at Columbus for many years. He is senior partner of the firm Rogers & Schoenover Company, who have the Hudson-Essex agency in Bartholomew County.

Mr. Rogers was born in White County, Indiana, September 3, 1878. His grandfather, Nathaniel S. Rogers, settled in White County as a pioneer in 1840, coming from Hampshire County, Virginia, now West Virginia. C. Earnest Rogers is a son of N. S. and Lucenia J. (West) Rogers, the former a native of White County and the latter of Johnson County, Indiana. His father was a contractor. C. Earnest Rogers has one brother, E. W. Rogers.

Mr. Rogers attended school in White County, the Johnson County High School and his first business employment was as manager of the local exchange of the telephone company of Franklin. He remained there ten years and then came to Columbus, as manager of the Crump estate. That property remained under his direction and care for eighteen years.

In 1925 he organized the Rogers-Schoenover Automobile Company, starting with the Page-Jewett franchise.

Subsequently he took over the Hudson-Essex franchise and since 1926 has handled the Hudson-Essex cars exclusively. The company does a business selling 200 cars annually in their territory and have six persons employed, including expert mechanics. Their office, shop

Charles Roll

and storage rooms have 1,100 square feet of floor space and every type of modern machinery and equipment are installed for perfect and adequate service on these very popular and high class cars.

Mr. Rogers married Lulu Taylor, and by this marriage has a son, Charles, who graduated with the A. B. degree from Franklin College in the class of 1927. Later Mr. Rogers married Mary M. Morton, and to this Union were born two children, Robert E. and Betsey E., both attending school at Columbus. Mr. Rogers is an active member of the Columbus Chamber of Commerce, of which he was one of the charter members in 1921. He is affiliated with the B. P. O. Elks and is a member of the Hoosier State Automobile Association.

WILLIAM P. WALTER has been engaged in the practice of law in the City of Fort Wayne since the year 1916, maintains his offices in the Farmers Trust Building and has a substantial law business of representative order.

Mr. Walter was born in the City of Massillon, Stark County, Ohio, January 17, 1879, and is a son of William B. Walter, who was born at Lancaster, Pennsylvania, March 15, 1845, and whose father, Jonas R. Walter, was there born in 1820, the family having early been established in that section of the old Keystone State. The marriage of William B. Walter and Mary Alice Donat was solemnized at Massillon, Ohio, November 12, 1872, and it was in that city their son William P., of this review, was born and reared, his public school education having there included the curriculum of the high school, and he having later attended the Heidelberg Teachers Training School in his native state. In preparing for his chosen profession he availed himself of the advantages of the law department of Tri-State College, at Angola, Indiana, and prior to engaging in the practice of his profession he had been employed in the Government post office service five years. In 1916 he established his residence in Fort Wayne, and here he has since been successfully established in the general practice of law.

December 25, 1900, marked the marriage of Mr. Walter to Miss Elsie Ruch, who was born at Canal Fulton, Ohio, where she was reared and educated, the date of her birth having been July 2, 1881, and she having died in 1902, at Massillon, Ohio, her only child, Chester W., having there been born August 10, 1901. Chester W. Walter gained his early education in the public schools of Massillon and Fort Wayne, in which latter city he had his high school training, and thereafter he studied electrical engineering in the Edison testing laboratory in New York City, he being now in the employ of the Westinghouse Electric Company, with his residence and headquarters in Milwaukee, Wisconsin. April 10, 1921, he married Teresa Fehrenbaugh, and their one child, William Joseph, was born March 3, 1928.

On the 2d of August, 1910, was solemnized the marriage of William P. Walter to Virginia Bortel, who was born at Massillon, Ohio, December 14, 1888, and the one child of this marriage is Mary Alice, who was born April 25, 1918, in Fort Wayne.

Mr. Walter has manifested no ambition for political office. He is a member of the Allen County Bar Association and the Indiana State Bar Association, and he and his wife have membership in the Reformed Church in their home city.

CHARLES ROLL, A. B., A. M., historian, author and editor of *History of Indiana, One Hundred and Fifty Years of American Development*, has been a teacher of history in the Indiana State Teachers College since 1913. He is a native of Indiana, born in Vigo County, August 8, 1883, a son of John Aaron and Mary Jane (Shaw) Roll. His grandparents came to Vigo County from Ohio and Kentucky in early days. Professor Roll is therefore of old Indiana stock and has spent practically all of his life in the state.

From boyhood Professor Roll has been deeply interested in history. He graduated from the Indiana State Normal School at Terre Haute in 1906 and from Indiana University with the Bachelor of Arts degree in 1910. He received the Master of Arts degree from the University of Wisconsin in 1912. During the year 1912-13 he served as Fellow in American History at the University of Wisconsin. He came to the Indiana State Normal School as assistant professor of history in 1913, later becoming associate professor. He has written numerous historical articles for periodicals and is accounted an authority on Indiana history. Professor Roll is a member of the American Historical Association, Mississippi Valley Historical Association, Indiana Historical Society, Society of Indiana Pioneers, National Education Association and Indiana State Teachers Association. He is a member of the Christian (Disciples) Church.

Professor Roll married Miss Opal McShane, of Tipton, Indiana, June 21, 1911, and they are the parents of two children: Charles Robert, born March 20, 1913; and Helen Marguerite, born November 29, 1916.

ORA A. DAVIS. No name has been more steadily honored in the legal profession in Warrick County than that of Davis. One of the oldest members of the Boonville bar is James W. Davis, who is still practicing law and who has lived in Warrick County practically all his life. His son of the second generation of the family, Ora A. Davis, has also played a notably successful part in the professional, civic and business life of that community.

James W. Davis married Mary F. Barnett, a native of Indiana. Of their seven children two died in infancy and those living are: Ethel V., Opha O., Herbert L., Ina M., and Ora A. Ethel is the wife of Eli Rose, partner in a lithographing corporation of Chicago, and has a son, Samuel W., born in 1928. Opha is the wife of Ed Heidt, an Evansville musician. Herbert L., bookkeeper and clerk for the Pigeon Creek Coal Company of Warrick County, married Maud Whittaker and has two children, Wanda L., born in 1915, and William, born in 1920. Ina married Roland R. Richardson, a chiropractor at Murphysboro, Illinois, and has a daughter, Mary Janette, born in 1919.

Ora A. Davis received his first educational advantages at Chandler, Indiana, and was graduated from the Boonville High School in 1900. He was a school teacher for nine years and for two years taught in country districts and for seven years at Chandler, where for six years of the time he was principal. In the meantime he was studying law in his father's office and in 1907 was admitted to the bar. The first case he had in court was defending a deaf and dumb man on the charge of drunkenness. His father was then deputy prosecuting attorney and had charge of the prosecution. The result was a hung jury and the case was dismissed. Mr. Davis in 1909 went in the office of Thomas W. Lindsay and in 1910 made the race for prosecuting attorney of Warrick County. He was elected for three consecutive terms, and gave a vigilant and vigorous administration. All the while he was conducting an independent law practice. Mr. Davis opened his law office May 4, 1910, under the firm name of Davis & Davis, in partnership with his father. They dissolved partnership in 1915 and he has given his full time to his law practice.

Mr. Davis is a real estate owner at Evansville. He owns the most beautiful home in Boonville.

He married at Chandler, Indiana, April 28, 1901, Miss Ethel C. Baum, daughter of William and Hattie (Huber) Baum. Her father was a coal miner and engineer, and died in Warrick County. By his first marriage Mr. Davis has four children: Elbert A., born in October, 1902; Claire N., born May 2, 1905; Frank E., born August 2, 1907, and Raymond F., born January 8, 1909. Elbert is cashier of the Southern Indiana Gas & Electric Company at Boonville. Claire married Paul A. Routh, an accountant in Chicago, and she was a teacher before her marriage. Frank, an electrician and superintendent of construction for the Southern Indiana Gas & Electric Company at Boonville, married Grace Wooley, of Warrick County. Raymond is a bookkeeper in the office of the Shaw Coal Company at Boonville.

Mr. Davis second wife was Anna Dilday, daughter of Joseph R. and Susie (Archer) Dilday. They were married in March, 1916. Mrs. Davis is also a lawyer, and helps her husband in his office. She was admitted to practice before the Warrick Circuit Court in 1915. Mr. Davis is a Democrat in politics. He is a past exalted ruler of the Elks Lodge and has filled all the chairs in the Independent Order of Odd Fellows, being a past noble grand and member of the Grand Lodge. He is a member of the Kiwanis Club and the American Legion. In 1918 he joined the colors, waiving his privilege of deferred classification, and entered as a private. He was trained with the Twenty-sixth Training Battery, Ninth Battalion, at Camp Taylor, Louisville, Kentucky, until after the armistice.

WILLIAM L. JONES, manager of the Furnas Ice Cream Company at Fort Wayne, has had over thirty years' experience in the business of manufacturing and distributing ice cream. Ice cream is one of America's unique products, and it might well now class as one of the big industries. During Mr. Jones' personal experience the business has expanded enormously. When he started, in the late '90s, there were very few commercial plants except in the larger cities, and such has been the demand for this popular and substantial article of diet that hundreds of millions of dollars are invested in plants and facilities for its manufacture and sale.

Mr. Jones was born in Howard County, Indiana, September 10, 1877, a son of Dougan and Lydia (Hobson) Jones. His family on both sides were Indiana pioneers. His grandfather, Alfred Jones, was a farmer in Southern Indiana and married Sarah Trogden. The maternal grandfather, Elihu Hobson, who married a Miss White, was an early settler in Howard County, where both of them died. Dougan Jones was born near Bedford, Indiana, July 12, 1847, and his wife in Howard County, June 14, 1849. They lived together fifty-six years, until the death of the good wife and mother in 1927. All of their four children are living. Dougan Jones spent his active career as a farmer and is now living retired. Both parents were members of the Friends Church.

William L. Jones grew up on an Indiana farm, attended public school in Howard County, the New London High School, and was graduated A. B. from Indiana University in 1905. As a youth he began teaching in country schools, later taught in the schools of Valley Mills and was principal of the high school at Bloomfield, and after completing his university career was principal of the Bedford High School for two years. Mr. Jones graduated from the Indiana Law School at Indianapolis in 1908, and his knowledge of the law has been valuable to him in his business career, but he has never seriously considered engaging in practice. While in school he taught during several summer terms, and before he entered university he worked for the Furnas Ice Cream Company at Indianapolis and Terre Haute. Mr. Jones in the spring of 1909 came to Fort Wayne to organize a branch of the Furnas Ice Cream Company, and has been the active manager and responsible for the great growth of the business of this plant over Northeastern Indiana. His first work for the Furnas Company was done at Indianapolis in 1898.

Mr. Jones is one of Fort Wayne's well-to-do and substantial business men. He is a thirty-second degree Scottish Rite Mason, member of

Gaylard M. Leslie

Mizpah Temple of the Mystic Shrine, belongs to the Fort Wayne Country Club, the Chamber of Commerce, and though reared as a Friend is now affiliated with the Plymouth Congregational Church at Fort Wayne.

He married in 1914 Miss Emma Ringenberg, of Fort Wayne. She was a Methodist. Mrs. Jones died in October, 1915, leaving one daughter, Mary Alice, who was born February 26, 1915. This daughter attended the West Town, Pennsylvania, Friends School and is now a sophomore in high school at West Town. Mr. Jones by a second marriage has two other children: Robert, born September 13, 1922, and Virginia Lydia, born September 21, 1924.

REV. CONRAD URBACH. Among the spiritual leaders of Warrick County, few are held in greater veneration and respect by the people than Rev. Conrad Urbach, priest of St. Rupert's Church, which is located eight miles east of Newburg. Coming to the United States in 1913, as a youth of eighteen years, he was ordained in 1924, and since 1926 has labored with zeal and enthusiasm in his present parish, winning the admiration and friendship of people of all creeds because of the genuineness of his faith and the worth of his accomplishments.

Father Urbach was born November 23, 1895, in Germany, and received his early education in the public schools of his native country. After coming to the United States in 1913 he continued his studies, and completed his theological work at St. Meinrad, Spencer County, where he was ordained in 1924. His first charge was at Terre Haute, where he spent one year, then being transferred to Lawrenceburg, where he passed a like period, and in 1926 took up his work at St. Rupert's, where he has since remained.

St. Rupert's parish was established in 1858, as a mission, being taken care of by the Benedictine Fathers from St. Meinrad. The first of these was Abbott Martin Marty, who was followed by Father Joseph. In 1875 Father Brooks, of Rockport, began to fill this charge, and continued to do so until 1885, in which year the parish was furnished its first regular pastor, Father Zogelmann. He was succeeded in 1886 by Father Charles Wagner, who served from 1886 until 1902, and was succeeded by Father Michael Wagner, who remained until 1903. In the latter year Father Mathias Schmitz took charge and remained until 1911, when he was suceeded by Father Zerkelbach, who, in turn, was replaced by Father Bleuel, who remained until 1920. The next priest to take charge was Father August Riehl, who remained until 1926, in which year Father Urbach assumed the duties.

Father Urbach has become widely and favorably known to the people all over Warrick, Spencer and Vanderburg counties, as a man of great piety, untiring industry, sound intellectual attainments and a love for the calling to which he has consecrated his life. Under his leadership the parish is prospering, both spiritually and in temporal affairs, and those of all denominations recognize in him a modest but really earnest man whom they welcome into movements making for the welfare of the community in every way.

GAYLARD MILLARD LESLIE, M. D., is a graduate of the old Fort Wayne Medical College and practiced his profession in Fort Wayne for several years. The present generation of Fort Wayne citizens know him chiefly for his executive connections with some of the city's oldest and best established industrial enterprises and business organizations, including the Bass Foundry & Machine Company, of which he is president.

Doctor Leslie was born at Van Wert, Ohio, January 19, 1878, son of Dr. B. F. and Adelaide Leslie. His father was a very fine doctor of the old school, and the son at an early age made a definite choice of his profession. He was graduated from the high school at Convoy, Ohio, in 1895, and soon afterward entered the Fort Wayne Medical College, which held its classes and had its laboratories in the old McCulloch homestead. He graduated M. D. in 1898, at the age of twenty, and being too young to practice independently had the training of an interne with the staff of the old Hope Hospital for one year. In 1899 he engaged in practice, and in a few years had a reputation as one of the ablest younger members of his profession in Fort Wayne.

On May 14, 1903, Doctor Leslie married Miss Laura Grace Bass, daughter and only living child of John H. and Laura H. Bass. The name of Bass for many years has been a conspicuous one in Fort Wayne's industrial and financial life. Since his marriage Doctor and Mrs. Leslie have lived at the beautiful and dignified old country home of the Bass family, known as "Brookside."

John H. Bass at this time was growing old and was gradually seeking relief from the heavy business responsibilities he had long carried. He had first known Doctor Leslie as a capable family physician, and as son-in-law he placed in him his confidence as a trusted business associate. In time Doctor Leslie assumed more and more of the management of the extended Bass interests, and thus circumstances opened for him a career as one of the prominent Indiana industrialists. Doctor Leslie in addition to being president and treasurer of the Bass Foundry & Machine Company is president of the Fort Wayne Foundry & Machine Company, is president of the Rock Run Iron Company at Rock Run, Alabama, is vice president and director of the First & Tri-State National Bank & Trust Company of Fort Wayne, a director of the Old National Bank, and spends most of his business time at his offices at 1602 Hanna Street, where the Bass Foundry & Machine Plant is located.

Doctor Leslie through the years has willingly accepted a more than nominal part in Fort Wayne's vital community and civic interests. He has been vice president and assistant treasurer of the Lindenwood Cemetery Association and is a former president of the Fort Wayne Employers Association. He was a leader in the old Commercial Club and helped reorganize it as the Chamber of Commerce, with increased membership and broader scope. He was one of the team workers in the campaign of 1926 to build the new home of the Chamber. His principal work with that body has been with the Industrial Bureau. Doctor Leslie was a contributor of his personal leadership and means in the original Y. M. C. A. campaign of 1916 and again in the Enlargement Fund campaign of 1925. He is a member of the Credit Men's Association. He was a contributor to the Catholic Community Center Building fund in 1924, to the various Red Cross campaigns, the Christmas Seal Kiddie Camp, the Fort Wayne Anti-Tuberculosis League, and all the Boy Scout and local hospital drives. He is a member of the National Aeronautical Association, the Fort Wayne Country Club, and a trustee of the Pixley Relief Home. During the World war Doctor Leslie was identified with the Fort Wayne Council for patriotic service, which preceded the Council of Defense, of which he was made a member of the citizens committee to provide war funds for carrying out the purpose of providing teachers for the Signal Corps and other purposes. He was in the different Liberty Loan drives, and was one of the executive committees of the Fort Wayne branch of the Fatherless Children of France. He was on the advisory board of the Officers Reserve Corps and had considerable to do with the local fuel administration. Some of his most valuable war service was given as one of the nine captains of the American Protection League, an auxiliary of the Federal Department of Justice. This league comprised a notable group of about 250 business and professional men at Fort Wayne. Doctor Leslie since boyhood has been interested in music and has been a member of numerous choral and similar organizations. He was one time president of the old Apollo Club, which during its existence included nearly all the male singers of note in the city. He is a director of the Fort Wayne Art School and Museum and has served as one of the trustees and a member of the music committee of the First Presbyterian Church.

Indianians all over the state comprising the Masonic constituency are familiar with Doctor Leslie's high attainments and great services to this ancient craft. He is affiliated with Summit City Lodge, A. F. and A. M., and in 1913 was awarded the supreme honorary thirty-third degree in Scottish Rite Masonry. For three years he was commander in chief of the Fort Wayne Consistory and in 1924 was grand commander of the Knights Templar of Indiana. He is a member of Mizpah Temple of the Mystic Shrine, a trustee of Fort Wayne Commandery No. 4, Knights Templar, on the board of trustees of the Scottish Rite Cathedral. He was appointed deputy for Indiana at the Boston, session of the Supreme Council of Scottish Rite Masons in September, 1927, this being

the highest honor that can be conferred by a state jurisdiction.

Doctor and Mrs. Leslie are the parents of five children: Mary Laura, now the wife of John D. Haynes, Linda Adelaide, now the wife of Edmund Seidel, John Bass, Grace Charlotte and Gaylard Franklin.

DONALD WILLIAM SCHAFER, M. D. One of the younger professional men of Fort Wayne, Indiana, is Dr. Donald W. Schafer, physician and surgeon and a veteran of the World war. Doctor Schafer enjoys the universal confidence of his fellow citizens and medical associates because of his professional qualifications, his bravery as a surgeon-soldier, his sterling personal character and his steadfast citizenship as a native of the great State of Indiana. Reared on his father's farm during his boyhood school period, he later had still better educational advantages and early began to cherish hopes of a medical career. In the meantime, however, the spirit of enterprise that he has cherished all of his life led him to seek independence in business channels, and it was not until 1916 that he found himself able to enter the medical department of the University of Indiana. The World war then interrupted his career, but in 1923 he received his medical degree and since that year he has been located at Fort Wayne in the enjoyment of an excellent practice.

Donald W. Schafer was born July 17, 1894, at Inwood, Marshall County, Indiana, and is a son of William L. and Jennie (Girard) Schafer. His grandfather was one of the early settlers of Marshall County, where from small beginnings he built up an extensive lumber business and was one of the substantial and highly-respected citizens of his community at the time of his demise. William L. Schafer was born in Marshall County, where he was reared and educated and spent his entire life. He was engaged in the lumber business for some years with his father, but eventually disposed of his interests therein and turned his attention and energies to farming, in which he is engaged at present, he and Mrs. Schafer living on a valuable and highly-developed property in Marshall County. They are the parents of three children: Mrs. C. W. Thresh, of Fort Wayne; Mrs. J. O. Morgan, of South Bend; and Dr. Donald W.

After attending the public school at Inwood, Donald W. Schafer entered the high school at Argos, Indiana, from which he was graduated in 1913. Although he had yearnings for a professional career, his financial resources were limited, and in 1914 he accepted a position with a vacuum cleaner manufacturing concern, as Indiana State crew manager on the road. In 1915 he entered the office of the Grace Construction Company of Fort Wayne, and in 1916-17 attended Indiana University. In the latter year he enlisted for service in the Medical Corps, and was assigned to Base Hospital No. 13, at Camp Taylor, Kentucky, and while serving there was the victim of an accident which incapacitated him from field

service and he was given his honorable discharge. Later he did work for the United States Government as a civilian, inspecting ammunition steel at Indiana Harbor, Indiana. In 1919 Doctor Schafer attended Valparaiso University, and in the fall of the same year entered the medical department of Cincinnati (Ohio) University, from which he was duly graduated with the degree of Doctor of Medicine in 1923. Coming immediately to Fort Wayne, he spent his interneship at Saint Joseph Hospital, and since then has engaged in a general medical practice here of an honorable and substantial character. Doctor Schafer maintains well appointed offices at 315 Wayne Pharmacal Building, and resides in his pleasant home at 1317 Maple Avenue, where he spends much of his leisure time in gardening and raising flowers, of which he makes a hobby. He stands high in the confidence of his professional associates and acquaintances and is a member of the Allen County Medical Society, the Indiana State Medical Society and the American Medical Association. He is a thirty-second degree Scottish Rite Mason and has several other connections, and in addition has taken an active interest in progressive civic movements.

On September 18, 1917, the day before he enlisted for military service, Doctor Schafer was united in marriage with Miss Neoma Pontius, a graduate nurse of the Illinois Post-Graduate Hospital, and to this union there have come two children: Donald W., Jr., born October 19, 1920; and George I., born August 9, 1922, both attending school.

ORVILLE W. McGINNIS, a member of the Evansville bar, where he has practiced his profession for over thirty years, was born at Owensville in Gibson County, Indiana, December 3, 1869. Mr. McGinnis is a highly educated attorney, and has practiced his profession largely to the exclusion of any political interests save that of good citizenship.

His father, the late Richard P. McGinnis, who died in 1905, was born in Illinois and from early manhood lived in Indiana. He was a farmer, merchant and banker. His wife, Margaret Pollard, was born in Indiana. There were two children, Orville W. and Roscoe C. McGinnis, who died February 16, 1906, was a banker at Princeton, Indiana.

Orville W. McGinnis attended public schools in Gibson County, and was graduated with the A. B. degree from DePauw University at Greencastle, Indiana, in 1892. Soon afterward he began the study of law in Cornell University of New York, but his course was interrupted by ill health and he spent considerable time recuperating on the home farm. He then returned to complete his law studies and about the time he was ready to practice his father's associate died and Orville McGinnis spent about two years with his father in the bank. In 1897 he formally began the practice of law at Evansville. For some time he acted as United States referee in bankruptcy. Much of his work as a lawyer has been as legal counsel for business organizations, and among others he is now general counsel for the Citizens National and the Citizens Trust & Savings Banks of Evansville, and is a director in both institutions. Mr. McGinnis is a Republican in politics and a member of the Methodist Episcopal Church.

He married at Owensville, Indiana, June 27, 1900, Miss Anna Robinson, daughter of James A. and Louisa (Benson) Robinson. They have three children, Richard R., born April 17, 1901; Allan O., born July 5, 1903, and Rossanna, born December 30, 1905. Richard, who is unmarried, graduated with the A. B. degree from DePauw University in 1922, took his law course at the Harvard Law School, and has been associated with his father in practice since 1926. The son Allan, who is connected with the Postum Food Company of New York City, married Dorothy Campbell, of Columbus, Ohio, and has a daughter, Dorothy Ann, born in 1928.

JOHN WALLACE CASWELL. No minor degree of the marked precedence now held by the City of Huntington, judicial center of the Indiana county of that name, as one of the industrial and commercial centers of major rank in the Hoosier State, has been gained through the medium of the Caswell-Runyan Company, of which John Wallace Caswell was the organizer and of which he has been the secretary-treasurer from the time of its incorporation, in 1907. This was the first industrial concern to be established in Huntington after the city made available its factory fund and adopted as its municipal motto "Opportunity's Gateway," —a motto that has been amply justified in practical results.

It is not within the province of this personal review to outline the history of this splendid industrial-commercial organization of Huntington, but it may be stated that the company now ranks as one of the nation's foremost in the manufacturing of cedar chests and radio cabinets of the highest grade. Under normal conditions the company retains a large force of employes, including many highly skilled mechanics, and the plant itself has gained recognition as one of model order as gauged by the best modern standards. The diversified products of this splendid Huntington institution find demand in all parts of the United States, shipments are made in carload lots, radio cabinets have become an important feature in the manufacturing activities of the company, and the operations of the corporation are based on a capital stock of $1,000,000.

John Wallace Caswell, who has translated constructive thought into constructive action that has made him a representative American captain of industry, is a native son of the Hoosier State, to which his loyalty has never faltered, as it is based on his full appreciation of the manifold advantages and attractions of this commonwealth. He was born in the City of Fort Wayne, Indiana, October 6, 1870, and there he continued his studies in the public schools until he had profited by the advantages of the high school. There he gained his initial experience in practical mechanics and in business through his association with the Bass Foundry & Machine Company, and later he was one of the principals of a company engaged in manufacturing wooden novelties at North Manchester, Wabash County. His next forward venture was made in his organizing, in 1907, the Caswell-Runyan Company, of Huntington, of which he has since continued the secretary-treasurer, Winfred Runyan being president of the company, John A. Snyder, vice president, Frank J. Book, vice president and superintendent, while Mr. Caswell functions not only as secretary-treasurer but also as general manager.

Mr. Caswell has not only been a potent figure in the development and upbuilding of the substantial industrial and commercial enterprise now controlled by the Caswell-Runyan Company, but is also president of the Women's Wear Service, Inc., another important Huntington commercial organization; is a director of the First National Bank of Huntington; and in his native City of Fort Wayne is a director and vice president of the Capehart Corporation. He is chairman of the Board of Utah Products Company, Chicago, Illinois. His civic and business progressiveness is further indicated in his being president of the Huntington Auto Transit Company, the Huntington Specialty Company, and the Firetuff Manufacturing Company. He was vice president of the Michigan & Erie Barge Canal Association, the object of which is to effect the construction of a barge canal between the cities of Toledo and Chicago. He is ever at the forefront in supporting measures and enterprises that are projected for the civic and material advancement of his home city.

The political alignment of Mr. Caswell is with the Republican party, in the Masonic fraternity he has completed the circles of both the York and Scottish Rites, in the former of which he retains affiliation with the Commandery of Knights Templar in Columbia City, and in the latter of which he has received the thirty-second degree, in the Consistory of the Valley of Fort Wayne. He is affiliated also with the Benevolent and Protective Order of Elks, is a former president of the Huntington Commercial Club, is a loyal and influential member of the local Chamber of Commerce and the Rotary Club and was its first president, is a trustee of the Huntington Y. M. C. A. and raised the first funds for the first building erected. He is president of the Masonic Realty Company, which raised the funds and built the Masonic Temple at Huntington.

On the 13th of March, 1894, Mr. Caswell was united in marriage to Miss Ruth Hemmick, of Columbia City, and they have two children: Mary Minot is the wife of Basil Brewer, a representative newspaper editor in the City of Lansing, capital of the State of Michigan, and their two children are John C. and Alice C. David, younger of the two children, is a student of the Principia College, St. Louis, Missouri.

Mr. and Mrs. Caswell are not only popular figures in the representative social and cultural life of their home city but have also indulged in extensive travel. Their attractive home in Huntington is known for its gracious hospitality and also for its fine flowers, lawns and gardens, in which Mr. Caswell takes the deepest interest and through which he finds much of recreation.

ANDREW F. GUGSELL, M. D., has not found it necessary to go forth from the boundaries of his native county to find a field for loyal and successful service in the work of his profession, and as one of the able and representative physicians and surgeons of Dubois County he has here been engaged in practice somewhat more than twenty years, his residence being now maintained in the attractive little city of Ferdinand.

Doctor Gugsell was born in Jasper on the 30th of June, 1876, and is the only survivor of a family of nine children born to Matthew and Margaret (Melchir) Gugsell, the former of whom was born in Germany and the latter at Jasper, Dubois County, Indiana, where their marriage was solemnized. Matthew Gugsell was a child when his parents came from Germany and made settlement in Dubois County, where they passed the remainder of their lives. Matthew Gugsell was here reared and educated and here he was long engaged in the retail shoe business, of which he continued a representative until his death, in 1902. His widow still resides at Jasper, the county seat, and she celebrated on July 20, 1929, the seventy-ninth anniversary of her birth. Her parents were born in France and her paternal grandfather was a soldier in the army of the great Napoleon, in which connection he participated in the historic siege of Moscow and was one of the 10,000 Napoleonic soldiers who escaped death in that great conflict.

Doctor Gugsell acquired in the public and parochial schools of Jasper his early education, and in the medical department of the University of Louisville, Kentucky, he was graduated as a member of the class of 1907. After thus receiving his degree of Doctor of Medicine he continued in the active general practice of his profession at Jasper until 1916, when he transferred his residence to Ferdinand, where he now controls a substantial and representative practice. At the county seat he served nine years as city health commissioner and there he held the office of postmaster under the administration of President Taft. When the nation entered the World war Doctor Gugsell enlisted for service in the Medical Corps of the United States Army, in August, 1917, and he had the distinction of becoming a member of the Fifty-eighth, one of the oldest organized regiments of officers in the entire United States. He was commissioned captain in the Medical Corps and was the senior medical officer of his regiment. He continued in service until the armistice brought the war to a close and received his honorable discharge in the early

Sam'l M. Foster

part of the year 1919. The Doctor is now affiliated with the American Legion and also with the famed World war organization known as the Society of Forty and Eight. He has membership in the Dubois County Medical Society, Indiana State Medical Society and the American Medical Association, is a stalwart in the local ranks of the Republican party, he and his wife are communicants of the Catholic Church, and he is affiliated with the Knights of Columbus.

On the 30th of June, 1896, was solemnized the marriage of Doctor Gugsell to Miss Nora Berger, of Jasper, and their one child, Evangeline, who was born in September, 1897, is the wife of Edwin Schlegel, D. D. S., who is engaged in the practice of his profession at Ferdinand. Doctor and Mrs. Schlegel have one child, Richard.

SAMUEL M. FOSTER is a citizen whose loyalty and manifold services of constructive order mark him as one of the most influential men of Northern Indiana and one of the most liberal and progressive citizens of Fort Wayne. To enumerate the agencies through which he has contributed to the civic and material progress and prosperity of his home city would be to catalogue the major number of important enterprises that have been here projected and carried to successful culmination within the many years of his residence in Fort Wayne.

Mr. Foster was born at Coldenham, Orange County, New York, December 12, 1851, and is a son of John L. and Harriet (Scott) Foster, he being the youngest in a family of six sons and one daughter. At the age of fourteen years, after due preliminary education in the public schools, Mr. Foster became a clerk in the dry-goods store conducted by his older brothers in New York City, and three years later he went to Troy, that state, where, at the age of twenty-one years, he and his brother Albert Z., now deceased, formed a partnership in the retail mercantile business. His ambition to advance his education found expression two years later by his entering Yale University. While a student in that institution he was one of the editors of the *Yale Courant*, was appointed to the junior exhibition, had the distinction of being chosen one of the Townsend men from a class of 132 members and was named by the faculty as one of the ten men to appear on the platform at the commencement exercises when his class was graduated, June 26, 1879. He received the degree of Bachelor of Arts and ranked fourteenth in class student honors in a class that originally had 200 members, and is a member of the Phi Beta Kappa.

In the autumn of 1879 Mr. Foster came to Fort Wayne, Indiana, and entered the law office of Robert S. Taylor. His health having become somewhat impaired through his close application while a student at Yale, he held in abeyance for a time his selection of vocation. After giving a period to the study of law he turned his attention to the newspaper business. He established the *Saturday Eve-*

ning Record at Dayton, Ohio, and became its editor. In 1880 he and his associates sold the plant and business, and this paper was the nucleus of the present *Dayton Daily Herald*. At this juncture in his career Mr. Foster returned to Fort Wayne and became associated with his brothers in the retail mercantile business. In 1882 the firm of Foster Brothers was dissolved, when one of its principals, Scott Foster, went to New York City and became president of a bank in the national metropolis. In the dissolution of the firm Samuel M. Foster continued the dry-goods department of the business, and it was while financial reverses were attending this enterprise that he became the originator and first manufacturer of shirt-waists for women. The innovation met with most favorable reception on the part of women throughout the United States, and it was through the medium of this line of manufacturing that Mr. Foster laid the foundation of his substantial fortune. He initiated the commercial manufacturing of shirt-waists in December, 1886, and the industry eventually became one of the largest and most important in Fort Wayne. Eventually Mr. Foster left to his associates the executive management of this large and prosperous business, and in 1904 he became one of the founders and also the president of the German-American National Bank of Fort Wayne, from which has been evolved the present Lincoln National Bank & Trust Company, one of the largest and most influential financial and fiduciary institutions in Northern Indiana and one of which Mr. Foster continued the president until he resigned the office and assumed his present position, that of chairman of its board of directors.

Mr. Foster gave prolonged service as president of the Wayne Knitting Mills, and from this position retired to assume that of chairman of the board of directors. He is now a large stockholder in many of the leading financial and industrial corporations of Fort Wayne, including the Fort Wayne Box Company and the splendid Lincoln National Life Insurance Company, of which he became president at the time of its organization and of which he is now the chairman of the board of directors.

Outstanding features in the career of Mr. Foster have been his loyal and determined efforts to protect and forward the interests of the people of his home city. He has reason to take special pride in the work that he accomplished as advocate of the principle that interest on public funds should not pass into the hands of officials but should belong to the people and be used for public benefit. On this issue Mr. Foster was elected a member of the Fort Wayne board of education, and the splendid campaign that he initiated resulted in legislative enactment of the Indiana law that requires interest on all public funds to be turned back to the public. He thus served as a trustee of the board of education one term, and it is worthy of special note that the interest received on school funds was supplemented by his donating his official salary and made possible the purchase of the site of the present public library of Fort Wayne, in 1895.

Mr. Foster has been a stalwart in the ranks of the Democratic party, and in 1914 President Wilson tendered him the diplomatic post of United States Ambassador to the Argentine Republic, an honor that he was constrained to decline, for private reasons. In 1907 Mr. Foster and his wife made an interesting tour of Southern Europe, and in 1909 they visited the Scandinavian countries and familiarized themselves with the fair Norseland.

Mr. Foster's civic loyalty and liberality have found many avenues of expression. In 1911 Governor Marshall appointed him a trustee of Purdue University, a position in which he continued to serve a number of years, and in 1916 Governor Samuel M. Ralston appointed him a member of the Indiana Centennial Commission. In the Masonic fraternity he has received the thirty-second degree of the Scottish Rite, besides being a Noble of the Mystic Shrine, and he is affiliated also with the Benevolent and Protective Order of Elks and the Loyal Order of Moose. In 1915 Mr. Foster sold his fine home to the local lodge of the Loyal Order of Moose, and then proceeded to erect his present beautiful residence and also one for his daughter, both being situated on Fairfield Avenue.

The civic pride and generosity of Mr. Foster found a most noteworthy exemplification in 1909, when he became associated with his brother, Col. David N. Foster, in presenting the idyllic Foster Park to the City of Fort Wayne, this being the largest, and in many respects the finest, of the city's public parks and its title serving as an enduring memorial to the two public-spirited citizens who made it possible. The travels of Mr. Foster have been made to include a trip around the world, this pleasing diversion having been enjoyed by him and his wife and daughter in 1912.

In June, 1881, was solemnized the marriage of Mr. Foster to Miss Margaret Harrison, of Fort Wayne, and their only child, Alice Harrison, is now Mrs. Thomas H. Mullins. He has one grandchild, wife of Dr. Arthur F. Hall, Jr., and two great-grandchildren, Arthur Fletcher Hall the Third and Samuel Foster Hall.

LAWRENCE R. MILLER, M. D. One of the best-known medical men of Pike County, Indiana, is Dr. Lawrence H. Miller, physician and surgeon, and owner and operator of the Miller Hospital at Winslow. Doctor Miller was born in Pike County, a member of one of the prominent old county families, and the greater part of a life of eminent service to humanity has been spent here. Of studious habit and with scientific leanings, medical science began to make an appeal to him early, and in 1907 he was graduated from Kentucky School of Medicine at Louisville with his degree. Further preparations for practice followed and he then came to Winslow, which

city has remained his chosen home ever since, finding here public appreciation, and the personal esteem that is one of the compensating factors of a life so busy and unselfish as his. In addition to his professional work, both medical and surgical, in his own model hospital at Winslow, Doctor Miller is on the staff of Saint Mary's Hospital, Evansville, Indiana, and is frequently invited to nearby cities as a consultant.

Doctor Miller was born in Pike County, Indiana, February 9, 1881, a son of Peter R. and Eliza J. (Camp) Miller. Peter R. Miller was a native of Pike County, and was reared within its confines, and here he became a farmer and politician. For two terms he served Pike County as sheriff. His death occurred October 19, 1926. The Miller family was established in Pike County by the grandparents of Doctor Miller, and they came from North Carolina. The maternal grandfather enlisted for the war between the states and was killed in action at Perryville, Kentucky. The Doctor's mother, Mrs. Eliza J. (Camp) Miller, died in Pike County, June 30, 1923. Mr. and Mrs. Miller had nine children: Doctor Miller, Hershel P., Noble C., Clarence E., Arval H., Cleva, deceased, and Eva, twins. Maud and Stella, who died in infancy.

In order to continue his own studies begun in Pike County schools, Doctor Miller taught school, at different intervals, for nine terms, after he was graduated from high school, and he took his degree of Bachelor of Science and that of Doctor of Medicine from the Kentucky School of Medicine, in 1907. His interneship was taken in the City Hospital, Louisville, Kentucky. In 1912 he did post-graduate work in the Louisville Medical College. His hospital is one of the best in this part of Indiana, and is well patronized. The people of Pike and surrounding counties, as well as members of the profession, feel that it is a great convenience, as well as a place in which proper scientific care can be given to the patients.

Doctor Miller was married to Miss Bess Barnett, a daughter of Marshall and Sarah (Adams) Barnett, old and prominent people of Pike County. Doctor and Mrs. Miller have one child, Jack Barnett, who was born July 17, 1918. He is a graduate of the Junior High School at Petersburg, Indiana, and of the Summer School of Woodcraft at Culver Military Academy in the class of 1931 and is now enrolled at the Kentucky Military Institute at Lyndon, Kentucky. In political faith Doctor Miller 'is a Democrat. The Christian Church holds his membership. He belongs to the Knights of Pythias; the D. O. K. K., having passed all of the chairs in the latter, and is the only man in Indiana that is as high in the order as he; the Modern Woodmen of America; the Independent Order of Odd Fellows. He holds membership in the Pike County Medical Society, the Indiana State Medical Society and the American Medical Association. In addition to the Miller Hospital, Doctor Miller owns city property at Winslow and a citrus grove in the Rio Grande Valley

Elmer E. McCray

at Harlingen, Texas. The qualities which have won professional advancement and made Doctor Miller a leader in his community have also gained him both the confidence and good will of the people. In the different movements of his neighborhood he is not only a factor, but in many cases the leader, and he takes pride in doing solid and substantial work for this region, as well as giving close attention to his professional responsibilities.

ELMER ELLSWORTH McCRAY. Ambition, thrift, integrity and persistence are the foundation stones in the character of Elmer E. McCray, president of the McCray Refrigerator Company, Incorporated, of which he is also owner, and one of the most prominent business men of Kendallville, Indiana. These above-mentioned qualities he has woven into the warp and woof of the great business he has reared, from the humblest beginning to an outstanding position of leadership, not only in the community but in the entire refrigerator industry.

From his father, the late Hiram McCray, he inherited the excellent basic patents upon the McCray system of refrigeration, and more important still, those sterling traits of character which enabled him to put those patents into practical application, to develop them to such a point that he may be rightfully called the founder of modern sanitary refrigeration.

His capital was the result of his thrift—five hundred dollars saved from earnings during his twelve years' association with his father in the produce business, and deposited in regular weekly installments with the local business and loan association. Add to this modest financial beginning the characteristics, infinitely more important in those pioneer days—industry, integrity, foresight and persistence—and you have the sum of the resources upon which this great business has been erected.

His hand has guided the destinies of the business from that early beginning to the present. He has steered a steady course, holding fast to an ideal of service and fair dealing, both to the public and his employes. The result is a business which sustains one-third of the families of its home community, which has made the name McCray synonymous with efficient refrigeration, and brought a food-saving and health-protecting service into homes, stores and institutions throughout the country and in many foreign lands as well.

Elmer E. McCray was born at Reynoldsburg, Ohio, June 20, 1860, a son of Hiram and Amanda (Reynolds) McCray. Hiram McCray was born in Licking County, Ohio, in 1829, and the wife and mother was born at Reynoldsburg, Ohio, which town was named in honor of her father, a pioneer of Ohio. Hiram McCray and Amanda Reynolds were married in Ohio, in 1857, and located at Reynoldsburg, where he was in the egg and butter business, although a carpenter by trade. In February, 1868, he brought his family to Kendallville,

Indiana, and continued in the same line of business. He was also the owner of a cooper shop, in which he manufactured barrels in large quantities. In the course of time the business so expanded that he had erected a building for storing his eggs, in which he specialized. It was in fact a mammoth refrigerator, holding several hundreds of barrels of eggs at a time. His market was principally New York City, although sales were made elsewhere.

When Elmer E. McCray was eighteen years old his father made him a partner in the butter and egg business, the name becoming H. McCray & Son. Hiram McCray was active in civic affairs and served for two terms as a member of the common council. A high Mason, he was advanced to the Commandery. He was the inventor and patentee on a cold storage plant which was the first to be built west of Pittsburgh, Pennsylvania, and was of a decidedly more efficient type than those made in the East. His patent covered what is known as the side method refrigeration.

Five children were born to Hiram McCray and wife, namely: Homer; Elmer Ellsworth, whose name heads this review; John, who lives in California; Cora, who is the widow of J. P. Stahl and resides in Kendallville, and Lena, who is the wife of H. H. McComer, of Kendallville. Hiram McCray died in 1888, and his wife is also deceased.

Elmer E. McCray, in spite of his remarkable business success, received only such an education as was afforded by the common schools of Kendallville in his youth. He left school when seventeen years old to devote all his time to his father's business, and, as already stated, from the time he was eighteen, was a partner in the business. In 1890 the McCray Refrigerator Company was organized, and, although he continued the butter and egg business for a year longer, in 1891 Mr. McCray closed his interest in that line so as to devote all of his time to what he felt was the more important undertaking.

Since he was eight years old Mr. McCray has lived at Kendallville, and naturally has played a very important part in its growth and expansion. One of the most charitable of men, his benefactions are beyond computation. When the new Lakeside Hospital was built he donated one-half of the money necessary for its erection, and the city paid the other half. In fact, of late years this has become his habit; to donate one-half if the other half is raised, and in this way Kendallville has some very excellent improvements, buildings and utilities far better than any other city of its size in the state. He is an ardent Republican, but has never aspired to or held a public office. Fraternally he is prominent in Masonic circles, having membership in all bodies of Masonry, and is also a member of Mizpah Temple, A. A. O. N. M. S., of Fort Wayne, Indiana. He also belongs to the Benevolent and Protective Order of Elks, and is as generous to his fraternities as he is along other lines.

On June 1, 1910, Mr. McCray was married to Miss Lena Orr, of Atlanta, Georgia, and they have one daughter, Sarah Amanda, who was born April 10, 1912. She was graduated from the Kendallville High School in 1930.

With the organization of the McCray Refrigerator Company Mr. McCray began to put to practical use the ideas which had been finally developed, and he produced the first of what may be called "modern, sanitary refrigerators," so that the company may be said to have made refrigerator history. The basic patents obtained by Hiram McCray and developed by Elmer E. McCray established a new standard of refrigeration, and the leadership which this superior refrigerator gave to McCray has been maintained consistently to the present day. McCray stands today as the outstanding manufacturer of refrigerators for all purposes.

In the factory which turned out the first McCray there was less than 2,500 square feet of floor space. The power was supplied by an old second-hand threshing machine. Today the floor space of the McCray plant is more than one hundred times that of the original—310,000 square feet; the old threshing machine has given way to the very latest equipment of electrical engines. While many changes have been made, and different plants erected, the same site has been retained, comprising seven acres.

The remarkable growth of the company is intimately connected with the development of Kendallville, for at least one-third of the population of the little city work in some capacity or other for the McCray people; and in addition there are over 350 persons employed in the outside territory. Always a public-spirited citizen, as well as a successful manufacturer, Mr. E. E. McCray has held the interest of his home city close to his heart. The esteem in which he is held by his fellow citizens, as well as by those associated with him in business, constitute a significant tribute to his character as a man, to his foresight and ability as a builder.

In December, 1926, Mr. McCray wrote an article which appeared in the magazine *System* of that month, under the title: "After Nearly 50 Years in Business I've Come to Know That——." It so clearly set forth his own business, and what he had learned from its conduct, and from his connections with other enterprises, that it was republished in the *McCray News* of that month. It is for the same reason quoted below:

"'The Decision of Kalamazoo' is the name I have given to one of the biggest of my business milestones. It dates back to 1895. Our plant had been shut down for want of business to keep the men busy, and I had gone fishing—to think. Homeward bound, our train stopped to pick up a car of celery at Kalamazoo—and there in the Kalamazoo yards I found myself literally standing up to a decision which is expressed—minus the expletives—in the following:

"'You control this business and from now on you are going to run it, regardless of what the other fellow says or thinks, and no matter what happens.'

"Just then the switching was climaxed with a suddenness common to railroading of that day, and I sat down—hard. The statement of an underlying business policy that has been a guide to this day was thus fittingly punctuated, even if a neck was nearly broken in the process.

"Successful business leadership demands courageously independent action. Advice and counsel are all well and good and at times necessary; but in the end the head of any business or department must proceed on his own, accepting the full responsibility for his acts and exerting the complete authority of his position.

"Nearly fifty years of active business life teach one many things—at a cost of thousands of dollars. Success, however, is based on the net, and the man who is right more often than he is wrong, whose mistakes are outnumbered numerically, and from the standpoint of effect, by right decisions and proper actions, is bound to attain it. A few men are lucky; the majority win through work.

"We have heard a lot lately about the butter-and-egg man. I started as one. In fact my father, Hiram McCray, founded a butter-and-egg business which served the prosperous and populous East back in 1868, when the handling of eggs, meat, poultry, fruit and butter was much more of a gamble with spoilage than it is today. In those days eastern distributors actually warned against cooling butter before shipping, on the grounds that cooling would ruin it. There was no storage of eggs in time of plenty against months of scarcity.

"Then, if a produce jobber made a few thousand one month, he usually lost it in the next. If butter showed a profit, eggs were almost certain to show a loss. The producer and wholesaler lost great sums of money in their transactions, and the public suffered internally through spoiled foodstuffs.

"Father's invention of a cold-storage plant—the first west of Pittsburgh and of a decidedly more efficient type than those in the East—was a response to economic necessity. In the first place, he had to find a way of protecting his own profits; in the second place, he was concerned over the condition in which produce reached the market of consumption.

"On the basis of Hiram McCray's patents—which covered what is known as the side method of refrigeration—the Kendallville Refrigerator Company was organized. My brother-in-law joined me in purchasing the balance of the stock not held by our family, for $1,350. This was followed by the organization of the McCray Refrigerator and Cold-Storage Company—the McCray Refrigerator Company of today.

"Politicians cannot run an army. The War Department cannot direct maneuvers in the field. Nor can stockholders in mass run a

SAINT MARY-OF-THE-WOODS

business, or a board of directors and an executive committee do more than form and lay down policies which must be executed by the man directly in charge of the particular element of endeavor concerned with those policies. A successful army must have a good general. A successful business must have a responsible and authoritative head. Both must operate on the basis of actual conditions as they themselves see them, and each must be capable of courageous, independent action.

"They told me that it was unnecessary for an executive to go over the mail any more; that reports would suffice. But the mail is a symptom-expressing pulse beat of this business, and as long as I am at the head of this business I want to see it. Not that I want to digest the details of its contents, or to follow through on its suggestions. Mine is a hasty scanning of the correspondence with an eye for complaints; and as long as this business or any business goes on there will always be some complaints. It is through correcting these that we perfect our operations.

"We want our branches and our branch salesmen to make money. There is no advantage of the opportunities offered them. With a salary and a bonus, they sit complacently under the protection of the salary. Practically every concern with which I have talked is in the same condition. They need men.

"The fourth of my fundamentals is that quality merchandise adequately and fairly priced is the soundest merchandise for long-swing progress. Again I must of necessity 'talk' in terms of my own business—we make it a policy never to—and we never have and never will under my direction—sacrifice quality to permit competitive pricing. Our drive is to keep ahead of competitors in quality, and in line with them in price. Today we are taking in many commercial refrigerators on trade at the figure they were bought for twenty-five years ago.

"Quality and price are two major considerations for today's and tomorrow's business men. Price selling should not require salesmanship. Quality merchandise contributes to long-swing success. I believe this to be fundamental.

"During the fiscal year which closed in October, 1926, our advertising department sent out 3,105,000 pieces of direct-mail matter. Over 2,000,000 of these were broadsides directed at specific markets, and 541,000 were letters sent out by our sales promotional department. All this is in addition to a definitely delegated national advertising program which directs so much against the general market, and a definite percentage against each individual field in which we sell.

"This advertising, our general accounting, our buying, our producing are all in capable hands whose responsibility and authority both are complete. Just as long as theirs is efficient, progress—net increase on the records which come to my desk—just as long as their inter-relations are what they should be, and our users are satisfied with what we are selling them, how it is being sold, and the manner of its servicing, mine is a simple task of keeping posted on what is going on and helping where I can.

"They say I am not wont to praise work well done. If a fault, it is one of bringing up. But why should competent operation demand praise beyond the personal satisfaction of having done the good work expected of one?

"There is a right and a wrong way of doing everything. There are also two kinds of decisions—correct and incorrect, There are two ways to go—ahead or back. How to do things, when to do them, and the course to follow are up to the heads of business—no matter what business it is.

"Business leadership—to be successful—means being on the job, developing that job, grooming men to succeed you at it, maintaining high standards at reasonable prices, and operating toward definite and always greater sales goals against which every selling resource, cloaked in the specificness of its particular audience, is consistently and determinedly directed."

SAINT MARY OF THE WOODS is one of the pioneer institutions for the higher education of women in the Middle West. Ninety years have crowned and abundantly blessed the self-sacrificing labors and ideals of the gracious Mother Theodore, who with five companions instituted the school in the heavy forests of the west bank of the Wabash River. Continuous harvests of the fruits of intellect and spirit have come from the original impulse and have given dignity and beauty to the institution as it has grown and developed in an environment which has been carefully adopted as the needs of modern civilization have taken away the forests, leaving enough of the primeval touch of the wilderness to justify the title of the school.

In the beginning it signified a retreat in the wilderness as secluded as any found on the rugged shores of Northern France, from which its founders came. Even now, to quote a writer of recent years, "the sylvan quiet and the religious peace that we like to associate with such institutions have not departed from Saint Mary's, despite the nearness of electric and steam roads, and by natural situation and because of its buildings and improved environments Saint Mary's is the most beautiful institution of Vigo County." The situation of the college is four miles west of Terre Haute and only two hours ride from Indianapolis. The date of the founding of Saint Mary's was October 22, 1840. From a religious community founded on the banks of the Loir in Central France in 1806, and which developed finally into the Order of the Sisters of Providence, came in 1840 Mother Theodore Guerin and her five companions, at the invitation of the Bishop of Vincennes, Rt. Rev. Celestine de la Hailandiere. Saint Mary's Chapel, which they found waiting for their accommodation, was a rough log cabin fourteen by twelve feet. It was under the impression of the majesty of the forest which stretched unbroken in every direction that the name was chosen of Sainte Marie des Bois, or Saint Mary-of-the-Woods. Although Mother Theodore brought to her work splendid intellectual ability, and a mind trained to direct others, she met difficulties that seemed almost insurmountable. At that time Indiana as a whole was largely frontier, and civilization was in its early material stages. For sixteen years she continued her labors at Saint Mary's, until her death on May 14, 1856. The first convent for the Sisters was a frame house which was purchased for them, and under its rude shelter the first winter was passed, the Sisters doing their cooking out of doors. The first school, a two-story brick structure twenty-five by forty, was occupied in 1841, and the first pupil was enrolled on the Fourth of July of that year. Thus was opened the first Catholic academy in the state. In 1845 additions were built to the academy, and in 1852 work was begun on a new convent, which was occupied in August, 1854.

Mother Theodore while in France had been awarded the Medallion decorations of the French Academy for proficiency in teaching. Her early associates were also women of learning and refinement, and thus from the first Saint Mary's was conducted according to the high standards of culture. Mother Theodore was in addition a superior organizer. The Medallion decorations awarded her by the French Academy are still cherished possessions of Saint Mary's. The ideals and standards set by Mother Theodore in these early days were extended to many other cities and towns, wherever the influence of the Sisters of Providence penetrated.

Saint Mary-of-the-Woods was started in January, 1846, as an institution of higher education. The school grew rapidly, demanding continuous enlargement and addition of buildings. In 1867 a three-story brick structure, with accommodations for 300 pupils, was completed. It was enlarged by the present beautiful front of Central Hall, in the Renaissance style of architecture and built of Indiana Bedford limestone. The Gymnasium and Natatorium were built in 1910. In 1913 the Conservatory of Music and the Anne Therese Guerin Hall were opened to students. Le Fer Hall, a residence hall for students, was occupied for the first time in September, 1923. Today Saint Mary-of-the-Woods has seventeen large buildings, situated on a spacious campus, a wonderful parklike environment, with gardens, tennis courts and golf course. The original charter of 1846 was amended in March, 1873, again in March, 1909, and the institution was re-chartered in 1928.

Saint Mary-of-the-Woods is recognized as an accredited standard college by the Indiana State Department of Education and Indiana State University; is affiliated with the Catholic University of America, and holds membership in the North Central Association of Colleges, the Association of American Colleges, the Catholic Education Association, the American Council on Education, the American Association of University Women, the American Medical Association, the Liberal Arts College Movement, and is registered by the Regents of the University of the State of New York.

The curriculum was of a collegiate and academic character until late in the '80s, when a preparatory department was opened and continued for about thirty years. The institution is now strictly a standard college, all high school and preparatory work instruction having been dropped in 1931. The courses lead to the Bachelor of Arts and Bachelor of Science degrees.

AMOS CARTER, M. D., is an Indiana physician and surgeon with more than fifty years of service and practice to his credit. Doctor Carter's experience gives him many interesting recollections of the pioneer circumstances under which the older doctors practiced. There were no telephones, good roads or automobiles for a number of years after he received his medical license. He rode horseback or drove buggies over miles of rough country roads to attend his patients. Doctor Carter for the past ten years has been superintendent of the Indiana Tuberculosis Hospital at Rockville, Parke County.

He was born at Plainfield, Indiana, September 28, 1852. His father, Newlin Carter, who was born in North Carolina, in 1829, came to Indiana at an early date and spent his active life as a farmer. He passed away in 1912. The mother of Doctor Carter was Beulah Hunt, also a native of North Carolina. She was two years of age when her family came to Indiana. The Carter family were Quakers, and both the Carters and Hunts were part of an extensive migration of Friends from the Carolinas to Indiana. Mrs. Beulah Carter died in 1902. She was the mother of eight children: Doctor Amos; Lydia, wife of Townsend Cope, of Plainfield; Mord, of Indianapolis; C. H., of Plainfield; Margaret, wife of E. S. Mills, of Indianapolis; Sarah, wife of D. B. Elliott, of California; Alonzo, who lives at Yorba Linda, California; and one other child who is deceased.

Dr. Amos Carter had the early experiences of an Indiana farm boy. He attended school at Plainfield, continued his education in the Hopewell Academy and spent one year in the Ohio Medical College. On February 28, 1878, he was granted his M. D. degree from the Indiana Medical College at Indianapolis. For two and a half years he practiced at Crawfordsville and then returned to his old home community of Plainfield, where he carried on his work in town and country for over thirty-five years, from 1882 to 1919. In 1919 he accepted the appointment of superintendent of the State Hospital at Rockville, and in this work he rounded out a full half century as an Indiana physician.

Doctor Carter has very high standing in medical circles in Indiana. He is a member of the Parke County, Indiana State and

William C. Mitchell

American Medical Associations, is a member of the Hospital Medical Association, and during the World war did patriotic service as an examiner for the draft board. He is a thirty-second degree Scottish Rite Mason, member of the Independent Order of Odd Fellows and Knights of Pythias. In politics he has always supported the Republican party and is a member of the Friends Church.

Doctor Carter married, February 21, 1878, Miss Elva Taylor, daughter of A. and Mary E. (Griest) Taylor. To their marriage were born four children, and the three living are Bertha, Helen and Charlton. Bertha is a college graduate and is engaged in library work in Illinois. Helen married D. B. Spradling. D. B. Spradling and Charlton Carter are associated in business as public accountants at Indianapolis. Charlton Carter married Rell Scott, of Indianapolis.

WILLIAM CAMPBELL MITCHELL, of Lafayette, is a veteran member of the Indiana bar, having been in active practice for over forty years. His name has been identified with many activities outside his profession. For over forty years he has conducted the Mitchell Abstract & Title Company of Lafayette.

Mr. Mitchell was born in Montgomery County, Indiana, July 9, 1854. The family has been in Indiana for nearly a century. His great-grandfather, Robert Mitchell, served as a drummer in a Scotch regiment, and after coming to America settled in Virginia and during the Revolutionary war was drum major of Captain Peter Bruin's Company in the regiment of riflemen commanded by Col. Daniel Morgan. He was at different times in the Eleventh, Fifteenth and Seventh Virginia Regiments. The war records at Washington show that he enlisted November 27, 1776, and his name still appeared on the rolls in May, 1779. As a Revolutionary soldier he was issued warrants for western lands.

His son, William Mitchell, was born in Winchester, Virginia, June 18, 1779, and at the age of sixteen years he left the parental home and journeyed into the Northwest Territory. In 1800 he secured a position as a helper on a flat-boat, in which he proceeded down the Ohio and the Mississippi Rivers to New Orleans, then up the Red River and into Texas. For four years he lived among the Indians, hunting and trapping. In 1804 he returned to Virginia, later coming to Ohio, where he met and married Sarah Myers, who was born in New Jersey, and had been brought when a child to the western country. In 1833 William Mitchell brought his family to Indiana, taking up land in Boone County, under a patent issued by President Jackson. He was a farmer, and in the early days, before the building of railroads, carried on a freighting business, hauling goods from Chicago to this section of Indiana. He was a soldier in the War of 1812 and was also with the volunteers in the war with Mexico.

Joseph Mitchell, father of William C. Mitchell, was born in Champaign County, Ohio,

March 4, 1817, and while still but a boy accompanied his parents to Indiana in 1833. His early life was spent in Montgomery County but about 1858 he moved to Tippecanoe County. He was a prominent character among the pioneers and during the early days of railway construction was a contractor during the building of the Lafayette & Indianapolis, the J. M. & I. Railways and the New Albany & Salem Railway. He was a farmer and after moving to Tippecanoe County conducted a general store and during the Civil war was made postmaster of Battle Ground, an office he held until 1880. He was also a justice of the peace and was widely known as Squire Mitchell and was credited with marrying more couples than any other justice in the county. He was the first candidate elected in Tippecanoe Township on the Republican ticket. In Montgomery County, Indiana, January 30, 1845, he married Louise M. Kendall, and to them were born ten children. Joseph Mitchell died March 8, 1880, his widow surviving him until October 11, 1896. She was a native of Virginia, and had come West with her parents in the pioneer days.

William C. Mitchell was educated in one of the oldest schools of Tippecanoe County, later attended the Battle Ground Collegiate Institute and on going to Lafayette worked in the recorder's and clerk's offices at the courthouse, utilizing his leisure time to take up the study of law. In 1882 he was elected clerk of court, serving four years. At the close of his term in this office he was admitted to the bar and in 1887 began the practice that has been continued without interruption for the past forty-three years. In 1887 he started his abstract business, which he has conducted in connection with his law practice. Mr. Mitchell was the first police commissioner of Lafayette under the Metropolitan police law, holding that office for eleven years. Upon several occasions he was appointed and served as judge pro tem, of the Tippecanoe County Circuit Court.

For forty years he has served as a director of the First Merchants National Bank of Lafayette, being now the sole survivor of the original board of twenty-one directors of that institution. For a similar time he has served as a director of the Star City Building & Loan Company. He was one of the organizers of the Purdue State Bank and is still on its board of directors and is a director of the Purdue Building & Loan Company.

On April 4, 1883, Mr. Mitchell married Miss Amelia Schweitzer, of Lafayette, a daughter of Eugene and Adalaide Schweitzer. They have a daughter, Miss Roe Mitchell, who finished her education in Purdue University. Mr. Mitchell is affiliated with Lodge No. 123 of the Masonic Order, the Royal Arch Chapter and Council and Knights Templar Commandery, is a thirty-second degree Scottish Rite Mason and member of Murat Temple of the Mystic Shrine at Indianapolis. For two years he was honored with the office of president of the Tippecanoe County Bar Association and is a member of the Indiana State and American

Bar Associations, the Episcopal Church and the Chamber of Commerce. He early became identified with the Indiana National Guard and still holds a commission as captain, issued by Governor Isaac P. Gray, in 1888. He also served for a time as military instructor at Purdue University, as professor of military tactics, and still maintains his interest in military affairs. During the World war he took an active part in the drives for the sale of Liberty Bonds and also did special work in the intelligence department of the United States army. Mr. Mitchell has always been a staunch and loyal Republican, has served as Republican precinct committeeman and was chairman of the central county and city committee.

GUILFORD L. RYKER was born in Jefferson County, Indiana, April 13, 1900. Though under age he was in service with the colors during the World war, and after the armistice took up the study of law and is now well established in the work of his profession at Indianapolis.

Mr. Ryker, who is a son of David C. and Eva (Imel) Ryker, attended public schools and business college. In 1918, at the age of eighteen, he was enrolled with the colors and assigned duties in the field ordnance department of the United States Army. Mr. Ryker after the war entered the Benjamin Harrison Law School at Indianapolis, was graduated in 1927 and for the past three years has been steadily working out for himself a large and satisfactory measure of general law practice, with offices in the When Building.

Mr. Ryker lives in the country, on Rural Route No. 10, at Washington Place. He is a member of the Young Lawyers Club of Indianapolis, Warren Township Republican Club and is a member of the Modern Woodmen of America.

He married in 1920 Miss Mary L. Hawkins, of Shelby County, Indiana, daughter of Samuel A. and Nona (Barnett) Hawkins. They have one daughter, Mary Alice, born in May, 1921.

ALBERT JORDAN. In Pike County the Jordan family have been known as people of very substantial qualities of citizenship for many years. They have been identified with farming, have taken an interested part in educational work, and one of the present representatives of the family, Mr. Albert Jordan, is well known as a banker, being president of the First National Bank at Spurgeon.

He was born in Pike County May 25, 1881. His father, Thomas Jordan, was a native of Lincolnshire, England, and came to the United States in 1852. He possessed many of the industrious traits of the typical Englishman, and spent many years as a farmer in Southern Indiana. He died there in 1909. After coming to the United States he married Matilda Kitchen, who was born in Indiana, of Welsh ancestry. She passed away in 1924. Of their thirteen children one died in infancy

and three when still young. The nine surviving children are William, a teacher in the Oakland City College; Elijah, of Indianapolis; John, connected with his brother's bank at Spurgeon; Albert; Martha, Mrs. Charles Green; Loualla, Mrs. L. H. Burdette; Maggie, Mrs. H. W. Bryant, of Marshall, Illinois; Bennie, a teacher in Oakland College; and Floyd, who served overseas in France during the World war and is now an instructor in Syracuse University in New York.

Albert Jordan grew up on a farm and completed his education in the grade and high schools of Pike County at Spurgeon and Oakland City. His business and financial talents were early in evidence, and a number of years ago he organized the First National Bank of Spurgeon and has been president of the institution from the beginning. He is also owner of real estate and farm land and does business in insurance. Mr. Jordan is a Democrat in politics.

JOHN A. CAMPBELL, retired business man at Orangeville, is one of the most highly esteemed citizens of Orange County. His life has been one of fair dealing and strict integrity in every relationship.

He was born in Martin County, near Natchez, Indiana, August 3, 1860, but grew up in Orangeville, attending school there. When a boy he found employment as clerk in a general store owned by his uncle. When his uncle died, in 1902, the store was taken over by the widow of Mr. Noblitt (his uncle) and was successfully continued by her under the firm name of Mrs. Van R. Noblitt, Mr. Campbell managing the business until her death in 1907, when our subject became the owner and successfully carried it on until he retired in 1924.

Mr. Campbell has always been interested in local affairs and for four years during the administration of President Harrison held the office of postmaster at Orangeville. He was appointed postmaster of Orangeville May 8, 1889, serving one term. He installed new equipment and boxes and other improvements. His successors from time to time continued the improvements. The postoffice was continued until March 30, 1907, when it was discontinued and rural service established. The quarter ending March 30, 1907, showed twenty per cent gain over the same quarter one year back and the quarter ending September 30, 1906, was forty-seven per cent gain in business over the same quarter one year back. But the will of the people for continuing the postoffice was overruled by politicians.

Mr. Campbell is a Republican. He has never married. His uncle was the late Van R. Noblitt, who was one of the very early settlers at Orangeville. In 1853 he established a store there, and conducted it for nearly fifty years, until his death in 1902. A while before his death a look over the county tax records showed him to be the largest individual taxpayer in Orange County. His parents came from Virginia.

SANFORD FORTNER TETER during his active lifetime was one of the foremost business men and merchants of Bloomington, a man of fine commercial standing and high character as a citizen.

He was a son of Newton and Susan (Adkins) Teter and a grandson of Thomas and Mary (Rockhold) Teter. His father was educated in Indiana University and spent the greater part of his life as a farmer. Sanford F. Teter attended school at Noblesville and in 1889 entered Indiana University at Bloomington, taking the full four years' course. After graduating in 1893 he entered the Showers Brothers Furniture Company, and to this organization he devoted the best years of his life. He retired about fifteen years ago, being at that time secretary and treasurer.

Mr. Teter was a Knight Templar and thirty-second degree Scottish Rite Mason and Shriner, was a member of the Phi Kappa Psi and the Methodist Episcopal Church. At one time he was president of the Bloomington Chamber of Commerce, was a member of the Rotary Club, served on the City Council and at all times was deeply interested in civic movements.

Mr. Teter married in 1895 Miss Nellie Showers, daughter of William N. and Hannah (Hendricks) Showers. Mrs. Teter resides at 528 N. Walnut Street in Bloomington. She is the mother of two children, Mary L. and William. Mary is the wife of C. W. Hare and has a son, William H.

ROBERT INGALLS. Among the many industries which are being extensively carried on in Indiana, not the least in importance is that of stone quarrying, which furnishes a prominent item of export and gives employment to a large number of people. A successful and very productive stone quarry is found at Romona in Owen County, which is advancing in productiveness and value under the expert superintendency of Robert Ingalls. Mr. Ingalls has been identified with this line of business all of his life, and while he is still a young man is proving himself an excellent executive and one who can secure results.

Robert Ingalls was born November 29, 1902, at Binghamton, New York, and is a son of Charles C. and Mary (Walford) Ingalls. His father, a sketch of whose career appears elsewhere in this work, was for many years a prominent business man of Bedford, Indiana, now deceased, Mrs. Ingalls still surviving him there. Robert Ingalls attended the public schools of Bedford, Indiana, having been still a lad when brought by his parents to Bedford, where he attended the high school one year. He then pursued a course at the famous Culver Military Academy, at Culver, this state, and graduated at the end of three years, in 1921. In that year he became associated with his father's various interests, principally in mill work and quarrying, and worked at various places, thus obtaining first-hand knowledge and experience. After working for a time on the night shift at the Mc-

Claren Mill he was transferred to the Ingalls Mill, and finally to the main office at Bedford, where he was made assistant treasurer of the Ingalls Company. Leaving this position, he came to Romona as superintendent of stripping, and in October, 1928, was made superintendent of the Romona Quarry, one of the principal and most valued possessions of the company. Mr. Ingalls is known as an energetic and industrious business man and one who has won the full confidence and cooperation of his workmen and the friendship and esteem of the people among whom he has come to make his home. He is a Blue Lodge, Royal Arch and a thirty-second degree Scottish Rite Mason and belongs to the Benevolent and Protective Order of Elks and the Lions Club. His religious faith is that of the Presbyterian Church. He has found little time for politics, but is a good citizen who supports all worthy measures.

On January 17, 1925, Mr. Ingalls was united in marriage with Miss Osie Alice McDowell, who was born, reared and educated in Indiana and is a daughter of Gurney and Iva (Cain) McDowell, the former of whom came from Oolitic, Lawrence County, Indiana, and is now a planerman in the employ of the Indiana Limestone Company. Mr. and Mrs. Ingalls reside in a pleasant and comfortable home at 358 North Main Street, Spencer, Indiana.

JOHN R. ROACH, proprietor of the Funeral Home at I and Tenth streets, Bedford, represents the third generation of the Roach family in the undertaking business in Indiana. He and his father have made up a succession of able men in this line of work, and their experience has included every successive improvement in the practice of handling and caring for the dead during a period of more than half a century.

Mr. Roach was born in Martin County, Indiana, in 1876, son of George and Catherine (Sargent) Roach, and grandson of Isaac Roach. Isaac Roach was a farmer, and also owned and conducted a general store. He is buried at Owensburg in Greene County, Indiana. George Roach was born in Greene County and was a soldier all through the Civil war with the Thirty-first Indiana Infantry.

John R. Roach attended the common schools in Martin County and as a boy went to work for his father in the general store and undertaking establishment. After the death of his father he carried on the business. His establishment was completely ruined by the great flood in 1913, but as soon as possible he put in new stock, and on December 23, 1915, opened his present place of business, one of the largest in Lawrence County. He has complete facilities, including funeral home and morgue, complete motor equipment, including ambulance.

Mr. Roach married Miss Leona McCormick. They have three children, Catherine, George and John C. John is now in business with his father, making the fourth generation of the family in the work. They all attend the Baptist Church. Mr. Roach in addition to his practical experience attended the Barnes Embalming School of Chicago, and both he and his wife are graduates of the Askin Training School at Indianapolis.

LEROY C. HANBY, who was overseas during the World war with the Motor Transport Corps, joined the colors soon after getting his college degree. After his return home he studied law and for the past seven years has made an enviable record in his profession in Connersville. He is now prosecuting attorney of Fayette County.

Mr. Hanby was born at Middletown, Indiana, February 26, 1896, son of Elisha and Matilda E. (Wisehart) Hanby. His father was born in Butler County, Ohio, and his mother in Henry County, Indiana. Elisha Hanby was with an Indiana regiment in the Union army during the Civil war and spent his active life as a farmer and cement contractor. He is a retired resident of Middletown. He has served as justice of the peace and postmaster.

Leroy C. Hanby attended grade and high schools at Middletown, graduating in 1914 and was awarded the A. B. degree at Butler University, Indianapolis, in 1917. After the war he completed his law course in the Indiana Law School, graduating LL. B. in 1922. He was admitted to the bar February 26, 1921. While in law school he was employed at a salary in an Indianapolis law office. He entered private practice in 1922 at Connersville.

Mr. Hanby married, June 15, 1921, Miss Ida Gustin, who was born in Henry County, Indiana, a daughter of Smith and Sally (Hupp) Gustin. They have a daughter, Sarah Eleanor, born August 25, 1922. Mr. Hanby and family are members of the Disciples of Christ Church, of which he is one of the board of deacons and a Sunday School teacher.

He has enjoyed various public responsibilities in connection with his private practice, having served by appointment as judge of the City Court in 1925. On January 1, 1928, he entered upon his duties as prosecuting attorney of Fayette County, to which office he was elected in 1926, and in the fall of 1928 was reelected for a second term, which expires January 1, 1932. He has been secretary of the Democratic party central committee. Mr. Hanby is a Royal Arch and Council degree Mason and member of the Square and Compass Club.

While working in a bank at Middletown he enlisted in October, 1917, and was mustered in at Fort Thomas, Kentucky, November 1, 1917. He was in training at Camp Johnston, Jacksonville, Florida, became a corporal and truck driver with the Motor Transport Corps and on May 26, 1918, sailed from New York for overseas. He was employed in emergency work in Champagne-Marne defenses, the Aisne-Marne offensive and the Aisne-Oise drive at Fisne. After the armistice he was kept in France, assisting in burying the dead

and in constructing cemeteries, including one of the largest in which the dead of the American Expeditionary Forces were buried. He was a member of Motor Truck Company Four Hundred and Eleven, but during most of the time was with the Second Army Corps. Mr. Hanby arrived in New York July 26, 1919, and was mustered out with the grade of corporal at Camp Sherman, Chillicothe, Ohio, August 5. While at Middletown he was an adjutant of American Legion Post No. 216, and has been adjutant of Post No. 1, at Connersville. He is a member of the auditing committee of the Loyal Order of Moose, is a member of the Lambda Chi Alpha national college fraternity, the Sigma Delta Kappa law fraternity, the Connersville Country Club, the Kiwanis Club, is president of the Fayette County Bar Association, a member of the Indiana State Bar Association, and the Commercial Law League of America. Mr. Hanby and family reside at 1800 Indiana Avenue.

ROBERT ARVIL SMITH, physician and surgeon at Newcastle, is doing capable work in a profession which has been honored by successive representatives of his family in Indiana since pioneer times.

Doctor Smith was born at Greensboro, Indiana, in 1902, son of Dr. George H. and Laura V. (Cook) Smith and grandson of Robert A. and Mary Jane (Evans) Smith. His great-grandfather, John Cook, was born in Henry County, Indiana, and was a son of Levi Cook, who established the family in Indiana, coming from Ohio and as a pioneer claimed a tract of Government land and improved a farm. Doctor Smith's father and grandfather were physicians and both of them were born in Hancock County, Indiana. Dr. Robert A. Smith, the grandfather, served with an Indiana regiment in the Union army during the Civil war. Dr. Robert A. Smith married Mary Jane Evans, who was born in London, England, while her parents were on their way from Wales to the United States. Dr. George H. Smith, who died in 1925, became widely known as a specialist in eye, ear, nose and throat. During his career as a physician he practiced at Greensboro, Knightstown and Newcastle. He was at one time county coroner of Henry County, an office which his father, Robert A. Smith, had also held.

Dr. George H. Smith's wife, Laura V. Cook, who died in 1904, was born at Greensboro, Indiana, daughter of Seth and Minerva (Hiatt) Cook, natives of Henry County.

Dr. Robert Arvil Smith has two brothers: George Murray, who was overseas during the World war with the Eleventh United States Marines, and Dudley A., who is associated with the *Indianapolis News*.

Robert Arvil Smith was educated in the grade and high schools at Knightstown and Newcastle, took his Bachelor of Science degree at Indiana University and was graduated from the medical department in 1926. He had one year of hospital training and expe-

L. Wallace Wible

rience as an interne in the Methodist Hospital in Indianapolis, and for two years was connected with the Indiana Village for Epileptics. In September, 1929, he began eye, ear, nose and throat practice at Newcastle, where his offices are at 1205 Race Street. He is a member of the Henry County, District and Indiana State Medical Associations and has kept in close touch with medical science ever since leaving college.

Doctor Smith married at Newcastle, November 28, 1929, Miss Margaret Carpenter, who was born at Newcastle, daughter of Orville and Myrtle (Hewitt) Carpenter, both natives of Henry County. Doctor Smith is a birthright Friend and Mrs. Smith is a Methodist. He is a Republican, a member of the Phi Delta Theta and Phi Rho Sigma college fraternities and belongs to the Newcastle Rotary Club.

LUTHER WALLACE WIBLE. About three miles southwest of Kendallville is located the home farm of L. Wallace Wible, a place interesting for the enterprise of its owner, who ranks as one of Indiana's largest onion growers and shippers. His father raised and shipped the first carload of onions from Noble County. That was in 1887, and onion growing has been a part of the Wible family industry for over forty years. His father set an example which in after years stimulated onion growing on a commercial scale. For many years Northern Indiana has ranked as one of the leading sections in the Union in the production of onions, and in Noble County no one has contributed more to the promotion of this branch of agriculture than the Wibles.

Mr. L. Wallace Wible was born in Allen Township, Noble County, December 7, 1880, son of C. L. and Verda (Halferty) Wible. His father died in 1909 and his mother in 1925. The founder of the Wible family in Noble County was John Wible, who came from Pennsylvania to Indiana after his marriage, and settled in Allen Township in 1850. He married Lucinda Varner. Their son, C. L. Wible, was born May 26, 1852, and lived an industrious life as a capable farmer. He was an official in the English Lutheran Church and a Republican in politics. The two sons were L. Wallace and Roy E. Roy was for a number of years in the service of the United States Government in Colorado.

L. Wallace Wible has always lived at the old Wible homestead. He was educated in local schools, and after reaching his majority he bought the home farm of eighty acres, and he owns another farm in the same township, comprising 160 acres, and thirty acres in Jefferson Township of Noble County. Mr. Wible is one of the recognized authorities on everything connected with the growing, handling and marketing of onions. Part of his land has always been in that crop and for several years his average production has been taken from about 180 acres. At his home he has an onion storage house and owns another large plant for storage purpose, located on the Penn-

sylvania Railroad at Lisbon, a half a mile from his farm. From these storage plants his onions are shipped to all parts of the United States. Mr. Wible is a Republican in politics and is a citizen whose public spirit has led him to participate in many movements for the betterment of the schools, the roads and the general improvement of country life conditions.

He married, March 23, 1902, Miss Minnie Pearl Rimmel, daughter of A. J. Rimmel. Their only child, Orville Ronald, born April 23, 1904, was drowned at Skinner Lake in 1921.

MRS JESSIE M. MAUCK is librarian of the Owensville Public Library and has lived all her life in that community.

She is a daughter of William Henry and Victoria Montgomery and a member of one of the old families of Gibson County. Mrs. Mauck attended the grade and high schools of Owensville, the Princeton Normal, and was a teacher for seven years. She was married to Mr. A. V. Mauck, of Owensville, and has one daughter, Myra J., who is now Mrs. Maurice Davis, living near Owensville.

The assistant librarian at Owensville is Mrs. M. P. Boren, daughter of James C. and Elizabeth (Stone) Pruitt, both of whom were born in Gibson County. Mrs. Boren is a graduate of the Owensville High School and the University of Indiana. She has two daughters, both graduates of the State University, Martha and Alice, graduating with the class of 1929. Mr. M. P. Boren was postmaster of Owensville for eight years. He died in September, 1928.

The members of the first board of the public library at Owensville were C. B. Smith, president, David Wallace, vice president, A. W. Thompson, secretary, R. W. Speck, Grant Teal, Larkin Mauck and J. W. Mauck.

The present library board membership is: Dr. G. B. Brasford, president, Charles N. Emerson, vice president, Mrs. W. B. Johnson, secretary, R. A. Smith, Miss E. M. Gregroo, Mrs. Florence Leonard and Clifton Wheelhouse.

REV. BASIL HEUSLER, O. S. B. One of the scholarly divines of the Roman Catholic Church in Indiana, Rev. Basil Heusler, O. S. B., dean of the Jasper district, pastor of Saint Joseph's Catholic Church, was born at Laufen, Canton of Berne, Switzerland, December 25, 1860. When he was ten years old he was brought to the United States by his parents, who located at Milwaukee, Wisconsin. He attended the parochial schools, the Saint Lawrence College in Wisconsin and the seminary at Saint Meinrad, Indiana, and was ordained to the priesthood May 20, 1883. His first parish was at Saint Anthony, Dubois County, Indiana, where he remained from 1885 to 1898, during that period building up the church both spiritually and materially. In 1898 he came to Jasper and here he has since continued his good work, making the parish of Saint Joseph one of the most important and influential ones in the diocese.

There are two assistants at Saint Joseph's Church, Rev. Roman Roeper, O. S. B., and Rev. Fintan Baltz, O. S. B.

Rev. Roman Roeper, O. S. B., was born November 28, 1877; ordained May 28, 1904, and has been assistant to Father Heusler since 1915.

Rev. Fintan Baltz was born at Nashville, Tennessee, August 24, 1894; ordained June 7, 1927, and has been assistant to Father Heusler since September 1, 1927.

The church property, including the church edifice, priest's residence, the parochial school building and the new Sisters Home, are valued at approximately $500,000, and the pupils of the school have a high standing· in other institutions of learning. The membership of the parish is being augmented in a most gratifying manner, and the finances are well regulated. The parish ministers to 1,062 families and 4,851 souls according to the 1931 church report. Six hundred and seventy children receive instruction in all grades in the Church School. Fifteen Sisters of St. Mary's of the Woods and one lay teacher are required for the teaching staff. The school is of the most modern type in design and equipment, and the newly completed Sisters Home is one of the most attractive buildings of Jasper.

When Father Huesler came to Saint Joseph's the parish consisted of only about 400 families and the buildings at that time were old and dilapidated, and the present splendid equipment is the result of many years of tireless effort on the part of Father Huesler. The school building now contains a large assembly hall and dining room, used not only by church groups but by civic clubs and other groups of townspeople as well.

CARL M. CLARK, physician and surgeon at Oakland City, was born in Southern Indiana and is one of the young men of sound education and ability who comprise the modern generation of doctors in this section of the state.

He was born in Pike County, Indiana, June 5, 1899. His father, Henry O. Clark, was a native of Vinton County, Ohio, and was brought to Pike County, Indiana, when four years of age. The Clarks came originally from Virginia. Henry O. Clark, now sixty-nine years of age, has followed the contracting business for many years. He married Lana A. McLaughlin, who was born in Pike County and died May 8, 1928. There were two children, Gertrude and Carl McLaughlin. Gertrude is the wife of William F. Sutton, of Pike County, living near Spurgeon.

Doctor Clark attended public schools in Pike County and after his high school course entered Oakland City College, where he was graduated Bachelor of Science. He completed his professional preparation in the University of Indiana School of Medicine, graduating M. D. in 1927. His interne experience was gained in the Saint Francis Hospital, and after practicing for a short time at Petersburg he located at Oakland City in February, 1928, and has rapidly gained favorable recognition for his talents and earnest work.

During the World war Doctor Clark was enrolled with the Students Army Training Corps in Oakland City and was given a commission as first lieutenant in the Medical Reserve Corps. He is a member of the Gibson County, Indiana State and American Medical Associations, is a Republican and Royal Arch Mason and is a member of the American Legion.

Doctor Clark married, June 5, 1923, Miss Mary Miller, of Vevay, Indiana, daughter of James D. and Mary (Joyce) Miller. They have one daughter, Ruth Ann, who was born July 14, 1928. An uncle of Mrs. Clark owned and for a number of years Mrs. Clark lived in the historic house at Vevay which was the birthplace of the author of *The Hoosier Schoolmaster*, Edward Eggleston.

SCHULTZ BROTHERS, of Elberfeld, are the millers of that community, carrying on an industry that has been long established and in former years was conducted by their father.

Their father was the late William Schultz, who was born in Germany and was brought to America when a child by his parents. The Schultz family have lived near Elberfeld in Gibson County and has given three generations of hard working, earnest and high minded citizens to that community. William Schultz though a native of Germany proved his loyalty to American institutions by serving four years in the Union army during the Civil war. His business interests covered a wide field. He was a farmer, a saw mill owner and thresherman, and for many years operated the flour mill which is continued under the capable management of his sons. William Schultz died in 1911, at the age of sixty-nine.

He married Carrie Geörge, also a native of Germany, who was brought to this country when a girl. She passed away in 1884, the mother of thirteen children, the last two being twins, who died at birth. The other children were: Tena, Alvina, Mary, Ferdinand, who died in 1926, Rose, Henry, Fred, Tilly, Lyda, Adolph and Edward. Tena is the wife of Henry Bond, and her four children are Millie, Mary, Margaret and William. Alvina became the wife of Henry Schopjohn and has a family of six children, named Flora, Lena, Margaret, Freda, Rose and Selma. Mary is the wife of George Manka and has two children, Esther and Arthur. Rose is the wife of Andrew Flitter, and they have twin daughters, Verdina and Oleta. Henry married Bertha Susott and has a family of five children, Alfred, Leodia, Virgil, Virles and Walter. Tilly is the wife of Louis Dassel, and their three children are Lorana, Cecil and Hirshell. Lyda became the wife of Al Speer and has a son, Melvin. Fred married Nora Susott and has two children, LeRoy and Norma. Edward married Alta Brown and has a son, Glenn. Adolph is unmarried and lives at home.

The firm of Schultz Brothers is made up of Edward, Henry and Fred Schultz, all of them

practical business men, with a long active experience in the milling business. They operate a mill with a daily capacity of seventy barrels, and the output of flour and feed milled from soft winter wheat is sold and distributed all over Southern Indiana and adjacent states.

RALPH N. TIREY, who in 1929 was chosen president of the Indiana State Teachers Association, has been a man prominent in educational affairs for many years and is well known over the state through the positions he has held and as a writer and lecturer on educational subjects.

Mr. Tirey, who is superintendent of city schools at Bloomington, was born at Mitchell, Indiana, November 10, 1882, son of William H. and Nancy (Gorges) Tirey. His grandfather, Joseph Tirey, came from North Carolina to Indiana in 1835 and was a pioneer farmer. William Tirey was a child when the family came to Indiana and when the Civil war came on he entered Company I of the Fiftieth Indiana Infantry and served four years with the Army of the Cumberland. It was the hardships of the war that eventually caused him the loss of his eyesight. After the war, until disabled, he engaged in farming and stock raising.

Ralph N. Tirey attended common and high schools at Mitchell, for one year was in the Southern Indiana Normal at Mitchell, pursuing the scientific course. In 1901 he began teaching in Lawrence County, and for three years was principal of the Springville School. For about two years he had charge of the school at Oolitic, near Bloomington, and was then elected county superintendent of schools. He held the office of county superintendent five years and from 1911 to 1918 was superintendent of schools at Vevay. In the intervals of his teaching he did work in Indiana University, won his B. A. degree in 1918 and in 1927 the State University conferred upon him the Master of Arts degree. He also completed a course in school administration in Harvard University during 1916.

Mr. Tirey was superintendent of schools at Washington, Indiana, for four years and in 1922 became superintendent at Bloomington. The several communities where he has been official head of the schools have set a high degree of appreciation on his constructive abilities. He is in every sense the practical educator, and he has made some valuable contributions to methods of teaching. He has prepared a series of textbooks for the lower grades, comprising exercises for developing the silent reading abilities, these to be brought out in public form in the near future. He is author of a monograph, "The Effect of Acceleration in Public Schools," which was published at Bloomington, and another special article that appeared in an educational magazine is a "Study on Character Education." Mr. Tirey married, September 15, 1909, Miss Io Short, daughter of Rev. Quincy and Alice (Dye) Short. Mrs. Tirey passed away June 30, 1920, and was buried at Mitchell. She left three

children: Alice N., a sophomore in Indiana University; Dorothy, in high school; and Billy, a student in the grades. On November 11, 1922, Mr. Tirey married Inez Bonhan, daughter of C. O. and Martha (Carnahan) Bonhan, of Washington, Indiana.

Mr. Tirey is a member of the Kappa Sigma fraternity, the Phi Delta Kappa National Educational fraternity, is affiliated with the Masonic Lodge, the Rotary Club, is a life member of the National Education Association and the National Department of Superintendent of Schools. He is an elder in the Christian Church, sings in the choir and teaches a men's class in Sunday School.

JOHN FOSTER BROOKS. The history of roadbuilding, as appertaining to artificial pathways formed through a country for the accommodation of travelers and the carriage of commodities, is a highly interesting one. Although the Romans set an example as roadbuilders, some of their public highways being still serviceable, the roads throughout Europe were in a wretched condition until toward the end of the eighteenth century, and in the United States real road construction, improvement and maintenance did not come for many years later. When the movement started, however, it progressed rapidly, and was given great impetus by the advent of the automobile, with the accompanying necessity for more, better and broader highways. Into this question also entered the matter of paving, for no road bed, however well it is constructed, can be considered complete if it is not given proper paving. In this connection may be mentioned the work of one of the foremost paving companies in Northern Indiana, the Brooks Construction Company, Inc., of Fort Wayne, the president and founder of which is John F. Brooks.

Mr. Brooks was born at Dunkirk, Indiana, September 29, 1882, and is a son of James Albert and Helen (Foster) Brooks, natives of Ohio. James Albert Brooks was born in 1857 and received a public school education until he was twelve years old. At the age of twenty-one years, in 1878, he left the parental roof and went to Dunkirk, Indiana, where he embarked in a modest produce business. Under his energetic and able management this grew and prospered, and eventually he found it necessary to seek a broader field for his operations. Accordingly he moved with his family to Logansport, Indiana, where he established a wholesale produce business, with which he was identified until his death in 1909. Mr. Brooks possessed all of the qualifications for success in a business of this character, and extended the scope of his operations all over the state, where he was widely known for his strict integrity and high character. He was a citizen of public spirit, but never sought public honors, and his only political connection was as a voter in support of the principles and candidates of his party. He married Miss Helen Foster, who was born in 1861 and died in 1917. They became the parents of two children: John F., of this review; and Rose, who died at the age of eleven years.

John F. Brooks was a child when taken by his parents to Logansport, where he received a grade and high school education. This was followed by a course at Culver Military Academy, at Culver, Indiana, and he then entered Purdue University. After leaving that institution he was employed from 1900 to 1902 by the Pennsylvania Railroad, and in the latter year became superintendent for the Moellerings Construction Company, of Fort Wayne. Resigning in 1905, he became assistant city engineer of Grand Rapids, Michigan, in which office he remained until 1908, then going to Manistee, Michigan, as city engineer, whence he then settled permanently at Fort Wayne, where he founded the Brooks Construction Company, Inc., paving contractors. During the more than twenty years that this business has been in existence it has carried through some of the largest paving contracts let in the state. Public confidence has been gained by the excellence and lasting qualities of the work done, as well as by the expeditious manner in which contracts are handled. As its president and founder Mr. Brooks epitomizes the successful business man of substantial character, great energy and sound integrity, and has gathered about him as associates other capable business men of Fort Wayne, including L. E. Ginn and Bruce C. Wilson, vice presidents, and Lillian E. Marsh, secretary-treasurer. Mr. Brooks is a thirty-second-degree Mason and a member of Mizpah Temple of the Mystic Shrine, and belongs to the Fort Wayne Country Club. His religious connection is with the Congregational Church.

On February 28, 1920, Mr. Brooks was united in marriage with Miss Emma S. Scheumann, of Fort Wayne, and to this union there have been born two sons, twins: James Edward and Robert Foster, born in 1923. The attractive family residence is situated at 4209 Drury Lane, and Mr. Brooks maintains commodious and well-appointed offices at 1123 Barthold Street.

JAMES EDWARD GUDGEL, M. D. The passing of forty-eight years brings changes to individuals and communities, but Dr. James Edward Gudgel, who came to the pleasant little City of Cynthiana, Indiana, as a young medical practitioner and has made his home here ever since, finds the old-time spirit of the place just the same in fact, though possibly newly named, as was the neighborly kindness that cheered and encouraged him with appreciation during those early days. Doctor Gudgel has been at the head of his profession here for many years, known, honored and trusted all over Posey County for his sound medical knowledge and surgical skill. Like many another eminent professional man, he was born and spent his boyhood on a farm, but educational advantages were not denied him. Following the example of his eldest brother, who became distinguished in medicine, he directed his studies to medical science, applied himself closely, won his degree of Doctor of Medicine in early manhood, and in 1883 established himself in practice at Cynthiana. He is a member of the Ohio Valley Medical Association and of other scientific bodies, and is an authority on some laboratory work, having always kept abreast of the times professionally. He is one of the city's substantial and public-spirited men and gives generously to charity.

Doctor Gudgel was born on his father's farm in Gibson County, Indiana, March 10, 1858, a son of Andrew Gudgel, the latter of whom was also born in Gibson County, in which he continued to farm from young manhood until his death. The grandfather of Doctor Gudgel was born in Kentucky, while his father was a Pennsylvanian by birth, so that the family is shown to have been one of the early ones to be established in this country. Andrew Gudgel was one of the young patriots who responded to the call of President Lincoln for troops at the beginning of the war between the states, and enlisted, being one of the Fifty-eighth Indiana Volunteer Infantry Regiment, and served for three years and three months, when he was seriously injured by the bursting of a shell during the battle of Stone River. While it incapacitated him for further military service, he finally recovered, and lived to reach the advanced age of eighty-six years. He married Miss Alvira Wallace, a native of Gibson County, who died at the age of seventy-three years. Eight children were born to them, of whom two died in infancy, the others being: William H.; Dr. John F., who is now deceased; Levin W.; George; Doctor Gudgel; Elinora. William H. Gudgel was a graduate of DePauw University, practiced law at Evansville many years and died in Washington State about 1919. Levin Gudgel was an attorney of prominence, but is now living retired in Gibson County. George Gudgel died at the age of eleven years. Elinora Gudgel married Jesse Muck, they have no children.

While Doctor Gudgel of this review secured his degree from the Evansville, Indiana, Medical College in 1882, he did post-graduate work in the Saint Louis, Missouri, College of Physicians and Surgeons, and spent one year in the City Hospital, Evansville. While he has never sought political honors he has been active in the Republican party at Cynthiana. The Presbyterian Church has held his membership since boyhood, and he is now one of its pillars. High in Masonry, he has been advanced to the thirty-second degree in that order, and he also belongs to Hadi Temple, A. A. O. N. M. S. Having made his money in this section Doctor Gudgel has felt that it was only right to invest it in local enterprises and realty, and has many important financial interests. During the World war he volunteered for service, enrolling October 8, 1918, but was not called, owing to the declaration of the armistice making unnecessary any further military operations.

On September 3, 1885, Doctor Gudgel married Miss Lizzie T. Smith, and they had four children born to them, namely: Eva, who died at the age of four years; Harold O., who is an official with the Indiana Oil Company lives at Vincennes, Indiana, and married Miss Ada Litsinger, no children; Marjorie, who died at the age of six months; and Helen, who is employed by the Indiana State Insurance Company, is unmarried, and resides at Indianapolis, Indiana. After the death of the first Mrs. Gudgel, on April 18, 1919, Doctor Gudgel married, in 1921, Miss Mabel Stinnett at Mount Vernon, Indiana. There are no children by the second marriage.

Doctor Gudgel is regarded among his professional associates and friends as a man of the highest character and his more than forty years of residence at Cynthiana has been a period of constant and honorable advancement in every relation which he has sustained, as well as in the city itself.

IVAN W. BLASE. There are two kinds of men who make money. Those who make money only, and those who make money and make good as citizens, and Ivan W. Blase, postmaster of Cynthiana, is one of the latter. The first class is worth but little to the country; while from the earliest days in the commercial history of the nation the latter have been mighty contributors to the progress of the people. Postmaster Blase, within his sphere of action, has been as useful to his community and its people as conditions have permitted, has lived and worked honorably, and no higher praise can be given any man. He is a native son of Posey County, born here September 22, 1890.

Through his mother Postmaster Blase is descended from James Whiting, a native of Wales, who established his line in the American colonies in 1617. She was Clara M. Whiting before her marriage, and was born in 1870. The father, Charles L. Blase, was born at Indianapolis, Indiana, and is in the furniture business at Richmond, Virginia. Two children were born to the parents: Fred and Ivan W. Fred Blase was graduated from Leland Stanford University, California, but he took courses in Harvard University, the University of California, is also a graduate of DePauw University, and had a short course at King's College, London, England. During the World war he was in the service for two years, for one year of that time being in France with Company K, Col. Theodore Roosevelt's regiment, One Hundred and Eighty-eighth Division. At present he is a professor in Redwood, California, High School. He married Miss Vivian Benson, of Owensville, and they have one child. The erudition and high scholarship of this gentleman makes him a most noted educator, and his future stretches out before him with bright promises.

While his brother from earliest childhood has displayed a scholarship that was most unusual, Postmaster Blase, on the other hand, showed his aptness for business life, and when he had completed his work in the common and high schools of Cynthiana he entered a local store, and continued as a member of its selling force for three years. In the meanwhile he used his leisure time to improve himself, and, taking up civil engineering, was able to secure a position on the surveying force of the Big Four Railroad Company, and held it for four years. Returning then to Cynthiana, he went into business for himself, handling produce of all kinds, and building up wide connections all over Posey County, and continued in that line until his appointment as postmaster, in 1926, by President Coolidge, which office he still retains. Under his able and businesslike administration the affairs of the office have been brought into splendid condition and the satisfaction with him is universal. In addition to other public work he has performed Postmaster Blase was town clerk of Cynthiana for eight years, and president of the water board. He is a director of the Mutual Building & Loan Association of Cynthiana, and is interested in other local undertakings. All his life he has been a Republican and a staunch party man. High in Masonry, he has been advanced in the Scottish Rite, and he belongs to Hadi Temple, A. A. O. N. M. S., of Evansville, and is a member of the local camp of the Modern Woodmen of America. The Methodist Episcopal Church is his religious home, and he is active in church affairs.

In May, 1914, Postmaster Blase was married to Gertrude F. Taylor, a daughter of Daniel and Laura (Williams) Taylor, and they have one child, Rex Eugene, who was born in February, 1915. From the above brief record it is easy to determine that Postmaster Blase is a man who represents what is highest and best in American citizenship. He has been and is successful, and his success is of his own making.

JOHN JOHNSON, of Bedford, is one of that class of men who constitute the foundation of the industrial prosperity of this stone city of Indiana. His father was a quarryman and John Johnson early learned the trade of stone cutter, and in the course of his experience has traveled widely over the Middle West, but always returning to Bedford, where he is now superintendent and general manager of the Donnelly Mill of the Indiana Limestone Company.

Mr. Johnson was born at Carbondale, Illinois, February 6, 1871, son of David and Ella (Walker) Johnson. His father was a native of Belfast, Ireland, and on coming to America first located at Philadelphia. He was in the stone business there for a short time, and later operated a stone yard at Louisville, Kentucky, in what is now the center of that city. During the Civil war he was enlisted in the Home Guards. Afterwards he removed to Carbondale in Southern Illinois, and a year after the birth of his son John, located at Bedford, Indiana, where he and a brother operated a stone quarry. For a time he was at Indianapolis and later at St. Louis, and on returning to Bedford became superintendent of the Hollowell plant. For three years he was superintendent of the Isaac Davidson Cut Stone Company at Cincinnati and then removed to Louisville, where he spent the rest of his life and where he is buried in Cave Hill Cemetery. He was a member of the United Presbyterian Church. The seven children in the family are named Kate, Edward, William, Harrison, Ella, John and Marion.

John Johnson was educated in the grade schools of Indianapolis, at Bedford, and finally at Louisville, Kentucky. When seventeen years of age he was working for his father at Louisville and his first employment as a stone cutter was with the Bedford Stone Works. His journeyman experience took him to many parts of the country and in 1895 he returned to Louisville and conducted a stone mill of his own. For about three years his business headquarters were at Lafayette, Indiana, and then again at Bedford, from which point he worked out over the country. Among other contracts on which he worked was that for the stone works at the state capitol at Frankfort, Kentucky. Mr. Johnson became superintendent and general manager of the Donnelly Mill at Bedford in 1927.

He married in 1916 Miss Caroline Wallhieser, daughter of Jacob Wallhieser. He and his wife are affiliated with the Church of Christ and fraternally he belongs to the B. P. O. Elks.

CHARLES E. BICKENHEUSER, superintendent and general manager of the McMillen Mill of the Indiana Limestone Company, has spent more than a quarter of a century in work with the great stone industries of Indiana, and his father before him was a pioneer in the business which more than anything else has contributed to the growth of the stone city of Bedford.

Mr. Bickenheuser was born at Bedford, Lawrence County, Indiana, December 5, 1887, son of Frank and Kate (Knorr) Bickenheuser. His grandfather, Jacob Bickenheuser, came from Southern Germany, and lived in Cincinnati, where he was connected with the brewing business for many years. He died there and was buried in the Spring Grove Cemetery. Mr. Bickenheuser's mother was born in the mid-Atlantic Ocean while her parents were on the way to America. Frank Bickenheuser was born at Cincinnati, in 1856, learned the trade of stone cutter and carver, and in 1879 located at Bedford, being one of the first men of special skill and artistic ability to work in the famous limestone of this region. During the rest of his active life he followed that work. He and his wife had a family of five children: Clifford, superintendent of the Strubble Mill; Frank, of Tulsa, Oklahoma; Charles E., Hilda, deceased; and Freda, wife of Leonard George.

Charles E. Bickenheuser had the advantages of the grade schools in Bedford until he was fifteen years of age. When he went to work as an apprentice in the stone industry he was with the George Dugan organization, which at that time was cutting its largest contract, supplying Indiana limestone for the state capitol at Frankfort, Kentucky. After the completion of his apprenticeship he became a foreman in the G. Ittenbach Stone Company at Indianapolis, and after two years was promoted to general superintendent and remained with that organization thirteen years. For two years he was with the J. Hoadley Stone Company at Bloomington, as superintendent of one of its plants. Then returning to Bedford, he took charge of the plant then being erected by W. McMillen & Son, who had just entered the cut stone business. Mr. Bickenheuser had designed this mill, which, like many others in the Bedford district, was combined in the merger of 1926, when all the mills became subsidiary operating plants of the Indiana Limestone Company. Mr. Bickenheuser has been retained as the superintendent and general manager of the McMillen Mill.

He married, November 14, 1907, Miss Nellie Naugle, daughter of John and Mary (Bishop) Naugle. Her father was also one of the early men in the stone industry of Bedford. Mr. and Mrs. Bickenheuser have three children, Robert, William and Esther. The two youngest children are attending school. Robert married Gertrude Book and has a son, Frederick. Mr. Bickenheuser is a member of the First Christian Church and the B. P. O. Elks.

ANTHONY STEVENSON. The distinction of being the oldest individual in active service in any sheriff's office in the State of Indiana was held by Anthony Stevenson, of Rockport, former sheriff of Spencer County, and more recently deputy sheriff. Although he has reached the age of eighty-eight years, this remarkable man is still active in both mind and body and carries on his daily routine of duties with the energy, ability and enthusiasm of men many years his junior. He has led an extremely active and useful life and has earned a rest from his labors, but his spirit and vitality will not allow him to cease being an active factor in the busy affairs going on about him.

Mr. Stevenson was born January 17, 1843, near Huntingburg, Dubois County, Indiana, and is a son of John and Elizabeth (Madison) Stevenson. His father, John Stevenson, was born in Scotland, February 27, 1812, and came to the United States at the age of nineteen years, after a stop-over of one year in Nova Scotia. A mining engineer by profession, he resided in Pennsylvania for some time, and in 1837 opened the first coal mine on the Ohio River, at Hawsville, Kentucky. Later he opened the coal mines at Bonharbor and in 1846 constructed a railroad thereto, but subsequently sold these to Barrett & Triplett, and in 1854 settled on a farm in Spencer County. In 1861 Mr. Stevenson opened the coal mines near Rockport, which he sold to Spear, Ross & Company, of Evansville, in 1864, and then settled in Rockport, where he continued to make his home until his death in 1881. Mr. Stevenson was a man of the highest character,

HIRAM DANNER

V. T. DANNER   MRS. L. S. BUMGARDNER
                      BETTY JANE BUMGARDNER

who bore an excellent reputation in business circles and took a helpful and constructive part in civic and public affairs. He married Elizabeth Madison, who was born in Devonshire, England, and was brought to the United States in girlhood, and they became the parents of nine children, of whom two are still living: James, born in 1844, who is now a resident of Texas, and Anthony, of this review; Anna, born in 1846, was the widow of James Taylor and died in 1930, as did also Elizabeth, born in 1848, the wife of John Feher.

Anthony Stevenson received his early education in the public schools of Indiana and Kentucky, and this was supplemented by a course in bookkeeping at Poughkeepsie, New York, following which he secured employment as superintendent of a coal mine at Rockport, owned by his father, and held this position for four years, or until the mines were sold. He was eighteen years of age at the outbreak of the war between the states, and he greatly desired to join the Union army in the field, but the Government was greatly in need of coal at the time, and Mr. Stevenson was prevailed upon to join the Home Guard and exert his energies in coal production. For two years Mr. Stevenson was engaged in the produce business at Rockport, and then began steamboating on the Tennessee River, being superintendent of the line and first clerk of the S. S. Rapidan No. 1. He then took charge of his father's farm and was engaged in agricultural pursuits for five years, and in 1872 was elected sheriff of Spencer County, holding office for two terms of two years each by reason of his reelection in 1874. Mr. Stevenson, at the expiration of his term, bought a farm six miles from Rockport, on which he lived for thirty years and was very successful as an agriculturist. In the meantime he also engaged in the business of flatboating, and from 1877 until 1887 was the owner of fifty-one flatboats and during this time never had an insurance claim. In 1886 Mr. Stevenson again entered public life, having been elected auditor of Spencer County, a capacity in which he served with the greatest efficiency for four years. In 1891 he was appointed examiner in the department of justice, where his duties included the examining of clerks, district attorneys, United States commissioners and other officials, acting in that capacity for four years. After buying more land he returned to his farm, where he remained until 1910, and then sold his property and settled permanently at Rockport, where he was engaged in the tobacco leaf business from 1906 to 1920. In 1927, his grandnephew, who was then sheriff of Spencer County, was shot and wounded while in the performance of his duty, and was in an Evansville hospital for several months and later committed suicide as a result of mental depression growing out of his injuries, and Mr. Stevenson took charge of the office. He continued as deputy to March, 1930, and performed all of the clerical work of the office. Mr. Stevenson is a stanch Democrat in his political allegiance, belongs to the Christian Church, and is a member of Rockport Lodge No. 112, A. F. and A. M. He owns his own home and other real estate, as well as city and road bonds, and is accounted one of the financially strong men of the community.

On December 16, 1863, at Rockport, Mr. Stevenson was united in marriage with Miss Fannie D. Bullock, daughter of George B. and Emmeline (Druery) Bullock, the former a native of Virginia and the latter of Maryland. Mr. Bullock, who was for many years engaged in contracting and building, was also prominent in public affairs and served at various times as township trustee and county commissioner. To Mr. and Mrs. Stevenson there have been born nine children: Emma, born in 1865, who married George E. Feltman, of Evansville; Elizabeth, born in 1867, the widow of Herbert Wells, a civil engineer, county surveyor and agriculturist; Anna, born in 1869, the wife of Samuel Shoemaker, a farmer of Spencer County; Archibald, born in 1871, who died at the age of fifty-four years; George B., born in 1873, who is engaged in agricultural pursuits; Robert, born in 1875, who makes his home with his father; Edward, born in 1879, who died at the age of five years; Jennie, born in 1880, the wife of Jacob T. Harrison, a foreman on construction work for the United States Government; and William, born in 1883, who is engaged in farming in Spencer County. Most of the family belong to the Methodist Church.

HIRAM DANNER. Belonging to that type of individuals who have exercised industry and native talent in the development of their lives, Hiram Danner, of Fort Wayne, can accurately be called a self-made man. He began his independent career with only ordinary advantages, a public school education and a firm determination to make the most of his opportunities, and through the possession of the qualities noted, along with perception, judgment and quick action, has built up what is probably the largest house-moving, wrecking, raising and shoring business in Northern Indiana, and likewise is a dealer in building material, a realtor and a home builder.

Mr. Danner, the son of V. T. Danner, was born on a farm in Paulding County, Ohio, July 17, 1878, and his education was acquired principally in the rural schools of his native community. He was reared to agricultural pursuits, but he had no liking for the life of a farmer, and when he reached the age of twenty-one years left the parental roof and came to Fort Wayne, where, being willing and industrious, he soon found work and was variously employed during the next six years. At the end of this time, in 1905, he decided on a business venture of his own, and invested his small, hard-earned capital in a modest dairy business, retailing milk and butter to the residents of the city. So excellent was the quality of his product and so industrious, faithful and obliging did he prove himself that he soon found his patronage growing by leaps and bounds, and he added to and modernized his equipment and hired assistants. Eventually he became the owner of a large and important dairy enterprise, which came to be considered as one of Fort Wayne's valuable community commercial assets, and this he operated until 1920, when the magnitude of his other interests made it necessary for him to dispose of his retail dairy products business.

In 1915 Mr. Danner embarked in the real estate business and in the buying and selling of homes. He soon found that it was less expensive to move buildings and residences himself than to hire others to do it and accordingly he purchased moving equipment. In time he was being called upon by others to do their moving for them, and this formed the nucleus for his present large and prosperous business. At this time he makes a specialty of house moving, the wrecking of old buildings, raising and shoring, and the handling of new and used building material of all kinds. His equipment is now thoroughly motorized and his operations extend far beyond the limits of Fort Wayne, where he maintains offices and an up-to-date plant and yard at 2529 East Pontiac Street. Mr. Danner is the owner of several homes and has built and sold many new residences at Fort Wayne. He has been a very busy man during his entire career, but is not merely a business drudge, for he enjoys the companionship of his fellows and belongs to a number of organizations. He has always shown himself a man of public spirit.

On August 22, 1901, at Fort Wayne, Mr. Danner was united in marriage with Miss Martha Barnhart, who was born here, a daughter of C. W. Barnhart. To this union there have been born four children: Bernice, the wife of L. S. Bumgardner, who has five children, Betty Jane, Marjorie Mae, Mildred Irene, Delores Ann and Mary Louise; Irma, the wife of A. M. White, who has two daughters, Ellen Elain and Miriam Lou; Everett, at home and attending public school; and Annabelle, also at home and a public school student.

ROBERT W. RICHARDS. Of the men who have contributed to the prestige and prowess of Spencer County as an industrial, commercial and agricultural center during recent years, few are entitled to greater recognition than Robert W. Richards, oil operator, promoter, grain farmer and public-spirited citizen of Rockport. Mr. Richards has led a singularly busy life and his career has led him into various avenues of activity, in which he has shown his versatile abilities, sound judgment and far-sightedness. Moreover, he has won success with honor and without animosity, and has managed to hold the friendship of even his most determined adversaries in the business world.

Mr. Richards was born May 27, 1870, on a farm in Spencer County, Indiana, and is a son of Robert M. and Harriet (Kerns) Richards. His father, a native of Ohio, was but a young child when brought to Indiana by his parents, who were among the earliest settlers of Spencer County, in 1849. He was educated and reared in the rural districts and toward the close of the war between the states, while serving as a member of the Home Guard, was wounded in a skirmish. He passed the rest of his life in agricultural operations, and died in 1888, greatly respected and esteemed. Robert M. Richards married Harriet Kerns, a native of Spencer County, and they became the parents of ten children: One who died in infancy; Ellen, who died at the age of sixteen years; John, a farmer, who died at the age of seventy-one years; George, who died on the home farm when twenty-one years of age; Hiram, who was associated with his father in farming on the home place until his death at the age of twenty-eight years; Frank, who was a real estate man and died when sixty-nine years of age; William, born in 1866, who is engaged in the real estate and loan business at Chickasha, Oklahoma: Kate, who died at the age of twenty-six years, as the wife of Wayne Martin; Fredonia, born in 1859, who is the widow of N. E. Palmer, a brick and tile manufacturer, and has two children; and Robert W., of this review.

The eighth in order of birth of his parents' children, Robert W. Richards acquired his early education in the public schools, and was reared on the home farm, where he took charge when about eighteen years of age, at the time of his father's death. When he was about twenty-two years of age he began the operation of a grain elevator in partnership with the late P. R. Hardy, and following his partner's death took over the business, which he operated alone, in addition to buying and marketing all of the tobacco raised by the farmers of his locality. He has continued to be engaged in this line of work ever since, and with the passing of the years has acquired other interests, at this time being the owner of large oil interests and much real estate. He was likewise president and principal stockholder of the old Rockport State Bank, and is one of the soundest men financially in his part of the state. He has a splendid reputation for integrity in his business dealings, and as a citizen has given his unqualified support to every movement making for the betterment of Rockport and Spencer County. A Republican in his political allegiance, he has been in no sense an office-seeker, but has not been indifferent to the responsibilities of citizenship, and for four years served capably in the capacity of auditor of Spencer County. Fraternally he is affiliated with Rockport Lodge No. 112, A. F. and A. M., and the Knights of Pythias, in both of which he has numerous friends.

On March 4, 1894, in Spencer County, Mr. Richards was united in marriage with Miss Maud M. Rhodes, daughter of Charles L. and Nancy (Johnson) Rhodes, the former a native of Warrick County, Indiana, who spent his career as an agriculturist. Mr. and Mrs. Richards are the parents of two children: Arnett E., born in 1897, manager of his father's office, who married Mary Guard Kellams, daughter of W. W. Kellams, retired owner of the *Rockport Democrat;* and Lucille, born in 1907, a graduate of Northwestern University, who took a degree in dramatic art, was a teacher in the Rockport public schools, in 1929 became a student in the School of Speech of the University of California, at Berkeley, and is now teaching in the Rockport High School.

MARSHAL H. HALL, who is now successfully engaged in the insurance and bond business at Mount Vernon, judicial center of Posey County, was born on the parental home farm, in Black Township, this county, December 16, 1859. He is the youngest in a family of six children, and was doubly orphaned when he was about ten years of age. He is a son of John T. and Lavina (Bradley) Hall, the former of whom was born in North Carolina and thence came to Indiana when he was sixteen years of age, and the latter of whom passed her entire life in Posey County, where she died in 1862, when her son Marshal, of this review, was not yet three years of age. John T. Hall continued as a substantial exponent of farm enterprise in Posey County until his death, April 7, 1869. The six children were Medora, Lawrence, Edward, Mary E., William and Marshal H., and all are deceased except Marshal H. Mary E. became the wife of Marion Whipple, and after his death became the wife of Aaron Greathouse, who likewise is deceased, and she died in November, 1929.

Marshal H. Hall was about ten years of age at the time of his father's death and was reared to manhood on the home farm in Black Township, where also he received the advantages of the schools of the period. He continued his active alliance with farm industry until 1866, when he found employment in a planing mill. Later he became custodian of the county courthouse at Mount Vernon, and after serving as deputy sheriff of his native county he was elected, in 1912, to the office of county sheriff, in which his loyal and efficient administration continued until January 1, 1918, when he retired. He has since been engaged in the general insurance and bond business at Mount Vernon, and his operations have been successful, both by reason of the effective service and his hold upon popular confidence and esteem in the community.

Mr. Hall gives his political allegiance to the Democratic party, he and his wife are members of the Methodist Episcopal Church in their home city, and in the local lodge of the Independent Order of Odd Fellows he has passed the various official chairs. In the World war period he served as chairman of the Posey County draft board and was otherwise influential in local patriotic activities.

On February 20, 1884, Mr. Hall was united in marriage to Miss Ruth Russell, daughter of John and Ellen (Darwood) Russell, who were born in England and who became honored citizens of Posey County, Indiana. Mr. and Mrs. Hall had three children: John W., who was born in 1884 and who is engaged in the cleaning and pressing business at Mount Vernon, married Miss Nettie Raben, and their one child, Ruth, was graduated in the Mount Vernon High School as a member of the class of 1929. Ina B., born in 1889, the second child, died in 1926. Orvan R., who was born in the year 1900, and who is now city editor of the *Mount Vernon Daily Democrat,* married Miss Elzada Burrows, and they are popular factors in the social life of their home community.

ELDREN E. FIELD. The many industries and large farm interests of Gibson County, Indiana, demand sound banking institutions to insure continued commercial prosperity, and one of these held especially trustworthy is the National Bank of Patoka, of which Eldren E. Field, one of Patoka's substantial young business men, is cashier. Mr. Field is a descendant of one of the old pioneer families of Gibson County and has practically spent his life here, and for twenty years has been identified with the National Bank of Patoka.

Eldren E. Field was born on his father's farm in Gibson County, April 3, 1889, second son of Robert A. and Fanny (Newsum) Field, both of whom are deceased, the father dying in 1921 and the mother in 1914. Mr. Field has three brothers: Elmer, Miletus and Walter, all well established business men and respected citizens. He received a public school education and then spent several years as a farmer. In November, 1909, he found an opening as a clerk in the National Bank of Patoka, and has continued with this financial institution ever since, each year becoming more and more a necessary factor in the management, and in 1920 was made cashier. His sound business reputation and high personal character being known all over the county, his occupancy of his present position gives the bank added prestige. In addition to his financial interests Mr. Field owns a valuable farm of 500 acres.

The marriage of Mr. Field took place April 22, 1914, when he was united with Miss Lillian Stalcup, a daughter of Eli Stalcup, of Gibson County. Mr. and Mrs. Field have two children: Byron, who was born January 11, 1915; and Billie J., who was born January 17, 1917, both of whom are attending school, and giving promise of developing into young people of decided talents. It is the intention of their parents to give them excellent educational advantages, and they are being reared with watchful care.

During the World war Mr. Field was a zealous participant in the different drives of Gibson County, and worked hard for the Liberty Loan and other war securities, the Red Cross and all war organizations, and his own contributions and purchases were unusually generous. He and his wife are consistent members of the Presbyterian Church of Patoka, and active in all of the good work carried on by that body. Fraternally he is a Blue Lodge Mason and a Woodman of the World. Mr. Field numbers among his friends a goodly number of the entire population of the county, as his banking connections have brought him into personal contact with so many, as have his social and fraternal activities. He is a straight, up-standing business man of the type that make themselves felt in any community by sheer force of character, and who always forge ahead no matter what the obstacles. He is honored and respected for his integrity and worth, and his popularity is well deserved.

BENJAMIN FRANKLIN HUFFMAN. A member of one of the oldest families of Southern Indiana, Benjamin Franklin Huffman, manager of the Waterworks Company at Rockport, is a man of versatile accomplishments. He was trained for the law, which he practiced with much success during his earlier years, but more recently has used his knowledge thereof only in the proper handling of large and complicated business affairs. His career has been an active one, in which he has never neglected the duties of citizenship.

Mr. Huffman was born March 16, 1874, at Huffman, Spencer County, Indiana, and is a son of Lemuel Q. and Amanda (Chewning) Huffman. His father was born June 21, 1850, in the same locality, which, named after the great-grandfather of Mr. Huffman, had been the home of the family for many years. Lemuel Q. Huffman, like his father and grandfather, was brought up to the pursuits of agriculture, which he followed throughout the active period of his life, but is now living in retirement at Tell City. He married Amanda Chewning, a native of the same community, and they became the parents of four sons: Dr. Logan, born in 1872, a successful practicing physician and surgeon of Oklahoma City, Oklahoma, who is unmarried; Benjamin Franklin, of this review; John M., born in 1876, a druggist of El Paso, Texas, who married Grace Conner, daughter of Sam Conner, of Troy, Indiana, and had two sons, Harrison, born in 1909, a high school graduate, and John, born in 1915, who is attending high school; and Lemuel Q., Jr., born in 1878, a farmer in Arkansas, who is married.

Benjamin Franklin Huffman attended the district school at Huffman, Indiana, and spent two years in the public school at Troy, following which he pursued a teacher's course at the Danville (Indiana) Normal School. For the next three years he was engaged in teaching school, but finally entered the law department of the University of Indiana, from which he was graduated with the degree of Bachelor of Laws, as a member of the class of June, 1897. Immediately thereafter he took up his residence at Rockport, which has since been his home, and began the practice of his profession. He soon attracted a good clientage and became known as a lawyer of sound and practical ability, which led to his election to the office of prosecuting attorney in 1904. At the expiration of his term of office he returned to private practice and continued therein until July, 1917, when he retired therefrom to

take over the management of the Rockport Water Company, which furnishes power, light and heat to Rockport and the surrounding communities. He is the directing head of this concern, of which he is the principal stockholder and a member of the board of directors. In addition thereto he is the owner of valuable real estate and has other financial interests. Mr. Huffman is an active member in the local councils of the Republican party and is now district chairman of the eighth district of the state Republican central committee, and for two terms, or seven years, represented the board of commissioners of Spencer County in the capacity of attorney. He still takes a keen and helpful interest in all civic affairs, and there are few movements promulgated that he is not consulted upon. His religious connection is with the Christian Church, of which he has been a generous supporter, and as a fraternalist he is a thirty-second degree Scottish Rite Mason, a Shriner of Hadi Temple, Evansville, and a member of the local lodge of the Independent Order of Odd Fellows. He still maintains membership in the Spencer County Bar Association, the Indiana State Bar Association and the American Bar Association, among the members of which he has numerous friends. His well-appointed offices are situated on Main Street.

On June 28, 1906, at Rockport, Mr. Huffman was united in marriage with Miss Alberta M. Kennedy, who was born here, a daughter of Prof. A. H. and Emma (Tennant) Kennedy, of Rockport, where Professor Kennedy is a well-known educator. Mr. and Mrs. Huffman have no children.

WESLEY W. KELLAMS. Among the veteran newspaper men of Indiana, and particularly those who have conducted publications in the smaller cities, probably none is better known or more greatly esteemed and respected than Wesley W. Kellams, former publisher and editor of the *Rockport Democrat*. Mr. Kellams became one of the owners of this newspaper in 1893, and was its sole proprietor from 1898 to 1929, having developed it to important proportions both as a party organ and a moulder of public opinion. During his career he has also been the incumbent of numerous public offices, including a seat in the Indiana State Legislature, and his record therein is one of loyal, constructive and conscientious service.

Mr. Kellams was born December 9, 1857, on a farm in Spencer County, Indiana, and is a son of Col. Gideon R. and Maria (Egnew) Kellams. Col. Gideon R. Kellams received a good educational training in his youth and for a period practiced law, but was more interested in farming, in which he spent the greater part of his life, although he was a capable attorney and could have had a large practice had it been his wish. During the war between the states he enlisted in the Forty-second Regiment, Indiana Volunteer Infantry, and through meritorious service rose to the rank of colonel. After the war he returned to farming and his law practice, in

CHRISTIAN J. ULMER

which he continued to be engaged until his death at Gentryville, Indiana, in 1902, at the age of about seventy-three. He married Maria Egnew, a native of Spencer County, Indiana, and they became the parents of eleven children: One who died at the age of three years; one who died at the age of sixteen years; Francis A., born in 1849, who spent his active years as an agriculturist and is now serving as an attendant at the State Hospital at Evansville; Henry L., born in 1851, who is engaged in the lumber business at Evansville; James C., born in 1853, a farmer, and died about 1925, at the age of seventy-two years; John S., born in 1855, during his active career was a timberman, but is now retired in Arkansas; Wesley W., of this review; Elizabeth, who died at Louisville, Kentucky, April 1, 1925, at the age of sixty years, was the wife of Jacob Lacer, a chiropractor, also deceased; Kate, born in 1864, is the widow of Herbert Rundell, a painting contractor in Newton, Kansas; Fronia, born in 1869, is the wife of J. Monroe Adams, a farmer near Aurora, Indiana; and Martha, born in 1871, is unmarried and a trained nurse.

The early education of Wesley W. Kellams was acquired in the public schools of Spencer County, following which he pursued a course at the State Normal School, a training which equipped him for the profession of teaching. This he followed for some years or until he was elected county surveyor, in which office he served for four years, this being followed by four years as county auditor. In 1893 Mr. Kellams became one of a company of eight men who bought the *Rockport Democrat* newspaper. Subsequently, with Robert W. May, he bought the interests of the others, but after one year Mr. May sold out to Ralph E. Roberts, a well-known Rockport attorney, who after one year disposed of his holdings to Hiram B. Wilson. In 1898 Mr. Kellams bought Mr. Wilson's interest, and from that time until 1929 was sole owner, publisher and editor of the *Democrat*, which prospered greatly under his management. It circulates throughout Spencer County and the adjacent countryside and is a well-edited, well-printed and interesting publication, sound in its views and practical in its policy. Mr. Kellams is widely known in journalistic circles, and belongs to the leading organizations of his profession. He is a staunch Democrat in his political views, and in addition to serving as county surveyor and county auditor, accomplished much as a member of the City Council for a number of years, and in 1912 was elected representative from Spencer County to the Indiana Legislature, where he worked hard and effectively for his constituency and state. He is a Lutheran in his religious faith, and fraternally is affiliated with Rockport Lodge No. 112, A. F. and A. M., and the Royal Arch Chapter of Masonry.

On October 2, 1887, Mr. Kellams was united in marriage, in Spencer County, Indiana, with Miss Josie Burkhart, daughter of Benjamin F. and Laura (Powell) Burkhart, natives of Spencer County, where Mr. Burkhart was engaged in farming for many years. To Mr. and Mrs. Kellams there have been born five children: Wayne, born in 1888, an electrical engineer in Saint Louis, who married Mary Wandel, of Grand View, and has two children, Sue, born in 1917, and Sarah, born in 1920; Ruple D., who died at the age of eight years; Mary Guard, who married Arnett Richards, an oil operator of Rockport, and she attended the University of Indiana, taking a course in journalism, after which she actively assisted her father in editing and managing the *Democrat;* George Robert, who died at the age of twenty-four years, leaving a widow, Madge (Allen) Kellams, and one child, Mary Jo, born in 1924; and Jo, who is a graduate of the University of Indiana and was a teacher in the public schools of Rockport, and later married Dr. Harry H. Alexander, Jr., of Princeton, Indiana.

ENNO J. ULMER. Among the old-established and reliable business establishments of Fort Wayne, one that has gained public confidence is the undertaking and funeral directing business at 1449 East Lewis Street, which is now conducted by Enno J. Ulmer. Founded in 1905, for a quarter of a century it has rendered faithful, considerate and conscientious service to the people of Fort Wayne, who have found consolation during the dark days of their bereavement through the kindliness, sympathy and tact of its members. The present proprietor, son of the founder of the business, is one of Fort Wayne's highly-respected citizens, and a veteran of the World war, in which he received three wounds during overseas duty.

Enno J. Ulmer was born at Fort Wayne, Allen County, Indiana, December 20, 1897, and is a son of Christian J. and Elise (Scherer) Ulmer. His father was born at New Haven, Allen County, where he received a public school education, and in young manhood settled at Fort Wayne, where he learned the undertaking business and in 1905 founded an establishment of his own, which he conducted under his name until his death in 1921. He was a man of high character and personal probity and was held in esteem by those who came into contact with him. His widow, also born in Allen County, is now a resident of Fort Wayne, and of their six children four survive.

The third in order of birth of his parents' children, Enno J. Ulmer attended the public schools of Fort Wayne, and after graduating from high school commenced to learn the undertaking business under the able preceptorship of his father. In order further to prepare himself for his calling he pursued a course at the Worsham Training School of Embalming, at Chicago, and for a time was associated with his father. Later he took an advanced course in embalming at Indianaoplis, and then again became associated with his father, at whose death, in 1921, he succeeded to the ownership of the business. Mr. Ulmer has a beautiful funeral home at 1449 East

Lewis Street, and his equipment, all motorized, includes everything necessary for the proper and reverent care of the dead. He stands high in his calling and belongs to a number of its organizations, is secretary and treasurer of the Fort Wayne Walther League, and an active member and vice commander of Fort Wayne Post, No. 47, American Legion.

During the World war Mr. Ulmer enlisted in the United States army, and after intensive training in various camps in this country went overseas as a member of the Fifty-sixth Heavy Field Artillery, a part of the First Division. The Fifty-sixth experienced some of the hardest fighting of the war, in which it won undying glory for valor and unfailing effectiveness. Mr. Ulmer participated in the battles of the Cantigny sector, was in the Aisne-Marne offensive, on the St. Mihiel front and took part in the stupendous engagement of the Argonne-Meuse, where the Fifty-sixth was engaged in one of the most hotly-contested parts of the battlefield in this sector, Mr. Ulmer receiving three flesh wounds. He remained with his regiment and following the signing of the armistice went with his command to Coblenz, Germany, with the Army of Occupation. In 1919 he returned to the United States, received his honorable discharge, and again took up the duties and responsibilities of a civilian.

On August 8, 1925, Mr. Ulmer was united in marriage with Miss Mildred Hildebrand, who was born at Fort Wayne, April 6, 1900, a daughter of Charles H. and Lena Hildebrand. Mr. and Mrs. Ulmer have one daughter, Lois Eline, born February 10, 1930.

VICTOR LEMME is a native of Gibson County, Indiana, whose career has been associated with the business and civic interests of his community for many years. Mr. Lemme resides at Mackey, where he is cashier of the Mackey State Bank.

He was born in Gibson County September 14, 1873. His father, William G. Lemme, came from Germany to the United States in 1857, locating near Evansville, and devoted an industrious life to his farm. He died in 1915. His wife, Maria Burton, was born in Gibson County and died in 1924. Of their three children Victor was the oldest. The son Charles, of Ogden, Utah, married Ada Shipp and has one child. Herbert, a civil engineer living at Jasper, Indiana, married Kingie Kumple and has two sons.

Victor Lemme was reared on a Southern Indiana farm, received his educational advantages in grade and high schools, and also attended the Oakland City College and the Central Normal College at Danville, Indiana. For fifteen years he was a school man of Gibson County, teaching in various localities, and his work set a high standard and contributed to the educational progress of the county. In 1908 he was given a still more responsible post when elected township trustee, and for the next six years diligently administered his office in charge of the schools of the township and the roads and other community matters. Mr. Lemme was one of Gibson County's leading farmers from 1914 until 1922, and in the latter year he entered the Mackey State Bank as cashier and has given his best time and energies to that institution. He still owns farm lands in Gibson County. Mr. Lemme is a Democrat in politics and is a Royal Arch Mason and Knight of Pythias.

He married, April 6, 1898, Miss Minnie Miller, daughter of Samuel Miller. They have a son, Maurice M., born in 1905, a graduate of the University of Indiana.

WILLIAM C. MASON. From the time of his admission to the bar, in 1885, William C. Mason has been engaged in practice at Rockport, where he has grown in prestige, prosperity and position to become one of the leading lawyers of his part of the state. Retained as counsel by large litigated interests at various times, he has fought his cases, usually with success, into the highest courts of the country, where he has shown a mastery of his profession that has decided the outcome of important contests against some of the most distinguished and eminent practitioners of the country.

Mr. Mason was born at Grandview, Spencer County, Indiana, September 28, 1863, and is a son of Dr. Ferdinand and Ada (Niles) Mason. His father was born, of English extraction, near Little Pigeon Church, Spencer County, Indiana, in 1827, and was trained for the medical profession. He was engaged in an excellent practice at the time of the outbreak of the war between the states, and volunteered his services, being assigned to the Medical Corps as a regimental surgeon. For three years he labored faithfully in the cause, and his health then broke down, causing him to be paroled home on a furlough. Late in the war he rejoined the army, and at the close of the struggle resumed his practice at Grandview, but his army experience had undermined his constitution, and he died in 1870, when he was only forty-three years of age. He married Ada Niles, a native of Perry County, Indiana, of Irish extraction, and they became the parents of two children: William C. and Annie L. Annie L. Mason, now deceased, married the late Liggett Shannon, and they had two children, the eldest of whom, William C., is a rancher in Texas. The other child, Eloise, married Wallace Richardson, a garage owner of Washington. Mrs. Richardson is possessed of considerable literary ability, and prior to her marriage was on the staff of the *Denver Post* for several years, and is still a contributor of stories and special articles to magazines.

After attending the public schools of Grandview, William C. Mason entered the University of Indiana, receiving the degree of Bachelor of Arts in 1885. At that time there was no established law school at the university, but Professor Newkirk, an experienced lawyer, conducted law classes as well as history and it was under his instruction that Mr. Mason received his initial training. Mr. Mason recalls with great satisfaction his associations with

E J Ulmer

several famous members of the faculty under whom he studied, among them being Dr. Daniel Kirkwood, David Starr Jordan and Dr. Thomas Van Nuys. In 1885 he entered upon the practice of his profession at Rockport, where he has since been located, with a constantly increasing professional business. Unlike many of his professional contemporaries, Mr. Mason did not give up his studies when he left college, but has all of his life been a close student, and is the owner of one of the largest and most complete law libraries in the state: He is a member of the Spencer County Bar Association, the Indiana State Bar Association and the American Bar Association, and is held in esteem by his fellow members, who admire him for his undoubted talents and for his strict observance of the ethics of his calling. Politically he is a Republican, and his religious connection is with the Methodist Church. During his long career he has become acquainted with some of the most famous of Indiana's sons, including the beloved poet, James Whitcomb Riley. While he has not been a seeker after public honors, Mr. Mason has kept in close touch with affairs, and in 1896 was a McKinley elector. He belongs to Rockport Lodge No. 112, A. F. and A. M., the Independent Order of Odd Fellows and the Knights of Pythias, and also holds membership in the local Kiwanis Club. In addition to his law practice he is a stockholder and director in the old Rockport State Bank, the First National Bank and the Grandview Bank, and is financially interested in several local business enterprises at Rockport.

On December 16, 1900, at Rockport, Mr. Mason was united in marriage with Miss Gertrude Feigel, a daughter of John and Barbara (Elzer) Feigel, natives of Germany, both of whom came to the United States as children. Mr. Feigel was for many years engaged in the livery business at Rockport, and he and Mrs. Feigel were the parents of three children, of whom Gertrude was the second in order of birth. Mr. and Mrs. Mason are the parents of two children: Alice, born in 1904, a graduate at Monticello and of the University of Indiana, from which institution she received the degree of Master of Arts, and is now a teacher in the high school at Rockport; and Paul F., who received his law degree at Indiana University in 1931 and is now associated with his father.

JOHN WILLIAM McGOWAN, M. D., has been a representative of the medical profession at Oakland City since 1881, and since his father, who was also a doctor, located there before the close of the Civil war the name McGowan enjoys an especially high and honorable prestige in medical circles in Southern Indiana.

Dr. John William McGowan was born at Monticello, Kentucky, January 22, 1854. His father, William Jefferson McGowan, was also a native of Kentucky, studied medicine in early life, and during the Civil war had charge of a Government hospital at Vicksburg, Tennessee, during 1863. In 1864 he moved to Oakland City, Indiana, and practiced there and over a large part of the surrounding country until his death on March 13, 1895. He married Delilah Jane Ramsey, also a native of Kentucky. She died in 1926. Of their four children two died in infancy and one at the age of nine years, leaving John William the only one to grow up. The McGowan family is of Scotch and Irish ancestry.

John William McGowan attended school in Oakland City and Owensville and completed his medical course in the University of Louisville, at Louisville, Kentucky, in 1881. He at once returned to Oakland City, and in a few years had justified the confidence of a people who had long learned to respect the name McGowan in a professional capacity. With the exception of one year he has practiced at Oakland continuously. During that year he was at Deer Lodge, Montana, as physician to the state penitentiary. Doctor McGowan is a very able surgeon as well as a highly qualified physician. He is a Democrat in politics, a member of the Methodist Church, a Scottish Rite Mason and Shriner, and a member of the Knights of Pythias. He has membership in the Gibson County, Indiana State and American Medical Associations. Doctor McGowan has long been a lover of trotting horses, being a true Kentuckian in that respect. For some years he owned one of the best stables of trotters in this section of the state.

Doctor McGowan married Miss Audie May Traylor, daughter of Alvin and Ellen Traylor, of Winslow, Indiana, where Mr. Traylor, who died in 1917, was a farmer. They have one son, Paul, a radio operator on an oil ship operated by the Continental Oil Company between New York, Texas and Mexico. During the World war he served as a radio operator on a submarine chaser, having enlisted for service in the navy in the summer of 1917, being the first volunteer from Oakland City and on one of the first three submarine chasers to reach France.

ULYSSES S. LINDSEY. The career of Ulysses S. Lindsey, of Rockport, has been substantially free from the monotony that often occurs when an individual applies himself unrestrictedly to a given line of work. His activities have entered the fields of education, agriculture, real estate and loans and public affairs, and at present he is publisher and editor of one of the thriving newspapers of Spencer County, the *Rockport Journal*. It has been his fortune to prosper in the varied enterprises with which he has been identified, and to hold the respect and confidence of his fellow-citizens.

Mr. Lindsey was born November 24, 1869, a native of Spencer County and a son of James and Lucinda (Overall) Lindsey, the latter likewise born here. His paternal grandparents were born in Kentucky and took up their residence in Spencer County about 1820, spending the rest of their useful, active and honorable lives in the development of a farm. James Lindsey was reared on his father's farm and received a district school education, following which he took up the vocation of farming, although he also worked at flat-boating to some extent when that occupation was in its hey-day. At the outbreak of the Civil war he and three brothers enlisted for service in the Union army, and for three years James Lindsey was a private in the Forty-second Regiment, Indiana Volunteer Infantry, under Capt. Alfred Myler. He saw some of the hardest fighting of the great struggle and after being wounded in the neck and being seriously injured in the back, received his honorable discharge at the close of the war, and returned to his home, where he passed the remainder of his life in farming and became a well-to-do and highly respected citizen of his locality. In 1866, in Spencer County, Mr. Lindsey was united in marriage with Miss Lucinda Overall, and they became the parents of eight children, of whom three died in infancy, the others being: Dora A., born in 1867, who married Charles Deschler, a farmer of Spencer County; Ulysses S., of this review; Ollie, born in 1872, who married Emanuel Wallace, a farmer of Posey County, Indiana; Lola B., born in 1876, who married Eugene Hartley, a farmer of Warrick County, this state; and John W., born in 1881, an insurance man of Washington, Daviess County, Indiana.

Ulysses S. Lindsey attended the public schools of Grass Township, and subsequently completed a teacher's course at the Central Normal College, at Danville, Indiana. He began his career in 1890, as a teacher during the winter terms, while farming during the summer months, and became well known as an educator, serving two terms of four years each, from 1907 until 1911 and from 1921 to 1925, as superintendent of schools of Spencer County. In the meantime, in September, 1919, he purchased the *Rockport Journal*, of which he has since been editor and publisher. He has developed this into one of the leading country papers in his part of the state and has a large circulation throughout Spencer, Warrick, Vanderburg and the adjacent counties. Mr. Lindsey furnishes his subscribers with a clean, reliable, newsy and interesting paper, which contains the latest national and local news, snappy editorials on timely subjects and important issues, feature matter, etc. It is well printed and well edited and has its full share in forming or swaying public opinion. Mr. Lindsey is a Republican in his political views, and this is the policy of his paper, although he endeavors to give his readers an unbiased and accurate view of the political situation, both local and national. He is a consistent member of the Methodist Church, and as a fraternalist is affiliated with the Knights of Pythias and the Independent Order of Odd Fellows. In addition to owning his modern newspaper plant and equipment he possesses a well-developed farm situated near Chrisney, is the owner of extensive city real estate, and is interested in a building and loan enterprise.

On October 2, 1901, in Spencer County, Mr. Lindsey was united in marriage with Miss Grace Atwood, a daughter of Jefferson and Amanda (Woodward) Atwood, the former a native of Ohio. Jefferson Atwood was reared in the Buckeye State, where he began life as a teacher, and as such moved to Missouri, from which state he enlisted for service in a volunteer infantry regiment during the war between the states. Following the war he settled in Spencer County, Indiana, where for a time he was engaged in teaching and farming, but finally removed to Gentryville, this state, where he followed general merchandising until his death in 1918. Mrs. Atwood survived him until 1921. To Mr. and Mrs. Lindsey there have been born two children: James J., born October 12, 1903, a clerk in the postoffice at Rockport, who married Maude Ritchie, a native of Spencer County, and has two children, Dorothy Ellen, born in 1923; and Sydney R., born in 1925; and Warren F., born October 19, 1908, a graduate of the University of Kentucky (class of 1929), who majored in journalism. He is now editor and business manager of *The Rockford Journal*.

JAMES R. MONTGOMERY, M. D., has spent a quarter of a century in a professional capacity and relationship with his native community in Gibson County. Doctor Montgomery is a man of education, has had a long and successful experience in his work, and has won civic esteem as well as business and professional success.

He was born at Owensville, September 16, 1879, son of S. N. and Melissa (Redman) Montgomery. His father was a native of Gibson County and his mother of Posey County. S. N. Montgomery followed farming all his active life. He died in 1916 and his wife in 1913. There were five children: Essie, wife of C. M. Wilkenson, and mother of one child; Otis L., unmarried, living at Owensville; Dr. James R.; Ruby, wife of Willis E. Roe, of East Chicago, and they have a family of three girls; and David, a doctor of dental surgery at Owensville, married Ethel Williams and has three children.

James R. Montgomery attended the grade and high schools of Owensville, graduated Bachelor of Science from Valparaiso University, and in 1904 took his medical degree at the College of Physicians and Surgeons of the University of Illinois. He at once returned home and has steadily practiced at Owensville for a quarter of a century. For four years he held a commission in the Reserve Corps of the United States Navy.

Doctor Montgomery is a member of the Gibson County, Indiana State and American Medical Associations. He is a director of the old State Bank of Owensville, is a Republican, a Presbyterian and a York Rite Mason and Shriner. His father was a Union soldier, being a member of Company F of the Eightieth Indiana Volunteers, and was wounded in the battle of Perryville, Kentucky.

Doctor Montgomery married in August, 1905, Miss Cora A. Knowles, daughter of I. N. and Martha (Cantrell) Knowles. Both her

Arthur D. Sayler

parents were born in Gibson County. They have one child, Arvid N., born August 11, 1909, a graduate from Purdue University at Lafayette, Indiana, in the class of 1930. He is now associated with the American Telephone & Telegraph Company at New York City, in the research and development laboratory.

ARTHUR DAILY SAYLER. Although he began his career as a newspaper man and life insurance salesman, Arthur Daily Sayler has been engaged in the practice of law at Huntington since 1920 and has gained a high standing in his profesion. He is a lawyer by inheritance and training, by experience and by native ability, and since applying himself to this vocation has, through industry and application, drawn to himself a large and representative clientele and has been identified with much important litigation that has come before the courts.

Mr. Sayler was born at Huntington, Huntington County, Indiana, January 18, 1894, and is a son of the late Hon. Samuel M. Sayler, whose death occurred April 12, 1920. Mr. Sayler's mother is still living and a resident of Huntington. Arthur Daily Sayler attended the grade schools of Huntington, and after spending three years in high school, completed his high school course at Phillips-Andover Academy, Andover, Massachusetts, in 1911. He next attended Oberlin College, Oberlin, Ohio, and received the degree of Bachelor or Arts from Beloit (Wisconsin) College in 1915, after which he pursued his law course at the Indiana Law School, Indianapolis, Indiana, and was graduated with the degree of Bachelor of Laws in 1917.

From 1917 until 1920 Mr. Sayler was identified with the Indianapolis News and with the Travelers Insurance Company for two years, but at the time of his father's death returned to Huntington, where he has since been engaged in the practice of his profession, having taken over his father's clientele and added greatly thereto, his offices being situated in the Citizens State Bank Building. He has won recognition as a sound, reliable and practical lawyer, and is well grounded in principles and precedents, being a constant student, well versed in all branches of his profession. During 1925 and 1926 he served as prosecuting attorney of Huntington County, and discharged the duties of that office in a highly capable manner. He is a member of the Huntington County Bar Association, the Indiana State Bar Association, and the American Bar Association, and in his profession is respected for his adherence to the best ethics and tenets of his calling. He belongs also to the La Fontaine Country Club, the Benevolent and Protective Order of Elks and the Knights of Pythias, and is an Episcopalian in his religious faith. Mr. Sayler has one brother, Oliver M., a resident of New York City.

On December 30, 1915, at Minneapolis, Minnesota, Mr. Sayler was united in marriage with Miss Helen Knight Stout, who was born at Minneapolis and is a graduate Bachelor of Arts of Beloit (Wisconsin) College, class of 1915. She is a daughter of the late William O. Stout, and her mother still survives and is a resident of Idaho. Mrs. Sayler, who is a woman of superior intellect and talents, taught school in Indianapolis and Huntington for several years after her marriage. Mrs. Sayler is active in church and charitable work and is popular in club circles of the city. She and Mr. Sayler had one daughter, Mary Knight, who died at birth, November 12, 1927. They have an adopted son, David Knight who was born June 7, 1929.

GUY H. WALKER, for nine years postmaster at Rockport, Indiana, and for many years one of the prominent business men of the city, is a member of one of the old and substantial families of Spencer County. His grandfather, Richard A. Walker, Sr., operated flatboats on the Ohio River and was also in business in Rockport. Guy H. Walker's father, the late John H. Walker, who was commercially inclined, founded solid business enterprises at Rockport, his native city, and later was elected its first mayor. After completing his educational training Guy H. Walker went through a period of business instruction under his father that served to equip him for a responsible position in the far West, but in 1904 he returned to Rockport, where his unusual capacity for business soon became evident and public approval rested upon his undertakings. Politically active in the Republican party, he has been tendered many positions of responsibility, but has never accepted any public office except that of postmaster, although few matters of civic importance at Rockport are completed without his judgment being consulted.

Guy H. Walker was born at Rockport, Indiana, October 29, 1875, and is a son of John H. and Ida (Bodenhamer) Walker. John H. Walker was born at Rockport, where he received a public school education and for many years was engaged in the grocery business, in which he met with success and prosperity because of the possession of good judgment, industry and sound ability. He was one of his community's most active citizens in public affairs, serving as Rockport's first mayor and as president of the City Council, and establishing a splendid record for high and valuable public service. In his death, which occurred February 17, 1929, his community lost one of its most public-spirited citizens. Mr. Walker married Miss Ida Bodenhamer, who was born in Ohio, and was brought as a child by her parents to Rockport, where she graduated from the public high school and subsequently took a college course. She and her husband were the parents of two children, of whom one died in infancy.

Guy H. Walker received his early education at Rockport, and following his graduation from high school was sent to the New York State Military Academy, at Cornwall, New York, from which he was graduated as a member of the class of 1894. Returning then to Rockport, he was for a time associated with his father in the grocery business, in 1902 going to California to represent the firm of Bishop & Company. In 1904 he again returned to Rockport, where he was engaged in the wholesale confectionery business until 1923, when he was appointed acting postmaster, and January 23, 1924, was appointed postmaster, a position he held until November, 1930. He proved himself a capable and conscientious public official and during his administration instituted a number of reforms and improvements that have elevated the standard of the mail service at Rockport. Mr. Walker is also the directing head of the grocery business which was founded by his father, and continues to operate a confectionery store, being known as one of the substantial and capable business men of his community. Mr. Walker is a staunch Republican and in Methodist circles is a generous contributor to all religious movements and a consistent attendant at services.

On May 11, 1904, at Rockport, Mr. Walker was united in marriage with Miss Elinor Sibert, a daughter of Thomas and Hannah (Garrison) Sibert, the former a native of Indiana and a flour mill owner, and the latter a native of Ohio. Mrs. Walker had one brother, who died while serving in the American army during the World war, and a sister, who survives. Mr. and Mrs. Walker have two children: John H. S., born August 2, 1905; and Mary Garrison, born February 1, 1914. Mrs. Walker has been very prominent in public affairs, and for two terms was chairman of the Republican First District Committee. She is also a competent business woman and a stockholder in two leading banks of Rockport.

FREDERICK WILLIAM PELZER had been a resident of Warrick County more than sixty years when death put its seal on his mortal lips, and here he had lived and wrought to worthy ends, had proved a citizen of influence, had identified himself with productive farm industry, and had in earlier years followed his trade, that of blacksmith. He was born at Osnabruck, Kingdom of Hanover, Germany, October 10, 1843, and his death occurred at his home in Boonville, Indiana, November 9, 1923, so that his life span had covered a period of over eighty years.

Mr. Pelzer received the advantages of the schools of his native place and also served an apprenticeship in the blacksmith shop of his father. In 1859, after the death of his parents, he came to the United States, accompanied by his youngest brother, Hon. Clamor Pelzer, to whom a memoir is dedicated on other pages of this publication. Mr. Pelzer was about sixteen years of age when he thus came to this country, where he and his brother, then a lad of seven years, landed in the port of New Orleans, Louisiana, whence in the following year they came to Warrick County, Indiana, where both remained until their death. On his arrival in Warrick County Mr. Pelzer found employment on the farm of a man named Stone, near Boonville, and in addition to his service on the farm he worked also at his trade, that of blacksmith. The passing years rewarded his earnest and honest endeavors with substantial prosperity, and at the time of his death he was the owner of valuable farm property in both Warrick and Pike counties, as well as real estate in Boonville, including the attractive home in which he passed the closing years of his life and in which two of his daughters still reside.

Unqualified was the loyalty of Mr. Pelzer to the land and state of his adoption, and he was known and valued as one of the liberal and progressive citizens of Warrick County. He was influential in public affairs of local order, was a stalwart supporter of the cause of the Republican party, was affiliated with the Masonic fraternity, and he and his wife, who preceded him to eternal rest, were earnest members of the Methodist Episcopal Church.

At Boonville, on the 9th of June, 1872, Mr. Pelzer was united in marriage to Miss Amelia Goettlich, who was born on Long Island, New York, and whose parents soon afterward came to Indiana and established their home in Warrick County, where they passed the remainder of their lives. Mrs. Pelzer was a daughter of Charles and Charlotte (Zohner) Goettlich, who were born and reared in Germany and who thence came to the United States soon after their marriage. Of the eleven children of Mr. and Mrs. Pelzer Marie died in infancy, and Elizabeth at the age of fourteen years. Charles, who died at the age of fifty years, a bachelor, was associated with his father in the hardware and plumbing business at Boonville at the time of his death. William, who died in March, 1928, virtually sacrificed his life on the alter of patriotism, as his death was the direct sequel of his loyal overseas service in the World war, he having been a member of a machine-gun battery of the American Expeditionary Forces in France, where he was in active service six and one-half months. On the voyage to France Mr. Pelzer responded to a marine night call and in the darkness fell and injured one of his eyes. A tumor formed back of the eye and he became blind after his return to his home, the injury having been the direct cause of his death, which occurred March 24, 1928. He was engaged in the hardware business at Vincennes at the time of his death, was a bachelor, and his sisters Emma and Freda were the chief beneficiaries of his estate. These sisters inherited also farms owned by their father, and these various properties they rent to desirable tenants. Emma, eldest of the surviving children, resides with her sister Freda and their bachelor brother Ernest in the attractive home at Boonville, where Ernest is successfully engaged in the gents furnishings business. Gertrude is the wife of John Wilke, who is a civil engineer and as such is in Government service in Washington, D. C. They have no children. Miss Clemintine is employed in the Government treasury department in Washington, D. C. Ernest, the one surviving son, is a representative business man of Boonville, as previously noted. Helen is the wife of Eurah Day, who is engaged in the grocery business in the village of Pelzer, Warrick County, a place named in honor of her father and his brother Clamor, the latter of whom was one of the most substantial capitalists of the county at the time of his death and a former member of the State Senate. Mr. and Mrs. Day have four children, whose names and respective ages, in 1929, are here recorded: Charles, twenty-one years; George, seventeen years; Dorothy, fifteen years; and Charlotte, eleven years. Blanche, next younger of the children, is the wife of William Veeck, who is an insurance man at Charleston, Illinois, and they have no children. Miss Freda is the youngest of the children and resides with her brother Ernest and sister Emma in their pleasant home at Boonville, as previously stated in this memoir to their honored father.

WILLIAM STILLWELL ENNES, former mayor of the City of Princeton, Gibson County, has lived all his life in that section of Indiana, and always in close touch with its educational, commercial and civic interests and welfare.

He was born in Gibson County, November 28, 1862, and his parents, Embree E. and Martha J. (Kirk) Ennes, were natives of the same county. He was their only child. His father died while serving in Company B of the Sixty-fifth Indiana Infantry during the Civil war. The widowed mother survived for many years, passing away at the age of eighty-four on September 10, 1927. It is interesting to note that Mr. Ennes' maternal grandmother died in 1925, at the extraordinary age of 104 years, having been born in 1821.

William Stillwell Ennes attended public schools in Gibson County, completed the teachers' course in the Indiana Central Normal College at Danville, and immediately began teaching in Gibson County. After three years he entered the grocery business, and in 1889 became deputy county treasurer. In 1898 he was elected deputy county treasurer, serving two terms. After the close of his second term, in 1905, he resumed his active connection with the grocery business, but since 1914 his business energies have been chiefly taken up by his farm interests in Gibson County.

Mr. Ennes was elected mayor of Princeton in November, 1925, serving four years, to 1930, and set a fine example of able and systematic management of the municipal affairs. He is a Republican in politics, a member of the Methodist Episcopal Church, is president of the Community Club and is a Scottish Rite Mason.

Mr. Ennes married in November, 1889, Miss Lucy Kightly, daughter of Josiah and Sarah J. (Roe) Kightly. Her father was born in England and came to Gibson County many years ago. Mr. and Mrs. Ennes had a family of four children: V. Dale, born in 1891, now living at Columbus, Indiana, married Florence Nicholson and has a daughter, Jeanne; Darle,

born in 1893, lives at South Bend, Indiana; Raymond died in infancy; and Lowell K., born in 1907, graduated from DePauw University with the A. B. degree in 1929, and is now associated with the General Electric Company at Fort Wayne, Indiana.

MRS. ANNA M. ALLEN, the loyal, efficient and popular librarian of the public library in the attractive little City of Newburg, Warrick County, was born and reared in this community, where her venerable father, Frederick Frank, now lives virtually retired, he being the oldest male citizen not only of Newburg but also of the township in which the village is located. He will be ninety-one years of age on October 21, 1931.

Frederick Frank was born in the vicinity of the City of Berlin, Germany, and was a youth when he came to the United States, he having become a resident of Warrick County, Indiana, a number of years prior to the outbreak of the Civil war, and his loyalty to the land of his adoption having been significantly shown in his service as a valiant soldier of the Union during virtually the entire period of that great conflict. He served in the command of General Ulysses S. Grant and later in that of General William T. Sherman, with whose forces he participated in the historic march from Atlanta to the sea. Among the early engagements in which he took part was the battle of Shiloh. He was one of nine men who simultaneously enlisted from the vicinity of Newburg, and all the others of the number met their death in battle. He was a member of the Twenty-fifth Indiana Volunteer Infantry and with that command lived up to the full tension of conflict in the many engagements in which it was involved. He is now one of the comparatively few remaining members of the Grand Army of the Republic in his home community. After the close of the war Mr. Frank engaged in the dry goods business at Newburg, and this old-established enterprise is now conducted under the management of his daughters. Though he still figures as its head, he has lived retired from active business during the past several years. He is one of the veteran business men and honored and influential citizens of Newburg and is the oldest living member of the local Evangelical Church. His wife, whose maiden name was Margaret Nester, likewise was born in Germany, and she also is a devoted member of the Evangelical Church. Of the six children three are living, two having died in infancy and Frederick, Jr., having died at the age of ten years. Misses Elizabeth and Lena remain with their venerable father in the old home at Newburg and have the active management of his mercantile establishment.

Mrs. Anna (Frank) Allen received her early education by attending the Newburg public schools and was a member of the first class to be graduated in the high school in the City of Newburg. She later took extension work in Evansville College, and has taken a summer library course in the City of Indianapolis since assuming her present position, that of librarian of the Newburg Public Library. Mrs. Allen is one of the influential women representatives of the Republican party in her native community and has been vice chairman of the party committee of Warrick County. She is a zealous member of the Presbyterian Church at Newburg, and is active in its Ladies Aid Society and its Missionary Society. She is an influential member of the Newburg History Club and has much of leadership in the social and cultural life of her home community. She has been deeply interested in the affairs of the Newburg Public Library from the time of its organization, in 1907, and her service as its librarian has been notably loyal and constructive. She is a member of the County and District Historical Societies and a member of the district library staff. Mrs. Allen has retained ownership of the home farm near Newburg since the death of her husband, in 1923.

March 28, 1905, marked the marriage of James L. Allen and Anna M. Frank, and the gracious marital bonds were severed by the death of Mr. Allen, March 18, 1923. He was born in Vanderburg County, Indiana, and a few weeks later his parents, Mr. and Mrs. Augustus Allen, who had come from Ohio to Indiana, removed to Warrick County, where they passed the remainder of their lives on their old home farm. James L. Allen was reared and educated in Warrick County and was one of the substantial and progressive farmers of this county at the time of his death, his civic loyalty having been significantly shown when he effected the construction of the first improved road of modern order in Ohio Township. Margaret Jane, elder of the two children of Mr. and Mrs. Allen, was born in the year 1908 and is now the wife of Floyd E. Long, a prosperous young farmer in Vanderburg County, their one child, Charles Allen Long, having been born July 31, 1928. Virginia, the younger daughter, was born in 1914 and remains with her widowed mother, she being a student in the Newburg High School in the class of 1932, after which she plans to attend Evansville College.

ERNEST C. PURDUE. In his administration as postmaster of Newburg, Warrick County, Mr. Purdue is giving effective and popular communal service in the attractive little city in which he was born and reared and in which he still resides in the family homestead that was the place of his birth, the date of his nativity having been March 28, 1885, and he being a representative, in the third generation, of one of the old, influential and honored families of this county.

Samuel D. Purdue, father of the Newburg postmaster, likewise was born and reared in this town. A man of fine intellectuality and distinctive civic loyalty, he gave forty-three years of service as a teacher in the public schools, and during thirty-five of these years he held the office of superintendent of the Newburg public schools. His was large and benig-

nant influence in training the youth of his native county, and here his name and memory are held in lasting honor, his death having occurred May 7, 1922. He gave six years of service as township trustee and was the incumbent of this office at the time of his death. His brothers Jarrott and William went forth as gallant young soldiers of the Union in the Civil war, and in that conflict the former sacrificed his life in battle. Mrs. Mary E. (Castle) Purdue, widow of Samuel D., still maintains her home at Newburg, where she was born and reared and where she is held in affectionate regard by all who have come within the compass of her gracious influence. She is a devoted member of the Methodist Episcopal Church, as was also her husband, and he was a Republican in political adherency. Of the seven children Dora died at the age of eighteen years; Grace is the wife of H. H. Stone, who is engaged in the dairy business in the City of Louisville, Kentucky; Ernest C., of this review, was next in order of birth; Nettie died at the age of fourteen years; Bertha is teaching in the public schools of Newburg, she being the wife of William Seybold, who is a farmer in this county, and their one child being a daughter, Grace Mary; Bernice is the wife of Armstrong Forster, who is engaged in the plumbing business in the City of Evansville, and they have two children, Hugh and Rodger; Samuel, the youngest of the children, is a salesman in the employ of a New York book-publishing concern, he having married Miss Marie Cann, of Frankfort, Indiana, and their one child being a son, John.

In the Newbury public schools Ernest C. Purdue continued his studies until he was graduated in the high school, as a member of the class of 1902. He soon afterward entered the employ of a telephone company, and by study and practical experience he became in time a skilled electrical engineer. He was manager of a local telephone company one year, and thereafter passed a year as an electrician in a leading shipyard in Chicago. He then returned to Newburg and became shipping clerk for the Ryan-Hampton Tobacco Company, with which he remained two years. His impaired health then led him to pass six months on a western ranch, where his vigorous activities enabled him to recuperate his physical powers. Upon his return to his native place he here assumed the position of assistant engineer with the Tennis Construction Company, with which concern he continued his service as a civil engineer nine years. During the ensuing fifteen years he was identified with the coal mining industry in this section of Indiana, and in 1922 he was appointed postmaster of Newburg, he having been reappointed in 1926 and again in 1930, and thus being in his eighth year of consecutive service in this office, in which his administration has been signally efficient and popularly satisfactory.

Mr. Purdue is a stalwart in the local cohorts of the Republican party, he is affiliated with the Independent Order of Odd Fellows, and in

Wm Fisher & Wife

their home community he and his wife are zealous members of the Methodist Episcopal Church, of which he is a trustee.

April 23, 1908, marked the marriage of Mr. Purdue to Miss Myrtle Vonderscher, daughter of Frank and India (Dodds) Vonderscher, of Newburg, and of the nine children of this union all are living except Bernard, who died at the age of three years. The names and respective dates of birth of the other children are here recorded: Bertha, born July 25, 1910, is serving with her father as assistant postmaster; Harold, March 23, 1914, will graduate from high school with the class of 1932; Kenneth, born May 15, 1916; is in the high school class of 1934; William Samuel (better known as Bill Sam), was born April 6, 1918; Mary, March 25, 1920; Paul, December 23, 1921; Bernice, April 18, 1924; and Jack, May 8, 1925.

WILLIAM FRANKLIN FISHER has been long and prominently identified with the textile industry and is now president of the Columbia City Woolen Mills, at the judicial center of Whitley County, he having been the virtual founder of this concern and having developed it into one of the great textile manufacturing corporations of Indiana, besides which he has become a prominent figure in farm enterprise in Whitley County, with special attention given to dairy farming. Here he has three finely improved farms, with respective areas of 270, 160 and 126 acres, and all situated near Columbia City. He operates his farms under effective partnership alliances, utilizes three tractors, maintains an average of sixty milch cows in the dairy department of the enterprise, and has brought his farms to model status, the properties representing an investment of $6,500 and his progressive policies of operation having resulted in the rendering of substantial dividends on the investment. Mr. Fisher has thus proved that under proper management farm enterprise may still be made substantially profitable.

Mr. Fisher was born on a farm in Noble County, Indiana, January 21, 1865, and is a representative of one of the old and honored families of that county. His public school studies were carried forward to the fifth grade, and as a boy he had his share of active fellowship with the work of the farm. After leaving school he found employment in the woolen mill operated by his father at Baintertown, a rural hamlet near New Paris, Elkhart County. At the start he received thirty cents a day and worked sixty-six hours a week. He acquired a thorough knowledge of the textile trade, and as a young man became a journeyman at his trade. In 1891 he became superintendent of the Menig Woolen Mills, at Danville, Illinois, and this position he retained four years, the mills having manufactured cassimer worsteds. During the ensuing four years Mr. Fisher was manager of the George Merritt Company's woolen mills at Indianapolis, Indiana, and he next gave two years of service as manager of the Rochester Woolen Mill, at Rochester, Minnesota. He then became manager of the Zanesville Woolen Mill, Zanesville, Ohio, manufacturers of dress goods, and with this concern he thus remained three years. He then returned to Indiana and at South Bend became general manager of the South Bend Woolen Mill, devoted to the manufacture of fabrics for men's apparel, and after nine years with this concern he came to Columbia City and, in 1914, organized the Columbia City Woolen Mills, of the controlling corporation of which he has since continued the president and general manager. He supervised the erection of the plant and operations were initiated on the basis of $6,000, though he soon affected the sale of preferred stock to the amount of $80,000. The manufacturing plant now covers an area of two acres, and the assets of the concern are now nearly $500,000, Mr. Fisher's stockholding in the corporation having a valuation of $175,000. The Columbia City Woolen Mills have been developed into a large and important industrial concern, and the products are principally uniform cloth for Railroad men, letter carriers, policemen and firemen. Both through this enterprise and those involved in his farm operations Mr. Fisher has made large and valuable contribution to the industrial and commercial prestige and advancement of Whitley County, and he is in the fullest sense a loyal and liberal citizen. His political allegiance is given to the Republican party, and he is affiliated with the Masonic fraternity. In his character, his ability and his achievement Mr. Fisher has signally conferred honor on his native state, and his success has been won entirely through his own efforts.

On the 5th of May, 1895, Mr. Fisher was united in marriage to Miss Mary Loutsenhiser, of Danville, Illinois, and they have two sons and one daughter. Merle M., the elder son, was born November 4, 1899, and was graduated in the University of Michigan as a member of the class of 1921 and with the degree of Bachelor of Arts. He is now secretary and assistant manager of the Columbia City Woolen Mills. The maiden name of his wife was Louise Erdman and their marriage was solemnized in 1924. Richard R., the younger son, was born March 4, 1907, and after completing his studies in the Columbia City High School he graduated at the University of Michigan, class of 1924, and thereafter he was a student one year in a textile school in Philadelphia, Pennsylvania, he being now treasurer and office manager of the Columbia City Woolen Mills. Vera, the only daughter, was born May 26, 1896, and supplemented the discipline of the South Bend High School by a course in Oberlin College, Oberlin, Ohio, she having been there graduated in the conservatory of music as a member of the class of 1919 and having thereafter been a successful teacher of music in the public schools until her marriage. She has two sons, William Howard and John, and one daughter Mary Alice.

John R. Fisher, father of the subject of this review, was born in England, in 1837, and in 1843 came with his widowed mother to the United States, the home having first been established at Akron, Ohio, where he later was united in marriage to Elizabeth Rider. In 1863 he and his wife came from Ohio to Indiana and settled in Noble County, he having been employed in various woolen mills before he initiated the operation of the mill in which his son William, of this sketch, served his apprenticeship, at Baintertown, Elkhart County. He and his wife were residents of Indiana at the time of their death. John R. Fisher depended entirely upon his own resources in fighting the battle of life, he and his mother were poor in the early period of their residence in the United States, and he worked loyally and earnestly to advance himself and provide also for his loved mother, while later he manifested the same spirit in providing for his wife and children.

MRS. NORA CHADWICK FRETAGEOT occupies, with characteristic graciousnes, a prominent place in the social and cultural life of the community in which she was born and reared, that of New Harmony, Posey County, where she has given more than a score of years of service as librarian of the Workingmen's Institute, one of the important educational and economic institutions of Indiana.

Mrs. Fretageot was born in the fine old family homestead in which she still resides in New Harmony, and the date of her nativity was April 27, 1858. She is a daughter of James and Mary Foster (Piper) Chadwick, the former of whom was born in Manchester, England, in January, 1815, and the latter of whom was born at Royalston, Massachusetts, August 17, 1816, she having been a daughter of Luke and Betsy (Cole) Piper, the former of whom was born in 1793 and the latter in 1791. Luke Piper was a farmer by vocation, as was also his father, Josiah Piper, who was born in 1768.

James Chadwick was a son of James Chadwick and a lineal descendant of Jordan Chadwyk, who went from his native Normandy to England with William the Conqueror. James Chadwick was reared and educated in his native land and there learned the trade of saddler. In 1837, shortly after attaining to his legal majority, he became a resident of New Harmony, Indiana, and was a charter member of the Workingmen's Institute, which was organized in the following year, a noble institution that has continued to function effectively during the long intervening period of more than ninety years, and of which his daughter Nora has been the librarian fully twenty years. James Chadwick played a large and worthy part in the interesting civic and industrial history of the New Harmony community and here he and his wife remained until their death, secure in the respect and high regard of all who knew them. The staunch building that was provided by James Chadwick as the family home and that is still

occupied by his daughter Nora, of this review, stands as one of the interesting landmarks of this section of the state, as the year 1930 marked the one hundredth anniversary of its erection. Of the three children who attained to maturity Mrs. Nora Fretageot is the youngest and now the only survivor. The son, Charles, was born at New Harmony, in the year 1842, and represented his native county as a gallant young soldier of the Union in the Civil war. His active career connoted his service as clerk and steamboat man, and he continued his residence at New Harmony until his death. In 1880 was solemnized his marriage to Miss Helen Robb, who likewise was born and reared in Posey County, and their children are four in number: Charles Robb, an accountant; Maurice Foster, a draftsman; Nellie Browning, a dietician and social worker; and Mildred, wife of H. G. Ranger, of Indianapolis. Mary Elizabeth, elder daughter of James and Mary F. (Piper) Chadwick, was born at New Harmony in the year 1846, and in her native town her death occurred in 1878. In 1865 she became the wife of Louis Pelham, who was born in 1838 and died in 1912, and they are survived by two children, Caroline Creese Pelham, born in 1867, and died in February, 1931, and Charles Louis Pelham, born in 1874, and still a resident of New Harmony. Charles Louis Pelham married Miss Mary Etta Lichtenberger.

The earlier education of Mrs. Nora C. Fretageot was acquired through the medium of public and private schools at New Harmony and in the preparatory department of the University of Indiana. Thereafter she took library courses at Earlham College, Richmond, Indiana, and at Chautauqua, New York. She has been librarian of the Workingmen's Institute at New Harmony since 1908, and hers is deep and abiding interest in all that pertains to this old and historic institution of which her father was one of the founders. She has membership in the Woman's Club of New Harmony, the Indiana State Historical Society, the Southwestern Indiana Historical Society and the Indiana Library Association, besides which she is vice president of the Posey County Historical Society at the time of this writing, in 1931. Mrs. Fretageot now assigns much of the detail service of the library of the Workingmen's Institute to the assistant librarian, Miss Louise M. Husband, who is represented in a personal sketch on other pages of this publication.

On the 5th of May, 1887, was recorded the marriage of Achilles Henry Fretageot to Miss Nora Chadwick, immediate subject of this review, and the one son of this union died in infancy.

Achilles Henry Fretageot, long a successful merchant and grain dealer at New Harmony, was here born October 16, 1842, and here his death occurred in 1906. He supplemented the discipline of public schools by instruction received under the direction of a private tutor, and by foreign travel and study. Four generations of the Fretageot family utilized the same business building at New Harmony, a structure dating back to 1822, when the historic New Harmony community was in its inception. Mr. Fretageot was a son of Achille Emery Fretageot and Cecelia (Noel) Fretageot, the former of whom was born in Paris, France, in 1813, and the latter of whom was born in that country in 1822, her death having occurred at New Harmony, Indiana, in 1853. Achille Emery Fretageot came to the United States in 1825, with his Paris school class and their teacher, and in the following year all made settlement in the New Harmony community, his mother, Madame Marie (Duclos) Fretageot, having become a teacher in the Maclure School of Industry in the Owen community, she having been a widow when she came to Indiana and her husband having been a colonel in the army of the great Napoleon in the historic march from Moscow. After the death of his first wife Achille Emery Fretageot eventually wedded Mary Alexander, who was born in Posey County, in 1833, and whose death here occurred in 1919. Of the children of the first marriage the first was Alexander Maclure Fretageot, who was born in 1840 and who died while serving as a Union soldier in the Civil war, in 1862; Eugene was born in 1845 and was drowned in the Wabash River in 1852; Oliver Noel, who was born in 1850 and died in 1922, was identified with steamboat navigation on the Wabash River and served as county clerk of Posey County, he having married Mary Ella Highman and their one child being a daughter; Eliza Sampson, who was born in 1847 and died in 1918, was the wife of Dr. Frederick Gundrum, and their two children are Fredrick Fretageot Gundrum and Eloise Fretageot Gundrum. Six daughters were born of the second marriage of Achille Emery Fretageot: Louise, born in 1856, married Eugene V. Johnson; Frances, born in 1859, became the wife of Percy Bennett; Mary, born in 1860, married John Hale, an Indian agent; Nancy, born in 1862, married William Boren; Sarah, born in 1865, married Hiram Lamar; and Isabella, born in 1868, died in childhood.

In 1870 Achilles Henry Fretageot married Miss Mary Kate Bolton, and they became the parents of two sons: Frank Pooley, who was born in 1871, was graduated in the Miami Medical College, Cincinnati, Ohio, and was engaged in the practice of his profession at the time of his death, in 1895. Arthur Emery, the younger son, was born in 1873, and received the advantages of DePauw University and the University of Michigan, he being now established in the mercantile business at New Harmony and being here owner of the ferry line across the Wabash River, with ten boats of various kinds in commission. He is affiliated with the Phi Gamma Delta college fraternity, is a Knight Templar Mason, and has membership in the Knights of Pythias and other fraternal and civic-social organizations. He married Stella Spencer, of Mount Vernon, the county seat of his native county, and they had two children: Cecelia, who died at the age of three years, and Mary, who was born November 24, 1905, who received from DePauw University in 1928 the degree of Bachelor of Arts, and who had previously had a year of study, 1926-27, in the celebrated Sarbonne in Paris, France.

The late Achilles Henry Fretageot was a Democrat in politics, was a member of the Methodist Episcopal Church, and was affiliated with the Masonic fraternity and the Knights of Pythias. He was one of the substantial citizens and business men of New Harmony, had valuable real estate holdings in his native town, as well as farm lands in Posey County, and gave loyal and constructive service in the upbuilding and civic progress of New Harmony.

ROBERT REED, who died January 12, 1929, was for over forty years identified with the stone industry around Bedford. He was a master craftsman, and also had exceptional gifts as an organizer and business manager and was associated with several of the largest plants in the Bedford district.

Mr. Reed was born at Carlisle, England, May 14, 1859, and he inherited some of the great traditions of the English stone workers. His parents were John and Jane (Bailey) Reed. The father was a sculptor who spent all his active life in the stone business. He made his home in England.

Robert Reed was educated in England and was sixteen years of age when he came to America in 1875. For a time he lived in Philadelphia and then joined his uncle, David Reed, at Chicago, where he learned his trade as a stone cutter. During his apprenticeship he attended night school and acquired a substantial education not only from books but from contact with men and affairs. For a time he was a student in the Valparaiso University of Indiana.

On coming to Bedford he was employed by the firm of Tomlinson & Reed, and soon took charge of the plant. In 1883 Mr. David Reed acquired control of this business, while Robert Reed was given some stock in the company. Later they bought the quarries at Oolitic and Sanders and also acquired the Peerless Mill. About that time David Reed died and Robert Reed assumed the full control of the various holdings. He was the leading spirit of the organization that built the Black Diamond Mill, one of the largest and most important, but subsequently sold out to Chicago interests. After being retired from active business for about two years he formed the organization known as the Reed & Powers Cut Stone Company and in 1922 built the Reed-Powers Mill, in the management of which he was active until his death. Mr. Reed was a Knight Templar Mason, a member of the B. P. O. Elks and the Episcopal Church.

He married, December 21, 1887, Miss Anna Thedora Reath, daughter of Jacob and Thedora (Hoffman) Reath. Her father was one of the earliest merchants of Bedford and for many years carried on a banking business there. In the Reath family were seven children: Henry, Theodore and Albert, all deceased; Miranda, wife of Sewell Avery; Lula, a widow, whose first husband was Frank Owens and her second husband, D. Leforce; Mrs. Anna Reed; and Charlotte, wife of Albert Dunihue.

Mrs. Reed, who resides at 1228 West Sixteenth Street in Bedford, is vice president of the Reed-Powers Mill, though not active in the business. She is a graduate of Bedford High School. She is the mother of four children, Anna E., Thedora R., Mary Ellen and David. Anna is in the Reed-Powers Company. Mary Ellen was first married to Clifford Dean and is now the wife of Carlton Klaus. By her first marriage she has four children, Robert R., Clifford Henry, David Neal and Annabelle.

BERNARD D. McCARTNEY, who has been a stone worker for thirty years, came to Indiana about 1907, and has filled many responsible positions in the great stone working industry around Bedford. He is now general manager and superintendent of the Donato Mill of Heltonville.

Mr. McCartney was born at Rahway, New Jersey, June 17, 1882, son of James B. and Margaret (Casey) McCartney. His father was a native of Boston, and both he and his wife were of Irish parentage. James B. McCartney learned the trade of spring maker, but for many years, until his death, was in the mail service with the Pennsylvania Railway. He and his wife are buried at Rahway. They had seven children: Bernard D., Lucy, John, Mary, William, Margaret, who became the wife of Thomas Trotter, and James.

Bernard D. McCartney attended St. Mary's School at Rahway through the grades and at the age of eighteen went to New York City, learning the trade of stone cutting with the John Henline Cut Stone Company. After his apprenticeship he spent two years in Texas and Mexico, being located at Monterey, Mexico, one year. As a stone cutter he did work at various places in the South, Nashville, Louisville and Memphis, and then went back to New York. On coming to Bedford in 1907 Mr. McCartney first worked at the old Salem Mill as a planer foreman. After two years he joined the Black Diamond Mill of Shea & Donnelly and in 1926, after a brief period at Detroit, became general manager and superintendent of the Donato Mill. He stands in high favor among the executives in the stone industry around Bedford.

Mr. McCartney married, June 1, 1908, Catherine Culhan, a daughter of James and Kate (Murphy) Culhan. Her father was one of the old time stone workers in this district. Her parents are buried in the Green Hill Cemetery. Mr. and Mrs. McCartney have two children, Mary and Gertrude, both attending school at Bedford. The family are members of Saint Vincent de Paul Catholic Church and Mr. McCartney is affiliated with the Knights of Columbus and B. P. O. Elks.

ELIAB PATTISON learned the stone cutter's trade while a boy in England. For the past twenty years he has been in the Bedford district of Indiana, where he is now superintendent and general manager of the Ingalls Mill No. 3.

Mr. Pattison was born at Leeds, England, October 16, 1882. His parents, William and Emma (Mouldin) Pattison, still live in England, where his father for many years has followed the business of merchant tailor. There are four children in the family, Florence, Eliab, Harry and Jack.

Mr. Pattison had only the advantages of grade school and was twelve years of age when he began his apprenticeship to learn the stone cutting trade. This apprenticeship was served through four years, and as a journeyman he went about to different places in England for about five years.

Mr. Pattison arrived in America in 1904. Failing to find work at his trade, he spent the next four years working on the docks in New York Harbor and was promoted to the responsibility of boss stevedore. In 1910 he came to Bedford, Indiana, and his first job here was with the Ingalls Company. Later he spent a short time with John A. Rowe and then returned to the Ingalls organization. He was a stone cutter, later was promoted to foreman, and has had a practical experience in nearly every line of the industry at Bedford. As general manager and superintendent of Ingalls Mill No. 3 he has the distinction of being in charge of the largest individual cut stone plant in the Indiana limestone district.

Mr. Pattison married, June 6, 1909, Miss Nellie Summerville. She came from the North of Ireland and they were married in Fall River, Massachusetts. They have seven children, Ethel, a graduate of the Bedford High School, Emma, Edith, Helen, William, Harry E. and John D. All the younger children are attending school at Bedford. Mr. Pattison is a member of the Masonic Lodge and for a number of years has been an influential worker in Saint John's Episcopal Church at Bedford.

CHARLES M. WILHELMUS, M. D., has proved in his ability, loyalty and effective service the integrity of his professional purpose, and his success is attested in the substantial and representative practice that he retains at Newburg, an attractive and prosperous little city in Warrick County.

Doctor Wilhelmus was born in Spencer County, Indiana, October 4, 1880, and is a son of Michael and Frances (Meyers) Wilhelmus, both natives of Germany, where the former was born at historic Bingen-on-the-Rhine and the latter in Baden. Michael Wilhelmus was a lad of twelve years when he came with his parents from Germany to the United States, the family home having been established in Spencer County, Indiana, and the father having continued to follow his profession, that of architect, during the remainder of his life, be-

sides becoming a farm owner in the county mentioned. Michael Wilhelmus completed his youthful education by attending the schools of Spencer County and also learned much of architectural art and science by assisting his father along that line and in building enterprise as a stone mason. He eventually gave his attention to farm industry, was long owner and active manager of one of the fine farm estates of Spencer County, and there he died in 1900, at the age of sixty-four years. His children by his first marriage are three in number: Emma is the wife of George Herr, a farmer in Spencer County; Edward likewise is a prosperous farmer; and Simon is employed as a salesman. The second marriage of Michael Wilhelmus was with Mrs. Frances (Meyers) Kaiser, who came from Germany to the United States when she was twenty-two years of age, her first husband having been Martin Kaiser and one child having been born of that union, Frances, who is the wife of Jacob Raibley. Of the seven children of Michael and Frances Wilhelmus. Dr. Charles M. was the second in order of birth; Otto, a farmer by vocation, died at the age of thirty-four years; Katie died as a child of eleven years; Clara is the wife of Porter Brown, who is identified with the mining industry; Miss Mary resides in the home of her sister Clara; Fred was engaged in farm enterprise and died at the age of thirty-eight years; Henry is a dentist by profession and is established in practice in the City of Evansville.

In the public schools of Spencer County Doctor Wilhelmus continued his studies until he had duly profited by the advantages of the high school, and in preparing for his chosen profession he went to the metropolis of Kentucky and completed the prescribed course in Louisville Medical College, in which he was graduated as a member of the class of 1907. After thus receiving his degree of Doctor of Medicine he was engaged in practice at Raywick, Marion County, Kentucky, two and one-half years, and he then returned to Indiana, where he has been established in successful general practice at Newburg since March 15, 1910. He is serving as health officer of his home community at the time of this writing, and his is distinct prestige as one of the representative physicians and surgeons of Warrick County. The Doctor has membership in the American Medical Association, the Indiana State Medical Society and the Warrick County Medical Society. His political allegiance is given to the Democratic party, he and his wife are communicants of the Catholic Church, and he is affiliated with the Knights of Columbus. The interests of Doctor Wilhelmus include his ownership of farm property and his association with agricultural and horticultural industry.

On the 12th of August, 1902, was solemnized the marriage of Doctor Wilhelmus to Miss Myrtle Meyers, who was born and reared in Spencer County and who is a daughter of the late Lemuel and Sarah (Oldham) Meyers, her parents, who were farmers, having died when she was very young. Beatrice, eldest of the children of Doctor and Mrs. Wilhelmus, was born February 13, 1905, and is a successful and popular teacher in the public schools of Newburg, having graduated from Evansville College in 1929. Irene, born April 10, 1907, was graduated in the University of Indiana as a member of the class of 1929, and is a teacher at Owensboro, Kentucky. Coriene, born December 27, 1908, is a graduate in the class of 1930 from the University of Indiana and is also a teacher. Kenneth, born September 6, 1914, is a student in the Newburg High School, in the class of 1933, and the two younger sons, Gilbert, who was born November 8, 1920, and Robert, who was born March 8, 1922, are in the grades.

PETER MARIA LA CAVA, well known Mishawaka attorney, is a man of very interesting accomplishments and talents. He has gained a substantial clientage as a lawyer, but many thousands outside of Mishawaka have heard and enjoyed the rich qualities of his singing voice.

Mr. La Cava was born at Hartford, Connecticut, May 4, 1896. His parents, Rocco and Rose (Montano) La Cava, came from Italy and located at Hartford, Connecticut, in 1884. They are still living in that city, his father retired. Peter La Cava was the thirteenth in a family of fifteen children, six of whom are living.

He was educated in the grade and high schools at Hartford and during the World war served thirteen months overseas with the Three Hundred Tenth Field Artillery in the Seventy-ninth Division. After having fulfilled his patriotic duty he took up the study of law, spending one year in New York University and in 1922 came to South Bend to enter Notre Dame University, where he was graduated LL. B. in 1926. Mr. La Cava practiced law in South Bend two years and on February 1, 1928, was appointed justice of the peace at Mishawaka. On November 4, 1930, he was elected for a full term of four years as justice of the peace on the Democratic ticket.

He is a member of the St. Joseph County, Indiana State and American Bar Associations, and is eligible to practice before the Supreme Court of Indiana. He belongs to the Mishawaka Exchange Club. He has been an ardent devotee of music since boyhood. Radio fans familiar with his singing know him as the "silver-toned tenor of the East," as he is usually introduced that way. For several years he has organized church choirs and since 1925 has been director of St. Mathew's Catholic Church choir at Mishawaka. Mrs. La Cava is organist at this church.

Mr. La Cava married, January 31, 1924, Miss Ann Elizabeth Arnot. She was born at South Bend, daughter of Mr. and Mrs. Asbury Arnot, deceased. They have three children: Rose Marie, born November 10, 1924; Betty Lou, born August 4, 1926, and Roxy Ann, born June 17, 1928.

JOSEPH L. QUINN, superintendent and general manager of the McLaren Mill of the Ingalls group in the Independent Limestone Mills of the Bedford district, learned his trade as a stone worker in the East, and his experience has been with a number of notable stone working organizations over the country.

Mr. Quinn was born at Newark, New Jersey, November 15, 1878, and is a son of Hugh T. and Catherine (McKee) Quinn. His father came from Scotland to America in 1872. He had grown up in the famous district of Paisley, Scotland, where he learned the trade of calico printer. He followed his trade at Newark for many years and is buried in the Holy Sepulcher Cemetery in that city. His wife, Catherine McKee, was a daughter of James and Sallie (Toner) McKee, who came to America in 1880. James McKee was a shoemaker living at Brooklyn, New York, and both he and his wife are buried in the Calvary Cemetery in that city. The children of Hugh T. Quinn and wife were: Hugh and James, now deceased; Rose, of Newark; Sarah, William, John, Mary, all deceased; Joseph L.; Stephen, of Newark, who married Alice Brennan; and Catherine, deceased.

Joseph L. Quinn was a student in Saint Michael's School at Newark from the age of seven to fourteen. His people were in very modest circumstances and for that reason and because of his self reliant spirit he was working to earn money as a small boy, carrying and selling papers when not in school. After leaving school he became an employee of the Street Railway Company, being what was known as tow boy, having charge of the extra horse used to pull the street car up a hill. Mr. Quinn by attending evening classes made up many of the deficiencies of his education resulting from his leaving school so early. He began his apprenticeship as a stone cutter with Barney Gerberich, being with him two years, then spent a year with J. J. Spurr & Sons, and when that plant went on a strike he finished his apprenticeship with the Passaic Quarry Company of Avondale, New Jersey. After two years there he was employed as a journeyman by William Gray & Sons of Philadelphia, returned to Newark and was with the George Brown & Company there from 1903 to 1913, and during the last eight years of this period was planer foreman.

Mr. Quinn came to Bedford, the capital of the Indiana limestone region, in January, 1914. His first work here was as planer foreman in Mill No. 3, and from there he was transferred to the McLaren Mill of the Ingalls group as superintendent and general manager.

Mr. Quinn married, June 24, 1903, Miss Anna Muir Mackechnie, daughter of George and Mary (Allen) Mackechnie. Her parents are buried in the Arlington Cemetery in New Jersey. Mr. and Mrs. Quinn have had four children: Joseph L., Jr., who after graduating from the Bedford High School spent two years in Purdue University and is now assistant engineer of the City of Bedford; Miss Kathryn, a graduate of high school, is an employee of the Indiana Limestone Company; Russell is deceased; and James is a student in the Bedford High School. Mr. Quinn is a member of the Independent Order of Forresters and the Catholic Benevolent Legion, and the St. Vincent de Paul Catholic Church.

JOE ARMSTRONG, retired resident of Bedford, was at one time one of the largest individual land owners in Southern Indiana. Most of his large holdings have been sold and he is now satisfied with the ownership of a small tract of a hundred acres near Bedford, land covering valuable stone deposits in this famous limestone district.

Mr. Armstrong was born April 24, 1854, near Springville, Indiana. His birthplace was his father's farm. He was a son of Ari and Mary (Short) Armstrong. The Short family was an old and prominent one. John Short was a soldier of the Revolution, enlisting as a private in August, 1776, at first under Capt. William Nail and later under Captain McCutcheon. On November 12, 1832, he was awarded a pension for his Revolutionary services. John Short had the following children: Wesley, born December 20, 1780, Sarah, September 15, 1782, William, October 9, 1784, John, November 11, 1786, Thomas, June 6, 1789, Samuel, March 13, 1792, Reuben, October 15, 1794, Ezekiel, December 12, 1797, and Hansford, July 12, 1800. Of these children John, or Jack, Short married Avy Owens, and by this union there were eleven children: Washington, born December 3, 1808, Nancy, April 12, 1810, Samuel, July 14, 1812, Polly, February 15, 1814, Wesley, May 10, 1816, Martin O., May 12, 1820, Jeal, September 15, 1822, Hansford, January 14, 1825, Maurel, March 12, 1827, Hubbard, September 12, 1828, and Hugh L., May 28, 1832.

Ari Armstrong was born November 4, 1814, and died November 29, 1905. His son, Joe Armstrong, grew up at Springville, attended the old academy there, later the Beaty School, where he completed the common branches of learning, and was also in a private school and had a course in the Normal School at Bedford. At the age of eighteen he took up teaching and taught two terms at Goose Creek and one term in Perry Township. Mr. Armstrong when twenty-one years of age made his first important investment as a land owner. He paid nine thousand dollars for 411 acres, at that time considered a very high price. In his investments he showed a great deal of wisdom and foresight, and from the proceeds from his energetic business career he steadily invested his surplus in land until he had accumulated about two thousand acres. Part of this land was in Texas and he had about 400 acres in the cotton belt. His son Dennis had charge of the southern plantation. On his Indiana lands and even on part of his Texas properties he carried on stock raising, and that was a business that supplied him a large part of his competence.

Mr. Armstrong has been retired for the past twenty years. He married, September

27, 1877, Miss Lizzie Oliphant. To their union were born seven children. The oldest, May, is the widow of Charles Moore and has four children, named George, Joseph, Milfred and Virginia. The oldest son, Dennis, married Luela Rush, and they had five children: Joyce, Rush, Ruth, Lois and Joe, the latter of whom is deceased. Lydia married Elijah McKnight. Cleo married Stanley Frazier and has four children, Eureta, Elizabeth, Robert and David. Ruth Armstrong is the widow of Quincy Rainbolt, and their two children are Richard and Elizabeth. Blain married Mary Holmes, and they have three children, Louise, Stewart and Freeland. Felix, the youngest, married Eula Rush and has two sons, Don and Harry.

Mr. Joe Armstrong on December 27, 1893, married Fannie Culmer, daughter of William and Susanna (Catherwood) Culmer. William Culmer was born at Canterbury, County Kent, England, in 1822, was brought to America when a child by his parents, Stephen and Sarah (Knight) Culmer, first living near Pittsburgh, Pennsylvania, and about 1846 came to Indiana and settled three miles north of Springville. By his second marriage Mr. Joe Armstrong has three children: Shirley, an A. B. and M. D. graduate of the University of Indiana and now a member of the faculty of Ohio State University; Spain, who married Mary Duncan, and their children are Mary J., Robert S., Helen E. and Phyllis; and the youngest is Helen Armstrong, who completed her education here, and is now engaged in welfare work at Columbus, Ohio. Mr. and Mrs. Armstrong are members of the Christian Church.

ELMER R. CONNER has lived practically all his life in close touch with the stone industry of Southern Indiana. As soon as his education was over he went into the quarries and mills, and has had a working experience that has taken him throughout this district and over the country at large. Mr. Conner is now superintendent of the Black Diamond plant of the Indiana Limestone Company at Bedford.

He was born on a farm in Monroe County, near Bloomington, in 1888, son of Tarence and Nancy (Hanson) Conner, and grandson of Alexander and Eliza (Pope) Conner. His grandfather was a Virginian, went to Kentucky and from there to Indiana, and became a large land owner and farmer in Monroe County. He and his wife are buried in a cemetery about fifteen miles from Bloomington. Tarence Conner was also a farmer, but has spent half a century in touch with the practical workings of the stone business as quarryman and in other interests. He is now living retired at the age of seventy, and his wife is sixty-seven. They have had seven children: Ida, wife of William Smallwood; Janie, widow of Max Neskie; Chessie, wife of Charles Neskie; Elmer R.; Russell, who married Naomi DeFord; Ivy, wife of Riley Mansfield; and one that died in infancy.

Elmer R. Conner attended the Patton School near his old home in Monroe County,

and received most of his schooling at Oolitic, where he finished high school and at the age of eighteen began learning the trade of planerman in the Hoosier Mill. He was there two years, then worked with the Reed-Powers Mill at Bedford, was with the Strubble Mill and four years with the Shea and Donnelly organization. For a short time he was at Louisville and as a stone cutter did work at Detroit and other places. However, most of his time has been spent in more or less executive duties in connection with various mills, being planer foreman in the Donato, Shea & Donnelly, McMillan mills. He was made superintendent of the Black Diamond Mill in 1926, just before the general merger that resulted in the organization of the Indiana Limestone Company.

Mr. Conner married, February 4, 1904, Miss Edith Miller, of Springville, Indiana, daughter of James and Eliza (Ford) Miller, her father deceased, and her mother is still living. Her father is buried in the Christian Cemetery at Springville. Mr. and Mrs. Conner have two children, Robert D., a graduate of DePauw University, and Helen, wife of Gayle Gabbert. Mr. and Mrs. Gabbert have a daughter, Mary Margaret. Mr. Conner was for two years a deacon in the Baptist Church and is member of the Industrial Club of Bedford.

MISS GENEVIEVE MACDONALD WILLIAMS. Enjoying innumerable benefits and advantages, the opening months of 1922 found the pleasant little City of Huntingburg, Indiana, still lacking a civic enterprise greatly desired by her resident scholars and her intelligent and progressive people generally, a public library. Nine years finds this lack remedied, and perhaps to no one is more credit due for the initial planning than to Miss Genevieve Williams, the present librarian. Miss Williams is a highly educated, cultured lady, an experienced teacher familiar with the world's best literature, and for a considerable period she spared no effort in furthering the founding of the public library in her native city. She is not only librarian, but is also a member of the library board, offices of responsibility which she has filled with marked efficiency since the library was founded, April 24, 1922. An indication of her good management is shown in the aroused and continued civic interest and in the increase and value of the books secured by purchase and otherwise.

Miss Genevieve Williams was born at Huntingburg, a daughter of Dr. Gershom P. and Alice (Macdonald) Williams, the latter of whom was born in Pennsylvania. The former was for many years one of the prominent physicians and surgeons of Huntingburg, but died in 1904. Mrs. Williams survived her husband until 1914, and then she, too, passed away. Five children were born to them, one of whom died in infancy, the others being: Grace, who married James O. Chaille, has three children, and they all reside at Fort Branch, Indiana, where Mrs. Chaille is on the library board; Frank, who resides at Louisville, Kentucky, married Lona Kaegin, and they have two children; Ross, who resides at Princeton, Indiana, is married and has two children; and Genevieve.

Her early education acquired in the common and high schools of Huntingburg, Miss Williams subsequently attended DePauw University and the Indiana State Normal School, after which she taught school at Huntingburg for ten years, and, although all admit that she is the ideal librarian, she is missed in her former occupation, for she was one of the best beloved educators of Dubois County.

The following history of the library was taken from the 1928 Industrial and Trade Edition of one of the local newspapers:

"Among her civic enterprises Huntingburg is justly proud of her public library.

"In the spring of 1922 several progressive and public-spirited citizens, realizing the need and advantages of a public library, started a movement to found one. A solicitation was made to secure enough cash subscriptions to raise the amount necessary to get legal enactment for the founding of a library. The people responded splendidly and the necessary subscriptions were secured. The list was promptly filed with the county clerk and the following persons were appointed as the library board by the circuit judge, the City Council and the city board of education: Miss Genevieve Williams, Louis Wagner, J. W. Finke, Mrs. Louis Lukemeyer, J. V. Stimson, Mrs. Ed. Dufendach and W. E. Menke.

"The newly appointed board took their oath of office April 23, 1922. The founding of the library was publicly celebrated in a meeting of citizens held in the City Hall Sunday afternoon, April 30, of that year, at which W. J. Hamilton, state secretary and organizer of the Puiblic Library Board of Indiana, was the speaker. The new board immediately took up the preliminary work of establishing the library. Two rooms were secured in the old Phoenix Hotel Building, which have since been the home of the institution. Joseph W. Schwartz, the proprietor, was kind enough to donate three months' rental to help the young enterprise. Miss Genevieve Williams, who had taken an active part in the movement to found a library, was chosen as librarian, a position for which she was exceptionally well fitted by reason of her many years of experience in the study and teaching of literature in the local high schools.

"The next problem confronting the board was the ways and means of securing books, as there were as yet no funds from taxation. Accordingly the board planned to solve the problem by means of a book shower. A call was issued for all citizens who had any books in their homes which they would be willing to donate to the library to do so. The work of collecting books was also taken up by the schools, churches and other organizations. In the upper grades and high school competition between the various classes proved a stimulant to the movement, and in the lower classes the movement took the form of a competitive penny shower. Through the schools alone 756 books were contributed and many others through the churches, clubs and individuals. Arrangements were also made to take advantage of the service of the state traveling library, whereby a collection of books can be borrowed from the state library for a definite period. The library was opened to the public June 29.

"From the start the young institution prospered and a great deal of interest was manifested in it, especially by the younger folk. A report of the librarian in the early part of February, 1923, showed that the library consisted of 1,700 books, 300 of which were loaned from the state library commission. One hundred and twenty new books had been purchased by the board, including the 1922 edition of the American Encyclopedia.

"At the present time there are 3,900 books in the library, 100 of which are borrowed from the Indiana state library commission."

The increase in the number of the books, while gratifying, in no way expresses what has been accomplished by this library. In having free access to good literature many youthful minds have been expanded, potentialities have been developed into actualities, and countless hours have been spent in pleasant occupation in this library that might otherwise have been wasted or have been harmfully employed. The general cultural outlook of Huntingburg has been broadened, the people are better informed, and the schools encouraged since the public library of the city was opened.

WILL F. WHITE has been a member of the Muncie bar since 1900. His name has been associated with a number of civic and public matters in his home city, but doubtless his outstanding service has been as a member of the Muncie Board of Education, of which he is president.

Mr. White was born in Saginaw County, Michigan, and he has the greater interest in the magnificent educational program of Muncie because during his own early years he had to start work without completing even a common school education, making up for his deficiencies long after he had become self supporting. He was born February 6, 1871, son of Andrew and Margaret (Previard) White. His father, a native of New Brunswick, Canada, spent all his active life in the lumber industry, being an all around woodsman and in later years a logging contractor. When a young man he went to Saginaw, and was with several of the great lumber firms operating in that section of Northern Michigan. He died in 1898. His wife, Margaret Previard, was born in Ireland and was taken to New Brunswick when a child. She passed away in 1876. Will F. White was one of a family of five sons and three daughters: Mina, James, Catherine (deceased), Lester, Ida, Nettie, Will F. and Elizabeth.

Will F. White attended school in Saginaw County only until he was eleven years of age.

J.E. Lawrence M.D.

He went to work in lumber mills, also did farm labor, and when nineteen years of age, in 1890, he enlisted in the regular army. He served his three years, his term expiring in the spring of 1893. During the rest of that year he was one of the Columbian guards at the World's Fair in Chicago, and when the Fair was over he entered Valparaiso University of Indiana, and during the next two and a half years studied hard to round out his educational equipment. While attending school he became a teacher and he was for six years a school man in Delaware County. While thus engaged he was making effective progress in his law studies and in 1900 was admitted to the bar and immediately opened an office in Muncie. He practiced alone until 1904, when he formed a partnership with Edward M. White, and in 1906 joined James Bingham and William T. Haymond. In the fall of that year Mr. Bingham was elected attorney general of Indiana. For twenty-four years Mr. White and Mr. Haymond have been associated in a partnership which is recognized as one of the strongest law firms in this section of Indiana.

Mr. White is a director of the Mutual Home & Savings Association, of the Citizens Finance Association. For eight years he served as county attorney and for six years was on the City Council. He is a former president of the Muncie Chamber of Commerce, is a director of the Muncie Community Chest, and during the World war was chairman of the County Council of Defense. He is major judge advocate of the Officers Reserve Corps and in 1929 was elected to an honorary membership in the Veterans of Foreign Wars. Mr. White is a former president of the Rotary Club, is a member of the Dynamo Club, and fraternally is affiliated with the Independent Order of Odd Fellows, both in the Lodge and Encampment, and the B. P. O. Elks. He is a Republican and a member of the First Presbyterian Church.

He married at Valparaiso, Indiana, October 11, 1894, Miss Ida May Wirt. She attended school in Elkhart County and was a student at Valparaiso University. Her father, Cyrus Wirt, was a well to do farmer and stock man in Elkhart County. Mrs. White passed away September 8, 1915, and is buried in Beech Grove at Muncie. She was the mother of six children: Helen M., wife of Frank Sheffield, an oil operator at Houston, Texas, and has three children, Cynthia, Jean and Frank H.; Miss Lillian A., of Washington, D. C.; Walter D.; Miss Florence W., of Muncie, a teacher in the Central High School; Charles W., a law student at Indiana University; and Robert W., in the School of Journalism of Columbia University, New York City. Walter D. White, who was born August 20, 1900, attended school at Muncie, for several years was a court reporter, attended the law school of Indiana University and was admitted to the bar in 1926, since which time he has been associated with his father's law firm. He married Catherine Hedden, of Muncie, and has four children, William H., Edwin, Jane Ellen and James.

Mr. Will F. White married, June 1, 1918, Mrs. Nellie K. Bales, of Columbus, Ohio, daughter of Charles and Catherine Keener and widow of Julian Bales, formerly of Winchester, Indiana. Mrs. White attended school at Winchester. She is a member of the Presbyterian Church and the Woman's Club and Y. W. C. A.

ISAIAH ESAES LAWRENCE, M. D., is one of the venerable and honored representatives of the medical profession at Columbia City, judicial center of Whitley County, where he is still engaged in active practice, though he celebrated in the summer of 1929 his eighty-fourth birthday anniversary. The Doctor has not only given distinguished service in his profession, both as practitioner and educator, but his is also the honor of having given loyal service in defense of the Union during the period of the Civil war.

Doctor Lawrence was born August 1, 1845, at the home of his parents, who were then living five miles west of Wooster in Plain Township, Wayne County, Ohio. His parents were natives of Pennsylvania, his father, John Abner Lawrence, having been born at Middletown, January 18, 1808, and went to Wayne County, Ohio, with his father's family in 1823. At the time of his death he was ninety-one years, nine months, twenty-four days old. He married, September 20, 1827, Sarah Rouch, who was born in Franklin County, Pennsylvania, June 1, 1807, and came to Plain Township, Wayne County, Ohio with her parents in October, 1819. She lived to the age of eighty years, eight months, four days. Her parents were Phillip and Elizabeth Rouch. All the grandparents of Doctor Lawrence were natives of Germany and were Protestants in religion. Doctor Lawrence was the eleventh child of his mother. The first born, Elizabeth, died soon after birth. The others were: Mary Ann, who married Will Mowrey; Malinda, who married Samuel Rouch; George W., who married Eve Ann Mowrey; Sarah became the wife of Joseph D. Wagner; Margaret was married to James E. Kelly; Priscilla married Austin McManus; John F. married Eliza Penland; Henry H., married Eunice Maurer; Lehannah was the wife of Elmer McManus; then came Isaiah E.; and the youngest of the family was Levi Abner, who married Catherine Bierce. Doctor Lawrence is the only survivor. Sarah was buried at Warsaw, Indiana, Margaret, at Alliance, Nebraska, Priscilla, in Michigan, Lehanna, at Wooster, Ohio, and the others are in the cemetery at Columbia City.

When Doctor Lawrence was nine or ten years of age he was sent out one day by his father to a neighbor to bring home a sum of money with which his father purposed to purchase some land in Indiana. This money comprised $1700 in gold, including two fifty-dollar pieces and the rest in tens and twenties. Doctor Lawrence's mother sewed these coins into a gusset, which fitted around his body like a vest underneath his shirt and other clothing, and he carried this on his trip by horseback to Indiana and purchased 160 acres for the son George and eighty acres for the daughter Malinda, wife of Samuel Rouch. Not long afterward the sister Mary Ann and her husband, William Mowrey, also came and acquired 160 acres, all of these being in Union Township, Whitley County. Doctor Lawrence grew up on the farm where he was born, and his advantages in the rural schools were supplemented by two years of study in Wittenberg College at Springfield, Ohio. He began the study of medicine at Wooster under Doctor Hunt and attended a medical college in Chicago one year. He was not yet sixteen when the Civil war broke out, and subsequently he enlisted in Company E, 169th Indiana Infantry, being assigned to the medical department. He was detailed at the headquarters of Gen. T. B. Vanard, who was then quartered in the old home of Gen. Robert E. Lee, across the Potomac River from Washington. Captain Lawrence had an important part in laying out the Soldiers' Cemetery at Georgetown, D. C. For his activities he was awarded a certificate of meritorious service signed by President Lincoln.

After getting his honorable discharge at the close of the war he entered Bellevue Hospital Medical College in New York, was graduated M. D. with the class of 1869, and then established himself in practice at Roanoke, Huntington County, Indiana. In April, 1870, he moved to Columbia City and for twenty years carried on a general practice, doing a great deal of country as well as town work, involving almost constant riding and driving.

In 1890 Doctor Lawrence moved to Chicago, and was in that city for eight years, during the first year being associated with the Mutual Medical Aid Association, one of whose sponsors was the elder Carter Harrison, then mayor, and two other well known citizens interested in the work were Oscar DeWolf and Samuel Crawford. Following that Doctor Lawrence had executive charge of the Illinois Institute of Physicians and Surgeons, and for six years was in charge of Doctor Bassett's Museum of Anatomy, a Chicago institution that contained some four hundred plaster casts exhibiting the different stages of disease in the genito-urinary organs, and the special service of the organization directed by Doctor Lawrence was in treating genito-urinary and venereal diseases. While in Chicago Doctor Lawrence was also associated with Dr. Oscar DeWolf and Dr. Frank Billings in the capacity of consulting physician to the various divisions of the city. All this constituted an experience that brought him in contact with the lowest elements in the social scale and enabled him to realize, as only such an experience could, the far reaching damage to society not only in a city but everywhere derived from perverted instincts. Ever since Doctor Lawrence has felt he had a great moral duty as well as a professional one to perform in using the full power of his abilities to overcome and modify the "brute beast" element in humanity.

In 1898 he returned to Columbia City, and for more than thirty years has carried on a general practice. Through these years it has been possible for him to regard as a hobby as well as an essential part of his vocation to help educate the public to the evils of selfishness, and particularly those arising from sex desire and sex perversion. In reviewing his long life Doctor Lawrence finds satisfaction not only in work done, but in his faithfulness to some of the rules of life, most especially in insisting upon the sacredness of his word, and making good his promises verbal equally with written, even to his own loss.

Doctor Lawrence is a member of the Whitley County Medical Society, Indiana State and American Medical Associations, and is a member of the New York University Alumni.

He was twice married and on August 11, 1914 married Miss Grace Coyle. Her father was Dr. William H. Coyle, of North of Ireland ancestry, who served during the Civil war as a member of Company K, Eighty-eighth Indiana Infantry. After the war he practiced medicine many years at Aetna, Whitley County, Indiana. He died July 29, 1903. He was a faithful member of the Grand Army of the Republic, as is also Doctor Lawrence, one of the last survivors of the war.

JOSEPH FORSYTHE. With the exception of one year, when he was identified with the Mercantile Trust & Savings Bank of Evansville, Joseph Forsythe has been cashier of the Grandview Bank, Spencer County, since its organization, in the development of which he has played the leading role. This institution has always claimed his chief attention, but he likewise has other large and important interests of a financial and business nature, which combine to make him one of the leading men of his community, and since the start of his career he has also contributed materially to the growth and development of his native place by his support of beneficial and progressive civic movements.

Mr. Forsythe was born at Grandview, February 21, 1872, and is a son of William and Margaret C. (Anderson) Forsythe. His father, who was born, reared and educated in Kentucky, came to Indiana in boyhood and settled at Grandview, where for half a century he was the proprietor of a mercantile enterprise and one of the most substantial men of the town. He died in 1908, and his wife, a native of Indiana, passed away in 1925. There were four children in the family: Samuel, who died in 1888; Ida, who died in 1918; Joseph, of this review; and William, a resident of Spencer County.

Joseph Forsythe attended the public schools of Grandview, and pursued a course at Nelson's Business College, Cincinnati, Ohio. With this preparation for a business career he joined his father in the mercantile business, in which he remained for ten years, during which time he familiarized himself thoroughly with business and financial methods as learned behind the counter of a flourishing store in a thriving community. In 1903 he became one of the organizers of the Grand-view Bank, and with the exception of the time above mentioned has been the cashier of this institution ever since. His good business methods have served to make this one of the prosperous institutions of Southern Indiana, and his well-known ability and personal integrity and probity have served to instill confidence in the patrons and to increase the bank's deposits. Mr. Forsythe is also secretary of the Grandview Building & Loan Association. He is a Republican in his political convictions but has not sought public office, and his religious affiliation is with the Lutheran Church. Fraternally he belongs to the Modern Woodmen of America at Grandview, to the I. O. O. F. Lodge No. 300 at Grandview and to the Benevolent and Protective Order of Elks at Evansville. He is also secretary of the Grandview Chautauqua and a man who is interested in everything that makes for higher standards of education, morality and good citizenship.

In November, 1897, Mr. Forsythe married Miss Mamie Knight, of Grandview, daughter of William Knight, and a member of an old and honored pioneer family of Perry County. To this union there have been born three children: Harold, a graduate of Indiana University, now an investment banker at South Bend, Indiana, who married Mary R. Sargeant, of Newburg, Indiana, and had two children, who are now deceased; Mary, who married George A. Rinker, of Indianapolis, Indiana, and has one child, Mary Jo, born in 1926; and William Joseph, who died on August 7, 1920.

The following information concerning the early history of these families in this section is included here for reference: Mrs. Forsythe's grandfather, J. B. Livingood, came to this county about 1850, settling at Newhope, and when Grandview was founded, in 1853, he and his family moved to the new townsite and he served as the first postmaster, having previously been postmaster at Newhope. Mrs. Forsythe's mother is of pioneer Kentucky stock from across the river near Grandview. Mr. Forsythe's mother is of Revolutionary stock, tracing the line back to a John Lamb of early days.

WILLIAM EDWARD POWERS is a master craftsman in the cut stone industry. Men all over the country in that line of business know him personally or by reputation. He has spent many years in the Indiana limestone district, and has been connected with some of the largest plants in this section.

Mr. Powers was born at Detroit, Michigan, May 18, 1878, son of John and Bridget (McInnery) Powers. His father came from County Kilkenny, Ireland, while his mother was born in Troy, New York. John Powers for many years was in the employ of the Lake Shore & Michigan Southern Railway, and lived at Chicago, where he was yardmaster. Both parents are buried in Chicago. They had eight children, Tom, Andrew, Frank, Bridget, Mary, Nellie, Catherine and William E.

William Edward Powers completed his grade school work in the Keith School of Chicago. He then went to work, but more or less regularly for eight years attended night school and in that way supplemented and broadened his educational training, studying subjects of direct practical value to him and his work. For five years he attended night school in Chicago and three years in Boston. All of the time he was in Chicago after leaving public school he spent learning his trade as a stone cutter. Other intricate technical branches of the business have been mastered by him as he has gone along, and he knows everything connected with the industry from the quarrying of the stone to its preparation and laying in building construction. He first came to this section of Indiana in 1905, and was made foreman and later superintendent of the Dugan Cut Stone Company. After this company sold out he went to Oolitic and became superintendent for the Central Oolitic Company of Bloomington. Later he returned to the Consolidated Stone Company at Bedford as general manager. Mr. Powers is now president and general manager of the Reed-Powers Mill, one of the largest of the independent mills operated in Lawrence County. It was formerly the Wallner Mill. He went with this business at first as vice president and since the death of Mr. Reed has been president of the company.

Mr. Powers married, June 23, 1908, Miss Elizabeth Schmidt, daughter of Ernest and Elizabeth (Mansing) Schmidt. She is a member of one of the oldest families in Bedford and Lawrence counties. Mr. and Mrs. Powers have two children: Mary Elizabeth, attending the Conservatory of Music at Cincinnati; and Margaret Frances, in the Bedford High School. Mr. Powers is a member of the B. P. O. Elks, Knights of Columbus, and is active in the Saint Vincent de Paul Society of the Catholic Church.

RALPH N. SMITH has been connected with the great limestone industry of Southern Indiana since he was sixteen years of age. His work has been in the quarries and mills, and his familiarity with the technical work of preparing and building is supplemented by a high degree of executive talent. Mr. Smith is now superintendent and general manager of the Donato Mill of the Indiana Limestone Company at Bedford.

He was born on his father's farm near Shoals, Indiana, January 8, 1884, son of McClure and Mary (Barker) Smith, and grandson of Thornton Smith, who came from Ohio and was an early settler in this part of Indiana. Thornton Smith was a Union soldier in the Civil war. McClure Smith was also born on a farm near Shoals, and during his active life followed farming and the trade of carpenter. He and his wife are buried in the Green Hill Cemetery. There were nine children: Clyde, who married Etta Kitchen; Ethel, who became the wife of Phillip Harris; Ralph N.; Ida, wife of Ely R. Clifton; Pulaski E., who married Effie Hill; Walter E., who died when eighteen years old; Fred W., who married Corinne Simon; Hobart T.; and Addie, wife of Oliver Rayburn.

Ralph N. Smith had all his early school advantages at Mount Union, Indiana. His subsequent education, including some technical and business studies, was acquired by night study after he began work. When he was sixteen years old he became a laborer in the P. M. B. Quarry, one of the deep workings in the vicinity of Bedford. Later he was put in the P. M. & B. Mill at Bedford and there spent two years learning the trade of planerman. About that time he became interested in local politics and was elected city clerk, and was reelected, but soon resigned in order to give his full time to his business. Later on he built up a successful side line in insurance, but sold his interest. Mr. Smith in 1924 was made planer foreman of the Donato Mill, and about a year and a half later was promoted to superintendent and general manager. He is a member of the Bedford Industrial Club, made up largely of superintendents, general managers and foremen in the stone industry.

He married, August 19, 1908, Miss Ruby Denniston, daughter of W. C. and Etta (Eller) Denniston. Her father is a retired farmer and her mother died in 1913. Mr. and Mrs. Smith have two daughters, Alah and Elizabeth, both graduates of the Bedford High School. Alah married, August 25, 1929, Opal F. Wilson, who is also a graduate of the high school at Bedford. Mr. Smith is a Republican voter, is a member of the Masonic Lodge, the Independent Order of Odd Fellows, and all his family are active in the Methodist Episcopal Church.

BENJAMIN F. TEETOR, inventor and manufacturer, is one of a group of men of mechanical genius comprising the Teetor family whose enterprise has been a powerful factor in the industrial development and prosperity of the City of Hagerstown, Wayne County.

Benjamin F. Teetor is a son of Zachariah and Barbara (Hoover) Teetor. The Teetor family has been in Wayne County, Indiana, since pioneer times. Benjamin F. Teetor attended public schools, grew up on an Indiana farm, worked as a farm hand between school terms, and when he was fourteen years of age he was working in a bicycle shop at Muncie. His brother Charles, now president of the Perfect Circle Company at Hagerstown, was one of the owners of that shop. It was while in the bicycle business that Charles Teetor invented a railroad car for inspection purposes that was propelled like a bicycle, and types of that vehicle are still being manufactured and used.

In 1895 the Teetor brothers began the manufacture of special railroad equipment and supplies at Hagerstown, under the name of Railway Cycle Manufacturing Company. There have been several changes in the name of the business during the thirty odd years of its existence. These changes in name reflect in a measure the differing emphasis placed upon articles of manufacture. The second name was the Light Inspection Car Company. That was succeeded by the Teetor-Hartley Motor Company, and a few years ago the company sold the motor portion of its plant and has since specialized in the manufacture of piston rings. The business became the Indiana Piston Ring Company and is now the Perfect Circle Company.

Benjamin F. Teetor was employed by and financially interested in this firm thirty-one years, until April 1, 1927, when he discontinued his active relations and has since engaged in experimental work, owning a shop for that purpose at Hagerstown. He has made a special study of design and construction for the railway motor car, different from the automobile, since it has no springs or tires, and at the same time is light in weight, so that it can readily be moved from the rails. The essential principle of the type of construction finally determined upon was one with vertical crank shaft and opposed cylinders, which has worked out very satisfactorily, employing the gyroscope principle, thus eliminating vibration. At the same time the car construction is very light and powerful. The United States patent office issued a patent on this car to Mr. Teetor, April 23, 1929, and patents have also been issued by Great Britain and Canada.

Mr. Teetor married, July 19, 1905, Miss Mabel Brower, who was born at Losantville, Indiana, daughter of Lewis and Lucinda (Parker) Brower. Their only child, George Henry, died at the age of one year. They are rearing two daughters, nieces of Mrs. Teetor, Josephine and Madeline, twins, born October 16, 1916. Mr. Teetor has served as a member of the Hagerstown City Council. He was reared a Republican, but is an independent voter, and is a member of the Masonic fraternity, Independent Order of Odd Fellows and Knights of Pythias.

CHARLES T. BAKER. The career of Charles T. Baker, owner and publisher of the *Grandview Monitor* since 1905, is an expression of practical diversified activity, and in its range has invaded the realms of journalism, education, politics and society, all of which have profited by the breadth and conscientiousness which are distinctive features of his work and character. Identified with newspaper work for about forty years, he has established a high reputation among the journalists of Southern Indiana, and in addition is probably one of the best-versed men as to the Spencer County life and history of Abraham Lincoln in the state.

Mr. Baker was born at Norwalk, Ohio, February 5, 1871, and is a son of H. Carlton and Mary Elizabeth (Zeller) Baker. His father was born July 6, 1847, at Norwalk, a son of

Dayton F. Abbott.

James W. Baker, who came from New York State, as a babe in arms to Ohio and who was born May 11, 1819, and died May 19, 1917. The Baker family trace their ancestry to Edward Baker, who came from England to Massachusetts in 1630. A genealogical record of the family was compiled and published in 1867 by Nelson M. Baker, of Lafayette, New York. H. Carlton Baker was reared and educated at Norwalk, and in early life adopted the vocation of farming, which he followed with success throughout a long and useful career, his death occurring at Norwalk, Ohio, in 1904. Mrs. H. C. Baker was also born in Ohio, her parents having gone to that state from Pennsylvania. She and Mr. Baker were the parents of five children: Charles T., of this review; Frank, born in 1873; Cora, born in 1876; Ella Grace, born in 1878; and Raymond W., born in 1883.

Charles T. Baker attended the public schools of Norwalk, Ohio, and spent a part of his boyhood and youth on the home farm. He was a delicate lad, however, and it was decided by his parents to send him to North Carolina for his health, and while there he made friends with the proprietor of a printing business, in whose shop he learned the trade. Upon his return to Norwalk he secured work in the shop of the Fair Publishing House, of Norwalk, and remained there until some time in 1898, when he came to Rockport, Spencer County, and went to work on the *Journal* and later on the *Democrat*, with which he was identified for six years. He was also employed on the *Baptist Observer*, of Greensburg, Indiana, for a short time, but in 1904 took up his permanent residence at Grandview, where he bought the *Monitor*. He has made this one of the leading papers in this part of the state, conducts a flourishing job department, and does all of his own work. Mr. Baker has been very actively interested in historical work and through his writings appearing in his own paper and others has become known as an authority upon that part of the life of Abraham Lincoln spent in Spencer County, his written comments upon this subject having been widely quoted and accepted as authoritative. He is one of the pillars of the Baptist Church at Grandview, where he serves as a member of the board of deacons and has also been superintendent of the Sunday School. Few men have done more for the development of their territory. He is a member of the library board, assistant secretary of the Chautauqua, secretary of the Grandview Lincoln Trail Club, and a director of the Grandview Building & Loan Association. A Republican in his political allegiance, he has served capably in the capacity of town clerk, and as a fraternalist has been affiliated with the Knights of Pythias. He is the owner of a farm and a pleasant and attractive home in Grandview.

Mr. Baker married Miss Anna Craig on December 9, 1902, the daughter of Captain Joe Craig, a steamboat man, and she died in 1916. On August 16, 1917, Mr. Baker married Miss Gertrude Barker, and they have two daughters: Annie May, born June 1, 1920, and Betty June, born June 19, 1925.

DAYTON FRANKLIN ABBOTT is president and general manager of the Abbott Detective Agency, with headquarters in the Standard Building at Fort Wayne. Mr. Abbott has had an extended experience as an investigator and law officer, and has made his organization one of the most complete of its kind in Northern Indiana.

He was bron in Wabash County, Indiana, December 29, 1877, son of Frank and Mary (Baer) Abbott, his father a native of Wabash County and his mother of Whitley County, Indiana. Mr. Abbott's paternal grandparents came to Indiana at an early date. The maternal grandparents were Amos R. T. and Sarah (Summers) Baer. Frank Abbott had a public school education in Wabash county and combined the occupations of farming and well drilling. He was a member of the Christian Church. He passed away February 1, 1929, when seventy-five years of age. His wife is a member of the Dunkard or Brethren Church. They had just two children: Dayton F. and Albert A. Albert was a road contractor and was serving as sheriff of Allen County when he was killed in 1923. The mother of these children died in 1918.

Dayton F. Abbott attended the North Manchester High School in Wabash County and in 1895, when he was eighteen years of age, went to work for the Telephone Company. His experience in the telephone business covered a period of fourteen years and in 1901 he moved to Fort Wayne, where he was associated with the Bell Telephone interests until 1906. From 1909 to January, 1911, he was in the service of the Pennsylvania Railway and in February, 1911, was appointed chief of police of Fort Wayne. He served four years, under the administration of Mayor Grice, and during the four-year period, 1914-18, he was with the Fort Wayne Transfer Company and the Grace Construction Company. Mr. Abbott was again called to the duties of the chief of police in 1918, serving during the four-year term of Mayor Cutshall. In 1922-1923 he did work with the Bureau of Investigation, in the Federal department of justice, and in 1923 established the Abbott Detective Agency, of which he is president and general manager.

Mr. Abbott is a Spanish-American war veteran. He was a sergeant in Company D of the 157th Indiana Volunteers during that war. He has membership in the Spanish-American War Veterans, and his family attend the Catholic Church, while he is liberal in his religious views.

Mr. Abbott married, September 30, 1913, Miss Grace A. Baker, daughter of Killian Baker. Her father died in 1911. Her mother, whose maiden name was Ann Daugherty, died in 1927 when eighty-nine years of age. Mr.

and Mrs. Abbott have four children: Ann Daugherty, born in June, 1917; Mary Frances, born in July, 1920; Dayton F., Jr., born in August, 1922; and Margaret Jean, born in May, 1924.

CLIFFORD W. BICKENHEUSER was born in the City of Bedford, grew up in the atmosphere of the stone-working industry and almost as a matter of course found his life work in the business that has its capital at Bedford. Mr. Bickenheuser is superintendent and general manager of the Struble Mill, one of the mills comprised under the ownership of the Indiana Limestone Company.

Mr. Bickenheuser was born June 13, 1882, on what was then High Street, now F Street, in the City of Bedford. As a boy he attended the common schools, being a pupil in the East Side School and later the West Side, where he entered the sixth grade and continued until he was about fourteen years of age. When he left school he learned the trade of stone cutter, and from cutting stone took up the branch of the business known as planerman. For several years he worked on the outside, helping with the stone work on the Southern Indiana Railway Shops at Bedford and Terre Haute for a year. He then resumed his work in the mills, spending three years in the Hoosier Mill, was with the Furst & Kerber Cut Stone Company until 1910 and since then has been with the Henry Struble Cut Stone Company, starting as a planerman, was promoted to planer foreman and since July, 1926, has been superintendent and manager of the Struble Mill.

Mr. Bickenheuser is a member of the Christian Church, and is affiliated with the Masonic fraternity and Modern Woodmen of America. He married, September 17, 1903, Miss Maud Teague, daughter of Mollie (Ikerd) and James E. Teague. They have three children, Helen Thelma, James Phillip and Mary Catherine. James Phillip married Eva George, and they have a daughter, Martha Lou.

TIMOTHY K. DONOVAN, of Bedford, knows the stone industry from the standpoint of nearly forty years of practical working experience. He is one of the important men in the business, being superintendent and general manager of the Shea Mill, a subsidiary of the Indiana Limestone Company.

Mr. Donovan was born in the City of Cork, Ireland, September 21, 1868, son of Michael and Mary (O'Keefe) Donovan. His parents lived all their lives in Ireland, and of their eight children three grew up, Timothy being the only one to seek the opportunities of America. His brother Daniel and his sister Hannah are still in Ireland. Timothy Donovan attended Irish schools and for several years studied with a view to entering the English civic service. When he was nineteen years of age, after completing his schooling, he came to America. His first location was at Lynn, Massachusetts, where he spent two and a half years learning the leather finishing trade. Mr. Donovan in 1892 entered the employ of the Shea & Donnelly Company at Lynn, Massachusetts, and his first work was as a truck driver for the company. After three years he was put in charge of the laborers of the mill, and from that learned the trade of planerman, was made planerman foreman and later superintendent. The mill where he was working was destroyed by fire in 1910, and soon afterward he was sent to Bedford to take charge of the holdings of the firm in that city and has been over the mill here for the past twenty years. This was one of the mills included in the merger of 1926.

Mr. Donovan married in 1899 Sue W. Dowling, of Prince Edward Island, Canada, daughter of James and Margaret (Kelly) Dowling. Mr. and Mrs. Donovan have four children: Mary, born in November, 1899; Rickard, born in August, 1902; John, born in March, 1904, married Louise Stueglitz and has a daughter, Margaret Louise; and Clarence, born in February, 1908. The family are all active members of the St. Vincent De Paul Catholic Church. Mr. Donovan is a member of the Knights of Columbus, the B. P. O. Elks and the Industrial Club, and is a member of the Bedford Country Club.

WILLIAM CUTHILL learned his trade as a stone cutter in Scotland. Nearly twenty-five years ago he came to the limestone district of Southern Indiana. His service has been continuous in and around Bedford except for two or three years during the World war. Mr. Cuthill is superintendent and general manager of the A. W. Stone Mill, formerly the Hoosier Cut Stone Company, now a subsidiary of the great organization known as the Indiana Limestone Company.

Mr. Cuthill was born in Scotland, October 21, 1884, son of James and Marion (Stirling) Cuthill. His parents lived all their lives in Scotland, where his father was a baker by trade. There were nine children, John, James, Tom, Alexander, Harry, Christina, Maynard, William and Robert.

William Cuthill is the only member of the family to come to America. He had an eighth grade education in his home town, leaving school at the age of fourteen, and for a time was employed in a grocery store and for over a year was a messenger in the Government service. After completing a four-year apprenticeship at the stone cutting trade he came to America in 1906. Mr. Cuthill as a youth had played football and has always been an ardent follower of athletic sports. About the time he arrived in this country there awoke a wave of popular appreciation of soccer football, and Mr. Cuthill played that game as a professional, being captain of the Newark, New Jersey, team. In later years he has kept up a strong interest in college sports.

In May, 1908, Mr. Cuthill came to Bedford and followed his trade in the stone mills until 1917, when he went to Canada and joined a regiment known as the Forty-eighth High-

landers. He was sent overseas to France, and saw a great deal of the hard service of the last two years of the war. For six months of the time he was laid up in a London hospital. After being relieved of military duty he came back to Bedford and was made foreman of the A. W. Stone Mill and later appointed its superintendent and general manager. He is one of the very popular executives in the stone industry.

He married in 1907 Miss Janet Hamilton, daughter of Ferguson and Janet (Patterson) Hamilton. Her parents lived in the same town in which Mr. Cuthill was born. They have a daughter, Janet, a graduate of the University of Indiana. The family are members of the Presbyterian Church.

GEORGE A. BALL is the youngest of the group of brothers whose activities have been such a great contribution to Indiana's industrial prosperity, and has contributed in full measure to the technical ability and sound business sense to the wonderful success of the organization.

Mr. Ball, like his brothers, was born on a farm in Trumbull County, Ohio, November 5, 1862, son of Lucius Styles and Maria (Bingham) Ball. The history of his family in detail is given on other pages of this publication. Mr. Ball in recent years has been given many honors and responsibilities in his home community of Muncie. In 1929 he was reelected president of the Muncie Chapter of the American Red Cross. He is a member of the Rotary Club, the Union League and Grolier Clubs of New York, Congressional Country and Army, Navy and Marine Clubs of Washington, and the Bibliophile Society and Omar Khayyam Club of Boston. If he has any hobby it has been books, of which he has been a collector of old and rare items for several years. He has fully cooperated with his brothers in their extensive donations to educational and other institutions, including the disposition of the funds and property that made possible the Ball State Teachers College at Muncie, and the James Whitcomb Riley Hospital for Children at Indianapolis. Mr. Ball is a thirty-third degree Scottish Rite Mason. His only daughter, Elisabeth Ball, was graduated from Vassar College in 1923.

JOHN H. TAYLOR, county auditor of Lawrence County, is a native of Kentucky, but has lived most of his life in this Indiana county, and before taking up his duties at Bedford was a carpenter and farmer in Bono Township.

He was born in Taylor County, Kentucky, October 16, 1872, son of Charles and Margaret (Cleaver) Taylor. Three years after his birth his parents came to Indiana. Charles Taylor during the Civil war was a member of the Twenty-seventh Kentucky Infantry in the Union army, serving with the Army of the Cumberland. In one battle he was wounded in the hand. By occupation he was a farmer, and both he and his wife lived out their lives in Lawrence County.

John H. Taylor grew up in Bono Township, attended the common schools there and finished a course in the Southern Indiana Normal School at Mitchell. As a young man he engaged in educational work for two years at Marshalltown and Bono. He learned the trade of carpenter, engaged in the building business and also owned and operated a farm in Bono Township.

Mr. Taylor since early manhood has been interested in community affairs and local politics. He was elected and served two terms as township assessor, and came from that office to the position of county auditor. He was appointed county auditor to fill the unexpired term of William M. Denniston.

Mr. Taylor married, June 13, 1895, Miss Cora Murray, daughter of Milton and Eliza (Todd) Murray. They are the parents of four children: Ruby, Clyde, Mabel and Teddy. Ruby is the wife of Noble Tanksley, and their children are Rollan, Ruth, Rolina, Ronald, Raymond and Ray. Clyde married Ann Allen. Teddy Taylor married Hazel Marshall and has a daughter, Evelyn Marie. Mr. Taylor and family are active members of the Church of the Nazarene.

ARTHUR EDWARD SMITH, who is filling the office of purchasing agent for Allen County, is a native of Fort Wayne, and for many years had an interesting commercial experience as a traveling salesman, building up a large acquaintance and commercial connections throughout Indiana and adjacent states.

Mr. Smith was born at Fort Wayne, August 14, 1872, son of Edward C. and Carrie (King) Smith. His father was born in Pontiac, Oakland County, Michigan, and moved to Fort Wayne in 1868, and was married the following year. His wife was a native of Adams County, Indiana. Edward C. Smith was in business as a manufacturer of wagons and carriages at Fort Wayne until his death. His widow now resides at Fort Wayne, at the age of eighty-five. Their three children are Arthur Edward, Harry Alexander, of West Virginia, and Mrs. John H. Vesey, of Fort Wayne.

Arthur Edward Smith attended school at Fort Wayne, and his early commercial training was gained while working for a Fort Wayne hardware company. His chief business experience, however, was as salesman for women's ready to wear goods, and for twenty-one years he was connected with the firm of George G. Wood & Company, of New York, traveling over the territory of three states, Indiana, Ohio and Michigan. During these years Mr. Smith has made his home in Fort Wayne, and is a popular citizen of Allen County. He was appointed purchasing agent for the county in July, 1928.

He has been quite active in politics for twenty years. During the World war he had charge of the first drive for the Y. M. C. A., and also was chairman for the last Red Cross drive during the war. He has been team captain in numerous other Red Cross and civic drives. Mr. Smith is a York and Scottish Rite Mason and Shriner, member of the Fort Wayne Country Club, Chamber of Commerce, and the First Presbyterian Church. His favorite pastime is golf.

He married at Fort Wayne, April 20, 1911, Miss Katherine B. Chapin, who was born at Kendallville in Noble County, Indiana, daughter of Judge Agustus A. Chapin, of Fort Wayne. They have one son, Franklin Chapin, now attending the University of Michigan, class of 1931. In his junior year he received the Phi Beta Kappa.

EDWARD TUHEY is a native son of Muncie, and for many years has been actively identified with the business affairs of that city. For fifteen years he has been a member of the Muncie board of education and much of the time secretary of the board.

He was born in Muncie January 10, 1856, son of Patrick and Anna Tuhey. His parents were natives of Ireland, and his father came to the United States when about twenty-one years of age, while his mother was brought over when a child by her parents. They settled at Muncie in 1854. His father was a laboring man, an honest and industrious citizen who made every effort to provide for the proper education and training of his children. He died in 1899 and is buried in the Beech Grove Cemetery. The mother passed away in 1900. There were five children: Edward; John Patrick, deceased; Blanche, deceased, who married John C. Greisheimer; Anna, widow of John Sweigart; and Mary, wife of Henry Omera, of Muncie.

Edward Tuhey attended public schools in Muncie, also for a time attended a country district school. During his early manhood he taught for eight years, and ever since has had a keen interest in the educational progress of his community. When he was twenty-five he took up farming as a vocation, and later engaged in the contracting business, putting up buildings and doing sewer work. After five or six years he entered the iron business, operating the Muncie Iron & Steel Company for about ten years. His interests in this were sold to a consolidation of iron dealers. In recent years his name has been chiefly identified with the canning industry and the wholesale and retail coal business. Mr. Tuhey is president of the Tuhey Canning Company and president of the Tuhey Coal Company.

Fraternally he is a member of Delaware Lodge No. 433, A. F. and A. M., and in former years was active in the Independent Order of Odd Fellows. In a public way he is remembered for two terms in the office of mayor. As a member of the school board for fifteen years he has been a prominent part in the reorganization and development of Muncie's magnificent physical plant for educational purposes. He has been especially interested in the vo-

cational program that has been made an integral part of the instruction in the junior and senior high schools. Mr. Tuhey is a Democrat in politics. He was much interested in the movement for the adoption of the blossom of the tulip tree as Indiana's state flower.

Mr. Tuhey first married Miss Mary Edna McKinley, of Delaware County. Her father, Alexander McKinley, was a prominent farmer of the county, and the McKinleys have lived in this section of Indiana since pioneer days. Mrs. Tuhey left two children, Carl and Earl, both of whom are associated with their father in business. Mr. Tuhey's second wife was Mary Sabine McKinley, daughter of Joseph W. McKinley, of Delaware County. Her father was also a farmer. Mrs. Tuhey was educated in the schools of Delaware County and was an active member of the High Street Methodist Episcopal Church. She died December 16, 1917. By his second marriage Mr. Tuhey has eight children: J. Walter, a resident of Salt Lake City; Nellie, Mrs. Ernest Krug, of Los Angeles; Raymond, of Muncie; Erma, wife of Forest Fillman, of Detroit, Michigan; J. Edward; Henry Arthur; Miss Blanche Elizabeth, a teacher in the high school at Muncie; and Frederick, who is also a member of the faculty of the Muncie High School.

CAPT. F. M. VAN PELT was one of the last of the old soldiers of the Union to answer the roll call of death, passing away suddenly at his home in Anderson on January 21, 1930.

He was born at Anderson, August 15, 1838, son of Uriah and Almira (Daugherty) Van Pelt. His early life was spent on his father's farm in Madison County. His education was the product of attending district schools during a few terms, and otherwise his training for life was the work and routine of the home farm. His apprenticeship at the carpenter's trade was interrupted by the outbreak of the Civil war.

In April, 1861, he enlisted, being mustered in at Indianapolis as a private in Company G of the Seventeenth Indiana Infantry. He saw service for three years, eight months, being honorably discharged at Nashville in January, 1865. His battle record included Chickamauga, Hoover's Gap, siege of Chattanooga, Farmington, Tennessee, and others. For meritorious service at Shiloh he was given two promotions, duty sergeant and later first lieutenant. In the fight at Farmington he was in command of his company, which made a splendid charge, capturing three Confederate field pieces and shattering the members of the battery and driving them across the Tennessee River. After the battle of Chickamauga in November, 1863, he was detailed for recruiting service by order of Governor Morton of Indiana. He was on recruiting duty until April, 1864, when he rejoined his regiment. While at Louisville, Kentucky, he was detailed to command sixty men and pursue a group of guerillas, and in the chase he was thrown from his horse and quite severely injured. After a period in a convalescent camp at Columbia, Tennessee, he rejoined his company and remained in command until January, 1865.

Following the close of the war Captain Van Pelt lived at Galesburg, Illinois, an employee of the Burlington Railway until 1870. He then became connected with a publishing house at Atlanta, Georgia, was in the railway mail service, and in 1880 was appointed deputy collector in the Internal Revenue Bureau, with headquarters at Atlanta. In 1889 he was made superintendent of the registry department of the Atlanta postoffice. He continued in this position until 1894, and after a year of residence at Lincoln, Nebraska, returned to Anderson in 1895.

During the last thirty-five years of his life Captain Van Pelt found interesting work and opportunities for contact with his fellow men. For many years he held the office of justice of the peace, and was succeeded in that position by his daughter, Minnie Van Pelt. He was commander of Major May Post, Grand Army of the Republic, and in 1924 was chosen state commander of the Grand Army. He was for two years, up to the time of his death, state commander of The Loyal Legion, composed of commissioned officers of the Civil war.

Captain Van Pelt married, December 24, 1868, Miss Amanda M. Slater, of Galesburg, Illinois, a teacher in the city schools. The Slaters were a New England family, and were represented by soldiers of the Revolutionary war. The children of Captain and Mrs. Van Pelt were Minnie A., Frances M. Bilyeu, Ada M. Phipps, of Indianapolis, and Myra S. Kegereis, of Anderson. They all completed their education in the Western Normal College at Lincoln, Nebraska. Miss Minnie had for a number of years been associated with her father in handling the duties of justice of the peace and is also a pension attorney and for eight years was a teacher in the Indiana S. & S. O. Home. Mrs. Van Pelt passed away in 1917. She had been prominent in the Woman's Relief Corps of the state and in civic affairs.

HON. ROBERT FRANK MURRAY, present judge of the Superior Court of Delaware County, Indiana, and for three consecutive terms judge of the Grant-Delaware Superior Court, district in said state, is a native of Delaware County and member of an old and honored family in Eastern Indiana.

He was born on a farm in the vicinity of Selma, in Liberty Township, August 1, 1884, son of Capt. William H. and Margaret Jane (Orr) Murray. His mother was born at Selma, October 13, 1844. Her father, James Orr, was a leading figure in Delaware County political life, serving in both Houses of the Legislature.

Judge Murray's first American ancestor in the paternal line was William Murray, who came from Ireland and joined the colonists in their war for independence against Great Britain. After the war he lived in Western Pennsylvania, and his son, Cornelius B. Murray, was born in Westmoreland County, that state. Cornelius B. Murray was a pioneer settler in Eastern Indiana and married Lucinda Burroughs, a native of Madison County, Indiana. Cornelius B. Murray and wife were married in Randolph County in 1836, and about two years later settled on a farm in Henry County, but in 1864 returned to Randolph County, where his wife died in 1873. Cornelius B. Murray spent his last years in Wayne County, Indiana. His son, the late Capt. William H. Murray, former auditor of Delaware County, was born in Henry County, Indiana, January 11, 1840, grew up on a farm and at an early age began teaching school. On July 4, 1861, when he was twenty-one years of age, he enlisted as a private in Company K of the Nineteenth Indiana Infantry. He was with that regiment for over three years, receiving his honorable discharge September 4, 1864, as a result of wounds. He was honored with the brevet title of captain.

Captain Murray on February 16, 1865, married Miss Margaret Jane Orr. During the next five years he devoted his time to farming in the summer and teaching school in the winter. In 1870 he sold his farm and established himself in the mercantile business at Selma. Two years later he was elected trustee of Liberty Township and in 1878 was chosen county auditor of Delaware County. After his four years in that office he returned to Selma and he and his wife lived out their lives in their country home there. His wife died October 12, 1912, and he passed away March 15, 1915. They are buried in the Beech Grove Cemetery at Muncie. The seven children were Robert Frank, Lula M., James O., Donn P., Margaret M., Arthur L. and Edna K.

Robert Frank Murray spent most of his childhood and youth on a farm. He was educated in the public schools of Selma, graduating from high school there in 1902. In 1908 he graduated from the law department of Indiana University, was admitted to the bar and began practice at Muncie, and for ten years was one of the busy members of the bar of Delaware County.

In 1918 he was elected judge of the Grant-Delaware Superior Court District, was reelected in 1922 and again in 1926, serving twelve years in that office. In 1930 he was elected as judge of the Superior Court of Delaware County, Indiana, for a term of four years and is now serving in that office.

Judge Murray has shown a public spirited attitude in every way to his community, and through his profession and as a private citizen his influence has always been for good. He is a member of the First Presbyterian Church, is a Knight Templar and thirty-second degree Scottish Rite Mason and Shriner, member of Muncie Lodge No. 245, B. P. O. Elks, and was formerly affiliated with the Loyal Order of Moose. He is a member of the college fraternity Sigma Nu and was the first president of the Muncie Kiwanis Club.

Judge Murray married at Muncie, June 10, 1911, Miss Charline R. Knapp. She died June

30, 1922, and is buried in the Beech Grove Cemetery. On January 21, 1928, Judge Murray married Miss Marie Underwood, who was reared and educated in Muncie, attended high school and musical college, and has been one of the leaders in musical affairs at Muncie and taught music for several years. She is a member of the Jackson Street Christian Church. Her parents are Philip and Lillie Underwood, of Muncie. Her father for many years has been connected with the Muncie Malleable Foundry Company. Judge and Mrs. Murray have one son, Robert Frank, Jr., born January 6, 1929.

HON. WILLIAM O. BARNARD of Newcastle, who has given over half a century to the cares and responsibilities of the profession of the law and public office, is a native of Indiana, his grandparents having been pioneers of the state. The Barnards represented the sterling Quaker stock which has been such a valuable element in the citizenship of Eastern Indiana.

Judge Barnard was born in Union County, October 25, 1852, son of Sylvester and Lavina (Myer) Barnard. His grandparents, William and Matilda (Gardner) Barnard, came from New York State, driving overland to Union County, Indiana, in 1816. Here William Barnard entered government land. He and his wife had a family of ten children, all of whom married and reared families, constituting an important contribution to the citizenship of the state. Judge Barnard's maternal grandparents were Jacob and Sarah (Landis) Myer, Pennsylvanians who were early settlers in Fayette County, Indiana. Sylvester Barnard was married in Union County, and after a few years moved to Fayette County and in 1864 to Henry County. He died in January, 1914, and his wife in April 1908.

William O. Barnard was reared on a farm, attended the common schools and Spiceland Academy and for five years alternated between teaching winter terms of school and attending school himself. When he was twenty-four he began the study of law in the office of James Brown, at Newcastle. In 1877 he was qualified as a member of the Indiana bar, and since that date he has given an almost uninterrupted service in his profession. For a few years he practiced with Captain Chambers, was then alone and from 1886 to 1892 performed the duties of prosecuting attorney. In 1896 he was elected judge of the Henry County Circuit Court, serving until November, 1902. He left that office by no means richer in this world's goods but with the satisfaction of having performed his duty in a manner that reflected his learning and his devotion to the right. In 1908 Judge Barnard was chosen representative from his Indiana district to the Sixty-first Congress, but was defeated for reelection in 1910. He then resumed his practice as a lawyer, and for fifteen years had as his partner William E. Jeffery. In 1917 his own son came into the office with him, but from 1921 to 1926 he

again practiced alone, after which George R. Jeffery, son of his former partner, joined him. Mr. Jeffery in March, 1929, was appointed United States district attorney of Indiana.

Judge Barnard married, December 27, 1876, Miss Mary D. Ballinger, who was born in Henry County, Indiana, daughter of Nathan H. and Margaret (Hubbard) Ballinger. Her father was born in North Carolina and her mother in Henry County, Indiana. Judge and Mrs. Barnard have four children: Paul, of Hagerstown, Indiana; George M., with the law firm of Van Nuys, Barnard & Walker at Indianapolis; Ralph W., of Kansas City, Missouri; and Ruth, Mrs. Herbert Griffith, of Los Angeles, California.

Judge Barnard is a trustee of the Friends Church of Newcastle, he is also a trustee of Earlham College at Richmond, is a Republican, in Masonry has affiliations with the Lodge, Royal Arch Chapter, Council and Knights Templar Commandery, has held chairs in the Knights of Pythias, is a member of the Improved Order of Red Men, is an honorary member of the Rotary Club, and is a director of the Henry County Building & Loan Association.

ASBURY W. PEASE is superintendent and general manager of the Hoosier Mill at Oolitic, Lawrence County, this being one of the oldest in the group of stone mills comprised in the Indiana Limestone Company. Mr. Pease has been identified with the stone industry since early boyhood, when he learned the cutter's trade. His experience embraces every phase of the industry, from cutting the stone on the job to executive responsibilities in the quarries and mills.

Mr. Pease was born at Louisville, Kentucky, March 13, 1862, son of Charles and Emma (Grimes) Pease. His father, a native of New York, was left an orphan when a boy and soon afterward went to sea, sailing before the mast for several years. Nature endowed him with a remarkable physique. When he was grown he stood six feet seven inches high and weighed about 280 pounds. One employment offered him by reason of his physical stature was in the famous old Dan Rice Circus. During the Civil war he became color sergeant in the Fifty-ninth Indiana Infantry, serving in the Army of the Cumberland. He and his wife had three children, Asbury W., Lottie and Edward.

When Asbury Pease was six years of age he entered the public schools at Louisville. About two years later the family moved to Orleans, Indiana, and after one term of school there the home was moved to Bedford, about 1869. Mr. Pease attended school later at Orleans and Mitchell. His father engaged in the stone business at Mitchell and when Asbury was fourteen years of age he left school and began learning the trade of stone cutter. He worked in a number of the plants around Bedford, and also cut stone for the Government canal locks. He was at Bloomington for a time and in 1900 came to the Hoosier Mill

D.O.McComb

at Oolitic as night foreman of the planer-men. He was promoted to superintendent and general manager, and is one of the best known and most capable superintendents of the various plants that make up the corporation known as the Indiana Limestone Company.

Mr. Pease is a member of the Industrial Club, the Knights Templar Masons, the Independent Order of Odd Fellows and Knights of Pythias. He married, May 24, 1888, Miss Lillian Conner, daughter of Abner and Miranda (Henry) Conner. They have one daughter, Catherine.

DAVID OLIN McCOMB is a native son of Allen County, and to that county he has given almost a lifetime of service in its educational interests. He began teaching in country schools more than thirty-five years ago, and for the past eighteen years has held the office of county superintendent.

Mr. McComb was born on a farm in Perry Township, Allen County, June 11, 1872. His father, James McComb, was a native of Ireland, of Scotch ancestry, was brought to America when three years of age, and during part of his boyhood was bound out to a family in Southern Ohio. He had only limited educational opportunities. He married Margaret Simonton and soon afterward, about 1850, came to Allen County, Indiana, and began his life as a farmer on 200 acres of wild land. He was long a substantial citizen of Perry Township, was elected in 1888 and served two terms as township trustee, was a leader in the United Brethren Church, and he reared a family of children whose careers have honored their parents.

The youngest of this large family is David O. McComb. He grew up on a farm, attended public schools there, spent one year in Taylor University at Upland, and was also a student in the Tri-State Normal at Angola. He began teaching in 1894. His work as a teacher brought him in close touch with the educational affairs of the county, and that early experience has been constantly utilized by him during the long period of years in which he has been the official head of the county system of schools. He has several times filled the office of justice of the peace, and in 1911 became deputy county auditor. Mr. McComb in March, 1913, was elected county superintendent of schools, and the splendid work he has accomplished in that office has well justified his repeated reelections.

Mr. McComb married, December 25, 1900, Miss Anna C. Matsch, of German ancestry. She was born and reared in Allen County. They have three children, James Christopher, Walter Allen, and Dorothy Mae. Mr. McComb and his sons, Walter and James, conduct a prominent business as undertakers in Fort Wayne, at 1140 Lake Avenue, known as McComb & Sons, of which Mr. McComb is president.

Mr. McComb is a Democrat in politics, is affiliated with the Masonic fraternity, and has been president of the Fort Wayne Council of the National Union. He has served on the board of trustees of the Crescent Avenue Evangelical Church, has taught a class of boys in Sunday School, and is now the superintendent of the Sunday School. For many years he has participated in civic, benevolent and war time campaigns as a team worker. For two years he was a chairman of the rural Red Cross membership campaign, captained a team in the Red Cross drive of 1917, was captain and township director of the Red Cross Christmas roll call of 1918, and has rendered similar assistance in subsequent years. He was during the war, Allen County director of the Boys Working Reserve, and while the normal quota for the county was 1660, he succeeded in enrolling 2459 boys in the organization, the largest enrollment of any county in the state, and Indiana was the leader of the nation in this particular auxiliary agency during the war period. After the armistice he was named on the special committee to assist returning soldiers and served on the Allen County rehabilitation committee to provide vocational training for disabled men. Mr. McComb was active in organizing and became the first president of the Northeastern Indiana Teachers Association, organized in 1922, and has been chairman of its executive board. He is a member of the State Teachers' Reading Circle Board.

BERT O. COOK. One of the substantial and well conducted financial institutions of Parke County is the Bank of Mecca, and of this valued communal institution the efficient and popular cashier is Bert O. Cook, who stands forward also as one of the loyal and progressive citizens of the attractive little City of Mecca.

Mr. Cook was born in Indiana, July 16, 1879, and is a son of Andrew and Martha Cook. He received the advantages of the public schools and in his native state he has found ample opportunity for gaining success and prestige in business life, as is attested by his incumbency of his present position of cashier of the Bank of Mecca.

Mr. Cook gives his political allegiance to the Republican party, in the Masonic fraternity he has received the thirty-second degree of the Ancient Accepted Scottish Rite, besides being a Noble of the Mystic Shrine, and he is affiliated also with the Knights of Pythias. Both he and his wife are zealous members of the Methodist Episcopal Church in their home community.

On the 20th of September, 1899, Mr. Cook was united in marriage to Miss Minnie Puntenney, daughter of John G. and Margaret Puntenney, the former of whom was long numbered among the representative farmers and citizens of Parke County, where the original representative of the Puntenney family made settlement more than a century ago, the old homestead place having remained in the possession of the family during all the long intervening years and being the present place of residence of Mr. Cook and his family. Mr.

and Mrs. Cook have three children: Bernice, who was born June 18, 1900, is the wife of George Richardson, of Mecca, and they have two children, Theron and Mark A. Maxine, who was born February 11, 1903, is the wife of Walter Murphy, and they likewise reside in the Mecca community, their one child being a daughter, Rosemary. Madonna, youngest of the children, was born May 18, 1909, remains at the parental home and is now assistant cashier of the bank of which her father is the cashier.

EDWARD VALENTINE TRAUTMANN, owner and proprietor of the Miami Electric Company at Peru, has built up that business from an enterprise that was started by himself and another electrician while both of them were employed on a salary for other companies. It has become one of the largest electrical contracting firms in Northern Indiana.

Mr. Trautmann was born at Peru, March 15, 1884. His father, Andrew Trautmann, a native of Bavaria, Germany, came to Indiana in 1870. He married Margaret Kolb, also a native of Germany.

Edward V. Trautmann was one of a family of seven children. He attended public schools but was only fourteen when he began earning his own living. He was employed in a wood working factory for a time and in 1905 took up electrical work. His experience was an opportunity in which to exercise his keen powers of observation and he has studied all phases of electrical engineering. His promotion was rapid while with the electrical department of the Indiana Manufacturing Company at Peru and he rose to the post of chief engineer. When the company moved its business to Richmond, Indiana, he was assigned the responsibility of installing the electrical machinery.

In the meantime, in 1911, he and his partner had started a small business of their own as electrical contractors. To buy the original stock of equipment Mr. Trautmann had to borrow the sum of $10. They took various jobs after working hours, such as house wiring and installation of electrical fixtures. In 1913 they rented a small room to carry a stock of fixtures and in 1914 they began giving all their time to the business, then known as the Miami Electric Company. The business steadily grew and in 1920 Mr. Trautmann bought out the interest of one of his partners and since 1927 has been sole owner. The first shop was at 9 West Second Street, then moved to 12 West Second Street, next to 19 West Second Street, from there to 63 South Broadway and to 4 South Broadway, and in February, 1925, to the present location, at 18 West Main Street. These changes were all made in response to a growth in the volume of business which demanded increased quarters and a better position in the business district. The Miami Electric Company, at 18 West Main, has a very attractive shop with show rooms and repair department, the entire business requiring over 11,000 square feet of floor space. Fourteen people are employed, and as electrical contractors they have done important work all over the State of Indiana. They handled the electrical work for the Rochester City Hall, for the Beverly Terrace Company Apartment Building at Anderson, the McCordsville School, the Wabash County Loan & Trust Company Building and many others.

Mr. Trautmann for several years was a director of the Peru Chamber of Commerce, is a member of the Kiwanis Club, the National Association of Electrogists, the Indiana Electrical Association, Association of Building Contractors of Indiana, the Miami County Jefferson club, Columbia Club of Indianapolis. He is a Lutheran and in politics exercises his independent judgment as a candidate. During the World war he assisted in all the war drives and helped raise funds for the Red Cross and Y. M. C. A.

Mr. Trautmann married Albertina Butzin, who was born at Peru. Her parents, Carl and Bertha Butzin, came from Germany to Indiana about 1880. Both are living in Peru, the father a highly respected citizen who until he retired was a cabinet maker. Mr. and Mrs. Trautmann have two children, Oscar Herman and Florence Ottilie. Florence is a graduate of the Peru High School and is assisting in her father's business.

HARRY KENNETT CUTHBERTSON, prominent Peru attorney, was born in Chicago, Illinois, October 13, 1882, was reared and educated in that city, and came to Peru in 1914. All his professional career has been spent in Indiana.

Mr. Cuthbertson is of Scotch ancestry. His grandfather, Edwin Cuthbertson, was a professor in Edinburgh University. About 1834 he crossed the Atlantic and settled in Canada. The father of Harry K. Cuthbertson was John Cuthbertson, a Chicago business man, who married Josephine Cornwell.

Harry K. Cuthbertson attended grammar and high school in Chicago and was graduated from the La Salle Extension University of that city, in the law course, in 1914. On coming to Peru he was admitted to practice in the Indiana courts, and has since been admitted to practice before the Supreme Court and the Federal courts.

He had made a promising beginning of his professional work when America entered the World war. On May 4, 1917, he enlisted in the Second Engineers, with the rank of master engineer, and later was assigned to the Twelfth United States Engineers, going overseas in July, 1917. He was brigaded with the British troops at San Quentin and Cambrai, and participated in both of the Cambrai battles in 1917. He was with the British general, Bain, in the counter attack against the German drive and in the Somme offensive, beginning in March, 1918. In June, 1918, he was transferred to the Second American Army and was in the St. Mihiel and Meuse Argonne campaigns and was near Metz when the armistice was signed. General Pershing gave him a citation for exceptional merit and conduct at the battle of Cambrai. Mr. Cuthbertson was overseas until April 29, 1919, and received his honorable discharge on the nineteenth of May, 1919.

Since the war he has taken an active interest in the American Legion and has served as adjutant of the post at Peru. He is a member of the Miami County, Indiana and American Bar Associations. Along with his law practice Mr. Cuthbertson has rendered valuable service to the Democratic party organization. He was nominated candidate for Congress from this district in 1920 and in 1930 was candidate for state senator from Miami and Howard counties, and was elected in November, 1930. He has served on the executive committee of the county organization.

Mr. Cuthbertson married June E. Wood, who was born in Butler Township, Miami County. Two sons and one daughter were born to their marriage, Robert Wood, deceased, Harry Kennett, Jr., and Joella.

RICHARD ROSENCRANZ represents a notable line of industrial and commercial figures in the life of Evansville and is head of one of the city's most substantial industries.

He was born in Evansville, November 11, 1879. His paternal grandfather, Carl Frederick Rosenkranz, came with his family to America in 1850 from Germany. He was a watchmaker and jeweler, and that was the trade and business he followed during his remaining years in Evansville. Mr. Rosencranz' maternal grandparents were William and Mary (Jenner) Heilman. William Heilman was a foundryman, head of the Heilman Machine Works, and had a conspicuous part in Southern Indiana affairs. He was a railroad builder and at one time represented the first Indiana District in Congress.

Richard Rosencranz after two years of high school work entered the foundry of the Vulcan Plow Company, and served successively as iron molder, pattern maker and foreman, thus getting a fundamental knowledge and experience in the business of which he is now the active head. He then spent three years as a student in DePauw University at Greencastle, Indiana, and at Cornell University at Ithaca, New York. On the death of his father in 1920 Mr. Rosencranz succeeded to the presidency of the Vulcan Plow Company. During the past ten years this industry has made steady progress in its manufacturing facilities and in the range of distribution of its products. In 1930 the Vulcan Plow Company acquired control of a number of established lines related to its own manufacture and reorganized, by consolidation, under the firm name of Farm Tools, Incorporated.

Mr. Rosencranz was on the original committee of the Evansville Chamber of Commerce to secure a college for the City of Evansville. Through the efforts of this committee one of Indiana's noted older institutions of learning, the Moore's Hill College of Moore's Hill, was moved to Evansville and has since been known as Evansville College. Mr. Rosencranz has served as a trustee and secretary of the board of trustees of the college since its establishment at Evansville in 1919. He has had a constant contact with the important civic, educational and benevolent affairs of his home city. He is a director of the Central Union Bank, member of the Rotary Club, is a Republican in national politics, independent locally. He has done considerable work in Inter Racial and boy welfare movements. Mr. Rosencranz is a lover of music and outdoor activities.

He married in 1915 Miss Margaret Eberle, of Watertown, Wisconsin. She is a graduate of the University of Wisconsin and is a daughter of Herman T. and Ida Louise (Oehler) Eberle. Her father was a druggist, postmaster of his town, and served on the library and school boards. The four children of Mr. and Mrs. Rosencranz are Richard, born in 1916, Albert and Allen, twins, born in 1919, and Joan Eberle, born in 1925.

HERBERT ERICKSON. Prominent among the officials who have contributed to the upbuilding, development and progress of Gary is Herbert Erickson, who has occupied the office of building commissioner for two terms. A resident of Gary since 1908, he has been engaged in the profession of architecture since the time of his arrival and in numerous ways has added to the beauty of the city of his adoption through his professional skill and capable workmanship.

Mr. Erickson was born at Fort Wayne, Indiana, June 22, 1885, and is a son of John and Anna (Fries) Erickson. John Erickson was born in Sweden, where he received good educational advantages, including a course in the University of Upsala, following which he became a designer and engineer in his native land. There he met and married Anna Fries, also born in Sweden, who was educated at Stockholm, and not long after their union they immigrated to the United States and about 1870 settled at Fort Wayne. There John Erickson continued to be employed as a designer and engineer until his death in July, 1929, having also been active as a member of the Masonic fraternity and as a public-spirited citizen interested in civic affairs. Mrs. Erickson died November 4, 1924, and both are buried at Fort Wayne. There were nine children in the family: Emil, who died at the age of thirty-five years; Richard, of Chicago, Illinois; Capt. Marshall, U. S. N., retired, of Seabeck, Washington; Herbert, of this review; Miss Ida, of Fort Wayne, Indiana; Nannie, the wife of Nestor Fries, of Fort Wayne; Maria, now Mrs. Lenz, of Montpelier, Ohio; and Misses Esther and Vivian, of Fort Wayne.

Herbert Erickson attended the public schools of Fort Wayne and after his graduation from high school, as a member of the class of 1904, secured a position with Charles Kendrick, an architect of Fort Wayne. He spent two years in the drafting department, and then entered the engineering department of the Wabash

Valley Traction Company, where he continued for a like period. His next three years were passed in the engineering department of the Clover Leaf Railroad Company, and in 1908 he came to Gary, where he opened an office and entered upon the practice of his profession as an architect. He has continued in this line to the present and has advanced steadily to a commanding position in the ranks of his profession. In 1922 Mr. Erickson was appointed a member of the board of city building commissioners, serving in that capacity for four years, and January 6, 1930, was again appointed to this office for another four-year term. He has discharged the duties of his office in a highly capable and commendable manner and has the full confidence and esteem of his associates and the public in general. Mr. Erickson is a member of Gary Lodge No. 677, A. F. and A. M., and for some years was active in the Benevolent and Protective Order of Elks, in which order he held several offices. He is also a member of the Optimist Club and the Gary Country Club. A Republican in his political views, Mr. Erickson was a member of the county council for a number of years and was the first president of the Gary Republican Club. Recently he was elected president of the Harrison Republican Club, and at all times he has been a leader in the ranks of his party. Mr. Erickson is a member of the English Lutheran Church.

At Delphi, Indiana, August 15, 1908, Mr. Erickson was united in marriage with Miss Grace Sines, a daughter of Edward and Emma (Jakes) Sines, of Delphi, the former of whom was for years a prominent merchant of that place, where he now lives in retirement. He has been active in civic affairs, and he and Mrs. Sines are consistent members of the Methodist Episcopal Church. Mrs. Erickson is a graduate of the Delphi High School, is a member of the Methodist Episcopal Church, and is active in club circles. She was county chairman of the Red Cross and Liberty Loan drives during the World war, and is a member of the Daughters of the American Revolution. Two children have been born to Mr. and Mrs. Erickson: Herbert, Jr., who died at the age of two years; and Jerry David.

SAMUEL NUSSBAUM was born and grew up near Berne in Adams County, and as an active citizen has found some connection with nearly every line of business in that community. He has been in insurance and real estate, a manufacturer, and has helped create new resources and opportunities for this enterprising city. Mr. Nussbaum was born near Berne, October 15, 1880. His father John P. Nussbaum, came from Switzerland, where he was born October 14, 1844. The Nussbaum family settled in Adams County, Indiana, in 1852, when he was eight years of age. He is now eighty-five and enjoying well earned retirement at Berne. John P. Nussbaum married in February, 1866, Virginia Mazelin, who was born near Berne, Adams County, October 15, 1845. Her people were among the very early settlers, coming from France. She is now eighty-four years of age and a very active woman for her years. The children were all born at Berne: Levi, born in 1869, since twenty-two years of age has lived in the West, is a contractor at St. Mary's, Idaho, and has never married; Peter, born in March, 1870, went west with his brother Levi and for many years has been a gold miner and prospector in Canada and Alaska, and like Levi, has never married; Sarah, born October 7, 1871, married Rudolph Wyss, of Chehalis, Washington, who died in 1918, and she is now living with her parents at Berne; William, born December 24, 1873, a farmer four miles from Berne, married Lena Stauffer; John, born October 9, 1877, went to North Dakota, where he married Cora Camel, and they now live at San Diego, California, where he is an employee of the municipal government; and Samuel, the youngest of the family.

Samuel Nussbaum grew up on a farm, was educated in local schools and at the age of twenty began teaching in country districts of Adams County. He continued his own education in Valparaiso University, graduating in 1903. For two years Mr. Nussbaum was on the road as a traveling salesman and in 1906 entered the clothing and shoe business at Berne. In 1908 he was elected township assessor, holding that office for six years. In 1914, after selling out his clothing store, Mr. Nussbaum took up real estate and insurance and that has been one department of his varied business enterprises during the past fifteen years. In 1913 he was elected manager of the Berne Supply Company, and as active head of that business he has made it an organization covering a wide range, handling supplies for schools, and also supplies for road and bridge contractors.

Mr. Nussbaum in 1924 started the Nussbaum Novelty Company, of which he is president and manager. The former purpose of this business was making cedar chests of cedar wood for the holiday trade. Mr. Nussbaum organized a small stock company and capitalized it at $12,000 and at first nearly all the work was done by hand. Larger quarters were secured, a heavy investment of wood working machinery installed and the force has been steadily increased until now about 100 people are employed, manufacturing an exclusive line of Cedar boxes and chests, which are shipped and sold in every state of the Union and in many foreign countries.

Mr. Nussbaum in 1922 acquired eighty acres of the Emanuel Leichty farm and laid it out into a splendid residential subdivision of Berne. From it he donated generously lots for school purposes and in every way handled the project to reflect credit upon his public spirited citizenship. Mr. Nussbaum for fifteen years has been an active member of the Berne fire department and for several years was secretary of the Berne Business Men's Associ-

H. A. White

ation. He is a Republican in politics and a member of the Mennonite Church.

Mr. Nussbaum married, February 6, 1906, Miss Mary Leichty, who was born in Switzerland and was two years of age when her parents came to America. She died May 20, 1916, and is buried at Berne. There were three children of this marriage: Hazel born September 7, 1907, was reared and educated in Berne, spent five years in her father's office and is now the wife of Dora Brewster, of Berne. Lester, the second child, was born April 5, 1911, and is with his father's manufacturing business. Florine, the youngest was born May 20, 1915, and is attending the Berne High School. Mr. Nussbaum on June 20, 1919, married Miss Ida Zumbrum, of Pierce, Nebraska. She was reared and educated in Nebraska. Her father, a farmer, died in 1917 and is buried in Nebraska and her mother now lives in Berne.

HARRY ORVILLE WHITE in point of years and continuous service is the oldest undertaker in Miami County. He has been in business at Converse for thirty-two years.

Mr. White was born in Wayne County, Eastern Indiana, August 17, 1871, and is a member of an early family of that section of the state. His grandfather, Nathan White, was born in Kentucky and moved to Indiana prior to 1816, using Government script with which he acquired some of the public lands. White is one of the old and honored names in Wayne County. The Whites were originally Virginians and followed westward over Boone's trail to Kentucky, where they settled about the close of the Revolutionary war. The father of Harry O. White was Thomas P. White, a blacksmith by trade, who served as deputy sheriff of his native county of Wayne. He married Orpha Blose, who was also born in Wayne County.

Harry O. White was one of four children. He attended school in Wayne County, and first prepared himself for the duties of educational work. After taking a course of training in the Central Normal College at Danville he taught school three years in Randolph County. He left school work to serve a practical apprenticeship of four years with an undertaking firm at Richmond, and in 1898 came to Converse and started the undertaking business he has carried on continuously. He has been successful in his aim to give this community a thoroughly progressive service. He has made provisions for a funeral chapel, has a combination coach and hearse and other equipment. In connection with the undertaking business he has been a dealer in monuments since 1902. For this he has provided a complete shop with skilled workmen and facilities for the carving and inscribing of monuments.

Mr. White has served as a member of the Miami County Council, and has been on the city advisory board at Converse. During the World war he was put in charge of Jackson Township drives for the sale of Liberty Bonds, the raising of funds for the Red Cross and

Y. M. C. A., and was also a member of the local sugar commission. Mr. White is past master of Converse Lodge No. 601, A. F. and A. M., member of the Royal Arch Chapter and Council, is a past commander of the Knights Templar Commandery at Marion, and a member of Fort Wayne Consistory of the Scottish Rite and Murat Temple of the Mystic Shrine at Indianapolis. He also belongs to the Independent Order of Odd Fellows and Knights of Pythias.

Mr. White married Miss Mattie E. Conley, a native of Wayne County, Indiana. They have one child, Naomi Emma, who graduated from the Converse High School and from the Metropolitan School of Music at Indianapolis. She is the wife of Fred Hankins, of Omaha, Nebraska. Mr. White is a member of the Lions Club and its treasurer, and is a member of the Monument Dealers Association.

MISS EUNETTE BUCK is librarian of the Kentland Public Library and has given her talents and services to that institution since it was founded, January 19, 1910. She has been librarian since 1928.

The Public Library at Kentland was established from a fund raised locally, and later benefited by a contribution by the Carnegie Library Fund and is now a standard Carnegie Library. The members of the board are: Charles Rinard, president; James Illingworth, vice president, secretary and treasurer; Clyde Hurt, W. O. Schanlaub, E. Griffin, Mrs. Virginia McCray, Mrs. Birdie Sharp and Mrs. O. E. Glick.

EDWIN GERHARDT VON FANGE was born in Bartholomew County, Indiana, December 17, 1875, and represents a family that was established in that section of Indiana ninety years ago. Mr. Von Fange is owner of the Von Fange Monument Works at Peru.

His grandfather, Gerhardt Von Fange, came from Hanover, Germany, and settled in Bartholomew County about 1840. He was a farmer, and had much to do with the establishment of the White Creek Lutheran Church in his community and was one of its most liberal supporters. He married Wilhelmina Ohmann, also a native of Germany. The father of the Peru business man was Herman C. Von Fange, a native of Bartholomew County, who married Wilhelmina Bode of the same county. They were substantial and respected farming people in that community.

Edwin G. Von Fange grew up on a farm, attended grade schools and lived with his father and was more or less closely identified with farm work and management until 1924. During that time he also sold farm implements and from 1912 to 1923 conducted a monument business at Seymour. When he sold his interest in that enterprise he moved to Peru and bought the Frank Cheeseman Monument Shop. Mr. Von Fange is a member of the National Memorial Craftsmen of America and the Indiana Craftsmen. He has a shop and show room at 19 West Canal Street, with a large amount of fine work on display, and has the technical facilities and the skilled craftsman capable of doing the finest type of work.

Mr. Von Fange had the contract to execute the markers and place them on several of Indiana's historical landmarks, including the ten o'clock line marker near Seymour.

For a number of years he represented the Federal agricultural department as a crop and farm condition reporter for Jackson County. During the war he assisted in all the drives for funds in his locality. He married Miss Emma Knott, a native of Jackson County. They were the parents of five children: Walter, Minnie who died in 1929, Carl, Alvin and Edward.

GEORGE SMITH, a resident of Goodland, is one of the oldest men in the service of the Chicago, Attica & Southern Railway on this division. He has earned the respect and frequent commendation of superior officials and is a man noted for his thoroughness and his ability to get work done under unfavorable as well as favorable circumstances.

Mr. Smith was born in Kentucky, March 17, 1879, and was a child when brought to Newton County, Indiana. His father was Samuel Smith, who died when his son George was an infant. The mother, Mrs. Helen (Jenks) Smith, was born in Kentucky and lives at Goodland. They had three children, Alva, William and George. Alva lives in Portland, Oregon, and William is deceased.

George Smith was educated in public schools in Newton County and followed farming during his early life. About thirty years ago he became an employee of the Pennsylvania Railway, and for the past fifteen years has been trackman of the track work for the Chicago, Attica & Southern. Mr. Smith is unmarried and resides with his mother at Goodland. He is a Republican in politics and is affiliated with the Independent Order of Odd Fellows.

JAMES M. KNAPP, of Hagerstown, has had an important role in the civic affairs of Wayne County for a number of years. He has served in the Legislature and has been identified with practically every movement for better advantages and progress at Hagerstown.

He was born there December 11, 1876, son of Charles T. and Inez Allen (Stombaugh) Knapp. His father was born in Ripley County and his mother in Henry County, Indiana. His father was a lumber dealer in Hagerstown. James M. Knapp attended grade and high schools at Hagerstown and as a boy served an apprenticeship to learn the marble cutting trade. That trade has been the basis of his permanent business, and since 1917 he has managed the monumental works at Hagerstown.

Mr. Knapp married, May 10, 1896, Miss Ethel J. Fox, who was born in Jefferson Township, Wayne County, daughter of Minus T. and Della (Petty) Fox. They have two children. The son, Wilfred T., connected with the Standard Oil Company at Richmond, married Elizabeth McLear and has a son, Donald Eugene. The daughter, Pauline, is the wife of Howard Klute, with the Dickinson Trust Company at Richmond.

Mr. Knapp has long been a leader in the Methodist Episcopal Church and for twenty-five years was superintendent of the Sunday School. In 1897 he served one year as truant officer for five townships of the county, and he was town clerk from 1908 to 1912. During 1905-07 he was clerk in the postoffice of the National House of Representatives at Washington. He served six years on the local school board. In 1919 he was a member of the General Assembly, and served on several important committees, being chairman of the cities and towns committee and the education committee. Mr. Knapp served seven terms in the Indiana House of Representatives and was speaker in the 1929 session and Republican floor-leader in 1931. He is a Republican and since 1905 has been a member of the Independent Order of Odd Fellows. Mr. Knapp was one of the men mainly responsible for building up a Chautauqua organization at Hagerstown. He is a member of the George Rogers Clark Memorial Commission. Mrs. Knapp died October 20, 1928.

HON. WILLIAM F. HODGES was one of the first attorneys to establish practice and office at Gary, locating there a few months after the founding of the city. He has been one of the outstanding members of the bar, also prominent in Masonry, in Chamber of Commerce and civic work and in politics. From 1926 to 1931 he was state senator from Lake County.

He was born at Hiseville, Kentucky, March 3, 1877, son of Edmond and Theodosia (Turner) Hodges. His grandfather, Alford Hodges, was born and reared in North Carolina and moved to Kentucky in 1850. He fought for the Union at the time of the Civil war. He owned a farm, and before railroads were built in his locality he was a wagoner, driving a six-horse team, freighting goods from Louisville to Glasgow and other points in Kentucky. He died about 1890 and is buried at Summershade, Kentucky. The Hodges family on coming to America first settled in North Carolina. Edmond Hodges was born in Johnson County in East Tennessee and was two years of age when his parents moved to Kentucky, where he grew up, was educated in common schools, and has spent a long and active career as a farmer. He supervises his farming interests, though now living retired at Hiseville at the age of eighty-two. He and his wife are members of the Christian Church. His wife was born in Kentucky and is seventy-six years of age. They had four sons: Joseph A., deceased; William F.; Thomas; and Harry B., deceased.

William F. Hodges was educated in public schools in Kentucky and in 1898 graduated with the Bachelor of Science degree from Valparaiso University of Indiana. In 1904 he

Chas V Postill

completed the law course there and during the years he was in Valparaiso he completed courses in civil engineering, commercial work and oratory. In 1903 he was admitted to the bar at Valparaiso and for one year practiced at Rensselaer, Indiana. After a trip over the West he settled at Rensselaer, in January, 1906. In September, 1906, he came to Gary, and he and Claude V. Ridgeley, now judge of the Superior Court, formed a partnership that continued to their mutual advantage and profit until May, 1927. For twenty years they constituted one of the strongest law firms in Northern Indiana. After this firm dissolved Hershell B. Davis became a partner of Senator Hodges, and the latter's son has recently become junior member of the firm of Hodges, Davis & Hodges, with offices at 607 Broadway.

Senator Hodges is a member of the Indiana and Gary Bar Associations. He owns real estate in Gary and for many years has been in close touch with the civic and industrial progress of the community. Fraternally he is affiliated with Gary Lodge No. 677 A. F. and A. M., Gary Chapter, Royal Arch Masons, Knights Templar Commandery, Ancient Accepted Scottish Rite, South Bend, Orak Temple of the Mystic Shrine at Hammond, is a member of the B. P. O. Elks, a life member of the Loyal Order of Moose, was president for 1929-30 of the Gary Rotary Club and district governor of the Twentieth District Rotary International in 1930-31. He is a former president of the Chamber of Commerce, member of the Gary Country Club, Gary Republican Club, Lincoln Club of Hammond.

His activity in politics has been incidental to his studious devotion to his professional practice. In 1909-10 he served as deputy prosecuting attorney of Lake County, was city attorney of Gary in 1914-15, and mayor of the city from 1918 to 1922. He has been president of the Municipal League of Indiana. From 1926 to 1931 he was a member of the State Senate. Senator Hodges is a member of the official board of the Congregational Church.

He married at Hiseville, Kentucky, January 3, 1901, Miss Cassie Vernon Newberry, daughter of Dr. Thomas L. and Jennie (Pemberton) Newberry. Her father served as a surgeon in the Confederate army and for many years did the work of a country physician over Barren and adjoining counties in Kentucky. He died in 1905 and the mother in 1885. Mrs. Hodges attended school at Hiseville, the Jessamine Institute, a girls' school at Nicholasville, Kentucky and in 1904 was graduated from Valparaiso University of Indiana. She was a teacher in Kentucky and for a time was one of the instructors in Valparaiso University. Mrs. Hodges for two years was president of the Gary Woman's Club and is a member of the Daughters of the American Revolution. They have two children. Their son, Thomas M., graduated from the Emerson High School of Gary in 1923, took his A. B.

degree at the University of Wisconsin in 1927, and graduated in 1930, with the degree Doctor of Laws, from the University of Chicago, immediately afterward joining his father in law practice. Senator Hodges' daughter, Jennie Theodosia, graduated from the Emerson High School in 1925 and from the University of Wisconsin in 1930, with the A. B. degree.

REV. CHARLES WALTER POSTILL, whose home is at Rensselaer, is a retired minister who has devoted his leisure to some very interesting and important studies and investigations, particularly the study of Indiana birds. He is probably the leading living authority as an ornithologist, and has amassed and collected a great mass of data which he has been preparing for publication and which bird lovers all over the Middle West will welcome as a mine of scholarly information on the bird life of this state. Mr. Postill out of a long and busy life has generated a wholesome philosophy and has propounded the interesting thesis that Indiana, with its wonderful beauties and resources of trees, flowers and birds, would have paid better dividends to Ponce de Leon in his search for the Fountain of Perpetual Youth than Florida.

Mr. Postill's father, William H. Postill, was born in Alexandria, Canada, and came to Indiana in pioneer times. He was an officer in the Civil war, serving with Col. Robert Milroy's men, known as the Ninety Day Men. He was wounded in the battle of Pittsburgh Landing. He was a farmer by occupation, and died in 1872. William H. Postill married Mary Ann Snodgrass, daughter of William Snodgrass, of Morgan County, Indiana.

Charles W. Postill received his early education in Jasper County and graduated with the degree Bachelor of Divinity from DePauw University in 1895. He became a member of the Northwest Indiana Conference and for three years was a pastor at Fontanet, six years at Wingate, three at Remington, five at Fowler, and at Attica three years. While at Attica his health failed and he gave up his pastoral duties. Coming to Rensselaer, he built in 1913 the handsome home which he has since occupied. In 1916 he retired from the ministry permanently.

Mr. Postill was appointed township trustee in 1917 to fill out the term of Harvey W. Wood and was subsequently elected for a term of four years. He is now chairman of the Jasper County Hospital Board and since 1913 has served as a member of the board of the Monett School for Girls at Rensselaer. Rev. Mr. Postill was appointed chairman of the Jasper County Red Cross in 1922. In 1929 he was elected president of the Rainbow Garden Club, and is now serving his second term as secretary-treasurer of the Jasper County Farm Bureau. He is secretary of the Rensselaer City School Board. All of these have been positions where he has had opportunity for constructive service and through which he has at the same time been able to pursue his hobby as a student of outdoor life. He also owns and operates a farm of 200 acres.

Mr. Postill married, September 3, 1890, Rebecca Elizabeth Richardson, daughter of Daniel and Elizabeth Jane Richardson, of LaPorte County. Their only child died in infancy. Mrs. Postill is a member of the Foreign Missionary Society and both are active members of the Methodist Church and are Republicans in politics.

EDWARD HARRY MILGRAM has distinct precedence as a pioneer shoe merchant in the City of Gary, where he has maintained his residence since 1909, and where his success and his popularity indicate the communal estimate placed upon him as a sterling citizen and representative business man. Of the family history due record is given on other pages of this work, in the personal sketch of his brother Samuel H., the two having long been associated in business in Gary and each having here continued independently in the shoe business since the dissolution of their partnership.

Edward H. Milgram was born in Odessa, Russia, July 2, 1887, and is a son of Harry and Dora (Springberg) Milgram. In the schools of his native land Mr. Milgram continued his studies until he was fourteen years of age and he then, in October, 1901, came to the United States and established residence in Wisconsin. He supplemented his education by attending a business college at Merrill, that state, and thereafter was employed a few years as mercantile clerk, at Merrill and Wausau. In this connection he gained his initial experience in the shoe business, and he was an ambitious and self-reliant youth of twenty-two years when he came to Gary, Indiana, in 1909, the following year having marked his engaging independently in the retail shoe business here. His brother Samuel H. later was admitted to partnership in the business, and in 1915 another brother, David H., likewise became associated with the enterprise, which continued to expand in scope and importance until commercial expediency led to a dissolution of the partnership, the firm having in the meanwhile opened two other stores in the city. The firm dissolved partnership in 1920, and Edward H. Milgram at that time assumed individual ownership of the store at 686 Broadway, where he has since continued to maintain a substantial and representative business, his establishment being known as the M. B. Boot Shop and being one of the finest in Northern Indiana.

Mr. Milgram has entered fully and loyally into the communal life of Gary and as a citizen and business man has exemplified effectively the progressive spirit that has ever animated this wonderful industrial city. He was for seven years a director of the Peoples State Bank, and is now president of the Buchanan Realty Company. He has membership in the Gary Chamber of Commerce and Commercial Club, his political support is given to the Republican party, and in their home city he and his wife are active members of Temple Israel. His ancient craft Masonic affiliation is with Gary Lodge, No. 677, A. F. and A. M., and in this great fraternity his Scottish Rite affiliations are with the Consistory in the City of Fort Wayne, in which he has received the thirty-second degree and has thus become a sublime prince of the royal secret. In the City of Hammond he is a Noble of Orak Temple of the Mystic Shrine, and he is affiliated also with the Benevolent and Protective Order of Elks and with the B'nai B'rith. He is a popular member of the Woodmar Country Club and the Turkey Creek Country Club.

At Wausau, Wisconsin, on the 26th of July, 1915, Mr. Milgram was united in marriage to Miss Anna F. Brenner, who was born and reared in that state and who received the advantages of the public schools of Wausau, including the high school. Mrs. Milgram is a daughter of D. J. and Rose (Chaimson) Brenner, who now reside in the City of Milwaukee, Wisconsin, Mr. Brenner having been engaged in the mercantile business a number of years and having thereafter been a traveling commercial salesman for a wholesale clothing house. He is now living virtually retired. Mrs. Milgram has membership in leading women's clubs in her home city and also in a local chapter of the Order of the Eastern Star. Mr. and Mrs. Milgram have three children, Hortense Madelin, Dorothy Jane and Jerome Charles. The elder daughter is, in 1931, a student in the Horace Mann High School of Gary, and the other two children are pupils in the public schools of their home city.

Mr. Milgram finds his chief recreation through the medium of golf, in which he is an enthusiast and indulgence in which he finds through the links of the two country clubs with which he is identified, as previously noted. He takes deep and loyal interest in all that concerns the welfare and progress of his home city, which he appreciates as having offered to him the opportunities through which he has gained substantial success in business, and in the World war period he was an earnest supporter of the various patriotic activities of Lake County.

LOUIS C. CHRISTOPHER has been a resident of Gary since 1916, and here has been consecutively associated with the advertising and newspaper business, in connection with which his initiative and administrative ability have enabled him to gain a position of prominence and influence. Mr. Christopher is here president and manager of the Printcraft Service Company, the well equipped headquarters of which are established at 739 Washington Street, and is also president of the Gary News Corporation, which publishes the *Glen Park News*, a well ordered weekly paper that effectively represents the varied interests of the attractive suburban district of Glen Park. As a member of the Gary City Council he is giving definite expression to his civic loyalty and progressiveness.

Mr. Christopher was born at Saint George, Serbia, August 28, 1894, a son of Charles and

Theodora (Subick) Christopher, who were there born and reared and who came with their children to the United States in 1903, the family home having been established in the City of Chicago, where Charles Christopher was engaged several years in the retail grocery business and where his death occurred February 26, 1914, his widow being now a resident of Gary, Indiana, which city likewise is the home of her three children, of whom the eldest is Louis C. Christopher, of this review; Stephen, the next younger son, has here been variously engaged, his activities having included service as teller in one of the local banking institutions; and Philip is here in the employ of the Illinois Steel Company.

Louis C. Christopher was a lad of about nine years when the family home was established in Chicago and there his public school advantages included those of the Lane Technical High School, in which he was graduated as a member of the class of 1913. Thereafter he completed a course in the Koester Advertising School of that city, and during the ensuing three years he was retained in the advertising department of the A. M. Rothschild Company, which at that time conducted one of the large department stores of Chicago and which was virtually succeeded by the present Davis Company. In 1916 Mr. Christopher came to Gary, Indiana, and during the first year he was here in the employ of the *Gary Post*. During the next four years he was similarly associated with the *Gary Tribune*, the pioneer paper of the city and one that eventually was consolidated with the *Post*, under the present title of *Gary-Post Tribune*. After severing his direct alliance with newspaper service, in which he had been a representative of the advertising department, Mr. Christopher organized the Indiana Advertising Service. For this concern he developed a prosperous and important business in the general newspaper advertising field, and after the passing of two years he amplified the enterprise by organizing the Printcraft Service Company, of which he has since continued the president and manager and to which he has drawn a substantial and representative clientage. The well ordered printing establishment and general offices of this progressive corporation are located at 739 Washington Street.

On the 12th of April, 1928, Mr. Christopher gave further evidence of his initiative ability and his progressiveness by founding the *Glen Park News*, which has been successfully published as a modern weekly paper, by the Gary News Corporation, of which Mr. Christopher is the president. As a member of the City Council Mr. Christopher has the 1931 assignment to its buildings and grounds, public welfare committee and special police investigating committee. He is a loyal and valued member of the Gary Chamber of Commerce and Commercial Club. His basic Masonic affiliation is with Mizpah Lodge, A. F. and A. M., in the City of Chicago, and in his home city he has membership in Gary Chapter, R. A. M., and Gary Commandery, Knights Templar. In the time-honored fraternity he has received the thirty-second degree of the Scottish Rite, besides being a Noble of the Mystic Shrine, in Orak Temple, at Hammond. He is affiliated also with Gary Lodge No. 1152, B. P. O. E., and with the local organization of the Loyal Order of Moose. His political allegiance is given to the Republican party, and he retains the ancestral religious faith, that of the Greek Orthodox Church. His wife likewise is an active communicant of this church and is affiliated with the Order of the Eastern Star.

July 20, 1924, recorded the marriage of Mr. Christopher to Miss Louise Gaitz, daughter of Dushan and Anna (Knezevich) Gaitz, who were born and reared in Serbia, where their marriage was solemnized and whence they came to the United States about 1900. After having been engaged in business some time in Philadelphia, Pennsylvania, Mr. Gaitz removed with his family to Detroit, Michigan, where his death occurred in 1914, his widow being now a loved member of the family circle of Mr. and Mrs. Christopher, in Gary. Mrs. Christopher received the advantages of the public schools of Philadelphia and Detroit, and prior to her marriage she had served a few years as bookkeeper in the offices of the General Motors, in Detroit. Mr. and Mrs. Christopher have two children: Louis C., Jr., and Nattalie.

RUDOLPH CONRAD MOHR has given excellent account of himself in the land of his adoption, is a skilled artisan in the cut stone industry, and along this line has become one of the leading contractors in the City of Gary, where he has maintained his residence since 1908 and where he has developed a large and important business in general contracting in stone construction work. His partner in the business is Willibald Dittrich, and the well equipped plant headquarters of the business are established near Third and Virginia streets, on the right-of-way premises of the Baltimore & Ohio Railroad. When the operations of the firm are at the maximum in rush periods it is found essential to retain an average of about twenty employes.

Mr. Mohr was born in Austria, February 19, 1876, and is a son of Ferdinand and Anna (Florian) Mohr, the former of whom passed his entire life in Austria, where his death occurred June 21, 1921, and where his mortal remains rest in the cemetery at Sandhübel, he having long been engaged in the bakery business in his native land, where his widow still resides. Of their seven sons one died in infancy, and of the survivors the subject of this review is the eldest; Joseph is a resident of Denver, Colorado; Julius has residence in Milwaukee, Wisconsin, as does also Raymond; Prof. Franz Karl Mohr is a member of the faculty of the historic old University of Virginia, at Charlottesville; Robert remains at the old home in Austria.

Rudolph C. Mohr received his early education in the excellent schools of his native land, including a trade school in which he gained a thorough knowledge of all details of the stone industry. After becoming a skilled workman at the trade of stone cutter and carver Mr. Mohr continued to follow the work of his trade in Austria until 1893, when he came to the United States and established residence in the City of Columbus, Ohio. After following his trade three years in the capital city of the Buckeye State he returned to his native land, where he served three years in the Austrian army. Upon coming again to the United States he located at South Bend, Indiana, where he followed his trade until 1908, which year marked his removal to Gary, where he has since continued to be independently established in business as a stone contractor and where he has a good measure of pioneer precedence in this important field of enterprise. Here his record has been one of marked success and he has gained rank among the substantial and representative business men of the great industrial metropolis of Lake County. Mr. Mohr is a valued member of the local Chamber of Commerce and Commercial Club, is a Republican in political alignment, and he and his wife are popular in social life in their home city, he being a talented pianist and being also skilled in the playing of band and orchestra instruments. Mr. Mohr is a communicant of the Catholic Church and his wife holds the faith of the German Lutheran Church.

At Gary, on the 31st of December, 1928, was solemnized the marriage of Mr. Mohr to Mrs. Margaret M. (Weisser) Schuster, who was born and reared in Germany, her father, Julius Weisser, having long been engaged in the bakery business in the City of Breslau, where he still resides and where occurred the death of his wife, Anna. Mrs. Mohr came to the United States in 1914 and had resided in Chicago a few years prior to her establishing residence at Gary. By her former marriage she has one son, Paul Theodore. Mr. and Mrs. Mohr have one son, Rudolph Ferdinand, born February 21, 1930.

RUSSELL E. WARREN. The county superintendent of schools of Randolph County, Indiana, Supt. Russell E. Warren, is a man of practical ideas, and a thorough knowledge of the requirements of the schools under his charge. His life has been spent in schoolteaching, he loves his work, but possesses the decision and persistence to enforce discipline; the patience and industry to impart knowledge, to reason and analyze, and the progressiveness to adopt new methods when he is certain that they will prove effective. His record in educational work is exceptionally good, and the results he is securing in his present office are very acceptable to the people of the county.

Superintendent Warren was born in Randolph County, November 2, 1889, a son of Joseph and Martha E. (Sarff) Warren, natives of Indiana, he born in Randolph County and she in Adams County. All his life a farmer, the father served for some years as township road supervisor, and was a man of standing in his community, and when he died, in July, 1918, his loss was mourned by all who knew him and appreciated his many excellent traits of character. The mother survived him until May, 1927, when she, too, passed away, leaving behind her fragrant memories of kindly deeds and Christian living.

After the usual educational training of a farmer's son Superintendent Warren had three years in the Terre Haute, Indiana, State Normal School; one year at Ball's Teachers College, Muncie, Indiana; six weeks at the University of Wisconsin, Madison, Wisconsin, and twenty-five hours at Adrian College.

In the meanwhile, at intervals between his own studies, he taught in the district schools for two years and a grade school for one year. Then for four years he was principal of the township high school of Ward Township, Randolph County, Indiana, going from there to the township high school of Green Township. His next school was that of Nettle Creek Township, where he remained for three years. Leaving Randolph County, he then taught for two years at Cowan, Delaware County, Indiana, and in February, 1926, assumed the duties of county superintendent of schools of Randolph County. Mr. Warren holds an A. B. degree from Ball's State College and a Master's degree from Indiana University.

In 1915 he was married to Miss Edna Wallace, who was born in Wayne County, Indiana, a daughter of William and Eva (Adams) Wallace, natives of Wayne County. There are no children. Superintendent Warren is a consistent member of the Methodist Episcopal Church. He is a Democrat in a Republican stronghold, and is the only Democrat to hold his present office in Randolph County, his personal popularity having elected him. He is a Chapter Mason, and belongs to the Kiwanis Club, the National Education Association, the Indiana State Teachers Association, the County Superintendents Association and other organizations, in which he is as popular as he is in everything with which he is connected. In addition to his official duties he is interested in farming, owning two farms, one of 135 acres and the other of fifty-six acres. He owns the Branham Hotel in Union City, Indiana, where he now lives, and also owns a one-half interest in the Hoosier Hotel in Danville, Indiana.

CHARLES H. ALLISON, whose home is in Russiaville, Howard County, has been a member of the county bar for over a quarter of a century. Mr. Allison is especially well known over Indiana through his official work in connection with the Independent Order of Odd Fellows.

He has lived practically all his life in one community. He was born November 5, 1872, in a log cabin which stood on the site of his present modern home at the western edge of Russiaville. Mr. Allison's great-great-grandfather, Charles Allison, with his brother James, natives of Holland, came to America

when young men and were soldiers on the American side in the Revolutionary war. The original Allison stock came from Northern England and moved to Holland on account of religious oppression in England.

Charles H. Allison is a son of Martin and Mary E. (Smithson) Allison. His father was born in York County, Pennsylvania, January 13, 1836, and his mother in Highland County, Ohio, August 30, 1837. They were married at Russiaville, Indiana, in 1859. Martin Allison came to Indiana in 1848. The old Madison & Indianapolis Railroad had not yet been completed to Indianapolis. While living with John Kessler in Lafayette he learned the wagonmaker's trade. For a short time his home was at Paris, Illinois, and in 1857 he bought the land at Russiaville comprising the Allison homestead, a large portion of which is owned by Mr. Charles H. Allison. Martin Allison from 1860 to 1866 was kept very busy building army wagons. All the woodwork had to be fashioned from the rough timber by hand skill.

Charles H. Allison attended the local schools at Russiaville and in May, 1890, was graduated from the high school of Delphi in Carroll County. Later he spent two years in Butler College at Indianapolis and one year in the Indiana Law School at Indianapolis, graduating in 1893. His experience as a lawyer has brought him in contact with a large amount of litigation and he has represented many of the citizens of Russiaville in business before the courts at Kokomo. While he still carries on a general law practice he has devoted much time to the building up of a general insurance agency. Mr. Allison is a lawyer who has had no aspirations for public office. In politics he is usually aligned with the Republican party.

In Odd Fellowship Mr. Allison was grand patriarch of the Grand Encampment of Indiana for the years 1916-17, was a representative to the Sovereign Grand Lodge at St. Louis in 1918 and at Boston in 1920. He has attended eleven sessions of the Sovereign Lodge. He was state field supervisor for the Independent Order of Odd Fellows from 1922 to 1927 and at the present time is special deputy grand master of Indiana. Since 1922 he has been one of the three directors of the State Odd Fellows Home at Greensburg, and is treasurer of the Odd Fellows Home Association. Another fraternal organization in which he has been deeply interested is the Knights of Pythias. He has held most of the offices in the local lodge, for a number of years was keeper of records and seals, and on two occasions was representative to the Grand Lodge. Mr. and Mrs. Allison are members of the Methodist Church of Russiaville.

He married, December 24, 1892, at Delphi, Indiana, Miss Carrie B. Kerlin. They have occupied their home at Russiaville practically ever since their marriage. Mrs. Allison is a daughter of James Calvin and Mary Magdaline (Pennybaker) Kerlin, natives of Pennsylvania, who came to Indiana when children.

Mr. Allison's only son, Grant E. Allison, is connected with the Chevrolet Automobile Sales Company at Kokomo. He married, June 7, 1914, Miss Beryl Davis, of Russiaville, and they have a pleasant home near Mr. Allison. Mrs. Grant Allison is an active worker in the Russiaville Methodist Church.

CLARE WILLIAM HOBART BANGS. In the allotments of human life few individuals attain to eminent positions. It is an interesting and curious study to note how opportunity waits on fitness and capacity, so that all at last fill the places for which they are best qualified. In the legal profession there is no royal road to promotion. Its high rewards are gained by diligent study and long and tedious attention to elementary principles, and are awarded only to those who develop, in the arena of forensic strife, characters of integrity and moral worth. All individuals fall into the niches in the elaborate edifice of life that they are qualified to fill. However marvelously "natural selection" may work in the production of species, there is a wondrous selection in the sifting out of the fittest from the mass of common material that crowds all the avenues of the law. In that most difficult and perplexing profession, the very occupation of superior position argues for its possessor solid ability, signal skill, sound learning, untiring industry and uncompromising integrity. In this connection extended mention is due Clare William Hobart Bangs, of Huntington, who is not only a leading lawyer of his state, but well known as an educator and successful as a business man.

Mr. Bangs was born on a farm in Richland Township, near Auburn, DeKalb County, Indiana, May 5, 1890, and is a son of Charles Henry and Virginia H. (Reynolds) Bangs. His father still operates the homestead farm on which he was born in DeKalb County, and for thirty years has been the Government crop reporter for his county, where Mrs. Bangs also was born. There were five children in the family, all of whom have taught school.

The third in order of birth of his parents' children, Clare William Hobart Bangs attended the public schools of DeKalb County, where he was reared on the home farm, and in 1912 received the degrees of Bachelor of Pedagogy and Bachelor of Arts from the Tri-State College, at Angola, Indiana. He then attended Indiana University and the University of Chicago and King's School of Oratory, Pittsburgh, Pennsylvania, this being followed by a correspondence school course in civil engineering. He received his degree of Master of Arts from Huntington (Indiana) College in 1913, his Bachelor of Laws degree from Columbia University, New York, in 1922, and from 1922 until 1924 attended the University of Paris, France.

Mr. Bangs commenced his career as an educator in 1909, when he became superintendent of high schools in Steuben County, Indiana, continuing to be thus engaged until 1912, when he became professor of sociology and philosophy at Huntington College. He was elevated to the presidency of that institution in 1914 and continued as such until his resignation in 1919. During his period as president he was an investigator of social problems at Chicago and Saint Louis at various times, and also a Chautauqua and commencement lecturer, in addition to which he did his share in promoting the various war movements, particularly at the students' military training camps. After his return from Paris, in 1924, Mr. Bangs entered upon the practice of his profession at Huntington, where he has since risen to an acknowledged position among the leaders, and now has offices at 48 Franklin Street. He has been identified with much important litigation that has come before the courts, and has shown himself a thoroughly capable, learned and reliable attorney. He belongs to the Huntington County Bar Association, the Indiana State Bar Association and the American Bar Association. Mr. Bangs has several business connections and is president of the Mutual Savings & Loan Association and treasurer of Huntington Pure Milk, Inc. Politically he is a Republican. He is a member and a past president of the Exchange Club and belongs to the Edward Bangs Descendants, of which he is a charter member. His religious connection is with the United Brethren Church, of which he was formerly a member of the board of trustees.

On July 18, 1917, Mr. Bangs was united in marriage with Miss Nellie A. Binning, who was born in Nebraska, and was teacher of English and oratory at Huntington College for nine years. She is a daughter of the late Edward Binning, a native of Illinois, who later moved to Kansas and Nebraska and became a prominent rancher and one of the influential citizens of his community. Mr. and Mrs. Bangs are the parents of two children: Charles Edward, born October 12, 1918; and Sarah Virginia, born December 8, 1921.

JOE HENRY WILDERMUTH has proved his ability and resourcefulness both as a teacher in the public schools and as a professional exemplar of the art and science of architecture, of which he is now a prominent representative in the great industrial City of Gary, Lake County, with office headquarters at 673 Broadway.

Mr. Wildermuth was born on the parental home farm near Star City, Pulaski County, Indiana, July 6, 1897, and is a son of Elias and Olive (Herrick) Wildermuth, of whom more specific mention will be found on other pages of this publication, in the personal sketch of an older son, Judge Ora L. Wildermuth. The public schools of Star City were the medium through which Joe H. Wildermuth acquired his earlier education, and in 1915 he was graduated in the Emerson High School in the City of Gary. In advancing his education he went to the West and entered the University of Arizona. In this institution he was graduated as a member of the class of 1919 and with the degree of Bachelor of Science. Subsequent post-graduate work gained to him in the following year the degree of Bachelor of Arts from the University of Illinois. It has been noted that he was graduated in the Emerson High School at Gary, and after his graduation he gave a year of characteristically effective service as a teacher in this school. His collegiate studies embraced work that specifically fortified him for technical and professional service as an architect, and since 1921 he has been one of the successful and representative exponents of this profession in Gary. Mr. Wildermuth has designed and supervised the erection of many important buildings in Gary, including the fine Municipal Auditorium, the Emerson Grade School, the Lew Wallace Public School, besides about twenty of the other public school buildings of the city, three Gary public libraries, and numerous business and residence buildings of the best modern type. His reputation as an architect of school buildings has extended beyond the limits of Indiana, and he is the only Gary architect whose name is listed on the membership rolls of the American Institute of Architects, the nation's organization of architects. He is one of the most prominent representatives of his profession in this part of the state and the year 1931 finds him in service as vice president of the Indiana Society of Architects.

Mr. Wildermuth was a student in the University of Illinois when the nation entered the World war, and he there entered the Officers Training Camp and was duly enlisted for service in the United States Army. He was not called to overseas service and he received his honorable discharge in December, 1918, about a month after the now historic armistice had brought the war to a close. He is now an appreciative and popular member of Gary Memorial Post of the American Legion.

Mr. Wildermuth was one of the real pioneers of the City of Gary. When he was a small boy his father brought him here in a two horse wagon, traveling a distance of seventy-five miles, which took three days to make the trip. His father built a small shack on Fifth Avenue and from this little home the lad witnessed the real start of Gary. He saw the grading shaft for what is now the Monmouth steel plant, and witnessed also the grading of the first streets. His part in the pioneer start of this now thriving city was that of a newsboy, he having been the first newsboy in the place.

Mr. Wildermuth is loyal and progressive in his civic attitude, is independent in politics, is enrolled as an active member of the Gary Chamber of Commerce, as well as the local Kiwanis Club, he has membership also in the Gary Country Club, the Lincoln Hill Country Club and the University Club of his home city, where also he is affiliated with Gary Lodge of the Benevolent and Protective Order of Elks. Both he and his wife are zealous members of the Methodist Episcopal Church, both are popular figures in the representative social activities of their home community, and Mrs. Wildermuth is active in women's clubs, besides being affiliated with Beta Gamma college sorority.

At Gary, on the 10th of January, 1923, was solemnized the marriage of Mr. Wildermuth to Miss Madeleine Havens, daughter of Daniel F. and Lola (Bassett) Havens. Mr. Havens was engaged in the sheet metal business in Indianapolis many years and he now resides at Gary, where he is living virtually retired, his wife having died in 1922. Mrs. Wildermuth completed her high school course in Indianapolis, and thereafter was a student in Northwestern University, Evanston, Illinois. Mr. and Mrs. Wildermuth have two children, Richard Lee, born June 22, 1924, and Dorothy Ann, born January 5, 1926, and the son is at the time of this writing a pupil in the Gary public schools. Mrs. Wildermuth has proved a solicitous and devoted wife and mother, is the gracious chatelaine of her attractive home and has found time and opportunity to identify herself actively with the church, cultural and social activities of her home community, where she is in the fullest degree *persona grata* in the various circles in which she moves.

LOUIS BOHREL RODIN has gained rank among the progressive business men and loyal and substantial citizens of Gary, where he has maintained his residence since 1920 and where he became the founder of the substantial business now conducted under the title of Calumet Glass Works. He is the owner and active manager of this prosperous business, the headquarters of which are established at 628 Washington Street.

Mr. Rodin is a member of a family of eight children, all of whom were born in Russia and all of whom are now residents of the United States, as citizens fully appreciative of the advantages and attractions of the land of their adoption. Mr. Rodin was born in Russia on the 21st of February, 1889, and is a son of Bohrel and Bernice (Bernstein) Rodin, who were born and reared in Russia and who there maintained their home throughout their entire lives, their mortal bodies having been laid to rest in a cemetery at Olito. Bohrel Rodin became in his native land a successful contractor in road construction, and he was able to make, in 1910, a visit to the United States and to his son Louis B., of this review, who had come to this country about five years previously. Bohrel Rodin did not long survive after his return to his native land, for there his death occurred in 1911, on the 25th of October, his wife having passed away in 1891 and both having been devout members of the Jewish synagogue in their home community in Russia. Of their eight children the subject of this sketch was the fourth in order of birth.

Louis B. Rodin received his youthful education in a private school in his native land and was an ambitious and self-reliant lad of about seventeen years when he severed the home ties and voyaged across the Atlantic ocean to the United States, in 1905. He established residence in Brooklyn, New York, where he gained practical experience in the glass business, with which he was there identified until 1911, when he came to the West and associated himself with the same line of business in the City of Chicago, where he remained until 1920, the year that marked his founding of the Calumet Glass Works at Gary, Indiana. With marked progressiveness and with effective service he has since continued this enterprise, the present scope and importance of which mark him as one of the successful and representative business men of the city.

Mr. Rodin has gained success through his own ability and efforts and has stood forward as a loyal and liberal citizen who is deeply interested in all that concerns the civic and material welfare of his home community. He has membership in the Gary Commercial Club and Chamber of Commerce, and is affiliated with the Masonic fraternity, the Independent Order of Odd Fellows, the Benevolent and Protective Order of Elks and the B'nai B'rith. He is a member of the Turkey Creek Country Club, and he and his wife are zealous members of Temple Israel and Beth El in their home city. In politics he maintains an independent attitude and gives support to men and measures meeting the approval of his judgment.

In the City of Chicago, on the 10th of October, 1917, Mr. Rodin was united in marriage to Miss Hannah Wolf, daughter of William and Rebecca Wolf, who there continued to maintain their home until their death. Mr. and Mrs. Rodin have three children: Bernice, Walter Herbert and Jacqueline Cherie. The year 1931 finds the two older children ambitiously pursuing their studies in the Gary public schools.

EDWIN F. SCHOENBECK, county surveyor of Lake County, was educated for a technical profession, and before his entrance into politics was in the engineering department of one of the great industrial corporations of Lake County.

Mr. Schoenbeck was born at Beatrice, Nebraska, March 8, 1900, son of Herman and Caroline (Goehring) Schoenbeck. His grandfather was John Schoenbeck, a native of Germany, who brought his family to America about 1872 and settled on a farm at Rochester, New York. Later he moved to Nebraska, living in the country near the Kansas line, and he is buried in the Bethlehem Cemetery near Odell, Nebraska. Herman Schoenbeck was born in Germany and was twelve years of age when the family came to America. He continued his education, begun in Germany, at Rochester, learned the trade of carpenter, but about 1880 moved to Nebraska and spent the rest of his life as a farmer. He died in February, 1924, and is buried in the Bethlehem Lutheran Church Cemetery near his old home. His wife, Caroline Goehring, was born near Waverly, Ohio. Her parents, Gotthold Goehring and wife, moved from Ohio to Illinois and later to Nebraska. Caroline Schoenbeck was a devout Lutheran. She died in November, 1924. There were five children: Walter, who died in 1918 at the Fort McHenry Hospital at Baltimore, Maryland, while enrolled in service as a soldier during the World war; Mrs. Helen Koenig, of Gering, Nebraska; Elmer, of Gering; Miss Martha, of Gering; and Edwin F.

Edwin F. Schoenbeck attended public school at Odell, Nebraska, graduating from high school in 1919, following which he spent two years in the college at Hastings, Nebraska, and in 1925 was graduated in the engineering course from the University of Nebraska. In the same year of his graduation he came to Gary, and entered the engineering department of the American Bridge Company, starting in the drafting room. He was with the bridge company until January 1, 1931.

Mr. Schoenbeck on November 4, 1930, was elected county surveyor of Lake County. His office is in the courthouse at Gary. He was elected as a Democrat and is a member of the Gary Democratic Club. He is a member of the Sigma Xi Society and the Trinity Lutheran Church. He plays golf, but his chief hobby is amateur photography.

CHARLES AUGUST BUBLITZ, Gary manufacturer, is president of the Calumet Sash & Door Company. This is one of the extensive industries of the city, with plant and yards at 2051-55 Adams Street.

Mr. Bublitz has had a long and successful experience in the woodworking business. He was born in Chicago, Illinois, October 31, 1887, a son of Carl A. and Katharina (Sommer) Bublitz. His parents were born and educated in Germany. His father was a young man when he came to America and located in Chicago. By trade he was a wagon maker, and that occupation he followed with different plants in Chicago until his final years. He died in 1918 and he and his wife are buried in the Waldheim Cemetery, Forest Park, Illinois. Both were devout members of the Holy Cross Evangelical Lutheran Church. Katharina Sommer came to America when a young woman and located in Chicago. She died December 28, 1929. Of their four children one died in infancy. Those living are Charles A., Mrs. Lillian Gehle, of Chicago, and Rudolph, an automobile worker in Chicago.

Charles A. Bublitz attended the grammar schools of Chicago and left school to become a salesman with Chicago mercantile houses. After a year and a half of this work and another year with the Reid Murdock Company, wholesale grocers, he started in a new line of experience in 1905, as an employee of the True & True Company, a sash, door and millwork plant in Chicago. He was with that firm for twelve years and during the latter part of the service was plant superintendent.

His first connection with the business affairs of Gary was made in 1915, when he accepted the place of head estimator for the Gary Mill Work Company. After a year and a half he returned to Chicago and was with the Quist & Becker Company, stair manufacturers, until 1919.

In 1919 Mr. Bublitz established himself in business at Gary, founding the Calumet Sash & Door Company. He has been president of the company since it was started, and has had the satisfaction of seeing the business grow and prosper. He employs on the average about thirty persons. Mr. Bublitz is also a director of the Industrial Finance Company and of the Home Savings & Loan Company.

His other affiliations indicate some of his public spirit and readiness to cooperate with organizations for the general welfare. These include the Commercial Club and Chamber of Commerce, Gary Country Club, Lions Club. In Masonry he is affiliated with Roosevelt Lodge No. 766, A. F. and A. M., Gary Chapter, Royal Arch Masons, Knights Templar Commandery, Orak Temple of the Mystic Shrine at Hammond. He is a member of the Loyal Order of Moose, a Republican, and is vice president of the church council of the Grace English Evangelical Lutheran Church. During the World war he helped in the various drives. His recreations are golf and fishing.

He married at Milwaukee, Wisconsin, June 4, 1913, Miss Hilda Kuchenbeiser, daughter of Emil and Anna (Beimdeike) Kuchenbeiser. Her father was born and reared in Milwaukee, while her mother was born at Beaver Dam, Wisconsin. Her father was an iron moulder and followed that trade for many years. He died about 1899 and her mother passed away December 7, 1925; both are buried at Milwaukee. Mrs. Bublitz attended school in her native city. She is a member of Gary Chapter of the Eastern Star and of the same church as her husband. Their two sons are named Charles August, Jr., a student in the Horace Mann High School, and Robert Harold, in grade school.

FRANK BORMAN, Gary business man, was born within the present city limits of this wonder steel city of Northern Indiana. Among his many property interests he still retains a portion of the old family estate, which was acquired when his father entered Government land in this part of Lake County three-quarters of a century ago.

Mr. Borman was born at Tolleston, now Gary, January 9, 1875, son of Christopher and Wilhelmina (Kurth) Borman. His parents were born and reared in Germany, attended public schools in that country, and his father came to America in 1855. At that time little had been done toward developing the northern or lake shore region of Lake County. He acquired land from the Government at two dollars an acre, and for many years was one of the leading citizens of Tolleston. For twenty-five years he was postmaster of the village. He also owned a grocery store and meat market, which was the first business of that kind established in Calumet Township. He possessed much talent as a musician. He and his wife were married in Tolleston and both are buried in the Waltheim Cemetery. His

M. L. Sterrett

wife was educated in Germany and came to America about 1860 with her parents. The Kurth family also took up land in northern Lake County. She was an active member of the Lutheran Church. She died in 1900 and is buried beside her husband. These parents had nine children: Christopher, deceased; Mathilda, widow of Fred Findling, of Hammond; Elbert, of Gary; Dorothy, deceased; Emma, deceased; Laura, deceased; Fred, deceased; Frank; and Otto, deceased.

Frank Borman spent his childhood and youth in the village of Tolleston and after leaving school took up the same line of business his father had followed and was a grocery merchant and meat dealer for twenty-two years. In the meantime Gary had been established and in its growth had absorbed the original village of Tolleston. On tracts of land which he owned he started building houses and other structures, and contributed in important measure to the upbuilding of the city. He is still the owner of considerable property in the Tolleston district. One of his buildings is the Borman Building and another is the Safeway Garage, owned and operated by Borman & Son. Mr. Borman is vice president and a director of the First State Bank, the oldest bank in Gary.

Probably any one acquainted with Gary business and civic affairs during the past quarter of a century is aware that Mr. Borman has been one of the outstanding leaders in the community. For fifteen years he has been vice president of the Gary park board. He is a Lake County jury commissioner, a Democrat, and a member of the church of his parents, the Lutheran.

He married at Tolleston, June 6, 1896, Miss Louisa Kunert, daughter of Charles and Augusta (Arich) Kunert. Her father was another early settler in Tolleston, where for many years he was in the general mercantile business, and both he and his wife are buried in the old cemetery. Mrs. Borman attended public schools at Tolleston. She is a member of the Lutheran Church, the Woman's Club and the Ladies Aid Society. The children of Mr. and Mrs. Frank Borman are Meta, Edwin O. and Florence. Meta was educated in public schools and in the Froebel High School at Gary, is a graduate of the Gary Business College and until her marriage was a clerical worker for the Gary Motor Truck Company. She is the wife of Arthur L. Krueger, who has charge of the insurance department in the First State Bank of Gary. Mr. and Mrs. Krueger have a daughter, Marylin. The son, Edwin O. Borman, graduated from the Froebel High School in 1920, was a member of the class of 1924 in Wittenberg College at Springfield, Ohio, and since the close of his college career has been associated with his father in business, in the firm of Borman & Son, operating the Safeway Garage. Edwin Borman married Margie Ann Pearce, of Dayton, Ohio, and they have a son, Frank II. Edwin Borman is a Phi Gamma Delta and one of the popular young business men and citizens. The daugh-

ter Florence graduated from the Emerson High School and from the Gary Business College. She is the wife of Walter McLean, formerly of Rockford, Illinois, now connected with the Cudahy Packing Company and a resident of Gary. They have one daughter, Bonnie May.

The civic interests of the community have always attracted a share of Mr. Borman's attention and energies. During the World war he helped in all the drives, being captain of one of the bond teams at Tolleston. His favorite recreation is hunting.

MORGAN LEE STERRETT since 1917 has been county superintendent of schools of Jasper County, with offices in Rensselaer. Mr. Sterrett is a well known Indiana educator, having held positions from teacher of a country school to his present post, over a period of thirty years. He was educated for the law, but practiced only a brief time.

Mr. Sterrett was born in Carroll County, Indiana, in 1880. His father Wilson Sterrett, also a native of Carroll County, is now eighty-two years of age. His mother, Jennie (Clark) Sterrett, died in March, 1919. These parents had thirteen children, Louis, Morgan L., Floyd, Maude, Jud, Ruby and Pearl, twins, Icie, Bud, Vance, Jennie, Ruth and Gaylord. Eleven are living, the two deceased children being Louis and Gaylord.

Morgan Lee Sterrett attended public schools in Carroll County, finished his high school course at Rockfield, and had two years of training in the Indiana State Normal at Terre Haute. He began teaching in 1899. After teaching for a few years he entered Indiana University School of Law, was graduated LL. B. in 1909 and practiced for a time with his brother Floyd at La Fayette. He gave up the law to return to his first love, educational work. He has done post-graduate work in the University of Chicago. He was principal of several schools, being located at Delphi, North Manchester, Carmel, and five years at Wheatfield.

Mr. Sterrett became county superintendent of schools of Jasper County in 1917. During the fourteen years he has been the official head of the school system of the county he has carried out a program which has brought the county a very favorable standing among Indiana counties in the matter of educational efficiency. After the war the county undertook a building program as requested by the governor, and has eliminated practically all the old and obsolete types of school buildings. Under Superintendent Sterrett the consolidation of individual school districts has been pushed, and the result is that the number of schools in the county has been reduced from seventy-three to fifteen. There are now eight high schools, affording the children advance educational opportunities in practically every community of the county.

Mr. Sterrett is a member of the Masonic fraternity, the Dywyki, which later became the Sigma Alpha Epsilon, and is a Republican and a Presbyterian. He married, June 13, 1909, Miss Nellie May, daughter of James A. May, of Wolcott, Indiana. They have one son, Morgan Lee, Jr., born November 4, 1911, now a student of law at the University of Chicago.

GEORGE BRUNO BEHNKE. Among active business men of Gary today, one whose life began in this section of Northern Indiana and who has lived in the vicinity of the site of the steel city all his years is George B. Behnke, who was born at Clark's Station in Tolleston, now Gary, December 16, 1887.

His father, Edward Behnke, came to Clark's Station about 1885, when he was twenty-three years of age. He was a native of Germany, where he was reared and educated, and on locating at Tolleston he engaged in the grocery business and was also a sand and gravel contractor. He was a devout Lutheran. He died in 1915 and is buried in the Waltheim Cemetery. His wife, Lena Schreiber, was born in Germany and came to America with her mother when eleven years of age. She finished her education in the Lutheran parochial schools of Indiana. She resides in Gary.

George B. Behnke was the only child of his parents. After getting his early education in the Lutheran parochial schools he attended Concordia College at Fort Wayne. Returning to Gary, he engaged in the coal and grain business in 1908, a business which his father had established in 1906. After his father's death in 1915 Mr. Behnke took over the enterprise under his individual responsibility, and carries it on today at 2134 West Tenth Avenue in Gary. He is also a director of the First State Bank. He is one of Gary's progressive and public spirited citizens, always ready to lend his hand in any community or welfare undertaking. He is a member of the Commercial Club and Chamber of Commerce, the Cressmore Country Club, is president of the Sixth Ward Welfare Association. He is a Republican and for a number of years has been a member of the board of the Lutheran Church.

Mr. Behnke married at Gary, December 31, 1908, Miss Gertrude Kunert, daughter of William C. and Anna (Diedel) Kunert. Her father was an early settler of Gary, and for many years has been connected with the Wonder Bakeries in that city. His father, Charles Kunert, and wife, Augusta (Arich) Kunert, were among the pioneers of Tolleston. William C. Kunert resides at Tolleston and his wife died about 1925. Mrs. Behnke attended the public and Lutheran parochial schools, and has been active in church work since girlhood. Mr. and Mrs. Behnke have two children, Helen Anna and George Edward. Helen was educated in the public and parochial schools, graduated from the Emerson High School, after which she spent two years in Valparaiso University. She is the wife of Fred Finger, formerly of Dubois Pennsylvania, who is a salesman for the Wonder Bakeries at Gary. George E. Behnke graduated from the Emerson High School and is taking the pre-medical

course in Valparaiso University. During the World war Mr. Behnke was a contributor to the loan and other drives. Outside of business he finds his chief recreation in duck hunting and golf.

CHESTER JAMES DUNN, prominent Indiana banker, is president of the First State Bank of Gary. His connections as a banker and as a citizen have made him widely known over the state.

Mr. Dunn is a native of Michigan. He was born at Muskegon, November 6, 1891. His father was a Michigan lumberman, Ernest G. Dunn. Ernest G. Dunn was born at Torquay, England, attended school there and in 1870 came to America. He lived in Chicago for some years, engaged in the wholesale lumber business, and in 1885 transferred his headquarters to Muskegon. In 1896 he moved to Michigan City, Indiana, and for many years has been retired from active business. Ernest G. Dunn married Leonora Gray, who was born in Brown County, Indiana, daughter of Elisha Gray, a pioneer Indiana citizen. The Gray family subsequently moved to Chicago and her parents were buried in that city. Mrs. Leonora Dunn was educated in Chicago She is an active member of the Episcopal Church, the Woman's Club, the Chapter of the Daughters of the American Revolution at Michigan City. She was the mother of eight children: Emma, deceased; Eunice, now Mrs. Frank Carr, of Chicago; Ernest, deceased; Chester J.; Mabel, wife of John Woodring, of Michigan City; Howard, of Saint Louis, Missouri; and twins, Marion and Dorothy, both of Michigan City.

Chester J. Dunn grew up in Michigan City, graduated from the high school there in 1910, and throughout the twenty years since he left school his energies have been directed in the banking field. He was with the First National Bank of Gary and with the Gary Trust & Savings Bank until 1920. At that time he became cashier of the First State Bank of Gary and in 1925 was promoted to the executive duties of president. He is on the board of directors and is vice president and director of the Gary Bankers Mortgage Company, is a member of the Indiana State and American Bankers Associations. Mr. Dunn lends his cooperation through the Commercial Club and Chamber of Commerce and from 1926 to 1930 was president of the Gary Board of Works. He acts independently in politics, is a member of the Knights of Pythias and Christ Episcopal Church.

He married at Furnessville, Indiana, July 21, 1914, Miss Martita Furness, daughter of Leigh and Mary (Barnard) Furness. Her father was a prominent farmer and stock raiser in that locality, the town Furnessville being named in honor of his father, Edwin L. Furness, the pioneer of that region. Leigh G. Furness died in 1927 and his widow now resides at Miami, Florida. Mrs. Dunn attended school at Michigan City, graduating from high school there, and later graduated from the

University of Chicago. She was a teacher in Furnessville for several years before her marriage. She is a member of the Gary Woman's Club. Mr. and Mrs. Dunn have three sons, Chester James, Jr., Leigh Ernest and Robert Furness, all of whom are attending the public schools at Gary. During the World war period Mr. Dunn spent much of his time in handling the work of the drives for the sale of Liberty Bonds.

CLARENCE RICHARD BROWN, mortgage banker, secretary-treasurer of the Gary Bankers Mortgage Company, was born in Northern Indiana, and is a member of a well known family around Valparaiso.

He was born at Valparaiso, November 19, 1893, son of Matthew and Emma (Podell) Brown and grandson of John Brown. John Brown was a native of Glasgow, Scotland, and about 1856 settled in Porter County, Indiana. He was a Union soldier in the Civil war and after the war resumed his life as an industrious farmer near Valparaiso. Both he and his wife are at rest in the Valparaiso Cemetery. Matthew Brown was born and reared at Valparaiso, and attended the public schools there. For practically all his active life, thirty-eight years, he has been connected with the police force of Valparaiso and during part of that time was chief of police. He is a member of the Sons of Veterans. His wife, Emma Podell, was born and reared at Winamac, Indiana, and attended school there. She is a member of the German Lutheran Church and the Ladies of the Maccabees. Clarence R. Brown's brother and business partner is Floyd M. Brown, a resident of Valparaiso. Floyd Brown married Miss Esther Beach, and they have children named Miriam and Gerald.

Clarence R. Brown was graduated from the Valparaiso High School in 1912, attended Valparaiso University, completed a commercial course there in 1914, and ever since leaving school has been in the banking business. For eleven years, except for the time he was in service during the war he was connected with the First National Bank of Gary and was assistant cashier when he resigned in 1927. For the past three years he has been in the mortgage bond business, the offices of the Gary Bankers Mortgage Company being in the Gary State Bank Building. He is director as well as secretary and treasurer of the company and is also a director in the Park View Building Company, in the Graham Development Company, the Engleside Realty Company, the Municipal Realty & Investment Company, the Woodbury Development Company and the Grant Park Development Company.

Mr. Brown is a member of the Commercial Club and Chamber of Commerce, the Gary Country Club, B. P. O. Elks, and takes an active part in civic affairs. He plays golf. He is a member of Gary Memorial Post No. 17 of the American Legion.

Mr. Brown enlisted in the navy soon after America joined the allies, on June 14, 1917, and was sent to the Great Lakes Naval Training Station, where he remained until transferred to a receiving ship at Philadelphia. He was at the United States Naval Base No. 2 at Inverness, Scotland, and later at Cardiff, Wales, was on board the U. S. S. *Black Hawk* for service in the North Sea as a first class yeoman. He was on that ship at Scapa Flow when the German fleet was sunk. He received his honorable discharge October 2, 1919, and on returning to Gary resumed his connection with the bank until 1927, when he joined the corporation of which he is secretary and treasurer.

Mr. Brown was the Republican nominee for joint representative in the State Legislature in 1930. He is a member of Saint Marks Catholic Church.

At Chicago, February 12, 1922, he married Miss Genevieve Hannon, daughter of John Hannon, formerly of Porter County, who for years was a well known farmer and stock raiser in that county. Mr. Hannon died March 27, 1927, and his wife in March, 1922, and they are buried at Valparaiso. Mrs. Brown attended school at Hammond, graduated from the Catholic High School, and is an active member of Saint Marks Church and the Catholic clubs and sorority. Mr. and Mrs. Brown have one daughter, Eleanor Joan, born February 8, 1924, now a student in Saint Marks parochial school.

OTTO V. GRAY. Many and varied have been the expressions of the civic loyalty and progressiveness of this sterling and popular citizen of Gary, and in this great industrial community he is, in 1931, serving his third term as a member of the City Council, of which municipal body he is president at the time this personal review is in process of compilation. Mr. Gray is likewise one of the outstanding industrial executives of the wonder steel city, where he holds the office of assistant manager of the American Sheet & Tin Plate Company, in charge of the Gary sheet mill of this great corporation.

Mr. Gray was born in Belmont County, Ohio, August 30, 1873, and is a son of Harvey B. and Mary J. (Young) Gray, who were born and reared in that county, where they received the advantages of the public schools, where their marriage was solemnized and where they passed their entire lives, Harvey B. Gray having long been one of the successful and honored exponents of farm industry in his native county and having been seventy-nine years of age at the time of his death, which occurred about 1915, his wife having passed away in 1907 and both having been earnest members of the Methodist Episcopal Church in their home community. Nathan B. Gray, grandfather of the subject of this sketch, was numbered among the pioneers of Ohio and there lived out his earnest and useful life as a farmer, both he and his wife having attained to advanced age and their mortal remains having been laid to rest in a cemetery in Guernsey County, not far distant from their old home farm. Of the seven children of

Harvey B. and Mary J. (Young) Gray the eldest is Mrs. Sarah E. Spring, of Barnesville, Ohio; George Oliver likewise resides at that place; Mrs. Mary T. Stephens likewise resides at Barnesville; William L. is a resident of Cadiz, that state; Omer C. resides in Columbus, Ohio, and is a bank superintendent; Otto V., of this sketch, was next in order of birth; and Nathan D. died at the age of twelve years.

After profiting by the advantages of the Ohio public schools Otto V. Gray continued his studies in the Ohio State Normal School at Franklin. After leaving school he went to Wheeling, West Virginia, where he was employed eighteen months with the Wheeling Traction Company. In 1896 he found employment with the Aetna Standard Iron & Steel Company of Bridgeport, Ohio, and in 1901 this concern was taken over by the United States Steel Corporation, with which Mr. Gray remained, with headquarters at Wheeling, West Virginia, until 1911, when he was transferred to Gary, Indiana, to initiate the operations at the local plant of the American Sheet & Tin Plate Company, one of the consituent units of the United States Steel Corporation. He became superintendent of the plate and jobbing-mill department, later became superintendent of the sheet-plate and jobbing department, and since 1928 he has here been the efficient and popular assistant manager of the company's sheet mill.

Mr. Gray has been thoroughly interested with the splendidly progressive spirit that has characterized the upbuilding of this great industrial city, even from the time of its inception, and has found many opportunities to give expression to his civic loyalty and appreciation. It has already been stated that he is now serving his third consecutive term as a member of the City Council, and his high place in the esteem of his associates is attested by his having been made president of the council, the office of which he is the present incumbent. He is influential also in the affairs of the Gary Chamber of Commerce and the local Commercial Club, and maintains a thoughtful and conservative outlook upon all projects and measures that have to do with the general wellbeing and advancement of his home city. Mr. Gray is unswerving in his allegiance to the Republican party, though he had neither time nor inclination to enter the arena of so-called practical politics. His influence has been made to count constructively in connection with civic affairs, and in his home community he has won inviolable place in popular confidence and esteem. He is a member of the local Young Men's Christian Association, in the affairs of which he takes deep interest, and he is a zealous member of the Methodist Episcopal Church, as was also his wife, whose death occurred February 5, 1930, and whose gracious personality had endeared her to the people of Gary, where she was a popular factor in social, cultural and church circles.

In Belmont County, Ohio, on the 8th of July, 1895, was solemnized the marriage of Mr. Gray to Miss Louise W. Wallace, who was reared and educated in West Virginia, where she received the advantages of the public schools. She was a daughter of the late David and Mary Wallace, who long maintained their home near Saint Marys, West Virginia, where Mr. Wallace was a progressive exponent of agricultural and live stock industry, as the owner of one of the valuable farm estates of Pleasants County, both he and his wife having there passed the closing years of their lives and their mortal resting place being the cemetery at Saint Marys. The death of Mrs. Gray occurred February 5, 1930, as previously stated in this context, and she is not survived by children.

Mr. Gray was a zealous worker in behalf of the various patriotic movements and drives in Lake County in the World war period, and the same spirit of loyalty has been his in connection with general civic affairs. He is a citizen upon whom high valuation is placed in the City of Gary, where his circle of friends is coincident with that of his acquaintances.

WILLIAM MATTHEW DUNN, lawyer, realtor and for many years closely identified with the business, professional and public life of the City of Gary, located in that city just as the community was rising to prestige as a manufacturing center of Indiana, and when he himself was a young and recently qualified member of the bar.

Judge Dunn was born at New Haven, Connecticut, June 14, 1878, son of Matthew and Kate E. Dunn. He acquired his early education in public schools, attended the Hillhouse High School of Connecticut, and before he was twenty years of age he enlisted for service in the Spanish-American war. He became a member of the Third Connecticut Regiment of United States Volunteers and was in service until honorably discharged. Afterwards he became the first president of the Gary branch of United States Volunteers, Spanish-American war.

After this military service he went south and completed his college education in Grant University in Tennessee, from which he was graduated in 1905. Two years later he completed his law course in Yale University. He was admitted to the Tennessee bar in 1905 and in the fall of 1907 was admitted to practice in the Indiana courts. Since that date his name has been one of increasing prestige in the legal profession at Gary. He was the attorney for the Wabash & Pennsylvania Railroad until 1914. In January, 1914, he began a four-year term as city judge of Gary and was reelected in 1918, serving until 1922. For the past eight years he has continued a law practice in connection with his business as a Gary realtor.

Judge Dunn is a member of the Lake County and Gary Bar Associations. He is affiliated with the Loyal Order of Moose, B. P. O. Elks,

Knights of Columbus, the University and the Harrison Clubs, the Brotherhood of Railroad Trainmen. He was at one time president of the Gary branch of the National Association for the Advancement of the Colored People. He is a member of the Saint Luke's Catholic Church at Gary. He served as one of the first trustees of the Holy Angels Church.

Judge Dunn married Deloma M. Clifford, daughter of John Clifford, of Valparaiso. They have three children: William Eustice, John Robert and Deloma Katherine. The two sons are students in the public schools at Gary. Judge Dunn is a member of the Gary Pioneer Club.

JOHN C. BRECKENRIDGE, D. D. Of the men who have contributed to the religious and educational advancement of Northern Indiana, few can lay claim to longer or more effective terms of accomplishment than Dr. John C. Breckenridge. Commencing his career as a country school teacher, his natural inclinations drew him into the ministry of the Presbyterian Church, in which he labored for long years with the zeal and ardor of a crusader. After achieving numerous beneficial works of a varied character he is now living in comfortable retirement at his home at Winona Lake in Kosciusko County.

John C. Breckenridge was born at North Liberty, Mercer County, Pennsylvania, October 19, 1858, and is a son of James and Mary (Glenn) Breckenridge, and of Irish-Scotch descent on both sides of the family, his maternal grandfather having been Valentine Glenn, who was born in 1807, in Mercer County, Pennsylvania. His father was born in Mercer County, Pennsylvania, May 3, 1828, a son of John Breckenridge, who was born in 1799. James Breckenridge married Mary Glenn, who was born September 3, 1833, in Mercer County, Pennsylvania.

The public schools of Mercer County furnished John C. Breckenridge with his early educational training and for a time he was a country school teacher. In 1877 he entered the Grove City Normal School and prepared to enter college, but due to impaired health he left school and was employed by a lumber concern at Grayson, Kentucky. In 1890 he was graduated from Wooster College, Wooster, Ohio, with the degree of Bachelor of Arts, subsequently receiving the degree of Master of Arts in 1893, in which year he graduated from McCormick Seminary with the degree of Doctor of Divinity. In 1910 this latter degree was conferred upon him by Wooster College. Doctor Breckenridge began his labors in the Presbyterian ministry as pastor at Somers, Wisconsin, in 1893, and January 1, 1899, was called to Bourbon, Indiana. From 1900 until 1903 he served the Bethany Presbyterian Church at Fort Wayne, Indiana, and in September of the latter year became secretary of the Winona Assembly and Bible Conference. In 1905 he was made assistant manager of the Winona Assembly and Bible Conference, which position he retained until 1907, the major part of his

work being as secretary. Doctor Breckenridge then organized the Winona College of Agriculture, which had a two-year course, and was its president until 1916, the last class to graduate being in 1917, when it was closed because of the entrance of the United States into the World war. Each student was required to pursue the two year course in Bible study. It shut its doors with all indebtedness cleared, and had a record of having graduated from thirty to thirty-five pupils each year. In 1918 Doctor Breckenridge was placed in charge of the dependent churches of Northern Indiana, but resigned this position December 29 to accept the position of secretary and general manager of the Winona Assembly and Bible Conference, serving in this capacity until January 1, 1928. At that time he organized the extension school of the State University, in association with Doctor Linton of the State University and Doctor Brandenberg of Purdue University, and this was carried on as a part of the Winona Assembly, with an enrollment of a student body of 500 members. Doctor Breckenridge brought about the sale of the Kosciusko Lodge Building to the Presbyterians of Indiana for religious work, and this is now a permanent institution. The purchase of the grounds was made possible by generous donations of Rev. William A. (Billy) Sunday and Mrs. Sunday, the famous evangelists, and under Doctor Breckenridge's administration there was completed the W. A. Sunday Tabernacle, with a seating capacity of 8,000. The cost of the building was $100,000, and $30,000 more was needed for its equipment. Rev. and Mrs. Sunday were generous contributors also to this project, and gave $12,000 toward the installing of the roque courts. These courts meet all the requirements of the National Roque Association, which body holds its annual tournaments thereon. Doctor Breckenridge, although now retired from active labors, continues to take a deep and helpful interest in all matters pertaining to the spiritual and educational welfare of his community and his advice is invariably sought on all matters of importance. He is a Republican in his political allegiance, but has never been lured into the maze of politics.

On July 12, 1883, Doctor Breckenridge was united in marriage with Miss Emma Bagnall, who was born December 12, 1857, at Millbrook, Pennsylvania. She was graduated from the Grove City Normal School in 1881 and was a teacher of mathematics at that institution until her marriage. Doctor and Mrs. Breckenridge are the parents of three children, Karl Bland Breckenridge was born November 2, 1885, graduated from Wabash College in 1907, with the degree of Bachelor of Arts, and then entered the College of Osteopathy, at Los Angeles, California, from which he graduated, practicing his profession at Bath, Maine, until his death in 1917. He married Gladys Dobbins, and they have two children: Karl B., born October 4, 1913, and John D. born April 30, 1915. Grace Breckenridge, second child of Doctor Breckenridge, was born July 13, 1894, and attended Winona College and Western Seminary of Ohio. She married R. K. Schmidt, a building contractor of Berkeley, California, and they have four children: Helen Glenn, born November 21, 1917; Richard K., born February 21, 1919; Dorothy Jane, born March 8, 1920; and Mary Elizabeth, born November 23, 1921. Helen Glenn Breckenridge, the youngest child of Doctor Breckenridge, was born January 2, 1897, and attended Winona College and Western Seminary. She married John M. Stroup, formerly a professor of chemistry, and now assistant secretary of the Empire State Pickling Company, of Phelps, New York, and they have two adopted children: Margaret G., born March 16, 1923; and Robert B., born August 16, 1925.

CHARLES ERNEST EURIT, D. D. S. There are two very distinct division in the art of cleaning and extracting teeth, of repairing them when diseased and replacing them when necessary by artificial ones. The first requires an extended medical knowledge on the part of the practitioner, as, for instance, a knowledge of diseases the effects of which may reach the teeth, of the connection between the welfare of the teeth and the general system, etc., as well as ability to discern latent oral diseases, calculate the effects of operations, etc. The second department, mechanical dentistry, is concerned with the construction of artificial teeth and requires much mechanical science, it being a very delicate work to give artificial teeth a perfectly natural appearance in shape and color. In both of these departments Dr. Charles Ernest Eurit is acknowledged to be an expert, and this fact explains in some degree the reason for his present standing as one of the leading dental practitioners of Lake County, with a large and lucrative practice at Gary.

Doctor Eurit was born at Logansport, Indiana, June 5, 1890, and is a son of Charles M. and Bertha (Rimpler) Eurit. His paternal grandfather, Stephen Eurit, was born in Virginia, where he was educated, and in young manhood came to Indiana to become one of the early settlers of Twelve Mile, Cass County. He engaged in agricultural pursuits and became the owner of an extensive property, a part of his original farm being now included within the corporate limits of the town, where he and his worthy wife are buried. Charles M. Eurit was born at Twelve Mile, where he received his education in the little schoolhouse situated near his father's farm, and later was given the added advantage of attendance at college at Terre Haute. For many years he was connected with the Pennsylvania Railroad, and died while still in the service of that company, in 1902, being buried at Logansport. He married Bertha Rimpler, who was born at Plymouth, Indiana, and educated in the public schools. Later, after her father had sold his hotel at Plymouth, the family moved to Twelve Mile, and there she met and married Mr. Eurit. She was active in the Presbyterian Church at Logansport, where she taught

in the Sunday School for a number of years, but for the past ten years has lived with her son at Gary.

The only child of his parents, Charles Ernest Eurit attended the public schools of Logansport and after graduation from high school there attended night high school at Indianapolis. He graduated from the dental college of Indiana University as a member of the class of 1919, receiving the degree of Doctor of Dental Surgery, and for about ten months was engaged in practice at Rushville, Indiana, but in May, 1920, moved to Gary, where for the past ten years he has carried on a very extensive and representative practice, his offices being located at 790 Broadway, corner of Eighth Avenue, where he has every known modern dental appliance. He is a constant student of his calling, keeping fully abreast of its recurring developments, and belongs to the various organizations of dental practitioners. If he may be said to have a hobby it is hunting and fishing, but he has been too busy to indulge himself greatly to these recreations. During the World war he offered his services to the Government, but was rejected because of a slight physical disability. Doctor Eurit belongs to Roosevelt Lodge No. 716, A. F. and A. M., of Gary; Logansport Chapter No. 2, R. A. M; and Council No 11, R. and S. M. He is the owner of some property at Gary and takes a helpful part in civic affairs. He holds membership in the Lincoln Hill Country Club, is independent in his political views, and as a churchman belongs to the First Presbyterian congregation.

On May 29, 1920, at Gary, Doctor Eurit was united in marriage with Miss Margaret Hulburd, a daughter of Willis and Delia (Dunn) Hulburd, of DeQuincy, Louisiana, where Mr. Hulburd has been for years an active and successful agriculturist. Mrs. Eurit was educated in the public schools of Arkansas and Kansas City, Missouri, and is a qualified stenographer, having been employed in that capacity for a time before her marriage. She is an active member of the First Presbyterian Church of Gary and of the Order of the Eastern Star. There is one daughter: Margaret, who is attending the Horace Mann School of Gary, and who has been given every advantage by her parents in the way of proper training.

CHARLES FRANKLIN KENWARD, D. D. S. Prominent among the dental practitioners of Lake County is found Dr. Charles Franklin Kenward, who has followed his profession for a period of twenty-eight years and has been located at Gary since 1918. Doctor Kenward has built up a large professional business through ability, close attention to the advancements made in his calling and great industry, and occupies a leading position among the dental surgeons of his part of the state.

Doctor Kenward was born at Watford, Ontario, Canada, January 1, 1876, and is a son of Frank and Martha (Eccles) Kenward. His grandfather, Thomas Kenward, was born in

England and in young manhood emigrated to Canada, where he became an early settler of Watford and there passed the remainder of his life as a merchant, both he and his wife passing away and being buried there. Frank Kenward was born and reared at Watford, where he received a public school education, and as a young man became interested in financial affairs. For many years he was identified with the Merchants Bank of Watford, which is now a branch of the Bank of Montreal. He was active in the Masonic Order and in civic affairs, and died in the faith of the Episcopal Church about 1923, being buried at Watford, where he had been known as a substantial and reliable citizen. He married Martha Eccles, who was born and reared near Watford and received a public school education. She died at Watford March 31, 1931. She was an active member of the Congregational Church. There were three sons in the family, all of whom are doctors of dental surgery: Dr. Charles Franklin, of this review; Dr. Burton, of San Francisco, California; and Dr. Edward, of Lacon, Marshall County, Illinois.

Charles Franklin Kenward attended the public schools of Watford, where he was graduated from high school as a member of the class of 1896, and then went to Lake Forest University, Chicago, now the Chicago College of Dental Surgery, from which institution he received his degree as a member of the class of 1902. For two years thereafter he was engaged in practice at Chicago, but in 1905 moved to Hobart, Indiana, where he bought the practice of Doctor Nixon and continued to conduct it until 1918, in which year he came to Gary, now occupying offices at 673 Broadway. Doctor Kenward's operating room is equipped with every modern appliance known to modern dental surgery and he keeps in constant touch with the developments of his profession, being thoroughly equipped in all the branches of his calling and possessing the technical and mechanical skill so necessary in these days of modern dental practice. Doctor Kenward is a member of the Gary Dental Society, the Indiana State Dental Society and the National Dental Association, the Benevolent and Protective Order of Elks and the Commercial Club and Chamber of Commerce. He is a Republican in politics and his religious affiliation is with the Catholic Church, he being a member of the Holy Angels congregation.

On June 27, 1911, at East Jordan, Michigan, Doctor Kenward was united in marriage with Miss Mabel Monroe, a daughter of John and Catherine Monroe, Mr. Monroe having been for many years a contractor and builder of East Jordan. He died in 1927, at East Jordan, where he is buried and where Mrs. Monroe still survives him. Mrs. Kenward attended the public schools of East Jordan and Detroit, and, as an accomplished musician, taught music in Michigan and in the public schools of Hobart for several years prior to her marriage. She is an active member of Holy Angels Catholic Church and of the Woman's Sodality. Six children have been born to Doctor and Mrs. Kenward: John, a graduate of Horace Mann High School, class of 1931; Martha, who is attending high school; and Frank, Charles and James and Jane, twins, who are attending grammar school.

Samuel Peretz Schorr has effectively proved his resourcefulness in the practice of his profession and is one of the representative and highly esteemed members of the bar of Lake County. He has made the City of Gary the central stage of his law practice from the time of his admission to the bar, in 1913, and his success and prestige are specially noteworthy by reason of the fact that when he came to the United States from his native Rumania, as a young man of twenty-three years, his knowledge of the English language was very limited, a handicap that he overcame with marked facility, as he had received advanced education in his native land, besides having been reared in a home of culture and refinement.

Born in Piatra Neamtz, Rumania, on the 3d of April, 1884, Mr. Schorr is a son of Peretz and Amelia (Dumchick) Schorr, who were likewise born and reared in Rumania and both of whom there received excellent educational advantages. Peretz Schorr has been for many years a successful merchant in Piatra Neamtz, a town situated in the Carpathian Mountains, and he is still active in the supervision of his business, though he celebrated in 1930 his eighty-third birthday anniversary. He is influential in the Hebrew Church of his community, as was also his wife, whose death there occurred in September, 1920, she having served as nurse in a local hospital during the progress of the World war and both she and her husband having been otherwise earnest and active in various phases of patriotic service in their home community. Of their six children one died in infancy; Faibish continues a resident of Piatra Neamtz, the old home city; Samuel P., of this review, was next in order of birth; Betty is the wife of Velvel Smil, and they reside in Berlin, Germany, as does also her next younger sister, Miss Pauline; and Miss Henrietta remains with her father at Piatra Neamtz.

After having profited by the advantages of the schools of his native city Samuel P. Schorr completed a course and was graduated in the University of Bucharest, in which fine old institution he was a member of the class of 1905. In 1907 he severed the ties that bound him to home and native land and came to the United States, he having been twenty-three years of age at the time, as previously noted in this review. After remaining a few months in New York City he removed to Cleveland, Ohio, and there he wisely supplemented his education by completing a course in the Central High School, in which he was graduated as a member of the class of 1908, his collegiate education in his native land having enabled him to complete his high school course in far less than the prescribed time. In 1909 he went to

Lima, Ohio, and found employment with the Lima Locomotive Works, and in the following year he came to Indianapolis and entered the Indianapolis College of Law, in which institution he was graduated as a member of the class of 1913, his admission to the Indiana bar having been virtually coincident with his reception of the degree of Bachelor of Laws. He received this degree on the 15th of June and soon afterward established his residence in Gary, whre he has continued in the practice of his profession to the present time and where he maintains his offices at 1071 Broadway. Mr. Schorr has proved a vigorous and resourceful trial lawyer, and has a substantial and representative practice, and in the same he gives major attention to criminal law. His political allegiance is given to the Democratic party, and as a citizen he is loyal and progressive.

HARRY AUGUST SCHIESS, D. D. S., has the technical skill and loyalty that mark him as one of the able and successful representatives of his profession in Lake County, and his well appointed offices in the Gary State Bank Building in the City of Gary provide the best of modern equipment and service in both operative and laboratory departments.

Doctor Schiess was born in the City of Philadelphia, Pennsylvania, November 28, 1893, and is a son of Walter and Agatha (Noser) Schiess, who were born and reared in Switzerland, whose marriage was there solemnized, and who thence came to the United States, about 1885, their home having been established in Philadelphia a number of years and removal having then been made to Paterson, New Jersey, where Walter Schiess is now living retired, after many years of close association with the silk manufacturing industry. He is a Republican in politics, is affiliated with the Masonic fraternity and the Benevolent and Protective Order of Elks, and his religious faith is that of the German Lutheran Church, in which his wife likewise was a zealous communicant, her death having occurred January 9, 1928, and her mortal remains having been laid to rest in beautiful Cedar Grove Cemetery at Paterson. Of the five children Dr. Harry A., of this review, was the third in order of birth; Walter, Jr., eldest of the number, is now a resident of Albany, New York; Fred is following in his father's footsteps and is actively concerned with silk manufacturing at Paterson, New Jersey; Edith was for a number of years in active service as a trained nurse and is now the wife of Dr. Orman Gregersen, a representative physician and surgeon engaged in practice at Jamaica, Long Island, New York; and Leah is the wife of William Newkirk, who is manager of the Knox Hat Company establishment at Forty-fifth and Madison Avenue in New York City, while he and his wife maintain their home at Jamaica, Long Island.

In the public schools of Paterson, New Jersey, Dr. Harry A. Schiess continued his studies until he was graduated in the high school, in 1914. He was thereafter a student in a collegiate preparatory school in New York City, and his preparation for his chosen profession was made through the medium of the Indiana Dental College, in the City of Indianapolis, this being now the dental department of the University of Indiana. He was graduated as a member of the class of 1918. Soon after the nation entered the World war Doctor Schiess went to Fort Benjamin Harrison, near Indianapolis, and enlisted for service in the Medical Corps of the United States Army, but he was reassigned to his studies in the dental college, in order that he might complete his course, and was thus engaged at the time the armistice brought the great world conflict to a close, he having soon afterward received his honorable discharge. After acquiring his degree of Doctor of Dental Surgery he came to Gary, where for the first year he was associated in practice with Dr. J. H. Long. Here he has since continued in individual practice, and that practice has shown a constantly cumulative trend, with the result that it is now one of broad scope and gives him place among the representative dental practitioners in Lake County. The Doctor has made judicious investment in Gary real estate and has developed a substantial business in the sale of realty thus owned by himself. He has membership in the Lake County Dental Society, the Northwest Indiana Dental Association and the Indiana State Dental Association.

Doctor Schiess is a Republican in political alignment and in 1929 was made a candidate for member of the City Council, his defeat having been compassed by political exigencies but the vote tendered him having shown popular appreciation of his loyalty and public spirit as a citizen of the Lake County metropolis. He is affiliated with Gary Memorial Post of the American Legion and with the local lodge of the Benevolent and Protective Order of Elks. He and his wife are communicants of the German Lutheran Church.

August 31, 1926, recorded the marriage of Doctor Schiess to Miss Emma Garber, who was born at Berlin, Wisconsin, a daughter of Frederick Garber, who was there engaged in the shoe business many years and whose death there occurred in 1927, his wife having passed away about three years previously. After completing her studies in the high school of her native place Mrs. Schiess entered Ripon College, at Ripon, Wisconsin, and from this institution she received in 1917 the degree of Bachelor of Arts. Prior to her marriage she had made a notably successful record as a teacher in the public schools, and in this connection had taught at Rockford, Illinois; Green Bay, Wisconsin; and Ironwood, Michigan, as well as Gary, Indiana, in which city she is still retained as the efficient and popular teacher of English in the Horace Mann High School, both she and her husband being popular figures in the social and cultural activities of their home city.

FRANK CARLETON JEWART. Although he is still one of the younger generation of business men of Gary, Frank C. Jewart has made rapid strides toward the attainment of position and success, and as owner of the Gary Blue Print Company is directing an enterprise that is forging its way consistently to the forefront. Mr. Jewart has been the architect of his own fortunes, having received no outside aid or been given the advantages of adventitious circumstances or conditions, and the manner in which he has conducted his activities has been such as to gain for him the respect of his business contemporaries and the confidence of the public.

Mr. Jewart was born November 3, 1897, in Pittsburgh, Pennsylvania, and is a son of A. P. and Sarah (Carpenter) Jewart, and a member of an old and honored pioneer family of the Keystone State which has contributed numerous men and women to fill positions of responsibility and trust in various walks of life. A. P. Jewart was born at Atwood, Pennsylvania, where he was given a common school education, and in young manhood took up teaching as a vocation. He rose rapidly in his calling and served capably as superintendent of schools of Carrick, a suburb of Pittsburgh, for years, but in 1911 came to Gary and entered the employ of the American Sheet & Tin Plate Company, being at present a foreman in that plant and one of the company's capable and trusted employes. He is a devout and active member of the Presbyterian Church and a man who is held in high esteem and respect. Mr. Jewart married Miss Sarah Carpenter, who was born and reared at Atwood, Pennsylvania, and educated in the public schools, and who was a school teacher for a few years prior to her marriage. She was always active in the work of the Presbyterian Church, and died in that faith in 1922, being buried in Oak Hill Cemetery, Gary. Mr. and Mrs. Jewart were the parents of two children: Frank C., of this review; and Ruth, the wife of Ward Hile, of the Illinois Steel Company, Gary, who has one child, Robert.

Frank C. Jewart attended the public schools of Pittsburgh, where he graduated from high school as a member of the class of 1911, and on coming to Gary in the same year secured a position with the American Sheet & Tin Plate Company, by which concern he was employed for a few years. Later he formed a connection with the National Tube Company, and continued with that concern until 1920, when he found himself prepared to embark in business on his own account and founded the Gary Blue Print Company, of which he has since been the president. From small beginnings this has grown to be an enterprise of recognized importance, and through prompt and efficient service and high-quality workmanship is adding steadily to its long list of patrons. Mr. Jewart has become an expert in his line, and his commodious plant, at 743 Washington Street, is fully equipped to turn out all kinds of first-class blue print work and photographic copy printing. This is a highly specialized field in which only those with a comprehensive knowledge of the art can hope to arise above mediocrity, and the fact that Mr. Jewart has attained an outstanding success argues strongly for his ability. Mr. Jewart has always been active and constructively helpful in matters of civic import and is an enthusiastic and working member of the Commercial Club and Chamber of Commerce and the Rotary Club. Fraternally he is affiliated with the Independent Order of Odd Fellows. He is a Republican, but not a politician, although he has borne his full share of the responsibilities of citizenship, and during the World war was active in all patriotic movements. He belongs to the First Presbyterian Church.

On November 27, 1919, Mr. Jewart was united in marriage, at Carlisle, Sullivan County, Indiana, with Miss Hester Land, daughter of J. I. and Anna (Cox) Land, of Carlisle, the former of whom was for years a prominent farmer and stock raiser of Sullivan County and still resides on his farm at the edge of Carlisle, although now in retirement. He is active in the Modern Woodmen and other fraternities and is known as a man of public spirit and sound views. Mrs. Jewart was educated in the public schools of Carlisle, where she graduated from high school, and was a member of the Presbyterian Church. She is a member of the Presbyterian Church of Gary and assists her husband materially. Mr. and Mrs. Jewart are the parents of one son: Eugene Francis, who is attending the Horace Mann School.

SCHUYLER C. IRWIN, prominent Indiana attorney, has practiced his profession at Rensselaer for over thirty-five years. He has found ample satisfaction of his ambition within the strict limits of the profession, and has been in politics only for the opportunity of making his influence felt in behalf of good local government.

Mr. Irwin was born in Jasper County, Indiana, February 4, 1867. His father, James F. Irwin, was a native of Hamilton County, Indiana, and during the Civil war was enrolled as a soldier in Company F of the One Hundred and Thirty-second Indiana Volunteers. He died May 12, 1912. James F. Irwin married Mary J. Ravenscroft, daughter of Edward Ravenscroft. They were the parents of three sons and four daughters, Schuyler C., Edward W., Frederick A., Frances, Mrs. A. E. Wallace, Mrs. I. N. Warren and Mrs. Earl Parsons.

Schuyler C. Irwin was educated in district schools in Jasper County, growing up on a farm, and was graduated from the Rensselaer High School in 1888 He took up the study of law, pursued it diligently and in 1893 was qualified for and admitted to the Indiana bar. He has handled his share of important litigation in the courts of Jasper County through all the years since he began practice. He has also been in the real estate business.

In the line of public service he was city clerk, justice of the peace and was one of the first officials chosen to office when the City of Rensselaer was incorporated, becoming city clerk.

He is a Republican voter, a member of the Christian Science Church and is affiliated with the Masonic Lodge, Independent Order of Odd Fellows and Modern Woodmen of America.

He married, October 13, 1894, Effie Stillwell Plummer, daughter of M. C. Plummer. They have a daughter, Genevieve, a student of music and art at Minneapolis and a musician whose work has been appreciated by that great audience of radio listeners. She has frequently been on the broadcast programs of stations at Minneapolis and Chicago.

ROBERT H. MOORE. In the selection of their counsel the great financial and business institutions of the country employ the utmost caution and careful judgment, the requisites for such identification being substantial legal ability, absolute rectitude of character and a broad experience of the world and men. All of these qualities are found in the personality of Robert H. Moore, of the firm of Moore, Long, Chudom & Johnson, of Gary, who, although now limited to corporation practice, has had sufficient experience therein to command a large and important clientage in that field of his calling.

Mr. Moore was born between Dundee and Maybie, near Detroit, Michigan, May 27, 1886, and is a son of David A. and Ida (Robbins) Moore. David Alonzo Moore was born and reared in the same community, but removed to Michigan City, Indiana, some years after his marriage, and there spent the remainder of his life. He will be remembered by many as a man of wonderful poetical imagination and one who possessed the rare faculty of extemporaneous poetry. Many of his productions were real gems of poesy, wit and beauty, and although he never sought their complete publication they were, nevertheless, widely recognized for their worth. He gathered together a number of these in his later years, but death overtook him before he could finish his self-appointed task.

Robert H. Moore was a young child when taken by his parents to Michigan City, where he attended the public schools and graduated from Saint Mary's High School as a member of the class of 1904. He then entered Valparaiso University, from which he received the degrees of Bachelor of Laws and Bachelor of Oratory, and in 1907 entered upon the practice of his profession at Michigan City. He continued to follow his calling with success until the United States entered the World war, when, in 1917, he entered the Officers Training Camp at Camp Zachary Taylor, where he remained in training until after the signing of the armistice, not being called for active service in the field. Upon receiving his honorable discharge Mr. Moore returned to his practice at Michigan City and in 1920 was appointed county attorney of Lake County, but resigned that office to accept that of city deputy prosecutor, the duties of which he dis-

charged to the full satisfaction of his fellow-citizens. Mr. Moore came to Gary March 1, 1928, and has since been engaged successfully in the practice of his profession. On September 1, 1930, he formed a partnership with Harry Long, Morris Chudom and City Attorney Roswell B. Johnson, under the firm style of Moore, Long, Chudom and Johnson, with offices on the eighth floor of the Gary State Bank Building, and this is already recognized as one of the strongest legal combinations in Northern Indiana. Mr. Moore is a member of the Indiana State Bar Association; the Gary Commercial Club and Chamber of Commerce; the Long Beach Country Club, and is a great golf enthusiast. He resides at the Gary Hotel, but owns a beautiful summer home at Michigan City and has another home at Long Beach. Mr. Moore has been very active in the ranks of the Republican party and has been devoted to the interests of his party.

Mr. Moore comes of sterling ancestry. His paternal grandfather, Thaddeus Moore, was a native of Monroe County, New York, and married Miss Nancy Scott, a descendant of the distinguished Scott family. His maternal grandfather, H. R. Robbins, was for years a well-known resident of Knox County, Indiana, a lawyer of distinguished attainments, and a public-spirited citizen who was largely responsible for the draining of the Kankakee marshes, which opened up a vast area for agricultural cultivation. He married a Miss Mary Miskell.

In McLean County, Illinois, Mr. Moore was united in marriage with Miss Nell Crate, a charming woman of many graces and accomplishments, a talented musician and vocalist and one of the most popular members of social circles and of the Long Beach Country Club. In addition to the connections before mentioned, Mr. Moore belongs to Gary Memorial Post No. 17, American Legion, and the Independent Order of Odd Fellows, and to the Ameaka Bogardus Society.

BARNEY JOSEPH SABLOTNY. In the career of Barney J. Sablotny, president of the Gary Paper & Supply Company, of Gary, there is to be found something of an encouraging character for the youth of any land who feels himself handicapped by lack of education, finances or friends. Mr. Sablotny, a poor German immigrant boy, began his independent life in the coal mines of Illinois at the tender age of twelve years. Many, in these circumstances, would never have emerged from obscurity, but such has been Mr. Sablotny's determination, spirit and ability that he has risen steadily to become one of Gary's leading and influential citizens, a force in business, political, social and fraternal circles.

Barney J. Sablotny was born at Stephansdorf, Germany, May 5, 1891, and is a son of Anthony and Frances Sablotny, natives of Germany. Anthony Sablotny, who passed his entire career as a farmer, was wounded in the knee during the Franco-Prussian war, and was a partial invalid all of his life, dying in 1902.

By his first wife he was the father of two sons: William, deceased; and Leon, a retired manufacturer of Chicago, Illinois. By his second wife he had six children: Louis, at one time a member of the Uhlans, a crack regiment of the Germany army, who died shortly after the World war, from the effects of his military service, and is buried at Stephansdorf, Germany; Valerie, now Mrs. Kamasa, of Germany, whose son, Joseph, was captain of a German ship during the World war and is now director-general of education of Poland; Frank and Frances, who are residents of Chicago; Barney J., of this review; and Joseph, of Chicago. After the death of her husband, in 1902, the mother of Barney J. Sablotny immigrated to the United States and first settled at Spring Valley, in the coal region of Illinois, but later moved to Chicago, where she spent the remainder of her life and died in 1913, being buried in Mount Olivet Cemetery.

Barney J. Sablotny attended public school in Germany from the time he was six years of age until he was about twelve, when he was brought to the United States by his mother and immediately went to work in a coal mine at Spring Valley, Illinois. That he was a precocious and somewhat unusual lad is seen in the fact that he had become such an influence by the time he was fifteen years of age that he was elected a representative of the United Mine Workers of America under Pres. John J. Mitchell, and served in that capacity for a period of three years. In 1908 he moved to Chicago, where he secured a position as fireman on the Nickel Plate Railroad, and likewise served as safety director and as representative of the Brotherhood of Locomotive Firemen. After about seven years he left railroading to engage in the retail grocery and meat business at Chicago, continuing in this line until 1917, when he accepted a position with the Tapajna Paper Company as salesman, and in 1919 took charge of the business at Gary, where he has since made his home and where he increased the sales of the company materially, making it one of the important enterprises of the city. On November 15, 1930, he severed his connection with the Tapajna Paper Company and formed the Gary Paper & Supply Company, of which he is the president and principal stockholder. Mr. Sablotny's interests have increased amazingly and have spread out in every direction. He is a member of the advisory board of the Salvation Army; a director of the Glen Park Building & Loan Association; helped organize the Lions Club of Gary, of which he is an officer; is a member of the Gary Commercial Club and Chamber of Commerce; a member of the Glen Park Republican Club, the Young Men's Christian Association, the Glen Park Boosters Association, the Lincoln Hills Country Club and other organizations, and has been active in the Izaak Walton League. He is an enthusiastic football fan, and during the season attends all of the big games that he can possibly reach. In politics he is a stanch supporter of the Republican party, and his religious affiliation is with the Forty-third Avenue Methodist Episcopal Church.

At Knox, Indiana, August 8, 1914, Mr. Sablotny was united in marriage with Miss Esther Garner, daughter of H. W. and Mattie (Hepner) Garner, of Gary, who make their home with Mr. and Mrs. Sablotny, Mr. Garner being a retired carpenter and a veteran of the Spanish-American war. Mrs. Sablotny, who graduated from Knox High School, is active in community life, a worker in the Methodist Church, and a member of the Parent-Teachers Association of Glen Park and the various women's clubs of the city. To Mr. and Mrs. Sablotny there have been born two children: Dorothy Marie and William Robert, both born at Chicago, the former of whom is in her second year at the Lew Wallace High Schol, and the latter in his first year in the same school at Gary.

WILLIAM ALEXANDER POZZO is one of Gary's enterprising business men, and has had more than twenty years of active experience in the automobile business. He was overseas during the World war and for the past ten years has had the Lake County agency for the Mack truck.

Mr. Pozzo was born in Italy, October 27, 1889. His parents, John and Illumanata (Caneparo) Pozzo, were natives of Italy, were reared and educated in that country and have spent all their lives there. His father, who died in 1896, owned and operated a woolen mill. The widowed mother is still living in Italy. Of her nine living children William was the sixth.

Mr. Pozzo while a youth in Italy attended parochial and private schools. He was about sixteen years old when, in 1905, he came to America. For seven years he lived in New York City, and there had a long course of training and experience in the automobile business. From New York he went to Chicago, where he also spent seven years.

He was in Chicago when America entered the World war and he enlisted in 1917. He received his training at San Francisco, in the Coast Artillery Corps, and went overseas with the Sixty-second Regiment, Coast Artillery Corps. He had charge of the automobile school at San Francisco, with the rank of corporal. In France he was located on duty near Bordeaux. On getting his honorable discharge, January 20, 1919, he spent two months traveling in France and five months in his native land.

After his military service he returned to Chicago and in 1921 came to Gary, where he acquired the Mack Truck Agency in Lake County. He owns a fine business, including a large shop and show room at 1100 Madison Street. He represents one of the oldest and largest of the commercial truck manufacturers in America.

Mr. Pozzo has been very active in civic affairs, is a member of the Rotary Club, Commercial Club and Chamber of Commerce. He is president of the Gary Italian Education

Association, Incorporated, and treasurer of the Eleventh Avenue Sub-Division and Improvement Association. He is a member of Gary Memorial Post of the American Legion, the Sons of Italy, in politics is an independent voter and is a member of the Catholic Church. Mr. Pozzo is one of the church committeemen at the Judge Gary Bishop Alerding Settlement Church.

He married in Chicago in January, 1921, Miss Rita Barili, daughter of Peter and Santina Barili. She was born in Italy, was reared there, and came to America in 1920. Mr. and Mrs. Pozzo have two children, Arnold Gianpier and Adrian Eleonor. Both children are attending one of the public schools of Gary.

EMIL M. T. NALLINGER. A resident of Gary since 1923, Emil M. T. Nallinger is identified with several of the leading financial institutions of the city and is likewise one of the best known members of the Loyal Order of Moose in the state. Mr. Nallinger started his career as a school teacher, but soon outgrew the environment of the schoolroom, turned his attention to financial affairs, and is now president of the Lake County Savings & Loan Association and has numerous other important connections which serve to make him one of the most substantial citizens of his adopted city.

Mr. Nallinger was born at Sturgis, Saint Joseph County, Michigan, March 25, 1888, and is a son of Albert and Mary (Kalberer) Nallinger. His father, a native of Germany, was reared and educated in that country, whence he immigrated to the United States in young manhood and settled at Sturgis, Michigan, where he secured land, developed a farm, and through industry and able management became one of the successful farmers and stock raisers of his community. He was a man of high and substantial character, who was highly thought of by his fellow-citizens, and a devout member of the Lutheran Church, to which Mrs. Nallinger, also a native of Germany, and who came to the United States in girlhood, also belongs. Mr. Nallinger died June 18, 1918, and was buried at Sturgis, where Mrs. Nallinger still makes her home. There were five children in the family: Emil, of this review; Carl, who died at the age of eighteen years; Dora, now Mrs. Morris Johnston, of Gary; Gustav, of Aurora, Illinois; and Esther, now Mrs. Cecil Green, of Sturgis.

Emil Nallinger received his education in the public schools of Sturgis and the Michigan State Normal School of Kalamazoo, this being supplemented by a commercial course at the Elkhart (Indiana) Business College. For two years he was a teacher in the public schools of Michigan, following which he became an instructor in the Elkhart Business College, but at the end of two years severed his connection with that institution to accept the post of chief auditor of the Loyal Order of Moose, at Mooseheart, Illinois. Mr. Nallinger remained in that capacity until 1923, in which year he came to Gary, where he has since served in the capacity of district supervisor for the order in Northwestern Indiana, with offices at 700 Adams Street. He has proved himself a great organizer as well as a careful and efficient executive and has done much to increase the membership of the Moose in his district. In 1926 Mr. Nallinger accepted the position of secretary of the Lake County Savings & Loan Association, and upon the death of John W. Thiel, in April, 1930, succeeded the latter in the presidency. He is likewise president of the Gibraltar Bond & Mortgage Company of Gary and has various other connections and holdings. Mr. Nallinger occupies a high place in the esteem and confidence of his associates and fellow-citizens and is known as a man of ripened judgment, enlightened views and rare foresight. He is a valued member of Jerusalem Temple Lodge No. 90, A. F. and A. M., of Aurora; the Independent Order of Odd Fellows, at Elkhart; the Loyal Order of Moose, the Knights of Pythias, the Modern Woodmen of America and the Benevolent and Protective Order of Elks of Gary. He also takes an active part in civic affairs as a member of the local Kiwanis Club. In politics he maintains an independent stand, voting rather for the man than the party, and his religious affiliation is with the Central Christian Church. He belongs likewise to the Gary Commercial Club and Chamber of Commerce and the Cressmore Country Club.

At Elkhart, Indiana, February 1, 1911, Mr. Nallinger was united in marriage with Miss Florence Taska, daughter of Otto and Hannah (Rose) Taska, of that city, where Mr. Taska has been foreman at the New York Central Railroad shops for many years. Mrs. Nallinger was educated in the public grade and high schools of Elkhart and the Elkhart Business College, and for a few years prior to her marriage was engaged in clerical work. She is active in the Central Christian Church, Olive Chapter of the Order of the Eastern Star, the Mooseheart Legion and the Pythian Sisters. Mr. and Mrs. Nallinger are the parents of three children: Earl M. T., born in 1913, who graduated from Emerson High School as a member of the class of 1929, and is now taking post-graduate work at Emerson School and extension work at the University of Indiana; Agnes M. L., who is attending high school; and Glenn O. W., who is in eighth grade of the public schools. The pleasant family home is situated at 772 Georgia Street, Gary.

JOHN THOMAS DENNIS is a Gary business man, active in local affairs and a citizen of public spirit and willingness to cooperate in every move for general advancement.

Mr. Dennis is a native of Kentucky, born in Montgomery County, that state, December 10, 1892. The Dennis family came to Kentucky in pioneer times. His great-grandfather crossed the mountains from Virginia to Kentucky and was a surveyor by profession. The grandfather, John Dennis, was a Kentucky farmer and stock raiser. J. Thomas Dennis,

John W. Kitch

father of John T., spent his active life as a farmer and stock man in Kentucky. He died in 1892, the same year his son was born, and is buried in the family cemetery near Mount Sterling. His wife, Betty Radcliffe, was born and reared in Kentucky, attended school there, and after her husband's death served for a number of years as postmaster of a village near Mount Sterling. She is a member of the Christian Church and now resides at Lexington, Kentucky. She is the mother of three sons: Henry W., a resident of Indianapolis; Austin, of Lexington, Kentucky; and John Thomas. By a second marriage the mother of these sons has a daughter, Bertie, now Mrs. John W. Crow, of Nashville, Tennessee.

John T. Dennis was educated in public schools near Mount Sterling Kentucky, and immediately after leaving school found work in the mercantile line, his employer being the John Hutchinson Grocery Company of Lexington. He remained with that concern for five years. In 1912 Mr. Dennis entered the service of the S. S. Kresge Company at Cincinnati, Ohio, and during this first period of service with this widely known chain store organization he was transferred for varying lengths of time to Louisville and Lexington, Kentucky. Following that he was with the Kerr Dry Goods Company of Oklahoma City for two and a half years.

On rejoining the Kresge organization he was located at Chicago for a year and a half, from 1922, was then sent to Toledo, Ohio, for ten months, and in 1912 opened the Kresge store at Aurora, Illinois, where he remained for over two years. In January, 1927, he was made district manager of the Kresge Company for the Philadelphia district, but in July, 1928, came to Gary, where he has since been manager of the Kresge Dollar Store.

Mr. Dennis is an active member of the Commercial Club and Chamber of Commerce and the Rotary Club. He is a member of the B. P. O. Elks, a Democrat in politics and a member of the Christian Church.

JOHN WALTER KITCH. In John W. Kitch the bar of Plymouth and Marshall County have a man who fully recognizes the fact that he is an officer of the court as well as a private practitioner, so that although he accepts his clients' instructions with his retainer, he regards himself nevertheless subject to the higher obligations of professional ethics. Probably because of this, in addition to his undoubted ability, both natural and acquired, he had from the start of his career a following, and today enjoys a very large and valuable practice, and has been the recipient of high political honors.

John W. Kitch was born at Bremen, Indiana, June 8, 1866, a son of Martin V. Kitch, born in Crawford County, Ohio, August 3, 1839; grandson of John B. Kitch, born in Tuscarawas County, Ohio, in 1810; and great-grandson of Martin Kitch, a German by birth in all probability, who with his father settled in Lancaster County, Pennsylvania. The mother of John W. Kitch bore the maiden name of Amanda M. Lehr, and she was born in St. Joseph County, Indiana, November 12, 1844, a daughter of Samuel Lehr; great-granddaughter of Samuel Lehr; and great-great-granddaughter of John Heinrich Loehr, born at the village of Wallahausen, Prussian-Saxony, who came to the American colonies in 1777 as a bond servant for passage money. He settled near Germantown, Pennsylvania. The mother of Mrs. Amanda M. (Lehr) Kitch was Malinda Geiselman; and Mrs. Kitch's grandfathers were Michael Geiselman and Samuel Lehr, and one of her grandmothers was Elizabeth Lehr. Martin V. Kitch's mother bore the maiden name of Sarah Doebler.

John W. Kitch attended the common schools of Marshall County, Indiana, and Valparaiso University, from which he received the degrees of Bachelor of Arts and Bachelor of Science. He began the study of law at the university and continued it in the offices of Frank E. Gates, Adair, Iowa; George B. Lynch, Adair, Iowa; and Mr. Lee of Coon Rapids, Iowa. While he was preparing himself for professional work Mr. Kitch taught school, for four years in the country schools of Marshall County and then during 1890 and 1891 he was principal of the high school at Holland, Michigan. From Holland he went to Adair, Iowa, as principal of schools, and held that position for two years, and then for two years he was superintendent of the schools of Coon Rapids, Iowa. At the same time, during 1892, 1893, 1894 and 1895, he was also publishing the *Adair News*.

In 1898 Mr. Kitch was admitted to the bar at Plymouth, Marshall County, Indiana, and was engaged in practice at Bremen, and later at South Bend, Indiana, remaining in the latter city for fifteen years. Since February, 1916, he has been in practice at Plymouth. During the sessions of the Indiana State Legislature in 1923 and 1925 Mr. Kitch represented Marshall County in that body, and in the former session was a member of the budget committee. He is a trustee of the Indiana School for Feeble Minded Youths and the Indiana Farm Colony for Feeble Minded.

Mr. Kitch has been twice married, his second wife having been Miss Mae Southworth prior to her marriage. There are two children: Lorene R., who married Clement Fox and lives at Gilbert, Arizona, where her husband is superintendent of schools; and Don F., who is associated with his father in the practice of law. Mrs. Fox is a graduate of the South Bend High School, the University of Chicago, where she took the degree of Bachelor of Arts; and the American Conservatory of Music, Chicago. She and her husband have three children: Arlene, Barbara H. and Don Fox. Don F. Kitch married Marie Clossen, of Kit Carson, Colorado, and they have three children, Robert J., Beryl Jean and Lora Leah. He was educated in the high school of Cheyenne Wells, Colorado, and the University of Colorado, Boulder. During the World war Don F. Kitch served for twenty-six months with the One

Hundred and Ffteenth United States Engineers, participating in the offensives of Saint Mihiel and the Argonne Forest, and was with the Army of Occupation, stationed near Coblenz, Germany.

Mr. Kitch of this review is not a member of any religious organization, but he attends the Episcopal Church. He is a member of the York Rite and Shrine in Masonry, and also belongs to the Knights of Pythias, the Fraternal Order of Eagles, the Kiwanis Club, the Chamber of Commerce and the Plymouth Country Club. His Masonic connections are as follows: Plymouth-Kilwinning Lodge No. 149, A. F. and A. M.; Plymouth Chapter, No. 49, R. A. M.; Plymouth Council No. 18, R. and S. M; Plymouth Commandery No 26, K T.; and Mizpah Temple, A. A. O. N. M. S., of Fort Wayne, Indiana. He is a Democrat in politics. In golf and fishing and the reading of history and biography Mr. Kitch finds recreation and pleasurable relaxation from his heavy professional responsibilities. Of a literary turn of mind, he wrote, in 1916, *Centennial History of Indiana*, a burlesque, which was well received.

JAY F. GRANTHAM. A resident of Gary since 1911, Jay F. Grantham has been identified with a number of lines of business activity during the past two decades, but for the greater part of this time has centered his interest in the automobile industry. In this field he is now a recognized leader, the Grantham Motor Sales Company, of which he is president, being sole agents for the Chevrolet automobile at Gary. He is also identified with a number of other enterprises and is a citizen of public spirit and civic pride who has contributed materially to the progress and growth of his community.

Mr. Grantham was born at Scottdale, Westmoreland County, Pennsylvania, and is a son of James W. and Julia (Schrader) Grantham. The Grantham family has carved a special niche in the history of Gary, for this family has very conspicuously identified itself with the business life of the city for a number of years. The family had its origin in England, and there is a family tradition that the immediate Grantham ancestor was a friend and follower of Thomas Fairfax, sixth baron of Cameron, who was born in England in 1691, educated at Oxford and was a contributor to Addison's *Spectator*. Disappointed in England, he came to America and settled on a vast landed estate in Virginia which he had inherited from his mother, a daughter of Lord Culpepper. There, in the midst of 10,000 acres of land, he built an unpretentious lodge, in which he lived a solitary and secluded life, taking no part in public affairs. It was there, at Greenway Court, that Washington met him. Between the two there sprang up a warm friendship, and when years later he learned that Washington had captured Cornwallis, he was overcome with emotion and called to his body-servant to carry him to his bed, "for I am sure," he said, "it is time for me to die." He

passed away at his lodge, in Frederick County, Virginia, December 12, 1782. Members of the Grantham family resided in Frederick County and later in Jefferson County, Virginia, where was born the paternal grandfather of Jay F. Grantham, John S. Grantham, who married Lucy Scharff, also a native of that county. John S. Grantham was a soldier of the Confederacy during the war between the states, and served with gallantry in a number of the hard-fought engagements of that struggle, following the close of which he established himself in the undertaking business at Middleway, where he passed the remainder of his life.

James W. Grantham was born at Middleway, West Virginia, where he acquired his education in the public schools, and later moved to Connellsville, Pennsylvania, where he learned the trade of carpenter, becoming very proficient in drawing plans and specifications. Eventually he entered the contracting business at Scottdale, Pennsylvania, and followed it there for many years, and in 1911 came to Gary, where he continued to be active as a contractor and builder until his retirement in about 1924. At one time he secured a huge contract from one of the steel concerns for the erection of 365 houses of concrete to be used as homes by the employes, and fulfilled this and other big contracts most satisfactorily. He retains his interest in business affairs as treasurer of the Grantham Motor Sales Company, and is likewise treasurer of the Oak Hill Cemetery Association. He married Miss Julia Schrader, who was born, reared and educated at Madison, Pennsylvania, and following their marriage removed to Scottdale, where she was active in the United Brethren Church until her death in 1900. To Mr. and Mrs. Grantham were born the following children: Lucy D., the wife of Rev. C. W. Snyder, a minister of the United Brethren faith at Lebanon, Ohio; Bettie, the wife of W. A. Gordon, of Scottdale; Rankin F., of Scottdale; John, also of Scottdale; Joseph P., who is engaged in the real estate business at Gary, where he is president of the Oak Hill Cemetery Association, and a review of whose career will be found elsewhere in this work; and Jay F., of this review.

Jay F. Grantham attended the public schools of Scottdale, Pennsylvania, where he was graduated from high school, and was an athletic enthusiast, being manager of the football and baseball teams of the class of 1905. Later he attended Pennsylvania State College, from which he was graduated as a member of the class of 1909, and this was followed by a year at Peterson's Business College, from which he was graduated in 1910. Upon leaving that school he became manager of the Scottdale Plumbing, Heating & Roofing Company, a position which he held for two years. On July 2, 1911, Mr. Grantham came to Gary, having secured the plumbing contract from the American Sheet & Tin Plate Company for the 300 homes they were building at Gary, and later secured the contract for roofing these 300 homes also. This work lasted for about one and one-half years, at the end of which time he organized a company known as the Motor Bus Transit Company, of which he was president, having secured an exclusive contract and franchise from the American Sheet & Tin Plate Company to operate buses over their property, carrying employes to and from their work at the rate of five cents per passenger. Mr. Grantham is credited with having brought the first five-cent motor transportation not only to this section of the state, but of the United States. He continued to be engaged in the same line of business until 1917, in which year he purchased one of the buildings at 529-535 Washington Street and launched the Gary Garage & Sales Company, of which he was president, carrying on a general garage business and taking over the sales agency for the Maxwell car. Later he was representative for the Dodge, Apperson, Scripps-Boothe, Nash and Chevrolet cars. During the year 1923 Mr. Grantham built a new building adjoining, which is known as 537 to 543 Washington Street, and discontinued the operations under the old firm name, taking on the exclusive franchise and sales of the Chevrolet cars. At the same time he formed a new company, known since then as the Grantham Motor Sales Company, of which he is president and his father treasurer. This is a $50,000 corporation, and the building covers a 150-foot front on Washington Street, with three outlet stores at different locations in the City of Gary, having a beautiful sales and show room at 543 Washington Street, where the main office is located. Seventy people are given employment in the business, which has a floor space of 14,400 square feet, commodious show rooms, storage rooms and service rooms, and is one of the largest and most important concerns in this field.

Mr. Grantham is vice president of the Gary Oak Hill Cemetery Association, president of the Washington Street Improvement Association and president of the Gary Automotive Association. He belongs to the Commercial Club and Chamber of Commerce, the Gary Country Club, the Benevolent and Protective Order of Elks, the Loyal Order of Moose, the Kiwanis Club, which he assisted to organize and is one of the present directors; the Lincoln Hill Country Club; and is a thirty-second degree Mason and Shriner and member of Gary Lodge No. 677, A. F. and A. M.; Gary Chapter, Commandery and Consistory; and Orak Temple, A. A. O. N. M. S., of Hammond. He is a Republican in his political allegiance, and a member and trustee of the First Presbyterian Church.

On November 25, 1926, Mr. Grantham was united in marriage with Miss Lillian Crossland, daughter of Homer and Violet (Harold) Crossland, formerly of Latrobe, Pennsylvania. Mr. Crossland, who was for many years a locomotive engineer on the Pennsylvania Railway, died several years ago and is buried in Pennsylvania, while Mrs. Crossland still survives and makes her home with her son, Dr. S. H. Crossland, of Gary. Mrs. Grantham at-tended the grade and high schools of Pitcairn, Pennsylvania, and the Indiana Conservatory of Music, and later pursued a course at the Sherwood School of Music, Chicago. Prior to her marriage she taught music for several years at Gary, where she is greatly popular in musical circles and is also active in the work of the Presbyterian Church. She is a past president of the Pi Sigma Phi sorority and active in the Woman's Club. Mr. and Mrs. Grantham are the parents of two sons: James Stewart, born September 8, 1927; and Robert Harvey, born June 12, 1930.

During the World war Mr. Grantham was active in the Red Cross and Victory Loan drives, and is still active in all civic affairs. He is a member of the "Old Scouts," and takes an interest and a constructive part in the Boy Scout movement, the Salvation Army and the Red Cross, and is a member of the University Club, a past president and a member of the board of directors.

AUGUST WILLIAM LAMP. The qualities of adaptability, perseverance, common sense and good judgment have prevailed in the energetic life of August W. Lamp, winning for him an enviable rank among the business element of Gary. A product of the agricultural reigons of Illinois, he first came to Gary in 1912 and in the following year became identified with the grocery business, in which line he has achieved recognition and position, meeting with the success which justly rewards an enterprising business career and consideration for the interests of his patrons.

Mr. Lamp was born in the vicinity of Iuka, Marion County, Illinois, January 4, 1891, and is a son of Fred and Ida (Behnke) Lamp. His father, who was born in Germany, was brought to the United States by his parents in childhood, and received his education in public schools at Chicago, in which locality he was reared to the pursuits of agriculture by an industrious father. On attaining man's estate Fred Lamp adopted farming and stock raising as his life work, and has continued therein, being at present the owner of a large and well-cultivated property in Marion County, where he is known as a substantial business man and public-spirited citizen. He married Miss Ida Behnke, who was born in Chicago, Illinois, and educated in the public schools there, and who is now active in the movements of the Lutheran Church at Iuka. There were seven children in the family: August W., of this review; Charles, who is deceased; Emil, a resident of Ladysmith, Wisconsin; Ida, now Mrs. Pardue, of Gary; Fred, of Chicago; Clara, who is deceased; and Eleanor, of Gary.

August W. Lamp attended the public schools of Iuka and was reared on his father's farm, but did not care for an agricultural career, and accordingly pursued a commercial course in a business college at Centralia, Illinois. In 1912 he came to Gary, where in the following year he embarked in the grocery business, and is now the proprietor of one of the I. G. A. chain stores, at 1625 Broadway, where he is doing a large and profitable business. In addition Mr. Lamp is a stockholder in the Gary Wholesale Grocery Company, of which he was secretary and a director for some years. He takes an active and constructive part in civic affairs as a member of the Gary Commercial Club and Chamber of Commerce, and belongs also to the Cressmore Country Club and the Lincoln Hills Country Club. Politically he is a Republican, but has never desired nor held public office. He belongs to Grace Lutheran Church, of which he has been a member of the official board for ten years, and for the past five years has acted in the capacity of financial secretary.

Mr. Lamp is unmarried. He is a golf and bowling enthusiast and is also greatly fond of hunting and fishing.

THE JAY GARMENT COMPANY, of Portland, is an industry with an interesting history, and is not only an important contribution to the prosperity of Portland but contributes to the diversity of Indiana as a great manufacturing state.

The owners of the business, Mr. J. A. Williams and Mr. O. R. Easterday, grew up together and have been friends from boyhood, and for years have been partners in their business undertakings. In 1921 they established the Jay Garment Company to manufacture work shirts and overalls and other garments from denim and similar materials. They are the manufacturers of a number of classifications of shirts, jackets and overalls, including the "Bob White Overalls," the "Booster" overalls and jackets, "Challenge" overalls and jackets, and other lines of work and outing shirts and garments.

The first garment was finished on September 12, 1921, having been designed and cut by William H. Teeters, a man of wide experience in the garment industry, who is superintendent of the plant today. From the first the Jay Garment Company was started with a vision of a service and certain policies, which have been modified but not especially changed. These policies were based upon the bedrock of commercial integrity and fair dealing, and also involved the making of garments a little better than the average value at the same price.

When the business was started in September, 1921, one room, thirty by seventy feet, was used. There were seventeen employees. After a few months the progress justified the purchase of a building 50 by 200 feet, and in spite of this addition the plant had to be expanded. In May, 1927, the company built an addition 48 by 140 feet, and in September of the same year put up a warehouse 30 by 100 feet. For a number of years the company distributed their product by the usual channels of distribution, relying upon a staff of salesmen, but about the close of 1928 they put into operation a plan of direct from the factory to the dealer sales, and this has resulted in such an increase of business as to more than justify the new policy.

While the company started in 1921 with 2,100 square feet of floor space, the product facilities of the factory today utilize nearly 52,000 square feet, and from seventeen employees the number has grown to over 500, comprising what the owners call their "Bob White Family."

PEARL RAYMOND SMITH. Of the followers of the skilled trades, the mere possession of a profitable and extensive contracting business in itself argues for superior ability and good workmanship. It is in the line of plastering that Pearl Raymond Smith has won a recognized and substantial position among the contractors of Gary, and perhaps heredity plays a part in his accomplishments, for his father and his maternal grandfather were both engaged in the same line of work. Mr. Smith has been engaged in business on his own account since 1912, and during this period has done the plastering and decorating in some of the finest buildings erected in the city.

Pearl Raymond Smith was born at Zanesville, Ohio, March 7, 1883, and is a son of Benjamin F. and Amelia A. (George) Smith. His paternal grandfather, William Smith, a native of Ohio, while he did not enlist in the Union army during the war between the states, saw service in that struggle as a wagoner and had many thrilling experiences and narrow escapes. Benjamin F. Smith was born in South Carolina, whence he moved to Zanesville, Ohio, and after following the trade of plasterer for some years as a journeyman, engaged in business on his own account as a contractor and continued as such until his death in 1926, being buried at White Cottage, Ohio. He married Amelia A. George, who was born in Pennsylvania, the daughter of a plasterer who served as a soldier of the Union army during the Civil war. She died in 1917 and was also buried in the White Cottage Cemetery, which is located near Zanesville, Ohio.

Pearl Raymond Smith received only ordinary educational advantages in the public schools of Zanesville, Ohio, which he attended until reaching the age of thirteen years, at which time he began to learn the trade of plasterer under the preceptorship of his father. He was joined in this by his brothers, Edwin, of Zanesville; Arthur E., of Glasgow, Montana; John A. and William R., of Zanesville; and Herbert B., of Columbus. He has one sister, Rose, the widow of Charles Hamilton, of Gary. One child died in infancy, Elsie died at the age of ten years, Seymour died at the age of fifteen years, and Pearl Raymond was the ninth child in order of birth.

Mr. Smith learned all the details of the plastering business, and October 3, 1911, came to Gary from Akron, Ohio, and in 1912 established himself in business as a plastering contractor, a business in which he has continued to the present. Among his larger accomplishments in the way of contracts may be mentioned the Palace Theatre; the Bath House and Pavilion at Miller, Indiana; the

F. D. Stanton D. C. Ph. C.

Tube Mill, the Grand Beach Hotel, a number of school buildings, the Gary City Hall, Mercy Hospital and the Dalton Apartments. He is president of the Metropolitan Securities Company, and owns a number of Gary properties, including the two buildings at 125 West Eighth Avenue, the yard at 2516 Peirce Street, and several vacant lots. Mr. Smith is prominent in fraternal circles, being a member of Roosevelt Lodge No. 716, A. F. and A. M.; Gary Chapter; Gary Commandery; Fort Wayne Consistory; and Orak Temple, A. A. O. N. M. S., of Hammond; the Loyal Order of Moose and the Benevolent and Protective Order of Elks. He likewise is a member of the Medinah Athletic Association, the Gary Rotary Club, Lincoln Hills Country Club, of which he is president (1931), Gary Commercial Club and Chamber of Commerce and the Contracting Plasterers Association. During the World war he was very active in all patriotic drives, and in times of peace has been a constructive and public-spirited supporter of good civic movements. Politically Mr. Smith gives his allegiance to the Republican party, and his religious connection is with the Methodist Episcopal Church.

At Roseville, Ohio, May 21, 1910, Mr. Smith was united in marriage with Miss Ruth Brummage, daughter of Eugene and Hannah (Tipton) Brummage, of Roseville, the former of whom was for years an agriculturist and a manufacturer of clay products and pottery. He died in 1915 and his widow died two years later, and both rest in the cemetery at Roseville. Mrs. Smith was educated in the public schools of Roseville and has been active in the Methodist Episcopal Church, the Woman's Club, the Order of the Eastern Star, the Oriental Shrine and the Woman's Relief Corps.

RAY A. BARWICK is one of the chief figures in the little business community of Judyville, Warren County, where he owns the R. A. Barwick general mercantile store and also performs the duties of postmaster.

Mr. Barwick was born in Warren County, February 7, 1897. His grandfather, Nicholas Barwick, came to Warren County from Maryland. Frank Barwick, father of Ray A., was born in Warren County and was a carpenter and contractor. He married Nettie Benett, who was born in Warren County, daughter of James Benett, a veteran of the Civil war. Frank Barwick and wife had three children: Lucy, wife of Claude Autar, of Warren County; Ray A.; and Agnes, wife of Charles Reynolds, of Warren County.

Ray A. Barwick was educated in public schools and as a boy learned telegraphy. He became a telegraph operator and that was his chief line of work until after the war. During the war he enlisted, in July, 1918, and was assigned duty as a radio and wireless inspector. He was given his honorable discharge in January, 1919. While in the service he was located at Pittsburgh, Pennsylvania. After the war he resumed his previous line of work, but in 1921 established his general store at Judy-

ville and in the same year was appointed postmaster, and has rendered a capable service in both these capacities.

Mr. Barwick is a Republican, is a member of the Masonic Lodge and the American Legion Post. He married in October, 1917, Miss Hazel Zenor, of Harrison County, Indiana. They have one child, Rex, born in 1919.

FREDERIC D. STANTON, Doctor of Chiropractic, has built up a successful practice and has done much to establish his profession in favor among the people of Remington and surrounding territory.

Doctor Stanton was born in Johnson County, Indiana, son of Oscar and Martha (Rutherford) Stanton. His father passed away at Danville, Illinois, recently. His mother is a daughter of John Rutherford. There were nine children in the family: Albert, Ira, Eli, Clinton, Frederic D., Ralston, Corella, Mary and Lena. All are living except Mary.

Frederic D. Stanton was educated in the public schools of Greenwood, Indiana, and later took up the study of chiropractic. After graduating at the National College of Chiropractic of Chicago he was in practice in Chicago until 1924, when he located at Remington, and is one of the busy professional men of that community. Doctor Stanton is a member of the professional organizations, also a member of the Masons, Knights of Pythias, Fraternal Order of Eagles, a Republican and a member of the Christian Church.

He married in 1912 Miss Mary Wisler. They have two children, Fred D., Jr., an employee of Carson Pirie Scott & Company of Chicago, and Lydia Marie, a graduate of the Indiana State Normal School at Terre Haute and now a teacher at New London, Indiana.

EDWARD SCHLEICHER. Among the numerous large interests that have been attracted to Gary during recent years, because of the ideal location and unsurpassed facilities of this thriving industrial city, one of the most prominent is the Schleicher Incorporation, of which Edward Schleicher is president. Mr. Schleicher is a self-made man, having commenced his career at the age of fourteen years as a Western Union Telegraph messenger boy, and now finds himself, by reason of his industry and business capacity, at the head of an enterprise which is one of the largest and most prominent in its field.

Edward Schleicher was born at Louisville, Kentucky, August 20, 1873, and is a son of Charles and Christine (Echsner) Schleicher. Charles Schleicher was born in Germany and came to the United States in young manhood, settling at Louisville, where he secured employment as a mechanic. Possessed of great inventive genius, he invented the first automatic car coupler, as well as a lathe machine which was adopted by the Brennan Southwestern Agricultural Works, in addition to which he did considerable research work for the Kentucky Wagon Works. He died in 1893 and his wife, a native of Saint Galen, Switzerland, died in 1898, and both are buried in a cemetery at Louisville. There were nine children in the family: Charles and Henry, who are deceased; Robert, a resident of Louisville; Frank, a retired cigar box manufacturer of Maplewood, New Jersey; John, who is engaged in the box manufacturing business at Saint Louis, Missouri; Mrs. Mary Hopenjon, of Kansas City, Missouri; Emma, the widow of C. M. Ross, of Louisville; Anna, who died in December, 1929, as the wife of Charles E. Laufer, of Louisville; and Edward, of this review.

Edward Schleicher attended the public schools of Louisville, and at the age of fourteen years secured a position as messenger boy for the Western Union Telegraph Company. He remained with that company until 1901, gradually advancing in position because of his ability and fidelity, but in the year mentioned resigned a responsible post to engage in the brokerage business at Louisville. In 1909 he went to Chicago, Illinois, where he engaged in the insurance business, and was successfully engaged therein until 1917, when he founded the business of which he is now the head. This company operated with success at Chicago until 1924, when he and E. P. Hettiger purchased the plant of the old National Steel Door Company, at 3824 Georgia Street, Gary. The present commodious and modern plant of 40,000 square feet of factory surface has been made since October, 1924. Improvements which have been completed in 1930, at a cost of $75,000, include new offices, recreation grounds, cafeteria, parlors for conferences, a suite of rooms for the accommodation of visiting dealers, extensive show rooms, landscape gardening and additional factory equipment. The plant is a model industry, in that latest devices provide for the comfort and safety of employes at all times. Shower rooms, tennis courts, putting greens and convenient sanitary arrangements are provided. At present the plant is giving employment to nearly 100 people.

The Schleicher plant, which is trademarked "Slyker," is at present the largest manufacturer of all-metal radiator coverings. A large assortment of designs is offered, period designs, the new mottled, rough finish that is proving so popular, imitation wood and cane coverings. Its officers are: Edward Schleicher, president; P. E. Schleicher, vice president, inventor and designer of most of the covers; and C. E. Bergren, treasurer. The covers are sold to hotels, apartment buildings, theatres and clubs, and are usually retailed through furniture stores. They consist of ornamental coverings which completely conceal the ordinary coil heating radiator and at the same time moisten the atmosphere of the room and protect walls and draperies. The general construction is pressed steel, annealed, welded and riveted. The finish is a variety of forms, all baked enamel and Duco. Each piece of metal before it is finished has been enameled and run through nine baking processes. Among the most beautiful of finishes are the natural wood patterns, made in imitation of walnut and mahogany grains. The pattern is transferred by means of a photo-engraving process, insuring absolute accuracy in imitating the natural grain of the wood. The mottled and rough finished tinted designs are mostly hand work, the rough surface carefully built up and hand painted by an artist from his palette.

As president of this concern Mr. Schleicher occupies a high standing among Gary's business men. He is a member of the Commercial Club and Chamber of Commerce, the Gary Country Club and the Builders Club of Chicago, and for a number of years was active in Louisville Lodge No. 8, B. P. O. Elks. He takes only a good citizen's part in politics, but is progressive in his views as to needed developments and beneficial movements.

At Louisville, Kentucky, October 10, 1894, Mr. Schleicher was united in marriage with Miss Irene Hecht, a daughter of Charles and Justine (DeLoi) Hecht, the former of whom was for years a prominent merchant tailor at Louisville, where he died in 1900, Mrs. Hecht having passed away in 1894. Mrs. Schleicher was educated in the public schools of Louisville, where she graduated from high school, and for years was active in the Dominican Catholic Church. To Mr. and Mrs. Schleicher there have been born three children: Alice Justine, the wife of J. E. Johnson, of Gary, who has three children, Joseph Owen, Justine Alice and Mark E.; Charles Henry, educated in the public schools of Louisville and high school at Chicago, who is now a manufacturers' representative at New York City, married Miss Evelyn Delanoie, and has two children, Alice and Charles H. Jr. (Sonny); and Paul E., born November 11, 1900, was educated in the grade and high schools of Kentucky, and spent two years at Loyola University, Chicago. Since that time he has been identified with his father's business at Gary, of which he is vice president, designer and inventor. He married, July 1, 1922, Miss Marguerite Whipple, of Chicago, daughter of Dennis and Mary Louise (Anderson) Whipple, of Chicago, the former of whom was for years engaged in the automobile business at Chicago, where he died in 1920, his wife now residing at Evanston, Illinois. Mrs. Paul E. Schleicher was educated in the public schools of Chicago and at Principa University, Saint Louis, and is active in the First Church of Christ, Scientist, and in club and social circles. Mr. and Mrs. Schleicher have three children, Paul E., Jr., Robert E. and Marguerite E.

During the World war Charles Henry Schleicher enlisted in the United States Army, and after training at Camp Thomas, Kentucky, was assigned to a tank company, with which he served eleven months in France. Paul E. Schleicher was in training at Camp Polk, Raleigh, North Carolina, at the time of the signing of the armistice, and therefore was not called into active service. Paul E. Schleicher is known as one of the energetic and progressive young business men of Gary, where he is a member of the Commercial Club and Chamber of Commerce and active in civic affairs. He belongs to Gary Post, American Legion and the Gary Country Club.

CARL HOCKER. In an industrial city of the size and prominence of Gary it is but natural that electric power should have a prominent place. Of the numerous enterprises connected with this phase of the city's activities none has gained a greater degree of leadership than the Hocker Electric Company, of which Carl Hocker is president. Still a young man in years, Mr. Hocker has had long, thorough and varied experience.

Mr. Hocker was born at Beaver Dam, Kentucky, July 22, 1896, and is a son of William D. and Mary (Stevens) Hocker. The Hocker family is of English origin, and was founded in Kentucky in 1790, by the great-great-grandfather of Carl Hocker, who was an early pioneer of the Blue Grass State, coming from Baltimore, Maryland, to the new country, where he secured land from the Government which still belongs to members of the family. The old log cabin in which this hardy pioneer made his home is still standing, in a fair state of preservation, and is one of the historic spots of the state. William D. Hocker was born at Beaver Dam, where he received a public school education, and was reared to the pursuits of agriculture. He has been a farmer and stock dealer all of his life and is now one of the substantial citizens of his community, where he is held in high respect and esteem for his many sterling qualities. Mr. Hocker has been content with the life of a private citizen, never having cared for public office, but has always supported good public measures and enterprises and has contributed his share to the furtherance of worth while projects. He married Miss Mary Stevens, who was born, reared and educated in the same community as her husband, and was active in the work of the Methodist Episcopal Church up to the time of her death in 1923, when she was buried in the cemetery at Beaver Dam. She likewise belonged to a pioneer family which has resided for many years in Kentucky. There were seven children in the family, of whom three died in infancy, the living being: Calvin, who is now a resident of Arizona; Fred, who still resides on the old home property at Beaver Dam; Carl, of this review; and Clayton, of Detroit, Michigan.

Carl Hocker was reared on the home farm and attended the public schools of Beaver Dam, where he graduated from the high school as a member of the class of 1914. He then finished a three-year course at the Evansville (Indiana) Technical School, and during this period was employed at times by contracting firms up to 1917. In that year he joined the emergency fleet of the United States Shipping Board, under Chairman E. N. Hurley, with which he remained until April, 1919, and at that time came to Gary to begin his service with an electric company. He belongs to the Commercial Club and Chamber of Commerce,

and is chairman of the Lions Club for 1930-1931; and belongs to Gary Lodge No. 677, A. F. and A. M.; Gary Chapter, R. A. M., and Gary Council No. 103, R. and S. M.; Gary Lodge No. 1152, B. P. O. Elks; the Electrical Craftsmen; Gary Chapter, O. E. S., of which he is patron; and Gary White Shrine No. 3. He is a Republican in his political allegiance, and his religious affiliation is with the First Methodist Episcopal (City) Church.

At Richmond, Virginia, December 17, 1917, Mr. Hocker was united in marriage with Miss Grace Ferguson, a daughter of John and Martha Ferguson, of Evansville, Indiana, where Mr. Ferguson was engaged in the lumber and sawmill business for many years, until his death in 1922. His widow still resides at the old home at Evansville. Mrs. Hocker was educated in the public schools of Evansville, where she graduated from high school, and has been active in the work of the Methodist Episcopal Church, the Eastern Star, the Women's Relief Corps, the White Shrine and the Woman's Club.

CHARLES E. SPAULDING, superintendent of schools at Plymouth, Marshall County, is a native of Southern Indiana, and his people have been in the state since pioneer times.

His great-grandfather came from England. His grandfather was born at Bardstown, Kentucky, January 6, 1802, and died in Indiana January 8, 1873. Charles E. Spaulding was born at French Lick Springs, Indiana, January 13, 1869. His father was also a native of Indiana and died March 13, 1896. The mother of Professor Spaulding was Ann Moore, who was born July 19, 1832, and died June 3, 1906. She was of English and Dutch ancestry.

Charles E. Spaulding attended country schools, the Paola High School, and was graduated from Indiana University in 1897. During the past thirty years he has taken a great deal of additional work in colleges and universities, being at the University of Chicago in 1905 and also in post-graduate study at Indiana University, and has completed several courses by correspondence. He was granted his first certificate to teach at the age of fifteen. He taught in French Lick Township, for several years was principal of the high school at Hagerstown, was superintendent of schools at Orleans for four years, at Converse five years, Winnemac six years, three years at Decatur, five years at Columbia City and three years at Tipton. He came to Plymouth in 1924 and is now on his second three-year contract.

Mr. Spaulding's father, Richard A. Spaulding, who was born in 1830, was a farmer, grain and live stock dealer. For five years he held the office of township trustee and during that time he rebuilt all the school houses in his jurisdiction. He was also a Civil war veteran, being a member of Company G of the Forty-ninth Indiana Infantry. He entered the service August 1, 1861, served in the ranks and was mustered out in 1865. While he was in the army his wife remained at home looking after the farm and her five children.

Mr. Charles E. Spaulding married Nora Alice Faucett. They have one son, Wayne Faucett Spaulding, born July 20, 1901. He graduated from the Columbia City High School in 1919 and completed the course in electrical engineering at Purdue University in June, 1923. He is now a traveling salesman for the General Electric Company. Wayne F. Spaulding married Eva Lawrence on September 3, 1922, and has two children, Katherine, born June 23, 1924, and Charles David, born April 18, 1926.

Professor Spaulding is a member of the Methodist Church, belongs to the Masonic Lodge at Decatur, Indiana, and is a Kiwanian. His hobby is philosophy and poetry.

IRA J. BIESECKER is a veteran Indiana banker, and has been active in the banking affairs of Morocco for thirty years. He is cashier of the Farmers State Bank of that city.

Mr. Biesecker, while a native of Illinois, is a member of one of Newton County's oldest families. His grandfather, Joseph Biesecker, came to Indiana and acquired by homestead and purchase from the Government a section of land located seven miles from Morocco, in Beaver Township, Iroquois County, Illinois. Ira J. Biesecker is today the owner of this land, which has long constituted one of the valuable farms of Iroquois County.

Ira J. Biesecker was born April 7, 1855. His father was also named Joseph and died many years ago. The mother of the Morocco banker was Genevieve Myers, whose father, Conrad Myers, came from Germany and settled near Lafayette, Indiana. Ira J. Biesecker has one brother, Joseph.

He was educated in public schools in Illinois and has lived at Morocco since 1900. For a number of years he was president of the State Bank and in 1920 became cashier of the new Farmers State Bank. Mr. Biesecker is a Republican in politics and a member of the Knights of Pythias.

He married, September 26, 1875, Miss Florene Archibald, daughter of James Archibald. The one child of their marriage is Laura Gertrude, the widow of Albert Grant. She has two children, Vera, who married Van E. Cox, and they have one son, David, and Clifford Grant. The son, Clifford, who lives at Gary, Indiana, married Elva Hammer.

ROBERT LEE STONE, an active young automobile man at Evansville, has had an interesting diversity of business experience and since early youth has been associated with Big Springs and with big men.

Mr. Stone was born at Lyndon, Vermont, December 4, 1898. His father, Benjamin F. Stone, is also a native of Vermont, for a number of years was in the automobile business and is now retired, living in Florida. He

married Lucretia M. Gregwire, who was born at Victory, Vermont.

Robert Lee Stone was the only child of his parents. He attended grammar and high schools in Vermont, completing his regular high school course at the age of fourteen and then remained two years in post-graduate study. After leaving high school he became secretary to the road master of the Boston & Maine Railway Company for two years. He left that to become secretary to the general manager of the Mathews Smith Chain Grocery business, one of the pioneers in chain store operations, a concern then doing $6,000,000 of business annually. For three years Mr. Stone had charge of the employment in this organization. For two years he was associated with the Piggly-Wiggly Chain Stores Company as general manager and buyer at Cleveland, Ohio. For a year and a half he was acting general manager of the Gammeter Mercantile Company at Akron, Ohio.

Mr. Stone for one year was secretary of the Guardian Realty Company of Chicago and in 1927 came to Evansville to become manager for a chain tire and automobile accessory concern, but resigned in November, 1928, to establish a service company for automobiles, and his business, located at 413 Sycamore Street, has become very popular among motorists. Mr. Stone is a Republican, a Catholic and is affiliated with the Loyal Order of Moose. During the World war he was enlisted in the navy from June, 1917, until January, 1919.

He married in May, 1928, Miss Lovena M. Hare, daughter of James and Mary Hare, of Mount Carmel, Illinois. They have one son, Robert Lee, Jr.

RICHARD E. KEMPER is a prominent Evansville citizen whose career has been distinguished by long and faithful service for one corporation, the Louisville & Nashville Railroad Company, and in more than forty years of active work he has risen from telegraph operator to division superintendent.

Mr. Kemper was born in Laurel County, Kentucky, May 17, 1872, son of John R. and Frances (Calloway) Kemper. His parents were born in Kentucky and his father spent his active life as a merchant. He is now eighty-three years of age and his wife passed away September 10, 1900. Of their nine children three died in infancy. The children, with the dates of birth were: Richard E., May 17, 1872; Leila M., October 23, 1874; Keonard K., October 3, 1876; Nora L., November, 1878; Della L., February, 1881; E. Belva, September 24, 1884; Fred L., March 6, 1887; Ruby C., September 13, 1894; and Roland A., August 18, 1896. Leila is the widow of Otis Mouser, who was president of a large coal company, with holdings in Virginia and Pennsylvania, and lives at Philadelphia, Pennsylvania. To this union were born two children, Otis, Jr., and Vivian, the latter dy-

George A Cobb

ing from being gassed in the World war. The daughter Nora married Edward B. Mouser, of Riley, Kentucky, and has a daughter, Sarah. Fred, a bond salesman in Louisville, married Evelyn King. The two youngest children Ruby and Roland, are unmarried.

Richard E. Kemper attended public schools in Laurel County, Kentucky. As a boy he learned telegraphy, and that was the means of getting into the railroad service, and hard work and faithfulness have been the means of promoting him through successive grades of responsibility. He was telegrapher and station agent from 1886 to 1892 and on October 8, 1888, was transferred to Evansville, which has been his home ever since. From 1894 to 1903 he was a train dispatcher and chief train dispatcher. From 1903 to 1920 he was master of trains. In 1920 he was made assistant superintendent and on April 22, 1929, was made superintendent of the Henderson & St. Louis divisions at Evansville for the Louisville & Nashville Railroad.

Mr. Kemper is one of the best known railway officials of Southern Indiana. He is a member of the Rotary Club, Transportation Club, the Evansville Chamber of Commerce, is a Methodist and a Republican.

He married, December 27, 1894, Miss Josephine Hawley. She died December 12, 1926, leaving a daughter, Ruth K., who is the wife of Norman Beach, of Evansville. On October 17, 1928, Mr. Kemper married Jennie Bush, daughter of Judge Charles H. Bush, of Hopkinsville, Kentucky.

HON. GEORGE CHRISTIAN KOPP. A lawyer by education and training, Hon. George C. Kopp, judge of the Fourth District Court, has been identified with such a variety of interests as to have become known as one of Southern Indiana's most versatile and capable citizens. His entire career has been a busy and interesting one. As a lawyer, in the preparation of his cases he was careful and painstaking and his thoroughness inspired confidence in his clients. As a judge he has been dignified, impartial and resolute. As an organizer of large enterprises and activities his executive ability has rarely been surpassed, and in citizenship he has established a record that may well be emulated.

Judge Kopp was born March 23, 1877, in Clark County, on his father's farm in Jeffersonville Township, and is a son of Christian and Catherine Wiedner (Warren) Kopp. His father, who was born in Bavaria, Germany, came to the United States at the age of fourteen years, and first settled in Kentucky, where, at sixteen years, he enlisted in Company B, Twenty-second Regiment, Kentucky Volunteer Infantry, for the duration of the war between the states. Following the close of his military services he came to Clark County and settled on the farm in Jeffersonville Township, on which he still lives in comfortable retirement at the advanced age of eighty-seven years. In the fall of 1864 Mr.

Kopp married Miss Catherine Wiedner, also a native of Bavaria, Germany, and of their nine children Judge Kopp, of this review, is the fifth in order of birth.

George C. Kopp attended the grade schools of Jeffersonville, and then entered the law department of the University of Louisville, from which he was graduated with the degree of Bachelor of Laws as a member of the class of 1903. Admitted to the bar in the same year, he immediately began practice at Jeffersonville, and January 1, 1908, was elected prosecuting attorney for the Fourth Judicial District. He was reelected in 1909 and served in that office in 1910 and 1911, following which he resumed his private practice, although he acted as city attorney of Clarksville for eleven years, Claysburg eighteen years and Sellersburg twelve years, all of these being towns near Jeffersonville, in Clark County. In 1926 he was elected judge of the Fourth Judicial Circuit Court and assumed the bench January 1, 1927, for a term of six years. In 1909, when the Clark County Bar Association was threatened with dissolution, it was Judge Kopp who brought about a reorganization that placed the body upon a firm and substantial basis, and he still holds membership therein, as he does also in the Indiana State Bar Association and the American Bar Association. As an organizer and executive of large enterprises Judge Kopp has had few equals. He was one of the organizers of the Clark County State Bank, of which he was a director until the time of his election to the bench. He was one of the organizers and is vice president and a director of the Switow Theatrical Corporation, which controls eleven theatres, including houses at Jeffersonville, New Albany, Bedford, Paoli and Salem. He also organized and is president and a director of the United Home Furnishing Company, founded in 1921, which has been developed into the largest complete home furnishing house in Southern Indiana, with two stores at Jeffersonville, one at Sellersburg, one at Salem and one at Scottsburg. He organized the City Ice Company and the Clark Realty Company, of which he was president and a director, but has disposed of his interests therein, and the Indiana Braid & Cabinet Company, at Borden, Indiana. He also organized the Young Men's Business Association, out of which grew the present Chamber of Commerce of Jeffersonville. During the World war Judge Kopp was a committeeman in the Liberty Loan drives, chairman of the Clark County Americanization committee and a member of the food committee, and was very active in various other ways. Fraternally he is affiliated with Jeffersonville Lodge No. 340, A. F. and A. M., the Independent Order of Odd Fellows, and Kwsind Tribe, Improved Order of Red Men. A Democrat in his political views, he is known as one of the leaders of his party in Clark County, and his religious connection is with St. Luke's German Lutheran Church of Jeffersonville. His po-

sition in the community is that of a man who
has lived according to the best that he has
known, whose abilities have been trained upon
the things that are worth while, and whose
general character is such as to win him those
most splendid and satisfying rewards, the
consciousness of well-doing and the esteem of
his fellow-men. He started the movement and
personally raised the subscription of $50,000
for the election of the Clark County orphan-
age. This home will be built entirely by public subscription and will afford a home for
fifty children.

Judge Kopp married Miss Frances Murphy,
November 10, 1910, she being a native of Indiana and a daughter of J. B. Murphy, general superintendent of the Pennsylvania Railway, and a member of an old and honored pioneer family of Indiana. Judge and Mrs. Kopp
have no children. They reside in a beautiful
home at 1507 Spring Street.

PATRICK JOSEPH KILROY. The early spirit of
personal independence that carried the men
who dwelt in Erin to far-away places continues, in a great degree, to individualize the
sons of Ireland. Isolation, dependence upon
their own resources, and the combativeness always developed by being the smaller, numerically, in great combinations of people, have,
doubtless, had much to do in giving to these
people their personal characteristics. Wherever they are found, in the army, in the professions, in business or in politics, there is a
spirit and a manner that tells us whence they
came and who their fathers were.

Patrick J. Kilroy, secretary of the Washington Street Improvement Corporation of
Gary and a large dealer in real estate and
insurance, is an Irishman, born at Foxfard,
County Mayo, Ireland, March 1, 1885, a son
of John and Bridget (Walsh) Kilroy. His
parents were born, reared and educated in the
same county, where they were married, and
about 1890 immigrated to the United States
and settled in Eel River Township, Hendricks
County, Indiana, where John Kilroy was engaged in farming and stock raising during the
remainder of his life and died January 26,
1922, being buried in Calvary Cemetery, East
Gary. He had spent the last three years of
his life in partial retirement at Gary. His
wife, who was an active member of Saint
Luke's Catholic Church, Gary, died October 2,
1926, and was buried beside her husband.
There were five children in the family: Mary,
now the wife of Dennis Rouse, of Castle Connor, County Sligo, Ireland; James, who died
at the age of fourteen years and is buried in
Calvary Cemetery, Chicago; Patrick J., of this
review; Catherine, now Mrs. Patrick Walsh,
of Foxfard, County Mayo, Ireland; and
Thomas, who died at the age of twenty-four
years and is buried at Toomore, Ireland.

Patrick J. Kilroy was educated in the public schools of County Mayo and at Royal College of Science, London, from which he was
graduated as a member of the class of 1907.
At that time he entered the service of the
British Ordnance Survey, in which he spent
two years, and in 1909 came to the United
States and first settled at Indianapolis, where
he was employed for some time by the Spiker
Engineering Company, of Vincennes, Indiana.
For two years he was connected with the
Bowen Publishing Company, and helped produce their road maps of Indiana and Michigan, being the producer of the data and drafting some of the maps for that work. Later
he joined the Eastern Rock Island Plow Company, in the capacity of cashier and accountant, positions which he occupied for four
years, and subsequently joined the biological
laboratories of the Pittman & Moore Company,
at Louisville, Kentucky, where he was in
charge of the accounting department until
1922. Upon the death of his father Mr. Kilroy came to Gary to settle up the estate, and
since then has been connected with the C. H.
Maloney Plumbing & Heating Company, contractors. He is also the owner of a real estate
and insurance business and has several pieces
of valuable Gary South Side residential and
business property, resides in his own home at
3861 Jefferson Street, and is secretary of the
Washington Street Improvement Corporation.
He belongs to the Open Forum Club and the
Gary American-Irish Literary Society, of
which latter he was one of the organizers and
is secretary and treasurer, and was for years
a member of the Republican Club. He likewise is interested in the Boy Scout movement,
and one of his hobbies is amateur astronomy
and field geology. He is active in civic affairs
and a constructive supporter of worthy municipal enterprises.

At Great Grimesby, England, July 16, 1908,
Mr. Kilroy was united in marriage with Miss
Annie Sophia Price, daughter of Thomas and
Eliza (Davenport) Price, of Ashby, De La
Zauche, Leicestershire, England. Mr. Price
was for many years manager and purchasing
agent for collieries at Moira and Coalville,
England, and was also extensively engaged in
farming, having a tract of 250 acres in Leicestershire. He died about 1905 and Mrs. Price
in 1912, and both are buried in Donisthorpe
Cemetery, Leicestershire, England. Mrs. Kilroy was educated in a young woman's boarding school in London, England, and for many
years has been active in the work of the Episcopal Church at Donisthorpe.

FRANK MELVILLE MACCONNELL. Well known
and esteemed highly at Warsaw, Indiana, and
in other sections of the country in which his
personal and business interests at times have
made him a resident, is Frank M. MacConnell,
an able member of the Warsaw bar. Mr. Mac-
Connell is also a registered pharmacist and in
that relation was long identified with several
of the largest drug houses of the country. By
the time he was thirteen years of age he had
made most satisfactory progress at school, for
he has always been an eager student, and
about that time he began to add materially
to the family income by working at night and
Saturdays and holidays in a drug store at

Warsaw, his native city. He applied himself closely, not because he liked the drug business, but because he loved learning, and thus acquired a clear, comprehensive knowledge of chemistry, botany and other branches without ever having had collegiate scientific advantages. He remained in the drug business until 1895 and then cultivated his talent for the law and was admitted to the bar. In 1901 he accepted a position with a large bond house at Detroit, Michigan, and continued there until 1910, when, overcome by an overwhelming nostalgia, he resigned his lucrative position and returned once more to Warsaw, where he has since been conducting a law practice very successfully. To him there is no city to equal Warsaw, no friends like the oldtime ones here, no life so full of quiet usefulness and content as in the honorable practice of his profession. Mr. MacConnell is little past middle age in years, and sometimes, in friendly converse, he paraphrases a line from one of Indiana's beloved poets and smilingly murmurs: "And one grows old very slowly in Warsaw."

Frank M. MacConnell was born at Warsaw, Indiana, January 1, 1866, a son of Nathan Bowman and Melissa C. MacConnell. He attended the grade and high schools for three years, and Cowan Seminary for two summer terms, and during about his thirteenth year began working nights, Saturdays and holidays in a drug store owned by Charles V. Pyle, where he remained for about six years. In 1886 he accepted employment with the Pottinger & Pyle Drug Company, of Hiawatha, Kansas, this store invoicing $20,000 and being known as "The Big Drug Store." It did an enormous prescription business and had a great territory to draw from, and as head of the prescription case Mr. MacConnell occupied a decidedly responsible position for eight years. In 1894 he purchased an interest in this store, and at this time it became, for the first time, necessary for him to be registered as a pharmacist, although this had not been necessary before, under the law. The examination was held at Hutchinson, Kansas, and out of forty-two applicants but seven passed. Mr. MacConnell stood 100%. This was the first time that such a mark had been made in Kansas, and Mr. MacConnell understands that it stood as a record for many years. Within the year 1894, while he was at the new store, he lost both wife and young daughter by tuberculosis, and his own health was impaired, so seriously that it seemed necessary to change entirely his occupation. He had remaining to him two children, who are still living: Mrs. Isaac E. Hire, of Warsaw; and Charles E. MacConnell, of Chicago, Illinois, an advertising manager. The mother of these children, whom Mr. MacConnell had married in 1887, bore the maiden name of Fredericka Röhl.

In 1895 Mr. MacConnell returned with his children to Warsaw, and shortly thereafter entered the law office of Judge Hiram S. Biggs and studied law for about three years. He then went to the office of Judge Edgar E. Haymond for a like period, and was admitted to the bar, but did not practice to any extent. In 1901 he went to Detroit, Michigan, on a visit, and so liked the city that he remained there, securing employment with the H. W. Noble Company, selling bonds. He had met and married his second wife in 1899, and in October, 1904, was born his third child, Kathleen E., now Mrs. Charles H. Campbell, a very prominent musician of New York City.

Mr. MacConnell's experience with the Noble Company was of great value to him, it being the only contact with the world of big things and big men that he ever had. But it was simply the reading of a great new book to him and, growing tired of the monotony of the money game, he resigned his position in 1910 and returned to his beloved Warsaw and to his law. Mr. MacConnell considers that he has led a very uneventful life and that his present existence is a quiet and commonplace one. But it suits him to be among his friends and among those who admire him not for what he has but for what he is.

CHARLES C. LEISURE, prominently connected in a business and public way with Earl Park, Benton County, is a native of Indiana, and is a veteran of the Spanish-American war.

He was born in Grant County, December 10, 1867. His father, Benjamin N. Leisure, and his grandfather, William Leisure, were natives of Kentucky. The Leisure family settled in Grant County about 1859. Benjamin N. Leisure married Jane Compton, a native of Adams County, Ohio. Of their seven children Charles C. was the oldest, and the others were Thomas and Pearl, deceased, Esta, Grace, Myrtle and Raymond.

Charles C. Leisure was educated in public schools in Grant County, and as a young man devoted his energies principally to farming. In 1895 he enlisted for a term of service in the regular army, and by reenlistment served for six years. He was an enlisted man when the Spanish-American war broke out, and he was sent to the Philippine Islands, and had some arduous service and exciting and dangerous duties incident to the Philippine insurrection.

After leaving the army in 1901 Mr. Leisure located at Earl Park, Benton County, Indiana. He was associated with a hardware business there until 1913, when he was appointed postmaster. He served two terms, eight years, throughout the Wilson administrations. Since 1922 he has been manager of the Wilbur Lumber Company of Earl Park. In 1922 also he was elected trustee of Richland Township, and has devoted much of his time to the management of the schools and the other duties included in the office of trustee. Mr. Leisure is a Democrat in politics. He has no formal church affiliation, but his family attend Catholic services. He is affiliated with the Knights of Pythias.

Mr. Leisure married in June, 1911, Miss Millie Flinn, who was born in Benton County, Indiana. They have one son, Charles Daniel, born November 29, 1922.

HON. LEW M. O'BANNON. Few men during
the past thirty years have had a wider and
more interesting connection with politics, public
affairs and other activities in Southern Indiana
than Mr. Lew M. O'Bannon, lawyer and editor
at Corydon.

Mr. O'Bannon was born on a farm in Harrison County, Indiana, August 18, 1864, and
is a descendant in the sixth generation from
Brian O'Bannon, a native of Ireland, who settled at Harpers Ferry, Virginia, in 1719. His
son, John O'Bannon, was a native of Ireland.
The great-grandfather of Lew O'Bannon, was
William O'Bannon, and the grandfather also
had the name of William. Both these ancestors were natives of Virginia. Mr. O'Bannon's
father, Presley Neville O'Bannon, was born
in Kentucky, July 29, 1824, in Breckenridge
County, and came to Indiana about 1849. He
died in Harrison County, January 25, 1881.
Presley Neville O'Bannon married Christiann
Ferree, who was born in Harrison County,
Indiana, February 1, 1830, and died at Corydon February 16, 1911. She was a daughter
of Jacob and Rachael Ferree and granddaughter of Joel Ferree, who gave up his life during
the War of 1812 at Zanesville, Ohio. Both
Jacob and Joel Ferree were natives of Pennsylvania. Jacob Ferree became a colonel in
the Indiana Home Guards during the Civil
war and was killed in the battle of Corydon,
Indiana, July 9, 1863.

Lew M. O'Bannon's early education was the
product of a few terms in rural schools. His
father had a plant for the manufacture of
shingles, and it was in this factory that Lew
M. O'Bannon trained his hand and eye until
his father's death in 1881. For nine years
his occupation was teaching country schools
in winter terms, the intervening summers being
spent in farm work. Out of a varied experience he trained himself for larger responsibilities. While he is largely self-educated, he
has constantly reached up to the broader hori-
zon of intellectual interests.

Mr. O'Bannon served as surveyor of Harrison County in 1887-90, was county recorder
in 1890-94, being elected to both offices on
the Democratic ticket. While in office he took
up the study of law, and has been an active
member of the bar at Corydon since January,
1895. He was fortunate in his association
as a law partner of Judge Robert S. Kirkham
until the latter's death on December 24, 1927.
Since then he has continued in individual law
practice.

Other business interests have occupied much
of his time, frequently to the exclusion of
his law work. Since October, 1910, he has
been secretary of the Savings & Loan Association of Corydon. He has been first vice
president and in 1927-29 was president of the
Savings & Loan League of Indiana. Mr.
O'Bannon has been owner and publisher of
the *Corydon Democrat* since January 1, 1907,
nearly twenty-five years. The *Corydon Democrat* is a newspaper with a great and loyal
following in Southern Indiana. It was established in 1856. Mr. O'Bannon is a former

president of the Indiana Democratic Editorial
Association.

He has had a number of honors within his
own party and also as a non-partisan ap-
pointee. From March 4, 1897, to March 4,
1907, he served as private secretary to the
late Congressman William Taylor Zenor, who
represented the Third Indiana District in Congress during these ten years. In the campaign
of 1924 Mr. O'Bannon was Democratic nominee for lieutenant governor of Indiana, and
in 1928 he was the permanent chairman of
the Indiana Democratic State Convention, held
at Indianapolis. He served as a member of
the Indiana Historical Commission during the
ten years of its existence, from 1915 to 1925,
being appointed by the successive Governors
Samuel M. Ralston, James P. Goodrich and
Warren C. McCray. Mr. O'Bannon is a member of the George Rogers Clark Memorial
Commission of Indiana and the George Rogers
Clark Sesquicentennial Commission, which was
created by act of Congress. He is deputy
district governor of the Lions Club of Southern Indiana. He belongs to the Masons, Elks,
Knights of Pythias, Modern Woodmen of
America fraternities, and the Christian
Church.

JOHN A. SZIKORA was one of the earliest
residents of Gary. He is remembered as a
sterling business man, an influential figure
among the Slovak people of that city, and
as a result of his industrious career and ability he left a splendid and growing business to
his family, several of whom are still active
in its management.

He was born in Austria-Hungary, February
8, 1870, son of Frank and Anna (Etsal)
Szikora. His parents lived out their lives in
their native land and are buried there. Of
their twelve children five sought home and
fortune in America. These were: John A.;
Charles and Frank, both of Gary; Mrs. Agnes
Korcek, of Detroit, Michigan; and Mrs. Matilda Slobodnick, also of Detroit.

John A. Szikora was reared and educated
in his native country, and came to America
in 1904. For three years he lived in Chicago
and in 1907 moved to Gary and was one of
the early grocery merchants in that rapidly
expanding steel city. He built up a great
trade and a splendid business and was active
in its supervision until his death. He also
owns farming lands and other property in the
city. Mr. Szikora died November 11, 1929. He
was a member of several of the lodges and
club organizations of Gary.

He married in Austria-Hungary in 1894
Miss Agnes Hittmar. She and her husband
were members of the Holy Trinity Church of
Gary. She died December 4, 1924. These parents had a family of seven children, Margarette, Elsie, John A., Jr., Agnes, Stephen (who
died when only one year old), Frank and
Joseph. All attended public schools and the
Emerson High School.

Miss Margarette Szikora, the oldest child,
is a thoroughgoing business woman, and for a

number of years has been the active manager of the Oak Park Grocery Company, the title of the business established by her father. She is also well known in local politics, and in 1930 was Republican candidate for township trustee of Calumet Township. She is a member of the Woman's Club, the Harrison Club, the Business and Professional Women's Club, the Hungarian Woman's Social Club, the Woman's Slovak Political Club, the Slovak Sokol, the Cosmopolitan Club, the Lincoln Hills Country Club and the Holy Trinity Church.

Elsie, the second daughter, is the wife of Julius Domonkos, of Gary. They have two children, Olga and Paul.

John A. Szikora, Jr., after graduating from the Ross Township High School entered the store of his father, and has been one of the hard workers in that establishment ever since. He is a member of the Harrison Club, the Slovak Political Club, the Lincoln Hills Country Club. He is unmarried.

Agnes is the wife of Ernest Woods, of Gary, who is also connected with the Oak Park Grocery Company. Their children are Richard and Audrey, and the Woods family are members of the Harrison Club.

Frank Szikora is unmarried, and is associated with the business established by his father. He is a member of the Lincoln Hills Country Club and Slovak Social Club.

Joseph, the youngest of the family, is also a popular figure in the business and is active in local clubs at Gary.

DORSEA W. ZOOK for over a quarter of a century has furnished that indispensable service of humanity, involved in the responsibilities of the undertaker and funeral director, to the community of Converse in Miami County. Mr. Zook is a man of fine character, whole souled and sympathetic, an ideal man for his service and profession.

He was born in Wabash County, Indiana, April 4, 1876. His father, Jacob B. Zook, was born in Ohio and came to Wabash County just before the Civil war. He married Lide E. Eckelberger, who was born in Wabash County.

Dorsea W. Zook is one of two children. He attended school near his father's farm and helped his father until he was twenty, when he left home to become a farmer on his own account. While thus engaged he took up the study of embalming and in 1902 was issued a license to practice. In 1903 he moved to Converse and in July of that year opened his undertaking parlors. He has been in business now continuously for twenty-seven years and along with his competent experience he has kept his facilities up to date. Supplementing his funeral service is a funeral chapel, and he has hearses, ambulances and funeral cars.

Mr. Zook in 1915 was elected a town councilman and was also elected a member of the advisory board of the city. By appointment he served as a member of the Converse school board from 1923 to 1927. During the World war he did his part in selling bonds, raising funds for the Red Cross and assisting in the food administration. He is now a member of the health board of Converse. He is a Democrat, he and his wife are members of the Christian Church, and he has affiliations with a number of social and fraternal organizations, including the Lions Club, Masonic Lodge, Independent Order of Odd Fellows, Improved Order of Red Men, Modern Woodmen of America. His wife is a member of the Rebekahs and the Eastern Star.

He married in 1898 Miss Zadia Lawshe, who was born in Wabash County. Her father, Thomas Lawshe, was the pioneer undertaker of the town of Somerset. Mr. and Mrs. Zook have two daughters, Miss Beatrice L. and Berniece. Berniece is the wife of Mr. Reno Tibbetts, of Converse, and they have three children, Wilma Dean, Rex Edward and Darrell William.

LEO JOHN CHELMINIAK, who was born at South Bend, April 9, 1895, has during the past ten years come rapidly into prominence in the financial life of the community. He is secretary and treasurer of the Kosciusko Building & Loan Association.

Mr. Chelminiak's parents, Lawrence and Antonette (Beyer) Chelminiak, were born in Poland. His mother was a child when her parents came to South Bend, about 1860, and she was a resident of that city for many years, passing away January 23, 1915. Lawrence Chelminiak came to South Bend in 1879, when a young man. In his native country he had learned the trade of painter and paper hanger, and in South Bend he conducted a paint and wall paper store on West Division Street, and for thirty years did a successful contracting business. He died October 3, 1922. These parents had a family of nine children, five of whom are living: Stanley J.; Leo J.; Aloysius and Walter, both of whom are railroad clerks; and Hattie, wife of Casmer Roznakowski, of Cleveland, Ohio.

Leo J. Chelminiak was educated in Saint Hedwig's Parochial School, attended the South Bend High School and the Thomas Commercial College, and was just getting established in a business career when the World war came on. He was in the Officers Training School at Fort Benjamin Harrison, later at the Great Lakes Naval Training Station, and finally an instructor in the Government Radio School at Harvard University.

Following the armistice and his release from military duty Mr. Chelminiak gave six months to his father in the paint and wall paper business, and on November 1, 1919, became secretary and treasurer of the Kosciusko Building & Loan Association. This is one of the oldest building and loan associations in Saint Joseph County, having been founded in 1884, and for over forty-five years has been an important factor in inculcating thrift and home ownership. The institution is now housed in a fine new bank building at 423 South Chapin Street.

Mr. Chelminiak married, September 30, 1919, Miss Theresa D. Urbanski, who was also born in South Bend, where her mother, Mrs. Stephen Urbanski, resides. Her father is deceased. Mr. and Mrs. Chelminiak have five children, Clement John, Gertrude Marie, Helen Marie, John Henry and Thaddeus Stanley. Mr. Chelminiak and family are members of Saint Stanislaus Polish Church and he is active in all Polish-American societies, being financial secretary and a director of the M. Romanowski Polish Falcons.

HUBERT MORTON ENGLISH, chairman of the medical staff of the Methodist Hospital at Gary and member of the staff of the Mercy Hospital, has achieved high rank and has won notable success in his profession since coming to Gary.

He was born at Marshall, Illinois, July 30, 1890, and represents the fourth generation of a family that went to Illinois nearly a century ago. His great-grandfather, Rev. Abel English, was descended from a Colonial family of New Jersey, and the family had representatives in the Colonial army during the War of the Revolution. Rev. Abel English moved west to Indiana in 1835, and in 1837 established a home at Marshall, Illinois. He was a pioneer Methodist minister, helped establish the first church of that denomination in Marshall and carried on the work of the ministry over a large part of the Illinois River Valley. He married Margaret Babcock and both are buried in a cemetery at Livingston, Illinois. Their son, Isaac English, was born in New Jersey, in 1821, and was fourteen years of age when the family moved to Indiana. He attended school in New Jersey, in Indiana, where the family home for two years was near Indianapolis, and completed his education in Illinois. He became a farmer, and spent an active life in that vocation. He died in 1896 and his wife, whose maiden name was Sarah Black, passed away in 1892. These were the grandparents of Doctor English of Gary.

Doctor English's parents were John A. and Marietta (Clemings) English. His father lived all his life at Marshall, Illinois, was a farmer and stock man and was in his fifty-third year when he died in 1900. His wife, Marietta Clemings, was born and reared near Newark, Ohio, attended school there and taught school in Ohio and Illinois before her marriage. She died September 7, 1927, at the age of seventy-nine, and she and her husband are buried at Marshall. Her parents were James and Rosana (Barclay) Clemings. Doctor English is one of a family of seven children. One child, Ferman, died in infancy. John William is a farmer at Paris, Illinois; Raymond C. is a railway mail clerk, with home at Decatur, Illinois; Ava is Mrs. Albert Hall, of Marshall, Illinois; Mark H. died at the age of seventeen; and Charles W. is with the Gary Railways Company at Gary.

Hubert Morton English grew up on an Illinois farm, attended district schools and was graduated from the Marshall Township High School in 1910. He then entered the University of Illinois, graduating in 1914, and completed his professional training in the Harvard Medical School, taking his M. D. degree in 1918. On July 1, 1918, he joined the colors as a first lieutenant in the Medical Corps, serving two and a half months in an officers training camp at Camp Greenleaf, Georgia, and for two and a half months was assigned duty at Saint Elizabeth's Hospital in Washington, D. C. He was given a discharge December 13, 1918, and then for three years engaged in a general practice at Anawalt, West Virginia. Returning to Chicago, he was for fifteen months connected with the Augustana Hospital as interne and in post-graduate study, and after this special training came to Gary in 1923, opening an office, and has enjoyed a rapidly growing practice in medicine and surgery. His offices are at 673 Broadway. Doctor English is a fellow of the American College of Physicians and since 1925 has given part of his time to his duties as an instructor in the medical department of Northwestern University at Chicago. He is a member of the Lake County, Indiana State and American Medical Associations. Doctor English is a member of the Masonic fraternity, is a Republican, member of the First Methodist Episcopal Church, and belongs to Gary Post of the American Legion.

He married at Ironwood, Michigan, January 11, 1923, Miss Esther Holmgren, daughter of John A. and Tolina (Gunderson) Holmgren. Her father has for many years been connected with the iron mines at Ironwood, and is superintendent in one of the large mines in that district. He is a member of the Masonic fraternity and a deacon in the Lutheran Church. Mrs. English attended school in Ironwood, graduated from high school there, and is a graduate of the nurses training class in the Augustana Hospital at Chicago, with the class of 1919. For four years after graduating she was surgical nurse at this hospital. She is a member of the Methodist Church in Gary and the Gary Woman's Club. They have one son, Hubert Morton, Jr., born July 2, 1925.

ALFRED PEARMAN DRAPER. Among the younger generation of attorneys practicing at the bar of Lake County, one who has made rapid strides in his calling and who has demonstrated the possession of the qualities which make for success therein is Alfred P. Draper, of Gary. During his comparatively short but prosperous career he has been identified with much important litigation, and as a citizen has attracted favorable attention by his readiness to support those movements which have been promulgated for the betterment of the community.

Mr. Draper was born at Baldwinsville, New York, December 29, 1891, and is a son of Russell J. and Ena (Pearman) Draper. This branch of the Draper family was founded in America by the great-grandfather of Mr. Draper, a native of England, who upon his arrival in the United States took up his residence at Hannibal, New York, where he passed the remainder of his life and where he and his wife are buried. Alfred Draper, the grandfather of Alfred P. Draper, was born near Hannibal, New York, where he was reared on

John L Seick

a farm and received a country school education. At the outbreak of the war between the states he enlisted in a New York volunteer infantry regiment, with which he served valiantly until the close of the struggle, when he received his honorable discharge and returned to his home near Hannibal, where he passed the remaining years of his life in agricultural operations until his retirement to the town of Fulton, New York, several years ago. He has the reputation of being a man of integrity and high character and has always taken a good citizen's part in movements which have been beneficial to his locality. Mr. Draper married Miss Ena Pearman, who was born in England and was brought to the United States as a young woman by her parents, receiving her education in the public schools of Fulton, New York. She was active in Baptist Church work and died in 1919, being buried in the cemetery at Mount Aduah, New York. Mr. and Mrs. Draper became the parents of two children: Alfred P., of this review; and Floyd S., an attorney, formerly of Gary, but now of Crown Point, Indiana, who in 1930 was the successful nominee for prosecuting attorney of Lake County on the Republican ticket.

Alfred P. Draper attended public school at Watertown, New York, where he was graduated from high school as a member of the class of 1911, and from 1913 to 1916 took a course in mechanical designing at Providence, Rhode Island, with the Brown & Sharp Manufacturing Company. He followed that business until 1919, but during the World war was in the Government service, designing tools for the manufacture of such articles as Liberty motors, howitzers and other machines of war. In 1919 Mr. Draper entered Valparaiso University, from which institution he was graduated with the degree of Bachelor of Laws as a member of the class of 1922, but was admitted to the bar prior to his graduation, in November, 1921. On leaving college he established himself in the practice of law at Gary, where he has since built up a large and representative clientele, and maintains a suite of offices at 522 Broadway. He is a member of the American Bar Association, the Indiana State Bar Association and the Gary Bar Association. In addition to his large law practice he is interested in a number of business and financial ventures and is a member of the board of directors of the Fifth Avenue Bank and of the Character Finance & Thrift Corporation. Fraternally he is affiliated with Valparaiso Lodge No. 137, A. F. and A. M., and he likewise belongs to the University Club, the Commercial Club and Chamber of Commerce and the Lake Hills Country Club. While he has always been interested in politics and civic affairs, he has never sought the candidacy for any office, but exercises his right of franchise as a Republican. He is a member and elder of the Forty-third Avenue Presbyterian Church.

At Syracuse, New York, May 24, 1923, Mr. Draper was united in marriage with Miss Leontine Porter, daughter of Frank and Louise (Fuller) Porter, of Syracuse, where for years Mr. Porter was prominent in business circles as a dealer in coal, building supplies, cement, etc., although now living in retirement. Mrs. Porter died in 1917 and is buried in the cemetery at Fulton. Mrs. Draper, who is a graduate of the Fulton High School, has been active in the work of the Forty-third Avenue Presbyterian Church and the Gary Woman's Club. There are two children: Donna Norene, who is attending public school; and Russell Porter.

JOHN LUCIUS SLICK is actively concerned with the directing of what is a virtual public-utility service in the City of Fort Wayne, where he is treasurer and manager of Slick's Family Washing & Ironing Company, the well equipped headquarters of which are established at 226 Dalman Street and the concern now ranks as one of the largest and most metropolitan of the kind in the city.

Mr. Slick was born in the City of South Bend, Indiana, March 13, 1889, and is a son of Thomas J. and Laura A. (Whitten) Slick, the former of whom was born in Lancaster, Pennsylvania, and the latter at South Bend, Indiana, where their marriage was solemnized. Thomas J. Slick was a boy at the time of the family removal from the old Keystone State to St. Joseph County, Indiana, where the home was established near South Bend, in the early '40s. He represented the Hoosier State as a gallant young soldier of the Union in the Civil war, and as a member of the Twenty-first Indiana Volunteer Infantry he participated in the various engagements in which that valiant command was involved, he having been actively affiliated with the Grand Army of the Republic in later years and having thus maintained his association with his old comrades of the Civil war. He founded and long conducted Slick's Laundry in the City of South Bend, and there his death occurred in 1919, his widow having passed away in 1926, and John L., of this review, being the youngest of the seven children, all of whom survive the honored parents.

John L. Slick supplemented the discipline of the South Bend public schools by there attending fine old Notre Dame University, in which he was a student about four years. He early gained practical experience in connection with his father's laundry business in South Bend, where he remained until 1911, when he became manager of the Slick Laundry at Gary, Indiana, in which city he was thus engaged until the nation entered the World war, in 1917, when he enlisted for service in the United States army and soon gained the rank of first lieutenant. He was assigned to the management of the Government laundry service at Camp Custer, Battle Creek, Michigan, and was there stationed until he received his honorable discharge, in the early part of 1919. Thereafter he was identified with the laundry business in the City of Terre Haute, Indiana, until January, 1925, when he came to Fort Wayne and founded Slick's Family Washing &

Ironing Company, of which he has since continued treasurer and manager, the company still continuing the laundry business in South Bend and having also two laundries in the City of Gary. Mr. Slick is one of the progressive citizens and business men of Fort Wayne, is here a director of the East Creighton Avenue Trust Company, is president of the Fort Wayne Better Business Bureau, is a loyal and valued member of the local Chamber of Commerce, is a director of the Fort Wayne Y. M. C. A. and the Rotary Club, and has membership in the Orchard Ridge Country Club. He is actively identified with the Indiana Laundry Owners Association and the National Laundry Owners Association, his political allegiance is given to the Republican party, and he and his wife have membership in the Congregational Church in their home city. Mr. Slick is affiliated with the American Legion, and in the Masonic fraternity has membership in the Scottish Rite bodies, as well as the Mystic Shrine.

At South Bend, this state, in 1912, Mr. Slick was united in marriage to Miss Harriet M. Barber, who was born at Hanna, La Porte County. She was graduated in the high school at South Bend and the college at Goshen, and was, prior to her marriage, for two years a popular teacher in the public schools of South Bend. Mrs. Slick is a daughter of the late Daniel Barber, whose death occurred in 1919 and whose widow passed away in 1918. Mr. and Mrs. Slick have one child, John L., Jr., born September 26, 1914, and the attractive home of the family is at 4210 Drury Lane.

JOHN BERNARD MONAHAN. Although he has been actively engaged in the real estate and insurance business at Gary for only four years, John B. Monahan has already made his name well known in realty circles as that of a shrewd operator of careful judgment and much acumen. His has been a career in which he has been engaged in a number of capacities in various sections of the country, and the variation of his employment and his numerous travels have served to add to his equipment and to give him a clear insight into human nature and character.

Mr. Monahan was born January 10, 1868, at Dwight, Illinois, and is a son of John B. and Bridget (Reynolds) Monahan. John B. Monahan, the elder, was born and reared in County Leitrim, Ireland, where he received his education in the public and parochial schools, and there met and married Bridget Reynolds, who was born and educated in the same community. Soon after their marriage, in 1860, they immigrated to the United States, landing at New Orleans, where they remained for about three years, and then going to Dwight, Illinois. In 1875 the parents removed with their family to Joliet, Illinois, where Mr. Monahan followed contracting and building, and several years later moved back to Dwight, where Mr. Monahan died in 1878, burial being made at Dwight. Mrs. Monahan passed away in October, 1925, and was buried at Joliet, at

which time her husband's remains were taken to Joliet and laid beside her. They were honest and honorable people who had the fullest respect and esteem of the people of the communities in which they made their home. Mr. and Mrs. Monahan were the parents of six children: Edward, who died in 1929, at the age of sixty-eight years; James P., of Chicago, who carried on the business of Monahan Brothers, plastering contractors, his partner having been his brother, the late Edward, who died in August, 1930; John B., of this review; Frank J. and David D., who are partners in an automobile business at Chicago; and Miss Elizabeth, who resides at Joliet.

John B. Monahan of this review received his education in the public schools of Joliet and on leaving school secured a position with the Illinois Steel Company, by which concern he was employed nine years. He then entered the service of Robert W. Hunt & Company, of Chicago, as inspection engineer, and during the nine years that he was engaged in this capacity was in charge of inspection work for the Colorado Fuel & Iron Company, Pueblo, Colorado. Later he was with that corporation in charge of their merchant mills for five years, returning to Joliet to spend two years with his brothers in municipal contract work. Subsequently he rejoined Robert W. Hunt & Company, Chicago, in charge of the southern district, located at Birmingham, Alabama, for five years, and in 1912 came to Gary with the Illinois Steel Company as superintendent of the rail mill, a position which he held until November, 1926. At that time he resigned and embarked in the real estate and insurance business, with offices at 757 Broadway, and under the firm style of J. B. Monahan has built up a large and profitable enterprise and carried through to a successful conclusion a number of transactions of great importance. He is the owner of much land of his own, including some of the Ogden dunes and considerable city realty, particularly on Harrison Street. Mr. Monahan is a charter member of the Gary Country Club, in which he has been active for years, and belongs to the Benevolent and Protective Order of Elks and the Knights of Columbus. His religious connection is with Holy Angels Catholic Church, and he has always been a generous supporter of worthy civic measures and enterprises which attract his enlightened views and good judgment.

At Pueblo, Colorado, November 28, 1906, Mr. Monahan was united in marriage with Miss Anna Dempsey, daughter of James K. and Mary (Garrity) Dempsey, the former of whom was for years a real estate operator of Pueblo, and was also interested in Democratic politics. Mr. Dempsey died in 1919 and his wife in 1907, and both are buried at Pueblo. Mrs. Monahan was educated in Loretta Convent, Pueblo, Colorado, and is active in Catholic Church work, in the Catholic Woman's League and the Woman's Club of Gary. She and Mr. Monahan have had six children: Marietta, a graduate of Emerson High School, who spent two years at Saint

Mary's South Bend, Indiana, graduated from the University of Chicago with the class of 1929, and is now a public school teacher at Gary; David D., a graduate of Emerson High School, who is now a sophomore at Notre Dame University; Eleanor E., a graduate of Horace Mann High School, class of 1930, who is now a student in the University of Wisconsin; Anna R. and Dorothy, who are students in Horace Mann High School; and Katherine, who is attending grade school, at Holy Angels School, Gary.

WILLIAM JOHN SCHROEDER. The building of the City of Gary, Lake County, upon the sandy wilds of the Lake Michigan area has constituted one of the marvels in American industrial and urban development, and in the passing years the original spirit of constructive progressiveness has here continued in force, for the city has gained and retained men of thought and action and of noteworthy loyalty and initiative, so that the march of progress has not faltered. In the Gary metropolitan district today William J. Schroeder is a liberal and influential business man who has been able to make important contribution to civic and material advancement through his active association with real estate development and control, especially through the medium of organizations formed for the normal and direct encouragement of building operations. Thus it is to be noted that he is president of the Glen Park Building & Loan Association, through which has been compassed the developing of the fine Glen Park suburban district, and he is also general manager of Park Manor.

Mr. Schroeder was born in the City of Chicago, October 3, 1885, and is a son of Frederick and Albertine (Zahlmann) Schroeder, who were born and reared near Danzig, Germany, where their marriage was solemnized, and whence they came to the United States and established residence in Chicago, Illinois, in 1881. In his native land Frederick Schroeder had been an exponent of farm industry, but upon becoming a citizen of Chicago he effectively adjusted himself to urban conditions by turning his attention to contracting and building, of which important line of enterprise he continued a successful representative during the remainder of his active career. He died October 13, 1929, at his home in Elmhurst, one of the attractive suburbs of Chicago, and there his mortal remains rest in Mount Emblem Cemetery, which is maintained under the auspices of the Masonic fraternity, he having long been affiliated with that time-honored fraternal order. His widow now resides in the home of her daughter Clara (Mrs. John Zimmerman), at Lombard, Illinois. Of the children the following brief record is available: Albert and Frederick, Jr., still reside in Chicago; Anna became the wife of Herman Tapel, of Chicago, and in that city her death occurred; William J., of this review, is the next younger of the children; John resides at Lombard, Illinois; Otto died at the age of

three years; Walter is a resident of Ontarioville, Illinois; Charles resides at Lombard, a virtual suburb of Chicago; and Clara is the wife of John Zimmerman, their home being at Lombard.

In Chicago the public-school education of William J. Schroeder culminated when he was graduated in the Holden High School, as a member of the class of 1902, his studies there having included a commercial course. In 1904 Mr. Schroeder enlisted in the United States Army, and at the expiration of his three years' term of enlistment he received his honorable discharge and passed two and one-half years in the purchasing department of the Nebraska Bridge Supply & Lumber Company, with headquarters in the City of Omaha. He then, in the spring of 1909, came to Gary, Indiana, and engaged in the real-estate and building business. His initial service was in the selling of realty for the First State Bank of Hobart, another of the cities of Lake County, and he then became sales manager in connection with the real-estate operation of George and William Earle. With this firm he remained eleven years, and he then, in 1920, effected the organization of the American Pure Paint Company, which erected a factory on Park Road and the tracks of the Michigan Central Railroad, Gary, where for the ensuing two years the company manufactured natural paint pigments. Mr. Schroeder then resumed his alliance with the real-estate business, organized a syndicate by which was purchased the Park Manor subdivision of Gary, at Broadway and Thirty-fifth streets, and proceeded to exploit and develop this tract of eighty acres. The best type of modern improvements was installed, in the matter of streets, sidewalks sewerage and lighting systems, etc., and a restrictive provision was made that none but brick or stone buildings were to be erected. On this tract about $2,500,000 was eventually expended in the erection of buildings and the making of general improvements, and Mr. Schroeder has continued as general manager of the Park Manor corporation. In the fall of 1922 he became associated with the organizing of the Glen Park State Bank, of which he was the first secretary and of which he became a director. In 1925 he was concerned in organizing the Glen Park Building & Loan Association, of which he became vice president, and two years later he was elected its president, the office which he still retains. The offices of this association are established at 3662 Broadway. Mr. Schroeder is a director of the Gary Commercial Club and Chamber of Commerce. He was influential in effecting the reorganization of the Chamber of Commerce, and served two years as its secretary.

The political allegiance of Mr. Schroeder is given to the Democratic party, and he has shown his civic loyalty in effective service in various avenues of service. He was a member of the city park board of Gary in 1914, the preceding year having marked his candidacy for membership in the City Council. In 1917 he was Democratic candidate for city clerk, and in 1928 as his party's candidate for the office of county recorder he ran more than 2,000 votes ahead of the party ticket, normal political agencies having compassed his defeat for this and the other positions, as the Democratic party is in the minority in Gary and in Lake County in general. In November, 1930, he was elected a member of the Lake County Council and when the Council was organized, he was elected president.

In 1927 Mr. Schroeder was deputized to organize the "Vigilantes of Lake County," and this body did successful service in capturing a number of desperadoes who were preying on banks and commerce in Indiana and Illinois. Mr. Schroeder is now chairman of the Lake County Protection Association and the Lake County Bankers Association. His basic Masonic affiliation is with Gary Lodge No. 677, A. F. and A. M., and in the Scottish Rite Consistory at Fort Wayne he has received the thirty-second degree, while as a Noble of the Mystic Shrine he has membership in Orak Temple at Hammond. In his home city he is a member of the representative organization known as the Sand Fleas, and in Chicago he has membership in Medinah Athletic Club.

At Huntsville, Alabama, on November 10, 1907, Mr. Schroeder was united in marriage to Miss Anna L. Harley, daughter of Russell and Louise (Cole) Harley, her mother having been in line of kinship with Daniel Boone, the historic Kentucky frontierman. Russell Harley was born in Ohio and represented that state as a gallant young soldier of the Union in the Civil war, he having participated in many engagements and having been wounded in the battles of Winchester and Stone River. After the war he gained pioneer honors in Arkansas, where he obtained land and where, as a skilled civil engineer, he was prominently concerned with railway building and general surveying work of important order. His death occurred about 1905 and that of his widow about 1922. Mrs. Schroeder received her youthful education mainly at Judsonia, Arkansas, and Huntsville, Alabama. Like her husband, she is deeply interested in the affairs of the Masonic fraternity, as a member of the Order of the Eastern Star and of the White Shrine of Jerusalem, besides which she is a popular figure in the social life of her home community. Mr. and Mrs. Schroeder have two fine sons: William Russell Schroeder was born at Huntsville, Alabama, January 13, 1909, and in 1928 he was graduated in Onarga Military School, with the rank of major. He thereafter was a student in the Chicago Art Institute and he is now a talented commercial artist. Earle, the younger son, was born at Hobart, Indiana, October 1, 1910, and received the advantages of the Glen Park public schools of Gary, where he had also two years of high-school work. In 1928 he was graduated in Onarga Military School, with rank of first lieutenant, and he is now a member of the class of 1932 in DePauw University. Both sons are affiliated with college fraternities, William R. being a member of Theta Chi Phi and Earle of the Phi Delta Theta.

JOHN CHRISTIAN PERRY, formerly secretary and treasurer of the Glen Park Building & Loan Association, which is one of the well ordered, progressive and valuable concerns of the City of Gary, with headquarters at 3662 Broadway, is able to claim the historic old Keystone State as the place of his nativity, for his birth occurred at Norristown, Pennsylvania, September 28, 1883. He is a son of William E. and Emma (Stump) Perry, both of whom were born and reared at Norristown, where they passed virtually their entire lives, the death of Mrs. Perry having there occurred in 1887 and her husband having survived her more than thirty years, his death having there occurred in the year 1921. William E. Perry was a son of John Perry, who was born and reared in the North of Ireland and who was a youth when he came to the United States and established residence at Norristown, Pennsylvania, where he was engaged many years in the livery business and where both he and his wife remained until their death, their marriage having there been solemnized. In the earlier part of his active career William E. Perry was associated with his father in the livery business at Norristown, and thereafter he passed many years in the service of the Philadelphia & Reading Railroad. Of the two children John C., of this review, is the elder, and the younger is Miss Jane M. Perry, a popular teacher in the public schools of her native City of Norristown. The mother was a devoted communicant of the Lutheran Church, in the faith of which she had been reared.

In the high school at Norristown, Pennsylvania, John C. Perry was graduated in 1901, and thereafter he completed a course in chemistry and mechanic arts in Drexel Institute, Philadelphia, in which institution he was graduated as a member of the class of 1906. Thereafter he held for three years a position in the laboratories of the Allen Wood Iron & Steel Corporation, in Pennsylvania, and in 1909 he came to Gary, Indiana, and became an assistant to H. C. Thomas, who was then chief chemist for the Illinois Steel Company. Mr. Perry continued his service with this great industrial corporation until 1912, when he assumed the position of deputy city comptroller of Gary, he having later become deputy city treasurer and having served in this capacity until 1922, when he engaged in the real-estate and insurance business, to which he continued to give his attention until 1925. He then became one of the organizers of the Glen Park Building & Loan Association, of which he continued as secretary and treasurer until January, 1931. At that time he became general agent for the Fidelity Health & Accident Company for Lake County.

A Knight Templar Mason, Mr. Perry has received also the thirty-second degree of the Scottish Rite, in the Consistory of the Valley of Fort Wayne, while as a Noble of the Mystic Shrine he has membership in Orak Temple in the City of Hammond. He is a charter member of Roosevelt Lodge No. 716, A. F. and A. M., of which he was the first secretary, and he is a past high priest of Gary Chapter, R. A. M. His political allegiance is given to the Republican party and he and his wife are members of the Methodist Episcopal Church.

In Los Angeles, California, January 26, 1923, Mr. Perry was united in marriage to Mrs. Daisy D. (Cross) Perry, daughter of Christopher Cross, who was for many years engaged in the meat market business at Tuscola, Illinois, where both he and his wife died. Mrs. Perry was reared and educated in Illinois and there occurred her marriage to Floyd Perry, who there died when he was a young man, no children having been born of this union. Mrs. Perry has been a popular figure in church and social circles in Gary, is a member of the Phi Sigma Pi college sorority and is an active member of the Gary Woman's Club.

Mr. Perry was animated by utmost loyalty in his association with patriotic activities in the World war period, and was influential in furthering the drives for sale of Government war bonds, the advancing of Red Cross work, etc. He is one of the progressive and loyal citizens and business men of Gary and is always ready to give his influence and cooperation in the furthering of civic movements and enterprises of value to the community.

BYRON WILLIAM MARSHALL, M. D. Since his advent at Gary in 1927 Dr. Byron W. Marshall has fully lived up to the reputation that he had established during twenty years of practice in the State of Wyoming as a thoroughly reliable and capable general physician and surgeon. Doctor Marshall entered upon his life work with an excellent education, an inherent love of his profession and a fulsome fund of sympathy. During the years that have passed he has added to his equipment broad experience, much study and steadfast attention to the broadening horizons of medical and surgical science, all of which combine to make him a useful member of his adopted community.

Doctor Marshall was born at Nashville, Indiana, October 9, 1878, and is a son of Jesse B. and Elizabeth (Woods) Marshall. His great-grandfather, a native of Tennessee, became one of the pioneer residents of the vicinity of Nashville, Indiana, where he hewed a farm from the timber and became a substantial citizen, and the old homestead is still in the possession of members of the family. Robert Marshall, the grandfather of Doctor Marshall, was born in Tennessee and was a child when brought to Indiana by his parents. He acquired a country school education and was working on the home farm when the call came for troops to serve in the Mexican war. He volunteered for this service, following which he returned to the farm, but again was called from his peaceful pastoral pursuits by the outbreak of the great war between the states, in which he enlisted, becoming a private in the Eighty-second Regiment, Indiana Volunteer Infantry, with which command he served valiantly until the close of the struggle. He again returned to his home, applied himself assiduously to his farming and stock raising operations and became one of the large land-owners of the community. He died near Nashville, where he and his wife are buried.

Jesse B. Marshall, father of Dr. Byron W. Marshall, was born and reared at Nashville, where he received a public school education, and early in life adopted the vocation of his father. A man of sound judgment, great industry and progressive ideas, he succeeded in his agricultural operations and eventually branched out into mercantile operations at Nashville, a venture in which he likewise was successful. He was a member of the Independent Order of Odd Fellows and of the Baptist Church, and as to politics espoused the cause of Democracy. He died in July, 1927, and was laid to rest in the cemetery at Nashville. Mr. Marshall married Miss Elizabeth Woods, a daughter of Jackson Woods, who enlisted in the Union army during the Civil war, was taken prisoner, and died of starvation in the terrible Andersonville Prison. Mrs. Marshall was educated in the public schools of Nashville and at the age of seventy-five years makes her home with her daughter at Indianapolis. She is still active in the work of the Baptist Church, of which she has been a lifelong member. There were seven children in the family: Nettie, now Mrs. T. J. Henderson, of Nashville, Indiana; Dr. Byron W., of this review; Winnie, now Mrs. J. B. Seitz, of 4049 Ruckle Street, Indianapolis; Jessie, who is married and also a resident of Indianapolis; Cleveland, who died at the age of three years; Dr. Clarence E., a successful practicing dentist at Livingston, Montana; and Pearl, now Mrs. Samuel Rednor, of Columbus, Indiana.

Byron W. Marshall attended public school at Nashville, Indiana, and after his graduation from the high school entered the Indiana Medical College, from which he was graduated with the degree of Doctor of Medicine as a member of the class of 1906. In 1919 he took post-graduate work at the New York Postgraduate Medical School and Hospital and at the Lying-In Hospital of New York City. His interneship was passed at Deaconess Hospital, Indianapolis, and in 1907 he went to the State of Wyoming, where for twenty years he was engaged in successful practice. While in Wyoming he was district surgeon for the Union Pacific and the Oregon Short Line Railroads, serving for a period of twenty years. In July, 1927, Doctor Marshall returned to Indiana and took up his permanent residence at Gary, where he now has a splendid suite of offices at 3776 Broadway, corner of Thirty-eighth Street. He has built up an excellent practice and is accounted a capable diagnostician, able practitioner and reliable surgeon, and a man who lives up to the strictest interpretation of professional ethics. He is a member of the American Medical Association, the Indiana State Medical Society and the Lake County Medical Society, and has attended numerous lectures and clinics in addition to spending much time in personal research and investigation. Fraternally he is affiliated with Pinebluff Blue Lodge, A. F. and A. M., of Pinebluff, Wyoming; the Consistory at Cheyenne; and Korein Temple, A. A. O. N. M. S., Rawlins, Wyoming, and for some years has been active in the Independent Order of Odd Fellows and Cheyenne Lodge No. 660, Benevolent and Protective Order of Elks. He belongs also to the Commercial Club and Chamber of Commerce of Gary, and in his religious faith is a Baptist. Doctor Marshall is independent in politics, and while a resident of Pinebluff, Wyoming, served as a member of the City Council for seven years, while since locating at Gary he has displayed a commendable interest in civic affairs. His hobbies may be said to be hunting and golf, but his practice has become so extensive that he finds little time to engage in either.

In 1904, at Indianapolis, Indiana, Doctor Marshall was united in marriage with Miss Sarah E. Deist, daughter of John and Louisa (Feber) Deist, the former a farmer of near Nashville for a number of years and also active in political circles. Mr. Deist died several years ago, while his widow survived him until February, 1930, and both are buried in the Nashville Cemetery. Mrs. Marshall was educated in the public schools of Nashville and after graduating from high school taught school for several years previous to her marriage. A woman of superior attainments and numerous graces, she has been active in the work of the Presbyterian Church, and is also active and popular in the Woman's Club and the Order of the Eastern Star.

HANS OLAF EGEBERG. Perhaps there is no position in the industrial life of our country that demands greater tact, diplomacy, courage and knowledge of general conditions and of human nature than that of the individual who must act as the intermediary between the employer and the employe. There are, as there always have been and always will be, differences between those who control our large corporations and those who are of the so-called working class. So to keep the machinery of trade and industry oiled in a manner that there will be no great friction and that it will continue to function in a smooth-running way is no light task, and in this connection mention should be made of Hans Olaf Egeberg, who in the capacity of superintendent of employment of the Illinois Steel Company, at Gary, has established a record for his ability in averting serious labor troubles.

Mr. Egeberg was born in Norway, February 1, 1875, and is a son of Ove and Pauline (Kausebohl) Egeberg. Ove Egeberg was born in Norway, where he acquired a high school education, and as a young man engaged in farming for his life work, being occupied

therein with success for many years. He was a man of importance in his community, where he served as a member of the Municipal Council, and was also active in the movements and charities of the Lutheran Church. He died in 1920, his wife having passed away in 1912, and both are buried in the Trogstad Cemetery, Norway. There were ten children in the family, of whom seven died in infancy, the three surviving being Hans Olaf, of this review; Tora, who is now Mrs. Kvilesjoe, of Norway; and Laurentze, now Mrs. Golden, of Norway.

Hans O. Egeberg was given good educational advantages in his youth, his father being a man of substance, and after graduating from high school pursued a course at the University of Norway, Oslo, from which he was graduated as a member of the class of 1895. This was supplemented by a course at the University of Dresden, Germany, and he then came to the United States and entered Cornell University, from which he received the degree of Civil Engineer as a member of the class of 1900. In that year Mr. Egeberg accepted a position with the Scherzer Rolling Mills, Chicago, with which he was identified for one year, and in 1901 became identified with the South Chicago Works of the Illinois Steel Company, in the capacity of inspector. He remained in that capacity until February 1, 1907, when he came to Gary to engage in construction work for the same company, and also traveled for some time in the inspection of construction materials. Mr. Egeberg next joined the operating department, which employment he retained until 1914, when he was made superintendent of the employment department, with offices on Virginia Street, and this post he has held to the present. Labor, in political economy, may be defined as effort for the satisfying of human needs. It is one of the three leading factors in production, the other two being land and capital, and in the vast circle of industry labor has a great variety of functions. The solution of the questions connected therewith is now universally regarded as a most pressing duty of statesmen and economists, but there must also be men, like Mr. Egeberg, who come into direct contact with the problems, and who have first-hand knowledge of how to meet crisis or to avert them in the way of an amicable settlement. It has been Mr. Egeberg's fortune to have gained and held the respect of the employes of the company, while at the same time protecting the interests of the concern which he represents. Fraternally he is affiliated with Roosevelt Lodge, A. F. and A. M., and South Chicago Chapter, R. A. M.; and also belongs to the Commercial Club and Chamber of Commerce of Gary, the Gary Country Club and the Young Men's Christian Association. Politically he is a Republican, without desire for public preferment. He is active in civic affairs as a good citizen and during the World war took a prominent part in all drives.

At Chicago, Illinois, August 14, 1897, Mr. Egeberg was united in marriage with Miss Ulrikka Christine Nielsen, daughter of Harald

C. J. Wadskier

and Fredrikke (Jensen) Nielsen. Mr. and Mrs. Nielsen were actors who were well known in their day, particularly in Norway, where they had a wide vogue in Ibsen dramas. Mr. Nielsen died in 1880, while his widow survived him until 1912, and both are buried in Bergen, Norway. Mrs. Egeberg received a high school education in Norway, and at Chicago became a private instructor in physical education. For a time after her marriage to Mr. Egeberg she continued her work in this direction, but has since abandoned it and now devotes herself to her home, although she is also active and popular as a member of the Woman's Club. To Mr. and Mrs. Egeberg there were born three children: Ove, who died at the age of one year; Dr. Roger Olaf and Gudrun. Roger Olaf Egeberg attended the public schools of Gary and Francis Parker High School, Chicago, following which he entered Cornell University and graduated with the degree of Bachelor of Arts as a member of the class of 1925. He then enrolled at Northwestern University, Evanston, Illinois, from which he was graduated with the degree of Doctor of Medicine as a member of the class of 1928. He pursued his internship at Wesley Hospital and Passavant Hospital, both of Chicago, and is now a medical instructor at the University of Michigan, although his home is at Chicago. He is a member of the leading organizations of his profession and has already displayed the possession of qualities that should carry him far in the vocation of his choice. Doctor Egeberg married Miss Margaret Chahoon, of Grandmire, Quebec, Canada. Miss Gudrun Egeberg, only daughter of Mr. and Mrs. Egeberg, attended Francis Parker High School, Chicago, and the University of Chicago, from which she was graduated with the degree of Bachelor of Arts as a member of the class of 1928. She is now engaged in investigation work for the Illinois State Hospital, located at (Dunning) Chicago, an institution for those who are mentally deranged.

HOWARD H. HAYDEN, a resident of Indiana since 1913, was for a number of years with the steel mills at Gary, and since coming to South Bend has established and is proprietor of the popular Morning Side Hotel, at 413 West Colfax Street.

Mr. Hayden was born in New York City, April 25, 1890. When he was a child his parents moved to Bath, Maine, where he received his early educational advantages. He afterwards attended school in Massachusetts and in 1913, on coming to Indiana, entered Purdue University. Before graduating he went to work in the steel mills at Gary, and was there until 1923. As a steel worker he contributed his bit to the winning of the war, since his work in the mills was considered more essential by the Government authorities than anything he could do as an enlisted man. Mr. Hayden in 1923 moved his family to South Bend and established the Morning Side Hotel. He has brought to this establishment a thoroughly business-like management and his personal popularity has also had much to do with its very unusual success.

Mr. Hayden is a thirty-second degree Scottish Rite Mason, is a member of Orak Temple of the Mystic Shrine at Hammond, has been active in the Rotary Club and the South Bend Chamber of Commerce. While a student in Purdue University he met and on June 24, 1913, married Miss Mary E. Adams. She was educated at Earlham College at Richmond, Indiana. They have three children: Louise, born in Gary, August 21, 1918; Charles, born March 13, 1921, at Gary; and Dorothy, born at South Bend, December 31, 1923.

CHARLES FREDERICK WEDEKIND is one of Logansport's prominent business men, has been active there for over a third of a century, and is manager and one of the owners of the Lake Maxinkuckee Ice & Coal Company, at 824 Michigan Avenue.

Mr. Wedekind was born in Logansport, April 27, 1863. His mother, Hannah Kerlin, was from New Jersey. His grandfather Wedekind was a native of Germany and settled at Richmond, Indiana, in 1840. He was a physician, and that was also the profession of Charles F. Wedekind's father.

Charles F. Wedekind was two years of age when his father died and from an early age he had to make his own way in the world. He had a common school education. He worked on a farm, but later returned to his native city and for thirty-seven years has been identified with the ice business. After many years as manager of the Lake Maxinkuckee Ice & Coal Company he acquired an interest in the business and is one of its owners. Mr. Wedekind is a Republican and a member of the Knights of Pythias.

He married Marian Skelton, who died in 1904, leaving three children. His second wife was Gertrude Puterbaugh, who passed away December 25, 1920. Mr. Wedekind has two daughters and one son by the first marriage: Earl F.; Alice, who married Homer Hawkens; and Eva, who married John Miller. To the second marriage was born a son, Charles J., who married Louise Clegg.

JAMES ROBERT DOTY, M. D. In the broad, difficult and interesting field of obstetrics and gynecology, few Indiana men of science are better or more favorably known for their numerous accomplishments than Dr. J. Robert Doty, of Gary. While he is one of the younger men of his calling, and has been located at Gary only since July, 1928, his training, natural ability and broad experience have been such as to give him high rank and standing and to place his name among those who are gaining fame in their chosen field of endeavor.

Doctor Doty was born at Willow Hill, Jasper County, Illinois, June 18, 1897, and is a son of S. O. and Maggie (Steele) Doty. Four generations of the family have been honored residents of the Willow Hill community, where they have contributed materially to the welfare and development of their locality and have furnished men who have been prominent in professional, business, agricultural and public affairs. Jeremiah Doty, the grandfather of Doctor Doty, was born in Ohio and was a child when taken to Illinois, where he engaged in agricultural pursuits, developed a valuable property and became one of his locality's substantial men.

S. O. Doty was born at Willow Hill, where he was reared, and was given excellent educational advantages. In addition to the public schools he attended McKendree College, at Lebanon, Illinois, and at the outset of his career adopted the profession of teaching. In 1911 he embarked in the dairy business at Daytona, Florida, and has continued in that line to the present, having met with honorable and well-merited success. Mr. Doty has always been a public-spirited man who has been willing to accept the responsibilities of good citizenship, and while residing in Illinois served for several terms in the capacity of township assessor. Mr. Doty married Maggie Steele, who was born in Ireland and was a child when brought to the United States by her parents, the family settling on a farm about twenty miles southeast of Willow Hill, Illinois. Reared on the home farm, she attended the country schools, following which she pursued a course at McKendree College, Lebanon, and then taught school for two years prior to her marriage. She died in 1903, in the faith of the Primitive Baptist Church, of which she had been a lifelong member, and was buried at Willow Hill. She and her husband were the parents of four children: Fleta E., J. Robert, Connie V. and Esther, the last named of whom died in infancy.

J. Robert Doty acquired his early education in the public schools in the vicinity of his birth and in Arkansas, completed his high school work at Daytona, Florida, and for two years was a student at Valparaiso (Indiana) University. In 1923 he took the degree of Bachelor of Science from the University of Chicago, where he had been enrolled as a member of the Students Army Training Corps during the World war, and his professional training was acquired at Rush Medical College, Chicago, from which famous institution he received the degree of Doctor of Medicine as a member of the class of 1926. During the following eighteen months he served as interne at the Rochester (New York) General Hospital, and for four months acted as resident physician to the Infants Summer Hospital of the same city, and his hospital training was rounded out with a year at the Presbyterian Hospital, Chicago. In these institutions he paid special attention to obstetrics and gynecology, and since locating at Gary, in July, 1928, he has specialized along these lines. He maintains well-appointed and commodious offices at 602 Broadway, and stands high in the estimation of his fellow practitioners and the general public. He is a member of the Lake County Medical Society, the Indiana State Medical Society and the American Medical Association. He is a member of the Commercial Club and Chamber of Commerce and the Phi Chi fraternity and secretary of the Gary Exchange Club, and during his college days was very active in the Young Men's Christian Association. He is a Republican in his political allegiance and a member of the Baptist Church.

At Gary, Indiana, June 18, 1920, Doctor Doty was united in marriage with Miss Gertrude R. Jenner, daughter of James B. and Amy (Pitkins) Jenner, Mr. Jenner having been a brick mason contractor at Gary for a number of years. He is a member of the Harrison Republican Club and the Westminster Presbyterian Church. Mrs. Doty was a member of the first class to graduate from the Froebel High School of Gary, in 1917, is active in the Presbyterian Church, and is widely known in musical circles, being one of Gary's talented vocalists. Doctor and Mrs. Doty are the parents of two sons: James Robert, Jr., born May 24, 1927, and George Richard, born April 11, 1930.

FLOYD HENRY BRETSCH. Two vocations, those of the attorney and the realty man, have occupied the chief interests of the life of Floyd H. Bretsch, who has gained not an inconsiderable fortune and a place of prominence in the professional and business world of Gary. At present, while he is giving his law practice all due attention, he is largely interested in a number of land development projects. During his career Mr. Bretsch has been the incumbent of a number of offices, in all of which he has displayed the possession of ability and conscientious devotion to duty.

Mr. Bretsch was born at Fishers Landing, Jefferson County, New York, November 22, 1878, and is a son of George W. and Sabrina (Robbins) Bretsch. His paternal grandfather, Henry Bretsch, was born in Germany, where he received a public school education, and, in young manhood, deciding that there were greater opportunities to be found in America than in the Fatherland, immigrated to the United States and took up his residence at Omar, New York, as a pioneer. There he continued to make his home during the remainder of his life, and he and his worthy wife were buried at Omar.

George W. Bretsch was born at Omar, New York, where he received his education in the public schools, and as a young man was engaged in agricultural operations. Subsequently he turned his attention to the general merchandise business, to which he gave his attention until 1890, and in that year embarked in the hotel business in Fishers Landing, New York, and later as proprietor of a hotel at Theresa, while two years later he opened a summer hotel at Fine View, New York. A few years prior to his death he disposed of his hotel interests and returned to the mercantile trade, in which he was engaged until his demise, May 26, 1928, when he was laid to rest in Oakwood Cemetery, Theresa, New York. Mr. Bretsch married on December 8

1875, Miss Sabrina Robbins, who was born and reared at Fishers Landing, New York, where she secured her education. She was a great home maker and home lover, and a woman who won and held the affection and esteem of her friends. She died March 19, 1926, and was buried in Oakwood Cemetery, Theresa. There were four children in the family: Clarence, a leading lawyer and deputy prosecuting attorney of Lake County, with offices at Gary; Floyd H., of this review; Albion, who died at the ago of two years; and Nellie Pearl, the wife of Harry E. Horner, of Syracuse, New York.

Floyd H. Bretsch attended the public schools at Fishers Landing and Theresa, New York, and began the study of law at the latter place. During the Spanish-American war he enlisted in Company E, Two Hundred and Third New York Volunteer Infantry, and upon receiving his honorable discharge returned to Theresa, where he was associated with his father in the hotel business, in the meantime continuing to prosecute his law studies. His advent in Gary occurred in 1919, and he continued as a law student until 1920, when he was admitted to the bar of Indiana and commenced practice in association with his brother. For two years he served as deputy prosecutor of Lake County, and in the meanwhile the brothers maintained their office at 690 Broadway, but since January 1, 1929, Floyd H. Bretsch has occupied offices at 504 Broadway, in the Gary State Bank Building, where he is now located. He has built up a large and lucrative practice, particularly in real estate law, and has appeared in much important litigation that has come before the courts. He belongs to the Indiana State Bar Association and the Gary Bar Association and occupies a high position in the esteem and respect of his fellow-practitioners, among whom he has established a reputation for integrity and high professional ethics. Of more recent years Mr. Bretsch has been largely interested in real estate development and has been identified with several large projects. He is also vice president and a member of the board of directors of the East Over Subdivision Company of Gary, which is another big project and one which is doing much to encourage the growth and development of the city Fraternally he is affiliated with Theresa (New York) Lodge No. 174, A. F. and A. M.; and B. P. O. Elks of Gary No. 1152. As a public-spirited citizen he has supported faithfully the work of the Gary Commercial Club and Chamber of Commerce. He likewise belongs to the Spanish-American War Veterans. He has practically only a good citizen's interest in politics, although a stanch Republican, and for two years served in the capacity of deputy prosecuting attorney of Lake County.

On September 14, 1925, Mr. Bretsch was united in marriage with Miss Grace McNab, of Gary. Mrs. Bretsch received her early schooling in the public schools of Hammond, Indiana, following which she applied herself to the study of law and was admitted to the Indiana bar in 1920, the same year as her husband. She has enjoyed an excellent practice, and at this time is court reporter of the Superior Court at Gary. She belongs to the Gary Bar Association and is active in the Business and Professional Women's Club.

RUFUS FOREST EAST. In insurance and loan circles of Gary the name of Rufus F. East has become increasingly well known with the passing of the last few years. Educated for the law he has never followed that calling save in the interest of his own business affairs, and his career has been a varied one. Ever since locating at Gary, in 1918, he has occupied a prominent place in civic circles and on several occasions, as at present, has been a candidate for important public offices.

Mr. East was born near Bloomington, Indiana, May 31, 1885, and is a son of William H. and Mary (Conder) East. He belongs to an old and honored family which settled in this country many years ago, becoming particularly known in North Carolina. In that state was born William H. East, who was brought as a child to Indiana by his parents and secured his preliminary educational training in the public schools. As a youth he applied himself to the study of law, was admitted to the bar, and for thirty years practiced in partnership with his brother, Hon. John R. East, who was for years a member of the Indiana State Legislature. This was one of the most prominent and successful law firms of Bloomington and took part in much litigation of importance that attracted widespread attention. Mr. East was a member of the Lake County Bar Association, the Indiana State Bar Association and the American Bar Association, and also belonged to numerous fraternal and social organizations. He was likewise active in civic affairs, and in his death, which occurred in 1915, Bloomington lost one of its most highly valued citizens. Mr. East married Mary Conder, who was born in White County, Indiana, where she was educated in the public schools. At the ripe age of seventy-one years she still resides at Bloomington, where she is active in the work of the Methodist Episcopal Church. There were seven children in the family: Austin, Daisy and Ethel, deceased; Ernest, of Marion, this state; Miss Ida, of Bloomington; Rufus F., of this review; and Earl, of Bloomington, who conducts an art store in partnership with his sister, Ida.

The public schools of Bloomington furnished Rufus F. East with his early education, and after he graduated from the high school, as a member of the class of 1904, attended the University of Indiana, where he pursued studies in both the literary and law departments. For twelve years he was a teacher in the high schools of Indiana, and then became manager of the Canadian branch of the Wayne Oil, Tank & Pump Company. In 1918 he located at Gary and for six years was a clerk in the employ of the Illinois Steel Company, resigning to become private secretary to Mayor R.

O. Johnson, a position which he held four years. In 1926 he entered the life insurance and mortgage loan business as representative of the People's Life Insurance Company, of Frankfort, Indiana, and has continued in the same line to the present, with constantly increasing success. He occupies well-appointed offices at 738 Broadway, and has a high standing in business circles. Mr. East is a Mason and member of the Loyal Order of Moose, and for years was active in the Knights of Pythias, the Independent Order of Odd Fellows and the Optimist Club. A stanch Republican in his political allegiance, in 1926 he made a strong race for the office of city treasurer and in 1930 became a candidate on his party's ticket for the State Legislature. He is a member of the First Methodist Episcopal Church, and for years was teacher of the boys' class in the Sunday School. In every way he has shown himself a dependable and reliable citizen.

At Decatur, Indiana, June 24, 1916, Mr. East was united in marriage with Miss Etta Brandyberry, a daughter of Simon and Elizabeth (Trim) Brandyberry, of Fort Wayne, Indiana, formerly of Decatur, where Mr. Brandyberry was for many years engaged successfully in the contracting business as a carpenter. Mrs. East was educated in the grade and high schools of Decatur, and for several years prior to her marriage was a public school teacher there and elsewhere in the state. She is a woman of superior intellect and has been helpfully active in the Central Baptist Church, the Order of the Eastern Star and several women's clubs. Mr. and Mrs. East are the parents of two sons: Robert (Bobby) and William (Billy), both of whom are students at the Horace Mann public school. The family resides in a pleasant and attractive home at 535 McKinley Street.

JAMES MURICE WHITE, M. D. Among the younger members of the medical profession of Lake County, one who has won prominence in his calling and popularity as a citizen is Dr. James M. White. Commencing his career as a school teacher, he subsequently attended medical college and received his degree, and since 1926 has made his headquarters at Gary, where he has well-appointed offices in the Gary State Bank Building. He has found the time to take an active part in community affairs and is president of the Gary Exchange Club.

Doctor White was born at Mount Ayr, Iowa, April 20, 1898, and is a son of Elmer E. and Anna (Bevington) White. His paternal grandfather, Hugh White, was born in Pennsylvania, and shortly after the close of the war between the states moved with his family to Ringgold County, Iowa, where he became a pioneer agriculturist. He was one of the substantial and highly esteemed citizens of his community and for several years served in the office of sheriff of Ringgold County. He and his wife are buried in the Mount Ayr (Iowa) Cemetery.

Elmer E. White was born in Pennsylvania and as a child was taken by his parents to Iowa, where he obtained a public school education. Mr. White was a merchant practically all of his life at Mount Ayr, although he also conducted a merchandise business at Guilford, Missouri, where he was a member of the school board and active in community affairs. He was a Mason and a member of the Independent Order of Odd Fellows, and throughout his life was a pillar of the Methodist Episcopal Church. He died in 1919 and was laid to rest in the cemetery at Mount Ayr. Mr. White married Miss Anna Bevington, who was born and reared at Mount Ayr, where she was educated in the public schools and for some years previous to her marriage was a teacher. Coming to Gary in 1926, with her son, Dr. James M. White, with whom she still lives, she has been active in the work of the Methodist Episcopal Church, the Order of the Eastern Star and the Gary Woman's Club. Three children were born to Mr. and Mrs. White: Orr B., engaged in the insurance business at Mount Ayr, who married Carrie Bruce and has four children, Doris, Anna and Arline and Maurine, twins; Dr. Hugh Carl, born May 30, 1889, a graduate Doctor of Dental Surgery of Drake University, class of 1912, who has done post-graduate work at Northwestern University, now engaged in an excellent practice at Gary, with offices with his brother in the Gary State Bank Building, married Miss Mildred Harper; and Dr. James M., of this review.

James M. White attended the public schools of Mount Ayr, Iowa, graduating from the high school with the class of 1916. He then spent one year at the Maryville (Missouri) State Teachers College, following which he was engaged in teaching school for three years at Guilford and Burlington Junction, Missouri, and then resumed his own educational training at the University of Chicago, where he received the degree of Bachelor of Science as a member of the class of 1922. He pursued his medical studies at Northwestern University Medical School, from which he was graduated as a member of the class of 1926, with the degree of Doctor of Medicine, then doing interne work at Harper Hospital, Herman Kiefer Hospital and the Children's Hospital, all of Detroit, Michigan. In the latter part of 1926 he settled at Gary, where he has been engaged in the general practice of medicine and surgery and has built up a large and lucrative professional business.

Doctor White has a splendidly equipped suite of offices in the Gary State Bank Building, 504 Broadway. For one and one-half years after his arrival he was associated in practice with Dr. A. A. Watts, but this partnership was dissolved and Doctor White now practices alone. He is a member of the staff of Mercy Hospital and secretary of the staff of the Methodist Hospital, and belongs to the Lake County Medical Society, the Indiana State Medical Society and the American Medical Association. He belongs to Guilford (Mis-

Morton Lamb

souri) Lodge No. 343, A. F. and A. M., the South Bend Consistory, thirty-second degree, the Phi Rho Sigma fraternity and the Pi Kappa Epsilon honor medical fraternity, is president of the Exchange Club and an active member of the Gary Commercial Club. Doctor White is a consistent Methodist and a Republican in politics.

HON. RALPH WIANT PROBST. The brilliant young prosecuting attorney of Noble County has made a name for himself that will long stand as a record one. In his office he has been ready to undertake the most unpopular prosecutions the moment he believed they were right, regardless of the personal consequence. He has not hesitated to attack guilt, in no matter how high a place it stood intrenched, and to bring down the guilty, no matter how powerful the influence that stood behind them. While, personally, he has many warm personal friends, he does not allow these bonds to influence him in any way, for he recognizes the fact that he is under obligation only to the law of the state and nation, and the light for his feet is his oath of office.

The birth of Ralph W. Probst occurred on a farm near Garrett, Keyser Township, DeKalb County, Indiana, May 24, 1900, and he is a son of George W. and Lydia (Wiant) Probst. The father was born on the same farm as his son, February 29, 1868. Growing to useful manhood on that farm, he conducted it for many years, but when he was elected county treasurer he moved to Auburn. His term of office covered the period from 1902 to 1906, inclusive, and at the termination of his term of office he removed to his farm near Garrett. There he resided until his death, which occurred in 1911. He was a son of Henry Probst, also a native of DeKalb County, born August 12, 1846, and he, too, served as treasurer of DeKalb County, his period in office being in the early eighties. It is somewhat remarkable that he succeeded his father, Charles Probst, a native of Pennsylvania. The Probst family has always stood very high in public esteem, and the fine homestead in DeKalb County affords wholesome recreation from professional cares to Attorney Probst, who makes superintending it his hobby. The mother of Attorney Probst was born in Butler Township, DeKalb County, Indiana, September 18, 1867, and she is now residing at Kendallville, Indiana, having survived her husband. She is a woman of superior mentality, and is vice chairman of the Noble County Democratic Woman's Association, as well as an active figure in the Indiana State Democratic Woman's Association. She and her husband had three children, namely: Henry Earl, who is a farmer; Wanda Rose, who is deceased; and Attorney Probst, who is the youngest.

Carefully educated, Attorney Probst completed his grade and high-school work at Garrett, and was graduated from the University of Indiana in 1925, since which time he has been engaged in the practice of law at Kendallville. In 1929 he was elected prosecuting attorney of Noble County, and, as already stated, he is proving himself one of the best and most fearless officials the county has ever had in the office. Two of his cases that became nationally known are the Lloyd Crench case of Columbia City, bank embezzler, and Joseph Saraceno case, bank robber of Columbia City, each of which were successfully prosecuted and resulted in convictions. He is a very active Democrat, has served as a justice of the peace, and is a member of the Allen Country Club and the Jefferson Club. He belongs to the Ancient Free and Accepted Masons, the Benevolent and Protective Order of Elks and the Knights of Pythias. The Methodist Protestant Church holds his membership, and he is regarded as one of its leaders.

On November 15, 1928, Mr. Probst was married to Miss Gertrude Bungartner, born near Avilla in Noble County. Mr. Probst is an able lawyer, a scholar and a gentleman, and there is no one who comprehends the ethics of his profession better than he. His reputation is widespread, not only over Noble and Whitley counties, which he represents, but his part of Indiana, and all who know him appreciate his many admirable characteristics.

MORTON LAMB, postmaster of the City of Kokomo, is a native of Howard County, and for many years was engaged in educational work. As a teacher his name is known and respected all over the county.

Mr. Lamb was born near Greentown, Howard County, Indiana, September 11, 1875. His parents, William and Artie (Silvers) Lamb, were also born in this section of Indiana, where the two families were pioneers. Mr. Lamb's mother is still living. His father, who died in 1913, was an old time boot and shoemaker. He did much of his work in the days when the making of boots and shoes was to satisfy individual patrons. It was long before the machinery for this work came into general use. Most men in those days wore boots, and every man had his particular fancy and taste, and William Lamb was a real artist in being able to satisfy the discriminating tastes of his clients. William Lamb was also a Union soldier, serving in Company I of the One Hundred Eighteenth Indiana Volunteers.

Morton Lamb grew up in eastern Howard County, attended local schools there and was still a very young man when he was put in charge of his first school as a teacher. His work as an educator continued over a period of twenty-three years. He taught in the common schools and in high schools and in the meantime was going on with his individual education. In 1908 he graduated from the Indiana State Normal School at Terre Haute. Mr. Lamb while engaged in teaching took a considerable interest in local affairs and politics as a Republican. In 1925 he was appointed deputy revenue collector, and served in that capacity until he became postmaster. His appointment to the office of postmaster at

Kokomo was given him by President Coolidge in 1926 and he was installed in office in March, 1927. Mr. Lamb is a member of the Friends or Quaker Church, his membership being with the church at Kokomo. He is affiliated with the Masonic fraternity, the Independent Order of Odd Fellows and the Knights of Pythias.

In 1895 he married Miss Erma Brown, of Howard County. The children of their marriage are Ross H., Ralph, Burcha, Mignon, Daniel, Charles and June. All are living except Daniel, who passed away in 1927.

WALTER ELBRIDGE HADLEY. Since 1918 the assistant general superintendent of the Gary Works of the Illinois Steel Company at Gary, Walter E. Hadley is one of the most capable and energetic officials of this great industry, of which he has become an essential integral part. His career, while somewhat varied in character, has been along the general line of his present activities, although his early training was such as to give him a somewhat broader knowledge than is possessed by many men who have confined their energies wholly to one line of endeavor. He is an able executive and devotes himself strictly to business, but finds time to take a helpful part in civic affairs, although he has never sought nor wished public office.

Mr. Hadley was born at Cambridge, Massachusetts, January 24, 1882, and is a son of Elbridge J. and Mary J. (Wood) Hadley. Elbridge J. Hadley, the first of the seventh generation of Hadleys in New England, was born at Charlestown, Massachusetts, and traces his ancestry far back in the history of this country. Among other famous members of this family may be noted Arthur Twining Hadley, the great American educator, president of Yale University; and James Hadley, the American philologist. Mr. Hadley's mother was related to the Rebecca nurse of old Salem (Massachusetts) witchcraft fame. In this connection a note or two pertaining to witchcraft may not be inapropos. It was first practiced in America in 1692, at Salem, where it broke out in the home of Mr. Parish, a minister. A company of girls had been in the habit of meeting a West Indian slave to study "black art." They suddenly began to act mysteriously, bark like dogs and scream at something unseen. An old Indian servant was accused of bewitching them, and the excitement spread and impeachments multiplied. A special court was formed to try the accused, and as a result the jails rapidly filled and many were condemned to death. It was unsafe to express a doubt of a prisoner's guilt and fifty-five persons suffered torture and twenty were executed. Common sense finally prevailed, but it was many years before many could be thoroughly convinced that witchcraft did not exist.

Elbridge J. Hadley received his education in the public schools of Charlestown, and at the outbreak of the war between the states enlisted as a private in the Sixteenth Regiment, Massachusetts Volunteer Infantry, with which he served until the close of the war. Returning to Cambridge, he engaged in the builders' supply business, in which he continued for many years, until his retirement, and became one of the substantial and highly respected men of his community. He was active in civic affairs and as a member of the Knights of Honor, and died in 1927, at the ripe age of eighty-five years, being buried in the cemetery at Cambridge. Mr. Hadley married Mary J. Wood, who was born in England and came to the United States as a child with her parents, who settled at Cambridge, where her father was engaged in the glass making business for many years. After the death of his wife, who was buried at Cambridge, Mr. Wood moved to St. Louis, Missouri, where his own death occurred. Mrs. Hadley was educated in the public schools of Cambridge, and for many years has been active in the work of the Methodist Episcopal Church. She still survives and is a resident of Randolph, Massachusetts. To Mr. and Mrs. Hadley there were born the following children: One who died in infancy; Camille, who also died in infancy; Miss Alice M., who resides with her mother at Randolph, Massachusetts; Adelaide E., now Mrs. Walter Rockwell, of Randolph; Charlotte A., now Mrs. Leon Crothers, of Randolph; and Walter E., of this review.

Walter E. Hadley acquired his education at Cambridge, where he was graduated from the manual training school in 1900, supplementing this by a course in the Massachusetts Institute of Technology, from which he was graduated in 1904. On leaving school he secured a position as assistant superintendent of blast furnaces of the National Tube Company, of McKeesport, Pennsylvania, and remained in that capacity for a period of seven years, when he joined the Tennessee Coal, Iron & Railroad Company and took up his headquarters at Ensley, Alabama, where he resided until 1916. In that year Mr. Hadley removed to Chicago, Illinois, where he established himself in a business of his own as president of the Trojan Electric Steel Company, but two years later disposed of his interests therein to come to Gary as assistant general superintendent of the Gary Works of the Illinois Steel Company, a position which he still occupies and in which, as noted, he has achieved marked accomplishments. Mr. Hadley has always been a public-spirited citizen, and during the World war was an active worker and generous contributor in behalf of the various drives. He is a member of the Commercial Club and Chamber of Commerce of Gary and the University Club. Politically he is a Republican, and his religious connection is with Christ Episcopal Church.

At Norwell, Massachusetts, September 10, 1913, Mr. Hadley was united in marriage with Miss Alice Faulkner, whose parents were residents of Lowell, Massachusetts, where her father was the owner of textile mills for many years and prominent as a citizen. Both parents are deceased and buried in the cemetery at Lowell. Mrs. Hadley was given her early education in public and private schools, following which she entered Smith College, at Northampton, Massachusetts, from which she was graduated as a member of the class of 1907. She has been very active in the various movements of Christ Episcopal Church, and is president of the Tri Kappa sorority and the Gary Service Club. To Mr. and Mrs. Hadley there have been born two children: Barbara, a graduate of Emerson High School, Gary, class of 1930; and Cornelia Kathryn, who is attending public school.

VERNON H. KRIDER was born on a farm in Washington Township, Elkhart, County, Indiana, July 13, 1876, son of Samuel L. and Leticia Jarvis Krider.

Samuel L. Krider was born in Lancaster County, Pennsylvania. He served in the Civil war, nine months in the infantry and three years in the cavalry, and came west and settled in Elkhart County, marrying Leticia Jarvis, then a school teacher at Dunlaps, Indiana.

Vernon H. Krider, the second in a family of four children, attended school at Bristol, Indiana, finishing the high school there in 1892, attended the high school at LaGrange, Indiana, during the winter of 1892 and 1893, graduating therefrom in 1893; studied medicine in 1894 and 1895, kept books for the Frisco Railway Company during the winter of 1896 and 1897 at Lebanon, Missouri, and taught school at Adamsville, Michigan, from 1897 to 1900. In the fall of 1899 Mr. Krider purchased a fruit farm south of Bristol and started in a small way in the nursery business, teaching in the schools of Middlebury Township during the winters of 1899, 1900, 1901 and 1902.

He served as trustee of Middlebury Township from 1909 until 1913 and from 1917 until 1925.

Mr. Krider was married to Erma M. Artley in 1902, and in 1903 purchased a farm in Middlebury Township, consisting of thirty-nine acres, and started the Krider Nurseries, as a mail order business, the first catalogue going out in the fall of 1903. In 1907 this was increased to one hundred acres and in 1922 another farm, of 128 acres, in the corporation of Middlebury was acquired, the company was incorporated, and the acreage increased to 225 acres. Another large farm was added in 1929, until the Krider Nurseries now consist of 420 acres in one block, located at Middlebury, Indiana, thirty miles east of South Bend, fourteen miles east of Elkhart, ten miles northeast of Goshen, ten miles south of White Pigeon and seventeen miles west of LaGrange.

This nursery at the present time is the largest and best equipped of any nursery between Cleveland and Chicago.

The Krider Nurseries sell direct both wholesale and retail, shipping stock annually into every state in the Union and many foreign countries. The Krider Nurseries, Inc., are members of the American Association of Nurserymen.

Vernon H. Krider is a member of the Knights of Pythias, Blue Lodge of Masons, and Knights Templar, also a member of the Saint Paul's Lutheran Church.

WALTER D. ELLIOTT has for many years been custodian of the Gen. Lew Wallace properties at Crawfordsville, including one of the most attractive shrines of Indiana literary people, General Wallace's Studio and Library, where that classic of American literature, "Ben Hur," was written.

Mr. Elliott was born in Greencastle, Indiana, June 20, 1856. His father, Dr. Dorcey O. Elliott, was a native of Maryland, and was one of the early settlers in Putnam County, Indiana, where for many years he practiced medicine and conducted a drug business in Greencastle. Doctor Elliott married Elizabeth Bagley, also a native of Maryland. She died in 1888 and his wife lived to be ninety-nine years of age. They had nine children, Pat B., Serving, Ann, Laura, Edward, Ehols, Walter D., Lula and Lawrence. All are now deceased except Pat B., who lives in Brookston, and Ann, wife of Howard Ehols, of Brazil, Indiana.

Walter D. Elliott was educated in the public schools of Greencastle. As a youth he clerked in a store, was in business for a number of years and for a time was city marshal of Brazil. He came to Crawfordsville in 1902, and at the request of General Wallace assumed charge of the Wallace properties. He has given a thoroughly businesslike administration and has also earned the good will of thousands of Indiana people who every year come to visit this literary shrine.

Mr. Elliott is a Democrat, is a member of the Christian Church and is affiliated with the Improved Order of Red Men and Loyal Order of Moose. He married, in 1880, Miss Bessie Rastry. They have a daughter, Zety, wife of Frank Stigler and living in Texas.

MISS MARY NEWLIN. The list of those to whose lot it falls to play a leading part in the dramas of national or civic life is comparatively short. Yet communities are made up of individuals, and the aggregate of achievements, no less than the sum total of human happiness, is made up of the deeds of those men and women whose primary aim through life is faithfully to perform the duty that comes nearest to hand. Individual influence upon human affairs will be considered potent or insignificant according to the standpoint from which it is viewed. However, there are some individuals whose labors are so generally accepted as being beneficial that their influence is never doubted, and this applies in the case of Miss Mary Newlin, township trustee of Calumet Township and one of Gary's most progressive and public-spirited citizens.

Miss Newlin was born at Homestead, Pennsylvania, and is a daughter of Robert S. and Hettie (Irwin) Newlin. Her grandfather was Richard Newlin, a native of Westmoreland County, Pennsylvania, of Quaker descent, who passed his life as an agriculturist and who, with his wife, is buried in the cemetery of the Quaker meeting-house near Millvale, Westmoreland County. Robert S. Newlin was born on his father's farm in Westmoreland County, Pennsylvania, where he received a country school education, and married, at Elizabeth, Pennsylvania, Hettie Irwin, who was born in Westmoreland County, of Scotch-Irish descent. Mr. Newlin was taught to be a mechanic in his youth and for some years was employed by the Clairton Steel Company, at Clairton, Pennsylvania, and later by the Illinois Steel Company, at Gary, and for years was with the Railway Spring Steel Company of Chicago Heights, Illinois. He moved with his family to Gary in 1907 and still makes this city his home. Mr. Newlin is a member of the local lodge of the Benevolent and Protective Order of Elks, which he joined at the time that body secured its charter, in 1907, and is one of the city's public-spirited and highly respected citizens. Mrs. Newlin was educated in the public schools of Irwin, Pennsylvania, and is a daughter of William and Charity (Saunders) Irwin, natives of Westmoreland County, where they are buried. Both sides of her family trace their ancestry back in this country to the sixteenth century, and both had representatives in the War of the American Revolution. Mrs. Newlin's parents were members of the United Presbyterian Church and she is a charter member of the First Presbyterian Church of Gary. Mr. and Mrs. Newlin had four daughters: Ruth, who died in infancy; Lucy, the wife of Carl Lehman, connected with the Illinois Steel Company, of Gary; Mrs. Alice Cothery, of Gary; and Miss Mary, of this review.

Mary Newlin attended the public schools of Clairton, Pennsylvania, and following her graduation from high school pursued a course at California State Normal, from which she was graduated as a member of the class of 1909. She later attended the Valparaiso University. For four years she taught school, two years each in Pennsylvania and the Froebel School, at Gary, and in 1915 became deputy township trustee under W. J. Williams, trustee of Calumet Township, a position which she held for eight years. In 1922 she was the successful candidate for the office of trustee of this township, assuming her duties in the spring of 1923 and was reelected for another term of four years, starting in 1927. She has discharged the duties of her office in a highly capable manner and has won the full confidence of the people of this enlightened and progressive community.

Miss Newlin is a charter member of the First Presbyterian Church of Gary. She is historian of the Pottawatomie Chapter, Daughters of the American Revolution, and a member of the Daughters of Veterans, an auxiliary of the Civil War Veterans, and of the Auxiliary of the Spanish-American War Veterans. She likewise belongs to Genesis Chapter of the Daughters of Rebekah, was for some years active in the Gary Woman's Club, and is a past president of the Lake County Tuberculosis Association. A woman of superior intellect and accomplishments, she is justly accounted one of Gary's valued and valuable citizens.

JAMES CLARENCE VANDERBUR. One of the signs of progress is the attention paid by local, state and federal authorities to the safeguarding of the foodstuffs of the people. Formerly there was but little protection, not only for the customer, but the honest dealer; the first buying blindly what was offered; the second having to meet the competition of those who, because of the inferior quality of their goods, could quote lower prices. Today, while there is still some dishonesty, the different laws are drastic, and the penalties for their violation heavy. However, even among dealers today there are differences, and, while some live up to the letter of the laws, there are others who take pleasure in rendering a better service, and carrying out the spirit as well. One of these first-class merchants of Kendallville who draws his large trade from the very best and most discriminating people of Noble County, James C. Vanderbur, has given such careful attention to details in his meat market, handling only "quality meats," that his store has become known all over this region as synonymous with the best in every respect.

James C. Vanderbur was born at Greensburg, Decatur County, Indiana, February 28, 1891, a son of Elijah and Nettie (Jackson) Vanderbur, natives of Decatur County, where the father was born April 26, 1866. For a number of years he was engaged in farming in Decatur County, but is now living retired. His father, Henry Vanderbur, was born in Pennsylvania, but came to Decatur County when only seventeen years old, and there he continued to reside the remainder of his life. The maternal grandfather of James C. Vanderbur, John W. Jackson, pioneered to Decatur County from Kentucky, and he, too, was one of the early farmers of that part of Indiana.

The eldest of eight children, James C. Vanderbur attended the district schools of his native county and Greensburg High School, but left the home farm when only sixteen years old to go to work in a meat market at Greensburg. His initial position was a lowly one, but he learned the business from the bottom up, and this in part accounts for his present success. He thoroughly understands, through personal experience, every phase of the work. In 1915 he entered the employ of Nelson Morris & Company, of Chicago, proprietors of the Union Live Stock Company, and remained with that great corporation until his enlistment for the World war. Going overseas with the Forty-second Division, A. E. F., he was division meat inspector, first with his division at the front for eight months, and then for two months held the same position at Coblenz, Germany, with the Army of Occupation. Returned to the United States, he received his

W. J. Golightly

honorable discharge at Camp Sherman, June 28, 1919. Mr. Vanderbur went back to Nelson Morris & Company, but was transferred from Chicago to Fort Wayne, Indiana, and made head of the sales department of the company's branch in the latter city, and he continued there until 1924. In that year he came to Kendallville, purchased the Hossinger Meat Market, which he has since operated under his own name. His market is equipped with modern appliances, and is admitted to be the finest in the northern part of Indiana. The first year he was in business his annual sales aggregated $78,000; in 1928 they were $110,000, and in 1929 they were still higher, the increase proving that he is receiving a constantly augmenting patronage.

Mr. Vanderbur belongs to the Benevolent and Protective Order of Elks, the Knights of Pythias, the Rotary Club, the Kendallville Country Club, the Chamber of Commerce and the American Legion. He makes a hobby of feeding cattle and has many head among the farmers of the county.

On September 2, 1920, Mr. Vanderbur married at Fort Wayne, Indiana, Miss Minnie Caroline Bill, a daughter of Jacob Bill, of that city. Mr. and Mrs. Vanderbur have no children. Their residence, one of the best at Kendallville, is one of the most desirable in the city, and here they entertain their many friends, for they are very hospitable and are never happier than when they have those dear to them gathered about them.

WILLIAM J. GOLIGHTLY was for thirty years superintendent of the Kokomo plant of the Pittsburgh Plate Glass Company. His total service in the glass making industry covered a period of fifty-five years. It was a service distinguished by much more than routine accomplishment or sound administrative work. He helped perfect the technic of glass making. He was in fact a master of the processes of glass making, and it was this mastery that gained for him such an eminent position in the industrial circles of America.

It was genius and the sheer force of character that enabled him to rise from poverty and lack of opportunity to a place of wealth, esteem and to be marked as one of Kokomo's most valued and valuable citizens. He was born April 4, 1860, at South Shields, England, which was the native town of his parents, Benjamin and Sarah (Tompkinson) Golightly. Benjamin Golightly from his income as a sailor could maintain his family only to the point of providing the necessities of existence, and when he was lost at sea William Joseph Golightly, then eight years of age, had to take upon his own shoulders the burden of supporting his mother. His schooling up to that time had been irregular and his subsequent education was largely the result of practical experience. He became a worker in a plate glass factory, and that determined his permanent vocation. Early in his employment in the plate glass trade he began experimenting in processes of plate glass manufacture and

eventually perfected a formula of his own that made him a particularly valuable man to the glass manufacturers. It was his technical knowledge that first brought him to the attention of American manufacturers and it was technical skill that kept him at the fore-front of the industry the rest of his life.

Mr. Golightly came to America in 1891, and was first employed as a plate glass maker in the casting hall of a plate glass factory at Charleroi, Pennsylvania. Later for a short time he was at Butler, Pennsylvania, and in 1892 came to Kokomo, where he was employed in a minor capacity in the Diamond Plate Glass Company of that city. Soon afterward he brought his family from England and in April, 1893, established his home at Kokomo. After two years he moved to Elwood for a year and spent about two years at Alexandria, being connected with hte plate glass plants in these Indiana towns, but in 1898 he returned to Kokomo to become assistant superintendent of the plant which in the meantime had been taken over by the Pittsburgh Plate Glass Company. In the following year the local superintendent, S. E. Clark, was transferred to Elwood and Mr. Golightly succeeded him as superintendent in 1899. As executive head of that plant, one of the two largest manufacturing industries of Kokomo, he continued until his death on November 4, 1929. During that time he contributed perhaps more notably than any other figure in the plate glass industry to the development of the business and more than any other man was responsible for the permanence of the plant as an asset of Kokomo. He became a recognized authority in his field. All his knowledge was the product of his own efforts. He possessed an alert and able mind, and his success was due to an indefatigable industry.

Kokomo citizens recall gratefully his special services in keeping the industry in the city. He did this largely through adapting and changing the local plant to be able to challenge competition from other plants both at home and abroad. It was while under his supervision that the Kokomo plant was equipped with gas engines, which at the time were considered the latest thing in the production of electric power. This change was made after the directors of the company had resolved to dismantle the Kokomo plant and Mr. Golightly was offered the superintendency of another plant in Missouri. He finally overcame opposition and the company backed his judgment by voting $5,000,000 at his disposal to rebuild the plant at Kokomo. Then, following the close of the World war, the entire system of gas engines was removed and the most up-to-date and efficient steam electrical power house in Indiana was constructed near the factory under his direction. The introduction of electrical power produced by steam turbines enormously increased the efficiency of his plant.

To quote a portion of an editorial tribute from the *Kokomo Tribune*, "William J. Golightly's service to Kokomo, however, did not lie alone in the fact that he preserved and successfully administered the plate glass industry here. His influence and worth were felt far outside the confines of the big plant whose operations he has supervised for three decades. He had become one of the most helpful and outstanding civic leaders and community workers—a man who in the last few years had contributed of personal efforts as much perhaps as any other one individual here to the various civic movements and public undertakings here that have added so greatly to the general progress and welfare of Kokomo.

"As the years gathered William J. Golightly mellowed and broadened. The aloofness of his earlier years—his disposition to attend strictly to his own affairs and mix not at all in community enterprises—wore away. In time he became a constant student of public needs, the most potent influence towards meeting them. He wished to measure up to the best standards of citizenship, and to that end dedicated all he had of constructive capacity—all he had of hand and head and heart.

"It is a fine record—one in which his family and friends and business associates can take fullest pride—one to which the city he served so well will do full honor, one which will be an example of shining citizenship in far distant days, one on which to bestow the best we have of gratitude and one to keep ever green with the laurel of affectionate memory."

Mr. Golightly had been elected president of the Kokomo Chamber of Commerce in 1925 and was given the honor of a second term in that office in 1926. For several years he was president of the Howard County chapter of the Red Cross, was a charter member of the Kiwanis Club, was a thirty-second degree Scottish Rite Mason, the B. P. O. Elks and Modern Woodmen of America. For many years he was a member of the vestry of St. Andrew's Episcopal Church and was a supporter of all civic enterprises. In addition to his responsibilities with the glass company he was a director of the Howard National Bank, director of the Hoosier Iron Works, stockholder in the Malleable Iron Works and a director of the Lincoln Acceptance Corporation.

In 1881, when he was twenty-one years of age, Mr. Golightly married Miss Isabella Adams Sims, and three of his children were born in England: The mother of his children passed away in 1916 and in 1918 he married Mrs. Harriet Ovens, of Kokomo.

The oldest of his children, Sarah, was born April 6, 1882, and was married in 1908 to Mr. John B. Duret, connected with the Kokomo plant of the Pittsburgh Plate Glass Company. Mr. and Mrs. Duret have three children, Mary Isabella, Sarah Elizabeth and John B.

The oldest son, Joseph Golightly, who is assistant superintendent of the Pittsburgh Plate Glass Company at Kokomo, was born in England November 18, 1883. He married, June 15, 1911, Miss Ada Woodward, of Kokomo, and they have five sons: James Sidney, born January 11, 1914; Joseph Richard, born October 26, 1915; Robert Edward, born May 10, 1917; George Lewis, born March 17, 1921; and Thomas Woodward, born November 19, 1930.

The third child, William Golightly, who is also an assistant superintendent in the Kokomo plant, was born in England June 21, 1889. He married Josephine Favre, of Kokomo. He has four children, William Joseph, John Frederick, Richard, and Joan.

During the residence in America four more children were born to Mr. and Mrs. Golightly: Miss Ethel; Sidney, who married Ruby Pierce, of Kokomo, and has three children, Sidney, Jr., Ralph and Geraldine; Miss Hilda; and Harry, who died in 1906, when five years of age.

DAVID H. BLUMENTHAL. Among the commercial establishments around the public square at Marion one of the most conspicuous is the Blumenthal Department Store on the west side. It is an establishment with an interesting history, and reflects more than the commercial growth of this city during a period of sixty odd years. It is a business of character as well as of material facilities and service equal to much larger cities. The foundation of the business was fair dealing, good merchandise, and these qualities earned the early patronage of the store and they have continued as vital factors in the steady growth of the business through all the years.

The founder of the business was Morris Blumenthal, a son of Morris Blumenthal, who was born and died in Germany. Morris Blumenthal, Jr., when nine years of age was sent to America on a sailing vessel. He was sent very much as an express package would be sent today. This precious human package was consigned to a sister, Mrs. Baer, then living at Peru, Indiana. He arrived safely, found a home with his sister, attended schools in that city and had his early training as an American citizen there. When he was seventeen years of age his first opportunity came to learn business as an employee of the Falk Clothing Store of Peru. Three years later he secured a better job in the store of Mr. Kahn of Shawneetown, Illinois.

He was living in Southern Illinois when the Civil war came on and was one of the first young men from that section to volunteer. He became a private in a regiment of Illinois cavalry, and served throughout the long struggle of four years between the North and the South, participating in many bloody engagements. During a furlough from the army in 1863 he visited his sister, Mrs. Baer, then living at Marion. During the furlough he bought the small clothing store conducted by his brother-in-law. After the purchase he rejoined his command at the front and continued his service as a brave and loyal soldier until the end. He gave serious attention to his work as a soldier, studied and prepared himself for leadership and before the war was over had won a commission as a second lieutenant.

On the restoration of peace the veteran soldier returned to Marion and resumed his new responsibilities as a merchant. A picture of Marion during the '60s and '70s would present a view of a small village of several hundred, the main street during the summer deep in dust and in winter and spring ankle deep in mud. There were no sidewalks, flag stones being laid irregularly and serving as stepping stones. It was here that Morris Blumenthal elected to begin his career as a merchant, full of energy, with a sound sense of commercial standards and principles, and with a confidence that won patronage. Those who knew him intimately agree that he was a genius as a merchant. He kept his business steadily growing and building, and eventually it was the largest store in the city.

After establishing his business on a substantial footing Morris Blumenthal made a trip to Rochester, New York, where he married Miss Ida Marks, a pretty dark-eyed young woman who remained a loving wife until his death on December 24, 1903. It was a fortunate marriage in every way, not least because of the fact that it brought to his business at Marion two of his wife's brothers. About 1872 David Marks bought an interest in the store, retaining it until 1880, when he sold out his to his brother Louis S. Marks, of Rochester, New York, who for three years had been a clerk in the store. After the death of Mr. Blumenthal the business was continued under the able leadership of Louis Marks and David H. Blumenthal. Another interest in the business was owned by Minnie Blumenthal, now the wife of Maurice Blumenthal, a New York attorney. Mrs. Morris Blumenthal, who died at the age of seventy-nine, had made her home for a number of years with her son David.

When Louis Marks entered the partnership he was only twenty-three years of age. He and his brother-in-law, Morris Brumenthal, were of rather contrasted types. Morris Blumenthal was very lively in his social intercourse, had a genius for friendship and had a large following of warm friends throughout this section of Indiana. Louis Marks on the other hand was somewhat reserved, though people esteemed him both for his manner and character. He was the soul of courtesy, and his habits were such that in combination with his business ability and resourcefulness he became a very valuable factor in the growth of the business. Mr. Marks after the death of Morris Brumenthal became the active head of the business, his junior associate being David H. Blumenthal. They added different departments until they had brought the business to the status of a complete department store, one of the largest in Eastern Indiana. Mr. Louis Marks, who married Miss Mattie Strauss, of Lyons, New York, passed away in June, 1922.

Since that date Mr. David H. Blumenthal, who was born at Marion, January 11, 1870, has had the full management of the business. Several years ago a disastrous fire damaged the building, which was owned by Mrs. Ida Blumenthal. Not long afterwards Mrs. Louis Marks sold her interest in the business to the Blumenthal heirs. They erected the new Blumenthal Block, a building which is regarded in every way as a distinct credit to the city. Under the leadership of David H. Blumenthal and his son Morris D. this business has continued to grow, and in its service caters to the better class of trade. It employs seventy-five sales people and is probably the chief establishment in maintaining Marion's reputation as one of the best retail centers in Indiana.

Mr. David H. Blumenthal married Miss Jenette New, of Wabash, Indiana. Mr. David Blumenthal is a Republican voter and has always shown a public spirited and generous attitude toward community affairs. He had the distinction of being the first and second president of the local Lions Club, and takes an active interest in the Marion Public Library Association, serving on its board of trustees and treasurer for two years and four years as president of the board. He was for four terms president of the City Planning Association. He is a member of the Masonic fraternity, Independent Order of Odd Fellows, B. P. O. Elks, Loyal Order of Moose and the Phi Delta Kappa fraternity. Mr. David Blumenthal has generously given his support to philanthropic and charitable enterprises of different kinds, but his hobby has been along the line of rescuing and salvaging the good in characters of men committed to penal institutions. In a large number of cases he has carried out personal investigations and when convinced of the fitness of some prisoner for parole he has worked to restore such a man to his family and regulated freedom. Mr. Blumenthal has not put forth these efforts as a sentimentalist, but rather as a hardheaded business man inspired by a sense of duty to humanity at large. So carefully has he estimated the worth of the individuals whom he has thus benefited that in only one out of a number of paroled prisoners has his faith and judgment been disappointed. All others have through their conduct shown their earnestness in becoming honest citizens.

SAMUEL C. MALSBARY. The Malsbary family has been in Tippecanoe County for three-quarters of a century. They have been known as prosperous farmers and stock men, also represented in various lines of business and professional life. Of this family Samuel C. Malsbary continues the family tradition as a practical farmer and stock man. His home is in Randolph Township, near Romney.

His great-grandfather was Job Malsbary, whose home was in New Jersey. He was born at Trenton, Monmouth County, that state. His children were Samuel, Isaac, William and Sarah. William Malsbary was born in Monmouth County, New Jersey, in March, 1794. He married Elizabeth Bowman. From New Jersey he went west to Hamilton County, Ohio, and took up Government land. He and his wife reared a large family of children, named as follows: Elizabeth A., Job, Samuel B., Linda M., John, Sarah, William, Mary, Alfred and Jasper.

The father of Samuel C. Malsbary was John N. Malsbary, who was born in New Jersey. Five of his brothers and sisters were natives of that state and three others were born in Ohio. Three of his brothers, Samuel, Alfred and Jasper, were soldiers in the Civil war. John Malsbary was born June 18, 1829, and died December 27, 1908. He was a boy when the family came west and he received most of his education in Hamilton County, Ohio. He learned the trade of wagon maker. In 1853 he settled in Montgomery County, Indiana, and in 1857 moved to Tippecanoe County, where he lived out his life. He married Martha Berry, and the children of that union were: Martha E., wife of C. M. Liston, Leahada and Ruth. The second wife of John Malsbary was Sarah Johnson. They were married June 19, 1856, and had nine children: Eliza, wife of John Coyle; Linda Jane, who married Robert A. Bonwell and had two children, named Earl J. and Opal E.; William F., deceased; Alfred; Samuel C.; John M., who married Alice McClamrock and had a son, James S.; Mary Addie, deceased; Sarah Elizabeth, widow of Edward Hayward; and the ninth child died in infancy. The parents of these children are buried in the Sugar Grove Cemetery in Jackson Township. The mother died April 24, 1880.

Alfred Malsbary has been well known in Tippecanoe County both as an educator and business man. He graduated from the Indiana State Normal at Terre Haute in 1889, is also a graduate of Indiana University, and he taught school in Montgomery and Tippecanoe counties, was superintendent at Thorntown eight years, and superintendent at Peru for three years. On leaving school work he entered the grain business and also conducted an independent telephone business at Monon and Francisville. At the same time he engaged in farming in Jasper County. He was in the grain business at New Richmond about five years, then at Remington, and in 1912 moved to Lafayette, which has since been the headquarters of his business affairs. He is a Scottish Rite Mason and Shriner, member of the Lafayette School Board, president of the Sunday School Association. Alfred Malsbary married in 1905 Meta Horner, daughter of E. W. and Alice (Malcolm) Horner. They have two children, Dorothy Maxine, a graduate of Purdue University, and Keith.

The late Edward Hayward, who married Sarah Elizabeth Malsbary, was born May 27, 1867, and died September 20, 1930. He was a son of Enoch and Margaret (Reed) Hayward. He was educated in the Terre Haute Normal School and Purdue University and taught for four years. At one time he was a township trustee. Mrs. Hayward's two children are William Blair and Edward Francis. The latter married Ruth Willis.

Samuel C. Malsbary was born at the old homestead in Jackson Township, Tippecanoe County, was educated in country schools, and his experience as a farmer has been converted into the practical training he has used for his mature career. He took the agricultural course at Purdue University, and then settled down to the practical profession of farming. He is well known as a breeder of pure bred cattle, and his stock has frequently won prizes. At one time he had a grand champion in his herd.

Mr. Malsbary married, February 14, 1895, Miss Mary Leaming, daughter of Henry and Martha (Fox) Leaming. The first of their children died in infancy. Mary is the wife of Dr. Robert Millis and has a son, Samuel Clark. George Dale Malsbary is a student in Purdue University.

Samuel C. Malsbary is ruling elder in the Presbyterian Church. He has been on the advisory board of his township and is a member of Henry Clay Lodge No. 288, Knights of Pythias.

HON. LINDLEY P. LITTLE, county attorney of Fountain County, has a long record of public service as an educator, lawyer and public official.

He was born in White County, Indiana, December 25, 1868, son of John S. and Martha J. (Pope) Little, his mother being a daughter of John Pope of North Carolina. His father was born in Ohio, followed the occupations of farming and carpenter work, and died when sixty-five years of age. Mr. L. P. Little has two sisters, Mattie and Hettie.

He acquired his early education in the schools of White and Fountain counties and at the National Normal University, Lebanon, Ohio, being dependent upon his own efforts, and earning his way through school. For seven years he was engaged in the work of teaching, then took up the study of law and since his admission to the bar has enjoyed a steadily increasing practice. He has been one of the respected and popular officials in the courthouse at Covington for many years. For eight consecutive years he was county attorney, after which there was an interval of three years when he was out of office. He is now serving his tenth year in that position and is president of the Fountain County Bar Association. Mr. Little is a staunch Republican and is a member of the Improved Order of Red Men and the Christian Church.

He married in Fountain County, April 2, 1890, Miss Myrtle Musgrove, daughter of Isaac Musgrove. She died in January, 1917. Seven children were born to their marriage. Goldie, the oldest, is a music and art teacher in the high school of Greenwood, Indiana. Frank H. and Earl both live at Indianapolis and are married. Leslie E., also of Indianapolis, is married and has two sons, named Leslie, Jr., and Harold Gene. Ralph S., a traveling salesman, is married and has two sons, Ralph K. and Gordon. Martha Elizabeth is married to Harry E. Spindler, of Clarion, Pennsylvania. Mildred Lucile is a student in Indiana University and for two successive

K. K. Firwek

years was president of the Alpha Delta Pi sorority.

CHARLES A. MARSHALL learned the trade of printer when a youth, and printing and publishing have constituted the chief business of his career. He is manager and publisher of the *Darlington Herald* in Montgomery County.

Mr. Marshall was born at Darlington, October 10, 1884. His father, Flavious H. Marshall, was also a native of Indiana and spent practically all his life at Darlington. For a number of years he was a farmer, and left the farm to go on the road as a traveling salesman. He was seventy years of age when he passed away in 1924. Flavious H. Marshall married Sarah A. Armstrong, daughter of William Armstrong, of a pioneer family of Indiana. Of their children three are living: Minnie E. Newman, of Saint Paul, who has a daughter, Charlotte; Edith Weesner, of Denver; and Charles A.

Charles A. Marshall had the advantages of the grade and high schools at Darlington, and his apprenticeship at the printer's trade followed immediately after his school work. He is a skillful printer, and has had experience in several other lines of business. In 1916 he bought the *Darlington Echo* from Gertrude Cook, changing the name to the *Herald*, and has made it a paper representative of the best interests of the community, carrying all the local news and furnishing a valuable medium of publicity.

Mr. Marshall married, June 1, 1927, Miss Pauline Cox, daughter of Denton T. Cox, of Darlington. Mr. Marshall's mother was a descendant of Revolutionary ancestors. His wife's grandfather, E. H. Cox, was a lieutenant in the Union army during the Civil war. Her brother, Byron Cox, was a soldier in the World war and the American Legion Post at Darlington was named in his memory.

Mr. Marshall is a Republican in politics and is a member of the State Editorial and the National Editorial Associations. His fraternal connections are with the Masonic fraternity and Knights of Pythias.

THOMAS M. CAMPBELL. No citizen of Darlington has received a higher degree of esteem, justly earned, than Thomas M. Campbell, who has lived in that locality most of his life. He has a distinction which has perhaps not been given to any other citizen of Indiana, in the fact that for forty-eight consecutive years he has been kept in the office of justice of the peace of his township.

Judge Campbell was born in Fountain County, Indiana, November 4, 1850, son of Thomas N. Campbell, a native of Hamilton County, Ohio, and a grandson of John T. Campbell, who came from Scotland. Thomas N. Campbell was a cooper and carpenter by trade. At the very outset of the Civil war he enlisted, and was with the colors four years, four months and sixteen days. He was in Company G of the Twentieth Indiana Volunteer Infantry. He fought in a number of battles, was once severely wounded, and his death, in 1872, was no doubt brought on by his hard service as a soldier. He married Sarah Grimes, a native of North Carolina, who passed away in 1884.

Thomas M. Campbell was the only child of his parents. He grew up and received his early school advantages in Fountain County, attended the Waveland Academy, and in 1866, when a boy of sixteen, began learning the trade of barber. For a number of years he carried on a confectionery business. Part of his time has been taken up with his duties as justice of the peace.

Judge Campbell has made both a hobby and a business of his interest in poultry growing. He has studied poultry and has an encyclopedic knowledge of the standards, the types and the points of excellence in many of the poultry breeds, and as a licensed poultry judge of the American Poultry Association has traveled all over the country both in the United States and Canada, attending poultry shows and exhibitions. Judge Campbell is one of Indiana's leading poultrymen, and for years has carried on a profitable business as a breeder of poultry, specializing in the White Langshans and the Golden and Silver Sebright Bantams.

In politics he is a Republican and is a member of the Knights of Pythias, the B. P. O. Elks. He married, December 30, 1879, Miss Sattie Hollingsworth. Her father was a Civil war soldier. Judge and Mrs. Campbell have four children. Miss Zola is at home. Catherine married Bryant Walkup, a World war veteran who died from wounds and shell shock received during the war, leaving one child, Ben Walkup. The daughter Ruby is the wife of Doctor McLeroy, a World war veteran who is still in France, in charge of a veteran's hospital, and they have one child, Billie. Laurence Campbell, of South Bend, enlisted in the United States Army before America got into the war and served until after the armistice.

KAZIMIR KARL FIWEK was born in Poland, March 2, 1881. He has been an American since he was twenty-one years of age, and his career at South Bend has brought him many prominent and successful relationships with the commercial and civic life of that city. He is one of the outstanding representatives of Polish-American citizenship there.

Mr. Fiwek is manager and principal owner of the Fiwek Brothers, retail hardware and furniture merchants at 501-503 South Carlisle Street. His father, Thomas Fiwek, died in Poland in August, 1919. After the death of his father, Kazimir returned to his native country and remained there eight months, then he brought his widowed mother and sister to South Bend, where they are both living, the mother being seventy-nine years of age.

Kazimir K. Fiwek was educated in Poland, had some training in practical lines of work there, and it was in June, 1902, that he arrived in South Bend. During the next eight years he was an employee in the plant of the

Singer Manufacturing Company. While working during the day he attended night school and made every possible effort to equip himself for a career in business lines. From 1910 to 1917 he was in the saloon business at South Bend and was proprietor of a restaurant from 1917 to 1923.

Mr. Fiwek in 1922 put up a substantial two-story building, 120 by 50 feet, on South Carlisle Street, and in this building in January, 1923, he and his brother Stanley opened a stock of hardware and furniture, which has since been known as the Fiwek Brothers Store, one of the most complete mercantile houses in the city in its line. In addition Mr. Fiwek is a director of the Peoples State Bank and for several years has conducted a private real estate business. He owns a farm in Olive Township, St. Joseph County.

Mr. Fiwek is first vice president of the Polish American Central Civic Club, is active in the Z. Balicki Falcons and other Polish organizations, and St. Adalbert's Polish Catholic Church.

He first married Miss Anne Gruzinski, who was born in Litwa, Lithuania, but was reared in South Bend. She passed away in February, 1921, leaving three children, Sophia Anna, Clement Kazimir and Eleanor Dorothy. In 1924 Mr. Fiwek married Mrs. Helen Repczynski, of South Bend.

KOKOMO PUBLIC LIBRARY. A library is an essential part of the educational facilities of any community, but in places where its service has been developed to a point where it realizes the greatest opportunities of a library it goes beyond the work of the schools and is in an important sense an educational extension to people of all the years. It is in fact a people's university.

One of the Indiana libraries that have attained to this degree of importance as a source of culture to the community is the Carnegie Public Library of Kokomo. The pioneers of Howard County were people of cultivated taste as well as possessed of sturdy qualities that enabled them to battle with the harsh circumstances of life on the frontier. In December, 1844, less than a year after the county government was organized, the commissioners reserved ten per cent from the sale of lands to establish a public library. The first trustees of that pioneer undertaking were William H. Grant, Franklin S. Price, Austin C. Sheets, David Foster, William Grant and John Vaughan. The first librarian to act in that capacity was Austin North. When James McCool was appointed librarian, in 1850, the members of the library board consisted of Reverend Mr. McDade, C. Richmond, N. R. Lindsay and Adam North.

The income of the library was only $100. The board ordered the librarian to purchase books and, true to library ethics, he spent all but fifty cents. Unfortunately the titles of the volumes are not a matter of present record. Private donations also augmented the books purchased by the board and another

auxiliary of the service in that early day was the McClure Library. Since Kokomo was not as accessible from all parts of the county as in modern years, the library board deemed it best to divide the book collection among the various townships. The disbursion of the collection had the unfortunate effect of decreasing an interest which would have been maintained with a large and permanent central collection.

The next stage of development was reached in 1883 when Mr. J. C. Leach became librarian. The board, then consisting of A. F. Armstrong, Dr. L. C. Johnson and W. E. Blacklidge, at that time levied a tax of one per cent on $100, and this provided an income making possible some real library development. After a short time the principal duties of librarian fell upon Mr. Leach's assistant, Mrs. Olive Moreland Shaw. Since the year 1900 there have been four librarians: Mrs. Eva Fitzgerald Rouch, now of Cleveland; Miss Edith Trimble Gotschell, of Vincennes; Mrs. Idabelle Ford Jones, of Fort Wayne; and Mrs. Dana H. Sollenberger. The earliest assistant was Mrs. Nora Dixon Moore, who still lives at Kokomo and who worked for Mr. Leach during the years of 1892-97. Other assistants have been Mrs. Lelah Trees Louthe, Mrs. Bertha Morgan Gregory, Mrs. Bernice Moon Donahue, Mrs. Ruth Miller Dotterer, Mrs. Aileen Scott Weiland, Mrs. Katherine Kelvie Beeching, Mrs. Ginevra Barngrover Mills, Mrs. Etta Jones, Miss Alice Cullnane, Miss Virginia Armstrong, Miss Edith Armstrong, Miss Ruth McKorkle, Miss Edith Nation, and Miss Dorothy Merrell.

The bronze tablet in the vestibule of the library gives the names of Louis Mehlig, Richard Ruddell and W. E. Blacklidge as members of the board from 1903 to 1905. It was this board that built the handsome and beautifully designed structure, of the Roman type of architecture, that now serves the purposes of the central library, located at Mulberry and Union streets. It was Mr. Blacklidge who originated the inscription over the entrance dedicating the library "to the people of Kokomo." For many years a library had been maintained by local taxation, and early in the present century Kokomo was one of the first of Indiana cities to benefit from the special philanthropy of Andrew Carnegie. Mr. Kautz, of Kokomo, made a journey to New York to interview Mr. Carnegie personally, and as a result of this visit $25,000 was given for the library building.

The library board have always consisted of the board of education together with the superintendent of schools. The present library board consists of Mr. J. A. Kautz, president, who has served twenty years; Mr. K. H. Rich, treasurer, who has also served a number of years; and Dr. J. C. Stone, secretary. The library at the present time contains a collection of over 48,000 volumes, which are circulated to over half the population of Kokomo. In line with the principles of making the library perform the functions of a people's university, the library staff have put at the disposal of the patrons their service in cooperating with the correspondents and extension courses of Indiana University and in providing special help and advice to groups or individuals undertaking other study courses. The Kokomo Library has a very fine special collection of books by Indianans and concerning Indiana and Indiana people.

Many libraries are not only the literary but also the art center of the community. This has been peculiarly true of the Kokomo Public Library. Many art exhibits have been held there, including an exhibit of the Indiana artists before these pictures were sent to the Indiana Building at the St. Louis World's Fair, two of the pictures remaining as a nucleus of the Kokomo art collection, having been bought by subscription during the exhibit. The Kokomo Library has also functioned as a meeting place for notable organizations. In the south club room the W. C. T. U. organization has met continuously for many years, and this was also the meeting place of the famous equal suffrage and literary club. More than two score organizations have their headquarters at the library building.

One of the interesting features of the Kokomo Library is its creed of service, which reads as follows:

"I am free.
I am without red tape.
I offer opportunity.
I am the great store-house of knowledge.
I have books for all tastes and needs and creeds.
I have numbers of the best newspapers and magazines.
I am clean and quiet.
I open my doors as a great people's university.
I open my doors as a great mental recreation ground for leisure hours.
I require few qualifications—Decency and Courtesy.
I am in the care of courteous attendants whose duty is to help you understand me.
I am
THE
PUBLIC
LIBRARY."

The present library staff consists of Mrs. Dana H. Sollenberger, Miss Leona Watne, Mrs. Hilda Ramseyer, Miss Adeline Garrard, Miss Julia Ulrich, Miss Carolyn Lawrence. Former staff members who are in other positions are Miss Edith Armstrong, librarian at the Kokomo High School, Miss Alice Cullnane, field secretary for the Alpha Omicron Pi, Miss Elizabeth Nation, in the Michigan University Library. Those who took training at Kokomo but have never been employed in the Kokomo Library are Miss Edith Switzer, now in the Logansport Library, Miss Faye Cantrell, assistant librarian at Butler University, and Miss Judith K. Sollenberger, instructor in the English department at DePauw University.

CHARLES MARCUS MACKAY is a native of Canada, learned telegraphy during his youth, and has had a very busy and important career in railroad service. He is now the local freight and ticket agent for the Pennsylvania Railway at Gary. In addition to his connections as one of the leading transportation officials of the city he has numerous connections with the organized business and social affairs of the community.

Mr. Mackay was born at Simcoe, Ontario, in Norfolk County, Canada, July 22, 1869. His grandfather was an Englishman by birth and a pioneer of Ontario. His parents were William M. and Miriam (McDonald) Mackay. His father spent the active years of his life as a merchant at Courtland, Ontario. He was postmaster there for forty years and also held the office of township treasurer. His later years were spent at Gary, Indiana, and his death on October 20, 1927, at the age of eighty-seven, was the result of drowning when he fell in the Calumet River. His wife died in 1919 and is buried at Courtland, Ontario, and his body was taken back and laid beside hers. Of their three children Nettie died when fourteen years old, and the only son is Charles M. The daughter Ethel is the widow of William Fleming, of Burgessville, Ontario, and she has a son, Paul, now eighteen years of age.

Charles M. Mackay received his early educational advantages in the grade and high schools of Courtland. After mastering the telegraphic art he became an operator with the Michigan Central Railway, in whose service he remained five years, and then for a time was operator at Woodstock, Canada, for the Canadian Pacific. In the spring of 1893 he accepted transfer to Ithaca, Michigan, where for two months he was operator for the Ann Arbor Railway Company. In April, 1893, nearly forty years ago, he came to Lake County, Indiana, and has continuously been in the service of the Pennsylvania Railway Company since that date. After a few days at Hobart he was sent to Hegewisch, Illinois, as freight clerk and operator, three months later was advanced to relief agent on the division, with headquarters at Plymouth, and on September 1, 1895, was made agent at Columbia City, Indiana. On September 1, 1899, he was transferred to Valparaiso as freight and ticket agent, and on February 12, 1912, came to Gary, where for a number of years he has been local freight and ticket agent for the Pennsylvania.

Mr. Mackay is a Knight Templar Mason, a member of the Lodge and Encampment and a past district deputy of the Independent Order of Odd Fellows, member of the Modern Woodmen of America, and was president in 1924-25 of the Lions Club. He votes as a Republican, for two years was a director of the Gary Chamber of Commerce, is a member of the Commercial Club and the Christian Science Church.

He married at Plymouth, Indiana, February 24, 1895, Miss Margaret Maish, daughter of Daniel and Belinda (Baker) Maish. Her father was a merchant at Jewett, Ohio, where he died. His widow later married a Mr. Richey, who died and is buried in Ohio. She moved with her family to Plymouth, Indiana, locating on a farm, and she died in Valparaiso about 1910. Mrs. Mackay attended grade and high schools at Plymouth. For two years she was second reader in the Christian Science Church at Valparaiso and is an active member of that church at Gary. Mr. and Mrs. Mackay had four children: Ruth, Blanche, Lee (who died when nineteen months old) and Miriam. Ruth is the wife of Fred A. Ring, a resident of Gary, and their two children are Beverly and Miriam. Blanche was married to Charles E. Petillon, sales manager for W. T. Alexander & Company of Chicago, with home at Gary, and they, too, have two children, Don and Lee. Miriam is the wife of Forde L. Bruce, a salesman with the Calumet Supply Company at Gary.

GEORGE M. WELLS, M. D., is well established in his professional work at Lafayette, being one of the professional men with offices in the Lafayette Life Building.

He is a native of Kentucky, born at Glasgow in Barren County, June 29, 1887. The Wells family came from England and first settled in Virginia. The family was represented by soldiers in the War of the Revolution and later in the Civil war. They settled in Barren County, Kentucky, about ninety years ago.

The father of Doctor Wells was Joshua C. Wells, a native of Kentucky and a farmer in that state. He married Emma Piercy, and they had a family of eight children.

Dr. George M. Wells was educated in Barren County, attended high school at Glasgow, and completed his medical training in Loyola University at Chicago. He was graduated in 1916 and for a brief period practiced his profession in his home county in Kentucky.

In May, 1918, he enlisted in the Army Medical Corps, was assigned duty on the examination board, was sent to New Haven, Connecticut, and was given special training at Yale University in tuberculosis. In September, 1919, he was honorably discharged, with the rank of first lieutenant.

Doctor Wells on January 1, 1920, began practice at Chalmers in White County, Indiana, and from there in the fall of 1922 moved to Lafayette. While living in White County he served as a member of the health board. He is well liked, a man of pleasing personality, public spirited and willing to do his share in civic undertakings.

Doctor Wells married Miss Ollie Spear, of Barren County, Kentucky. They have two children, Opal C., a student in Purdue University, and George M., Jr.

Doctor Wells was secretary of the Barren County Medical Society while in that state. He is a member of the Tippecanoe County, Indiana State and American Medical Associations, the American Legion, Lafayette Lodge No. 492 of the Masonic fraternity, and is a Republican and a Baptist.

PERRY F. WRIGHT is founder and owner of the Wright Machine Company at Lafayette, a business which he has carefully developed with standards of thorough workmanship and service that have brought a constant flow of orders for its products.

Mr. Wright is a native of Indiana, and has been identified with the electrical and machinery industries since boyhood. He was born in White County, April 18, 1886, son of Theodore J. Wright and a grandson of James Perry Wright, the latter of whom came to Indiana and settled in White County before the Civil war. He was a soldier in the Union army. By profession he was a lawyer and was also an inventor, his mechanical genius having been transmitted on to his grandson. He married Martha Louden. Theodore J. Wright was a carpenter by trade and later was in the grain business. He was born in Jasper County, Indiana, and married Katherine Cartmill, of Chillicothe, Ohio.

Perry F. Wright was one of their five children and was educated in White County, attending grade and high schools there. When seventeen years of age he became an employee of the Sterling Electric Company. He was with that organization eleven years and resigned as superintendent to establish a business of his own in the fall of 1913. The Wright Machine Company, with plant at 14 South Third Street in Lafayette, operates a general machine shop, and does a large amount of custom business, making special tools, the equipment of the plant and the personnel of experts being capable of turning out finished products in this line. Mr. Wright has sixteen men in his employ.

He is also a director of the Rush Manufacturing Company. During the World war he turned his plant over to the uses of the Government, handling contracts for war material. During the last month of the war he was in the East, at the Watervliet Arsenal.

Mr. Wright married Miss Anna L. Brice, a native of Hamilton, Ohio. They have three children: Donald P., a graduate of Purdue University, with the Bachelor of Science degree and now associated with the Wright Machine Company, and Glenn C. and Virginia, both in school.

W. LYNN AGNEW, prominent Hammond business man, was born in that city November 29, 1897, but grew up in South Dakota. He returned to Hammond about the time of the World war, and has been one of the energetic and public spirited citizens of the community.

His grandfather was Captain Agnew, a Union officer of the Civil war, who was born and reared in Ohio and for a number of years was a merchant at Winamac, Indiana. After retiring from business he lived in Chicago, where he died about 1902. His wife passed away in the same year and both are buried at Maywood, Chicago. William H. Agnew, father of W. Lynn, was born in Ohio, was a child when brought to Indiana and acquired

Joseph Eckman

his early education in public schools and the State Normal School. He taught for several years near Winamac. His brother was the late Nate L. Agnew, a former member of the Indiana State Senate, and who was a teacher in the law department of Valparaiso University. William H. Agnew moved to Hammond in 1890 and was connected with the Hammond Packing Company until the plant was burned in 1900. He then took his family to South Dakota, settled on a homestead and was engaged in ranching until his death at his home on White River, near Pierre, on March 9, 1918. He was laid to rest in a cemetery at Winamac, Indiana. William H. Agnew married Clara A. Walburn, who was born and reared at Nappanee, Indiana, and attended school there. She is an active member of the Baptist Church and the Eastern Star. The first wife of William H. Agnew was Mary Overmeyer, of Winamac, who died in 1880. She was the mother of three children: Chester W., of Gary, a plasterer contractor; John C., probate commissioner of the Superior Court at Hammond; and Catherine. By the second marriage there were also three children: Adelaide, wife of George Hensley, of Belleville, Illinois; Frances, Mrs. C. S. Connor, of Minneapolis; and W. Lynn.

W. Lynn Agnew attended school in South Dakota, graduating from the Vivian High School. He completed his education in Creighton University at Omaha, Nebraska, and in 1918, after the death of his father, returned to Hammond with his mother. For about a year he was with the American Steel Foundry Company and in 1919 entered the automobile business at Gary. In 1921 he returned to Hammond and became sales manager for the E. L. Shaver Company. In 1928 he bought out the Shaver business and changed the name to the Agnew Motor Company, dealer in Hudson and Essex cars, of which he is owner. This is one of the leading sales organizations in Hammond, and his company has beautiful show rooms and offices at 5311 Hohman Avenue.

Mr. Agnew is active in social and civic organizations, including the Chamber of Commerce. He is a member of McKinley Lodge No. 712, A. F. and A. M., Hammond Chapter No. 117, Royal Arch Masons, Hammond Commandery No. 4, Knights Templar, Orak Temple of the Mystic Shrine, is a member of the Shrine Club and the Shriners Drum and Bugle Corps. He was formerly active in the Kiwanis Club, is a member of the Woodmar Country Club, a Republican and is affiliated with the Presbyterian Church.

He married at Hammond, October 3, 1925, Miss Virgene Hammond, daughter of Frank and Nellie (DeBow) Hammond. Her father was a grandson of Thomas Hammond, founder of the Hammond Packing Company and of the City of Hammond. Frank Hammond is a banker, formerly was vice president of the First Trust & Savings Bank and is now president of the Calumet Building & Loan Association. Mrs. Agnew was educated in the

Hammond High School and Indiana State University. She is a Delta Gamma and Kappa Kappa Kappa and member of the Presbyterian Church. They have three children, Claire Gene, and twins named Muriel and Lynelle.

JOSEPH ECKMAN is one of the older living native sons of St. Joseph County. He was almost old enough to have some memory of the first railroad line that went through this county. The country he grew up in was only one stage removed from that of the earliest pioneer. During his lifetime he has witnessed a remarkable series of developments that have completely changed the City of South Bend, from a town with a few manufacturing industries until it has become one of the big industrial centers of America. Mr. Eckman's occupation has alyaws been that of a farmer, but the growth of South Bend gradually encroached on his farming land, and eventually he saw the fields that he cultivated for many seasons absorbed into one of the industrial divisions.

Mr. Eckman was born in Center Township, St. Joseph County, December 1, 1847. His father, William Eckman, was born near Dayton, Ohio, and married, in 1843, Catherine Ullry, also a native of Southwestern Ohio. They came to St. Joseph County in the early 1840s and William Eckman died in 1857. Catherine Eckman's parents, Joseph and Catherine (Cripe) Ullry, on coming to St. Joseph County first settled in Clay Township and later on a farm in Center Township.

Joseph Eckman grew up with his widowed mother on the old homestead in Center Township, and his early advantages were those of the district schools. He took up farming as an occupation, and in 1874, three years after his marriage, he bought a farm of a hundred acres in Portage Township. This land adjoined the City of South Bend on the South, lying west of South Michigan Street. Here he was engaged in the practice and routine of a farmer for over forty years, until the World war. The tremendous growth of South Bend eventually made his farm too valuable as suburban property to keep it any longer for agricultural production, and Mr. Eckman disposed of most of it after planning it as a subdivision, and it is now completely covered with fine homes. He still owns several lots on South Michigan Street. His own home is at the corner of South Michigan Street and Eckman Avenue. It is the house which he built when he bought the land, though it has been remodeled and completely modernized. He has retained the ground, and his property is one of the most attractive in the entire subdivision. Though much of his time has been taken up in recent years by his real estate activities, Mr. Eckman still regards himself as a farmer. He owns another tract of forty acres of land that, with the extension of the city limits, now adjoins the city line on the south.

Mr. Eckman has always cast his vote as a Republican. From 1901 to 1909 he served as a member of the Portage Township advisory committee. He is a charter member of the St. Joseph Valley Grange, is a member of the Masonic Lodge, and is a Methodist.

He married, October 12, 1871, in Portage Township, Miss Anna M. Van Buskirk. She was born in Ohio and was two years of age when her parents came to St. Joseph County, Indiana. Her parents, Thomas and Susannah (Kollar) Van Buskirk, were married at Dayton, Ohio, her mother having been born near that city, while her father was a native of Bedford County, Pennsylvania. Mr. and Mrs. Eckman have four children, all of whom live in South Bend: Etta R., wife of Charles Whitmore and the mother of three children, named Donald E., Winifred Jeanette and Anna Virginia; Bessie, the wife of Eli Krow; William Eckman, who married Marie Fanning; and Arthur J., who is married and has a son, Arthur J., Jr.

PETER L. BISHOP, a nonagenarian, one of the oldest residents of Jay County, is an interesting link connecting the modern age with the pioneer epoch. He went through all the experiences of the pioneers in clearing up the wilderness and developing farms while Indiana was still a state depending almost altogether on agriculture. In his personal experience he has witnessed the improvement of roads, the growth of towns and cities, great industrial centers, the extension of railroads and he was past fifty years of age when the first automobiles were seen on the streets of Portland.

Peter L. Bishop was born in Bear Creek Township, Jay County, May 12, 1839, son of Thomas and Frances A. (Hossick) Bishop. His parents were natives of Germany, his father born in Darmstadt and his mother in Wuertemberg. Thomas Bishop after coming to America lived in Pennsylvania three years and in 1836 entered 160 acres of land in Bear Creek Township of Jay County. He made the preliminary improvements and in 1837 his wife joined him and for eighteen months they lived in a log cabin which had only a dirt floor, after which a floor of puncheon was laid. Their cabin was one of an increasing number that marked isolated clearings in the dense woods that covered this section. Mrs. Thomas Bishop once got lost in these woods. She had gone out to look for the cows, and becoming bewildered she went on, getting farther and farther away. Reaching a stream of water, she took off her shoes and walked down the bed of the creek for a mile and a half, until she came in sight of the house of Samuel Huey, near Portland. In the meantime her husband had aroused some of his neighbors but the search was fruitless through the remainder of the day and night and it was on the following morning that his wife was found. She was a fine type of the pioneer woman, untiring in her work, and a very earnest Christian, being a member of the United Brethren Church, while her husband was of the German Reformed. She lived to be eighty-two years of age and he passed

away at the age of eighty-seven, at their old home in Bear Creek Township. They reared a large family of children: Mrs. Caroline Smith; Peter L.; Catherine, who married William Prillaman and went to the State of Washington; George W., who in 1862 enlisted as a private in Company C of the Eleventh Indiana Cavalry, was wounded at the battle of Franklin, Tennessee, and died at Jeffersonville, Indiana; Benjamin F., who made his home at Indianapolis; John V., who also established his home in the State of Washington and spent some time in the Klondyke gold fields; Mary M., who became the wife of John Kunkle, of North Dakota; and Adam D., who stayed on the old homestead.

Peter L. Bishop came to manhood with the experiences of a pioneer community. He attended school a few months each winter, one of the old-fashioned schools of Indiana, where the teaching was confined to the rudiments of knowledge. As soon as his strength permitted he was called into the fields and to the woods to assist his father in breaking the soil, in cutting the trees and in clearing away the underbrush, and that was his best training for the duties and responsibilities of manhood. Farming has constituted his occupation, and he was active until advanced years brought him the ease he so richly deserved. He has been a worthy representative of a very worthy and important family in this section of Eastern Indiana. His father on coming to Indiana was accompanied by two brothers, Peter and George Bishop. They traveled overland from Bucyrus, Ohio, with oxen and wagons. The only sister of the family, Sophia, married Jacob Marshall and lived out her life in Seneca County, Ohio.

Peter L. Bishop has always voted as a Democrat and has been an earnest church member. He is an elder and former superintendent of the Sunday School of the Lutheran Church.

In December, 1861, he married Miss M. J. Grigsby. She was also born in Bear Creek Township, daughter of James and Rheney A. (Morgan) Grigsby. Her parents were natives of Muskingum County, Ohio, and during their residence in Bear Creek Township improved a farm, and later, in 1884, moved to Missouri, where James Grigsby died in 1893, having survived his wife one year. Peter L. Bishop after his marriage moved to Butler County, Ohio, and for fourteen years lived in that state. In partnership with Jacob Emerick he embarked on an extensive program of fruit growing, planting fifty acres of peach trees and ten acres of strawberries and, being pioneers in the production of fruit, they profited. Mr. Bishop continued active in the business until he sold his interests and returned to Bear Creek Township, where he bought 120 acres of land and subsequently added forty acres of adjoining land, giving him a well proportioned farm, which he improved with a commodious residence and other buildings.

Peter L. Bishop is a well loved old resident of Jay County, as was also his wife. He is now past ninety-two. Mrs. Bishop died July

2, 1930. They had a family of five children. Their first child, Theresa, died in infancy. Their son George W. is deceased. The other children are Charles G., who looks after his father's affairs and cares for him in his declining days, Giles F. and Nina G. Nina is the wife of R. D. Wheat, a well known attorney at Portland, and former judge of the Jay Circuit Court.

Charles G. Bishop has for many years been an outstanding citizen of the Bryant locality of Jay County. He has been reelected for a second term as trustee of the township and has taught in the public schools of this county for a quarter of a century. He was postmaster at Bryant and was also elected twice to the office of trustee of his township several years ago. Charles G. Bishop married Lillie Rae Foss. She was born at Cardington, Ohio, in 1881, daughter of Isaac Foss, now deceased, and his wife, Mrs. Eva Foss, who lives at Visalia, California. Mrs. Charles G. Bishop passed away December 3, 1925. Her only son, Claude F., born in September, 1905, is a linotype operator at South Bend and married Miss Marjorie McKee, of Portland, daughter of E. A. McKee, former editor of the *Portland Sun*. This union resulted in incompatibility after three years and Claude F. Bishop subsequently married Violet Butler, of Fort Wayne, Indiana.

Nina G. Bishop, wife of R. D. Wheat, has one son, Cree, who is a chemist. He is married and lives in Detroit, Michigan. George W. Bishop, who married Tavia Penney, of Hamilton, Missouri, and both now deceased had a son, Lee R., who is a public accountant, married and lives in Detroit, also a daughter, Freda, who is married and lives in Richmond, Indiana. Her husband is a grocery man. Giles F. Bishop married Miss Maid Milligan, of Portland, Indiana. Both are still living in Dayton, Ohio. Giles F. was a street railway conductor for twelve years and for eighteen years was deputy auditor and afterwards deputy recorder of Montgomery County, Ohio. They have three sons, all of whom are high school and university graduates. All were present at the old homestead on May 12, 1931, to celebrate the grandfather's ninety-second anniversary. On this occasion Peter L. Bishop, the grandfather, said: "I think the socks, shirts, sweaters and slippers I have now will be all I'll need for several years yet." Long may he live.

SAMUEL P. HOLLINGSWORTH, a retired business man of Russiaville, Howard County, has lived in that community all his life and has been known as a man of quiet and efficient action, honest and reliable, and doing his duty by himself and his fellow men.

He was born in Honey Creek Township, Howard County, March 5, 1861, son of Isaac and Penina (Cosand) Hollingsworth. His father was born in Ohio and came to Indiana as early as 1837, being an early settler of Monroe Township, Howard County. Some of the logs of the cabin where he first lived are in a building on the old homestead and are now almost a hundred years old. Penina Cosand was born at Salem, Washington County, Indiana.

Samuel P. Hollingsworth received his early education in the old Lynn schoolhouse, about two miles east of Russiaville. For a short time he was a student at West Middleton. The first opportunity for regular work came to him in his father's saw mill. Later he and his brothers owned and operated the mill, and eventually Samuel P. Hollingsworth took over the business and continued it alone, making it the chief factor in his business career. He was in business until the spring of 1929.

Mr. Hollingsworth is a Republican, but has never sought or held any public office. Fraternally he is affiliated with Russiaville Lodge No. 82, A. F. and A. M., is a member of the Knights Templar Commandery at Kokomo, and belongs to Russiaville Lodge No. 195, Independent Order of Odd Fellows. Mr. Hollingsworth is a birthright Friend. All his life he has had membership in the Russiaville Church. The new Friends Church at Russiaville was recently erected in the same block in which is located Mr. Hollingsworth's home, one of the modern residences of the town.

These brief facts give a general sketch of Mr. Hollingsworth's business and community relationship. Forty odd years ago he was a well known figure in the world of sports as an expert and champion bicycle rider. As a youth he was interested in mechanics, and, like thousands of other boys, was enthusiastic over every new development in the field of transportation. He and his brother Benny had a little blacksmith shop, and among other work they fabricated there was a bicycle, which they not only designed but even made the tools for its construction. Most of the material that went into this primitive bicycle was wood. It was, of course, of the old high wheel or "ordinary" type. Mr. Hollingsworth developed a considerable degree of expertness in the use of the clumsy vehicle, practicing on a track which he built on his father's farm. With this machine he won his first race at Middlefork in Clinton County. Bicycling was a popular sport in those days, though comparatively few engaged in it, and it was considerably more hazardous than the bicycle racing of modern times. Mr. Hollingsworth won a good deal of prize money, and in this way he was able to acquire a more expensive model. He did his most famous racing on a high wheel model of the Columbia bicycle, made by the Pope Manufacturing Company of Boston, Massachusetts. In 1886 he was crowned world's champion cyclist, after establishing a record of 283 miles in twenty-four hours. The course over which he won his title and nationwide fame was from the Guyman house in Greenfield to the toll gate east of Cumberland, Maryland, part of the famous old National Road, which in the early years of the last century was laid out and built from Washington through Cumberland, Wheeling, Indianapolis and on west toward Saint Louis. By his racing and road work Mr. Hollingsworth did much to make bicycling popular, and within six or seven years after he had won his great race bicycling was as much a rage as twenty-years later was automobiling. For several years he toured the East, racing to new records against crack competitors. During all these eastern tours he carried the colors of the Indianapolis Athletic Club, which he helped organize in 1886. The sporting pages of the *Metropolitan Press* as well as all the periodicals devoted to bicycling and similar sports during the '80s devoted a great deal of space to Mr. Hollingsworth's fame and achievements. When he gave up racing he returned to the quiet routine of the home farm in Howard County and took over the management of his father's saw mill.

The Hollingsworth family is a very ancient one. The first mention of the name appears about 1022 A. D. near Motram, Northeastern Cheshire, England. The derivation is from Holly, a tree, while "worth" means a farm or place. The old Hollingsworth estate contained 620 acres and remained in the family from one generation to another until the death of Robert Hollingsworth in 1865. The name was transplanted to America by Valentine Hollingsworth, who came to this country with William Penn in 1684.

Samuel P. Hollingsworth married, May 2, 1888, Miss Lottie Haun, daughter of George and Frances Haun, of Russiaville. To their marriage were born five children, one of whom died in infancy. Tracy Hollingsworth, born March 19, 1889, is cashier of the First National Bank of Russiaville. Lucille, born September 27, 1891, married Raymond Redding, of Russiaville. Teddy, born January 1, 1902, is county superintendent of public highways. Karleen, the youngest, born January 30, 1906, is the wife of Leland Wright, of Russiaville.

REV. JOSEPH SIMON RYDER. The Catholic clergy numbers among its members men of broad education, religious enthusiasm and enlightened views, men whose example and teaching exercise an influence for morality that must be counted as one of the great factors in advancing any community. Not alone must a Catholic priest be a spiritual guide to his people, but he also must possess a large measure of the practicality which will help him to advise and teach in the ordinary events of life and protect the interests of his parish while also promoting its temporal affairs. Much, in fact, is demanded of those who choose the unselfish life of the Catholic priest. Not all, as in other walks of life, are fitted by Nature for the same sum of responsibility and perhaps few, under the same conditions, would have so rapidly advanced to the important position now occupied by Rev. Joseph S. Ryder, pastor of St. Mark's Catholic Church of Gary.

Father Ryder was born at Columbia City, Indiana, September 8, 1887, and is a son of Simon J. and Mary E. (Reardon) Ryder. His paternal grandfather, Daniel Ryder, was born in Ireland, where he received a public school education and was apprenticed to the shoe and bootmaker's trade, which he mastered in every particular. Feeling that greater opportunities awaited him in the United States, he set sail for this country, but on the way over the ship was wrecked. Mr. Ryder not only saved his own life, but that of a young boy, whom he later adopted and named Barney Ryder. Daniel Ryder became one of the pioneer residents of Walkerton, Indiana, where he established himself in business as a boot and shoe maker, and the excellence of his workmanship made him renowned for many miles around. Frequently his boots and shoes brought as high as twenty dollars a pair, which was a phenomenal price in those early days, but his customers always felt that they received full value for their money. He became known as one of the substantial citizens of his community, a man of high character and one who had the universal esteem of his fellow-men. He and his worthy wife died at Walkerton, where they were buried.

Simon J. Ryder was born near Walkerton, where he received a public school education, and as a young man commenced his career as a teacher. For a number of years he followed the vocation of an educator, but turned his attention later to railway matters, and for a number of years was superintendent of the Fort Wayne Traction Company at Fort Wayne and other points in the state. He retired some years ago and he and his wife now reside at Fort Wayne, where he is active in the Knights of Columbus and the Catholic Benevolent League. Mr. Ryder married Mary E. Reardon, who was born at Donaldson, Indiana, and educated in the public schools of Donaldson and Plymouth, Indiana. She is a daughter of James Reardon, who came to America from Ireland with his wife, Elizabeth (Leighton) Reardon, early pioneers of Northern Indiana. They passed away at Columbia City, Indiana, where they are buried. To Mr. and Mrs. Ryder there were born five children: one who died in infancy; Rev. Joseph S., of this review; Rev. S. Joachim, of St. John the Baptist Catholic Church, at Fort Wayne; George W., auditor for General Motors Corporation, Memphis, Tennessee; and C. Florian, who is connected with the First National Bank of Fort Wayne.

Rev. Joseph S. Ryder attended the Brothers' School at Fort Wayne, graduating as a member of the class of 1904. In September of that year he entered St. Francis Seminary, Milwaukee, Wisconsin, where he completed classical and philosophical courses, graduating in 1911. In September, 1911, he entered Mount St. Mary's Seminary, Cincinnati, Ohio, where he was ordained to the priesthood in July, 1914, was sent to Holy Angels parish, at Gary, as assistant to Father Jansen. On June 23, 1923, he was appointed pastor of St. Mark's Church, Gary, which pastorate he still retains. He is a fourth degree member of the Knights of Columbus, belongs to the Catholic Order of Forresters and also is identified with the Cressmore Country Club.

At 10:00 a. m., Sunday, July 31, 1927, the Rt. Rev. Bishop John Francis Noll dedicated the new St. Mark's Church, assisted by local clergy. The genesis of St. Mark's parish may be traced back to the establishment of one of the centers of the Catholic Instruction League, in the latter part of 1921. A flourishing community had gradually been built up south of the river and a goodly number of Catholic families was to be found in the outlying section of the city called the Glen Park district. About 300 Catholic children attended the Glen Park School and as the distance to their respective parishes was over four miles it was hardly to be expected that they could attend the parochial schools. Hence the necessity of establishing a means of imparting religious instruction to the children. A committee was formed with the Rev. J. B. DeVille, director of the League, and it was decided to purchase the old Lutheran Church, situated in Tolleston, which had been closed after the tragic death of the Reverend Kayser, who was murdered during the war. The church, with all its appurtenances, pews, altars, etc., was moved and placed on a foundation which had been built on one of four lots previously acquired at Thiray-ninth Avenue and Broadway. Later on the Rt. Rev. Bishop Alerding permitted the celebration of Holy Mass on Sunday and the structure was formally dedicated as St. Mark's Church, October 2, 1921, with the Rev. Father DeVille temporarily in charge. Two Masses were celebrated every Sunday. Church school was held in the basement. However, the parish grew so rapidly in numbers and importance that an appeal was made to the Bishop to appoint a regular pastor for the parish who could devote all of his time and energy to it, Father DeVille being burdened with the Italian parish and the Settlement House at that time. Accordingly Father Ryder was appointed in June, 1923.

Father Ryder worked faithfully and hard at his new task and the parishioners, who had long and favorably known him when assistant for nine years at Holy Angels Church, responded generously. An attractive rectory was built adjoining the church and Father Ryder moved into it in September, 1923. During his pastorate an addition was build to the old church, with the hope that it might supply the needs for some years to come. However, the community kept on growing by leaps and bounds, and the old church was found no longer adequate to accommodate the people. In 1921 a block of land had been acquired on Ridge Road as a location for a future church, and in 1925 it was definitely decided to build. Both pastor and people enthused over the project of carrying out the splendid plans which had been submitted by C. L. Wallace, architect, of Joliet, Illinois, and accepted, worked incessantly to carry them to completion, and today can look upon the beautiful edifice with justifiable pride and gratification. The school was opened in the following September with the Dominican Sisters in

charge, the Poor Hand Maids of Jesus Christ, who formerly had charge of the children, having played a prominent part in laying the foundation for the school and which became an integral part of the parish.

The church is designed in Italian style of architecture, built of brick, trimmed in stone, with a green tile roof. It is situated on the south side of the Ridge Road between Jackson and Monroe streets. The building is designed in what is known as a combination building, containing a church, school, assembly hall and gymnasium. The central portion of the building is used as a church, with a seating capacity of 750. On each side of the church there are three class rooms, six in all. Across the rear of the building is the assembly hall, provided with a stage which is fully equipped to take care of the school entertainments, under the hall is the gymnasium, and adjacent to the gymnasium is the kitchen, service pantry, stairway, corridors, boiler room, etc., while on the main floor are the toilet rooms, corridors, office, vestibules, etc. The main entrance to the church is through three large double doors which open into a commodious vestibule which opens directly into the church auditorium. The ceiling of the church is vaulted in pure Italian style, with ribs and groyns supported by pilasters surmounted by ornamental caps. The radiators are recessed into the side walls and directly above these are the stained-glass windows. The sanctuary is extra large and will accommodate about fifty priests; the main altar and the side altars occupy the usual positions as in all Catholic churches, and a priest's sacristy and a boys' sacristy, connected by an ambulatory, will give all the necessary accommodations to the priests and acolytes.

The entrances to the schools are back on the sides of the church but facing the front and placed about forty feet from the front, thus keeping the children away from the front of the building. Corridors six feet wide surround the church and the class rooms are located on these corridors, each room being standard size, properly lighted and ventilated. The hall is so arranged that it can be converted into class rooms, the gymnasium is so arranged that it can be converted into a hall, and the stairs are so fixed and the walls so arranged that a second story can be put on the hall, providing four extra class rooms, which will probably be ample for all time. Ample arrangements are made for the organ loft and gallery, and the entrance to the latter is through the two towers.

The church stands on an elevated position on the Ridge which is ten or twelve feet above the Ridge Road. The towers, which are exactly alike in design, occupy the two main corners of the church proper and offer an imposing sight to the passers-by on the Ridge Road. The church is placed well back from the front on an auxiliary street about fifty feet south of the Ridge Road. This affords easy access for automobiles and pedestrians and eliminates all steps except the few at the entrance. Between the Ridge Road and the auxiliary road is a beautiful terrace, and the trees which adorn the ridge offer a beautiful perspective, perhaps none in the United States affording a more picturesque view of a Catholic Church.

The building was designed in true Christian art, the three front doors symbolizing the Trinity, the Rose window and its twelve circles around the outside and the large window in the center symbolizing Christ and the twelve apostles, and the two large towers, exactly alike, symbolizing the divine and human nature of Our Blessed Lord, the crosses surmounting both being the standard of Christianity. The vaulted ceiling represents the dome of heaven, the steps leading up to the front symbolize penance, the vestibule, purgatory, the auditorium of the church, heaven, and the sanctuary, the seat of the beatific vision. Five large windows above the altar in the sanctuary piercing the dome over the sanctuary represent the five wounds of Our Lord which were such an offense that they pierced the dome of heaven. The twelve large pilasters on the sides of the church stand for the twelve apostles, or the pillars of the Church.

Ample space is provided for the confessionals and the baptistarium. In designing the building nothing was lost sight of to make it a complete parish unit. The building is 112x175 feet, exclusive of the steps, and the church auditorium is about thirty-seven feet high.

WILLIAM LYNN PARKINSON, who has made his mark as a lawyer and citizen at Lafayette, is a member of a very old and influential family of Western Indiana, his people having been extensive land owners, stock raisers, and closely associated with business affairs and politics.

Mr. Parkinson was born at Attica, Fountain County, Indiana, September 18, 1902. His grandfather was Harvey Edward Parkinson, who was born at Rensselaer in Jasper County, Indiana, where he owned an extensive farm and held the office of township trustee. Harvey Edward Parkinson was a son of William Kenton Parkinson, whose father, John Graham Parkinson, married Matilda Kenton, a daughter of Simon Kenton, the first settler at Rensselaer, who located there about 1830. Many members of the Parkinson family have been especially well known in Jasper County because of their interest in and success with the live stock industry, their farms having been the home of many herds of pure bred cattle.

William Henry Parkinson was born and reared in Jasper County, made a choice of the law as his profession, and has practiced both in Jasper and Tippecanoe counties. He was prosecuting attorney of Jasper County. At the age of forty-three he enlisted for service in the army during the World war and was commissioned a second lieutenant in the Tank Corps. He married Emma Linn.

William Lynn Parkinson attended school at Rensselaer, completing his high school education there. He was a student in Purdue University and began his law studies under his father and was qualified for practice when only eighteen years of age, but was not admitted to the bar until he had reached his twenty-first birthday, on September 25, 1923. Prior to that time he had handled the legal work in a number of cases. He is a Republican, the same brand of politics that distinguished his father and grandfather. He was appointed junior chairman of the Tippecanoe County central Republican committee.

Mr. Parkinson married Elsie Ruth Bausman, daughter of Charles C. Bausman and granddaughter of Andrew Bausman, who was a member of the Indiana State Legislature and a pioneer of Tippecanoe County, coming from Pennsylvania in the 1830s. Mr. and Mrs. Parkinson have one son, William L., Jr. Mr. Parkinson is a member of the Tippecanoe County and Indiana State Bar Associations, is affiliated with the B. P. O. Elks, Knights of Pythias, Fraternal Order of Eagles. In 1929 he was president of the Exchange Club and is now district governor of the Exchange Club. He has been much interested in the Phi Delta Kappa and was national president for 1927-28. Mr. Parkinson is an energetic, active and ambitious young attorney, and his attainments so far give promise of a notable career in his profession.

ESTEN GOODIN, clerk of the Circuit Court of Fountain County, has won a strong hold on the popular confidence and esteem of the people of the county during his four years in office.

Mr. Goodin was born in the picturesque hill country in the northern part of Parke County, Indiana, August 10, 1899. His grandfather, William Goodin, was a Union soldier in the Civil war and participated with Sherman in the march to the sea. John C. Goodin, father of Esten, was born in Fountain County and is still living on his farm there. He has been a man of influence in county politics and is a stanch Democrat. He married Eva Eleanor Sampson, daughter of Thomas Sampson. They had a family of five children. William Thomas, the oldest living child is a merchant at Indianapolis. Charles L. is a farmer at the old homestead in Fountain County and married June Weaver. Susie, the only daughter, is the wife of Otto Stonebaker, of Indianapolis, and has two children. Paul, the oldest child, died when but four years of age.

Esten Goodin grew up on a farm and attended public schools in Jackson Township, Fountain County, being two years old when his parents moved to this county. He graduated from grammar school and from the Wallace High School in 1918, after which he spent the summer months in the Central Normal College of Danville, Indiana, and also for a time was a student in the Normal School at Muncie. During the winter he was a teacher in the Wallace School, Jackson Town-

Everett R Ellerman

ship, beginning in the fall of 1918. Mr. Goodin was a school teacher until 1923 and then engaged in farming, the occupation which he had learned as a boy.

In 1926 he was elected on the Democratic ticket to the office of clerk of the Circuit Court of Fountain County and began his duties in that office in 1927. In 1930 he was reelected to the office of clerk of the Circuit Court by one of the largest majorities ever received by a Democrat in Fountain County. His home has been at Covington since he became clerk. Mr. Goodin is a member of Wallace Lodge No. 495, A. F. and A. M., is a member of the Royal Arch Chapter and Council at Crawfordsville, and of Gao Grotto at Danville, Illinois, and is a member of Tidal Lodge, Knights of Pythias of Covington.

EVERETT ROY ELLERMAN. The biographies appearing in this work, illustrating the growth and progress of the State of Indiana, are largely those of early settlers or of the founders of great business enterprises, or of leaders in public life or in professional vocations. Such men, through the circumstances of their coming, or the period of their connection with affairs, possess a factitious advantage quite apart from their individual and intrinsic characters. Those following them, while they may possess equal or greater endowments, are in a measure overshadowed by the veneration in which men hold their elders, and are quite submerged in the vaster multitudes who, in a large city or state, compete with one another for prominence, crowding every avenue of business and filling every opening for fame. Nevertheless the life of the state cannot be adequately illustrated without taking into account those who have taken up the work of their fathers and carried it on with success. To this younger generation belongs Everett R. Ellerman, who has demonstrated himself as being one of the most capable as well as successful young contractors and builders of Fort Wayne. Mr. Ellerman was born at Huntington, Huntington County, Indiana, July 26, 1897, and is a son of Charles J. and Dessie (Stezel) Ellerman. His father was born at Brookville, Indiana, February 4, 1873, and his mother at Huntington, this state, December 12, 1877, and both still are residents of Huntington. Of their three children, all of whom are living, Everett R. is the second in order of birth.

Everett R. Ellerman received his education in the public schools of Huntington and following his graduation from high school became identified with the contracting and building business. He was variously employed by large concerns until November 1, 1923, at which time he located permanently at Fort Wayne, establishing a business of his own, with offices at 4538 South Lafayette Street. Since then he has built up a large and important business, and has risen rapidly to the front rank among the younger members of his vocation. A number of the substantial structures of Fort Wayne give evidence of his expert workmanship, and among the residences and commercial structures which have been constructed by him many have been built according to plans drawn by himself, for he makes a hobby of drawing and possesses considerable ability along architectural lines. Fraternally Mr. Ellerman is a member of the local Blue Lodge of Masonry, and he also belongs to the Fort Wayne Kiwanis Club. He is also a member of the Chamber of Commerce.

On April 28, 1917, at Adrian, Michigan, Mr. Ellerman was united in marriage with Miss Mabel L. Lindsay, who was born at Van Buren, La Grange County, Indiana, a daughter of Stephen J. and Maria (Garbet) Lindsay. Mr. Lindsay, who was born near Kokomo, Howard County, Indiana, is deceased. Mrs. Lindsay, a native of Tipton County, this state, resides at Kokomo. Mr. and Mrs. Ellerman are the parents of three children: Mary Maxine, born May 17, 1921; Charlotte June, born October 6, 1922; and Betty Rose, born March 25, 1928. Mr. Ellerman is the owner of an attractive home at 4538 South Lafayette Stret.

ANTONIO GIORGI, M. D. There is no profession to which men devote themselves more dignified in its ethics or more reasonably helpful to the world than that of medicine. Similar claims are made by the church and by the law, but they, while essentially true enough, are based on other foundations. The healing art demands of its real followers that natural reverence for the dignity of the human body that commands the exercise of all the skill that years of study and training have brought to them to cure its ills. Their scientific discoveries have not only eased the bed of former torture but have found the cure for almost every bodily affliction. Justly is this noble profession in the forefront. Methods may differ, systems may not be quite alike, and personality counts for much, but the aim and principle remain the same. Among the members of the medical profession well known in Lake County is Dr. Antonio Giorgi, whose skill and faithfulness, together with his determined hopefulness and cheerfulness, have made his presence valued in many households during the last twenty-one years, which period has covered his residence at Gary.

Doctor Giorgi was born in the City of Rome, Italy, March 28, 1861, and is a son of Joseph and Signiati (Antonio) Giorgi. Joseph Giorgi was a flour manufacturer and miller of Rome during his entire life and a man of high character and business standing. He died in March, 1880, his widow surviving him until 1883, and both are buried in a Catholic cemetery at Rome. There were seven children in the family: Two who died in infancy; Phillip, who died at Rome in 1927; Sebastian, who died in 1919 at Rome; Catherine, who died in 1926 at Rome; Mrs. Elizabeth Pelle, who resides at Rome; and Dr. Antonio, of this review.

From the Guido Pitoni Heraldic Library, 3 Walnut Street, Rochester, New York, it has been possible to draw the following interesting data concerning the Giorgi family, whose coat-of-arms still exists in the great collection of Crollalanza at the Heraldic Library.

The Giorgi family, which in ancient times bore also the name of Zorzi, originated from a Chevalier of Moravia (Austria) who established himself in the City of Venice, Italy, and who acquired dominion of several castles in the territorial area of the cities of Pavia and Placenza. With the passing of the years different branches of this ancient family settled from north to south in the Italian peninsula, where they still flourish. The family has produced many illustrious personages, among whom the following are worthy of special mention: Bernard Giorgi, who was a Ventian senator and one of the three reformators of the City of Padua; Marino Giorgi, who was the fiftieth Doge of the Republic of Venice, as the successor of Peter Gradenigo, in 1911; six members of the family surname were procurators of St. Mark's in Venice; several were Bishops of the cities of Bresci and Piacenza; one, Ottavian Giorgi, was captain of justice in the City of Siena; Ippolito Giorgi was doctor and professor of rights in the University of Ferrara in 1751; one, Cesar Giorgi, of the same city, was also a doctor, as well as counsellor of the second order, in 1787; Alexander Giorgi, abbot, of Venice, was literate in about 1770; one, Anthony Augustine Giorgi, of St. Mauro of Romagna, was Augustinian and Orientalist in 1790; Domenick Giorgi was achaeologist in Rome in 1746; one, George Giorgi, of Florence, was a celebrated jurist and counsellor of the state and later became senator, in 1792; Iacop Giorgi was a famous painter of Florence in the seventeenth century; Ignatius Giorgi, of Rome, was the chief librarian in the Casanatense Library; Louis Giorgi, of Luca, was a celebrated engraver of the past century; and Paul Giorgi is literate of the present time. Two branches of the Giorgi family belong to the Italian nobility, and, as before stated, the coat-of-arms is to be found extant in the Heraldic Library.

Antonio Giorgi attended a seminary at Rome, from which he was graduated in 1881, and after further preparation entered the famous Pavia University, from which he received the degree of Doctor of Medicine as a member of the class of 1891. From 1891 until 1903 he practiced medicine and surgery in his native city with Professor Doctor Baccelli, and in the latter year came to the United States and settled at Utica, New York, where he formed a partnership with Doctor Harrer, with whom he carried on his calling in that city until 1907, at which time he moved to Canton, Ohio. In December, 1909, he took up his permanent residence at Gary, where he has since been in the enjoyment of a large and profitable general practice of medicine and surgery. In 1914 Doctor Giorgi conceived and carried through the idea of the establishment of a private hospital, the St. Antonio Hospital, of Gary, located at 1837 Jefferson Street, which has been developed into a modern institution with accommodations for fifty patients. He is the sole owner of this hosptal, with seven gradute nurses in attendance, and from fourteen to sixteen skilled physicians and surgeons on the staff, with every conceivable appliance for the convenience and cure of those confined. Doctor Giorgi is a man of great and extensive experience, who keeps fully abreast of all modern advancements and spends much of his time in personal research and investigation. He has done much post-graduate work, has attended numerous lectures and clinics, and is a member of the American Medical Association, the Indiana State Medical Society, the Tri-State Medical Association and the Lake County Medical Society. He belongs to the Knights of Pythias and the Roosevelt Club and for some years was active in the Commercial Club and Chamber of Commerce of Gary. A stanch Republican in political allegiance, his only public office has been that of health officer, which he filled from 1926 to 1930. He belongs to the Roman Catholic Church.

On September 3, 1892, at Rome, Italy, Doctor Giorgi was united in marriage with Miss Victoria Anaclerio, daughter of Nicola and Angela (Giannini) Anaclerio, the former of whom was colonel of a regiment in the Italian army and for many years prominent in Government and army affairs in Italy. Both parents are now deceased and buried at Rome. Mrs. Giorgi received the equivalent of a normal school education in Italy, where she also attended Victoria Colonna, and for three years prior to her marriage was a teacher in the public schools. She was very active in church and charitable work at Gary, where she died August 30, 1928, and was buried in Calvary Cemetery. To Doctor and Mrs. Giorgi there were born five children: One who died in infancy; Antoinetta, now Mrs. Dr. Sirianni, of Milwaukee, Wisconsin; Joe, a merchant tailor of Chicago, Illinois; Angelina, now Mrs. Del Pianto, of Rome, Italy; and Paul, an attorney of Gary, who married Miss Le Bue, of Chicago, and has two sons, Antonio and Andrew.

MORRIS CHUDOM. Among the most successful and reliable practitioners at the Gary bar is Morris Chudom, a member of the firm of Moore, Long, Chudom & Johnson, who is likewise widely known in business and fraternal circles. He is a man of settled purpose, firm convictions and practical views, whether as an attorney or citizen, and has, therefore, advanced steadily to a lofty and substantial professional position, having been effective also in the furtherance of the projects which have been advanced by good citizens of modern tendencies.

Mr. Chudom was born at Poltava, Russia, July 23, 1891, and is a son of Jacob and Bertha (Leviant) Chudom. Jacob Chudom was born in Russia, where he received an excellent educational training and was graduated from the University of Petrograd at the age of twenty-three years. He immediately entered upon the practice of his calling, in which he has been engaged ever since, and still continues to carry on the business of a large and important clientage, although he has reached the age of seventy-three years. Mrs. Chudom also survives and both she and her husband are active in the community life in their part of Russia. There were nine children in the family: Abraham, now a commercial artist of Toronto, Canada; Samuel, a banker of Russia; Morris, of this review; Maurice, a commercial artist of Chicago; Dr. Wolf, a practicing physician and surgeon of Russia; Dr. Peter, also a physician and surgeon, who died in 1922; Anna, now Mrs. Sokal, of Russia; Miss Vivian, a high school teacher of Russia; and Leona, of Russia.

Morris Chudom attended the public and high schools of Russia and the art school at Kiev, and in 1912 immigrated to the United States and attended Cooper Institute, or Cooper Union College, New York City, and the New York University Law School. In 1918 he entered the United States Army and was in the training camp at Camp Upton, New York, as a member of the Seventy-first Regiment, recruited from New York City, at the time of the signing of the armistice. He was honorably discharged in 1919 and at that time made use of his knowledge of art to engage in commercial drawing work at New York City. In 1921 he removed to Chicago, where he remained one year and in 1922 went to Indiana Harbor, where he opened a photographic studio, which he conducted for three years. In 1925 he settled permanently at Gary, where he engaged in the practice of law in partnership with John H. Haller for two and one-half years, and then formed a connection with Robert H. Moore. This continued until September 1, 1930, when Harry Long and City Attorney Rosswell B. Johnson joined the firm, which is now known as Moore, Long, Chudom & Johnson and occupies commodious offices on the eighth floor of the Gary State Bank Building. Mr. Chudom has been one of the busy lawyers of Gary, and among the numerous and interesting cases which he has conducted to favorable conclusion it would be difficult to specialize. It may suffice to say that he is thoroughly grounded in principles, precedents and court procedure and possesses innate and acquired ability for one of the most difficult and intricate of the learned callings. He is a member of the Lake County Bar Association, the Indiana State Bar Association and the American Bar Association. He has been active in Masonry as a member of Indiana Harbor Lodge No. 686, A. F. and A. M., and belongs to the Order of B'nai B'rith and Gary Memorial Post No. 17, American Legion. Politically he is a Republican, but thus far in his career has found no time to engage actively in political affairs, although he has always been a willing and constructive supporter of all commendable civic movements.

At Chicago, Illinois, December 28, 1922, Mr. Chudom was united in marriage with Miss Katherine Logan, a daughter of Morris and Iris Logan, the former of whom was for years a merchant of Russia and died several years ago, while Mrs. Logan passed away in 1925, both being buried in Russia. Mrs. Chudom was educated in Russia and in the grade and high schools of Chicago, having come to the United States when about twelve years of age. She is active in the Jewish Hadassah and the Woman's Circle.

JOHN ADAM NOLDE. While John Adam Nolde has been a resident of Gary only since 1928, he has already become a leading figure in business circles of this thriving industrial city, where he is the owner and operator of the Dunes Tire Company. From the time that he left college, with the exception of a short period spent in the army during the World war, he has been connected with the automobile tire business, and at present, in addition to his main business at Gary, is operating flourishing branches at Hammond and Indiana Harbor.

Mr. Nolde was born at St. Louis, Missouri, December 17, 1897, and is a son of J. T. and Elsie M. (Bickel) Nolde. The Nolde family has been known at St. Louis for many years, the name having been established at that city by Mr. Nolde's great-grandfather, a native of Germany, who was a pioneer business man. John Nolde, the grandfather of John Adam Nolde, was born at St. Louis, where he was reared and received a public school education, and for many years was a well-known wholesale cigar dealer. J. T. Nolde, father of John Adam Nolde, was also born at St. Louis, and was educated in the public schools. A man of great business sagacity and executive capacity, he organized and for many years operated the J. T. Nolde Dental Supply Company, of which he was still president at the time of his death, March 15, 1914. He was also president of the Chippewa Bank, and as a public-spirited citizen was one of the prime movers in the Million Population Club, of which he was president. He was likewise active in politics, was a Mason and attended the Methodist Episcopal Church. Mr. Nolde married Miss Elsie M. Bickel, who was born at St. Louis and educated in the public schools, and is still a resident of the Mound City and active in the work of the Methodist Episcopal Church. To Mr. and Mrs. Nolde there were born two children: Elsie, who is now Mrs. Glen A. Brown, of St. Louis; and John Adam.

John Adam Nolde attended the public schools of St. Louis, where he was graduated from high school as a member of the class of 1915. He then attended Washington College, and on leaving that institution secured employment with the United States Tire & Rubber Company, being thus engaged when called for service in the United States Army during the World war. He joined the Aviation Corps, and was honorably discharged December 11, 1918. At that time he returned to his position as traveling salesman for the United States Tire & Rubber Company, with which concern he remained until 1924, when he joined the Goodyear Tire & Rubber Company, but remained only one year, when he embarked in the retail tire business at Columbus, Ohio, and continued therein for three years. On December 11, 1928, Mr. Nolde disposed of his Columbus interests and came to Gary, where he purchased the Dunes Tire Company, of which he has since been the proprietor. This he has built up to important proportions, and now has successful branches at Indiana Harbor and Hammond. Mr. Nolde is a Master Mason and a member of the Benevolent and Protective Order of Elks and the Gary Commercial Club and Chamber of Commerce, and was formerly a member of the Lions Club, at Columbus. He is a Republican in his political affiliation and a member of the Methodist Episcopal Church.

At Memphis, Tennessee, January 28, 1920, Mr. Nolde was united in marriage with Miss Annie Lee Johnson, daughter of W. A. Johnson, who for many years has been a prominent farmer, stock raiser and realtor of Jonesboro, Arkansas. Mrs. Nolde was educated in the public schools of Arkansas, where she graduated from high school, and is active in the work of the Methodist Episcopal Church.

FLOYD B. COTTRILL is successfully engaged in the coal business at Hartford City, Blackford County, where he conducts his substantial and prosperous enterprise under the title of American Coal Company. His well equipped yards occupy an area of one-half block, on West Franklin Street, with office at 1017 on that thoroughfare, and he specializes in the handling of high-grade Kentucky and West Virginia coal, his annual utilization of which averages 100 carloads. This business was founded in 1922, by S. L. Cork, from whom Mr. Cottrill purchased the plant and business in 1927, his vigorous and honorable policies having since effected a splendid expansion of the enterprise.

Mr. Cottrill was born in Buchanan County, Missouri, October 2, 1893, and is a son of Benjamin and Mary (Maryland) Cottrill, of whose three children he was the second in order of birth. Benjamin Cottrill became one of the substantial exponents of farm enterprise in Buchanan County, Missouri, was loyal and public-spirited as a citizen and he gave effective service as a member of the school board of his district. The Cottrill family gained Colonial prestige in the historic old State of Virginia and some of its representatives served as patriot soldiers in the War of the Revolution. Elias Cottrill, grandfather of the subject of this review, was born at Roanoke, Virginia, and was one of a family of twelve sons, three of whom became pioneers in Missouri and he having been one of this number. Elias and his brother John established permanent residence in Missouri, and the other brother, Watson, eventually became a resident of Texas. Elias Cottrill developed in Missouri the productive farm on which he passed the remainder of his life, and in that state his son Benjamin well up-

held the honors of the family name as a citizen and as an enterprising agriculturist and stock grower.

The public schools of his native county constituted the medium through which Floyd B. Cottrill acquired his early education, and in the meanwhile he assisted in the work and management of the home farm. He advanced his education by attending the Missouri State Normal School at Marysville, Missouri. With his family he removed to Emporia, Kansas, in 1914, where he was employed with the G. W. Newman Dry Goods Company. He was a resident of Emporia, Kansas, at the time the nation entered the World war, and he was one of the earliest volunteers from Kansas, his enlistment having occurred May 1, 1917,—less than a month after the United States formally declared war against Germany. He became a member of Company L, One Hundred Thirty-seventh Infantry, Thirty-fifth Division, from Emporia, and with this command he embarked April 25, 1918, for overseas service. He was in active service in France at the time of the signing of the armistice and there he remained until April, 1919, when he returned to his native land and received his honorable discharge, with rank of sergeant. After visiting the home in Emporia, Kansas, Mr. Cottrill passed a year in New Mexico, and he then came to Indiana, where he was soon afterward married, at Muncie. He was thereafter a traveling salesman of coal during a period of five years, with residence at Muncie, and in October, 1927, he purchased at Hartford City the business that he has since continued under its original title of American Coal Company.

Mr. Cottrill is a Democrat in politics, has membership in the local Kiwanis Club and the Hartford City Chamber of Commerce, and he is affiliated with Emporia Lodge No. 12, Ancient Free and Accepted Masons. He is a member of the American Legion and is adjutant of Paul O. Moyer Post No. 159.

At Muncie, this state, was solemnized the marriage of Mr. Cottrill to Miss Leona Nabring, and the one child of this union is a son, Richard Madison. Mr. Cottrill has gained secure standing as one of the progressive and popular business men of the younger generation in Blackford County.

HARRY LONG, who for eight years was assistant general counsel to the United States Shipping Board at Washington, and is now practicing law at Gary, was born at Eaton, Delaware County, Indiana, July 26, 1881, and spent his early life in a community where his people were among the earliest settlers.

The town of Eaton was laid out and platted on land which his grandfather had entered from the Government in 1837. His grandfather was William A. Long, who was born in Ohio, November 16, 1815, son of Robert Long, a native of York, Pennsylvania. William A. Long came to Indiana with his father and settled in Delaware County in 1837, entering land covered with timber, on which one

L. W. McGann

of the first improvements was a log house. William A. Long married, October 28, 1841, Anna McLaughlin, who was born in Ohio in 1823 and died in 1864. Their son, John W. Long, was born April 19, 1846, and when he was twelve years of age he carried the chain helping the surveyor lay out the town of Eaton from a part of his father's homestead. John W. Long spent most of his life as a farmer at Eaton. He was one of the local men who when natural gas was discovered helped finance the Eaton Gas Company. He was also one of the organizers of the Farmers State Bank in 1894, serving as vice president and from 1898 as president for a quarter of a century. He was active in politics, serving as a member of the county advisory board and was a member of the Christian Church. He died in October, 1922, and is buried at Eaton. His father, William A. Long, had been active in the anti-slavery movement and assisted in the operation of one of the stations of the "underground railroad" at Eaton. John W. Long married, in 1876, Miss Rufina Smith, who was born in Iowa, in 1854, and was a small child when her parents, Stephen J. and Susan Smith, settled in Indiana, returning to Delaware County after a brief residence in Iowa. Mrs. Rufina Smith Long is now seventy-six years of age and resides at Eaton. She was the mother of three children: William A., who died at the age of seventeen; Harry; and Robert W., a farmer and banker at Eaton, who married Mary Peterson, member of another old family of Delaware County, and has two daughters, Helen Hope and Mary Catherine.

Harry Long as a boy witnessed some of the feverish activities due to the natural gas discoveries in Delaware County. He graduated from the Eaton High School in 1900, spent four years in Indiana University and in 1905 graduated from the Indiana Law School with the LL. B. degree. He belongs to the Phi Delta Theta fraternity. He was admitted to the bar, and until 1921 was in practice at Muncie, associated as a partner with George W. Cromer, former congressman from the Eighth Congressional District. In 1921 Mr. Long was appointed assistant general counsel to the United States Shipping Board, and his duties kept him in Washington until September, 1929, when he resigned. On returning to Indiana he located at Gary, where he joined R. B. Johnson in partnership. Later the law firm of Moore, Long, Chudom & Johnson was founded, which commands a very large and important practice. Their offices are in the Gary State Bank Building.

Mr. Long has been active in Republican politics and was formerly district chairman of the Eighth Indiana District. For four years he served as prosecuting attorney of Delaware County. He is a member of Eaton Lodge No. 606 of the Masonic fraternity and Muncie Lodge No. 245, B. P. O. Elks.

He married in Wells County, Indiana, October 31, 1905, Miss Clara R. Davis, daughter of Leander and Mary (Behner-Eichhorn) Davis. Her father was a farmer and stock man of Wells County and her parents are buried at Markle. Mrs. Long graduated from high school at Bluffton, attended Indiana University and taught school at Bluffton until her marriage. She is a member of the Christian Church, the Eastern Star and Kappa Kappa Gamma sorority. They have two children, John Robert and Mary Virginia. John Robert was educated in public schools at Muncie and Washington, graduated from the Charlotte Hall Military Academy in 1928, subsequently attended Maryland University and is now attending the University of Indiana, where he belongs to the same fraternity as his father, the Phi Delta Theta. He was born in 1911, and is a youth of unusual intellectual capacity. The daughter, Mary Virginia, is attending public school at Gary.

Lewis William McGann has been a resident of South Bend since 1911, and is well known over St. Joseph County as a funeral director, owning and conducting one of the best establishments of the kind in South Bend.

Mr. McGann was born at Macomb, Illinois, March 25, 1883, son of James H. and Anna (Von Rospatch) McGann. His father was born in New York City, April 19, 1855, and two years later, in 1857, his parents moved to Macomb, Illinois. He grew up on a farm there and as a young man acquired land of his own and followed farming and stock raising until his death. His wife was a native of McDonough County, Illinois, and is now living at South Bend. All her six children are living, Lewis being the second in age.

Mr. McGann had all the experiences of boyhood and early youth at Macomb, where he attended grade and high school and the Illinois State Normal School. His first work was teaching, beginning in 1904, when he was twenty-one years of age. For three years he taught in his home town. When he left teaching he began an apprenticeship in the undertaking business with James Hainline, then the leading undertaker of Macomb. After two years he entered the Hoenshue Embalming School at Peoria, was graduated in 1910 and at once went east to take a position in New York City and did work in a number of eastern cities before his return to his native state.

On coming to South Bend, in November, 1911, Mr. McGann bought what is known as the Notre Dame Undertaking Establishment. He moved it to 333 North Michigan Street and in 1925 to his present location at 424 North Michigan Street. Here he has a complete funeral home and chapel. Mr. McGann is a member of the Indiana State and National Funeral Directors Associations, is a member of the Knights of Columbus, the B. P. O. Elks and the South Bend Country Club.

He married, June 15, 1915, Miss Catherine A. McIlwee. Mrs. McGann was born at Denver, Colorado. They have two children, Lewis William Jr., born June 5, 1920, and Margaret Elene, born October 30, 1925.

JAMES J. CARROLL, district commercial manager of the Illinois Bell Telephone Company, of Gary, has been identified with this great corporation for nearly a quarter of a century, during which time he has won steady promotion through individual merit and great industry. Since locating at Gary, in 1919, he has interested himself actively in civic affairs and at present is a member of the City Planning Commission.

Mr. Carroll was born at North Judson, Indiana, December 29, 1884, and is a son of Michael and Hannah (O'Brien) Carroll. Michael Carroll was born in Queens County, Ireland, and was an infant of one year when brought to the United States by his parents, the family settling at San Pierre, Starke County, Indiana, where he received a public school education and in young manhood secured employment with a construction crew in railroad work. He was thus employed for a number of years with various companies and later removed to Hammond, Indiana, where his death occurred in 1916, burial being made in Calvary Cemetery, near Gary. His father was James Carroll, a native of Ireland, who was a pioneer of San Pierre, and for years was identified with the Monon Railroad. He died at San Pierre about 1890, while his wife survived until 1913, passing away at the advanced age of ninety-five years, being laid to rest at his side in the family burial ground at San Pierre. Mrs. Hannah (O'Brien) Carroll was born at Lexington, Kentucky, where she was educated in the public schools, and throughout her life was an active member of the Catholic Church. She died February 23, 1930, and is buried at the side of her husband in Calvary Cemetery, near Gary. All seven of the children of Michael and Hannah Carroll are living: John, of Hammond, this state; Margaret, the widow of Jerome Ball, of Plymouth, Indiana; James J., of this review; Hugh E., of Hammond; Leo F., of East Chicago, Indiana; Eugene C., of Hammond, who was a member of the United States Navy during the World war; and Gerald M., of Chicago, Illinois, who was a member of the United States Signal Corps during the World war and saw eighteen months of overseas service.

James J. Carroll attended the public schools of North Judson, Indiana, after leaving which he secured employment with the G. H. Hammond Packing Company, of Hammond, with which concern he remained for one and one-half years. For the two years that followed he was in the employ of the Erie Railroad Company, at Hammond, and following this was employed in the traffic department of Williams & Peters, of Chicago, for one year and eight months. On November 6, 1907, Mr. Carroll entered the service of the Chicago Telephone Company (now the Illinois Bell Telephone Company), in the capacity of chief clerk at the Hammond district office, and October 15, 1919, was appointed manager of the Gary area. On April 1, 1929, he was promoted to his present position as district commercial manager of District No. 4, which includes all Indiana properties and a part of Illinois, comprising twenty-three exchanges. This is an exceedingly important post and one in which Mr. Carroll has been able not only to carry on the regular duties in a highly commendable and expeditious manner, but also to improve the service materially through the introduction of newer methods and by his own executive ability. Mr. Carroll is a member of the board of directors of the Home Building, Loan & Savings Association of Gary. He is fraternally affiliated with the Knights of Columbus an the Benevolent and Protective Order of Elks, and belongs also to the Rotary Club, of which he was secretary for one year; the Gary Country Club, the Gary Commercial Club and the Chamber of Commerce and the City Planning Commission. He is a Republican in his political allegiance and his religious connection is with Holy Angels Catholic Church.

At Hammond, Indiana, June 27, 1917, Mr. Carroll was united in marriage with Miss Eileen K. Foley, daughter of John J. and Nellie (Cramer) Foley. Mr. Foley, who was for years a locomotive engineer on the Erie Railroad, died at Hammond, May 27, 1930, Mrs. Foley having passed away January 12, 1930. They are buried in a Marion (Ohio) cemetery. Mrs. Carroll was educated in the public schools of Hammond, where she graduated, and the parochial school at Huntington, this state, and for a few years was employed in the office of the Illinois Bell Telephone Company. She takes an active part in the work of Holy Angels Catholic Church and in the Catholic Women's League. Mr. and Mrs. Carroll live in an attractive home at 701 Polk Street.

JOSEPH ARDAPPLE. The Ardapple Storage & Warehouse Company, at 1128 Main Street in Lafayette, is a business to which members of three generations of the Ardapple family have contributed. Though not under the name of the present corporation, the business has been in existence for over sixty-five years.

The founder was Andrew Ardapple, who came to Indiana in 1855, and a few years later began a service in Lafayette using teams and drays for local transportation of goods. Mr. Joseph Ardapple, who was born at Lafayette, February 5, 1870, is a son of Andrew and Sophia Ardapple. As a boy he attended the Jenk School at Lafayette, and when he was eighteen began helping his father. His father at that time was doing considerable contract work, utilizing a force of teams and drivers, and Joseph Ardapple assisted in concentrating the material for the first brick paving on Main Street. Later he hauled all the brick for the construction of the plant of the Lafayette Steel Products Company. Since 1907 the business has been known as the Ardapple Storage & Warehouse Company. The first location was on Ninth Street, afterwards at Cincinnati and Erie streets, then at 1338 Main Street, and finally the present headquarters at 1128 Main Street. Mr. Ardapple has three warehouse buildings and a service garage, and the company uses over 123,000 square feet of floor space. There are ten employees and they use seven trucks, handling large special contracts, and also operating a daily and hourly service for the convenience of local customers.

Mr. Joseph Ardapple married Katherine Garrison, also a native of Lafayette. They have three children, two daughters and a son, all of whom were educated in Lafayette.

The son, Walter Ardapple, was born at Lafayette, January 19, 1896, and was educated in the grade and high schools and also attended the Lafayette Business College. At the age of sixteen he became bookkeeper in his father's establishment and on May 3, 1917, enlisted for service in the World war. He was overseas ten months and after his release from military duty rejoined his father's business, in which he has a responsible part. Walter Ardapple married Dorothy Irvin, who was born at Oxford, Indiana. They have two children, one born in 1923 and the other in 1924, and both are now in school.

ROSE GRAY DOUGAN is one of the very interesting and cultured women of the City of Denver. She has spent much of her life in travel over the United States and abroad, but her home is at Denver, where her family has been prominent for many years, since 1875.

She was born at Richmond, Indiana, daughter of David Henry and Rosanna (Lamm) Dougan, her father a native of Niles, Michigan, and her mother of Wayne County, Indiana. Her mother was a daughter of Isaac and Rebecca Lamm, of Wayne County, and a granddaughter of Thomas and Sarah (Smith) Lamm, who were married August 4, 1813. Miss Dougan's paternal grandparents were William and Ann (Gray) Dougan, who came to Michigan from Ireland, and Mrs. Dougan settled in Wayne County, Indiana, in 1856, after the death of her husband in Niles. The Lamms were early day farmers in the county. Isaac Lamm was also a dealer and shipper in furs, and during the 1850s he built at Richmond a large brick home at the corner of Third and National Road, where Miss Dougan spends several months during the year.

Among her ancestors were the Smith family, who owned a large tract of land in the southeastern part of what is now Richmond, and there employed David Hoover to survey the tract, known as Smithville. Another early pioneer was Jeremiah Cox, who owned the land across the road and founded what he named Jericho. These two men were unable to agree as to a joint name for their community and consequently David Hoover was called in and named the place in honor of John Smith's ancestral home, Richmond, England. John Smith came from Guilford Court House, North Carolina. He was a lifelong Quaker, was a slave owner in the southern states, and when fifty years of age he refused to remain a slave owner, but the law forbade freeing slaves, so he gave them to the Quaker meeting, to be freed as soon as the South became "civilized" (he was sure it would sometime) and came to Indiana in 1804-05. He left behind a large number of his negroes and came north, some of his faithful slaves accompanying him. He was one of the early pioneers of Wayne County.

Miss Dougan's parents were married at Richmond in 1867. Her father graduated from the Bellevue Medical College in 1874, and in 1875 went west to Colorado, practicing two years at Alma, and then located at Leadville, where later he engaged in banking. He died at Richmond in 1919, though his home at the time was at Denver. He 's buried in the Earlham Cemetery. Miss Dougan's mother now divides her time between Richmond and Denver.

Miss Dougan attended public and private schools in Denver. She traveled extensively and studied music in Paris. Miss Dougan is a linguist and is a woman of many interests. One of her hobbies is the collection of native finger rings. She has deeply interested herself in the pueblo Indians' arts and crafts, and has particularly striven to get recognition for some of the artistic talents of the Red Men. Miss Dougan is a member of the Richmond Garden Club, National Audubon Society, National Travel Club, American Museum of Natural History, Archaeological Institute of America, and a life member of the American Red Cross.

EDWARD PAYTON MOORE lived his life at Mitchell in Lawrence County. That community knew him as a highly valuable citizen on account of his banking experience, his judgment in all financial matters and the wisdom with which he guided an enterprise that involved important interests for hundreds of customers and clients.

Mr. Moore was born September 11, 1869, and died September 17, 1924, at the age of fifty-five. His grandparents were Silas and Mary Moore. Silas Moore was of Virginia ancestry and came to Indiana from Kentucky. The old home he had at Mitchell is still standing and he was one of the early merchants of that community and had a great deal to do with making Mitchell one of the best small towns in this part of the state. He was one of the founders of the local Presbyterian Church. Milton N. Moore, father of the late Edward Payton Moore, was born in Orange County, Indiana, and when the Civil war came on joined an Indiana regiment. He left his store under the management of a brother while he was in the army. After the siege of Vicksburg he returned to Mitchell and resumed his mercantile business. In 1882 he organized the Bank of Mitchell and continued to act as its president until his death on June 1, 1904.

Edward Payton Moore received his formal education in the public schools and a normal college, also had a business course, but the fundamentals of his financial knowledge came to him during the years he was in close contact with his father. He entered his father's bank at an early age, and when his father died he took the post of president and was unfaltering in his devotion to his business duties until he passed away. For many years he was also in the insurance business, conducting the E. P. Moore Company, which probably handled a larger volume of insurance business than any similar organization in the county. Mr. Moore was affiliated with the Lodge of Masons, the Knights of Pythias, belonged to the Elks at Bedford and was very active in the Presbyterian Church, of which he was a trustee.

Mr. Moore married, December 28, 1892, Miss Elizabeth Hyatt, who survives him and continues to reside at their old home at 705 Warren Street in Mitchell. Mrs. Moore represents a long line of American ancestors. Her parents were Henry H. and Mary (Hoffmeister) Hyatt. Her father was born in Washington, Daviess County, Indiana, son of John Hyatt, who in turn was a son of Thomas and Elizabeth (McFerran) Hyatt. Thomas Hyatt was a son of Chadrack and Elizabeth Hyatt. Chadrack Hyatt was with a Maryland company and regiment in the Revolutionary war in 1776 and was wounded in the battle of Long Island, but made his escape through the swampy country. He was under the command of Capt. David Noble and Captain Cresap and Colonel Smallwood. He was a private in Washington's army and after the war enjoyed a pensnion from the Government. Mrs. Moore's grandfather, John Hyatt, came from Kentucky and acquired a large tract of land and opened up a plantation in Southern Indiana. Her father, Henry H. Hyatt, spent most of his life as a merchant at Washington, Indiana and he and his wife are buried in the Maple Grove Cemetery. They were the parents of six children: Clara, who became the wife of Charles Bareford; Harriet, Mrs. Charles R. Hudson; Mrs. Elizabeth Moore; Cameron, who married Laura Jones; Mary, who died in infancy; and Anna.

GEORGE REMINGTON CARTER. In the death of George Remington Carter, which occurred December 12, 1922, the City of Connersville lost one of its able men and public-spirited citizens. Beginning life with few advantages, through his own efforts he made himself one of the foremost figures in the leather industry, and at the time of his death was president of the George R. Carter Company, which still is operating at Detroit, Michigan. His career was a busy and useful one, full of good and kindly deeds and characterized by excellent public service, and although some years have passed since he was called to the Great Beyond his memory is still kept green and fragrant by the many who knew and appreciated his many sterling qualities of heart and mind.

Mr. Carter was born near Felicity, Clermont County, Ohio, January 4, 1854, and was a son of Henry and Anna (Trisler) Carter, the former a native of Pennsylvania and the latter of Ohio. Henry Carter was reared in his native community, where he received a public school education, and in young manhood adopted the vocation of farming, in which he was engaged throughout life, his death occurring in Clermont County, Ohio.

After attending the public schools of his native locality George Remington Carter began teaching school in the winter terms and following farming during the summer months. He then moved to Cincinnati, Ohio, where he took a position with the American Oak Leather Company, and later represented the large old leather house of James N. Duffy Leather Company for a number of years. Because of the failure of his health he spent one year in farming in Clermont County, Ohio, and then went to Williamsburg, Ohio, where he founded a business of his own in a room sixteen by twenty feet, cutting leather strips for different parts of buggies. The excellence of his goods, the uniformity of his workmanship and his own personal energy and good management soon attracted attention and patronage, and within four years he had a prosperous and thriving business. This became so large that it outgrew the town, and particularly the railroad facilities, and Mr. Carter moved his plant to Connersville where after various changes it confined itself, as at present, to automobile trimmings and findings. When Mr. Carter came to Connersville he founded the George R. Carter Company, a corporation, with himself as president; Henry Adrian Carter, vice president; Joel D. Bolender, treasurer; James R. Carter, secretary; and Claude Case, director. Following his death his widow became president and remained in that capacity until January, 1929, when the business was sold to the Vogt Manufacturing Company, of Rochester, New York. The business was conducted at Connersville until August, 1930, at which time it was removed to Detroit, Michigan, where it is still conducted under the name of The George R. Carter Company.

Mr. Carter was one of Connersville's most highly respected men. During his earlier years he had been a member and lay preacher of the Methodist Episcopal Church, but later adopted the faith of the Christian Science Church, which is that of his widow. He was a Republican in politics and a thirty-second degree Mason and Shriner.

In August, 1887, Mr. Carter was united in marriage with Miss Sarah Jane Ringold, who was born near Glendale, Ohio, daughter of John and Martha (McMillan) Ringold, the former born in Holland and the latter in the North of Ireland. Mrs. Carter, who is a high school graduate, is prominent in the Connersville Literary Club and in social circles of the city. She and her husband were the parents of the following children: Henry Adrian, who married Alta Isabelle Bilby and has two children, George Remington and Virginia Isabelle; Martha Anna, who married Joel D. Bolender and has two children, George William and Jean Ann; James Remington, who married Mary Agnes Elliott and has two children, Catherine Jane and Martha Susanne; and Iva Pearl, who married Claude Case and

John J. Kinsel

has three children, Sarah Maude, Martha Elizabeth and Robert. Mrs. Sarah Jane Carter resides in her own attractive home at 903 Lincoln Street.

JOHN J. HIMSEL was born and reared in Dubois County, Indiana, and his secure place in popular confidence and esteem in his native county needs no further voucher than the statement that he has held continuously since 1923 the office of postmaster of the City of Jasper, the county seat.

Mr. Himsel was born at Haysville, Indiana, June 8, 1873, and is a son of John and Katherine (Retsch) Himsel, both of whom were born in Germany and both of whom were children when the respective families immigrated to the United States and established residence in Indiana. John Himsel was reared on his parents' farm in Indiana and his youthful loyalty was shown when, at the age of sixteen years, he volunteered for service as a soldier of the Union in the Civil war. He became a member of Company K, Twenty-first Indiana Volunteer Infantry, and reenlisted at the expiration of his original term, so that he continued in active service until the close of the war, he having taken part in the many engagements in which his command was involved. After the close of his military career he resumed his active alliance with farm enterprise, with which he continued to be identified seven years. At his home in Haysville, Dubois County, he was foully murdered by two outlaws, David Devault and Benjamin Shipley, the latter of whom fired three shots into the body of the victim, and the two desperadoes having made their escape and never have been brought to the bar of justice. Within a comparatively short time after the close of the Civil war John Himsel was united in marriage to Mrs. Katherine (Retsch) Saurtich, widow of John Saurtich, who died while serving as a soldier of the Union in the Civil war, and one of whose children later met an accidental death, the surviving son being Martin Saurtich. Of the children of Mr. and Mrs. John Himsel the eldest is Thomas, who married Barbara Neukam, their home being at Jasper and their children being two daughters. Elizabeth, second of the children, like her father, met a tragic death, she having been so severely burned that her death soon followed. George, a resident of Sidney, Florida, married Mrs. Jane White, and they have one child, Glenn. John J., of this review, is the youngest of the four children, his father having been murdered on the same evening John was born.

The educational discipline that John J. Himsel received in the public schools of Martin County was advanced by his attending normal school in Dubois County and after four terms in the Central Normal College at Danville, Indiana, he taught nine seasons in the rural schools of his native county. He then completed a course in the Spencerian Business College of Louisville, Kentucky. In 1901 he became manager of the Dubois County Telephone Company, with which he continued un-

til the system and business were sold to the Southern Indiana Telephone Company, in 1926. By the latter corporation he was retained in the same executive capacity until the present time, completing thirty years of continuous service in the same position on May 20, 1931. In 1923 he initiated his administration as postmaster of Jasper, his appointment having been made August 1 of that year and he having been reappointed in 1927. His administration as postmaster has been notably loyal and progressive and has met with unqualified popular approval, constant progress having been made in the service.

The political allegiance of Mr. Himsel is given to the Republican party and he has been influential in its councils in Dubois County, having been elected county chairman four successive terms and being the first man in fifty years to have this honor conferred on him more than once. He is affiliated with both York and Scottish Rite bodies of the Masonic fraternity, as well as the Mystic Shrine, and has membership also in the Independent Order of Odd Fellows and the Modern Woodmen of America. He and his wife are members of the Evangelical Church in their home city.

June 18, 1899, was marked by the marriage of Mr. Himsel to Miss Katherine Dilly, daughter of Philip and Barbara (Leistner) Dilly, of Dubois County, and of this union have been born five children: Lester is manager of the Woolworth store in the City of Gary, Indiana, and formerly held the same position in their store at Cleveland; Miss Viola is employed as stenographer in the office of a hide and belting company in Indianapolis; Karl K. is employed by the Southern Indiana Telephone Company, with headquarters at Jasper; Elsa is a stenographer in the office of the Jasper Desk Company; and Katherine is a graduate of the training school for nurses that is maintained by Grace Hospital in Detroit, Michigan.

By way of summary it is interesting to note that Mr. Himsel was left homeless and penniless at the age of sixteen, and the extent of his education at that time was the completion of the fourth grade, home obligations having interfered with his schooling from the start. Left to shift for himself, he first decided he must have a better education and consequently worked at hard farm labor during summer months, at a salary of thirteen dollars per month, which earnings provided his meager necessities during the school terms. Unlike the average boy, whose every need is supplied by loving parents, he appreciated the value of every minute of his scant school opportunities and by long hours of study, in addition to chores done to augment his living expenses, he finished the next four years' grades in one, graduating from the common schools of Rutherford Township of Martin County at seventeen years of age, with the second highest grades. Encouraged by this success, he attended another winter of school and after the close of this term, entered Dubois Normal School, as already stated, which prepared him for teaching his first school the following winter, from which time he continued to teach and study at normal schools until married in 1899. After his marriage he taught two more winters, after which time he entered the telephone business, as before mentioned. Mr. Himsel has thus always known the meaning of hard work and frugal living and has suffered personal illness and the death of two children, the oldest, Chloea, and the youngest, Jeremiah. In spite of these many handicaps and with the ambition ever before him to give his children the best advantages of which he was capable, he has succeeded in affording them at least a high school education, sound bodies and a good name.

It is also interesting to note that three professional callings made strong appeals to Mr. Himsel, namely the medical, ministerial and legal, but lack of educational opportunities prevented him from entering any of these.

O. DALE SMITH, district manager at Muncie for the Equitable Life Assurance Society of New York, is a native of Delaware County and was connected with the clothing trade for a number of years, but found his real forte in insurance.

He was born in Delaware County, January 25, 1894, son of E. A. and Myrtie (Jones) Smith. His grandfather, William Smith, was born in Madison County, Indiana, May 9, 1850, and died December 8, 1897. William Smith married Amanda Smith, who was born October 21, 1853, and died in 1890. The father of William Smith came to Indiana from South Carolina. E. A. Smith was born and reared in Madison County, had a public school education, and has devoted his active career to farming and stock raising and to a mercantile business at Anderson. His wife, Myrtie (Jones) Smith, was born and reared in Delaware County, and died April 9, 1894. She was a daughter of Warren and Nannie (Woodring) Jones, Nannie Woodring being a daughter of William Woodring, an early settler of Delaware County. Mrs. Myrtie Smith was educated in public schools and was engaged in clerical work before her marriage. She was an active member of the Methodist Episcopal Church. She is buried in the Jones Cemetery in Delaware County.

O. Dale Smith was the only child of his parents. He was educated in public schools, including the Muncie High School, and then spent two years clerking for the Wolf Clothing Company, was also connected with a shoe business at Springfield, Illinois, for a time, and spent two years with the Bell Telephone Company at Indianapolis. From there he went to Gary and clerked in a retail clothing store until September, 1918, when he answered the call to the colors.

He was sent for training to Camp Grant at Rockford, Illinois, later to Camp McArthur, Texas, and from there to Camp Taylor at Louisville, Kentucky, where he received his honorable discharge January 1, 1919, having been a sergeant in the Regimental Headquarters Company. After the war he returned to Gary and was with the Acker-Schmidt Clothing Company in that city until 1923.

Mr. Smith then returned to Muncie, and after six months with the Greiger Clothing Company was made a partner and vice president of the organization, but disposed of those interests and until 1925 was with the Keller Clothing Company.

Mr. Smith retired from the clothing business to become agent for the Equitable Life Assurance Society of New York, and he found insurance such a fascinating occupation and so in line with his special abilities that after a year and a half he was promoted to manager of the Muncie agency and has made that one of the leading agencies of the company in Indiana.

Mr. Smith is affiliated with Marion Lodge No. 35, A. F. and A. M., at Indianapolis, belongs to the Fort Wayne Consistory of the Scottish Rite and Orak Temple of the Mystic Shrine at Hammond. He is secretary of the Eastern Indiana Kennel Club, is active in the Muncie Exchange Club, Delaware Post No. 19 of the American Legion, and is a Phi Delta Kappa. He is a Republican and is affiliated with the Friends Memorial Church at Muncie.

Mr. Smith married at Indianapolis, July 16, 1923, Miss Lucille Leffler, daughter of James Harve and Nettie (Sloniker) Leffler. Mrs. Smith graduated from the Muncie High School and is prominent in the social and club life of that city, being a member of the Friends Memorial Church, the Woman's Musical Club, the Kings Daughters and the Eastern Star.

James Harve Leffler, father of Mrs. Smith, was born on a farm near Muncie, June 23, 1862, son of Phillip and Mary (Garrard) Leffler. He was educated in public schools and the Central Indiana Normal School at Danville, after which he taught for a few years, also engaged in farming and stock raising, and left the farm to take up a business career as a hardware and implement dealer at Albany. After about nine years he traded his hardware store for an interest in the Albany Furniture & Manufacturing Company. Not long afterward the plant of this business was burned to the ground without insurance. Mr. Leffler in 1894 moved to Muncie, and for about seven years was deputy county clerk under Clerk John E. Reed. He resigned his work for the county to go with the Indiana Union Traction Company in its right-of-way and claim adjustment department, and while there helped secure the rights of way for the Indiana Northern Traction Company and the line between Newcastle and Middletown. In 1898 Mr. Leffler resumed his active connection with Muncie, where he engaged in the real estate and farm loan business with the firm of Garrard & Company. In 1908 he was nominated and elected county clerk, serving one term of four years. While in that office he became a member of the firm Miltenburger & Leffler, successors to Garrard & Company, and in 1927 he sold the real estate department to Mr. Miltenburger and then acquired an interest in the Ault Insurance Agency at Muncie. As president of this agency he has made it one of the largest in Eastern Indiana. Mr. Leffler helped organize the Western Reserve Life Insurance Company of Muncie, serving as vice president and a member of its board, and succeeded David P. Campbell at his death as president of the company. This insurance business was sold in 1927 to the Northern States Company of Hammond. In 1908 Mr. Leffler helped organize the People's Trust Company of Muncie and has been on its board of directors continuously.

He served one term as junior vice commander of the Indiana Division, Sons of Veterans. He is affiliated with Delaware Lodge No. 46, A. F. and A. M., is a Knight Templar and Scottish Rite Mason, a past chancellor of the Knights of Pythias, a past sachem of the Improved Order of Red Men, member of the Loyal Order of Moose, Sons of Veterans, Travelers Protective Association, and is a former vice president of the Kiwanis Club. He is a Republican and a member of the Friends Memorial Church, being on the board of trustees and the pastoral committee.

Mr. Leffler married at Eaton, Indiana, June 23, 1888, Miss Nettie A. Sloniker, who was reared and educated in Delaware County. She is a member of the Friends Memorial Church at Muncie, the Eastern Star and the Federation of Women's Clubs. Her parents were David W. and Elizabeth (Green) Sloniker. Her father died in 1917 and her mother in 1918, and they are buried at Beech Grove, Muncie. Mr. and Mrs. Leffler had one child, Josephine Lucille, who graduated from the Muncie High School in 1915, also took work in the Muncie Normal, now the Ball State Teachers College, and was a kindergarten teacher until her marriage to Mr. O. D. Smith.

REV. CHARLES E. WATKINS, of Muncie, is the possessor of many talents, which he has exercised in the field of practical business, in the ministry of the Baptist Church and in behalf of many worthy causes. He was formerly pastor of a church in Muncie, but most of his time in recent years has been taken up with organization and welfare work. He is now a representative of the American Cities Bureau of Chicago. He and his family have a beautiful home at 500 University Avenue, in Muncie.

He was born at Huntsville, Logan County, Ohio, May 26, 1876, son of William J. and Sarah (Kelly) Watkins. His parents lived all their lives in that section of Ohio. His father was a contractor and builder. He retired from busines about 1920, died at Dayton, Ohio, May 4th, 1930. The mother of Rev. Mr. Watkins died January 13, 1920, and is buried at West Liberty, Ohio. They were active members of the Methodist Episcopal Church. The children besides Charles E. were: Harry E., of Dayton; Kelly M. Watkins, in the automobile busines at Johnstown, Pennsylvania; Bessie, wife of John C. Licht, of Dayton; Ray, with the National Cash Register Company at Dayton; Miss Tempie A., with the Larkin Transfer Company of Day-

ton; and Miss Mattie B., a trained nurse at Dayton.

Charles E. Watkins attended the public schools in Logan County, Ohio. As a youth he gave evidence of talents for speaking and for activities requiring natural leadership among men. For six years he was an employe of the Barney & Smith Car Company, passenger car manufacturers at Dayton. During these years he was a student of theology and prepared himself for the ministry of the Baptist Church. Mr. Watkins came to Muncie in 1904, and for a short time was in the electrical business in that city. In 1906 he was made pastor of the Seventeenth Street Baptist Church, now the Walnut Street Church, and did some valuable work in building up that church during the six years he was pastor. In 1912 he was made superintendent of Evangelism for the Indiana Baptists, a work he continued until 1917.

Mr. Watkins left the active ministry during the World war and for two years acted as secretary of the local Y. M. C. A. at Muncie, and used his talents as a speaker in connection with many of the drives and campaigns both in Muncie and other sections of the state. In 1919 he was made director of personnel for the T. W. Warner Company, and when that business was taken over as a part of the General Motors Corporation his services were retained until February, 1925. Since leaving the General Motors Company Mr. Watkins has been associated with the American City Bureau of Chicago, an organization that sends him to different parts of the country to assist in campaigns under the auspices of Chambers of Commerce, in Community Chest drives and religious and other campaigns for the raising of funds.

Mr. Watkins is a member of the Muncie Rotary Club and was district governor in 1920. He also belongs to the Chamber of Commerce, is a Republican and a member of the First Baptist Church.

He married at Dayton, Ohio, September 1, 1899, Miss Cora Lee Baldwin, daughter of Alford and Molly (Finn) Baldwin. Her father was a farmer and stock raiser at Milldale, Kentucky, where he died in 1880, and her mother died several years earlier. Mrs. Watkins attended the public schools in Kentucky. She has always been an earnest worker in the Baptist Church and is a member of the Muncie Woman's Club.

James Elwood Watkins, only son and child of Rev. and Mrs. Watkins, was born June 7, 1900. He graduated from the Muncie High School in 1916, then entered Franklin College, but his education was interrupted when he volunteered at the age of seventeen during the World war. He received training at Fort Sheridan, Illinois, was commissioned a second lieutenant and was sent west to the University of California, at Berkeley, and assigned duty as an instructor. After the armistice he was transferred to the Utah State Agricultural College at Logan, and on resigning returned to Indiana and finished his education in Purdue University, graduating in 1922. During the following two years he was with the Merchants Trust & Savings Bank of Muncie and is now secretary and manager of the Elm Ridge Memorial Park. He belongs to the Chamber of Commerce, Dynamo Club, Muncie Club, and he and his wife reside at 912 Gilbert Street in Muncie. He married at Pittsburgh, Pennsylvania, October 14, 1925, Miss Margaret Ehrhardt, daughter of Mr. and Mrs. J. H. Ehrhardt, of Pittsburgh, where her father is a stock broker. Mrs. James E. Watkins is a member of the Xiota Psi sorority.

JAMES H. KENSLER, general merchant at Monroe City, has lived in Knox County all his life, and that county has been honored by the good citizenship of a number of members of his family.

He was born in Knox County January 26, 1887, son of Robert and Elizabeth (Shouse) Kensler and grandson of John Kensler. His grandfather was a Knox County farmer and was of French ancestry. Elizabeth Shouse was a daughter of J. H. Shouse, long one of the outstanding citizens of Knox County. J. H. Shouse was a farmer, was a trustee of Palmyra Township, served two terms as mayor of Vincennes, was sheriff of Knox County, and during the Cleveland administration was door keeper in the national capitol at Washington, and for a time was in the pension offices. He served four years as a soldier in the Union army. He died in 1926 on his farm in Knox County.

James Kensler was one of two children. He attended public schools in Knox County and was a farmer until 1919. For over ten years he has carried on a large and well stocked business as a general merchant at Monroe City. He still owns and operates his farms in Palmyra Township.

Mr. Kensler, on October 11, 1908, married Miss Flora Bonewits, of Knox County. He is affiliated with Monroe City Lodge No. 548, A. F. and A. M., attends the Cumberland Presbyterian Church, and is a Democrat. During the World war he had an active part in promoting the success of the Liberty Loan drives.

MATTHEW W. WELSH has marked with special versatility of achievement his career as a business man, his skill as an organizer and executive have come into play in the forming of various important corporations, and as financier and economist he has filled numerous positions of trust. In the handling of bonds and other high-grade securities the corporation of which Mr. Welsh is a principal, that of LaPlante & Welsh, has marked priority in the City of Vincennes, where its offices are established at 19 North Third Street. Mr. Welsh was one of the organizers of this representative corporation and is its secretary and treasurer.

Matthew W. Welsh was born in Jackson County, Indiana, September 9, 1886, and is a son of John E. and Ella (Robertson) Welsh.

John E. Welsh, who became a successful exponent of manufacturing industry, at Brownstown, Jackson County, was born and reared in Indiana and his father, Patrick Welsh, was born in County Clare, Ireland. Patrick Welsh was a young man when he came to the United States, and after residing some time in Boston, Massachusetts, he removed to Cincinnati, Ohio, from which city he came to Jackson County, Indiana, where he passed the remainder of his life, he having served as a loyal soldier of the Union in the Civil war.

Matthew W. Welsh, a member of a family of six children, was reared in his native county, and there his early educational advantages included those of both the high school and a business college. As a youth he there clerked several years in a general mercantile establishment and two years in a drug store. He was then appointed bailiff and later official court reporter of the Circuit Court of the Fortieth Judicial Circuit of Indiana, comprising Jackson and Scott counties, and his service continued during the period of 1907-10. In the meanwhile he applied himself to the study of law and was admitted to the bar of his native state in 1908. Upon retiring from the position of court reporter he went to Indianapolis, where he was associated two years in the practice of law with Carl E. Wood. He then became associated with Mr. Wood and others in organizing the Columbian National Fire Insurance Company, of Detroit, Michigan, and of this corporation he became secretary and treasurer. In 1915 he resigned this dual office and went to the City of Chicago, where he effected the organization of the Great Lakes Fire Insurance Company. He soon afterward returned to Brownstown, Indiana, to give attention to his interests in his native county, and shortly after the beginning of the World war he entered government service under the jurisdiction of the Department of Commerce, with executive headquarters in Chicago, until the armistice brought the war to a close. Thereafter Mr. Welsh gave personal supervision to his various capitalistic and property interests at Brownstown until 1920, and in the meanwhile he there organized the Brownstown Loan & Trust Company, of which he was president two years, he having resigned this office in 1920, afterward being associated with the Meyer-Kiser Bank at Indianapolis until October, 1924. In 1924 he moved his family to Vincennes, in which city he was one of the organizers of the corporation of La Plante, Welsh & Risacher, which was succeeded by La Plante & Welsh. He is now its vice president and the corporation controls a substantial business in the handling of bonds, investments and general securities of high standard. Mr. Welsh is a member of the Indiana State Bankers Association, the Mortgage Bankers Association of the United States, the Vincennes Chamber of Commerce, the A. F. and A. M., Vincennes Lodge No. 1, the B. P. O. Elks, the local Harmony Society of his home city, and was a director in the Vincennes Ro-

Walter J. Daumhauer

tary Club in 1931, the while his political allegiance is given to the Democratic party. On July 15, 1909, at Vallonia, Jackson County, Indiana, Mr. Welsh married Miss Inez Empson, daughter of William and Mary (Copeland) Empson, of Vallonia, and the children of this union are Matthew E., Mary, Virginia, John Edward and Margaret Louise. Matthew E. is a student in the Wharton School of Commerce of Pennsylvania University.

It has already been noted that the paternal grandfather of Mr. Welsh was born in Ireland, and it is interesting to record also that on the maternal side he is a representative of a family that was founded in Virginia in the Colonial period of American history.

CLARE B. CURREY is district manager at Connersville for the Remedial Loan & Finance Company, was in early life a teacher, and has made a most creditable record in business and financial affairs in his native County of Fayette.

He was born in Jackson Township, Fayette County, Indiana, December 5, 1889, son of Thomas E. and Hanna F. (Corbin) Currey, also natives of Fayette County. His grandparents were Thomas E. and Catherine (Whittaker) Currey, who came from West Virginia, while Alfred and Katherine (Meyers) Corbin were born in Fayette County, Indiana, where their parents were among the earliest pioneers of this section of the state.

Clare B. Currey grew up on his father's farm, was educated in the common and high schools and the normal schools at Marion and Muncie. For seven years when not in school himself he was a teacher. Mr. Currey's business experience prior to the war period was as a representative of the Prudential Insurance Company, and he was with that organization from 1913 until the fall of 1917. On October 5, 1917, he entered Camp Taylor at Louisville, Kentucky, in the quartermaster's department, and acted as officers pay voucher sergeant until after the armistice. He received his honorable discharge February 17, 1919, and at once resumed work for the insurance company. Mr. Currey was appointed manager of the Remedial Loan & Finance Company at Connersville in September, 1921. He also has supervision over the branch offices at Brookville and Rushville. He married, July 14, 1920, Miss Nola A. Siebethol, who was born at Vevay, Indiana, daughter of Andrew Jackson and Onisca (Netherland) Siebethol. Her father was born in Switzerland and her mother in Kentucky. Andrew Jackson Siebethol came to America with his parents, who settled in Kentucky, along the Ohio River. After reaching manhood he was responsible for starting the first water power flour mill in Switzerland County, Indiana. Mr. and Mrs. Currey have one son, Thomas Lane, born June 25, 1922. The family are members of the Christian Church, Mr. Currey is an independent Democrat, a member of the Lodge and Encampment of the Independent Order of Odd Fellows, the Loyal Order of Moose, and is a past commander of Reginald Fisher Post No. 1 of the American Legion.

HON. WALTER J. DAUNHAUER. Born, reared and educated at Ferdinand, Hon. Walter J. Daunhauer, postmaster of the same place, has all of his interests centered here, and naturally has the continued prosperity of his native place close to his heart, and he is willing to make any kind of sacrifice for its advancement. His birth occurred March 24, 1902, and he is a son of Joseph B. Daunhauer, who was born near Ferdinand, in Dubois County. For a number of years he has owned a grocery and bakery here, and he is numbered among the leading business men of the town. His father, John Daunhauer, was one of the very early settlers of Dubois County, coming here from Pennsylvania, and later moving to Spencer County, where he spent most of his life in farming and died at Ferdinand in March, 1928, at the age of ninety-two. Many others followed him and located in the region about Ferdinand. He owned the first threshing outfit in the county, and for some years operated it in the summer season. The mother of Postmaster Daunhauer was Ann Russ prior to her marriage, and she was also born in Dubois County. Eight children were born to the parents, namely: Postmaster Daunhauer, Myrtle, Earl, Cora, Mabel, Doris, Doherty and one who is deceased.

After he had attended the public and parochial schools of Ferdinand, Postmaster Daunhauer took a commercial course in the Lochyear Business College at Evansville, and was graduated therefrom, after which he returned to Ferdinand and became a clerk in a jewelry store. Still later he occupied a similar position in his father's store, and held it until he was appointed postmaster of Ferdinand by President Coolidge in 1928, which office he still holds.

In political faith he is a Republican and he is one of the active members of the local organization. He and his family are members of the Roman Catholic Church, and he is a Knight of Columbus. Postmaster Daunhauer is unmarried. Since he took charge of the postoffice its affairs have been admirably administered, and the service is proving satisfactory to all concerned. It is a source of pride to him that in a community where his name is an old and honored one, he is able to add to its distinction and prove that his generation is as progressive as those before him.

When the grandfather of Postmaster Daunhauer came to Dubois County this part of Indiana was almost entirely undeveloped, and if he had not been far-sighted and practical he might not have been willing to remain and contend with all of the pioneer conditions. However, he saw that Indiana was destined to become a great state, and that those who became its pioneers could achieve prosperity for themselves and their children, and he sent back such encouraging reports of the region that a number of his old neighbors in Pennsylvania migrated to the county, and they, too, became successful farmers and business men, and therefore from the initial settlement of the first of the name of Daunhauer has come, in large part, the wealthy and important Dubois County.

HENRY WYSOR MARSH, one of the active business men of Muncie today, has a name that constantly recalls to many of his fellow citizens historic characters, builders and founders, men interested not only in the early development of Muncie, but throughout the years in carrying on the good work they had started until one of the important cities of Eastern Indiana had been wrought out as a reflection in no small degree of their influence and energies.

In 1856 a newcomer arrived in Muncie named John Marsh. He had come from Cambridge City, Indiana. In association with John W. Burson he established the Muncie branch of the State Bank of Indiana. The establishment of this bank was in reality a mile post in the progress of Muncie as a commercial center. John Marsh before living in Indiana was a resident of Preble County, Ohio. He was born August 22, 1811, son of Timothy and Mary (Clawson) Marsh. Mary Clawson was born near the mouth of the Little Miami River in Ohio, August 22, 1787. Her father, John Clawson, had been a soldier with the Continental forces in the War of the Revolution, going from his home colony of New Jersey. His daughter Mary, it is claimed, was the first white child born in Southern Ohio. She died in September, 1877. Timothy Marsh was a native of Elizabeth, New Jersey, and was a descendant of Samuel Marsh, who came to America from England in 1632.

A son of the pioneer Muncie banker, John Marsh, was William M. Marsh, whose mother was Mary Mitchell Mutchner. William M. Marsh was actively identified with banking, manufacturing and other business enterprises at Muncie. One of his brothers was Charles C. Marsh, an officer in the United States Navy, and another was John R. Marsh. A sister was Harriet M. Marsh, who became the wife of John R. Johnston, who died leaving a son, Robert Marsh Johnston.

William M. Marsh married Martha Wysor, who was a daughter of Jacob Henry and Sarah (Richardson) Wysor. Among the names of the various men who are counted as constructive factors in the history of Muncie probably more could be said concerning Jacob Henry Wysor than any other.

He was born near Dublin in Pulaski County, Virginia, December 6, 1819, the only child of Jacob and Margaret (Miller) Wysor, who were also native Virginians. Jacob Wysor had served as a soldier in the War of 1812, while his grandfather, Henry Wysor, was a commissioned officer in the Continental Army in the Revolution. Jacob Wysor had died a short time before the birth of his son Jacob Henry, and his widow later married John Guthrie, and in 1834 they moved from South-

western Virginia to Indiana, locating in the Smithfield community in Eastern Delaware County. Jacob Henry Wysor was then fifteen years of age. Subsequently he was sent back to Virginia to complete his education. In 1841 he opened a general store at Muncietown, now Muncie, handling dry goods and groceries. The store was burned down with almost a total loss. Following that he went to work in the Gilbert Flour Mill, the first of Muncie's pioneer industries. After a few months he leased the mill and in 1843 two other conspicuous men in the early affairs of Muncie, John Jack and James L. Russey, joined him, and together they secured the capital to purchase the mill. In 1849 Jacob Henry Wysor left his business to join in the rush across the plains to California. The captain of the party was his partner, James L. Russey, who lost his life at the hands of Indians soon after reaching California. Mr. Wysor himself remained in the far West for three years and on returning to Muncie resumed business with his partner, John Jack. In 1854 the firm of Wysor & Jack erected a flour mill on North Walnut Street. This mill was kept in operation for over sixty years, its machinery being changed from time to time to correspond to new processes in flour manufacture. Finally the plant was sold to a power company and the old landmark was razed.

For years Jacob Henry Wysor's personal influence or his money were identified with nearly every constructive move made in Muncie. He took an active part in the building of some of the turnpike roads, being president of the Muncie & Granville Turnpike Company. In the course of time these pikes were turned over to the county. He was foremost among Muncie citizens in aiding the construction of the first railroad, what is now the Big Four line. Jacob Henry Wysor was well advanced in years when the natural gas discoveries were made in Delaware County during the '80s, but he came out of his retirement and as much as any other man used his capital and enterprise to utilize this new fuel resource to the advantage of Muncie's developments as a commercial and industrial center. He responded heartily to the appeals and the plans carried out through the Commercial Club, the Citizens Enterprise Company and similar organizations.

His name is especially familiar to the people of Muncie both of the present as well as a former generation in connection with buildings that are at the very heart of the city's commercial and cultural growth. In 1872, at the corner of Main and Walnut streets, he built an opera house, at that time one of the finest in Indiana. Twenty years later, in 1892, he gave Muncie a still more pretentious building, the Wysor Grand Opera House, at the corner of Jackson and Mulberry streets. The site of the old opera house eventually became the ground on which was erected Muncie's first modern office building, the business home today of many of the city's leading professional and business organizations, the Wysor Building. In estimating the importance of his character and influence in Muncie one writer said: "Upon three different occasions when efforts of Muncie citizens to carry the city forward seemed doomed to failure, Jacob Henry Wysor by his courage and example put renewed heart into the workers and crowned their efforts with success. When the Enterprise Fund was a practical failure he increased his subscription fourfold, quickly followed by James Boyce, A. F. Patterson, George F. McCulloch and others. When the stock of the old Natural Gas Company was about to be sold to out-of-town parties he bought the stock for home interests. During the panic of 1893, when one bank had closed its doors and a run was being made on the others, he headed a list of citizens guaranteeing against loss every depositor in every bank in Muncie. Thus confidence and enterprises were restored."

Jacob Henry Wysor was eighty-six years of age when he passed away January 18, 1905. For many years he had lived in a picturesque and beautiful home, a property he bought in 1866 at 418 North Walnut Street. It was the old Goldsmith Gilbert Home Square, and at the time he bought it was known as the John Jack homestead.

Jacob Henry Wysor married, April 6, 1854, at Peru, Indiana, Miss Sarah Richardson, who passed away November 6, 1893. She was born in Virginia, daughter of John and Martha Richardson. Their four children were: Harry Richardson Wysor; Martha, who became the wife of William M. Marsh; Virginia, who died when a child; and William H. Wysor, who died in 1894. Harry Richardson Wysor, who was born April 8, 1858, after completing his education joined his father in business at Muncie and in 1881 took over the management of the old opera house, and later the Wysor Grand Opera House until that property was leased. In 1906 he and his sister, Mrs. Marsh, tore down the original opera house and on the site put up the Wysor Office Building. Harry R. Wysor married, in 1884, Miss Jennie Kemper, daughter of William Kemper, of Iowa. They had two daughters, Sarah, who married Robert Carson, and Mary, who married Howard Keifer.

Henry Wysor Marsh was born at Muncie, July 18, 1884, and was educated in the schools of his native city, afterwards attended the University of Pennsylvania. From boyhood it was his ambition to become a farmer, and that is the business to which he has given most of his time since leaving college. For twelve years he was interested in farming in the locality that was the home of his ancestors in Southwestern Virginia, Pulaski County. In 1916 he returned to Muncie, and subsequently bought the old Dow farm on Wheeling Pike, north of Muncie, and the supervision of his farming and stock raising interests has made heavy demands upon his time. He is also manager of the Wysor Estate and as such has offices in the Wysor Building.

Mr. Marsh is treasurer of the Delaware County Farm Bureau. He is on the vestry of the Grace Episcopal Church. On March 6, 1907, he married, at Dublin, Virginia, Miss Cora Reid Wysor, daughter of Henry C. and Mary (Shipp) Wysor. Her father was a well-to-do farmer and stock man in Southwestern Virginia. He died August 28, 1928, and his wife in August, 1924, and both are buried at Dublin, Virginia. Mrs. Marsh was educated by private tutors and is a graduate of the Stonewall Jackson Institute at Abingdon, Virginia. She is a member of the Grace Episcopal Church of Muncie. Mr. and Mrs. Marsh have had four children: Martha Shipp; Mary Wysor, who died at the age of two years; Margaret Johnston; and Henry Wysor, Jr. The daughter Martha was graduated from the Muncie High School in 1929 and is attending the Ball State Teachers College. The two younger children are in grade school.

L. F. BLANN, Monroe City merchant, is a native of Knox County and is a successful representative of a family that has been in Indiana since early pioneer times.

The pioneer of the family was Marion Blann, who came from Kentucky and settled in Busseron Township, Knox County, more than a century ago. His son, S. G. Blann, was a Knox County farmer. S. G. Blann was the father of Edward P. Blann, who has been well known as a merchant and farmer and was township trustee of Harrison Township and county treasurer from 1914 to 1917. Edward P. Blann married Mattie Nolen, of Knox County, representing the Nolen family which came to Knox County about 1830. The Blanns are of old Virginia and English stock and were in Virginia in Colonial times. Edward P. Blann died in 1927. His first wife died in the early nineties and he later married Nannie Campbell, of a pioneer family of Knox County, and to this union were born two children.

L. F. Blann, son of Edward P. and Mattie (Nolen) Blann, was born in Weidner Township, Knox County, March 16, 1886, being the second in a family of two children. He attended public schools, and as a youth and young man assisted on the home farm and in his father's store. He has been in the hardware business at Monroe City since 1910, at which time he bought his father's stock of hardware. For seven years he was associated as a partner with C. A. Junkin, at the end of which time he bought the Junkin interest and has since continued the business under the name L. F. Blann, general hardware, agricultural implements and the local agent for the Chevrolet car.

Mr. Blann is a member of Monroe City Lodge No. 548, A. F. and A. M., a member of the Indiana Hardware Dealers Association, and a Democrat and Presbyterian. He married, August 20, 1905, Miss Charlotte Cooper, a native of Harrison Township, Knox County, and daughter of James L. and Charlotte (Myers) Cooper. Her father was a farmer, and died about 1915. Her mother resides at the old Cooper home in Harrison Township.

In 1930 Mr. Blann was elected on the Democratic ticket trustee of Harrison Township for a term of four years. Since early boyhood he has been interested in farming, and for a number of years has operated farming interests in Harrison Township.

JOHN M. GRAYSON, former mayor of the City of Vincennes and a former member of the Indiana State Legislature, is established in the practice of law as one of the constituent members of the representative Vincennes firm of Ramsey & Grayson, with offices at 118 North Seventh Street.

Mr. Grayson was born in Wabash County, Illinois, September 29, 1878, and is a son of Dr. Thomas J. and Harriet (Couch) Grayson, the former of whom was born in Kentucky and the latter in Wabash County, Illinois. The Grayson family was founded in Virginia in the Colonial period of American history and thence representatives of the same went forth to number themselves among the earliest settlers in Kentucky. Doctor Grayson was long and successfully engaged in the practice of medicine in Lawrence County, Illinois, and he gave loyal service in defence of the Union in the period of the Civil war, he having been assigned to the commissary department and having been in active service during virtually the entire period of the war. In this immediate connection it is interesting to record that his son John M., of this review, well upheld the military honors of the family name by service in the Spanish-American war and Philippine Insurrection.

John M. Grayson, one of a family of seven children, was reared and educated in Lawrence County, Illinois, where his advantages were those of the public schools. After his service in the United States Army during the period of the Spanish-American war and Philippine Insurrection he turned his attention to the real-estate business, of which he was a representative in Vincennes, Indiana, during the period of 1902-18. In the latter year he was elected representative of Knox County in the State Legislature, his record in which met with such popular approval that he was re-elected in 1920, from which he resigned in the latter part of 1921, shortly after his election to the office of mayor of Vincennes. His administration as mayor, constructive and progressive, continued from January, 1922, until 1926, and he has since been engaged in the practice of law in this city, with standing as one of the representative members of the bar of Knox County. Mr. Grayson prepared himself for the legal profession by private study under effective preceptorship, and was admitted to the bar in 1923. The firm of which he is a member controls a substantial and important law business of general order. He has membership in the Knox County Bar Association and the Indiana State Bar Association, is an influential figure in the Knox County ranks of the Republican party, and is affiliated with the Knights of Pythias and with Charles D. McCoy Camp No. 28, Spanish-American War Veterans. In the Spanish-American war period he was a member of Company I, Eleventh United States Infantry, his service covered a term of three years and within this period he was on active duty with his command in the Philippine Islands. He was a zealous worker in behalf of patriotic activities in Knox County in the interval of American participation in the World war, and served as captain of the Vincennes Township team that directed a splendid campaign in support of the sale of Government war bonds.

On December 7, 1903, at Bloomfield, Indiana, was solemnized the marriage of Mr. Grayson to Miss Jessie Clemmons, and they have three children: Jeannette Barrill is the wife of Lee Hindman, of Vincennes, who is a student in medical college at Indianapolis, and they have two children, Grace and Susanna. Dorothy is a graduate of the Vincennes University, class of 1931, and Harriet is a student in the Vincennes Junior High School.

FLOYD O. WERT, manager of the Home Lumber & Supply Company at Muncie, has had practically all his business training and experience in the lumber industry. His father before him was a lumberman, so that the vocation came natural to him.

Mr. Wert, one of the live and enterprising business leaders of Muncie, was born at Waynetown, Indiana, December 29, 1894, son of Austin E. and Hattie (Miller) Wert. His grandfather, John William Wert, was an early settler in Wayne County, Indiana, where he followed the business of a building contractor. He moved to Indiana from Ohio. He was killed about 1908 as a result of a fall from a cherry tree at his home. He is buried at Waynetown. Austin E. Wert was born and reared in Wayne County, had a public school education and during all his active life followed the business of forester and lumberman. He left July 4, 1912. His wife, Hattie Miller Wert, was born and reared at Waynetown, and was very attentive to her duties in the Baptist Church. She died December 12, 1923. Her three children were Floyd O., Russell E., of Indianapolis, and Catherine, Mrs. Ulysses Elmore, of Crawfordsville, Indiana.

Floyd O. Wert attended the grade and high schools of Waynetown and finished his education in a college at Danville, Illinois. On July 28, 1913, he came to Muncie, and has been continuously identified with the Home Lumber & Supply Company. He started as yard assistant and has mastered all phases of the business, both inside and outside. Larger responsibilities have been given him from time to time. He was made yard superintendent and for nine years acted as manager of the

Charles W. Brizius   Oscar C. Brizius

Norman J. Brizius   Walter W. Brizius

company's plant at Roachdale. On July 28, 1921, he was called back to Muncie and has since been local manager of the company.

Mr. Wert has been keenly interested in civic affairs, is active in the Chamber of Commerce and the Muncie Y. M. C. A., and is affiliated with the Knights of Pythias and Fraternal Order of Eagles. He is a member of the Retail Lumber Dealers Association, the Optimist Club, Dynamo Club, and is a Republican voter. He and his wife are members of the Avondale Methodist Episcopal Church.

He married, at Newcastle, Indiana, September 19, 1926, Miss Clara Hall, daughter of Joshua Hall and wife. Her father was a building contractor at Newcastle, and both her parents are deceased and are buried at Roachdale. Mr. Wert first married, November 26, 1914, at Waynetown, Miss Lura M. Yount, daughter of Walter and Florence Yount. Her father was a druggist at New Market, Indiana, and is buried in the Masonic Cemetery at Crawfordsville. Her mother still resides in New Market. Mrs. Wert passed away July 17, 1926, and is buried in the Masonic Cemetery at Crawfordsville. She left two children, Robert and John, both of whom are attending the grade schools at Muncie.

Mr. Wert's present wife was educated in the public schools of Roachdale. She is the mother of two sons, Charles and James.

AUGUST E. BOLK is the founder of the August E. Bolk Hardware Company, of Vincennes. This is a complete supply store for heavy hardware, a wholesale business shipping and supplying material over a wide extent of country, much beyond the normal boundaries of the Vincennes wholesale district.

Mr. Bolk was born at Vincennes, September 5, 1884, son of William C. and Mary (Steffen) Bolk. His father was born in Germany, located at Vincennes in 1880, and was in the liquor business for a number of years and was living retired at the time of his death in 1930. There were five children: William, Jr., Otto, deceased, Mary, August and Frank. All three of the living sons are associated as the August E. Bolk Hardware Company.

Mr. August E. Bolk grew up in Vincennes, attended the St. John's School and the public schools, and has been an active business man since early manhood. In 1918 he bought the A. B. Evering Hardware Company, a business that had been established in 1894. Since 1918 the business has been conducted as August E. Bolk & Company, with headquarters at 811 North Second Street. The company now employs a staff of from twelve to fifteen persons, and utilizes over 28,000 square feet of floor space, with switching facilities on the Baltimore & Ohio Railroad.

Mr. Bolk is a member of the National Supply and Machinery Distributors Association. He is one of the popular citizens of Vincennes, a member of the Order of Eagles, the B. P. O. Elks and Loyal Order of Moose, the Harmony Society and the Knights of Columbus.

He was elected to the City Council of Vincennes in November, 1929, on the Democratic ticket.

He married, June 29, 1907, Miss Hannah Miller, member of a family that settled in Vincennes before the Civil war. Their children are: Johannah, now Sister Frances Elvire, of the Sisters of Providence of Terre Haute, Margaret, Rosaline, Mary and William III.

CHARLES W. BRIZIUS is a native son of Warrick County, is a representative of the third generation of the family in this county, and in his activities as a loyal and progressive citizen and influential business man of Newburg he has well upheld the honors of a family name that has been prominently and worthily lined with the history of Warrick County since the pioneer days. Mr. Brizius is president of the Charles W. Brizius Company, which corporation is one of the important industrial and commercial concerns of the fine little City of Newburg, where its flour milling plant is of the best modern equipment.

Charles W. Brizius was born near Boonville, the judicial center of Warrick County, October 22, 1857, and is a son of Charles and Mary (Hermann) Brizius, both of whom were born in Germany. Charles Brizius was reared and educated in his native land and was one of the patriotic young men who took part in the revolution in Germany in the '40s, for which reason he there became persona non grata to the government and, like many others of his countrymen, came to the United States, where he was assured of freedom and independence in thought and action. He was one of twelve children and upon coming to this country he was accompanied by his parents, the family home having been established in Warrick County, Indiana, where his parents passed the remainder of their lives and where their remains rest in the cemetery at Newburg, as later the remains of Charles Brizius and his wife were also laid away. The father was a cooper by trade but becoming one of the substantial pioneer farmers of Warrick County, he having retired after his sons were equipped for taking charge of the old farm and the cooperage business that he had established.

Charles Brizius gave his attention to farm industry until 1865, when he established a brewery at Newburg. This he conducted until 1881, when he and his partner transformed the plant into a flour mill, this substantial old mill being that in which is installed the modern plant of the present Charles W. Brizius Company, the establishment having been at all times maintained at the highest contemporary standard. Mr. Brizius had as a partner in this enterprise Louis Pepmiller, his brother-in-law, and the business was conducted under the title of Pepmiller & Brizius Company, while eventually Charles W. Brizius, of this review, was admitted to partnership in the business. In 1894 John Raab, brother-in-law of Charles W. Brizius, purchased the Pepmiller interest, and the firm name was then changed to Charles Brizius & Company. After the death of Charles Brizius his son Charles W. and son-in-law, John F. Raab, purchased the interest of Mrs. Brizius and after the death of Mr. Raab Charles W. Brizius acquired his interest through purchase at appraiser's sale. The business was carried on under the title of Charles W. Brizius for several years until 1907, when Mr. Brizius admitted his three sons to partnership and the business was duly incorporated under the present title of The Charles W. Brizius Company. Of the eight children of Charles Brizius all but one are living: Mary C., who became the wife of John Raab, survived him until 1928, when she too passed away, survived by five children, of whom the son Adolph served in the United States Army in the World war period. Louis, next younger of the children of Charles Brizius, is associated with the Charles W. Brizius Company, he having married Carrie Cook, of Newburg, and their children being four in number. George H., next younger son, is one of the prosperous farmers of Warrick County. His first wife, whose maiden name was Rose Koehler, is survived by two children, and he later married Lydia Kuebler, the children of this marriage being four in number. Mary E. is the wife of Charles K. McDonald, a cigar manufacturer at Newburg, and they have no children. Rudolph G., manager of the Presbyterian Old People's Home, married Kate Johnson, and they have one child. Clara is the wife of J. W. Foltz, engaged in the dry-goods business at Newburg, and they have no children. Herman, youngest of the children, is engaged in the drug business at Newburg. The maiden name of his wife was Mattie Lant and they have no children.

Charles W. Brizius attended the Newburg public schools and also a local private school, and supplemented this youthful education by remaining two terms as a student in an academy at Elmhurst, Illinois. His initial business experience was acquired in his father's brewery, and when the same was remodeled and equipped as a flour mill he continued his active association with the business. The milling business has been continued during the long intervening period of nearly half a century, and he is now its executive head, as has been previously noted. On March 14, 1931, The Charles W. Brizius Company celebrated its fiftieth anniversary of operation in the milling business.

Mr. Brizius is a Democrat in political adherency and he and his wife are members of Zion's Evangelical Church in their home city. He is a Knight Templar Mason and is a Noble of Hadi Temple of the Mystic Shrine, in the City of Evansville, where likewise are maintained his Chapter, Council and Commandery affiliation in the York Rite of Masonry. He has membership also in the Liederkranz Society of Evansville. Mr. Brizius gave four years of characteristically loyal service as a member of the City Council of Newburg and an equal period of service as a trustee of the local board of education. He is president of the Newburg Building & Loan Association and is vice president of the Newburg State Bank. He retains controlling interest in the business of the Charles W. Brizius Company and is the owner of valuable real estate in his home city and native county.

November 27, 1881, marked the marriage of Mr. Brizius to Miss Philipine Folz, daughter of William and Barbara (Roth) Folz, of Warrick County, and the death of Mrs. Brizius occurred December 11, 1904, she being survived by three sons: Walter W., who was born December 12, 1883, and who is now vice president of the Charles W. Brizius Company, married Lucy Dodd, of Evansville, and they have one child, Walter J., who was born January 25, 1908. Norman J., the second son, was born November 6, 1886, and is now secretary of the Charles W. Brizius Company. He married Gertrude McMurtry, of Evansville, and they have no children. Oscar C., the youngest son, was born June 2, 1892, and is now treasurer of the Charles W. Brizius Company, besides which he has been a member of the City Council of Newburg more than three years and was its president in 1929. He was one of the gallant young sons of Indiana who represented this state in overseas service in the World war, he having been assigned to the One Hundred Twelfth Ammunition Train, Thirty-seventh Division of the American Expeditionary Forces, having left Philadelphia with his unit June 28, 1918, and having been in active service in France when the armistice brought the war to a close. At Camp Taylor, Kentucky, he received his honorable discharge April 29, 1919. He married Laurena Inderrieden of Boonville, Warrick County, and they have two children: Mary E., born October 29, 1924, and Charles O., born March 23, 1929.

The second marriage of Charles W. Brizius was solemnized September 20, 1907, when he wedded Mrs. Fannie L. Bell, no children having been born of this union. She had four children by her former marriage, the only one now living being Emmet Bell, chief of police of Evansville.

FRANK BASTIN is a native of Belgium, where he learned thoroughly the art of glass manufacture, and he came to America equipped with a knowledge and training which he has put to use as an American glass maker. Mr. Bastin is president and manager of the Blackford Window Glass Manufacturing Company, Incorporated, at Vincennes.

He was born October 15, 1872, and came to America in 1890. He had a number of years of experience in various glass plants all over the country and later organized and became manager of the Blackford Window Glass Manufacturing Company, with plant at Hartford City, Indiana. Later this plant was sold and dismantled and on January 5, 1903, the business was moved to Vincennes, where it has been in operation for over a quarter of a century.

Since 1924 the Vincennes factory has used the new sheet drawing process in the manufacture of sheet glass. It is a big and thriving industry, employing 225 men, working in shifts day and night, and employing the most modern processes of manufacture. The machinery of the plant was imported from Belgium. The grounds and plant comprise sixteen acres, with railroad switching tracks up to the doors for the bringing in of raw material and the shipping of the finished product, which goes all over the United States.

Of the corporation Mr. Bastin is president and general manager, Charles A. Weisert is vice president, R. J. Dognaux, secretary, and Ira G. Schaeffer, treasurer.

Mr. Bastin served two terms as president and as a director of the Vincennes Chamber of Commerce. He is a past president and charter member of the Rotary Club, member of the Harmony Society, B. P. O. Elks and Knights of Columbus. For twelve years he was councilman at large of Vincennes. He is a director of the Indiana Manufacturers Association and in 1929 was vice president of the Window Glass Manufacturers Association. During the World war he took a leading part in insuring the success of the Liberty Loan drives. He is a Republican.

Mr. Bastin's wife, Anna Bastin, is also a native of Belgium. They have two children, Nellie, wife of R. J. Dognaux, and Jules, factory representative of the Blackford Window Glass Manufacturing Company in Chicago, and who has three children, Mary Ellen, Rene J., Jr., and Dolores Anne. Jules was enrolled in service during the World war and R. J. Dognaux was also in an army camp during that period.

JOHN B. RICHARDSON, of Monroe City, is an Indiana man of interesting business achievement. He started literally with nothing, but the labor of his hands and ambition have carried him steadily forward from small beginnings until he now has active contact with several lines of business, being an undertaker and funeral director, in the road contracting business, and has also been interested in banking and farming.

He was born in Washington County, Kentucky, September 24, 1880, son of Thomas B. and Malvina (Mayes) Richardson. He was the only son in a family of seven children.

His education was supplied by the common schools of Washington County, Kentucky, and he was doing a man's work long before he attained his majority. For a time he was hauling goods a distance of fourteen miles, also did farming, and at the age of nineteen, in 1899, located at Monroe City, Indiana, where for two years he was employed as a painter and paper hanger. For six years he worked in a brick yard and for two years conducted a restaurant and confectionery. After selling out this business he became an undertaker, in 1914, buying the E. P. Blann Furniture and Undertaking Establishment, and has carried on that business, known as the Donaldson & Richardson Undertaking Establishment ever since. Mr. Richardson from 1921

to 1927 was assistant cashier of the Monroe City State Bank. Since 1927 he has been a member of the firm Byers & Richardson, road building contractors. In this time they have constructed gravel roads and about forty bridges in Illinois and Indiana. As a farmer Mr. Richardson has 150 acres devoted to wheat, corn, oats and live stock in Knox County.

During the early 1900s he served as city treasurer of Monroe City for six years, three terms. He is a past master of Monroe City Lodge No. 548, A. F. and A. M., is a member of the Independent Order of Odd Fellows. During the World war he did work in his community in promoting the success of the Liberty Loan drive. In political affiliation he is a Democrat.

Mr. Richardson, in October, 1901, married Miss Nina Bonewits, now deceased. They had two daughters, Miss Theatis and Miss Madge. Theatis was educated in Purdue University, Vincennes University, the Indiana State Normal at Terre Haute and Columbia University of New York City and is now the head of the economic department of the Wheatland High School. Madge graduated with the class of 1931 from the Vincennes University.

HERBERT MALES, former mayor of the City of Evansville, and former sheriff of Vanderburg County, has been in the intervals of his official experience an active business man of that city. It is doubtful if Evansville has ever shown more complete confidence and given higher honors to any one of its native sons than to Mayor Males.

He was born in Evansville, July 19, 1875, son of Thornton and Emma (Smith) Males. His great-grandfather was a Hollander and his great-grandmother an English woman. His grandfather was one of the early pioneers of Knox County, Indiana. Thornton Males was born in Indiana, served as a Union soldier in the Civil war, under Captain Hollingsworth, in Company F of the One Hundred and Thirty-sixth Indiana Regiment, with the rank of sergeant. After the war he followed mechanical trades, and died December 18, 1913. His wife, Emma Smith, was of English ancestry, and her father was one of the early settlers in Vanderburg County, a pioneer farmer, and became one of the county's largest land owners, having at one time 900 acres. He was a stock man and in the early days imported cattle from England. Thornton Males and wife reared six of their ten children. Edgar, who died at the age of fifty-one, had been a township trustee of Evansville, married Elizabeth Sauer and left two children, Clara, wife of Harry Geissler, and Miss Lillian, secretary to W. W. Gray, president of the City National Bank of Evansville. John, a machine molder, served in the Spanish-American war and was in the intelligence department of the American Expeditionary Forces during the World war. Isaac Males, who was born in 1872, is also a molder by trade and is unmarried. Anna, born in 1862, married August Lehnhard, a retired business man of Evansville, and they have a son, Elmer, born in 1893, a salesman, who married Nellie Cheesebro and has a son, Jack, born in 1924. The daughter, Mary Males, who died at the age of fifty-five, was the wife of John Blum, and left three children, Mary, born in 1899, Catherine, born in 1901, and Ruth, born in 1905.

Mr. Herbert Males grew up and attended public school in Evansville, graduated from business college, and after leaving school he spent twenty-five years with one firm, Lehnhard & Neitert, a well known wholesale produce and fruit business at Evansville. He was with that organization until 1914 and then engaged in business for himself by organizing the Chera Cola Bottling Company, in which he is still interested as a stockholder. He was manager of the business from 1914 to 1918. He also owns several productive oil wells and has been very fortunate in his oil investments and operations.

Mr. Males was elected sheriff of Vanderburg County in 1918, and served in that position four years. When he retired from office he went on the road as a traveling salesman for a wholesale produce house and continued traveling three years, until in 1925 he made the race for mayor. In the election he was accorded the largest majority ever given a candidate for that office in Evansville. Evansville is proud of the administration of its municipal affairs which he gave the city, and which is recognized as one of the most constructive administrations the city has had. Mr. Males is a Republican in politics, is a member of the Evangelical Church and is a thirty-second degree Scottish Rite Mason and Shriner. He also belongs to the Woodmen of the World and the B. P. O. Elks.

He married, in January, 1895, at Evansville, Miss Anna Griese, daughter of William Griese, of Evansville, a brick manufacturer. By this marriage there is one son, John C., born September 28, 1895, now chief clerk in the water works department at Evansville, and is married and has one child.

GUY R. DUNPHY is one of the prominent representatives of the automotive trade in the City of Vincennes, where he is president of the Dunphy Automobile Company, which here has the agency for the celebrated Cadillac and Pontiac cars and which maintains its metropolitan headquarters at the corner of Sixth and Vigo streets.

Mr. Dunphy was born in the State of Kentucky, October 9, 1873, and was a child at the time of the family removal to Illinois, where his father became a successful business man. He is a son of William Dunphy, who was born in Ireland and who was a young man when he came to the United States, where eventually was solemnized his marriage to Miss Elizabeth Jennings, the children of this union being five in number: Lena is the widow of O. O. Rice; Guy R., of this review, was next in order of birth; Charles W. resides in Chicago, in the employ of the International Har-

vester Company, and the maiden name of his wife was Edna Gordon; Jennie C., deceased, was the wife of C. P. Gordon; Carl E., and his wife, Effie, reside at Roanoke, Virginia, and he is there successfully established in business.

Guy R. Dunphy received his youthful education in the schools of Illinois and when about eighteen years of age he entered the service of the International Harvester Company, at St. Louis, Missouri, with which great corporation he continued his association until 1916, he having in the meanwhile won advancement through various departments and having finally been made the manager of the company's important branch in Cincinnati, Ohio. Upon resigning this office, in 1916, he came to Vincennes and effected the reorganization of the Hartman Manufacturing Company, manufacturers of farm implements. He was made assistant sales manager, as well as a director of the company, and with the concern he continued his active alliance until 1921, when its plant and business were sold to the Blount Plow Company of Evansville, this state. It was at this juncture that Mr. Dunphy turned his attention to the automobile business, by purchasing the Gibson Overland branch at the corner of First and Main streets, Vincennes. On May 15, 1922, he purchased also the business of the Fellwock Automobile Company, at the corner of Sixth and Vigo streets, the two enterprises having been consolidated at the latter location, where the business has since been continued as one of the most successful automotive agencies in this historic old city. In addition to handling the Cadillac and Pontiac cars the Dunphy Automobile Company has also the local agency for the LaSalle and Oakland cars.

Mr. Dunphy is a past director of the Vincennes Chamber of Commerce, is affiliated with the Masonic fraternity, in which he has the distinction of being a member of historic Vincennes Lodge No. 1, A. F. and A. M., and is a member of the Vincennes Harmony Club. His political allegiance is given to the Democratic party, and he was elected as councilman at large of the City of Vincennes in 1930, on the Democratic ticket. In the World war period Mr. Dunphy was active in support of patriotic movements of his home community and made liberal subscriptions to the Government war bonds. In the 1930-31 roll call he was chairman of the Vincennes Chapter of the American Red Cross. He has won secure vantage-ground as one of the progressive business men and loyal citizens of Vincennes, and gives his major attention to the affairs of the Dunphy Automobile Company, of which he is president and general manager.

Mr. Dunphy, on October 9, 1895, at Sumner, Illinois, married Miss Jessie M. Couchman, of Lawrence County, Illinois, and their only child, Ernestine, is the wife of George A. Mischler, who is assistant auditor of the Vincennes Bridge Company and who was in Government service in the World war period. They have one child, Guy W. Mischler.

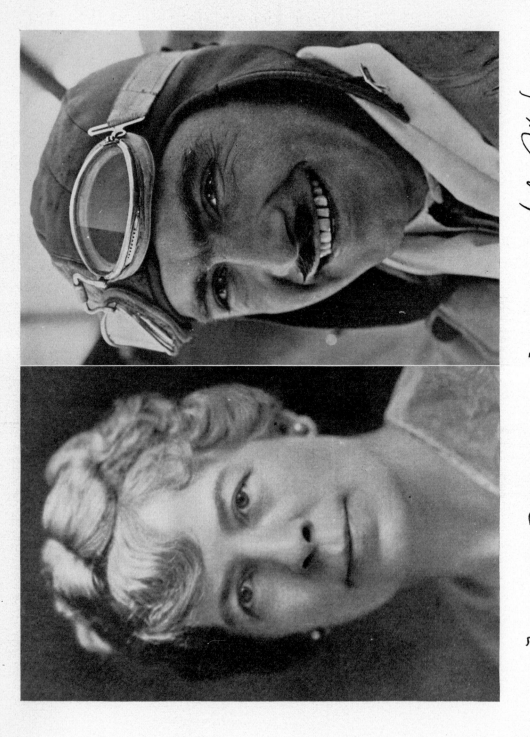

Margaret R. Wister   Major Wiley R. Wright

Anton Bohnert has been long identified with industrial enterprise in his native City of Vincennes, where he is now manager of the plant of the Central Foundry Company. His skill as a mechanic and executive has been enlisted at other places for varying intervals, but Vincennes has been the principal stage of his activities during the major part of his long business career, which had its inception when he was a lad of thirteen years. Mr. Bohnert has been in the fullest sense the architect of his own fortunes, even as his broader education has been acquired through self-discipline —well ordered reading and study during the passing years that have likewise fortified him in business experience.

Mr. Bohnert was born in Vincennes May 29, 1869, and is a son of Gottfried and Mary (Dutchman) Bohnert, the former of whom was born in Baden-Baden, Germany, and the latter in Alsace, France. Gottfried Bohnert made settlement in Vincennes, Indiana, prior to the Civil war, and here found employment in the boiler department of the Ohio & Mississippi Railroad, which is now a part of the Baltimore & Ohio system. Later he was similarly engaged with the Big Four Railroad and he continued his residence in Vincennes until his death, his wife having survived him a number of years and both having been earnest communicants of the Catholic Church. Their children were four in number: Theresa, Anton, Aloysius and Frank (deceased).

In Vincennes Anton Bohnert received his early education, which was very limited, as he was but thirteen years of age when he discontinued his studies in the parochial school of St. John's Church, German Catholic, and began to aid in the support of the family. His ambition led him to give time to home study and reading, and along this line he has continued until he has become a man of really liberal education. He was employed in a local dry-goods establishment until he was sixteen years of age, when he entered upon his apprenticeship to the machinist's trade in the local shops of Clark & Buck. At the age of twenty years he became a machinist in the local factory of the Bell-Armstead Manufacturing Company, and of the machine department he was made foreman when he was twenty-four years of age. In 1899 the plant and business of this company were sold to the Central Foundry Company of New York City, and with the latter Mr. Bohnert was retained as foreman of the machine shop until 1914, when the plant was closed. The same company then transferred him to its plant at Bessemer, Alabama, whence he was transferred six months later to Holt, that state, where he remained three months. He next passed three years in service with the Central Specialty Company in Detroit, Michigan, after the Alabama plants had been temporarily closed. In 1919 he returned to Vincennes and became manager of the reopened plant of the Central Foundry Company. In 1925 the plant was again closed, and Mr. Bohnert then returned to Michigan, where he remained as assistant foreman of the Ypsilanti Foundry Company, at Ypsilanti, until 1927, when he returned to Vincennes and reopened the plant of the Central Foundry Company, with which he has since remained as manager.

Mr. Bohnert is a Democrat in politics and he and his family are communicants of the Catholic Church. He is affiliated with the Fraternal Order of Eagles and the Loyal Order of Moose.

In Vincennes was solemnized the marriage of Mr. Bohnert to Miss Fannie M. Wise, daughter of Frederick and Rosalene Wise. Of the five children of this union four are living: Miss Rosalene remains at the parental home, as does also Miss Lucille, who is a deputy in the office of the county clerk of Knox County; Mary graduated with the class of 1931 in the Sister Academy; Joseph is a student; and Richard is deceased. The family home is maintained at 154 East Swartzel Street.

Mrs. Margaret Reed Wright is matron of Thornton Home at Newburg, Warrick County, Indiana. Mrs. Wright formerly lived at Evansville but since the death of her husband she has found opportunity for a useful work and interesting contact with people whom she loves and who in turn love her.

Mrs. Wright is the widow of the late Dr. A. C. Wright, a prominent physician and surgeon. Doctor Wright was born in Warren County, Kentucky, and died October 29, 1910, at the age of seventy-one. His father was Dr. Thomas B. Wright, also a native of Warren County, Kentucky. Dr. A. C. Wright was one of five children. His sister Mrs. Elizabeth Wright Thomas, who died March 1, 1931, at the age of eighty-nine, was active in literary and social clubs at Bowling Green, Kentucky. She had two sons, Thomas and Richard, both of whom were leading lawyers. Hon. Thomas Wright died March 4, 1930, at the age of sixty-three. Another son, Daniel Webster Wright, was a Kentucky lawyer and land owner and a member of the Legislature.

Mrs. Margaret Reed Wright is a daughter of Rev. Wiley Martin Reed, who was born in Giles County, Tennessee, entered the Confederate army, commanded a regiment as colonel and was mortally wounded at Fort Pillow while serving under General Forrest. General Forrest appointed a special escort to convey him to Jackson, Tennessee. He was also an intimate friend of General Jackson, who presented him with a beautiful horse when he joined the army. Prior to the war he had been pastor of the First Cumberland Presbyterian Church at Nashville, Tennessee. Rev. Wiley Martin Reed was distinguished in appearance and his abilities were in keeping. The mother of Mrs. Wright was Mary Caroline White, also a Tennesseean, daughter of John D. White, a pioneer of Shelby County, that state, and a very wealthy man. Mary Caroline White and Wiley Martin Reed were educated at Lebanon, Tennessee, and their romance began while in college there and they were married as soon as their studies were completed. In the Reed family were seven children: Edgar, Marshall, Erskine, Percy Ward, Mary, Margaret, now the only one living, and Wiley M., Jr. Edgar was for many years with the Louisville & Nashville Railroad. Marshall was educated for medicine but spent an active career as a railroad man. Erskine was connected with the Dun and Bradstreet Commercial Agencies. Mary married William H. Cook, of Smith's Grove, Warren County, Kentucky.

Miss Margaret Reed was educated at Nashville, Tennessee, and at New York City specialized in music and expression. Both she and her sister taught music and expression in the Cumberland Female College at McMinnville, Tennessee, for six years. Miss Reed and Doctor Wright were married at Smith's Grove, Kentucky, November 14, 1895. Mrs. Wright has one son, Wiley Reed Wright, who was born April 6, 1897, and was educated in Bowling Green, Kentucky, and the Castle Heights School, and during the World war was in training with the Aviation Corps, receiving a commission as first lieutenant and later was promoted to captain and finally to major of the Reserve Corps. He was for a time at Gerstner Field, Lake Charles, Louisiana, and after the war spent some time with the Clyde Steamship Lines. He is now under the United States Commerce Department, aeronautic branch, as inspector of aeroplanes and products. This line of service requires him to travel over the mountain and Pacific States and Alaska, establishing airports and reporting on various angles of aviation industry.

Mrs. Wright is a Democrat in politics, is a member of the Presbyterian Church of the United States, and belongs to the United Daughters of the Confederacy and Daughters of the American Revolution and the Newburg Literary Club.

The Thornton Place Home is an institution conducted for the benefit of disabled Presbyterian ministers, their wives, widows, missionaries and orphans. It was established at Evansville by the Cumberland Presbyterian Board, but in 1908 the board acquired the beautiful residence and country home of Mrs. Ames at Newburg in Warrick County. Other buildings have been added to supplement the facilities provided by the handsome residence and there are accommodations for forty guests, though at the present time only twenty-five are enrolled. Mrs. Wright handles all the financial affairs of the institution, which is supported by the church at large. She has the supervision of a staff of three nurses and other competent employees. Outside the buildings there are 110 acres of land. A motor bus was presented to the institution by a prominent Evansville philanthropist and other things that add to the comfort and entertainment of the guests are radio and piano. Mrs. Wright for the past seventeen years has been in full charge of the institution. She is called "mother" by all and she calls the guests her children, although some of them are much older than herself. These children idolize her.

Mrs. Wright is exceptionally well educated, a woman of fine culture and broad experience and has been an ideal person for the position she fills.

I. GRANT BEESLEY, president of the City Transfer Company, which virtually represents one of the important public-utilities of Vincennes, gives further evidence of his progressiveness by his loyal service as a member of the City Council, in which he is representative from the Fifth Ward, serving his second term.

Mr. Beesley was born in Lawrence County, Illinois, April 12, 1887, and is a son of William Penn and Mary (Brosa) Beesley, both likewise natives of Lawrence County, where they were reared to adult age, where their marriage was solemnized and where they long maintained their home, William P. Beesley having made a successful record as a teacher in the public schools and also as a merchant. In 1889 he moved his family to Vincennes, where he and his wife reside, and where since 1895 he has been a representative business man. Of the three children I. Grant, of this review, is the eldest; Everett I. is a civil engineer and as such is in the employ of the Mississippi Valley Steel Company, of St. Louis, Missouri; Oscar V., who is now identified with the Sterling Manufacturing Company, of Sterling, Illinois, was in overseas service in the World war, had active service in various conflict sectors and gained the rank of first lieutenant.

James Beesley, grandfather of the subject of this sketch, was born in England and was a child when the family came to the United States, in 1831, his father, Thomas Beesley, having kept the family in the State of New York the first year and then having come to the West and established the family home in Wabash County, Illinois.

I. Grant Beesley was a child of two years at the time of the family removal from Illinois to Vincennes, and in the public schools of this city his studies were continued until his second high school year. At the age of twenty years he here entered the employ of the American Express Company, and two years later he transferred his service to the Klemeyer Lumber Company, in the offices of which he remained nine years. He then, in 1920, became associated with E. C. Reel, C. R. Haartje and C. E. Travis in organizing the City Transfer Company, upon the incorporation of which he assumed his present dual office of president and general manager. In 1926 Mr. Beesley bought out the interest of E. C. Reel and C. E. Travis. The company controls a large and representative business in general draying, functions effectively in freight distribution in the city and as local agents for the Central Union Truck Terminal Company of Indianapolis, besides operating a line of trucks between Terre Haute and Evansville. The company has eight of the best of modern motor trucks in commission and retains a corps of fifteen employes.

Mr. Beesley is a member of the Indiana Motor Truck Association, is one of the progressive and loyal members of the Vincennes Chamber of Commerce and for the past four years a director in the Vincennes Kiwanis Club. His basic Masonic affiliation is with historic Vincennes Lodge No. 1, A. F. and A. M., he is a member of the Harmony Club in his home city, and his political allegiance is given to the Democratic party. He takes deep interest in all that concerns the welfare and advancement of Vincennes and at the time of this writing, in 1931, he is giving characteristically loyal service as representative of the Fifth Ward in the City Council. His church affiliations are with the Bethany Presbyterian.

Mr. Beesley married, November 16, 1910, at Vincennes, Miss Emma Hartje, of Grand View, Spencer County, Indiana, and their four children are daughters: Gretchen Christine, Doris Emma, Mary Roberta and Sarah Ella. Gretchen Christine will graduate from the Vincennes High School with the class of 1933 and Doris Emma with the class of 1934.

RALPH C. PHILLIPPE is a native of Vincennes, member of a family that has been in Knox County for a century, and his own particular achievements are represented by a group of organizations, insurance and advertising, that covers a large portion of Indiana and Ohio.

Mr. Phillippe was born in Vincennes October 29, 1891. His father, Peter Phillippe, was also born in Knox County, as was his grandfather, George W. Phillippe. The great-grandfather was a West Virginian, whose grandfather served as a soldier in the American Revolution. The great-grandfather came to Knox County, Indiana, about 1830, and in Washington Township, near Bicknell, acquired land which has ever since been referred to as the Phillippe homestead and which has come down through the different generations. Mr. Ralph C. Phillippe is a part owner of the land, and it has been in five generations of the family. George W. Phillippe spent his life as a farmer and married Mary Smith. Peter Phillippe was an educator, and served fifteen years as county superintendent of schools of Knox County. He married Lettie Huring, of Warrick County, Indiana, and they were the parents of seven children.

Ralph C. Phillippe attended school at Vincennes and completed his education in the University of Indiana in 1916. In the meantime he had been ticket agent for the Baltimore & Ohio Railway Company three years, 1911-14, and from 1915 to July, 1917, was manager of the insurance department of the Knox Bank & Trust Company.

He left the bank to join the colors as a private in the infantry, Company C, Eight Hundred and Thirteenth Infantry, attached to the Thirty-third Division, and in 1918 went to France. He had a series of promotions from private to corporal, to sergeant, to sergeant major, to second lieutenant, and when he was discharged, August 3, 1919, it was with the rank of first lieutenant. He is a member of the Officers Reserve Corps, with the rank of first lieutenant.

Soon after his return from overseas and his release from army service Mr. Phillippe organized the Bainum Phillippe Company, handling general insurance. In January, 1928, this firm was consolidated with the R. C. Mossman agency, the new organization taking the name of the Union Agency, Incorporated, of which Mr. Phillippe is president, M. D. Gould, vice president, H. M. Robbins, secretary, and R. C. Mossman, treasurer.

In addition to his activities in the field of insurance Mr. Phillippe has for several years been building up important relationships with the field of advertising, particularly outdoor advertising. He is vice president of the Saiter Morgan Company, Vincennes, Indiana, is president of the Indo Poster Advertising Company at Marion, Indiana, president of the Evansville Bulletin Service at Evansville, president of the Universal Advertising Service of Vincennes, president of the Wabash Poster Service at Mount Carmel, Illinois, president of the C. & H. Poster Advertising Company of Defiance, Ohio, president of the Indo Poster Advertising Company of Union City, Indiana, president of the Vicksburg Poster Advertising Company, Vicksburg, Mississippi. These various companies employ about a hundred persons and operate thirty-five trucks, doing poster work and advertising distribution throughout the states of Indiana and Ohio.

Mr. Phillippe, on September 7, 1918, at Chillicothe, Ohio, married Miss Helen Schumaker, of Vincennes. Her people have been in Knox County for several generations. Mr. Phillippe is a member of the Rotary Club, Harmony Society, member of Vincennes Lodge No. 1, A. F. and A. M., the B. P. O. Elks, Y. M. C. A., Vincennes and Old Post Country Club, and is city chairman of the Democratic committee. He is a charter member of American Legion Post No. 73 and also of the local Forty and Eight Society.

PHILIP KABEL. The banker of today, especially in the smaller cities and towns of the country, can render a most effective aid in presenting new business opportunities, or discharging the wornout ones, for he is of all men the best placed for such a service. He has the most intimate relations and also the final word; he keeps the money in circulation on good terms and at the same time contributes to the prosperity of his farmer neighbor as well as the city people, who in turn put their money back into the bank. Working along these lines Philip Kabel, president of the Farmers & Merchants Bank of Winchester, has built up a solid institution and a wide patronage.

Philip Kabel was born at Winchester, February 1, 1879, a son of John and Rebecca (Mendenhall) Kabel, natives of Randolph County; and grandson of Philip and Mary

(Goetz) Kabel, natives of Germany, who located in Randolph County at an early day and here became substantial farming people, and the grandfather also conducted a woolen mill. The maternal grandparents, Nathan and Maria (Larisen) Mendenhall, were also early settlers of Randolph County, and farmers. John Kabel and his wife located at Winchester after their marriage, and for some years he was a public school teacher. Later he went on the road, but throughout his life he was interested in farming. His death occurred in 1917, and his wife's in 1898.

After he had completed the work of the grade and high schools Philip Kabel attended Earlham College, and at the age of nineteen years began teaching school. For the following eight years he continued that calling, and then decided upon a business career and entered his present bank as assistant cashier. Three years later he was made cashier, and February 9, 1921, was made president. The bank is capitalized at $50,000, and has resources of $845,000. It is the oldest banking institution in Eastern Indiana, having been established in 1857, and from then on it has weathered all of the financial storms that have destroyed one or other of the earlier competitors. Its policies are conservative, its connections are important, and its investments are of the most solid. Some of the best business men in this part of the state are on its directorate, and its name back of any project is sufficient guarantee for discriminating investors.

On August 14, 1901, Mr. Kabel was married to Miss Alice Reynard, born in Randolph County, a daughter of Elisha and Martha (Adamson) Reynard, natives of Randolph County. Mr. and Mrs. Kabel have had the following children: Rebecca, who was born in January, 1903, was graduated from the Winchester High School and Earlham College, from which latter she took her degree of Bachelor of Arts, and she completed her Master's degree in the University of Indiana, and she has taught English in the McKinley High School since 1925; and Elbert, who was born November 15, 1910, was graduated from the Winchester High School, and is now a student of the University of Indiana. He was made a member of the Indiana University Band, which is called the All-American College Band of the United States. This band, of 100 members, is recognized as the leading organization of its kind in the country.

Philip Kabel is a Quaker, and is a member of the ministerial board of the Friends' Church, and he has held other offices in connection with it. His political belief makes him a Republican. Fraternally he affiliates with the Knights of Pythias. He is a past president of the Rotary Club; Fountain Park Cemetery Board has him as its president, and he has held the office for a long period, and at different times he has been on the school board of Winchester. He is an interested member of the American Historical Association and of the National Geographical Society. A well-educated man, he is interested in cultural subjects, and exerts himself to promote the advancement of the city along this line, as he does in a business way, and the results are gratifying and effective.

CHARLES H. GRIGGS is president of the C. H. Griggs Motor Corporation of Vincennes, and is effectively ordering the policies and directing the business of this company, which here has the agency for the celebrated and popular Graham-Paige automobiles. The attractive, spacious and well equipped sales and display rooms as well as the service department, of this agency are established at 601 Main Street.

Mr. Griggs was born at Bridgeport, Lawrence County, Illinois, September 27, 1882, and is one of the four children born to John V. and Cora Griggs, the former of whom was born in Perry County, Ohio, and the latter in Lawrence County, Illinois, where their marriage was solemnized and where John V. Griggs had established residence prior to the Civil war.

The early education of Charles H. Griggs was acquired in the schools of Bridgeport and Saint Francisville, Illinois, and at the age of fourteen years he became associated with his father's business, that of buying and shipping livestock, the father having also maintained a hardware store and grain elevator at Saint Francisville. Charles H. Griggs continued to be actively and constructively identified with his father's varied business operations until he attained to his legal majority, when he married and established his residence on a farm in his native county, where he continued his successful operations as an agriculturist and stock-grower until he was twenty-six years of age. He then purchased a half-interest in his father's hardware and grain-elevator business at Saint Francisville, and in 1909 he there initiated his connection with the automobile business, as agent for the Reo cars. After two years he transferred his base of operations in this line of enterprise to Lawrenceville, the county seat, and four years later he removed to Princeton, Indiana, where he maintained a Hudson and Buick agency three years, or until November 1, 1919, when he identified himself with the Vincennes Nash Motor Company, which here maintained a factory branch agency until 1922. The business was incorporated in 1922, and Mr. Griggs was elected president and general manager of the company and continued identified with the Vincennes Nash Motor Company until December 1, 1930. The C. H. Griggs Motor Corporation was organized December 2, 1930, and Mr. C. H. Griggs was elected president and general manager. The large and well equipped building was erected specially for the use of the corporation. This building was erected in 1925 and affords nearly 7,000 square feet of floor space. The agency is one of the foremost in importance in the City of Vincennes, covering the counties of Knox in Indiana and Lawrence County in Illinois, and

O. L. Belcher M.D.

is represented in membership in the National Automobile Dealers Association.

The political allegiance of Mr. Griggs is given to the Republican party. He is an active member of the Vincennes Chamber of Commerce, is president of the local Rod and Gun Club and the Two Eye Duck Club, which alliances indicate his deep interest in hunting and fishing, and in Lawrenceville, Illinois, he still retains membership in lodge No. 1208 of the Benevolent and Protective Order of Elks. His basic Masonic affiliation is now with Vincennes Lodge No. 1, A. F. and A. M., and he is also a member of the Scottish Rite Consistory at Evansville, besides being there a Noble of the Temple of the Mystic Shrine.

Mrs. Cora (Jordan) Griggs, first wife of the subject of this review, died at Saint Francisville, Illinois, and is survived by two children, Beulah May and John Albert. In 1916 Mr. Griggs was united in marriage to Miss Gladys B. Bramble, of Lawrenceville, Illinois, and she is the popular chatelaine of their attractive home in Vincennes, at 1152 East Sycamore Street.

HARRY R. ANDERSON, clerk of the Vanderburg Circuit Court of Vanderburg County, has been firmly established in public confidence and esteem at Evansville for a number of years, first as a business man and then as a public official.

Mr. Anderson was born in Pike County, Indiana, October 9, 1892, son of John L. and Louise (Sprinkles) Anderson. His parents were born in Warrick, Indiana, and his father died in 1906 at Evansville and his mother in 1894. John L. Anderson spent his active life as a farmer. There were two children besides Harry R. Clarence, born in 1888, a farmer in Warrick County, married Ethel Lawrence, who was born in that county, daughter of Peter Lawrence, a farmer. Eugene Anderson, who died at the age of thirty-one, was a cigar maker, and by his marriage to Olivio Cummings left three children, Charles, born in 1909, Mary, born in 1912, and Lena, born in 1911.

Harry R. Anderson attended the grade and high schools at Evansville, and graduated from business college in 1910. After a year of work as clerk in the sales department of the Hercules Buggy Company he went west on account of failing health, spent a year in recuperating, and on returning he was an employee of the Adams Express Company and filled several other positions, as bookkeeper, salesman, with Evansville business organizations. Mr. Anderson has some farming interests in Warrick County, growing cattle and hogs, and also has real estate in Evansville. In 1914 he joined the Evansville police department as a patrolman and later was promoted to motorcycle officer. He resigned in 1918 to join the colors and was with Headquarters Company in the field artillery at Camp Taylor, Kentucky, until discharged in 1919. For two years after the war Mr. Anderson sold automobiles at Evansville. In

1921 he went to the courthouse as deputy county clerk and served in that position five years, an experience that gave him a thorough knowledge of the routine of the county clerk's office. In March, 1926, came his appointment as chief of police of Evansville, and he was the police chief of the city until January 1, 1929, when he entered upon his duties as clerk of the Vanderburg Circuit Court following his election in November, 1928.

He married, at Evansville, August 11, 1918, Miss Bertha Ambrose, daughter of Julius Ambrose, a grocery merchant. Mr. Anderson is a Republican in politics and a member of the B. P. O. Elks.

OLIVER L. BELCHER, physician and surgeon at Monroe City, is a member of a family that has been in Indiana for considerably more than a century. The family for the most part has been substantial farmers. The two counties that have known members of the Belcher family have been Crawford and Knox.

Doctor Belcher was born in Harrison Township of Knox County, May 7, 1884, son of Joseph and Isabell (Helderman) Belcher, a grandson of Jeremiah Belcher and a great-grandson of the Belcher who came from Germany and settled in Crawford County in early pioneer times. Jeremiah Belcher was born in that county in 1820. Joseph Belcher was a native of Knox County, born in 1855, but spent the greater part of his active life on a farm in Knox County. He was a local leader in politics. His wife, Isabell Helderman, was descended from the Helderman family of North Carolina.

Doctor Belcher was the second in a family of nine children. He grew up on a farm, attended public schools in Knox County, spent two years in Vincennes University and one year in the State Normal College. His professional training was acquired in two institutions, the first two years at the University of Indiana and the second two years at the University of Louisville, Kentucky, medical department, where he was graduated M. D. in 1908. Doctor Belcher subsequently took postgraduate work in Rush Medical College of Chicago. He has practiced his profession at Monroe City since 1908, the only important interruption to his service among the people of that community being during the World war period.

He was with the colors a year and four months, connected with the Tenth Division at Camp Funston, Kansas, as first lieutenant, and was in the Hospital Ambulance Corps and Infirmary Division. He was ordered overseas but the order was cancelled. Doctor Belcher is a member of Monroe City Lodge No. 548, A. F. and A. M., is a Democrat in politics, and a member of the American Legion at Vincennes. He married on September 17, 1904, Gertrude Teverbaugh, of Knox County, daughter of Wesley and Sarah (Marsh) Teverbaugh. The Teverbaugh family is a pioneer family in Knox County, Indiana. Wesley Teverbaugh was a veteran of the Civil war serving with the Union Army, from Indiana. He followed farming all his life and died in 1901 and his widow survived until 1917. The two daughters born to Doctor and Mrs. Belcher are: Cecil Marie, a member of the class of 1932 of Indiana State Normal at Terre Haute in art and music, and Goldie Jewel, member of the class of 1933 in the same Terre Haute institution.

Doctor Belcher is a member of the Knox County, Indiana State and American Medical Associations. In 1927 the doctor visited Belgium, France and Switzerland and took a post-graduate course at Heidelberg University, Heidelberg, Germany.

DALE JAMES FERGUSON, an Indiana school man, has shown a rare capacity both for teaching and for the administrative detail work connected with a career as an educator.

He is a native of Indiana, born in Lancaster Township, Wells County, December 23, 1891, son of Albert C. and Nellie (Dailey) Ferguson. His father was born at Holden, Missouri, a son of Gideon Ferguson, whose original home was in North Carolina. Mr. Ferguson's mother was born at Bluffton, Indiana, daughter of James and Adeline (Niblick) Dailey. James Dailey was born at Paterson, New Jersey, in 1815, and his wife was a native of Marietta, Ohio, daughter of Robert Niblick, who came from County Claire, Ireland. Albert C. Ferguson is a retired plastering contractor now living at Ossian, Indiana.

Dale James Ferguson was educated in grade and high schools, attended Winona College and graduated from the Central Indiana Normal School at Danville. He has been teaching in public schools since 1912. The chief interruption to his career as an educator came during the World war, when he was with the colors. On May 1, 1918, he enlisted and was sent to Fort Thomas, Kentucky, later transferred to the Officers Training Camp at Camp Gordon, Georgia, as a bayonet instructor, and on October 15, 1918, was commissioned a second lieutenant in the infantry. He was with the Sixth Replacement Regiment at Camp Gordon and later in the Eight Hundred and Seventeenth Pioneer Infantry at Camp Greene, North Carolina.

He was discharged December 20, 1918, and at once resumed his school work. For two years he was principal of the Aetna Township High School in Whitney County, for three years was principal of the high school at Galveston, two years principal of the high school at Quincy, Indiana, and since 1925 has been principal of the high school at Lynn in Randolph County. Mr. Ferguson is a member of the Indiana State Teachers Association and the National Education Association. He is a Democrat in politics, a Presbyterian and a member of the Masonic fraternity and Eastern Star, Knights of Pythias and the American Legion Post.

Mr. Ferguson married, October 31, 1917, at Ossian, Indiana, Miss Georgiana Hostetler. Mrs. Ferguson was born at Evansville, Indiana, daughter of Charles A. and Bessie (Holland) Hostetler. Her father was a native of Milltown, Indiana, son of Edmond and Clementine (Powers) Hostetler, while her mother was born at Paola, Indiana, daughter of William and Mary Holland. Mrs. Ferguson is a high school graduate. They have two children, Dale Eugene, born April 4, 1921, and Cair Elaine, born September 8, 1923.

LOUIS L. KING. The growth and development of Winchester, Indiana, during the past half of the new century has been largely due to the enterprise and foresight of her real estate dealers, who are practically the best promoters of any growing and progressive town. The advantages which have made Winchester real estate desirable as an investment have been exploited in such a way by her realtors as to attract capital and additions to her citizenship. One of the foremost men engaged in this business is Louis L. King, who operates in partnership with Ulysses Grant Daly, the two also writing insurance and making collections, and having a very large connection. Mr. King was born in Randolph County, Ohio, October 17, 1879, a son of Benjamin and Hettie C. (Davis) King, he born in Preble County, Ohio, and she in Wayne County, Indiana. Benjamin King served in the Fifth Ohio Cavalry during the war between the states, and was so severely wounded with a sabre that he was rendered unfit for active business. He died in 1900. Mrs. King, who was a daughter of William H. Davis, died in 1924.

Louis L. King attended the public schools of Winchester until he was seventeen years old, and then learned the lathing trade, which he followed for four years. He then became an operator in a moving picture concern of Winchester, and traveled in its behalf until 1918. In that year he became connected with the Metropolitan Life Insurance Company, and was its representative for three years. His next business venture was the operation of a music and electrical appliance store for two years, but he sold it and entered his present field, in which he is accomplishing so much of constructive value.

In 1903 Mr. King was married to Miss Ruiah Edwards, of Adams County, Indiana, a daughter of Ross and Arminda (Syphers) Edwards, also of Adams County. Mrs. King died December 3, 1921, having borne her husband the following children: Lester C., who is in his father's office; Florence Helen, who is taking the nurses' course in Reed Memorial Hospital, Richmond, Indiana; and Mary B., who is a bookkeeper for a concern at Dayton, Ohio. The Kings are Quakers. A very active Republican, Mr. King has long been precinct committeeman, and has served as delegate to the state conventions of his party upon numerous occasions. Fraternally he maintains membership with the Masonic Order, the Improved Order of Red Men and the Sons of Veterans. His office is on West Washington Street, and his residence at 235 Carl Street.

Mr. King represents the type of man who both thinks and does, and has a practical business head, which he uses to excellent advantage not only for himself but the public as well.

CHARLES R. LENAHAN, member of the firm of Lenahan & Koken Company, of Vincennes, a prominent firm of road building contractors doing work on both side of the Wabash River, was born in Wabash County, Illinois, and for the greater part of his life his home has been in the historic City of Vincennes.

His father, Patrick W. Lenahan, was born at Hamilton in Butler County, Ohio, July 17, 1858, son of John and Mary (Hogan) Lenahan. John Lenahan was born in County Kildare, Ireland, and prior to the Civil war settled at Hamilton, Ohio. He and his wife had nine children. Of these Patrick W. grew up in Illinois, in the home of his uncle, John S. Garitson, until he was sixteen years of age, and then started out alone to earn his living and supplemented his educational opportunities. He worked after school hours, was a farm hand at thirteen dollars a month, and during the next seven or eight years she was attending school, working on farms in the summer and selling merchandise during the winter season. The next stage in his business experience was as a farm renter. He raised grain and live stock in Wabash County. In August, 1892, he moved to Vincennes, and during the past thirty-five years has supervised from that city his growing interests as a land owner, farmer and business man. He acquired some land opposite Vincennes, in Illinois, and has been a dealer in real estate, figuring as a medium in many transactions involving large acreage tracts. He still owns about 500 acres of land, all in cultivation. For a number of years Patrick W. Lenahan was in the contracting business, building roads, doing work in Knox County, Indiana, and in Wabash and Lawrence counties, Illinois. As a road contractor he completed 150 miles of gravel road in those counties. When he retired from contracting work in 1922 he turned his business organization over to his two sons and a nephew, and they make up the Lenahan & Koken Company, of Vincennes.

Patrick W. Lenahan has been in a very important degree one of Vincennes' most useful citizens. For six years he was secretary and treasurer of the local school board, is secretary of the North Side Building & Loan Company, and is a director of the First National Bank. He is a member of the Knights of Columbus, the Harmony Society, is a Republican. He was a prime mover in bringing about the reclamation work carried on by the Bevort, Spangler and Lenahan Levee Association, and was president of the association for over ten years. He was the third man to sign the petition for construction of reclamation work and the levee has protected and brought under cultivation about 50,000 acres of land in Knox County, south of Vincennes.

Patrick W. Lenahan's two oldest brothers were in the Civil war, James and Edward, both in Company I of the Seventy-fourth Ohio Infantry, Fourteenth Army Corps, under General Thomas. Edward was a color sergeant and was in seventeen hard-fought battles, and James was wounded in one action.

Patrick W. Lenahan married Euretta Higgins, of Allendale, Wabash County, Illinois, daughter of William and Sarah (Crane) Higgins. Her father was a farmer and during the Civil war held the office of postmaster. Patrick W. Lenahan and wife had three children: John W., associated with his brother in the road contracting business, is married and has three living children; Charles R.; and Ethel, wife of J. B. McCarthy of Knox County, Indiana, who has five children.

Charles R. Lenahan was educated at Vincennes and as a boy was employed by his father, thus learning the contracting business from the ground up. Later he and his brother bought the business from their father, becoming equal partners, with Mr. John G. Koken, who is a nephew of Patrick W. Lenahan. This company employs about eighty-five persons during the high point of the season's work. They have fifty acres of gravel pits and have all the machinery and equipment for prompt and efficient work, including eighteen gravel motor trucks and many other types of power machinery, including grade scrapers and tractors. This firm since it has been in existence has completed fifty miles of concrete highway and 200 miles of gravel road in three counties of Indiana and Illinois, Knox, Wabash and Lawrence. The best equipped machine shop in Vincennes is owned by this organization and keeps the machinery in complete repair.

Mr. Charles R. Lenahan is a member of the Harmony Society, is affiliated with the B. P. O. Elks, Fraternal Order of Eagles and Knights of Columbus, and votes as a Republican. He married Marceline DeLisle, daughter of J. E. DeLisle and member of one of the old French families of Vincennes. They have six children: Charles Bernard, Mildred Katherine, John Pat, Harold Robert, Charles R., Jr., and James Kenneth.

John W. Lenahan, the other Lenahan represented in the firm of Lenahan & Koken, married Mary Fatchett also of old French ancestry. They have three living children, John Dewit, Paul Richard and William, Jr.

HIRAM MCCORMICK. One of the veteran lawyers of the Indiana bar, Hiram McCormick, of Shoals, has been engaged in practice since 1871, and today is serving in the capacity of deputy prosecuting attorney of Martin County. Few are left of the men who were his contemporaries when he came to the bar, but he continues to carry on his private practice and fulfill his official duties with a clear mind and alert step that belie his years. The great confidence and esteem in which he has always been held by his fellow-citizens are evidenced by the number of offices to which he has been elected, and in which he has registered an honorable record for conscientious devotion to duty.

Mr. McCormick was born on a farm in Martin County, Indiana, February 28, 1847, and is a son of William and Susannah (Faris) McCormick. His paternal grandfather, William McCormick, senior, a native of Scotland, immigrated to America in young manhood, espoused the cause of the patriots and entered the Revolutionary army, and eventually became a colonel in the army of General Washington. In his later years he secured a land grant from the Government for his military services and moved to Tennessee, where he rounded out his career. William McCormick, the father of Hiram McCormick, was born in Tennessee, and was a soldier during the War of 1812, serving under Andrew Jackson and fought in three engagements, Horse Shoe Bend, Alabama, Pensacola, and the Battle of New Orleans, also in a number of Indian engagements. The greater part of his life was spent in agricultural pursuits in Martin County, where his death occurred in March, 1876, when he was eighty-nine years of age. By his first marriage he had ten children, and after the death of his first wife he married Susannah Faris, a native of Kentucky, who survived him until 1892. They became the parents of twelve children, of whom Hiram is the youngest.

Hiram McCormick acquired his early education in a log schoolhouse in Martin County, and while the methods were crude and primitive he became sufficiently educated to secure a position as a teacher. He was thus engaged until being elected township assessor in Martin County in 1867, and in the following year was elected sheriff of Martin County. While holding these offices he applied himself to the study of law, and in 1871, after successfully passing a strict examination, was admitted to the bar and at once settled at Shoals, where he has been engaged in active practice ever since. For many years Mr. McCormick has handled large interests, practiced actively at the bar and acted in behalf of prominent estates. He has not appeared so frequently in private cases recently, owing to his official duties, but still is numbered among the leading lawyers of Southern Indiana. For four years he served in the capacity of prosecuting attorney of Martin County, and for several years has acted as deputy prosecuting attorney, having obtained many convictions during his incumbency of these offices. He is a member of the Martin County Bar Association, the Indiana State Bar Association and the American Bar Association, and is a Democrat in politics. While a religious man by nature, he does not hold membership in any church. He has no fraternal connections.

In August, 1866, Mr. McCormick was united in marriage with Miss Rebecca Davess, and to this union there were born eight children: two who died in infancy; Nancy, the wife of Prof. Sherman Fortner, a college instructor,

and has no children; Stella, the wife of Charles W. Slates, president of the Martin County Bank, who has one child, Louise Slates; Annie Myrtle, unmarried, who is engaged in teaching school; Grover, a well-known attorney of Shoals, whose wife died without issue; Leona, the wife of J. R. Roach, of Bedford, who has three children, Catherine, George Hiram and John Chester; and Ephraim, who died in October, 1929, married Stella Chattin and one child, William Malcolm, was born to that union. Mr. McCormick took for his second wife, September 7, 1899, Matilda Martin, widow of Henry Zum Felde, a member of one of the pioneer families of Martin County, and they have had no children.

JAMES RUSSELL MARSHALL. Among the public officials of Southern Indiana who have contributed materially and substantially to the betterment and development of their respective communities, one whose official record is worthy of commendation and attention is James Russell Marshall, of Shoals, who since 1928 has been county treasurer of Martin County. Like many men who have risen to public office, Mr. Marshall began his career as a school teacher, subsequently became interested in mercantile affairs, and eventually attracted the interest and confidence of his fellow-citizens to such an extent as to warrant his election to a position of great trust and responsibility.

Mr. Marshall was born February 2, 1899, at Shoals, Martin County, Indiana, and is a son of James B. and Lillian (Luzadder) Marshall. James B. Marshall was born in Ohio, in 1857, and in that state was reared on the home farm, receiving his early education in the rural schools. Later he received training for the law, embarked in practice, and served as county surveyor of Martin County and prosecuting attorney. Subsequently he moved to Shoals, where he practiced during the remainder of his career and was known as a brilliant, reliable and successful member of his calling. He belonged to the Martin County Bar Association, the Indiana State Bar Association and the American Bar Association, and was universally esteemed because of his high character. His death occurred July 17, 1926, aged sixty-nine years, nine months. Mr. Marshall married Miss Lillian Luzadder, a native of Bloomington, Indiana, who still survives him, at the age of sixty-seven years, her home being at Shoals. Four children were born to this union: Gale, a resident of Indianapolis, who married O. H. Hershman; Lois, who is art supervisor of the high school at Bedford, Indiana; Ruth, a teacher in the public schools of Dana, Indiana; and James Russell, of this review.

James Russell Marshall attended the public schools of Shoals, following which he pursued a course at the Danville Central Normal College, at Danville, Indiana. For three terms he attended Indiana University, and then taught for one term in the public school at Trinity Springs. For the next three years he

Geo. E. Gardner

Dr. C. Gardner!

was a teacher in the high school at Petersburg, this state, but at the end of that period returned to Shoals and engaged in the lumber and automobile business, in which he still is interested. A Democrat in his political views, in 1928 Mr. Marshall was elected on that party's ticket to the office of county treasurer of Martin County, in which position he has since acted with commendable energy and ability. He belongs to the American Legion and the Lions Club and is one of the most popular citizens of Shoals. During the World war he served in the Student Army Training Corps, but the armistice was signed before he was called into active service.

On December 17, 1928, Mr. Marshall was united in marriage with Miss Laura Whitman, daughter of Calvin Whitman, a merchant of Petersburg, and to this union has been born one child, Patricia Ann, born October 29, 1929. Mr. and Mrs. Marshall occupy a pleasant residence at Shoals.

DEXTER C. GARDNER is the present head of an institution that was founded in 1816, the year that Indiana ceased to be a territory and became one of the commonwealth of the Union. It is most appropriate that this institution, which has represented the work and service of five generations of the Gardner family, should be located in historic old Vincennes, about which so many of the historic associations of the state cluster.

The present head of the business bears the name of his grandfather, Dexter Gardner, whose name for many years has been retained in the title of Dexter Gardner & Son. The Gardners were the pioneer undertakers at Vincennes. A complete account of this family business would represent a consecutive history of the profession of embalming and undertaking from the time that the cabinet maker supplied the most important service in a funeral down to modern conditions when the service not only demands men and women of the highest degree of technical training and professional skill, but large and valuable equipment represented in funeral home and chapel, ambulances, motorized equipment, all of which is found in the present funeral directing business of the firm of Dexter Gardner & Son.

The founder of the business at Vincennes in 1816 was Andrew Gardner, the great-great-grandfather of Dexter C. Gardner. The pioneer home of the establishment was a small frame building. Andrew Gardner was a man held in high esteem in the Vincennes of a century ago. He passed on his skill and experience to his son Elbridge Gardner, one of his two sons. Elbridge Gardner owned and conducted the business for a number of years and when he, too, paid the final debt of nature, the establishment was taken up by his son Dexter, whose methods and equipment were far in advance of the simple standards maintained by the originator of the house. Dexter Gardner took his son George E. into partnership and since that date the firm title

has remained Dexter Gardner & Son. Dexter Gardner, himself, was an outstanding citizen of Vincennes and continued to be the head of the business until his death in 1902. From 1902 until August, 1929, his son George E. Gardner was the sole owner and active manager. In 1916, on the centennial anniversary of the founding of the business, George E. Gardner admitted his son, Dexter Carl, into partnership, so that the continuity of the business was assured by this representative of the fifth generation of the family.

The location of the funeral establishment of Dexter Gardner & Son is at 505 Main Street. A number of years ago the firm acquired on that site one of the historic landmarks of Vincennes, the old Bonner Mansion. The building was erected as a home in 1795 by Jonathan Spinning. In the early half of the present century it became an inn, and among other noted guests who were entertained there was Abraham Lincoln when he visited Vincennes several times. Because of this association one room of the funeral home today has been fitted up and dedicated to the memory of the great prairie president. Among other tributes to the great martyred president is a bronze tablet appropriately inscribed, and many other valuable Lincoln relics and mementos have been collected in the room. As the residence and former inn were transformed for the present purpose of a funeral home a portion is set aside for a beautiful funeral chapel. One feature of the chapel are the four memorial windows, dedicated respectively to Andrew Gardner, Elbridge Gardner, Dexter Gardner and Fannie Gardner. Fannie Gardner was a daughter of the late Dexter Gardner.

All the members of the four generations of the family who have successively carried on the undertaking business since the time of the pioneer Andrew Gardner were born in Vincennes. George E. Gardner grew up in that city, attended the grammar and high schools, and accepted the opportunities for thorough training in the business, and then carried it on until his death in August, 1929. He was one of the liberal and pubic spirited citizens of the community, was a member of the Vincennes Chamber of Commerce, a Democrat in politics, and, like his father, was affiliated with historic Vincennes Lodge No. 1, A. F. and A. M. He was also a member of the Vincennes Commandery of Knights Templar and of the Mystic Shrine.

George E. Gardner married Miss Ella Whittic. She was a native of Pennsylvania. Her father was an artist and author and also a very successful man of affairs, having large interests in steamship companies, forge industries and other enterprises. Mr. and Mrs. George E. Gardner had two children, Ruth and Dexter Carl.

Ruth Gardner was graduated from Saint Rose Academy at Vincennes. She is the wife of Mr. Alfred Badolett. Mr. Badolett was born and reared in Vincennes and is a descendant of one of the distinguished old

French families who were in Vincennes from the time of its founding. His ancestor Jean Louis Badolett was the first United States land registrar of the Northwest Territory after Indiana was transferred by the treaty of 1783 to the independent American colonies. Jean Louis Badolett was also the first president of Vincennes University and was a close friend of that eminent Indiana patriot, Colonel Vigo. Mr. and Mrs. Alfred Badolett reside in Vincennes. He is a member of Vincennes Lodge No. 1, A. F. and A. M., the Royal Arch Masons, the Council of Royal and Select Masters, and Vincennes Commandery No. 20, Knights Templar.

Dexter C. Gardner, now the active head of Dexter Gardner & Son, is one of the very popular young business men of his native city, where he was born May 4, 1901. He was educated in public schools, attended Vincennes University, and was only fifteen years of age when, as a mark of the centennial celebration of the family business, he was taken into partnership. He acquired a thorough technical training and was his father's able assistant until the death of George E. Gardner in August, 1929, when he succeeded to the active management.

Mr. Dexter C. Gardner is a member of Vincennes Lodge No. 1, A. F. and A. M., the Scottish Rite Consistory and Shrine at Evansville, the B. P. O. Elks at Vincennes, and the Methodist Episcopal Church. He married, October 15, 1928, at Vincennes, Miss Hellen Tracy, daughter of O. H. Tracy, of Bridgeport, Illinois. They have one daughter, Edwina Gardner.

GLEN W. TURNER, whose people for several generations have been Indiana farmers, was born on a farm, but his active life has been devoted to the banking business. For a number of years he has been a resident of Farmland, Randolph County, where he is cashier of the First National Bank.

He was born at Muncie in Delaware County, February 10, 1891. His grandparents, Robert and Rebecca (Ogle) Turner, and Breckenridge and Euphemia (Gibson) Reynolds, were natives of Virginia and early settlers in Eastern Indiana, becoming farmers in Delaware County. Mr. Turner's parents, Philip E. and Indiana F. (Reynolds) Turner, were both born in Delaware County and live on a farm near Muncie.

Glen W. Turner received his early education in the grade and high schools at Cowan, Indiana, and after completing a course in the Muncie Business College came to Farmland, where for nine years he was assistant cashier of the Farmland State Bank. He left there to become cashier of the First National Bank, an institution capitalized at $25,000, with surplus of $6,500, total resources aggregating $275,000. The average deposits are $250,000.

Mr. Turner in 1917 married Myrtle Rinker, also a native of Delaware County, and her parents, Jacob E. and Alberta M. (Neff) Rinker, were also born there. Mr. and Mrs.

Turner have four children, Robert E., Dorothy M., James H. and Charles E. Mr. Turner is a trustee of the Christian Church. For six years he held the office of town clerk, is a trustee of the Chamber of Commerce, is a Republican and a member of the Masonic fraternity and Knights of Pythias.

VIRGIL GRANT TEAGAR, a Newcastle real estate man, was born at Tuscola, Illinois, October 23, 1900. In 1904 his parents, Otto Grant and Edith R. (Hodyshell) Teagar, moved to Newcastle, where the family have been well known in a business and civic way for a quarter of a century.

Otto Grant Teagar was born in Kentucky and his wife in Illinois. He was a professional photographer for many years and for ten years conducted a studio at Newcastle for the enlarging of pictures. Since 1907 he has been in the real estate business, handling farm and city property. There were three children: Vivian, wife of John A. Jacobs, of Newcastle; Virgil Grant; and Vera Leon, at home.

Virgil Grant Teagar attended the grade and high schools of Newcastle and at an early age took up a business career. For four and a half years he had charge of the junior department of the L. Straus & Company of Indianapolis, and for a time was in charge of the furnishing department of N. J. Pilger & Brothers of Anderson, Indiana. In January, 1929, he returned to Newcastle to become a partner with his father in the real estate business. They have a succesful organization, with offices in the Burr Building.

Mr. Teagar married, November 19, 1929, Louise Rieks. They are members of the Christian Church. Mr. Teagar was one of the active organizers of the Junior Republican Club during the city campaign of 1929. He is a member of the Beta Phi Sigma fraternity.

GUS BARFUSS, Rockville florist, is a master of his profession and business, and a long and thorough training and technical knowledge have enabled him to make a more than ordinary success in his work.

He was born in Germany, October 8, 1885, son of Amial and Anna (Finchel) Barfuss, who are still living in the old country. Gus Barfuss attended the German schools, and after his literary training had four years of study and experience in an agricultural and technical college. There he specialized in floriculture, both theoretical and practical, and the studies begun in college have been continued through a mature life, so that there are few points about the growth and development, the nature of plant life, particularly blooming plants, of which he has no knowledge.

As a young man Mr. Barfuss came to America for the purpose of finding here the opportunities to use his diversified training. The day after he landed in Baltimore he started to work for a florist, with whom he remained two and a half years. After that he was in Pennsylvania and New York State,

Victor C. Vaughan

and in 1919 came to Rockville, Indiana. Here he used his modest capital in putting up a small hothouse and nursery, and his business has been the result of a steady expansion, each increase justified by the volume of his transactions. More capital has been put into the business and he has a large amount of space under glass, and all the facilities and arrangements for growing and production of flowers and the handling of them in artistic floral designs. Shipments of cut flowers and plants are made from his greenhouses to several states. He is a member of the F. T. D. Florists Association, an organization of florists that makes possible the prompt delivery of floral orders in any part of the United States.

Mr. Barfuss married, November 27, 1916, Miss Catherine Bexta, daughter of John and Johanna Bexta, who were natives of Germany. Mr. Barfuss is a Democrat in politics and a member of the Lutheran Church.

VICTOR E. HARMAN for the past thirty years has been one of the most active business men of the community of Saratoga in Randolph County. He was formerly in the general merchandise business, and is one of the oldest established automobile dealers in this section of the state.

Mr. Harman was born in Randolph County September 10, 1881, son of Daniel and Mahala Harman, his father a native of Ohio and his mother of Indiana. His father spent his life as a farmer and died in 1910 and the mother passed away in 1907.

Victor E. Harman was educated in district schools and grew up on an Indiana farm. When he was nineteen years old he began clerking in a store at Saratoga, later for a time clerked at Portland, Indiana, and then joined his brother Henry E. in a general store at Saratoga. After six years he bought his brother's interest and in 1911 traded his business for a farm. He has been handling automobiles for over fifteen years and is one of the oldest dealers in the Overland and Willys-Knight cars in this section of the state. He built a well-equipped garage, 32 by 120 feet, in 1915 and in 1920 added an addition 35 by 120 feet. This is a fire-proof garage, providing ample space for sales and service, and his general repair department is one of the most popular institutions of the kind in Randolph County. Mr. Harman is a director of the Saratoga State Bank.

He married in July, 1904, Miss Bessie E. Fraze, who was born in Randolph County, daughter of Hiram C. and Jenetta (Holms) Fraze. They have two children, Cyrus Dale and Robert C. Mr. Harman is secretary of the United Brethren Church at Saratoga. For six years he was a member of the town council, is a Democrat, has filled chairs in the Improved Order of Red Men, the lodge of the Independent Order of Odd Fellows, is a member of the Encampment of the Odd Fellows and a thirty-second degree Scottish Rite Mason.

WESLEY W. RATLIFF, prosecuting attorney of Henry County, is a resident of Knightstown, and during the past eight years has established himself in a successful practice as a lawyer.

He was born at Lawrence, Indiana, June 30, 1900, son of Luther H. and Mary (Wilson) Ratliff. His father, a native of Marion County, Indiana, was an able physician and surgeon and stood high in his profession at Lawrence, where he practiced until his death on July 9, 1929. The widowed mother still makes her home at Lawrence.

Wesley W. Ratliff was liberally educated. After the public schools he entered DePauw University and while there was enrolled, in September, 1918, with the Students Army Training Corps. He received training as an infantryman until his honorable discharge on December 12, 1918, after the armistice. Mr. Ratliff in 1922 graduated LL. B. from the Indiana Law School and at once located at Knightstown, where his abilities and his personality won him friends and a rapidly growing law practice. Mr. Ratliff became prosecuting attorney of Henry County on January 1, 1930.

He is a Republican, a member of the Henry County and Indiana State Bar Associations, and fraternally is a Royal Arch and Council Degree Mason and a member of the Knights of Pythias. He and his family are members of the Methodist Episcopal Church.

They reside at 34 West Pine Street, Knightstown. Mr. Ratliff married, April 4, 1923, Miss Ruth Sherwood, who was born at Bedford, Indiana, daughter of Frank T. and Ida (Hatfield) Sherwood. Her father was born in New Jersey and her mother in Indiana. Mr. and Mrs. Ratliff have two children, Wesley W. and Christian.

VICTOR C. KNAUTH is owner and executive head of the Victor C. Knauth Company, which, with well equipped headquarters at 321 North Second Street in the City of Vincennes, controls a substantial and important leadership in the contract plumbing and heating business.

Mr. Knauth was born in France, June 9, 1885, and is a son of Martin and Dora (Gross) Knauth, both of whom were born in Germany. In 1886 Martin Knauth came with his family to the United States and made settlement at Brazil, Indiana, where he became identified with operations in the coal mines of that locality. Of the seven children in the family the eldest is Mrs. Dora Hand, a widow; Lang is a retired meat packer; Katherine is the wife of Albert Zinkler; Victor C., of this review, was next in order of birth ad was an infant at the time the family came to the United States; Louise is the wife of Ernest Loranze; Henry is deceased; and Freda is the wife of Leo Swettenam.

Victor C. Knauth received in his early youth the advantages of a Lutheran parochial school in the City of Terre Haute, where his parents then maintained their home, and he was but thirteen years of age when he there initiated his apprenticeship in the plumbing and heating trade. In this service he continued to be associated with the Prox & Brinkman Company of Terre Haute five years, and in 1904 he established his residence in Vincennes. Here he was associated with J. H. Sowden about three years, and in the period of 1908-12 he was here in the employ of the Buck & Boyd Company. In April of the latter year he became senior member of the firm of Knauth & Earson, which engaged in the plumbing and heating business at 305 North Third Street. In April, 1914, Mr. Knauth assumed full ownership of the business, which he continued in an individual way until after the close of the World war. He admitted his brother Henry to partnership in the business, and this alliance continued until the death of his brother, January 2, 1929. Mr. Knauth has continued as the owner and active executive head of the business, which is conducted under the title of Victor C. Knauth Company, the concern ranking as one of the foremost in Vincennes in the handling of plumbing supplies and in general contracting for heating and plumbing installation. The company utilizes at its headquarters 8,500 square feet of floor space, and owns the building in which the business is conducted—on a corner lot 130 by 65 feet in dimensions. All departments of the establishment are of the best modern equipment and the service of all is of the highest standard. The concern has handled many important contracts in plumbing and heating installation, including that of the six-story Oliphant Building, on Main Street; the Good Samaritan Hospital; the Gibault High School; the cathedral and school buildings of Sacred Heart Church; similar installation in connection with the remodeling of the courthouses of Knox and Sullivan counties; the new senior high school building in Vincennes, and many of the finer residences of this city. The business of the concern has been extended over a territory within a radius of 100 miles from Vincennes, and the company installed the first vapor heating system in Southern Indiana. A corps of skilled employes is retained and the substantial business has been developed on the basis of fair dealings and effective service.

Mr. Knauth is a member of the Indiana Engineering Society, was formerly a director of the Indiana Association of Sanitary Engineers, in 1926, is a member of Indiana Engineering Society, the National Association of Piping Contractors, the Associated Building Contractors and the Vincennes Merchant Plumbers Association. His political alignment is with the Republican party. He is a member of the local Harmony Society, he is a past president of Vincennes Aerie No. 384, Fraternal Order of Eagles, and is affiliated also with the Benevolent and Protective Order of Elks. His hobby is quail hunting and clay pigeon shooting.

Mr. Knauth in January, 1913, at Vincennes, married Miss Ethel Mann, who was born in Illinois and is a representative of a family that was founded in that state in the early pioneer days. Mr. and Mrs. Knauth have two children, Vivian Maxine and Betty Fay, both students in the Vincennes public schools.

While Mr. Knauth gained effective technical knowledge through his apprenticeship and practical experience in his trade, his ambition led him to broaden his fortification by completing a course in plumbing and heating, through the medium of the International Correspondence Schools, of Scranton, Pennsylvania, in which he was graduated in 1906 and duly received his diploma. He has won advancement and success through his own ability and efforts and has secure standing as one of the progressive business men of Vincennes.

SAMUEL H. ROSS. Few business enterprises can lay claim to a better record for sustained and continued public service or for more honorable methods than the drug business of Samuel H. Ross, which has flourished at Shoals, Martin County, for more than four decades. Since 1889 Mr. Ross has lived and labored among the citizens of this thriving community, and during this long period has not only become known as one of the most substantial and honorable merchants here, but also as a citizen who has borne his full share of public responsibilities.

Mr. Ross was born in the little community known as Hart's Mill, in Ripley County, Indiana, April 23, 1865, and is a son of Joseph A. and Emily (Savage) Ross. His grandfather, William T. Ross, was born in Scotland, and in young manhood immigrated to the United States and made his way to Dearborn County, Indiana, where he followed his trade as a cooper. Many still live who remember his sturdy industry and many sterling qualities of mind and heart. Joseph A. Ross was born in the village of Harrison, Indiana, where he was reared and given a good public school education. Early in life he took up teaching as a vocation and followed it in the rural schools for a long period, but in later years was identified with mercantile houses and financial institutions as a bookkeeper. A highly religious man, he was for many years a local preacher of the Methodist Church, continuing as such until his death, August 26, 1878. Reverend Ross married Miss Emily Savage, a native of Indiana, who died December 23, 1926, and to this union there were born eight children: Henry M., of Shoals, Indiana; Florence, deceased; Samuel H., of this review; Jennie; Charles, deceased; Laura; James, deceased; and Nina.

Samuel H. Ross attended the public schools of Huron, Indiana, but his father died when he was only thirteen years of age, which obliged him, as the eldest living son, to go to work and assist in the support of the family. His first employment was in a brick yard, but later he secured a position as clerk in the general merchandise store of Johnson & Chenoweth, at Shoals, where he remained for several years. He received his introduction to the drug business in the pharmacy of Benjamin C. Johnson, and in 1889 embarked for himself in the same line of business, in which he has continued without interruption to the present. During the passing of the years Mr. Ross has kept fully abreast of the advancements and progress of the business, and now owns one of the most modern drug stores in Southern Indiana, located at Shoals. He has a splendid record in business circles as a man of integrity and high character, and as a citizen has done his share in the upbuilding and development of the community. A Republican in politics, he has served ably as a member of the school board for nine years, and as a member of the board of trustees two and one-half years. Mr. Ross is a consistent member of the Methodist Church and was for many years a member of the board of trustees. Fraternally he is a Mason and a past master of the Blue Lodge of Shoals and belongs to the Knights of Pythias, of Shoals, the Order of the Eastern Star and Odd Fellows.

On February 25, 1897, Mr. Ross was united in marriage with Miss Margaret Allen and there have been born to this union three children: Dr. Harry P., a successful practicing physician at Richmond, Indiana, who married Beryl Barber and has three children, Ellen E., Margaret Ann and Eleanora Jean; Allen T., who is interested in the drug business with his father, married Mary Rogers, and has two children, Marion Allen and Betty M.; and Thelma, a graduate of the Indiana University Training School for Nurses at Indianapolis.

MISS HAZEL LETT. The public library as an institution has become generally accepted as one of the principal and most important factors in our country's educational system, and at present there are few progressive cities which do not possess an institution of this kind. All, however, are not as fortunate in the possession of a capable and efficient librarian as is the Washington Public Library, where Miss Hazel Lett is in charge. A college graduate and a former school teacher, Miss Lett is singularly equipped both by talent and training for her post, which she has held since 1925.

Miss Lett was born in Daviess County, Indiana, and is a daughter of Alvin P. and Cora (Russell) Lett, members of old and honored families of this part of Indiana, who came as pioneers from South Carolina in 1820. Most of their members have been agricultural people, but both the Lett and Russell families have had prominent representatives in business, professional, public and military life. John Russell, Miss Lett's maternal grandfather, enlisted in the Union army at the outbreak of the war between the states, and served as a private in the Forty-second Regiment, Indiana Volunteer Infantry, for two years, or until incapacitated for further active duty by a serious wound received in action.

Miss Lett received her education in the public schools of her native locality, following which she pursued a course at the Danville Normal College. She began her career as an educator following her graduation, and for five years was one of the most popular and efficient teachers at Washington, but in 1925 gave up her work in this direction to accept the appointment as librarian of the Washington Public Library, which position she has since retained. Miss Lett is thoroughly familiar with every branch of her work, and has systematized the details of the library so that all matters are handled expeditiously and without friction. Through her courtesy and obligingness and a pleasing personality she has attracted numerous new patrons to the institution, and has established innumerable friendships, as well as having won the confidence and regard of the people of Washington. In Miss Laura Routt she has an energetic and capable assistant.

The Washington Public Library was organized in 1901 and from small beginnings has grown in equipment and number of volumes to large proportions, offering its patrons a wide range of literature of all kinds. The present school board is composed of J. W. McCarthy, president; Lester Lee, vice president; and W. F. Axell, secretary, all of whom are prominent citizens of Washington.

ENOCH O. CHATTIN, D. V. S. In the extended and varied career of Dr. Enoch O. Chattin, of Washington, there has entered none of that monotony which often ensues as the result of the following of a single line of endeavor. A veterinary surgeon by profession, he has also followed contracting and road-building, and among his other interests are holdings in farms and city property. Likewise he has been prominent in public affairs for a number of years, and at present is serving his second term in the office of county treasurer.

Doctor Chattin was born on a farm in Daviess County, Indiana, September 20, 1877, and is a son of William and Eliza A. (Harris) Chattin. His father was born in Dubois County, Indiana, where he was educated in the country schools and reared on a farm, and at the outbreak of the war between the states enlisted in the Union army as a member of the Sixty-fifth Regiment, Indiana Volunteer Infantry, with which he served four years. After the war he came to Daviess County, where he was successfully engaged in farming and stock raising until his death in 1927, at the age of eighty-three years, at which time he was one of the well-to-do agriculturists and substantial citizens of his community. Mr. Chattin married Miss Eliza A. Harris, who survives him at the age of seventy-eight years, and they became the parents of five children: Dr. Robert A., a successful doctor of dental surgery at Richmond,

Indiana; Nathaniel H., who is engaged in farming in Daviess County; Elizabeth, the widow of Hawley Williams; Nettie, who is single and resides with her mother; and Dr. Enoch O., of this review.

Enoch O. Chattin attended the public schools of Daviess County, following which he pursued a course at the Indianapolis Veterinary College, from which he was graduated April 9, 1909, with the degree of Doctor of Veterinary Medicine. He commenced practice at Washington and devoted himself to his profession for several years, following which he became a contractor and built several roads in Daviess County. In 1916 and 1917 he occupied the post of county highway supervisor, and in 1926 became the Republican candidate for the office of county treasurer, to which he was elected by a gratifying majority. His services during his first term were so acceptable that in 1928 he was reelected to this office, in which he is acting at this time to the entire satisfaction of his fellow-citizens. Doctor Chattin is a religious man, although he has no avowed church affiliation, nor does he belong to any lodges, although appreciative of the companionship of his fellow-men. He has always had faith in the value, present and future, of property in this section, and owns city real estate and farm lands.

On December 1, 1899, Doctor Chattin was united in marriage with Miss Sarah Carroll, a native of Daviess County, and to this union there have been born two children: Oral C., of Indianapolis, Indiana, and Earl E., who is identified with farming in Daviess County and who married Hazel Wallick, of Oden, Indiana.

EDWIN M. ROWLETT, of Gaston, is one of the outstanding business men of Delaware County. His business activities have been centered at Gaston for a great many years. Since 1920 he has had the authorized Ford car agency, but his activities have not been confined to one line. He is the father of Mr. Charles E. Rowlett, a popular young business man of Muncie.

Edwin M. Rowlett was born in Blackford County, Indiana, February 26, 1872, son of David E. and Esther A. (Heaton) Rowlett. The Rowletts are a pioneer family of Indiana. His great-grandfather came from France, and settled in Eastern Indiana as early as 1817, when Indiana was a very new state. Mr. Rowlett's grandfather, Edwin Rowlett, was born and reared in Wayne County and spent his active life as a merchant and miller, his home for many years being at Pennville. Finally he moved to Nebraska, and died at Madison in that state, he and his wife being buried there.

David E. Rowlett was born in Wayne County and was a boy when his parents moved to Jay County. He had the distinction of being the youngest Indiana soldier in the Civil war, enlisting at the age of fourteen years, four months, eight days. He served in Company B of the Eleventh Indiana Cavalry and after the war for many years conducted a mercantile business and a mill at Pennville. From there he moved to Delaware County, settling on a farm, and also had a store at Gaston. He was a member of the Independent Order of Odd Fellows. He died September 5, 1920, and is buried in Beech Grove at Muncie. His wife, Esther A. Heaton, was born in Jay County, attended school at Trenton, and from childhood was a devout Methodist. She passed away January 5, 1878, and is buried in the Bethel Cemetery of Delaware County. She was the mother of five children: Mary Jane, wife of A. J. Brock, of Bristol, Indiana; John, who died in infancy; Edwin M.; George W., a merchant in Muncie; and Ida Belle, deceased, who was the wife of George W. Carnes, of Muncie, and left a daughter, Mrs. Eva Guinn, of that city. David E. Rowlett after the death of his first wife married Samantha A. Brock, of Gaston, and to this union three children were born, Orpha B., wife of Fred McIntosh, of West Alexander, Ohio, Arthur J., who died in infancy, and Mittie M., who died after her marriage.

Edwin M. Rowlett attended the grade schools at Gaston and as soon as he left school found an opportunity for a business career in association with his father. He started in his father's store but at the age of eighteen he started in business for himself and for over thirty years has been closely identified with general merchandising there. In 1920 he took the Ford agency for Gaston and has done a big business in that territory. He owns a well equipped shop and sales room and takes the responsibility of contracting for several hundred cars annually.

Mr. Rowlett was one of the men who brought about the establishment of a canning factory at Gaston. He owns a summer resort at Tippecanoe Lake, and is interested in real estate in Muncie and Gaston. He is affiliated with Mathews Lodge No. 650, A. F. and A. M., Sioux Tribe No. 123 of the Improved Order of Red Men, belongs to the Eastern Star and Tribe of Pocahontas. He has served on the local school board and has always played a helpful part in local affairs. He is a Republican and a Methodist. His grandmother was a sister of Bishop Wright, long a prominent figure in the United Brethren Church at Dayton and father of the famous Wright brothers.

Mr. Edwin M. Rowlett married in Delaware County, May 22, 1892, Miss Lydia F. Rector, daughter of Rev. James A. and Cordelia (Carey) Rector. Her father spent forty years in the ministry of the United Brethren Church and is now living retired at Gaston, at the age of seventy-seven, his wife being seventy-four. Mrs. Rowlett attended school in Harrison Township of Delaware County. For many years she was identified with the United Brethren Church, but is now a Methodist. She is a member of the Eastern Star and is a past great chief for the State of Indiana in the Tribe of Pocahontas. Mr. and Mrs. Rowlett had three children. Their daughter Iva Fern died at the age of two years, ten

Geo S Ingle

months, twenty-one days. The living children are Charles E. Rowlett and Ruth I. Ruth graduated from the Gaston High School, attended the Blaker School of Indianapolis, and taught at Muncie until her marriage to Mr. Robert O. Rinker, who is in the grocery and meat market business at the corner of Council and Howard streets in Muncie. Mr. and Mrs. Rinker have a daughter, Alice May, now a kindergarten pupil.

Charles E. Rowlett was born April 3, 1894, graduated from the Gaston High School in 1913, and in May, 1917, enlisted in the United States Marines. He was stationed at Washington with the Navy Yard Detachment and received his honorable discharge in February, 1919. On returning to Indianapolis he became a traveling salesman for Hibben & Hollweg for three years. In 1922 he moved to Muncie and has a splendid location on College Avenue, near the Ball State Teachers College, where he has built up a splendid business in a well appointed shop, handling confectionery and lunch service. Charles E. Rowlett is affiliated with Mathews Lodge No. 650, A. F. and A. M., Muncie Chapter No. 30, Royal Arch Masons, Lodge No. 245, B. P. O. Elks, and Delaware Post No. 19 of the American Legion.

JOSEPH CALVIN BLAKELY, president of the Muncie Electric Sales Corporation, has been a popular business man in that city for a number of years. He was in the newspaper business in various capacities until he took up his present line of work as a dealer in electrical appliances and radio equipment.

Mr. Blakely was born at Fostoria, Ohio, July 31, 1891, son of Carl Watson and Clara (Crooks) Blakely and a grandson of Joseph Blakely. Joseph Blakely was an early settler of Delaware County, Indiana, a farmer, and he and his wife are buried in the Bethel Cemetery of that county. Carl Watson Blakely spent many years as a farmer and stock raiser in Delaware County, where he was born and reared. He died in 1923 and is buried in the Union Cemetery. His wife, Clara Crooks, was born at Granville, Delaware County. She was a Methodist and took a keen interest in politics. She died in 1925 and is buried beside her husband. There were two children, one of whom died in infancy.

Joseph C. Blakely attended public schools and graduated from the Muncie High School in 1908. His newspaper experience began with the *Muncie Evening Press*, of which he was circulation manager and later advertising manager for thirteen years. He left that to take up photo engraving work and for four years was a traveling representative for the Delaware Engraving Company. Mr. Blakely in 1925 became associated with R. F. Bryan and L. B. Springer in establishing the Muncie Electric Sales Corporation, and they have enjoyed a very successful business as dealers in electrical appliances and radio apparatus, with an attractive shop at the corner of Walnut and Washington streets, in the heart of the down town business district. In addition

to being president of this company Mr. Blakely is president of the Washington Acceptance Corporation and is a director of the Credit Bureau of the Chamber of Commerce. He is a Republican in politics.

He married at Muncie, September 30, 1913, Miss Roxie N. DeWitt, daughter of Wesley and Eva (Austin) DeWitt. Her father, a Delaware County farmer and stock man, died in 1916 and is buried in the Union Cemetery near Desoto. Mrs. DeWitt lives with her daughter and son-in-law, Mr. Blakely, on a farm near Desoto. Mrs. Blakely graduated from the Desoto High School in 1909 and is also a graduate of the Conservatory of Music at Muncie, and has been an active figure in musical circles in that city. She is a Methodist. Mr. and Mrs. Blakely have four children: Walter, Josephine, Betty and Robert. The two oldest are attending school at Muncie.

GEORGE S. INGLE, a retired business man and property owner at Evansville, was born in Vanderburg County, October 17, 1847. He is a sterling representative of a family that has lived in this section of Southern Indiana since pioneer times, and has always enjoyed a reputation for industry, thrift and good citizenship.

The old town of Inglefield in Vanderburg County was named after his grandfather, who came to this county from England in 1818 and died in 1872. His father, William Ingle, was born in England and was two and one-half years old when brought to Vanderburg County. He died in 1900. William Ingle married Eliza Neil. The house her father built in the west end of Evansville more than a hundred years ago was still standing in 1930. George S. Ingle was one of seven children, one of whom died in infancy, and another was killed by the kick of a horse at the age of two years. The children who grew up were John, George S., Charles, Anna and Joseph. John served two years in the Union army in the Twenty-first Indiana Infantry, and participated in fourteen engagements. About the time the war closed he was drowned while bathing in Mobile Bay. Anna became the wife of Frank Stacer, a farmer in Warrick County, and they had four children. Charles, who farmed the old homestead, married a daughter of Doctor Allison and has three children. Joseph died while engaged in ranching east of the Cascade Mountains in Washington.

George S. Ingle attended public schools at Inglefield and after leaving school learned the trade of carpenter. For several years he was engaged in carpenter work and contracting in Vanderburg County. In 1875 he went west to California, and became a rancher and farmer in the Sacramento Valley. The first year he put in a crop of two thousand acres of wheat. The second year his planting was on four thousand acres, but before the crop was harvested the levee along the river broke and destroyed all his fields. For several years he was engaged in gold mining, saved a few thousand dollars, and, bringing his capital back to Indiana, set himself up in business at Evansville as a grain commission merchant. Some years ago he promoted the development of the Epworth coal mine in Warrick County, was president of the company and was a coal operator until he retired in 1925. Some of his investments have taken the form of purchases of farm land in Texas. Mr. Ingle has never been a seeker for the honors of politics, and the only office he ever held was that of constable, to which he was elected when he was twenty-one years of age, in Scott Township, and he also served as deputy sheriff under Frank Darling. Mr. Ingle married in November, 1877, Mary Corbiere, a native of California. Her first husband was Dr. Charles F. Diefendorf, and by that marriage she had one son, Charles F., Jr., now represented in the medical profession of Evansville. Mr. and Mrs. Ingle have one daughter, Della A., who is a graduate nurse, having completed her training course in the Mayfield Sanitarium at Saint Louis, did post-graduate work in the Presbyterian Hospital of Chicago, and for one year studied medicine. When she was twenty-one years of age she had charge of the Pacific Hospital in San Francisco. She is now the wife of Charles U. Smith, and they have a son, George Ingle Smith, who was born January 9, 1911, and spent a year at Purdue University and is now engaged in work with an aviation company at Murfreesboro, Tennessee.

ARTHUR E. FRAKES. The proprietor of the popular public outing place, picturesquely known as Magnolia Manor Resort, at Shoals, Arthur E. Frakes has led a career that has been varied and interesting and entirely free from the monotony that frequently is the result of following a single line of endeavor. Like many men who have risen to success in various walks of life, Mr. Frakes commenced his career as a school teacher, but his was not the nature to remain long in the dull routine of the school room and his subsequent activities were of a character that suited his fancy. He has owned his present establishment since 1928 and is making a success of his venture, having in the meantime gained and held the confidence of the people of his adopted community.

Mr. Frakes was born January 19, 1883, at Branchville, Perry County, Indiana, and is a son of John W. and Susanna (Esarey) Frakes, and a grandson of Thomas Frakes, likewise a native of Perry County, where the family were among the earliest settlers. John W. Frakes was born at Branchville, Perry County, October 7, 1857, and was reared in that county, where he received a rural school education and took up farming. During his career he was an agriculturist, a stockman and a merchant, and he died at Branchville, February 17, 1931, where he was known as one of the substantial and public-spirited men of his community. He married Miss Susanna Esarey, also of Perry County, who died January 19, 1931, and to this union there were

born six children, of whom three died in infancy; Mary E. died at the age of fourteen years; Ida Pearl married Charles Rissler, of New Albany, Indiana, and has four children; and Arthur E., of this review.

Arthur E. Frakes received his early education in the public schools of Perry County, following which he pursued a course in the normal school at Corydon, Indiana. With this preparation he was able to secure a teacher's certificate and for a time was an instructor of the young minds of the rural districts of Perry County, but eventually sought adventure and enlisted in the United States Army, in which he served for three years, receiving his honorable discharge in 1906. In the same year he went to Indianapolis, where he secured employment on the street railway, and remained there for one year, subsequently going to Louisville, Kentucky, where he was employed in a like capacity for five years. He then returned to Indianapolis and resumed work as a street car man, continuing as such for seven years or until 1924, in which year he embarked in the insurance business at Indianapolis. In 1928 Mr. Frakes came to Shoals and purchased Magnolia Manor, one of the most popular resorts in Southern Indiana, which he has since conducted with great success. Mr. Frakes is an ideal host and has installed numerous conveniences and comforts for his patrons at the establishments, which is located on Shoals R. F. D. Route No. 1, three miles west of Shoals. Mr. Frakes is a Republican and belongs to the Methodist Church and the Blue Lodge of Masonry, Evergreen Lodge, No. 703 at Indianapolis. Since locating at Shoals he has expressed his public spirit by assisting several movements for the betterment of his adopted community.

On September 3, 1908, Mr. Frakes was united in marriage with Miss Ada Prather, of Lancaster, Kentucky, and to this union there have come six children: Mary E., born in 1910, who married Horace Gaither and has one child, Betty Jean; William E., born in 1911, who is a member of the United States Army; Audrey P., born in 1913, married Theodore Melvin; Harold E., born in 1915, attending public school; Eva J., born in 1923; and Bruce D., born in 1926.

ROBERT E. ECKERT, county superintendent of schools of Dubois County, is a highly qualified and gifted educator and comes of a family of educators.

He was born June 4, 1884, son of Edward F. and Mary L. Eckert. Both his father and mother were teachers, and his maternal grandfather was one of the pioneer school men of Dubois County. Mrs. Mary L. Eckert gave forty-one years of her life to school work in that county, thirteen years of which were in the schools of Jasper.

Robert E. Eckert learned to read and write at the knee of his maternal grandmother. His first teacher was Mrs. Sarah Cooper, sister of Judge Hunter, of Jasper, and after that he had a succession of teachers, Mrs. M. A.

Gugsell, Dr. A. F. Gugsell, Hon. Frank L. Betz. In 1898 he was graduated from the eighth grade, under Prof. Phineas Clark, and graduated from high school in 1902, under Prof. E. F. Sutherland. He was one of the early high school graduates of Jasper. He attended two summer normal schools in Jasper, beginning his teaching at Dubois in 1903, and was with the public schools of that town eight consecutive years, until 1911. In the meantime, in 1905, he entered the Indiana State Normal School for the summer term, and went back each summer and spring until graduating from the "Old Four Year Normal Course" in 1913. In the summer of 1914 he was enrolled in the University of Indiana, and kept up his studies there at intervals until he was graduated with the Bachelor of Arts degree, majoring in education and with philosophy his minor, in 1926. At the close of the summer session of 1929 he received his Master of Arts degree in education at the State University.

Mr. Eckert taught in the French Lick public schools, eighth grade, two years, 1911-13, was then elected principal of the high school, but accepted an offer at Markleville, where he secured the commission for the high school and remained as principal of this semi-consolidated school four years, 1913-17.

Mr. Eckert has been continuously at the head of the system of county schools in Dubois County since 1917. Except for the first term he has received the entire vote of the board, and in 1929 was reelected for his fourth term of four years. He has the distinction of being entitled to his rank of superintendent from three different qualifications: by virtue of his Master's degree, by exchange of license and by virtue of holding office.

Mr. Eckert was chairman of the Third District County Superintendents Association five years, and has been treasurer of the Indiana County Superintendents Association since 1925. He was the first schoolman from Dubois County and the first county superintendent in Indiana to become a life member of the National Education Association, and in that organization served as a member of the committee on tenure. He was secretary of the resolutions committee of the State Teachers Association in 1926-28 and has also served on the auditing and nominating committees of the same association. He has served as a member of the executive committee, chairman of the executive committee, and as vice president and president of the Southwestern Teachers Association of Indiana, an organization made up of 1,600 teachers. He is a member of the Indiana School Men's Club, member at large of the Pi Gamma Mu, a national social science organization. He took his first Masonic degrees at Markleville, Madison County, in 1913. During the World war Mr. Eckert was a director of the Jasper Chapter of the Red Cross and a four-minute speaker, and carried on other war activities through the schools. He is also a member of the Indiana State Historical Society.

He married in the fall of 1905 Miss Kathryn A. Seng, of Dubois. They have three children: George, born in 1906, is a salesman at Jasper; Ruth, born in 1910, is a graduate of the Indiana State Teachers College at Terre Haute, in the class of 1930 and is now teaching school in the Richland Township High School, Fountain County; and Roberta, born in 1921, is attending the grade schools at Jasper.

SAMUEL ALBERT CHENOWETH. Although the career of Samuel Albert Chenoweth belongs to the past rather than the present of Martin County, his death having occurred March 29, 1904, his life was such a successful and honorable one and his accomplishments so numerous and varied that no work pertaining to the achievements of prominent men of the Hoosier State would be complete without at least a brief history of his activities. A resident of Shoals for many years, he was a leader in a number of lines of endeavor, and at various times was chosen by his fellow-citizens to represent them in important public offices.

Mr. Chenoweth was born March 13, 1856, in Washington County, Indiana, a son of Wilson and Mary (McIntosh) Chenoweth. The family traces its ancestry back to John Chenoweth, who was born at Martin, County Cromwell, Wales, in 1682, and was the founder of the family in America, being an early settler of Baltimore County, Maryland, where he passed the rest of his life as a planter. His son, John Chenoweth, was born in that county, in 1706. The next in the direct line of descent was also named John, as was the latter's son, and the last named also had a son named John, who was born December 16, 1765, in Hampshire County, Virginia, later West Virginia. Joseph Chenoweth, son of John just named, and grandfather of Samuel Albert Chenoweth, was born in the same county, March 8, 1799, and became an early settler of Washington County, Indiana, where he located a farm and passed his life in its cultivation. Wilson Chenoweth, son of Joseph, was born September 26, 1826, in Washington County, Indiana, where he was reared, educated and married, and early in life took up the business of flour milling. He subsequently became a pioneer of Martin County, where he built and operated the first mills at Shoals, became a prominent and substantial citizen, and rounded out a long and honorable career. He married Mary McIntosh, daughter of James and Winfred (Potter) McIntosh. James McIntosh was born in Virginia, the oldest son of John O. McIntosh, a native of Scotland, who came to America during the Revolutionary war.

Samuel Albert Chenoweth was educated in the public schools of Washington and Martin counties, and as a youth became associated with his father in the latter's flour milling operations. On entering upon his independent career he took up farming and stockraising and later milling, and became successful in all of these lines of activity. During his later years he was the possessor of large financial interests and president of the Martin County Bank of Shoals at the time of his death. Mr. Chenoweth was a leader in civic affairs and in the Republican party, being for some years chairman of the Martin County Republican committee. He served ably as county auditor and township trustee, and in all of his activities maintained a record for unquestioned integrity and probity. As a churchman he was allied with the Methodist Church, and his fraternal connections were with the Blue Lodge and the Independent Order of Odd Fellows. In his death his community lost one of its most valuable and highly-respected citizens.

On September 16, 1889, Mr. Chenoweth was united in marriage with Miss Susan Brooks Campbell, of Loogootee, Indiana, daughter of Dr. J. C. L. and Emily (Brooks) Campbell. To the union of Mr. and Mrs. Chenoweth were born four children: Ida Alberta, born June 14, 1890, who married Leon B. Rogers, in the insurance business at Bloomington, Indiana, and has one child, James C., born August 8, 1922; Laura A., born October 26, 1891, who married Reg B. Stull, cashier of the First National Bank at Bloomington, Indiana, and has two children, Mary S., born January 6, 1921, and Richard B., born October 31, 1923; Wilson, born June 29, 1893, who is in the rural mail service and married on February 1, 1930, Joice Furry, and they have one child: John W., born January 20, 1931; Ainslie C., born June 24, 1895, a salesman of fraternity jewelry, who is unmarried.

WARREN D. SHULTZ. Among the old-established and reliable manufacturing concerns of Indiana, one which for a half a century has held the confidence and patronage of a wide and representative trade is the Griffith Furniture Company, of Muncie. During this long period it has developed from modest beginnings to become one of the leading manufacturers of smokers' and novelty furniture in the country, principally through the fact that it has been in the hands of capable, energetic men of good judgment and absolute integrity. One of these men is Warren D. Shultz, who joined the concern, as an accountant, in 1927, and who now occupies the position of secretary, being also a member of the board of directors.

Mr. Shultz was born in Randolph County, Indiana, July 1, 1886, and is a son of Hon. George C. and Anna L. (Peacock) Shultz. His paternal grandfather, Peter Milton Shultz, was born in Pennsylvania, whence he came as an early settler to Spartansburg, Indiana, prior to the outbreak of the war between the states, during which he served as a soldier in an Indiana volunteer infantry regiment and won the rank of captain. Following the war he returned to Randolph County, Indiana, where he spent the remainder of his life and became one of the substantial members of his community. He and his worthy wife are buried at Winchester, this state.

George C. Shultz, the father of Warren D. Shultz, was born in Randolph County, and attended the public schools of Ladoga, Montgomery County, where he prepared for the law and was admitted to the bar. At one time he was a law partner of Sen. James Watson, of Winchester, but practiced for a few years only, his activities for twenty-six years being devoted to the cause of education as a teacher in various schools. He became widely known in educational circles for his progressiveness, judgment, farsightedness and learning, and won particular distinction as one of the earliest advocates of the consolidated schools. He was likewise prominent in civic and political affairs, and served one term each in the House of Representatives and the Senate of the Indiana State Legislature. His death occurred in 1923, and interment was made at Union City, Indiana. Mr. Shultz married Miss Anna L. Peacock, who was born and reared in Randolph County, where she received a public school education, and throughout her life has been active in the work of the Christian Church. She survives her husband and resides at the old Shultz home near Winchester. Her father was Hiatt Peacock, who married a Miss Pickett, of Randolph County.

The only child of his parents, Warren D. Shultz attended the public schools of Randolph County, and after his graduation from high school pursued a course in the Eastern Indiana Normal School at Muncie, where he was graduated in 1907. Two years later he completed his course in the Indiana Business College, and for five years following taught in public schools in Randolph County and two years in the Indiana Business College. He then secured an appointment in the United States postal service at Union City, Indiana, but in 1919 resigned to come to Muncie as an employe in the offices of the General Motors Corporation, where he remained two years. He next was employed by the Durant Motors Company for four years, subsequently opening an office as a public accountant. In 1927 Mr. Shultz formed his first connection with the Griffith Furniture Company, starting as an accountant and later being made secretary and a member of the board of directors. This company was founded about 1880, at Huntington, Indiana, by the late George Griffith, the plant being subsequently moved to Albany, Indiana, and finally to its present site at Muncie, where, as before noted, it has been developed into one of the largest manufacturers of novelty and smokers' furniture in the United States. Following the death of George Griffith the business was carried on by one of his sons, Edwin L. Griffith, who brought the plant to Muncie, and whose own death occurred in 1917. The latter's two sons then took charge of the business, these being F. Randolph Griffith and George Lytle Griffith, the former of whom died in September, 1928, and the latter in December, 1924. The business is now carried on by Verne G. De Camp, as vice president, plant superintendent and member of the board of directors, a sketch of whose career appears following in this work; Mr. Shultz of this review; and Miss Ethel Hartman. Mr. Shultz is acknowledged to be one of the capable and energetic business men of the city and one who is active and progressive in civic and political affairs. He is a member of the Knights of the Golden Eagle, the Modern Woodmen of America, the Muncie Chamber of Commerce and the Muncie Exchange Club. In politics he supports the principles of the Republican party, and his religious connection is with the Christian Church.

On August 20, 1913, at Union City, Indiana, Mr. Shultz was united in marriage with Miss Nellie Roe, of Union City, a daughter of Fred and Nettie (Alexander) Roe, of that place. Mr. Roe was for many years a prominent farmer and stock raiser of his community, but for the past twenty or twenty-five years has been engaged in mercantile activities at Union City. Mrs. Schultz was educated in the public schools of Union City, including the high school, and is one of the prominent women of Muncie, being active in the work of the Jackson Street Christian Church, the Order of the Eastern Star, the Woman's Club and the Matinee Musical Club. Mr. and Mrs. Shultz have one daughter: Marta Ruth, who is preparing her way for a comprehensive future education by attending kindergarten.

VERNE G. DE CAMP. The young and energetic generation which is contributing so greatly to the commercial and industrial prestige of the thriving City of Muncie finds an able and worthy representative in the person of Verne G. De Camp, superintendent and a member of the board of directors of the Griffith Furniture Company. A member of an early Indiana family, he is largely a self-made man and started his career before reaching his majority as a railroader, and his career has included overseas service during the World war. Since 1925 he has been identified with his present company, and in addition to discharging his duties therewith has a number of interests which lead him to touch life on many sides.

Mr. De Camp was born at North Judson, Indiana, March 16, 1894, and is a son of Abe and Margaret (Ford) De Camp. His paternal grandfather was one of the early pioneer settlers of Starke County, Indiana, where he carried on extensive operations as a farmer and stock raiser, and he and his worthy wife are now buried at North Judson, Indiana. Abe De Camp was born at North Judson, Indiana, where he acquired a rural school education, and when still a youth was attracted, like many other farm boys, by the romance of railroading. Leaving home in about 1889, he entered the service of the Erie Railroad, with which he has been identified for more than forty years, and now has a passenger conductor run out of Huntington, Indiana, where he makes his home. Mr. De Camp has a wide acquaintance among the traveling public

and there are few men who are more greatly esteemed, either by their fellow-citizens or by the company that has employed them for so many years. Mr. De Camp married Miss Margaret Ford, who was born and reared at Mount Vernon, Ohio, and educated there and in Indiana, where she came with her parents as a child, the family settling as agriculturists in Starke County. She also survives and is very active in church work as a member of the Presbyterian congregation at Huntington. To Mr. and Mrs. De Camp there were born two children: Verne G., of this review; and Donald, employed by the American Express Company at Huntington, who married Miss Avis Smuck, whose people are prominent agriculturists and stock-raisers near Huntington.

Verne G. De Camp attended the grade and high schools of Huntington, graduating from the latter as a member of the class of 1913. On leaving school he secured a position on the Erie Railroad as yard clerk at Huntington, and by industry, ability and fidelity worked his way upward to the responsible position of yardmaster. In 1914 Mr. De Camp resigned his position to enter the employ of the Caswell-Runyan Company, with which he continued until the United States entered the World war, and May 13, 1917, enlisted in the United States Army. He entered the First Officers' Training Camp at Fort Benjamin Harrison, where he remained three months and received his commission as first lieutenant, following which he spent a few months in southern training camps and went overseas July 31, 1918, in command of the Thirty-ninth P. O. D. Company. In this service he built and operated the woodworking section of the Ordnance Base Shops at Mehun-Suryebe, France, where he remained until July 3, 1919, and then sailed for the United States and was honorably discharged at Washington, D. C., August 1, 1919, after twenty-seven months of loyal service. Returning to Huntington, he rejoined the Caswell-Runyon Company, in the capacity of assistant superintendent, but February 1, 1925, resigned to accept the position of superintendent of the Griffith Furniture Company, of Muncie, which position he still fills, in addition to which he is a member of the board of directors and vice president of this concern. Mr. De Camp is known as one of the energetic and capable business men of the city, and one who is thoroughly informed as to every detail of his work. He is a thirty-second degree Mason and a Knight Templar, and has been active as a Shriner since reaching the age of twenty-one years. He belongs also to Muncie Post No. 19, American Legion, the Exchange Club and the Chamber of Commerce. Politically he is a Republican and has been active in a number of civic movements. His religious connection is with the Presbyterian Church.

On October 10, 1921, at Huntington, Mr. De Camp was united in marriage with Miss Marie Oswald, of Fort Wayne, Indiana, a daughter of Gabriel Oswald, who for many years has been an engineer in the employ of the Fort Wayne Electric Company. Mrs. De Camp is a graduate of the Fort Wayne High School, and is active in the work of the Presbyterian Church. She and her husband are the parents of one daughter: Yvonne Marie, who is attending public school.

HERMAN P. CAMPBELL, secretary and treasurer of the Evers Soft Water Laundry Company at Muncie, is a native of Indiana, and almost his entire business experience has been identified with laundry work. He is a master hand in directing the complicated processes of this business, which now ranks among the staple functions of service to the American home.

Mr. Campbell was born at Lebanon, Indiana, December 12, 1888. His grandfather, John Campbell, was an early settler in Boone County, Indiana, and acquired land from the Government, developing one of the substantial farms of that section. He and his wife are buried in the Hopewell Cemetery in Boone County. L. P. Campbell, father of Herman P., was born and reared at Lebanon, attended school there, and has been one of the leading farmers and stock men in that locality. He and his wife still reside on their farm near Lebanon. He married Laura E. Jarred, who was born in Kansas but was reared and educated in Illinois and Indiana. She is an active worker in the Christian Church. They had five children: Ora F., of Frankfort, Indiana; Agnes, wife of Charles Glen Beck, of Lebanon; Herman P.; Elza E., of Kokomo; and Alford Ray, of Detroit, Michigan.

Herman P. Campbell was reared and educated at Lebanon, completing his high school work there, and after a few years of experience on a farm went to work for the Lebanon Laundry. He learned the business with that institution. Later he spent three years at Los Angeles, California, and in 1921 he and Mrs. Charles C. Stucky bought the Evers Soft Water Laundry at Muncie. Mr. Campbell is not only an expert in laundry work, but a very efficient business organizer, and as secretary and treasurer of the company has contributed a great deal to its steadily increasing success.

He is affiliated with the Independent Order of Odd Fellows and Loyal Order of Moose, is a member of the Chamber of Commerce and Dynamo Club, the Muncie Y. M. C. A., and belongs to the National and Indiana State Laundry Owners Associations. He is a Democrat in politics and a member of the Baptist Church.

Mr. Campbell married, October 25, 1914, at Kokomo, Miss Vada M. Powell, of that city, daughter of Chauncey and Amanda (Ferguson) Powell. Her father for many years carried on a farm and stock ranch near Kokomo, and died in 1901. Her mother passed away November 16, 1929, and both are buried in the Sharon Cemetery near Kokomo. Mrs. Campbell completed her high school course at Kokomo. She is a Baptist, is a member of the auxiliary of the Order of Moose and the S. C. Club. Mr. and Mrs. Campbell have one daughter, Eva Lucille, now in high school at Muncie. Mr. Campbell during the World war did his part in the various drives, particularly in the Y. M. C. A. and Red Cross campaigns.

ROLLIE MARK MOREN, one of the most popular citizens of Daviess County, is an Indiana man who has rendered important service as an educator, in business, as a soldier in the World war and as a public official.

Mr. Moren, who is the present county auditor of Daviess County, was born at Plainville, Indiana, September 4, 1894. His father, Rev. William G. Moren, was born in Reeve Township, Daviess County, Indiana, and has given his active life to the ministry of the United Brethren Church. He married Sarah Ellen Wininger, of Reeve Township, daughter of John Wininger. Their children were: Alfred G., who lives at Seymour, Indiana; James E., of Washington; Ezra E., of Washington; Hattie, of Plainville; Inis, of Washington; Myrtle, of Washington; and Rollie M.

Rollie M. Moren was educated in the public schools of Plainville and the high school at Epsom. He is an A. B. graduate of the Indiana State Normal School of Terre Haute. He began teaching at Plainville and continued the routine of a school man until 1918, when he volunteered for service in the World war, in the Seventieth Field Artillery, and served with the A. E. F. in France.

Mr. Moren after his return and discharge from the army was in the service of the Commerce Coal Company at Washington, Indiana, and for a time conducted a grocery business at Washington. He has been interested in politics in Daviess County and in November, 1926, was elected county auditor on the Republican ticket and was reelected in 1930 for a term of four years.

Mr. Moren married, September 13, 1919, Miss Eulabelle Parsons, of Montgomery. They have two children, Wilma Jean, born December 16, 1924, and Mary Margaret, born February 12, 1926. Mr. Moren is a member of the United Brethren Church, the American Legion, Post No. 21, of Washington, Indiana, the A. F. and A. M., No. 30, of Washington, the R. A. C. No. 92 of Washington, and Washington Council No. 67 and Washington Commandery No. 33. He has served through all the chairs with the exception of the commandery. He is a Republican and is a past chairman of the Washington Township Republican committee. He also holds membership in the Odd Fellows fraternity.

FRANK W. BUDD is vice president and manager of the Central Indiana Gas Company at Muncie. His experience in public utility engineering and management has taken him to many parts of the country, but he is a native of Indiana, having been born in the City of Muncie, March 30, 1890.

Rollie M. Moren.

His grandfather, Samuel O. Budd, came from York State and was an early settler in Eastern Indiana. He was a gunsmith by trade and afterwards took up the profession of dentistry, which he practiced until his death about 1910, at the age of eighty-one. He and his wife are buried in Beech Grove Cemetery at Muncie. Chester A. Budd, father of Frank W. Budd, was a highly respected professional man of Muncie, where he practiced dentistry from the time of his graduation from the Cincinnati Dental College until his death in November, 1902. He is also buried in Beech Grove. He was born and reared at Muncie, and attended the grade and high schools, graduating from high school in 1875. He was active in Masonic circles, was a member of the Independent Order of Odd Fellows and for two terms before his death was in the City Council. His church was the Universalist. Dr. Chester A. Budd married Fannie Corbley, who was born at Mount Washington, Cincinnati, Ohio, attended school there and at Muncie. She was a member of the Universalist Church, though reared a Baptist, and they belong to the McRae Club. She died in July, 1918. Of her nine children one died in infancy; Alma S., deceased, was the wife of Harry E. Paris, of Muncie; William O. died while attending Purdue University; Ada Mae is the wife of Robert H. Crandall, of Miami, Florida; Chester F. lives at Denver, Colorado; Bessie L. is Mrs. Perry L. Manifold, of Newcastle, Indiana; Frank W.; Thomas Guthrie died at the age of twelve years; and Samuel D. is with the American Railway Express at Toronto, Ohio.

Frank W. Budd was educated in the schools of Muncie and after high school took extension courses in both business and engineering with the Alexander Hamilton Institute and the International Correspondence Schools. For two years he was in the shop of the Whitely Malleable Castings Company at Muncie, spent eighteen months with the Inland Steel Company at Terre Haute, for a year and a half was at Muncie with the Central Indiana Gas Company. Following that he spent a few months at Columbus, Ohio, with the Columbus Gas & Fuel Company, was at Spokane, Washington, with the Spokane Gas Company, for six months, and for four and a half years was located at Wallace, Idaho, with the Coeur D'Alene Hardware Foundry Company. In September, 1918, he returned to Muncie and joined the engineering staff of the Central Indiana Gas Company. Later he was a salesman, then became local auditor in the general office, and on July 1, 1928, was promoted to division manager, with headquarters at Muncie. He is also a director, vice president and treasurer of the corporation. Mr. Budd is well known in public utility circles, is a treasurer of the Municipal League of Indiana and secretary and treasurer of the Indiana Gas Association.

Fraternally he is affiliated with Delaware Lodge No. 46, A. F. and A. M., is a past president of the Kiwanis Club, member of the Chamber of Commerce, Delaware Country Club. He is a Republican, and has served consecutively eight years as a member of the Muncie City Council. He has been a member and vice president of the City Planning Commission since it was organized in 1923.

Mr. Budd married at Minneapolis, Minnesota, June 6, 1917, Miss Marie Hill, of that city, daughter of J. P. and Anna (Dallam) Hill. Her father for many years was in the banking and real estate business at Minneapolis, where he died in November, 1919. Her mother lives at Muncie. Mrs. Budd is a graduate of a high school at Minneapolis. She specialized in vocal music, is a member of the choir of the Grace Episcopal Church at Muncie, a member of the Delaware Country Club and the Woman's Literary Club. Mr. and Mrs. Budd are rearing one of his sister's children, Pauline Paris, whose mother died some years ago. Pauline is attending the Muncie High School.

ADAM J. KNAPP is a retired Evansville physician who has given more than thirty-seven years to the routine of his profession and has become one of the leaders in public health work in Southern Indiana.

Doctor Knapp was born in Tuscarora County, Ohio, in October, 1853. His parents, Frederick and Adelaide (Paul) Knapp, came from Germany, his father at the age of sixteen and his mother when a young girl. Frederick Knapp was a merchant and banker in Ohio, and died in 1909, his wife passing away in 1911.

Doctor Knapp was next to the oldest in a family of ten children. He attended public schools and graduated from the medical department of the University of Tennessee in 1893. He at once located in Evansville, where he has carried on the work of his profession ever since. Doctor Knapp was a teacher of successful experience before entering the medical profession, and while teaching he became interested in the problems of the children, particularly those who apparently from some physical or pathological cause had difficulty in making the grades. Shortly after getting established in his practice he accepted the opportunity to render some special service to the schools in the way of making free examinations of public school children for hearing and sight. In that work he had the cooperation of some other Evansville doctors. The chief result of their work was that many pupils with marked poor vision and poor hearing received special treatment. This paved the way for regular and permanent medical inspection and health work in the public schools, Evansville being one of the first progressive cities of the state to institute such a program.

A number of years ago Doctor Knapp, while attending a medical convention in Iowa, was greatly impressed by the discussion and practical demonstration of tubercular cows as the source of human tuberculosis. At that time Evansville was infected with tuberculosis cases, and when he returned to the city he immediately took steps to arouse the medical profession and the public in general to the possibility of the white plague being carried through infected milk. A great deal of praise was given him for his stand in that matter, though the praise was also accompanied by a great deal of criticism. At a meeting held in the Walker Hospital by the county medical association the resolution was adopted asking for the testing of all dairy cows supplying milk to Evansville. The test showed that a great number of cows in the local dairies were tubercular, and in the course of years the campaign has gone on until Evansville was supplied only with milk from tested herds and today Evansville is comparatively free from the scourge of tuberculosis.

Doctor Knapp is a successful physician with an interesting side-line and hobby as a floriculturist. About twenty-seven years ago he began growing peonies, and his hobby has developed into something more than a pastime. He has contributed to making Southern Indiana the greatest center in the United States for the propagation and breeding of peonies and his own farm, comprising 200 acres, is one of the largest commercial peony growing plants in the United States. From his beds he ships thousands of roots annually and also does an immense business in cut flowers. He established his own markets in the principal cities and was a pioneer in the practice of shipping the flowers and buds. On last Mother's Day Doctor Knapp shipped from one of his farms 48,000 dozens of peony blossoms.

Doctor Knapp married in October, 1876, Miss Barbara Wise, of Ohio. They have two children, Bleeker J. and Eva. Bleeker, a physician and surgeon, a well-known Evansville specialist, married Eleanor D. and has two children, Mary E. and Eleanor Gordon. The daughter, Eva, is the wife of Doctor Dyer, of Evansville, and has a son, Wallace Knapp Dyer.

S. WALLACE COOK has been one of the very active figures in the commercial life of Evansville for over forty years, an insurance man, banker and manufacturer, and is an American citizen whose people have been in this country for ten generations.

Mr. Cook was born at Evansville, April 20, 1863. His grandfather was a native of Massachusetts and his father, S. H. S. Cook, was born in Rhode Island, came to Indiana in 1857, was a school teacher, later a grocery merchant, served as a first lieutenant in the Union army during the Civil war and in the latter part of his life followed the insurance business. He died in March, 1910. His wife, Esther Jarvis, was born in Vanderburg County, Indiana. Her father was born in Aberdeen, Scotland, and her mother in Vanderburg County. Mrs. Esther Cook died September 23, 1923, at the age of eighty-one. Her children were S. Wallace, John, Nettie and Clarence A. John, in the insurance business, married Martha Jones and has two children. Nettie is the wife of William E. Nelson, of Evansville, former representative of the First Indiana District in Congress, and they have two children. Clarence, in the insurance business at Indianapolis, married Sadie Vickery and has one child.

S. Wallace Cook attended the grade and high schools at Evansville and was valedictorian when his class graduated, in 1880, from high school. After two terms of teaching he entered DePauw University at Greencastle, Indiana, but left in his junior year to take up insurance work, which he has followed steadily since July, 1883, and has one of the oldest agencies in Southern Indiana. Mr. Cook has been doing business with the National City Bank of Evansville since 1883 and for some years has been vice president of that institution and is also a trustee of the Peoples Savings Bank. His influence has always been constructive in the financial and industrial growth of Evansville. For thirty-five years he was president and is now vice president of the Stanley Clothing Company of Evansville.

Mr. Cook was Republican candidate for Congress from the First District in 1914 and 1915 and in the latter year was defeated by the narrow margin of 200 votes. He is a member of the Trinity Methodist Episcopal Church and is a Knight Templar Mason and Shriner, member of the Knights of Pythias and the B. P. O. Elks.

He married, at Kansas City, Missouri, January 9, 1887, Miss Isabelle McNutt, daughter of Patterson and Louisa (Slavin) McNutt. Her father was a scholar and educator and at one time was professor of mathematics in old Asbury University, before the name of that Indiana institution was changed to DePauw University. Mr. and Mrs. Cook had four children: Louisa, who died in 1914, Esther, Isabella, who died in infancy, and Stephen Wallace, Jr. Esther is the wife of John R. Stanley, who is manager of the Stanley Clothing Company, and has two children, Louisa, born in 1915, and John W., born in 1922. Stephen Wallace, Jr., graduated from Evansville High School and left his studies at the University of Illinois to enlist during the World war, became a first lieutenant and served one year overseas in France. He now owns the Peter Healy Brass Works. He married Edith Newman.

DR. GEORGE RICE PECKINPAUGH, a veteran physician, who has given nearly half a century of his lifetime to the task and responsibilities of a doctor of medicine, is a resident of Evansville, and is held in high esteem by prominent members of his profession throughout Southern Indiana.

Doctor Peckinpaugh was born at Alton, Indiana, June 5, 1854. His father, Nicholas Peckinpaugh, who was born at Hardin, Kentucky, in 1808, moved to Indiana when a

Vic F. Sturm

young man and had business interests that marked him as one of the prominent figures along the Ohio River. He was a member of a group of men who installed the first packet line between Louisville and New Orleans, his boats being the *Rainbow* and *Fawn*. He also owned extensive tracts of land, and had a large organization of workers getting out wood to fuel the steamboats along the Ohio River. He died in 1859. Nicholas Peckinpaugh married Eleanor Sheckell, who was born in Hardin County, Kentucky, in 1815 and died in 1890. Of their family of twelve children Doctor Peckinpaugh is the only survivor. He was next to the youngest.

Doctor Peckinpaugh attended grade and high schools at Alton, Indiana, continued his education in the University of Indiana, at Bloomington, and was graduated M. D. from the Ohio Medical College in 1882. Doctor Peckinpaugh from 1881 to 1907 practiced medicine at Mount Vernon, Indiana, and in the latter year moved to Evansville. He has his offices in the Mercantile Bank Building, and for several years his assistant has been his niece, Miss Maud Emmick, a daughter of Capt. John Emmick, who was captain of a company during the Civil war and later a captain on an Ohio River steamboat. Doctor Peckinpaugh married, in October, 1885, Rosemond Alexandra, but she died without children in 1892. Doctor Peckinpaugh is a Republican, a member of the Methodist Episcopal Church and the Masonic fraternity.

Many years ago Doctor Peckinpaugh's interest was aroused in special lines of research and investigation to afford his fellow doctors better means of coping with the treatment of disease, realizing that many of the pharmaceutical preparations prescribed by standard pharmacy were inadequate and ineffective. Doctor Peckinpaugh as a result of many years of study and experiment has introduced what is regarded as a profound if not revolutionary method of treating disease by internal hygiene through the application of a physiological system of plant pharmacy, and his work along that line has been given recognition and credit by many distinguished doctors.

The essential features of his treatment, which he and other doctors have used with particular success in cases of tuberculosis and auto-intoxication, are described in the following paragraph:

It is claimed that the superior merits of this Physiological System of Pharmacy consists in extracting and purifying medical properties of plants in a manner to retain the life principle of resuscitation of weakened organs, to retain the natural antiseptic properties for countering the ferment on which the germs subsist, also to retain food properties rich in ash or organic salts to supply chemical needs of the system in a form to be easily assimilated. Alcohol is not used or required in this system of pharmacy, neither as an extractor, preservative or vehicle. These medicines are preserved by natural antiseptic properties of the life principle of plants They are antiseptic, germicidal and eliminant, the combined effects of which are to promote nutritional functions, such as appetite, digestion and assimilation of food, to help the system generate "medicines" from food, also to counteract, destroy and eliminate poison.

VICTOR F. STURM, president of the Jasper Office Furniture Company, is a very alert and enterprising young business man of Dubois County. He is member of a family that has been prominent in Southern Indiana for several generations. Mr. Sturm was liberally educated, and his capacity for work has grown with his responsibilities.

He was born in Spencer County, Indiana, August 8, 1887. His father, Joseph M. Sturm, was a well known merchant in that section of the state, and from 1900 to 1905 held the office of county recorder. He was elected on the Democratic ticket. He married Mary C. Schuntermann, whose father was John Schuntermann, one of the pioneer physicians and country doctors of Southern Indiana. Victor F. Sturm has among his possessions the commission given his grandfather, Joseph G. Sturm, as a lieutenant in the Union army during the Civil war. Joseph M. Sturm and wife had a family of seven children, four of whom are deceased, Irene, Emil, Bertha and Mary, and those living are: Dr. E. A., a well known physician at Jasper, who married Mary Salb and has four children; Victor F.; and Albert, who married Eleanor Gossman and has two children.

Victor F. Sturm attended the common schools and the Jasper Academy of Saint Meinrad Seminary at Jasper. He spent the first two years of his high school course at Rockport and on June 15, 1906, graduated from Jasper College. His business career has been in one line. He joined the Indiana Desk Company as office boy, and later was promoted to manager. In 1922 he became secretary, manager and treasurer of the Jasper Office Furniture Company, of which he is now president and manager. This is a business that has grown and has reached out its trade connections over the entire United States and some of their products are exported.

Mr. Sturm married Miss Clara O. Rumbach, daughter of Christian and Mary (Hettich) Rumbach, of Jasper. Her parents came from Germany in 1881 and settled at Jasper, where Mr. Rumbach owned and operated a farm and died in 1910, at the age of sixty. They were married in Reuthe, Baden, Germany, in 1876. Mr. Rumbach was a soldier in the Franco-Prussian war. Mrs. Rumbach lives at Jasper. Mr. and Mrs. Sturm have four children: Mary Ann, born October 6, 1922, Ruth, born September 21, 1924, Patricia, born February 26, 1927, and George, born May 3, 1931. Mr. Sturm is a Democrat in politics and he and his family are communicants of the Catholic Church.

AUGUST PFAFFLIN, an engineer by profession, has spent most of his life in Evansville, and in a professional capacity has had an important and constructive part in the municipal development, particularly during the years he he served as city engineer.

Mr. Pfafflin was born in Cincinnati, Ohio, December 16, 1857. His father, August Pfafflin, was a native of Germany, and came to the United States in 1847 and died in 1882. He was also a surveyor and civil engineer. August Pfafflin married Emily Schneider, who was born in Paris, France, and was about a year old when her parents came to this country. She died in 1918. She was the mother of ten children, two of whom died in infancy and those who grew up were named Fredericka, Anna, August, Josephine, Fred, Eva, Emily and Theo.

Mr. August Pfafflin attended the grade and high schools at Evansville while a boy and had commercial training in the Kliner and Wright's Business College For a number of years he worked with his father and by practical experience acquired a fundamental knowledge of surveying and civil engineering. In his work he has also had the advantage of training and experience as a machinist. He served an apprenticeship at the machinist's trade with the Cox Machine Works. Many years of work and experience constitute the background of his professional attainments. For ten years he was county surveyor, being elected for the first time in 1890. He has been city engineer of Evansville during the administrations of Mayors Hawkins, Cavert, Hulman and Males.

Mr. Pfafflin is a real estate owner of Evansville. He is a Republican in politics, a member of the Presbyterian Church and is affiliated with the B. P. O. Elks, Fraternal Order of Eagles and Knights of Honor.

He married, November 18, 1885, Miss Anna Stenecker. They have three children, Edna, born in 1888, Florence, born in 1890, and William, born in 1893. Edna is the wife of Arnold Elemdorf, an Evansville furniture merchant, and they have one child. Florence married George Klippel and lives in California. William, who owns a seed store in Chicago, married Inez Spain.

WILLIAM NEAL WALDEN, of Evansville, was thoroughly grounded in the fundamentals of the fine arts before he took up what was then a little more than a skilled craft, photography, and he has been one of a group of American photographers who have elevated this medium through the plane of the fine arts.

Mr. Walden, whose studio at Evansville has become famous there and in many states, was born at New Albany, Indiana, March 26, 1861, son of Martin and Amanda Jane (Kepley) Walden. His father was born in Kentucky and his mother in Indiana, and she died in 1914, at the age of seventy-four. Martin Walden was a druggist, and early in the Civil war became a member of the Medical Corps of the Union army and died as a result of exposure. He had two children, Hattie and William N. Hattie married John H. Mason, who was born in Spencer, Indiana, and is now deceased, and Mrs. Mason lives at Columbus, Georgia, with her daughter Ellen, wife of Doctor Baird, a medical specialist there.

William Neal Walden attended grammar and high school at Evansville and in 1886 he went east to New York City and for five years carried on his studies with the Art Students League. After this period of training and apprenticeship he returned to Evansville and established a studio, teaching art classes, and for several years he did a great deal of work as a magazine illustrator. It was in 1897 that he turned to photography as his chief medium. Thirty years ago there were very few men who made any profession of photography as an art, and only a few had a vision of the possibilities which have been developed by Stieglitz and a few others. Mr. Walden was one of the first artistic photographers in Indiana, and his work has been given some of the highest awards by the American Photographers Association. He has one of the finest equipped studios in Indiana, and his equipment includes apparatus for the making of motion pictures. Mr. Walden is a Republican, a member of the Methodist Episcopal Church, the B. P. O. Elks and the Kiwanis Club. He also belongs to the Chamber of Commerce.

JAMES LOGAN BALLARD. The name of Ballard has been prominently identified with the hotel interests of Indiana and other states. The late James Logan Ballard was an Orange County man, very successful in his business career, and a man possessed of enviable personality, who had friends in many sections of the country.

He was born in Orange County, August 5, 1879. His brother, Edward Ballard, is owner of the West Baden Hotel. His early education was supplied by the grade and high schools of Orange County. As a young man he entered the hotel business, and at one time owned the Grand Hotel of Mackinac Island, Michigan, one of the finest of the summer resort hotels in America. He was also a dealer in real estate and left a large amount of busness property as well as farm lands.

Mr. Ballard, who died in 1923, married Bessie Duey, daughter of John and Katie (Dirr) Duey, of Cincinnati. Mrs. Ballard resides at West Baden. She is the mother of three children: Katherine L., born September 16, 1908; Jane L., born December 9, 1916; and James L., born June 3, 1919. Katherine is a graduate of Saint Mary's of the Woods at Terre Haute, and is the wife of Frank Dixon, of West Baden. The two younger children are both in school.

The late Mr. Ballard was a Republican in politics. He served as a soldier in the Spanish-American war. Mrs. Ballard is oracle in the Royal Neighbors and noble grand of the Rebekah Lodge.

WILLIAM G. FRENCH is an Evansville physician, has practiced there for twenty years, and is one of the scholarly and able men of his profession in Southern Indiana.

Doctor French is a native of Kentucky, born at Newport February 2, 1885. His grandfather served four years with the Union army in the Civil war. Doctor French is a son of Dr. Malachi R. and Sarah Bell (Woods) French, both of whom reside at Evansville, where his father for many years has practiced medicine. His father was born in Iowa and his mother in Illinois. There were four children: Dr. William G.; Stella, born in 1887; Robert L., born in 1888; and Stephen F., born in 1890. Miss Stella is unmarried and lives at Evansville. Robert, also a physician, is practicing in Oak Park, Illinois, and by his marriage to Mabel Clark has two children. Stephen F. is a dentist, located at Elmhurst, Illinois. He married Margaret Perkins and they have three children.

Dr. William G. French attended grammar and high schools in Chicago, continuing his higher education in Valparaiso University of Indiana, and was graduated M. D. from the General Medical College of Chicago in 1906. Doctor French had the benefit of three years of general routine practice in Chicago before coming to Evansville, where he located May 17, 1909. He is fellow of the American Academy of Proctology, and this is a line that represents his specialty. Doctor French was county coroner of Vanderburg County from 1922 to 1924, and for the past four years has been police surgeon. He is a member of the County, Indiana State and American Medical Associations, is a Republican in politics, a member of the Evangelical Church, and is a York and Scottish Rite Mason and Shriner and member of the B. P. O. Elks. He is also president of the Evansville Press Club.

Doctor French married at Chicago in June, 1913, Miss Sarah Ellen Young, daughter of Fred and Ellen Young. They are the parents of four children, Mildred Ellen, born in 1917, Russell Gayle, born in 1920, Stella Margaret, born in 1924, and William Clement, born in 1927.

HARRY MORTON GARRISON is a physician and surgeon practicing in Evansville, where he has been located since the close of the World war. His first years of practice were in Warrick County, the section of Indiana where he was born and reared and where his family have lived since pioneer times.

Doctor Garrison was born in Warrick County, son of Willard Garrison. Both his father and grandfather were born in Warrick County. His father was born in 1860 and died in 1901, and lived out his life on a farm near Garrison Chapel. He married Catherine Easley, who is now seventy-one years of age, and her family were also early settlers of Warrick County. Of the eight children two died in infancy, and those to grow up were Ora H., Dr. Harry M., Dennie T., Hubert W., Ethel and May. Ora, who was a railway

clerk, married Anna Taylor and has two children. Dennie lives in Ohio. Hubert, a member of the Evansville police force, died in 1927, leaving four children. Ethel is the wife of Ed Stephen, of Boonville, and has five children, and May is the wife of Elmer Walter, living in Wabash, Indiana, and has two children.

Harry Morton Garrison attended public schools at Dale, Indiana, and graduated from the Louisville College of Pharmacy. He was a drug clerk for several years and in 1911 graduated from the Southwestern School of Homeopathy. For one year he practiced at Dale, seven years at Selvin in Warrick County, and six months at Winslow.

He volunteered for service during the World war and was commissioned a first lieutenant in the Medical Corps just about the time the armistice was signed. On January 1, 1919, he moved to Evansville, where he has practiced with a steadily growing reputation for able work and conscientious devotion to his clients. He is a member of the Vanderburg County, Indiana State and American Medical Associations.

Doctor Garrison married in December, 1916, Gale Whittinghill, daughter of Wayne and Agnes (Spradly) Whittinghill, of Warrick County. They have one son, Harry M., Jr., born in November, 1918. Doctor Garrison is a Republican, a member of the Methodist Church, and is affiliated with the B. P. O. Elks and Independent Order of Odd Fellows.

JOHN GEORGE MALMBERG, who for a number of years was an active figure in the insurance circles in Wisconsin and at Chicago, since coming to South Bend has given that city one of its best known insurance organizations, the Income Guaranty Company, of which he is president.

Mr. Malmberg was born in Denmark, November 28, 1880, son of Nels and Johanna (Joergensen) Malmberg. His father was born in Sweden, in 1849, and his mother in Denmark, in 1852. In 1887 the parents came to the United States and settled at Oshkosh, Wisconsin, where Nels Malmberg was in business as a florist. He died in 1919. After acquiring American citizenship he was a staunch Republican and from early youth was a member of the Danish Lutheran Church. There were four sons in the family: Anton M., born in 1876; John G.; Emil C., born in 1882; and L. William, born in 1885. All the sons are living. Their mother, who passed away in 1915, had taught school during her early life in Denmark.

John G. Malmberg learned his letters and received his first instruction in the primary branches from his mother. He finished his public schooling at Oshkosh and at the age of eighteen went to work in a grocery business owned by his father. His active connection with the grocery trade continued from January 1, 1899, to April 10, 1905. He then entered the insurance field, at Oshkosh, where he was associated with the Union Accident & Benefit

Association until May 1, 1912. He then moved to Green Bay, Wisconsin, and assisted in the organization of the Badger Casualty Company. Later this company acquired the business of the Midland Casualty Company of Illinois, and with the consolidation of the assets and business of the two organizations headquarters were established in Chicago and Mr. Malmberg became secretary of the company.

On September 1, 1917, he moved to South Bend and took part in the organization of the Income Guaranty Company, which has enjoyed a steadily increasing volume of business and has become one of the well known and reliable insurance houses of Northern Indiana. Mr. Malmberg was secretary of the company when it was organized, later vice president and treasurer, and since March 1, 1929, has been president. The secretary and treasurer is his son-in-law, Mr. A. N. Hepler, Jr. Mr. Malmberg is also a director of the company and is a director of the Rotary Club.

He has been very prominent in Masonic affairs and is a past master of Lodge No. 294, A. F. and A. M., is a past sovereign prince of the Scottish Rite Council and second lieutenant commander of the Consistory. He is a member of Murat Temple of the Mystic Shrine at Indianapolis and is on the board of control and the board of representatives of the St. Joseph Valley Temple Association. He still has membership in the Green Bay Lodge of B. P. O. Elks. Mr. Malmberg is a member of the First Methodist Episcopal Church of South Bend. He is a past patron of the Eastern Star Chapter and a member of the Chamber of Commerce.

On June 25, 1902, he married Miss Jeanette Anderson, of Oshkosh. They have two children, Dorothy Jeanette, born April 7, 1904, and John Milton, born August 22, 1909. The son is a graduate of the South Bend High School and is a member of the class of 1931 in the University of Illinois and is preparing for the profession of the law. Dorothy Jeanette is a graduate of the South Bend High School, and assisted her father in the business office until her marriage to Mr. A. N. Hepler, Jr. They have two sons, Albert Newton Hepler III and Robert John Hepler.

WILLIAM M. WILHELMUS, M. D. The modern medical man shares in the progress of the age, for science has reached a degree bordering upon perfection in matters pertaining to his profession. Were it not that the man of the twentieth century is developing new diseases by reason of his complicated and unnatural mode of living, doubtless the scientists could prevent decay and prolong human life almost indefinitely. As it is miracles are being daily performed and methods approved that seem beyond the comprehension of the layman, however much he may benefit from their application to his individual case. One of the men of Indiana who has attained to a high position among his contemporaries in the medical profession, not only at Saint Wendell where he resides, but in the medical socie-

ties with which he is connected, is Dr. William M. Wilhelmus. He was born in Spencer County, Indiana, December 23, 1882, a son of Otto Wilhelmus, a native of Germany.

At an early day Otto Wilhelmus came to the United States, and, like so many of his fellow countrymen, upon coming here became a farmer. The great ambition of the immigrants of an early day was to secure land of their own, something only the wealthy or nobility could hope to have in their own country, and few there were who did not at one time or another become farmers. However, Otto Wilhelmus was willing to defend the country he had adopted, and when war was declared between the states, enlisted in the Union army, fought bravely, and was wounded in the shoulder during the great battle of Missionary Ridge, which was fought with such terrible losses on both sides. After the close of the war he resumed his farming, and continued in that calling until his death, in 1884. His wife, formerly Mary Kaiser, was born in Indiana, and she survived him many years, passing away in August, 1914. They had two children, namely: Doctor Wilhelmus and Charles.

Reared amid strictly rural surroundings, Doctor Wilhelmus was early taught to make himself useful, and to save the money his labor earned for him, and these early lessons have remained with him, and while he is engaged in a large practice he is also an extensive farmer of Spencer County. His early education was acquired in the country and high schools of Spencer County. Having made up his mind to enter the medical profession, he entered the Louisville Medical College, Louisville, Kentucky, and was graduated therefrom in 1908, with the degree of Doctor of Medicine, after which he established himself in practice near Boonville, Warrick County, Indiana. After a year there he moved to Powell, Wyoming, and was there engaged in practice for a year, but then came to Saint Wendell, in 1911, and here he has since remained, building up a large practice, which covers Armstrong and other portions of Vanderburg County.

Twice married, he was united first to Miss Retta Wallace, of Dale, Indiana, November 26, 1908, and they had one child, Dorothy, who was born October 14, 1910, and is now attending Evansville, Indiana, College, where she is taking a course in liberal arts, in the class of 1932. The first Mrs. Wilhelmus died February 5, 1921, and in October, 1923, Doctor Wilhelmus was married to Miss Rose Martin, of Saint Wendell. There are no children of the second marriage. Doctor Wilhelmus is a Democrat, but has never sought office, preferring to exert his influence as a private citizen. However, when he found that there was need of his professional services he accepted appointment as deputy health officer of his community. He is a member of the Roman Catholic Church and of the Knights of Saint John. While his time is occupied with the demands of his large practice, Doctor Wilhelmus is interested in those measures which tend toward a better education of the people to the necessity for more sanitary regulations and hygienic conditions. He is not bound by his professional knowledge, but is able to take a broad, humanitarian view of life and join with others in working to effect improvements that will raise the average man and woman and develop the best quality of citizenship.

EDWARD E. HIGHMAN was born and reared in Posey County, Indiana, is a scion, in the third generation, of one of the sterling and honored pioneer families of this county, and here he has long held prestige as an influential citizen and leading business man of Mount Vernon, the county seat, where he is president of the Old First National Bank and also of the Home Mill & Grain Company.

Mr. Highman was born on the parental home farm, in Lynn Township, this county, December 25, 1851, and thus became a welcome Christmas day arrival in the home circle of his parents, John and Mary A. (Wilson) Highman. John Highman was born in Pennsylvania and was a child at the time of the family removal to Posey County, Indiana, where his parents passed the remainder of their lives, his father having here gained a goodly measure of pioneer honors in farm enterprise. John Highman was reared and educated in this county and here he continued a substantial exponent of farm industry until his death, May 25, 1854. His wife, who was born in Pennsylvania, was a child when, in 1816, she came with her parents to Indiana, much of the journey having been made on a flat-boat down the Ohio River. Mrs. Highman survived her husband nearly forty years and was of venerable age at the time of her death, November 28, 1893. Of the eight children the eldest is Elizabeth, who is the wife of John Wilsey, a farmer in Lynn Township, two of their four children having died in infancy; Andrew, the second child, died in infancy, as did also the next child, Martha; Malinda died at the age of eighteen years; Elzina became the wife of Joshua Seward, who was a gallant soldier of the Union during virtually the entire period of the Civil war, he having been a member of the First Indiana Cavalry, and their children were four in number; Mara A. died at the age of fourteen years; Robert W., who resides at Mount Vernon, married Sarah Alexander, and they have two children; and Edward E., of this review, is the youngest of the number.

Edward E. Highman was reared to the sturdy discipline of the home farm and received the advantages of the public schools of his native county. He continued to give his attention to farm enterprise until 1888, when he was elected sheriff of Posey County. He retained this office two terms, gave an effective and loyal administration, and upon his retirement therefrom, in 1894, he engaged in the buying and shipping of grain, with headquarters at Mount Vernon. He continued his operations in an individual way until 1900, when he organized the Home Mill & Grain Company, of which he has since served as president and which is one of the leading industrial and commercial concerns at Mount Vernon. He is likewise president of the Old First National Bank of Mount Vernon. Mr. Highman is a stalwart in the local ranks of the Democratic party and is affiliated with the Knights of Pythias.

At New Harmony, Posey County, on December 25, 1884, his birthday anniversary, Mr. Highman was united in marriage to Miss Kate M. Schnee, daughter of David and Nancy (Travis) Schnee, and of this union were born five children: Fannie K., who was born January 15, 1886, is the wife of William Sonnerman, and they have one child, Martha, who is now (1929) eighteen years of age. Eugene, who was born February 3, 1888, and who is cashier of the Old First National Bank of Mount Vernon, married Miss Lucille Hardwick, and they have two children, Robert and Glenn, aged respectively eight and seven years. Helen, next youngest of the children, died at the age of two and one-half years. Annabel, who was born September 12, 1894, is the wife of George P. Guffin, of Gary, Indiana, and they have two children, George H., aged seven years, and Kathryn, aged five years. Edith, youngest of the children, was born August 12, 1896, and is the wife of S. C. Aldridge, who is engaged in the insurance business in Saint Paul, Minnesota. They have no children.

ALBERT GALLATIN HOLCOMB was for many years one of the outstanding citizens of Gibson County, a farmer and fruit grower, and from early manhood was the recipient of repeated honors from his fellow citizens, holding all the offices within their gift.

Mr. Holcomb was born in Johnson Township, Gibson County, March 7, 1858. His grandfather, Hosea Holcomb, came from Virginia and was one of the pioneers of Southern Indiana, entering land from the Government located three and a half miles east of Haubstadt. Here he cleared the timber, built a home, reared a fine family and was in every sense of the word a successful man. Albert G. Holcomb was a son of Silas Mercer and Nancy M. (Ralston) Holcomb, his mother being a sister of Doctor Ralston of Evansville. The parents had a family of five children: William R., of Vincennes; Albert G.; Minnie, deceased; Martha, of Fort Branch; and Andrew R., who died in Oklahoma.

Albert Gallatin Holcomb made good use of his early educational advantages, attending the district and high schools of Gibson County. Eight years of his early life were spent in teaching, and he always lived on a farm, his place adjoining the City of Fort Branch. He gave much attention to fruit growing, and took a active part in the Farmers Institute for many years.

When only eighteen years of age he was elected chairman of the Democratic township committee, and held that office thirty years.

He was also for four years chairman of the county Democratic committee. For two consecutive terms he served as township trustee, and it was his splendid adminstration of the schools and other duties included in that office that made him the choice of his district for the State Senate, as was his father, Silas Holcomb, before him. He was elected for one term, and in 1904 was Democratic candidate from this district for Congress, being defeated in the general landslide which occurred when Roosevelt was candidate for his second term. Mr. Holcomb was president for several years and director for sixteen years of the Gibson County Fair Association.

This greatly beloved citizen of Gibson County passed away October 12, 1928, when seventy years of age. He married October 27, 1881, Miss Alice M. Hull, who survives him and continues to occupy the old homestead near Fort Branch. This farm comprises about 200 acres, and is an important unit in the fruit growing interests of this section of the state. Mrs. Holcomb is a daughter of Thomas Hull, a pioneer of Gibson County. She is the mother of two sons, Thomas and Harold. Thomas, a graduate of the University of Georgia in 1908 and of the Yale Law School in 1909, is now practicing law. He served as a first lieutenant in the Ninety-first Division during the World war and previously in the Philippine Constabulary. He married Miss Sarah E. Whittemore, of Evansville. He was retired from the army service on December 7, 1928, with the rank of first lieutenant. The son Harold, a fruit grower near Fort Branch, is a graduate of Purdue University and served as a second lieutenant in the war, being in France for eleven months and participating in the Meuse Argonne drive. He married Mary E. Martin, of Terre Haute, and has one child, Dorothy Alice, born in 1925.

AUGUST J. ZILIAK is head of the Ziliak flour mills at Haubstadt, an industry whose wheels have been turning and which has been manufacturing flour under brands that have become famous not only over Southern Indiana, but have been shipped extensively for both the domestic and foreign trade.

Mr. Ziliak was born at Haubstadt, July 3, 1875. His grandfather, Lawrence Ziliak, was born in Alsace-Lorraine and came to the United States when a young man. The father, Alois Ziliak, was born at Saint Joseph in Vanderburg County, Indiana, and was also a miller and grain dealer, a business he followed all his active life. He died April 1, 1926, when seventy-five years of age. Alois Ziliak married Caroline Wolf, who was born in Augusta, Georgia, in 1852, and is now seventy-nine years of age. These parents had a family of nine children: Lawrence A., born November 25, 1873, a physician practicing at Princeton, Indiana, married Emma Weidel and has five children; August J.; Joseph, born July 22, 1877, died in 1924, and by his marriage to Ida Wetzel has six children; Elizabeth, born August 1, 1879, is the wife of

August Schulthies and has two children; Margaret, born October 28, 1881, is the wife of John Singer, and they have a family of five children; Peter, born December 12, 1883, died in infancy; Olivia, born December 16, 1885, is the wife of Albert Lynn and has four children; Christina, born May 1, 1888, died in infancy; and Otto, born January 25, 1890, lives at Evansville, married Clara Vervain and has one child.

August J. Ziliak attended the grade and high schools at Haubstadt and from boyhood was working in his father's flour mills. He has had a responsible relationship with those mills since 1890, a period of forty years, and after his father retired he took the active management. Under his management the mills have been constantly improved, and their equipment is equal to that of any mills in the southern part of the state. The product of the Ziliak mills is sold extensively through branch selling agencies in Mobile, Alabama, and Evansville, Indiana.

Mr. Ziliak married, May 19, 1896, Miss Julia Singer, daughter of Joseph and Margaret (Halbig) Singer. The children of their marriage were: Stella, deceased, Oliver, Lorana, Helen, John, Raymond, Beatrice, Henry, Frank and Woodrow. Helen is the wife of Andy Graubal, of Evansville, and has two daughters, Wanda May and Colleen. Raymond is a graduate of Notre Dame University, and is now representing the Midland Flour Mills of Kansas City and expects later to take over his father's mill. Lorana, now deceased, was a graduate nurse. Oliver and John are associated with their father in the mill. Beatrice married James Davis, and they live at Lawrence, Kansas, where Mr. Davis is with a construction company. They have one son, Vernon Larue. Henry is preparing for the priesthood at Saint Meinrad's Seminary. Frank is attending an academy at Jasper, Indiana. Woodrow is attending school at home.

Mr. Ziliak is a Democrat in politics, is a Catholic, a fourth degree Knight of Columbus, and belongs to the Elks Lodge at Princeton. In addition to his business as secretary-treasurer of the Haubstadt Milling Company he is a director in the Haubstadt Bank.

ERNEST E. TANKSLEY. One of the representative citizens and prominent business men of Orange County, Indiana, is Ernest E. Tanksley, of French Lick, president of the town board and owner of the French Lick Monument Works, one of the community's most important business enterprises. Mr. Tanksley is a native of Lawrence County, Indiana, and his boyhood was passed in an agricultural atmosphere, so that it was but natural that he should commence his own career as a farmer on the home place. His natural inclination for mechanics, however, led to his learning the stone-cutting and polishing trade, in which for many years he has shown remarkable talent, taste and skill. In 1910 he founded his present business, and during the two decades that have passed he

Adolph E. Haller.

has built up an extensive patronage, not only the perfect workmanship but the variety of the tasteful designs coming from this establishment having brought patrons from all over the country.

Ernest E. Tanksley was born April 5, 1871, in Lawrence County, Indiana, and is a son of Miles and Sarah C. (Weise) Tanksley. Miles Tanksley was also born in Lawrence County, where he attended the public schools, was reared a farmer, and subsequently studied and practiced law and served capably as a justice of the peace for two terms. At the outbreak of the war bewteen the states he was still a youth, but enlisted in Company H, Seventeenth Regiment, Indiana Volunteer Infantry, and was attached to the command of Gen. U. S. Grant, under which great commander he served until hostilities between the North and the South ceased. When peace was declared the young soldier returned to his home with an excellent military record and resumed activities on the farm, in which vocation he never lost interest, although he was also known as one of the skilled, reliable and capable lawyers of his day and could have had a large and lucrative law business had he so desired. He was a man of the highest character and his service on the bench was such as to place him substantially in the confidence and esteem of his fellow-citizens. His death occurred in 1905, when he was seventy-two years of age. Judge Tanksley married Miss Sarah C. Weise who was born in Lawrence County, and died in 1923, at the age of seventy-eight years, and to this union there were born five children: Hattie, deceased; Cora, deceased; Joseph, deceased; Howard, a farmer in Lawrence County; and Ernest E., of this review.

The rural schools of Lawrence County furnished Ernest E. Tanksley with his educational training, and for several years he applied his energies to farming. He learned the stone-cutting and polishing trade, and in 1891 began working for different monument concerns, making an effort to learn every possible detail of the business. In 1910 he founded the French Lick Monument Works, of which he has been the proprietor to the present, and which, as above noted, has grown to be one of the leading and most prosperous concerns of its kind in this part of the state. Mr. Tanksley is widely and favorably known in business circles, and in addition to his regular business is interested in real estate, of which he owns much in this locality. He is a Democrat in his political views and is influential in the ranks of his party, having been president of the town board for the past six years. While not a professed member of any religious denomination, Mr. Tanksley is a religious man and a willing contributor to worthy movements. He is fraternally affiliated with the Independent Order of Odd Fellows, of which he is a past grand.

In November, 1892, Mr. Tanksley was united in marriage with Miss Isis Palmer, and to this union there were born four children: One who died in infancy; Nellie, the wife of Mike Stipp, a farmer of Lawrence County, who has two children: Ruby, who married Charles Pruitt, and has one child; and Ralph, who is unmarried and resides at Lawrenceville. After the death of his first wife Ernest E. Tanksley married Miss Nellie Rainey, in 1907. They have no children.

ADOLPH E. HALLER. The modern baking plants have lifted a heavy burden from the shoulders of the housewife, and, by releasing her from the drudgery of preparing her bread and pastry herself, have given her added years of enjoyment of life. Not only this, but these plants, equipped with the latest of modern machinery, are sanitary as no home can be, and their products are uniformly excellent because experts conduct the operations with scientific exactness. One of the men who, with his brothers, owns one of the above-mentioned plants is Adolph E. Haller, of Haller Brothers, proprietors of one of the finest plants of its kind in Southern Indiana, located at Jasper.

Adolph E. Haller was born at Jasper, January 7, 1893, a son of Joseph and Magdeline (Eckstein) Haller, both natives of Indiana, he, born in Dubois County and she in Ripley County. By trade the father was a building contractor, and many of the best construction work done at Jasper and the surrounding country stands to his credit. His death occurred in 1913. Eleven children were born to Joseph Haller and his wife, namely: Mamie, who married John Schnaus, of Jasper, has six children; Martin, who lives at Saint Louis, Missouri, married Helen Jones, and they have two children; Oscar, who also lives at Saint Louis, married Madge Ayres, no children; Felix, who died in 1915, was married and had one child; Albert, who lives at Jasper, married Delphine Roelle, has two children; Viola, who married Dr. John Casper, of Louisville, Kentucky, has one child; Ray, who lives at Jasper, married Florence Judy, and they have two children; David, who married May Long, has no children; Adolph E., whose name heads this review, and two who are deceased.

Adolph E. Haller attended the parochial school at Jasper, and when old enough to work commenced clerking, which occupation he followed for three years. In 1911 he embarked in the bakery business for himself, and in 1912 took his brother Albert in with him as a partner, the two remaining in the business together until 1915, when Albert sold his interest and went into the grocery business. In the meanwhile Adolph continued the bakery until 1917, when he enlisted in the army, and another brother, Ray, took charge.

Upon his induction in the Federal service, in Battery C, Adolph E. Haller was sent to Camp Custer, as part of the Fourteenth Division. There he was retained until after the armistice, when he was honorably discharged, and returned to Jasper. Here he resumed his business connections, and has as his partners Ray and David Haller. This business has had a remarkable growth, and great attention is paid to maintaining the excellence of the product. The territory is a wide one, and orders come in from surrounding towns, as well as from local regions.

Adolph E. Haller was married to Miss Anna Fromm, a daughter of Fred Fromm, of Mount Carmel, Illinois. They were married May 20, 1919, and have two children, William, born in 1921, and Robert, born in 1925. Mr. Haller is a Democrat, but has not gone into politics actively, his business responsibilities occupying his time. He is a member of the Catholic Church, his parish being Saint Joseph's, and the Knights of Columbus. When the local post of the American Legion was organized Mr. Haller became a charter member, and he was commander from 1929 to 1930, during which time the membership of the post increased from 125 to 334, thus becoming the largest post in the Third Indiana District and merited a citation from the National Commander. The post has grown steadily since. He also belongs to the Forty and Eight Society of which he has been treasurer since its organization. In addition to his interest in his flourishing business Mr. Haller owns city realty, for he believes in investing his money in the town in which he makes it, and he is properly regarded as one of the most prosperous of the young business men of Dubois County.

PETER WALTER, of Mount Vernon, now retired, is a man who has lived a long life, one of unusual experience, and is well known along the Ohio River Valley in Southern Indiana and elsewhere.

Mr. Walter was born in Germany, April 20, 1846. His parents, Valentine and Barbara (Diefenbach) Walter, lived all their lives in Germany, where his father died at the age of seventy-two and his mother at eighty-one. They were farmers in the old country. Of their ten children only two are now living, Peter and his brother Valentine, whose home is in Erie, Pennsylvania, and who enjoys good health at the advanced age of ninety-four.

Peter Walter attended school in Germany and as a youth learned the trade of baker and confectioner, serving a thorough apprenticeship. In 1865, when he was nineteen years old, and just as the American Civil war was closing, he arrived in this country and for the first two years worked at his trade at Erie, Pennsylvania. For one year he was at Louisville, Kentucky, and he then was employed as cook and baker on some of the large river steamboats operating on the Ohio.

Mr. Walter located at Mount Vernon, Indiana, in 1880 and for five years was proprietor of the St. Nicholas Hotel. When he left the hotel business he carried on a bakery and confectionery establishment for forty years, finally selling out and retiring from active business in 1925. He owns business property at Mount Vernon and also has some real estate in Tulsa, Oklahoma. In politics

he has voted as a Democrat, is a member of the Catholic Church and the Knights of Columbus.

Mr. Walter married, October 1, 1871, Miss Margaret Moll, a native of Mount Vernon, Indiana. They enjoyed a long married life of over half a century. Mrs. Walter passed away in April, 1923. There were seven children: Henry, Charles, Martin, Edward, Lena, John and Fred. Henry, who lives at Mount Vernon, married Miss Wisesinger and has a son, Harry. Charles and Martin are in the real estate business at Tulsa, Oklahoma, and the former married Miss Newbert, and the latter Miss Wilson, who died, leaving two children. Edward is in the bakery and confectionery business at Tulsa, Oklahoma, and is married and has one child. Miss Lena is with her father at Mount Vernon. Fred, connected with the oil interests of Oklahoma, with home at Tulsa, married Pauline McFarlin and has a daughter, Mary Frances.

HENRY T. DIXON, M. D., who is now one of the veteran and honored physicians and surgeons in the City of Evansville, has been engaged in the practice of his profession during the long period of half a century, and his technical ability and loyalty have been on a parity with the success that has attended his faithful ministrations.

Doctor Dixon was born in Henderson County, Kentucky, March 20, 1850, and is a son of Charles C. and Isabella (Clay) Dixon, both of whom were likewise born and reared in Henderson County, where they passed their entire lives, Charles C. Dixon having marked his active cereer by close and effective association with farm industry in his native county. He was a son of Capt. Hal Dixon, who was born in North Carolina and whose father, a native of Ireland, was a patriot soldier in the War of the American Revolution. The mother of Doctor Dixon was a kinswoman of the great American patriot Henry Clay, her father being first cousin of Henry Clay. Charles C. and Isabella (Clay) Dixon became the parents of eleven children, namely: Roger, Betsy, Henrietta, Isabella, Charles, Susanna, Henry T., Robert, Winn, Clay and Mary.

Doctor Dixon passed the period of his childhood and early youth on the old home farm that was the place of his birth, and he supplemented the discipline of the common schools by attending Hart's Academy, Corydon, Kentucky. In 1879 he was graduated in the college that is now the medical department of the University of Louisville, Kentucky, and in the passing years he has kept in touch with advances made in medical and surgical science, both by study of the best standard and periodical literature of his profession and also through post-graduate work at Paulo Clinic, Chicago, in 1893, in which year he had the privilege also of attending the great World's Columbian Exposition in that city.

After receiving his degree of Doctor of Medicine Doctor Dixon was for three years established in practice in Posey County, Indiana, and he then returned to his native county in Kentucky, where he continued in practice until 1884, since which year he has maintained his home and professional headquarters in Evansville, Indiana, where he has secure prestige as one of the able and representative physicians and surgeons of Vanderburg County. He has membership in the Vanderburg County Medical Society, the Indiana State Medical Society and the American Medical Association.

Doctor Dixon was reared in the faith of the Democratic party and has never deviated from the line of strict allegiance to that party. He is affiliated with the Masonic fraternity and the Independent Order of Odd Fellows, and he and his wife have membership in the Presbyterian Church.

In October, 1878, was solemnized the marriage of Doctor Dixon to Miss Amelia Wilson, who was born in the City of Louisville, Kentucky, and who is a daughter of the late William S. and Narcissa Wilson. Dr. Percy Dixon, only child of Doctor and Mrs. Dixon, is a dentist by profession and is established in successful practice in Evansville, the maiden name of his wife having been Lillian Kargis, and their two children being Barney, born in September, 1912, and William (Billy), born in March, 1919.

THOMAS GIFFORD ELLIS, former county clerk of courts in Orange County, has been a prominent business man of French Lick, and is now president and general manager of the Mackinac Island Hotel Company at Mackinac Island, Michigan.

Mr. Ellis was born in Dubois County, Indiana, May 11, 1880. The Ellis family have been in Southern Indiana since early pioneer times. His great-grandfather, David Ellis, was one of the very early settlers of Orange County and is buried in the old Newbury Cemetery. Mr. Ellis' grandfather, Marvin Ellis, was an early day Methodist minister. James M. Ellis, father of Thomas G., was born in Dubois County in 1842 and died at New Haven, Florida, in 1914. He was a Union soldier, serving in Company A of the Forty-ninth Indiana Volunteer Infantry. He was under General Grant in the Vicksburg campaign, and at the battle of Champion Hill was wounded and never completely recovered from these injuries. His active life was spent as a merchant. He married Mary A. Beaty, who was born in Orange County in 1843 and died in April, 1927, when eighty-five years of age. Of their seven children two died in infancy. Those living are: Ulysses M., of Orange County, married Emma Lane and has two children, Mary and Olive; Elsworth E. married Sophia Whittinghill and they have a large family of ten children; Ida, who died in 1909, was the wife of Joe Eicher and left five children; Thomas Gifford, of this review; and Joseph A., of Orleans, has three children by his first marriage and two by his present wife, who was Miss Grace Alexandra.

Thomas Gifford Ellis was educated in grade and high schools and as a boy did work clerking in a store. While a clerk he studied bookkeeping and for ten years his chief work was that of bookkeeping. During this time he also studied law and was admitted to the Orange County bar in 1909 and to practice before the treasury department of the United States Government on April 1, 1931. Later he joined W. W. Cave and A. C. Smith in the mercantile business, the firm being known as the Smith, Cave & Ellis Mercantile Company. Selling out after three years, Mr. Ellis built a flour mill, was busy with its management for three years and then traded the mill for a store and stock of goods at Paoli. He was in active charge of this business from 1913 to 1920.

Mr. Ellis was elected clerk of court in 1919, and served in that official capacity for two terms, until January, 1927. In the meantime he had become financially interested in the Dixie Garage, the French Lick Garage and Automobile Service. In 1927, on retiring from office, he sold his interest in the French Lick Garage and Auto Livery and then acquired the entire business of the Dixie Garage, in connection with which he operated the West Baden Cab Service.

In January, 1930, Mr. Ellis became interested in the Mackinac Island Hotel Company and was elected president and general manager of the company and in June, 1931 arranged to devote his full time and attention to this business along with his minor investments. Mackinac Island, located in the straits of Mackinac near the junction of the three Great Lakes, Superior, Huron and Michigan, is eight miles in circumference; its main plateau is 150 feet above the level of the lakes and some of the higher points tower 300 feet above the water level. The primitive grandeur of the island remains undisturbed. No motor cars are allowed on the island. The horse and buggy is the only mode of travel over the miles of gravel roads that encircle and thread the woodlands in every direction.

Riding, golfing, tennis, yachting, canoeing, fishing, and swimming are the chief diversions. Among the points of interest are Fort Mackinac, built by the British more than a century ago.

The Grand Hotel, of which Mr. Ellis is manager, is a palatial summer home for elite vacationers consisting of 400 rooms, with the finest appointments and a dining room of exquisite design and a cuisine unexcelled in the world, the chef having formerly served at Buckingham Palace. A fourteen-piece orchestra and special entertainers delight the guests daily. Across the front of the hotel is a wide veranda, 780 feet in length, with impressive pillars and other architectural design. Beautiful and spacious formal gardens grace the grounds, while seventy-eight acres of golf course and woodland provide ample recreation facilities.

Mr. Ellis is also owner of real estate in French Lick. He has always been a loyal supporter of the Republican party. He is a member of the Masonic Lodge.

He married Miss Amanda L. Whittinghill, daughter of Dr. B. F. and Matilda (Weller) Whittinghill. Her people lived in Warrick and Spencer counties. Mr. and Mrs. Ellis have four children: Arnold, born June 23, 1904, graduated from the College of Music at Cincinnati, a five year course, in 1928 and is now an accomplished musician and associated with his father in the entertainment department of the Grand Hotel. Vivian, born November 9, 1905, graduated from Indiana University in 1927, taught English, Latin and journalism for two years in the Mount Morris, Illinois, High School and married in August, 1929, Vane R. Howard of Remington, Indiana, who is one of three owners and sales manager of the Indian Rubber Company at Indianapolis, where they live. They have one son, Ellis Vane, born January 26, 1931. Rose, born March 9, 1911, is a student in the class of 1933 at the State University of Indiana. Frank, born September 4, 1912, is also attending the State University, class of 1935.

DANIEL BENTON CAIN is one of the honored members of the professional fraternity of Evansville, where for over thirty years he has performed the routine and special service of a physician and surgeon, a man of skill, and one of the most useful members of the community.

He was born in Warrick County, Indiana, November 6, 1863. His father, Henry H. Cain, was also a native of Indiana, and until he was seventy-five years of age gave his labors to the farm. He died March 11, 1931, at the age of 100 years, two months and eight days. Henry H. Cain married Elinor E. Hudson, who died in 1897, at the age of sixty-three. Of her nine children two died in infancy, and the seven to grow up were Martha, Lucinda, John, William, Daniel Benton, Rachael and Lida. Doctor Cain is the only surviving son, and his two surviving sisters are Rachael and Lida. Rachael is the widow of James Perry and has four children, and Lida is the widow of Thomas Wilder and is the mother of five children.

Doctor Cain attended public schools in Warrick County, finishing his high school work at Boonville, and continued his education in the Indiana Normal School at Terre Haute. For seven years he was a school teacher, and from his earnings as a teacher paid his way through medical college at Louisville, Kentucky, where he was graduated M. D. in 1893. Doctor Cain first practiced at Newburg, remaining there until 1897, when he removed to the City of Evansville. He has enjoyed an extensive general practice and is a member of the staff of Saint Mary's Hospital. He belongs to the County, Indiana State and also to the Ohio Medical Associations. Doctor Cain is a Democrat in politics, is a member of the Central

Methodist Episcopal Church, and is a thirty-second degree Scottish Rite Mason and member of Hadi Temple of the Mystic Shrine. He also belongs to the Fraternal Order of Eagles.

Doctor Cain married, February 10, 1889, Miss Lillie Hedges, daughter of Allen and Sadie Hedges. They were married in Boonville and have two sons, Burton U., born in 1890, and Howard B., born in 1893. Both sons were with the Aviation Corps during the World war, and Howard piloted a plane thirty miles out to sea as one of the air escorts to the ship carrying President Wilson to Europe. Burton, who is president of a bank at Hollywood, California, married Lida Webber, of Evansville, and has two children, Mary K., born in 1913, and Janet, born in 1917. Howard, in the real estate business at Glendale, California, married Thelma Harris, a native of Kentucky, and has a son, Howard B., Jr., born in 1923.

BRUCE H. BEELER, surgeon, whose attainments have given him a reputation on both sides of the Ohio River, is successor in practice at Evansville to his father, Dr. Jerome S. Beeler, who also made a fine name in his profession.

Dr. Jerome S. Beeler was born in Warrick County, Indiana, in 1849, was a graduate of the University of Cincinnati, and practiced at Boonville until 1898, when he moved to Evansville. He was one of the first physicians to specialize in diseases of the rectum. He was a homeopath, and a member of the American Institute of Homeopathy. He was a Knight Templar Mason and Shriner and member of the Independent Order of Odd Fellows. Dr. Jerome S. Beeler, who died at Evansville December 10, 1922, married Sarah Florence Barrett, of Pike County, Indiana. She died in 1901. Dr. Bruce H. is the only surviving son. One daughter became the wife of the prominent Evansville hotel man, Harold Van Orman.

Dr. Bruce H. Beeler was born in Warrick County, Indiana, in 1888, attended school there, and after the age of ten continued his education in Evansville. Part of his preparatory education was acquired in one of the most exclusive preparatory schools of the East, Phillips-Exeter Academy. Doctor Beeler was graduated in medicine at the University of Louisville in 1915. The following years he was in the East getting hospital experience at Philadelphia and Wilmington, Delaware. At Wilmington he was the youngest surgeon on the staff of the Delaware Hospital. During that time he also joined the colors, enlisting in 1917, went overseas in 1918 and was attached to the Eighth French Army. He received his honorable discharge in March, 1919, and the following year returned to Evansville to take over his father's practice. Like his father he has specialized in the treatment and cure of diseases of the rectum and is now rectum surgeon for the Deaconess and St. Mary's Hospitals. He is a member of

Geo. R. Dale

the Vanderburg County, Indiana State and American Medical Associations, being a fellow of the latter. For four years he has been chairman of the Citizens Military Training Camp. His offices are in the Central Union Building at Evansville.

Doctor Beeler is a thirty-second degree Scottish Rite Mason and Shriner. He married at Wilmington, Delaware, Miss Eleanor Graves, who died August 12, 1920, leaving a son, Bruce H., Jr., who was born June 13, 1918, when his father was overseas. Doctor Beeler on March 22, 1922, married Miss Dana Wolvin, of Pike County, Indiana.

HON. GEORGE R. DALE, mayor of the City of Muncie, which since the publication of the book *Middletown* has become the best known American city to students and readers of serious literature, is a newspaper man, and a few years ago was a national figure in the anti-klan fight.

Mayor Dale inherits his personal courage and fighting instinct from a long line of ancestors, in which the blood of English, Scotch and Irish mingled. His grandfather was William Dale, a pioneer settler of White County, Indiana, who came from Virginia. He died when about thirty-five years of age. The father of Mayor Dale was Capt. Daniel D. Dale, who was born and reared in White County, attended public schools there and was an officer in the Union army during the Civil war, captain of Company K of the Nineteenth Indiana Regiment. This was the regiment that was almost wiped out during Grant's bloody battles in the wilderness of Virginia. After the war Mr. Dale took up the practice of law at Monticello, served as county clerk, as clerk of the State Senate, and was a close personal friend of Senator Turpie. He died in 1886 and is buried at Monticello. Captain Dale married Ophelia Reynolds, who was born and reared at Monticello and was a staunch Presbyterian. Her people came from Ireland and the family was represented in service in the Revolutionary war. She died in 1887. There were four children: Charles H., editor of the Troy, Ohio, *Democrat*; George R.; Bertha M. and Ida Dale, who are in the real estate and insurance business at Hartford City, Indiana.

George R. Dale attended school at Monticello and as a young man acquired a practical newspaper experience at Hartford City, where he and Charles Wigmore published the *Hartford City Press*, the first daily paper in that town. Later he sold out and established the *Hartford City Journal*, of which he was publisher until 1915, in which year he came to Muncie. At Muncie he was the editor of the *Muncie Post* until that well known old paper was discontinued.

In 1921 Mr. Dale established the *Post-Democrat*, a weekly newspaper, the only Democratic newspaper published in Delaware County.

To tell the subsequent career of Mr. Dale as it should be told resort should be had to quotations from an article that appeared in a Pennsylvania publication shortly after Mr. Dale was elected mayor. It reads as follows:

"The past seven or eight years have been most tempestuous ones for George Dale, an old Indiana journalistic war horse, and that he has finally emerged completely victorious over as rascally a gang of Ku Klux politicians as ever disgraced any city or state is indeed cause for great rejoicing on the part of his old friends, and the friends of decency everywhere. When the Klan started to get a strangle-hold on Indiana state and local governments, it fastened its tenacles first on Muncie, putting a corrupt gang of thugs in various municipal positions. George Dale, a non-Catholic, launched a weekly paper which he called the *Muncie Post-Democrat* and started in to tan the hide off the Ku Klux Klan, its principles, if any; its practices, its officials and members, and everything in any way connected with that odoriferous organization.

"Presently a bomb was exploded under his printing shop, then at his home, despite the presence of six or seven children and their mother. Then he was slugged, blackjacked, beaten and told to get out of town and stay out. For reply, he came back in the next issue of his paper with an editorial which shook the whole Klan organization in the Hoosier state. He was arrested on trumped-up charges of having liquor in his possession. Immediately thereafter he printed another blistering editorial, accusing the presiding judge of moral turpitude, citing names, dates and places. He was promptly re-arrested and at once found guilty of contempt of court by the very judge he had accused. He appealed his case to the Indiana State Supreme Court which later on rendered its notorious decision that the "truth was no defense." In other words, what Dale said about the presiding judge being a scoundrel was all true, but he shouldn't have printed it even to bolster his case against that judge, who was also an officer of the Klan in Muncie and one of the high officials of the organization in Indiana.

"By this time the persecution of Dale by the Klan in Muncie and Indiana had become national news. It became known that Dale was at the end of his financial resources and that he'd probably have to go to the Indiana state prison to serve harsh sentences unjustly imposed after convictions on trumped-up charges. At this point, the *New York World*, the *Chicago Tribune* and the Hearst paper entered the picture. They sent reporters to Muncie to investigate the Dale story, and the subsequent dispatches appearing in those papers aroused the entire East and Middle West to rally to the aid of Dale. Before the resources of those powerful and wealthy newspapers could be thrown into the fight for Dale, the latter's bitterest enemies had themselves run afoul of the law and were in disgrace. Some were sent to prison, some fled from Muncie and Indiana under cover of darkness, some are still under indictment for various offenses against the moral and civil codes, and others retired under a cloud. The Governor of Indiana granted Mr. Dale full pardons, and now the fiery, courageous and unrelenting foe of the Klan when to fight the Klan in Indiana took courage of a high order, has lived to see the day when he is honored with the highest office within the gift of the people of his home town; a complete vindication of his efforts in fighting, exposing and routing one of the most abominally corrupt political organizations which has ever been spawned upon an American state or city."

Mr. Dale was elected mayor of Muncie in November, 1929, by a majority of 1,349 votes. His election was not only a vindication for the ill usage and abuse to which he had been subjected, but even more it expressed a determination upon the part of the decent people of Muncie to put a new broom to work in municipal affairs. Mr. Dale was inaugurated mayor on January 6, 1930, for a term of four years. Mr. Dale is a Democrat in a city that is normally 5,000 Republican.

He married at Hartford City, Indiana, January 14, 1900, Miss Lena Mohler, daughter of Henderson S. and Mary E. (Cantwell) Mohler. Her uncle, Sidney Cantwell, was at one time speaker of the House of Representatives of Indiana. Mary E. Cantwell's father was a leading Hartford City attorney. Henderson S. Mohler was for many years a contractor and builder and erected many of the larger buildings in Hartford City. He died November 20, 1901, and his wife, February 15, 1917, and both are buried at Hartford City. Mrs. Dale is a graduate of the Hartford City High School with the class of 1900 and was married shortly afterward. She has been a most effective aid to Mr. Dale in his newspaper work and has stood loyally by him in all the vicissitudes of his career. Mr. and Mrs. Dale have seven children: Mary O., Elizabeth, George R., Jr., Martha Ellen, Virginia Ruth, Daniel D. and John Henderson. The three oldest all attended school at Hartford City. Mary graduated from the Muncie High School in 1918 and was married May 18, 1927, to Glen Butts, formerly of Battle Creek, now of Muncie, and they have a daughter, Joan, who was born at Battle Creek November 18, 1929. Elizabeth graduated from the Muncie High School in 1926 and is the wife of Lester E. Holloway, and they have two sons, Charles Edward and Larry Eugene. George R., Jr., graduated from high school in 1924, was formerly in the city engineer's office at Muncie, was later with the state highway department and is now assistant city engineer of Muncie. He married Majorie Heath, daughter of Arthur Heath, of Muncie, and they have a daughter, Edna Jean. The four younger children of Mr. and Mrs. Dale are all in school at Muncie, Martin being in high school and Virginia in junior high school.

LESTER E. HOLLOWAY, city comptroller of Muncie, has for several years had an active part in the business and civic affairs of that community.

Mr. Holloway was born at Pontiac, Illinois, March 19, 1904, son of Charles E. and Minnie C. (Unzicker) Holloway. His grandfather, Edward T. Holloway, was a pioneer Illinois farmer and stock man, and he and his wife are buried at Pontiac. Charles E. Holloway was born and reared in Illinois, had a high school education, supplemented by attending Valparaiso University, and for a number of years was in business as a grain dealer and elevator operator. He died July 15, 1917, and is buried at Pontiac. His wife, Minnie C. Unzicker, was born and reared near Pontiac, where she still resides and is an active member of the Presbyterian Church. There were four children: Erma, wife of Morris Veatch, of Chicago; Lester E.; Elden, of Pontiac; and Miss Agnes, of Pontiac.

Lester E. Holloway attended the grade and high schools of Pontiac, completing his high school work in 1922, and in 1926 was graduated from the University of Illinois. After a brief experience as a traveling salesman he came to Muncie and took a place with the *Post-Democrat*, and since 1927 has operated an automobile paint shop. He was appointed city comptroller November 11, 1929, and has held the office since January 6, 1930.

Mr. Holloway is a Royal Arch Mason, member of the Sigma Pi fraternity, is a Democrat and belongs to the First Presbyterian Church.

He married in Chicago, Illinois, September 30, 1928, Miss Elizabeth Dale, daughter of Mayor George R. and Lena (Mohler) Dale, of Muncie. Mrs. Holloway is a graduate of the Muncie High School and also attended the Ball State Teachers College. They have two sons, Charles Edward and Larry Eugene.

BENJAMIN J. PURLEE. Since the pioneers, pressing wastward toward the setting sun, reached that part of the Mississippi Valley now known as Indiana, this region has been noted for its fertile soil, and for the crops it produces. Many of the most prosperous and influential of the residents of the state still till the land, and furnish the people with food and many of the industries with raw products necessary for their operation. Orange County has a number of these agriculturists, but few as progressive and scientific as Benjamin J. Purlee, whose finely cultivated farm of 300 acres lies one mile from Orangeville.

Benjamin J. Purlee was born in Washington County, Indiana, in July, 1888, a son of Orange G. and Mary E. Purlee, both of whom also were born in Washington County. He died May 5, 1924, aged sixty-seven years, as he was born in 1857, and his wife died February 4, 1931, at the age of seventy-five years. By occupation he was a farmer. The parents had three children born to them: Blanche, who married Elmo Zink, of Indianapolis, Indiana, and has three children; Benjamin J.; and Ethel, who died at the age of twenty-six years.

Growing up in his native state, Benjamin Purlee attended the district and high schools of Orange County, and was in high school at Orleans. His first employment was secured as a clerk in a hardware store, and he held it for three years, after which he purchased his present farm, and has continued to operate it ever since according to modern methods, and has today one of the best properties in this part of Indiana. He is a Republican, and served for some years as township trustee, and during the period he was on the board he secured the passage of the measure which provides school buses for the high school children. In this he has the honor of being the first trustee in Orange County to take such a stand, although his example has been followed all over this region, as its desirability has been recognized. For years he has been a member and pillar of the Christian Church. In fraternal affiliations he is a Blue Lodge Mason.

On January 10, 1914, Mr. Purlee married Miss Jessie Hall, a daughter of David and Lillian (Speer) Hall, and they have four children, namely: Evelyn L., who was born April 9, 1915, and Lela Mae, who was born January 12, 1917, both of whom graduated from Orleans High School in 1931, Lela being the youngest high school student in the state for 1931 and one of the youngest on record; Benjamin J., Junior, who was born December 30, 1920; and Mary E., who was born January 6, 1922. Mr. Purlee is known as a man of high character, who lives up to his promises, is full of enterprise and energy, and never relinquishes his efforts in any undertaking until he has pushed it through to success, so that he has been and is a great factor in the growth and development of his home neighborhood.

MANSON J. STALKER is owner of one of the flourishing mercantile enterprises of the City of Orangeville. in Orange County. He took up a business career after having spent his early life as a farmer, and has made a more than ordinary success.

He was born, of Scotch-Irish ancestry, near Salem in Washington County, Indiana, July 25, 1889. His father, John M. Stalker, was also born in Washington County, and was a highly respected farmer of that section of the state, where he died in 1926. John M. Stalker married Florence M. Floyd, who was born in 1865 and is now sixty-six years of age. She was the mother of five children, Clyde M., Manson J., Ethel I., Fred and Charles. Clyde, a resident of Orange County, married Sally Landrath, by whom he has five children. The daughter, Ethel, died in 1914. Fred, who lives near Bedford, married Elsie Smith and has two children. Charles is a resident of Bedford and married Alberta Sheeks and has one child.

Regarding the earlier ancestry of the family, the Stalker family came from Scotland to the United States in 1808. Manson Stalker's great-grandfather having settled in Washington County, Indiana, in that year. The Floyd family came from Ireland in the early nineteenth century, settling in North Carolina, and thence migrating to Floyd County, Indiana, which was named for them. Manson Stalker's grandmother on his father's side was a Clark, being a great-niece of George Rogers Clark of historic fame.

Manson J. Stalker grew up on a farm, attended schools in Washington and Orange counties, and followed farming as his vocation for fifteen years. In 1924 he located at Orangeville and has built up a very extensive trade as a general merchant. He owns a well stocked store. Mr. Stalker is a Republican in politics and a member of the Independent Order of Odd Fellows.

He married January 6, 1910, Miss Neva A. Hughes, daughter of William and Jessie (Edwards) Hughes, of Lawrence County, Indiana. They have one daughter, Ethel Louise, born January 11, 1913, a graduate of the Orleans High School in 1930 and of the Bedford Business College in 1931.

EMMERT BROTHERS. JOHN A. EMMERT and PETER J. EMMERT, druggists, are among the old and honored business men of Haubstadt, Gibson County. Their father, Adam Emmert, was a native of Bavaria, Germany, and came to Indiana when seven years of age. He served in the Union army as a soldier in Company F of the Eightieth Indiana Volunteer Infantry and participated in several engagements, being present at the fall of Atlanta. He was one of the old time and substantial residents of Haubstadt. He married Mary Wolf, also a native of Bavaria, Germany, who come to Indiana when a year old. She died May 7, 1927. There were seven children in the family, John A. being the oldest, he having been born September 1, 1867. Magdalen, the second child, is the wife of John Adler, a farmer near Haubstadt, and has four children. Anna married Frank Brenner and has two children. Lonie married Adam N. Adler, of Evansville, and has three children. Mary is the wife of Henry Schiff and the mother of one child. Katherine married Ben E. Meny and has two children. Peter J. is the youngest.

John A. Emmert was in the drug business at Haubstadt for forty-eight years, finally, in 1913, selling his store to his brother, continuing, however, to be active as a pharmacist. He is a member of the American and Indiana Pharmaceutical Association and of the Knights of Columbus. He has never married.

His brother, Peter J. Emmert, was born at Haubstadt January 5, 1887, and attended the public and parochial schools of that town. As a boy he worked in his brother's store, afterwards passed the state board and became a registered pharmacist, after thorough scholastic training. In 1913 he bought the business from his brother and is giving his close attention to its management. He is a member of the American and Indiana Pharmaceutical Association, is a Democrat, a Catholic and a fourth degree Knight of Columbus.

Peter J. Emmert married Elnora Schafer, daughter of Martin and Rose (Ziliak) Schafer, of Haubstadt. They were married November 6, 1912, and have an interesting family of nine children, the oldest being seventeen years of age. Their names are Mary Rose, who graduated in 1931 from Haubstadt High School, Rita, Paul, John, Roger, Norma, Ruth Lee, Robert and Edwin Bernard. Rita is attending Benedictine Convent at Ferdinand, Indiana, in preparation for taking the vows of a nun.

JOSEPH RODOLPHUS DILLINGER, M. D., of French Lick, is a specialist in eye, ear, nose and throat, a doctor of wide experience and attainments that have well earned him the splendid reputation he enjoys in this section of the state.

Doctor Dillinger was born at Chambersburg in Orange County, Indiana, October 11, 1875. His grandfather, Nicholas Dillinger, came from Virginia to Indiana with his parents as a young man and served in the Black Hawk war. He was engaged in farming in Harrison County, and he married Margaret Mayall, of Harrison County. They had seven children. The Dillinger family is of German origin. The Doctor's great-great-grandfather immigrated from Germany to England and his great-grandfather came from England to Virginia in Colonial days. Doctor Dillinger's father, Rodolphus S. Dillinger, was born in Harrison County, Indiana, and was a soldier in the Union army at the time of the Civil war. He was with the Thirty-eighth Indiana Volunteers and was under the command of Generals Sherman and Hooker. He was slightly wounded in one battle. After the war, until a few years before his death, he followed the business and trade of blacksmith and machinist. He passed away December 17, 1901. Rodolphus S. Dillinger married Nancy Jane Osborn, member of a pioneer family of Orange County. She died in 1883. Of her ten children two died in infancy and those to grow up were Theresa, Amy, Ida, Emma, Allie, Stella, Mary and Joseph Rodolphus. Doctor Dillinger has only three living sisters, Amy, Stella and Allie. Amy is the wife of John M. Boyd, of Indianapolis, and has four children. Stella is the wife of Q. W. Lomax, of Cherryvale, Kansas, and Allie married William Carson, of Irvington, New Jersey, and is the mother of three children. In 1885 R. S. Dillinger married Esther Ann Moorman, and she died in August, 1901, leaving no children by this marriage.

Joseph Rodolphus Dillinger attended the grade and high schools of Orange County at Paoli, took work in the State Normal School and as a young man devoted eight years to teaching. Teaching was the stepping stone to his professional work. He pursued the course of preparation in the Louisville Medical College and Medical Hospital, from which he was graduated M. D. in 1903. Doctor Dillinger for a number of years engaged in general practice, and that experience has furnished the background for his specialty. During 1921 he was a post-graduate student at the University of Pennsylvania and in 1922 took special work in the Knapp Eye Hospital of New York City. Doctor Dillinger is a member of the Orange County, Indiana State and American Medical Associations and is a member of the Association of Ophthalmology and Otolaryngology. During the World war he enlisted and was commissioned a first lieutenant in the Army Medical Corps and was discharged with the rank of captain. He is a member of the American Legion, of which he was the organizer and first commander of W. W. Benson Post No. 76 at French Lick, Indiana. He is also a member of the Kiwanis Club at French Lick, is a Scottish Rite Mason and Shriner, member of the Independent Order of Odd Fellows, Knights of Pythias and Modern Woodmen of America. Politically he has always supported the candidates of the Republican party. He served six years as county coroner. He is railway surgeon for the Monon Railroad and the Southern Railroad.

Doctor Dillinger married, December 25, 1901, Miss Lula Charles, daughter of George A. and Sarah (Dalton) Charles, members of old and respected families of Orange County. Doctor and Mrs. Dillinger have three children. Their son, Dr. George R., born September 30, 1902, graduated in medicine from the University of Indiana in 1929, and took postgraduate work in the City Hospital of Indianapolis, receiving his Cum Laude in 1930, and is now practicing in French Lick. He married, in September, 1928, Margaret Kosht, of Butler, Indiana, also a graduate of Indiana University Nurses' Training School and who died April 2, 1931, leaving one son, David R., born February 27, 1930. The two daughters are Marcia M., born December 21, 1907, a graduate of the University of Indiana, who is now taking nurse's training at the University Hospitals at Indianapolis; and Amy Irene, born December 12, 1909, who is taking the regular liberal arts course at the State University at Bloomington, Indiana, in the class of 1933.

CHESTER A. THOMAS, county clerk of Madison County, has a wide experience in business, and was still a boy, several years under his majority, when his interest in politics and public affairs was aroused and many have looked upon him as one of the most efficient leaders of the Republican party in the county.

Mr. Thomas was born at Anderson. He represents the third generation of the Thomas family in Madison County. His grandfather, Benjamin Thomas, was a native of Seven Acres, Wales. After completing his apprenticeship at the trade of stone cutter he came to the United States, located in Anderson, and subsequently engaged in contracting work and built up a profitable business. After some years he made preparations to go back to

C. F. Oneall.

his old home in Wales, and while on the journey he died. He left children named Andrew, Carrie and Minnie.

Andrew Thomas was born at Anderson, was twelve years of age when his father died, and he went on with his education in the public schools and then learned the trade of stone cutter. He likewise entered the contracting business and continued active therein until his death in 1908. He married Alice Robinette, who was born on a farm in Jackson Township, Madison County, where her parents, Cornelius and Emeline (Cannon) Robinette, were early settlers. Mrs. Alice Thomas was educated in rural schools and taught in a one-room school house for a time. She now lives at Anderson. Her five children were Chester A., Frank, Emma, Hallie and Benjamin.

Chester A. Thomas was reared and educated at Anderson, graduated from high school in 1912, after which he entered upon a business career. He was for a time in the factory of the Rotary Valve Company, then with the Remy works, and left that to go on the road as a traveling salesman. He was on the road until elected county clerk.

Mr. Thomas cast his first vote for the Republican party and has been a staunch upholder of the principles of the party and has contributed a great deal of valuable work to the party organization in Madison County. In 1921 he was chosen chairman of the Anderson City Republican committee. By reelection he has been kept at his duties as county clerk and is one of the most popular men in the courthouse at Anderson.

Mr. Thomas married Miss Georgia Gustin, daughter of Hallie Gustin. They are members of the Central Christian Church. He belongs to the Y. M. C. A., Lodge No. 187 of the United Commercial Travelers, Mount Moriah Lodge No. 177, A. F. and A. M., and has membership in several other branches of Masonry, including Murat Temple of the Mystic Shrine at Indianapolis.

JOHN ALVIN BRUMFIELD, Doctor of Dental Surgery, has been practicing that profession in Gibson County for the past thirty years. Doctor Brumfield is a native of Gibson County and his home is at Fort Branch.

He was born in February, 1875. His father, Richard Brumfield, was a native of Kentucky, where the name is associated with the early period of settlement. Richard Brumfield came to Indiana when a young man and spent his life as a farmer in Gibson County, where he died in 1909. He married Matilda Knowles, a native of Indiana, who died in 1922. They reared a large family of children, named Henry, Laura, Ella, Rosina, John Alvin, Victor, Mary P., Melvin, Wilford, Florence and Clara.

John Alvin Brumfield was educated in public schools at Haubstadt, grew up on his father's farm, and completed his literary education in the Indiana Normal School at Terre Haute. After leaving there he taught for three years and completed his professional preparation in

the Ohio Dental College at Cincinnati, where he was graduated with the degree D. D. S. in 1900. Doctor Brumfield for eighteen years practiced his profession at Princeton and since 1919 has been located at Fort Branch, where he is the leading representative of his profession. He is a member of the District, Indiana State and National Dental Associations. During the World war he was enrolled six months, on duty as a Y. M. C. A. secretary at Camp Dodge, Iowa. Doctor Brumfield is a Democrat, a Methodist, is a Scottish Rite Mason and member of the Knights of Pythias.

He married, June 27, 1900, soon after graduating from dental college, Miss Myrtle D. Smith, a daughter of Noah and Martha (Emerson) Smith. They have two sons, Paul E., born in 1903, and Richard M., born in 1910. Paul is a graduate in the class of 1924, from DePauw University with the A. B. degree and in the class of 1930 from the Carnegie Institute of Technology at Pittsburgh, and is now teaching at Utica, New York. Richard is a graduate, in the class of 1931, from Purdue University at Lafayette, Indiana.

CHARLES F. O'NEALL was one of Tippecanoe County's best known farmers and stock men. His home was in Lauramie Township, where he lived all his life. He was born there September 28, 1856, and died February 24, 1914, at the age of fifty-eight.

Mr. O'Neall was a son of Kelly and Margaret (Ritchie) O'Neall. His grandfather, Abijah O'Neall, came from Virginia to Ohio and then to Indiana, locating in Wea Township of Tippecanoe County, where he lived out his life. Kelly O'Neall was born in Wea Township, being the oldest child of his parents. He was a man of prominence in business and politics. His business was farming and stock buying and he bought and shipped thousands of mules. At one time he represented the county in the State Legislature. There were four children: Charles; Mrs. Alice Backus; Anna, who married Nate Sefton; and Robert, deceased.

Charles F. O'Neall was educated in the Gladden School and in school at Stockwell and was brought up and trained from boyhood to the routine of farm duties. He began his career as a renter on some of his father's land, and he also had the trading genius of his father. For many years he was engaged in the business of buying cattle, mules and hogs. Mr. O'Neall had a taste for politics, and would willingly work for any community cause and for the election of his friends for office.

He married, January 1, 1883, Miss Mabel Kirkpatrick. Mrs. O'Neall is a daughter of Porter and Rozilla (McLean) Kirkpatrick and a granddaughter of George and Catherine (Porter) Kirkpatrick. George Kirkpatrick was one of the first settlers in Wea Township, Tippecanoe County, locating there in 1825. Porter Kirkpatrick was born in Pickaway County, Ohio. He was a prominent farmer, served as justice of the peace, was a charter member of the Lodge of Odd Fellows and always keenly interested in politics and a thorough Bible student. Mr. and Mrs. O'Neall had no children. Mrs. O'Neall was the oldest of four children. Her sister Lilly became the wife of C. W. Landis. Her other sister was Ida Adella. Her brother, Fairfax, now deceased, married and had two children, named Ruth and Porter.

CHARLES J. CLAXTON made pharmacy his business and profession until 1930. He was proprietor of one of the best appointed drug stores in Orange County, at West Baden, and is one of the prosperous younger business men of that locality.

He was born at French Lick, Indiana, December 15, 1900. His father, Edward L. Claxton, is a French Lick Business man, an ice and coal dealer, and has been prominently identified with local politics and public affairs, serving on the town board eleven years, and is chairman of the Orange County Republican committee. The grandfather of Charles J. Claxton was a soldier in the Civil war, serving under General Sheridan. Edward L. Claxton married Ora Newton, who was born at French Lick. Of their family of seven children two died in infancy and those to grow up are Louis, Charles J., Chapell, Cora and Edward, all of French Lick.

Charles J. Claxton was educated in public schools, graduating from the high school at French Lick in 1919. He then entered the Indianapolis College of Pharmacy, and received the degree of Graduate Pharmacist in 1922. While attending school he worked in drug houses at Indianapolis and remained there altogether for four years. At West Baden he was with the Moore Drug Company until 1927, when he used his capital and experience to establish himself in business.

Mr. Claxton married in March, 1926, Miss Madge Ballard, of West Baden, daughter of Harry Ballard, a cousin of Edward Ballard, owner of the famous West Baden Springs Hotel. Mr. Claxton is a Republican, a member of the Methodist Episcopal Church, and is affiliated with the Masonic Lodge, Independent Order of Odd Fellows and Knights of Pythias.

WILLIAM W. CAVE. During all the years that French Lick has enjoyed its world-wide reputation as a great watering resort, William W. Cave has been one of the most active of the local business men of the community. Mr. Cave is president of the French Lick Bank and one of the very generous and public spirited citizens of the town.

He was born in Dubois County, Indiana, January 25, 1873. His father was born in Indiana and his grandparents came from South Carolina. His father, Thomas Cave, now living retired at French Lick, at the age of eighty-seven, is one of the last survivors of the Army in Blue. He was for four years, two months, in the Union army, a member of the Eighteenth Indiana Volunteer Infantry. He saw active service under General Grant and later under Sherman. His life since the war has been spent as a farmer. He married Mary C. Kirkland, who was born in Hawkins County, Tennessee. She is now eighty-five years of age. Her parents moved to Indiana in 1850. Thomas Cave and wife had four children: William W., Stella, Bell and Isis. Stella married Albert Kirby and had four children. She died in 1915 and Mr. Kirby lives at French Lick. Bell married Arthur Wells, of French Lick, and they have two children. Isis is the wife of Clark Hill, of French Lick, and they have one son.

William W. Cave attended public schools in Orange County, completed a normal course at Paoli, and six years of his early manhood were devoted to teaching. For a time he was a student in the University of Indiana, and is a man of liberal education. After giving up school work he entered the mercantile business at French Lick, and later conducted the Wells Hotel. He still has mercantile interests and is one of the large real estate owners of the town. Mr. Cave has been engaged in banking since 1905 and is president of one of the most substantial financial institutions of Orange County, the French Lick Bank.

For eight years he was a member of the local school board and he held the office of postmaster four years during the Taft administration. Mr. Cave for two terms, 1920-27, was a trustee of the Indiana State Reformatory.

He married, October 10, 1899, Miss Cora Wells, daughter of Hiram E. and Mary J. (Hill) Wells. Her people were an old and respected family of French Lick. Her father served in the Twenty-fifth Indiana Infantry during the Civil war, and was wounded and never completely recovered from his injuries. Mrs. Cave passed away June 6, 1929.

Mr. Cave is a Republican, a member of the Methodist Episcopal Church, and is affiliated with the Masonic Lodge. During the World war he was chairman of the local chapter of the Red Cross.

WILLIAM F. GRUBER, manager of the *Springs Valley Herald* at French Lick, is a comparatively young man but has a veteran's experience in the printing and newspaper business, starting to learn it when a boy of fourteen.

Mr. Gruber was born in Martin County, Indiana, February 18, 1889. His father, William C. Gruber, was born in Ohio, in 1861, came to Indiana in early life and was engaged in farming until 1903. In that year he moved to French Lick and established a printing business. In October, 1904, from his plant was published the first issue of the *Springs Valley Herald*. Some years ago he turned his printing business over to his sons and is now conducting one of the widely known chicken hatcheries, the Hoosier Hatchery, at French Lick. He married Elizabeth Decker, who was born near Jasper in Dubois County, Indiana, in 1870. They have four children: Burt C., of French Lick; William F.; Clarence E., of Canton, Ohio, married Maude

Eugene O. Burger

Hauger and has two children; and J. Earl, associated with the *Springs Valley Herald*, married Grace Liffler and has one child.

William F. Gruber attended public schools in Martin County. When his father moved to French Lick he at once entered his father's printing shop, and has a thorough technical master of the printing art. He has been for a number of years manager of the *Springs Valley Herald*, in which he is associated with his brother. Mr. Gruber is a member of the Indiana Weekly Press Association. He has served as city clerk and treasurer of French Lick, is a member of the Kiwanis Club, a Democrat, a supporter of the Methodist Church and is a Royal Arch Mason.

He married in 1909 Maona Milburn, of Dubois County, niece of Attorney-General Milburn and daughter of James and Jane (Dooley) Milburn. By this marriage there were three children, Francis, Eugene and John. Mr. Gruber on August 29, 1925, married Mary C. Reynolds. They have two sons, Gordon L. and R. Glenn. Mrs. Gruber is an active member of the Christian Church.

MRS. MAUDE A. BEATY, who served for ten years as librarian of the French Lick Public Library, is a native of Orange County, and was actively identified with the library at French Lick from the time it was founded in 1920.

Her father, Thomas Lane, is a well known citizen of Orange County, a retired farmer. He was born in this section of Indiana, his parents coming here from South Carolina. Thomas Lane married Rachael Hobson, a native of Orange County. Of their ten children one died in infancy and the others are: Lucy, William, Maude, Pearl, Grace, Sampson, C. Ann, Ruth and Noble.

Mrs. Beaty was educated in the grade and high schools at French Lick. It was in 1920 that the public library was organized, and she was one of those chiefly interested in projecting the institution as a community enterprise and has served as librarian since the library was opened.

She was married in 1905 to Dr. Grant S. Beaty. Doctor Beaty served a year as captain in the Medical Corps during the World war.

The French Lick Public Library board comprises the following members: C. E. Ellis, president; N. B. Mavity, vice president; Mabel Collins, secretary and treasurer; Cora Adkins, Mrs. Grace Pruett, Clarence Tolliver, Hulda Hancock and John Stack. The present librarian is Mrs. Sarah Melton.

DR. GUY H. WILSON is a physician and surgeon at Bicknell in Knox County, where he has enjoyed favorable prominence as a professional man and citizen since 1917.

Doctor Wilson was born in Vigo County, Indiana, August 31, 1889, son of William M. and Nancy C. (Parker) Wilson and a grandson of William Wilson, a native of Putnam County. The Wilson family settled in Northwest Territory, in what is now Putnam County, soon after the armies of George Rogers Clark had cleared the way for peaceful advance of Americans from the East. The Wilsons were a Colonial family of Virginia. Doctor Wilson's grandfather, William Wilson, was a Union soldier in the Civil war and a farmer and cattleman, the occupation which was also followed by William M. Wilson.

Dr. Guy H. Wilson attended school at Terre Haute, spent two years in the University of Indiana and graduated in 1916 from Saint Louis University, where he took his Bachelor and Doctor of Medicine degrees. He was in the Saint Louis City Hospital and for one year was resident physician of the Lutheran Hospital of Saint Louis, and with this unusually thorough training and broad experience he took up the work of his profession at Bicknell in 1917. Doctor Wilson was city health officer of Bicknell from 1924 to 1928. He is a member of the Knox County, Indiana State and American Medical Associations, and in 1931 served as president of the Knox County Medical Society.

He married in September, 1917, Miss Maud E. Ecker, of Collinsville, Illinois, and they have one daughter, Dorris Mae. Doctor Wilson is a member of the Phi Chi college fraternity, the Phi Rho Chapter, is affiliated with Bicknell Lodge No. 535, A. F. and A. M., the Knights Templar Commandery at Vincennes and the Scottish Rite bodies and Mystic Shrine at Evansville.

EUGENE O. BURGET was born at Burget's Corner in Clinton County, Indiana, January 5, 1869. His fellow citizens in Clinton County have followed with a friendly interest his career, made up of successive chapters as a teacher, county official, financier and insurance executive. Mr. Burget is president of the People's Life Insurance Company of Frankfort, one of the most successful organizations of the kind in the state.

He is of English ancestry and of Revolutionary stock. One of his forefathers, Emanuel Burget, was a soldier of the Revolution, went as a pioneer to Southern Ohio, settling in Butler County, and was killed by Indians while trying to reach his block house after swimming the Big Miami River. The grandparents of Eugene O. Burget were William and Lydia (Keever) Burget, substantial and highly respected people of Butler County, Ohio, and Clinton County, Indiana, where they were pioneers in Johnson Township, where their daughter Elizabeth had the distinction of being the first white child born in the township.

William M. Burget, father of Eugene O., was born in Clinton County, Indiana, June 28, 1844, and the first break in the quiet routine of existence on the home farm came when he enlisted, August 13, 1862, in Company H, Eighty-sixth Indiana Infantry. He was with the Army of the Cumberland in campaigns through Kentucky, Tennessee, Georgia and Alabama, being a participant in the battles of Stone River, Chickamauga, Missionary Ridge and Knoxville, and later in the battles of Franklin and Nashville, which completed the rout and dissolution of Hood's Confederate forces. He served until honorably discharged, June 6, 1865. He was three times married and was the father of nine children. His first wife and the mother of Eugene O. Burget was Permelia Mott, daughter of Sayres Mott. Eugene was the second of her four children.

Eugene O. Burget supplemented his advantages in the local schools by attending the Indiana State Normal at Terre Haute, and for several years was a successful teacher, being principal of schools at Scircleville and Hillisburg. In 1894, at the age of twenty-five, he was appointed deputy county auditor of Clinton County and in 1902 was elected chief of that office for a term of four years. After leaving the auditor's office he was assistant cashier of the Clinton County Bank, resigning to become secretary and general manager of the People's Life Insurance Company in 1907. He has had the general management of this insurance organization for twenty-three years, and since July 1, 1926, has also served as president. Mr. Burget has a sound knowledge based on long experience of the insurance business, and has been satisfied to see his own company steadily increase its resources and extend its service until it now has over $54,000,000 of insurance in force and assets of over $8,000,000.

Mr. Burget is a director and former president of the Frankfort Chamber of Commerce, is a past eminent commander of the Knights Templar Commandery at Frankfort and also belongs to other bodies of York and Scottish Rite Masons, and Murat Temple of the Mystic Shrine at Indianapolis. He is a member of the Knights of Pythias, Independent Order of Odd Fellows, B. P. O. Elks, Improved Order of Red Men. He is a Republican and a Methodist.

Mr. Burget married at Frankfort, June 28, 1899, Miss Carrie Boyle. She was born at Michigantown, Clinton County, Indiana, daughter of Josiah L. and Mary Boyle.

THOMAS ERROL THERIAC, manager of the personal loan department of the First National Bank of Vincennes, judicial center of Knox County, is a representative of one of the sterling French families that was founded in this city about the year 1812. He is a son of Thomas and Clara (Inderrieden) Theriac, the former having been the fourth child of Mitchell and Elizabeth (Mominee) Theriac, and Mitchell Theriac having been a scion of the third generation of the original ancestor who came from France and made settlement in Vincennes about 1812, the family name having been worthily identified with the history of this fine old city during the passing years, as one generation has followed another on to the stage of life's activities.

Thomas Theriac was born and reared in Vincennes and here passed his entire life, he having here been in the Government postal service during a period of seventeen years and

in his character and achievement he worthily upheld the honors of the family name. His father, Mitchell Theriac, served as a gallant soldier of the Union during virtually the entire period of the Civil war, he having been a member of the Fourteenth Indiana Volunteen Infantry and having participated in many engagements, including a number of major battles. He specially distinguished himself at the battle of Chickamauga, where he was with the forces commanded by General Thomas. Mitchell Theriac was long one of the influential business men and representative citizens of Vincennes, and here was engaged in the manufacturing and repairing of carriages long prior to the advent of the automobile.

The history of the Theriac family is one of interesting order. The first representatives in America made settlement in Canada, and there, in the City of Montreal, a French soldier, Francois Tiriac (original spelling of the family name) was united in marriage, in January, 1743, to Magdelene Benard, daughter of Jean Batiste and Marie Magdelene (Pesillard) Benard. Francois Tiriac was a son of Jacques and Marie Agnes (Monigan) Tiriac, whose home was in the parish of St. Sulpice Church in Paris, France. He was a soldier in the company of the famous M. Linctot, who was destined to become a prominent figure in the intrigues that eventually led to the gaining of the great northwest possession of the United States. Linctot was a soldier and trader and figured prominently in early French history on the continent of North America. Francois Tiriac and his wife became the parents of six children, and about 1751 the family removed from Montreal and made settlement near DeRepentigny, in the District of Joliette. There was born the son Mitchell. The family thereafter followed the French settlers southward, and in January, 1796, as shown by records still extant, was solemnized the marriage of this son Mitchell to Therese Andre, of Vincennes, the ceremony having occurred at St. Francis Xavier Cathedral and Rev. Jean Francis Rivet having been the officiating priest. Mitchell and Therese (Andre) Tiriac (or Tiriaque) became the parents of Joseph Tiriac, who was born April 13, 1803, and this son married Ellen Villeneuve, a direct descendant of Mathurin Villeneuve, who made settlement in Canada in 1669, though the Villeneuve family had come to Vincennes, Indiana, prior to 1764, as shown by a land grant of St. Agne. Representatives of this family assisted General George Rogers Clark in his historic capture of Vincennes, and in recognition of this service they were accorded land grants.

Thomas Errol Theriac, immediate subject of this review, was born in Vincennes, on the 30th of July, 1897, was eldest in a family of six children and was about nineteen years of age at the time of his father's death, so that practical responsibilities soon fell upon him and he was denied higher educational advantages, his youthful education having been acquired in the St. Francis Xavier parochial school in his native city. The next younger of the children is Mitchell, who attended Jasper College, at Jasper, Indiana, and who is now identified with an enterprise in the City of Chicago, where he married Miss Mary J. Ashcroft. Miss Pauline Theriac still resides in Vincennes. Frances M. is the wife of Morris H. Reel, of Vincennes. Martha is here attending school, and John S., youngest of the children, died at the age of two.

Thomas E. Theriac, as the eldest child, began to contribute to the support of his widowed mother and the other children when the father passed away. He found employment in a local drug store, and in his native city he continued to be identified with this line of business ten years. In the interests of a New York City corporation he opened and assumed management of the branch Morris Plan Bank established in Vincennes, and several years later this branch was sold to the Morris Plan Corporation of Evansville, Indiana. Mr. Theriac continued in that management until 1931, when he assumed his present position with the First National Bank of Vincennes. He is a member of the local Chamber of Commerce and the Rotary Club, is a member of the Harmony Society in his home city and was its director five years, and is a popular member of Old Post Country Club. His political allegiance is given to the Republican party and, holding the religious faith in which he was reared, he is an earnest communicant of the St. Francis Xavier Catholic Church. Mr. Theriac was married at Indianapolis, Indiana, by Bishop Chartrand, on October 24, 1923, to Estella M. Recker, daughter of Henry M. and Mary C. (Frund) Recker, of Vincennes. They have four children: Thomas H., born September 7, 1924, Mary Claire, born January 19, 1927, Owen Clinton, born December 23, 1928, and Carolyn Ann, born February 19, 1930.

HON. JOSHUA L. BLAIZE, county clerk of Knox County, and a man known all over this part of Indiana, has long held the confidence and respect of his fellow citizens, and has added to his prestige by the manner in which he is discharging the duties of his important office. He was born in Pike County, Indiana, September 28, 1881, a son of John B. Blaize, of Pike County, the latter a farmer and educator, and for years county superintendent of schools, and for a much longer period a school trustee. John B. Blaize was a son of Isaac Blaize, a native of North Carolina, who located in Pike County, Indiana, prior to the war between the states, and there he became a farmer. All his life he was a devout Christian. Five children were born to John B. Blaize and his wife, formerly Mary S. Hoover, of Indiana, namely: Sallie, who married Robert Grubb; Rufus, who is an educator of Terre Haute, Indiana; Joshua L., who was the third in order of birth; Guy Hoover, who married Grace Rumble; and Victor S., who died May 19, 1930, and who was principal of

the Vincennes High School, married Jewel Sandige.

From childhood Joshua L. Blaize has been interested in intellectual matters, and after he had completed the public school work he entered Oakland City College and later was a student in the Indiana State Normal School, Terre Haute. Taking up the study of medicine, in Louisville, Kentucky Medical School, he was graduated therefrom in 1907, with the degree of Doctor of Medicine. Immediately thereafter he returned to Indiana, and until 1911, was engaged in practice at Stendal, but in the latter year moved to Oaktown, where he continued in practice until 1923, when he was elected clerk of the Circuit Court of Knox County and moved to Vincennes to assume the duties of his office. In 1926 he was reelected for a second term. A close student, he has not only pursued his own studies but has educated others, beginning to teach school at the age of eighteen years, and continuing in that calling from 1899 to 1906. While he was a student of the Louisville Medical College he also taught school. During a portion of his career he studied law through a course in the Hamilton College of Law, and this knowledge is proving very valuable to him in his present office. He is a member of Vincennes Lodge, No. 1, A. F. and A. M., and the Modern Woodmen of America. In political faith he is a Democrat, and he is very active in party matters. The Baptist Church holds his membership and receives his generous support. During the World war he enlisted in the Medical Reserve Corps, was called three times, and as many times ordered to remain at Oaktown, where his services were so needed.

Doctor Blaize married, July 19, 1918, Grace E. Mason, of Missouri, and they have one living child, Floyd Luther Blaize, now attending school. In his office Doctor Blaize is proving the contention that no course of study is taken in vain; that each one develops some faculty that otherwise might have remained latent, and thus is a man enabled to be of further service to mankind.

EDWARD F. STEFFEN is secretary and general manager of the Vincennes Rose Gardens, Inc., a concern that gives both industrial and aesthetic prestige to the fair and historic City of Vincennes, judicial center of Knox County.

Mr. Steffen was born in Vincennes, December 13, 1893, and is a son of Edward F. and Julia (Hamke) Steffen, both likewise born in Vincennes. Edward F. Steffen, Sr., was long and successfully established in the retail grocery business in Vincennes. His father, Albert F. Steffen, was born and reared in Germany and settled in Indiana prior to the Civil war, his children who attained to mature years having been four in number. Of the children of Edward F. and Julia (Hamke) Steffen the first born, Carl, is deceased. Marie is the wife of Joseph Lutzinski, of Marion, Indiana. Henry A. and Edward F., Jr., are twins, the former being a resident of Bicknell, Indiana, and connected with the American Mining Company, and the latter being the immediate subject of this review. Henry A. Steffen married Miss Carmen Byers, of Monroe City, Knox County, and his twin brother, Edward F., married, April 3, 1923, Miss Bernice C. Childress, of Lawrence County, Illinois, the two children of this union being Martha Jean and Lyda Lou.

The early education of Edward F. Steffen, Jr., was acquired in the Lutheran parochial school of Vincennes, and while still attending school he and his twin brother, Henry A., gained practical business experience and also contributed to the family revenue by selling on the streets of Vincennes the excellent bread and cakes baked by their mother.

After leaving school Edward F. Steffen entered upon an apprenticeship in the Emil H. Younghans cigar factory, and he there continued to be employed for about eighteen months. In August, 1908, he became associated with the Paul C. Schultz Greenhouse Company, with which he was here connected until 1912. He then passed a year in Indianapolis, in greenhouse work for Bertermann Brothers, and after his return to Vincennes he became again associated with the Schultz greenhouse business, to partnership in which he was admitted in 1920. He thus continued until January, 1927, when he sold his interest in this concern, and in the following April effected the organization of the Vincennes Rose Gardens, Inc., the headquarters of which, of the best modern standard, are situated at 310 Busseron Street. B. F. Nesbitt is president of this corporation and Mr. Steffen is secretary and general manager. The concern ranks among the foremost in the domain of floriculture in this section of the state and has a large and representative patronage, as its products are of the finest type and uniformly challenge popular appreciation. The company specializes in the growing of all varieties of roses for the wholesale market, and it is interesting to record that in the year of 1930 it produced more than 750,000 roses, part of which were consumed locally, but the greater part shipped in wholesale lots. The fine rose gardens of this progressive Vincennes corporation have an area of two and one half acres, the general equipment being of the most approved modern order, and the best scientific methods are utilized. The company has twenty-five acres of land that is of the best in Knox County, located on the old Bruceville Road, four miles northeast of the business section of Vincennes. Much of its wholesale trade is centered in Cleveland, Ohio; Dayton, Ohio; and Indianapolis, Indiana.

Mr. Steffen is affiliated with the Democratic party and as a citizen he takes loyal interest in all that touches the welfare of his native city and county, while as a business man he is distinctly progressive. He served as a member of the City Council from 1925 to 1929, as representative of the Fourth Ward. The attractive family home is maintained at 615 North First Street. Of the marriage and children of Mr. Steffen mention has been made in a preceding paragraph.

ROBERT G. MOORE, M. D. In medical science the name of Moore carries distinction with it throughout Indiana, and the City of Vincennes is proud to record that it has been the birthplace and home within the last half a century of three generations of the name whose professional achievements have been notable. The present representative, Dr. Robert G. Moore, physician and surgeon, is a worthy successor of his father and grandfather, and is universally recognized as a leader at Vincennes in advanced medical and scientific work. From boyhood his heritage as well as his natural urge inclined him toward medical science in his studies, reading and investigations, and in 1924 he was graduated from the Indiana University School of Medicine, at Indianapolis, and in 1925 he established himself in medical practice at Vincennes. He has a wide professional connection and is considered an authority on various medical questions. Doctor Moore is a member of the Knox County Medical Society, and a past secretary thereof, 1925-31, and also has membership in the Indiana State Medical Association and the American Medical Association. He is secretary of the Vincennes Board of Health, medical director of the Vincennes Medical Laboratory, member of the Indiana X-Ray Society and of the Radiological Society of North America. Additionally, Doctor Moore is an overseas veteran of the World war, in active service in France for eleven months, with base hospital units, connected with the Medical Corps at Camp Shelby Mississippi, for thirteen months, and at Fort Benjamin Harrison, Indianapolis, Indiana, for three months. After his honorable discharge he completed his education in the University of Indiana.

Doctor Moore was born at Vincennes, March 1, 1898, a son of Dr. Maurice Gardner Moore, whose death occurred January 27, 1911, and whose birth took place in Indiana. Dr. Maurice Gardner Moore was a graduate of Jefferson Medical College, Philadelphia, Pennsylvania, after which he was engaged in professional work until his death, specializing in surgery. He married Miss Flora Krueger, of Bloomington, Indiana, and although they had two children but the one reached maturity. Dr. Maurice Gardner Moore was a son of Dr. Reuben Gardner Moore, also a physician of Vincennes. He was a graduate of the Ohio Medical College, Cleveland, Ohio, and established himself in practice at Vincennes at a date prior to the opening of the war between the states. He married Miss Sarah Celine Burns, a graduate of Moorehill College, Indiana.

Dr. Robert G. Moore was graduated in medicine in 1924, from Indiana University School of Medicine, after which he served his internship in the Indianapolis City Hospital for a year, and then, in September, 1925, commenced his practice at Vincennes. He is a member of Vincennes Lodge, No. 1, A. F. and A. M., the

Phi Rho Sigma, Phi Kappa Psi, and is active in fraternal matters. The First Presbyterian Church of Vincennes holds his membership, as does also the American Legion Post, No. 3, of Vincennes.

The wife of Doctor Moore bore the maiden name of Gertrude Benner, and she was born at Burlington, Iowa. Doctor and Mrs. Moore have three children: Mary Ellen, Joanne and Robert Gardner, Junior. It is a source of pride to Doctor Moore that he and his can trace back their line of ancestry to Daniel and Lucy Moore, of the distinguished Moore family of Virginia, which contributed valiant soldiers to the American Revolution, as well as notables in private life during the Colonial epoch in the country's history.

WILLIAM F. HOLLAND, president of the W. F. Holland Company, a leading concern in the wholesale produce business in the City of Vincennes, was born in Somerset County, Maryland, March 29, 1889, and is a son of James A. and Ella E. (Hickman) Holland, both likewise natives of Maryland and representatives of sterling old families of that historic commonwealth. There James A. Holland was born in Somerset County, and in the years of his active business life he gave major attention to enterprise along the line of his dual trade, that of blacksmith and wheelwright. Of the two children William F., of this review, is the elder, and James A., Jr., is a manufacturing cabinet-maker in Baltimore, Maryland.

William Holland received his early education by duly profiting by the advantages of the schools of his native state, and there also he acquired his initial business experience. He was an ambitious youth of twenty years when, in 1909, he came to Indiana. After passing a short period of time in Indianapolis, he became a salesman for a wholesale produce commission concern in Terre Haute, and in January, 1917, he transferred his residence to Vincennes and initiated a produce business for Joseph Diekenper. On the 6th of March, 1921, he engaged in the same line of enterprise in an independent way. His thorough knowledge of and former experience in the business, as coupled with careful and honorable policies, caused the enterprise rapidly to expand in scope, and September 1, 1923, as a matter of commercial expediency, he effected the incorporation of the business, under the title of Holland-Cook Company, which continued until December, 1929, at which time the present corporation was formed as the W. F. Holland Company. Mr. Holland is serving as president of this substantial and progressive corporation, and Kenneth Waters is the secretary and treasurer. The company specializes in the handling of fruits of vegetables, and in addition to its trade in Knox, Daviess and Gibson counties, Indiana, its operations are extended into Wabash and Lawrence counties, Illinois. The company buys produce from all sections of the Union, retains a corps of about twenty employes, and has in commission a battery of eleven motor trucks.

Mr. Holland has impressed himself as one of the forceful and progressive business men of Vincennes, is an active member of the local Chamber of Commerce, is affiliated with Vincennes Lodge No. 1, Ancient Free and Accepted Masons, is a Republican in politics, and he and his wife have membership in Bethany Presbyterian Church.

At Terre Haute, on July 28, 1910, was solemnized the marriage of Mr. Holland to Miss Letha McCoskey, who was born and reared in Indiana, and the children of this union are five in number: Charles F., Bessie E., James Raymond, Alice May and Dorothy Marie.

The well equipped headquarters of the W. F. Holland Company in Vincennes are established at 2 North First Street, and Mr. Holland and his family have an attractive home on Hart Street Road.

GEORGE C. CULLOM, prominent business man of Frankfort, is an alumnus of two of Indiana's best known higher institutions of learning, Butler and Purdue, and has had thirty-five years of active business experience, at first as a druggist at Frankfort and for the past fifteen years as an executive of the wholesale house of W. M. Shafor & Company.

Mr. Cullom was born on a farm near Culver's Station in Tippecanoe County, Indiana, November 23, 1872, son of W. H. and Mary (Bausman) Cullom. His early environment was a farm, with attendance at rural schools, and in 1889, at the age of seventeen he entered Butler College. He was there three years, and contributed to the budding prestige of Butler College athletics, being a member of the football team of 1890 and 1891, a championship team both years. In 1892 he entered the School of Pharmacy of Purdue University at Lafayette, graduating in 1894. At Purdue he also played baseball and football and was a member of the Purdue championship football team of the early 1890s, and it was thirty-five years before the university was able to repeat and again claim the honors of a championship in Middle West football.

Mr. Cullom after graduating from Purdue became a member of the firm Cullom & Rous, druggists at Frankfort. He sold his interest to Mr. Rous in 1900 and following that was a partner with Charles Ashman in the drug business until 1914, when he sold out. Leaving the drug field, he became associated with the W. M. Shafor & Company, wholesale grocers. He acquired a financial interest in the corporation, was made secretary and treasurer, and still holds those executive offices, and is also sales manager.

Mr. Cullom through the years has been a leader in organized commercial, civic and social activities at Frankfort. He helped organize the first Chamber of Commerce and was its president two years, and is now vice president of the Rotary Club. In 1928 he was one of the local men who founded the Country Club, and in 1929 he succeeded E. O. Burget as president of the club. He is a member of the

Masonic fraternity and B. P. O. Elks, is a Republican, and he and his family are Presbyterians.

He married, November 22, 1899, Miss Maude Coulter, daughter of David Alexander and Mary (Depew) Coulter, of Frankfort. Their only child is Paul Coulter Cullom, who was born February 11, 1904, and is now connected with the Fletcher-American Company of Indianapolis. Paul C. Cullom married in September, 1928, Miss Esther Harding, of Des Moines, Iowa.

DAVID ALEXANDER COULTER was for nearly three-quarters of a century a resident of Clinton County, Indiana. When he died at Frankfort, June 11, 1928, he left an impressive record of constructive business achievement, sound and public spirited citizenship and a relationship with his community and fellow men that deserve the memorial of a record that can be read by future generations. He was a man of very strong character, and it was his character that gave his material achievements added value and influence.

He was born in Juniata County, Pennsylvania, December 21, 1846. His grandfather Coulter was a native of Ireland and came to America when a young man, locating in Juniata County where he married and reared his family and where for many years he was distinguished as an eloquent, earnest and scholarly minister of the Presbyterian Church. His son, John Coulter, Jr., father of David A. Coulter, was born in Juniata County in 1813, and in 1854 brought his family to Indiana, locating on a farm in Ross Township. He died at Rossville, September 24, 1864. John Coulter, Jr., married in 1836 Margaret Given, daughter of James and Nancy (Enslow) Given, of Juniata County. Her father followed the Coulters to Clinton County Indiana, in 1856, and he and his wife spent their last years at Frankfort.

David Alexander Coulter was eight years of age when his parents moved west to Clinton County, but he remained there, completing his education, and it was in 1863 that he came to Frankfort, where for a short time he was clerk in the firm of A. B. and B. Given, his uncles. In the spring of 1864 he enlisted in Company H of the 135th Indiana Infantry and served until September 29, 1864. Most of the time he was on garrison duty and several times came in contact with the Confederate cavalry under General Forrest. After his military service he was clerk for John Brown, a Logansport merchant, until 1867, when he returned to Frankfort and joined his brother, J. W. Coulter, in the firm J. W. Coulter & Brother, clothing merchants. During these early years the community was given evidence of his unusual business capacity and leadership. He helped organize the First National Bank of Frankfort and became a member of its first board of directors. In 1871, disposing of his interest in the clothing business to his brother, he moved to Rockville and for a short time gave his attention to coal mining

operations there, and also assisted in establishing the Parke Banking Company of Rockville. After his return to Frankfort he rejoined his brother and they erected a new business block for their store. In 1878 he acquired his brother's interest in the clothing business, but in 1881 disposed of his mercantile interests and then entered the Farmers Bank of Frankfort.

The later generation of Frankfort citizens remember him chiefly for his activities as a banker and financier. He was cashier of the Farmers Bank until 1904, when he became its president. He was president of the Waterworks Company of Frankfort, and was auditor of the American Life Insurance Company of Indianapolis. These and many other activities occupied him and made of his career one of usefulness and service until his death.

David A. Coulter for eight years was commissary general of the Indiana State Militia, with the title of colonel, on the staff of Governors Mount and Durbin. He rendered some valuable service as trustee of the Indiana State Prison at Michigan City. During the nine years he was president of the Frankfort School Board the new high school building was erected, at that time one of the largest and finest high schools in the state. He was for two terms a member of the council. He was deeply attached to the principles as well as the personnel of the Republican party. He took a large measure of satisfaction in having served as a delegate to the national convention at St. Louis in 1896, when William McKinley was nominated to run against the free silver champion, William J. Bryan. His public services as well as his private business career were guided by strong convictions, positive character and integrity. He was a member of the Grand Army of the Republic, the B. P. O. Elks and the Presbyterian Church.

David Alexander Coulter married in January, 1874, Miss Mary Depew, of Parke County, Indiana. She survives him and resides at Frankfort. Three children were born to their union, the only one living being Maude, wife of George C. Cullom, of Frankfort.

DAVID INGLE, Evansville coal operator, is a great-grandson of John Ingle, who arrived at Evansville August 1, 1818, direct from England, and whose family through four generations, covering more than a century, have provided personal leadership, business resourcefulness and vision in the enlargement and growth of Evansville's destiny as a commercial and civic center.

John Ingle was born in Huntington County, England, in 1788, was an English farmer and left his country largely as a result of the heavy losses to English agriculture during the Napoleonic wars. In Southern Indiana he bought a farm, establishing the country home since known as Inglefield. He served as country postmaster, and died at the age of eighty-six. His son, John Ingle, Jr., was born January 12, 1812. His early education was largely the result of reading his father's li-

David A. Coulter

brary in the log cabin home in Southern Indiana. He learned the trade of cabinet maker, and while employed in Philadelphia studied law in the office of Thomas Armstrong. Two of his fellow students were George R. Graham, who subsequently became editor of *Graham's Magazine*, and Charles J. Peterson, founder of *Peterson's Magazine*. He was admitted to practice and opened an office in Evansville in 1838, but in 1850 gave up law in order to devote his time to business. John Ingle, Jr., is credited with supplying the enthusiasm, the organization and other resources which made possible the construction of the Evansville & Terre Haute Railroad, one of the pioneer railroad lines of Southern Indiana. He was president of the company until 1873, two years before his death. In 1866 he organized John Ingles & Company, coal mining operators, and that company started the mining industry in Southern Indiana. John Ingle, Jr., was the first president of the Evansville Library Association. He was an intense patriot during the Civil war, and throughout his life he practiced and set a splendid example of Christian manhood and conduct. While he was head of the railroad he permitted the operation of the road only six days of the week in order that the railway employees might have their Sunday for rest. John Ingle, Jr., married Isabella C. Davidson, whose father, William Davidson, was a native of Scotland.

One of their seven children was David Ingle, Sr., who died October 18, 1909, and who for many years was active in the coal mining industry, being founder of the Ayrshire Coal Company. David Ingle, Sr., married Fanny Burbank, who is a resident of Evansville, now seventy-four years of age. Their children were David, Frances, wife of William Bebb, William D., who married Grace Ross and has five children, and Katherine.

David Ingle, Jr., was born in Evansville October 25, 1875, attended grammar and high schools and graduated as a mining engineer from the Rose Polytechnic Institute at Terre Haute, Indiana, in 1897. His active experience, covering over thirty years, has been in coal mining, as an engineer and operator, and he is now operating the Ayrshire Coal Company, founded by his father in 1880. Mr. Ingle is a member of the American Mining and Metallurgical Engineers, is a member of the Chamber of Commerce, the Masonic fraternity and in politics is a Republican.

He married, October 5, 1904, Miss Effie Hughes, daughter of R. P. and Effie (Rose) Hughes, of an old Evansville family. Her father was president and active head of the William Hughes Company. Mr. and Mrs. Ingle have two children, David III and Thomas H. These sons, born in 1906 and 1920, represent the fifth generation of the Ingle family at Evansville. David III graduated from the Massachusetts Institute of Technology in 1928 and is now associated as an engineer with his father in the coal industry. On April 6, 1931, David Ingle III married Miss Susan Hopkins, of Evansville, daughter of John Stuart Hopkins, a prominent Evansville business man and political leader.

THOMAS M. MARTIN is the resourceful and popular chief of the police department of the historic old City of Vincennes, judicial center of Knox County. His has been long and efficient service in connection with this important municipal department. His first appointment to his present office was made in April, 1917, and he served a term of four years. In July, 1926, he was again appointed for a term of four years and in January, 1930, was reappointed under the J. W. Kimmell administration.

Mr. Martin was born in Lawrence County, Illinois, June 15, 1879, and is a son of John M. Martin, who was born and reared in Ohio and whose father, Micheaux Martin, was born in Virginia, of French ancestry, he having removed from the Old Dominion State and become a pioneer settler and farmer in Washington County, Ohio, much of the land that is now the site of the City of Marietta, the county seat, having been a part of his original farm estate. John M. Martin gave the greater part of his active life to farm industry and specialized in the raising of live stock. He supplemented his industrial activities in Lawrence County, Illinois, by there serving a number of years as postmaster of Bridgeport. He married Miss Mary Ann Scalley, of Louisville, Kentucky, and they became the parents of seven children: Byron P., is deceased; John E., who married Miss Nellie Carney, resides in Vincennes; William D., is deceased; Anna, who resides at Vincennes, Indiana, is the widow of C. H. Bubenzer, who was here a member of the City Council, in 1917, during the J. D. McDowell Administration; Thomas M., of this review, was next in order of birth; Margaret is the wife of Henry E. Sandifer, of Vincennes; and Mary is the wife of Frank Smith, of Walbach County, Illinois.

Thomas M. Martin received his early education by attending the public schools of his native county, and as a youth he became identified with railroad construction work, in the capacity of fireman of a steam-shovel. He was thus engaged several years, and thereafter he was engaged in the meat-market business in Illinois during a period of six years. In the initial period of his residence in Vincennes, Indiana, the city's present chief of police was here concerned with business affairs, and he later passed a number of years in the western states. He was first appointed Chief of Police of the Vincennes department in April, 1917, and served until 1921. In the latter year came a change in the administration of municipal affairs and he retired from the police service. During the ensuing three years he was employed at Universal City, California, and he then returned to Vincennes and again became a member of the police department, of which he was made the chief in July, 1926, his administration in this office having fully justified his reappointment in January, 1930. He has the work of his department thoroughly systematized and has the confidence and loyal cooperation of the other members of the department—eighteen in number. He was elected president of the Indiana Association of Police Chiefs in 1928, and was made a life member of that association.

Mr. Martin married at Vincennes, Indiana, July 11, 1921, Augusta Rush, daughter of Samuel and Hattie Rush, of Vincennes. Mr. and Mrs. Martin have one child, Mary Ann, born September 24, 1924. In his political affiliation Mr. Martin is a strong Democrat, and he is a chartered member of the Jefferson Club of Knox County.

CHARLES POOLE CLEMENS. In 1927 one of the prominent business men of Princeton passed from the companionship of friends and kindred into the unseen world to which all mankind is hastening. Through six and fifty years, rich in the fruit of good deeds, Charles Poole Clemens discharged every duty of life, as citizen, son, brother, philanthropist and Christian. A true patriot, an ardent though not blatant reformer, a faithful friend, loving and beloved.

Mr. Clemens was born at Greensburg, Indiana, November 25, 1871. Left an orphan at an early age by the death of his parents, he was reared in the home of his grandmother and acquired a public school education. When about seventeen years of age he became identified with the stone-cutting trade and subsequently with the business of building monuments. From Greensburg he moved to Oakland City with his family and there made his home until 1913, when he settled permanently at Princeton and became founder and owner of the Princeton Memorial Works, with which business he continued to be identified until his final illness, his death following about two weeks later as a result of heart disease and other complications. Mr. Clemens was early trained to habits of industry, strict economy and perfect integrity, enduring qualities which he carried with him through life. He made himself the friend and helper of those in his employ and those who were associated with him. Much might be said of his benevolence. He regarded himself as a steward indeed, and he was a faithful one. He was a member of the Blue Lodge of Masonry, a past worthy patron of Golden Fleece Chapter of the Order of the Eastern Star and a member of the Modern Woodmen of America. In 1902 Mr. Clemens was united in marriage with Miss Ollie M. Clark, of Greensburg, who survives him, and they became the parents of six children: Poole, Charles O., Ora, Lloyd, Nellie Mae and Mildred Virginia, all of Princeton. Mr. Clemens is also survived by a sister, Mrs. James Ayers, of Denver, Colorado.

Since the death of Mr. Clemens the business has been owned and occupied by Poole and Charles O. Clemens, under the style of Princeton Monument Works, Clemens Brothers, proprietors. Both are college men and progressive and enterprising business citizens. Charles O. Clemens was attending Oakland City College when his father was stricken with his fatal illness, and gave up his studies to hasten home to assist in the business. Both of the sons had their business training when young under their father, who taught them the art of stone-cutting, and some of the most beautiful and massive monuments to be found at Princeton and near-by communities have come from the modern plant at the corner of Spruce and Prince streets, where pneumatic tools and appliances are used in all the work done. Both brothers are Masons and Mrs. Charles P. Clemens belongs to the Order of the Eastern Star and the Daughters of the American Revolution. The family is widely known and greatly respected throughout the county.

WILBUR C. PATTERSON is known and valued as one of the progressive citizens and business men of Indianapolis, where he is owner and manager of the prosperous enterprise that is conducted under the title of the Patterson Shade Company, with headquarters at 132 North Delaware Street. Mr. Patterson was born at Morristown, Shelby County, Indiana, January 22, 1887, and is a son of Homer S. and Ollie (Fox) Patterson, both likewise natives of Indiana, where the former was born at Kokomo. The Patterson family was early founded in Pennsylvania and from that state came the first representatives in Indiana, where was gained a goodly measure of pioneer precedence.

Wilbur C. Patterson received the advantages of the public schools of Alexandria, Tennessee, and Memphis, Tennessee, and after completing his high school studies he found, at the age of nineteen years, employment as clerk in a leading department store in Memphis. He was thus engaged ten years and in the meanwhile gained a thorough and valuable business experience. At the time of severing his connection with this line of service he initiated his independent business career, by forming a partnership with R. L. Williams in the window-shade business. This firm established its business at Memphis, Tennessee, and the partnership continued five years in the original location and removal was then made to Indianapolis, where the business has since been successfully continued, at first under the title of Patterson-Williams Shade Company and later under the present title of Patterson Shade Company, Mr. Patterson now having sole ownership of the large and prosperous business built up by the company.

In the World war period Mr. Patterson enlisted for service in the Ordnance Corps of the United States Army, in which he gained the rank of sergeant, and with which he continued in service until the armistice brought the war to a close, though his unit was not called to overseas service. He duly

received his honorable discharge and he is now an active member of the American Legion. His political allegiance is given to the Republican party and he and his wife are members of the Meridian Street Methodist Episcopal Church in their home city. Mr. Patterson has received the thirty-second degree of the Ancient Accepted Scottish Rite of the Masonic fraternity, besides being a Noble of the Mystic Shrine. He is an active member of the Indianapolis Chamber of Commerce, is a director of the Hoosier Motor Club, and has membership in the Optimist Club.

The year 1920 marked the marriage of Mr. Patterson to Miss Bertha Louise Maxwell, who was born in Ohio, and the one child of this union is a winsome daughter, Mary Louise, born in the year 1927.

WILLIAM LANE EWING. In Knox County, three miles east of Vincennes, on U. S. Highway No. 61, is located the Mont Clare country estate of the Ewing family. This is one of the show places of Indiana, a practical farm and also a country place of great beauty that for many years has been carefully parked and landscaped. There is a beautiful house, and the entire environment shows the care and labor of more than a century, during which it has been in the Ewing family.

This was the birthplace of William Lane Ewing, Sr., who was born there in 1812 and when a boy was taken to Saint Louis, where he grew up and became one of the most conspicuous citizens of that city. He was in the wholesale commission business for many years and a prominent leader in public affairs. He delivered the opening address when the famous Eads bridge was opened to traffic across the Mississippi River.

His son, William Lane Ewing, Jr., was born in Saint Louis March 16, 1843, was educated at Saint Louis, completing his training in the Christian Brothers College. He then joined his father in the wholesale commission business, and was elected and served as mayor of Saint Louis in 1882-1884. When he retired from business he returned to the old home, Mont Clare, at Vincennes, and devoted the last years of his life to the improvement and cultivation of the farm. He died at Vincennes June 4, 1904.

The founder of the Mont Clare estate was Nathaniel Ewing, a native of Pennsylvania and of Scotch ancestry. He established Mont Clare at Vincennes while Indiana was still a part of Northwest Territory. Nathaniel Ewing was a banker and lawyer, and for a number of years was connected with the Government land office at Vincennes. William Lane Ewing, Sr., married a member of the Berthold family of Saint Louis, connected with the Chotoes of that city.

William Lane Ewing, Jr., married in July, 1883, at Vincennes, Miss Mary Flemming, who survives him and continues to occupy the Mont Clare estate. She is a daughter of John and Harriett (Schafer) Flemming. The Flem-

mings came from Ireland and settled in Virginia and about 1642 moved to Frederick, Maryland. The Flemming colonial farm home during the Civil war was used as a hospital. Mrs. Ewing was one of a family of seven children. Her sister Clara married Charles Heyman of Indianapolis, Indiana. Her brother John has been active in public affairs in Saint Louis and her other living sister, Alice, is the wife of T. C. Whalen, of Indianapolis.

Mrs. Ewing has one son, William Le Clede Ewing. He married for his first wife Ola Du Kate, who died at Biloxi, Mississippi, leaving two children, William L. and Nathaniel D. Mrs. Ewing is a member of the Methodist Church and the Fortnightly Club of Vincennes.

OLIVER W. MCGAUGHEY is a prominent Fountain County attorney, member of the law firm of Wallace & McGaughey at Veedersburg.

He was born in Putnam County, Indiana, December 20, 1870. The McGaughey family came from County Down, Ireland, being Scotch-Irish, and first settled in Virginia, in the village of McGaheysville, the landmark of his family's settlement there. Mr. McGaughey's father, Jacob McGaughey, was born in Putnam County, Indiana, and during the Civil war was with a regiment of Indiana Infantry. He enlisted at Greencastle, was sent to Camp Morton and served until the close of the war, when he came out with the rank of sergeant. He spent his active life as a farmer and died in 1924. Jacob McGaughey married Mary A. Leonard. They had a family of three sons and one daughter. The son, G. Stanley, is a minister of the Christian Church, Saint Paul, Indiana, and is married and has two children. Charles McGaughey, an attorney practicing law at Greencastle, is married and has one child. The daughter is Mrs. Minnie Call, who lives south of Greencastle.

Oliver W. McGaughey grew up on a farm and was educated in the public schools of Putnam County, attended the Shurtleff College Academy School at Upper Alton, Illinois, and in 1899 was graduated with the A. B. degree from Wabash College. His first profession was the ministry of the Christian Church. For three years he was with the Sixth Christian Church of Indianapolis, spent two years in the Central Christian Church at Columbus, Indiana, for two years was pastor of the First Christian Church at Everett, Washington. He still does occasional preaching and is a splendid example of Christian manhood and conduct.

While in the ministry he prepared himself for the law, taking post-graduate work in Butler University and completing his law course with the American School of Law. He was admitted to the bar in 1909 and has had a busy practice for twenty years. For two years he was honored with the office of president of the Fountain County Bar Association and in 1909 was elected as a Republican to the office of mayor of Veedersburg. He is a member of the Masonic fraternity, the Independent Order of Odd Fellows, Knights of Pythias, the Tribe of Ben Hur, the Modern Woodmen of America, and was a member of the Indiana House of Representatives in the session of 1931.

Mr. McGaughey married, November 1, 1899, Miss Alberta Booe, daughter of Arthur Booe, of Veedersburg. To this union one son, Gilbert, was born, who is now in business at San Diego, California, and is married and has one son. Mr. McGaughey, on September 17, 1911, married Miss Ardella Inlow, daughter of John B. Inlow and granddaughter of J. M. Livengood. Mr. and Mrs. McGaughey have two children, John Max and Martha Alice, both attending school at Veedersburg.

GEORGE R. ALSOP, president of the American National Bank in the historic and picturesque old City of Vincennes, Indiana, has the further distinction of being a scion of one of the old and honored families that was founded in Virginia in the early Colonial period of American history.

Mr. Alsop was born at Sperryville, Rappahannock County, Virginia, December 19, 1851, and is a son of Dr. William S. and Lavinia H. (Amiss) Alsop, both of whom were born in Rappahannock County, and both of whom passed their entire lives in Virginia, where Dr. William Alsop was for many years a leading physician and surgeon of Rappahannock and Spottsylvania counties, he having received his technical education in historic old Jefferson Medical College, Philadelphia, Pennsylvania. Doctor and Mrs. Alsop became the parents of seven children, of whom George R., of this review, was the third in order of birth. Four of the children died in infancy. The son, John W. was long in service as general baggage master of the Chesapeake & Ohio Railroad, and the son Dr. Thomas E., was graduated in a Southern medical college, he having thereafter been engaged in the practice of his profession in Indiana and later at Carlisle, Illinois.

George R. Alsop was reared and educated in his native state of Virginia and has been a resident of Indiana since he was seventeen years of age. In the earlier period of his residence in Knox County, of which Vincennes is the metropolis and county seat, he gave his attention to educational work, and also taught in the schools of Sullivan, Indiana. He served four years, 1878-82, as trustee of Widner Township, and in the period of 1884-88 he was clerk of the Circuit Court for Knox County. In the spring of 1875 George Alsop graduated from the University of Louisville, with the M. D. degree, and from 1875 to 1883 was engaged in the practice of medicine. In April, 1888, he became one of the organizers of the German National Bank of Vincennes, and he served as cashier of that institution from the date of organization until 1911. In 1911 he was elected president of that institution, which position he has continued to hold. Mr. Alsop has long been one of the able and

representative exponents of banking enterprise in this section of Indiana and his policies have been well ordered in connection with the substantial and important institution of which he continues the executive head. In the World war period he was instant and influential in the furthering of local patriotic movements and enterprises and was specially active in the Knox County campaigns in the sale of the Government war bonds, he having been a member of the committee in charge of the drives in support of these war loans, Red Cross work, etc.

The political allegiance of Mr. Alsop is given to the Democratic party, he and his wife are members of the Christian Church, he has been a trustee of the Vincennes Y. M. C. A., from the time of its organization to the present, he is a trustee also of Vincennes University, his basic Masonic affiliation is with historic Vincennes Lodge No. 1, A. F. and A. M., and in his home city he has membership in the Chamber of Commerce and the Harmony Society.

The year 1875 was marked by the marriage of Mr. Alsop to Miss Nancy J. McClellan daughter of the late Abraham McClellan, who gave prolonged service as treasurer of Sullivan County, this state. Of the seven children of Mr. and Mrs. Alsop five are living: William M., was graduated in the University of Indiana, and thereafter served as superintendent of the public schools of Knox County. He is now engaged in the practice of law in this city, and he is president of the Vincennes Savings & Loan Association, the maiden name of his wife having been Cora J. Meyer. Eustis F., resides in Vincennes and is engaged with the Central Fiber Products Company. Byrd became the wife of Benjamin B. Sproat, who is now deceased, and she maintains her home in Vincennes. Edith V. is the wife of Meredith P. Reed, of Vincennes. Jane is the wife of George G. Graham, who is now county superintendent of the public schools of Knox County.

Mr. Alsop has marked the passing years with large and worthy achievement and his activities as a citizen and man of affairs have inured greatly to the benefit of the community in which he has long maintained his home.

LEANDER J. CULLY. The business interests of Brownsville are of sufficient importance to engross the attention of some men of more than ordinary ability, and among them none stands any higher than Leander J. Cully, merchant and banker, and one of the prime movers in everything that looks toward the advancement of the town and Union County. He is a native son of the county, born in Brownsville Township, October 26, 1864.

The Cully family was established in Union County at a very early day by the paternal grandfather of Leander J. Cully, Joseph Cully, a native of North Carolina, who married, after he located here, Sarah Elizabeth Levison, born in Union County. The maternal grandparents were Maj. William and Rhoda (Sea-ton) Watt. Major Watt was born in Lancaster County, Pennsylvania, December 6, 1776, and he was a hatter by trade. Coming to Brownsville when it was the county seat of Union County, he became the first hatter of the place, and was engaged in this line of business for many years.

The parents of Leander J. Cully are Leander and Margaret (Watt) Cully, both born in Union County, he in 1838, and she in 1836. They were farming people, and he died in 1882, and she in 1911.

Growing to manhood amid strictly rural conditions, Leander J. Cully attended the district schools and learned to farm, and later was a student of the Brownsville schools. When he was twenty-four years old Mr. Cully embarked in a general mercantile business at Brownsville, and has built up a large and valuable trade which extends over a wide territory. He also owns a fine farm of 160 acres in Liberty Township, and bank stock. In fact it has been his practice to invest his earnings in local enterprises, as he believes all good citizens should do, in this way building up strong home concerns.

In 1888 Mr. Cully was married to Miss Carrie E. Bell, born in Union County, a daughter of Jacob and Margaret (Thomas) Bell, of Union County. The paternal grandparents, John F. and Anna (Carr) Bell, were early settlers of Union County. The maternal grandparents were John and Margaret (Whitinger) Thomas, of Welsh descent. The Whitingers are prominent in Pennsylvania, and have been for several generations. Mr. and Mrs. Cully have no children.

The Methodist Episcopal Church holds Mr. Cully's membership, and he served it as trustee for many years. Always taking an active interest in Democratic politics, he. has been elected to a number of local offices, and served as treasurer of Brownsville from 1901 to 1903, and he has also represented the city or county in party conventions a number of times. A Mason, he served as worshipful master of the Blue Lodge ten terms. He represented Union and Franklin counties in the State Legislature, 1901 and 1903, sixty-second and sixty-third sessions of the General Assembly.

As a matter of history it is interesting to note in connection with Mr. Cully's biography, because of the long residence in Union County of his people on both sides of the house, that the land on which Brownsville now stands was bought from the United States Government by Aaron Ashbrook and Charles McCathlin, in October, 1815. The town was platted and laid out in 200 lots for Thomas Constant by James Levison, surveyor. Later a Mr. Smith made an addition to the town. This town of Brownsville was the first laid out in Union County, and belonged to Fayette County until 1821, when, from Franklin, Fayette and Wayne counties, Union County was created. Bazilla Trail, with a band of men, began cutting the timber for the houses of Brownsville in 1818, and the town continued to be the county seat from December 31, 1821, until 1824, when the county offices were moved to Liberty by act of Legislature. A jail was built at Brownsville in 1822, by order of the county commissioners, and it cost $246. The town was incorporated December 24, 1853. In many of these proceedings, and all of the later ones, members of Mr. Cully's family participated, and he is continuing the good work today of furthering the town's interests as far as lie in his power.

JOSEPH MICHAEL DATTILO. The produce business has one essential advantage—it is an absolute necessity. Nevertheless, too many individuals trade upon this fact, and, as a consequence, are a long way removed from the hustling resourceful citizen known the world over as the twentieth-century produce man. As in all lines of business, a financial creed is necessary in order not to fall behind in the procession. No one is better qualified to advise on the subject than Joseph Michael Dattilo, president of the Dattilo Wholesale Produce Company, of Vincennes, and his experience should be worth much to the young man who thinks he fits into a similar groove in business life.

Mr. Dattilo was born in Sicily, Italy, August 13, 1879, where he attended public school until reaching the age of eleven years. In 1890 he came to the United States and first settled at Harrisburg, Pennsylvania, where he completed his education, his next location being Nashville, Tennessee, where he remained for three years. Subsequently he lived for a time at Hopkinsville, Kentucky, and then took a trip to Europe, but returned to the United States in 1900 and remained at Hopkinsville until January, 1902. In that year he engaged in the wholesale and retail fruit business, under the firm style of J. M. Dattilo Wholesale Fruit Company, at Vincennes, Indiana, and three years later became the prime mover in founding the firm of Dattilo Brothers, with his brothers, Charles S., and Anthony. This connection flourished until 1926, when Joseph M. Dattilo sold his interests and founded the wholesale produce business of Dattilo & Balsamer Company, which has since been changed to its present style, Dattilo Wholesale Produce Company, of which he is the president. This has been developed into one of the largest enterprises of its kind in the state, and the company ships in car-load lots only. Early in his career as a produce merchant Mr. Dattilo found that there was money to be made in specialization, and for some years he has specialized in new turnips and early tomatoes grown in Knox County. Other produce favored by him include canteloupes, watermelons and New Jersey sweet potatoes, and at the peak of the season he ships apples and peaches in 200 car-load lots. He has a large trade at Milwaukee, Wisconsin, and also ships to eastern and northern markets, and is widely and favorably known to the trade as a business man of high character and honorable dealing. He maintains his business office at 920 Vigo Street, and has large warehouse facilities at Vincennes. Quick turnover, cool judgment, quick grasp of opportunities and hard, earnest work have achieved a full meed of well merited success, and Mr. Dattilo is accounted one of the leading business men of his city. He is a Republican in politics, but has not troubled with political affairs, although maintaining a high position as a citizen of public spirit and civic pride and a contributor to all worthy movements. His religious faith is that of the Catholic Church, and he is a past navigator of the Knights of Columbus, fourth degree, belonging also to the Benevolent and Protective Order of Elks and the Fraternal Order of Eagles, in all of which he is very popular. During the World war he was a generous contributor to the loan drives, buying heavily of Liberty Bonds and being active in all community war work. During an active and varied career he has touched life on many sides, and in each of his connections has maintained a reputation for honorable and upright conduct.

Mr. Dattilo on April 25, 1900, in Sicily, Italy, was united in marriage with Miss Maria Lazzara, of Sicily, Italy, and to this union there have been born three children: Marguerite, who married Charles Panzica, of Chicago Heights, Illinois, and Augustine and Maria. Augustine is a graduate of the Catholic high school at Vincennes and Maria is a student in the St. Rose Catholic Academy at Vincennes.

LOUIS L. ROBERTS was born in the interesting old town of Carlisle in Sullivan County, Indiana, April 26, 1891. His father, James Nelson Roberts, was a native of Virginia, followed merchandising, and died May 2, 1922. His mother, Caroline Long, was born in Evansville and is still living. There were three children. The son Raymond R., born in 1889, is a farmer in Sullivan County, and Charles E., born in 1894, is in the investment department of the Northwestern Life Insurance Company, in charge of their Saint Louis office.

Louis L. Roberts attended public school at Carlisle, the Assumption Parochial School, the Evansville High School and Culver Military Academy. From there he entered Wabash College at Crawfordsville, graduating A. B. in 1912. At Wabash he was a member of Phi Delta Theta and Tau Kappa Alpha, and was elected to the honorary scholastic fraternity, Phi Beta Kappa. After college he taught two years, and in 1914 was awarded, after competitive examination, the first Knights of Columbus scholarship for Indiana at the Catholic University of America at Washington. In 1915 he was awarded the Master of Arts degree, and during the following year continued graduate study and was instructor in American constitutional history. He received his law degree in 1916.

He resigned in April, 1917, to enter the First Officers Training Camp at Fort Meyer, Virginia, and was commissioned a captain of the Three Hundred and Fifteenth Field Artillery, Eightieth Division, and in May, 1918, was overseas with the division. In October, 1918, he was returned to the United States to assist in training field artillery, and was enroute to France when the armistice was signed. He was honorably discharged at Camp McClellan, Alabama, and in March, 1919, came to Evansville, where he began the practice of law, with the firm Veneman & Welborn. In the same year he was taken into the firm as junior partner. In 1924 Frank H. Hatfield, W. C. Welborn and he formed a new partnership, and since January 1, 1929, he has practiced as a law partner of Mr. Hatfield, the firm name being Hatfield & Roberts.

Captain Roberts in 1921 organized at Evansville the first unit of the new National Guard, Battery F, One Hundred and Thirty-ninth Field Artillery, and is now the senior reserve national guard officer in Southern Indiana, with the rank of lieutenant-colonel. Colonel Roberts is a Democrat, a member of the Catholic Church, and for several years was district deputy of the Knights of Columbus. He is a member of the Veterans of Foreign Wars, the American Legion, is a former vice president of the Chamber of Commerce and was elected its president in January, 1928, but was obliged to decline the honor. He is a director of the local chapter of the American Red Cross and a director of the Vanderburg County Anti-Tuberculosis Society.

Colonel Roberts married, April 27, 1920, Miss Pauline Molony, daughter of James S. and Mary (Sullivan) Molony, of Crawfordsville, Indiana. Four children were born to their marriage: Caroline Mary, born September 1, 1921; Pauline, born October 2, 1922, and died the same day; Louis Nelson, born November 30, 1925; and James Alan, born July 12, 1930.

ALONZO ERWIN is in the fullest sense worthy of special recognition in this history of Indiana, as he is one of the venerable native sons of Posey County, is a representative of families that were here established in the early pioneer days, and here he has marked the passing years with earnest and worthy achievement, through which he is well fortified in prosperity that enables him to pass the gracious evening of his life in retirement. He is one of the honored pioneer citizens residing at Mount Vernon, the county seat, where in former years he held various official positions and where he was engaged in business during the long period of over forty years. His is the further distinction of having represented his native county and state as a gallant young soldier of the Union in the Civil war.

On the parental home farm near Mount Vernon the birth of Alonzo Erwin occurred April 17, 1842, and in this county likewise were born his parents, John Howard and Elizabeth (McKinney) Erwin, of whose four children he is the eldest and the sole survivor; the daughter Penelope died in 1862, at the

Charles W. Dockins

age of sixteen years; Caroline died at the age of twenty-seven years; Lawrence died at the age of thirty years. Caroline became the wife of Julius Patmore, a Posey County farmer, and they had three children. Lawrence Erwin was a farmer by vocation and was still a bachelor at the time of his death, when a young man. Both the paternal and maternal grandparents of the subject of this sketch were numbered among the early settlers of Posey County and through farm enterprise contributed their share to civic and industrial development and progress, the paternal grandfather, Samuel Erwin, having come to Indiana from his native State of Tennessee.

The early education of Alonzo Erwin was obtained mainly through the medium of the old-time private or subscription schools, and he was a sturdy youth of nineteen years when the Civil war was precipitated. His youthful patriotism moved him to almost immediate enlistment in a regiment of volunteer infantry that was recruited in this part of Indiana, and during his first two years at the front he served in turn in the commands of General Grant and General Fremont. Among the various engagements in which he took part was the historic and early battle of Shiloh. He and most of the other members of his regiment were poisoned by drinking from a spring into which the enemy had placed the poison, and the disability that he thus endured resulted in his receiving an honorable discharge at Sedalia, Missouri. After the close of the war he remained some time on the old home farm, and he also learned and followed the trade of carpenter. He remained on the farm until 1867, when he traded his farm for city property in Mount Vernon, where he established his home and engaged in business as a carpenter and builder. He here gave three and one-half years of service as jailor of the county jail, and he gave intervals of service as deputy sheriff. In 1891 he also engaged in the retail grocery business, and in this line of enterprise he was successfully established twenty years, at the expiration of which he sold the business, though he still owns the building in which the enterprise was conducted. He has since lived retired and is enjoying the rewards of former years of earnest endeavor. In addition to his attractive home he is the owner of other residence properties, as well as store buildings and lots in Mount Vernon, and he still takes vital interest in all that concerns the welfare and progress of his home city and native county. He is one of the few remaining veterans of the local post of the Grand Army of the Republic, his political alignment is with the Democratic party, he is affiliated with the Independent Order of Odd Fellows, and he has his membership in the Baptist Church, as did also his wife, who died July 26, 1928.

At Mount Vernon, on the 11th of October, 1863, was solemnized the marriage of Mr. Erwin to Miss Angeline McFadin, who was born February 27, 1846, in Posey County and who was a daughter of the late Zimri McFadin, a representative farmer in his day and generation, the family name of his wife having been Kennedy. Of the two children of Mr. and Mrs. Erwin one, a son, died in infancy. Amos was born April 1, 1869, was reared and educated in his native county and is now a successful and popular commercial traveling salesman. He married Miss Ida Mendenhall, of Evansville, Vanderburg County, and they maintain their residence in Mount Vernon, the elder of their two children being John Alonzo, born October 27, 1906, who is a medical student, and the younger being Robert Amos, born October 10, 1908, who is a newspaper correspondent. By a former marriage Mr. Amos Erwin has another son, Edson L., born September 12, 1897, who has a responsible position with the Western Electric Company in New York City and has a Master's degree from Chicago University.

CHARLES W. DOCKINS is an Indiana school man, has been a teacher for fifteen years and is superintendent of schools at Veedersburg, Fountain County.

Mr. Dockins was born in Orange County, Indiana, August 8, 1890. His father, John S. Dockins, was also born in Orange County, spent his active life as a farmer and died in 1914. He married Emily Pinnick, daughter of Volney Pinnick. They had three children: Volney T., of Bloomington, Indiana; Cora, wife of F. Roark, of Bloomington; and Charles W.

Charles W. Dockins was educated in the grade and high schools of Orange County, took some work at Indiana University, and was graduated with the A. B. degree from the Central Normal College at Danville, Indiana. Later he won the Master of Science degree at Purdue University.

Mr. Dockins began teaching in 1916 and has been superintendent of schools at Veedersburg since 1926. He is a member of the National Education Association, the Indiana Superintendents Association. He is a Methodist, and his fraternal affiliations are with Tippecanoe Lodge No. 452, A. F. and A. M., Lafayette, Indiana, the Scottish Rite Consistory and Shrine at Indianapolis.

He married, June 9, 1920, Miss Rosborough S. Kerlin, daughter of Wilson S. Kerlin, of Tippecanoe County. She was graduated from Purdue University in 1913 and for several years was a teacher in the public school. Her grandfather was a soldier in the Civil war.

ELLIS H. TADE, Doctor of Medicine, has been engaged in the work of his profession in Southern Indiana for a quarter of a century. His home is at Bicknell in Knox County.

Doctor Tade was born in Knox County, Indiana, October 27, 1878, son of Samuel T. and Louisa C. (Williams) Tade, his mother being a daughter of John Williams, of a pioneer family of Knox County. His father was a son of John and Mary (Small) Tade, and John Tade was a son of Martin Tade, who came from Virginia and was a pioneer of Indiana. John Tade spent his active life in the milling business at Bruceville and Wheatland in Knox County. Samuel T. Tade was a farmer and cabinet maker, and died December 1, 1896. His widow still survives and resides in the old place three and one-half miles north of Wheatland.

Doctor Tade was the oldest and only son of three children. His two sisters are Fannie E., wife of Walter Hicks, and Anna, wife of Charles Myers. Doctor Tade was seventeen years old when his father died, and as the only son he had to take upon himself the responsibility for supporting the family. He conducted the farm, and it was only after discharging all his obligations to his family that he was able to carry out his cherished purpose of going to medical college. While in college he worked during the summer months to pay part of his expenses. Doctor Tade attended public schools in Knox County, the Wheatland High School, and was graduated in medicine from the Indiana Medical College, now the medical department of the University of Indiana, with the class of 1905, M. D. degree. Doctor Tade for twelve years practiced at Wheatland and since 1917 has practiced at Bicknell. While at Wheatland he served six years as township trustee and was health officer of Bicknell from 1920 to 1924. He is a member of the Knox County Medical Society and served one term as its president, a member of the Indiana State Medical Association, is a Democrat, is affiliated with Lodge No. 535 of the Masonic fraternity, and with the B. P. O. Elks of Bicknell.

Doctor Tade on August 17, 1904, married Ethel P. Black, of Knox County, daughter of Henry C. and Amanda (Donaldson) Black, both now deceased. Doctor and Mrs. Tade have four children: Lillian E. is the wife of Carl Jessup, of Frankfort, Indiana, and has a son, Billie Gordon; Marguerite is the wife of James Lawson, of Spencer, Indiana; Ellis Harold is a pre-medical student at the Indiana University; and Woodrow Wilson is a high school student.

CHARLES C. SUTTER, physician and surgeon, is a professional man well known throughout Vanderburg County, and particularly in the City of Evansville and in his old home community of Howell.

Doctor Sutter, whose professional work gains added distinction by his service during the World war, was born at Evansville, November 8, 1888. His father, Charles I. Sutter, now living retired at Howell, is a veteran locomotive engineer. He was born in Illinois and entered the service of the Louisville & Nashville Railway Company in 1881. He had the distinction of piloting the first train over the Henderson bridge between Evansville and Henderson. He married Martha E. Culley, who was also born in Illinois. Of their five children three are living: James died at the age of three and a half years, and the youngest, Eugene, at the age of ten; Enola, born in 1886, is a teacher at Evansville; Doctor Sutter is the only living son; and Flora, born in 1890, is the wife of Fred Ware, a locomotive engineer, and they have a daughter, Martha Jane, born in 1923.

Dr. Charles C. Sutter attended public schools in Evansville, and was graduated from the medical department of the University of Indiana in 1910. He then returned to his home community and engaged in a general medical practice. From 1914 to 1917 he practiced at DePauw, Indiana, from there he joined the army for service in the World war on December 10, 1917, and went overseas with Unit I Hospital and was on duty at Base Hospital in France. He returned home after the armistice and received his honorable discharge at Camp Sherman, Ohio, July 21, 1919, with the rank of first lieutenant. Since the war he has given ten busy years to his professional duties in and around Howell and in Evansville.

Doctor Sutter is a director of the Howell State Bank, a director of the Howell Building & Loan Association, and is a real estate owner in Howell. He is a member of the Indiana State, Vanderburg County and the American Medical Associations, is a member of the staff of Saint Mary's Hospital, and is now president of the Lancet Club of Evansville. He belongs to the American Legion Post and the Kiwanis Club.

Doctor Sutter married at Evansville, June 12, 1923, Miss Margaret Blackman. Her father, J. W. Blackman, an Evansville merchant, was born in that city, and her mother, Virginia Bell (Vick) Blackman, was born in Tennessee. Doctor and Mrs. Sutter have one daughter, Virginia Bell, born October 10, 1925. Doctor Sutter is a Republican in politics, a member of the Methodist Episcopal Church, is a thirty-second degree Scottish Rite Mason and member of Hadi Temple of the Mystic Shrine.

LLOYD J. VOYLES, Evansville attorney, with offices in the Mercantile Bank Building, was overseas during the World war, and completed his legal education after returning home. He practiced at Saint Louis for one year.

He was born in Edwards County in Southern Illinois, December 1, 1899, and his parents, Lloyd F. and Lura (Melrose) Voyles, were born in the same county. His father is a retired real estate man.

Lloyd J. Voyles, the only child of his parents, attended public schools in Edwards County and in 1918 completed his preparatory work in the McKendree Academy at Lebanon, Illinois, the oldest academy in the Northwest Territory. As soon as he was out of school he enlisted in the army and went overseas in the summer of 1918, remaining in France about a year. He became a student in the University of Illinois, but completed his education and took his law course at Washington University in Saint Louis, in 1922. After being admitted to the Missouri bar, July 18,

Everett A. King M.D.

1922, he remained in Saint Louis, for six months associated in practice with Nathan Frank and for six months was with the legal department of the Travelers Insurance Company. Mr. Voyles came to Evansville in September, 1923, and for two years was associated with the law firm of Walker & Walker. He has been practicing alone since 1926. He is a Democrat in politics, but his whole time and exertions are given to his business as a lawyer.

Mr. Voyles married at Saint Louis, November 18, 1922, Miss Grace Spencer, daughter of Albert B. and Anna M. Spencer. Mr. and Mrs. Voyles have two children, Patsy, born February 6, 1924, and Lloyd, Jr., born September 15, 1928.

THOMAS HUNNELL, a retired business man of Evansville, has lived in that city all his life, and his own work and influence have contributed to a very honorable family record, so that the name Hunnell has a substantial influence wherever spoken in that community.

Mr. Hunnell was born at Evansville April 3, 1854. His father, William Hunnell, located in Evansville in 1834. He conducted a planing mill and for many years took an active part in the upbuilding of the city. For twelve years he was a member of the City Council. He died across the Ohio River at Henderson, Kentucky, in 1909. William Hunnell married Mary E. McCorkle, a native of North Carolina. They were the parents of nine children, David, Henry, Elizabeth, James, John, Rachael, Thomas, Jacob and Lida. Mr. Thomas Hunnell is the only surviving son, and two of his sisters are living, Rachael and Lida. Rachael is the widow of Henry Haynie, lives in California, and has a daughter, Emma. Lida is the wife of Fred Tennemyer, a retired building contractor of Evansville.

Thomas Hunnell attended public schools in Evansville and as a youth learned the painting and decorating business. He did the work of a journeyman until 1894, when he took up the contracting business for himself and was probably the leading painting and decorating contractor in the city until he retired from the business in 1922. He now looks after his investments, including several business buildings, and is also a stockholder in the Sonntag Hotel and Lowes Theater. Mr. Hunnell is a Republican in politics.

WILLIAM F. MORRIS, physician and surgeon, is a native of Gibson County, Indiana, and it is to his home community and his home people he has devoted his active years as a professional man. Doctor Morris resides at Fort Branch.

He was born in Gibson County, September 14, 1875. His father, John T. Morris, was a native of the same Indiana county, and was a Civil war soldier with Company F of the Fourth Indiana Cavalry. He participated in several battles and was once slightly wounded on the jaw. John T. Morris was born in 1838 and lived to be eighty-four years, eleven months of age, passing away in December, 1922. He was one of the last survivors of Grant's armies. After the war he followed farming and also operated saw mills. John T. Morris married Elizabeth Miller, who was born in Gibson County and died in 1917. They were the parents of six children: George T., of Elberfeld, Indiana, married Mary Heldt and has four children; Dr. J. L., a physician practicing at Princeton, Indiana, married Artie Epperson and has one child; Silas, of Elberfeld, married Augusta Ebracht and has two children; R. B. Morris, of Elberfeld, married Lula Smith and has four children; Dr. William F.; and Eva May, wife of W. C. May.

William F. Morris grew up in a rural locality in Gibson County, attended the common schools and high school, and had work in the Princeton Normal School. He completed his professional education in one of the oldest and best medical colleges in the country, Jefferson Medical College at Philadelphia, where he was graduated M. D. in 1900. Soon after getting his diploma he located at Fort Branch, and has been a reliable doctor in that community for the past thirty years. He is a member of the Gibson County, Indiana State and American Medical Associations. During the World war Doctor Morris spent much time in helping raise funds and in other work of a patriotic nature. He is a Republican in politics, a member of the Methodist Church, and is affiliated with the Independent Order of Odd Fellows.

He married in September, 1902, Miss Ercel Arburn. They have one son, Ludson D., born in September, 1907. He graduated from Evansville College with the A. B. degree and in 1929 entered Chicago Medical College, with a view to following the same profession as his father.

DR. EVERETT ALLEN KING, physician and surgeon in Fort Wayne, has brought to the important work of his profession a thorough training and also the indispensable requisites of youth, enthusiasm, high ideals and a tremendous energy which accounts for his rapidly increasing popularity.

Doctor King was born in Crawford County, Indiana, October 28, 1901. His parents, Joel V. and Dora (Allen) King, were also born in Crawford County, his father in 1878 and his mother in 1880. The grandfather, George King, was an early settler of Indiana and is now eighty-eight years of age, a resident of Orange County. The maternal grandfather, Archibald Allen, was a Union soldier in an Indiana regiment in the Civil war and died in 1927, at the age of eighty-two. Joel V. King is a retired farmer, a member of the Independent Order of Odd Fellows and the Christian Church.

Dr. Everett A. King graduated from high school at English, Indiana, in 1920, took his pre-medical course in Valparaiso and graduated from the Eclectic Medical College of Cincinnati in 1925. His work in medical college was supplemented by practical training and experience as an interne in the Methodist Hospital at Fort Wayne during 1925-26, and when he left his duties as interne he immediately engaged in private practice. He is a member of the Allen County, Indiana State and American Medical Associations. He also belongs to the Phi Alpha Gamma medical fraternity. In 1928 he was candidate for the Republican nomination for county coroner and took defeat by a narrow margin of three votes. In 1930 he was appointed deputy coroner of Allen County. Doctor King is a member of the B. P. O. Elks, Fraternal Order of Eagles, the Orchard Ridge Country Club and the Trinity Lutheran Church.

He is most happily married and has a wonderful wife and daughter. He married, May 16, 1927, Miss Margaret Louise Simminger, of Fort Wayne. Their daughter is Sylvia Louise, born July 6, 1928.

JOSEPH W. SMADEL, M. D., has been established in the practice of his profession in the historic old City of Vincennes during a period of more than thirty-five years, and his personality, ability and successful achievement mark him as one of the representative physicians and surgeons of his native state.

Doctor Smadel was born at New Albany, county seat of Floyd County, Indiana, December 5, 1871, and is a son of Tobias and Magdalena (Schau) Smadel, who were born and reared in Baden Baden, Germany, where their marriage was solemnized. Tobias Smadel received his youthful education in the excellent schools of his native land and was a self-reliant and ambitious young man of twenty years when he came to the United States. He was long and successfully established in the mercantile business at New Albany, Indiana, and in the period of the Civil war he there served as a member of the Indiana Home Guard. He and his wife continued their residence at New Albany until their death and they are survived by three children: William M. is still a resident of the old home City of New Albany; Dr. Joseph W., of this review, was next in order of birth; and George, who was a retired farmer, and died at Auburn, Indiana, in 1929.

Doctor Smadel received the advantages of the public schools of New Albany, including the high school, and in preparation for the profession of his choice he went to the metropolis of Kentucky and entered the medical department of the University of Louisville. In this institution he was graduated as a member of the class of 1896, and in the year that he thus received his degree of Doctor of Medicine he established his residence at Vincennes, in which city he has continued in active general practice during the intervening years, with standing as one of the leading physicians and surgeons of Knox County. He has insistently kept in touch with the advances made in medical and surgical science, has been a close student of the best standard and periodical literature of his profession and has taken effective post-graduate courses in

the New York Post Graduate School of Medicine and in the Peter Brent Brigham Hospital in the City of Boston, Massachusetts. In the period of continuous service Doctor Smadel now ranks as the second oldest physician in Vincennes, and he has continuously maintained his office headquarters at 729 Main Street during a period of over a quarter of a century. He controls a large and representative practice, has given several terms of service as a member of the city board of health, and he is one of the honored and influential members of the Knox County Medical Society, having served the society two terms as president, besides maintaining active membership in the Indiana State Medical Association and the American Medical Association. As a member of the State Medical Association he was for six years counselor for the Second Congressional District of Indiana.

Doctor Smadel is unswerving in his allegiance to the Republican party, and while he has had no desire for political preferment he is known and valued as a liberal, progressive and public-spirited citizen. The Doctor is affiliated with both York and Scottish Rite bodies of the Masonic fraternity, as well as the Mystic Shrine, and his is the distinction of having his basic affiliation with Vincennes Lodge No. 1, A. F. and A. M., the oldest in the State of Indiana.

The first marriage of Doctor Smadel was with Miss Clara Green, of Detroit, Michigan, she having died in 1905, and the one surviving child being Joseph E., who received his B. A. degree in 1927 from the University of Pennsylvania, and his M. D. degree from Washington University of Saint Louis with the class of 1931. For his second wife Doctor Smadel wedded Miss Fannie E. Stitzel, of Louisville, Kentucky, and she likewise is deceased, no children having been born of this union.

PHILIP E. ROWE, postmaster of his native City of Mount Vernon, judicial center of Posey County, was here born on the 18th of July, 1897, and he is a representative of one of the old and honored families of the Hoosier State. He is a son of Isaac A. Rowe and Ottillie (Prenzel) Rowe, the former of whom was born in Harrison County, this state, and the latter in Posey County, at Mount Vernon, where they still maintain their home. Isaac A. Rowe served at one time as sheriff of Posey County, but the major part of his active career has been devoted to the L. & N. Railroad Company as bridge foreman. Of the four children the eldest is Maurice P., who is a telegraph operator by occupation and who married Miss Mary Gill, their two children being Phyllis and Robert. Lester G., who is now one of the progressive dairy farmers of New York State and who is a former county surveyor of this county, married Miss Margaret Zerbe, and their one child is a daughter, Elizabeth Caroline. Philip E., of this review, is next younger of the children. Charles T., who is claim adjuster for the Fidelity

Casualty Company of New York, married Miss Vivian Coers, and they maintain their residence in Indiana's capital city.

After being graduated in the Mount Vernon High School Philip E. Rowe was for a time employed as clerk in a local mercantile establishment, and later he was associated with his father in the contracting and building operations on the L. & N. Railroad until there came to him the call of patriotism, when the nation became involved in the great World war. He was but eighteen years of age when he enlisted in the Indiana National Guard, and in his World war service he became a second lieutenant in Company L, One Hundred Fifty-second United States Infantry, from which he was transferred, in 1918, to Company G, One Hundred Fifty-first Infantry, and advanced to the rank of first lieutenant. With this latter command he served as divisional bombing officer, he having been sent overseas in September, 1918, as a member of an advance school detachment of the Thirty-eighth Division, and having thus attended the bombing school at Chatillon-sur-Seine, where he was appointed an instructor at the completion of his technical course and where he continued his service in such capacity until the school was closed, in 1919. He had formulated plans for continuing in service in the United States Army, but abandoned this purpose. After his return to his native land he received his honorable discharge, at Camp Jackson, South Carolina, June 20, 1919.

After terminating his military career Mr. Rowe was for several months associated with one of his brothers in the garage business at Ziegler, Illinois, and he next gave a year of service as a specialty salesman for the great Chicago meat-packing concern of Swift & Company. During the ensuing two years he was engaged in the clothing business at Mount Vernon, as junior member of the firm of Lowenhaupt & Rowe. He then sold his interest to his partner, and thereafter he was a traveling salesman for the Crown Chair Company until 1925, in which year he was appointed acting postmaster at Mount Vernon, to fill the vacancy caused by the death of the regular incumbent, A. W. Mackey. He thus initiated his service on the 1st of September, and on the 15th of the following December he was given official appointment as postmaster, of which position he has since continued the incumbent and in which he is giving a most effective and loyal administration.

Mr. Rowe is a stalwart in the local ranks of the Republican party, and he and his wife are members of the Methodist Episcopal Church in their home city. In the Masonic fraternity his basic affiliation is with Beulah Lodge No. 578, A. F. and A. M., at Mount Vernon, and in the Scottish Rite he has received the thirty-second degree, besides which he is a Noble of Hadi Temple of the Mystic Shrine, in the City of Evansville. He has membership in Mount Vernon Lodge No. 277, B. P. O. E., is actively affiliated with the American Legion, and has membership in the Mount Vernon Chamber of Commerce and the local Kiwanis Club.

Mr. Rowe still retains vital interest in military affairs and in addition to being a member of the Officers Reserve Corps of the United States Army he is an officer in the Indiana National Guard, in which he is captain of Battery E, One Hundred Thirty-ninth Field Artillery, he having organized this battery, which has its headquarters at Mount Vernon, and having been its captain from the beginning. The battery enjoys the use of a fine state-owned armory and stables, as well as a large drill field in the city. Mount Vernon also has the only tax-built World War Memorial in Indiana, a beautiful monument secured through the untiring efforts of the American Legion Post. Mr. Rowe was president of the Kiwanis Club of Mount Vernon for the year 1929, and through service of ancestors he is eligible for affiliation with the Sons of the American Revolution. Mr. Rowe is the owner of real estate in his native city and is a stockholder and a vice president of the company that owns and operates the toll-bridge at New Harmony, Posey County. He is also chairman of the Disaster Preparedness Committee of the American Red Cross for Posey County.

At Evansville, Indiana, on the 20th of September, 1923, Mr. Rowe was united in marriage to Miss Margaret Cuyler Holton, daughter of the late William E. Holton, who was a prominent banker at the time of his death and whose father, Dr. William M. Holton, was long a leading physician and surgeon of Posey County. Mrs. Otillie (Brinkman) Holton, widowed mother of Mrs. Rowe, is a daughter of the late Henry Brinkman, who was a prominent merchant in Posey County many years. Mr. and Mrs. Rowe have one child, William, born June 11, 1924.

LOUIS W. THOMAS is a loyal and efficient arbiter of law and order in his native county, and his secure place in popular esteem is shown in his having been elected to his present executive office, that of sheriff of Posey County. He is a representative of the third generation of the Thomas family in this county, his birth having here occurred on the parental home farm in Black Township, August 3, 1880. In this county were likewise born his parents, Miles W. and Mary J. (Lewis) Thomas, and the respective families established residence in Posey County in the pioneer days. Miles W. Thomas was long numbered among the substantial exponents of farm industry in his native county, was influential in community affairs and served six years as trustee of Black Township. He and his wife now reside in the City of Evansville, where he is living virtually retired, and of their six children two died in early childhood and Minnie at the age of fourteen years. Of the three surviving children Louis W., of this review, is the eldest. Elizabeth, who is thirty-eight years of age at the time of this writing, in 1929, is the wife of William Woodward, a painter by trade and vocation, and they reside in Mount Vernon, judicial center of Posey County. They have no children. Thompson, who is twenty-seven years of age, is successfully engaged in farm enterprise in Kentucky, he having married Miss Minnie Loveland, of Posey County, and their two children being Betty Ann and Dorothy May.

The childhood and early youth of Louis W. Thomas were compassed by the invigorating influences of the home farm, and he continued to be associated with its operations until he was twenty years of age, his educational advantages in the meanwhile having been those of the public schools. At the age noted he engaged in farm enterprise in an independent way, and he continued in the active management of his farm, in Black Township until 1927, when he sold the property, he having been elected county sheriff in the preceding November and having removed to Mount Vernon and assumed his official duties January 1, 1927. He is giving a most efficient administration in this position, and is thus giving further evidence of his loyalty to and interest in his native county. His political allegiance is given to the Democratic party, he is affiliated with the Modern Woodmen of America, and he and his wife have membership in the Baptist Church.

At Mount Vernon, on the 13th of October, 1907, Mr. Thomas was united in marriage to Miss Myrtle M. Crunk, who likewise was born and reared in Posey County and who is a daughter of Joseph and Elizabeth (Barnett) Crunk, her father having been one of the prosperous farmers of this county at the time of his death. Mr. and Mrs. Thomas have three children: Thelma Elizabeth, who was born December 5, 1909, is the wife of Edward Kingsley, a progressive young farmer of Posey County, and they have one child, Zeltha Jean. Dorothy Olivia, born December 16, 1911, and Louis Lee, born November 5, 1920, are attending the Mount Vernon public schools and represents much of juvenile buoyance in the parental home.

WILLIAM MICHAUX FORD left a large and worthy impress upon the civic and material history of his native town and county, was in the most significant degree loyal, progressive and public-spirited as a citizen, and the community manifested its sense of loss and bereavement when he was called from the stage of life's mortal endeavors, his death having occurred at New Harmony, Posey County, June 19, 1923. Mr. Ford had large and varied property and capitalistic interests in this community and was president of the Mount Vernon National Bank, at the county seat, at the time of his death.

Mr. Ford was born at New Harmony on the 19th of January, 1846, and was a son of Richard and Prudence (Birkbeck) Ford, whose marriage was here solemnized, the latter having been born in the State of Illinois. Richard Ford became a leading merchant at New Har-

mony, and was a large land owner both in Posey County and in the State of Illinois, he having been eighty-two years old at the time of his death, in 1901, and his wife likewise having passed the closing years of her life at New Harmony—the family home for many years. She was ninety-one years old when she died in 1915. Of the eight children two died in early childhood; William M., of this memoir, died at the age of seventy-seven years; Morris died at the age of seventy-two; George was seventy-six years of age at the time of his death; Charles is seventy-eight in 1931; Ann B. is seventy-two and Lincoln R. is sixty-eight years of age at the time of this writing, in 1931. Morris married Helen Chaffin, and he is survived by one son, Edwin C., a Posey County landowner. George, who was a representative farmer, married Eliza Lichtenberger, and he is not survived by children. Charles is an exponent of farm industry both in Posey County and Illinois, the maiden name of his wife was Mollie Wiley and they have no children; Miss Ann B. resides in the home of the widow of her brother William M., of this review; Lincoln R. is a substantial farmer in Posey County, the maiden name of his wife was May Rose Husband, and they have no children.

The schools of New Harmony afforded William M. Ford his youthful education, and after leaving school he became actively associated with his father's mercantile business. He long continued in the general merchandise business at New Harmony, where he also owned and operated the flour mill of which his only son and child is now in charge. For forty years Mr. Ford was associated in the mill with John Corbin, who was president until he died in 1911 and Mr. Ford bought it in 1916. He organized and was president of the Mount Vernon and Evansville Traction Company, that operated cars between those points for many years. He was associated with Braddock McGregor in promoting the installation of well equipped electric light plants at both New Harmony and Mount Vernon, and after operating the plant at the county seat a number of years they sold it to the city, as did they later sell the New Harmony plant, which likewise became a municipal concern. Mr. Ford was the owner of several valuable farms in Posey County and, as before stated, was president of the Mount Vernon National Bank at the time of his death. He had important real estate holdings in New Harmony, including the beautiful seventy-four year old home still occupied by his widow, who has lived in the house since it was built, and the mill operated by their son. He was a Republican in political allegiance and was affiliated with the Benevolent and Protective Order of Elks and the Knights of Pythias. He was one of twenty-six members of the Workingmen's Institute, which is a highly important institution in New Harmony, described more fully elsewhere in this work and membership in which was and is regarded as a distinct honor and

Ethel A. Glascock, D.C.

responsibility. He was too young to enter military service in the earlier stage of the Civil war, but was in the 100-day service in the closing part of that conflict.

At New Harmony, on the 15th of November, 1871, Mr. Ford was united in marriage to Miss Mary T. Lichtenberger, who was here born and reared and who is a daughter of the late Adam and Caroline (Beal) Lichtenberger, her father having owned and operated a flour mill at New Harmony many years—until it was destroyed by fire. Mrs. Ford still resides in New Harmony, where she has long been a gracious and popular figure in social and cultural circles. The only child, Harry Cuyler Ford, was born September 9, 1873, and he gives supervision to his farm interests and also to the operation of the well equipped local flour mill that is an integral part of his father's estate. He married Miss Marcia V. Corbin, daughter of John and Mary (Truscott) Corbin, of New Harmony, and they have three children: Richard C., born September 23, 1904, John Birkbeck, born December 4, 1906, and died November 25, 1928, and William Michaux II, born November 3, 1909. Richard C. attended the University of Pennsylvania, later took a course in business college, and he is now associated with the Pittsburgh Plate Glass Company at Baltimore. William is in Lehigh University at Bethlehem, Pennsylvania, in the class of 1933.

WILLIAM H. BOETTICHER, a native of Evansville, has long been regarded as one of that city's most progressive business men. His name is officially identified with several business organizations, including the Boetticher-Kellogg Company, of which he is president.

Mr. Boetticher was born in Evansville December 6, 1860, son of Edward and Amelia Boetticher. His father was born in Ohio, January 7, 1837, and came to Evansville in 1868. He had learned the hardware business in Ohio and in Evansville he joined the old hardware house of Wells, Kellogg & Company. Three years later he bought the interest of Wells and was actively associated with Mr. Kellogg in the business until 1903. He died in Germany, while on a tour, in 1912. His wife was born in Cincinnati and died in 1910. Of their family of eight children five died in infancy. The three living sons are: William H.; Oscar, born in 1868, first vice president of the Boetticher - Kellogg Company, married Georgia Naas, of Evansville; and Carl F., born in 1872, vice president and sales manager for the company. William H. Boetticher attended public schools and Commercial College at Evansville and since early manhood his chief interest has been in the business built up by his father and Mr. Kellogg. He started as a clerk, later was a traveling salesman, and up to a few years ago, he continued business trips every third week. In that way he built up a large and loyal following all over the territory served by the Boetticher-Kellogg Company, wholesale dealers and manufacturers of hardware, automobile accessories, sporting goods and electrical goods. He became a partner in the business in 1897 and has been the directing head since his father retired.

Mr. Boetticher is a forceful busines executive and is regarded as the chief factor in the expansion of the prosperous business of the Boetticher-Kellogg Company. In addition he is also president of the Advance Stove Works of Evansville, vice president of the Monitor Furniture Company, a director in the Claimer Furniture Factory and a director of the National City Bank and the Lincoln Savings Bank.

He married at Evansville, February 27, 1890, Miss Ida Griener, daughter of Roman R. and Anna Griener. Her father was a leading furniture manufacturer of Evansville and both parents were born in Germany. Mr. Boetticher is a Republican but has steadfastly refused all political honors, none the less exercising an important influence in his home locality. He is a Presbyterian, a member of the Knights of Pythias and B. P. O. Elks, and for three years served with the Evansville Riffles in the Indiana National Guard.

ETHEL AMANDA GLASCOCK, Doctor of Chiropractic at Veedersburg, is an Indiana professional woman who has won success in her chosen vocation and enjoys the distinction of being secretary of the Indiana Alumni Association of the Palmer School of Chiropractic.

Doctor Glascock was born in Fountain County and is of Colonial Virginia stock, where several generations of the Glascocks were plantation owners and people of wealth and aristocratic connections. Her great-grandfather, Joseph Glascock, was born in Fauquier County, Virginia, December 24, 1791. Her grandfather was Harrison Glascock. The Glascocks came originally from Scotland, and the family was represented in the Revolutionary war.

Doctor Glascock's father, George Glascock, was a Fountain County farmer and for a number of years did a considerable business as a contractor for road work and street building. He was an influential member of the Democratic party. He died in 1913. Doctor Glascock's mother is Siddie Ellen Hesler, daughter of James Hesler, whose people came from Pennsylvania. Doctor Glascock has one brother, Dr. Clinton Harrison Glascock, who is a graduate of the Indiana University School of Dentistry, practices at Indianapolis and married Anna May Martin.

Ethel A. Glascock was educated in the grade and high schools of Fountain County. In the matter of getting a living and making a place of usefulness for herself in the world she entered the Palmer School of Chiropractic at Davenport and was graduated in 1924. For a short time she practiced in Indianapolis and then located at Veedersburg, where a large patronage has responded to her skillful ability. She owns a home and modern offices. She is secretary of the Sigma Phi Chi sorority, a Chiropractic organization, is a member of the

Eastern Star, the Christian Church and a member of the Daughters of the American Revolution.

LOLA NOLTE. The executive and cultural details involved in the practical management of the well equipped public library in the City of Mount Vernon, county seat of Posey County, are entrusted to an efficient and popular librarian, Miss Lola Nolte, whose study of library methods and policies, as combined with her keen literary appreciation, make her an ideal official and one who is doing admirable work in directing and expanding the influence of the library.

Miss Nolte was born at Mount Vernon, and thus her interest in the city and county is that of a loyal native daughter. Her father, Frederick Nolte, was in earlier years a traveling salesman for a wholesale dry goods house, and thereafter he was a representative exponent of farm industry in Posey County, his death having occurred at Mount Vernon, in the year 1899, and his widow, whose maiden name was Mary Ann Evison, being still a resident of this city, where she was born and reared. Frederick and Mary A. Nolte became the parents of six children, all of whom survive the honored father: Mary is the wife of Elijah M. Spencer, who is a prosperous farmer near Mount Vernon, and they have two children, of whom the elder is Mrs. Mark Crunk, of Indianapolis, and the younger is Jane, born in 1919. Lola, the subject of this review, is the second eldest. Lucy Belle, next younger of the children, is the wife of Kenneth Weyerbacher, a city official of Boonville, Indiana, and their two children are William and Gayle. Emily is the wife of Walter Thoma, who is in the service of the Standard Oil Company, their home being maintained in Mount Vernon and their children being Mary Ann and Walter, Jr. Frederick, elder of the two sons, who resides in Mount Vernon and is one of the progressive farmers of his native county, married Miss Evelyn Wheaten, of Elberfeld, Warrick County, and their two children are Ellen and Frederick, Jr. James is employed as buyer for the firm of Belknap & Company, of Louisville, Kentucky, and the personal name of his wife is Myrtle.

Miss Nolte continued her studies in the Mount Vernon public schools until she had duly profited by the curriculum of the high school, and thereafter she passed one year as a student in the Great Chicago Art Institute. Her special training for library work was received in the City of Indianapolis, and she has been librarian of the Mount Vernon public library since 1920. In addition to giving loyal and enthusiastic service as librarian Miss Nolte also has no minor leadership in general cultural and social activities in her home community, where her circle of friends is virtually coincident with that of her acquaintances. In 1928 Miss Nolte had the distinction of serving as president of the State Library Association of Indiana, she is president of the Tuesday Literary Club of Mount Vernon and of the Gamma Psi chapter of the Kappa Kappa Kappa sorority, a state organization.

The Mount Vernon public library, the corporate title of which is the Alexandria Free Public Library, was founded by Mrs. Mathilda Alexander, a cultured, gracious and public-spirited woman of Mount Vernon, and her private library was donated as a nucleus for the now large and well ordered library. The fine library building was erected through the medium of the Carnegie library fund, and the institution now has on its shelves fully 10,000 volumes.

The father of Miss Nolte was long prominent and influential in the Posey County councils and campaign activities of the Republican party, and was a liberal and progressive citizen who commanded unqualified popular esteem. His widow is now the oldest native daughter of Posey County residing in Mount Vernon, and she is loved by all who have come within the compass of her gracious influence.

ELISHA A. WILSON has been for more than thirty-five years actively identified with the mercantile business in the City of Boonville, county seat of Warrick County, and his successful achievement and secure civic and business standing are specially pleasing to note by reason of his being a native son of this county and a representative of one of its sterling and influential families. His venerable father, Rice Wilson, was long and prominently concerned with farm industry in this county. He was born in Kentucky and was a youth when he became a resident of Warrick County, where he now resides at Boonville and where in his years of retirement he enjoys peace and prosperity and the high regard of all who know him. His wife, whose maiden name was Charlotte Madden, passed her entire life in Warrick County and her death occurred in 1903. Rice Wilson gained status as one of the most progressive exponents of farm enterprise in Warrick County and was the founder of the Boonville Fair Association, which for sixty-five years maintained one of the largest and best county fairs in Indiana. In former years Mr. Wilson was influential in public affairs in his county and he gave eight years of service as county recorder.

Of the three children of Rice and Charlotte (Madden) Wilson the youngest, and only survivor, is Elisha A., of this review. James R., who died at the age of sixty-two years, became a prominent member of the bar of his native county and was engaged in the practice of law at Boonville at the time of his death, several years ago. He married Miss Natalia Brown, who survives him, as does also one child, John M., who is a salesman for the great mercantile house of Montgomery Ward & Company in the City of Chicago. John W., next older brother of the subject of this review, died in 1924, at the age of sixty-two years, the two having been partners in the dry-goods business at Boonville. John M. Wilson married Miss Flora Stuckey, who survives him, no children having been born of their marriage.

The public-school discipline of Elisha A. Wilson culminated in his graduation in the Boonville High School, in 1884, and he continued to be associated with the work and management of the old home farm until he was nineteen years of age, when he married and also initiated his independent career as a farmer. He was thus engaged three years, and during the ensuing two years he was employed in the coal mines of this locality. In 1893 he and his brother John established themselves in the drug-goods business at Boonville, and fair and honorable methods and effective service resulted in the upbuilding of a substantial and representative business. Upon the death of his brother, in 1924, Elisha A. assumed individual control of the prosperous business, but he soon admitted William L. Roth to partnership in the enterprise, which has since been continued under the firm name of Wilson & Roth.

Mr. Wilson has ever taken loyal interest in all that concerns the welfare of his home city and native county, his political allegiance is given to the Democratic party, he is affiliated with the Independent Order of Odd Fellows, and in their home city he and his wife are zealous members of the Presbyterian Church, in which he is an elder.

December 31, 1886, marked the marriage of Mr. Wilson to Miss Nannie Gough, who likewise was born and reared in Warrick County and who is a daughter of the late Robert and Elizabeth Gough, her father having been a coal-mine operator in this county. Helen, first born of the two daughters of Mr. and Mrs. Wilson, died at the age of sixteen years. Robert R., who was born August 2, 1887, is one of the principals in the George J. Roth Company, which conducts a leading department store at Boonville, he having married Miss Ida Roth, daughter of his partner, George J. Roth, and the one child of this union being Charlotte, who is fifteen years of age at the time of this writing, in the summer of 1929. Ruth, youngest of the children of the subject of this sketch, was born September 20, 1893, and is now the wife of Thomas C. Mullins, who was born in Arkansas, and who is now associated with coal-mining operations in Warrick County, with the Sunlight Coal Company, the headquarters of which are maintained at Boonville. Mr. Mullins was in active service in the United States Army in the World war period, was commissioned captain of the Thirty-fourth Engineers, and now has the rank of major in the Officers Reserve Corps of the United States Army. He is affiliated with the American Legion and also with the Masonic fraternity, including the Temple of the Mystic Shrine in the City of Evansville. Robert R. Wilson, son of the subject of this sketch, likewise is a noble of this temple of the Mystic Shrine, his York Rite affiliations being in his home City of Boonville. Mr. and Mrs. Mullins have three children: Jean, Thomas C., Jr., and William W.

LOUISE M. HUSBAND. One of the finest libraries of the State of Indiana is that maintained at New Harmony, Posey County, in connection with the historic Workingmen's Institute. Here Mrs. Nora C. Fretageot has held the office of librarian somewhat more than twenty years, and she counts herself fortunate in having as her efficient, popular and valued coadjutor Miss Louise M. Husband, who has been the assistant librarian since 1909. On other pages of this work individual recognition is given to Mrs. Fretageot, and to that personal sketch reference may be made for further record concerning the library.

George Husband, a native of Albion, Illinois, came to Indiana in the early '40s and established his residence at New Harmony, the center of a remarkable community whose history has been one of marked interest in the annals of the Hoosier State. Mr. Husband was a speculator along real estate and industrial lines, and he long figured prominently and worthily in civic and business activities in this community, where his death occurred in 1886, he having been born in the year 1825. Here was solemnized his marriage to Miss Elizabeth Williams, who was born and reared at New Harmony, a representative of one of its sterling pioneer families, she having been born in 1839 and her death having occurred in 1917. Of the three children of this union one died in infancy; Mary, elder of the two daughters, was born March 18, 1870, and her death occurred in 1895, she having been the wife of Rev. William H. Newkirk, who was born in Illinois, who is a clergyman of the Methodist Episcopal Church and who now resides at Tampa, Florida, no children having been born of the union; Louise M., of this review, is now the sole surviving member of the immediate family. By a former marriage George Husband had a son, Harry Carrol Husband, who was active many years in the grain and merchandising business at New Harmony and died in April, 1910. He married Miss Lena Robb, daughter of a pioneer Posey County family, and they had one daughter, Mrs. Hazel C. Daily, who lives in Chicago. His comradeship is among his sister Louise's most pleasant memories.

Miss Husband was born at New Harmony, September 16, 1877, and here she continued her studies in the public schools until she had profited by the advantages of the high school. Later she completed a course in library training, at a leading Indiana school. Hers has been a place of prominence and influence in connection with social and cultural affairs in her native city and state, and her activities have been of diversified order. As a staunch advocate of the principles of the Republican party Miss Husband was chairman of the Hoover Club for Posey and Gibson counties in the national campaign of 1928. She is a member of the Woman's Library Club of New Harmony, is treasurer of the Posey County Historical Society, is a member of the Southwestern Indiana Historical Society, was incumbent of the office of guardian for Camp Fire Girls, and she has gained reputation as a writer of marked literary ability, in which connection she has been associated with the *New Harmony Times* fully seventeen years. She is an earnest communicant of Saint Stephen's Church, Protestant Episcopal, and is an active and popular member of the parish Guild. She was president of the Woman's Library Club in 1904-05, and again from 1918 to 1920. At the age of thirteen years Miss Husband was made an honorary member of the Posey County Teachers Association, in appreciative recognition of her extraordinary analysis of a poem presented by Professor Dodson in illustrating his method of normal instruction. Miss Husband has taken active part in amateur theatrical productions, and she is in the fullest sense persona grata in the community in which she was born and reared and in which she owns and occupies the home in which her birth occurred—a place endeared to her by many hallowed memories and associations. She is a life member of the Indiana Library Association and in her native commonwealth she stands forth as a gracious and cultured gentlewoman.

GEORGE W. WARD is one of the efficient and popular officials of his native county, where he is giving a characteristically loyal and effective administration as sheriff, with executive headquarters in the courthouse at Boonville, the vital little city that is the judicial center of Warrick County.

Mr. Ward was born on the parental home farm in Lane Township, this county, July 26, 1888, and is a son of George W. Ward, Sr., and Margaret Angeline (Bass) Ward, both likewise natives of Warrick County, where the respective families gained much of pioneer precedence. George W. Ward, Sr., who was familiarly known as "Wash" Ward, from an abbreviation of his second personal name, Washington, passed his entire life in Warrick County and was long numbered among its substantial farmers and popular and enterprising citizens, his political allegiance having been given to the Democratic party and he and his wife having been members of the Baptist Church. Of their eleven children eight are living, and all of the number attained to maturity. James W., who died at the age of thirty years, was a farmer by vocation and was survived by his wife and their two children. Clara A., who died at the age of forty years, was the wife of Thomas B. Taylor, who is still engaged in farm enterprise in Warrick County, his wife being survived by four children. Audie became the wife of Arlos Siebe, a farmer in this county, and was twenty-five years of age when she died, at the birth of her only child, which likewise died. Frank, eldest of the surviving children, is a progressive farmer in Gibson County. He married Ludie Welty and they have six children. Pervis, who is one of the enterprising farmers of Warrick County, married Sarah Oxley, who died in 1928 and who is survived by two chil-

dren. Cardie is the wife of Norman Fisher, a farmer in Warrick County, and they have two children. Dora is the wife of James Williams, who is engaged in the blacksmith business at Madison, Illinois, and they have two children. Ida is the wife of Rudolph Ruble, who is engaged in the furniture business at Boonville, and they have one child. Minnie is the wife of Frederick Edwards, who is now engaged in ranch enterprise in Colorado, and they have two children. Jennie is the wife of Clifford Julian, of Boonville, and they have no children. George W., Jr., of this review, is the youngest of the children. His early education was acquired in the schools of his native township, where he continued to be associated with the work and management of the old home farm until he attained to his legal majority, when he there engaged in the same line of enterprise in an independent way.

Mr. Ward continued to give his active attention to the management of his farm until 1924, when he was appointed deputy sheriff. He made an excellent record in this position and thus was recognized as the most eligible candidate for the office of sheriff in the election of 1926, when he was made the candidate on the Democratic ticket and was elected by a majority that attested his secure place in popular esteem in his native county. His administration as sheriff has fully justified this popular confidence. Sheriff Ward has been active and influential in the councils and campaigns of the Democratic party in Warrick County, he and his wife are members of the Baptist Church, and he has passed various official chairs in the local lodge of the Independent Order of Odd Fellows, of which he is warden in 1929. He still retains ownership of valuable farm property in his native county.

At Spurgeon, Pike County, on the 4th of June, 1910, Mr. Ward was united in marriage to Miss Emma Lance, and their one child is a daughter, Imogene, who was graduated in the Boonville High School as a member of the class of 1929, her birth having occurred April 30, 1911.

WALTER ALONZO HALL, M. D. The medical profession at New Albany, Indiana, or elsewhere could scarcely be more ably represented by a general practitioner than in the case of Dr. Walter A. Hall, physician and surgeon, a man of long and comprehensive medical experience and an ex-president of the Floyd County Medical Society. Interested from boyhood in books and study rather than in work on his father's farm, Doctor Hall chose preferably the life of the physician, applied himself closely and was graduated with honors from the medical department of the University of Kentucky. After several years of country and village practice he located at Borden, Indiana, where he continued for sixteen years, and then came to New Albany, seeking a wider field of opportunity and usefulness. He belongs to many representative medical bodies, frequently contributes to their literature and has served as an official at times.

Walter E. Helmke

Doctor Hall was born at Becks Mill, Washington County, Indiana, January 2, 1880, and is a son of William A. and Laura E. (Mitchell) Hall. The Hall family originated in England and during Colonial times came to America and settled in North Carolina, while the Mitchell family were Colonial settlers in Virginia. William A. Hall, the grandfather of Doctor Hall, was born in Virginia, and came to Indiana among the pioneers of 1825, subsequently passing his life here in the pursuits of farming, in which he was engaged during the remainder of his life. He was a man of ability and judgment, and through good management and great industry built up a considerable competency. William A. Hall, the son of William A. and father of Doctor Hall, was born in Indiana, and early in life adopted the vocation of farming, to which he devoted his entire career. At the time of his wife's death, in 1902, he was superintendent of the county poor farm and was a man of high integrity who had the well-earned confidence of the people of his community. He married Laura E. Mitchell, daughter of John and Camilla Mitchell, the former of whom was a captain in the Union army during the war between the states and assisted in suppressing the raids of General Morgan and his Confederate troops into Salem, Indiana. He was a farmer who had settled in Indiana about 1825.

One of a family of five children, Walter A. Hall attended the public schools of Livonia, Indiana, and then entered the medical department of the University of Kentucky, from which he was graduated with the degree of Doctor of Medicine as a member of the class of 1904. Following this he spent two years at the Louisville City Hospital, and later at Upland, Indiana, where he practiced two years, his next location being at Borden, where he remained for sixteen years, built up a large and representative practice and became widely known as well as greatly popular. In 1923 he settled permanently at New Albany, where he has become a leader in his profession. Doctor Hall is known as a man who is capable in every way in his profession. He is an expert surgeon, a thorough practitioner and a diagnostician of highly trained faculties, and is frequently called into consultation by his fellow physicians in difficult cases of obstinacy and long standing. During the World war he tendered his services to the United States Medical Corps, but was not called to join the colors, although he assisted in many ways in making sure the cause of American arms. He is a member of the Floyd County Medical Society, of which he was formerly president; the Third District Medical Society, of which he was secretary; the Indiana State Medical Society and the American Medical Association. A Democrat in politics, he served for some time as health officer of Ward Township, Clark County, Indiana, and while at Borden was postmaster at that place during a part of his residence. He has several business and

civic connections and as a fraternalist is a popular member of the Masons, the Independent Order of Odd Fellows, the Junior Order United American Mechanics and the Benevolent and Protective Order of Elks. His well-appointed offices are situated at 511 Elsby Building.

Doctor Hall has been twice married. His first wife was Miss Olive Genevieve McKinley, who is deceased, a member of an old family of Indiana. The present Mrs. Hall was before her marriage Miss Anna Josephine Day, of New Albany, a member of a prominent Southeastern Indiana family.

WALTER EDWARD HELMKE. Among the younger generation of attorneys practicing at the Fort Wayne bar, few have made more rapid or permanent strides towards a place of leadership in their profession than Walter E. Helmke, junior member of the firm of Douglass & Helmke, with offices in the First and Tri State Bank Building. Since the outset of his career, in 1925, he has been identified with a large and lucrative practice, has been prominent in many organizations, and in 1928 was elected prosecuting attorney for Thirty-eight Judicial District of Indiana, comprising Allen County and the City of Fort Wayne.

Mr. Helmke was born in Allen County, Indiana, December 17, 1901, and is a son of Herman and Mary (Engel) Helmke. His paternal grandfather, Frederick William Edward Helmke, was born in 1842, in Germany, and when sixteen years of age came to the United States, coming to this locality directly from New York, where he arrived May 21, 1861. For three years he drove mules on canal boats on the Erie Canal, out of Fort Wayne to Toledo, and then enlisted in the Union army for service during the war between the states, carrying arms until the close of that great struggle and taking part in a number of hard-fought engagements. At the close of his military service he returned to Fort Wayne, and, having learned the shoemaker's trade in his youth, began the manufacture of footwear, in which he continued to be engaged successfully during the remainder of his life, his death occurring in 1916. He was a man of high character and good business ability, and had the esteem and respect of the people of his adopted community. Mr. Helmke married Miss Margaret Kiefer, who was born in Adams County, Indiana, in 1841, and died at Fort Wayne in 1913.

Herman Helmke, the father of Walter E. Helmke, was born July 5, 1867, in Allen County, Indiana, where he received his education in the parochial school of the Lutheran Church. As a youth he entered his father's shoe factory, where he learned the business in all of its details, and was engaged therein until 1900, when he transferred his attention to the grocery business, conducting a large and successful enterprise at Fort Wayne until his retirement in 1910. He then lived quietly until his death July 25, 1927. He was well and widely known in business circles and as a public-spirited citizen, but never sought public office or political preferment. In Allen County, September 1, 1888, Mr. Helmke was united in marriage with Miss Mary Engel, who was born November 12, 1866, at Asmushausen, Hessen, Nassau, Germany, and was about seventeen years of age when he came alone to this county. Her parents were George and Anna Engel, the former of whom died in 1871 and the latter in 1888. Mrs. Helmke still survives her husband and is a resident of Fort Wayne. There were three children in the family: Millie, who is unmarried and resides with her mother; Arthur F., chief clerk at the Wabash freight office at Fort Wayne; and Walter E., of this review.

Walter E. Helmke attended the parochial schools of his native community, from which he was graduated in 1916, and then entered the Central High School, Fort Wayne, from which he was graduated in 1920. After two years of literary work at the University of Indiana he entered the law department of that institution and received therefrom the degree of Bachelor of Laws as a member of the class of 1925. Immediately thereafter he entered upon the practice of his profession at Fort Wayne, where he is now junior member of the firm of Douglass & Helmke, with offices at 608-609 First and Tri State Bank Building. He is accounted an able, thoroughly learned, versatile and soundly grounded attorney, and has already been identified with much important litigation, the firm controlling the legal business of a number of important interests. Mr. Helmke is assisted materially in his practice by the possession of oratorical powers and debating ability, and while at college was a member of the Tau Kappa Alpha honorary debating society and won the Niezer medal for debating in 1923. He belongs to the Phi Delta Phi law fraternity, the Phi Kappa Psi national social fraternity, the Allen County Bar Association, the Indiana State Bar Association and the American Bar Association. A Republican in his political views, he has been active in the ranks of his party and in 1928 was elected prosecutor for the Thirty-eighth Judicial District of Indiana, comprising Allen County and the City of Fort Wayne. He is very fond of fishing and hunting and is an active and enthusiastic member of the Izaak Walton League. He likewise belongs to the University Club of Fort Wayne; the Friars Club; the Fort Wayne Young Men's Christian Association; the Junior Chamber of Commerce, of which he served as one of its first board of directors; the LL. B. Club, of which he is president; the Walther League; and the Lutheran Young Peoples Society, of which he is a member of the international board of directors. His religious connection is with St. Paul's Lutheran Church of Fort Wayne.

On June 3, 1926, Mr. Helmke was united in marriage with Miss Wilma L. Wehrenberg, and they are the parents of one son, Walter, born December 28, 1927, and one daughter, Mary Ann, born November 16, 1930.

JESSE W. EVANS, factory manager for the Graham-Paige Body Corporation at Evansville, has been connected in one capacity or another with the Graham Brothers, motor truck and car manufacturers, for many years.

Mr. Evans was born at Richwood, Illinois, September 19, 1892, son of Silas and Elizabeth (Hyatt) Evans. His parents were born in Illinois, where his father was a merchant. There were five children in the family. The daughter Clara, who died at the age of thirty, was the wife of Tuck Davis, and left two children. The four living children are: Effie, born in 1887, wife of William Carroll, a barber at Loogootee, Indiana, and mother of five children; Asa, born in 1890. chief engineer of the body plant of the Graham-Paige Corporation in Michigan, married Clara Brown and has five children; Jesse W.; and Floyd, born in 1896, painting foreman for the Graham-Paige Company at Evansville.

Jesse W. Evans attended school at Vincennes, Indiana, graduating from high school in 1908. For six months he worked in a paper mill, and for twelve years was with a glass factory at Loogootee, Indiana. This factory was owned by the Graham Brothers and thus from a trade worker he became identified with the automobile industry. In 1918 he was transferred to the Graham Brothers plant for the manufacture of trucks. His first service there was in axel assembly, and later he had other responsibilities in truck building, being eventually put in charge of the paint, truck assembly and body mounting in the new plant on Hidelbach Street in Evansville. In 1923 he was sent to Detroit to take charge of the plant of the corporation there and in 1926, with the merger of the Graham Brothers and Dodge Company's business, he was returned to Evansville. In 1927 the Graham Brothers acquired the Paige Motor Car interests, and at that time a new body plant was started at Wayne, Michigan, and Mr. Evans was put in charge. After a year a new plant for the construction of bodies was erected at Evansville, and Mr. Evans returned to the city to take charge of building operations and after the plant was finished he remained as factory manager. This is one of the largest industries of Evansville and is an important source of prosperity to the city. Mr. Evans is a stockholder in the Graham-Paige Company and also owns real estate at Evansville.

He married at Loogootee, Indiana, February 12, 1911, Miss Ada Mary Rawlings, daughter of Ezra and Dora (Slater) Rawlings. Both parents were born in Ohio and her father was a farmer in Martin County, Indiana. Mr. and Mrs. Evans had five children: Walter, born February 6, 1912, Lester, born in August, 1913, Robert, born in May, 1916, Norma, born in October, 1921, and Jesse, Jr., born in September, 1925. Walter is a graduate of Jasper Academy at Jasper, Indiana, and is now working in the Graham-Paige Body Plant under his father. Lester is a graduate in the class of 1931 at Bosse High School at

Evansville and plans to take up a college course. Mr. Evans is independent in politics, is a member of the Christian Church and is a thirty-second degree Scottish Rite Mason and member of Hadi Temple of the Mystic Shrine at Evansville.

GEORGE E. SLOATS has been identified with electric public utilities for many years, and the routine of his work eventually brought him to Southern Indiana, where he is general superintendent of power stations for the Southern Indiana Gas & Electric Company, with home and headquarters at Evansville.

Mr. Sloats was born in Chicago, March 22, 1866. His father, Andrew Sloats, a native of Germany, was brought to the United States when a boy by his parents and grew up in Wisconsin. He was in that state when the Civil war came on, and he served as a sergeant in the Union army. He died at Waterville, Wisconsin, December 22, 1920. Andrew Sloats maried Minnie Wagner, a native of Wisconsin. Of their four children two are living, Lillian and George E. Lillian is the widow of a Mr. Roach, a musician and barber at Los Angeles, and she and her daughter, Merlie, born in 1909, now operate a restaurant in that city. One son, William, who was born in 1869 and died in 1919, was assistant manager of the Chicago Beach Hotel, and had married about two years before his death.

George E. Sloats attended public school in Chicago. When he was fourteen years old he began his practical career, and his education after that was the result of practical work and connection with men and affairs. For two years he was employed in railroad shops at Kaukauna, Wisconsin, then became a steamfitter's helper in Chicago, a trade he followed three years. For three years he was assistant engineer of one of the large buildings in Chicago, the McCormick Building, and then became assistant engineer of the wholesale warehouse of Carson, Pirie, Scott & Company. He left there to become an assistant engineer with the Central Electric Light Company of Chicago, and in the course of one year was promoted to chief engineer and served in that capacity for three years, until this utility was taken over by the Commonwealth Edison Company. He has had a long and interesting service with the electric public utilities. For two years he was with the National Light Company as chief engineer, leaving that to join the General Electric Company in overhauling and repair work, being sent about over the country to different plants while the equipment was being changed and brought up to modern standards. For a time he was in New York State, and after returning to Chicago he supervised the construction of an electric light plant at Hammond, Indiana. Mr. Sloats is also a stockholder in the Southern Indiana Gas & Electric Company and has had the general supervision of its power plants during the years this company has undergone a rapid development and extension of its facilities. Mr. Sloats also has a fruit farm in the Rio Grande Valley of Texas and owns real estate at Evansville.

He has been three times married. His present wife was Miss Emma Victoria Ryemers, a native of Chicago. By his first wife, Clara Caterbau, of Chicago, he has one son, Richard, born in 1900, an artist in Chicago, who is married and has a son, Warren, born in 1927. Mr. Sloats is a Republican in politics, is a York Rite Mason and member of Hadi Temple of the Mystic Shrine at Evansville, and also belongs to the B. P. O. Elks.

HILBERT P. KLEIN, M. D. Prominent in the medical profession of Gibson County, Indiana, is Dr. Hilbert P. Klein, physician at Fort Branch for almost a quarter of a century, and a substantial and dependable citizen who has had much to do with advancing the welfare of the community. He enjoys a large general practice that is not confined to Gibson County, and is a member of several medical organizations of note.

Doctor Klein was born in December, 1875, at Huntingburg, Indiana, and is a son of Charles C. and Anna Mary (Dufendacher) Klein. His father, who was born in Germany, was a young man when he came to the United States in 1860, and for a short time served as a soldier in the Union army during the war between the states. In Germany he had learned the trade of shoemaker, and following the war established a business of his own at Huntingburg, Indiana, where he became a substantial shoe merchant and a reliable citizen. His death occurred in 1919, while his widow, a native of Indiana, survives him at the age of eighty-six years. They were the parents of eight children, of whom three died in infancy, the others being: Lydia, who married S. H. Wulfman, of Huntingburg, and has three children; Florence, who married C. E. Doane, of Boonville, Indiana, and has three children; Dalia, the wife of Dr. C. M. Dowell; Charles H., a contractor and interior decorator of Huntingburg, who married Ella Berger and has three children; and Hilbert P., of this review.

Hilbert P. Klein received his early education in the public schools of Huntingburg, and following his graduation from high school entered Northwestern University, Evanston, Illinois, where he spent two years. He then entered the Eclectic Medical College, at Cincinnati, Ohio, from which he was graduated with the degree of Doctor of Medicine as a member of the class of 1899, following which he commenced practice at Ferdinand, Indiana, and remained at that place for three years. In 1902 he became interested in the coal business and temporarily gave up his practice to become a local operator, but after five years disposed of his coal interests and resumed his medical practice at Fort Branch, where he has since been in the enjoyment of a large and lucrative professional business. Doctor Klein is thoroughly grounded in all branches of his profession and has specialized along no particular line. He is held in high esteem by his fellow-practitioners, and is a valued member of the Eclectic State Medical Society and the National Eclectic Medical Association. A Republican in his political allegiance, he has not sought political honors, but has kept himself fully abreast of public affairs and developments and since locating at Fort Branch has shown his civic pride and public spirit in a number of ways. He belongs to the Presbyterian Church and is a York Rite Mason.

In 1919, at Rockport, Indiana, Doctor Klein was united in marriage with Miss Beatrice Biggs, daughter of John and Lula Biggs, of Rockport, and to this union there has been born one son: John B., who is attending public school.

OSCAR ANDERSON. Well known in military, business and social circles at Princeton, Indiana, is Oscar Anderson, of the One Hundred and Thirty-ninth Field Artillery, United States Reserve Corps, who is owner and proprietor of the leading drug store and has additional business interests in this city. Mr. Anderson is a veteran of the World war, in which his rapid promotion from a private in the ranks to a captaincy gave evidence of his high personal character and recognition of his military knowledge and soldierly qualities.

Mr. Anderson belongs to a substantial old family of Gibson County, Indiana, and was born at Princeton, August 14, 1895, only child of Dr. Robert S. and Lizzie (McCoy) Anderson. The latter, a native of Blue Mound, Illinois, still survives. The father of Mr. Anderson died at Princeton, December 22, 1915. He was a very prominent citizen, an eminent citizen widely known in Gibson County, where he was born in 1861, and he was one of the three medical men who promoted and built the Princeton Hospital.

Oscar Anderson was reared at Princeton, where he had both social and educational advantages. Upon completing his high school course he spent three years as a student in Wabash College and one year in Culver Military Academy. Then came the World war and January 11, 1917, Cadet Anderson enlisted, as a private, in the Fourth Indiana Infantry. He was stationed at Indianapolis until September, when he was transferred to Hattiesburg, Mississippi, and remained at Camp Shelby until July, 1918, when he was transferred to the Fourth Officers Training Camp at Louisville, Kentucky. In the meanwhile the Fourth Infantry had been transferred to the One Hundred and Thirty-ninth Field Artillery, and in August, 1918, Private Anderson was commissioned a second lieutenant. He was then assigned to the Tenth Division, Tenth Brigade, Thirteenth Regiment, with which he served until his honorable discharge February 1, 1919, as lieutenant.

Upon his return to civilian life Mr. Anderson completed a course in the Embalming School of the University of Indiana, after which he was in the undertaking business at Evansville for three years. He then disposed of his interests there and returned to Princeton and bought his present drug store, which he is conducting in the same vigorous thoroughness that has always been characteristic of all that he has undertaken.

He married Georgia Lee Ballard, of Princeton, Indiana, April 28, 1930. Since he cast his first vote he has supported Republican candidates. The Methodist Episcopal Church holds his membership. High in Masonry, he has been advanced in the Scottish Rite and Shrine. In addition he belongs to the Benevolent and Protective Order of Elks and the Country Club. For several years he has served on the Armory Board, and he is now its president. In addition to his drug store he is a stockholder in several local concerns.

HON. GEORGE W. DONALDSON, who died December 29, 1929, was a lifelong resident of Knox County and for nearly half a century had been closely identified with business, financial and political affairs. He conceived the idea which later formed into the Federal Reserve System and made several speeches in its behalf. He was a close friend of Thomas Marshall, who became the father of the Federal Reserve System which is in effect today. Mr. Donaldson lived a fearless, hopeful and conscientious life, and the record of his career is vital with meaning to all who knew him.

He was born on a farm near Wheatland, Knox County, February 11, 1856, son of Winthrop F. and Jency Ann Donaldson. His father was born in Scotland and on coming to America settled on a farm in Knox County. George W. Donaldson was one of the four children of his parents. After his mother's death his father married Susan Staley, and there were also four children by this union.

His early life spent as a farmer and school teacher, George W. Donaldson became well known to the people of Knox County before his entry into public life, which began in 1888, with his election to the office of county treasurer. He was reelected in 1890. On retiring from office he organized, in 1893, the Second National Bank, and was its president for twelve years. He resigned on account of ill health in 1905 and after a year of rest returned to business as a member of Robinson-Donaldson Buggy Company. For fifteen years he was its vice president. For thirty-five years Mr. Donaldson was treasurer of the People's Building & Loan Association of Vincennes, resigning that office shortly before his death.

In 1922 he was elected county auditor and was reelected in 1926. He held this position until his death, and as a mark of respect for his official standing all the county offices were closed on the day of his funeral. He also served three years as a member of the Vincennes Board of Public Works. In Masonry he was affiliated with the lodge at Bicknell, the Royal Arch Chapter, Council and Knights Templar Commandery at Vincennes and the Scottish Rite Consistory at Indianapolis. He

M. F. Worthman

was a member of the Harmony Society, and for four years was president of the Chamber of Commerce. In politics he was a Democrat.

Mr. Donaldson married, September 8, 1878, Miss Sarah A. Gilmore, of Knox County. She and four children survive. The oldest daughter, Myrtle, is the wife of Robert N. Foulks, of Indianapolis, and has a daughter, Mary Alice. Bessie is the wife of James Byron Blair, of Lynn, Indiana, and has two sons, Donald and William Kelly. Madie is married to Bert C. Fuller, of Indianapolis, and has a son, George E. Fuller. The only son, George Raymond Donaldson, lives with his mother at Vincennes, is married and has a son, George R., Jr.

To supplement this brief account of experiences, accomplishments and public and business services of Mr. Donaldson are the even more significant facts brought out in the following editorial published at the time of his death:

"The passing of George W. Donaldson after a brave fight for his life is another example of eminent men of this community whose public careers are an eloquent sermon pointing the way to honorable success and distinction.

"He was never brilliant or daring in his pursuits for the rewards of service in business and politics, but ever possessed courage and persistency and by his devotion to duty, his industry, his good common sense and honesty he was enabled to steadily ascend the ladder of success.

"We hear much these days about the right kind of literature for 'the new boy,' who does not take any interest in the tales of Indians and pirates. Therefore, the written and unrecorded stories of poor, plain boys who have achieved success as citizens and become factors in the industrial and political spheres of a community, such as that of George W. Donaldson, are examples for the rising generation —as well as the rest of us—to contemplate and profit thereby. Such lives restore a sense of proportion, of true values, of the things that give real meaning to life and rob death of its victory.

"Mr. Donaldson was a man of gentle disposition and although suffering for years, he bore his illness with remarkable fortitude, never complaining. He was recognized as a faithful and efficient official in the discharge of the duties imposed upon him during his terms as an elective officer and in his association with business men lived up to the golden rule: 'Do unto others as you would they do unto you.'

"His religious connections were with the First Christian Church and for many years he was a faithful member of the official board of that congregation. Amidst its associations he spent many of the brightest and happiest hours of his life. His familiar figure will be seen no more in the offices at the Knox County Courthouse, nor upon the streets of the city he loved so well, and he will be missed by all who knew him."

MARTIN FREDERICK WORTHMAN, city superintendent of schools at Decatur, was born in Adams County, and at an early age found his life work and vocation in the field of education. He has been connected with the Decatur schools for over twenty years.

Mr. Worthman was born in Preble Township, Adams County, Indiana, April 20, 1883. His Worthman ancestors came from Lienen, Kreis Tecklenburg, Westphalia, Germany, where they had lived for generations. His grandfather, Ernest Worthman, was born in that locality of Germany and after his marriage came to America, making the passage across the ocean on a sailing vessel that took fourteen weeks from the German port to New Orleans. He first went to Cincinnati, crossed the country by wagon to Fort Wayne and in 1855 settled in Adams County, where he paid five hundred dollars for eighty acres of unimproved land. During the next eight years his time and energies were fully consumed in clearing away the woods, putting part of the land under cultivation and establishing a comfortable home for his family. He was called from the farm in 1864 when drafted for service in the Union army, and after reaching the camp at Indianapolis was stricken with an illness from which he passed away, leaving his widow and a large family of children, comprising three sons and three daughters.

Lewis Worthman, father of Professor Worthman, was born on the old homestead in Adams County in 1860 and is now in his seventieth year. He was a small boy when his father died and in after years he bought the old home and has been not only a successful farmer but a very substantial citizen in every other way. He is a Democrat in politics and all the members of the family belong to the Reformed Church. Lewis Worthman married Miss Sophia Bloemker, who was born in Adams County in 1861 and passed away November 15, 1915. Of their eleven children Martin F. was the oldest. Three are now deceased. Of those that grew up, two became ministers of the Gospel, two teachers, and the others farmers. The two ministers are Rev. Edward and Rev. Mathew, both of whom graduated from the Mission House College at Plymouth, Wisconsin, and then entered the ministry of the Reformed Church.

Martin, F. Worthman while a boy on the home farm attended country schools in Preble Township and completed his high school work in the Marion Academy in 1901. He took the standard four year course in the Indiana State Normal College at Terre Haute, graduating in 1911. Mr. Worthman has the natural tendencies and habits of the student, and in the course of his long experience as a school man has constantly broadened his knowledge. He has done a great deal of post-graduate work at the University of Chicago. He began teaching in a country school in Washington Township, in 1902, later taught in his home township, and for a short time was principal of a village school at Clarkshill, Tennessee. His first work in the Decatur schools was as principal of the West Ward School. He took charge of that school in 1908, and in 1909 was made principal of the grammar grades in the Central School Building. In 1911 he became teacher of mathematics in the Decatur High School, and in 1912 was promoted to high school principal. He succeeded Mr. C. E. Spaulding as superintendent of schools of Decatur in 1916. Decatur, like other progressive Indiana cities, has greatly expanded its school plant and carried out a general reorganization of its school facilities in the past twelve or thirteen years, and in that work Mr. Worthman has proved invaluable through his long experience in school administration and as a practical business man.

Mr. Worthman votes the Democratic ticket and affiliated with the Masonic fraternity, being a thirty-second degree Scottish Rite Mason, also a member of the Knights of Pythias. He and his family are members of the Reformed Church. He married Miss Lydia Fruechte, who was born and reared in Preble Township of Adams County, daughter of Henry Fruechte, a farmer. Mr. and Mrs. Worthman have three children, Mildred Susanna, Lillian Sophia and Robert Kenneth. Mildred is attending the Ball Teachers College, taking a course in applied music, and the younger daughter, Lillian, is completing a nurses training course in Indiana University Hospitals at Indianapolis. The son, Robert, born in 1920, is in the sixth grade of the Decatur public schools.

ALBERT W. FUNKHOUSER has exemplified many fine abilities and has rendered many distinguished services while a member of the Evansville bar. He has been a public official, is a banker and business man, and a citizen of exalted patriotism. He was the father of two of Indiana's favorite sons who gave up their lives as supreme sacrifices during the World war.

Albert W. Funkhouser was born in Harrison County, Indiana, October 4, 1863, son of Jacob and Mary L. (Winder) Funkhouser. He is a descendant of John Funkhouser, who came from Switzerland, about 1700. John Funkhouser was the father of Christian Funkhouser and was the grandfather of Moses Funkhouser, who was born in Shenandoah County, Virginia, in 1794, and at the age of seventeen took part in the famous battle of Tippecanoe, when General Harrison destroyed the power of the Indian confederacy in Northern Indiana. Moses Funkhouser was the grandfather of Albert W. Funkhouser.

Jacob Funkhouser was born in Harrison County, Indiana, June 21, 1821, and had the advantages of pioneer schools and spent all his active life as a farmer. He was a very devout Methodist. His wife, Mary L. Winder, was also born in Harrison County. They reared a family of seven children: James L., who died at the age of eighty-two, Zachary T., who died at the age of sixty-five, Hugh C., born in 1854 and died November 10, 1929,

William H., born in 1857, Laura E., who died at the age of forty-one, Albert W., and Arthur F., born in 1866. James L. graduated from Hartsville College, was professor of Latin and Greek in that institution from 1874 to 1886, later entered the Methodist ministry, and retired fifteen years ago, spending his last years at Hartsville, where he died in November, 1927. In his will he bequeathed six thousand dollars to the Methodist Church and also deeded his home to the church. The son, Zachary T., was a graduate of Hartsville College, a doctor of dentistry, and practiced at Columbus, Indiana, and twenty-five years in Evansville. He left a son, Albert T., also a dentist. Hugh C. Funkhouser graduated from Hartsville College, and was in the insurance business until he retired five years ago. His son, William Delbert, is a widely known scientist, an entomologist. William H. Funkhouser graduated from Hartsville College and is a retired physician at Evansville, and has never married. Laura E. married Frank Turner, in the grain business, and their two children are Claud, a banker at Sweetzer, Indiana, and Mary, wife of Harry Duerstalk, connected with the Western Union Company at Fort Wayne. Arthur F. Funkhouser graduated from the law department of DePauw University in 1888, served as prosecuting attorney at Cannelton, and for thirty-five years has been associated with his brother Albert in the practice of law. He is a director of the Howell State Bank and of the Central Union Bank.

Albert W. Funkhouser attended country schools in Harrison County and was graduated with the A. B. degree from DePauw University in 1885. He studied law in the office of Robert J. Tracewille at Corydon, and shortly afterward was elected prosecuting attorney, while in 1888 his partner was chosen a member of Congress and afterwards was for seventeen years comptroller of the United States Treasury by appointment of President McKinley. In 1888 Mr. Funkhouser began practice alone, and in 1891 joined his brother in practice at Evansville. He was city attorney of Evansville for five years, from 1901 to 1906. Mr. Funkhouser is a director of the Mercantile Commercial Bank, the Indiana Trust & Savings Bank, is vice president of the Owensboro City Railroad Company, director of the Evansville, Ohio, Valley Railway Company, and is chairman of the board of directors of Evans Hall. In politics he is a Republican, is chairman of the board of trustees of the Bayard Court Methodist Episcopal Church. Mr. Funkhouser has long been prominent in the Masonic fraternity and was grand master of the State of Indiana in 1925-26, and in September, 1928, at Atlantic City, was given the supreme honorary thirty-third degree in Scottish Rite Masonry. He is a trustee of the Indiana Masonic Home, at Franklin, Indiana.

He married at Leavenworth, Indiana, January 21, 1891, Miss Alta Craig, who is a graduate of the University of Indiana. She is a daughter of Robert M. and Sarah (Breeden) Craig, both natives of Harrison County. Her father was a captain in the Union army. Mr. and Mrs. Funkhouser had a family of six children, and four grew to mature years: Albert Craig, born March 23, 1893, Paul Taylor, born February 21, 1895, Alta, born November 27, 1900, and Ruth, born November 15, 1907. Ruth graduated with the A. B. degree from the University of Indiana in 1927, and from the University of Illinois, and is assistant librarian of the Evansville Public Library. Alta is an A. B. graduate of the University of Indiana, spent one year in the New York Library School, and is the wife of Hubert Arnold, district manager for the Remington-Rand Company, Incorporated.

In the Superior Court room at Evansville is a tablet dedicated to members of the Vanderburg County bar who volunteered their services to their country in the World war, containing thirteen names, and at the head of the list the one Gold Star member is that of Albert C. Funkhouser. Albert C. Funkhouser was born at Leavenworth, Indiana, March 23, 1893, attended the Evansville High School and DePauw University, and was admitted to the bar November 14, 1914. He practiced two years and on April 17, 1917, applied for admission to the Signal Corps of the Aviation School, and a few days later to the First Officers Training Camp at Fort Harrison. Subsequently he volunteered and was with the motor truck company until sent to Camp Bowie at Fort Worth, October 17, 1917. On April 19, 1918, he graduated from the Third Officers Training Camp, was commissioned a second lieutenant May 18, and on September 25, 1918, was assigned to Company B of the 144th Infantry. He embarked for France July 17, 1918, was graduated September 21 from the First Corps Training School at Gondrecourt, and on October 27 was commissioned first lieutenant. He was in the Thirty-sixth Division, bridged with the Fourth French Army, under General Gouraud, and participated in the great Champagne advance from October 6 to October 28, and subsequently in the Meuse Argonne. In a brilliant movement on the night of October 6-7, which brought a citation to the Thirty-sixth Division, Lieutenant Funkhouser was wounded in the right knee and in the right hand, but continued in action. He was awarded the Croix de Guerre by the French Republic for gallantry. On May 25, 1919, he embarked from Brest in charge of a casual company, landed at Newport News June 9, 1919, ill of lobular pneumonia, and died June 15, 1919, at the Embarkation Hospital, Camp Stewart, from the combined effects of pneumonia and poisonous gas inhaled on the battlefield. He was buried with full military honors in Oak Hill Cemetery, Evansville, June 19, 1919.

He was the second occasion of bereavement for the City of Evansville and the Funkhouser family. His younger brother, Paul Taylor Funkhouser, had been killed in action October 20, 1918. Paul Taylor Funkhouser was born February 21, 1895, at Leavenworth, Indiana, attended the Evansville High School, was a student in Northwestern University in 1915-16, and in the Law School of Indiana University in 1916-17. He was chosen a member of the Indiana All-Star High School Foot Ball Team for 1915.

Paul Taylor Funkhouser entered the First Officers Training Camp at Fort Benjamin Harrison, May 12, 1917, being discharged August 14, 1917, to accept commission as second lieutenant in the Infantry Officers Reserve Corps, and on August 27, 1917, was assigned to Company C, Fifty-ninth United States Infantry, Third Division. On January 5, 1918, while at Camp Greene, he was assigned to Company B, Seventh Machine Gun Battalion, Third Division, and proceeded with the battalion to Camp Merritt, March 25, 1918, embarking April 1, 1918. He arrived at Liverpool April 11, reached LeHavre April 15, and on May 30 was ordered to Chateau-Thierry. He remained with the Seventh Machine Gun Battalion continuously during his entire military service in France, participating at Chateau-Thierry, in the Marne offensive and in the St. Mihiel and Meuse Argonne campaigns. He was killed in action in Clire-Chenes Woods while leading an attack on Hill No. 299, October 20, 1918, after having captured the enemy machine guns and at his own request having been assigned to lead Lieutenant Wood's Platoon after that officer had been wounded. In this action every commissioned officer of Company B except Lieutenant Hose was killed or wounded. This was the last action in which the battalion was engaged.

Lieutenant Funkhouser was cited for gallantry—"Kept up liaison with infantry under heavy shell fire," by Major General Robert L. Howze.

Funkhouser Post No. 8 of the American Legion at Evansville is named in honor of Lieutenants Albert C. and Paul T. Funkhouser.

THE WILLARD LIBRARY, one of the most interesting of the institutions expressing the will and purpose of a wealthy Indiana citizen to contribute something permanent to the culture and education of the state was given to the City of Evansville by Willard Carpenter. In 1876 he conveyed to trustees selected by himself property estimated to be worth at that time $400,000. The building was to be located on a tract known as Carpenter's field, the remainder of the tract to be forever kept as a public park. The first board of trustees consisted of Thomas E. Garvin, Alexander Gilchrist, Henry F. Blount, John Laval, Matthew Henning and Charles H. Butterfield.

The foundation of the building was constructed in 1877, but financial troubles interfered with further work until 1882. The building was completed in the fall of 1884, and the library was opened March 28, 1885, more than a year after the death of Mr. Carpenter.

The library has been in continuous operation since its opening. Its circulation has grown with the growth of the city, the number of books distributed last year being 103,-703. The library contains 67,263 volumes.

As a reference library the Willard is second to none in this section of the country. The collection contains many valuable old books and many definite editions of great use to students. The library is in possession of almost complete newspaper files since 1843.

The first librarian was Miss Otilda Goslee. Associated with and succeeding her have been Miss Lou Scantlin, Miss Katharine Imbusch, Mrs. Mary Flower and Mrs. George K. Denton.

The members of the present board are S. G. Evans, A. J. Veneman, D. H. Ortmeyer, S. M. Rutherford, Mrs. James T. Cutler and Mrs. George K. Denton.

The present library staff comprises Mrs. George K. Denton, Miss Mary Gertrude Veneman, Miss Mary Smythe and Miss Mary Van Cleve.

Mrs. George K. Denton, librarian, was born in Boston, is a graduate of Boston University, and married Mr. George K. Denton, former member of Congress from the First Indiana District. Mrs. Denton has two children: Winfield K., an Evansville attorney, is married and has a daughter, Bethia; and Helen is Mrs. George Allen, of Evansville, and mother of two children, Glenn and Linda Mae.

Miss Katharine Imbusch, who has been connected with the Willard Library at Evansville since 1893, was born in that city. She grew up and acquired her schooling in Evansville, and in 1893 became a member of the staff of the Willard Library, and was librarian from November, 1921, until her death, December 8, 1930.

CHARLES PETER LEUTHART, M. D. Good birth and breeding, augmented by comprehensive general and professional training, contribute to the present success and future of Dr. Charles P. Leuthart, a medical and surgical practitioner of New Albany who has followed his calling at this place and Galena, Indiana, for three decades. During his long and active career he has been honored by appointment to numerous offices, and since 1924 has been a member of the board of health of Floyd County.

Doctor Leuthart was born on a farm in Floyd County, Indiana, May 18, 1873, and is a son of Charles and Mary (Rosenberger) Leuthart, both of whom are now deceased. His father, a native of Switzerland, came to the United States in young manhood and secured land in Floyd County, where he passed the remaining years of his life in farming and became one of the highly esteemed citizens of his adopted locality. He married Miss Mary Rosenberger, who was born in Harrison County, and they became the parents of seven children.

Charles P. Leuthart attended the public schools of Floyd County, following which he entered the Kentucky School of Medicine, now the University of Louisville, and was graduated therefrom as a member of the class of 1901, receiving the degree of Doctor of Medicine. In the same year he commenced the practice of his profession at Galena, Indiana, where he remained for twenty-four years, and then removed his residence to New Albany, where he maintains his office at 1410 East Spring Street, although continuing also his practice at Galena. He has a high standing and a large and lucrative practice, is genial and approachable in manner, skillful in diagnosis and treatment, and has completely won the confidence of the most conservative members of the community. Doctor Leuthart was United States pension examiner under President Wilson from 1912 until 1918, and from 1924 to the present has been a member of the Floyd County Board of Health. He is treasurer of the Academy of Medicine, and a member of the Floyd County Medical Society, the Indiana State Medical Society and the American Medical Association, and has several civic and fraternal connections.

Doctor Leuthart married Miss Barbara Best, a native of Indiana, and they are the parents of two children: Valeria Louise and Woodrow Charles, both of whom are attending school.

RUDOLPH W. MEISINGER has been the county engineer under whose technical supervision all the hard surfaced paved roads of Vanderburgh County have been constructed. Mr. Meisinger has had a wide experience in his profession and has been in construction work at many different times over the country.

He was born in Pekin, Illinois, February 15, 1882. His parents, Adam and Elizabeth Meisinger, came from Germany, were married in this country, and his father, now eighty-two years of age, has spent the greater part of his active life as a contractor and builder. There were four children in the family: Alma, Rudolph, John and Roy. Alma is the wife of George Kickler, of Pekin, Illinois, and John and Roy live in Ohio. Roy was in France eighteen months during the World war.

Rudolph W. Meisinger attended grade and high schools at Pekin, Illinois. His engineering training was acquired in practical work for his father in the contracting business. For two years he was a draftsman at Terre Haute, Indiana, and for four years assistant city engineer, from 1906 to 1910. His engineering work has taken him to all parts of the United States. During 1910-11 he was engineer of construction for the Big Four Railway Company. During 1912-13 he was general foreman for the Ohio River Contracting Company, and in 1916-17 was construction foreman with the Arnold Construction Company of Chicago. He was doing essential work when America entered the World war, and in 1918 he was transferred to the direct service of the Government at Nashville, Tennessee, in charge of the skilled mechanics at the powder plant, having the responsibility of overseeing 3,500 men in the mechanical division there. After the close of the war and the shutting down of this plant

John A Newhouse M.D.

he took up work for the State Highway Commission as a locating engineer one year, during 1920 was construction engineer for the Standard Oil Company, and in 1921 was appointed special engineer for Vanderburg County for hard road construction. All of the modern highways of Vanderburg County have been built since the close of the war, and Mr. Meisinger has been the official who has supplied the technical planning and supervision for practically all of that work. In November, 1922, he was elected county engineer, and has been reelected to that office in 1924, 1926 and 1928.

Mr. Meisinger is a Republican, is a member of the Evangelical Church, and is a Lodge and Royal Arch Chapter Mason. He married in July, 1911, Miss Carrie Seiffer, daughter of August and Elizabeth Seiffer. Their two children, both attending school, are Elizabeth C., born September 8, 1913, and Katherine L., born April 15, 1915.

SAMUEL CHESTER WENTZELL. Well known in Floyd County, Indiana, is S. Chester Wentzell, one of the younger members of the bar at New Albany, a graduate of the University of Kentucky, at Louisville, a lawyer of recognized ability, and something of a leader in civic matters in his community. Although born in Kentucky, most of his life has been passed in the Hoosier State. He is of Colonial settlement and Revolutionary stock and can trace an ancestral line back to the Empire of Austria, whence his paternal forefathers came to America and became residents of Pennsylvania as early, perhaps, as 1682. In after years their descendants migrated to Virginia and many served under General Washington in the War of the American Revolution. In still later generations the Wentzells became people of importance in other states, and in 1907 the parents of S. Chester Wentzell came to New Albany from their old home of many years in Kentucky. On the maternal side, also, Mr. Wentzell can claim ancestral distinction, for his mother's people, the Lords, belong to the same branch of a sturdy old English family that gave to the world that immortal poet, Alfred Tennyson.

S. Chester Wentzell was born at Louisville, Kentucky, May 24, 1905, and is a son of William A. and Emily (Lord) Wentzell. The family first settled in Pennsylvania, but moved to Kentucky about 1849, and in that state William A. Wentzell was born. In young manhood he became identified with the tobacco industry, in which he became a prominent figure, and for a number of years made his home at Louisville. He became vice president of the Tobacco Rehandling Company of Louisville, and still retains that position, although since 1907 he has made his home at New Albany, where he likewise has large and important interests. He married Miss Emily Lord, and they became the parents of six children.

S. Chester Wentzell was about two years of age when brought by his parents to New Albany, where he attended the parochial and high schools. Subsequently he entered the University of Kentucky, at Lexington, from which he was graduated with the degree of Bachelor of Laws as a member of the class of 1925, and in 1926 was admitted to the bar. Since then he has been engaged in the practice of his profession, with an office in the Second National Bank Building, and has been successful in building up a large, important and representative clientele. In the litigation in which he has been engaged as counsel he has shown the possession of marked ability, and is making rapid strides in his calling. He is a member of the Floyd County Bar Association, Indiana State and the American Bar Associations. An ardent Democrat in politics, he was appointed, in 1931, city attorney.

JOHN A. NEWHOUSE, physician and surgeon, has built up a successful practice and enjoys some prominent associations with the professional life and community affairs of Hammond, and is a member of the staff of St. Catherine's Hospital of East Chicago. Doctor Newhouse came to Hammond from Chicago and earlier was a professional man of Ontario, Canada.

He was born at Brampton, Ontario, March 22, 1898, and is descended from one of the oldest of the French families of Montreal. His great-grandfather was Antoine Maisonneuve, which is the French form for the word Newhouse. The Maisonneuve family history runs back to the very beginning of Montreal and the old French regime in the Saint Lawrence Valley. Doctor Newhouse's father was John Newhouse. Antoine Maisonneuve had a grant of land given him for his service as a soldier in the War of 1812.

The parents of Doctor Newhouse were lifelong residents of Ontario, and his father was a farmer there and quite active in local politics. He held the position of reeve in his township for a number of years, and later for one year was warden of the county. He was a Baptist. He died November 7, 1924, and the mother of Doctor Newhouse passed away September 22, 1924. They are buried at Snelgrove, Canada. Jessie (Groat) Newhouse was also of a pioneer Canadian family. There were two children, Dr. John A. and Wilfred, the latter of whom died in 1929, at the age of twenty-nine years.

John A. Newhouse attended school in his native community, graduating from the Brampton High School in 1914, and completed his professional preparation in Toronto University in 1921. In the meantime, during the World war, he was enrolled in the Officers Training School at Toronto University and his time was taken up with military training until after the armistice, when he resumed his medical studies. He had his interne work in Toronto General Hospital. Doctor Newhouse practiced medicine and surgery in Northern Ontario, until 1924. During 1925-29 he was located in Chicago and in the latter year moved to Indiana Harbor and Hammond, becoming one of the physicians of the Indiana Harbor Clinic. His offices are at 6445½ Kennedy Avenue, where he also has his home. He is a member of the Lake County Medical Society. Doctor Newhouse is independent in politics and is a member of the Baptist Church and a Mason.

He married at Toronto, September 22, 1923, Miss Madeline McConnell, daughter of William and Amelia (Evans) McConnell, formerly of Toronto, now of Chicago. Her father spent many years with the Ellis Brothers establishment of Toronto, but since 1928 has been in the mercantile business in Chicago. Mrs. Newhouse attended public school at Toronto, completing the work of the High School of Commerce there. She is a member of the Ladies Clubs of the United Presbyterian Church at Hammond. Doctor Newhouse's favorite sports are golf, baseball, fishing and hunting. They have two children, John Robert and William Eugene, both students in the Hammond public schools.

WILLIAM FRANCIS EDWARDS, M. D. Among the various branches of professional knowledge on which civilized humanity is more or less dependent for the maintenance of healthful conditions and for exemption from physical distress, medicine and surgery play a leading part. Careless habits of living, indulgence in articles of food and drink that are detrimental to the bodily organs, and the changed conditions of modern existence make the physician and surgeon indispensable. Moreover, the doctor of today must keep fully abreast of the latest achievements in his profession. He must add skill to thorough research and combine close application to his task with the ability gained through experience. Such a practitioner is Dr. William Francis Edwards, a specialist in the treatment of the eye, ear, nose and throat, who has been attached to the staff of Saint Edward's Hospital, at New Albany, since 1929.

Doctor Edwards was born January 4, 1901, at Anniston, Alabama, and is a son of William Thomas and Laura Frances (Coker) Edwards. The family originated in England, whence came the first American progenitors in Colonial days, taking up their homes in Virginia. Later members of the family migrated to various parts of the United States, following the close of the Revolutionary war, and for the most part have been business and professional men.

William Francis Edwards received his early education in the public schools of Alabama, and after his graduation from high school entered the University of Alabama, where he completed his literary course and received the degree of Bachelor of Arts in 1921. He then enrolled as a student of the medical department of Emory University, from which he was graduated with the degree of Doctor of Medicine in 1925, but was not yet satisfied with his preparation for his profession, and therefore spent more than three years of internship, one year of general work, at the Grady Hospital, Atlanta, Georgia, and eighteen months at the Piedmont Hospital, Atlanta, in special work. This was followed by postgraduate work in eye, ear, nose and throat at several Florida state institutions, and April 1, 1929, he settled permanently at New Albany, Indiana, where he has been engaged in practice of a private character and also as a member of the staff of St. Edward's Hospital, confining himself to his specialty, in which he has acquired a broad and substantial reputation. Through hard work and close application Doctor Edwards has won a recognized position among medical men of Indiana, and it has likewise been his fortune to gain the confidence and esteem of the people of his adopted community. He is a member of the Aesculapius Medical Society, the Indiana State Medical Society and the Floyd County Medical Society, the Phi Chi medical fraternity and Anniston, Alabama, Lodge No. 700, A. F. and A. M. During the World war he was a member of the Student Army Training Corps. In politics a stanch Democrat, he has been steadfast in his support of the principles and candidates of his party, but has never sought office or preferment.

Doctor Edwards was united in marriage with Miss Lucy Elizabeth Moore, a native of Georgia, and a direct descendant of the distinguished old Colonial Virginia family of that name. Their attractive home at New Albany is situated at 2408 East Spring Street. They have one daughter, Dorothy Ann, born March 15, 1928.

CHARLES D. KNOEFEL. As a community passes out of its embryo and assumes a stable position, when the frontier settlement has become one of the leading centers of a great and productive region, there arises an insistent call for banking and trust institutions with large capital, carefully guarded by law, and for managers learned in the principles of monetary science and trained in the intricate business of the bank. With this mode of growth and such management one would look, as the community increased, for greater stability and wiser management, and when it had grown to the dimensions of a commercial and financial center, one would expect to find solidity, permanence and solvency in banking institutions, and matured experience and trained and expert skill in their management. The evolution of banking at New Albany is but a process of such natural growth and a realization of such expectations, and this applies emphatically to the New Albany Trust Company, the able president of which is Charles D. Knoefel, one of Floyd County's leading citizens.

Mr. Knoefel was born at New Albany, in December, 1858, and is a son of Dr. August and Wilhelmina (Merker) Knoefel. His father, a native of Germany, left the Fatherland about the time of the overthrow of the revolution in that country, in 1848, when such noted patriots as Carl Schurz and others sought sanctuary in the United States. For a time August Knoefel lived at Pittsburgh, Pennsylvania, but in 1857 moved to New Albany, Indiana, where he passed the remaining years of his life in the drug business. He was a man who was held in the highest esteem in his community, was well read and highly intelligent, and took an active part in civic betterment. He and his wife, who was also born in Germany, were the parents of seven children.

Charles D. Knoefel attended the public schools of New Albany, after leaving which he pursued a course at the College of Pharmacy, at Louisville, Kentucky. Returning to New Albany, he became associated with his father in the drug business, and remained with the elder man until 1885, at which time he established a pharmacy of his own. During the next twenty-eight years he built this up to large proportions and developed one of the most modern drug stores in the state, at the same time establishing himself firmly in the confidence of his fellow citizens as a man of honor and high character. When he retired from this enterprise, in 1913, it was a wholesale and retail business employing eighteen people and shipping its products all over the state. It is still in business but operating under a different name and management. Mr. Knoefel is a man of great organizing ability and was organizer and first president of the Louisville Home Telephone Company, and was a member of the board of directors and president of the New Albany Home Telephone Company from the time of its organization until it was sold to the Bell Telephone Company. He was elected president at the time of the organization, in 1921, of the American Securities Company, and occupied that position until the time of his retirement from the company in 1928, and was a director of the Seelbach Realty Company up to the time of its selling out. In 1914 Mr. Knoefel was made president of the New Albany Trust Company, and has remained in the same capacity to the present, this being an institution with a capital of $50,000. He is also a member of the board of directors of the Second National Bank of New Albany, chairman of the board of trustees of the Masonic Temple Association and for several years was commissioner of the sinking fund of New Albany. He is a past president of the Commercial Club, and although he has reached the age when most men are willing to give over life's tasks to those of the younger generation, is still possessed of an active body and an alert mind that allow him to participate fully and constructively in all movements fostered for the benefit of the community and its people. He is a thirty-third degree Mason, being a member of De-Pauw Lodge, A. F. and A. M.; New Albany Chapter, R. A. M.; Indiana Council, R. and S. M.; New Albany Commandery, K. T.; Indiana Consistory, S. S. R. M., and Knights

of Constantine, thirty-third degree, and Murat Temple, A. A. O. N. M. S., of which he is jester. He has passed through all the bodies and offices of Masonry and is one of the best known men of this order in the state, having been a past grand illustrious master of the Council in 1913. He is also a past exalted ruler of the Benevolent and Protective Order of Elks and a former president of the Hall Maenerchor Company. He is past president of the New Albany Rotary Club and one of its organizers. He maintains offices in the New Albany Trust Company Building.

Mr. Knoefel's first wife was Miss Mary Lang, who died in 1920, without issue. The present Mrs. Knoefel was formerly Miss Teckla Henry, of New Albany.

BENJAMIN LEWIS HARRISON, physician and surgeon, is a native of Indiana, and has earned a high reputation in his profession since locating at Newcastle.

He was born at Danville, Indiana, May 23, 1898, son of Francis Marion and Hattie May (Thomas) Harrison. His parents were born in Hendricks County, Indiana, and his father is a retired farmer at Danville. Doctor Harrison was educated in the grade and high schools and the Central Indiana Normal College at Danville. He was graduated with the A. B. degree from Indiana University and took his degree in medicine in 1924. For one year he was an interne in the Indianapolis City Hospital and remained with that institution two more years as resident surgeon. In March, 1927, he engaged in private practice at Newcastle, where his offices are in the Jennings Building.

Doctor Harrison is a member of the Henry County, Indiana State and American Medical Associations. During the World war he was sent for training to the Great Lakes Naval Training Station near Chicago in May, 1918, and was assigned duty in the Hospital Corps. He received his discharge in August, 1919, as a third class pharmacist's mate. Doctor Harrison is a member of the American Legion, the Sons of the American Revolution, is a Methodist, a Republican, a Scottish Rite Mason, member of the B. P. O. Elks, Modern Woodmen of America, the Columbia Club of Indianapolis, is a director of the Kiwanis Club, and his college fraternities are the Phi Beta Phi and Alpha Omega Alpha.

Doctor Harrison married, September 12, 1928, Miss Florence Catherine Bufkin, who was born at Middletown, Indiana, daughter of Samuel J. Bufkin.

Mr. Samuel J. Bufkin, postmaster of Newcastle, was born at Zionsville, Indiana, June 20, 1874, son of Oliver and Catherine (Thornton) Bufkin, both natives of Henry County. His paternal grandparents, Samuel and Catherine (Kinnick) Bufkin, came from Pennsylvania to Henry County and were members of the Quakers or Friends Church. Mr. Bufkin's grandfather, George Thornton, was born in Henry County, Kentucky, and settled at Flat Rock in Henry County, Indiana. Oliver Buf-

230

INDIANA

kin was a carpenter. He died in May, 1900, and his wife in September, 1929.

Samuel J. Bufkin attended public schools and at the age of fourteen began learning the cigar maker's trade. This was his working occupation for six years, and for eight years he worked as a heater and rougher in a rolling mill. He then established a cigar factory in Newcastle and conducted that business for eighteen years. Mr. Bufkin was appointed postmaster in 1922 and was reappointed for a second term in 1926. He has always taken an active part in Republican politics and for eight and a half years was a member of the City Council. He is a member of the Friends Church, belongs to the B. P. O. Elks, Knights of Pythias, Fraternal Order of Eagles, the Rotary Club and the Chamber of Commerce.

He married, January 1, 1900, Alegra Parker, who was born at Lewisville in Henry County, daughter of Benjamin F. and Hulda (Vickersham) Parker, both natives of Henry County. Mr. and Mrs. Bufkin have two children, Florence Catherine, wife of Doctor Harrison, and Samuel Parker. Mrs. Bufkin has been a leader in woman's club work and is secretary of the Newcastle Historical Society.

RICHARD WOOD HARRIS, M. D. The dean of the medical profession in Pike County, is Dr. Wood Harris, of Algiers. Doctor Harris has to his credit a career of professional activity covering more than half a century. All that time he has been the devoted doctor and friend of the community where he now resides.

Doctor Harris was born at Dale, Spencer County, Indiana, October 28, 1848. His father William G. Harris, was a Virginian by birth, and was an early settler in Spencer County, locating there about 1832. He was a cabinet maker by trade, and one of the worthy and industrious citizens of that community. He lived to be eighty-four years of age, passing away in 1886. The mother of Doctor Harris was Isabelle McQuon, who was born in Kentucky, and also lived to be eighty-four years of age, passing away in 1901. Of her eleven children three died in infancy, and those to grow up were George W., Edward J., Benjamin F., deceased, Dr. Richard W., William M., James F., deceased, Sarah E., and Samuel deceased. George, a resident of Gentryville, Spencer County, married Nancy Daniels and has seven children. Edward, of Petersburg, married Sarah Brown and had one child. William, of Gentryville, is married and has six children. Sarah E., is Mrs. Milton Lemon and the mother of four children.

Richard Wood Harris derived his early advantages from the public schools at Dale, attended high school at Huntingburg, and largely through his own efforts and earnings paid his way through the Louisville Medical College, where he was graduated with the M. D. degree in 1877. On getting his medical diploma Doctor Harris located at Algiers, and that community has known him as its stanch friend in time of need for more than fifty-three years. He has always had a large medi-

cal practice, and has worn out many horses, vehicles and in later years automobiles in attending to his work. He still drives his own car and he works, acts and looks like a man only fifty instead of only four score. Doctor Harris married, June 8, 1880, Miss Loualla A. Lett, daughter of Isaac and Elizabeth (Traylor) Lett. She was born in Pike County, Indiana. By this marriage Doctor Harris has eight children: Maude, John, Audrey (who died at the age of eighteen months), Sarah J., Ben F., Ruth, Simon and Virgil. On April 27, 1901, Doctor Harris married Ada Hall, and of this marriage there are two children, Lena and Harry.

Doctor Harris has always voted the Democratic ticket. For eleven years in addition to his duties as a doctor he served as township trustee. He is a member of the Presbyterian Church, is affiliated with the Independent Order of Odd Fellws and Knights of Pythias, and belongs to the Pike County, Indiana State and American Medical Asociations. Doctor Harris owns and supervises 200 acres of farming land in Pike County.

GROVER E. SALB, member of one of Dubois County's best known families, his father and several of his brothers having attained eminent positions in the medical profession, was liberally educated but chose a business rather than a professional career. Mr. Salb has been the man largely responsible for the building up of an important manufacturing industry at Jasper, the Indiana Desk Company of which he is manager.

He was born at Jasper, November 6, 1892, son of Dr. John P. and Margaret (Bell) Salb. His father for many years practiced as a physician and surgeon at Jasper, and his great skill as a surgeon earned him election as a fellow of the American College of Surgeons. He and his wife had the following children: May, Dr. John A., Dr. Leo A., Dr. Oscar G., Vic M., Grover E., Ardella, Aurelius (now deceased,) and Dr. Max. Dr. John A., is practicing medicine at Indianapolis and is a graduate of Purdue University. Dr. John A. and Vic M., were both World war veterans. Dr. Leo A., also a World war veteran, is an able physician at Jasper. Dr. Oscar G., a graduate of St. Louis University, practices at Seymour. Vic M., is a graduate of Purdue University and is in business at Jasper. Dr. Max graduated from the medical department of Indiana University and is practicing at Indianapolis.

Grover E. Salb attended public schools in Jasper and attended Purdue University in 1911-12. The first line of work he took up was the automobile business. He became widely known as a skillful driver, and engaged in automobile racing and was one of the drivers in the 500-mile races at the Indianapolis Speedway in 1913 and 1914.

Mr. Salb in 1915 joined the Indiana Desk Company at Jasper. His father was one of the chief owners of this business and industry. With the death of his father in 1927 Mr. Salb

Francis J Dorsey

succeeded to the active management and control of the business, being now secretary and general manager of the Indiana Desk Company. His work with this company was interrupted by his participation for fifteen months in the World war, assigned to the Ninety-first Division, overseas, and seven months in the Army of Occupation.

Mr. Salb married, September 4, 1919, Miss Lucille Beckman, daughter of Henry Beckman. They have four children: Thomas, born in 1920; Earl, born in 1924; Mary Jane, born in 1926; and John P., born in 1928.

Mr. Salb is a Democrat, is a member of the Catholic Church, and has affiliations with the B. P. O. Elks, also with the American Legion, of which he has served as post commander. He is also a member of La Societé de 40 Hommes et 8 Chevaux. He has also served as a director of the local Chamber of Commerce. In addition to his active connection with the Indiana Desk Company he is a director of the New Indiana Chair Company.

FRANCIS J. DORSEY has won a prominent position in the Hammond bar. However, his first association with Hammond, and one long continued, was in the railroad service. He has a veteran's record as a railroad man, having given a quarter of a century to his work in connection with the great industrial and belt line railways of Northern Indiana and the Chicago industrial area.

Mr. Dorsey was born at Chatham, Ontario, Canada, of American parentage, July 21, 1879. The Dorsey family came from Ireland, and lived for many years at Brooklyn, New York. His grandfather, John Dorsey, was born in that city, attended school there and for many years was connected with the industry of white lead manufacture. He was killed in an accident in a lead plant. He and his wife are buried at Brooklyn. Joseph Dorsey, father of the Hammond attorney, was born and reared at Brooklyn, attended public and parochial schools there, and graduated from St. Xavier's College. His permanent home for many years was at Detroit, Michigan. He was in the lumber industry, and logged off great tracts of timber land in Canada. He married in Detroit and his home for only a few years was at Chatham, Ontario. He was a member of the Catholic Mutual Benefit Association of Detroit. During the World's Fair in 1893 he moved to Chicago and in 1903 to Hammond. He has been retired for a number of years and since 1930 he and his wife have lived with their daughter in Milwaukee, Wisconsin. Joseph Dorsey married Magdalen Pickard. The Pickard family were among the first settlers of what is now Detroit, locating there when the central feature of that settlement was Fort Gratiot. Mrs. Dorsey is a daughter of Amos and Susan (McMullen) Pickard, and the McMullens were also early settlers of Detroit. Her father was a stationary engineer. Mrs. Joseph Dorsey attended public school in Detroit. She was a Methodist until her marriage and since then has been a loyal Catholic convert. Her four children are: William W., of Berwyn, Illinois; Francis J.; Marie Theresa, wife of A. J. Buck, of Milwaukee; and Joseph Alphonsus, a contractor in plumbing and steam fitting in Hammond.

Francis J. Dorsey attended public school both in Detroit and Canada and in 1894 was graduated from the high school of Niles, Michigan. Mr. Dorsey has always had the habit of work, has been actuated by a high purpose and ambition, and has shown the disposition to make the most of his opportunities and advantages in whatever situation he has been. When only nine years of age he began working after school hours and in vacations as water boy and timekeeper for Roadmaster Hagan of the Toledo Division of the Michigan Central Railway. Subsequently he became a clerk under his uncle, Alonzo Pickard, then superintendent of bridges and buildings for the railroad. After completing his high school work he continued railroading. When the Michigan Central built the Chappel yards on the Chicago West Side he was sent there as clerk in the transportation department. The terminal facilities of the Michigan Central and other roads were eventually consolidated as the Indiana Harbor Belt Railway Company, and Mr. Dorsey was promoted from time to time until he was made joint agent for the Michigan Central, Chicago Junction Railway, Chicago Terminal Transfer Company, now the Baltimore & Ohio Chicago Terminal, the Chicago, Peoria & Western, Santa Fe, and Dolese & Shepherd Terminal Railway. In 1903 he came to Hammond as accountant for the Chicago Junction Railway, now the Indiana Harbor Belt, and in 1905 was sent to Indiana Harbor as agent. In 1906 he was transferred to Gibson in the same capacity, and continued there until 1912. This completed a quarter of a century of work for railroad companies, starting from the age of nine years. While at Gibson he performed the duties of auditor, paymaster (without bond) and handled millions of dollars of funds for the road, and for several years signed all the checks for pay day.

His railroad career came to an end in 1912, merging immediately into the professional career of a lawyer. While working in railroad offices he took up the study of law, attended night school in Chicago and also at Hammond, and in 1912 was graduated from the Lincoln-Jefferson College of Law at Hammond. The instructors in this college were also members of the faculty of Valparaiso University, and eventually that university took over the Law College. Mr. Dorsey began practice at Hammond and is a member of the firm McAleer, Dorsey, Clark & Travis, with offices in the First Trust Building.

Mr. Dorsey is a third and fourth degree Knight of Columbus, being a member of Unity Council No. 726, and Abraham Lincoln General Assembly. He is a member of the Order of the Alhambra, Boabdil Caravan No. 9 at Chicago and the Catholic Order of Forresters,

Court Luers No. 111 of Hammond. He belongs to Hammond Lodge No. 570, Loyal Order of Moose, the Mooseheart Legion of the World, Victory Legion No. 48, is a member of Hammond Lodge No. 485, B. P. O. Elks. He votes as a Republican and is a member of All-Saints Catholic Church. He is a sports fan, particularly outdoor athletics, and personally enjoys fishing. In younger years he displayed much talent as a musician, and played the violin and banjo. His fellow members of the bar have a high degree of confidence in Mr. Dorsey, one tribute being that he is an "honest and square shooter."

He married at Hammond, October 12, 1904, Miss Anna Kunzmann, daughter of Fred and Marie Kunzmann. Her father was a Hammond merchant and died in 1912, and his wife in 1927, being buried in the Oak Hill Cemetery. Mrs. Dorsey attended public school at Hammond. She was reared a Lutheran, but became a Catholic. She died on Thanksgiving Day, November 28, 1918, and is buried in Oak Hill Cemetery. She left a daughter, Marie Lydia, who is now Mrs. Joseph Millstone, of Hammond. Mr. Millstone is sales manager for the Gary Heat, Light & Water Company at Gary, but resides in Hammond. Mr. and Mrs. Millstone were married in December, 1930. She is a graduate nurse of St. Margaret's Hospital of Hammond and is classified as a registered nurse.

Mr. Dorsey on July 14, 1923, at Hammond, married Miss Florence O. Ramsey, of Harrisburg, Illinois, daughter of Walter and Margaret Pearl (Fox) Ramsey, who now reside at Omaha, Illinois. Mrs. Dorsey attended public school in Harrisburg, including high school, and is a graduate trained nurse and practiced her profession in Illinois until her marriage. She was formerly a member of the Christian Church, but became a convert to the Catholic faith and is now a member of All Saints Church of Hammond. Mr. and Mrs. Dorsey have three children, Francis Joseph, Jr., a pupil in the All Saints parochial school, John Walter and Margaret Pearl.

ZEPH E. KELLER is an Indianapolis attorney, has practiced law in that city for the past fifteen years, and came to Indianapolis from Western Indiana, where he was born and reared and where his people have lived since pioneer times.

He was born in Clay County, December 26, 1878, son of Alfred and Malinda (Orman) Keller. His father was born in Owen County, Indiana, and his mother at Ormanville, Iowa, a little community named for her family. She was a daughter of David and Nancy (Houck) Orman, early settlers of Iowa. Mr. Keller's paternal grandparents were Henry and Elizazeth (Minnick) Keller, the former a native of Putnamville, Indiana, and the latter of Virginia. Henry Keller was a pioneer tanner at Putnamville. Alfred Keller is a retired farmer living at Howesville, Indiana. His wife died in 1887.

Zeph E. Keller was educated in district schools, was an Indiana farm boy, and at an early age learned to rely upon his own initiative for his education and advancement. He had one year of high school work in the Central Normal College at Danville. Among other early experiences he spent four years with the *Clay City Democrat* and at the same time studied law. His work in the offices of Gardner and Storm was supplemented by courses in the American Central Law School at Indianapolis, where he was graduated in 1914. Mr. Keller first practiced with offices in the Hume-Mansur and is now located in the Inland Bank Building. He is a member of the Indiana Bar Association and for a time acted as deputy prosecuting attorney of Clay County. He is a Democrat, a Royal Arch Mason and a Sigma Delta Kappa.

He married, in June, 1905, Miss Lena Benham, who was born at Clay City, daughter of Jesse R. and Flora (Goshorn) Benham, her father a native of Ripley County and her mother of Owen County, Indiana. Mr. and Mrs. Keller have six children, Paul B., William W., Jessie M., Eleanor Alice, Robert R. and James Robertson. The family are members of the Presbyterian Church.

DR. EDWARD H. WHITE, osteopath, is one of the ablest representatives of his profession in Henry County, Indiana. Doctor White was born in Hendricks County, Indiana, in 1907, son of Arthur and Nell (Chambers) White. His father was born at Greenfield, Indiana, and his mother in Hendricks County, and his father has spent his active life as a farmer.

Edward H. White was graduated from high school in 1925. This was followed by a course in osteopathy and surgery and in June, 1927, he completed his preparation as an osteopath. He began practice with Dr. Milton C. Hanmer at Newcastle, with offices in the Union Building. Doctor White is a member of the Friends Church, is a Republican in politics and is affiliated with the Masonic fraternity.

ALBERT A. O'BRIEN was an Indiana florist, and for many years carried on his business at Union City. Since his death this business has been continued under the competent direction of Mrs. O'Brien, who had worked with him and is a thoroughly qualified florist.

The late Mr. O'Brien was born in Darke County, Ohio, in 1868. His father, Cornelius O'Brien, came from Ireland. He married after coming to the United States, his wife being an English woman. They then settled on a farm in Darke County, Ohio, where their son, Albert A., spent his early years.

Mr. Albert O'Brien had a common school education. The first occupation he took up was the trade of florist. After learning it he went to Denver, Colorado, and operated a greenhouse at University Park in Denver. About 1899, returning to Indiana, he went to the rose city of Newcastle and was employed in the extensive greenhouses of Heller Brothers. From there he came to Union City, where

H A Johnson

he established a business of his own. Mr. O'Brien had an expert knowledge of the production of flowers, and he specialized in the growing of flowers for funeral designs. In 1905 he built the greenhouse at 907 West Pearl Street in Union City, and the business has been carried on there for a quarter of a century. Mr. O'Brien passed away November 20, 1924.

He married in 1909 Miss Anna Zicht, who was born in Union City, daughter of Henry Zicht. Her father came from Germany and was a bricklayer by trade. Mrs. O'Brien was educated in public schools. She is a member of the Lutheran Church, and is an independent voter with leanings toward the Republican party.

WILLIAM N. McMAHAN was born at Lawrenceburg, Indiana, the son of Rev. S. S. and Victoria (Boulware) McMahan, he born in Union County, Indiana, and she in Clermont County, Ohio. The paternal grandparents, Elijah B. and Charity (Beck) McMahan, were born in North Carolina, and he was a son of Morgan McMahan, the latter of whom came to Union County, Indiana, from Salisbury, North Carolina, about 1819 and here bought a tract of land, his brothers at about the same time making entries of Government lands.

This was before the creation of Union County, the territory now included within the county lines being attached to other counties. The maternal grandparents, Benjamin and Ann Boulware, natives of New Jersey, came as far west as Clermont County, Ohio, and there the remainder of their lives was passed. The parents of Mr. McMahan moved about considerably, as this was the custom of the Methodist ministry. Both father and mother died at Liberty, however, the former in 1882; the latter in 1916.

William N. McMahan having prepared himself for a teacher began his work as such at nineteen years of age, and has continued in this profession for thirty years, with the exception of 1914 to 1918, when he held the office of county treasurer. For the past thirteen years he has been superintendent of the Union School of College Corner, Ohio.

Mr. McMahan is an official member of the Liberty Methodist Episcopal Church, a trustee of the Public Library, and a member of the Indiana and the Ohio State Teachers Associations.

ALBERT T. RUMBACH, who was an Indiana soldier overseas during the World war, has during the decade since the close of the war found opportunity for usefulness in his native community of Jasper, Dubois County, as manager and editor of the *Jasper Herald*.

Mr. Rumbach was born at Jasper September 14, 1895. His father, Christian Rumbach, was a native of Germany and was a soldier in the Franco-Prussian war of 1870-71. In 1880 he brought his family to America, and from that time until his death, thirty years later,

was a prosperous and influential farmer at Jasper, Indiana. He died in 1910. He married, in Germany, Mary Hettich, who is still living. They were the parents of twelve children, two born in Germany and ten in Dubois County, Indiana.

Albert Thomas Rumbach was the eighth in this large family of children. As a boy he attended parochial schools, and completed his literary work in St. Meinrad College in Spencer County, and after graduating there took a course in journalism at Marquette University at Milwaukee.

During the World war Mr. Rumbach enlisted with the engineers and was sent overseas, spending eleven months in France, attached to the general headquarters. He returned home and received his discharge at Camp Grant, Illinois, April 1, 1919, and just a month later, on May 1, returned to Jasper and took charge of the *Jasper Herald* as manager and editor. His training in journalism, his experience as a man among men have enabled him to give to the *Herald* unusual qualities as a newspaper. The *Herald* was established in 1895.

Mr. Rumbach is a member of the Indiana Weekly Press Association, and has found various opportunities of expressing his civic interests in the community. He is a member of the Chamber of Commerce, the American Legion, of which he has served as commander, is a Democrat, a Catholic and Knight of Columbus. On October 20, 1920, he married Miss Cecilia Kramer, of Chicago. They have three children, John Thomas, born July 24, 1923, Edwin Joseph, born November 19, 1925, and Margaret Mary, born April 17, 1927.

HANS A. JOHNSON is a Hammond business man who has raised himself from the obscurity of a worker in the ranks to success and influence. Mr. Johnson is a native of Norway, but came to America as the land of opportunity and has found in this country the opportunities for individual initiative and has made his name respected and honored in Hammond, where he is president and the principal stockholder in the Johnson Transfer & Fireproof Storage Company.

He was born at Oslo, Norway, August 1, 1874, son of John and Andrina (Olson) Johnson. His parents spent all their lives in Norway. They were educated in public schools, and his father was a dairy farmer. His father died in 1902 and his mother in 1910. Of their eleven children one died in childhood, and Anna Olson passed away in 1929. All the others are living.

Hans A. Johnson was the fourth in this large family. He acquired a public school education in his native country. At the age of eighteen he came to America. His first location was at Minneapolis, Minnesota, where for four years he was an employee of the Street Railway Company. He then returned to Norway, but after five years in his native land again sought the opportunities of the new world in 1905, and this time he located at Hammond, Indiana. Here because of his previous experience he found employment with the Street Railway Company. He resigned in 1917 in order to establish the Johnson trucking business. He has built this up, gradually extending the service and increasing his facilities. In 1927 the company built a large fireproof storage warehouse on Douglas Street, with railroad switching facilities. The Johnson Transfer & Fireproof Storage Company now has one of the best equipped plants in Northern Indiana, with 45,000 square feet of floor space.

Mr. Johnson is active in the Hammond Chamber of Commerce. He is affiliated with the Knights of Pythias and B. P. O. Elks, is a member of the Lake Hills Country Club, votes as a Republican, and he and his family are members of the Trinity Lutheran Church. He is an animal lover, and all his life he has been very fond of horses.

Mr. Johnson married at Hammond, December 22, 1917, Mrs. Anna Prohl. She is a daughter of Herman and Anna Werner, formerly of Riverdale, Illinois, where her father was one of the early settlers and for many years in business as a general merchant. Both her parents are buried in Riverdale. Mrs. Johnson attended public school at Riverdale and has always been a loyal Lutheran in religion. Her first husband, John Prohl, died in 1913 and was buried at Hammond. By this marriage she had two children, John and Virginia Prohl. John spent two terms in the Valparaiso University, and is now associated with Mr. Johnson in the storage and transfer business. He is unmarried. Miss Virginia, now at home, is a cultured and highly educated young woman. After graduating from the Hammond High School she attended the Rockford College for Women at Rockford, Illinois, and finished her education in Indiana University.

DANIEL W. BELL, M. D. A well-known and highly valued member of the medical profession in Pike County, Indiana, is Dr. Daniel W. Bell, physician and surgeon at Otwell, a veteran of the World war, and now a major in the United States Medical Reserve Corps. Doctor Bell is a native of Indiana, a descendand of old pioneer families, and the greater part of his busy, useful life has been spent in his native state. Son of a veteran of the war between the state, and one of a large family, his early educational opportunities were confined to the local schools but, largely through his own determined efforts, he was graduated with honor from a well-known medical school when but twenty-six years old. From that time until the present he has been devoted to his profession, and for twelve years the residents of the pleasant, thriving little City of Otwell have profited by his sound medical knowledge, surgical skill and general good citizenship.

Doctor Bell was born in Pike County, Indiana, January 28, 1878, a son of William M. Bell, the latter of whom was born in 1840, in the same county as his son, was a farmer by occupation, and died in 1899. During the war between the states he served in the One Hundred and Forty-fourth Indiana Volunteer Infantry. The Bell family migrated from North Carolina to Indiana prior to the birth of William M. Bell, and were pioneers of Pike County. The mother of Doctor Bell, Mrs. Mary J. (Lomax) Bell, was born in Pike County, in 1840, and died in 1908, having borne her husband twelve children, three of whom died in infancy, the others being: William A., who died in 1925, lived at Texico, New Mexico, and was the husband of L. (Minion) Bell; James Z., who is deceased; Nannie E., who married George P. C. Selby, of Pike County, has no children; Rebecca, who married J. R. Chew, is a widow, Mr. Chew having died in 1900, leaving four children; George W., who lives at Clovis, New Mexico, is a widower and has seven children; Minnie A., who married William H. Stewart, is a widow with five children; Dr. Daniel W.; Clarence, who lives on the old homestead, married Miss Nannie Robinson, had two children, but only one is living; A. Howard, who lives at Gary, Indiana, and is auditor for the city schools, married Miss Nina Maple.

Doctor Bell attended the common and high schools of Pike County, and took his medical training in Hahnemann Medical College, Chicago, Illinois, from which he was graduated in 1904, and immediately thereafter he began the practice of his profession at Williamsport, Indiana, but a year later moved to Glendale, Indiana, and remained there for seven years, after which he went to Winslow, Indiana, for four years. At the termination of that period, in 1916, he located permanently at Otwell, and has here built up a very large and augmenting practice.

During the World war Doctor Bell enlisted in 1918, and was commissioned a first lieutenant of the Medical Corps. His service was confined to this country, and he was honorably discharged in March, 1919, and placed in the Reserve Corps, with the rank of captain, and was promoted to the rank of major in March, 1932.

On June 1, 1904, Doctor Bell was married to Miss Cora T. Thomas, a daughter of Frank and Margaret (Hollon) Thomas, also natives of Pike County. Three children have been born to Doctor and Mrs. Bell, one of whom is deceased: William F., who was principal of the Otwell public schools and is now manager of the leading mercantile store at Otwell, married Edna Craig, and they have two children, William F., Junior, and Roger Craig Bell; and Violet E., a graduate nurse, makes her headquarters at Otwell. Doctor Bell has been much interested in the training of young ladies for nursing and has often sponsored local girls in that noble calling, having at one time a class of eight girls at Walker Hospital, Evansville.

In political faith Doctor Bell is a Democrat. He belongs to the Baptist Church, and is one of its valued members. Fraternally his

affiliations are with the Odd Fellows, Modern Woodmen of America and the Order of Ben Hur. Professionally he belongs to the Pike County Medical Society, the Indiana State Medical Society, and the American Legion. In addition to his practice Doctor Bell owns farm land and real estate and is accounted one of the men of means in his community.

GEORGE B. DE TAR, M. D. The medical profession in Pike County, Indiana, includes many learned and experienced practitioners whose qualifications fit them for high standing in medical science. One of these is found in Dr. George B. De Tar, physician and surgeon at Winslow, where he has large property interests, and he is a veteran of the World war. In boyhood he attended the public schools at Winslow, where his father, also a physician, still resides; later he had college advantages, and in 1904 he was graduated from the Louisville Medical College, with the degree of Doctor of Medicine. However, he continued his medical studies, taking post-graduate work in the Chicago Polyclinic and the Chicago Post Graduate schools. An enthusiast in his profession, he has continued to study as well as practice and has attended many conventions and clinics in different medical centers. His first year of practice was with his father at Winslow, to which field of work he returned in 1916, after a practice of ten years in Spencer County, Indiana. In 1918 Doctor De Tar enlisted for service in the World war, was commissioned a first lieutenant in the United States Medical Corps, and was stationed at Fort Sherman. He is a member of the American Legion.

Dr. David De Tar, father of Doctor De Tar of this review, enlisted for service in the war between the states when he was but fifteen years old, and served as a drummer boy under the command of General Grant and Gen. Lew Wallace. Doctor De Tar, the elder, married Miss Willie B. Bouldin, a native of Missouri, who died in 1886, aged thirty-two years, leaving two children: Dr. George B. De Tar; and De Orr, who is an automobile dealer of Los Angeles, California. He is married and has three children.

Dr. George B. De Tar first attended the public schools of Winslow, later was a student of Danville, Indiana, Normal School, completing his education as already stated.

On December 31, 1894, Doctor De Tar married Miss Viola Bartley, of Harrison County, Indiana, and three children have been born to them: Marion D., who is an oil salesman in Philadelphia, Pennsylvania, married Helen Barnitz, of New Oxford, Pennsylvania, no children, and during the World war he was in France for eleven months as a member of the Tank Corps, and after the Armistice he remained in Paris for eighteen months as vice consul, and for a year held the same office in Palermo, Island of Sicily; Harold E., who is an oil man at Bristow, Oklahoma, married Miss Ruth Crawford, of Oklahoma, and they have two children, George and David;

and Mary Bell, who married Maurice Turner, of Rising Sun, Indiana, and they have a daughter, Barbara Jane.

Doctor De Tar is a Democrat, but is not active in politics. He is a consistent member of the Christian Church, and he belongs to the Knights of Pythias, the Woodmen of America, the Pike County Medical Society, the Indiana State Medical Society and the American Medical Association. In addition to his large practice he owns property at Winslow, and is a man of ample means and one who takes a deep and constructive interest in civic affairs.

HON. GEORGE W. DEFFENDALL, a leading citizen of Pike County, and a member of one of its old and substantial families, served the City of Petersburg as mayor from 1926 to 1930, to which office he was elected on the Republican ticket. Mayor Deffendall was born, reared and schooled in Pike County, and as an educator for many years, and as a successful business man and upright citizen for many more, formed and promoted personal friendships all over Pike County that no circumstances will ever be able to break. Since coming to Petersburg as a permanent resident his active interest in civic affairs relating to the substantial welfare of the city has been notable, and the confidence and esteem of his fellow citizens could scarcely have been shown in a more definite way than when he was chosen, in 1925, for the highest municipal honor within their gift and made mayor of Petersburg, which prospered under his wise business administration, founded on honesty and economy.

Mr. Deffendall was born December 19, 1873, a son of James Deffendall, also a native of Pike County, in which locality his father, a native of Germany, settled upon coming to the United States in young manhood, at which time he accompanied two brothers. James Deffendall was a farmer all his life, and was a highly esteemed citizen, whose death occurred in February, 1904. He married Susan Hoover, whose father was a second cousin to President Herbert Hoover. Mrs. Deffendall died in November, 1913, having borne her husband fourteen children, one of whom died in infancy, and John, Sarah, Mary, Marion, Abraham and William died later on in life. The others were: Lucy, who married George Blaiza, of Pike County, has three children; Elizabeth, who married Newton E. Carr, of Pike County, has seven children; Loren, who lives in Pike County, married Rose Robling, and they have two children; Julia, who married Morton Trusler, has two children, and lives at Oakland City, Indiana; George W.; Ida, who married Lawrence Skinner, has four children, and lives in Pike County; and Prentice, who lives at Saint Louis, Missouri, married Miss Wallace, and they have no children.

George W. Deffendall attended the schools of Pike County, and when he secured a certificate, taught school for ten years. Leaving the educational field, he entered that of business, and owned and conducted a grocery store at Hosmer, Indiana, for twenty years. When he sold it was at a substantial profit, and in 1918 he began selling insurance, which work occupied him for two years. He then became bookkeeper and accountant, and was so engaged until 1925, when he was elected mayor of Petersburg, taking office January 4, 1926, and which office he held until January, 1930. He is now practicing law at Petersburg. He was admitted to the Indiana bar in December, 1929.

In December, 1894, Mr. Deffendall was married to Elizabeth De Jarnett, a daughter of Daniel and Mary (Quiggins) De Jarnett, natives of Pike County. Mr. and Mrs. Deffendall have four children, namely: Leona, who is a school teacher at Evansville, is a graduate of Blaker's Teachers College, Indianapolis, and is unmarried; Grace, who is also a teacher in the Petersburg High School, lives at home, is unmarried, and a graduate of the Indiana State Normal School; Denver, who lives at Indianapolis, married Miss Dorothy Lentze, and they have two children, Robert and Richard; and Hugh, who is at home.

In political faith Mr. Deffendall is, and always has been, a Republican, as his father before him. He has been advanced through all of the bodies of the York Rite in Masonry, and also belongs to the Shrine at Evansville, being now its oldest member in point of membership. He is a director in the Petersburg Building & Loan Association. While, aside from a patriotic participation in local war work, Mr. Deffendall has had no military experience, two of his father's brothers and three of his mother's brothers served in the war between the states as Union soldiers, and rendered an excellent account of themselves.

WILLIAM DIXON CROW. Although he commenced his career as a lawyer and still retains a knowledge of that calling which is of inestimable value to him in his present vocations, it is as a newspaper man that William Dixon Crow is best known to the present and rising generation at Petersburg. Since 1907 he has been owner, editor and publisher of the *Petersburg Press*, a Republican weekly newspaper which has a large circulation in Pike and the surrounding counties and which wields a strong influence in the molding of public opinion as to movements of general importance. He has likewise born his full share of responsibility as a citizen, and on various occasions has served his community capably in public offices.

William Dixon Crow was born May 23, 1871, at Petersburg, Pike County, Indiana, and is a son of John and Tennessee (Traylor) Crow. He was graduated from Petersburg High School in 1890, and then entered Indiana University, from which he was graduated as a member of the class of 1894, being the recipient of the degree of Master of Arts. Even thus early he displayed a predilection for the profession of journalism and during the terms of 1893 and 1894 served in the capacity of editor-in-chief of the *Indiana Student*, the university students' paper. During the next three years Mr. Crow was variously employed, principally in the study of law, and then returned to the University of Indiana for a one-year legal course. He was admitted to the bar and commenced the practice of his profession in 1898, and not long thereafter was elected city and county attorney and continued to act in these capacities until 1907. Although he had an excellent and remunerative practice and was acknowledged to be a capable and thoroughly informed lawyer, the urge toward a journalistic career was too great to withstand, and in the year above mentioned he purchased the *Petersburg Press*, a Republican weekly, which he has published continuously since that time. He is giving his readers a well-printed, attractive and well-edited newspaper, handling news of a national as well as a local character, timely editorials and features. A stanch Republican in his political views, Mr. Crow served as supervisor of the census for the First Congressional District in 1910, and occupied the position of postmaster of Petersburg from 1922 until 1927. He was a member of the advisory committee of the state Republican committee during the campaign of 1928, and always has wielded a strong influence in his party. Mr. Crow belongs to the Methodist Episcopal Church, the Phi Delta Theta fraternity, the Modern Woodmen of America and the Kiwanis Club of Petersburg, and formerly was a member of the Indiana Bar Association and the American Bar Association.

In 1900 Mr. Crow was united in marriage with Miss Lula May Harris, daughter of Doctor and Sarah (Brown) Harris. Two children have been born to this union: Mrs. Elizabeth Von der Lehr, of Chicago, who has one son, William N.; and Mrs. Margaret Meinerding, of Columbus, Ohio. Mrs. Crow has long been prominent in civic and social circles and in church work, and is secretary of the Southwestern Historical Society and a member of the Daughters of Veterans of Wars.

EMERY VIRGIL COUTS, A. B. Not only is Pike County a leading section of Indiana in industry and commerce, but it can lay claim also to being one of the foremost in encouraging and maintaining excellent public schools, many of which, at the present time, are under the capable direction of her native sons. One of these, Prof. Emery Virgil Couts, county superintendent of schools, is widely known as a man of real scholarship and an experienced teacher, and belongs to Pike County's honored group of overseas veterans of the World war. His boyhood was spent on his father's farm while attending the country schools. Collegiate advantages awaited him when he left the local high school, and perhaps his future career had already been determined upon, as immediately after his graduation and winning of his degree of Bachelor of Arts he entered the educational field. As a matter of choice he remained in Pike County for a

Howard A. Bounder.

number of years, giving his best efforts to build up a high educational standard in the schools. In 1925 he was called into public life as county superintendent of schools, and is still serving in this important office, for which he is so well qualified.

Superintendent Couts was born in Pike County, November 3, 1893, a son of James M. and Mary E. (Connor) Couts, the latter of whom was born in New York City, where her parents had settled upon coming to this country from Ireland. James M. Couts was born in Pike County, Indiana, and has spent his life in farming. Both he and his wife are living. Nine children have been born to them, namely: James A., who resides in Gibson County, Indiana; John E., who lives in Pike County; Mary, who lives in Ohio; Emery V., of this review; William C., who resides in Pike County; Wilford, who is a teacher in Illinois; Cecil T., who is a teacher in the Pike County schools; George H., who is a teacher in Pike County; and Edith, who lives at home. All are graduates of the Oakland City College.

Superintendent Couts took his degree of Bachelor of Arts from Oakland City College, after which he was a student of Indiana State Normal School at Terre Haute for two terms, or one year. He has also studied at the Indiana State University and expects to receive his M. A. Degree in 1932, along with his brothers, Wilford and Cecil. His period of service as a public-school teacher in Pike County covered fourteen years, and he is continuing his fine work upon a wider scale in his present office.

On November 24, 1920, Superintendent Couts was married to Miss Agnes Hyneman, a daughter of Robert and Lillie (Thornton) Hyneman, of Pike County. Their one child died in infancy. In politics he is a Democrat. While a man of high moral character, he does not affiliate with any church. He belongs to the Modern Woodmen of America and the American Legion.

In October, 1917, Superintendent Couts was inducted into the United States Army, was sent to France after due training, as a member of the Three Hundred and Thirty-fifth Infantry, Eighty-fourth Division, and after eleven months overseas was returned to the United States, and honorably discharged in July, 1919. With his return to civilian life he resumed his educational work both of teaching and studying. Truly it may be said that teachers, like poets, "are not made, but born." This truism may be properly quoted with reference to Superintendent Couts, for few men of his profession in Pike County can be said to possess in higher degree the qualities which combine to make the successful educator. The best recognition of his ability in this respect was shown in his election to the office of county superintendent of schools, in which he has served with marked efficiency, proving himself to be not only an advanced scholar and profound student and thinker, but an executive of superior talents.

HOWARD A. BOENDER, Hammond insurance man, well known for his constructive thought and action, is a native of Holland, in which country he was born May 4, 1888.

The Boender family have lived in Holland for many generations, where they have been active in commercial life. His parents, K. J. and Anna (Baunch) Boender, were both born in Holland. His father was a flax buyer with his father on the Board of Trade. K. J. Boender was also educated for the profession of veterinarian. When he brought his family to America he settled at Harvey, Illinois, in 1895, and for about ten years was in the dairy business. He lived for several years at Galveston, Texas, and then moved to the far Northwest, locating at Wenatchee, Washington, where he and his wife reside. He and his sons have engaged extensively in the fruit growing business, making a specialty of the famous Delicious apples. The parents are members of the Dutch Reformed Church. The children are: Howard A.; Lizzie, wife of George Heyen, of Wenatchee; K. J. Boender, Jr., who has two large apple orchards at Wenatchee; Anna, wife of Carl Anderson, of Wenatchee; Richard, an apple rancher at Wenatchee; and John A., a newspaper man at Baltimore, Maryland. One son, John, lost his life in 1900, following the Galveston tidal wave.

Howard A. Boender received his early advantages in private schools in Holland, afterwards attended public school at Harvey, Illinois, and when he left school he became a clerk in the contract department of the New York Central lines, where he remained five years, three years at Kankakee, Illinois, and two years at Gibson, Indiana, his home being at Hammond. Since 1913 he has been in the insurance and real estate business. His business is conducted under his individual name, with offices in the First Trust Building.

Mr. Boender is a member of the Chamber of Commerce, is a Republican in national politics, but votes independently in local affairs. In 1917 he enlisted and became a member of the Ambulance Corps of the American Red Cross. He was stationed at Camp King, Sound Beach, Connecticut, until after the armistice. He held the rank of sergeant. Mr. Boender is a member of St. Paul's Evangelical Lutheran Church of Hammond.

He married at Kankakee, Illinois, February 22, 1910, Miss Anna Radzom, daughter of Robert and Adeline (Radzom) Radzom. Her father for many years was with the car department of the Illinois Central Railway. The Radzom family came from Germany. There were five children, Carl, Anna, Ernest, Lizzie and Lillian, all of whom were born at Kankakee. Mrs. Boender attended public and parochial schools at Kankakee. She is a member of the Ladies Aid of the St. Paul's Evangelical Lutheran Church.

Mr. Boender while not a native American has been an ardent student of American history, and has been a great admirer of the

famous statesmen of this nation, Washington,
Lincoln, Roosevelt and others. He has delivered many patriotic addresses and recently
he was a speaker before the Chamber of Commerce at Lansing, Illinois, in the course of
which he declared: "Our great republic means
nothing unless it means triumph of a real
democracy, popular government, and an economic system under which each man shall be
guaranteed the opportunity to show the central feature of the history of the world, and
all nations look for hope to our democracy."

Mr. Boender has especially interested himself in constructive measures to relieve the
great employment depression of 1930-31. He
helped organize the Municipal Tax Payers
League of Hammond and secured a working
cooperation between the taxpayers of the
Calumet district with a view to lightening
the burdens of government charges and a
greater efficiency in expenditures. Mr.
Boender gained national recognition for his
proposal early in 1931 that the resources of
the states and nation be employed to construct
a magnificent super-highway eighty feet wide
from the Atlantic to the Pacific coasts, with
an intersecting highway from Canada to the
Gulf, a project which he estimated would require five years to complete, would employ
100,000 men directly in the labor of construction and many others in the supply of material, and would not only supply transportation arteries which sooner or later must be
built, but would stimulate business activities
throughout the nation.

JOHN THOMAS KIME, M. D. For many years
the family name of Kime has been a familiar
and honored one of the medical profession in
Pike County, and the line has been unbroken.
A present worthy bearer of the name and
title is Dr. John Thomas Kime, physician and
surgeon at Petersburg, successor of his prominent father, the late Dr. John Kime, who came
early to the county and spent his life in the
work of his noble profession.

Dr. John Thomas Kime was born at Union,
October 27, 1866, and had excellent early
school advantages, supplemented later on by
a university course at Bloomington and a
thorough medical education in the University
of Louisville, Kentucky, Medical College,
Louisville. He came back to Petersburg after
graduating and has continued in medical practice here ever since. He commands the confidence and enjoys the esteem of his fellow citizens and is favorably known professionally
all over and beyond Pike County.

The elder Doctor Kime continued in practice at Union, Indiana, until his death in
1886, when he was but fifty-five years old.
He married Cassandra Jones, and they had
six children: Gardner, who is in the real estate business, married Jennie Thompson, and
they have two children; Dr. John Thomas was
the second; Azel F. is a merchant living in
Union, Indiana, who married Ada Lindsey,
and they have one child; William M., who
lives at Saint Cloud, is married and has four

children; Marshall M.. who is deceased, married Grace Stuckey, and they had two children; and Laura E., who died in 1918, was
the wife of James Billings and the mother
of three children. There were two children
by a former marriage: R. R. Kime, M. D.,
deceased, and James F. Kime, of Pasadena,
California.

Graduated in medicine March 1, 1889, with
the degree of Doctor of Medicine, and, returning to Petersburg, Dr. John T. Kime has
built up a practice in his native city that is not
only large and valuable, but one that is constantly augmenting.

On October 30, 1894, Doctor Kime was married to Miss Effa Posey, a daughter of Richard and Jennie (Gray) Posey, all natives of
Pike County and descendants of an old Revolutionary family and of one of the oldest families in Southern Indiana, after whom a county
was named. Mrs. Kime is a member of the
D. A. R., in which she has held several offices.
Doctor and Mrs. Kime have four children:
Posey T., who is an attorney of Evansville,
Indiana, and now judge of Indiana Appellate
Court, married Margaret Bollenbacker, and
they have one child, Helen Aileen; Harold R.,
who is a graduate of Northwestern College,
is a realtor of South Bend, Indiana, and is
unmarried; Aileen, who is deceased; and Allen, who resides at Petersburg, is engaged in
the ice business. He married Edith B. Col-
vin, and they have one child, Carolyn C. Doctor Kime is a Democrat in his views and has
been honored by his party. For two terms he
was county health officer, and for two terms
more he was coroner. The Cumberland Presbyterian Church holds his membership, and he
is highly valued in that body. He belongs to
the Independent Order of Odd Fellows, Modern Woodmen, the Pike County Medical Society, the Indiana State Medical Society and
the American Medical Association.

LEWIS JOHNSON EARLY. Among the citizens of marked enterprise and public spirit
at Petersburg stands Lewis Johnson Early,
owner and publisher of the *Pike County Democrat*, a leading Democratic newspaper of
Southern Indiana. Mr. Early is a native of
Kentucky and received his early education in
Ohio County, that state, and later was graduated from the Western Kentucky College, in
which he subsequently was an instructor for
some years, in the meanwhile having learned
the printing business. The educational field
as a permanency did not altogether satisfy
Mr. Early's ambition, however; in fact even
then he found himself best contented when
engaged in newspaper work, and after considerable experience in various city offices in
Kentucky he purchased a newspaper, *The
Cannelton Telephone*, at Cannelton, Indiana,
and conducted it for thirty years, 1892 to
1922, during which long period he became
well and favorably known in journalism in
this state. On becoming a citizen of Petersburg he bought the *Pike County Democrat*,
the oldest newspaper in Pike County and this

part of the state. As an earnest citizen and seasoned newspaper man he has conducted his publication most efficiently, and, in association with his eldest son as publisher, has made it not only a convincing exponent of the principles of the Democratic political party, but also a world-wide news visitor into homes all over the state.

Lewis Johnson Early was born in Ohio County, Kentucky, February 2, 1865, and is a son of James and Sarah A. (Miller) Early. His father, who was born at Hardinsburg, Kentucky, passed his entire life in the occupations of farming and stock raising in Ohio County, where he died in 1889, while his mother, a native of Davis County, Kentucky, still survives at Los Angeles, California, aged ninety-one years. There were six children in the family: Emmett, deceased; Alice, deceased; Walter, a resident of Los Angeles, California; Clara, the wife of J. W. Dillon, of Terre Haute, Indiana; and Mrs. L. B. Evans, deceased.

Lewis Johnson Early, as noted above, received his early education in the rural and high schools of Kentucky, following which he took a business course at the Western Kentucky College, and also attended the Danville (Illinois) Normal School and Valparaiso (Indiana) College. During this period he had taught school for one year, and after leaving Valparaiso College he taught in the Western Kentucky College for five years. Giving up educational work, he entered the newspaper field and worked in offices at Lewisport, Hawesville and Owensboro, Kentucky, and in 1892 went to Cannelton, Indiana, where he purchased a newspaper, of which he was the proprietor for thirty years, during which time he gained recognition and prosperity. In 1922 he disposed of his interests and went to Los Angeles, but after remaining in California for one year returned to Indiana and settled at Petersburg, where he purchased the *Pike County Democrat*. This is the oldest paper in the county, having been established in 1856, and is one of the oldest in the southern part of the state. The paper is modern in every respect, has a wide circulation, and connected therewith is an up-to-date job printing department which is fully equipped to turn out the highest grade of work. Mr. Early has always been a Democrat, is public-spirited and possessed of civic pride, and gives his unswerving aid to beneficial civic movements. He holds membership in the Chamber of Commerce and the Kiwanis Club, but has no fraternal connections, while his religious affiliation is with the Methodist Church.

In 1895 Mr. Early was united in marriage with Miss M. Baker, of Hawesville, Kentucky, who died in 1905. In October, 1906, Mr. Early married Miss Margaret Blake. Mr. Early is the father of three sons: Justin Lee, of Petersburg, who is publisher of the *Pike County Democrat* and married Muriel McLellan, October 13, 1930; Shannon Bruce, assistant general manager for a paper mill at Monroe Bridge, Massachusetts; and Robert, who is a graduate of Bosse High School at Evansville and is now associated with his brother Shannon in the paper mill at Monroe Bridge.

SYLVANUS RICHARD CLARK, M. D. A prominent and substantial citizen of Pike County, Indiana, and one of the leading medical practitioners, was Dr. Sylvanus R. Clark, physician and surgeon at Petersburg, secretary of the board of health and president of the Petersburg school board. He was a native of Ohio, but his home had been in Indiana practically all his life and Pike County claimed him, for it was here in his infancy that his soldier father settled after the close of the war between the states, of which he was a veteran. Doctor Clark's medical education was secured in the Ohio Medical College at Cincinnati, from which he was graduated in 1890, and immediately afterwards he returned to Indiana, being anxious to begin his practice in familiar and friendly surroundings. It was not until 1912, however, that the advantages of Petersburg so impressed him that he came to this city to establish a permanent home. He had also studied at the Kentucky School of Medicine at Louisville and took post-graduate work in surgery in Saint Louis.

Doctor Clark was born in Vinton County, Ohio, February 25, 1864, a son of John F. and Margaret (Gardner) Clark, the latter of whom died in February, 1902, the former in April, 1898. During the war of the sixties John F. Clark served in the One Hundred and Forty-eighth Ohio Volunteer Infantry, and after the close of the war and his honorable discharge he located on the farm in Pike County, Indiana, on which he subsequently died. He and his wife had twelve children, four of whom died in infancy, the others being: Mary, Isaac, Oliver, Doctor Clark, Newton and his twin sister, Alice, Ellen and John.

Graduated from medical college in 1890, with the degree of Doctor of Medicine, Doctor Clark went to Otwell, where he remained for twelve years. He was at Union for five years, at Glezen for five years and from 1912 he practiced at Petersburg until his death, by automobile accident, on October 5, 1929. During the World war Doctor Clark was appointed examiner of the draft board, and when he was through with its work he enlisted in the Medical Corps, was commissioned a captain, and served with that rank at Fort Harrison Base Hospital Number 25, and at Camp McLellan, Alabama, to which he was transferred on November 11, 1918, the day the armistice was signed.

In November, 1896, Doctor Clark was married to Miss Sarah V. Elliott, a daughter of James and Nancy (Ball) Elliott, of Connersville, Indiana. There are three children: Margaret, who married Thomas Ogden, of Petersburg and has three children, Thomasina Louise, Richard Gene and Lola Faye; Myrtle, who married Ernest Brown, has no children and lives at Lewistown, Montana; and Helen, who married George McLellan, lives at Dallas,

Texas, and has one child, Kathryn Mary. Doctor Clark was a Republican. The Presbyterian Church held his membership. He was a Scottish Rite Mason, and he also belonged to the American Legion, the Pike County Medical Society, the Indiana State Medical Society and the American Medical Association. He was also a member of the Odd Fellows for thirty-five years and of the Modern Woodmen for about thirty years.. In addition to his practice, with which a large and valuable one, Doctor Clark owned the post office building at Petersburg and other valuable real estate in the city of which he was so valued a factor. He also owned and operated the only hospital of the town, which was the result of a life long dream.

To give a truer picture of Doctor Clark's life we quote from an editorial in the *Winslow Dispatch* written by one who knew him well: "The love and esteem in which Doctor Clark was held has been manifested since his death by the constant stream of people from all stages of society who have filed past his casket.

"A good man has gone to his reward. The torch of life has been snuffed out just when the dreams of a lifetime were being realized and a philanthropic venture to which he had dedicated his life was reaching consummation.

"The passing of Doctor Clark is a great loss to Petersburg and Pike County. He was one of the county's foremost citizens."

EZRA P. MATHERS, a veteran of the Civil war and one of the last surviving members of the Indiana troops who fought for the Union, also has to his credit a veteran's record as a locomotive engineer. Mr. Mathers is now enjoying retirement from active service and for many years has been a resident of Greencastle.

He was born in Monroe County, Indiana, March 11, 1845. His father, James P. Mathers, was born in Kentucky, came to Indiana in 1818, only two years after the territory was admitted to the Union, and spent his active life as a farmer. He died in 1868. James P. Mathers married Elizabeth Vandivar, also a native of Kentucky, who passed away in 1858. Ezra P. Mathers was one of the older of a family of ten children. He was thirteen when his mother died. After a public school education in Monroe County, he went to work on a farm and was eighteen years of age when, in November, 1863, he enlisted in Company I of the Tenth Indiana Cavalry. He saw active service all during the last two years of the war, participating in several battles, but was never wounded. He received his honorable discharge at Vicksburg, Mississippi, in August, 1865, and was soon again mustered into civilian activities, at first as a farmer and later as a brick maker.

Mr. Mathers in 1870 took up railroading as a career and for fourteen months was a fireman with the L. N. A. & C. He then transferred his services to the Big Four Railway as an engineer and was with that company nearly forty years, being retired on the pension rolls in 1918. He also gets a pension from the Government for his service as a soldier. Mr. Mathers has been post commander of the Grand Army of the Republic for four years. He is a member of the Brotherhood of Locomotive Engineers, is a Republican voter and a member of the Christian Church.

He married, July 6, 1868, Miss Rachael Harrell, of Bloomington, Indiana. The three children born to their marriage were Katherine, Elizabeth and Luella. Katherine is the wife of L. Frank Treat and has two children, Mary E. and Charles H. Elizabeth married P. R. Christie, of Greencastle. Luella is the widow of Dr. E. G. Fry, of Greencastle, and has a son, Raymond E. Fry, of Rochester, New York, and a daughter, Nellie, who is the wife of J. H. Taylor, of Kalamazoo, Michigan, and has two children, George E. Taylor and James Franklin Taylor, who are great-grandsons of Mr. Mathers.

DANIEL E. TAYLOR as a physician and surgeon has given the resources represented by thorough training, good natural ability and by conscientious service to the community of Velpen, Pike County, for nearly thirty years.

Doctor Taylor was born in Pike County, Indiana, February 16, 1869. His father, Andrew Jackson Taylor, was born November 1, 1835, near Millersburg, Indiana. His grandfather was a native of Kentucky and married Rebecca Perry, who was born in Warrick County, Indiana. Andrew Jackson Taylor when a boy was a driver on the towpath at the old canal and spent his mature years as a Pike County farmer. He died November 26, 1918, at the age of eighty-three. Andrew Jackson Taylor married Eunice J. Risley, who was born December 25, 1835, in Pike County and died on March 5, 1871. Her father, James Risley, was a native of Virginia, born in 1809, and married Patricia Miller, also a native of that state. Doctor Taylor was one of three children. His brother Henry, a resident of Los Angeles, California, married Jane Davis, of Chandler, Indiana, and has a family of four sons and one daughter. His other brother Joe J., married Flora B. Harris, and they have six children.

Dr. Daniel E. Taylor grew up on a Pike County farm, attended the grade and high schools of the county, and as a young man qualified as a teacher. He spent eleven years teaching in different localities, and this work enabled him to carry out his long standing ambition to become a physician. Doctor Taylor in 1903 was graduated from the Louisville Medical College, with the degree of Doctor of Medicine, and at once located at Velpen, where he has carried on a general town and country practice. He is a member of the Pike County and Indiana State Medical Associations, and enjoys very high standing both as a professional man and citizen. He is a Democrat, a Baptist, and is affiliated with the Independent Order of Odd Fellows and Knights of Pythias.

Doctor Taylor married, October 3, 1894, Miss Jessie Bottom. She died March 26, 1909,

JAMES C. PELTIER III   WILLIAM H. W. PELTIER
LOUIS PELTIER

leaving a daughter, Bernice, born August 23, 1895, who is the wife of L. O. Brown of Owensboro, Kentucky, and has a son, Robert, who was born July 19, 1920. Doctor Taylor's second wife was Mattie E. Osborn, born February 29, 1884. They were married June 26, 1912, and they have one child, Dorothy, born November 21, 1918.

WILLIAM H. W. PELTIER carries on the traditions of Fort Wayne's oldest family and also of the oldest established business as undertakers and funeral directors.

His great-grandfather, James Peltier, was a French Canadian, one of those hardy, daring men of the woods and the rapid flowing streams who made up the picturesque characters of the eighteenth century. For some time he was a courier carrying mail and express by horse or pirogue from the military post at Detroit westward through the southern end of Lake Michigan. He established his home at old Fort Wayne in 1787. His wife was Angeline Chapeteau, who as a girl and orphan came by pirogue to Fort Wayne in 1804 with her uncle and aunt. Her red hair made a great impression upon the Miami Indians, who straightway baptized her "Golden Hair." Soon after her arrival she became the bride of James Peltier. They as time went on became great favorites with the Indians. Because of her popularity with them she and her family were allowed to live outside of the Fort, where in the capacity of accepted go-between she rendered valuable service to the garrison, the settlers obliged to live within the fort and the besieging Indians. The prolonged siege had so depleted the Fort's stores that venison given Mrs. Peltier by the Indians was of vast assistance to those in the Fort and salt obtained at the fort by Mrs. Peltier was gratefully received by the Indians. Eventually the siege became so bad the family were ordered into the fort. While they were living at Fort Wayne a son, Louis Peltier, was born to them on March 15, 1813. He had the distinction of being the first white child born within the limits of the present City of Fort Wayne.

Louis Peltier was the first man to make a business of undertaking. He engaged in that line of work in 1832, nearly a century ago, and throughout all the years the name Peltier in Fort Wayne has had its chief business significance in association with the duty of caring for and burying the dead. During the years before Louis Peltier engaged in the business the only persons officially concerned with funerals were a minister or priest, and sometimes the local cabinet maker, though frequently the coffins were also the product of volunteer friendly labor on the part of a carpenter. For a number of years after Louis Peltier set up in business it was customary for all coffins to be made as needed, and consequently were of crude and hurried workmanship. Practically all the developments and changes in the undertaking business during the past century have been part of the experience of the three generations of the Peltier family at Fort Wayn. The most marked changes have come within the time of Mr. James C. Peltier, son of Louis, involving the introduction of the modern processes of embalming, the improvement of the mechanical facilities, particularly the use of automobile equipment.

William H. W. Peltier was born at Fort Wayne March 1, 1869, son of James C. and Selina (Wadge) Peltier. His father had represented the second generation of the family in the undertaking business. William H. W. Peltier grew up in Fort Wayne, attended the Clay Street School, also the Sihler German private school, where he learned to speak the tongue of so many citizens of Fort Wayne. He also attended the old Methodist College at Fort Wayne, the Shattuck Military Academy at Faribault, Minnesota. Mr. Peltier as a boy and youth enjoyed all the manly sports of his generation. For several years he played semi-professional baseball, and his greatest thrill in sport, as he recalls it, was a day when, playing with the team of the University of Michigan, he brought in the winning run that broke a tie score, and was carried off the field by the cheering Michigan students. When the bicycle was at the height of its popularity as a vehicle of speed he was in the ranks of the professionals as a rider, and was employed regularly for advertising and demonstration purposes by one of the companies making a popular model of that time. Another interest of those earlier years was military training. He enlisted in a Fort Wayne company of the Indiana National Guard, Company B of the Second Regiment, has commissions as captain bearing the signatures of former Governors Hovey and Mount.

When he graduated from the bicycle it was only natural that he became one of the first enthusiasts for the motor car, and he had the distinction of owning and operating the first automobile in Fort Wayne, and the newspapers of that city and surrounding towns where he made startling appearances in his horseless carriage kept him almost daily before the public eye by stories recounting the marvelous performance of his gasoline buggy.

After taking over the management of his father's business he was constantly studying methods of improving the service, and was one of the first funeral directors in Northern Indiana to introduce motor equipment. For years he has been an advocate of good roads construction, and for a number of years served as chairman of the Good Roads Bureau of the Fort Wayne Chamber of Commerce. For thirty years his name has been linked with all progressive matters in his home city. He was one of the twelve founders of the first chapter of the Red Cross at Fort Wayne. He is a York and Scottish Rite Mason and Shriner and a member of the Royal Order of Jesters, made up of Shriners. He is also a member of the Knights of Pythias and Elks and belongs to the Y. M. C. A., the Rotary Club, Izaak Walton League, the Hoosier Automobile Association, Fort Wayne Country Club, the Orchard Ridge Country Club and the National Selective Morticians. He was given the appropriate honor of being selected the first president of the Fort Wayne Historical Society, a tribute to his descent from the oldest family of the city. Mr. Peltier and family are members of the Episcopal Church. He married, January 29, 1908, Miss Isabel Elizabeth McClure, daughter of Mr. and Mrs. Rosser McClure.

THOMAS W. BASINGER, M. D. One of the representative citizens and prominent medical practitioners of Pike County, Indiana, is Dr. Thomas W. Basinger, physician and surgeon at Petersburg, and formerly, for twenty years, health officer of Pike County. After a period in the public schools of Perry County he became a teacher, and in this way earned the necessary capital to take him through his medical course. A practitioner since 1880, his career has been a long, useful and honorable one, and there are few men in the county who are held in higher esteem.

Thomas W. Basinger was born in Perry County, Indiana, May 6, 1854, a son of Joseph S. and Philadelphia (Chewning) Basinger. His father, who was born in 1832, in Kentucky, came to Indiana in young manhood and settled in Perry County, where he was engaged in agricultural pursuits at the outbreak of the war between the states. He served two years in the Union army, as a private in an Indiana volunteer infantry regiment, and upon receiving his honorable discharge returned to Perry County, where he resumed his agricultural operations. He was thus employed until his retirement, and died July 18, 1918, at the advanced age of nearly eighty-seven years, having been born January 25, 1832. Mr. Joseph S. Basinger married Philadelphia Chewning, of Rockport, Indiana, and of their five children three are still living: Thomas W., of this review; Lavina, wife of William W. Lawrence, of Pittsburg, Kansas, and Dr. John H., a physician and surgeon of Oklahoma City.

Thomas W. Basinger attended the public schools of Perry County and was reared in the midst of agricultural surroundings, but in early life decided upon a professional career, and accordingly secured a teacher's certificate and for seven years instructed the young minds of the rural districts of his native locality. During this period he applied himself to preliminary study in medicine and at the same time saved his earnings carefully, finally enrolling as a student at the Louisville University of Medicine, Louisville, Kentucky, from which institution he was graduated with the degree of Doctor of Medicine as a member of the class of 1880. In the same year he commenced practice at Oatsville, Pike County, where he remained until 1892, and in the latter year changed his residence and scene of practice to Petersburg, where he has followed his calling for a period of forty years. During this time he has attracted and held a large and lucrative practice and built up a firm reputation as a diagnostician, practitioner and operator. He is a member of the Pike County Medical Society, the Indiana State Medical Society and the American Medical Association, and served as health officer for twenty years. A Republican in his political views, he has taken an interest in public affairs and for one term was county auditor. His religious affiliation is with the Methodist Episcopal Church, while fraternally he belongs to the Independent Order of Odd Fellows and is a Mason. In addition to his large medical practice Doctor Basinger has other interests, and is president of the Pike County Building & Loan Association.

On September 14, 1876, Doctor Basinger was united in marriage with Miss Mary E. VanWinkle, of Perry County, Indiana, and to this union there were born seven children: Ida M., deceased, who married Owen J. Neighbors, a native of Maryland, now superintendent of public schools at Wabash, Indiana, who has four sons; Homer, an oil man of Indiana, who married Elizabeth Hammond and has five children; Dr. H. R., engaged in a successful veterinary practice at Wheatland, Indiana, who married May Overbay; Doris, who married William C. O'Brien, an electrical engineer in charge of the installation of a large electrical plant at Grand Rapids, Michigan, and they have two boys; and three of the doctor's children are deceased.

ORACE D. HARRIS. Progress is the order of the day; in every profession mighty strides forward are being made; business has been so reorganized that conditions have completely changed within the present century, and the outlet of the people and their viewpoint are altered. However, unchangeable, unaltered and rigidly permanent is the reverence paid to those who, passing from this mortal sphere, await consignment to their narrow resting place in one or other of "God's Acres." As far back as there are any records respect for the dead has been a distinguishing characteristic of man as compared to the lower animals. The manner of caring for the dead, however, has changed, and greatly for the better. The modern funeral director has to be a man who has been graduated from a college of his profession, with a state license to practice, and if he is a business man of any pride and repute he has an equipment that insures a dignified and adequate service that will reflect credit upon the dead and the living as well. Such a man is Orace D. Harris, of Petersburg, Indiana, who for nearly thirty years has been in the undertaking business in this city.

Orace D. Harris was born in Dubois County, Indiana, February 11, 1874, a son of Nicholas and Martha (Hogland) Harris, both of whom were born in Dubois County. The father was a carpenter and contractor, and, when the need arose, made coffins. For forty years he lived in the vicinity of Lemmon's Church, but

at the close of that period moved to Otwell, Pike County, and engaged in the undertaking and furniture business, in which he continued until his death in 1927. He and his wife had eight children, three of whom died in infancy, the others being: Orace D., who is the eldest; Bell, who resides at Otwell, married Sherman Scraper, and they have three children; Ovid, who died at Boerne, Texas, aged twenty-three years; May, who married Clarence Ayres, lives at Otwell; and Grace, who is unmarried, lives at Otwell.

After attending the Lemmon School in Dubois County Orace D. Harris was associated with his father in the furniture and undertaking business, and in 1900 took a course in Clark's School of Embalming at Louisville, Kentucky, from which he was graduated, and he received his license from the State of Indiana in 1901. In 1902 he came to Petersburg, established himself in business, and for six years carried it on in a dignified manner. With his election to the office of county treasurer of Pike County he left the undertaking business, and served his term of two years most successfully. Once more he became an undertaker, and has continued to so serve the people ever since.

On August 20, 1896, Mr. Harris was married at Petersburg to Miss Lilla A. Dillon, a daughter of W. Curran and Malinda (Rogers) Dillon, members of old and honorable families of Indiana, and of this country. The great-great-grandfather of Mrs. Harris, Lieutenant Dillon, served under the direct command of Gen. George Washington in the American Revolution. Mr. and Mrs. Harris have three children: Owen Dillon, born October 20, 1898, is a mortician and resides at Petersburg, where he is associated with his father, and has served as county coroner continuously for ten years, since January 1, 1922. He married Miss Clara Heldt, of Evansville, Indiana, and they have one son, William Owen, born October 9, 1929. Lee N., born December 23, 1900, is unmarried, and is also a mortician, associated with his father at Petersburg. Fay, born September 27, 1904, is attending the University of Indiana.

Mr. Harris is a Democrat, but is not in politics. He belongs to the Presbyterian Church. With his two sons he belongs to the Masonic Order, his sons belonging to the Mystic Shrine, and he is also an Odd Fellow, Modern Woodman and Red Man, and belongs to the Indiana State Embalmers Association. Mrs. Harris belongs to the Daughters of the American Revolution, the Eastern Star and the White Shrine.

LEO A. SALB and three of his brothers are representatives of the medical profession in their native State of Indiana and he himself has been since 1910 established in successful practice as a physician and surgeon at Jasper, Dubois County, at which judicial center of the county his loyal professional activities have been interrupted only during the period of his service in the Medical Corps of the United States Army in the World war interval.

Doctor Salb was born in his present home City of Jasper, November 4, 1886, and is a son of Dr. John Salb and Margaret (Betz) Salb, both likewise natives of this state. Dr. John Salb was long numbered among the representative physicians and surgeons in Dubois County and was engaged in practice at Jasper until his death, in 1925, his widow being still a resident of this city. Of the nine children eight survive the honored father, in whose professional footsteps four of the sons are following. May, eldest of the children, is the wife of E. Sturm, M. D., and they reside at Jasper; Dr. John, Jr., is a physician and surgeon and is engaged in practice in the City of Indianapolis; Dr. Leo A., of this review, is the next younger; Oscar S. likewise is a physician and surgeon and is established in practice at Seymour, Indiana; Victor M. is engaged in the insurance business at Jasper; Grover E. is factory manager of the Indiana Desk Company; Dr. Max was graduated in the medical department of the University of Indiana as a member of the class of 1929 and is practicing now at Indianapolis; Ardella is the wife of L. G. Bohnert, and they have one child.

After completing his studies in the Jasper High School Dr. Leo A. Salb entered the medical department of the University of Indiana, in which he was graduated as a member of the class of 1908. After thus receiving his degree of Doctor of Medicine he further fortified himself by the valuable clinical experience he gained as an interne in a leading hospital in the City of Terre Haute, and in 1910 he engaged in the active general practice of his profession in his native City of Jasper, where he has since continued his earnest and effective ministrations save for the period of his service in the Medical Corps of the United States Army during the time of the nation's participation in the World war, he having been called to overseas duty, and having been in service in France eleven months, with rank of captain in the Medical Corps. His brothers John, Victor and Grover likewise were in service in the World war period. Doctor Salb received his honorable discharge in August, 1919, and then resumed the practice of his profession at Jasper. He has membership in the Dubois County Medical Society, the Indiana State Medical Society and the American Medical Association, is a Democrat in political alignment, is affiliated with both York and Scottish Rite bodies of the Masonic fraternity, as well as its Mystic Shrine, and has membership also in the American Legion and the Benevolent and Protective Order of Elks.

On the 8th of February, 1917, Doctor Salb was united in marriage to Miss Lena Joseph, daughter of Frank Joseph, a representative citizen of Jasper. The one child of Doctor and Mrs. Salb is a fine son, Robert Lee, who was born August 27, 1918, while his father was in service in France. Doctor Salb was thus not permitted to see his son until the latter was one year old, and he relates that in response to a letter from his wife in which she mentioned that the son had received a haircut, he manifested his longing to see the youngster and hoped this would be possible before the youthful scion of the Salb family began to shave his face. Doctor and Mrs. Salb are popular figures in the representative social life of the community in which they were reared and in which they continue to maintain their home.

MRS. MARGARET JEAN. Prominently concerned in much that adds to the civic welfare of Petersburg, Indiana, is Mrs. Margaret Jean, librarian of the Petersburg Public Library, member of the library board, secretary of the Red Cross for this district and secretary of the Children's Board of Charities. She has been long well known at Petersburg and in other parts of Pike County through her musical gifts, as she is an artist in proficiency and for twelve years was a popular teacher of music. In almost every community may be found, in these modern days, a group of earnest, educated women who, often with great unselfishness, devote time, means and effort to public-spirited movements, and Mrs. Jean is one of this body at Petersburg. Fully realizing, as one of her cultured tastes and training could do, the inestimable benefit that a public library would be to her city, she was a not inconsiderable factor in bringing about the founding of this institution in 1923, of which she has been the librarian ever since. The library is in a very prosperous condition and has become, under Mrs. Jean's capable management, a source of civic pride and congratulation.

Mrs. Jean was born at Martinsville, Indiana, a daughter of John and Sarah (Graham) Story, the former of whom was born of Irish parents, and the latter of Scotch-Irish ancestry. Both parents of Mrs. Jean, however, were born in Morgan County, Indiana. The father died in 1867 and the mother in 1873. They had two children, Mrs. Jean and her brother, William Edward.

Carefully educated in the grade and high schools, Mrs. Jean displayed such unusual talent for music that she was given the opportunity of perfecting herself in her art in the New England Conservatory of Music at Columbus, Indiana, and she was graduated therefrom with honors. For the succeeding twelve years she was engaged in teaching music, and made a most remarkable success in her profession, her own talent enabling her to stimulate her pupils with some of her love for what she taught, and some who came under her instruction later rose to high position in the musical world.

Francis N. Jean, husband of Mrs. Jean, died at his home at Petersburg, Indiana, in 1921, leaving his widow and one daughter, Aline Elizabeth, now the wife of Dr. Walter E. Treanor, judge of the Indiana Supreme Court. Judge and Mrs. Treanor have one child, Rosemary, now nine years old.

In addition to her duties as librarian Mrs. Jean is a member of the Woman's Club, has served as secretary of the local chapter of the American Red Cross, is a member of the Cradle of Liberty Chapter of the Daughters of the American Revolution at Petersburg. and is secretary of the Children's Board of Charities. She is one of her sex who is proving the fact that women do take an interest in civic affairs, and that they can be depended upon to do their duty as citizens. In her work in the library Mrs. Jean is supported with a very strong library board, composed of Mrs. Anna Flemming, president; Mr. Hershel Johnson, vice president; Mrs. Effie Kraig, secretary; and Gus Frank, L. L. Dearing, Mrs. A. E. Davis and Frank Burger, directors.

CHARLES O. SCHOIER, M. D., has been established in the practice of his profession in the City of Jasper, judicial center of Dubois County, since 1921, and he has gained specially high reputation as a skilled surgeon.

Doctor Schoier was born in the historic old City of Munich, Germany, where his father was a manufacturer of astronomical instruments. The Doctor is a son of John and Adele (Christen) Schoier, the former of whom was born in Germany, where he passed his entire life, and the latter of whom was born in France. The death of John Schoier occurred in 1910, and that of his widow in 1917, both having been devout communicants of the Catholic Church. Of the five children two died young; Rev. Eugene Schoier, elder of the two surviving sons, is a priest of the Catholic Church and has a pastoral charge at Watkins, Minnesota; Emil was editor of a paper at Saarbrüeken, Germany, at the time of his death, in 1918; and Dr. Charles O., of this review, is the youngest of the five children.

The excellent schools of his native city afforded Doctor Schoier his early education, which included the curriculum of the gymnasium, an institution comparing with the high school of the United States. He served the prescribed period in the German army, and in 1913 he came to the United States. Here he was able to initiate studies in consonance with his long cherished ambition— that of preparing himself for the medical profession. He was a student two years in the college at Pullman, Washington, and in the period of 1917-20 he was a student in the University of Kansas, where he availed himself of the advantages of the medical department. In 1920 he entered the medical department of the University of Louisville, Kentucky, and in that institution he was graduated as a member of the class of 1921. In the year that thus marked his reception of the degree of Doctor of Medicine he established his residence at Jasper, and here his ability and personal popularity have gained to him a notably large and representative

Thomas J. Martinson

practice. The Doctor keeps in close touch with the advances made in medical and surgical science, avails himself of the best standard and periodical literature of his profession and has taken effective post-graduate work in the medical department of Tulane University, New Orleans. He has active membership in the Dubois County Medical Society, the Indiana State Medical Society and the American Medical Association. His political allegiance is given to the Democratic party, he is a communicant of the Catholic Church, and is affiliated with the Modern Woodmen of America. The early military service of Doctor Schoier included two years with the field artillery of the German army, in which he served as a supervisor.

In the year 1900 Doctor Schoier was united in marriage to Miss Anna Hoidl, and her death occurred in 1917. Of the children of this union the eldest is Adella, who is the wife of Carl Holcer, their children being two in number; Fanny, the next younger daughter, is the wife of O. Fritch, and they live at Munich, Bavaria; Emil and Eugene reside in the City of Chicago; Miss Anna lives with kinsfolk in Munich, Germany; and Miss Sally is training as a nurse at Saint Mary's and Elizabeth Hospital at Louisville, Kentucky.

THOMAS J. MARTINSON, chief of the police department of the City of Hammond, has been a member of the department since 1922 and his advancement to his present office has been a normal result of efficient service and civic loyalty.

Mr. Martinson was born at Goole, England, on the 17th of October, 1888, and is a son of John D. and Elizabeth (Leggett) Martinson, who were born and reared in England and who thence came to the United States, with their family, in 1889. The family home during the first year was maintained at Clifton, Illinois, and removal was then made to the City of Kankakee, that state, where the parents have since continued to reside. John D. Martinson is a skilled workman at the trade of carpenter and since 1890 has been in the service of the New York Central lines, on the Western division of which he holds the position of foreman in the bridge and building department. He has membership in various organizations of railway employes, is affiliated with the Knights of Pythias, and he and his wife are communicants of the Protestant Episcopal Church. They became the parents of seven children: James, Thomas J., Sarah Elizabeth (deceased), one who died in infancy, Martha Victoria (Mrs. Tracy Williams of Kankakee), Cornelius (a resident of Kankakee), and Alfred (deceased).

Thomas J. Martinson was an infant at the time of the family removal to the United States and was reared and educated in Kankakee, where he supplemented the discipline of the public schools by taking a course in the Kankakee Business College. While still in school he served as a newsboy in his home city, and during the period of 1904-06 he there held a position in the bookkeeping department of the Paramount Knitting Mills. In the latter year he entered upon an apprenticeship to the trade of machinist, in the Kankakee shops of the New York Central Railroad. He was there in service until 1910, when he went to Birmingham, Alabama, and passed a year as a machinist in the shops of the Alabama-Great Southern Railroad. He next passed a few months at Joliet, Illinois, in the employ of the Elgin, Joliet & Eastern Railroad. In 1911 he came to Hammond, Indiana, where he engaged in railroad work and in 1919 became round-house foreman for the Indiana Harbor Belt Railroad, and he was thus engaged until 1921, when he engaged in the garage and general automobile business at Kankakee, Illinois, though still residing in Hammond. A few months later he disposed of his interest in this business, and he then passed about six months in the employ of the Universal Portland Cement Company, at Hammond. In 1922 Mr. Martinson became a member of the Hammond police department, in which his service as patrolman continued two and one-half years. During the ensuing five years he held the office of sergeant in the detective division of the department, and the record of efficiency that he made in the service had much to do with the official recognition of his eligibility for the office of chief of police, to which he was appointed January 9, 1930, and in which he has given the excellent administration that has met with unqualified popular commendation.

Chief Martinson is a member of the Hammond Safety Council, and is vice president of the Tenth Congressional District Police Association. He also holds membership in the Indiana Police Association and is treasurer of the Fraternal Order of Police, Hammond Lodge No. 51. He is a Master Mason in McKinley Lodge No. 712, A. F. and A. M., of Hammond, his political allegiance is given to the Republican party, and in their home city he and his wife attend the Christian Church.

In the World war period Mr. Martinson was notably active and loyal in the promotion of various patriotic movements and agencies. He was made chairman of the railroad employes department of the Seven Federated Shop Crafts of the Indiana Harbor Belt Railroad, controlled by the New York Central lines, and in this connection he attended various conventions and was concerned in the formulating of the national agreement that was eventually presented to Mr. McAdoo, then the federal director of the railroads of the United States, under governmental war-period control. Mr. Martinson likewise served as chairman for the Government war loan drives of the Seven Federated Crafts, was a resourceful four-minute speaker and was financial secretary of the local machinists union. A devotee of athletic sports, Chief Martinson manifests special predilection for football and baseball.

At Kankakee, Illinois, on the 13th of July, 1911, Mr. Martinson was united in marriage to Miss Doris M. Byrnes, who was reared and educated at Bradley, that state, and who is a daughter of George W. and Elizabeth Anne (Colberg) Byrnes. Mr. Byrnes was long engaged in farm enterprise near Kankakee, and was a resident of Bradley, Illinois, at the time of his death, his widow being now a loved member of the family circle of Chief and Mrs. Martinson, of whose four children the eldest is Olive Elizabeth, who was graduated in the Hammond High School as a member of the class of 1928 and who is now bookkeeper for the Elliott & Daniels Automobile Sales Agency in the City of Gary. Doris Victoria is now a student in the Hammond High School. Muriel Roberta died at the age of ten years. Thelma Joan is a student in the Hammond public schools.

RALPH E. ROBERTS. For more than thirty-five years Hon. Ralph E. Roberts has been engaged in the practice of law in Spencer County, and during this long period has held a soundly established position as a capable, reliable and industrious attorney whose clientage has been of the most acceptable kind. A thorough master of the intricacies and perplexities of his profession, he has been connected with much important litigation, and likewise has occupied a position on the bench. As lawyer, judge and citizen he has so comported himself as to deserve fully the confidence and esteem in which he is held.

Judge Roberts was born January 22, 1868, on a farm in Jackson Township, near Gentryville, Spencer County, Indiana, and is a son of John and Nancy Louisa (Tuley) Roberts. John Roberts was born January 2, 1834, in Jackson Township, where he received a district school education and on reaching his majority centered his activities in farming. He was thus engaged when the differences between the North and the South brought about the war between the states, and he volunteered and was accepted as a private in Company K, Forty-second Regiment, Indiana Volunteer Infantry. After serving for two years he contracted illness, which rendered him unfit for service in the field, he being sent home on a furlough. The disease proved an obstinate one, needing long and patient care, and by the time Mr. Roberts had recovered the war had come to a close. He then returned to his agricultural operations, in which he continued to be engaged until his retirement, several years before his death, which occurred April 12, 1912. Mr. Roberts was a Democrat in his political views, and served as township trustee for at least twelve years. He was a member of the Grand Army of the Republic and had the respect and esteem of the people of his community. Mr. Roberts married Miss Nancy Louisa Tuley, who was born April 24, 1834, in Jackson Township, Spencer County, and died January 9, 1892, and of the six children born to this union, one, Kelso K., died at the age of three years, the others being: James W., a farmer, who died at the age of thirty-eight years;

John J., born in 1866, who was engaged in farming up to the time of his retirement and his death occurred in 1922; Henry H., born in 1864, and died August 9, 1929, at Kingman, Arizona, where he is buried, was for many years connected with mining; George S., born September 19, 1865, is still engaged in farming and stock raising on the old home place in Jackson Township; and Ralph E. of this review.

Ralph E. Roberts attended the public schools of Jackson Township, under the preceptorship of Prof. C. C. Hinkle, one of the well-known educators of his day, and others of that day, and when still a young man secured employment as a teacher in the rural schools, a vocation which he followed until 1888. With the money thus earned he attended the University of Indiana for two years, and then came to Rockport and took the position of deputy auditor of Spencer County, Indiana, December 5, 1891. While thus engaged he bought an interest in the *Rockport Democrat* and conducted this for a time, but in 1896 disposed of his holdings therein and since then has devoted himself to the practice of his profession, having been admitted to the bar of Indiana in 1895. His work has carried him into the higher courts, where he has demonstrated his ability, sound logic, knowledge of principles and precedence and power of expression in placing his facts before court and jury. For six years he served in the capacity of judge of the Circuit Court of Warrick and Spencer counties, this being the Second Judicial District, and his record in that capacity was one of conscientious service. Judge Roberts is a Democrat in politics. His family belong to the Methodist Church, but he has no particular religious connection, although he has always supported worthy movements. Fraternally he is a past master of Rockport Lodge No. 112, A. F. and A. M. In addition to his large law practice he is the owner of a valuable and well-developed farm in the vicinity of Gentryville and extensive real estate within the limits of the city. He has been a member of the Spencer County Bar Association, the Indiana Bar Association and the American Bar Association.

On November 29, 1896, in Spencer County, Judge Roberts was united in marriage with Miss Alice E. Saunders, who was born in Ohio Township, seven miles from Rockport, and to this union there have been born five children. Ralph R., born October 16, 1897, is a former executive secretary and at present an employee of the Democratic Congressional Committee at Washington, D. C. He was in his second year at the University of Indiana when he left school to accept an appointment at Annapolis Naval Academy, where he remained for about a year, resigning to enlist in the United States Marines and was sent to Paris Island, where he underwent intensive training, and was soon to be sent to the frontline trenches in France with the Eleventh Regiment of Marines at the time of the signing of the armistice. He was attending an officers training school at Langres when the armistice came and was from there sent to West Point Academy, where he remained nearly a year, and in 1919 returned to his home and in 1922 was appointed private secretary to Hon. William E. Wilson, at that time United States congressman from this district. Graduating from the National University of Law, at Washington, D. C., he was admitted to practice before the Supreme Court of the United States and local courts of the District of Columbia January 21, 1929. He had previously been admitted to the local and Supreme Courts of Indiana. He is also admitted to the Federal Court of Indiana and the Federal Court of Appeals at Chicago. He is unmarried and resides at Rockport. Olive L. Roberts, the second child, was born October 28, 1899, and in young womanhood taught four years in the United States and one year in Canada during the World war. She married George E. Stevenson, a civil engineer, who served three terms of two years each as county surveyor of Spencer County, and is now deputy surveyor of Vanderburg County. They are the parents of one child, Alice Louise, born April 6, 1926. Marguerite Roberts, the third child, was born March 15, 1904, and graduated from the Rockport High School at the age of fifteen years, receiving the degree of Bachelor of Arts from Evansville College before she was twenty-one years of age. For two years she taught school at McLeansboro, Illinois, and then went to Radcliffe College, Cambridge, Massachusetts, and took all her work under Harvard University professors, where she received the degree of Master of Arts. In 1930 she finished her third year as teacher of English at the Central High School, Evansville, Indiana, a position to which she was reappointed. In 1929 she took leave of absence to go to Cambridge University, England, for a short course, and made a tour of Europe, after which she taught another year at Central High School at Evansville and is now on leave of absence at Radcliffe College, preparing for her Ph. D. degree. John L. Roberts, the fourth child, was born November 20, 1907, spent one year at Bloomington and one year at Evansville College, and then pursued a course at Lockyear's Business School. During the winter of 1928-29 he attended the Western Union Telegraph School, Chicago, and was a member of the communication branch of the United States Army Coast Guard service, assigned to the Flagship *Argus*, with base at New London, Connecticut, until the fall of 1930, when he was admitted to practice in the Indiana courts and is now associated in practice with his father, having been admitted to practice in all of the courts in Indiana. Alice, the youngest child, was born February 25, 1910, and after graduating from the Rockport High School spent one year at Evansville College. She also took a three-year course in the music department, part of the time while she was attending high school, and from July, 1928, to June, 1930, studied voice culture and music in Berlin, Germany, under the famous Maestro Bachner, in preparation for a musical career in grand opera. She is now at home in Rockport, pursuing her work in music.

JOHN LAVAL was a physician and surgeon of Evansville, and he returned to that city, where he was born, after several years of preliminary training and experience in his profession in other localities.

Doctor Laval was born at Evansville April 23, 1893, a son of Charles F. H. and Theresa (Doyle) Laval. His father was also born at Evansville and his mother was a native of Indiana. Charles Laval, now deceased, was a druggist for many years. Dr. John Laval was five years old when his mother died. The older son was Charles Laval, who owns a newspaper at Shanghai, China, and has for a number of years been correspondent for the Associated Press. He married Adelaide Killoge.

Dr. John Laval attended grammar and high schools at Evansville and graduated Bachelor of Science from the University of Chicago in 1917. He took his pre-medical work at the university and finished his course in the Rush Medical College of Chicago, where he was graduated in 1919. After an internship in the Saint Francis Hospital at LaCrosse, Wisconsin, Mr. Laval practiced three years at New Albin, Iowa, and in 1923 returned to his home City of Evansville, where he had a fine reputation and a large practice. He was a member of the Vanderburg County, Indiana State and American Medical Associations.

Doctor Laval married, September 18, 1915, Miss Margaret Thompson, daughter of J. E. Thompson. They had a son, John F., born January 16, 1917, now in school. Doctor Laval was a Republican in politics, was a member of the Knights of Columbus, Fraternal Order of Eagles, for which he served as examining physician, and was a member of the Catholic Church. On February 6, 1930, Doctor Laval died, after a brief illness, of pneumonia.

JOSEPH KORDES, former sheriff of Dubois County and a popular and efficient member of the official family of the county at Jasper, its judicial center, was born on the parental home farm in this county, May 9, 1872, and is a son of the late Valentine and Philamina (Stratmann) Kordes, both of whom were born in Germany. Valentine Kordes was a young man when he came to the United States, and he was one of the substantial farmers of Dubois County many years, his death having occurred in 1911 and that of his wife in 1917. Of the children of the family the eldest is John, who resides in Kentucky; Theresa is the wife of August Blumé, their home being in San Antonio, Texas, and their children being ten in number; Casper died at the age of twenty-seven years and Adam at the age of forty-eight years; Philamina is Sister Superior in the Catholic convent at Ferdinand, Dubois County; Joseph, of this review, was next in order of birth; Emil and his wife, whose family name was Wahr, reside in Louisville, Kentucky, and they have eight children; Frank, who resides on the old home farm of his parents, married Miss Lillian Brosmer, and they have three sons and one daughter; Anton, now a resident of Lawrence, Nebraska, married Miss Sophia Reining, and they have five children.

Joseph Kordes was reared in the faith of the Catholic Church and his early education was acquired in a Catholic parochial school in his native county. After leaving school he found employment in the general store conducted by his uncle at Schnellville, a village in Dubois County, and in 1903 he engaged in the hardware business at Huntingburg, this county. He finally sold this business and for several years thereafter he owned and operated a planing mill at Huntingburg. He next turned his attention to contracting and building, and with this line of enterprise he continued to be identified until 1927, when he was elected county sheriff. The popular estimate placed upon his administration was shown by his reelection in the spring of 1929, his second term expiring January 1, 1931. Mr. Kordes is a staunch supporter of the cause of the Democratic party, he and his family are communicants of the Catholic Church, and he is affiliated with the Woodmen of the World.

On the 9th of November, 1905, was solemnized the marriage of Mr. Kordes to Miss Rose Schnaus, daughter of Agat and Mary (Buchart) Schnaus, and the three children of this union all remain at the parental home, namely: Marsella, Louella and Antonetta. The two older daughters are employed at the Newberry Store at Jasper.

EUGENE D. ROGERS, the oldest living native son of Boonville, has spent the greater part of his life in that Warrick County community and where he is now living in honored retirement.

He was born there December 23, 1845. His father, David Rogers, a native of Connecticut, possessed the Yankee genius of invention and invented and manufactured a stomach pump that made him considerable money. He died in 1855. David Rogers married Paulina Williams, a native of Pennsylvania, and of their four children the twins died early, and Eugene D. and Ida grew to mature years. Ida married Edward Gough, district judge and president of the City National Bank of Boonville. Judge and Mrs. Gough had seven children, five now living, and one son, Eugene, is a deputy comptroller of currency at Washington, D. C.

Eugene D. Rogers attended private and public schools at Rising Sun, Indiana, was a student in Holbrook's famous Normal School at Lebanon, Ohio, and the first regular employment he had after finishing his education was as a grocer's clerk in a store owned by the father of Senator James A. Hemenway of Boonville. After two years he engaged in the dry goods business, and during the Civil war he was with a regimental sutler in the Union army. Following the war Mr. Rogers attended normal school nine months and in 1865 became bookkeeper and a shipping clerk in a flour mill at Newburg. After eighteen months he engaged in the dry goods business for himself and remained there until 1868. Following that he spent five years on a Kansas farm, and on returning to Indiana clerked in a dry goods store at Evansville ten years. He and E. H. Stephens were associated as partners in a general merchandise establishment for nineteen years, and after that he was alone in business until 1902.

Mr. Rogers in that year went to Kansas, where his wife's father was ill. Mrs. Rogers died while in that state, and was laid to rest in Warrick County, Indiana. Since then Mr. Rogers has lived retired at Boonville. He finds occupation for his leisure time in looking after his flowers, garden and other work around the home and is an ardent disciple of Izaak Walton.

He married at Newburg, Indiana, February 6, 1868, Miss Mattie Lewis, daughter of John B. and Minerva (Anderson) Lewis. Her father was born in Warrick County and spent his life as a farmer. Her mother was a niece of Bailey Anderson, one of the prominent pioneers of Warrick County. Mr. Rogers is a Republican, and has been affiliated with the Independent Order of Odd Fellows and Tribe of Ben Hur.

Mr. Rogers has many interesting memories of the early days in Boonville, and by way of indicating the great changes that have occurred in his life time he recalls seeing wild deer running through the streets. At the time of the Civil war the rebels made a raid into Indiana at Newburg, and he was sworn into service to join the party that ran them out. These indicate only a few of his early recollections.

NORMAN M. SPRADLEY, M. D., has been long and successfully established in the practice of his profession at Boonville, judicial center of his native County of Warrick, and is distinctly one of the representative physicians and surgeons of this county. In his substantial and important practice he now has an effective coadjutor in the person of his younger brother, Dr. Louis G. Spradley, of whom individual mention is made on other pages of this publication.

Dr. Norman M. Spradley was born on the parental home farm in Warrick County November 24, 1860, and is a son of William T. and Hannah (Roberts) Spradley, the former of whom was born in one of the counties in Eastern Tennessee and the latter of whom was born in Indiana. William T. Spradley was five years of age when his parents came from Tennessee and established their home on their pioneer farm in Warrick County, Indiana, where they passed the remainder of their lives. William T. Spradley was reared in Warrick County, where he received the advantages of the public schools of the period and where he early had fellowship with the

Bessie B. Ross.

activities of the home farm. He not only gained eventual status as one of the substantial farmers of this county but also became a successful lawyer at Boonville, where also he gave sixteen years of service as city assessor and two years as county assessor. Here his death occurred March 16, 1894, and his wife survived him several years. Of the eight children James A. died at the age of three years and Andrew B. at the age of eighteen years. Temperance, now seventy years of age (1929), is the widow of M. M. Rice, her husband having given prolonged service as a teacher in the Indiana public schools. Dr. Norman M., of this review, is next younger. William B., who is now a carpenter and builder in the City of Pensacola, Florida, married Clara Jones, of Spencer County, Indiana. Agnes is the widow of D. W. Whittinghill, who was a merchant in the City of Evansville, Indiana. Dr. Louis G. is the subject of individual mention elsewhere in this publication. Charles, who is engaged in the restaurant business at Tennyson, Warrick County, married Miss Norris and they have three children, Mildred, Gilbert and Woodrow.

The public schools of Warrick County afforded Dr. Norman M. Spradley his early education, and in preparing for his chosen profession he went to the metropolis of Kentucky and completed a course in Louisville Medical College, in which he was graduated February 18, 1890. After thus receiving his degree of Doctor of Medicine he was engaged in the practice of his profession at Selvin, Warrick County, eleven years, his professional headquarters during the ensuing eight years having been at Tennyson, this county, and he having then established his residence at Boonville, the county seat, where he served four years as county auditor, and in the meanwhile continued in the practice of his profession. He is now one of the leading physicians and surgeons of Boonville and has as a valued associate his brother Dr. Louis G. He has membership in the Warrick County Medical Society and the Indiana State Medical Society. His political allegiance is given to the Democratic party, he is affiliated with the Masonic fraternity, the Independent Order of Odd Fellows and the Modern Woodmen of America, and he and his wife are active members of the Methodist Episcopal Church, as was also his first wife.

October 18, 1884, marked the marriage of Doctor Spradley to Miss Mary Springstun, and her death occurred in 1908. Of the nine children of this union three died in infancy, and Carl was killed in an accident while employed in one of the great steel mills at Gary, Indiana, he having been twenty-seven years of age. Lois, wife of Loren Hobbs, a farmer in Warrick County, died December 28, 1928, and is survived by five children. Earl M., eldest of the surviving children, resides at Boonville, where he served four years as county sheriff and one year as chief of police and is now auditor in the gasoline tax department for the State of Indiana, working under State Auditor Floyd Williamson. He married Delores Frahlich, and they have three children—Earl Wylie, Margaret Elizabeth and Norman Mountford II. Narl A., next younger of the children, is a popular teacher in the Vanderburg County public schools, and the maiden name of his wife was Ivy Mae Kain. Lolin is the wife of Ira Shelton, who is a carpenter by trade and vocation, and they maintain their home at Boonville.

The second marriage of Doctor Spradley was solemnized November 24, 1910, when he wedded Miss Mina Wilke, daughter of William Wilke, of Warrick County. Of this union there are three children: Wilma, Lela and Norma. Wilma was graduated in the Lockyear Business College at Evansville as a member of the class of 1929 and Lela graduated from the same school in 1931. Wilma is now employed as secretary in the office of the law firm of Folson & Lindsey at Boonville.

MRS. BESSIE B. ROSS, county recorder of Lake County, has the distinction of being the first woman elected to a county office in Lake County, and she was also the first woman to hold the position of city clerk of Gary.

Mrs. Ross was born in Muncie, Indiana, daughter of Thomas and Florence (Blount) Blease. Her father, a native of Cincinnati, Ohio, was educated in Richmond, Indiana, and went to Muncie when a young man. For many years he was boot and shoe merchant. For twelve years the family lived in Kansas, and while he was there he served as judge of the Police Court at Weir City. From Kansas the family went back to Muncie, where he resumed his active connections with mercantile affairs. He died in 1919 and is buried in the Beech Grove Cemetery at Muncie.

Mrs. Ross' mother, Florence Blount, was born May 2, 1877, and reared in Muncie, and was a great-grandchild of William Blount, who took up the first tract of land in Delaware County, Indiana. The mother of Mrs. Ross was reared and educated in Muncie and still lives in that city, where she takes an active interest in the work of the Methodist Church and in the Woman's Club. Mrs. Ross is the youngest of three children. Her older brother, Charles F. Blease, is a merchant at Muncie and a member of the City Council. He married Miss Pansy Guthrie and they have two children, named Cole and Sara Jane. Tom Blease, the younger brother, is associated with Charles Blease, in the mercantile business at Muncie. He married Miriam Wright.

Mrs. Ross received most of her early education in the schools of Kansas. She graduated from the Newton High School there and after the family returned to Muncie, Indiana, she completed a course of work in the Cook County Normal School at Chicago. For five years she taught in the public schools of Muncie and for three years was a reporter for the *Muncie Star.*

On December 25, 1903, she was married to Ralph W. Ross, who at that time was deputy prosecuting attorney of Delaware County. Mr. Ross represented an old and prominent pioneer family of the county. He had attended high school at Muncie, studied law and was admitted to the bar, and while practicing at Muncie served as president of the Chamber of Commerce. In 1909 Mr. and Mrs. Ross moved to Hammond, Indiana, where he continued the practice of law and for five years was chief deputy prosecuting attorney of Lake County. In 1915 they established their home in Gary, where Mr. Ross continued his law practice until his death in 1921. He is buried in the Beech Grove Cemetery at Muncie. Mr. Ross was a Mason, member of the Independent Order of Odd Fellows, B. P. O. Elks and Loyal Order of Moose. During the World war he did much work as a member of a registration committee. He was a member of the Commercial Club of Gary. During the war Mrs. Ross was county chairman of the women's organization in the war work drives.

She became interested in public affairs and politics before her husband's death and served as chairman of the woman's Republican organization of Lake County. After the death of Mr. Ross she was appointed by Mayor William Hodges as city clerk, and at the next general election was chosen to that office, leading the ticket. This gave her the distinction of being the first woman in Indiana to hold an elective office in a city government. While city clerk she was made secretary of the State Municipal League, and continued in that position until the close of her term. Mrs. Ross is a thorough business woman, and enjoys the contacts of business and political life. After leaving the office of city clerk she was secretary of a building and loan association in Gary and was manager of the boys' department in Gary's largest clothing store.

In the general election of 1928 Mrs. Ross was elected recorder of Lake County. That office has had a highly systematic and efficient management since she took control. There is probably no more popular woman in Lake County than Mrs. Ross. She is a director of a building and loan company of Gary.

Mrs. Ross is a member of the Eastern Star, is corresponding member of the Muncie Woman's Club, member of the Hammond Woman's Club, the Gary Woman's Club, the Parent-Teachers Association, the League of Women Voters, Business and Professional Women's Club, and was the organizing chairman and is now a director of the Gary Y. W. C. A. She is a Republican and a member of the Episcopal Church of Gary.

Mrs. Ross has two children, Ralph Blease and Florence Elizabeth. Ralph graduated from the Emmerson High School and from the Idaho State University and is now with the United States International Ice Patrol, with base operations at Saint Johns, Newfoundland. The daughter graduated from the Emmerson High School in 1926 and received her A. B. degree with the class of 1931 in Northwestern University, where she specialized in journalism.

PHILIP LUTZ, JR., is a lawyer practicing in his native community of Boonville, Warrick County, where the Lutz family has lived and given their substantial influence to business, professional and civic affairs for over fifty years. While he has achieved a commendable reputation as a lawyer Mr. Lutz is probably more widely known as a horticulturist, being owner of the Phil Lutz Peony Farm, with sixty acres devoted to the propagation and culture of peonies, said to be the largest peony farm in the United States.

Mr. Lutz was born at Boonville August 28, 1888, son of Philip and Barbara E. (Billman) Lutz. Both parents were born in Germany and came to the United States in 1865. His father for many years was in the grocery business at Boonville, where he died in May, 1924. The family household consisted of twelve children, five of whom died in infancy and a daughter, Katie, who died at the age of fourteen. The living children besides Philip, Jr., are Louise, born in 1885, wife of Charles Hartinger, a merchant at Cincinnati; George, born in 1887, a merchant at Boonville, married Mabel Hartloff, of Chandler, Indiana; Carrie, born in 1891, is the wife of Dr. C. B. Ferguson, an osteopathic physician and surgeon at Miami, Florida; Ernest, born in 1897, is a florist at Boonville; and Anna, born in 1903, is the wife of Perry Lowell, a farmer and merchant at Boonville.

Mr. Philip Lutz, Jr., attended grade and high schools at Boonville and completed both the academic and law courses at the University of Indiana in 1912, receiving the A. B. and LL. B. degrees in the same year. He has been in the practice of law at Boonville since July, 1912. He has had no partnership, and has had a successful volume of general law practice.

Mr. Lutz is a local leader of the Democratic party. He was elected a member of the Indiana Legislature in 1914, serving during the session of 1915. He was county attorney in 1928 and 1931, and is now Democratic District chairman for the Eighth Indiana District.

Mr. Lutz married at Saint Paul, Indiana, June 16, 1914, Miss Lois Vane (Ryse), of Saint Paul, Decatur County, daughter of Gus and Lavira (Shelhorn) Ryse, both natives of Indiana. Mr. and Mrs. Lutz have one son, John Philip, born August 20, 1915, now a senior in the Boonville High School.

The family are members of Saint John's Evangelical Church. Mr. Lutz is a Scottish Rite Mason, a member of the B. P. O. Elks, Woodmen of the World, and was president of the Kiwanis Club of Boonville in 1928 and in 1929 lieutenant governor for the Fifth Indiana District. Mr. Lutz is president of the Boonville Building & Loan Association, president of the Monarch Finance Company, vice president of the La Salle Finance Company and is a director of the First National Bank and several other business organizations.

Mr. Lutz's mother had the faculty of making flowers and plants bloom and flourish, and her native faculty as a horticulturist has been inherited by the Boonville attorney. He has always been interested in gardening as an amateur and some years ago entered work on a commercial scale as a breeder and grower of peonies for the Chicago, New York and other markets. The Phil Lutz Peony Farms are the propagating grounds of perhaps as large a variety of the choice species of peonies anywhere found, and Mr. Lutz has searched the world over for many rare specimens, his grounds containing the descendants of many of the oldest of the best known stocks as well as some of the latest developments. Visitors come from widely different localities to the Lutz Peony Farms. His brother Ernest is also a successful man in the flower business, operating Maple Wood Gardens, of Boonville, which does a big business throughout southern Indiana. Mr. Lutz has done much to promote the development of this section of Indiana as the largest center of peony culture in the United States.

LESLIE H. HENDRICKSON is one of the representative younger members of the bar of Warrick County, his residence and professional headquarters are maintained at Boonville, the county seat, and the election of November, 1928, brought him to service as prosecuting attorney of his native county.

Mr. Hendrickson was born at Folsomville, this county, March 22, 1896, and is a son of S. H. and Miranda (Scott) Hendrickson, the former of whom was born near Huntingburg, Dubois County, this state, and the latter at Stendal, Pike County, their home being now established at Folsomville, Warrick County, and Mr. Hendrickson having long been one of the substantial and representative exponents of agricultural and live stock industry in that part of the county. Leslie H. Hendrickson, of this review, was the second in a family of six children, of whom the eldest is Capt. Charles W., who is a captain in the National Guard and who holds the office of shipping inspector for the port of Seattle, Washington, in which city was solemnized his marriage to Miss Minna Eccles. J. Harold, who is still a bachelor, resides in the City of Indianapolis and is assistant state superintendent of public instruction. Harvey K., likewise a bachelor, is superintendent of the public schools of New Palestine, Hancock County, at the time of this writing, in the summer of 1929. Gladys is the wife of Loren Hesson, who is actively associated with the automobile business in the City of Evansville, and they have two children, Betty Jean and William. Hazel is the wife of Leonard Freudenberg, superintendent of the public schools of Freelandville, Knox County.

Leslie H. Hendrickson continued his studies in the public schools of Warrick County until he was graduated in the high school at Tennyson, in 1914, and later he was graduated in the Central Normal College of Indiana, with the degree of Bachelor of Arts. He was a student in the law department of that institution when the nation entered the World war, in the spring of 1917, and he forthwith volunteered for service in the United States Army. He received due preliminary training and August 31, 1918, he embarked with his unit for overseas service and was later granted a commission as first lieutenant and with his command he was in active service in France at the time of the termination of hostilities by the signing of the historic armistice. June 1, 1919, he embarked for the return voyage, and at Camp Sherman, Ohio, he received his honorable discharge on the 6th of the same month. He still retains commission as first lieutenant in the Officers Reserve Corps of the United States Army, and it is to be noted that in 1928 he was district commander of the American Legion.

After the conclusion of his World war service Mr. Hendrickson resumed the study of law, and in May, 1920, he was admitted to the bar of his native state. He was actively and successfully established in the practice of his profession at Boonville at the time of his election to his present office, that of prosecuting attorney of his native county, in November, 1928, and his administration is distinctly adding to his reputation as a resourceful and vigorous trial lawyer. Mr. Hendrickson is unwavering in his allegiance to the Republican party, is a member of the Warrick County Bar Association and the Indiana State Bar Association, and both he and his wife have membership in the Methodist Episcopal Church in their home city.

June 11, 1921, recorded the marriage of Mr. Hendrickson to Miss Hazel Madden, who was born at Lynnville, Warrick County, the second of the eight children of M. L. and Eva (Holder) Madden, who still reside at Lynnville, Mr. Madden being a representative farmer in that locality. Mr. and Mrs. Hendrickson have two children: Leslie H., Jr., born June 13, 1922, and Paul Eugene, born July 29, 1924.

ALDEN J. HEURING, newspaper publisher, has for over thirty-four years given Pike County one of its best newspapers, the *Winslow Dispatch*, of which he is proprietor and editor.

Mr. Heuring was born at Spurgeon in Pike County, Indiana, December 19, 1873. His father, Frank E. Heuring, a native of Baltimore, Maryland, came to Indiana in 1869, and his home was at Winslow from 1884 until his death in 1922. Frank E. Heuring married Eliza Richardson. The Richardsons were of old Colonial and Revolutionary stock. Her father was a pioneer minister of the Primitive Baptist Church in Pike County. Mrs. Eliza Heuring is now seventy-seven years of age. She is the mother of three children, Alden J., Margaret and Edward. Margaret is the wife of Walter Shiver, of Evansville, Indiana, and has one child, while Edward, who also lives at Evansville, Indiana, married Elizabeth Dillon, and they have a son and daughter.

Alden J. Heuring was educated in the grammar and high schools of Pike County and also attended the Indiana State Normal School. The basis of his business as a newspaperman was acquired in a printing office at Vincennes, where he learned his trade. After some years of working for others he established the *Winslow Dispatch* in March, 1898, and has been in the newspaper business continuously down to the present time.

Mr. Heuring married, October 15, 1899, Miss Georgia Shugert. She died March 12, 1920, and of the three children born to their marriage two died in infancy. The surviving son is Frank, who was born February 17, 1905, and is now a capable assistant and partner with his father in the newspaper business. Mr. Heuring on April 3, 1924, married Beulah Woodford. By this marriage there are two children, Patty Ann, born April 30, 1927, and Richard L., born June 30, 1928. Mr. Heuring is a staunch Democrat in politics, and at present is Democratic county chairman of Pike County. He is a York Rite Mason and Shriner, member of the Kiwanis Club, Knights of Pythias and the Winslow Chamber of Commerce.

JESSE FRANK KIMMEL, proprietor of the J. F. Kimmel furniture and undertaking business at Gaston, is a native of Indiana, where his people have lived for several generations, being an old and honored family of Henry County.

He was born on a farm in that county, January 19, 1890, son of Joseph W. and Mary (Burns) Kimmel. His grandfather, Michael Kimmel, was a Pennsylvanian by birth and an early settler in Henry County, where he spent his active life as a farmer and stock raiser, owning a farm of several hundred acres. He was progressive in everything whether it concerned his own business or the community. One instance was the fact that he introduced the first threshing machine into that vicinity. He died in 1900 and he and his wife are buried in the old Lutheran Church Cemetery near Hagerstown, Indiana. Joseph W. Kimmel was born and reared in Henry County, and he and his wife still live on their farm in that part of the state. They are active members of the Christian Church. His wife, Mary Burns, was also born in Henry County and attended school there. She is a daughter of Calvin J. and Nancy (Nation) Burns, well-to-do farmers of Henry County, who are buried in the New Lisbon Cemetery. Jesse Frank Kimmel has one brother, Carl J. Kimmel, a farmer in Henry County, who married May Ridgeway and has two daughters Mary and Catherine.

Jesse Frank Kimmel attended public schools in Henry County, including the Newcastle High School, and in 1908 was graduated in the Barnes Embalming School of Indianapolis. For two years he was associated with W. A. Fox, a Newcastle undertaker, and he also worked at his profession in Cambridge City and Goshen, Indiana. Mr. Kimmel in 1915 located at Gaston and established the

J. F. Kimmel furniture and undertaking house. He is an able merchant and a splendid representative of his profession, both as to his personal character and his skill and ability. He carries a fine stock of reliable furniture and house furnishing goods. In addition to this business he is vice president of the Gaston Banking Company, and he owns a farm in Henry County. Mr. Kimmel is a member of the Indiana State Association of Embalmers. Since early manhood he has been active in the Masonic fraternity, being affiliated with Matthews Lodge No. 640, A. F. and A. M., Muncie Royal Arch Chapter and Knight Templar Commandery, the Scottish Rite bodies at Indianapolis. He is a Republican, and for the past twelve years has served as city treasurer of Gaston. He was reared in the Christian Church, but in the absence of a church of that denomination at Gaston he joined with the Methodists in worship and is a member of the official board of the church.

Mr. Kimmel married in Henry County. Indiana, February 17, 1909, Miss Mary Lillian LaBayteaux, daughter of James and Margaret (Alger) LaBayteaux. Her father was of French ancestry. He was a farmer and stock man in Henry County and is now living retired, at the age of eighty-six. Her mother died in 1920 and is buried in the Batson Cemetery near Newcastle. Mrs. Kimmel attended the schools of Henry County, graduating from the New Lisbon High School. She is a member and a past matron of the Eastern Star Chapter at Gaston, belongs to the Woman's Club, and is a member of the Methodist Church.

LOT W. OWENS, Boonville druggist, where he has been a substantial factor in the commercial affairs of that town for over thirty years, is a native of Kentucky and has spent his life largely in three states, Kentucky, Illinois and Indiana.

He was born in Kentucky September 10, 1850, son of William and Susan P. (Ringo) Owens. Both parents were born in Kentucky, where his father was a farmer. His father died in 1878. His mother was descended from a drummer boy in the American Revolution, who also rendered service as a dispatch bearer. After the war he came west and became owner of the Belgrave Springs in Kentucky and had numerous slaves. William Owens and wife had a family of nine children. The seven now deceased were: Augustine, John, Avon, Burt, Jerry, Sally and Mollie. Mr. Lot Owens has a brother, Francis R., a retired farmer at Manchester, Ohio, who married Lynie Davis, of Kentucky, and they reared a family of seven children.

Lot W. Owens attended school in Kentucky, completed a commercial college course at Bloomington, Illinois, and then took up pharmacy as a business and profession. He was in the drug business in Grayville, Illinois, until coming to Boonville in 1897, and here he established a store that has been one of

the institutions of the city for over thirty years. He owns a fine business, also has local real estate, including his home in Boonville. Mr. Owens is a Republican in politics, and is an elder in the Presbyterian Church.

He married at Albion, Illinois, January 15, 1880, Rosamond Wood, who was born in that state, of English parentage. They have three children, Mary Bertha, Elise and Neva. Bertha is the widow of Percy Ferguson, who died of the influenza in 1919, while sales manager of the Des Moines division of the Standard Oil Company, and left two children, Owen, born in 1910, who has completed a business college course, and Martha, born in 1914, a high school girl. Miss Elise Owens assists her father in his drug business. Neva, who has two children, Peggie Ann, born in 1924, and Dale, born in 1926, is the wife of Ralph Richardson, formerly of Spencer County, Indiana, now conducting a fine business as a fruit broker in the State of Washington.

ARTHUR MORTLAND CLEVELAND. To be descended from honorable forebears in an unbroken line, whose deeds are written on the pages of the country's history, is a distinction not given to everyone, and therefore when it is possessed, it is cherished more than any mundane honors or material riches. To mention the name of Cleveland is to call to mind a long line of men of stability and integrity dating back to Moses Cleveland, the founder of the family in the New World in 1635, and including, among others of high distinction, a President of the United States. The representative of the name at Plymouth, Arthur M. Cleveland, president and general manager of the Edgerton Manufacturing Company, is living up to the family prestige, and enjoys the full confidence not only of his associates in business, but of the public at large.

Arthur M. Cleveland was born at Plymouth, Indiana, July 24, 1896, a son of the late Arnott Morrill Cleveland. He was graduated from the Plymouth High School, after which he had two years of work in the University of Illinois, one year in Columbia University and one year in Roger W. Babson's School of Business. With his completion of the latter, he entered his father's business as manager of the plant of the Edgerton Manufacturing Company at Paoli, Indiana, and continued to operate it until his father's death, January 14, 1925. At that time he was made president and general manager of the entire business, and has inherited many of the characteristics of his father, being a fine executive and manager, and a recognized leader. He is deeply interested in civic and political affairs, but does not seek office, although his party has made him the nominee for mayor of Plymouth. He is a member of the Sigma Chi fraternity and all of the Masonic bodies. Mr. Cleveland was a lieutenant during the World war.

Arthur M. Cleveland and Josephine Ramage, of Dallas Texas, were married, July 13, 1923. Mrs. Cleveland was educated in the schools of her home city. While she was born in Texas, she is of German and French parentage. Mr. and Mrs. Cleveland have two children, Charles Arnott Cleveland, born December 14, 1924, and Sara Jane Cleveland, born February 4, 1931.

The record of the Cleveland family in brief is as follows:

Moses Cleveland, of Woburn, Middlesex County, Massachusetts, according to family tradition, sailed from London, England, and arrived in Massachusetts, probably Plymouth or Boston, in 1635. He was born at Ipswich, England, in 1624. Married Ann Winn, daughter of Edward and Joanne (Moses) Winn. Family of children consisted of Moses, Hannah, Aaron, Samuel, Marian, Joanne, Edward, Josiah, Isaac and Enoch.

Of the above children Samuel Cleveland was a sergeant in King Philip's war, he married Jane Keyes, of Newberry, Massachusetts, October 25, 1680.

Joseph Cleveland married first Abigail Hyde, and, second, Sarah Ainsworth, and she was the mother of Samuel Cleveland, who married first Ann Welch, and, second, Ruth Darby, and she was the mother of William Darby Cleveland. He married Phebe Abbott, daughter of Nathaniel Hatch, and mother of Pliny Cleveland, whose first wife was Rachel Ketchum, who bore him three children, Emma, William and Charlotte, and whose second wife was Elizabeth Holt, daughter of Asa Holt. She bore him Augusta, Louisa, Adelia Ann, Celia L., John M., Mary, Kelsey P., and Charles S. Cleveland, and they are descendants of the following ancestry—Edward Winn, Keyes, Grant.

Governor Alvin P. Hovey, died at Denison Hotel, 1891. Horace Gillet Cleveland, one of the compilers. Thomas A. Edison, No. 2967, 2970, 8098. Hugh Compton, 3101. Lee Ensign No. 8462. Mills 3107. Gabriel Huff 19623. Priscilla Compton 8448. Keyes 13973. Edward Winn. Joseph V. No. 499. Jedediah No. 501. Revolutionary Army.

Brothers of William Darby:

Nehemiah V. No. 748. Roswell V. No. 750. Revolutionary Army. Lieutenant Joseph Winn, Revolutionary Army. Sylvester 5513. David 6. 19438 shooting.

1—Moses' wife, Ann Winn.

2—Samuel's wife, Jane Keyes.

3—Joseph's wives, Abigail Hyde, Sarah Ainsworth.

4—Samuel's wives, Ann Welch, Ruth Darby. William Darby's wife Phebe Abbott Hatch. Pliny's wives, Rachel Ketchum, Elizabeth Holt.

Members of the family who held prominent positions:

1 Fellows of the Royal Society.

2 Fellows of the Society of Antiquaries.

3 Soldiers and Sailors of King Philip's war.

3 Indian war 1688.

4 Old French war, 1745-48.

16 French and Indian war 1748-63.
7 Colonial Militia.
149 Colonial Army, Revolutionary war, 1775-83.
7 United States Navy.
2 British Army.
2 Leaders Whiskey Rebellion 1794.
31 U. S. Army War 1812.
3 U. S. Navy War 1812.
3 Creek Indian War 1813-14.
1 Black Hawk war 1832.
3 Texan Army 1835.
3 Cherokee war 1837-8.
2 Canadian troubles 1837.
1 British Soldier Canadian Rebellion 1840.
13 Mexican war 1846.
345 Army War Between States 1861-65.
7 Navy War Between States 1861-65.
1 President of the United States.
4 Governors.
1 Lieutenant governors.
3 United States Senators.
7 United States Congressmen.
1 Cabinet Ministers, United States.
5 Presidential Electors.
1 Member Original Republican Committee, National.
18 State Senators.
61 State Representatives.
1 Territorial Representative.
10 State Officers.
34 Judges.
49 County Officers.
12 Mayors.
2 Village Presidents.
81 City and Town Officers.
51 United States Government Officers.
5 Canadian Parliament.
2 Canadian Government Officers.
4 Great Britain Parliament.
167 Clergymen and Bishops.
269 College Graduates.
2 College Presidents.
16 College Professors.
196 Doctors.
130 Lawyers.
2 Members Chicago Board of Trade.
1 Member Chicago Stock Exchange.
3 Members New York Chamber of Commerce.
6 Members New York Produce Exchange.
2 Members New York Stock Exchange.
94 Confederate Army 1861-65.
1 Confederate Navy 1861-65.
1 Modoc war 1873.
1 Indian war 1877.
6 Spanish-American war April to August, 1898.
5 West Point Graduates.
14 United States Regulars.
7 United States Navy.
6 British Army Officers.
7 British Navy Officers.
143 Authors and Writers.

2040
In different wars—741.
No history of the Cleveland family, nor of

the City of Plymouth, would be complete without extended mention of the late Arnott Morrill Cleveland, and all of the obituaries published following his demise in the prime of useful manhood, January 14, 1925, none met with greater appreciation than that which appeared in the columns of the Plymouth *Daily Pilot*, and was later issued in pamphlet form as a tribute to his memory. It is given below because it is the best expression of the prevalent feeling with regard to his loss at the time of his death.

"Arnott Morrill Cleveland, only child of the late Charles S. Cleveland, former mayor of Plymouth, and Mary A. Cleveland, was born at McKean, Pennsylvania, on June 22, 1875, and departed this life at his home in Plymouth, Indiana, on January 14, 1925.

"Death was due to Bright's disease, which began its imprint upon him almost fifteen years ago. Long under the shadow of broken health, at times plunged to the depths of suffering, he struggled heroically against his constitutional frailty and renewedly entered into enterprises that drew heavily upon his strength.

"Mr. Cleveland at the time of his death was president of the Edgerton Manufacturing Company, Plymouth's oldest industry, and for more than thirty-three years had been an outstanding figure in the civic and business life of the community. He ended his four-year term as state senator for Marshall and St. Joseph counties in January, 1925.

"'Arnie,' as he was known to his wide acquaintances, came to Plymouth in October, 1891, with his parents, and assisted his father in the establishment of the Edgerton Manufacturing Company, which has since grown to be the largest basket and fruit package plant in the world.

"The industry, during the past fifteen years, acclaimed him as its most outstanding figure and authority. He was a firm believer in cooperation. He founded the industry's first organization, the National Basket and Fruit Package Manufacturers' Association, and became its president. After his father's retirement from active business, in 1910, he assumed general control of Plymouth's oldest industry and directed it through an era of great progress.

"Characteristic of his great foresight, he established the first fruit package factory in the South, in the great fruit and vegetable belt. This concern, the Marshall Manufacturing Company, at Marshall, Texas, has proved to be the most remarkable success of the industry and Mr. Cleveland has served as its president since its inception.

"Mr. Cleveland later became president of the Texas Crate and Basket Company, Rusk, Texas; the Package Sales Corporation, South Bend, Indiana; the Indiana Land and Timber Company, Paoli, Indiana; and the Indiana Veneer and Package Company, Paoli, Indiana, the latter now a part of the Edgerton Manufacturing Company.

"A man of sterling integrity, of sound business judgment, with the power of keen and accurate analysis and decision, virile and yet kindly, cautious yet courageous, genuine, hating sham and pretense, bouyant in spirit, always with the forward look, spreading cheer and hope wherever he went, he was a tower of strength as a director, as a counselor and as a friend.

"Arnott Cleveland loved and believed in Plymouth. In all progressive movements his name was always at the head of the list.

"He was the second president of the first of our business organizations, the Plymouth Commercial Club, and during his administration it was largely through his personal efforts that an agreement was reached between the Bell and the Independent telephone companies which gave the city the single line.

"Although largely a self-educated man, he was vitally interested in education. He was a member of the board of education of Plymouth for three years, serving one year as its president. He took genuine pride in giving his three children a complete course at the University of Illinois, and in sending his two sons to Babson Institute in Massachusetts, a business school with the highest tuition in the United States.

"He was one of the chief factors in the building of the Plymouth Country Club at Pretty Lake, and served as its president during its first two years. It was at Pretty Lake that he spent the most of the last six months of his life, finding great pleasure in the large model garden adjacent to the Cleveland Summer home, the most beautiful on the lake.

"Although always a worker in Republican politics, he never sought office. In 1920, however, he was persuaded to allow his name to appear as a candidate for state senator for Marshall and Saint Joseph counties, and in the election that followed he was swept into office with a vote that eclipsed that of President Harding in the district.

"Although broken in health, he distinguished himself in the Senate. He was chairman of the cities and towns committee, and was a member of the committees on education, judiciary, military affairs, manufactures, swamp lands and drains, and telephones and telegraphs.

"Last spring on account of his illness, he declined renomination.

"Fraternal affairs held a keen interest for him. He was a member of all the Masonic bodies of Plymouth, and was a past eminent commander of the Knights Templar. He was a thirty-second degree Mason, holding membership in the Scottish Rite at Indianapolis; he was also a Shriner of Murat Temple at Indianapolis.

"He also held membership in the Odd Fellows, the Elks, the Kiwanis Club and the South Bend Country Club. He was a member of the First Presbyterian Church.

"With his parents he lived for some years in Columbia City, Indiana, Leipsic, Ohio, and at Edgerton, Ohio, until 1891, when they moved to Plymouth, which has since been the home of the family.

"Mr. Cleveland was married at Walkerton, Indiana, on December 24, 1895, to Laura Groshans. To them were born three children, Arthur M., of Plymouth, who succeeded his father as president and general manager of the Edgerton Manufacturing Company; Chester W., editor of *The Magazine of Sigma Chi*, with headquarters in Chicago; and Mary Jane, at home. His wife, children, mother and one grandson, Charles Arnott Cleveland, born December 14, 1924, survive.

"Funeral services were held at the home at 2:30 o'clock, Friday afternoon, January 16, in charge of Plymouth Commandery, Knights Templar. As a mark of respect the Indiana State Senate adjourned and the banks and business houses of Plymouth closed during the funeral hour.

"The steadfast fealty with which he held himself to his numerous duties despite an almost constant physical distraction was indicative of his high sense of responsibility. The long list of activities bearing his name stands as a tribute to his unfaltering courage."

Hundreds of letters and telegrams were received by the bereaved family following the death of Senator Cleveland, from all parts of the United States. Governor and Mrs. Emmett Branch, of Indiana, telegraphed to Mrs. Cleveland:

"Are greatly shocked and grieved to read of Senator's death. Send sympathy and love."

The State Assembly Woman's Club telegraphed Mrs. Cleveland:

"With deep regret and sorrow we learn of the death of your husband. We send our sincere sympathy to you and ask God's blessing and comfort for you."

U. S. Lesh, attorney general, State of Indiana, wrote Mrs. Cleveland:

"We are deeply pained to learn through the press reports in the morning papers that Senator Cleveland had passed away. We did not know of the illness from which he was suffering for some weeks, according to reports.

"Arnott Cleveland was a man of rare character. Seldom has it been my privilege to know a man to whom nature had given such a perfect blending of social and business talents.

"He was equally gentle and courageous and his private and public course of life will leave a permanent imprint for good on the community and State.

"Mrs. Lesh joins me in extending sympathy to you and the children. Except for her own precarious health Mrs. Lesh would go to be with you in these trying hours."

F. Harold Van Orman, lieutenant governor of Indiana, wrote to Mrs. Cleveland:

"It was with deepest regret that we learned of the death of your dear husband, and immediately upon receiving the news a Resolution of Condolence was passed, and a committee of Senators sent to Plymouth.

"I know our sorrow cannot be measured with yours at your great loss, however, I do wish you to know that I stand ready to aid you in whatever manner possible to make the burden lighter."

Oscar Ratts, attorney of Indianapolis, and for several sessions president pro tem of the Indiana State Senate, serving in that capacity during Senator Cleveland's tenure of office, wrote to Arthur M. Cleveland:

"Your telegram contained very sad news and I sympathize more deeply with you and your mother because I know you both so well and I realize what a great loss you have sustained, and only those who have sustained a great loss can appreciate the load you carry today.

"Your father was a kind man and a loyal friend. I served with no one in the Senate in all my time toward whom I felt so tender a relation.

"We could not bear such troubles if we could possibly avoid them, but as it is we can only struggle on and emulate the good example.

"My health will not permit my attendance at the funeral and I regret it very much. However, the tenderest feelings of my heart are with you in your bereavement, and in your renewed efforts to continue the battles of life."

The Resolution passed by the Indiana State Senate referred to by Lieutenant Governor Van Orman, dated January 15, 1925, is given below:

"At a regular session of the Indiana State Senate held on the fifteenth of January, nineteen hundred and twenty-five, the following resolution was unanimously adopted:

"Mr. President:

"I offer the following resolution and move its adoption: Whereas, The membership of this body learned with unfeigned regret of the untimely death on yesterday, of Arnott M. Cleveland, a revered and beloved former member of the Indiana State Senate from the counties of Marshall and St. Joseph, And, as a token of respect, and in his memory, did thereupon adjourn until this day.

"BE IT NOW RESOLVED, that his presence at our deliberations during his incumbency of office has proven most valuable, and his counsel has ever represented great wisdom, and deepest sympathy. Urbane, conscientious, thoughtful, wise and just, his legislative endeavors will long remain to occasion merited praise.

"We bow to the Infinite God who has called him hence.

"To his family we extend our tenderest sympathy over the loss of a most lovable husband and father. May God give them sweetest peace in this hour of affliction, and bring into highest relief his many virtues to always minister consolation.

"BE IT FURTHER RESOLVED, That a copy be entered on the minutes; a copy transmitted to the bereaved family; and a copy given to the press.

"L. A. Bradford
"Howard A. Cann
"Andrew E. Durham
"Senators
"(Signed) F. Harold Van Orman
"Lieutenant Governor
"(Signed) Zell C. Swain
"Secretary of the Senate."

In addition to the above and many others from political conferes of Senator Cleveland, the business world also contributed its share to the messages to the family. The following telegram was received by Arthur M. Cleveland from E. B. Hayes, general manager, Texas Crate & Basket Company, Rusk, Texas:

"I deeply sympathize with you in the death of your father. He sacrificed his health and life for the benefit of others."

W. L. Pitts, secretary, The Marshall Manufacturing Company, Marshall, Texas, telegraphed:

"Even knowing that the end was near your telegram that 'A. M.' had passed away was a great shock to us. We have lost a kind, loving, unselfish friend, and know that his family will miss him greatly. God's will must be done and all of us who have loved him must carry on as we know he would have us do. Wire hour of funeral as we wish to close plant here."

George L. Barden, of the Barden & Robeson Corporation, Penn Yan, New York, wrote Mrs. Cleveland:

"Word has just reached me of your intense sorrow and it has produced a particular saddening in my own heart.

"Few men I have known have had Mr. Cleveland's genial good nature or his ability to plan and execute work. It was a rare privilege to know him intimately. I will miss his companionship, and trust that you may be given strength to endure the strain."

The National Basket & Fruit Package Manufacturers Association, through their secretary, C. H. Rodehaver, St. Louis, Missouri, issued the following bulletin:

"A few days ago there came into my office the information that A. M. Cleveland was dead and I am giving the notice to you just as it came to me, as it is a great deal better than I could write it. I know that every member of our Association and the package industry as well will feel the loss of Mr. Cleveland.

"'Andy' is dead.

"'Arnott M. Cleveland, president of the Edgerton Manufacturing Company, Plymouth, Indiana, passed away at his home January 14, 1925. in his forty-ninth year, of Bright's disease.

"'He was for many years one of the outstanding figures in the fruit package industry of the United States, and was one of the principal organizers and first president of both the National Association of Basket & Package Manufacturers and the Package

Sales Corporation. He was an aggressive business man and had many firm friends, and some enemies, as any aggressive man will, but it is a notable fact that many who were formerly unfriendly to him in later years and on closer acquaintance came to recognize his better qualities of character and are glad to be numbered among his friends, to whom he was familiarly known as 'Andy' on account of his rather unusual first name.

"'He was not great of stature, but he had a really great and brilliant mind and will be much missed in the fruit package industry as well as business and social circles of his home locality.

"'The sympathy of his many friends is extended to the sorrowing family.'"

The Union Trust Company of South Bend, Indiana, through J. E. Neff, vice president, wrote Arthur M. Cleveland as follows:

"Your telegram informing us of your father's death comes to the management of the Union Trust Company and to myself as particularly saddening news. It seems a premature ending of a useful and constructive life.

"Our sincere sympathy goes out to all the members of his family and to his immediate business associates."

The Meridian Club of Paoli, Indiana, through its president, E. L. Throop, wrote Arthur M. Cleveland as follows:

"The Meridian Club wishes to extend sincere sympathy and express its profound regret in the death of your father, and while we realize that nothing we can say or do can mitigate the grief and loss you must feel, we believe it to be a privilege and a friendly duty to pay our tribute of respect and esteem.

"He has been our guest at our meetings, and his talks on those occasions revealed to us his friendly spirit, his civic pride and his confidence in his fellow men, and we consider it a pleasure and honor to have been his host at numerous times.

"This community has suffered a distinct loss in his demise, and we again assure you of the sympathy of all members of the organization."

The Orange County Bank, Paoli, Indiana, through its cashier, Raymond Stout, wrote Arthur M. Cleveland:

"I realize what a great responsibility your father has left for you, but I feel certain that you will be able to handle it well.

"Your father was a wonderful man in many ways. His host of friends all over Indiana and in many other states will deeply regret his passing away. His personality and his work will live on with much credit to his family."

Fuller & Sons, manufacturers and mill agents, Los Angeles, California, through B. H. Fuller, wrote to the Edgerton Manufacturing Company:

"We have lost a friend and you have lost a good counselor. Please convey my heartfelt sympathy to his family."

The St. Louis Box & Basket Company, St. Louis, Missouri, through A. E. Steideman, expressed sympathy to Mrs. Cleveland as follows:

"We have just learned this morning of the passing away of Mr. Cleveland, and we can sincerely extend to you our heartfelt sympathy in your bereavement.

"Our president, Mr. Johnson, is away, but we will convey this sad news to him and we know his sorrow will be deep because he always thought so much of Mr. Cleveland, both in a personal way and for his straightforwardness in business transactions."

The St. Joseph Iron Works, St. Joseph, Michigan, through W. E. Hatch, secretary-treasurer, communicated with Arthur M. Cleveland as follows:

"Your wire giving news of your father's death was received with considerable shock by us here.

"Practically everyone in our organization knew Mr. Cleveland personally, and the expression of sorrow throughout our shop was universal.

"I know well the loss you feel, and I realize that nothing I could say could assuage your grief. I cannot refrain, however, from stating that the Company feels it has suffered a loss, and the writer realizes that he has suffered a very definite personal loss.

"We arranged to have some flowers sent to the funeral, and we trust they will arrive on time."

ELIJAH JEFFERSON WHITELOCK is one of the very successful citizens of Pike County, Indiana. His interests are represented by active farming operations on several hundred acres and also in the grain and milling business at Petersburg, where he resides.

Mr. Whitelock was born in Franklin County Indiana, February 27, 1860. His father, Joseph Whitelock, was a native also of Franklin County, and spent his career as an industrious farmer. He died in 1898. His wife Elizabeth Childras, was born in Kentucky, and died in 1897. Of the seven children born to the parents one died at the age of eleven years, and four others are now deceased, named Rusha Ann, John W., Edward J. and Charles W. The two surviving children are Elijah Jefferson and Walter, the latter a Pike County farmer.

Elijah Jefferson Whitelock grew up on an Indiana farm, made good use of the opportunities of the local schools, and since early boyhood has been familiar with the tasks and routine duties of farming. For many years he has carried on his farming operations on a large scale. Since 1898, a period of over thirty years, he has been connected with the milling business, and his industry at Petersburg has afforded a continuous market for the grain growers of this locality.

Mr. Whitelock married, March 21, 1883, Miss Louisa Foust, who was born in Pike County, and died at Petersburg, April 8, 1913.

Of the five children of their marriage two died in infancy. The three surviving sons are Fred, Hooker and Herman, Fred and Hooker being connected with their father's milling business, while Herman is cashier of the Citizens Bank of Petersburg. Fred married Ada Malott and has two sons, Horace and Harold. Hooker married Bessie Smith and has four children, Leland an electrical engineer, Myron, Dorothy and Herbert. Herman is married and has one son, Donald. Mr. Whitelock is a Democrat in politics, is affiliated with the Independent Order of Odd Fellows and is a member of the United Brethren Church.

CLARA COMSTOCK, who now holds the chair of physical education in Earlham College in her native City of Richmond, is one of the loyal, talented and popular members of the faculty of this fine old institution, which has been from its founding maintained under the auspices of the Society of Friends.

Miss Comstock received the advantages of the public schools of Richmond, including the high school, Richmond having long numbered among its honored citizens her parents, Daniel Webster Comstock and Josephine (Albright) (Rohrer) Comstock, of whom more specific mention is made on other pages, in the personal sketch of their son Paul. Daniel W. Comstock was born at Germantown, Ohio, a representative of one of the old and sterling families of the Buckeye State. Miss Comstock has been an enthusiastic student and teacher. She has taken courses of study in the University of Chicago, in which great institution she was retained three years as instructor, and her educational advantages included also those of Earlham College and the New Haven Normal School of physical education, in the City of New Haven, Connecticut. She was for a time a teacher in the high school of Richmond, where she has held since 1916 her present professorship of physical education in Earlham College.

Miss Comstock gives to the Republican party her political allegiance and in her home city is a zealous member of the First Presbyterian Church. She is affiliated with the Altrusan Club and the local Woman's Club as well as with other civic, educational and social organizations in Richmond, and is a member of the American Physical Education Association, the United States Field Hockey Association, the American Posture League, and the Association of Directors of Physical Education for Women of Colleges and Universities.

LEWIS S. BOWMAN, former state auditor of Indiana has lived all his life in Wayne County and has an interesting record of service in business as well as in public affairs.

He was born near Hagerstown, July 31, 1867, son of Solomon and Christina (Schultz) Bowman, natives of Henry County, and grandson of Benjamin and Mary (Bell) Bowman who were also born in Henry County, Benjamin Bowman being a son of Benjamin, Sr., a native Virginian, who came north to Ohio and then to Indiana. The maternal grandparents were Martin and Christina (Klapper) Schultz.

Lewis S. Bowman worked on his father's farm in Jefferson Township, attended country schools, the Hagerstown High School, spent two terms in normal school instruction, and from the time he was twenty-one years of age his abilities were directed to teaching for fifteen years, from 1888 to 1903. From 1904 to 1911 he spent seven years in the boot and shoe business at Hagerstown.

Mr. Bowman has always manifested a strong interest in community affairs. For seven years, from 1901 to 1908, he was town clerk of Hagerstown and served four years as township trustee of Jefferson Township, 1905-09. In 1910 he was elected auditor of Wayne County, holding this office for seven years, until 1918. He was county chairman of the Republican committee eight years, 1908-09 and 1914-19. For one year he was president of the Richmond Chamber of Commerce and was on the board of directors for six years, 1912-17. During the World war he was a member of the County Council of Defense.

Mr. Bowman resigned as county auditor to become deputy state auditor on December 1, 1918, and served through the years 1919-20. In the spring of 1920 he was defeated for the nomination for state auditor. From 1921 to 1924 he was treasurer of the American Trust & Savings Bank of Richmond. Mr. Bowman was elected auditor of the State of Indiana in 1924, for a term of two years, and in 1926 was reelected. He held the office until December 1, 1928, and left the State House at Indianapolis to return to Hagerstown, where he is now secretary and auditor of the Perfect Circle Company, an old established industry that has been manufacturing products of national and international distribution for many years.

NOBLESVILLE PUBLIC LIBRARY is one of the very interesting institutions of its kind in Indiana, serving not only merely the immediate locality of the City of Noblesville, but all of Noblesville Township. It was formerly a county library, and it was much to the regret of the people of intelligence and culture throughout the county when, through the efforts of a few dissatisfied tax payers, the county wide system was abolished.

The library contains a collection of about 15,000 volumes and also numerous current magazines. Under the county system before it was abolished an automobile was used to carry books from the library to the patrons over the county. This automobile was named "Parnassus." It made daily trips over the roads taking and returning books to the homes of farmers and other residents who were patrons. In this way the facilities of a high class library were made available to many small communities as well as individual homes.

Myrtle G. Meara

"Parnassus" still visits the homes of the farmers in Noblesville Township and the township schools.

The board of directors of the library at the present time is made up as follows: Paul Michaels, president; H. H. Thompson, secretary; Fred Starr, superintendent of the Noblesville schools; G. E. Jones, Mrs. Earl S. Baker, Mrs. R. O. Morris, Mrs. A. W. Truitt and Mrs. Raymond Horney.

The annual library budget is approximately $6,000. Since the organization of the library it has been under the efficient management of Miss Lulu M. Miesse, librarian, and her interests, enthusiasm and earnest efforts have been largely responsible for the splendid service rendered, which in proportion to the amount of money available and the number of volumes is probably not excelled by any similar institution in the state. Miss Miesse has interested herself in the desires and the needs of the children as well as the adult patrons of the service, and her efforts have gone a long way toward educating the people of the county to appreciate the value of this cultural factor in their midst.

Miss Miesse is a member of the Indiana State Library Association and for one year was secretary. She was born in Noblesville, attended school there and completed her professional training in the Library School at Chautauqua, New York. Under her direction the library compiled the records of Hamilton County in the World war, these records comprising four volumes of clippings, illustrating every essential feature of local activities during the war period.

WILLIAM F. GRAHAM is one of the active young business men of the City of Anderson, proprietor of a successful industry as an ice cream manufacturer.

He was born at Anderson, son of Amery Graham, also a native of Madison County. His grandfather Graham was a native of Scotland and came to the United States when a young man, settling in Madison County. Soon after locating there the Civil war broke out and he joined an Indiana regiment that went to the front and with it he saw active duty in several battles and campaigns. After his honorable discharge he returned to Madison County and lived for a number of years at Pendleton. Later he went to Indianapolis, where he spent his last years and where he is buried in the Crown Hill Cemetery.

Amery Graham is now in the real estate business at Jacksonville, Florida. He married Christina Guenthenspberger, who was born in Madison County, daughter of Vincent and Barbara (Scheidecker) Guenthenspberger William F. Graham is one of two sons, having a brother, Fred.

Mr. Graham was educated in the public schools of Anderson, and on leaving school he worked on one of the local industries. When he was eighteen years of age he formed a partnership with William Purnell to manufacture ice cream. They have been going steadily ahead with their industry, improving their facilities, keeping their plant thoroughly up-to-date and producing a quality of product which is sold and distributed throughout the Anderson trade territory.

Mr. Graham married in 1915 Miss Zeota Pfaff, who was born in Anderson, daughter of Louis and Amelia (Hieden) Pfaff. Mr. and Mrs. Graham have a son, William. They are members of the Christ Lutheran Church and he belongs to the United Commercial Travelers.

MRS. MYRTLE G. MEARA, of Hammond, has the distinction of being one of the few women in Indiana who have been honored with the office and responsibilities of township trustee, an office which under the Indiana system of local government carries responsibilities and duties of the highest importance.

Mrs. Meara was born in Hamilton County, Indiana, a daughter of Richard Newton and Emily Jane (Manford) Young. Her maternal grandparents were John and Susan Manford, who came from England and were early settlers of Hamilton County, where her grandfather followed the business of farming and stock raising. Mrs. Meara's paternal grandmother was Diana Creekmore, daughter of Thomas and Lydia (Olvey) Creekmore, who were among the very first settlers of Hamilton County, Indiana, coming overland in pioneer times from North Carolina. Richard N. Young was born and reared in Hamilton County, and taught school there for a number of years. Later he was in the ministry of the United Brethren Church. His business during his later years was as a contractor in the construction of oil and gas pipe lines. He was always deeply interested in politics, and from him perhaps Mrs. Meara inherits the flair for politics. Mr. Young died in January, 1916. His father, Jacob Young, was born in Ohio and attended school there, and was an early teacher in the schools of Tipton, Indiana, where he had lived. His death was the result of an accident, a fall from a tree. His widow survived him and passed away in 1926, at the age of ninety-four. They are buried in Hamilton County. Mrs. Emily J. (Manford) Young lives at Hammond. She has always been a devout member of the United Brethren Church. The Manford family settled in Hamilton County about 1824.

Dr. Alva A. Young, only son of Richard N. and Emily J. (Manford) Young, is a prominent physician and surgeon at Hammond. He attended public schools in Hamilton County, graduated from high school there and took his degree Doctor of Medicine at the University of Indiana in 1905. He also received a diploma from the University of New York in 1915. His interne work was at Indianapolis and he practiced there for a year. Since 1908 he has had a commanding place in his profession at Hammond. In 1917 he entered the United States Medical Reserve Corps, received training at Camp Travis, Texas, was commissioned a first lieutenant and was on duty for a year and a half, being discharged at the close of the war with the rank of first lieutenant. He is a member of Hammond Post No. 16 of the American Legion, the Lake County, Indiana State and American Medical Associations, and is city chairman of the Democratic party at Hammond. He is a Royal Arch Mason, member of the Independent Order of Odd Fellows and B. P. O. Elks, and teaches a class in the Sunday School of the Episcopal Church.

Doctor Young married at Indianapolis, July 8, 1907, Miss Lillian Fellows, daughter of Mr. and Mrs. Harry Fellows. Her parents came from England, and her father died in Chicago in 1915. Mrs. Young attended grammar and high school in Chicago. She is a member of the Episcopal Church, is president of the Parent-Teachers Association at Hammond, and member of the Hammond Woman's Club. Doctor and Mrs. Young have one son, Harry Newton, now a sophomore in the Hammond High School. Doctor Young has always been greatly interested in athletics and out-door sports in general and was the organizer of the National Foot Ball League, being chairman of the committee on rules and by-laws.

Myrtle G. Young attended District School No. 2 in Fall Creek Township, Hamilton County, continued her education at Noblesville and in 1896 was married to Mr. Thomas G. Meara, of Madison County. His parents were Michael and Elizabeth (Dodd) Meara. His father came from Ireland and his mother from Delaware, and they lived out their lives in Madison County, Indiana. Thomas G. Meara was educated in Madison County, and began his business career with the Trust Gas Company at Indianapolis. For eight years his home was in Hamilton County and in 1908 he moved to Hammond, where he became connected with the Public Service Company of Northern Indiana, at first as plant superintendent and is now inspector. He is a Master Mason, member of the Improved Order of Red Men and a Democrat in politics.

Mrs. Meara since childhood has been a member of the United Brethren Church. She belongs to the Eastern Star, Daughters of Pocahontas, the Hammond Woman's Club. She is Tenth District vice chairman of the Democratic party and was a charter member of the first Women's Franchise League, and served as Lake County chairman. She was elected township trustee of North Township, Lake County, November 4, 1930. This township includes Hammond, East Chicago, Indiana Harbor and Whiting. She was the first woman to hold the office in the township and began her four year term January 1, 1931.

Mr. and Mrs. Meara have one son, Lester Richard Meara, who was graduated from the Hammond High School in 1915, afterwards spending two years in the University of Chicago. He is now safety first engineer for the International Lead Company at East Chicago, a subsidiary of the Anaconda Company. He is married and has two children, Richard and Thomas, both of whom are attending school at Hammond.

UNION W. YOUNGBLOOD is conferring distinct honor on his native county and state by his service on the bench of the Circuit Court, and his administrative headquarters are maintained in the City of Boonville, the judicial center of Warrick County, he having here been established in the successful practice of law at the time of his election to his present office.

Judge Youngblood was born on the parental home farm, four miles distant from Boonville, on the 4th of September, 1872, and is a scion of the third generation of the Youngblood family in this county, where his paternal grandfather made settlement upon coming here from his native State of South Carolina, he having been a young man at the time and having become one of the county's representative farmers in his day and generation. Judge Youngblood is a son of William B. and Mary (Patten) Youngblood, the former of whom was born and reared in Warrick County and the latter of whom was born in Ohio. William B. Youngblood gave his active life to productive farm industry in his native county, served as a member of the Home Guard in the Civil war period, and was a substantial and loyal citizen who held inviolable place in popular confidence and esteem. His political allegiance was given to the Republican party and he and his wife were members of the Baptist Church. Of the eight children only three are living: Melissa died at the age of six years. Alonzo L., who died at the age of sixty-eight years, was a successful school teacher in earlier years, later was influential in politics and held local offices of public trust, and thereafter he gave prolonged service as a traveling salesman of agricultural implements. He married Samantha Whitmer, who was born in Kentucky, and of their children two are living, Nathaniel H., who is engaged in the practice of law in the City of Evansville; and Carl W., who is engaged in the insurance business. Dr. Eli L., a successful and honored physician and surgeon, was engaged in the practice of his profession at Boonville at the time of his death, when he was sixty-eight years of age. He married Nera Masters, and the one surviving child is Leland M. Morton, who died at the age of twenty-one years, had been a popular teacher in the public schools and was preparing himself for the medical profession when death terminated his exceptionally promising career. He married Rose Boyer, who survived him, as did also their one child, Orion, who is now about forty-four years of age. Jerusha Lowell, the one surviving daughter, is the wife of James E. Lowell, a farmer in Warrick County, and their four children are Lyman, Earl, Mary and Emma May. Lucian D. is a clergyman of the Methodist Episcopal Church and is assigned to pastoral service in the Vincennes district of the Indiana Conference of his church. He married Ella Schwartz and they have three children—Laverne, Alleene and Crystal. Judge Union W., of this review, was the next in order of birth.

Galien, youngest of the children, died at the age of twenty-three years.

After his studies in the Boonville High School Judge Youngblood attended a business college at Fairfield, Illinois, and in preparing for his chosen profession he completed a course in the law department of the National University, of Washington, D. C., in which he was graduated as a member of the class of 1907, with the degree of Bachelor of Laws. He had previously begun the study of law in the law office of James R. Wilson, of Boonville, and later in the office of former Judge Edward Gough, of Boonville. He was admitted to the bar of Indiana in 1898 and was elected prosecuting attorney of the Second Judicial Circuit in 1902, serving two years. In 1901 he had formed a partnership with Mr. Wilson, in whose office he had first studied law. This partnership dissolved when Mr. Youngblood was elected as prosecuting attorney. He afterward practiced alone until 1908, when he returned from Washington and formed a partnership with M. R. Tweedy, who was afterward, in 1916, elected judge of this circuit and served until 1922. In the period of 1906-1908 Mr. Youngblood served as secretary to the comptroller of the United States Treasury, and in his professional activities he has continuously maintained his residence at Boonville. Here he held for ten years the office of city attorney, and here he continued in the successful practice of his profession until his election to his present office of judge of the Circuit Court, a position which he assumed on January 1, 1929.

Judge Youngblood is a stalwart in the ranks of the Republican party, has membership in the Warrick County Bar Association and the Indiana State Bar Association, and is affiliated with the Independent Order of Odd Fellows, in which he is a past grand conductor of the Indiana Grand Lodge, and with the Woodmen of the World and the Order of Ben Hur. He and his wife are members of the Main Street Methodist Episcopal Church of Boonville, Indiana. In the World war period Judge Youngblood was active and influential in local patriotic movements, he having been chairman of the legal advisory board of Warrick County and also chairman of the committee that directed the work of the four-minute speakers in this county.

On the 26th of May, 1901, was solemnized the marriage of Judge Youngblood to Miss Neta Bernice Youngblood, the two being of distant kinship, as both are lineal descendants of Samuel Youngblood of South Carolina. Mrs. Youngblood was born and reared in Warrick County and is a daughter of John W. and Mary (Taylor) Youngblood, both likewise natives of this county, where the respective families were founded in the pioneer days, Mary (Taylor) Youngblood being a descendant of Hubbard Taylor, who here established residence in the year 1814. John W. Youngblood has long stood forth as one of the sterling and prosperous exponents of farm industry in Warrick County and is eighty-two years of age at the time of this writing, in 1929. He is a grandson of Rev. John W. Youngblood, who was a pioneer clergyman of the Methodist Episcopal Church in Indiana. Of the children of Judge and Mrs. Youngblood the first born is Mary Maurine, who has received the degree of Master of Arts from the University of Michigan, at Ann Arbor, and is teacher of Romance languages in the Mississippi State College for Women. William W., next in order of birth, is a skilled civil engineer and as such is retained as the engineer in charge of the Midland Electric Coal Company's mine at Atkinson, Northern Illinois. He married Miss Mildred McCool and they maintain their home at Geneseo, Illinois. Hyatt, next younger son, was graduated in De-Pauw University as a member of the class of 1929 and is now in the employ of the American Telephone & Telegraph Company. Thomas E. was graduated in the Boonville High School as a member of the class of 1929 and is now engaged as an expert advertising copy writer in Indianapolis. Roy is a graduate of the same high school in 1931 and is now pursuing an engineering course in college, as is also his brother William.

HENRY E. EDEN is an active young business man of Muncie, one of the partners and the active manager of a prosperous business located at 108 West Washington Street, specializing in the handling of automobile parts and accessories.

Mr. Eden was born in Muncie, May 11, 1906. He is a son of William L. and Josephine (Koons) Eden. His grandfather Eden was a Kentuckian, moved to Indiana about 1877, and after a year or so went to Kansas, where he lived on a farm for three years. He then returned to Kentucky and in 1890 established his home in Muncie, Indiana, where he and his wife lived out their lives. Both are buried in the Beech Grove Cemetery. William L. Eden was born April 3, 1878, at Losantville, Indiana, attended public schools and for forty years has been a resident of Muncie. For over thirty-three years he has been with the Ball Brothers Company, as operator of one of their machine shops in the plant at Muncie. He is a member of the Loyal Order of Moose and Modern Woodmen of America, and the Christian Church. His wife, Josephine Koons, was born and reared near Mooreland, Indiana, and attended school there. She was an earnest member of the Jackson Street Christian Church of Muncie. She died October 4, 1921, and is buried in the Beech Grove Cemetery. Her parents were John L. and Ellen Koons, of Henry County, Indiana, where her people were very early settlers. William L. Eden had two children, Madeline and Henry E. Madeline is the wife of E. C. Payne, connected with the Muncie Products Division of the General Motors Company.

Henry E. Eden was educated at Muncie, graduating from high school in 1926, and also attended Saint Xavier College at Cincinnati, Ohio. He is a member of the Beta Phi Sigma fraternity. In 1927 he returned to Muncie, and became associated with Wiley Spurgeon and William E. Hitchcock, Jr., in the automobile parts business. In June, 1929, he was made manager and since the death of William E. Hitchcock, Jr., on December 29, 1929, has been in full charge of the business.

Mr. Eden is unmarried. He is a member of the Delaware Country Club, is a Republican in politics and belongs to the Jackson Street Christian Church.

GOLDSMITH GILBERT WILLIAMSON. One of the oldest families in Delaware County is the Williamsons. They have been in this section of the state for over a century. James Williamson was a New Jersey man, and on coming to Indiana took up land from the Government, brought it under cultivation, and his thrift and industry enabled him to accumulate over a thousand acres before his death. His land was in the Yorktown community of the county and he and his wife are buried in the cemetery at Yorktown.

A son of this pioneer was Jesse H. Williamson, who was born and reared in the county, had a public school education and for many years gave his attention to his business as a miller and merchant, both at Yorktown and Muncie. He died in April, 1916, and is buried in the Beech Grove Cemetery. Jesse H. Williamson married Julia Andrews, member of another conspicuous pioneer family of Delaware County. She was born at Muncie, attended the public schools of that city, and passed away October 3, 1928, being buried beside her husband in Beech Grove. She was a daughter of Dr. D. H. and Mary Jane (Gilbert) Andrews. Mary Jane Gilbert was the first white child born on the site of the modern City of Muncie. Her father, Goldsmith Gilbert, has the historical distinction of being the founder of Muncie. Coming to Indiana almost with the first opening of the lands of this region to settlement, he acquired several hundred acres, and on the south side of his tract he donated half of the land now in the courthouse square at Muncie. He owned nearly all the land north of this line, comprising the north half of the city. Goldsmith Gilbert in pioneer times had a post where his principal customers were Indians. Later he conducted a store, operated flour mills, was an extensive farmer and his name was associated with many of the early enterprises of the village. His daughter, Mary Jane Gilbert, married Dr. D. H. Andrews, who was prominent in the early days of Muncie as a physician and surgeon.

The only child of Jesse H. and Julia (Andrews) Williamson is Goldsmith Gilbert Williamson, who was born at Yorktown, Delaware County, November 28, 1867. He attended public schools in Muncie and finished his education in Indiana University, after which for a quarter of a century his work was with the Delaware County Bank at Muncie. For four years he served as county treasurer of Delaware County. On leaving the bank he took charge of the J. H. Williamson Company, a mercantile enterprise that was established by his father in 1885. This business now occupies his full time and attention. He is a dealer in flour, feed and seeds, both wholesale and retail.

Mr. Williamson has never married. He is a popular citizen of Muncie, being a member of Silver Shield Lodge, Knights of Pythias, and Muncie Lodge No. 245, B. P. O. Elks. He is a Democrat in politics.

LLOYD H. CLARK is a native of Delaware County and has a prominent reputation as an educator in that section of the state. He is superintendent of schools and principal of the high school at Yorktown.

Mr. Clark was born at Selma, Indiana, June 23, 1892, son of P. G. and Delilah Leora (Tharp) Clark. His grandfather, Charles Clark, was a pioneer farmer near Selma, where he and his wife are buried. P. G. Clark was born in Maryland, was twelve years of age when his parents came to Delaware County, Indiana, and after completing his schooling took up farming as a career. He is now practically retired, employing his time during most of the year as driver of a school bus. His home is at Selma, where he is a member of the Methodist Episcopal Church. His wife was born and reared at Mount Pleasant, near Selma, and was a very earnest worker in the Methodist Episcopal Church. She died in April, 1928, and is buried in the Maxville Cemetery near Farmland. Of her six children two died in infancy and the others are Chester, Raymond, Lloyd H. and Wilma.

Lloyd H. Clark attended school at Selma, graduating from high school in 1911 and soon afterward took up the work which has engaged his energies, with brief exceptions, to the present time. In the intervals of school work he went on with his higher education and in 1926 received the A. B. degree from Ball State Teachers College. He graduated from Indiana University in 1930, taking the Master of Arts degree. He has done considerable work on his Ph. D. degree in Indiana University since receiving the M. A. degree. Mr. Clark has been an active school man for seventeen years. During 1912-13 he taught at Hebron, North Dakota, and for one year, 1913-1914 was principal of the high school at Delaware, Oklahoma. With those exceptions his educational activities have been in his home county in Indiana.

On April 5, 1917, the day that America declared war against the Central Powers, he enlisted and received his training at Fort Hamilton and Fort Wadsworth, New York. He went overseas with the Seventieth Coast Artillery Corps and was stationed at Brest, Angers, St. Nazaire and La Meignanne, France, until after the armistice. He received an honorable discharge at Camp Sherman, Chillicothe, Ohio, March 12, 1919, with the grade of corporal. He was with the colors nearly one year. As soon as released from

Albert L. Doyle

military duty he returned to his school work in the Whittier School in Muncie, Indiana. Mr. Clark is a member of Delaware Post No. 19, of the American Legion.

For several years he taught in the public schools at Muncie and has been principal and superintendent of the Yorktown schools since 1927. He is a member of the Indiana State Teachers Association, is a Republican, and he and his wife are active members of the Friends Memorial Church at Muncie, at which place Mr. Clark is assistant teacher of the Golden Band Class.

At Farmland, Indiana, October 29, 1919, he married Miss Mildred Branson, daughter of W. M. and Ella (Diggs) Branson. Her father is a substantial farmer at Farmland and both he and his wife are members of the Friends Church. Mrs. Clark graduated from the Farmland High School in 1911, following which she spent a year in the Marion Normal School and one year in the Eastern Indiana Normal School, now Ball State Teachers' College. She teaches a class in the Sunday School of the Friends Memorial Church, is a member of the Woman's Club, a member of the Fourth Division Ladies Aid, and of the Friends Missionary Society. Mr. and Mrs. Clark have one daughter, Mary Alice, aged nine, a pupil in the McKinley School at Muncie.

KARL EUGENE PUTERBAUGH is a physician and surgeon, a young man of thorough education and fine professional qualifications who is practicing in Delaware County, with home at Albany.

Doctor Puterbaugh was born at Greenville in Darke County, Ohio, February 4, 1898. He is a son of Harrison and Lucinda (Potter) Puterbaugh. His grandfather, David Puterbaugh, was a native of Pennsylvania and spent his active life as a farmer near Greenville, Ohio, where he and his wife are buried. Harrison Puterbaugh was born and reared in Darke County, followed farming and stock raising, and died in 1916 and is buried at Greenville. His wife, Lucinda Potter, was born and reared at Greenville, attended public schools there, and is an active member of the Christian Church.

Karl Eugene Puterbaugh was the only child of his parents. He was educated in the public schools of Greenville, graduating from high school in 1916. This was followed by normal instruction in Earlham College at Richmond, Indiana, and in Defiance College at Defiance, Ohio, after which for two years he taught as principal of the high school of Hollansburg, Ohio. His pre-medical course was taken in the University of Chicago and the Armour Institute of Technology of Chicago. He was graduated in 1922 and then entered Indiana University in the School of Medicine, taking his M. D. degree in 1926. Doctor Puterbaugh had additional training as an interne in the Grant Hospital at Columbus, Ohio, and in 1927 established his home at Albany, Indiana. His offices are in the Albany State Bank Building. He has made himself a valuable factor in the community through his abilities as a general practitioner. He is a member of the Delaware-Blackford Counties, the Indiana State and American Medical Associations and the Muncie Academy of Medicine. Doctor Puterbaugh is very much interested in the work being done by the Kiwanis Club. He is affiliated with the Masonic fraternity, is an independent voter and a member of the Christian Church.

He married at East Liverpool, Ohio, November 26, 1921, Miss Sylvia Claire Davis. Doctor Puterbaugh and Miss Davis first met while both were teachers at Hollansburg, Ohio. She is a daughter of Thomas A. and Maude (Whitehill) Davis. Her father for many years was in the wholesale produce business, at first at Pittsburgh, Pennsylvania, and later at Liverpool, Ohio. He is now a retired business man at East Liverpool. Mrs. Puterbaugh was educated in public schools at Pittsburgh and East Liverpool, graduating from the high school of the latter place and was graduated in 1922 from the Kent State Normal School of Ohio. She taught at Hollansburg for two years. Mrs. Puterbaugh is a member of the Twentieth Century Club and Pollyanna Club and the Eastern Star Chapter at Albany. To the marriage of Doctor and Mrs. Puterbaugh was born one daughter, Betty Jean.

JUDGE ALBERT LORING DOYLE, city judge of Mishawaka, has distinguished himself as a very capable attorney since his admission to the bar and in a few brief years has become established as a progressive leader in the affairs of his community.

Judge Doyle was born at Buffalo, New York, March 15, 1904. His parents are William and Cora (Pattison) Doyle, his father a native of New York State and his mother of Missouri. In 1912, when Judge Doyle was eight years of age, his parents moved west to Minneapolis, Minnesota, and since 1914 they have resided at Fargo, North Dakota. William Doyle was in the hotel business there until he retired. There were three sons, the first two, twins, being John W. and Welcome P.

Albert L. Doyle graduated from the Fargo High School in 1922. He subsequently came to Indiana and entered Notre Dame University at South Bend, where he completed the course of the law school and took his law degree in 1927, being admitted to the Indiana bar in July of the same year. In his practice he has been an associate of C. W. Bingham at Mishawaka. Judge Doyle was deputy prosecuting attorney of St. Joseph County from 1927 to 1929. On November 4, 1929, he was elected city judge and has shown a rare capacity in handling the work of his court.

Judge Doyle is interested in welfare work, particularly among younger boys. For the past six years in addition to his legal work he has been public speaking instructor at Notre Dame University. He is a past president of the Mishawaka Exchange Club and former district governor of the Exchange, a member of the Knights of Columbus, Fellowship Club, Eagles, St. Joseph County, Indiana State and American Bar Associations and is a Democrat. He is a member of the Catholic Church.

Judge Doyle married, June 10, 1931, Miss Loretta Irene Leddy, daughter of Mr. and Mrs. John J. Leddy, of 91 Whitney Avenue, Elmhurst, Long Island, New York.

WILLIAM H. BALL, secretary of the Ball Brothers Company of Muncie, is a son of the late William C. Ball, one of the five brothers whose partnership relations began in early manhood and whose collective genius made the name and business of Ball Brothers of national scope and importance. William C. Ball for many years remained as representative of the family interests at Buffalo, New York, but spent his last years in Muncie, where he died April 30, 1921, and is buried in the Beech Grove Cemetery. The fame of the Ball Brothers as manufacturers has reached into every corner of the civilized world. During the past ten years their contributions and practical work in the field of education and philanthropy promise no less rich returns for the world at large. The Ball Brothers have given millions of dollars to education, benevolence and general welfare work, distributed among institutions in different parts of the country, and Muncie has been particularly fortunate through the support of the Ball Brothers of such institutions as the Ball Memorial Hospital, the Ball Teachers College, the Y. M. C. A. and other objects.

When it was formally opened, on August 4, 1929, the Ball Brothers Memorial Hospital was pronounced by hospital authorities from different parts of the country as an unsurpassed physical plant for its use and purpose as a general hospital. It represented an outlay of more than a million dollars and its location adjoins the grounds of the Ball Teachers College. The building realizes not only all of the requirements for A standard hospital construction, but in many features represents the last word in architectural details, the mechanical and technical facilities, and also the achievement of harmony in material arrangement and atmosphere which put this institution a long step in advance of the conventional type of hospital.

One of the auxiliary features of the hospital is a plant built for the sole purpose of producing milk and other dairy products for its use. The hospital is, in fact, an almost self-contained institution, having among its many departments a butcher shop, laundry, drug store, bakery. The dairy plant, which is the particular hobby of Mr. William H. Ball, is located ten miles north of Muncie, on a farm of 320 acres. A herd of sixty Guernsey and Holstein cattle, practically all pure bred, were brought from the heart of the Wisconsin dairy belt. The dairy barn, 80 feet wide, 100 feet long and 50 feet high, was designed and constructed with the single purpose of securing utmost cleanliness in the production of milk products for the hospital use. The mechanical equipment includes not only elaborate ventilating devices and methods that prevent the contamination of the milk, but also milking machinery, cooling apparatus and prompt delivery service to the hospital, where there is equipment for pasteurizing, grading and testing for all the requirements of the dietary.

Mr. William H. Ball is the only child of William C. Ball and his wife, Emma (Wood) Ball. Mrs. Emma Wood Ball resides in the beautiful family home in Muncie. She has been very active in the work of the Universalist Church, in the Federation of Women's Clubs, and is a past regent and for over twenty years has been chaplain of the local chapter of the Daughters of the American Revolution.

William H. Ball was born at Buffalo, New York, October 28, 1893, but was reared and educated in Muncie, attending grade and high schools there, and was graduated in 1911 from the Howe Military Academy. He took his A. B. degree at Hillsdale College at Hillsdale, Michigan, one of the institutions to which the Ball Brothers have made large gifts. After leaving Hillsdale he specialized in chemical engineering at Cornell University. In 1917 he enlisted, was in training at Fort Oglethorpe, Georgia, and at Camp Logan in Eastern Texas where he was put in the Fifth Division. With that division he went overseas in April, 1918, and took part in the St. Mihiel campaign from September 14 to September 26, and was in the Argonne from November 2, to November 11. After the armistice his division became part of the Army of Occupation. He received his honorable discharge on July 7, 1919.

Mr. Ball on his return to Muncie became identified with Ball Brothers Company, being a director, and after the death of his father was chosen secretary of the corporation, the office he now fills. He is also a director of the Merchants Trust & Savings Bank, the Merchants National Bank, the Peoples Home and Savings Association, and the First Rural Loan & Savings Association. He is a past master of Muncie Lodge No. 433, A. F. and A. M., belongs to the Royal Arch Chapter and Knights Templar Commandery, and is a thirty-second degree Scottish Rite Mason. He has filled chairs in all the Masonic bodies at Muncie. He is a director of the Kiwanis Club, a member of Muncie Post No. 19, American Legion, belongs to the Delta Tau Delta fraternity, is a Republican, and, like other members of the family belongs to the Universalist Church. He was in the church choir for nine years.

He married at Muncie, November 11, 1917, Miss Agnes Medsker, who attended school in Muncie and has likewise been identified with the Universalist Church since early girlhood, and for a number of years was in its choir. She is an accomplished musician, having carried on her studies in Chicago. She is a member of the Psi Iota Xi sorority. Her father C. L. Medsker, has for many years been a leading member of the Muncie bar. Mr. and Mrs. Ball have two children, Lucina and William Hudson.

HARRY L. STONECIFER is an Indiana railway man, has been in railroad service for over thirty years and has had many promotions to larger responsibilities with the Nickel Plate system. He is now division superintendent, with headquarters at Muncie.

Mr. Stonecifer was born at Cambridge City, Indiana, February 7, 1876, son of B. F. and Elizabeth (Ensminger) Stonecifer. His grandfather, Jonathan Stonecifer, came to Indiana from Virginia and was a pioneer farmer and stock raiser near Cambridge City, where he and his wife are buried. B. F. Stonecifer was born and reared at Cambridge City, was educated in private schools and when a young man took up railroading and for forty-nine years was a railway passenger conductor. He began his service for the Fort Wayne, Cincinnati & Louisville, which afterwards became a part of the Lake Erie & Western. He continued active at his duties until his death in June, 1928, at the age of seventy-seven. He is buried at Fort Wayne. B. F. Stonecifer was a thirty-second degree Scottish Rite Mason. His first wife, Elizabeth Ensminger, was born and reared at Laurel, Indiana, and died there in 1882. She was educated in public schools and she and her family were active Methodists. She was the mother of twin sons, Doctor Herbert and Harry L. Dr. Herbert Stonecifer practiced his profession as a dentist at Los Angeles, California, until his death in 1913. He is buried at Fort Wayne, Indiana. He left a widow and one child, Francis, who continue to make their home at Los Angeles. B. F. Stonecifer's second wife was Melissa Philpot, of Anderson, Indiana, who died leaving one son, B. Paul, who is now manager of the Inter-Department Stores Company at Springfield, Massachusetts.

Harry L. Stonecifer attended the grade and high schools of Fort Wayne and was a student in the Indiana Dental College until 1896, when he gave up the idea of a professional career to go to work for the Nickel Plate Railway Company as a brakeman. He has earned many successive promotions. From brakeman he was made freight conductor, then passenger conductor, later was yardmaster and trainmaster on various divisions. He has been a division superintendent since 1921, having successively had his headquarters at Peru, Indiana, Tipton, Indiana, Lima, Ohio, and since August, 1927, at Muncie, where he is superintendent of the Fort Wayne and Sandusky division.

Mr. Stonecifer has taken an active part in the community affairs of the various cities where he has had his home. He is a Knight Templar and thirty-second degree Scottish Rite Mason, member of Mizpah Temple of the Mystic Shrine, and for a number of years was active in Rotary clubs. He was a member of the Rotary Club and Chamber of Commerce at Lima, Ohio. He is a Republican and a member of the High Street Methodist Episcopal Church at Muncie.

Mr. Stonecifer married at Fort Wayne, June 20, 1900, Miss Helen Birbick, daughter of William and Isabella (Dickey) Birbick. Her father was also in the railway service, being for many years foreman in the Wabash Railway shops at Fort Wayne, where he died in 1923. Her mother still lives in Fort Wayne. Mrs. Stonecifer was educated in the grade and high schools of Fort Wayne and is an active member of the Presbyterian Church.

DONALD H. BINFORD is the active partner in the Muncie Sand & Gravel Company, an organization that has supplied immense quantities of material for road building and other construction purposes in Eastern Indiana. Mr. Binford has been connected with road building during most of the years since he came home from France after his service overseas during the World war.

He is a member of an old and prominent family of Hancock County and on both sides is of sterling Quaker ancestry. The Binford and Hill families came from North Carolina, joining in the migration of Friends that left that portion of the South and came to the Northwest beginning in the early years of the nineteenth century.

Mr. Binford was born at Greenfield, Indiana, September 29, 1895, son of N. C. and Sarah (Hill) Binford. His grandfather, Robert Binford, came to Indiana from North Carolina and was an early settler in Rush County, where he followed the business of farmer and stock raiser. He and his wife are buried in the Walnut Ridge Cemetery in Rush County. N. C. Binford was born in Rush County, attended school there and for many years has been a prominent banker of Greenfield, where he is still active as president of the Capital State Bank. The chief business of his early years was farming and cattle raising, and he still owns 400 acres of land and supervises these interests from his home at Greenfield. His brother, John H. Binford, wrote a history of Hancock County. Mrs. Sarah Hill Binford was born and reared in Rush County, where her people were early settlers. Mr. and Mrs. N. C. Binford are prominent members of the Friends Church of Greenfield.

Donald H. Binford was the only child of his parents. He attended public schools in Hancock County, the Friends Boarding School at Westtown, Pennsylvania, and spent two years in the University of Chicago. He left the university in 1917 to join the colors, enlisting in the United States Marine Corps and was sent to Paris Island, South Carolina. He was given the duties of drill sergeant, and helped train three companies at Paris Island. He went overseas with Company C of the Eleventh United States Marines, an organization that furnished replacement troops for different parts of the front. He remained in France, with this organization, and in August,

1919, after his return to the United States, received his honorable discharge at Norfolk, Virginia.

After his war service Mr. Binford spent several years managing his father's farms in Rush County. He then became associated with Mr. C. M. Kirkpatrick, and they were awarded a contract for the hard surface paving for the twelve miles of the National Road. In November, 1923, he and Mr. Kirkpatrick bought the plant and business of the Delaware Sand & Gravel Company, and since that time Mr. Binford has made his home at Muncie and has been giving his personal attention to the operation of the business. The firm has offices at 205 South Jefferson and its plant is located on the McGolliard Road. The business employs from twenty-five to thirty-five persons, and represents a large investment in machinery and equipment, including a fleet of trucks for prompt supply of material to contractors and builders.

Mr. Binford is a member of the Muncie Chamber of Commerce, the Dynamo Club and for several years was active in the Kiwanis organization. He is a Republican and a member of the Friends Church and belongs to Delaware Post No. 19 of the American Legion.

He married at Greenfield, Indiana, October 27, 1922, Miss Martha Kirkpatrick, daughter of C. M. and Susan (Knight) Kirkpatrick. Her father, who was born in Henry County, Indiana, has for many years been a prominent contractor and is a senior partner in the Delaware Sand & Gravel Company. but has been practically retired from active business for several years. He and his wife reside at Greenfield. At Greenfield Mrs. Binford grew up and attended the grade and high schools and was graduated from Earlham College of Richmond in 1918. For several years she was a teacher, teaching at Fountain City and Manilla. She is a member of the Methodist Episcopal Church of Greenfield, and belongs to the Psi Iota Psi sorority and the Women's University Club. Mr. and Mrs. Binford have three children, Joe Kirk, Sarah Susan and Martha Ann. Joe Kirk is attending grammar school and Sarah is a kindergarten pupil.

C. HERBERT LAUB, Ph. D., is acting head of the department of history in the Ball State Teachers College at Muncie. Doctor Laub is an Indiana man and part of his early education was acquired in the Indiana Teachers College at Terre Haute.

He was born in that city September 11, 1898, son of Carl A. and Helene (Scheurman) Laub. His father was born in Wuerttemberg, Germany, in 1870, was fifteen years of age when he came to this country and for many years has had his home at Terre Haute. He has been a traveling dry goods salesman. He is a Methodist. Helene Scheurman was born in Terre Haute and attended school there, preparing for work as a teacher in the Indiana Normal School. She taught for several years before her marriage. There are two children, C. Herbert and Miss Hilda H. Hilda

is a graduate of the State Teachers College at Terre Haute and is now supervisor of art in the public schools of Springdale, Pennsylvania.

C. Herbert Laub was graduated from the Garfield High School of Terre Haute in 1917. This was followed by two years of study in the State Teachers College and two years in DePauw University, where he was graduated with the A. B. degree in 1921. Doctor Laub did his graduate work in the University of Wisconsin, where he came under the inspiring influence of some of the ablest historical scholars in the country. He received his Master of Arts degree at the university in 1922 and continued his graduate studies there in the intervals of other work, being awarded the Doctor of Philosophy degree in June, 1929. Doctor Laub was assistant in history at Wisconsin and during his last year of graduate work was fellow in American history. For two years he was instructor in American history at New York University.

He came to the Ball State Teachers College in September, 1929, taking the position of acting head of the history and social science departments during the leave of absence of Doctor Lafollette. Doctor Laub is a member of the American Historical Association and is a Methodist. Among Doctor Laub's literary contributions are: *William and Mary College Quarterly*, January, 1930, *British Crown Lands in the West*, 1773-1775; *William and Mary College Quarterly, Virginia and the Crown Lands*, 1775-1784, are to be published.

WESLEY P. MARKS is a Muncie business man, one of the partners in the Birch Contracting Company, a firm that specializes in asphalt street paving. Mr. Marks has lived all his life in Delaware County and is a member of one of the old and substantial families of that section of the state.

He was born September 6, 1870, son of F. J. and Agnes (Arbuckle) Marks. His grandfather, Charles Washington Marks, moved to Delaware County from Ohio and was a farmer. He and his wife are buried in the Union Cemetery. F. J. Marks was born in Ohio, was a boy when brought to Indiana, attended public schools in this state and followed farming and stock raising in Delaware County. He died in 1920 and his wife in 1927, and both are buried in the Union Cemetery. His wife, Agnes Arbuckle, was born in Missouri, attended school there, and was visiting relatives in Delaware County when she met F. J. Marks, whom she married. They had seven children: Charles W., one of the Birch Contracting Company at Muncie; Wesley P.; John Carl, deceased; George Edgar, also of the Birch Contracting Company; Adam W., Henry F. and Mary Bertha, all deceased.

Wesley P. Marks was reared on a farm, had the advantages of the public schools and has been a hard worker since early manhood. In 1914 he joined the Birch Contracting Company and has been one of the very active members of that organization. Mr. Marks is

Raymond A. Brooks

a Democrat in politics and is a member of the High Street Methodist Episcopal Church.

He married at Albany, Indiana, April 5, 1895, Miss Minnie Dowden. She died in 1920, being buried in the Beech Grove Cemetery. She was the mother of two children, Bly and Vivian. Bly is engaged in clerical work at Muncie. Vivian is the wife of Bernard Swerking, of Muncie, and has two sons, Bly Edward and Charles Robert. Mr. Marks on March 4, 1921, married, at Muncie, Mrs. Pearl McGill, daughter of Rufus and Eliza (Falls) Hunter. Her father was a leading farmer of Delaware County and died in 1926. He is buried at Germantown, Indiana. Mrs. Marks' mother lives in Muncie. Mrs. Marks is also an active Methodist, and both she and her husband participate in the social and community life of the city.

DAVID F. BROOKS has been for thirty-five years one of the honored and influential members of the bar of Wabash County, is a man of high professional attainments and achievement, as indicated by his having received the honorary degree of Doctor of Laws, and he has been continuously engaged in the practice of law at Wabash, the county seat, since 1895, besides which he is here founder and general manager of the Brooks Loan Company.

Mr. Brooks was born in the picturesque little mountain City of Staunton, Virginia, March 17, 1866, and it may be noted in this connection that Staunton was likewise the birthplace of the late President Woodrow Wilson. Mr. Brooks is a son of Richard G. and Elizabeth (Kennedy) Brooks, both of whom passed their entire lives in Virginia, where the active career of the father was marked by association with farm industry. Richard G. Brooks was a son of Silas Brooks and a member of a family of thirteen children. The original American representatives of the Brooks family made settlement in Virginia in the Colonial period of our national history, and members of the family represented the Old Dominion as loyal soldiers in the War of 1812.

David F. Brooks was born in the year following the close of the Civil war and in Virginia was reared under the somewhat depressed influences that marked the so-called reconstruction period. He was not denied educational advantages of excellent order, however, as he supplemented the discipline of the Virginia Common schools by completing there a course in Trickling Spring Academy. He was nineteen years of age when he came to Indiana, in 1885. and here continued his studies in the State Normal School at Portland, while later he completed a course in the law department of what is now Valparaiso University, at Valparaiso, this state. In that institution he was graduated as a member of the class of 1895. He received at that time the degree of Bachelor of Laws, and on June 15, 1919, he had the distinction of receiving from his alma mater the honorary degree of Doctor of Laws, the twelfth degree

of this order to have been granted by that university during a period of fully sixty years.

In the year of his graduation Mr. Brooks was admitted to the Indiana bar and initiated the practice of his profession at Wabash, where he has continued his professional activities during the long intervening period of fully thirty-five years and where he has appeared prominently in much of the important litigation in the various courts of this section of the state. Mr. Brooks is now one of the veteran members of the Wabash County Bar Association and the Indiana State Bar Association. His political allegiance is given to the Republican party, and while he has been active and influential in political affairs in his county he has manifested no desire for public office, he has considered his profession worthy of his undivided fealty. In the Masonic fraternity he is a member of the local Blue Lodge, Chapter and Council of the York Rite, and he is affiliated also with Wabash Lodge, B. P. O. E. Mr. Brooks has ever been loyal and progressive in his civic attitude and is still an active and valued member of the Wabash Chamber of Commerce. In the World war period he gave earnest cooperation in all patriotic work in Wabash County, was a member of the legal advisory board of the county in connection with the selective drafting of recruits and he did constructive service as a speaker in connection with the local war-bond drives, etc. Mr. Brooks is the owner of valuable farm and dairy interests in Wabash County, and was the founder of the Brooks Loan Company, in 1907, he having since continued to supervise the business of this company, the concern having gained high reputation for its reliable and effective service and the enterprise being one of representative order.

Mr. Brooks married Miss Anna Cale, of Warren, Huntington County, in which county she was born and reared, the Cale family having gained pioneer precedence in Indiana, and prior to that in the vicinity of Dayton, Ohio. Mr. and Mrs. Brooks have seven children: Laila, Vada, Everett, Harry, Raymond A., represented in a personal sketch following, Virginia and Mary. Miss Virginia received the advantages of the University of Indiana and at the time of this writing, in 1930, is a successful and popular teacher in the public schools of Bryan, Ohio, while her sister Mary is a student in the University of Indiana.

RAYMOND A. BROOKS is engaged in the practice of law at North Manchester, Wabash County, and is one of the representative younger members of the bar of his native County. He was born in the city of Wabash, judicial center and metropolis of Wabash County, and the date of his nativity was February 10, 1903. He is a son of David F. Brooks, who is one of the veteran members of the Wabash County Bar and the active executive head of the Brooks Loan Company, at Wabash, of which his son Raymond A. is president. A brief review of the career of David

F. Brooks appears in the preceding sketch, so that further reference to him or to the family history is not here demanded.

In the public schools of the City of Wabash Raymond A. Brooks continued his studies until he was graduated in the high school, and thereafter he pursued courses in both the academic and law departments of the University of Indiana, in which institution he was graduated as a member of the class of 1926 and from which he received the degree of Bachelor of Arts. He had profited simultaneously by the curriculum of the law department, besides having previously pursued his law studies under the able preceptorship of his father, his admission to the bar of his native state having occurred in 1925, the year prior to that in which he received his academic degree at the university.

In July, 1926, Mr. Brooks established his residence in the City of North Manchester, and in this community of his native county he has since been established in the active practice of his profession, with a success and prestige that mark him as one of the leading lawyers of the younger generation in Wabash County. As before stated, he is president of the Brooks Loan Company, at Wabash, this company having been founded by his father, who has active supervision of the business.

Mr. Brooks is aligned loyally in the ranks of the Republican party, has membership in the Wabash County Bar Association and the Indiana State Bar Association, his Masonic affiliations are extended also to the order of the Eastern Star, and he is an active member of the Kiwanis Club of North Manchester. His wife, whose maiden name was Beatrice Churchill, likewise was born and reared in Wabash County, and their one child is a fine little son, R. Ned. The North Manchester law office of Mr. Brooks is at 103½ East Main Street, and he has already built up a substantial and important law business.

FREDERICK FAY REASONER, cashier of the Lincoln Bank & Trust Company of Muncie, is a former county treasurer of Delaware County and has been well and favorably known as a banker, business man and citizen of that community for many years.

Mr. Reasoner was born in Blackford County, Indiana, August 21, 1883, son of John B. and Catherine (Jones) Reasoner. His grandfather, Peter Reasoner, came from Ohio and settled in Blackford County about 1833 and did the pioneer work of developing a farm in the wilderness. His son, Noah Hill Reasoner, was the first white child born in Blackford County. Peter Reasoner and other members of his family are buried in the Elizabethtown Cemetery. John B. Reasoner was a native of Blackford County, grew up on a farm and devoted his life to farming and stock raising. He also did a considerable business as a road builder, being a road contractor and for a number of years was superintendent of gravel roads. He had to his credit a record of three

years of service in the Union army as a member of the Ninth Indiana Cavalry. John B. Reasoner died May 4, 1926, at the age of eighty years, seven months, and is buried at Elizabethtown. His wife, Catherine Jones, was born in Grant County, Indiana, attended school there, and she died October 8, 1929. She and her husband were lifelong members of the Presbyterian Church. They had a family of eight children: Alta, William G., Lillian E., Nellie D., Frederick F., Earl, and Harry B. and Homer H., twins. All are living except Lillian.

Frederick Fay Reasoner was educated in public schools in Blackford County, graduating from the Hartford City High School in 1904, and completed his education in the Eastern Indiana Normal School, now the Ball State Teachers College at Muncie. Soon after leaving school he became messenger and clerk in the Delaware County National Bank, and was assistant cashier of that institution when he resigned in 1921 to begin his duties as county treasurer of Delaware County and city treasurer of Muncie. He was elected county treasurer in 1920 and gave a very businesslike administration to the affairs of the office until 1926. Since leaving the office of county treasurer he has resumed his active connection with banking, joining the Farmers Savings Bank, which is now the Lincoln Bank & Trust Company of Muncie. He has held the office of cashier for the past four years. The bank is a member of the State and American Bankers Associations.

Mr. Reasoner has been active in civic affairs through the Chamber of Commerce and other organizations. He was a charter member of the Kiwanis Club, is affiliated with Muncie Lodge No. 245, B. P. O. Elks, is a member of the Y. M. C. A., and is president of the board of trustees of the First Presbyterian Church. Mr. Reasoner is a Republican in politics.

He married at Hartford City, June 26, 1912, Miss Lydia A. Chapman, daughter of James and Sarah (Pickett) Chapman. Her father for a number of years was a millwright with the Hartford City plant of the Dupont Powder Company. He also held the office of postmaster there. He died in 1922 and her mother in the fall of 1914, and both are buried at Hartford City. Mrs. Reasoner attended the grade and high schools of her native town. She is a Presbyterian and is vice president of the Sorosis Women's Civic Club. Mr. and Mrs. Reasoner have one daughter, Sarah Catherine, a student in the Muncie High School.

ELMER J. GLASER has been identified since leaving school with the building and contracting business of his brother, Albert J. Glaser. In that work he is following in the same line as his father and grandfather, both of whom were builders.

His grandfather was Fred Glaser, a mason contractor who spent most of his life in Franklin County, Indiana. The father of the Muncie contractor was Michael Glaser, who was born and reared in Franklin County, Indiana, and from boyhood was familiar with the work of the building trades. He married Cecilia Ertel, a native of Franklin County, and after his marriage he made his home at Batesville, where he was a building contractor until 1892. In the meantime the discoveries of natural gas in the Eastern Indiana fields had brought a great boom to Muncie as an industrial center, and Michael Glaser moved to that city and found a large amount of business as a builder of houses, industrial plants and other structures. He continued active in his business until his death on January 5, 1911. He is buried in the Beech Grove Cemetery. Both he and his wife were zealous communicants of Saint Lawrence Catholic Church. His widow still resides at Muncie, at the corner of Madison and Sixth streets. They had a family of five children: Albert J., of Muncie; Laura, the wife of Jay Adams, formerly in the grocery business, now connected with the Glaser contracting firm, and who during the World war was with the army, and is a member of Delaware Post No. 19 of the American Legion and a Knight Templar and thirty-second degree Scottish Rite Mason and Shriner, and Mr. and Mrs. Adams have one daughter, Mary Doloris. Arthur Glaser, also connected with the Glaser contracting firm as a foreman, married Miss Fay Bond, of Muncie; Harry J. Glaser, who died in 1926, at the age of thirty-three; and Elmer J. Glaser, also with the Glaser contracting organization.

Elmer J. Glaser was born at Muncie, May 30, 1896, four years after the family established their home in that city. He was educated in public schools, in the Lawrence parochial school, and on leaving school he began an apprenticeship to learn the trade of bricklayer. He was employed by his oldest brother, Albert J. Glaser, who took up and carried on the contracting and building business after the death of the father. Mr. Elmer Glaser has been associated with his brother's business as a general contractor and since 1916 has been foreman of the organization.

On September 1, 1917, he joined the colors, being sent to Tampa, Florida, and was in training at Camp Wheeler at Macon, Georgia, until discharged in January, 1918, because of disability. After recovering he reenlisted, in May, 1918, and was with the trops at Camp Sheridan in Alabama until honorably discharged in February, 1919.

After the war he resumed his work with his brother. Mr. Glaser is a member of Delaware Post No. 19 of the American Legion, belongs to the Forty and Eight military society, and is an independent voter.

He married at McKeesport, Pennsylvania, September 24, 1923, Miss Mildred Mongrain, daughter of Edward and Clara (Mercer) Mongrain, of Delaware County. Her parents live at Muncie, where her father for a number of years has been master mechanic at the plant of the Republic Iron & Steel Company. Her mother is a past matron of the Eastern Star and a member of the Woman's Club. Mrs. Glaser graduated from the Muncie High School in 1917. She is a member of the Woman's Auxiliary of Delaware Post No. 19 of the American Legion.

GEORGE W. GUNDER, of Brownstown, has had a notable career. His talents have impressed themselves in many directions and he has been an educator, newspaper editor, writer, lecturer, lawyer, and his life and work have made him well known in a number of cities and communities, east, south and west.

Mr. Gunder was born in Preble County, Ohio, January 12, 1859, a descendant of William Gunder, a Pennsylvanian who moved to Ohio in pioneer times. George Gunder's uncle, George W. Gunder, was a soldier in the Civil war and afterwards held the rank of colonel and was brevetted brigadier-general in the Spanish-American war. Mr. Gunder's father was Henry Gunder, who for many years was a professor of mathematics and at one time superintendent of schools at Greenville, Ohio, North Manchester and Newcastle, Indiana, and also did a great deal of organization work in Indiana schools. He married Catherine Chase, of Preble County, Ohio, and they had a family of eight children.

George W. Gunder attended grade school in Preble County, high school at Greenville, Ohio, and graduated in 1873, when fourteen years of age, and went to Indianapolis and spent a year clerking in a grocery store. Through the influence of the Indianapolis attorney, Benjamin Harrison, who later became President, he was, at the age of fifteen, given a job in a drug store in Indianapolis. He began teaching in Wabash County, Indiana, at sixteen, taught one country school, then acted as principal of a consolidated school, and at the age of eighteen was made superintendent of schools at Roann in Wabash County, Indiana. He held this position four years and when twenty years of age was president of the County Teachers Association of Wabash County and lectured over a wide area in county institutes. While teaching he studied law with Judge T. B. Redding at Newcastle, Indiana, and at the age of twenty-one was qualified and admitted to the Indiana bar. While superintendent of schools at Roann, he was a candidate for county superintendent of Wabash County schools, but having a tie vote for three days, he yielding to his opponent when promised the nomination of prosecuting attorney.

In 1885 Mr. Gunder went to Kansas City, Missouri, and entered real estate, and later became connected with an abstract company and was made head of the abstract force in the courthouse. From there he removed to Fort Smith, Arkansas, and for a number of years remained in Arkansas. At Fort Smith he conducted a real estate business and in 1889 managed the *Fort Smith Evening Call* and was its editor for one year. He proved his enterprise as a business man and citizen in many ways while at Fort Smith. As head of the Commercial Club he brought much influence to bear in behalf of paving streets and brought about the organization of a paving brick plant to supply material for paving. He became city editor of the *Arkansas Gazette* at Little Rock in 1892, and started an illustrated magazine, called *The Bee*, and while it was not financially profitable it did a great deal to encourage young writers in the South. While there he also acted as a staff correspondent for the *Saint Louis Republic*, and was prominent in the Press Association and a representative of the Associated Press. From 1892 to 1897 Mr. Gunder was at Little Rock, associated with the *Arkansas Gazette*, one of the oldest newspapers in the South, founded in 1819. While there he headed the movement for the establishment of a city park and the securing of a regimental post at Little Rock, Fort Logan H. Roots, and in other ways proved himself a live and forceful factor in the community.

After leaving Arkansas Mr. Gunder went to New York City and entered the insurance business reorganizing and being for three years superintendent of agencies of the New York Casualty Company. Resigning that office, he returned to Wabash, Indiana, was engaged in organization work for several years in Michigan and Georgia, and later bought an insurance business at Ewing in Jackson County, and since 1907 has owned and conducted the leading general insurance business at Brownstown.

Mr. Gunder married Miss Jessie Rhodes, of Wabash. She died, leaving one daughter, Jessie, who is the wife of Harry Gray and has four children. Mr. Gunder's second wife was Amiee Robertson, of Jackson County, Indiana, a woman of rare intellectual attainments. By this marriage there is one child, Georgia, formerly wife of G. Montague Taylor, a business man at Salem, Indiana, now deceased, and in January, 1931, she was married to Elmer L. Stephenson, president and manager of the Fidelity and Casualty Company at Indianapolis.

Mr. Gunder is a charter member of the Lions Club of Brownstown, is active in the Knights of Pythias and was instrumental in organizing the first Commercial Club, now the Chamber of Commerce. He was one of the pioneer advocates of hard road construction in the state and his influence with the Chamber of Commerce was instrumental in bringing about the construction of the first concrete road in Jackson County. He is secretary of the Southern Indiana Good Roads Association, was formerly president of the Dixie Hoosier Scenic Route from Indianapolis to Louisville, Kentucky, which he sought to be incorporated in the Dixie Highway. He is a charter member of the Jackson County Historical Society.

During the campaign for raising funds for the Lincoln Memorial in Spencer County, Indiana, Mr. Gunder was made chairman of the Jackson County Memorial Committee. Mr. and Mrs. Gunder are now completing a Colonial home in Brownstown, where they hope to make comfortable their remaining years, rearing and educating their little granddaughter, Janet Taylor.

RALPH E. STOUT, a Muncie business man, was born in Delaware County, and has had an interesting range of business experience and responsibilities.

He was born August 26, 1882. The Stout family were among the earliest settlers in this section of Eastern Indiana. His grandfather, James R. Stout, came from North Carolina and was the first white man to settle west of Killbuck Creek in Delaware County. He secured land from the Government and developed a large and well-improved farm of 350 acres. He reared a family of seven sons and three daughters, the youngest of the children being John Stout, who was born and reared in Delaware County and was a loyal soldier of the Union during the Civil war. He first served in the Thirty-eighth Indiana Infantry and later in the One Hundred Fortieth Indiana Volunteers. He was in the service three years, participated in the battle of Antietam, was with Sherman's forces in the Atlantic campaign and took part in some of the bloodiest battles of the war. After the war he became a stationary engineer, and as chief engineer was employed by some of the largest organizations operating in the eastern Indiana natural gas field. He died in the spring of 1919 and he and his wife are buried in the Jones Cemetery of Delaware County. James R. Stout and wife are buried in the old Bethel Church Cemetery. John Stout married Serena Sears, daughter of Increase Sears, who was one of the first justices of the peace in Delaware County outside of Muncie and served in that office for over thirty-five years. He owned a farm of 240 acres in Delaware County. Mr. and Mrs. Sears are buried in the Nottingham Cemetery. Mrs. Serena Stout attended public schools and was an active member of the Methodist Episcopal Church. She died March 15, 1926. Her three children are Ralph E., Miss Stella, of Muncie, and Harley, who is connected with the Guarantee Tire & Rubber Company of Muncie and by his marriage to Lena Mitchell has three children, Mary, Howard and Eugene.

Ralph E. Stout received his education in the public schools of Delaware County. Immediately after leaving school he entered upon a business career. His work from the first has been largely identified with manufacturing corporations. He has worked in plants and offices, as traveling salesman. His first connection was with the Midland Steel Company, with which he remained two years, and for four years was with the canning industry of S. H. Dragoo & Company. He then spent seven years with the American Insulating Company of Yorktown, Indiana, and for two years was on the road for the Chicago house of Bromen & Company. Mr. Stout for five years was connected with the live stock commission business, buying and shipping live stock to domestic and foreign markets.

Since 1920 he has been an automobile dealer at Muncie, where he owns the General Motors Truck Sales Company, at 814-16 South Walnut Street. He has the leading sales service for

Albert A. Watts M.D.

the General Motors trucks and commercial cars and also owns and operates the large garage, storage and repair shops.

Mr. Stout has been active in the Chamber of Commerce, is a Republican, a Methodist and for twenty years has had membership in the Improved Order of Red Men and for fifteen years has been affiliated with Muncie Lodge No. 245, B. P. O. Elks.

He married, November 19, 1900, in Delaware County Miss Sarah A. Petty, daughter of Lewis Napoleon and Hulda (Williamson) Petty. Her father was a farmer and stock man of Delaware County. He died in 1922 and his wife in 1927 and both are buried in the Jones Cemetery. Mrs. Stout attended public schools in Delaware County, is active in the Methodist Church and the Ladies Aid Society. Mr. and Mrs. Stout have three children: Charles E., Ruth and Ruby. Charles attended the grade and high school of Yorktown, is with the Standard Auto Company of Muncie, and married Miss Helen Oland, daughter of Mr. and Mrs. Thomas A. Oland, at Muncie. The daughter Ruth attended school at Yorktown and Muncie, is the wife of Forest E. Mitchell, who assists Mr. Stout in the automobile business, and they have a son, Ralph E. Mitchell. The daughter Ruby was educated at Muncie and is the wife of Eugene Karl, employed in the Remy Products Company, a unit of the General Motors Corporation. Mr. and Mrs. Karl have two sons, Robert Eugene and Charles Edward.

ALBERT A. WATTS, coroner of Lake County since 1926, is head of a distinguished professional firm of Gary, comprising a group of physicians and surgeons of the highest ability and specialists in several fields.

The offices of the firm are at 749 Broadway in Gary. Doctor Watts is the senior partner. His associate Dr. Walter M. Behn is secretary of the Gary Board of Health, Dr. James B. Burcham is coroner's physician, Dr. M. C. Marcus is an eye, ear, nose and throat specialist, and another member is Dr. Ed Gaebe. They also employ a staff of trained nurses. Doctor Watts is a lifelong resident of Lake County and was about nineteen years old when the City of Gary was founded. He was one of the first three public school teachers in Gary. He was born at Hammond, Indiana, September 21, 1887, son of William H. and Paulina (Daumer) Watts. His father was born in England and was five months old when his parents came to America and settled in Northern Indiana. Doctor Watts' grandfather, William Watts, was a native of England, born at Sutton, December 16, 1820, and when a boy went to sea. He became captain of a sailing vessel, and for thirteen years lived on the high seas and visited many ports of the world. In his later years his grandchildren heard from his lips many thrilling stories of his adventures and experiences. He endured shipwreck three times, and once was tossed out in a broken life boat for five days before being picked up by a fishing ves-

sel. In his time it was customary for a sailing ship to cross the Atlantic in about twenty-five days, a voyage that has been cut down by the fastest steamship to less than five days. Captain Watts came to this country in 1861 and settled at Gibson Station, a flag stop on the Michigan Central Railway. Two miles south of the railroad he settled in the midst of the heavy timber and underbrush, where he hewed out a home and developed a farm, and there his three sons and five daughters grew up. The locality later became known as Hessville. It was about thirty miles from Chicago, and the surrounding country was filled with wild game and much of the transportation to market was done by wagons drawn by oxen, several days being required in going and returning from Chicago. Captain Watts and wife are both buried in the Hessville Cemetery near Hammond.

William H. Watts grew up at the home farm near Hammond, attended school in that city and for many years carried on a business as a truck farmer. For over twenty years he held the office of justice of the peace in Calumet Township. He was a member of the Maccabees, the Ross Community Church, and a Republican. He died in March, 1928, and is buried at the Ridge Lawn Cemetery at Gary. His wife, Paulina Daumer, was born and reared in Germany, attended school there and finished her education after coming to America. She passed away in March, 1929. These parents had a family of eight children: Mrs. Rose Good, who is the mother of three children; Dr. Albert A.; Benjamin; Mrs. Lucy Ott; Mrs. Lillie Waite, who has two children; Mrs. Nettie Owen, mother of two children; Henry, Jr., who has one child; and Dr. Elmer Watts.

Albert A. Watts attended public school Ross, graduating from high school in 19 and while getting his bearings as to his manent career he took up school teac and, as noted above, was employed as o the first teachers at Gary when that was founded in 1906. He went on thro the higher branches in Valparaiso Univers where he graduated in 1911, and in 1915 to his degree in medicine from the Chicago College of Medicine and Surgery. He had further training as an interne in the Saint Elizabeth Hospital of Chicago. During the World war he was enrolled in the Medical Corps, serving a year and a half with the rank of captain, and during part of the time was overseas and on duty in the front line trenches. He was near the front line in some of the hardest fighting of the war. During the past ten years Doctor Watts has been engaged in a busy general practice at Gary, and his individual attainments have contributed much to the high standing enjoyed by the firm comprising himself and his associates.

His great public service has been rendered in the office of county coroner, to which he was first elected in 1926. He has introduced a number of changes to bring about a better system and increased efficiency in his office and has at all times shown himself an advocate of safety measures on the highways and railroads which would safeguard human life in Lake County. Doctor Watts is a member of Gary Memorial Post No. 17 of the American Legion, is a member of Gary Lodge No. 783, Loyal Order of Moose, Gary Commercial Club, Harrison Club, Gary Republican Club, Young Men's Christian Association, Gary Lodge No. 1152, B. P. O. Elks, and Gary Lodge No. 677 of the Masonic fraternity. He is a member of the Lake County, Indiana State and American Medical Associations and the Gary Country Club.

He married in October, 1928, Miss Mayme Fyffe, daughter of Mr. and Mrs. Oscar Fyffe. Her father was a farmer at Sumner, Illinois, where Mrs. Watts received her early education. She is a graduate nurse of the Cook County Hospital of Chicago and has been active in church and social life at Gary, being a member of the Woman's Club and the Eastern Star. Doctor and Mrs. Watts have one daughter, Alberta.

DON A. BOLLINGER. The entire career of Don A. Bollinger, from the time that he left college halls until the present, has been identified with the Seymour Woolen Mills, to the growth and development of which he has contributed in no small degree, and in which he has risen from the position of salesman to that of president. In addition to being prominent as a business man, he has likewise taken a leading part in public affairs and is justly rated as one of the community's most valued citizens.

Don A. Bollinger was born April 12, 1887, at Seymour, Jackson County, Indiana, and is a son of Albert and Anna (Schneck) Bollinger. His father, a native of Switzerland, was still a boy when brought by his parents to the United States, the family settling at Seymour, where the youth learned the trade of shoe-making. For a number of years he occupied a cobbler's bench, during which time he saved his earnings carefully, so that in time he was able to establish himself in the shoe and boot business on his own account in a modest way. Industry and good management brought their just reward, and he became one of the substantial and highly-respected merchants of the city. He married Miss Anna Schneck, who was born in Jackson County, Indiana, and they became the parents of two children: Lynn, who died in 1918; and Don of this review.

Don Bollinger attended the public schools of Seymour and after leaving high school enrolled as a student at DePauw University, as a member of the class of 1908. Almost immediately after his graduation he secured a position as traveling salesman for the Seymour Woolen Mills, with which he has been identified to the present, rising step by step through the various departments and positions to the post of president, a position to which he was elected in 1919. Mr. Bollinger is authoritatively rated as one of the best-informed men in his line in the country. He is a member of the Wool Blanket Manufacturers Association, and the company belongs to the Indiana Manufacturers Association and the Indiana State Chamber of Commerce, leading societies of this line of business. The Seymour Woolen Mills had its inception at the close of the war between the states and was incorporated in 1866, at which time the factory was a small frame establishment with not much to support it but hope, ambition and ability. About 1870 Mr. Bollinger's grandfather, Louis Schneck, became interested in the woolen mills and served as president until his death in 1905. He was succeeded by his son, Benjamin F. Schneck, who retained the office of president until his passing in 1919. In that year as previously mentioned, Mr. Bollinger became the president of the mills. During the more than six decades that have passed, the plant has grown to be an enterprise covering 150,000 feet, a plant that is equipped with every modern convenience and device. The working force consists of 200 skilled people, all expert in his line, and the plant turns out about 125,000 pairs of blankets and from 5,000 to 10,000 pieces of flannel annually. During the World war period the plant was engaged 80% in war production, furnishing blankets. Mr. Bollinger is a member of the board of directors of the First National Bank. He is intensely interested in a public spirited way in the welfare and progress of his community and is an enthusiastic member of the Rotary Club, of which he was formerly president. Politically he is a Republican, and his fraternal affiliation is with the Benevolent and Protective Order of Elks. He is president of the school board of Seymour, a member of the board of trustees of Schneck Memorial Hospital, a director of the Cooperative Building & Loan Association, and a member of Trinity Methodist Church. Although he is still a young man, his career has touched life on many sides, and he has shown himself capable of meeting and overcoming the obstacles that have arisen in his path.

Mr. Bollinger married Miss Hannah Mills, of Seymour, Indiana, and to this union there have been born five children: Don Mills, Carolyn, Louise, Richard and Roger. The family occupies a pleasant and attractive home at Seymour.

WILLIAM C. BALL is head of the William C. Ball & Son, lumber dealers, the oldest and largest organization of its kind in Jackson County.

Mr. Ball was born at Madison in Jefferson County, Indiana, September 27, 1865. His parents were James M. and Eliza A. Ball and his grandfather was Spencer Ball, who came from Delaware to Indiana. Spencer Ball was a building contractor. When the Jefferson, Madison & Indianapolis Railway was built he was a contractor for its depots, round houses and other buildings and later in life became a coach builder. His son, James M. Ball, followed in his example as a building contractor.

William C. Ball was one of five children. He was educated in the grade schools at Madison until fifteen, completing his schooling at Brownstown. Like his father and grandfather before him he learned the trade of carpenter, but when he was twenty years of age, in 1884, he started in the lumber business and that has absorbed his energies and activities almost wholly for the past forty-five years. William C. Ball & Son now have a place of business occupying an entire block of land at Ewing, Brownstown, and handle everything needed in the building line. In former years the firm did considerable service in contracting, building a number of churches in Indiana, but the activities of the firm are now confined strictly to dealing in building material.

Mr. Ball is a member of the Brownstown Chamber of Commerce and during the World war took an influential part in the Liberty Bond, War Stamps and Red Cross drives. He is a member of the Masonic fraternity and Knights of Pythias and is a trustee and deacon of the Christian Church. Politically his activities have been with the Democratic party.

Mr. Ball married Alice Humphrey, of Washington County, Indiana. They became the parents of eight children, all of whom graduated from the Brownstown High School. The oldest, Stella V. is now in charge of the primary department of the Brownstown public schools. Ethel is the wife of George H. Conner, a Brownstown business man. Clarence B. is associated with his father as a junior member of William C. Ball & Son. The younger children are Grace Ann; Dr. William L., a dentist; Ester E.; Kenneth H., a student of aviation; and Charles L., who attended Butler University, and is now at the University of Louisville, Louisville, Kentucky.

JOSEPH M. ROBERTSON. One of the leading citizens and vigorous and far-sighted business men of Southern Indiana is Joseph M. Robertson, of Brownstown, president of the Jackson Brick & Hollow Tile Company of Brownstown, and of the Medora Brick Company, of Medora, with farming and other interests. For many years the family name of Robertson has been a respected and familiar one in Jackson County, where its founder, the great-grandfather of Joseph M. Robertson, settled in 1816. Acquiring a large amount of Government land, he became an extensive farmer in Hamilton Township and a man of importance. A Virginian by birth, his early years were passed in Kentucky.

Joseph M. Robertson was born October 9, 1876, in Jackson County, Indiana, and is a son of Hon. Jonathan and Carrie (Miller) Robertson, a grandson of John Blaze Robertson, and a great-grandson of Andrew Robertson, the pioneer of the family in Indiana. John Blaze Robertson, a lifelong resident of Jackson County, was a farmer of ability, resource and great industry, and also a civil engineer who made an established place for himself in that difficult calling. He was active in public affairs, and served two terms each as county surveyor and county clerk. Jonathan Robertson, the father of Joseph M. Robertson, was born in Jackson County, where he was reared and educated, and chose the life of an agriculturist, being engaged in tilling the soil throughout his career. He became prominent and influential in public affairs, representing Jackson County in the House of Representatives of the State Legislature from 1901 until 1903, and also being president of the County Council for ten years. He had extensive interests in several lines, and at one time was the owner and operator of a mill. Mr. Robertson married for his first wife Miss Carrie Miller, who died, leaving two children: Amy Robinson, who married George W. Gunder; and Joseph M., of this review. After the death of his first wife Mr. Robertson married Mary E. Swain, and they became the parents of two children: Genevieve, who married Dr. Joseph McNinch; and Carrie B., who married Harry Mather.

Joseph M. Robertson, who traces his ancestry back to a Robertson who was at one time secretary to a governor of Virginia in Colonial times, attended the public schools of Jackson County and the high school at Brownstown. He commenced his career at the age of eighteen years, as an employe in his father's flour mill and grain elevator, and in 1903 bought an interest therein, which he still retains. In 1920 Jonathan Robertson retired from active business and sold his interest in the mill to R. M. Robertson, a cousin of Joseph M. Robertson, and at this time they are the proprietors. In 1906 Mr. Robertson of this review became one of the founders of the Jackson Brick & Hollow Tile Company, of Brownstown, and served as its treasurer until 1920, in which year he was elected president, and has remained in this capacity. In 1923 the company bought the Medora Shale Brick Company, and is still its president. The Jackson Brick & Hollow Tile Company manufactures brick and building and drain tile, employing thirty-five people and shipping its product throughout the central states territory meeting with a ready market in six states, its output being over 100 tons daily. The Medora company, operating at Medora, manufactures common, face and paving brick, its output being 50,000 bricks daily, manufactured in down draft kilns, and its market being the central states territory. Mr. Robertson is one of the best known and most thoroughly informed men in his line in the state, and is a member of the National Face Brick Manufacturers Association and the Structural Tile Manufacturing Association. He is also active in farming and at present has 600 acres of fertile Jackson County soil under a high state of cultivation. Fraternally he belongs to the Masons, the Benevolent and Protective Order of Elks and the Knights of Pythias. He is also active in civic affairs, and during the

World war served as food administrator for Jackson County, being also active in the Loan, War Stamps and Red Cross drives.

Mr. Robertson married Miss Bessie Burrell, of Jackson County, a daughter of John B. Burrell, who for many years was a prominent merchant of Brownstown and a substantial agriculturist of Jackson County, as well as president of the County Council. Mr. and Mrs. Robertson have one daughter: Carolyn, a student.

MOODY I. MASSENA. In the world changes that have taken place in comparatively recent years through war and subsequent adjustments, many sections of different counties have become familiar names in innumerable households; but still, Napoleon and the battle of Waterloo of a past century have not lost their historical interest. It is possible, however, that very few of the veterans of that great battle spent their last days in peace on a quiet farm in Pennsylvania, as did the brave French General Mazzine, who was the grandfather of Moody I. Massena, former postmaster and prominent citizen of Medora, Indiana.

Moody I. Massena was born at Lexington, Scott County, Indiana, April 8, 1878, a son of Uriah Massena, as the family has written it since it became a family name early in 1800. Uriah Massena was born in Pennsylvania, where he was reared, receiving his education in the public schools, and in his youth learned the trade of carpenter, subsequently developing into a building contractor. When the war between the states was precipitated, in 1861, he enlisted in Company K, Twenty-sixth Regiment, Pennsylvania Volunteer Infantry, and loyally and bravely served his country for three years and three months. After the close of the war he moved with his family to Scott County, Indiana, and his ten children were reared there and in Lawrence County. The father continued to be engaged in the contracting business until his death and was one of his community's highly esteemed citizens.

After acquiring a public school education in Scott and Lawrence counties, Moody I. Massena secured employment in a sawmill, and continued to be engaged in that business until 1918, when he was elected township trustee of Carr Township. He discharged the duties of that office ably until 1921, in which year he was appointed postmaster at Medora by President Harding, and in June, 1926, was reappointed to this position by President Coolidge. During his incumbency he did much to improve the service in the way of efficiency and expeditiousness in the correct handling of the mail, and at all times proved himself a courteous and capable official. He belonged to the Tri-State Postmasters Association, was a Mason, and passed through the chairs of the Independent Order of Odd Fellows and the Knights of Pythias. He had various business interests and was a member of the board of directors of the Medora Building & Loan

Association. Politically he was a stanch Republican and wielded a distinct influence in his party in Jackson County. During the World war Mr. Massena was greatly active in the various movements for the success of American arms, and was so successful in his efforts in selling Liberty Bonds that he was awarded a medal by the United States Government, which trophy was fashioned of metal taken from a captured German cannon.

Mr. Massena married Miss Stella Russell, a native of Jackson County, and to this union there were born three children: Wilma, a graduate of the high school at Medora, who attended Danville College one term and the Indiana University two terms, and was engaged in teaching in the public schools until her marriage to Ernest J. Mason, a veteran of the World war who saw active service in France as a member of the Aviation Corps; Eula Mae, who attended Indiana University, married John W. Hill, of Medora, and they have a daughter, Donna C.; and Ruth, a graduate of Medora High School, is now the wife of Len Shipley. Moody I. Massena died November 2, 1930.

VIRGIL T. ABEL, M. D. The medical profession in Jackson County, Indiana, can justly claim many able and widely-known practitioners, men of stable characters who are valued members of representative medical organizations, and who, as laymen, are foremost in serving the best interests of their communities. Not a few of these are native sons of Indiana and descendants of her pioneers. One of these is found in Dr. Virgil T. Abel, a capable and thorough physician and surgeon for many years at Vallonia.

Doctor Abel was born September 12, 1877, at Jonesville, Bartholomew County, Indiana, and is a son of John and Maria (Thomas) Abel. The founder of the family in Indiana was his great-grandfather, Pollard Abel, a native of Virginia, who paused first in Kentucky but was yet a young man when he settled permanently in the Hoosier State, where he rounded out his career as an agriculturist. His son was Francis Abel, also an Indiana farmer, and John Abel, the father of Doctor Abel and a native of Bartholomew County, also spent his life in the tilling of the soil. The latter married Maria Thomas, of Jackson County, this state.

Dr. Virgil T. Abel passed his boyhood on his father's farm and was one of a family of thirteen children, all of whom were reared comfortably and all had school opportunities, but Doctor Abel was the only one to devote his life to medical science. Almost from early youth his natural inclination was in this direction, and ultimately the goal of his ambition was reached when he was graduated from the medical department of the University of Cincinnati, with the degree of Doctor of Medicine, being a member of the class of 1901. He chose the pleasant little City of Vallonia, Indiana, as his first field of practice, and here, more than a quarter of a century

later, he is found, now one of the leading men of his profession in Southern Indiana and universally honored and trusted by those he has faithfully served so long. Although interested in civic politics to some extent and a member of the Pension Board, he has never accepted an office that would absorb too much of his time from his medical work. He is a constant student of his profession and a member of the Jackson County Medical Society, the Indiana State Medical Society and the American Medical Association, and occasionally contributes to their literature. Fraternally he is a Mason and a member of the Knights of Pythias, and is active in the latter order, of which he is chancellor commander.

Doctor Abel was united in marriage with Miss Mabel Hunsucker, of Vallonia, and to this union there have been born two children: George Emerson and Joseph Neal, both of whom are attending school.

HON. WILLIAM P. PATTERSON, president of the Gary board of public works, has several times been called upon for important service in the great steel city of Northern Indiana, though he has never been classed as a politician and has never been an office seeker. His citizenship in Gary has been a source of sound civic influence and public benefit, almost from the time that Gary was started on the sand dunes. He is perhaps Gary's oldest realtor, and through his own business he has been able to realize some of his ideals in the development of a community which is unique in the history of American municipalities.

Mr. Patterson is a member of an old Indiana family. He was born on a farm about twenty-six miles east of Vincennes, in Daviess County, near the town of Washington, February 28, 1864. His parents were William P. and Elizabeth (Padgett) Patterson. His grandfather, Joseph Patterson, went from West Virginia to Kentucky and later to Daviess County, Indiana, locating on land in the woods four miles from the nearest neighbors. He and his wife are buried in the Loogootee Cemetery in that county. William P. Patterson, Sr., was a native of Kentucky and was a child when the family moved to Daviess County, Indiana, and during much of his life he lived on the old homestead which has been in the family possessions for fully a century and has never had a transfer recorded against it since it was taken up from the Government. He died in 1892, at the age of seventy-eight, and is buried at Loogootee. His wife, Elizabeth Padgett, was also a native of Kentucky, was reared and educated in that state and taught school there for a time. She was a devout Catholic. She died in 1881. There were eleven children in the family, six sons and five daughters: Presley, Mary Ann, George, Mrs. Ellen McCauley, Charles, Joseph, William P., Malinda, Mrs. Alice Norris, of Loogootee, Eva and Lawrence. Only three are now living, Mrs. McCauley, the Gary realtor and Mrs. Norris. The member of the family occupying the old homestead in Daviess County is Mrs. McCauley.

That old homestead is a place of particular interest to students of the life of Lincoln. The *Gary Post-Tribune* on Lincoln's birthday in 1930 published an interesting feature story from information supplied by Mr. Patterson and serving to supplement the rather meager information concerning the movements of the Lincoln family during their life in Indiana. The Lincolns, it will be recalled, left their old home in Spencer County, Indiana, and started for Illinois in the spring of 1830. Young Abe was then just twenty-one years of age. The route they followed was the old Buffalo trail through Daviess County and at the close of a cold, rainy day in March the oxen stopped in front of the Patterson home and the Patterson's welcomed these forlorn travelers and made them comfortable for three days, during which time, according to the family tradition, young Abe made friends with everybody and with every animal on the farm, and when he went away he wore a sleeveless coat of the kind known as "wampus," which one of the Patterson family gave him after noting how thinly clad he was.

It was in that rural environment in Southern Indiana that William P. Patterson grew to manhood. He walked back and forth during the winter to a country schoolhouse four miles away, getting up long before daylight in order to help with the chores and hurrying home after school session to take care of the stock before dark. Mr. Patterson at the age of twenty-one went to Indianapolis, served an apprenticeship in a mercantile house and when he was thirty years of age established himself in business as a general merchant at Alexandria. He built up a big and flourishing trade there, and enjoyed prosperity and contentment until his continued application to the work of the store brought about a serious condition of health so that on the advice of a physician he sold out in 1904 and moved to Indiana Harbor. There he resumed his connection with merchandising on a more modest scale, but after two years was again threatened with a complete breakdown. The decision was made to get into some line that would keep him out of doors.

It was on February 26, 1906, that Mr. Patterson paid his first visit to the steel town that was growing up on the site of Gary. His companions were Mayor A. F. Knotts, of Hammond, and his brother, Tom Knotts, the first mayor of Gary. Soon afterward Mr. Patterson rented an office over Sam Miller's clothing store and established a fire insurance business, being able to make a complete canvass of the scattered business houses and homes of the city every thirty days. In 1908 he and Carl Stout, another Gary pioneer, formed the partnership of Patterson & Stout, with offices at 664 Broadway and doing a real estate brokerage and loan business. They became local representatives for the Union National Savings & Loan Association of Indianapolis, which made their first loans on

Broadway through this office. Mr. Patterson in 1921 joined Samuel Muscat in organizing the first successful Chamber of Commerce in Gary. Over a period of twenty-five years his operations in real estate have made him a continued factor in the growth and development of the city. In many ways he has been able to influence the trend of appropriate civic planning and bring about an improvement vital to the future development of the city. Mr. Patterson first served on the board of public works for four years during the second administration of Mayor R. O. Johnson. In 1922 he and Mr. Stout established a branch office for their business in South Bend. The following year Mr. Patterson acquired his partner's holdings and has since conducted business alone. His offices are at 113 West Sixth Avenue.

Mr. Patterson is individually a large property owner in the Gary district. He was appointed president of the board of public works January 6, 1930. On different occasions he has made public-spirited efforts to cooperate in behalf of some special improvement demanded or needed by the community, and since becoming head of the board of works he proposed to donate a portion of lake frontage owned by him to the west of Grand Boulevard as part of a site to be developed by the city as a harbor for pleasure boats. Mr. Patterson is an active member of the Chamber of Commerce, the B. P. O. Elks and in politics has always been a staunch Republican.

He married at Washington, Indiana, in June 1890, Miss Roberta Rodgers, a native of Tennessee. By this marriage he has a daughter, Mildred, now the wife of Robert Patterson, of Chicago, Illinois. Mr. Robert Patterson was for some years in the service of the city government at Chicago and is now looking after his oil interests there and in California. Mr. and Mrs. Robert Patterson have two children, Robert, Jr., and Patty Ann. Mr. William P. Patterson married at Gary in 1920 Miss Effie Kain. She is active in the Presbyterian Church and various social clubs of Gary.

FRANK L. RANDALL, general manager of the Randall Mills, is an energetic representative of the business interests of Delaware County. He is a man of liberal education and of unusual business training and experience.

Mr. Randall was born at Anderson, Indiana, February 2, 1904, son of William and Anna (Thompson) Randall. His father was a lifelong resident of Madison County and had a farm near Anderson, but later gave most of his time to the management and development of the oil wells brought in on his own land. He died in 1906 and is buried at Anderson. His wife, Anna Thompson, was born and reared near Elwood, attended school there and now resides at Muncie, where she is an active member of the Methodist Episcopal Church. She is a daughter of Frank and Sarah Thompson, the former being identified during his active life with farming interests. Both her parents are buried at Elwood. William Randall and wife had three children: Raymond, of Auburn, Indiana; Lawrence, of Chicago; and Frank L.

Frank L. Randall attended public schools at Gaston, graduating from the high school there in 1921. For three years he was a student in what is now the Ball State Teachers College at Muncie, and in the intervals between his school terms he taught for two years at Gaston and one year at Matthews, Indiana. After giving up school work he went to Chicago and spent four years with Montgomery Ward & Company and one year with Bell & Howell.

Mr. Randall returned to Gaston in February, 1930, and acquired the Gaston Roller Mills and is now giving his entire time and attention to the management of the Randall Mills. Mr. Randall is a member of the Methodist Episcopal Church.

He married in Chicago, March 20, 1925, Miss Mabel DeGries, daughter of Ralph and Kate (Terbourgh) DeGries. Her father was an accountant in Chicago and died in 1929, being buried in that city. Mrs. DeGries resides with Mr. and Mrs. Randall. Mrs. Randall graduated from the Schurz High School of Chicago in 1922 and from the Metropolitan Business College of that city in 1925. She was a stenographer in the offices of Montgomery Ward & Company until her marriage. She is a Methodist. Mr. and Mrs. Randall have two children, Ruth Evelyn and Robert William.

Mr. Frank L. Randall acquired his knowledge of the milling business during his youth as an employee of the Gaston Roller Mills, then owned by his uncle and benefactor, the late Dr. George W. Huber. Mr. Randall was in many ways befriended by Doctor Huber, who was one of Gaston's outstanding citizens.

Doctor Huber was born at Gaston, May 2, 1867, and lived there all his life. He died February 2, 1930, at the age of sixty-two years and nine months. His parents were Frederick and Susan (Boyle) Huber. Doctor Huber was educated in the grade and high schools at Gaston, attended the old Muncie Normal School and in 1894 was graduated from the American Medical College of Cincinnati, and subsequently took a degree from the Eclectic Medical College of Indianapolis. He had an extensive medical practice, but much of his time was also given to business affairs. He was identified with the Gaston Milling Company from 1882. This industry was established by his father as a carriage making shop in 1860, at a time when Gaston was known as New Corner. In 1880 a saw mill and flour mill were added to the equipment and Doctor Huber took charge of the flour mill in 1882. After the death of his father, in 1898, he owned and conducted the business under his personal supervision. He was a member of the Indiana Millers Association and from boyhood was a devout communicant of the United Brethren Church. He made his religion a part of his every day life, and the community of Gaston will always respect his memory as that of a sincere Christian, an able physician and a citizen of utmost public spirit.

Doctor Huber married, March 2, 1890, Miss Corrina May Barrett, daughter of Samuel and Lana Barrett, of Delaware County. She died December 9, 1898, leaving two children, Alderd W. and Beatrice B., of Gaston. Doctor Huber on December 25, 1900, married Miss Nannie Thompson, a daughter of Frank and Sarah Thompson. She survives him. Doctor Huber was also survived by four brothers and one sister, James F., William E., Frederick, Jr., Frank and Amanda C. Huber.

HORACE M. PAYNTER, physician and surgeon at Salem, is a native of Washington County, Indiana, and has distinguished himself by many loyal services in private practice and in the opportunities for work open to a skilled representative of his profession.

Doctor Paynter was born at Salem, November 2, 1865. His great-grandfather was a native of England, of German ancestry, and was sent to Quebec, Canada, with some British troops at the time of the war with the American colonies. Learning the true inwardness of the war, that the Americans were fighting for freedom, he crossed the Saint Lawrence River and joined the American troops and fought for independence. After the war he moved to Virginia, and from that state the Paynters went west to Kentucky about 1795, and a few years later came to Indiana. Doctor Paynter's grandfather was John R. Paynter, a native of Virginia, who was a child when taken west to Kentucky. He married a Miss Etzler, of Virginia. Doctor Paynter's father, Dr. C. L. Paynter, was a pioneer physician of Washington County, Indiana, where he practiced forty years. He was born in that county and married Sarah J. Smith, who was born at Elizabethtown, Kentucky. Dr. C. L. Paynter served as a first lieutenant in the medical department, under General Taylor, in the war with Mexico. Horace M. Paynter was one of four children, three sons and one daughter.

Doctor Paynter attended grade and high schools at Salem, and in 1890 was graduated from the medical department of the University of Louisville. For one year he practiced in Omaha, Nebraska, where he became a member of the Omaha Medical Society and the Douglas County Medical Society. For eight years he was in practice at Bedford, Indiana, and since then his professional duties have been in his old home community. Doctor Paynter during the Spanish-American war was Government examining surgeon. During the World war he was issued a certificate, authorized by the National Council of Defense, on October 8, 1918, for valuable services rendered. The Government Treasury Department also awarded him a special certificate for his valuable work during the influenza epidemic of 1918-19. He is a member of the Lawrence County Medical Society and the University

of Louisville Alumni. Doctor Paynter has been affiliated with the Independent Order of Odd Fellows since 1893 and the Knights of Fythias since 1895, and was a member of the Elks while at Bedford.

He married Miss Jessie Trotter, of Valley City, Harrison County, Indiana. They have four children: Eva, wife of J. Marly Hall, of Eagle Grove, Iowa; Grace, wife of Joe Killeen, of Detroit; Howard, who is married and living in Milwaukee, Wisconsin; and Margaret, wife of Charles Pitts, local agent at Salem for the Standard Oil Company.

ANDREW J. BRODHECKER is one of the veteran newspaper men of Southern Indiana, president and active head of the *Brownstown Banner*, which has been officially as well as popularly recognized as the best weekly paper in the state.

The *Brownstown Banner* was founded in April, 1869, and has rounded out 62 consecutive years of useful service as a newspaper. William Frysinger, its founder, issued it as a five-column, four-page weekly, all home print. The plant was burned down in 1898. Within less than a year after, Mr. Brodhecker became owner, but the paper never missed an issue, as for two issues the paper was printed at Cincinnati while equipment was being assembled for the new plant. The plant today, thoroughly modern in every way, has frequently been called a model newspaper plant. The Indiana journalistic fraternity awarded the *Banner* a silver cup as a symbol of its exceptional qualities as a weekly newspaper. It has a circulation of three thousand copies, and is published from a plant with 1800 square feet of floor space and with nine employees.

Mr. Brodhecker has been a printer and journalist all his life. He has had the loyal cooperation of his family, including his sons, and since 1887 his twin sister, Margaret Brodhecker, has also been with him continuously as assistant local editor. She was graduated from the Brownstown High School in 1887.

Mr. Brodhecker was born in Jackson County, Indiana, April 27, 1869. His father, Conrad Brodhecker, came from Saxony, Germany, and settled in Brownstown Township, Jackson County, Indiana, soon after 1840. He was a merchant tailor. His wife was Louise (Seidel) Schaferman, a native of Leipsic, Germany, who was thirteen years of age when she accompanied one of her brothers, Edward Seidel, to America, leaving their parents and several brothers and sisters in the old country.

Andrew J. Brodhecker attended grade schools, was graduated from the Brownstown High School in 1887 and during his last year in high school was working in the printing establishment of which he afterward became owner. He started as a printer's devil and has never for any length of time been away from the smell of printer's ink since he was nineteen years of age. In 1890 he was made stock foreman of the *Banner*, in 1897 became managing editor and in 1898 bought the business, and for thirty-three years the *Banner* has responded to his particular genius as a newspaper man. Mr. Brodhecker for thirty-three years has been a member of the Indiana Democratic Editorial Association, is a member of the Indiana Weekly Press Association, and the Brownstown Chamber of Commerce. He is a member of the Jackson County Historical Society and for many years has been the official publisher of the Democratic party in the county. He has been president of the Brownstown Commercial Association and Fairview Cemetery Association and has taken an active part in many civic movements and industrial propositions.

Mr. Brodhecker married, November 1, 1894, Miss Cora D. Shepard, a native of Kansas. They are the parents of four children. The son Claude Giles is a graduate of Indiana University, majoring in economics and sociology and minoring in journalism, was associated with and part owner of the *Banner* until he sold his interest in 1924, and is now advertising manager. He is president of the Indiana Democratic Editorial Association and during the world war spent nine months at Lafayette, Indiana, with the Motor Transport Corps. He married Catherine Lucas in 1917. He has two sons, Curtis II, and Robert VIII.

The second son, Rolland Andrew, is also a graduate of Indiana University, where he was a member of the Phi Delta Theta fraternity and of Sigma Delta Chi, professional journalistic fraternity. He now owns a one half interest in the *Banner* and with the exception of three years on the Kokomo, Indiana *Dispatch*, he has been connected with the *Banner* since his graduation from high school. He was with the Students Army Training Corps at Indiana University during the World war. The third son, Lou Allen, was educated at Hanover College, is assistant reporter on the Brownstown Banner, and married Blanche Gibson, of Richmond, Indiana. The only daughter of Mr. and Mrs. A. J. Brodhecker, Miss DeAlba, is a graduate of the school of Music at DePauw University at Greencastle.

Claude Broadhecker was publicity director of the Indiana Weekly Press Association in 1928 and was reelected for 1929, but resigned. Rolland had a prominent part in the organization of the Weekly Press Association in 1925 and was its secretary in 1926. Claude is now chairman of the combined legislative committees of the Indiana Democratic, Republican and Weekly Press Associations, and during the 1927, 1929 and 1931 sessions of the Indiana General Assembly was legal representative of Indiana newspapers. These two sons were made editors-in-chief of the *Indiana Daily Student*, the university publication, during their senior years and Claude organized and instituted the printing department of the Bloomington High School at Bloomington, Indiana. Rolland, while editor-in-chief, held the first Associated Press membership for the *Indiana Daily Student*. Claude helped organized the State Fair Edition of the *Indiana Daily Student*.

Mr. Brodhecker and his sons Claude and Rolland are all affiliated with the Knights of Pythias, and he has been through the chairs and is a past chancellor of the Lodge. Rolland is a member of the Masonic and Elks lodges. Mr. Brodhecker and Claude are deacons in the Presbyterian Church, while Mrs. Brodhecker and her son Lou Allen and daughter DeAlba are Methodists. Claude Brodhecker was one of the organizers and became a charter member of Camp Jackson Post No. 112 of the American Legion, and Rolland was post historian. Claude at the present time is liaison officer of the post. He is a member of the 125-piece Indiana State Legion band.

HON. THOMAS H. BRANAMAN is a Jackson County man who has become well known over the state, a very able lawyer, spent several years in Indianapolis in the attorney-general's office, and the members of his profession look upon him as thoroughly qualified for the highest honors open to a lawyer.

He was born in Jackson County, May 5, 1884, son of Frank and Ada (Burrell) Branaman, and is a descendant of Christian Branaman, who represented a Pennsylvania Dutch family and who three times enlisted with Pennsylvania troops for service in the war for independence. Christian Branaman after the war came to Indiana to receive his land bounty, which was located in Owen Township, Jackson County. This old soldier married Mary Cresner. One of their sons was Abraham Branaman, a native of Jackson County, who married Susan Kindred. Abraham Branaman was the father of Christian Branaman, who married Mary Wells, and they were the grandparents of Thomas H. Branaman. The latter's father, Frank Branaman, was a leading lawyer and served as a member of the Indiana State Senate from 1885 to 1889. For twenty years he was on the school board. He and his wife had two sons, John C. and Thomas H.

Thomas H. Branaman attended grade and high school at Brownstown, was graduated with the A. B. degree from Indiana University in 1905, and took his law degree at the Harvard Law School in 1909. In 1907 he was admitted to the Indiana State bar and in 1909 engaged in practice at Brownstown. During 1911-14 he was deputy attorney-general and in 1916 was promoted to assistant attorney-general of Indiana. During these years he spent most of his time at Indianapolis. Since 1917 he has been busy with an extensive general practice. In 1924 he was elected a member of the State Senate and was renominated for that office, but resigned to accept the nomination for justice of the Indiana Supreme Court. He is a member of the Delta Tau Delta fraternity, is a Knight Templar Mason at Seymour, member of the B. P. O. Elks, the Chamber of Commerce, was the second president of the Brownstown Lions

Berenice M. Harrison

Club, and is a member of the Jackson County, Indiana State and American Bar Associations.

Senator Branaman married Miss Blanche Cunningham, of Jackson County, daughter of James W. and Mary Cunningham.

THE SEYMOUR PUBLIC LIBRARY, an institution that has functioned as an important source as well as a center of the literary and artistic culture of that community for a quarter of a century, was organized in 1904. A gift from Andrew Carnegie of $10,000 made possible the original building, which was formally opened January 5, 1905. The members of the original library board were: Harry M. Miller, president; Henry Siebenburgen, vice president; C. S. Mercer, secretary; Miss Nina Ewing. Dr. J. M. Shields, Mrs. Lynn Faulkoner and Mrs. Zoe St. John Williams.

The library when it was opened had only 2,066 volumes and during the first year the statistics of use indicated 988 readers and a circulation of 17,031. The library became increasingly popular and useful during the succeeding years until the building became entirely inadequate for the service demanded of it. Finally the library board issued bonds to the amount of $17,000 for additions and improvements and on November 22, 1928, the new building was dedicated, providing double the capacity of the old, and appropriate structures to house the collection of 14,500 volumes and to provide the varied service demanded of a modern library. Besides the main building the library affords a service to the district and city schools and a branch at Schneck Memorial Hospital.

At the time the rebuilding work was done there was also constructed a special new wing, known as the H. Vance Swope Memorial, a room to be used entirely as an art gallery. This was erected with an endowment of $3,000 given to the Seymour Art League by the late H. Vance Swope, a celebrated New York artist and a native of Indiana. The art room is devoted exclusively to the exhibition of pictures, including a large number of fine canvases bequeathed to the Art League by Mr. Swope at the time of his death.

The Seymour Public Library in per capita circulation of books ranks very high among Indiana cities with library facilities. Much of the good work done by the library has been credited to its librarian, Miss Katherine Frazee, who brought to her work not only sound technical training but a fundamental appreciation of literary and artistic things and a zeal for improving and broadening the application of the library to the cultural interests of the community. Miss Frazee was born in Hamilton County, Indiana, and was graduated from the Indiana Library School in the class of 1913. In 1914 she came to Seymour and has been active head of the library for the past fifteen years except during the year 1915-16. She is a member of the Seymour Tuesday Study Club.

The members of the library board at the time the new building was dedicated were:

R. A. Cox, president; T. A. Mott, vice president; Mrs. Lynn Faulkoner, secretary; Mrs. J. H. Carter, Mrs. O. O. Swails, C. D. Billings and John H. Conner.

BERENICE M. HARRISON is an Indiana woman who has had a successful career as an attorney at law and court reporter. Her home is at Angola in Steuben County.

Mrs. Harrison was born at Three Rivers, Michigan, May 23, 1890. Her parents now reside at Mishawaka, Indiana. Her father, Alva Stephen Hodges, was born in LaPorte, Indiana, June 6, 1869, and his vocation is that of a machinist. Her mother, Hattie (Norton) Hodges, was born at Plymouth, Indiana in October 1873. Mrs. Harrison has one brother, Warren Alva Hodges, who was born at Three Rivers, Michigan, July 26, 1894, and is a radio salesman.

Mrs. Harrison attended the common schools of Mishawaka, the South Bend Business College, and was married, April 26, 1913 to Mr. Herbert E. Harrison.

Mrs. Harrison was graduated from the law department of the Tri-State College of Angola with LL. B. degree in 1923. She has enjoyed a very satisfactory career in the legal profession and as a court reporter. She is a member of the Commercial Law League of America, the Indiana State, District and County Bar Associations, having been secretary of the county association since its organization. She is an honorary life member of the Blackstone Law Club, is a member of the Eastern Star, the White Shrine of Jerusalem, the Woodmen's Circle, is a past chief of the Pythian Sisters, a member of the King's Daughters Association and of the Delphian Society. She belongs to the American Legion Auxiliary, is state vice president of the American Rose Society, state president of the National Shorthand Reporters Association, member of the Indiana Historical Society, the National Geographic Society, American Forestry Association, all of these indicating some of her active interests. She is a past president of the Steuben County Business and Professional Woman's Club and state recording secretary of the Indiana Federation of Business and Professional Women's Clubs. She is a member of the Occupational Advisory Committee of the National Federation of the Business and Professional Women's Clubs, and is also regional secretary and publicity chairman of the organization.

F. J. BOWLING is a Jackson County business man, owner of the Willys-Knight Automobile Agency at Brownstown. He became interested in the automobile industry when a boy, and his enterprise has put him into the ranks of the substantial business men of this community.

Mr. Bowling, who is a son of George K. Bowling, was born in Nelson County, Kentucky, April 6, 1898. He attended school in Kentucky and at the age of twenty-one established a vulcanizing and battery shop, where the postoffice is now located in Brownstown. His business soon became well established and after four years he began handling automobiles. During the past seven years he has been located at his present location, at the west end of Brownstown, and since 1924 has had the Willys-Overland agency.

Mr. Bowling has a large plant, with over nine thousand square feet of floor space, and has abundant space for store room, shop and storage. His shop has all the modern machinery for handling any kind of repair job. He has five people employed and is doing a very prosperous business.

Mr. Bowling is a member of the Brownstown Chamber of Commerce. He was the third president of the local Lions Club and is a member of the Knights of Columbus. He married Miss Ora Gilkey, also a native of Nelson County, Kentucky. Their two children are Mary and Donald.

CHARLES H. COX, president of the First National Bank of Brownstown, is a native of Jackson County, Indiana. He left his home community when a young man and was in business in St. Louis and other places for a number of years, and then returned to Brownstown, where he has been a merchant, banker and a prominent figure in civic and business organizations.

He was born in Jackson County February 25, 1866. His father, R. M. J. Cox, was a native of Kentucky and was one year old when his family settled in Jackson County, Indiana. He spent his active life as a farmer and civil engineer. R. M. J. Cox married Silistus Wort, of Brownstown, and they had a family of ten children.

Charles H. Cox attended the grade and high schools at Brownstown and during his boyhood had a very thorough training in civil engineering under his father. In 1892 he went to St. Louis and established himself in the retail grocery business, and for a time he was located at Fowler, Indiana. From 1894 to 1899, he conducted a grocery business and was a manufacturing confectioner in Indianapolis. On being elected president of the First National Bank of Brownstown, in 1924, he retired from the manufacturing confectionery business and has given all his time to the affairs of this bank since 1925.

Mr. Cox is a member of the Jackson County and Indiana State Bankers Association, is a Royal Arch and Scottish Rite Mason, member of the Knights Templar Commandery at Seymour, and Murat Temple of the Mystic Shrine at Indianapolis. He is a member of the Jackson County Historical Society, was one of the organizers and for three years was president of the Brownstown Chamber of Commerce, and is a member and one of the organizers of the Lions Club. He is an elder in the Presbyterian Church and in national affairs votes the Republican ticket.

Mr. Cox married Marie Stilwell, of Brownstown. They have a son, Richard M. J. Cox, who was educated in the Indianapolis High School, is married and is now in California, being an inspector in the state highway department there.

LOUIS H. OSTERMAN, one of the valued physicians and surgeons of Jackson County, returned to his native community to take over the work of his father, who for almost half a century had been one of the outstanding representatives of medicine and surgery at Seymour.

Dr. Louis H. Osterman was born in Jackson County, September 15, 1896. His father, Dr. A. G. Osterman, was born in Germany, and a year after his birth his parents came to America and settled at Louisville, Kentucky. He was educated there, graduating from the Louisville Medical College, and devoted all the rest of his lifetime to his professional duties in Jackson County. He married Henrietta M. Goecker, a native of Indiana, where her people were early settlers.

Dr. Louis H. Osterman was one of a large family of eleven children. He attended grade and high schools in Jackson County, and was graduated M. D. from the University of Indiana in 1925. He also took special training in the Indianapolis City Hospital and completed a course in clinical work in the Fifth Avenue Hospital of New York City in 1926. After this preparation he located at Fort Wayne, Indiana, and became assistant to Dr. Charles G. Beall, an eminent authority on internal medicine. He was there eighteen months, and on the death of his father, on October 13, 1927, returned to Seymour and has brought additional prestige to the name of Osterman in the medical profession in this county.

During the World war period Doctor Osterman was for eighteen months with the military forces on the Mexican border. He is a member of the American Legion, belongs to the Theta Kappa Psi medical fraternity, the Jackson County and Indiana State Medical Associations, and is a fellow of the American Medical Association.

THEODORE O. PLUMMER, one of the prominent younger business men of Seymour, is founder and active head of the T. O. Plummer Insurance Agency.

He was born in Jackson County, Indiana, April 10, 1901. The Plummer family has been in Indiana for four generations. His grandfather, Scott Plummer, was born in this state and spent his active life as a farmer. Mr. Plummer's father, T. J. Plummer, was born in Jackson County, is a substantial farmer resident of the county, and has been a leader in the Republican party. T. J. Plummer married Carrie Sullivan, a native of Jackson County, and of their five children four are living.

Theodore O. Plummer attended public schools at Medora in Jackson County, and after high school took a course in the Seymour Business College. He was graduated in 1918, and for several years was an automobile salesman. He took up insurance work in 1923,

and during the past seven years has made the T. O. Plummer Insurance Agency one of the leading business establishments of its kind in Southern Indiana. He handles all kinds of insurance, including life, fire and casualty, and bonding. Mr. Plummer, like his father, has a deep interest in local politics and at the present time is Republican city chairman at Seymour and fourth district chairman of the Republican Junior organization. He is president of the Seymour Lions Club, and has since been elected and is now serving Indiana Lionism as district governor of the state.

Mr. Plummer married Catherine Carmine, of Seymour, whose people were pioneers of Franklin County, Indiana. Her father was a manufacturer. Mr. and Mrs. Plummer have one son, Thomas, who is a member of the B. P. O. Elks and is a member of the Seymour Country Club.

HARRY FINDLEY, an insurance man, is one of the most popular citizens of Seymour. He has lived in that section of Indiana nearly all his life, and has a host of friends to appreciate his sterling qualities as a business man and his public spirit as a citizen.

He was born in Jackson County, March 9, 1871. His grandfather, Hugh A. Findley, was born in Westmoreland County, Pennsylvania, and in coming west traveled on the Ohio River until he reached Indiana. He settled in Jackson County and took up a homestead and secured the patent from the Government in the early 1830s. He developed a farm and also followed the trade of gunsmith. He was of Scotch-Irish ancestry. He married Rebecca Coons of Clark County, Indiana. William A. Findley, father of Harry, was born in Jackson County and married Sara Durland, of that county. They had a large family of twelve children.

Harry Findley attended the grade schools of Jackson County and lived on a farm during his youth. For four years he was with the Adams Express Company and then entered the railway train service and was a railroad man until 1907. He still holds his card of membership in the Brotherhood of Locomotive Engineers and has been secretary of the local branch of that organization for the past eighteen years.

Mr. Findley in 1907 located at Seymour and became a solicitor for life insurance. In 1913 he bought a general agency and has conducted that business, together with loans and bonds and investments, making it one of the best organizations of the kind in Jackson County. Mr. Findley has always been responsive to calls upon his civic support for worthy measures. In 1917 he was elected city clerk of Seymour. He is a Republican, a member of the Masonic fraternity, B. P. O. Elks, Loyal Order of Moose, Independent Order of Odd Fellows and Knights of Pythias.

Mr. Findley married Margaret Heuser, of Jackson County. They have two children, Mylrea and Miss Madeline. Mylrea is the wife of Ralph Schafer.

MILTON DUDLEY HEINY. Among the men who, because of the extent and importance of their holdings and interests, are accounted leaders in financial and business circles of Gary, few are held in greater esteem than Milton D. Heiny, one of the largest road, sewer and street contractors in Indiana. A product of the farm, at the time he gained his majority he embarked in business on his own account, and during his career has been identified with several lines of activity, in all of which he has achieved the kind of success that can be gained only by a man of versatile and uncommon abilities.

Mr. Heiny was born on a farm in Cass County, Indiana, March 6, 1875, and is a son of Jonathan and Mary (Ireland) Heiny. His paternal grandfather, Jacob Heiny, was born in Germany, and immigrated to the United States in 1834, taking up his residence in Pennsylvania, where he lived for several years. Later he moved to Cass County, Indiana, where he became a pioneer settler and took up farming land, being engaged in agricultural operations throughout the remainder of his life and acquiring a comfortable competence. During the last few years of his life he lived in retirement, and he and his worthy wife, also a native of Germany, are buried in the Cedarville (Indiana) Cemetery.

Jonathan Heiny was born in Germany, in 1830, and was about four years of age when brought to the United States by his parents. For a few years the family resided in Pennsylvania, where the lad received his early education, and this was completed in the public schools of the country districts of Cass County, Indiana, where he grew to manhood on the home farm. During the war between the states he enlisted in the Union army, becoming a private in the One Hundred Fifty-seventh Regiment, Indiana Volunteer Infantry, with which he served gallantly until the close of the struggle, following which he resumed his activities as a farmer and stock raiser. In the evening of his life he retired with a modest fortune, and lived to the remarkable age of ninety-six years, three months and one day, passing away November 23, 1927, and being laid to rest in the cemetery at Idaville, White County, Indiana. Mr. Heiny, who was one of the highly esteemed and public-spirited citizens of his community, married Miss Mary Ireland, who was born and reared in Carroll County, Indiana, where she received her education in the public schools. She was a faithful member of the Baptist Church and active in its work, and died January 7, 1915, being also buried at Idaville. The Ireland family is also one of the old and honored ones of Indiana. Mr. and Mrs. Heiny were the parents of fourteen children, of whom four died in infancy: Henry Markle, who died in 1929; Netta, now Mrs. Herman, of White County; James, also of White County; Mrs. Nella Jones, of Rockford, Illinois; Eva, now Mrs. Benjamin of White County; Charles, of White County; Milton D., of this review; Ora, of Cass County; Mrs.

Grace Leslie, of Lake County; and Bert, of Gary.

Milton D. Heiny attended the public schools of White and Cass counties, and on leaving school began to assist his father on the home place, continuing until he reached the age of twenty-one years. Not long thereafter he married and moved to Starke County, Indiana, where he established himself in the ice and trucking business, in which he continued to be engaged for twelve years. In 1907 he moved to Gary and began contracting in roads, streets and sewers, and with the passing of the years has built up the largest enterprise of its kind in the State of Indiana, with offices at 3804 Broadway, Glen Park, in the Glen Park State Bank Building. Mr. Heiny has contributed to the upbuilding of Gary a number of flat buildings, the Glen Park State Bank Building and a number of beautiful residences and also drew plans and outlined the architectural work for his own beautiful home at 3620 Jefferson Avenue, one of the show places of Gary. He owns a one-third interest in the Park Manor Land Company and is a director in a number of other companies and corporations and has a high standing in business and financial circles. Mr. Heiny has always taken a sincere and constructive interest in civic affairs and is a member of the Gary Commercial Club and Chamber of Commerce; the Gary Rotary Club, of which he is a member of the directorate; and the Gary Country Club. He is a thirty-second degree Mason and belongs to Gary Lodge No. 677, A. F. and A. M.; Fort Wayne Consistory, and Orak Temple, A. A. O. N. M. S., of Hammond. He is a Republican in his political allegiance and a Christian Scientist in religious faith.

Mr. Heiny married in White County, Indiana, April 11, 1893, Miss Mary Davis, daughter of Rev. William J. and Mary Jane Davis, the former of whom was for many years a Methodist Episcopal divine in the Indiana Conference. Both Reverend and Mrs. Davis are deceased and buried in Blue River Cemetery, near Columbus City, Indiana. Mrs. Heiny died in November, 1914, and is also buried in Blue River Cemetery. Of the two children born to that union one died at birth, and Ruth Irene is now Mrs. Glen S. Smith, of Gary, whose husband is associated with Mr. Heiny as superintendent of construction. Mr. and Mrs. Smith have one child, Glen Dudley. On April 10, 1918, Mr. Heiny was united in marriage with Mrs. Gertrude (Davis) Dagenhart, of Ohio, who had one child by her former marriage: William, who is attending high school at Gary. Mrs. Heiny was born and reared in Ohio, where she attended school, and as a proficient musician has been a teacher of music for some years, being especially gifted as a pipe organist. Mr. and Mrs. Heiny have three children: Frances Louise and Milton Dudley, Jr., who are attending school and studying music and dancing; and Johnathan (Jack) Weldon. Mr. Heiny is a member of the Turkey Creek and Crown Point Country Club.

VIRGIL H. FOUNTAIN, county clerk of Jackson County, came to that office after having gained a reputation as a substantial business man. Much of his early life was spent on the farm and later in banking.

Mr. Fountain was born in Jackson County, March 18, 1880. His great-grandfather, Stephen Fountain, came from the Carolinas to Indiana in 1818 and settled in Jackson County, near Leesville, where his industry and thrift enabled him to clear up and develop a good farm. He was the father of Abraham Fountain, who was born in Indiana, and Abraham was the grandfather of Virgil H. Fountain. John W. Fountain, his father, is also a native of Jackson County and served on the County Council and as trustee of Owen Township. He married a Jackson County girl, Miss Mary E. Hamilton, and they had a family of four children.

Virgil H. Fountain was reared on a farm, attended country schools, and up to the age of twenty-six spent most of his time assisting his father on the farm and in the mercantile business at Clear Spring. Mr. Fountain in 1906 removed to Brownstown, becoming assistant cashier of the Brownstown State Bank, and in May, 1916, was elected president of that institution. He resigned the following September and resumed farming. In connection with farming he performed the duties of cashier of the Citizens State Bank from May, 1923, until he entered the clerk's office in February, 1924. In 1922 he was elected county clerk and by reelection in 1926 holds that office today, being one of the very popular men in the courthouse at Brownstown.

Mr. Fountain is a member of the Masonic fraternity, Knights of Pythias, is a Democrat, a member of the Chamber of Commerce and the Baptist Church. He married Miss Nora E. George, of Jackson County, and they have a family of nine children, consisting of five sons and four daughters: Hugh, Ray J., Ross, Oren Woodrow and Virgil, Jr., Gladys, Helen, Ruth and Elizabeth.

ROSCOE W. HAGUE is proprietor of the third oldest automobile agency in Jackson County. Mr. Hague's business is at Seymour, where he owns the agency in the local territory for the Buick and Marquette cars.

Mr. Hague was born in Washington County, Indiana, February 26, 1899. His grandfather, Joseph D. Hague, was born in Tennessee and came to Indiana about 1860, his parents accompanying him. They settled in Washington County, where Joseph D. Hague for many years followed farming. He married Mary Collins, of Indiana. William L. Hague, father of Roscoe W., was born in Washington County and for many years has been active in the business of undertaking at Medora in Jackson County. He married Nellie M. Starr, of Washington County.

Roscoe W. Hague attended grade school in Medora, is a graduate of the high school there and at the age of fourteen began his business experience. For one year he was employed in a confectionery store at Bedford, Indiana, and for two years was a garage man at Seymour. He left that work to go on the road as a traveling salesman for the Tiona Refining Company, traveling over Central Indiana and Illinois for three years. On returning to Seymour he rejoined the garage with which he had been previously associated, but which in the meantime had changed ownership and was known as the Central Garage. In 1923 he spent a year with the Columbus Buick Company, at Columbus, Indiana, and then was awarded the Buick agency in Jackson County. There being no building available, he handled the business at Medora for a few months and then opened a sales room on South Chestnut Street in Seymour. After a year he moved to another location on that street and then moved into the Craig Building, on South Carter Street. From there he took up his present quarters, at 101-103 West Third Street, a building he has owned since 1926. The Buick Agency was first established in this building in 1917. Mr. Hague has 12,800 square feet of floor space for show room, office, storage and repair shops. It is a modern brick building, equipped with all the machinery and appliances to give it rating as a Buick specification repair shop. Mr. Hague has been handling over seventy-five new and used cars annually and keeps a full stock of parts for the Buick and the more recent product of the Buick organization, the Marquette car. Associated with him in the business is his brother, C. D. Hague, who has charge of the parts and stock department.

Mr. Hague married Mildred Paul, of Columbus, Indiana. He is a member of the Masonic fraternity and B. P. O. Elks.

FERNANDO C. FOSTER, manager of the Jackson County Farmers Mutual Insurance Company at Brownstown, is a member of one of the oldest families of Southern Indiana. The Fosters in all the generations since they came to America in the early Colonial period, have been characterized by the cardinal virtues of industry, honesty and frugality, and their strength of character has shown through all their deeds and personal relationships. Mr. Foster is a great-grandson of Hiram and Polly (Trumbo) Foster, two splendid pioneer characters of Southern Indiana whose descendants a few years ago organized the Foster Family Association, of which Fernando C. Foster was elected secretary and is now president of this organization.

Mr. Foster was born in Jennings County, Indiana, July 21, 1875, a son of Benjamin F. and Allie J. (Lewis) Foster, a grandson of Jacob Foster, a Jennings County farmer who married Margaret Fear. Jacob Foster was one of the children of Hiram and Polly (Trumbo) Foster.

Hiram Foster was born June 21, 1797, a son of Gabrielle and Permelia (Campbell) Foster. Gabrielle was a son of Timothy and Bethiah (Howell) Foster. Timothy was a son of Thomas and Hannah (Hildreth) Foster. Thomas Foster was born in 1691, son of John and Hannah (Abbott) Foster. John Foster was born February 8, 1662, a son of John Foster, who was born in England in 1634, son of Christopher Foster, who was born in England in 1603, and on June 17, 1635, sailed for America with his wife and three children. He settled on a farm on Long Island. Thus the Foster family has been in America almost three centuries.

Gabrielle Foster with his brothers, Zebulon and Luke, in the fall of 1788 settled in Hamilton County, Ohio. In 1803 Gabrielle Foster moved to Indiana, locating about twenty-five miles above the falls of the Ohio, and was one of the earliest settlers in the vicinity of Deputy, Indiana, in Jefferson County, where he cleared up and developed a farm, on which he lived out his life.

The oldest child of Gabrielle Foster and his wife, Permelia Campbell, was Hiram, who was about six years of age when the family came to Jefferson County. Hiram Foster lived to a good old age, passing away January 17, 1876. His wife, Polly Trumbo, whom he married December 24, 1818, died November 21, 1872. A record of the children of this worthy couple is as follows: Elvira, born October 7, 1819, married November 27, 1824, and died April 9, 1872; William, born June 11, 1821, married September 21, 1843, and died May 6, 1870; Jacob T., born January 4, 1823, married July 18, 1844, and died August 9, 1865; Henry C., born March 6, 1825, married April 15, 1847, and died April 27, 1870; Belinda, born November 25, 1826, married in September, 1848, and died in 1914; John T., born October 16, 1829, married August 18, 1853, and died January 12, 1912; Oliver S., born November 7, 1831, died February 1, 1843; Stephen, born March 17, 1836, married August 31, 1856; Benjamin F., born November 13, 1838, married March 1, 1860, and died July 3, 1887; Hannah, born July 7, 1841, died June 29, 1843; and Edward, born July 31, 1843, married October 10, 1867.

Fernando C. Foster, the oldest of nine sons, attended grade school in Jackson County, and took up teaching, a profession he followed for six years in Vernon Township. On locating at Brownstown, in 1900, he served four years as deputy county clerk and for three years was a rural mail carrier and for three years assistant cashier of the Brownstown State Bank. Mr. Foster has been in the insurance business since 1911 and for twenty years has been the very able manager of the Jackson County Farmers Mutual Insurance Company which has grown and prospered under his direction. He is also a director of the Indiana Mutual Fire & Cyclone Insurance Company of Indianapolis, and has charge of the work of that organization in eleven counties, being district adjuster. He is also a director of the Farmers Mutual Liability Company of Indianapolis. Mr. Foster for six years acted as agent of the Jackson County Board of Children's Guardians. He has been secretary of the Brownstown Chamber of Commerce, and a member of the Baptist Church. He has served as president of the State Association of Mutual Insurance Companies of Indiana, 1930-1931.

He married Vionesia Staples, daughter of Thomas J. Staples, a well-to-do farmer and banker in Jennings County, and an ex-county treasurer. Mr. and Mrs. Foster were married March 31, 1902, and have four children: Miss Helen, a graduate of Franklin College, married Harold E. Troyer, of Monroeville, Indiana, November 27, 1930; Thomas S., a mechanical engineer, married Elizabeth Ogle on May 12, 1928; Charles E., a graduate in civil engineering at Purdue University; and Dorothea, attending high school at Brownstown.

JOHN H. CONNER came in contact with newspaper work while in school, and though he went on with his education through universities, graduating from law school, he returned to his first love and has been a newspaper man rather than a lawyer.

Mr. Conner is editor and publisher of the *Seymour Daily Tribune*. This is a newspaper with half a century of history behind it. In its present form it represents the consolidation of the *Seymour Daily Republican* and the *Seymour Daily Democrat*. The *Republican* was founded in 1879, and the daily edition has been published for many years. After the merger of the *Republican* with the *Democrat* the name of the daily was changed to the *Tribune*, while the *Republican* continues as a weekly. The *Daily Tribune* prints from eight to sixteen pages, with Associated Press service, and approximately 3,000 copies are distributed throughout this section of Indiana. It is one of the most influential newspapers in the southern part of the state. As a business it employs twenty-two persons, and has a plant equipped with the most modern printing machinery, including equipment for commercial printing and a great deal of book work is done here. The owners of the newspaper and business today are John H. Conner and his brother-in-law, Dr. R. E. Harris, of Cincinnati.

Mr. Conner was born at Oakland City, Indiana, January 4, 1886. He is of Irish ancestry, his great-grandfather, John Conner, having been one of three brothers who left Ireland before or about the time of the Revolutionary war. John Conner became a colonel in the patriot army during the war for independence. Mr. Conner's grandfather was Isaac Conner, who married a member of the Nichols family, early pioneers of Scott County, Indiana, where they took up Government land about 1816. John W. Conner, father of the Seymour newspaper man, was born at Lexington, Indiana, and has been a resident of Seymour for over forty years, being one of the early clothing merchants of the city. He has served on the school board, as president of the Business Men's Association several times and has been active in civic affairs. He married Olive Thomas, of Washington County, Indiana, daughter of Hezekiah Thomas. Hezekiah Thomas was also born in Washington County and was a corn mill operator and about 1880 laid out a part of Seymour, known as the Thomas addition. John H. Conner was the only son of his parents. His sister, who is active in musical circles at Cincinnati, is the wife of Dr. R. E. Harris, of that city.

John H. Conner attended the grade and high schools of Seymour, graduated from DePauw University at Greencastle in 1907 and in 1909 was awarded his LL. B. degree by the Indiana Law School at Indianapolis. During vacations he had worked for the *Seymour Daily Republican* and immediately after completing his law course he returned to become associated again with that paper as editor. He held that post of duty until 1921, was then appointed business manager and on January 1, 1926, he and his brother-in-law bought the plant from the original owners and he is now the responsible manager and publisher.

Mr. Conner is a member of the Republican Editorial Association, Indiana Home League Daily, the Inland Press, the National Editorial Association, is a member of the Rotary Club, B. P. O. Elks, Masonic fraternity in the Lodge, Royal Arch Chapter, Knights Templar Commandery and Murat Temple of the Mystic Shrine at Indianapolis. Mr. Conner married Ethel McGrew, of Vanderburgh County, Indiana. They have one child, Thomas William, attending school at Seymour.

HASKELL LETT. Occupying a conspicuous place among the citizens of Jackson County who are rendering capable and conscientious service to their respective communities in positions of importance and responsibility is Haskell Lett, postmaster of the thriving City of Seymour. A member of a family which came to Indiana in 1824, he is of pure Revolutionary stock, which traces its ancestry back to Colonial Virginia. For many years he followed the profession of veterinary surgery, at one time being deputy state veterinarian, and during a long period has been a Republican party leader in the state.

Haskell Lett was born July 30, 1887, on a farm in Jennings County, Indiana, a son of Dr. William S. and Maude (Wilson) Lett. The Lett family originated in England, whence the first American ancestors came to this country in early Colonial times and took up their residence in Virginia, and from that colony enlisted Gen. Daniel Lett, who won distinction as an officer in General Washington's army during the War of the Revolution. He was the father of the great-grandfather of Haskell Lett, Daniel Lett, who came to Indiana from Kentucky with his family in 1827 and took up patents in Marion Township, Jennings County, where he passed the remainder of his life in the development of his property and was a man of substantiality and high character. His son, Fielding Lett, was born in Owen County, Kentucky, and was a youth when he accompanied the family to Indiana. He received a public school education and was reared to the pursuits of agriculture, in which he continued to be occupied during the remain-

der of his life, his property, consisting of some 2,000 acres, being mainly in Marion Township. He also took an interest in stock raising and shipping, and in 1835 was one of the constructors of the Madison Northern Railway. Mr. Lett first married Miss Diana Hoagland, and his second wife, Sarah Jane, was a member of the well-known Applegate family. William S. Lett, the father of Haskell Lett, was born in Jennings County, and spent the greater part of his active career on his farm, in addition to practicing veterinary surgery, a field in which he is still widely known. He married Miss Maude Wilson, a native of Jennings County, and they became the parents of four children.

Haskell Lett attended the public schools of Jennings County, following which he pursued a course at the Chicago Veterinary College, from which he was graduated with the class of 1909, receiving the degree of Doctor of Veterinary Medicine. In that year he commenced practice at Seymour, where he built up a large and profitable business, to which he gave his entire attention until the time of his appointment to the postmastership in 1922. He was again appointed to this office December 22, 1926, and has given his community the best of service, making numerous and lasting improvements in the service that have commended themselves to the people served by the Seymour office. From 1917 until 1919 Mr. Lett served in the office of deputy state veterinarian, and then was made a member of the Live Stock Sanitary Commission for the State of Indiana, remaining on this board until 1921. During this period he likewise was a member of the State Veterinary Examiners Board and president of that body, and during the war era was a member of various committees in the sale of bonds, stamps, etc. Doctor Lett is a member of the Presbyterian Church, a Mason and a Republican in politics. He was Republican city committee chairman in 1916, township chairman in 1917 and county chairman in 1918 and again in 1920, and in the latter year was elected delegate from the Fourth District to the Chicago National Convention of 1920.

Mr. Lett married in 1909 Miss Ethel Louise Klemme, who was born in Pike County, Illinois, and they have no children.

THOMAS HARVEY CANNON. In a lifetime of eighty-two years "Tom" Cannon, of Gary, has earned such titles of distinguished service and experience as are represented in the names journalist, soldier of fortune, Indian fighter, explorer, prospector, poet, philosopher, humorist, author, historian and reconteur.

His ancestors came from the Isle of Man, where they represented an infusion of Norse, Scotch, Irish and Celtic bloods. His father, Randall Portus Hays Cannon, was of Virginia stock, and his mother, Mary Jane (MacCampbell) Cannon, was of a Kentucky family, though the MacCampbells likewise had come out of Virginia and farther back from County Tyrone, Ireland. The first home of the Cannons in America was in Pennsylvania. Like many other families of that state they moved down the Valley of Virginia to North Carolina and thence to Tennessee. The late Joseph G. Cannon (Uncle Joe) was a native of North Carolina and was a third cousin of Tom Cannon. The latter's paternal grandmother, Margaret Hays, was born at Harrod's Fort, Kentucky, and she was held in the lap of Daniel Boone when the Indians attacked that Kentucky outpost.

Tom Cannon was educated in Indiana and after the age of nine years at Muscatine, Iowa, where he attended high school. In 1869 he entered Wabash College of Indiana, but left college two years later and went to Missouri. He completed a law course in the University of Missouri, practiced a short time and then became editor of the Greenfield, Missouri, *Advocate*. In 1874 he and a party of four young men crossed the plains in a wagon to Del Norte, Colorado, and there he organized a pack train to go over the mountains to the headwaters of the Uncompaghre River. There he founded the Town of Lake City and started the first newspaper west of the Rockies in Colorado. This was the *Lake City Silver World*. While in Western Colorado he held several offices, including deputy mining recorder, deputy postmaster, probate judge of Hinsdale County. Later he acted as a scout for the United States Cavalry during the Ute war, and had an interesting experience in the final campaign for the extermination of the Apache Indians in Arizona, under Chief Geronimo. In 1875 he was with the Wheeler and Hayden Federal exploring expedition in a survey of the peaks and deserts of Southwestern Colorado, Northern New Mexico and Northeastern Arizona.

Mr. Cannon in 1876 became a member of the staff of the *Rocky Mountain News* at Denver, but in 1878 returned to Missouri. He was associated with several Missouri newspapers, including the *Springfield Morning Herald*. His next important experience came in 1884, when he did right of way work through Indian Territory and Texas in the extension of the Frisco lines from Fort Smith, Arkansas, to Paris, Texas. One feature of this work was the establishment of a newspaper at Paris, through which a campaign was conducted resulting in the donating of the right of way from Red River to Paris, a distance of sixteen miles, in addition to land at the edge of the city for terminal yards. On leaving Texas, Mr. Cannon joined the editorial and news staff of the *Kansas City Times*. Here he had an unusual experience as a newspaper reporter. He was assigned the task of interviewing the eminent financier and railroad man, Jay Gould. He was permitted to enter Mr. Gould's private car. An engine was immediately attached and the car was taken out forty miles into Kansas, where the newspaper man was summarily dropped on the wide prairie and the train departed without him. It was afterwards explained that this action was taken to prevent the publication of Mr.

Gould's plans for the purchase of the Kansas City and Northwestern Railroad, in which the municipality of Kansas City held to the sum of $300,000. However, Gould did not outwit the resourceful Tom Cannon, who walked six miles to a little town and telegraphed his story to the Times, which made a big "scoop" in the matter. Another newspaper investigation by him at Leavenworth disclosed a complete census of "blind pigs" in that city and the publication of the story resulted in the discharge of the entire police department and the board of police commissioners. While there he also covered the original opening of Oklahoma Territory. He gave up his profession as night managing editor of the *Times* to go to Chicago in 1890 and became political editor of the *Chicago Times*. The *Times* was merged with the *Herald* and became the *Times Herald* in 1894, and Mr. Cannon remained with the new publication for several years as assistant to the publisher and editor, Herman H. Kohlsaat. For seven years he reported every session of the Illinois Legislature and nearly every national convention of the Republican and Democratic parties from 1890 to 1900. Governor John P. Altgeld, of Illinois, in 1892 appointed Mr. Cannon state canal commissioner in which office he served until 1896. In 1896 he reported the convention in the old Coliseum at Chicago when William J. Bryan was nominated. He also worked for the *Tribune* and for Hearst's *American*, later was chief editorial writer on the *Chicago Journal* until 1909, in which year his career became identified with Gary, Indiana.

Here he and Frank B. Patrick founded the *Gary Evening Post*, which in 1910 was sold to J. R. and H. B. Snyder, who retained Mr. Cannon. With the exception of a few intervals Mr. Cannon has remained with the *Post*, now the *Post-Tribune*, ever since. He conducts the "Flue Dust" in the *Post-Tribune*, and is widely known as one of America's famous "columnists." He is also well known throughout Northwestern Indiana under the pen name of "Lud Wrangler."

Besides his daily contributions to the press Mr. Cannon has written verse that has been published in many magazines. Some of his poems include such titles as "Over the Range," "Arms and the Man." "Ashes of Remembrance," "Songs of the Dunes," "Hills of the Ozarks," "A Valentine," "L'Envoi," "My Southern Indiana Hills."

After coming to Gary, Mr. Cannon took a personal interest in public affairs, especially in the construction of the Burns ditch which reclaimed 20,000 acres of overflown land; in the construction of the Dunes Highway and in the establishment of a state park in the Indiana Dunes. In 1912 Mr. Cannon, A. F. Knotts and others organized the National Dunes Park Association, with Mr. Knotts as president and Mr. Cannon as secretary. Their activities led to the creation of the park by the Indiana Legislature. Mr. Cannon has been a member of the Gary Rotary Club, B. P. O.

Elks, honorary member of the Gary Kiwanis Club, member of the executive council of the Gary Boy Scouts, member and a past president of the Izaak Walton League, honorary member of the Gary Real Estate Board and the Indian Hill Country Club; for two terms was a director of the Gary Chamber of Commerce; a member of the Gary Commercial Club and the Lake County Historical Society.

In his eighty-first year Tom Cannon wrote what many have regarded as his most notable work, the life story entitled *Old Frontiers and New*, which is a record of his colorful career from the time of the Civil war to the prsent day. He was chief editor of the *History of the Lake and Calumet Region of Indiana*, published in 1927.

He married in 1882 Glen Constance Cones, of Lamar, Missouri. She died in 1886, leaving one son. He married in 1895 Miss Ora Lee Bedwell. By this marriage he has a son, Edward Harvey Cannon, who is engaged in the publishing business in Chicago.

JAMES R. THOMPSON. Among the younger generation of business men who have attained positions as the heads of large and important enterprises formerly occupied only by men many years their seniors is James R. Thompson, president of the Thompson Dairy Company, of Seymour, and chief executive official also of the Seymour Ice Cream Company. These are enterprises which have been developed under his supervision from small and modest beginnings to business concerns of considerable size and importance, necessitating a steady and capable directing hand and mind to continue and further the course of their development. In the innumerable details that must be taken care of in the smooth running of business industries such as these Mr. Thompson has shown himself conservative and at the same time progressive, shrewd and able, and at all times honorable in his methods.

Mr. Thompson was born March 18, 1897, on a farm in Jackson County, Indiana, and is a son of J. B. and Mary (Holmes) Thompson. His grandfather, A. F. Thompson, was born in Bartholomew County, Indiana, a son of one of the first settlers of that region, and passed his entire life in agricultural pursuits. J. B. Thompson was born on a farm in Bartholomew County, and subsequently moved to Jackson County, where for many years he followed farming and later took up banking, being at present vice president of the Jackson County Loan & Trust Company of Seymour. He married Mary Holmes, of Jackson County, and they became the parents of five children.

James R. Thompson attended the public schools of Jackson County while assisting his father in the work of the home farm, and after his graduation from the high school entered the United States army, in 1917, for service during the World war. He was at first in the Marine Corps, but was subsequently transferred to the Aviation Corps, and was still in active training at the time of the signing of the armistice. He still maintains his interest in flying and watches with keen appreciation the constant developments being made in flying. In 1919 Mr. Thompson was graduated from Purdue University and returned to the vocation of farming, to which he applied himself energetically until 1924, when he bought out the Seymour Ice Cream Company and changed the name to the Thompson Dairy Company, Inc., consolidating the Newby Dairy Company with the Ice Cream Manufacturing Company. This company now manufactures ice cream, butter, cheese and all dairy products, doing a huge business all over South Central Indiana, with plants located at North Vernon and Bedford (the Bedford Dairy Company). These plants give employment to forty-five people, and have an annual output of 100,000 gallons of ice cream, 1,500 gallons of milk daily and 2,000 pounds of butter daily. The Seymour plant covers about 4,000 square feet and is equipped with the most modern machinery known to the business, and the North Vernon plant covers 1,800 square feet. In the regular procedure of its business the Thompson Dairy Company utilizes fourteen motor trucks and eight wagons and Mr. Thompson is president and general manager. He takes an active part in all matters pertaining to the welfare of his adopted city, and is a past president of the Rotary Club and a member of the board of directors of the Merchants Association. A great friend of education, he is a former member of the school board, of which he was treasurer one year and secretary two years. He belongs to Jackson Lodge, A. F. and A. M., the Scottish Rite at Indianapolis, and Murat Temple of the Mystic Shrine.

Mr. Thompson married Miss Helen Temple, of Frankfort, Indiana, and to this union there have been born two children: James and Jane.

FRANK J. VOSS is senior member of the F. J. Voss Company, funeral directors and undertakers at Seymour. This is a business which has been conducted by Mr. Voss for upwards of thirty years. He is a native son of Seymour and has been long and favorably known in business and civic affairs in that community.

He was born there September 14, 1865. His father, Fred Voss, came from Hanover, Germany, and locted at Seymour about 1853. He conducted a cooperage business. He married Catrina Siekendiecker, also of Hanover, and they had a family of five children.

Frank J. Voss attended the grade schools of Seymour, and left high school when about fifteen years of age to become a clerk in a local dry goods firm. At the age of twenty-two he became a partner in a men's furnishing goods store and tailoring business, and after three years went on the road, representing a prominent wholesale house of Cincinnati for five years.

At Indianapolis he learned the undertaking and embalming business, completing his education in Professor Clark's School at Cincin-

nati and in the Barnes College of Embalming at Chicago. He has been a funeral director at Seymour since 1898. Recently his company completed a modern funeral home, one of the best in this section of the state.

Mr. Voss in addition to conducting a successful business has been prominent in organizations representing his line of work. He served as treasurer of the Indiana State Funeral Directors Association in 1917-18. He is a member of the Seymour Retail Merchants Association, is a Rotarian and during the World war helped in all the drives for the sale of liberty Bonds, War Stamps and in raising funds for the Red Cross and other auxiliary war organizations. He is a member of the Masonic fraternity, Independent Order of Odd Fellows, Knights of Pythias and B. P. O. Elks.

Mr. Voss married Katrina Leininger, of Seymour. His only child, Walter Voss, is the junior member of F. J. Voss Company. He attended high school at Seymour, spent four years in the University of Indiana, two years in the medical department, and completed his training in the Askins School of Embalming at Indianapolis. Walter Voss married Helen Galbraith, whose father, Dr. Thomas A. Galbraith, was a prominent citizen of Jackson County, where he located about 1870. Walter Voss and wife have three children, one daughter and two sons.

NORBOURNE D. SHORT, member of an old and patriotic family of Jackson County, a World war veteran, is the active head of the N. D. Short Motor Sales Company of Seymour, one of the busiest and most prosperous motor sales organizations in Southern Indiana.

Mr. Short was born at Seymour, December 10, 1890. His great-grandfather was a pioneer of Jackson County, being of Virginia ancestry. Mr. Short's grandfather, Zachariah Short, was born in Jackson County and became a brick mason and contractor. Zachariah was a nephew of Aaron Short. Aaron Short was an Indiana man who went over the river into Kentucky to do some work in the building of a canal. He had a fight with an Irishman and after defeating the Irishman he was referred to by his comrades as the "Hoosier," and it is claimed that he was the first Indiana resident to be given this nickname that has since been applied generally to Indiana natives. The incident occurred in 1829, so that the word Hoosier has been in speech currency for over a century.

Norbourne D. Short is a son of Ransom R. and Esther (Robertson) Short. His father was a brick mason and contractor at Seymour and served as a member of the City Council. He died in 1918.

N. D. Short was one of a family of eight children. He attended grade schools in Jackson County, high school at Seymour, but at the age of fifteen was earning his own way. He was on the farm until the World war, when he enlisted and joined the Three Hundred Thirty-fifth Infantry, Eighty-fourth Division. He was with the colors altogether twenty months, and was in France nine months of that time. He served with the grade of corporal. On returning home and getting his honorable discharge in 1919 he located at Seymour, and in May, 1924, organized the N. D. Short Motor Sales Company, handling the Oakland, Pontiac and Nash cars. Since 1927 the company has represented the Nash Motor Company exclusively. His company has a complete show room, shop, storage and sales rooms, in a building at 313-315 North Ewing Street, with 10,000 square feet of floor space. Five employees are in the shop, which is equipped with the most modern machinery for the prompt and expert handling of every repair work.

Mr. Short is a member of the American Legion. His father was a soldier in the Union army during the Civil war. He is a member of the Hoosier State Automobile Association, and is affiliated with Jackson Lodge No. 146, A. F. and A. M., the Royal Arch Chapter and Council in Masonry. Mr. Short married Gertrude Hewitt. Their two children, Norbourne D., Jr., and Helen Rosemary, are both attending school at Seymour.

WILLIAM J. ABRAHAM, of Seymour, has been associated with the building trades since boyhood, and his knowledge of the mechanical side of the industry has been an important factor in his success as a general contractor.

Mr. Abraham was born at Lawrenceburg, Dearborn County, Indiana, August 31, 1880. His father, Frederick William Abraham, was a native of Neustadt, Germany, and settled at Lawrenceburg, Indiana, in 1850. He spent his active life as a farmer and dairyman. His wife was Amelia Rollfing, of Jennings County, Indiana.

William J. Abraham was one of a large family of ten children. As a boy he attended grade schools in Lawrenceburg and was thirteen years of age when he went to work in a cooper's shop. Later he learned the trade of carpenter, and after a journeyman's experience of several years began contracting in a small way, and has built up one of the best organizations of the kind in Southern Indiana. He began his business in Lawrenceburg, but for a number of years has been located at Seymour.

The character of his work and business can best be exemplified by noting some of the buildings for which he has been contractor in recent years. Those at Seymour include the home of the Eagles fraternity, the addition to the Seymour Library, the First Nazarene Church, the Emerson School, the high school at Freetown, the Greendale School at Lawrenceburg, the Union Township School and the Bell Telephone Company Building at Seymour.

Mr. Abraham is a Republican, but follows his independent inclination to vote for the best man. He is a prominent member of the Nazarene Church and has been trustee of the church and member of its building committee. He married Miss Lillian Seekatz, of Dearborn County, and they have four living children.

CLIFFORD R. JACKSON. From the time that he completed his education until 1918 Clifford R. Jackson, of Seymour, was engaged in educational work, a profession in which he established a record for ability and learning. In the year mentioned, however, he accepted an attractive offer to become identified with the milling business, and at this time is manager of the Farmers Hominy Mill Company, of which he was one of the organizers, and which is now owned by the Farmers Co-Operative Elevator Company, of which Mr. Jackson is a member of the directorate. He is also widely known in fraternal circles and is one of the strong and influential Republicans of this section of the state.

Mr. Jackson was born August 16, 1887, and is a son of Sherman and Rosie (Allen) Jackson. The family originated in North Carolina and was founded in Indiana about 1830, by the pioneer great-grandfather of Mr. Jackson. His grandfather was Rev. Henry Jackson, a native of Clark County, Indiana, who subsequently moved to Jackson County, and spent the rest of his life as a farmer, also at different times filling pulpits as a minister. Sherman Jackson was born in Jackson County, and has been a substantial farmer all of his life, a man of high character and sound principles, and one who takes a constructive interest in the welfare of his community. Mrs. Jackson is a native of Scott County, this state.

Clifford R. Jackson attended the graded and high schools at Freetown, Jackson County, the Central Normal School of Danville, Indiana, and the University of Indiana. After graduating from the last named institution he commenced his career as a teacher, spending four years in the graded schools, eight years as principal of the Cortland High School, and two years as principal of the high school at Vallonia. In 1918 he became one of the organizers, secretary and a director of the Farmers Hominy Mill Company, which bought the present mill at Seymour, and of which he has been in active charge to the present. In 1921, when this mill was sold to the Farmers Co-Operative Elevator Company, he was retained as manager of the mill and made a member of the board of directors of the new company. This company manufactures corn products, employing fifteen people, and ships its capacity of 400 barrels daily to the eastern states, under the well-known trade brand of "Apex." The company has established an excellent record for the purity of its products and belongs to the Indiana Grain Dealers Association and the National Corn Millers Federation. Mr. Jackson is known as a sound and reliable business man and one of the best informed in his line in the state. He takes a great interest in business and civic affairs and is a member of the board of directors of the Rotary Club, of which he was formerly vice president. Dur-

J. B. Burcham M. D.

ing the World war period he was chairman of the committees in charge of the drives of the American Red Cross, Young Men's Christian Association and War Savings Stamps. As a fraternalist he is a past master of Jackson Lodge No. 146, A. F. and A. M.; exalted ruler of the Benevolent and Protective Order of Elks; and a past chancellor commander and a member of the board of trustees of the Knights of Pythias. A stanch Republican in his political views, he is particularly prominent in the work of county organization as a member of the advisory committee. He likewise is a member of the Jackson County Historical Society, in the meetings and work of which he takes a helpful interest.

Mr. Jackson married Miss Carolyn Beatty, of Jackson County, a member of a pioneer family who settled in Indiana at an early date. She was active in the Home Economics Club and in religious work, and died in July, 1929, leaving two children: Robert, a student at Purdue University; and Eudora, who is attending high school at Seymour. The family home is located at 109 East Fourth Street.

JAMES BENJAMIN BURCHAM is a prominent physician and surgeon who is acting as coroner's physician and is one of the prominent men of his profession who are located at 749 Broadway in the City of Gary.

Doctor Burcham was born at Bloomfield, Indiana, November 10, 1901, son of Rolly and Alma (Carroll) Burcham, and member of an old and prominent family of Greene County, Indiana, where his great-grandfather, Rolly Burcham, was one of the early pioneer settlers. His grandfather, James Burcham, lived there, and during the last two years of the Civil war served in the ranks of the Union army. Doctor Burcham's father, Rolly Burcham, was born and reared near Bloomfield, and spent his active career as a farmer and stock man. He and his wife still live on the old home farm. He is a member of the Independent Order of Odd Fellows. His wife was born and reared near Bloomfield, attended school there and has always been active in the Methodist Church. These parents had a family of nine children: Mary, wife of Orla G. Stingel; Brantley, an attorney practicing law at Orlando, Florida; Miss Goldie, at home; James Benjamin; Mina, wife of Ralph Crane, of Flint, Michigan; Balis, a graduate of the Indiana University; Gilbert, of Orlando, Florida; Freeman, in Indiana University; and Harley, a high school boy.

James Benjamin Burcham had as his early environment an Indiana farm and the rural scenes and activities of the little community of Bloomfield, where he attended grade school, graduated from high school in 1920, and soon afterward entered Indiana University, where he received the Bachelor of Science degree in 1924. He had his pre-medical training in the university and in 1926 graduated M. D. from the Medical School of Indiana University. Following that came a year of post-graduate work and experience in Saint Joseph's Hos-

pital at Fort Wayne, and in 1927 he came to Gary, locating at 749 Broadway, where he is an associate of Doctor Watts. He is a member of the Lake County, Gary, Indiana State and American Medical Associations and belongs to the Phi Chi medical fraternity. He is a Republican and a Methodist.

Doctor Burcham married at Niagara Falls, New York, July 3, 1928, Miss Sara Huffman, daughter of Jason and Jane (Breeden) Huffman, of Bloomfield, Indiana. Her father is a well-to-do farmer in that locality. Mrs. Burcham attended school at Bloomfield, graduating from high school in the same class with her husband and also took her Bachelor's degree at Indiana University in the class of 1924. Prior to her marriage she taught in the high school at Salisbury a year, also in the Filmore High School and two years in the Bloomfield High School. She is a member of the Phi Omega Phi sorority, American Association of University Women, the Gary Woman's Club and the Pan-Hellenic Club.

SAMUEL PHILIP VOGT for a number of years has had an honored place in the Harrison County bar. The honors and responsibilities of public office have been bestowed upon him and he is a worthy representative of a family that has lived in the county for over three-quarters of a century. His father, Henry Vogt, has the distinction of having lived on one farm in that county for seventy years. Henry Vogt was born in Louisville, Kentucky. The Vogt family originated in Alsace-Lorraine. It was due to various difficulties of living in that country, partly religious, that they immigrated to America and eventually came out to Southern Indiana, crossing the country with wagon and team. Henry Vogt was a soldier in the Union army, in Company E of the One Hundred Forty-fourth Indiana Infantry. He has lived in Harrison County since 1852 and for forty years held the office of justice of the peace. He married Louisa Snyder, and they were the parents of eight children.

Samuel P. Vogt was born in Harrison County, November 5, 1876, grew up on his father's farm, attending district schools, and later was a student in the Central Indiana Normal College at Danville. He studied law with Dan F. Lemmon, of Corydon, was admitted to the bar in 1906, but did not engage in practice for a number of years after that. For four years he was in the mercantile business at Corydon, and then went to Jeffersonville as an instructor in the Indiana State Reformatory. Mr. Vogt in 1914 returned to Corydon and has since carried on a general law practice. In 1922 he was elected prosecuting attorney of the Third Judicial Circuit. He is active in politics as a Democrat, is a member of the Harrison County Bar Association and the Knights of Pythias and Modern Woodmen of America.

Mr. Vogt married Miss Georgia Hess Lemmon, of Harrison County. Her father, Amos Lemmon, compiled a volume of the history of

Harrison County. Mr. and Mrs. Vogt have one son, Samuel Harlan Vogt, who is now principal of the Port Fulton School. He married Isabel Buckley, and has one daughter, Julia Louise, born October 4, 1929.

IRVIN EUGENE HUCKLEBERRY, physician and surgeon, is a native of Washington County, Indiana, was overseas during the World war and for the past ten years has carried on a splendid practice at Salem.

He was born April 17, 1893, son of Sanford and Meda M. (Hodgins) Huckleberry, and grandson of John Huckleberry. His grandfather settled in Indiana on coming from England. Sanford Huckleberry and wife were natives of Washington County and spent all their lives as farmers.

Doctor Huckleberry after attending the grade and high schools of Washington County continued his education in Butler University at Indianapolis. His professional preparation was gained at the University of Louisville, where he was graduated M. D. in 1916. Before getting well settled into the routine of private practice he enlisted in the Army Medical Corps, was commissioned a first lieutenant, and was with the colors from 1917 to 1919. While overseas he was assigned duty with the British Army Medical Corps in France and Belgium. After returning from France Doctor Huckleberry located at Salem and is one of the busiest doctors in Washington County. He is a member of the County, Indiana State and American Medical Associations, belongs to the Lions Club at Salem, is a thirty-second degree Scottish Rite Mason and a member of Murat Temple of the Mystic Shrine at Indianapolis.

He married Miss Mayme Warren, who was born in Lawrence County, Indiana. They have one daughter, Marietta, born January 31, 1922.

ELVIS M. BOSS, president of the Boss Motor Company, Incorporated, at Brownstown, has been in the automobile business since early manhood. The only important interruption to his business career came during the World war, when he went to France.

Mr. Boss was born in Washington County, Indiana, August 24, 1896. His father, G. M. Boss, was also a native of Washington County, a substantial farmer there, and was a son of Simon Boss, who came to Indiana from the Carolinas. G. M. Boss married Susan Purlee, of Washington County, and they were the parents of five children.

Elvis M. Boss attended grade schools in Washington County, and after graduating from the Pekin High School taught for a year. He learned the automobile business at Salem, Indiana, and was with a firm there until he joined the colors for service in the World war. He was with the colors eighteen months, and ten months of that time were spent in France, where he was with the Fifty-eighth Balloon Company. On returning from France he resumed his connection with the automobile business and since 1921 has been the au-

thorized Ford agent at Brownstown. The Boss Motor Company is incorporated, with Mr. Boss president and general manager and Charles M. Osker secretary and treasurer. They have a sales room and shop with over eight thousand square feet of floor space and with all the modern machinery and appliances for expert handling of every type of repair work on Ford and other cars. They employ ten people and their business runs to about four hundred new and used cars annually.

Mr. Boss married Miss Mamie Davis, of Washington County. He is a member of the Chamber of Commerce and was the first president of the Lions Club at Brownstown. He is also a member of the American Legion and has been active in its affairs, having served for four years as vice commander and is now commander of Camp Jackson Post No. 112 at Brownstown.

WILLIAM JOSEPH BULLEIT. Harrison County people have given Mr. Bulleit their patronage as a business man for over a quarter of a century. He was born at New Middletown, that county, member of a pioneer family, and his career has been such as to deserve the confidence reposed in him and the success he has enjoyed.

He was born September 15, 1877, a son of V. H. Bulleit, also a native of Harrison County, and grandson of Augustus Bulleit. Augustus Bulleit came from Alsace-Lorraine and settled in Harrison County, Indiana, about 1825. He was a farmer by occupation. V. H. Bulleit as a young man learned the trade of blacksmith, and for many years carried on an implement and automobile business, beginning the sale of automobiles in Harrison County in 1911, as one of the pioneer dealers. He served as president of the Corydon Savings & Loan Association from the time of its organization until his death. V. H. Bulleit married Mahala Johnson, who was also born in Harrison County, and they had a family of six children.

William J. Bulleit was educated in the Corydon grade and high schools and also attended the Ohio Valley Normal College. In 1902 he joined his father in the implement and seed business, and has had an interested part in carrying on that business down to date. It is one of the oldest houses of its kind in this section of Indiana. In 1914, after the death of his father, Mr. Bulleit took over the local Ford car agency and is now general manager of the company at Corydon which has the agency for the Ford motor car products over Harrison County. His organization has placed as many as 265 cars a year. The business establishment at Corydon is a modern building with over 8,000 square feet of floor space, providing quarters for show rooms, storage and repair department, and with all the mechanical equipment required for the exacting work of automobile repairing. Fourteen persons are employed in the business.

Mr. Bulleit married Miss Louise M. Miller, of Corydon. They have four children, William

G. Kenneth Hubbard

V., Henrietta, Elizabeth and Frederic. Mr. Bulleit during the World war was with the committees and other organizations engaged in the bond and stamp drives. He is a member of the Hoosier State Automobile Association, is a director of the Lions Club, member of the Knights of Pythias and B. P. O. Elks and the Methodist Church.

BERNEY R. STEWART. Ever since 1820 the Stewart family has been well and prominently known in Indiana, and its members, since pioneer days, have been men and women who have maintained high principles of citizenship. For the greater part they have been agriculturists or merchants, but a number have also made their mark in professional life, and among the latter is Berney R. Stewart, principal of the Seymour High School.

Mr. Stewart was born October 19, 1886, on a farm in Jefferson County, Indiana, and is a son of James J. and Mary (Nay) Stewart. The family originated in North Carolina and was brought to the Hoosier State early in 1820, by the great-grandfather of Berney R. Stewart, who took up his residence among the pioneer settlers of what is now Jefferson County, developed a farm, erected a home, and passed an industrious, useful and honorable life in the pursuits of the soil. John H. Stewart, the grandfather of Berney R. Stewart, was born in Jefferson County, and like his father, was an agriculturist all of his life and a man who was held in high esteem in his community. His son, James J. Stewart, followed the family vocation, and is still engaged in farming in Jefferson County, where both he and his worthy wife were born.

Berney R. Stewart attended the public schools of Jefferson County, following which he entered the Marion Normal College and was graduated therefrom as a member of the class of 1912. He completed his education at Indiana University, with the class of 1915, and immediately entered upon his career as an educator, teaching two years in the Marion High School, in Grant County, and then becoming principal at Sweetser, where he remained for three years. His next position was that of principal of the high school at Madison, where he remained six years, and in the fall of 1926 was called to Seymour to become principal of the high school, a position which he has since retained. Mr. Stewart has become widely and favorably known as an educator, and is a member of the Indiana State Teachers' Association. During his incumbency he has introduced numerous improvements which have elevated the high school's standards, and has become popular with teachers, students and parents, at the same time gaining a firm place in the confidence of the general public. He has continued to be a scholar himself, and during the summer months makes it a practice to take special work at the University of Indiana. He is a member and secretary of the local Lions Club. During the World war period Mr. Stewart was active in all war drives, and did particu-

larly valuable work through his connection with educational institutions.

Mr. Stewart married Miss Marie Ratz, of Nebraska, and they have had five children: Mildred, Vivian, Thelma, James and Ruth, of whom James is deceased.

GEORGE KENNETH HUBBARD. Well established in the practice of law at Angola, Indiana, is G. Kenneth Hubbard, of the law firm of Hubbard & Hubbard. Although one of the younger members of his profession at Angola, his legal ability has been so generally recognized from the first that many of the most important cases of litigation in Steuben County during the past few years have been placed in his hands and have been satisfactorily disposed of. He is able to name among his clients many corporations and banks, together with personalities widely known in business circles in Indiana and Michigan, and, all in all, his career has had an auspicious start.

Mr. Hubbard was born June 28, 1902, at Stephenson, Menominee County, Michigan, and is a son of Edward R. and Alice (Sandall) Hubbard. Edward R. Hubbard was born at Newcastle, New Brunswick, Canada, where he received a public school education and in his youth learned the trade of carpenter. He eventually established a business of his own as a contractor and builder, which he followed for some years at Stephenson, Michigan, finally removing to South Bend, Indiana, where he had a large and profitable general contracting business, with offices at 311 Citizens Bank Building. He is now located at East Lansing, Michigan. He is one of the substantial citizens and successful business men of his community, and his prosperity is well merited because it has been self gained. On July 26, 1900, Mr. Hubbard married Miss Alice Sandall, who was born at Stephenson, Michigan, and to this union there have been born the following children: G. Kenneth, of this review; Harris W., born November 26, 1903, at Stephenson, Michigan, who graduated in law and is now a member of the firm of Hubbard & Hubbard, at Angola; C. Rogers, born December 6, 1904, who is engaged in the insurance business at Kenosha, Wisconsin; Byron J., born July 22, 1906, who is living at Chicago, Illinois, where he is connected with a publishing house; Edna B., born May 17, 1908, who married Charles Chisler, engaged in the automobile agency business at Lansing, Michigan; Carlton L., born September 11, 1912, at Stephenson, is connected with the Healthwin Hospital at South Bend, Indiana; Helen, born October 5, 1914, who is attending high school at East Lansing, Michigan; and Edward T., born September 30, 1915; Elton, born August 9, 1917; and Alice E., born in 1920, all of whom are attending public school at East Lansing, Michigan.

G. Kenneth Hubbard attended the grade and high schools at Stephenson, Michigan, and Marquette University, Milwaukee, Wisconsin, for one year, following which he pursued a full course of four years at Valparaiso (Indiana) University, and was graduated from that institution with the degree of Bachelor of Laws, class of 1924. He at once commenced practice at Angola, with offices at 119 Maumee Street, and thereafter formed a partnership with his brother, Harris W. Hubbard, forming the law firm of Hubbard & Hubbard, as at present. This is one of the strong and formidable combinations of the city and has been engaged successfully in much important litigation. Mr. Hubbard is a member of the Steuben County Bar Association, the Indiana State Bar Association and the American Bar Association, and in his profession is known as a man singularly qualified for his difficult and perplexing vocation. He is well grounded in all the departments of his calling and therefore has specialized in none, having been content to follow his calling as a general practitioner. He is a member of the Methodist Church and the Independent Order of Odd Fellows, and as a citizen has given his hearty support to all beneficial measures.

On March 23, 1925, Mr. Hubbard was united in marriage with Miss Marian C. Potter, who was born September 3, 1904, at Angola, where she was educated in the public schools. Her father, Alfred S. Potter, was for many years a substantial business man of Angola, and is now living in reirement at 217 North Superior Street, and her mother, a native of Angola, bore the maiden name of Iris Kemp. Mr. and Mrs. Hubbard have two children: Imogene Marian, born January 6, 1926; and George Kenneth, Jr., born July 23, 1927. Mrs. Hubbard is active in church work at Angola, where she is popular in social circles.

FRANK SELF, attorney, is the successor of his father, the late George W. Self, as editor and owner of the *Corydon Republic*. The *Republican* is one of the oldest newspapers in Indiana, having been established while Corydon still boasted the distinction of being the state capital of Indiana. For sixty years of the more than a hundred years of its existence it has been conducted by the Self family.

The late George W. Self was born in Hart County, Kentucky, and moved to New Albany, Indiana, about 1854. He also practiced law, and afterwards moved to Corydon and in 1869 took charge of the *Corydon Republican*. He served four years in the Indiana State Senate and for eight years was reporter for the Indiana Supreme Court. George W. Self married Addie Adams, a native of Harrison County and descended from the pioneer Heath family of that county.

Mr. Frank Self, one of the two children of his parents, was born at Corydon, April 6, 1875. He attended grade and high school there, the University of Indiana at Bloomington, and completed his law education at Georgetown University, Washington, D. C., graduating LL. B. in 1896. He was admitted to practice in the United States Supreme Court in 1899. Mr. Self in 1897 returned to Corydon and was associated with his father in law practice until the latter's death. He

also assumed an increasing share of responsibilities in the editorial management of the *Republican* and has continued his work as a newspaper man and lawyer.

Mr. Self is a former president of the Harrison County Bar Association. In 1919 he entered the Indiana Legislature, serving four years. He is a trustee of the Boy's School at Plainfield, Indiana, and is a member of the Southeastern Indiana Historical Society. During the World war both personally and through his newspaper he was a leader in the Loan and Red Cross drives. He is affiliated with Pisgah Lodge No. 32, A. F. and A. M., and the Royal Arch Chapter of Masons. Mr. Self married Miss Lida Marshall, of Harrison County.

THE CORYDON PUBLIC LIBRARY was established March 5, 1909. Several years later the sum of $7,500 was obtained from the Carnegie library fund for a building and in December, 1914, the building was completed at a cost of about $8,700. The total value of the real estate today is $10,500. The library contains approximately 4800 volumes. It is one of the valuable institutions of this historic old political and social center of Southern Indiana.

The librarian since 1911 has been Mrs. Georgia Stockslager Fisher, who was born in Corydon and finished her education in the University of Indiana. Her father was Hon. S. M. Stockslager, one of the distinguished public men of Harrison County. He was a Union soldier, captain in the Thirteenth Indiana Cavalry and afterwards represented his district in the Indiana State Senate, was a member of Congress and was commissioner of the General Land Office under President Cleveland. He was promoted to the rank of captain for gallantry under fire at the battle of Murfeesboro, and had his whiskers shot away and his sabre shot in two pieces. He died June 1, 1930, at the Naval Hospital at Washington, D. C., and was buried in Arlington Cemetery. Mrs. Fisher's mother was Kate Miller, a native of Harrison County.

STANLEY PFLANZ is proprietor of the Stanley Pflanz Chevrolet Company at Corydon. Mr. Pflanz has been in the automobile business for many years and is a member of a pioneer family of Louisville, Kentucky, where he was born January 15, 1891. His father was the late John R. Pflanz. His mother was Ida (Wilkes) Pflanz, who was born at Louisville. Her father was a steamboat pilot, running from Pittsburgh to New Orleans.

Stanley Pflanz grew up a Louisville, attended school there and learned the automobile business in that city. He was for seven years a dealer in Ford cars. On January 1, 1929, he organized the Stanley Pflanz Chevrolet Company at Corydon.

Mr. Pflanz married Nellis Housefield, of Campbellsburg, Washington County, Indiana. They have two children, Alice Josephine, born October 9, 1929, and Grace Artise, born December 1, 1930. Mr. Pflanz is a member of

Monroe G. Schuster

the American Legion. During the war he was in Company F of the Sixty-seventh Infantry, Ninth Division, and was located at Camp Thomas and at Camp Sheridan in Alabama, with the rank of sergeant.

The Stanley Pflanz Chevrolet Company owns the sales franchise for the Chevrolet car, and has a contract for placing 125 cars annually. His business is a modern new brick building with 9,000 square feet of floor space, affording ample facilities for shop and sales room. The shop is equipped with all the machinery required for special handling of the Chevrolet car. Mr. Pflanz employs seven people in the business at Corydon.

LEWIS EVERETT HANGER is an attorney at law, but during the greater part of his professional career has had his chief routine of duties as cashier of the Sellersburg State Bank.

Mr. Hanger was born in Clark County, December 12, 1881. His grandfather, David Hanger, was a native of Germany, who came to Harrison County, Indiana, about 1836 and settled on a farm. Mr. Hanger's parents were Jesse D. and Sarah Jane (Bottorff) Hanger. His father was born in Harrison County and spent his active life as a quarryman.

Lewis E. Hanger was one of a family of six children. He grew up on a farm, attended public schools and was graduated LL. B. from the University of Louisville in 1913. For three years he carried on a general law practice at Sellersburg, and he still handles cases of law in the courts of Clark County. In addition to his office as cashier of the Sellersburg State Bank he also conducts a general insurance agency and is one of the busy men in that community.

Mr. Hanger for four years was a member and president of the Sellersburg Town Board. He is a past president of the Sellersburg Chamber of Commerce, a member of the Indiana State and American Bankers Associations, and is admitted to practice in the Indiana Supreme Court. He is affiliated with the Masonic fraternity and Knights of Pythias.

He married Miss Hazel Hause Hinton, of Clark County. They have two children, Alice Jane and Nettabell.

SIMA SHAPINSKY, department store owner, is one of the oldest of the local business men of Scottsburg in point of continuous service, having been a factor in the supplying of necessities and luxuries to this community for a third of a century.

Mr. Shapinsky was born at Louisville, Kentucky, in February, 1875, a son of Aaron and Sarah Shapinsky. His parents had first settled in Scott County in 1865, shortly after the Civil war. His father was also a merchant, but his chief business was in contracting for and supplying oak staves and headings for cooperage manufacturers.

Sima Shapinsky was one of a family of nine children. He grew up and received his early education in Scott County, and when seventeen years of age became a clerk for his uncle, who was a general merchant and farmer. These years of working for his uncle he utilized to excellent purpose and in 1896, when he was twenty-one, started business for himself. For the past thirty-three years Scottsburg has known and patronized the establishment of S. Shapinsky, which in that time has grown to a general department store. He started it as a clothing and shoe business, and he now has a store with over 10,000 square feet of floor space, employing eight people and carrying a large general stock of shoes, clothing, dry goods, women's ready-to-wear garments and millinery.

Mr. Shapinsky is also interested in country life and is owner of two dairy farms, comprising 200 acres, stocked with forty Jersey cows and with three men employed in handling this branch of his business.

Mr. Shapinsky married Miss Mattie Wells, a native of Greensburg, Kentucky. Both of their children, Robert and William, are attending school. Mr. Shapinsky is a member of the Scottsburg Commercial Club and is affiliated with the Knights of Pythias and Improved Order of Red Men.

REV. MONROE GOEBEL SCHUSTER. The people who are designated as the Disciples of Christ constitute a communion of more than 1,000,000 members. This body, which has its greatest strength in the Middle West, is found in nearly all parts of the United States, in addition to which there are churches in Canada, England and Australia and a vigorous missionary program is being carried out in numerous foreign countries. The Disciples have various agencies for the promotion of missions, benevolences and education. Although they have not accepted a formulated creed, there are elements of faith which are generally believed that distinguish them from other communions. The fact that the Disciples have prevented their faith from becoming formulated in a written creed has made it easy for them to develop in their interpretation of religion. The fact that they have no written constitution, outlining the policy of the church, has made the development in organization inevitable. Because they have no written creed and constitution there are widely divergent elements in the church, but all feel that they are true Disciples.

Among the leaders of this great religious body in Indiana, one who has been untiring in his zeal and unfaltering in his piety is Rev. Monroe Goebel Schuster, pastor of the Central Christian Church of Gary. Reverend Schuster was born at Louisville, Kentucky, February 10, 1900, and is a son of Frank J. and Josephine (Unz) Schuster. His paternal grandparents, George Adam and Elizabeth (Korb) Schuster, were born and reared in Germany, and after their marriage immigrated to the United States, being among the early settlers of Louisville, Kentucky, where they located prior to the war between the states. They became well known and highly respected residents of their community and are buried in Cave Hill Cemetery there.

Frank J. Schuster was born at Louisville, where he acquired a public school education, and as a youth became identified with mercantile affairs. As the years passed he grew to be a leading wholesale grocery merchant and carried on a thriving and successful business for more than three decades, but is now retired from business affairs and is serving in the capacity of associate county clerk of Jefferson County, Kentucky. At the age of sixty-four years he is still active in mind and body and takes a great deal of interest in the work of the Benevolent and Protective Order of Elks and of Saint John's Evangelical Church. Mrs. Schuster, also a native of Louisville and a product of its public schools, is sixty-three years old and is likewise much interested in church work. Her father, John Unz, was one of the early hardware merchants of Louisville, and his son, Louis Unz, still carries on this business, which is one of the old and reliable concerns of the city. Three children were born to Mr. and Mrs. Schuster: Carlisle, who is engaged in the insurance business at Louisville; Evelyn, now the wife of Ernest Speckman, also of that city; and Monroe G., of this review.

Monroe Goebel Schuster attended the public schools of Louisville and graduated from Louisville High School as a member of the class of 1917. In that year he obtained a position as clerk in the general storekeeper's office of the Louisville & Nashville Railroad, a capacity in which he served for about two years, subsequently becoming associate secretary of the Railroad Young Men's Christian Association at Louisville. Two years later he entered Transylvania College, Lexington, Kentucky, from which he was graduated with the degree of Bachelor of Arts as a member of the class of 1925, and in 1926 graduated from the College of the Bible there with the degree of Master of Arts. He went then to Yale University and in 1928 received the degree of Bachelor of Divinity. In the meantime, in 1925, at Lexington, he had been ordained a minister of the Disciples of Christ Church, although he had been preaching for a number of years previous to that time. In 1921 he began his ministry at Ruddles Mills, Kentucky, where he spent five years, and while there was also pastor of the East Union Christian Church at East Union, Kentucky. After his first year at Yale he was pastor of the Main Street Baptist Church at Meriden, Connecticut, where he remained one and one-half years, and in 1928 came to Gary as pastor of the Central Christian Church, which ministry he still fills. Reverend Schuster has carried forward a great and good work. Connected with the church is the church school, which includes religious education, young people's department, intermediate department, junior department, primary department, beginners department and cradle roll department. There is also the Men's

Brotherhood Class, King's Daughter's Class, Service Class, Young Married People's Class, Truth Seekers Class, Faholo Class, Christian Endeavor, Girl's Circle, Triangle Girls and Boy Scouts.

Reverend Schuster is a Master Mason and belongs to the Loyal Order of Moose, the Kiwanis Club, Phi Kappa Tau fraternity, Aleph Theta Ze honorary ministerial fraternity, the Cressmore Country Club and the Lincoln Hills Country Club. Politically he is a Republican and takes an active and constructive part in all movements promulgated and fostered for the benefit of the community.

On June 4, 1931, he was united in marriage with Miss Lucille Russell Ingram, of Dayton, Ohio.

HENRY H. KASPERLAIN. The manufacture of furniture now covers such a broad and varied field that many of the men engaged in this line of business have limited their activities to specialization in some particular department, feeling that thus they can produce a better product and concentrate on bringing forth a more finished and acceptable article. An illustration is found in the Seymour Chair Manufacturing Company, at Seymour, which manufactures chairs exclusively and which is now a leading enterprise of the city. The growth of this factory is a testimonal to the business ability and aggressive industry of Henry H. Kasperlain, the present owner. It is not a product of a bonus or subscriptions, but represents only the capital and work of the man who owns it. It has a thoroughly substantial basis, growing from a small enterprise and expanding as the demands of an increasing business have justified.

Henry H. Kasperlain was born at Cincinnati, Ohio, December 21, 1859, and is a son of George and Magdelain (Wigle) Kasperlain. He attended the graded schools of that city and commenced work on a farm, leaving the parental roof at the age of twenty-three years to engage in farming on his own account. Not caring for an agricultural career, he secured employment in a furniture and cabinet factory, and at the age of twenty-eight years embarked in the manufacture of furniture, under the style of the Linwood Furniture Company, but in 1893 came to Seymour and became one of the organizers of the Home Furniture Company, being mill foreman and part owner. After two years this business was closed, and in 1896 Mr. Kasperlain engaged in the chair manufacturing business in a small building on Second Street, where he had 450 feet of floor space. Two years later he built an addition, twenty by eighty feet. In 1897 the present plant, corner Ninth Street and Shields Avenue, was acquired, this having been an old bicycle shop, which he rebuilt. This new plant was started about 1897. In 1906 Frank Patrick bought an interest in the business and with new additions to their factory the output by 1911 was 100 dozen chairs a week. A two-story addition, fifty by eighty feet in dimensions, was built at the south end of the factory, and, like the remainder of the large building of which it became a part, was constructed of brick. Preparations at the same time were made for the erection of another addition, on the west side, sixteen by forty feet. From that time to the present the plant has been constantly enlarged and improved, and now covers 30,000 square feet of floor space, being a brick building, two stories throughout. Seventy-five people are given employment in the manufacture of chairs, with a side line of made-to-order furniture, and the product finds a ready market throughout Indiana, Ohio and Kentucky, and also is shipped to Texas, New York and other states. Mr. Kasperlain is one of the best known and most highly esteemed business citizens of Seymour, and has always been ready to contribute materially to movements for the betterment of the community. He has been primarily a business man all of his life and has not sought public office. Fraternally he is identified with Jackson Lodge, No. 146, A. F. and A. M.

Mr. Kasperlain married Miss Edith Amann, and to this union there have been born three children: Anna, Will and Maggie.

JAMES M. HAMER. Among the sound and substantial business citizens of Seymour whose activities have served to contribute to the city's progress and prosperity, none has a better right to the esteem and respect of his fellow-men than James M. Hamer, owner of the builders' supplies business conducted under the name of J. M. Hamer Company. For a period of thirty-eight years this business has been carried on under the same direction and management, and during this long time its policies have been so straightforward as to have gained and held the full confidence of the community.

James M. Hamer was born near Mitchell, in Lawrence County, Indiana, October 26, 1854, and is a son of Joseph and Martha (Mattox) Hamer. His paternal grandfather was born in England, Hugh Hamer, and was brought as an infant to the shores of America, where later he participated as a soldier in the War of the Revolution. Joseph Hamer, the father of James M., was born in New York State, whence he came to Indiana in 1829, joining his uncle, Hugh Hamer, in the operation of a flour mill, near Mitchell, which the elder man had founded some two years before. This business was carried on for more than forty years, but in his declining years Joseph Hamer retired. He married Martha Mattox, who was born south of Bloomington, Indiana, and they became the parents of five children. Several of these were sons who fought in the Union army during the war between the states, one, Hugh Hamer, losing his life on the bloody battlefield of Missionary Ridge. Hugh Hamer had served as state senator and for a number of years was prominent in public life.

James M. Hamer attended the public schools of Lawrence County and remained under the parental roof until he was eighteen years of age, at which time he was attracted by the romance of the railroad, and became a water boy on a work train. For twenty-one years he was identified with the transportation department of the O. & M., B. and O. S. W. railroads, but in 1892 embarked in the building supplies and coal business at Seymour, founding the J. M. Hamer Company, of which he has been the head for thirty-eight years, and which under his wise and careful management, industry and honorable business methods has grown to be one of the leading enterprises of the city, with a large modern plant and yards at the conjunction of the Baltimore & Ohio and Pennsylvania Railways. Mr. Hamer is a member of Jackson Lodge No. 146, A. F. and A. M., the Chapter, Council and Commandery, the Scottish Rite at Indianapolis, Murat Temple of the Mystic Shrine and of the Methodist Episcopal Church. During the World war period he was very active and contributed liberally to all drives and movements for the success of American arms.

Mr. Hamer married for his first wife Miss Mary Dunkle, of Vincennes, Knox County, Indiana, who died leaving four children: James E., associated with his father, and a part owner of the J. M. Hamer Company, a veteran of the Spanish-American war, in which he served in Company F, Eighteenth United States Infantry, married Aline Brown; Laura Maude, the wife of Ferdinando W. Wesner, an attorney of Seymour; William E., a veteran of the Spanish-American war, who is interested in his father's business and also identified with the Baltimore & Ohio Railway, married Ora E. Russell; and Harry J., who is deceased. In 1897 James M. Hamer married Miss Emma G. Johnson, a native of Ohio, and to this union there was born one son: Harry L., deceased. The family residence is at 404 North Chestnut Street.

HON. GEORGE H. D. GIBSON, of Charlestown, is one of Clark County's oldest members of the bar, and his own record as a practicing lawyer combined with that of his father covers a period of nearly a century, leading back to the time of country law practice and the custom of attorneys and judges riding horseback from one court to the other.

His father was Thomas W. Gibson, a native of Philadelphia, and son of John Gibson, who was born at Dublin, Ireland, and came to this country and settled in Philadelphia a few years after the Revolutionary war. He married Sarah Clark. Thomas W. Gibson came to Lawrenceburg, Indiana, in 1821, and in 1837 located at Charlestown. He rose to distinction as a practicing attorney and for a number of years also practiced at Louisville, Kentucky. He served as a member of the Indiana Constitutional Convention, was in the State Senate in 1848-50. He was a graduate of West Point Military Academy, was a captain in the Mexican war, raising a company at Charlestown, and commanded a regiment as colonel of Kentucky troops in the Civil war, and for a time was provost marshal at Louisville. Col. Thomas W. Gibson married Mary W. Goodwin. Her father, Colonel Goodwin, was at the battle of Tippecanoe under General Harrison. One of the Goodwins had served under Gen. George Rogers Clark. The Goodwins were allotted land for their services, and George H. D. Gibson today has his home on a part of this original land grant.

·George H. D. Gibson was the youngest of a family of six children and was born at Charlestown, Clark County, September 9; 1851. He attended schools at Charlestown, graduated in 1872 from the Kentucky Military Institute at Frankfort and completed his law course at the University of Louisville in 1874. He was admitted to the Kentucky bar in 1873 and to the Indiana bar in 1874. He practiced law for three years at Charlestown, 1874-77, and from 1877 to 1892 had his law offices in Louisville. In 1892 he was elected judge of the Fourth Judicial District of Indiana, serving six years. His judicial service constitutes one of the high points in his long professional service. For the past thirty years he has devoted his time and talents to a general law practice at Charlestown. He also supervises the operation of his farm, comprising a section of land.

Mr. Gibson was a member of the Indiana State Legislature in 1881-83 and was prosecuting attorney of the district comprising Floyd and Clark counties in 1875-76. For many years he was head of the County Council, and has attended as a delegate two notable national conventions of the Democratic party, that at Chicago in 1884, when Cleveland was nominated, and the memorable New York City convention of 1924. During the World war Mr. Gibson was chairman of the Liberty Bond committee. For several years he was president of the City Council. He is a member of the B. P. O. Elks and the Sigma Alpha Epsilon college fraternity. Judge Gibson married Virginia C. Van Hook. She was born at Charlestown and is now deceased. There were no children.

MERTON L. HUGHBANKS is a native son of Scott County, was a merchant and banker in his home locality, and has become known all over the southwestern quarter of the state as the organizer and active head of the Farmers Investment & Loan Company of Scottsburg.

Mr. Hughbanks was born in Scott County July 2, 1883. His grandfather, William Hughbanks, was a native of Virginia, moved to Kentucky and from there came to Scott County, Indiana, about 1818. He was a pioneer, a large land owner and an early merchant at Austin, where he put up the first house, about 1820. David M. Hughbanks, father of Merton L., was born in Scott County, became a well-to-do farmer and for two terms was honored with the office of county treasurer and also served two terms as township trustee. He married Alice C. Whitson, a native of Scott County.

Merton L. Hughbanks was one of a family of eight children. He attended public schools in Scott County, and after completing a commercial course in Valparaiso University took up the work of teaching. He was in school work from 1902 to 1905, and in 1906 entered the mercantile business in his home town of Austin. He sold out in 1909 to assist in organizing the Austin State Bank, of which he was cashier until 1916.

Mr. Hughbanks in 1917 moved to Scottsburg and entered the general insurance business. In 1920 Mr. R. L. Whitson joined him and they organized the Farmers Investment & Loan Company, for the purpose of making farm loans and handling mortgages. The company was started with a capital of $37,500. The present capital is now $120,000, with total resources of $400,000, all built up within a period of nine years. The company is chartered under the laws of Indiana, with Mr. Hughbanks as president, J. G. Martin, vice president, and R. L. Whitson, secretary and treasurer. This company does much more than a local business, having clients all over the southeastern part of the state, in Scott, Clark, Floyd, Washington, Orange, Crawford, Lawrence, Jackson, Bartholomew, Jennings, Jefferson, Switzerland and Ohio counties.

Mr. Hughbanks' first wife was Avis Mann, who died in 1913, leaving two sons, Lester and Leland, both in school. In 1923 Mr. Hughbanks married Edna Killey, of Scott County.

During the World war and since Mr. Hughbanks has been active in various patriotic and charitable drives, having served as secretary of the Red Cross, as chairman of the County Red Cross and Charity Fund drives, has been president of the Commercial Club, was the first president of the Lions Club of Scottsburg. He is affiliated with Scott Lodge No. 120 A. F. and A. M., is a member of the Royal Arch Chapter, Council and Knights Templar Commandery, and Murat Temple of the Mystic Shrine at Indianapolis.

JONAS GEORGE HOWARD, president of the Clark County Bar Association, has practiced since his admission to the Indiana bar at Jeffersonville, where his offices are in the Citizens Bank Building.

There have been four generations of the Howard family in Indiana, and in each one the name Jonas appears. The first Jonas Howard was a Vermonter who came to Indiana and settled in Floyd County about 1816. The second Jonas G. Howard was born in Vermont and became a brick manufacturer in Southern Indiana. Jonas G. Howard III was born in Floyd County and for many years practiced law and had a variety of business connections as well. He was chosen representative of this Indiana district to Congress during Cleveland's first administration. He was a graduate of DePauw University and of the law department of the University of Indiana. His wife, Elizabeth Roswell, was a member of an old family of Clark County, the Roswells coming from Pennsylvania to this state about 1820.

J. D. Hodson

Mr. Jonas G. Howard IV, the Jeffersonville attorney, was one of three children and was born in Clark County February 2, 1886. He attended grade and high schools, for two years continued his studies in the University of Indiana, and in 1907 took his law degree at the University of Louisville, Kentucky. He was admitted to the Indiana bar in 1907 and from that date has been engaged in a general law practice at Jeffersonville. He has been admitted to practice in the Federal courts and is a lawyer of sound scholarship and with a reputation for thoroughness in everything he does.

For eight years he served as a member of the City Council and was appointed mayor for an unexpired term of eighteen months. He has been on various boards and during the World war was active in the Liberty Loan and Red Cross drives. He is a member of the board of directors of the library association, is a member of the Indiana State and American Bar Associations, was a director and second president of the Lions Club, and since early manhood has been a leader in the Democratic party, recognized as one of its ablest orators. He served two terms as city chairman, has also been district chairman and a member of the state Democratic committee. Mr. Howard is affiliated with the B. P. O. Elks. He married Helen Armstrong, of Clark County. They have one daughter, Janet.

FRANK OSWELL HODSON. A resident of Gary for nearly a quarter of a century, Frank O. Hodson is now one of the leading contractors and civil engineers of the state. Commencing his career as a school teacher, eventually he turned his attention to the business in which he is now engaged, mastered its many details, until he has attained at length a commanding position among the enterprising men of Gary, and has been able to hold it amid the strong competition which increasing capital and trade have brought to the city. His success has been due alone to his enterprising character and business capacity, for he began life without pecuniary assistance or the aid of family or other favoring influences.

Mr. Hodson was born in Howard County, Indiana, April 8, 1871, and is a son of Samuel and Hannah (Coyle) Hodson, and a grandson of a native Virginian who was a pioneer of Howard County, where he located prior to the war between the states and spent the remainder of his life in agricultural operations. The grandparents are buried in the cemetery at Russiaville, this state.

Samuel Hodson was born in Union County, Indiana, where he received a country school education and was reared on the home farm, and during the Civil war enlisted in the Union army, but was not called upon for active service in the field. He devoted his entire life to the pursuits of farming and stock raising and became a man of substance, dying on his farm in 1912 and being buried in the cemetery at Russiaville. He was a lifelong Democrat, but had no aspiration for public office, although always a good and public-spirited citizen. Mr. Hodson married Hannah Coyle, who was born in Shelby County, Indiana, and was a product of the public schools of that locality. She was a daughter of Francis and Nancy Coyle, pioneers of Shelby County, where Mr. Coyle was engaged in the manufacture of brick and was also a large landholder. The Coyle family, originally from Virginia, is one of the leading families of Shelby County, and a number of its members are buried in the cemetery near Wilson. Mrs. Hodson was active in community life and in the work of the Christian Church. She died in 1900 and is buried at Russiaville. There were three children in the family: George E., a blacksmith and carriage manufacturer of Elwood, who died in 1910, leaving a widow, formerly Miss Mollie Martin, and a son, Harry, one other child having died in infancy; Frank O., of this review; and Ada, who died in 1904, as the wife of Ellsworth Adair, formerly of Russiaville, who is now engaged in the insurance business at Frankfort, this state.

Frank O. Hodson attended the public schools of Howard County, after which he started his career as a teacher, teaching for three years in Howard County and for two years in Madison County. Giving up the profession of educator, he then turned his attention to contracting and civil engineering at Elwood, and in 1906 came to Gary as engineer for the Gary Land Company and assistant engineer to the chief engineer, Ralph E. Rowley, of the Illinois Steel Company and the Gary Land Company. Mr. Hodson continued in this position for one year and then entered the engineering department of the City of Gary, where he remained until 1910. That year saw his real entrance into the private field of contracting, in which he has attained a remarkable success, his offices being located at 128 West Ninth Avenue, corner of Adams. Mr. Hodson stands high in business circles and particularly so in his special line, being president of the American Asphalt Paving Association. He is a director in the Central Trust & Savings Bank and the Inland Bonding Company of South Bend; a past president of the Chamber of Commerce and a director in the Commercial Club and Chamber of Commerce of Gary; vice president and a director in the Lookout Mountain Cave Company, of Chattanooga, Tennessee; and secretary and treasurer of the Municipal Contracting Supply Company, of Gary, of which he is also a member of the directorate. He is a thirty-second degree Mason and Shriner, and a member of Gary Lodge No. 677, A. F. and A. M.; Gary Chapter, R. A. M.; Fort Wayne Consistory; and Orak Temple, A. A. O. N. M. S., of Hammond. He belongs also to Elwood Lodge No. 368, B. P. O. Elks, and for years was active in the Knights of Pythias, the Improved Order of Red Men and the Rotary Club. He is active in civic affairs as a member of the various organizations which are developing the city's resources. He also belongs to the Gary Country Club. Mr. Hodson is a Democrat in his political allegiance, and is a member and trustee of the First Presbyterian Church.

At Elwood, Indiana, May 8, 1895, Mr. Hodson was united in marriage with Miss Gertrude Bassett, daughter of Charles and Mary (Keyger) Bassett, the former of whom was engaged in the tinning business for a number of years, but retired some years ago when he and Mrs. Bassett began to make their home with Mr. and Mrs. Hodson. Mr. Bassett died May 9, 1929, and Mrs. Bassett in the following July, and both are buried at Elwood. They had been early residents of Union County, where the family was widely known and highly respected. Mrs. Hodson received her education in the public schools of Union County, Indiana, and is a woman of superior attainments. She is active in the work of the First Presbyterian Church and treasurer of the local Young Women's Christian Association. A member of the finance board of Gary Chapter, Daughters of the American Revolution, she was selected as a delegate to the national convention at Washington, D. C., in 1930, but illness prevented her attendance. She is a member of the Order of the Eastern Star and of the Woman's Club of Gary. Mr. and Mrs. Hodson are the parents of one son, Ralph Lorenzo, born at Elwood, Indiana, April 29, 1899. He attended the public schools of Gary, graduating from Emerson High School in 1917, following which he entered Purdue University, where he was a student of civil engineering when the United States was drawn into the World war. In 1917 he enlisted in the United States Navy and after a few months of training at the Great Lakes Naval Training Station, Great Lakes, Illinois, was sent back to Purdue University to undergo Government training at the Officers Training Camp, in civil engineering. He was thus engaged at the time of the signing of the armistice and shortly thereafter received his honorable discharge, although for a time he was a member of the Naval Reserves. He graduated from Purdue with the class of 1922, degree of Civil Engineer, and since then has been associated with his father in business at Gary, where he is vice president and a director in the Municipal Contracting Supply Company. Ralph L. Hodson is a thirty-second degree Mason and Shriner, and a member of Gary Lodge of Elks, the Gary Country Club, the Kiwanis Club, and Gary Memorial Post No. 17, American Legion. In politics he is a Democrat and his religious connection is with the Forty-third Avenue Presbyterian Church. Mr. Hodson married Miss Margaret Murphey, of Lafayette, Indiana, daughter of William J. Murphey, who is engaged in the general office supply book and stationery business. Mrs. Hodson is a graduate of Lafayette High School and of Purdue University, class of 1921. She is active in the Forty-third Avenue Presbyterian Church and a member of the

Kappa Kappa Kappa sorority and the Gary Garden Club. Mr. and Mrs. Hodson have two daughters: Nancy Jean and Patricia Ann.

ELWIN LOWELL HUGHBANKS, member of one of Scott County's oldest and most highly respected families, is the present county auditor of Scott County. For many years he was in the railroad service.

He was born in Scott County, March 4, 1866. His grandfather was William Hughbanks and his great-grandfather was David Hughbanks. William Hughbanks was born in Virginia, went to Kentucky in early life and about 1818 came to Indiana and settled in Scott County. He acquired land from the Government and built the first house at Austin in Scott County, about 1820. He was a merchant at Austin for many years. Elwin L. Hughbanks is a son of Thomas and Eliza (Montgomery) Hughbanks. His father was a merchant at Austin and was a brother of David M. Hughbanks, who served for two terms as county treasurer.

Elwin L. Hughbanks, one of a family of five children, grew up at Austin, attended public school there, and at the age of twenty was working in his father's business. When he was twenty-three years of age he began his service record with the Pennsylvania Railway Company. The first year he was baggage master at Seymour, then in the freight office there fourteen years, and in 1906 was transferred to Scottsburg as station agent. He continued this work until he resigned in 1921, and as a token of his more than thirty years of faithful service with the company was given an honor button. Mr. Hughbanks in 1922 was elected for his first term as county auditor and was reelected in 1926. During the World war he was in the railway service, an essential line of work, and participated in all the war loan drives during that period. Fraternally he is affiliated with Scottsburg Lodge No. 572, A. F. and A. M., Royal Arch Chapter No. 144, and is a member of the Commercial Club.

Mr. Hughbanks married Nora Buxton, a native of Scott County, daughter of Frank Buxton and descended from pioneers of Indiana. Mr. and Mrs. Hughbanks have one daughter, Halcy, who is the wife of W. L. Craig. Mr. Craig, now superintendent of the Scottsburg city schools, is a graduate of Wabash College and also attended Columbia University in New York.

LAWRENCE WINFIELD PAYNTER as a physician and surgeon has been numbered among Indiana's leading professional men for over thirty-nine years. The locality that has known him best both as a professional man and citizen is Washington County, and he was born in that county October 30, 1871.

His father, Jacob L. Paynter, was born in Washington County, son of John Paynter, who came from Virginia and settled in Washington County about 1822. He was a pioneer farmer. Jacob L. Paynter was one of a family of eleven children. Two of his brothers, George and Harry Paynter, were members of the Indiana Legislature. Jacob L. Paynter was a graduate of the University of Indiana, was a qualified attorney, but all his life lived on a farm and for ten years conducted a mercantile business. He married Sarah E. Barnett of Washington County, and they were the parents of seven children. There were four sons, two of whom, Lawrence W. and Claude B., became physicians, while Asa Lea is a pharmacist and Harry W. has followed business lines.

Lawrence W. Paynter was educated in public schools at Salem, and was graduated M. D. in 1893 from the medical department of the University of Louisville. For twenty-seven years he made his home and practiced medicine at Campbellsburg, and since May, 1920, has lived at Salem. Doctor Paynter was a member of the Medical Advisory Board during the World war and at different times has filled the office of county coroner, aggregating a service of fifteen years. He has been honored with the offices of president, secretary and treasurer of the Washington County Medical Society, is a member of the Third District and Indiana State Medical Associations. Doctor Paynter is a Scottish Rite Mason, member of the Knights of Pythias, Modern Woodmen of America, and the Methodist Episcopal Church.

He married Margaret Maude Strattan, who was born in Washington County and is of Colonial ancestry. The Strattans came from England to America about 1622. In the different generations for three centuries the family has been represented by soldiers in practically every war, including the Revolution. Doctor and Mrs. Paynter were the parents of four children: Marie, wife of William A. Finley, a business man, is a graduate of the Thomas Normal Training School at Detroit, Michigan; Leslie W., who died in 1922; Harry Strattan, a graduate of the New Albany Business College, now in business; and John J., a graduate of the Louisville School of Pharmacy.

JOHN MILLER MONTGOMERY, owner and president of the J. M. Montgomery Motor Company, is in point of continuous service the oldest automobile dealer in Scottsburg. He was trained as a machinist, and had a shop for general repair work at Scottsburg when the automobile made its appearance as a promising vehicle of transportation. Mr. Montgomery has probably repaired every make of car that has been on the road during the last twenty years.

He was born in Scott County, October 20, 1878, a son of W. D. and Hannah (Wardell) Montgomery. His father was born in Kentucky, and was brought to Indiana by his parents after the Civil war. He was a carriage maker by trade. John M. Montgomery was one of a family of ten children. His education was that supplied by the public schools, and when seventeen years of age he began working in a blacksmith shop. He has always been interested in everything mechanical, and he was the first man of Scottsburg to purchase an automobile. Soon after automobiles became something more than an object of curiosity he started doing general repair work for cars, and later began selling them. In the course of his experience he has handled the Hudson, the Overland, the Dodge, the Studebaker, and is now the Scottsburg selling agent for the Chevrolet, conducting the business as the J. M. Montgomery Motor Company. Mr. Montgomery's first repair shop was a log room fourteen by fourteen feet. His business has demanded steadily increased facilities, and he now has sales room and service shop affording 20,000 square feet of floor space. His business establishment is well equipped and has a force of expert workers to handle every class of repair job, and he also carries a large line of accessories. His company places about 250 new cars annually. In addition to the Chevrolet agency the company acts as agent for the Indian Refining Company. His business employs about fifteen persons.

Mr. Montgomery married Miss Carrie E. Yount, of Scott County. They have three children: J. Max, who was educated at the University of Indiana, married Alice G. McKinsey; Russell L., a graduate mechanical engineer of Purdue University; and J. Willard, who also attended Purdue University, is working for his father and is a member of the Citizens Military Training Camp.

Mr. Montgomery is a member of the Scottsburg Lions Club, the Commercial Club, and is affiliated with the Masonic fraternity. He has served as a city trustee and was president of the board from 1920 to 1924. During the World war he did his part in promoting the success of the loan and other drives for the Government.

GEORGE THEODORE HEMPEL. An impressive illustration of what may be accomplished within a score of years by industry, sobriety and persistent endeavor is furnished in the career of George Theodore Hempel, president and general manager of the Hempel Machine Company, Inc., of Jeffersonville. Without aid from adventitious sources and relying solely upon his own inherent energy, perseverance and sound judgment, he has built up a business that is highly creditable to himself and the community of which he is a worthy member.

Mr. Hempel was born at Louisville, Kentucky, March 9, 1887, and is a son of Theodore and Miranda (Francis) Hempel. He is of German descent, the family having established itself in Kentucky during the nineteenth century, and his father was born and educated at Louisville, where for many years he was an important figure in industrial circles. There were two children in the family: George Theodore, of this review; and Theodore, Jr.

George Theodore Hempel attended the public schools of Louisville until he was fourteen years of age, at which time he began to learn the trade of machinist. He proved an apt and retentive pupil, and after mastering his vocation worked as a journeyman machinist for some years, until becoming employed by the Bauer Machine Company, of Jeffersonville, in the capacity of manager. In 1921 Mr. Hempel bought this plant, changed the name of the company to the Hempel Machine Company, and moved the machinery into a new building, at Market and Broadway, where he has since replaced the former machines with the most modern to be secured. The firm is now incorporated as the Hempel Machine Company, Inc., with Mr. Hempel as president and general manager; Walter L. Eckhouse, vice president; and C. L. Kalmbach, secretary and treasurer. Among other articles this company manufactures lock-stitch harness, sewing machines, automobile piston pins, axle and drive shafts and automobile wheel pullers. The plant is located on a lot of 7,000 square feet, and eighteen skilled mechanics are given employment. The concern manufactures for jobbers, and its products find a ready market in Iowa, Nebraska, Oklahoma, Ohio, Indiana, Missouri, Kentucky, Illinois, Minnesota and Texas. Its plant is capable of producing a daily capacity of 600 wrist pins, 100 wheel pullers and 300 axles, and other articles in proportion. During the World war the factory was running 100 per cent day and night in the production of war materials. Mr. Hempel has been exceptionally busy with his business interests, but has always been cognizant of the duties and responsibilities of citizenship, and from 1920 until 1924 served as a member and treasurer of the Clarksville School Board. His name has been connected with all civic enterprises tending toward progress and enlightened views, and he can be counted upon to support worth-while measures of all kinds. As a fraternalist he belongs to Jeffersonville Lodge No. 340, A. F. and A. M., and is a York Rite Mason and a Knight Templar.

In 1907, at Jeffersonville, Mr. Hempel was united in marriage with Miss Lula A. Bartle. a native of Indiana and a granddaughter of a pioneer of this state. To Mr. and Mrs. Hempel there have been born two children: Theodore Franklin, a graduate of the Jeffersonville High School, who is now attending the University of Louisville;. and Ida May, a student at Jeffersonville. The family reside in an attractive home at 510 Montgomery Street.

JAMES EDMONDS HOWARD. From the year 1834 the name of Howard has been indissolubly identified with the business of shipbuilding at Jeffersonville, Indiana, where four generations of the name have added to the prestige and development of the city through their constantly increasing business operations in this field of industry. The present head of this firm, now known as the Howard Ship Yards & Dock Company, is James E. Howard, who has spent his entire life in this business and since 1925 has been its president. He is likewise a constructive and public-spirited citizen, a leader of far-sighted intelligence, and an ex-president of the local Chamber of Commerce.

Mr. Howard was born at Jeffersonville, Indiana, October 2, 1876, and is a son of Edmonds J. and Laura (Burke) Howard. His grandfather, James Howard, was born in England, and was a child when his parents brought him to the United States, the family first settling at Cincinnati, Ohio, where the youth became interested in shipbuilding. In 1834 he came to Jeffersonville, established modest yards and docks, and started business, as James Howard, by building his first boat, the steamer *Hiperion*, a 170-foot side-wheeler. From that time forward he built sixteen boats until 1848, and in the year mentioned he founded the firm of James Howard & Company, taking into partnership his brother, Dan Howard. The business was at that time removed to its present site, in the 800, 900, 1000 and 1100 blocks of East Market Street, and between 1848 and 1884 the firm built about 400 boats. In 1884 the name was changed to the Howard Ship Yard, Edmonds J. Howard becoming the active manager.

Edmonds J. Howard, was born at Madison, Indiana, and as soon as he had completed his education entered his father's business, of which he took charge at his father's demise in 1876. He was a man of business ability, a graduate of the Kentucky Military Institute, and was active in public affairs as a member of the City Council of Jeffersonville for several years. From 1884 until his death, January 30, 1919, the company built about 1,200 boats of all kinds, the firm in the meantime having been reorganized, in 1917, under the name of the Howard Ship Yards & Dock Company, its present style. During the war between the states James E. Howard was manager of stores at the Quartermasters Depot at Jeffersonville. E. J. Howard married Laura Burke, a native of Louisville, Kentucky, who died in December, 1919, and they had two children: Clyde Howard, the operator of the Mound City Marine Ways at Mound City, Illinois, who married Julia Thompson, of Jeffersonville; and James E., of this review.

James E. Howard and his brother attended the public schools at Jeffersonville and a preparatory school at Louisville, Kentucky, following which they entered their father's business and became identified with its every department. When the elder man died James E. Howard became manager, and was engaged as such until 1925, when he purchased his brother's interest and became sole owner and president, Loretta M. Howard being secretary and treasurer. The plant and yards cover about sixteen acres of land and 200 people are given employment in the manufacture of ships and boats of every kind. Since the death of Edmonds J. Howard about 1,200 boats have been constructed at the plant, which, during the World war, was worked 100 per cent for boats and supplies for the United States Government. During that

Thomas O'Brien

period James E. Howard was on various committees engaged in Liberty Loan, Red Cross and War Stamp drives in Clark County. He is a member and an ex-president of the Chamber of Commerce; a charter member of the Rotary Club, from which he recently resigned; and a member of the Indiana Manufacturers Association.

Mr. Howard married Miss Loretta Wooden, a native of Jefferson County, and to this union there have been born three children: Edmonds J., a student of the Manual Training School of Louisville, Kentucky, who is learning the business with his father, and is in the fourth generation; and the Misses Martha and Ruth, who are attending school. Mrs. Howard was formerly president of the Women's Civic Club of Jeffersonville, and is active and popular in social circles.

THOMAS O'BRIEN. The career of Thomas O'Brien is illustrative of what may be accomplished through the homely traits of industry, integrity and perseverance when backed by character and native ability to accept opportunities as they are recognized. He was a poor immigrant youth of nineteen years when he first came to the United States, and it took many years for him to work his way, step by step, to his present position, that of manager of the Gary Tin Mill, of the American Sheet & Tin Plate Company, one of the most important enterprises of this great industrial city.

Mr. O'Brien was born January 1, 1868, in Wales, and is a son of Thomas and Julia (Collins) O'Brien. His parents, who were born and reared in County Cork, Ireland, went to Wales as young people and were there married and spent a number of years. Eventually Thomas O'Brien, the elder, decided that America offered better opportunities for the gaining of independence of a financial character, and accordingly, in 1887, he brought his family to the United States and took up his residence at Pittsburgh, Pennsylvania. In Wales he had followed the calling of a miner and at Pittsburgh found employment of the same nature, remaining at that city until 1892, when he removed to Elwood, Indiana, and there spent the remainder of his life in following his occupation, with the exception of the last few years, when he was retired. He died in 1921, his worthy wife having passed away in 1918. Both are buried at the Elwood (Indiana) Cemetery. There were ten children in the family: Mary, of Elwood; Catherine, who makes her home in England; Bridget, who is deceased; Henry; Dennis, who is deceased; Thomas, of this review; Daniel, deceased; William; John, deceased; and Arthur, manager of the Bethlehem Steel Tin Plate Plant at Baltimore, Maryland.

The public schools and parochial schools of Wales furnished Thomas O'Brien with his educational training, and he was nineteen years of age when he accompanied the family to the United States. Not long after their arrival he secured employment in the Carnegie Steel Plant, at Pittsburgh, as a helper, and remained with that company until 1891, when he joined the P. H. Laughman Company, of Appollo, Pennsylvania. In 1892 he left this position to accompany the family to Elwood, Indiana, where he became a tinner in the tin plant, and remained with that concern for a period of twenty-eight years, gradually rising by promotion to a position of importance because of his natural and acquired ability, his faithfulness and his hard work. From 1906 until May 1, 1920, he served in the capacity of manager of that plant, and upon the latter date was transferred to the Farrell Works, at Farrell, Pennsylvania, as manager there. On August 1, 1929, he came to Gary as manager of the Gary Tin Mill, a position which he has since retained. Mr. O'Brien is admittedly one of the best informed men in his line in the country. As he has passed through the various grades and departments he has thoroughly assimilated all the details of each, and there is nothing about the mill that he does not know. He has gained his knowledge from first-hand contact and not through the medium of text books, and his associates have come to rely implicitly upon his judgment and acumen. While he has always been a strict disciplinarian, asking just as much from his men as he does from himself, he has an inherent sense of justice and he has experienced little labor trouble in his long and varied career. He has developed rare executive capacity, while at the same time making himself popular with his fellow-officials and the employes. Mr. O'Brien has of recent years found pleasure and relaxation in golfing. He is interested in civic affairs, belongs to the Commercial Club and Chamber of Commerce of Gary and the Gary Country Club, and is on the advisory board of Saint Mary's Mercy Hospital. Politically he is a Republican and his religious connection is with Holy Angels Church.

At Pittsburgh, Pennsylvania, October 8, 1891, Mr. O'Brien was united in marriage with Miss Mary Meany, daughter of John and Hannah (Taylor) Meany. Mr. Meany was a blast furnace man with a concern in Wales for a number of years, but after coming to the United States and settling at Pittsburgh, he lived in retirement until his death in 1918. Mrs. Meany survived him until 1926, and both are buried at Pittsburgh. Mrs. O'Brien was educated in the public and parochial schools of her native town in Wales and was twenty years of age when she accompanied her parents to the United States in 1887. For some years she was active in church and social life at Sharon and Farrell, Pennsylvania, and since coming to Gary has been a consistent and helpful member of Holy Angels Church. Six sons have been born to Mr. and Mrs. O'Brien: Thomas F., Jr., who attended the parochial school at Elwood, Indiana, and spent two years at Notre Dame University, now hot mill superintendent of the Sabraton plant of the American Sheet & Tin Plate Company, Morgantown, West Virginia, married Miss

Margaret Wander and has two children, Frances and Thomas III; John, who died at the age of twenty-two years; Dan, who died at the age of seventeen years; Leo, educated at the parochial school of Elwood and a graduate of the high school at Sharon, Pennsylvania, now a foreman in the hot mill department of the Gary Tin Mill; Maurice, a graduate of Sharon High School, who spent two years at Notre Dame University, now in the fuel engineering department of the Gary Tin Mill; and Joseph, a graduate of Sharon High School, who spent one year at Duquesne University and is now a student at Notre Dame University.

JAMES MARRA. In the ranks of the business men of Jeffersonville who have gained position and wealth through native and acquired ability, tireless industry and natural and acquired talent, one who stands out prominently as an example to the aspiring youth of any community is James Marra, president of the Jeffersonville Baking Company. His has been a long and varied career, in which he has had to meet and overcome a number of obstacles, but he has always retained faith in himself and has striven to gain the confidence of others by his honorable dealing, and he now finds himself, when in middle life, with many powers unimpaired, at the head of a large industry and in the midst of a circle of well-wishers and admiring friends.

Mr. Marra was born at Jeffersonville, Indiana, December 29, 1874, and is a son of Michael and Mary B. Marra. His father was born in County Tipperary, Ireland, where he was reared and given a country school education, and was still a youth when he immigrated to the United States and took up his residence at Jeffersonville about the year 1863. He soon found employment with the Jeffersonville & Indianapolis Railroad and continued to be identified with that line for some years, but at the time of his demise was employed in a responsible capacity by the Sweeney Iron Foundry at Jeffersonville. Mr. Marra married Miss Bridget Corrigan, of Cynthiana, Kentucky, and they were the parents of five children.

James Marra attended the public schools of Jeffersonville until he was thirteen years of age, at which time he began work as clerk in a local grocery store, with which he remained for eight years. In the meantime he improved himself by attendance at night school and supplemented this by a course in a business college, so that in 1895 he was ready to begin a career of his own and opened a modest grocery establishment at Court Avenue and Watt Street. He built up a successful and flourishing business there, but in 1913 sold out to his brother, Dan Marra. In the meantime, on April 14, 1910, he had founded the Jeffersonville Baking Company, Inc., of which he was treasurer and a member of the board of directors for six months, at the end of that time becoming president and treasurer, positions which he has retained to the present, a period of two decades. This concern manufactures all kinds of bread, rolls and biscuits, and now occupies one of the most modern plants in the state, with the latest automatic equipment and machinery. It was the first to completely modernize the baking business, the first to successfully wrap bread in this district, and the plant, which occupies 17,000 square feet of floor space, is absolutely dust-proof. Ten large motor trucks are utilized in the delivery of the company's product, and thirty-two people are employed in producing a capacity of 75,000 loaves weekly, the greater part of which find a market among the people of Clark County. Mr. Marra is widely known as a capable, energetic and honorable business man, and is president of the Mutual Loan Association No. 4 of Jeffersonville. He is a member of the advisory board of the Indiana Bakers Association, and during the World war was bakery advisor to the food administrator, as well as being active in the Liberty Loan, Red Cross and War Stamp campaigns. He takes an intense and constructive interest in all civic affairs, and is a member of the board of directors of the local Chamber of Commerce, a director of the Rotary Club, director of the Jeffersonville Recreation Club, and vice president of Clark County Aerie of the Boy Scouts of America. For over thirty years he has been a trustee of Saint Augustine's Church. Mr. Marra married Miss Alice R. Russell, of Clark County, and they reside at 917 East Seventh Street. They have no children.

Thomas H. Marra, a brother of James Marra, is president of George S. Anderson Company, founders and manufacturing machinists, of Jeffersonville. He married Miss Cora G. Lang, daughter of William Henry Lang, vice president of that old-established and substantial concern.

WILLIAM LEE HUBBARD is president and owner of the W. L. Hubbard Company at Scottsburg. He grew up in the atmosphere of the lumber industry, his father having been a pioneer saw mill man in Scott County. Later Mr. Hubbard established a hardware business, and in recent years resumed his connection with the lumber business as operator of a retail yard. He has a permanent and assured position in the business affairs of his native county and has been a leader in many lines of civic enterprise as well.

Mr. Hubbard was born in Scott County June 9, 1868, son of Madison Hubbard. His father, a native of Taylor County, Kentucky, came to Scott County during the Civil war. For many years he carried on a business manufacturing lumber and handling timber. He married Sicha Jane Richey, of Scott County. Her father, Richard Richey, was born October 9, 1812, shortly after the Pigeon Roost massacre, to escape which her parents had sought refuge in the block house at Charlestown, Indiana.

William L. Hubbard, the oldest of five children, was educated in common schools and as a boy worked for his father in the woods and lumber mills. In October, 1896, he became proprietor of a retail hardware business at Scottsburg, and has carried on that business now for thirty years. Since 1916 he has also been a dealer in lumber, his business being known as the W. L. Hubbard Company. Mr. Hubbard has enjoyed some interesting honors in connection with his business. From 1920 to 1926 he was a member of the National Board of the Hardware Dealers Association, in 1915 was president of the Indiana State Hardware Men's Association, has been on the advisory board of the state organization and is also a member and on the advisory board of the Indiana Lumber Dealers Association. He is president and senior member of the Baker Overall Company, a Scottsburg industry that affords employment to sixty-five workers. He is vice president and a director of the Citizens Security Company, and a director of the Scottsburg State Bank and of the Henryville Bank. He was the fourth president of the Scottsburg Lions Club and a member of the Commercial Club, and from 1908 to 1912 served on the City Council.

Mr. Hubbard married, February 23, 1897, Miss Florence M. Bailey, who was born in Scott County, Indiana. They have one daughter, Wilma, a student at DePauw University. Mr. Hubbard is a member of the executive committee and is now treasurer of the Hoosier State Automobile Association. During the World war he was fuel administrator for Scott County, managed the first war drive, and was active in the subsequent local program of war activities. For two terms he was a member and president of the school board and is a member of the Tuberculosis Association. Mrs. Hubbard's father, James P. Bailey, was born in Kentucky, came to Indiana in 1859 and was a soldier in the Civil war. During the World war Mrs. Hubbard was a member of the Council of Defense and on the executive committee of the Red Cross and county chairman of the food clubs. She is a member of the Scott County Historical Society. The family are members of Scottsburg Baptist Church.

HARRY A. CHRISTENSEN. In every thriving and growing community one of the most important assets for protection is the fire department. In this connection Jeffersonville is fortunate in having as chief such an able and experienced man as Harry A. Christensen, who possesses the requisites of courage, executive capacity, judgment, diplomacy and energy in no small degree. His career, which started in early boyhood, has been a long, honored and varied one, and in each capacity in which he has acted he has held the full confidence of those with whom he was connected.

Chief Christensen was born at Watson, Clark County, Indiana, September 6, 1872, and is a son of Peter and Pateria (Dall) Christensen, natives of Denmark. The parents were educated at Copenhagen, where they were married, and some time after the close of the war between the states, about 1869, immigrated to this country and settled in Clark County, Indiana, where Peter Christensen came a substantial and highly respected agriculturist and a citizen who had the welfare of his community at heart. He and his worthy wife were the parents of three sons and three daughters.

Harry A. Christensen attended the public school at Watson, which he left at the age of fifteen years, but though he has had no further school training he has been a great reader and student all his life, and thus has gained an excellent practical education and a broad knowledge of worth-while subjects. He began his career as the driver of a mule team at a cement mill, and from this humble position worked his way steadily upward by industry and fidelity until he became stationary engineer of the company, having worked through all the departments during his seven years of employment. In 1894 he resigned his position and went to Louisville, Kentucky, where he became hoister at the round-house of the Pennsylvania Railway Company. Later he was promoted to the position of night foreman at the round-house, but at the end of five years resigned to join the Louisville Gas & Electric Light Company on their spillway. His next position was that of engineer of the steamer pump engine of the Jeffersonville fire department, in 1918, and early in 1919 was made chief. He served in this capacity until 1923, when he became yard foreman for the P. F. Myers Lumber Company, but at the end of four years was recalled to the fire department and has served as chief to the present. Under his administration the department has been improved in many ways, and now consists of twelve men, operating three pieces of modern motorized fire apparatus. He is a strict disciplinarian, cool and collected in times of emergency, and a "smoke-eater" whose exploits are well known far beyond the immediate vicinity of Jeffersonville. He belongs to the Indiana State Police and Fireman's Association, and has been a member of the Modern Woodmen of America for a quarter of a century. The present fire house was originally erected in 1900, and since then at various times has been improved and made larger, until today it compares favorably with many stations located in the big cities of the state. Chief Christensen has always been interested in civic movements and his support can be relied upon when advancement and progress are at stake.

Chief Christensen was united in marriage with Miss Lucy Williams, an orphan, of Seymour, Indiana, and to this union there were born five children: Henry, of Jeffersonville, a veteran of the World war, who saw two years of overseas service in France with the Thirty-fifth Infantry, A. E. F., and married Mattie Adkins; Ernest, who married Ann McCarthy; Calhoun, who married Lena Shea; Ruth, who married William Cole; and Lucille, who is deceased.

JOHN NYE ROBERTS. Among the more uncommon branches of manufacture, that of the making of veneer is an interesting one. Veneer is a beautifully grained or figured wood, which is, owing to its cost, rarely used in the form of solid boards, but cut into thin slices. Veneers are cut from almost all the finer woods, both native and foreign, including American walnut, mahogany, birch, rosewood, ebony, satinwood, cedar, tulipwood, Hungarian ash, sycamore and others, being principally used on pianos and fine furniture. In Indiana a representative concern which earned a reputation for excellent workmanship and high principles was that of John N. Roberts & Son, manufacturers of lumber and veneer at Jeffersonville, Clark County, the owner of which, John N. Roberts, has been engaged in the business for a quarter of a century. In March, 1931, the firm was incorporated as the Roberts, Dulaney Veneer Corporation.

Mr. Roberts was born at Richmond in Wayne County, Indiana, March 28, 1863, and is a son of John and Mary (Nye) Roberts. His father, who was born at Cincinnati, Ohio, was brought to Indiana by his parents as a child, in 1840, and grew up on a farm, but later turned his attention to the manufacture of furniture, a field in which he gained much success. He was a man of good business judgment and sound ability and was known for his straightforward and honorable principles in business dealing. He married Mary Nye, who was born in Franklin County, Indiana, and they became the parents of five children.

John N. Roberts attended the public schools of Wayne County and Earlham College, and began to have an acquaintance with business affairs when he was only sixteen years of age, as a hand in his father's mill. He remained with the elder man until 1879, following which he was identified with various other mills of a like nature, learning the business in all its departments and particulars and carefully conserving his money with the idea in view of embarking in business on his own account. This ambition he realized in 1905, at which time he located at New Albany and erected a veneer mill, which he operated successfully for a period of thirteen years. In 1918 he sold out and came to Jeffersonville, where he organized the firm of John N. Roberts & Son and started the veneer mill which still bears his name, and which is known all over this section of the state for its fine work and the excellence of its material. This is now a partnership between father and son, and the business has been built up to large proportions and now employs some twenty-nine persons in the manufacture of lumber and veneer of American walnut for various large furniture companies. The plant covers ten acres and is furnished with all the modern machinery known to the trade. During the World war period it was engaged in 100 per cent war production. Mr. Roberts is a member of the local lodge of the Benevolent and Protective Order of Elks, and has several civic connections. He has not taken any active part in politics.

Mr. Roberts married Miss Amy Willard, of Indianapolis, and to this union there have been born three children: Amy Rosbrugh, who was educated in a private and public schools at Indianapolis, and is now a resident of New Albany, Indiana; Lydia Mary, educated in a private school at Orange, New Jersey, who is the widow of Dr. Thomas Farris Hale, a physician; and John Ralston, a graduate of Purdue University, who served eighteen months in the United States Navy during the World war, and is now his father's associate in business. The family home is situated on Silver Hill, New Albany.

MARK STOREN, of Scottsburg, has long enjoyed a statewide reputation as one of the eminent members of the Indiana bar. He has been a practicing lawyer nearly half a century. Mr. Storen has held various positions of trust and responsibility and for eight years was United States marshal of Indiana.

He was born in Columbia County, New York, April 12, 1857, and was a boy of about eight years when his parents, Michael and Mary Storen, came to Indiana. His father spent many years in the railroad service and afterwards settled on a farm. Mark Storen, one of six children, grew up in Scott County, had most of his school advantages there and for two terms attended the Terre Haute, Indiana, Normal School. While teaching for five years in Scott County he pursued the study of law under Judge J. D. New at Vernon, and in 1880 was admitted to the Indiana bar. Since that date he has had his law offices in Scottsburg, and has enjoyed many of the distinctions paid to the able lawyer and man of affairs. Many important cases have been intrusted to him in the course of his practice. In 1888 he was elected clerk of the Scott County Circuit Court and by reelection held that office eight years. He was also a member of the Indiana Legislature and representative of Scott and Jennings counties, and soon after the beginning of President Wilson's first term was appointed United States marshal for Indiana and in 1918 was reappointed by the president, serving until 1922.

When he became United States marshal he resigned the office of president of the Scott County Bank. He had been president of that institution for several years and is still on the board of directors. Mr. Storen for twelve years was a member of the Scottsburg School Board. He has been a leader in the Democratic party and served on the county and state committees. He was the third president of the Scottsburg Lions Club, and is a member of the Indiana State and District Bar Associations. He belongs to the Scottish Rite bodies of Masonry at Indianapolis, also Murat Temple of the Mystic Shrine, is affiliated with the Independent Order of Odd Fellows, Knights of Pythias, Modern Woodmen of

Raphael F. Donnelly

America and B. P. O. Elks. Scott County has no more disinterested and public spirited citizen than Mark Storen.

He married Miss Minerva E. Cravens, of Scott County, whose people were pioneers of this section of Indiana, coming from Kentucky and originally from Virginia. Mr. and Mrs. Storen have one daughter, Merle, wife of Lawrence E. Reeves, a business man of Columbus, Indiana.

REV. RAPHAEL FRANCIS DONNELLY. Among the many advantages that make Gary a pleasant place to have a home are its fine school facilities and its numerous church organizations, learning and religion permeating its business, civic and social life. Saint Luke's Catholic Church, with a large and devout congregation, is an example of church influence and is in a very prosperous condition under the pastorate of Rev. Raphael F. Donnelly, whose sound church doctrine is very acceptable to his parishioners. Reverend Donnelly is a man of broad mind, great humanitarianism, much learning and unusual organizing ability, and, perhaps due to the last-named gift, his field of active church service has been one of wider experience than often comes into the life of a priest in a similar space of time in regard to change of location and effective work done.

Father Donnelly was born in Huntington County, Indiana, February 24, 1889, and is a son of John and Mary (Moran) Donnelly, the former a native of Wooster, Ohio, and the latter of Birmingham, England. His maternal grandparents were Dominick and Catherine (O'Malley) Moran, natives of County Mayo, Ireland, who spent a short time in England and then came to the United States in 1881, settling in Ohio. The paternal grandparents of Father Donnelly were Ambrose and Bridget (McDermott) Donnelly, natives of County Langford, Ireland, who settled in Ohio in 1850.

Father Donnelly studied at Saint Patrick's parochial school at Fort Wayne, and afterward entered Saint Joseph's College, Rensselaer, Indiana, from which institution he was graduated with the degree of Bachelor of Arts, June 17, 1908. Having decided to devote his life to the Catholic priesthood, he became a student at Mount Saint Mary's Seminary, Cincinnati, Ohio, where he completed his theological course as a member of the class of 1913. On November 18 of the same year he was ordained a Catholic priest by the Rt. Rev. Bishop Herman Joseph Alerding, at the Cathedral of the Immaculate Conception, Fort Wayne, and his first charge was as assistant to Father E. F. Barrett, at All Saint Church, Hammond. He remained there for three years, and his next service was at Anderson, Indiana, as assistant to the Rev. Thomas Mungovan, of Saint Mary's parish, until December 13, 1919. Failing in health, due to too close attention to his ministerial work, he spent the next year and one-half at Tucson, Arizona, and San Antonio, Texas. On June 15, 1921, he assumed the pastorate of the Church of the Immaculate Conception, at Ege, Noble County, Indiana, remaining there until August 24, 1925, when he became resident pastor of Saint Luke's parish at Gary, which pastorate he has since held.

Father Donnelly has dedicated himself to his duties in association with this parish to the end that it has been constantly gaining in size, his work in spiritual ministry having borne much fruit. He is also a business advisor of his people, as well as guide and friend, and no man at Gary is held in greater respect or esteem. Father Donnelly is a fourth degree member of the Knights of Columbus and belongs to the Catholic Order of Forresters and the B. P. O. Elks.

WILLIAM MILTON GILMORE. Of the men of energy, perseverance and good judgment who have contributed to the advancement and development of Clark County, few have made more rapid strides or contributed more valuable services than William Milton Gilmore, who is engaged in the successful management of a prosperous real estate and insurance business at Jeffersonville. Although he is still to be numbered among the younger generation of men engaged in this prolific field, he has already been the medium through whom large transactions have been carried through to a successful and satisfying conclusion, and has likewise been the promulgator of movements of a development character that have added to his community's growth and population.

Mr. Gilmore was born December 27, 1894, on a farm in Clark County, Indiana, and is a son of Marryman and Carrie L. (Raymond) Gilmore. The Gilmore family is of Scotch and Irish extraction and were Colonial settlers who took part in the Revolutionary war and later in the War of 1812. The great-grandfather of William Milton Gilmore was John Gilmore, who was born in Virginia and in young manhood accompanied the first settlers into the new Kentucky country. After residing there for a few years, in 1802 he penetrated the wilderness of the Northwest Territory, settling on an unimproved farm in Indiana prior to statehood. There he worked industriously until he had prepared a good home and productive farm, and eventually became one of the substantial men of the community. William Milton Gilmore, the grandfather of William Milton Gilmore of this review, was born in Clark County, where he followed farming and the raising of live stock and was one of the locality's constructive citizens. He married Elizabeth Marryman, who was also born in Clark County, and they reared a large family to honorable man and womanhood.

Marryman Gilmore was reared in Clark County, where he received a subscription school education, and in young manhood began farming. In his later years he turned his attention to merchandising, and for many years was the successful and energetic proprietor of a general store at Jeffersonville, where he built up a large and loyal patronage.

He was never a man to seek office, but took an interest in public matters and gave his support to worth-while movements. Mr. Gilmore married Miss Carrie L. Raymond, a native of Kentucky, and they became the parents of four children: Raymond L., John M., William M. and Gordon.

William Milton Gilmore attended the public schools of Jeffersonville, following which he took a course at a local business college. He was twenty years of age when he embarked upon his independent career and was engaged in clerical work until September, 1917, at which time he joined the United States Marines, for service during the World war, and after going through a training period was assigned as drill instructor at Paris Island, South Carolina, where he remained for six months. He was next transferred to Cuba, where he remained four months, being connected with the coast defense, and finally went to France, where his contingent remained until after the signing of the armistice. He returned to Jeffersonville about one year after the close of the war and for something more than seven years was engaged in farming in Clark County. In 1927 he established his present business, which is conducted as William M. Gilmore, with offices located at 136 East Court Avenue. Mr. Gilmore is an excellent judge of realty values in this part of the country, where he has passed his entire career, and is known as a clever and persuasive operator who has a record for straightforward dealing and honorable accomplishment. In addition to his real estate interests he carries a line of general insurance, representing a number of the well-known old-line companies.

Mr. Gilmore is an active and constructive member of the Chamber of Commerce of Jeffersonville, and belongs to the Masons, Knights of Pythias and Benevolent and Protective Order of Elks. He is commander of Lawrence Capehart Post No. 135 of the American Legion.

ARTHUR ROSS MEAD, M. D. Aside from any distinction which may attach to being a member of one of the oldest and most highly respected families in Indiana, Arthur R. Mead, M. D., of Jeffersonville, is known for his high professional character and ability and for the success that has attended his labors in one of the most difficult of sciences. It is indicative of his ability and the confidence in which he is held that he has been a successful private physician and surgeon, has been active in the work of medical organizations, and is now attached to the staff of the Clark County Memorial Hospital.

Doctor Mead was born at Pekin, Washington County, Indiana, January 26, 1887, and is a son of Benjamin F. and Harriet Elizabeth (Diehl) Mead. The American ancestor of this family settled in North Carolina, where members distinguished themselves in the Colonial wars as well as civilians, and later generations moved to Kentucky, in which state was born David Mead, the great-grandfather of Doctor Mead. In young manhood David Mead came to the then wilderness of Indiana, where he hewed a farm and labored during the rest of his life in tilling the soil and in supplying the family larder with game through his skill as a hunter and trapper. Ben Mead, the grandfather of Doctor Mead, settled in Washington County, this state, about 1830, and passed his entire life there in agricultural operations. He was a man of high and sturdy character and one who commanded the respect and esteem of the entire community. Benjamin F. Mead, the father of Dr. Arthur R. Mead, was born in Washington County, Indiana, and acquired a common school education in the rural districts. Reared on a farm and belonging to an agricultural family, it was natural for him to take up the tilling of the soil as his life work, and during his active years he developed a fertile and well-developed farm. He is now living in comfortable retirement, having reached the ripe age of seventy-eight years. Mr. Mead married Harriet Elizabeth Diehl, also of Washington County and a member of an old and respected family of this state, and they became the parents of four children: Flora, Albert O., Mary and Arthur R.

Arthur R. Mead attended the grade school at Pekin, Washington County and the Central Normal Teachers' College at Danville, this state, following which he entered the medical department of the University of Louisville, Kentucky. He was graduated with the degree of Doctor of Medicine as a member of the class of 1911, following which he had two years of clinical work in the City Hospital, Louisville, and started practice at Pleasant Lake, Indiana. In 1913 he came to Jeffersonville, and here has been successful in the development of a large and lucrative practice, his well-equipped offices being located at 437 Spring Street. From the time of his arrival Doctor Mead impressed himself upon his adopted community as a man of personal reliability and proficiency in his profession, and attracted to himself the patronage of some of the leading families of the community. Later he was invited to become a member of the staff of the Clark County Memorial Hospital, and still retains this post. Being equally familiar with all departments of his calling, he has specialized in none. He belongs to the Clark County Medical Society and the Indiana State Medical Society, in both of which organizations he takes a prominent part, and is a tireless student and investigator. Fraternally he is a Mason and Knight Templar.

At Jeffersonville, Doctor Mead was united in marriage with Miss Pearl Bruner, who was born in Arkansas, a daughter of Dr. E. W. and Joetta (Brentlinger) Bruner. Her grandfather, Dr. Jacob Bruner, a physician and surgeon and an accredited minister of the Methodist Episcopal Church, came to Indiana about 1830 and spent the rest of his life in practicing medicine and preaching the Gospel at Bedford, Utica and elsewhere. Dr. E. W.

Bruner, the father of Mrs. Mead, was also a prominent physician and surgeon of Jefferson County. During the war between the states he served as a commissioned officer, and later, for five years, was employed by the Government as visiting physician to the surviving Creek and Cherokee Indians in the South. He returned then to Jeffersonville, Indiana, where he passed away after sixty years of medical practice. He married Joetta Brentlinger, and they became the parents of six children. One of these, Mrs. Mead's brother, is Dr. Ralph W. Bruner, a well-known physician and surgeon of Jeffersonville, a sketch of whose career will be found elsewhere in this work. Doctor and Mrs. Mead are the parents of two daughters, Gladah Elizabeth and Marjorie Ann, both attending school, and the members of the family reside in a pleasant and attractive home located at 911 East Court Street, Jeffersonville.

JOHN COURTLAND WORRALL. The entire career of John C. Worrall may be said to have been identified with the matter of transportation, for after twenty years of experience in railroading in the West during his younger years he returned to his native State of Indiana to become proprietor of an automobile business, the Worrall Motor Sales Company of Jeffersonville, exclusive dealers in Hudson and Essex cars. From a modest beginning, through industry and good judgment Mr. Worrall has built up a prosperous business, and now has a large and modern salesroom and repair plant, where he has installed every up-to-date contrivance for the care and repair of these makes of automobiles.

Mr. Worrall was born on a farm in Clark County, Indiana, December 25, 1888, and is a son of Oliver T. and Annie E. (Espy) Worrall. The Worrall family originated in Ireland, whence three brothers, Thomas, John T. and William Worrall, came to America on a sailing vessel and landed on the eastern coast. Seeking their fortunes further to the West, about 1795 they started on their long and perilous journey, coming down the Ohio River until they reached Harrod's Creek, Kentucky, where Thomas and John T. remained. William, however, pushed on further and finally reached Southern California, where his descendants are now the famous Worrall fruit-growing family. After a few years in Kentucky, Thomas Worrall went on to Iowa, where all trace of him was lost. In 1805 John T. Worrall established the first ferry across the Ohio River, from Harrod's Creek to Utica, Indiana, and operated it with success for many years. In 1817 he crossed over into Indiana, and spent the remaining years of his life as a farmer.

Curtis Worrall, son of John T. Worrall, and grandfather of John C. Worrall, was born in Indiana, where he attended the subscription schools and was reared on his father's farm. His entire life was devoted to the tilling of the soil and the breaking of new land for the production of produce, with the exception of the Civil war period, when he served as a soldier of the Union and was active in repelling the raids of Morgan. He was a man of reliability and high character and one who held the esteem and respect of the community.

Oliver T. Worrall was born in Clark County, Indiana, and spent the active years of his career as a gardener. He never held office, but was accounted one of the reliable and constructive citizens of his community, noted for his fair dealing and personal probity. He married Annie E. Espy, a native of Chester, Illinois, who was a descendant of General Bartholomew, after whom Bartholomew County, Indiana, was named. Mr. and Mrs. Worrall became the parents of six children.

John C. Worrall attended the public schools of Clark County until he reached the age of fourteen years, in the meantime assisting his father in his work on the home place. Like many country boys of his day, he became attracted by the romantic life of railroading, and, leaving home, secured employment with the Pennsylvania Railroad. After twenty years of work as an engineer with this and other roads he resigned and returned to Jeffersonville, where he organized the Worrall Motor Sales Company, in February, 1928, taking over the franchise as exclusive dealer in his community of Hudson and Essex cars. He has a large and well-equipped showroom and warehouse at 430 Wall Street, which is so arranged as to do any kind of work on these cars, and during his first year of business put 110 cars in the hands of purchasers. Mr. Worrall is a business man of ability and one who has readily accustomed himself to the particulars of his present business. He has made and held many friends and patrons, and his excellent workmanship and fair dealing have combined to bring him into the confidence of the general public. He has a number of civic connections and belongs to Jeffersonville Blue Lodge, A. F. and A. M.

Mr. Worrall married Miss Maud Applegate, a native of Indiana, and they are the parents of three children: Miss Joyce Emmaly, Darcy Anderson and John David, all of whom are attending public school at Jeffersonville. The pleasant and attractive Worrall home is situated at 430 Watt Street.

EDGAR HINTON HUGHES. A prosperous business enterprise at Jeffersonville, Indiana, is the E. H. Hughes Company, the proprietor of which is Edgar Hinton Hughes, an experienced, qualified machinist, a military aviator and an overseas veteran of the World war. He comes from an old Welsh family of Colonial settlement in Virginia about the time of the Revolutionary war, where, like their kindred, the Buckners of Kentucky, they long maintained an almost feudal style of living on their great plantations. Prior to the changes brought about by the war between the states these families and many others of their class and sections were recognized people of wealth and social importance, as are many of these today with perhaps slightly changed standards. Jeffersonville has been Mr. Hughes' home all his life and since his youth he has been interested in mechanics, more especially in connection with the automobile industry and aviation.

Edgar Hinton Hughes was born at Jeffersonville, March 8, 1896, and is a son of George R. and Elizabeth (Rose) Hughes. George R. Hughes was born in Kentucky, and at the outbreak of the war between the states enlisted in the Confederate army and was with Morgan's men in their spectacular raids through Southern Indiana, Missouri and Illinois. At the close of the war he enlisted in the regular United States Army, with which he served for eight years, and then settled in Clark County, where he entered the building construction business, and during his career in that line of industry erected some of the finest buildings in this part of the state. He was known for his high character and personal and business integrity, and held the respect and confidence of his fellow-citizens in full degree. Mr. Hughes married Miss Elizabeth Rose, a native of Kentucky, whose father, Andrew Rose, was the first of the family to come to Indiana. To Mr. and Mrs. Hughes there were born eleven children.

The public schools of Jeffersonville furnished Edgar Hinton Hughes with his early education, and after he had graduated from high school he entered Purdue University. He left this institution to become identified with the automobile industry as a mechanic, and in the years that followed worked his way through all the branches of automobile building. In 1917 he enlisted in the United States Navy Aviation Corps, and was in active service for two years in France, receiving his honorable discharge in 1920, with the rank of warrant machinist and a splendid record for fidelity and gallant service. Returning to Jeffersonville, he entered the employ of the Chevrolet Sales & Service Company, with which he was identified for six years and then, in October, 1926, organized the E. H. Hughes Company, of which he has since been the proprietor. This at first was a service station and repair shop, handling General Motors trucks and the Durant line of cars. On January 1, 1927, he took over the Chrysler and Plymouth lines, and these he represents at present. Mr. Hughes' success may be judged by the fact that in 1928 he placed 194 cars, with the expectation of doubling this number in 1929. The show room, storage and shop cover 15,000 square feet of floor space, and ten skilled men are employed, able to do all kinds of work on these two makes of cars. Mr. Hughes carries a full line of accessories and tires, and in addition to his headquarters has established three agencies. Mr. Hughes is a member of the American Legion. Primarily a business man, he has always taken an interest in civic affairs and has served as committeeman on the election board and been a nominee for the office of councilman-at-large.

Mr. Hughes married Miss Avalina Nahstoll, of Clark County, a member of an old and prominent agricultural family of Indiana, and they are the parents of three children: George Edgar, Joan and James Bertram. The pleasant family home is located at 902 East Court Street.

WILLIAM HENRY LANG. One of the oldest and most reliable business concerns in the entire State of Indiana is that of George S. Anderson & Company, of Jeffersonville. Founded in a modest way in 1832, as a foundry and machine shop, during the years that have followed the company has undergone a number of changes in both name and ownership, but has never changed its policy of the highest grade of work and the strictest of integrity in its dealings. The guiding head of this large enterprise is now William Henry Lang, who is secretary and treasurer and leading owner, and who has been connected with the concern all of his life, starting as an apprentice machinist. Mr. Lang has been the architect of his own fortune and is now one of the most substantial business men of Jeffersonville, where he has been active in civic and public affairs.

Mr. Lang was born at Jeffersonville, Indiana, March 21, 1864, and is a son of Henry and Frances (Shoemaker) Lang. Henry Lang was born in Germany, and when he came to the United States, in 1836, was first a ship carpenter and later a brewer. Miss Shoemaker was his second wife and William Henry was one of their seven children. The parents were highly esteemed people of their community, and both died at Jeffersonville.

The public schools of his native place furnished William Henry Lang with his educational training, and at the age of sixteen years he became an apprentice machinist in the foundry and machine shop of C. C. Anderson. This had been founded by Mr. Anderson in 1832 and originally was located near Howard's Ship Yards, later moving to near Maple and Spring streets, and finally to its present location at 425 Watt Street. A short time later, in 1890, the firm name was changed to George S. Anderson & Brothers, and in 1899 to George S. Anderson & Brothers Company. In 1906 the firm was incorporated as George S. Anderson & Company, its present title, and at that time largely increased its capacity as founders and machinists, enabling the factory to do all kinds of work.

Upon completing his apprenticeship Mr. Lang began to exercise the most rigid economy and in 1899 was able to buy a one-fourth interest in the concern, and subsequently purchased another quarter. In 1918 he became full owner of the concern, but in 1921 sold a one-third interest to his son-in-law, T. M. Marra, who is his present partner. Mr. Lang has relied completely upon his own resource and ability in the working out of a successful and highly honorable career. He is known as a shrewd and capable business man of the highest character and as a citizen who commands the highest respect. He has served constructively and efficiently as a member of the

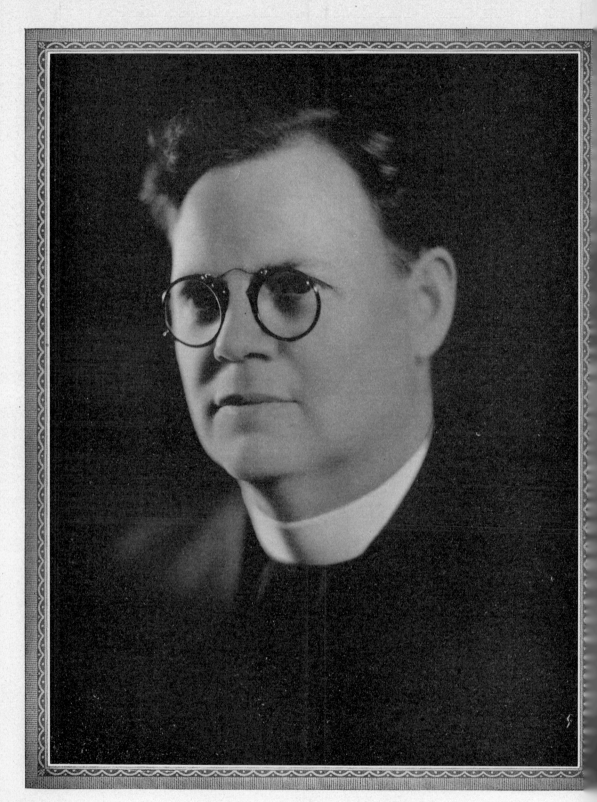

J. A. Costello.

City Council of Jeffersonville and in other capacities, and during the World war was very active in all drives for securing loans for the Government.

Mr. Lang married Miss Alice G. Howard, of Clark County, Indiana, and to this union there have been born two daughters: Mrs. Frances M. Yarber and Mrs. Cora G. Marra, the latter of whom died December 19, 1929. Mrs. Yarber resides at Jeffersonville. Mrs. Lang died April 1, 1928.

REV. JOHN ALOYSIUS COSTELLO. Few Catholic priests of Indiana have their time more fully occupied or are engaged in more extended and beneficial activities than Rev. John A. Costello, of Gary. For fifteen years past his missionary work has taken him all over the United States, for three years he has had charge of the propagation of the faith in the Diocese of Fort Wayne, and recently he added to his labors the management of the Judge Gary-Bishop Alerding Settlement House. His work has been uniformly successful and constructive and he is accounted one of the most vigorous and constructive priests of the church.

Father Costello was born at Anderson, Indiana, July 23, 1888, and is a son of John and Ann (Heenan) Costello. His paternal grandfather, John Costello the elder, was born in Ireland, whence he brought his family to the United States and became a pioneer resident of Anderson, where he passed the remainder of his life and was regarded as a good citizen and man of reliable character. He and his worthy wife are buried in the Catholic cemetery at Indianapolis. John Costello, the younger, was born in Ireland and was a lad when brought by his parents to Anderson, where he received his education in the public schools. In young manhood he engaged in work upon a farm and eventually, through industry and steady application, became the owner of a property of his own, upon which he raised the standard crops and also grew live stock. He was highly esteemed in his community and was held in confidence by his fellow-citizens, who elected him county commissioner for a number of years. His death occurred in 1896, when he was buried in Saint Mary's Cemetery at Anderson. Mr. Costello married Miss Ann Heenan, who was born in Ireland and as a child was brought by her parents, Patrick and Mary Heenan, to Rochester, New York. Patrick Heenan engaged in railroad work, first at Rochester, New York, and later at Logansport, Indiana, where, at the time of his death, he was superintendent of tracks of the Logansport Division of the Pennsylvania Railroad Company. Mrs. Costello was educated in the schools of Rochester, New York, and Logansport, Indiana, and prior to her marriage was engaged in social service work at Logansport. Following her marriage she gave a good deal of her time to this service and was always active in the Catholic Church, in addition to rearing a family of nine children. The death of this worthy woman occurred January 21, 1930, and she was laid to rest at the side of her husband in Saint Mary's Cemetery, Anderson. Of the nine children one died in infancy, the others being: Mary, Margaret, Anna, Josephine, James, of the Costello chain stores, Jeremiah, Rev. John A., of this review, and Patricia.

John A. Costello attended the public schools of Anderson and graduated from Dayton (Ohio) University as a member of the class of 1908. He then entered Cincinnati Seminary, where he pursued courses in theology and philosophy, and was graduated in 1913, in which same year he was ordained to the Catholic priesthood. For the next four years Father Costello was stationed at Muncie, this state as assistant to Father Schmidt, being then transferred to the Catholic University at Washington, D. C., where he took a graduate course as well as a missionary course. In 1918 he began his regular missionary work, in which he is still engaged, and which has made him a familiar figure in many parts of the United States. In 1927 Father Costello took charge of the propagation work in the Diocese of Fort Wayne, and this he has also carried on without interruption. In 1930, when Father John B. deVille, who was in charge of the Judge Gary-Bishop Alerding Settlement House, lost his health and was compelled to take a trip to Europe, Father Costello was asked to take over his labors. He has filled this assignment with the greatest of ability and is accomplishing a great and good work, in addition to his other manifold and arduous duties. A man of untiring energy, enduring faith and much executive capacity, he is one of the most highly considered priests of the Church of Indiana. He is a member of the Knights of Columbus.

LYNN CRAIG, president of the Citizens Security Company of New Albany, is descended from one of the oldest families of Scott County. His grandfather, James Craig, was a native of Kentucky, to which state the family had migrated from Virginia in pioneer times. James Craig came to Indiana and settled in Scott County about 1816, the year that Indiana entered the Union. He acquired a tract of Government land, part of which is included within the present City of Scottsburg.

Mr. Lynn Craig was born in Scott County, January 13, 1890, son of James B. and Anna (Gardner) Craig. His maternal grandfather, William Gardner, was another prominent early day resident of the county. He served with an Indiana regiment in the Union army during the Civil war and held offices as township trustee and county treasurer. James B. Craig was a lumber manufacturer and farmer.

Mr. Lynn Craig was one of the three children of his parents. He attended the city schools of Scottsburg, rounding out his education with three years in Wabash College, after which he taught in the Scottsburg High School for three years. He left school work to enter banking, as cashier of the Scottsburg Bank, in 1920, but in 1923 resigned to assist in organizing the Citizens Security Company. He was made vice president and since March, 1929, has been president of this organization, one of the substantial financial institutions of Floyd County. Mr. Craig is a member of the Indiana Bankers Association. During the World war he did his part in the Liberty Loan, War Stamp and Red Cross drives and was a volunteer in the Officers Training Camp. Mr. Craig is affiliated with the Masonic fraternity, being a Royal Arch Mason, and was the third business man of Scottsburg elected to the office of president of the Commercial Club.

He married Miss Bess Hubbard, of Scott County, daughter of William T. Hubbard and descended from a Hubbard who took up land in Scott County about 1816.

JOHN FREDERICK BEGGS, building contractor, was born and grew up in Scott County, has always lived there, but his business relationships in his contract work have covered an increasingly wide territory over Southern and Southeastern Indiana.

Mr. Beggs was born in Scott County February 15, 1881. His father, J. H. Beggs, was a Virginian by birth, lived for some years in Alabama and about 1880 came to Scott County, Indiana. He was an iron moulder by trade. His wife was Rebecca Aldridge, and they had a family of two children, J. Frederick and Etta.

J. Frederick Beggs acquired his literary education in the schools of Scottsburg, attending high school there until he was about nineteen. The basis of his business career was laid as a journeyman carpenter. From that he branched out in 1907 into building contracting. Scottsburg has been his headquarters in that work. Mr. Beggs has gained a reputation for prompt and reliable service, has been very successful in keeping together a fine organization and has repeatedly demonstrated his efficiency in handling large building enterprises. A few of his more notable contracts should be mentioned. They include the Harrison County courthouse, the Masonic Temple at Jeffersonville, the Baptist and Presbyterian churches at Lebanon, Kentucky, the high school and library at Scottsburg, grade school at Corydon, Methodist Church at Corydon, the Dubois County State Bank and the Greensburg National Bank buildings.

Mr. Beggs is an active member of the Scottsburg Commercial Club. He is a Democrat and a Baptist and is a past noble grand of the Scottsburg Lodge of Independent Order of Odd Fellows.

He married Miss Sarah Emma Bridgewater, a native of Scott County. They have two sons: Willard Maurice, a graduate of the University of Indiana, now associated with his father in the contracting business; and Lowell Frederick, a graduate of the Culver Military Academy, now a student of medicine at the Indiana University.

MARK HAYS, county clerk of Scott County, is one of the younger men in the political life of this section of the state. His people have been prominent in Scott County for several generations.

Mr. Hays' grandfather was Henry T. Hays, a native of Virginia and a first cousin of President Hayes, who spelled the family name somewhat differently. Henry T. Hays when a boy of fifteen ran away from home and went to Kentucky, and about 1847 settled in Clark County, Indiana. He was a river man in the lumber industry. In Indiana he married Tirzah Giltner, of a pioneer family of Bethlehem, this state.

The father of Mr. Mark Hays was Noble Jay Hays, a native of Scott County and a farmer and attorney by profession. He served as clerk of courts from 1897 to 1905, for two terms was prosecuting attorney of Jackson County, and was a member of the Seventysecond General Assembly as member of the Senate from the district comprising Scott, Clark and Jackson counties. Noble J. Hays married Susan Phillips, a native of Jefferson County, Indiana.

Mark Hays is one of six children. He was educated in Scott County, graduating from the Scottsburg High School in 1920. He learned the trade of baker and for several years was in the employ of Doctor Walker. In 1928 he was elected county clerk of Scott County for a four year term. He has been through the chairs of the local lodge of the Knights of Pythias and improved Order of Red Men, and is a member of Scottsburg Lodge No. 572 of the Masonic fraternity.

On June 29, 1930, he was united in marriage with Lucille Whitlock, of Scottsburg.

JOEL ATKINS HUNT. Prominent among the officials of Clark County who through energetic and capable discharge of duty are contributing to their community's welfare and prestige is Joel Atkins Hunt, of Jeffersonville, who occupies the post of county recorder. Although still a young man, his life has been a full and varied one, in which he has gained broad experience and ripened judgment, and at present is the proprietor of a prosperous real estate and insurance business.

Mr. Hunt was born in Clark County, Indiana, January 30, 1893, and is a son of Thomas Jefferson and Maggie Elizabeth Hunt, natives of Kentucky, his father being a painting contractor. The second in order of birth in a family of seven children, at the age of eight years he was contributing to the family support by working a newspaper route, although he continued his education, which was commenced in the public schools of Jeffersonville, by courses at the Jeffersonville Business College in 1915 and the Indiana University Extension course. When he entered upon his regular career it was as an inspector for iron manufacturing companies in Ohio, and in 1917 was appointed an honorary member of the United States Shipping Board, at Hoboken,

F. X. Guerre.

New Jersey. He was employed by the United States Government Quartermaster's Depot at Jeffersonville for six years as superintendent of the warehousing department, and was active as chairman of committees on Liberty Loans, Red Cross and War Savings Stamps. In 1921 Mr. Hunt embarked in the real estate and insurance business at Jeffersonville, in which he has been engaged to the present, with much success. He has placed many large and important risks with the old-line companies, and has also been the medium through which large realty negotiations have been transacted, and in all of his dealings has maintained a reputation for straightforward methods and honorable dealings. A Democrat in his political views, he has been the incumbent of several public positions, having served as deputy assessor in 1922, 1923, 1924 and 1925. In 1926 he was made attendance officer of the Clark County school board, and in 1927 was elected to the office of county recorder and in 1930 he was reelected for a second term. He has established a splendid record in this office. He is a Mason and a past master of Jeffersonville Lodge No. 340, A. F. and A. M., and is also an active member of the Knights of Pythias, in which he has passed through the majority of the chairs.

On February 16, 1921, at Jeffersonville, Mr. Hunt was united in marriage with Miss Carrie Varble Wyatt, of that city, a member of a pioneer family of Clark County which traces its ancestry in this country back to Colonial Virginia. Mr. and Mrs. Hunt have no children.

ODA L. PYLE held the office of deputy sheriff of his native county, with official headquarters in the City of New Albany, judicial center of Floyd County, and he proved a valued assistant to Sheriff William R. Helm, of whom individual mention is made on other pages of this publication. On January 6, 1929, he was appointed captain of police of New Albany.

Mr. Pyle was born on his father's farm in Floyd County and the date of his nativity was May 31, 1894. He is the sixth in a family of seven children and is a son of George and Eliza (Veron) Pyle, the former of whom was born in Kentucky and the latter in Indiana. George Pyle was reared and educated in his native state and was a young man when he came to Indiana, where he has long been actively engaged in farm enterprise in Floyd County.

Oda L. Pyle received the advantages of the district school of the home neighborhood and also those of the New Albany public schools. At the age of nineteen years he began his apprenticeship in an iron foundry at New Albany, and he continued to follow his trade sixteen years. In the early part of the year 1929 he was appointed to the office of deputy sheriff of Floyd County, and, as above noted, he is now captain of police.

To the lasting honor of Mr. Pyle will be the loyal and patriotic service that he accorded in the period of the nation's participation in the great World war. At Camp Taylor, Kentucky, he became a member of the Fifty-ninth Battalion of Light Artillery, from which he was subsequently transferred to the Six Hundred and Fifth Engineers and sent to Camp Forrest, Georgia. With his command he entered overseas service with the American Expeditionary Forces in France, where he remained eight months and where he was on active duty when the armistice brought the great world conflict to a close. After his return to his native land he received his honorable discharge, with the rank of sergeant. He is affiliated with the American Legion, the Veterans of Foreign Wars, the Junior Order United American Mechanics, and the Masons. He has membership in the union of iron, tin and steel workers and served five years as treasurer of the local union at New Albany. In a fundamental way he is a Republican, but in local affairs, where no national issues are involved, he supports men and measures meeting his approval, regardless of party lines. His name is still enrolled on the roster of eligible young bachelors in his native county.

REV. FRANCIS XAVIER GUERRE during the six years of his labors in the Gary district has demonstrated the abilities of the organizer and builder and is also a very popular churchman, with a large following of admiring friends throughout this industrial region of Northern Indiana.

Father Guerre was born at Saint Die, France, July 3, 1898, son of Alexander and Elizabeth (Jehlen) Guerre, who left France and came to America in 1907, when the son Francis X. was nine years of age. Alexander Guerre was a weaver by trade. He located at Kokomo, Indiana, and there became connected with the Pittsburgh Plate Glass Plant. He died May 20, 1929. He was active in church and a member of the Holy Name Society and Knights of Columbus. There were four sons in the family: William and Charles, both residents of Kokomo; Francis X. and George, who with their mother constitute the family circle in the priest's home at Miller, Indiana.

Francis X. Guerre attended public and parochial schools in Kokomo, and from boyhood his training was directed toward the priesthood. In 1918 he graduated from Saint Francis Seminary and in 1924 completed his theological training in Mt. St. Mary's Seminary. He was ordained a priest June 14, 1924, by Bishop Alerding, of Fort Wayne. For a short time he was assistant pastor in Saint Vincent's Church at Elkhart and on July 24, 1924, was assigned to Gary as assistant pastor of the Holy Angel's Church. On July 21, 1929, the bishop directed him to the pastorate of a new parish, called Saint Mary of the Lake, located at Miller. Here his tasks are those of building up a new congregation and parish, and in addition to his congregation at Miller he is assigned as a missionary at East Gary. Father Guerre is active in the Knights of Columbus and Catholic Order of Forresters, and while at Gary was for a time identified with the Kiwanis organization.

CHARLES F. C. HANCOCK, M. D. The Clark County medical fraternity is composed perhaps of as fine a body of members of their science as can be found anywhere. All are not as well equipped for the duties of their calling, however, as is Dr. Charles F. C. Hancock, of Jeffersonville, who has been engaged in active practice for more than forty years, and who has won a distinguished place in his profession. It is not only as a physician and surgeon that he has attained prominence and honors, but also as a participant in public affairs, to which he has given much attention during a long and successful career. He has been the incumbent of a number of offices and in 1904 was elected to the State Senate, serving with energy and ability for a term of four years in that body.

Doctor Hancock was born on a farm in Clark County, Indiana, February 3, 1867, and is a son of William and Catherine (Smith) Hancock. He belongs to one of this country's distinguished families and is a descendant of John Hancock, the Revolutionary patriot and president of Congress. John Hancock was born at Quincy, Massachusetts, January 12, 1737, and was a leading spirit in the inception of the Revolution. The attempt to arrest Hancock and Samuel Adams led to the battle of Lexington. Hancock was a member of the Continental Congress from 1775 to 1780, and from 1785 to 1786, serving as president of the body from 1775 to 1777. The Declaration of Independence as first published bore only his name. He served as governor of Massachusetts twelve years. As an orator he was eloquent, and as a presiding officer dignified and impartial. He died at Quincy, Massachusetts, October 8, 1793.

From the New England states members of the Hancock family moved to Pennsylvania, and later to Kentucky, from which state came Hardin Hancock, the paternal grandfather of Doctor Hancock. He penetrated the wilderness of Clark County, Indiana, some time during the late '40s, hewed himself a farm from the forests, and became one of that locality's early citizens in the development and progress of what was to become, in later years, one of the most productive sections of the state. His son, William Hancock, was born in Kentucky and was brought as a child to Clark County, where he was educated in the rural schools and reared to the pursuits of farming. A man of high character and sound intelligence, he took his natural place as a leader in public affairs and served many times in the offices of county commissioner and township trustee, as well as in other capacities. Mr. Hancock married Miss Catherine Smith, who was a native of Plymouth, England, and they became the parents of six children.

Charles F. C. Hancock attended the graded schools of Clark County, the high school at Seymour, Indiana, and Eikosi Academy, at Salem, Indiana, from which institution he was graduated as a member of the class of 1883. He completed his medical education at the Ohio Medical College, class of 1887, when he received the degree of Doctor of Medicine, and his first location was at Jasper, Indiana, where he remained in practice for fourteen months. In 1888 Doctor Hancock settled permanently at Jeffersonville, where he has become one of the leading physicians and surgeons of this part of the state. He is equally proficient in all branches of his calling and has a practice that is prominent and gratifyingly remunerative. He has been local surgeon for the Pennsylvania Railway for thirty-five years, and for many years has occupied a like position for the New York Central Railway Company, and has served at various times as a member of the Jeffersonville Board of Health. He is a member of the Clark County Medical Society, the Indiana State Medical Society and the American Medical Association. Since young manhood he has been an active member of the Republican party, occupying various offices, and in 1904 was sent to the State Senate, where he served in a constructive and energetic manner for four years. Fraternally he is a Mason and a member of the Knights Templar.

Doctor Hancock was united in marriage with Miss Nora Duffy, daughter of James T. Duffy, a native of Clark County, where for many years Mr. Duffy was engaged in agricultural operations, and to this union there have been born the following: James Duffy, a graduate Doctor of Medicine, University of Louisville, Kentucky, who spent his interneship at the Post-Graduate Hospital, New York City, and is now enjoying a large medical and surgical practice at Louisville; James Reynolds, a graduate of Boston Technical College, degree of Mechanical Engineer, who is now identified in an important capacity with the Murphy Construction Company, of Louisville, Kentucky; Catherine Virginia, the wife of Norman Guernsey; William, a business man of Jeffersonville, Indiana; and Charles F. C. Jr., a student at the University of Louisville. Doctor Hancock occupies splendidly appointed offices and a modern operating room at 329 Spring Street, where he also has a large and comprehensive medical library, to the perusal of which he has given much of his time, having always been an indefatigable student and tireless investigator in the realms of his science. It has been his fortune to surround himself with many congenial friends, who always meet with a warm welcome at the pleasant home of Doctor Hancock at 131 West Chestnut Street.

RALPH WALDO BRUNER, M. D. An old and professionally prominent family of Indiana, founded here in 1830, bears the name of Bruner, one that is familiar in both Jefferson and Clark counties as ably representing the medical profession. Almost a century ago Dr. Jacob Bruner came to Clark County from Tennessee, not only as a medical practitioner but also as an accredited minister of the Methodist Episcopal Church, and in both beneficent capacities he spent a long and useful life. No less prominent was his son, the late Dr. E. W.

Bruner, a native of Indiana. During the war between the states he served as a commissioned officer and later, for five years, was employed by the Government as visiting physician to the surviving Creek and Cherokee Indians in the South. He returned then to Clark County, where he passed away after sixty years of medical practice.

Succeeding his father and grandfather and preserving their high ideals of medical service and ethical principles is Dr. Ralph W. Bruner, physician and surgeon at Jeffersonville, Indiana, member of the staff of the Clark County Memorial Hospital, former health officer and an ex-president and ex-secretary of the Clark County Medical Society. Doctor Bruner was born in the State of Arkansas, February 10, 1890, and is a son of Dr. E. W. and Joetta (Brentlinger) Bruner. His grandfather, as before noted, came to Indiana about 1830, and spent the rest of his life in practicing medicine and serving as a minister of the Methodist churches at Bedford and Utica. His son, the late Dr. E. W. Bruner, married Joetta Brentlinger, and they became the parents of six children.

Ralph W. Bruner attended the public schools of Jeffersonville, and, following the tendency of the family, early took a deep interest in the science of medicine. He received careful and comprehensive training under the able preceptorship of his father, and then entered the University of Indiana, from which he was graduated as a member of the class of 1919, receiving the degree of Doctor of Medicine. During the year 1920 Doctor Bruner was an interne in the University of Louisville, Kentucky, and to prepare himself further spent about a year as a country physician near Maysville, Kentucky. During the latter part of 1921 and the year 1922 he was engaged in practice at Sellersburg, and in the latter year settled permanently at Jeffersonville, where he has since been engaged in practice. He has shown himself to be a capable diagnostician, able practitioner and skilful surgeon, and has built up a large and lucrative practice, with modernly-equipped offices at 437 Spring Street. During the World war Doctor Bruner rendered highly valuable services at the civilian hospital at Camp Knox, Kentucky. From 1926 until 1929 he served as city health officer, and at present is a member of the staff of the Clark County Memorial Hospital. He belongs also to the Clark County Medical Society, of which he formerly served as president and secretary on separate occasions; the Indiana State Medical Society and the American Medical Association. Fraternally he is a Mason and Knight Templar. Doctor Bruner is a man of public spirit and civic pride and has identified himself with many civic movements for the public welfare.

Doctor Bruner married Miss Ruth Ann Sagebiel, of Indiana, and they have three children: Ralph Waldo, Jr., John Jacob and Ruth Ann.

JULIUS CHARLES MOSER, vice president of the George Moser Leather Company, one of the substantial business concerns that give industrial and commercial precedence to his native City of New Albany, is known and valued as one of the progressive and alert business men of the younger generation in this vital city of Southern Indiana.

Mr. Moser was born at New Albany on the 24th of June, 1893, and is one of the five children born to George and Josephine (Buche) Moser, the former of whom was born in Germany and the latter in Indianapolis, Indiana. George Moser was reared and educated in his native land and was a young man when he came to the United States, after the close of the Civil war, and made settlement in Floyd County, Indiana. Here he was employed several years in a tannery, and about the year 1879 he organized the George Moser Leather Company of New Albany. The business had a modest inception, as his financial resources were limited at the time, but his careful and able direction of the enterprise in the passing years brought to it consecutive expansion in scope and importance, with the result that at the time of his death, in 1914, the company had gained rank as one of the leading industrial and commercial concerns of New Albany—a rank that it continues to maintain. George Moser was not only a successful man of affairs but also a loyal and public-spirited citizen. While he had no desire for political preferment, his civic loyalty was shown in his constructive service as a member of the local board of education, of which he was chosen the president. He was president of the George Moser Leather Company, a wholesale and jobbing concern, at the time of his death, and his sons proved worthy successors in ordering the affairs of the business. His widow still resides in New Albany. Julius C. Moser, whose public-school advantages in his native city included those of the high school and who later completed a course in the New Albany Business College, became associated with his father's business when he was eighteen years of age, and with same his brothers George, Jr., and Karl F. likewise became actively allied, the latter when he was twenty years of age. George, Jr., is now deceased; Karl F. is secretary and treasurer of the company; Julius C., as previously noted, is its vice president, and Charles E., eldest of the brothers, is the president. Karl F. married Miss Margaret Marquette, who likewise was born and reared in Indiana, and Julius C. married Miss Irma T. Morgan, who was born and reared in this state, the one child of this union being a winsome daughter, Miriam Juel.

The George Moser Leather Company controls a substantial general leather and saddlery business, with the best of modern facilities for the curing and tanning of hides, and the wholesale trade of the concern has been extended into various states of the Union aside from Indiana. The manufacturing plant of the company utilizes an area of about seven acres, the corps of employes averages about seventy, and about 100,000 hides are handled annually. The late George Moser, Sr., was president of the New Albany Trust Company at the time of his death, and had much of leadership in both civic and business affairs in the city that long represented his home and to the advancement of which he contributed in generous measure. His only daughter, Anna, is the wife of Charles P. Tighe, of New Albany.

Julius C. Moser, like his parents and other members of the family, is a communicant of the Catholic Church, and he is affiliated with the local council of the Knights of Columbus. He is a loyal and valued member of the New Albany Chamber of Commerce. When the nation became involved in the World war he enlisted for service in the United States Army and was assigned to an infantry regiment. He continued in service six months, during which he was stationed in turn at Camp Taylor, Kentucky, and Camp Pike, Arkansas.

WILLIAM ALEXANDER MARTIN. In any growing, active and thriving city one of the most important departments in the community government is that of police chief. It was not so long ago that the mention of the chief of police of a community would bring the thought of a brutal, burly and self-asserted individual, more than often intensely ignorant and at all times basking in the light of self-esteem and extreme egotism. But times have changed with the growing of a national intelligence. The successful police official, and particularly the chief, must be a man of intelligence if not of higher education. He must be able to act promptly in times of danger or public panic, must be cool-headed and deliberate in rendering his decisions, and must be possessed of a migh order of moral and physical courage; yet at the same time be a diplomat, a tactician and an executive that can handle a large body of men in a manner that will keep the machinery of law and justice moving in an orderly and smooth-running manner. Such an official is William A. Martin, who since 1902 has been identified with the police department of New Albany and who has occupied the post of chief since March 19, 1928.

Chief Martin was born on a farm in Floyd County, Indiana, May 20, 1862, and is a son of John A. and Susan (Johnson) Martin. He belongs to one of Indiana's old and honored families, which has resided in the state through five generations, or over a period of more than ninety years. His grandfather, a native of Pennsylvania, came to Indiana during the early '40s and settled on a farm in Floyd County, where he developed a good property and was known as a man of high character and sound business integrity, as well as an agriculturist who was far-sighted and progressive in his methods. John A. Martin was born on his father's farm and received a common school education, following which he learned the trade of cooper, and was em-

ployed at this occupation until the outbreak of the war between the states, when he enlisted in an Indiana volunteer infantry regiment and fought with gallantry until the close of the struggle. He then returned to his native community and followed his trade and farmed until his demise. Like his father he was held in high esteem and respect and took a good citizen's part in civic affairs. He married Miss Susan Johnson, a native of Indiana, and to this union there were born three children: William A., of this review; and Frank and Ollie, both deceased.

William A. Martin attended the graded schools until he was fifteen years of age, at which time occurred the death of his father, whose life was undoubtedly shortened by the privations and hardships of his military service. Young William, being the eldest child, left school at that time and began to shoulder the burdens and hardships of manhood in assisting in the support of the family. He continued to be engaged in farming for the next eight years, but in 1885, when twenty-three years of age, was attracted by the romance of railroading and took a position with the old Air Line Railway, in the service of which he remained for three years. His next connection was with the K. & I. Terminal Railway, and when he left that road had won promotion to the position of yardmaster. In 1895 he joined the Monon Railway, and won advancement with that line through ability, fidelity and industry until 1900, at which time his railroading career was cut short by a serious injury and for the next two years he was compelled to live retired. Having recovered from his accident, in 1902 he was appointed a patrolman of the New Albany police department, and later was advanced to captain, subsequently passing through higher grades until March 19, 1928, when he was made chief of police, which position he has since held. During the twenty-seven or more years of his service Chief Martin has established an excellent record as a fearless officer and a capable enforcer of law and order. Since assuming the duties of chief he has improved the department in a number of ways, both as to efficiency and strength and as to morale of the men who compose the force. New Albany is a well-policed and law-abiding community, and much of the credit for this desirable state of affairs is due to the energy and executive capacity of Chief Martin. He has established stanch and lasting friendships with the leading business and professional men of the community, who have placed their faith in the protection of the police and who have not been betrayed. The force consists of fifteen men and constitutes one of the best drilled and disciplined bodies of its kind in the state. Chief Martin belongs to the International Association of Police Chiefs; Pythagoras Lodge No. 355, A. F. and A. M., and the Improved Order of Red Men.

Chief Martin married Miss Mary Cook, a native of Floyd County, and to this union there have been born two daughters: Miss

Ollie, a successful business woman of Louisville, Kentucky; and Blanche, the wife of R. M. Sloan, a railroad man of New Albany, who has two children, Ollie and Katherine.

LOUIS THORN. While Louis Thorn has been a resident of Floyd County for many years and among its most enterprising and substantial citizens, his business interests have been so extensive and widespread as to entitled him to claim identity with the great State of Indiana. For a long period he has been connected with the cement products business in several states and among the largest dealers of the enterprising men whose vigor and energy have made this one of the leading industries of the state. The career of the president and owner of L. Thorn & Company, of New Albany, adds another to the many illustrations which Indiana has furnished to the world of the results which are attained by intelligence, tact and perseverance when applied to the building up of a business under favoring conditions. It is true that during this period unusual opportunities have opened to business men, but they have only yielded the meed of success to those who have had the sagacity to perceive them and the boldness to push them to their best results.

Mr. Thorn was born at Sellersburg, Clark County, Indiana, October 11, 1875, and is a son of Charles and Katharine (Schaffer) Thorn. His grandfather was Frank Thorn, a native of Germany, who immigrated to the United States as a young married man and settled in Indiana, where he passed the remainder of his life in agricultural operations. Charles Thorn was born in Germany and was a young child when brought by his parents to Indiana, where he was educated in the common schools and as a youth took up farming, a vocation in which he was engaged in Clark and Harrison counties during the remainder of his active career. He married Katharine Schaffer, who was born in Harrison County, and they became the parents of four children.

Louis Thorn attended the public schools of Floyd County and was reared on the home farm, but subsequently became interested in the cement business, and for sixteen years was employed by various construction companies in building all manner of structures, including the cantonments at Camps Taylor and Knox during the World war. In 1923 he founded the firm of L. Thorn & Company, of New Albany, of which he has been the owner and active manager to the present. This concern manufactures cement products, including ornamental cement articles and cement blocks, and gives employment to sixteen people, its territory covering the State of Kentucky and the southern part of Indiana. Mr. Thorn enjoys an excellent reputation in business circles as a man of good judgment and high integrity. He is a member of the Chamber of Commerce and the East End Civic Club, and as such takes an active part in all worth-while movements. His modern plant, located at 1319 Vincennes Street, covers about 20,000 square feet of ground, and is equipped with the latest machinery and improvements. Mr. Thorn is an active and influential Republican, but has never sought public honors.

He married Miss Elizabeth Linnert, of Floyd County, Indiana, and they have five children: Charles, a graduate of the New Albany High School and a business college, who is now associated with the Ford Motor Company of Detroit, Michigan, married Marjorie Blackston, and has two children, Aletha and Doris; Roy, a graduate of the New Albany High School, who is associated in business with his father as a member of the firm of L. Thorn & Company; Pearl, also educated at that school and likewise associated with her father; and Willard and Lavena, who are still attending school.

JAMES WITCOMB BURNS. The legal profession of Lake County contains its full quota of brilliant members of the profession, who have devoted their lives to the law and its interpretation and have lent charm and dignity to a somewhat dry and often tiring calling. Prominent among this class is found James W. Burns, who has been engaged in a constantly growing practice at Gary for nearly two decades, and who as a lawyer and citizen has developed his abilities and activities until he has become a prominent figure for great usefulness.

Mr. Burns was born at Fremont, Sanilac County, Michigan, May 16, 1874, and is a son of Moses and Bridget (O'Connor) Burns. His parents, natives of County Wexford, Ireland. accompanied their respective parents to the United States, and here grew to manhood and womanhood and were educated in the public schools of Michigan, where they were married. For many years Mr. Burns carried on farming and stock raising in Fremont Township, Sanilac County, also serving capably as state agent and as superintendent of the poor farm. capacities in which he showed himself capable, active and humane. One of the foremost Republicans of his locality, his home was the meeting-place for governors, senators and other high officials, and at all times he himself was active in public and civic affairs. Mr. Burns was a faithful member of the Roman Catholic Church. He was fond of travel, and in 1907 made a trip back to his old home in Erin, making the journey with his son James W. He died in 1912 and was buried in the cemetery at Croswell, Michigan, and his worthy wife, who followed him to the Great Beyond in 1925, rests at his side. They were the parents of seven children: W. E., a retired business man of Croswell, Michigan, who died in April, 1931; John V., deceased; Anna, the widow of Bartley McNulty; Moses, who is deceased; Thomas, who is deceased; Lawrence, of Detroit, Michigan; and James W.

James W. Burns acquired his education in the public schools of Michigan and Illinois, where he attended the township schools of

Fremont Township and Bryant and Stratton's Business College. He likewise took a special course in English at Chicago and then entered the law department of Georgetown University, Washington, D. C., from which he was duly graduated with the degree of Bachelor of Laws as a member of the class of 1908. Two years later the degree of Master of Laws was conferred upon him by the same institution. Admitted to the bar in Chicago in 1911, he moved to Gary in the same year and has been engaged constantly in practice of the highest and best kind, having been admitted to the Supreme Court in 1913. He belongs to the American Bar Association, the Indiana State Bar Association, the District Bar Association and the Gary Bar Association and is accounted one of the most learned, alert and shrewd lawyers engaged in general practice at Gary, where he has well-appointed and commodious offices at 738 Broadway. Mr. Burns' practice has carried him into all the courts, in which he has been identified with some very important litigation. A leading member of the Knights of Columbus, he is president of the Knights of Columbus Noonday Club, and likewise belongs to the Benevolent and Protective Order of Elks, the Loyal Order of Moose, the Harrison Republican Club, the Kiwanis' Club and the Press Club of Lake County. His religious affiliation is with Holy Angels Catholic Church.

Mr. Burns is single. He is active in civic affairs and was deputy prosecuting attorney for four years, from 1916 to 1920. He was assistant city attorney for five years, under Mayor R. O. Johnson's second and third terms, and in 1920 was originally a candidate for the office of prosecuting attorney, but withdrew from the race. During the World war he was active in all the drives, Red Cross, Liberty, etc., and did his full duty as a patriotic citizen.

JAMES LEWIS BOTTORFF. While the bar at Jeffersonville, Indiana, perhaps lays no claim to being made up entirely of John Marshall's, it is able to point with pride to a membership far beyond the ordinary equipment in legal matters, and one of its able and valued members is James L. Bottorff, twice prosecuting attorney of Clark County. Mr. Bottorff comes from an old and patriotic family of America, one of his ancestors, Henry Bottorff, fighting at Bunker Hill, Brandywine and Germantown during the war of the American Revolution, enduring the rigors of Valley Forge with General Washington, and who penetrated into the Indiana wilderness in 1785 and met his death from wild animals or savage Indians. Another, Henry Bottorff, Jr., stood side by side of William Henry Harrison at the battle of Tippecanoe. Mr. Bottorff is a native of Indiana, has mainly passed his life here, and Jeffersonville has been his home for many years. In addition to handling the responsibilities of a large and remunerative law practice he takes an active part in civic matters, is a member of the Chamber of Commerce, and during the

World war was food administrator for Clark County and served in many other important capacities.

James L. Bottorff was born January 6, 1886, on a farm in Clark County, Indiana, and is a son of Moses E. and Amanda (Hill) Bottorff. He comes of a family which was founded in America in its early Colonial history by Adam Bottorff, the great-great-great-great-grandfather of James L. Bottorff. The latter's great-great-great-grandfather was Martin Bottorff, who lived for some years in Pennsylvania, where was born Rev. John Henry Bottorff, the great-great-grandfather of James L. Bottorff. Rev. John Henry Bottorff was a minister of the Reformed Church and came as an early pioneer to what was then the wilderness of the Northwest, making a home in Jefferson County in 1785. There he passed the remaining years of his life, tilling the soil and preaching among the early settlers and endeavoring to make Indian converts. He met a martyr's death in 1805, being killed either by wild animals or the red savages.

Henry Bottorff, the great-grandfather of James L. Bottorff, was born in Indiana, and became one of the early millers of the state. In 1811 he joined the forces of William Henry Harrison and took part in the famous battle of Tippecanoe, in which the white frontiersmen defeated decisively a much larger number of Indians. He came by his military courage naturally, as his father had been a soldier under Washington at Bunker Hill, Brandywine and Germantown. Lewis Bottorff, the grandfather of James L. Bottorff, was born in Indiana, where he was engaged in farming throughout his life, and also took part in flatboat trading prior to the war between the states. He married Mary C. Congleton, of Roanoke County, Virginia, and among their children was Moses E. Bottorff, who was born in Indiana and spent his entire life in agricultural operations in Clark County. He married Amanda Hill, and they became the parents of five children.

James L. Bottorff attended the public schools of Clark County, including the high school at Utica, and pursued his law education at the Jefferson School of Law, Louisville, Kentucky, from which he was graduated in 1910 with the degree of Bachelor of Laws. Prior to this, in order to earn the money for his professional tuition, he had served as a telegraph operator for the Baltimore & Ohio Railway, at Watson, Indiana. Although he had been admitted to the bar May 18, 1909, prior to his graduation, he did not settle down permanently to practice at Jeffersonville until January 1, 1912, but since then has built up a large and important clientele, with well-appointed offices in the Beck Building. He is recognized as a thorough and capable legist, and in 1920 and again in 1922 was elected to the office of prosecuting attorney of Clark County. He is attorney for the Clark County State Bank, local attorney for the Baltimore & Ohio Railway, town attorney for the town of Clarksville and a member of the Clark

County Bar Association and the Indiana State Bar Association. He is a Mason and a member of the Chamber of Commerce. As a member of one of the old and honored families of the state he takes a great interest in the affairs of the Indiana Historical Association, to which he also belongs. He is also a member of the Indiana Pioneer Association. Mr. Bottorff is also eligible to membership in the Sons of the American Revolution, being able to trace his ancestry back in a straight line to Ensign Henry Bottorff, who in 1780 was a member of Capt. Michael Wolf's Company of Berks County (Pennsylvania) Militia. During the World war he served as food administrator for Clark County and chairman of the War Savings campaigns in Jefferson and other townships.

On November 28, 1912, Mr. Bottorff was united in marriage with Miss Edna Lewis, daughter of Doctor Lewis, a native of Clark County, and to this union there were born two children: James Montgomery, born February 25, 1915, and Robert Graham, born July 18, 1917, both of whom are attending school. Mr. Bottorff is a member of the Christian Church.

JOSEPH M. WALTERMANN is a member of the firm Unser & Waltermann, funeral directors at Richmond, Indiana, and it was in that city that he was born and reared. His people were among the pioneer Catholic citizens of Wayne County.

Mr. Waltermann was born at Richmond March 24, 1884, son of Henry A. and Gertrude (Theobold) Waltermann. His father was born in Richmond, Indiana, while his mother was a native of Mount Morris, New York. The paternal grandparents were Frederick and Johanna (Brockamp) Waltermann, natives of Germany, Johanna being a daughter of Joseph Brockamp. In 1841 the Brockamp family settled at Richmond, Indiana, and Joseph Brockamp built the house on South Fourth Street in which mass was first said for Catholic services in this community. Frederick Waltermann came to this country in 1852 from Germany. The maternal grandparents of Mr. Waltermann were George and Genevieve (Rist) Theobold, also natives of Germany, who settled at Mount Morris, New York. George Theobold was a stock buyer, and after moving to Saint Louis, Missouri, enlisted in the Union army. After the war he came to Wayne County, Indiana, and lived at Richmond until his death. One sister, Mrs. Helen van Nuys, also lives in Richmond.

Henry A. Waltermann after his marriage in Richmond followed the trade of casket varnisher for the J. M. Hutton Casket Company until appointed market master in 1907. At the time of his death in 1909 he was city market master. He was survived by his widow, who makes her home with her son.

Joseph M. Waltermann, who has never married, grew up in Richmond, attended Saint Andrews parochial school and the Finley public school. At the age of seventeen he learned the trade of casket trimmer. After the death of his father he filled out the unexpired term of market master for one year, returning to the casket company and remaining until 1915. Mr. Waltermann has been in the undertaking business since 1915, at first as a member of the firm of Jordan, McManus, Hunt & Waltermann, and now as Unser & Waltermann. Their establishment, at 32 South Eleventh Street, represents a complete home for funerals, with display room and room for visitors. It is beautified with large colonial columns, the finest in the city, and funeral services are held in the spacious rooms. Mr. Waltermann is a member of Saint Andrew's Catholic Church and has been sacristan of the church since 1899. In 1913 he was elected a member of the City Council from the First Ward and has been the representative of the First Ward's interests in the city legislative department consecutively to the present time. Mr. Waltermann is a Democrat, and a member of the B. P. O. Elks, Fraternal Order of Eagles, German Beneficial Union, Knights of Columbus, Knights of Saint John, is president of the Young Men's Institute, and a member of Saint Joseph's Benevolent Association.

NEWTON AUGUST GREENE is expressing in his administration as mayor of New Albany, the fine little city that is the judicial center of Floyd County, the same vital and resourceful loyalty that has marked his achievement in connection with business affairs. He has been a resident of New Albany since his boyhood and when he was a lad of ten years he aided in the support of the family by daily service in making deliveries on a local newspaper route. That the former newsboy of New Albany has become mayor of this city indicates how well he has wrought out his career of usefulness in the passing years and also determines the high estimate placed upon him in the community in which he is best known.

Though he is a scion of one of the pioneer families of Indiana, Mr. Greene reverts to the old Bluegrass State as the place of his nativity. He was born at Hawesville, Hancock County, Kentucky, July 24, 1866, and is a son of Prof. George K. and Molly (Lewis) Greene. Prof. George K. Greene was a man of remarkable intellectuality and high scientific attainments, as is evidenced by the fact that he was credited as being one of the twelve foremost geologists of the world. The Professor was born in Clark County, Indiana, a son of George and Eunice M. (Parker) Greene, the former a native of England and the latter of Scotland. George Greene became a pioneer shipbuilder at Jeffersonville, Indiana, on the Ohio River, he having there settled in 1818, and having become one of the influential citizens of the community, as attested by his having been one of the early mayors of that city.

Prof. George K. Greene acquired his advanced scientific education almost entirely by self-application to reading, study and research, and he gained wide reputation in the domain of geology and paleontology, in which he became an authority. He wrote twenty volumes on paleontology and geology, served as a collegiate professor along these lines, and in the period of the '70s held the office of state geologist of Indiana, a position that he retained about ten years, besides being a teacher of geology at Corydon, the pioneer capital city of Indiana. He received high recognition by the English Society for the Advancement of Science, as well as by the great British Museum and by leading scientific societies in other countries, including the United States. Both he and his wife passed the closing years of their lives in their native State of Indiana, their children having been eight in number. Like many others who have devoted their lives to science and to educational work of enduring value Professor Greene never achieved more than limited financial success, but his success was greater than this, for he gave much to the store of human knowledge and to the advancement of science.

Newton A. Greene was six years of age when his parents returned from Kentucky to their native State of Indiana, where they finally established the family home at New Albany. Here he profited by the advantages of the public schools, including the high school, while his was the further privilege of being reared in a home of distinctive culture. It has already been noted that he early assumed his share of individual responsibility in aiding in the support of the family, and when he was sixteen years of age he here engaged in the produce business on a most modest scale. Two years later, when he was but eighteen years of age, he amplified his enterprise into one of wholesale order, and he continued a leading representative of this line of business at New Albany during the long period of twenty-six years.

Mr. Greene proved progressive and resourceful not only as a business man but also as a public-spirited citizen, and he has ever been a stalwart in the local ranks of the Democratic party. He gave effective administration as mayor of New Albany during the period of 1910-14, and the people of the community were mindful of this when he was again made candidate for and elected to this office in 1926, his present term as mayor expiring in December, 1929. During his membership in the City Council Mayor Greene represented the Fifth Ward—1907-08—besides having previously served one term. As mayor he is ex-officio judge of the municipal Police Court, and as a jurist he is called upon also to try cases pertaining to violations of the Federal prohibition laws. In the Masonic fraternity he is affiliated with the four York Rite bodies, including the local Commandery of Knights Templar, besides being a Noble of the Mystic Shrine. He has been active in politics in this section of Indiana and has served as a member of the Democratic committee of Floyd County. His wife, whose maiden name was Lesa Taylor, was born in the State of Arkansas, her father and one of her brothers having become clergymen of the Methodist Episcopal Church, and her father having received the honorary degree of Doctor of Divinity. Lesa, only child of Mr. and Mrs. Greene, died at the age of nine years.

MARION BURCH, county treasurer of Monroe County, is a member of a family that has been in this section of Indiana for nearly a century. The farm on which Mr. Burch was born was taken up by his grandfather as a Government claim.

Mr. Burch was born August 13, 1866, in Indian Creek Township, son of Hiram and Nancy H. (Sparks) Burch and grandson of Joel and Matilda (Burch) Burch. His grandparents were of the same name but their families were not related. Joel Burch came from North Carolina to Indiana in 1836 and entered the land which has been in the possession of his descendants for nearly a century. Both Hiram and Nancy Burch are still living, having reached very advanced years. Hiram was born on the old homestead October 22, 1840, and his wife was born in 1838. Hiram Burch grew up under pioneer conditions, had a limited education, but made a success of life and developed a well-improved farm of 200 acres. The old log cabin is still standing on the farm.

Marion Burch attended the Big Springs School in Indian Creek Township and the Yo Ho School, where he completed his education. All the time he was in school he had a regular routine of duties on his father's farm. After he was twenty-two he began working out among neighboring farmers and when he was twenty-six he engaged in the mercantile business at Sanford. He was there two years and in 1901 came to Bloomington. In 1903 he went with the Neeld Hardware Company and was with that business twenty-two years, its manager for twelve years of this time.

Mr. Burch in May, 1928, accepted the Democratic nomination for the office of county treasurer and was elected in the following November. By appointment he served as a member of the first County Council of Monroe County. He was also appointed and served four years as a member of the Bloomington police force. He has been very active in the Baptist Church, of which he is a deacon, and is a member of the Knights of Pythias.

Mr. Burch married, September 29, 1892, Miss Lillian H. Pofford, daughter of S. E. and Mary (Hostetter) Pofford. Her mother is deceased and her father still lives on his farm a mile east of Sanford in Van Buren Township. Mr. and Mrs. Burch have four children and several grandchildren: Irene is the wife of John R. East, and their children are John E., Robert G. and Frederick B.; Clifford married Mayme Skelton; Cledith is the wife of W. W. Franklin and has two children, William D. and Hannah Sue; and Miss Bernice, a graduate of Indiana University, is now teaching at Knightstown, Indiana.

Robert N. Wimmer M.D.

ROBERT NORRIS WIMMER, M. D. The medical fraternity of Gary has in the person of Robert Norris Wimmer, M. D., an able representative and one who has gained his present prominent position through none of the arts of the charlatan, but by reason of native and acquired talent, deep study and thorough keeping abreast of the advancements made in modern medicine and surgery. His career has been a useful one, including service in the Medical Reserve Corps during the World war, and his professional standing and personal reputation are high.

Doctor Wimmer was born at Lamar, Missouri, December 20, 1886, and is a son of Dr James Monroe and Carrie (Norris) Wimmer. His paternal grandparents, James and Ma thilda Wimmer, natives of New York State, came as a young married couple to Grant County, Indiana, where James Wimmer was engaged in farming for some years, subsequently moving to Marion County, this state, and eventually to Lamar, Missouri, where he rounded out a successful and honorable career. He and his wife were the parents of five sons and one daughter: Dr. James Monroe, William, Glenn, Scott, Newton and Adeline.

James Monroe Wimmer was born on his father's farm at Lamar, Missouri, where he attended the public schools, subsequently becoming a student at Hobart University, Washington, D. C., where he graduated with the degree of Doctor of Medicine. With the exception of a short time at Lamar, Missouri, his entire professional career was passed at Marion, Indiana, where he built up a large and profitable practice and won the confidence and esteem of the people of the community. He was a member of the various organizations of his profession, had several social and fraternal connections, and was known for his public-spirited identification with and support of numerous measures for the public benefit. His death in 1900 removed one of his community's sterling citizens. In 1859, in Cass County, Indiana, Doctor Wimmer was united in marriage with Miss Carrie Norris, who was born near Logansport, Indiana, a daughter of William Norris and his wife, natives of Pennsylvania, who migrated to Cass County during the pioneer history of that locality and there passed the remainder of their lives. They were the parents of four children, of whom Carrie was reared and educated at Logansport. She still survives her husband as a resident of Gary and is active in the work of the Methodist Episcopal Church. She and her husband became the parents of three children: Nell, teacher of mathematics at Emerson High School, Gary; Harry, who died at the age of eighteen years; and Dr. Robert Norris, of this review.

Robert Norris Wimmer acquired his early education in the public schools of Marion, graduating from high school as a member of the class of 1904. At that time he took a position as chemist in the soap department of Swift & Company, Union Stock Yards, Chicago, remaining two years, following which he entered the employ of the Bell Telephone Company, Chicago, and worked as an auditor three years. Feeling that he was not making satisfactory progress, Doctor Wimmer then entered the preparatory college of the Young Men's Christian Association, at Chicago, and graduated from the University of Chicago with the degree of Bachelor of Science in 1918. In the meantime, in 1917, he had enlisted in the Medical Reserve Corps. and when he was honorably discharged, a few days after the armistice, he had gained much knowledge and information that were greatly to help him in his professional career. His medical education was completed at Rush Medical College, from which famous institution he was graduated in 1920 with the degree of Doctor of Medicine, but he continued his work and studies for two years at the Presbyterian Hospital, then serving an eighteen months' internship at Michael Reese Hospital, also of Chicago. In 1923 he took up his permanent residence at Gary, where he has since built up a large and lucrative general practice in medicine and surgery, with well-appointed offices at 600 Broadway. Doctor Wimmer is acknowledged to be an expert diagnostician, an able practitioner and a skilled and steady-handed surgeon and has gained an enviable standing in his calling for high professional ability and ethics. He belongs to the Lake County Medical Society, the Indiana State Medical Society and the American Medical Association. Fraternally he is affiliated with Cornerstone Lodge No. 875, A. F. and A. M., of Chicago, and likewise holds membership in the Gary Country Club and the Commercial Club and Chamber of Commerce. In his political faith he remains independent, voting for the man and measure rather than for the party. His religious connection is with the First Methodist Episcopal Church.

At Crown Point, Indiana, February 21, 1925, Doctor Wimmer was united in marriage with Miss Marguerite Zeitsch, a daughter of Julius and Sophia (Knorr) Zeitsch, of 2809 Logan Boulevard, Chicago, natives of Germany. Mr. Zeitsch taught a boys' school in London, England, for some years. Mrs. Zeitsch came to the United States as a child with her parents and received her education in Chicago, where she had resided for the past fifty-seven years. After settling in Chicago Mr. Zeitsch embarked in the mercantile business, and is now engaged with a large wholesale house and is a prominent resident of the Windy City. He is very active in the Masons and the Independent Order of Odd Fellows and a citizen of public spirit and civic pride. Mrs. Wimmer enjoyed unusual educational advantages, and after graduating from high school specialized in music at the Chicago Conservatory of Music. She is active in musical circles of Gary, where she taught music for several years, as she did also at Chicago, and is popular in club affairs. Showing her versatility is the fact that for several years she was private secretary to the president of the Universal Portland Cement Company. To Doctor and Mrs. Wimmer there have been born two children: Barbara Jean and James Robert. As has been before noted, Doctor Wimmer has been prominent in various civic affairs. When he can spare the time from his professional and other duties he enjoys a game or two of golf, but probably is more greatly interested in fishing and is an enthusiastic member of the Izaak Walton League of America. He is an alumnus of Michael Reese Hospital, Chicago, belongs to the Phi Chi medical fraternity, and is active in the Gary Country Club.

WILLIAM ROBERT BAKER. The individual who works perfunctorily may attain a certain degree of prosperity and even some reputation, but it is the man who exerts his every effort and who is in sympathy and understanding with his labor who will be found occupying a real position in his chosen field. The foregoing is one of the reasons for the undeniable success of William R. Baker, who within the space of a few short years has developed a large and lucrative patronage in the business of dealing in contractors' supplies. From modest beginnings he has worked his way steadily and faithfully upward, and while gaining material prosperity and success has secured and held the confidence and friendship of his associates and those who have come into contact with him.

William R. Baker was born at Omaha, Nebraska, August 15, 1897, and is a son of Samuel and Sallie (Lohrman) Baker. His father, a native of Russia, was a child when he was brought to the United States by his parents, who settled at Omaha, where the grandfather was engaged in the grocery and market business in a small way. Samuel Baker received a common school education and when still a youth began to assist his father in the elder man's business operations. When he came into control of the enterprise he enlarged it gradually, as his financial condition would permit, and eventually became one of the substantial men of his community, and a valued, desirable citizen who supported with enthusiasm all measures for the welfare of his community. He died in 1905 and was buried at Saint Louis, where he had been in the same line of business since 1900, while his worthy widow still survives him and makes her home at the Mound City. There were twelve children in the family, of whom William R. was the eleventh in order of birth.

One of the younger of a family of numerous children, William R. Baker had only ordinary advantages in his youth, but applied himself assiduously to his studies and took advantage of all his opportunities, with the result that he obtained a good practical working education in the grades and Fisher High School of Saint Louis. On leaving school he became associated with his father in the grocery and meat market business, and continued with the elder man for a number of years. He then joined his brother-in-law, L. Weiss, of Chicago,

in the leather goods manufacturing business, and after familiarizing himself with this line of work was in charge of the factory in the Illinois metropolis for five years. In 1924 Mr. Baker severed his connection with this concern and located at Hammond, where he became a salesman and junior partner with the McLaughlin Mill Supply Company, with which concern he remained three years. At the end of that period he decided to engage in business on his own account and accordingly came to Gary, where he established himself in business in the line of handling building specialties and contractors' supplies. The firm is William R. Baker & Company, of which Mr. Baker is president, and the commodious office and display and stock rooms are located at 735 Washington Street. This is the only business of its kind at Gary, and Mr. Baker has built up a large patronage which extends over a wide area of country. He has been prompt in the fulfillment of his contracts and honorable in all of his dealings and thereby has won prestige and the confidence of those with whom he has had dealings. Mr. Baker has always taken an active part in civic affairs, and is vice president of the Young Men's Hebrew Club of Gary and a member of the B'nai B'rith and the Lincoln Hills Country Club. His political allegiance is given to the candidates and principles of the Republican party, but he has not sought nor cared for public office or political preferment. During the World war he was active in all of the various drives working for the support of American arms and was, although married, subject to the draft and had passed the physical examination for the army. He had already received his railroad ticket and had made all preparations to go to the training camp when the armistice was signed and therefore he was not called for duty.

On September 29, 1918, at Chicago, Illinois, Mr. Baker was united in marriage with Miss Celia Meizel, daughter of Joseph and Reva (Bruce) Meizel, both of whom were born and reared in Russia, where they received public school educations. Shortly after their marriage in Russia Mr. and Mrs. Meizel immigrated to the United States and settled at Chicago, where Mr. Meizel established himself in the tailoring, cleaning and dyeing business. During the many years that he was engaged in this line of effort he built up a large and lucrative business through industry and integrity, but for a number of years has lived in retirement, enjoying the fruits of his early labors. Mrs. Meizel died March 6, 1921, and is buried in Waldheim Cemetery, Chicago. Mrs. Baker received her education in the public schools of Chicago, and after her graduation from high school secured a secretarial position, in which she was employed for several years prior to her marriage. She takes an active part in the business of her husband and is a member of the Sisterhood of the Bethel Temple, Gary. Mr. and Mrs. Baker are the parents of three children: Arthur Sheldon, born March 11, 1920, attending the Horace Mann School; Regina, born December 7, 1921, also attending that school; and Leighton, born June 10, 1929.

WILLIAM METTLER. The magic growth of Gary from an unimportant straggling village to a great industrial, commercial and financial center created a need for men of the greatest ability in every line and furnished ample opportunity for the development of every latent ability and energy there was in those who sought the city as the scene of their activities. In few cities have there been won more notable successes, and the successful men are not confined to the professions, to commerce, to finance or to industry, but uniformly extend all along the line in every calling where intellect, enterprise and energy may with reward. The rapidity with which the city's commerce and manufactures increased and leaped into importance paved the way for a demonstration of the very best skill and ability among the financiers, and that they were equal to the occasion the record shows. With the growth and development of the automobile industry many of the younger generation have turned their attention to this line, and one who has won well-merited success is William Mettler, proprietor of the Packard Auto Agency.

Mr. Mettler was born May 5, 1893, at Hammond, in Lake County, Indiana, and is a son of John J. and Elizabeth (Staub) Mettler. His father, a native of Switzerland, received his education in that country's public schools and accompanied his parents to the United States when still a youth, the family settling at Chicago some time after the close of the war between the states. Mr. Mettler established himself in the bakery and confectionery business at Chicago, and there married Elizabeth Staub, who was also born in Switzerland and came to the United States in young womanhood with her parents. For a time they resided at Chicago, but subsequently went to Hammond, Indiana, where Mr. Mettler continued in the same line for about thirty years. In 1914 he retired from active participation in business and returned to Chicago, where he died in 1917. Mrs. Mettler afterward resided at Van Nuys, Colorado. They were devout members of the Methodist Eiscopal Church, to which they were generous contributors all their lives, and Mr. Mettler was a member of the Masonic fraternity. To Mr. and Mrs. Mettler there were born three children: Elizabeth, the wife of Frederick Becker, of Chicago, Illinois; Ernest J., who is connected with the New York Central Railroad at Hammond, Indiana; and William, of this review.

William Mettler attended the grade and high schools of Hammond, graduating from the latter as a member of the class of 1912, and immediately thereafter secured employment with the New York Central Railroad, with which he was identified for three years. He then embarked in the wholesale grocery business at Chicago, and continued to be engaged therein for five years, but in 1922 disposed of his interests to engage in the automobile business at Gary and Hammond, under the firm style of William Mettler Packard Automobile Agency, with offices, plants and salesrooms at 121 East Fifth Avenue, Gary, and 429 Fayette Street, Hammond. He has beautiful show rooms and sales and service departments at both addresses and has built up a splendid business through industry, energy and good executive management. Mr. Mettler is one of the thoroughly informed men of his line of business and stands high in the estimation of his business associates, who have found his integrity and probity beyond reproach. He has formed an indissoluble connection with the buying public of the two cities in which his business interests lie, and this has its foundation in confidence and genuine friendship. Mr. Mettler has several business connections and is a member of the board of directors of the Beneficial Loan Association. He stands high in Masonry, belonging to McKinley Lodge No. 712, A. F. and A. M.; Hammond Chapter No. 117, R. A. M., the Scottish Rite, at Fort Wayne, Indiana, thirty-second degree, and Orak Temple, A. A. O. N. M. S., of Hammond, and belongs also to Hammond Lodge No. 485, Benevolent and Protective Order of Elks, the Gary Country Club, the Gary Commercial Club and Chamber of Commerce and the Midland Club of Chicago. For several years he was also active in the Gary Kiwanis Club, but has given up his membership in that organization. Politically he is a Republican and his religious faith makes him a Christian Scientist. During the World war he was active in the sale of Liberty Bonds and in all war activities, and in peace times has given his moral, physical and financial support to all worthy movements of a civic, educational or religious character.

On September 17, 1916, at Hammond, Mr. Mettler was united in marriage with Miss Lytta Grace McMahan, who was born in Indiana, a daughter of Asa C. and Margaret (Chase) McMahan. Mr. McMahan, who was for years a conductor in the service of the New York Central lines, died about 1920 and was laid to rest in the cemetery at Meadville, Pennsylvania, while Mrs. McMahan still survives and makes her home with her daughter and son-in-law, Mr. and Mrs. Mettler, of this review. Mrs. Mettler attended the grade and high schools of Hammond and is an earnest Christian Scientist and a popular member of the Gary Woman's Club. To Mr. and Mrs. Mettler there has been born one daughter: Lytta Jane, who is attending Horace Mann School at Gary.

ANTHONY G. BIEBERICK. Not the least in importance of the activities which occupy the attention and labors of mankind are those which cater to our aesthetic natures. Among these there is none which contributes in a greater or more beautiful degree to the pleasures of existence as the vocation of the florist, and in this connection mention is due to the career of Anthony G. Bieberick, who has spent the entire period of his active life in this vocation and who is now the owner of the largest greenhouses in Huntington County, situated in Huntington.

Mr. Bieberick was born at Fort Wayne, Indiana, September 18, 1883, and is a son of Henry Bieberick, an early pioneer of Fort Wayne, who is now deceased. Anthony G. Bieberick attended the public schools of Fort Wayne and commenced work as a youth as an employe of the Vesey Greenhouse of his native city, where he remained for several years. From Fort Wayne he went to Columbia City, Indiana, where he was associated with a florist for three years, and in 1908 took up his permanent residence at Huntington, which has since been his home. At the time of his arrival he embarked in business on his own account in a modest way, but soon found it necessary to enlarge his greenhouses, and from that time to the present he has been constantly developing his business until he now has 25,000 square feet under glass, this being the largest greenhouse in Huntington County, located at 407-17 Graystone Avenue, the office and retail store being at 12 West Market Street. Mr. Bieberick's business is not merely a local one, as he ships plants, shrubs, trees, flowers, seeds, etc., all over Indiana and to other states, his product having gained a splendid reputation. He has established himself strongly in the confidence of the public as a man of integrity who makes no false representations and who lives strictly up to the letter of his contracts. Promptness in delivery, adequacy of service and high quality of goods have combined to gain him success and reputation, and what prosperity he has secured, and it has not been inconsiderable, has come through the medium of his own efforts. Mr. Bieberick is a member of the National Association of Florists, the Benevolent and Protective Order of Elks and the Loyal Order of Moose. As a hobby he is greatly fond of fishing, and whenever his business can spare him he takes trips, armed with rod and reel, to the streams, lakes and rivers. He has been active in civic work in a number of movements, and is a consistent member of the local Christian Church.

Mr. Bieberick married Miss Lillian Clark, a native of Whitley County, Indiana. They have no children and reside at 531 West Park Drive.

LE ROY POPE is an Indiana business man, representative of a family that has been in the state since pioneer times. Mr. Pope formerly resided at Williamsport, where for many years he has conducted a monument business. In 1931 he moved to Crawfordsville and established business there in addition to the Williamsport office. His first occupation was the trade of stone cutter, and he was an expert worker in stone and for many years superintended stone construction contracts.

He was born in Benton County, Indiana, February 11, 1886. His grandfather, Robert Morton Pope, came to Indiana from North Carolina. The father of Le Roy Pope is James F. Pope, who was born in Grant County and formerly was a blacksmith and machinist. James F. Pope married Harriet A. Anderson, who was born in Warren County, Indiana. Her father, James Anderson, came from Warren County, Ohio, to Warren County, Indiana, in 1853. James Anderson was a sergeant in Company D, Eighty-sixth Indiana Infantry, during the Civil war. He was wounded in one battle, was captured and spent a term of confinement in Libby Prison at Richmond. James F. Pope and wife had four children: Vaughn L., now deceased, Le Roy, Lanford C. and James. Both Lanford and James are World war veterans. Lanford, who is now a train despatcher at Thief River Falls, Minnesota, was in the wireless department of the army and for one year was a traffic chief in France. James was in the Ordnance Corps, and died while at the great testing grounds at Aberdeen, Maryland.

Le Roy Pope was educated in public schools and when a boy began an apprenticeship at the stone cutters' trade. After completing his apprenticeship he worked as a stone and marble cutter, and became a construction foreman and superintendent, a business that took him to all parts of the United States. In 1919 he established his monument business at Williamsport. Mr. Pope for a number of years has taken a great interest in marking with permanent memorials the graves of Civil war soldiers in this section of Indiana and has set up many such markers supplied by the Government. He also manufactures reinforced concrete burial vaults. Mr. Pope was a member of the Indiana National Guard, from January 1, 1901, to April, 1903. He is a Republican, a Royal Arch Mason, member of the Lions Club and is president of the Williamsport School Board.

He married, May 12, 1909, Miss Florence Levy, daughter of James and Lizzie Levy, of Chicago. They have two children, Isabella, born in 1916, and Le Roy, born in 1919, both attending school.

MRS. ELLA D. MCERLAIN, proprietor of the South Bend Engraving & Electrotyping Company, was called to the executive responsibilities of business after the death of her husband, and has shown a remarkable capacity for looking after executive details and supervising the work of the technical departments as well. Leaders in South Bend business affairs give her a very high rating as a successful business woman, and undoubtedly she owes her success largely to her habit of close attention and unremitting energy in the daily conduct of the business.

Mrs. McErlain was born in South Bend, February 5, 1883. Her parents were born in Germany, her father in 1841 and her mother in 1848. They were married in Saint Joseph County, Indiana, in 1871 and of their five children four are living. Mrs. McErlain's father was reared and educated in Germany,

JOHN W. THIEL

served his apprenticeship at the blacksmith's trade there, and this was his occupation after coming to Indiana. During his later years he was employed in the shops of the Studebaker Company. He died in 1903 and his wife in 1921. Both parents were charter members of Saint Peter's Evangelical Church.

Mrs. McErlain was educated in public and parochial schools, spent two years in the South Bend High School and also had a business college course. As a young woman she was employed in the South Bend Engraving & Electrotyping Company, and had acquired a considerable knowledge of the business before her marriage to its proprietor Mr. John J. McErlain. They were married July 30, 1921.

Mr. McErlain was a native of Missouri and of Scotch and German ancestry. He was brought to South Bend when a child and finished his education in Notre Dame University. His first business was manufacturing cigar boxes and later he organized the South Bend Engraving & Electrotyping Company, and he carried on that business until his death on October 23, 1926 at the age of fifty-seven. He was highly esteemed as a business man and citizen and was a member of the B. P. O. Elks.

Mrs. McErlain after the death of her husband at once took charge of the business, which has grown and prospered until it is one of the leading establishments of its kind in Northern Indiana. Mrs. McErlain is an active member of Saint Peter's Evangelical Church.

HON. JOHN WILLIAM THIEL. Since his arrival at Gary, early in 1916, Hon. John W. Thiel has advanced steadily to a leading position at the bar of Lake County and is now in the enjoyment of a large and representative law practice. As a citizen he has taken a prominent part in all movements which have made for the betterment of both Gary and Hobart, and likewise has been a leader in the Republican party, now serving his fourth term as a constructive and aggressive member of the State Legislature.

Mr. Thiel was born at Zurich, Ontario, Canada, September 22, 1877, and is a son of Louis and Caroline (Finkbeiner) Thiel. His father, who was born and reared in Ontario, received a public school education, and as a young man applied himself to mastering the trade of blacksmith. In 1886 he moved to Huron County, Michigan, where he bought a farm and continued its operation for many years, at the same time occasionally working at his trade in doing necessary blacksmith work for his neighbors. He was a skilled mechanic and a capable farmer, and was highly respected in his community as a man of integrity and high character. About the year 1914, having accumulated a competence, he retired from active pursuits and moved to Pigeon, Michigan, where his death occurred in 1919, burial being made in the cemetery there. Mr. Thiel married Miss Caroline Finkbeiner, who was born at Crediton, Canada, and edu-

cated in the public schools there. Born July 1, 1854, she died August 27, 1880, in the faith of the Evangelical Association, in which she had been active all her life, and was buried at Crediton. There were three children born to Mr. and Mrs. Thiel: Thomas H., who is identified with the Holland Furnace Company, of Elizabeth, New Jersey; John W., of this review; and Caroline, now Mrs. D. C. Houpe, of Albuquerque, New Mexico. After the death of his first wife Louis Thiel married Miss Amanda Allendorf, and they became the parents of six children: Flora; Edward (who is deceased), Aaron, Oscar, George and Samuel.

John W. Thiel attended the public schools of Huron County, Michigan, following which he took academic work at Steinman College, Dixon, Illinois, and the Dixon Normal School. He commenced his career as a teacher, being for some months located in South Dixon Township, and for five years following in Lee County, Illinois. He then commenced attending the summer school of Valparaiso (Indiana) University, in the meantime continuing his teaching in Huron County, Michigan, and for three years was teacher at Bay Port Quarters, Michigan. Returning then to Valparaiso University, he took a course in elocution and law, receiving the degree of Bachelor of Oratory in 1911 and that of Bachelor of Laws in the following year. Admitted to the bar in Porter County, Indiana, in 1912, he resumed teaching school, at Kouts, Indiana, for one year, and then spent three years at Hobart, Lake County. On June 1, 1916, Mr. Thiel settled at Gary, where he has since been in the enjoyment of a large and representative law practice, with offices at 800 Broadway. He has risen to a high and recognized position in his profession and is a member of the Gary Bar Association, the Indiana State Bar Association and the American Bar Association. He has various business and financial interests and is a director and president of the Lake County Savings & Loan Association and a director of the Gibraltar Bond & Mortgage Company. He is a member of Pigeon Lodge, A. F. and A. M.; the Independent Order of Odd Fellows and the Loyal Order of Moose. Mr. Thiel has been particularly prominent in the Moose, being former dictator of Gary Lodge No. 783, and a life member thereof. This lodge presented him with a gold card and case in appreciation of his work and services, and has already voted his son, John W., Jr., aged twelve years, a life membership in the order, in recognition of Mr. Thiel's work. He likewise belongs to the Fraternal Order of Eagles, the Rebekahs, the Order of the Eastern Star, the Commercial Club and Chamber of Commerce. Politically a Republican, Mr. Thiel has been one of the standard-bearers of his party, is now serving his fourth term as a member of the Legislature, and in 1930 was a candidate for reelection. He has been one of the working members of this body and has been instrumental in fostering and securing the passage of much needful and beneficial legislation.

Mr. Thiel belongs to the Methodist Episcopal Church of Hobart, Indiana, where the family home is located, although Mr. Thiel's activities are centered at Gary.

At Cass City, Michigan, June 10, 1910, Mr. Thiel was united in marriage with Miss Anna Zinnecker, daughter of John and Elizabeth Zinnecker. Mr. Zinnecker was for many years a shoemaker, following that occupation up to his death in 1926, when he was buried at Cass City, where lies also the remains of his worthy wife, who survived him one year. Mrs. Thiel is a graduate of the high school at Cass City, a member of the Rebekahs and the Order of the Eastern Star, and is serving her second term as senior regent of the Women of Mooseheart Legion. Three children have been born to Mr. and Mrs. Thiel: Caroline Elizabeth (Betty), a graduate of Hobart High School, class of 1930; Florence Lillian, in her second year of high school work; and John William, Jr., who is attending public school at Hobart.

JOHN EDWARD BEYER. Many years have passed since John Edward Beyer ceased his activities as secretary of Spring Fountain Park Assemblies, held on Eagle Lake, Warsaw, Indiana, but he has been spared to reach an honorable and useful age, and during the years stretching between 1895, when the park was sold, to the present time Mr. Beyer has been occupied with numerous undertakings of moment, and today is one of the most respected citizens of Winona Lake, where he is living retired, his leisure moments made comfortable and happy by the companionship of his beloved wife, who has stood back of him in all of his projects, and is herself known all over Kosciusko County because of her bountiful charities and warm sympathy for all in need or trouble.

John Edward Beyer was born in Gunsungen, Germany, March 6, 1858, and he was a student of its excellent schools until 1872, when he accompanied his brother, Cyrus C. Beyer, to the United States. They made Goshen, Indiana, their first stopping place, and for the succeeding summer worked on a farm adjacent to Goshen on the east, and in the winter months went to school, continuing this for three years.

The father, John August Beyer, a resident of Germany, with his wife, Maria Elizabeth Eckhart, whom he had married in 1847, bore him five children, the oldest of whom is John August Beyer, born May 2, 1849, now the head of the family in Germany, residing on the home farm. The second son, John Frederick, was born October 17, 1850, and he lives on his farm that is inside the city limits of Warsaw, and he is a very prominent citizen and business man of the city. The third son, Albert Frederick, was born November 20, 1852, came to the United States, and is a professor in a college at German Valley, Illinois, and a minister of the German Reformed Church. The fourth son, Cyrus Christian, was born February 13, 1855, and lives at Kendall-

ville, Indiana, where he is engaged in the wholesale grocery business. The fifth son is, of course, John Edward, whose name heads this review.

Having obtained a fair knowledge of the language and customs during the three terms he had attended school, John Edward Beyer, in 1874, entered the employ of George Freese, of Goshen, Indiana, his work being collecting country produce throughout the neighboring country, in connection with his brother Frederick. These young men were intelligent, observant and ambitious, and while performing their duties acquired a knowledge of the business. They also saved their money, and February 2, 1877, they, together with Cyrus, who had joined them, went into business at Warsaw as Beyer Brothers, wholesale produce. They began in a small way, not trying to undertake more than their capital justified, but were soon able to expand, and began establishing stations in different cities and towns in the Central West, until they had twenty-two of them at which produce was collected. They also established distributing houses in the East, two in New York City, one at Brooklyn, one at Providence, Rhode Island, and one at Boston, Massachusetts, all of which were opened and managed by John Edward Beyer until 1917, when the Beyer Brothers Company produce business was sold to Armour & Company.

Mr. Beyer was also in the banking field at Rochester, Indiana, and the public utilities business at Rochester, Bourbon, Tipton, Etna Green, Fulton, Argos and the surrounding country, but in 1922 sold these utility interests to the Samuel Insull corporation for $500,000.

In addition to these activities Mr. Beyer bought, in the spring of 1881, for Beyer Brothers, the large farm which surrounded the east end of Eagle Lake, east of Warsaw, and with characteristic foresight laid the foundations for the present Winona Assembly Institution. They developed and beautified the lake and made it into a park by planting shrubbery, flowers and trees. They opened springs and sunk flowing wells, built hotels, restaurants, cottages, piers, docks, bathing beaches and pavilions, laid out walks and roads, and provided launches and steamboats. In spite of all of the effort and money expended it was not primarily their idea to make it a financial proposition, but to provide a beauty spot where the people of that section could enjoy recreation and wholesome enjoyment without going far from home, with especial thought for the young people. With that end in view the best of musical talent was secured, lecturers of note and well-known entertainers procured, and entertainments of high class were given so as to raise the cultural tone of the rising generation. At first operations were carried on under the name of Spring Fountain Park on Eagle Lake.

The park was first opened to the public in the spring of 1884, and many Sunday Schools and secret fraternal organizations came on excursion trains from distant places for picnics, being induced to do so not only by the beauties of the park, but also because of the high moral tone of all of the entertainments, and the fact that the young people were carefully guarded by the owners from any suggestion of evil. The park soon became very popular with the home people, as well as those from a distance, and it was soon upon a paying basis.

The Spring Fountain Park Assembly was organized, and the first program was given July 16 to 28, 1890. The first officers were as follows: President and superintendent, Rev. D. C. Woolpert, M. D., D. D.; vice president, Hon. J. A. Funk, J. S. Baker and W. D Page; directors, S. W. Oldfather, P. L. Runyan, Silas W. Chipman, William B. Funk, E. F. Yarnelle; secretary, J. E. Beyer; treasurer, J. F. Beyer; and superintendent of grounds, C. C. Beyer. The musical director was D. A. Clippinger, of Chicago. Sermons and addresses were made by noted men, among them being: Rev. M. M. Parkhurst, D. D.; Rev. J. H. Potts, D. D., of Detroit, Michigan; Rev. C. H. Caton, of Denver, Colorado; Gen. W. H. Gibson, of Canton, Ohio; Gov. Will Cumback, and many others of equal ability, such as Prof. D. A. Clippinger, Rev. T. W. Brake, Rev. J. H. Wilson, Prof. T. J. Sanders, A. M., Ph. D., W. D. Pease, Rev. E. M. Baker, Rev. A. E. Mahin, Rev. C. E. Bacon, Rev. P. S. Henson, D. D., Rev. Joseph Cook, D. D., Prof. M. R. French, Rev. A. A. Willits, D. D., Rev. C. H. Caton, D. D., Prof. J. B. Demotte, A. M., Ph. D., Rev. J. DeWitt Miller, D. D.; Prof. Mark B. Beal and William Vanslyke.

In 1891 the assembly was held for four weeks, and the officers were: President and superintendent, Rev. D. C. Woolpert, D. D.; assistant superintendent, Rev. T. W. Brake; vice presidents, Hon. J. A. Funk, W. D. Page, J. S. Baker and Hon. R. W. McBride. The directors were: S. W. Oldfather, William B. Funk, Rev. W. D. Parr, Rev. J. Simons, Rev. William Vanslyke, Silas W. Chipman, E. F. Yarnelle, Rev. F. G. Browne, Rev. Somerville Light, C. W. Burkett and Rev. M. S. Marble. The secretary was J. E. Beyer; the treasurer, J. F. Beyer, and the superintendent of grounds, C. C. Beyer.

The lecturers were: Mrs. Josephine R. Nichols, Hon. George W. Bain, Orren B. Clark, Rev. J. P. D. John, LL. D., Rev. E. M. Baker, Bishop J. Weaver, D. D., Prof. D. A. Clippinger, Rev. C. C. McCabe, John Hogarth Lozier, Gen. William H. Gibson, Judge Allen Zollars, Judge Byron K. Elliott, Rev. W. D. Parr, Gov. Alvin P. Hovey, Gen. James R. Carnahan, Dr. Alice Stockham, Rev. Jahu DeWitt Miller, D. D., Rev. J. S. Wilson, Prof. James Clement Ambrose, Rev. Robert McIntyre, D. D., Mrs. J. Ellen Foster, Rev. A. A. Willits, D. D., Rev. J. H. Potts, D. D., Rev. J. F. Perry, D. D., Bishop I. W. Joyce, D. D., Rev. D. H. Moore, Rev. Robert Nourse, D. D., Col. Robert Dowden and Richard Lew Dawson.

In 1892 the Assembly was held for four weeks, and the following were the officers:

President and superintendent, Rev. D. C. Woolpert, M. D., D. D.; vice presidents, Hon. J. A. Funk, W. D. Page, J. S. Baker, Hon. R. W. McBride; directors, S. W. Oldfather, Rev. W. D. Parr, Rev. F. G. Browne, Rev. Somerville Light, Rev. M. S. Marble, Gen. James Carnahan, E. F. Yarnelle, William B. Funk, Rev. J. Simons, Rev. William Vanslyke, C. W. Burkett and Silas W. Chipman; secretary, J. E. Beyer; treasurer, J. F. Beyer; and superintendent of grounds, C. C. Beyer. The lecturers were: Busby Sisters, Miss Marion Harter, Mrs. Cecil Gohl, Rev. Dr. E. H. Richards, Bishop E. W. Arnett, Prof. S. H. Blakeslee, Rev. W. N. Bell, Bishop E. B. Kephart, Col. George W. Bain, Robert Nourse, Gov. Ira Chase, Rev. M. M. Parkhurst, Rev. Washington Gardner, Hon. R. G. Horr, Rev. J. W. Kain, Prof. J. Umbenhour, Mrs. Mary T. Lathrop, Rev. H. N. Herrick, Rev. J. F. Berry, Rev. A. A. Willits, Mrs. Josephine R. Nichols, Mrs. G. G. Hudson, Rev. Charles F. Deems, D. D., LL. D., Rev. W. L. Davidson, E. F. Williams, G. B. Shaw, Brooks and Robertson, Rev. Dr. E. L. Eaton, Rev. J. DeWitt Miller, D. D., Hon. Oliver T. Morton, Hon. Charles E. Griffin, Mary Wood Allen, Rev. Frank M. Bristol, and Rev. Russel N. Conwell.

In 1893 the Assembly held two weeks of Chautauqua and two weeks of Ministerial Institute, with the following officers: President and superintendent, Rev. D. C. Woolpert, D. D.; vice presidents, Hon. J. A. Funk, W. D. Page, J. S. Baker and Hon. R. W. McBride; directors, S. W. Oldfather, Rev. W. D. Parr, Rev. M. S. Marble, Gen. James R. Carnahan, Hon. J. T. Thayer, E. F. Yarnelle, Rev. F. G. Browne, Rev. J. Simons, C. W. Burkett, W. B. Funk, Rev. Somerville Light, Rev. William Vanslyke, Silas Chipman and H. P. Comstock; secretary, J. E. Beyer; treasurer, J. F. Beyer, and superintendent of grounds, C. C. Beyer. The following were the lecturers: Rev. A. E. Mahin, Rev. Russel H. Conwell, Rev. J. L. Leeper, Rev. J. M. Dickey, Mrs. J. R. Nichols, Rev. George Hindley, Rev. Dr. E. L. Eaton, Professor Blakeslee and Rev. J. P. D. Horn, D. D., LL. D. The ministers were: Revs. S. F. Harrison, W. C. Perry, G. W. Rench, J. A. Miller, A. D. Gnagey, S. H. Bashor, Z. T. Livengood, D. C. Christner, W. W. Summers, H. R. Holsinger, M. M. Sterling, J. D. McFaden, I. D. Bowman, B. C. Moomaw, W. L. Spanogle and J. H. Palmer.

In 1894 the Assembly held two weeks of Chautauqua, and the officers were as follows: President and superintendent, Rev. D. C. Woolpert, D. D.; vice presidents, Hon. J. A. Funk, W. D. Page, J. S. Baker and Hon. R. W. McBride; directors, S. W. Oldfather, Rev. W. D. Parr, Rev. M. S. Marble, Gen. James Carnahan, Hon. J. D. Thayer, E. F. Yarnelle, Rev. F. G. Browne, Rev. J. Simons, C. W. Burkett, W. B. Funk, Rev. Somerville Light, Rev. H. C. Smith, Silas Chipman and H. P. Comstock; secretary, J. E. Beyer; treasurer, J. F. Beyer; and superintendent of grounds, C. C. Beyer. The lecturers were: Smith Sisters, Col. George W. Bain, Quivey

Sisters, Rev. H. S. Riggs, Dr. E. L. Eaton, Hon. O. Z. Hubbel, Rev. Robert McIntyre, Prof. Lou Beaucamp, Doctor Reade and Rev. J. L. Leeper.

Great pains were taken with these institutes or assemblies and the programs were improved each year, and very large crowds attended them, and they were looked forward to with great interest by those to whom the cultural and highly moral programs appealed. However interesting as these gatherings were, Mr. Beyer did not neglect to secure activities for other seasons. The Uniformed Rank of the Knights of Pythias held their state encampments at Spring Fountain Park for three years. In 1890 a large panorama of the Battle of Lookout Mountain and Missionary Ridge painted on 15,000 feet of canvas by Mr. Kellog was a drawing attraction. In 1892 another large painting, on 15,000 feet of canvas, of the Life of Christ, was exhibited by Prof. E. J. Pine, of Mobile, Aalabama. Maj. Gen. James P. Carnahan, of Indianapolis, Indiana, and Maj. Gen. Ross, of Indiana, established a military park, in 1891, that was connected with the Spring Fountain Park, and called Carnahan's Military Park. In connection with this was General Carnahan's cottage and Housier Rest, and a large hotel called The Barracks. All of this property was later purchased by Beyer Brothers and added to their park. The Barracks is now known as The Inn Hotel. On May 10, 1895, Spring Fountain Park was sold to the Winona Assembly and Summer School Association by Mr. J. E. Beyer for the Beyer Brothers, at the Bates House, Indianapolis, Indiana. The Association was represented by its executive committee, composed of the following: Charles A. Conner, of Louisville, Kentucky, president; Rev. Dr. Saul C. Dickey, of Indianapolis; George W. Brown; E. F. Yarnelle, Fort Wayne, Indiana; and D. E. Scott, secretary. On May 15, 1895, the stockholders of the Assembly Association held a meeting at Warsaw, and approved the action of the committee; these stockholders attending were: Charles A. Conner, president; John Studebaker, George W. Brown, E. F. Yarnelle, William Johnson, Doctor Colter, Doctor Dickey and S. E. Scott.

On November 13, 1884, Mr. J. E. Beyer married in Kosciusko County, Miss Irene Oldfather, born in Wabash County, Indiana, August 14, 1860. She attended a country school, but made the best of her opportunities. Her father, Adam Oldfather, was born at Allentown, Pennsylvania, September 14, 1818, and died in Indiana in 1893, and he was a son of Frederick Oldfather, the latter born at Berlin, Germany, October 17, 1775. Mrs. Beyer's mother, Mrs. Caroline (Berger) Oldfather, was born January 26, 1823, and she was of German descent.

Mr. and Mrs. Beyer had two children: Earl Edward and Frank S. Beyer. Frank S. Beyer died in infancy, but Earl Edward Beyer survived, and was graduated from DePauw University in 1904. Afterward he attended Leland Stanford University, 1905 and 1906, and Yale University, from which he was graduated in economics in 1908. For several years he was employed in the National City Bank with Frank A. Vanderlin until the latter withdrew, when he too severed his connection with the National City Bank, and became a "Dollar-a-Year" man at Washington during the World war, in the employ of Hallgarden Company. After the close of the war he became a member of the firm of Campbell, Starring & Company in New York City. In June, 1911, he married Miss Zella Jones, of Greencastle, Indiana, graduated from De-Pauw University in 1908. They have one child, Edward Morton Beyer, who was born at New York City, December 1, 1914, and is now in a preparatory school in that city. During the World war Earl E. Beyer was in charge of production and distribution of the company with which he was connected, under the direction of Mr. Vanderlip, and in his position came into contact with the greatest men of the age, and formed many warm friendships which are still maintained.

Mr. and Mrs. J. E. Beyer are members of the Methodist Episcopal Church, and she is a devoted church worker, and is connected with various charitable organizations. While she is an intelligent lady, she is very modest and retiring, remarkably well-preserved for her years. Few homes are presided over with such grace and charm as hers, and she is noted for her housekeeping. In 1928 the Beyers took a trip around the world, and were accompanied by Ralph Parlette, of Chicago. Upon his return Mr. Parlette wrote the following letter to a mutual friend, Homer Rodeheaver, of Winona Lake, Indiana, in which he gives a fine characterization of these two, probably the best beloved couple of Winona Lake. It bears the date of August 13, 1928, and is as follows:

"I wish I could join in the throng tomorrow night in the Beyer Home. I'd like to tell them all more of the secret of the happiness of that magnificent home. It is a wonderful home because architect and artist have built it, but its glory is in the love there between two people who have hand-in-hand journeyed these years through upward, unfolding life.

"As you celebrate the birthday of the woman who presides over that home, let me tell you of a time just a little while ago when it seemed that she would not have another birthday on earth. It was on a ship going round the world. Mr. and Mrs. Beyer were on this ship and I had the honor of being with them for nearly five months. She was stricken by the tropic heat as we came across the equator. Up through the Philippines, through China, Korea, Japan and back across the Pacific her life hovered in the balance. I think the reason she remained with us was that Mr. Beyer sat day and night at her bedside, all else forgotten in the important task of keeping her here. And never was a man happier than he as he saw the pink again flushing her cheeks.

"Here are two wonderful comrades—Mr. and Mrs. Beyer. I rejoice that this is her birthday, and that she has so many friends to help her celebrate it. And I rejoice that we have two such people to show us the real foundations of the home and our civilization today. It is a fine thing to see a young boy and girl love each other and found a home, but it is an inspiring and re-assuring thing to see two people go many years through life in their home adoring comrades as their hair becomes silver. Our homes are saved by such examples.

"I know something of the secret of their success. It is love and loyalty. This man Beyer began his career as a poor boy with no chance. He made his chances by constant struggle and vision of better things. He succeeded in a material way. He has exalted character and religion. He visioned Winona Lake years ago and opened the gates for men and women to come here and develop it. He has been the friend to progress and idealism. And at his side this woman has stood helping in every effort.

"So, as we celebrate her birthday, it can well be the birthday of new inspiration in our own lives and larger achievement.

"Faithfully,
"Ralph Parlette,
"70 East Walton Place,
"Chicago, Ill."

As Mr. Parlette says, Mrs. Beyer has been at the side of her husband in all of his undertakings, encouraging, aiding and oftentimes prompting him, and today, although their period of active participation in the world's work is ended, there is still much of great value in life to them, and they have the satisfaction of knowing that wherever they are known they have warm, personal friends, and that the results of what they have accomplished remain as an inspiration, and will continue to do so long after they pass over to the other world, for it is founded on the bedrock of probity and Christianity raised to a high level.

JOHN PORTER RUDY is one of the influential figures in the industrial and commercial activities centered in the vital and progressive City of New Albany, the judicial center of Floyd County, where he is owner and executive head of the thriving meat-packing business conducted under the title of Frank Manus Company.

Mr. Rudy was born at Maysville, Mason County, Kentucky, December 29, 1883, and is a son of William Henry and Julia Frances (Shea) Rudy. He received the advantages of the public schools of his native state and as a youth he served an apprenticeship to the trade of carriage maker, to which he gave his attention a few years. He was a young man when he left his native state and came to Indiana, and here was solemnized his marriage to Miss May Manus, daughter of the late Frank Manus, who was founder of the business here still carried on under the title of Frank Manus Company. In 1876 Mr. Manus established a retail meat market at New Albany, and a few years later he amplified the enterprise into a wholesale business in the packing of pork products. He continued the active executive head of the business until his death, in 1926, but about two years previously his son-in-law, J. Porter Rudy, assumed much of the management of the varied details of the industry, of which he has maintained ownership and control since the death of its honored founder, and in connection with which he has rank as one of the most loyal and progressive business men of the younger generation in New Albany. The well equipped manufacturing plant of the Frank Manus Company is situated at 1418 State Street and here special attention is given to the packing of cured hams and smoked meats, the products being of the highest grade and the wholesale trade of the concern being widely extended through Southern Indiana. The establishment gives employment to a corps of skilled operatives and the enterprise has contributed definitely to the industrial prestige of New Albany.

Mr. Rudy is loyal and liberal as a citizen, is a Democrat in politics, and is affiliated with the local lodge of the Benevolent and Protective Order of Elks. In the World war period he was active in the advancing of local patriotic movements and enterprises, especially the campaigns in the sale of Government war bonds. Mr. and Mrs. Rudy have one daughter, Mary Rita, born June 4th, 1922.

FRANK JACOB RENN has found it neither necessary nor expedient to search outside the boundaries of his native City of New Albany for a field of successful business enterprise, and in that city, the judicial center of Floyd County, he is president of the Renn Aluminum & Brass Foundry, one of the well ordered industrial concerns that contribute to the commercial prestige of the city.

Mr. Renn was born in New Albany on the 30th of May, 1881, and is a son of Jacob J. and Elizabeth (Speth) Renn, who became the parents of three children. Jacob J. Renn was born and reared in Indiana, as was also his wife, and his father, who was born in the Rhine Province of Germany, became a pioneer settler in Indiana, where he established his home in the year 1825 and where he became one of the substantial farmers of his day and generation.

Frank J. Renn is indebted to the New Albany Catholic schools for his early education, and at the age of eighteen years he here entered upon an apprenticeship to the molder's trade, at the plant of the Anchor Stove Works. He thus continued to be employed at his trade until 1919, when he engaged independently in business by founding the substantial and well ordered industrial enterprise that he owns and conducts under the title of Renn Aluminum & Brass Foundry. The establishment is situated at 2505 East Elm Street, its facilities and general equipment are of the best modern order, and the business is represented primarily in the manufacturing of aluminum and brass castings for manufacturers and mechanics. He also manufactures modern aluminum cookware. Mr. Renn has depended upon his own resources in making his way forward to the goal of success and business prosperity, he is animated by a spirit of civic loyalty and progressiveness, and he takes deep interest in all that touches the well being and advancement of his native city. His political allegiance is given to the Democratic party, but in local affairs he votes for men and measures meeting the approval of his judgment, rather than being constrained by strict partisan lines. He and his wife, whose maiden name was Rosa Ringley, are communicants of the Catholic Church, and he is affiliated with the Knights of Columbus and the Fraternal Order of Eagles.

JOSEPH BENHART FLECK has been a resident of South Bend for thirty years, and his name in a business way is best known as the proprietor of the Fleck Plumbing Company, at 434 South Fellows Street. This is a company of contractors in plumbing, heating and ventilating, an organization that represents his long experience and practical skill in every branch of his business.

Mr. Fleck was born at Silver Lake, Kosciusko County, Indiana, July 21, 1885. His parents, Frank M. and Sarah (Fleck) Fleck, came from Europe, his father at the age of twelve years. Frank M. Fleck in 1861 enlisted from Seneca County, Ohio, in the Fourteenth Ohio Volunteer Infantry. He became a lieutenant in his company, was wounded in one battle and after the war moved to Indiana. For many years he conducted a butcher business at Silver Lake. He died in 1916, when eighty-nine years of age, and his wife passed away in 1920. One son, Christ Fleck, is now in the butcher business at Mentone, Indiana.

Joseph B. Fleck was educated in public schools at Silver Lake and Wabash and as a boy began his apprenticeship at the plumbing trade. He came to South Bend in 1901. In 1905 he became a member of the firm of Fleck & Ehrhardt, but in 1908 bought the interest of Mr. Henry Ehrhardt and since that time has carried on the business alone, in the name of the Fleck Plumbing Company. Mr. Fleck is a master plumber and building contractor, and real estate owner and industrial executives all over northern Indiana know the quality of his work and the reliability of his service. It would not be a difficult matter to compile a long list of important structures in the business district and residential sections of South Bend and in outlying cities exemplifying the contracting service of Mr. Fleck. He had the plumbing and heating contract for the Max Adler Building, for a number of schools and churches in South Bend and Mishawaka, and some years ago, when a company carried out an unusual program of costructing 100 houses at one time in South Bend, Mr. Fleck was awarded the contract for all the plumbing and heating installations. Mr. Fleck has as a side line been a dealer in real estate and owns several apartment buildings in South Bend.

He is a member of the St. Joseph County Society of Sanitary Engineers. Mr. Fleck has three children, Frank Michals, Joseph Benhart, Jr., and James Knox. His son Frank is a graduate of the University of Illinois and is now with the General Trust Company of Illinois at Chicago.

ARCHIE ROBERT HUNNICUTT in his business as a general contractor is following a line of work which has been in the family for at least a century. For four successive generations of families to carry on, from father to son, one line of business is very unusual in America.

Mr. Hunnicutt's great-grandfather, Samuel Hunnicutt, was a native and lifelong resident of Richmond, Virginia, where he did business as a general contractor in the early days and was also a merchant. Mr. Hunnicutt's grandfather was James S. Hunnicutt, who was born in Belmont County, Ohio, and also followed contracting work. In 1849 he went west to Iowa and was one of the pioneers of his business in that state. He lived to the remarkable age of 101 years, five months, passing away in 1923.

The father of Archie Robert Hunnicutt was James Clifford Hunnicutt, who was born in Tama County, Iowa, and for many years carried on a building contracting business in that section of the state. He is now living retired at Union City, Indiana. James Clifford Hunnicutt married Margaret Otto Davidson who was born at Madison, Wisconsin.

Their son, Archie Robert Hunnicutt, was born in Custer County, Nebraska, February 1, 1885. He attended the grade and high schools of Iowa and at the age of seventeen began learning the building trade. He worked as a journeyman over Iowa and other middle western states until 1911, when he located at Columbus, Indiana, and since 1920 has made his home at Union City. He is associated in partnership with his brother Ralph N. Hunnicutt, who lives at Marion, Indiana. These brothers have the benefit of the family traditions and long experience in the building business. They have handled large contracts all over Indiana and other states and have specialized in the building of hospitals and schools.

Mr. Archie Hunnicutt married Miss Ethel May Pentecost, who was born at Boston, Whitley County, Indiana, daughter of Lorenza B. and Mahalia (Busenburg) Pentecost. Mr. and Mrs. Hunnicutt have three foster children, Howard, Robert and Betty. They are members of the First Christian Church and he is chairman of its official board. Mr. Hunnicutt has been a member of the Union City Council and acting mayor. He is a Democrat, a thirty-second degree Scottish Rite Mason and Shriner

C. W. Yarrington M. D.

and member of the B. P. O. Elks, is a director of the Union City Country Club and for two years was vice president of the Rotary Club.

Mr. Hunnicutt, in May, 1917, enlisted in the Indiana National Guard at Shelbyville. He was in training during the World war period and following the war was called out with the guard for active duty during the prolonged strike in the steel mills at Hammond, Indiana Harbor and Gary. When he was discharged April 21, 1920, he held the rank of battalion sergeant major.

CHARLES WEBB YARRINGTON, M. D. Among the medical and surgical practitioners of Lake County none are held in higher esteem both for professional ability and stalwart and constructive citizenship than Dr. Charles Webb Yarrington, of Gary. Coming to this city February 1, 1912, he had the distinction of becoming the first public school physician, a position which he held for one and one-half years, since which time he has been engaged continuously in a constantly-growing private practice. Likewise he has been active and prominent in civic, fraternal and religious affairs, and for a long period served as coroner's physician.

Doctor Yarrington is of Welsh extraction and a member of an old and honored Vermont family which traces its ancestry back in this country for many generations. He was born at Norvell, Jackson County, Michigan, January 30, 1877, and is a son of Hon. Charles and Elavene Harriet (Bancroft) Yarrington, and a grandson of Edgar Strong Yarrington, who was born in 1792, at Norwich, Vermont. Edgar S. Yarrington was reared and educated in his native locality, but in young manhood braved the new country of Michigan, becoming one of the early pioneers of the Grass Lake community, where his death occurred in 1840, after some years of agricultural work. He and his wife are buried at Grass Lake.

Charles Yarrington was born in 1839, at Grass Lake, Michigan, where he received a public school education, and in young manhood secured a position as clerk in a drug store. After learning the drug business he secured a pharmacy of his own and during the remainder of his life conducted a substantial business at Norvell, where he reached the ripe age of eighty years, dying in 1919 and being laid to rest in the cemetery at Norvell. He was a man of sound and straightforward character, who had the respect and confidence of his fellow-citizens, and for several years served ably as representative from Jackson County in the Michigan Legislature. He married Elavene Harriet Bancroft, who was born at Brooklyn, Michigan, and educated in the public schools. Reared a Baptist, she was active in that church for some years, but eventually became a Presbyterian and died in that faith in 1914, aged sixty-five years. She was laid to rest in the same cemetery as her husband. There were three children in the family: Miss Ida May, born May 2, 1871, who has always been an educator and is now principal of the McKinley School, Toledo, Ohio; Nellie M., now the wife of R. W. Stevens, district principal of schools of Detroit, Michigan; and Dr. Charles Webb, of this review.

Charles Webb Yarrington attended the public schools of Norvell and the high school at Millford, Michigan, from which latter he was graduated as a member of the class of 1895. He received the degree of Doctor of Medicine from the University of Michigan as a member of the class of 1902, and during the following year did interne work at Dollar Bay, Michigan. While at the university he became a member of the Nu Sigma Nu medical fraternity. He then became physician and surgeon for the North Kearsarge Mining Company, of Calumet, Michigan, with which concern he was identified for two years, and for seven years thereafter was engaged in a like capacity by the Calumet & Hecla Mining Company, at the same place. These were years of hard work and poor remuneration, but they gave Doctor Yarrington experience of a varied character that he could have hardly acquired in any other way, and also bred in him an experience of self-confidence in any emergency which has been of the greatest value to him in later years. On February 1, 1912, Doctor Yarrington came to Gary as its first public school physician and held that post for one and one-half years. He then entered private practice and has since continued therein, having a splendidly equipped suite of offices at 607 Broadway. He has built up a well-merited reputation as a general practitioner who is familiar with every branch of his calling, and has won general confidence and esteem. Doctor Yarrington is a member of the Lake County Medical Society, the Indiana State Medical Society and the American Medical Association and is a fellow of the American College of Surgeons. For sixteen years he served as coroner's physician, and otherwise he has been active in civic affairs. He belongs to Roosevelt Lodge, A. F. and A. M.; Gary Chapter, Gary Council and Gary Commandery; Fort Wayne Consistory and Orak Temple, A. A. O. N. M. S., of Hammond; and Gary Lodge, B. P. O. Elks. He likewise holds membership in the Rotary Club, Gary Country Club, Gary Commercial Club and Chamber of Commerce. Politically he is a Republican. He is an Episcopalian in religion, and for a number of years was a member of the vestry of that church.

At Calumet, Michigan, June 30, 1906, Doctor Yarrington was united in marriage with Miss Bessie M. Kratz, a daughter of Prof. H. E. and Elizabeth (Deal) Kratz, of Calumet. Professor Kratz was one of the well-known educators of his day and locality and for some years occupied the chair of pedagogy at Mitchell, South Dakota. Subsequently he became superintendent of schools at Sioux City, Iowa, and later superintendent of schools at Calumet, Michigan, then going to Chicago, where for a time he was in charge of a teachers' agency. Finally he retired from active pursuits and moved to Gary, where he died in

1929, his wife having passed away two years previously, and both are buried in Woodlawn Cemetery, Gary. Mrs. Yarrington attended the public schools of Sioux City, Iowa, and then entered the University of Wisconsin, from which institution she was graduated as a member of the class of 1902 and was a member of the Alpha Phi. For a few years prior to her marriage she taught school at Calumet. She has been active in the work of the Episcopal Church, the Woman's Club and the A. A. U. W. To Doctor and Mrs. Yarrington there have been born two sons: Charles Webb, Jr., born June 6, 1908, a graduate of Emerson High School, Gary, and of the University of Michigan, Bachelor of Science, class of 1930, who is now preparing himself for his father's profession at the same institution; and Edouard Bancroft, born September 28, 1910, a graduate of Emerson High School, Gary, who is attending the University of Michigan.

During the World war Doctor Yarrington served as medical advisor on the draft board for some time and then entered the United States Medical Corps, receiving his captain's commission November 5, 1918. He went to Fort Riley, Kansas, but at the end of thirty days, the armistice having been signed in the meantime, received his honorable discharge and returned to Gary, again to take up his general practice. As will be noted in the foregoing, he has led an active and useful career. All civic movements have had his whole-hearted support, and for two years he worked constructively as a member of the board of directors of the Gary Chamber of Commerce. It has been his fortune to attract to himself numerous friends and to form connections that have been fruitful of much pleasure to himself and the members of his family.

VALERIUS PETER HOPE is one of the oldest residents of Morocco, Newton County, Indiana. He is now retired from business and is enjoying the fruits of earlier years of strenuous application to his duties.

Mr. Hope was born in Ohio, December 16, 1851, son of William K. and Eve Elizabeth Hope. His people were farmers in Van Wert County, Ohio. His father died about 1910. Valerius P. Hope is the only surviving child. His sister was Lydia Jane.

Mr. Hope attended school in Van Wert County, Ohio, grew up on a farm and in 1875 came to Indiana and located in Newton County. His home has been at Morocco for half a century. He was engaged in farming and also was active in the business life of Morocco until he retired. Mr. Hope is a Republican and a member of the Methodist Episcopal Church.

He married Maria A. Smart, daughter of John Smart. Their living children are Orval, Otho, Lucinda E. and Mary. Mary is the wife of Marion Robinson, of Compton, California, and they have two children. Orval, connected with the Government fish hatchery in Colorado, married Ada Tillot and has two chil-

dren. Otho is a farmer near Pearson, Indiana, married Cora Tracy and has five children. Lucinda E. is the wife of Max Levi, and they have an adopted child. Mr. Otho's son, Myron E., was in the World war and in France with a supply train and is now deceased. He married Mary Robinson, and they had one son.

RALPH ALBERT CONFER, whose home is at Greencastle, has devoted a number of years to study and research as a genealogist. His investigations have been centered on the families in his own line. One of these lines is that of the Burkes, traced back in America to the year 1725. Allied families are the Vaughans, McIninch, Burtons and others.

Mr. Confer has obtained his data from persons in California, Texas, Alabama, Kansas, Washington and the eastern states, including Pennsylvania and New York. In compiling his records he has examined data from twenty-five hundred people and has also gone to the monuments and cemeteries and the parish and court records of many localities.

Mr. Confer has an enthusiastic companion in research in the person of his wife, Mrs. Daisy Ethel (Dean) Confer. Her father was James Dean, and the Deans are a prominent old family of Indiana.

EARL L. ELDRIDGE, postmaster of Boswell, is a World war veteran, and throughout his business career has been identified with this little community of Warren County.

Mr. Eldridge was born in Benton County, Indiana, September 4, 1895. His father, William E. Eldridge, was a native of Rhode Island, and during his youth learned the trade of watch-maker. When a young man he came to Indiana and for a number of years carried on a prosperous business as a jeweler and optician at Boswell. He was a man of much influence in the locality, being president of the town board, and at the time of his death, on February 3, 1911, was secretary of the Masonic Lodge and the Independent Order of Odd Fellows. He married Ida F. Chaney, a daughter of John Chaney. She is still living. They had four children: Beeca L., wife of Dr. L. H. Conway, of Colorado Springs, Colorado, and mother of a daughter, Mary E.; Earl L.; Doris, wife of J. M. Doane, of Decatur, Indiana, and mother of two daughters, named Gladys and Anna Bell; and Miss Helen, a resident of Denver, Colorado.

Earl L. Eldridge was educated in the grade and high schools of Boswell. He took up the trade of painter and decorator, became an expert and developed a good business as a contractor in this line.

His business career was interrupted on December 11, 1917, when he joined the colors in the Aviation Corps, and received his training at a field in Texas, reaching the rank of first class sergeant. He received his honorable discharge at Battle Creek, Michigan, March 28, 1919.

Charles H Dooley

Mr. Eldridge married, February 4, 1923, Miss Anna Hackerson, daughter of John and Lena Hackerson. They have a daughter, Shirley Maxine, born in 1924. Mr. Eldridge was appointed postmaster of Boswell August 25, 1923, and has made his administration of the office very popular among the patrons. He is a Republican, belongs to the Masonic Lodge, is a Methodist and affiliated with his army comrades in the American Legion Post.

ROBERT HOLLOWELL, JR., attorney-at-law, is a resident of Danville, where he was born and where his father practiced law. Robert Hollowell, Jr., handles his professional work with an office in the Indiana Trust Building at Indianapolis.

He was born at Danville in Hendricks County July 3, 1899. His great-grandfather Hollowell came from Wales and settled in Indiana more than a century ago, taking up Government land in Parke County. The Hollowells were Quakers and were a very prominent family in the early days in Parke County. Robert Hollowell, Sr., when a boy accompanied his father to Kansas, living in that state for several years and getting some of his schooling there. He graduated in law from the University of Michigan, and spent all his active career in his profession at Danville. He married Mattie Ross, a native of Indiana and of Virginia and Kentucky ancestry.

Robert Hollowell, Jr., was the only child of his parents. He attended grade and high schools at Danville, had three years of work in Indiana University and one year in DePauw University, and in 1922 was graduated LL. B. from the law department of the University of Michigan. He graduated just forty-one years after his father took his law degree there.

Mr. Hollowell during the World war was with the Officers Training Camp at Indiana University from October 1, 1918, until December of that year. He is a member of the American Legion, is a Methodist, a Republican, affiliates with the Masonic Lodge at Danville and is a member of the Sigma Phi and Gamma Eta Gamma fraternities. He belongs to the Indianapolis Lawyers Club, and the Hendricks County and Indianapolis Bar Associations.

He married Miss Edna K. Hawley, a native of Danville, and they have two daughters, Joyce and Janet.

JOSEPH E. LEWIS, postmaster of Williamsport, Indiana, is a member of an Indiana family that has been in the state since pioneer times.

Mr. Lewis was born at Oxford in Benton County, Indiana, August 12, 1896. His grandfather, Isaac Lewis, was also a native of Oxford and was of Scotch and Irish ancestry. The father of the Williamsport postmaster was Homer W. Lewis, born at Oxford and a farmer by occupation. At one time he was chief of police at Mount Carmel, Illinois. He married Mary J. Julian, who was born at Independence, Indiana. They had eight children: William C., of La Juana, Mexico; Della, of Houston, Texas; Mayma, of Woodstock, Illinois; Jennie, of Indianapolis; Guy, deceased; Fred, of Danville, Illinois; Charlotte, of Chicago; and Joseph E.

Joseph E. Lewis received his grade and high school education at Indianapolis. He followed farm work until 1917. He enlisted and was assigned to Three Hundred and Thirty-fourth Regiment of Infantry at Camp Taylor, Kentucky. In February, 1918, he sailed with his regiment for France and was overseas seventeen months. While in France he was promoted to second lieutenant and at the present time holds a commission of first lieutenant in the Officers' Reserve Corps. Mr. Lewis returned home and received his honorable discharge in June, 1919. Since the war he has been a prominent worker in the American Legion, being a past commander of Warren Post No. 259 and since 1925 has been county chairman for the Citizens Military Training Camp.

Mr. Lewis was commissioned postmaster of Williamsport in 1926 by President Coolidge and has given a highly satisfactory administration of that office. He is a staunch Republican, a member of the Masonic fraternity and an elder in the Presbyterian Church. He married, September 10, 1916, a daughter of Daniel and Nellie Isabella (Carter) Fullienlove, natives of Kentucky. They have one son, Robert C., born April 11, 1925.

CHARLES HENRY DOORLEY. The career of Charles H. Doorley, superintendent of the Elgin, Joliet & Eastern Railroad, with headquarters at Gary, has been typical of the lives of railroad men of the older generation who fought their own way, unaided, up through the ranks into positions of authority and power. Mr. Doorley began his independent career as an engine wiper in a railroad machine shop, and each step upward has come as a direct result of hard work, loyalty and added value to his company, with which he has now been identified for a period of thirty-three years.

Mr. Doorley was born at St. Catharine's, Canada, March 24, 1866, and is a son of James A. and Mary (McCarthy) Doorley. His parents, natives of Ireland, were reared and educated in that country, whence they emigrated to Canada as a young married couple some years previous to the war between the states in this country. Mr. Doorley, who was a farmer and stock raiser in Canada, came to Elkhart, Indiana, about 1871, and from that time forward lived in retirement until his death about 1874, burial being made in the cemetery at Mishawaka. His wife died in Canada in 1867 and was buried at St. Catharine's. To Mr. and Mrs. Doorley there were born three children: James, who died in 1895, at Oak Point, Oregon; one child who died in infancy; and Charles H., of this review.

Charles H. Doorley attended the public schools of Indiana and Illinois and was graduated from the Douglas High School, Chicago. He immediately secured a position with the Grand Trunk Railway Company, March 24, 1884, starting to work as an engine wiper in the machine shops at Chicago. In February, 1885, he was advanced to the post of fireman for the same road, and in April, 1886, became engine hostler, a post which he held until May, 1886. He then was made switchman for the same road, remaining until December, 1886, and from January, 1887, until 1889 was switchman for the Chicago & Alton. In 1889 he was advanced to yardmaster for the latter line, remaining in that capacity until 1896, in February of which year he became yardmaster for the Chicago, Hammond & Western Railroad, remaining until March, 1898. Mr. Doorley was next a switchman for the Chicago, Lake Shore & Eastern Railroad, with which he remained from April, 1898, until August, 1899, at that time becoming assistant yardmaster for the same road. From September, 1901, until August, 1903, he was night yardmaster, from August, 1903, until December, 1908, general yardmaster (now a part of the Elgin, Joliet & Eastern Railway), from December, 1908, until April, 1915, was assistant superintendent of the same road; from April, 1915, to September, 1915, superintendent of terminals of the same road at Joliet, and from September, 1915, to date has been superintendent of the Gary Division of the Elgin, Joliet & Eastern Railway, with headquarters at Gary. Mr. Doorley has been with this road for a period of thirty-three years (up to 1931) and is one of its most trusted employes as well as one of its oldest in point of continuous service. Throughout his life he has taken his work seriously, having felt that the business of railroading was a highly important and dignified one and that rules were made to be followed, and as a result has been a strict disciplinarian, although never a martinet. By treating his men with fairness and justice he has been able to secure their loyalty and cooperation and thus has added to his value to his company. Mr. Doorley has invested his earnings carefully and with good judgment, and today is a member of the board of directors of the Fifth Avenue Bank of Gary and of the Gary Building & Loan Association. He is a trustee of the Young Men's Christian Association and the Knights of Columbus, and belongs to the Lions Club, the Gary Country Club, the Commercial Club and Chamber of Commerce. Politically he is a Republican, and his religious connection is with St. Mark's Catholic Church.

On May 24, 1888, at Chicago, Illinois, Mr. Doorley was united in marriage with Miss Della Zaremba, daughter of Major Zaremba, for years master mechanic of the Illinois Central Railroad, located at the Chicago shops. He died in 1908 and his wife in 1915, and both are buried in Calvary Cemetery, Chicago. Mrs. Doorley was educated in the public schools of Chicago, including high school, and has been active in the work of the Knights of Columbus Auxiliary, the Daughters of Isabella, and of St. Mark's Catholic Church. Six children have been born to Mr. and Mrs. Doorley: Charles M., educated at Chicago, where he holds a position with Franklin, McVeigh & Company, wholesale grocers, married Miss Annie Shannen; James A., educated at Chicago, and is now holding a position in the tube plant of the Illinois Steel Company, married, Louise Rabb and has one son, Billy; Hazel, a graduate of the Emerson High School, of Gary, who married R. J. Castle, connected with the home building department of Sears, Roebuck & Company of Chicago, resides at Gary and has three children, Dorothy May, Harriet and Ralph; Ralph M., educated in the public schools of Chicago, including high school, now in the real estate and insurance business, unmarried and active in politics and the Knights of Columbus; Sarah who died in infancy; and Florence, who died at the age of fifteen years.

BLISH TODD has had an experience dating from early manhood with the limestone industry of Southern Indiana. He knows the business from the standpoint of a practical expert in all the operations involving the quarrying and preparing of the stone for building construction, and he has been identified with a number of different organizations, at the present time being general manager and superintendent of the McGrath Mill, a subsidiary of the Indiana Limestone Company.

Mr. Todd was born October 14, 1889, son of William G. and Elizabeth (Miller) Todd and grandson of William and Sarah Todd. His grandfather came from Tennessee, locating on a farm seven miles east of Mitchell, Indiana, being one of the early settlers in that section of the state. He was a man of much prominence in local politics there. At the time of the Civil war he and his son, William G., enlisted and served in the same company and regiment. William G. after his first term of enlistment expired reenlisted for the remainder of the war. At the close of the war they moved to Lawrence County and William Todd spent the rest of his life on his farm. He and his wife, Sarah, are buried in the county. They were the parents of fourteen children. William G. Todd was a farmer for several years and then took up the profession of photographer, which he followed at Mitchell, Indiana. After selling his studio he returned to the farm, and he is buried at Liberty, Indiana. The widowed mother is still living. Their children consisted of one that died in infancy, and the names of the others are Archie, Effie, Malcolm, Ott, Roscoe, Blish and Cleo.

Mr. Blish Todd began his education at Mitchell. He was seven years old when his parents returned to the farm and during the next eight years he had the routine of an Indiana farm boy, attending country schools. When he was fifteen years old he started working in a quarry, later learned the trade of planerman and completed his apprenticeship while with the Indiana Quarry Company. Later he was with the Consolidated Stone Company at Bedford. When Morris McGrath organized the Interstate Cut Stone Company, Mr. Todd was one of the skilled workers who joined that organization, and he has been through the various departments, finally coming to his present position as general manager and superintendent of the McGrath Mill, which was one of the many mills embraced in the general consolidation under the Indiana Limestone Company.

Mr. Todd married, June 13, 1907, Miss Ona J. Harris. Her parents, Dan and Emma (Sellers) Harris, are members of well known Lawrence County families. Mr. and Mrs. Todd have four children: Clovis, a graduate of the Bedford High School, Geneva and Antoinette, in grade school, and Patricia Anna, who was born in 1929. The family are all interested members of the Christian Church, and Mr. Todd is a member of the Bedford Industrial Club.

MARTIN SMITH has in many respects justified his reputation as being one of the most valuable citizens of Lawrence County. He was left an orphan when an infant, had to work out his own destiny, has enjoyed increasing prosperity as a farmer, is also a banker and has had much to do with the public affairs of the county in recent years.

Mr. Smith, who resides in the town of Williams, was born September 3, 1883, son of Orrel and Elizabeth (Bowman) Smith. His grandparents were Hetch and Martha (White) Smith. His grandfather served in the Union army during the Civil war, owned a large amount of land in Lawrence County and afterwards moved with his family to Knox County. Orrel Smith was born in Lawrence County, and was a farmer and land owner in Knox County. Both he and his wife are buried in the Bruceville Cemetery of that county.

Martin Smith was about a year old when his parents died. For a few terms he attended the Kings Ridge School, but his most valuable lessons have been learned in the school of experience and practical work. During his boyhood and early manhood he worked out for other farmers, carefully saving his money until he invested in thirty acres of land. That constituted his real start in life. After selling his first land he bought what now constitutes his present farm, known as the River View Farm, comprising 213 acres. He also has another place, of 107 acres across the river. His farm is a mile and a half west and south of Williams, and Mr. Smith gives it his close personal supervision.

Mr. Smith has been president of the Williams Bank since it was established in 1923. He is a member of the Church of Christ. He married, August 10, 1904, Miss Eva Doane, daughter of Henry and Mary (Bex) Doane. They have one daughter, Helen, born in 1921, now attending the public schools at Williams.

Mr. Smith has given Lawrence County the value of his service as a county commissioner for the past six years. His term expires January 6, 1930. While on the board he has used his influence to reduce taxation and give an economical administration of county affairs and at the same time produce a constructive administration, including the building of the County Hospital, construction of concrete highways through the county, and he has energetically favored the proposition for a new courthouse. Mr. Smith is a Republican in politics.

JOHN A. RITTER, physician and surgeon, is the dean of the medical profession at West Baden, where he began practice fifty-seven years ago. His name is held in highest esteem throughout Orange County, where his father was a doctor before him.

Doctor Ritter was born in Orange County, August 7, 1849, of German ancestry. His grandfather came from Germany as a young man, and married in this county a Miss Butler, daughter of an Arabian-Turkish political refugee. He died one year after his son John was born, leaving no record of previous family history in Germany. Dr. John Ritter, father of Dr. John A. Ritter, was a pioneer physician of Orange County and practiced there until his death. During the Civil war he became captain of Company G of the Forty-ninth Indiana Infantry and later was transferred to the Medical Corps and became chief surgeon for General Asterhous' Division. He was once slightly wounded by a spent ball. Dr. John Ritter married Margaret Carter, who was born in Orange County and lived to a good old age, passing away in 1910. They were the parents of nine children: Dr. Theophilus, deceased; Harriet, who married L. P. Brown, and is now living at Orangeville, Indiana; John A.; William, a merchant at French Lick, who owns one of the best stores in Southern Indiana; Thomas, deceased; Mary, deceased; James, deceased; Doctor Henry, deceased; and Maggie, who married George Taylor and lives at South Bend, Indiana.

Dr. John A. Ritter was educated in public schools in Orange County, continued his education at Greencastle and took his medical course in the Louisville Medical College. He was graduated in 1874, and shortly afterward located at West Baden. He did the work of a pioneer doctor, riding horseback, traveling in buggies years before the advent of good roads, the telephone or the automobile. He has been prosperous in a business way and owns considerable real estate and is one of the owners of the Ritter Hotel. Doctor Ritter has always voted as a Republican, as have all the Ritters of whom the Doctor has knowledge. He has filled the chairs of the Independent Order of Odd Fellows and Knights of Pythias lodges.

He married, May 3, 1882, Miss Sally Jackman, daughter of George and Cynthia (Wolfington) Jackman. Her father died while in the Union army during the Civil war. Doctor and Mrs. Ritter have two children, Harry O., born September 21, 1885, and Pearl M., born August 21, 1890. Harry, a hardware merchant at West Baden, married Mattie Laws, and they have two children, Mary E. and Pearl M. Pearl Ritter became the wife of Grover Bedster, of West Baden, and they have a daughter, Betty Pearl.

As evidence of the physical vigor of the Ritter family, Doctor Ritter's grandfather was the champion wrestler of the State of Kentucky, as determined by a series of contests, and Doctor Ritter himself was acknowledged as the best wrestler among the 600 men in DePauw University at the time he was there. He graduated therefrom in 1871.

GEORGE BENTON HIBBS. Almost the entire career of the late George Benton Hibbs was identified with the business of hotel operation and restaurant keeping, in both of which fields of endeavor he became widely known to the traveling public of Indiana. His was a long, busy and successful life, in which he won honor and success solely through the medium of his own efforts, for he had but few advantages during his boyhood and was forced to depend upon his own resources. As the years passed he won, through industry and good management, the fruits that come through the possession and exercise of the modest virtues, and in his death, which occurred March 10, 1927, the City of Rockport lost one of its substantial citizens and highly respected men.

Mr. Hibbs was born at Madison, Indiana, December 15, 1848, a son of Hamilton and Nancy (Duffy) Hibbs. His father, a native of Scotland, was brought to the United States in boyhood, being about seven years of age, and settled with his parents in Kentucky. The family remained in the Blue Grass State only for a short time, however, moving then to Marion, Indiana, where Hamilton Hibbs learned the trade of carpenter, and eventually developed into a contractor and builder, a business which he followed during the remainder of his life. He was a man of high character and had the esteem and respect of his fellow-citizens. He married Nancy Duffy, who was born near Jeffersonville, Indiana, and of their six children five lived to maturity: Sally, Laura, Mary, Jess and George Benton, all of whom are now deceased.

George Benton Hibbs received his education at Madison and Columbus, Indiana, and began life on his own account as a wagon boy for an express company. Subsequently he became a bell boy at the Belvidere Hotel, Columbus, Indiana, and remained at that hostelry for eight years, rising to the position of clerk. In 1879 he took up his residence at Rockport, where he bought a pocket billiard and cigar store, and March 15, 1881, was united in marriage with Miss Eva Biedenkopl, a daughter of Henry and Catherine (Scherer) Biedenkopl, the former born in this country and the latter in Germany. Henry Biedenkopl was a general merchant and retail liquor dealer, and subsequently was connected with the Occident Hotel, which, with a restaurant, he operated until his death, when the business was taken over by his son-in-law, Mr. Hibbs. Four children were born to Mr. and Mrs. Biedenkopl, of whom three are living: Henry, born in 1867, who conducted the Occidental Hotel for twenty-four years and married Amy Ellis, of Rockport; Catherine, born in 1865, who married Kap Morris, a native of Mount Vernon, this state; and Eva, who became Mrs. Hibbs.

Ten children were born to George B. and Eva Hibbs, namely: Lillian May, born December 9, 1881, who married Harry Bawter, a traveling salesman, and has three children; George B., born October 1, 1883, who takes care of the restaurant business for his widowed mother; Mabel, born August 20, 1886, who died at the age of twenty years; Eva, born September 12, 1888, who married first Harry Chappel, who died of influenza during the World war, leaving two children, and she then married Leonard Marquardt, a mechanic, and has three children; William C., born May 27, 1891, who died at the age of three years; Helen, born June 23, 1893, unmarried and a trained nurse by profession, who served overseas during the World war; Caroline, born October 23, 1895, who died at the age of ten years; Edward J., born February 12, 1900, a clerk in the Rockport postoffice; Esther, born June 21, 1903, who married Byrnie McDaniel, who is employed by the local traction company; and Catherine, born May 17, 1907, who is unmarried and serves as cashier in her mother's restaurant.

After disposing of his pool hall and cigar business Mr. Hibbs purchased the hotel known as the Spencer House, which he renovated, repaired and renamed the Cottage Hotel, which became a very popular hostelry and was well patronized by the traveling public. He also continued to operate the Occidental Hotel, had various other interests, including much real estate at Rockport, and at the time of his demise was one of the three oldest business men in the city. He was a Republican in politics, but did not seek public office.

CHARLES P. WALKER is widely known as a business man in the Upper Wabash River Valley. His home is at Mecca, where he is general manager for the William E. Dee Clay Manufacturing Company.

Mr. Walker was born October 22, 1849. His parents were Christopher and Rachael Elizabeth (Wiltsey) Walker. His father was born in Ohio, May 4, 1812, and died January 14, 1869, and his mother was born in Pennsylvania, in 1820, and died in 1857. Charles P. Walker was one of a family of eight children. Christopher Walker was a merchant at Cincinnati, where the children grew up.

Charles P. Walker after attending public schools started his career as an office boy with a railroad company. Later he became cashier in an office of the Chicago & Great Eastern Railway, was promoted to paymaster, and when he finally left the railroad service he had special training and qualifications as a traffic expert. He turned this experience and his capital to account in the coal business at Clin-

ton, Indiana, where he was located for twenty-five years. While there he organized the Norton Creek Coal & Mining Company, acting as its general manager. From coal mining he turned his attention to the clay products manufacture in the Wabash Valley and during this period of thirty-one years has acted as general manager of the William E. Dee Clay Company, manufacturers of sewer pipe, tiling, fire brick and similar products.

Mr. Walker is a Democrat in politics and a member of the Masonic fraternity. He married, October 15, 1873, Miss Jeanie A. Sammis, who was born at Brooklyn, New York, April 8, 1851. Mrs. Walker passed away January 15, 1927. Mr. and Mrs. Walker had six children, six grandchildren and one great-grandchild. The three deceased children were Rachael, Fanny Frances and Charles P., Jr., the latter of whom died January 15, 1915. He had married Annett Cutler. The living children are: Antoinette Steward, of New York; Geneva H., wife of Charles H. Hughes, living in Michigan; and Jeanie A., wife of Samuel Cutler.

JOHN OLIVER BOWERS. A resident of Gary since 1910, during the two decades that he has spent in the city John O. Bowers has won a high and substantial position at the bar, and likewise is known for his achievements in the real estate investment field. A man of scholarly attainments and literary ability, he has taken a great deal of interest in the history of Lake County and the Calumet River region, and there are few men who are better posted on the matters pertaining to early growth and development in this locality.

Mr. Bowers was born in Bedford County, Pennsylvania, in 1860, and is a son of John and Sarah R. (Conley) Bowers. His father was a member of an old and honored family of the Keystone State and was born and reared in Bedford County, where he acquired a serviceable education in the public schools of his day. He was reared to the life of an agriculturist, and when the war between the states came on he, being still too young for enlistment, was called upon to remain at home and till the parental acres while several of his elder brothers took up the dangerous implements of war and saw active and gallant service in the field. He was not destined to live long, passing away during the '60s and being buried at New Paris, Bedford County, Pennsylvania. He married Sarah R. Conley, who was also born, reared and educated in Bedford County, where she taught school for several years prior to her marriage. She was also active in the United Brethren Church, in the faith of which she died March, 1910, and was laid to rest at the side of her husband at New Paris. They were honorable and God-fearing people who had the full respect and esteem of all with whom they came into contact. There were three sons in the family: George M., who died in infancy; John O., of this review; and Edward B., who has spent practically all of his life in Montana, but who is now a resident of Porter County, Indiana.

After attending the public schools of his native locality John O. Bowers pursued a course in the Central State Normal School, Lockhaven, Pennsylvania, from which he was graduated as a member of the class of 1886. Three years later he received his degree of Bachelor of Laws from the Valparaiso (Indiana) University, and in the same year was admitted to the state bar. For a few years thereafter, while further preparing himself for his profession, he taught school, and then went to Kansas, where he began his professional career. However, that location and the conditions surrounding did not satisfy him, and in 1894 he returned to Indiana and opened a law office at Hammond. That city continued to be his home until 1910, in which year he took up his permanent residence at Gary, where he has since become one of the community's most respected and substantial citizens. In his profession he is known as a man of versatility, equally proficient and learned in all lanes of legal lore, so that it has been unnecessary for him to apply himself to any single branch of his calling. He served in the capacity of referee in bankruptcy for the Twelfth Referee District of Indiana for twelve years, this comprising the counties of Lake, Porter, Newton, Jasper, Benton, Stark and White. At the time of his coming to Gary he resigned as referee and has largely given himself to his real estate investments, having been active in the building up and development of Gary, and himself at present the owner of two city blocks. His commodious law office is situated in one of his own buildings, at 542 Broadway, and he is a member of the Gary Bar Association, Indiana State Bar Association and American Bar Association. Among other public-spirited works, he was active in the promotion and substantiation of the Dunes State Park. Although liberal in his political views, he is apt to lean slightly toward the Republican party during national elections. His family attends, he helping to support, the Congregational Church. Mr. Bowers has given a great deal of time and attention to historical subjects. He was one of the organizers and for a time president of the Gary Historical Society, and for some years was also president of the Lake County Historical Society. In connection therewith he has written a number of articles and pamphlets which have been received by many of his fellow-citizens with much favor. Among the most ambitious of these interesting works is a little booklet entitled *Dream Cities of the Calumet*, published in December, 1929. The limits assigned to this sketch of Mr. Bowers are inadequate to permit of quoting this book in full, but some idea of his easy and interesting style may be gained through a few excerpts. In his foreword the author states: "In the publication of this little story no one will realize its shortcomings more keenly than the author. He is aware that the events of importance described in the story are comparatively few, and that even the most important have had little influence upon the developments that have succeeded the earliest attempts to build or establish cities. Yet beginnings, though followed by failures, are usually interesting, and are generally presented as prefaces to portrayals of subsequent successful undertakings of like character. For example: No one would assume to write a history of the Panama Canal without mention of the name Ferdinand de Lesseps and of his efforts, and no one could purport to write a history of the growth of chemistry without reference to alchemy and the alchemists. The writer does not assume the role of historian at all, but merely seeks to aid in the preservation of a few points and items of some interest in the present and probably of an increasing interest through the coming years, which will certainly witness such revolutionary transformation of the territory hereby covered that it will tax the imaginations of the minds most fertile in fancy to envisage the activities and the social environments of a period that will then have become a bygone age. At this late date little historical material relative to the adventures of those far days is really available. What details might yet be discovered by patient and persistent effort the writer does not know, but if there he extant any old documents or date pertaining to these projects, the historian of the future and his readers will surely welcome the preservation and the publication of the same. By him and them the small beginnings of the early days will not be despised." Then, with much grace of literary style, and with numerous anecdotes, Mr. Bowers sets forth an interesting narrative of a number of the smaller cities which at their outset had dreams of future greatness, but only succeeded in being the forerunners of the metropolises of today, among them Liverpool, Manchester, Indiana City, City West, Sheffield and Waverly. "Concluding," says Mr. Bowers, "let me add that there have been dreams hereabouts which were not all dreams. A little while ago there were some dreamers who dreamed not of the 'fountain of youth,' nor 'the pot of gold at the foot of the rainbow,' but of a place at which all the raw materials which enter into the production of steel could be assembled at a hitherto unknown minimum of cost; to which the ore, the heaviest of all, machinery-mined-and-loaded, could be transported without an iron rail or the touch of a human hand. They were captains of industry—descendants of old Tubal-Cain. They had both enterprise and capital. They dreamed of a great army of men daily making tons and tons of steel, while great towers were emitting smoke 'like incense from the altar of labor.' They awoke and sought the place of which they had dreamed. By and by they found the place on the banks of a sluggish, two-mouthed, sourceless, silent stream, skirting the shore of an inland sea. They sought the employment of many men, and had the means to satisfy the pay-roll. (Maybe that helped the dream to come true.)

They built furnaces, factories and mills. Thousands of men are at work, and the smoke ascends, and sometimes descends, but a city close by is building, still building—not built. Both site and city are unexampled and unrivalled. The incorporating citizens of the new town sought not the capitals or marts of the old world for a name; they just gave it the name of one of the dreamers—the outstanding figure in the world of steel—Gary. But I have wandered far from the subject of my story, for I have passed from dreams that did not come true to dreams that did. I leave the story of this adventure for some historian who shall chronicle achievements as well as aspirations—deeds as well as dreams. I revert, but just to say that, after all, those 'cities' whose prophets were false, or—came too soon, lie buried in a land of marvels, and sometime, we know not the day, they may yet arise, like the fabled phoenix, from their mouldering ruins, at the sounding of the trumpet of Progress, and those streets long ago dedicated but never used, marked or graded, may yet resound with the footsteps of a busy metropolitan population."

At Allegan, Michigan, October 25, 1894, Mr. Bowers was united in marriage with Miss Nellie A. Blackman, daughter of Henry Elijah and Lucy (Sherwood) Blackman, of Allegan County, Michigan. Mr. and Mrs. Blackman, who were farming people, both passed away in Allegan County in 1913, the former at the advanced age of ninety-three years, and were buried there side by side on the Blackman farm cemetery. Mr. Blackman was a pioneer of that region, coming thence about 1838 and settling on the road running from Allegan to Kalamazoo. His grandfather was Elijah Blackman, a captain during the Revolutionary war, and Mr. Bowers has in his possession the old Government commissions signed by John Hancock and others of the early Colonial governors. He also possesses a number of photostats of the old commissions and a list of the names of the men in the company which Mr. Blackman raised and commanded in the Revolution. Mrs. Bowers was educated in the public schools of Allegan County, and after graduating from the Allegan High School was a teacher in the public schools of Michigan and Indiana for several years. She is active in the work of the Congregational Church, and for some years was active in the Daughters of the American Revolution and the Woman's Club. She and her husband have had eight children, of whom two died in infancy, the others being: Sylvan Forrest, a graduate of the Michigan State Normal School and the law school of the University of Chicago, degree of Bachelor of Laws, now a lawyer in the employ of the West Publishing Company, of St. Paul, Minnesota, who married Miss Jessie Duncan, of Valparaiso; Harold Eldon, a graduate of the Indiana University, who is now taking postgraduate work at the University of Chicago; Marjorie Elizabeth, a graduate of Earlham College and the New York State Library

School, who now occupies a position in the Gary Library; John Oliver, Jr., a graduate of Purdue University, and now engaged in the real estate business at Gary, who married Hazel Knotts, daughter of former Mayor Thomas E. and Ella Knotts, and has two children, Martha ,Ann and John Oliver III; Dorothy Naomi, B. S., B. A., M. A., University of Illinois, now a teacher in the high school at Farmington, Illinois; and Sherwood.

JOHN W. LAMB is an Oakland City business man, carrying on the oldest undertaking and embalming establishment in Gibson County, a business that was founded by his father and has had most capable direction under the management of the son.

John W. Lamb was born at Oakland City, December 26, 1890. His father, Porter H. Lamb, was also a native of Indiana and lived at Oakland City from 1884. In the early part of his life in that community he was in the livery business and in 1891 engaged in undertaking and was active until his death on March 9, 1929. At the time of his death he was one of the oldest business men of Oakland City. He married Louisa Poch, who was born on German Ridge in Perry County, Indiana, and died in September, 1916. There were two children, Esther L. and John W. Esther is the wife of Alfa W. Woodruff, a merchant of Oakland City, and to their marriage were born four children, one of whom is now deceased.

John W. Lamb attended the grade and high schools of Oakland City and in 1908 was graduated from the Cincinnati College of Embalmers, the same institution where his father completed his professional preparation. On January 29, 1909, he entered his father's business, being at that time one of the youngest embalmers in the State of Indiana. He has carried on the business now for over twenty years, except for the time he was in the army during the World war. He takes pride in the service that has been associated with the name Lamb in this community.

Mr. Lamb served at Camp Custer, Michigan, from the date of his enlistment in August, 1918, until honorably discharged on December 20, 1918. He is a Republican in politics, is a member of the Independent Order of Odd Fellows, Knights of Pythias and Modern Woodmen of America, and donates liberally to churches and other worthy causes. He is a member of the Kiwanis Club and the American Legion. Mr. Lamb married, May 18, 1911, Adith L. Crawford, step-daughter of Doctor McGowan, of Oakland City. They have two children: J. P., born March 25, 1912, and Emalou, born January 18, 1920.

GEORGE L. ADAMS, trustee of Perry Township, Monroe County, has lived all his life on the old Adams homestead, a farm that has been in the continuous possession of the family since pioneer days in this section of Indiana. This farm is located five and a half miles from Bloomington, on Route 37.

Mr. Adams was born on this farm November 17, 1871. He has been in charge of the property for about thirty years, and the improvements and developments on this 132 acre place stamp him as one of the progressive men in this agricultural community.

Mr. Adams is a son of David and India (McQueen) Adams, and is a grandson of Samuel Adams, who came from South Carolina, where he was born and reared. He entered the land in Perry Township from the Government. The grandfather and both of the parents are buried in the Clear Creek Cemetery. David Adams was a child when the family came to Indiana. In addition to farming he was a very skilled cabinet maker.

George L. Adams as a boy attended the Handy District School, completing the common grades there, and by work at home was well qualified to become the successor of his father as a farmer. He was only a boy when his father died, and he grew up to responsibilities in advance of his years. He has never left the old home place.

Mr. Adams married Myrtle Prince, and his second wife was Bertha Waldon, daughter of George and Emma Waldon. His three children were all by his first marriage: Grace, wife of Ray Porter; Alvin L., deceased; and Georgia H.

Mr. Adams has given altogether thirteen years to the duties of township trustee. He served a term of six years a number of years ago. He has been township trustee for seven years, his term expiring December 31, 1930. He has the distinction of being the first Democrat elected to this office in the township during the past half century. His administration of schools and roads and other township affairs has been one to justify the confidence of his fellow citizens. He is a member of the Christian Church and has been active in committee work for the Democratic party.

ZANAS N. FINNEY. Contributing to the general commercial prosperity of Princeton, Indiana, as a sound, reliable, far-seeing business man is Zanas N. Finney, owner and prosperous proprietor of a first-class grocery store, in which he has been interested since 1922. Although not a native of Indiana, a large part of his life has been spent here. He came first to Gibson County over forty years ago, and later spent some years in business in the West, but eventually returned to the county named, and here his interests have been centered ever since. Mr. Finney has a wide acquaintance among substantial business men in several lines, owns property at Princeton, and is counted one of her leading citizens.

Zanas N. Finney was born in Morgan County, Ohio, January 24, 1853, and is a son of Thomas and Margaret J. (Nash) Finney. His father, who was born in Maryland, was reared to the pursuits of agriculture, and as a young man moved to Ohio, where he was engaged in farming at the outbreak of the Mexican war. He volunteered for service during this struggle, served valiantly, and at its close returned to the pursuits of peace, subsequently moving to Indiana, where he spent the remainder of his life in farming in Crawford County and became one of the substantial and highly respected men of his community. He married Margaret J. Nash, who was born in Pennsylvania, and died in Indiana, in 1906, and they became the parents of eleven children, of whom all grew to maturity except one who died in infancy.

Zanas N. Finney received his education in the public schools of Crawford, Indiana, where he was reared on the home farm, after leaving which he was for a time employed in a sawmill. In 1875, at the age of twenty-two years, he took up his residence in Gibson County, Indiana, where he established himself in business as the owner of a sawmill business, and later added a threshing outfit, which he operated for many years, all over the county. In 1901 Mr. Finney disposed of his interests and moved to Enid, Oklahoma, at that time a newly-opened section of the country, and for a few years found success in agricultural pursuits in that state, but subsequently returned to Gibson County, and went to work in the oil fields, where he was employed until 1922. In that year he embarked in the grocery business at Princeton, and has since built up a large and profitable patronage by reason of the superiority of his goods, his promptness and courtesy and the general confidence in which he is held by the people of the community. He carries a full line of groceries and general supplies and his business covers a broad territory. Mr. Finney is a stanch Republican and a public-spirited citizen, but has never sought nor cared for public office. He is a member of the United Presbyterian Church and is fond of his home, therefore having no club or fraternal affiliations.

On December 25, 1890, Mr. Finney was united in marriage with Miss Sarah Barnett, and to this union there were born four children: Bessie, who married R. C. Westerfeld, the proprietor of a grocerv at Princeton, and has one child; Jessie, who married J. M. Bishop, state mine inspector, and has five children; Edna, who married Carl M. Smith and lives near Princeton; and Mary, who is unmarried and makes her home with her parents.

ORA F. BRANT is one of the prominent representatives of the automotive business in the City of Fort Wayne, where he is vice president and manager of the South Side Chevrolet Company, the well equipped headquarters of which are at 2315 South Calhoun Street.

Mr. Brant was born at Columbia City, judicial center of Whitley County, Indiana, October 24, 1897, and is a son of Harvey H. and Amanda (Blair) Brant, both now deceased. Harvey H. Brant was born in Ohio and was a young man in Indiana when the Civil war was precipitated, he having served in that conflict as a member of an Indiana regiment of volunteer infantry. He was identified with farm enterprise many years and thereafter was engaged in the manufacturing of bedsprings, at Princeton, Gibson County. After retiring from active business he established his residence in the City of Lafayette, where he died in 1919, at the age of seventy-seven years. His wife likewise was born in Ohio, and she passed the closing period of her life in Fort Wayne, where her death occurred March 17, 1929. The parents are survived by two sons and six daughters, and of the number the subject of this review is the youngest.

Ora F. Brant was graduated in the high school at Wabash, this state, and since that time he has continued to be actively identified with the automobile business. He was in the employ of Greiger Brothers Motor Company in the City of Lafayette and thence came with C. A. Greiger to Fort Wayne, where a business was established under the same corporate title, that of Greiger Brothers Motor Company. He was thus engaged until March, 1927, when he established the South Side Chevrolet Company, of which he has since continued vice president and manager and the business of which has been signally prosperous under his progressive executive supervision. He is a member of the Fort Wayne Chamber of Commerce, and is affiliated with the Benevolent and Protective Order of Elks.

September 6, 1923, recorded the marriage of Mr. Brant to Miss A. L. Peavey, who was born at Clay City, Indiana, and they are popular in social circles in their present home community. They have no children.

WILLIAM P. KENNEDY. The Citizens Bank of Liberty, Indiana, is fortunate in having a man of the caliber of William P. Kennedy as its cashier, for his experience along diverging lines has been a broad and valuable one, and his pleasing personality adds to the volume of business of his banking house. He was born at Liberty, Indiana, March 30, 1866, a son of James P. and Lavinia W. (Dunbar) Kennedy, he born in Lancaster County, Pennsylvania, May 20, 1826, and she in Union County, Indiana, January 13, 1834. The paternal grandparents, John and Nancy Kennedy, natives of Ireland, and members of the same clan as Robert Emmett, took passage on the sailing vessel Venturn, bound for Philadelphia, Pennsylvania. On the voyage they became acquainted, and after landing were married. After several years spent in Pennsylvania they migrated to Franklin County, Indiana, arriving in the state in 1830.

James P. Kennedy's first work in Indiana was that of splitting rails, and he was paid sixteen and one-half cents per 100. Later he clerked in the Bevins Hotel at Cincinnati, Ohio, but was taken violently ill, and the young lady who was his nurse became his wife September 1, 1857. They lived for a short time at Oxford, Ohio, but went from there to College Corner and he worked for Jonathan Ridenhour, president of the old Junction Railroad, doing any kind of labor,

S. T. Martin

and receiving but a nominal salary. Three years later, with Dr. Andrew Hawley, he bought this railroad, but when they were refused switching privileges Mr. Kennedy came to Liberty, Indiana, arriving here in the latter part of 1862, and embarked in a mercantile business that he continued until 1871, when he sold it, and organized the First National Bank, in connection with Joseph Corrington, Michael J. Witt and others. Mr. Kennedy remained with this bank until his death, which occurred May 11, 1900. In addition to his other activities he had taught school in Franklin County, so that he had a varied experience. The maternal grandparents of William P. Kennedy were Andrew and Sarah (Stover) Dunbar, he born in Pennsylvania and she in Carter County, Tennessee. In 1811 they started for Indiana with two big wagons drawn by mules. On their journey they were ferried across the Ohio River, the ferry being drawn by twenty-four horses. At the place they landed there was a large two-story house, painted red, that was called the blockhouse, and was used as a refuge for the pioneers when attacked by the still hostile Indians. The site of that old blockhouse is now covered by the City of Cincinnati, Ohio. From there the Dunbars came on to Union County, Indiana, and settled on Whitewater River. Mrs. Dunbar's maternal grandfather, John Miller, died in 1814, and his wife, Mary, died in 1822. She, Mrs. Dunbar, told William P. Kennedy that John Miller had accompanied Lewis and Clark on their expedition into the "Northwest Territory," and that at the age of eighty-five years he could pick a squirrel from the tallest tree without using his glasses. He was three times married, reared twenty-seven children, and at one time took eighteen sons and went out against the Indians. Mr. Kennedy is proud of the fact that his grandmother thought he was like this sturdy old pioneer. He, himself, is one of six children, namely: Jinevra, who was a landscape artist, died at the age of sixty-nine years, April 1, 1927; L. M., who died January 30, 1927, married Flora Davis, was a tailor and manufacturer of Liberty, Indiana; Allevia, who married Saul Lambert of Liberty, was cashier of the First National Bank of Liberty for forty years, died March 15, 1928; William P., whose name heads this review; Adelaide, who is the wife of Franklin T. DuBois, of Liberty; and Emmazetta, who married Henry G. Bonnelle, was leading lady in Brady's productions.

William P. Kennedy was graduated from high school at the early age of sixteen years, and entered a bank at Hope, Indiana, that his father had helped to organize, and was its cashier until 1899, when he disposed of his interests there to come to Liberty as the cashier of the Citizens Bank of this city, and he is still serving in this capacity.

On April 5, 1899, Mr. Kennedy was married to Miss Alice K. Vogler, who was born at Hope, Indiana, a daughter of Louis and Roseltha (Lee) Vogler, natives of Hope, Indiana. Mr. and Mrs. Kennedy have no children. She

has always been very active in the Eastern Star, and in 1924 had the great honor of being grand matron of the Grand Chapter of Indiana. She has been trustee of the Masonic Home, and trustee and president of the board of Easthaven Hospital, Richmond, Indiana. In addition to these connections she belongs to various clubs and societies, and to the Moravian Church. Mr. Kennedy is a Republican. He is a thirty-second degree and Shriner Mason, and he also belongs to the Benevolent and Protective Order of Elks, the Independent Order of Odd Fellows, the Knights of Pythias, the Improved Order of Red Men and the Eastern Star. Both Mr. and Mrs. Kennedy are deservedly popular, and have a host of warm personal friends all over this part of Indiana.

STEPHEN THOMAS MARTIN has direct and important connection with the industrial and commercial interests of the City of Gary through his service as secretary, treasurer and general manager of the Clover Leaf Dairy Company, one of the leading concerns of this kind in Lake County.

Mr. Martin was born in Serbia, February 14, 1897, and is a son of Thomas and Gladys (Martin) Martin, who were born, reared and educated in Serbia, where their marriage was solemnized and whence they came to the United States in 1900. After passing a few years in Iowa the parents removed to the State of Washington, within whose borders they continued their residence until 1910. They then established the family home in the City of Chicago, there Thomas Martin was engaged in the retail grocery business a few years, and he then returned to Washington, in which state his attention was given to farm enterprise until 1915, since which year he and his wife have maintained their home in Gary, Indiana, where he is living virtually retired. Of the ten children three died in infancy; Mrs. Jennie Jankovic is a resident of Gary; Nicholas is a civil engineer in Serbia, native land of his parents; Mrs. Amelia Nickolich resides in Gary, as does also Robert, next younger of the children; Dorothy is a resident of Serbia; Stephen T. is the immediate subject of this review; and Miss Helen remains at the parental home in Gary.

In the public schools of Chicago Stephen T. Martin continued his studies until he had profited by the advantages of the high school, and he was not yet sixteen years of age when he came to Gary and entered the employ of the Illinois Steel Company. With this great industrial corporation he was connected three years, and he then became an employe of the Gary Sanitary Grocery Company, with which he remained one year in its establishment at Gary and the next year in that at Indiana Harbor. It was in the year 1917 that he identified himself with the Clover Leaf Dairy Company, the following year marked his advancement to the position of sales manager, in 1921 he assumed the office of secretary of the company, and since 1929 he has functioned as secretary, treasurer and manager, besides being a director of the company. He is a director likewise of the Printcraft Service Company and is treasurer and a director of the Milk Dealers Bottle Exchange of Northern Indiana. Mr. Martin has made the passing years count in worthy achievement and has gained secure place as one of the substantial and progressive business men of Gary. He here has membership in the Chamber of Commerce and Commercial Club, as well as the Lions Club.

The political views of Mr. Martin place him loyally in the ranks of the Republican party, his basic Masonic affiliation is with Gary Lodge, No. 677, A. F. and A. M., and he has membership also in a local chapter of Royal Arch Masons, in the Gary Commandery of Knights Templar and in Orak Temple of the Mystic Shrine, in the City of Hammond. He has membership also in the representative social organization known as the Sand Fleas. He retains the religious faith in which he was reared, that of the Serbian Church, his name is still enrolled on the roster of eligible young bachelors in the Steel City, and one of his chief diversions is found through the medium of occasional hunting trips.

ELBERT C. COOK, M. D. Of the medical men of Jefferson County who have gained recognition and position in their profession solely through the medium of their abilities and learning, Elbert C. Cook, of Madison, is an excellent example. He has gained broad information through varied experiences, has fought his own way to prominence, and the honors that have come to him have been deservedly won. In the various official capacities in which he has acted he has discharged faithfully the responsibilities which have attached to his offices, and in the meantime has won esteem with honor and without rancor.

Doctor Cook was born in 1877, on a farm in Athens County, Ohio, and is a son of W. I. and Polly (Beebe) Cook. His father, who followed farming and milling, was one of the highly respected residents and public-spirited citizens of Athens County, where he and his wife passed their entire lives and both were noted for their sterling qualities of mind and heart. Elbert C. Cook attended the public schools of Athens County and the high school at Stewart, Ohio, following which he entered the Kentucky School of Medicine and was graduated with the degree or Doctor of Medicine as a member of the class of 1906. He served his internship at Rosalia Maternity Hospital, Pittsburgh, Pennsylvania, and in 1907 settled permanently at Madison, where he has since been engaged in a constantly increasing general practice. Doctor Cook has a fine presence in the sick room, having been specially prepared for this by his early training. At the time that he graduated from high school his financial circumstances did not allow him to enter medical college at once, and he therefore took a course in professional nursing at Bellevue Hospital, New York City.

After he left that institution he was employed for some years as a professional nurse, and thus had the opportunity of gaining invaluable experience in the care and handling of patients. To this early training he attributes much of the success that has come to him. He is now accounted one of the most capable and thorough general practitioners in Jefferson County. He maintains well-appointed offices at the corner of West and Third streets, where he has every known appliance of the modern physician and surgeon. During the World war he was appointed Government referee of the draft board, and before the war had closed had his application in to join the Navy Medical Corps. He has since been designated as physician for the United States Bureau of Compensation, and has also served as secretary of the city health board of Madison. He is a member of the Jefferson County Medical Society, of which he was president in 1927; the Fourth District Medical Society and the Indiana State Medical Society, and fraternally is identified with Madison Lodge No. 2, A. F. and A. M., and the Knights of Pythias. Doctor Cook now owns and resides on the old "Vawter Homestead," one of the show places and landmarks of this section of the state. This comprises about sixty acres of the original land grant, and the home, built in 1804, is one of the oldest in Indiana, but is still in an excellent state of preservation. Doctor Cook is a busy physician, but has always found time to devote to civic interests and has won the right to be considered one of the most public-spirited men of Madison.

Doctor Cook married Miss Myrtle Baer, daughter of ex-Judge Baer, a well-known lawyer and jurist of Indiana, and to this union there have been born two children: Norma, who married Russell Kloepfer and has one child, Zonia Lee; and Rosamond, the wife of Don Hudson.

HARVEY C. SULLIVAN. For many years the virtue of the springs of West Baden, Indiana, have brought to this resort people from all parts of this and other countries, and have made necessary, in order to maintain the prestige thus gained, the operation of first-class hotels to entertain the many who seek relaxation and look for relief from disease. One of these hostelries whose fame is being carried to other lands is the Sullivan Hotel, formerly the Terrace Hotel, owned and operated by the late Harvey C. Sullivan, and now under the direction of Mrs. Sullivan. The slogan in this hotel is "service with a smile at pre-war prices." Mr. Sullivan passed away, after brief illness, on October 6, 1930.

Harvey C. Sullivan was born in Washington County, within two miles of Salem, Indiana, November 10, 1872, a son of James and Nancy Jane (Simpson) Sullivan, the latter of whom was born in Greene County, Indiana, and is still living at the age of ninety-one, but the former died June 10, 1925. He was born in Greene County, and was a farmer of Washington County. During the war between

E. E. Cook M.D.

the states he served in the Union army and was a brave and gallant soldier. The parents had fourteen children, namely: Mary who died in infancy, William L., James, Martha J., Charles C., George W., Laura L., Harvey C., Minnie, Robert L., Nannie J., Frank, Fred and Daisy.

The public schools educated Harvey C. Sullivan, and he remained in Washington County for some years. His first venture was farming, his second merchandising, and he conducted a store at Greenville, Indiana, in partnership with his brother William from 1894 to 1908, when on March 26, the store burned down and they moved their business to Pekin, Indiana, where they operated one of the best stores in that locality. Harvey C. Sullivan purchased his brother's interest soon after establishing at Pekin and continued as sole owner until 1919, when once more he sold, making money in the transaction.

While he was thus engaged Mr. Sullivan began to be interested in handling real estate, and was so successful in his first ventures that he decided to enter the field, with the object of handling hotel and apartment properties. At the same time he invested in some very valuable pieces of property, and in July, 1929, bought the Terrace Hotel at West Baden. Immediately thereafter he made some improvements, changed the name to the Sullivan Hotel, and infused every department with his characteristic energy and wholesome spirit of enterprise, and the effect has filled his house with contented guests who feel that in it they have home surroundings and food together with a perfect service no private home can achieve. Probably Mr. Sullivan was one of the most popular men in Orange County, and he knew people from all over the world.

On October 3, 1902, Mr. Sullivan was married to Miss Annice Gertrude Templeton, daughter of Robert P. and Sarah Ellen (Ransom) Templeton, the former a native of Pennsylvania and the latter a native of Bradford, Indiana, where they were married. Mrs. Sullivan has one sister, Mrs. Ora Smith, of Salem, Indiana, and one brother by a later marriage of her mother, Leyden Steele, of Bedford. Mrs. Sullivan was born at Floyd Knobs, Indiana, December 17, 1879. Mrs. Sullivan is now the friendly hostess who greets the guests at Sullivan Hotel and makes them feel at home. One child has been born to them, James Templeton, April 5, 1904. This young man attended the Scottsburg High School, where he specialized in agriculture. When he first left school he worked for his father in the store, later spent two years with the Francoise Products Company, Baltimore, Maryland, then operated the White River Casino, near Seymour, Indiana, for two years and in 1931 built his own modern oil station and lunch room near the same location, known as Sullivan Cafe, where he is enjoying a splendid business. In July, 1925, he was married to Miss Laura Betty Yanaway, of Casey, Illinois. They have no children.

Mr. Sullivan of this review was a Democrat, as was his father before him, and as is his son after him. For many years he was a strong supporter of the Methodist Church and other institutions for the public good. Fraternally he belonged to the Independent Order of Odd Fellows, to which he belonged twenty-five years and the Improved Order of Red Men.

Mr. Sullivan's death was a distinct loss to the whole community, he having been characterized by an editor who knew him as "one of the best known business men of Southern Indiana." His cheery smile and inexhaustible good will and energy are much missed by the regular guests of the hotel. The funeral was held at his mother's home near Salem, Indiana, and he was buried in Crown Hill Cemetery at Salem.

WILLIAM E. CARR. Prior to his election, in 1929, to the office of county treasurer of Jefferson County, William E. Carr had been known principally to the people of this community as a practical, progressive and successful agriculturist and raiser of live stock, and as a straightforward and public-spirited citizen of enlightened views and modern tendencies. During his short incumbency of the office, however, they have learned that he possesses also those qualities which make for capable and expeditious service in offices of public responsibility and trust, and in demonstrating these he has strengthened in no small degree his hold upon public confidence.

Mr. Carr was born on a farm in Jefferson County, Indiana, February 9, 1873, and is a son of James H. and Mary A. (Kessler) Carr. His paternal grandfather, John Carr, was born in Ireland, and immigrated to the United States in young manhood, settling on a Jefferson County farm during the early '40s. He became an ardent abolitionist in the years prior to the outbreak of the Civil war, and made his home a station of the "Underground Railway," that famous organization which, under cover of darkness, enabled thousands of fugitive slaves to escape to Canada. Mr. Carr became one of the substantial citizens of his community, where he spent the remainder of his life in farming, and died respected and esteemed. He married Miss Perminta Ryker, a native of England.

James H. Carr, father of William E. Carr, was born in Jefferson County, where he received a rural school education and was reared in the atmosphere of the farm. Brought up in a home where the mere thought of slavery was an outrage, it was but natural that he should enlist in the Union army at the outbreak of the war between the states, in which he saw three years of hard and valiant service as a private in an Indiana volunteer infantry regiment. Following the war he returned to the farm, where he spent the remainder of a long and useful career, and in his death left behind him a record of unsullied citizenship. He married Miss Mary A. Kessler, who was also born in Indiana, and they became the parents of eight children, of whom William E. was the fifth in order of birth.

William E. Carr attended the country schools of Jefferson County, but when sixteen years of age was compelled to give up his studies. The family was large and it was necessary for him to take his place as a contributor to the general income, which he did as an associate of his father, with whom he farmed until 1900. In that year he began farming on his own account, and through industry and the use of modern methods and machinery became, as he is today, one of the leading growers of corn and wheat and raisers of fine cattle in the county. Always a stanch and active Republican, in 1928 he became the candidate of his party for the county treasurership, to which he was elected, taking over the reins of office in 1929. Since he has assumed his official responsibilities he has shown himself competent, energetic and conscientious in the performance of his duties, leading the people to a confident belief that the finances of Jefferson County are in safe and capable hands.

Mr. Carr was united in marriage with Miss Mabel L. Ryker, who was born in Jefferson County, Indiana, where her father, an agriculturist by vocation, was also a toll-road operator during the greater part of his life. Mr. and Mrs. Carr are well and favorably known in social circles of Madison, where they are also active in church work. They are the parents of one daughter, Miss Mary Stella.

EUSEBIUS PHINEAS TRAPP. The business of banking at Vernon, like the art itself, has been a development springing out of the needs of accumulating wealth and diversified commerce. The bank does not come to an embryo town perfectly organized and fully capitalized. It does not come on the first boat nor build up its solid walls in a settlement of tents and camps. There must precede it some degree of maturity in business, some accumulation of wealth and an active commerce with distant regions. As the business of banking is the outcome of the need of its facilities, so the men who assume control of its operations are usually those as happen, by reason of natural aptitude and the circumstances surrounding them, to be drawn into the vocation. Thus the first bankers in a community are usually drawn from other callings, teachers, merchants, lawyers and men of versatility and ready adaptation. Such has been the case with E. P. Trapp, who was engaged in educational labors until 1895, at which time he became assistant cashier of the First National Bank of Vernon, of which he has been cashier since 1900.

Mr. Trapp has born in Jennings County, Indiana, October 29, 1871, and is a son of John H. Trapp. His paternal grandparents, John and Marguerite Trapp, were born in Germany, whence they came as young people to the United States, and for some years lived in Missouri. From that state they moved to Jennings County, Indiana, where John Trapp, who had been a bailiff in Missouri, spent the rest of his life in agricultural pursuits.

John H. Trapp was born in Jennings County, where he received a common school education, and was reared on his father's farm. He was thus engaged at the outbreak of the war between the states, during which he enlisted in Company K, One Hundred and Twentieth Regiment, Indiana Volunteer Infantry. Shortly after the war Mr. Trapp became interested in the business of brickmaking, and this he continued to follow, in connection with agricultural operations, until the close of his active career. He was a man of excellent business judgment and one who won and held the confidence of his fellow-citizens, who elected him to public office, he having served as township trustee from 1884 until 1888, and as county treasurer from 1894 until 1899. He and his wife became the parents of three children: E. P., of this review, Marguerite and Nellie.

E. P. Trapp attended school in Jennings County and was graduated from the high school at Vernon, following which he became a school teacher in Lovett Township and followed the educator's profession for four years. Appointed deputy county treasurer in 1895, he served in that capacity for four months, resigning that post to accept the position of assistant cashier of the First National Bank of Vernon. In April, 1900, he was made cashier, and has continued to act in that capacity to the present. The First National Bank was organized in 1886, as the Jennings County State Bank. In 1891 the bank became nationalized and was chartered, and in 1911 was rechartered. On December 27, 1930, it was consolidated with North Vernon National Bank of North Vernon, Indiana. Mr. Trapp continued with the reorganization. He is widely known as a capable, conservative and thoroughly learned banker, and has a number of connections with banking organizations. Fraternally he is affiliated with North Vernon Lodge No. 59, A. F. and A. M., and the Royal Arch Chapter of Masonry; and Mount Ida Lodge No. 73, I. O. O. F He served as a member of the school board of Vernon, and in every way has discharged the duties of good citizenship, particularly during the World war, when he was one of the most active men in his community in working for war funds

Mr. Trapp married Miss Ann Wenzel, of Jennings County, Indiana, of German ancestry, and to this union there have been born six children, including two sets of twins: Marguerite, the wife of Henry Hulse, a business man of Vernon; Florence, her twin, who married William H. Simpson, postmaster of Vernon and a veteran of the World war, who saw two years of convoy service in the United States Navy; John Wenzel, a graduate of Hanover College; Rachael, the wife of Carl Lunsford, a business man of Vernon; Ruth, her twin, who is deceased; and Mary, the wife of Robert Whitcomb, a graduate of Han-

George S. Silliman M.D.

over College and now a teacher in the public schools. Mrs. Trapp is prominent in social circles of Vernon, a popular member of the Woman's Club, the Jennings County Historical Society and Vernon Chapter of the Society of Colonial Dames, and is secretary of Rebekah Lodge No. 33, Vernon, and district president of the Sixth District, Rebekahs of Indiana.

JOHN H. GREEN, M. D. In the annals of medical science in Jennings County no name is better known or held in higher esteem than that of Green. Three generations bearing this name have practiced at North Vernon, where the family has been identified with the profession since 1859. The present representative is Dr. John H. Green, who is not only the possessor of a large personal practice in general medicine and surgery, but also surgeon for the Baltimore & Ohio Railway and United States Government medical examiner. His career has been an active and successful one, and his high character and talents are indicated in the fact that he is a member of the State Board of Health and president of the Jennings County Medical Society.

Dr. John H. Green was born at North Vernon, Indiana, in 1886, and is a son of Dr. James H. and Emma (Millizen) Green. His paternal grandfather was Dr. Charles H. Green, who was born in Columbiana County, Ohio, a member of one of the old and distinguished families of the Buckeye State. After attending the public schools he entered the Ohio Medical College (University of Ohio), at Cincinnati, Ohio, from which institution he received the degree of Doctor of Medicine, and in 1856 commenced practice at Butlerville, Jennings County, Indiana. Three years later he removed to North Vernon, where he was not only prominent in a professional way, but also in public affairs, contributing materially to the upbuilding and development of this part of the state during the period of its infancy. He was a physician of the old school who rode many miles on horse-back and in his buggy to attend to cases far from his home and whose benevolence and charity were by-words all over the countryside.

Dr. James H. Green, father of Dr. John H. Green, was born in Jennings County, not long after the arrival of his parents in this state, and from his father inherited an inclination for the profession of medicine. He was carefully trained under the preceptorship of the elder man, and was then sent for a full course to the Ohio Medical College at Cincinnati, from which he was graduated with his degree as a member of the class of 1884. He was a thoroughly capable member of his profession, who won success by sheer ability and industry, and like his father was a prominent figure in civic affairs, holding a number of offices and being held in high esteem by the people. He married Miss Emma Millizen, a native of Illinois.

After attending the public schools of North Vernon Dr. John H. Green pursued a course at Purdue University, and then entered the medical department of the University of Indiana, from which he was graduated with his degree of Doctor of Medicine in 1911. Immediately thereafter he settled down to practice at North Vernon, where he proceeded to assume the mantle of his father's and grandfather's ability, and is now in possession of one of the best practices to be found in the state in a city of this size. During the World war he served as a member of the Medical Advisory Board and later was commissioned a first lieutenant in the United States Medical Corps and was stationed at Fort Riley, Kansas, for four months, but was not called for overseas service. He was formerly health commissioner of North Vernon, and since 1923 has been a member of the Indiana State Board of Health, in addition to which he is president of the Jennings County Medical Society, surgeon for the Baltimore & Ohio Railway and United States medical examiner at North Vernon. He belongs also to the Fourth District Medical Society, the Indiana State Medical Society and the American Medical Association. He is commander of the local post of the American Legion for 1929, belongs to the Country Club, and is a member of North Vernon Lodge No. 59, A. F. and A. M.

Doctor Green married Miss Minnie Graves, who was born at North Vernon, daughter of Albert B. and Alzora Graves, and a member of an old and prominent family of Indiana, who settled here in an early day.

GEORGE STEPHEN SILLIMAN, M. D., a distinguished roentgenologist, saw active service with some of the American units in the World war, and has recently established his professional headquarters in Gary.

Doctor Silliman was born at Hoosick Falls, New York, December 26, 1882. His grandfather, Abraham Silas Silliman, was a Connecticut Yankee, from Fairfield, Connecticut, followed the business or occupation of farming and later lived at Hobart, New York, where he and his wife are buried. The father of Doctor Silliman was prominently and widely known throughout the East as a clergyman of the Episcopal Church. He was Rev. George D. Silliman, who was born and reared at Hobart, New York, was educated in St. Stephens College at Annandale, New York, and in the General Theological Seminary of New York City. After being ordained he was sent west and was for a time rector of the Trinity Church at San Francisco. He was rector of St. George's Church at Newburg, New York, and held several prominent pastorates in the Albany diocese, being rector of St. Mark's Church at Hoosick Falls and of Grace Church at Albany, and of St. John's Church at Stockport, New York. He died April 1, 1910, and is buried at Newburg. His wife, Mary Warren, was born at Newburg, New York, was educated in St. Gabriels School at Peekskill, New York, and after her marriage was heart and soul in sympathy with her husband's career. She died in November, 1897, and is buried at Newburg. Her children were: Cecelia, who died when twelve years old; Mary Warren, a very gifted concert pianist who died in New York City in 1917; Rev. William W., now rector of St. John's Church at Cambridge, Ohio; and George S.

George S. Silliman made the most of superior educational opportunities, attending the Albany Academy, graduated from St. Stephens College at Annandale in 1904, and took his degree in medicine at the Albany Medical College in 1908. Doctor Silliman for seventeen years carried on a general practice in medicine and surgery at Westbury, New York. He was located there when America entered the World war. On May 30, 1917, he was enrolled in the Medical Corps, received training at Fort Benjamin Harrison, Indianapolis, for two weeks and volunteered for immediate service in France. He went overseas, was attached to the British army and served as a medical officer in various units along the front line of the British armies until after the armistice. He was commissioned a first lieutenant and promoted to captain in July, 1918. After the armistice he was with the Army of Occupation near Cologne, Germany, until February, 1919. His honorable discharge came to him at Camp Upton, New York, May 6, 1919, and he then resumed his private practice at Westbury. Since the war he has been a member of the American Legion.

Having become deeply interested in X-Ray work and an expert roentgenologist, Doctor Silliman gave up his private practice at Westbury and for three years was associated with the Rutland Hospital at Rutland, Vermont, as pathologist. For one year he was roentgenologist at the United States Veterans Hospital at Aspinwall, Pennsylvania, and spent two years as roentgenologist at the Johnston Memorial Clinic at Abingdon, Virginia.

Doctor Silliman came to Gary May 1, 1929. Here his special service has been that of roentgenologist to the Methodist Hospital. He is a member of the Lake County, Indiana State and American Medical Associations, is a Mason, member of the Omega Upsilon Phi medical fraternity, is an independent Republican and member of the Episcopal Church.

He married at Westbury, New York, September 1, 1910, Miss Anne Margaret McConnell, of Philadelphia, daughter of Franklin and Margaret (Burke) McConnell. Her father was employed for many years as bookkeeper to the William and Harvey Roland Spring Corporation of Philadelphia, where he is now living retired. Her mother died a number of years ago, when Mrs. Silliman was about ten years of age. Mrs. Silliman attended grammar and high schools in Philadelphia, is a graduate of the Pennsylvania State Normal School and was a kindergarten teacher for several years before her marriage, doing this work in the public schools of Philadelphia. She has been active in church work and while at Westbury was a member of the Eastern Star Chapter.

To the marriage of Doctor and Mrs. Silliman were born six children, Margaret McConnell, George Stephen, Jr., Nancy Marion, Dorothea Janette, Elinor Warren and John Benjamin. Margaret was graduated from the Horace Mann High School in 1929, is the wife of William Nylec, who is now attending Indiana State University, and they have an infant child. George S., Jr., and Nancy are students in the Horace Mann High School, Dorothea and Elinor are in the Jefferson Grammar School.

SIMON W. TAYLOR, who at the time of his death was living retired in the attractive little City of Boonville, Warrick County, had in former years made a record of successful service as a teacher in the public schools and as one of the progressive exponents of farm industry in Warrick County. He was a scion, in the third generation, of a family whose name has been worthily identified with the history of this section of the Hoosier State since the early pioneer days. Simon W. Taylor died of heart trouble at Saint Mary's Hospital, Evansville, on May 28, 1931, at three a. m. and was buried at Boonville on Memorial Day, May 30, 1931.

He was born in Spencer County, Indiana, July 31, 1854, a son of Robert and Minerva B. (Burns) Taylor, both of whom were born in Warrick County, where the respective families were established in the pioneer period. Robert Taylor was born in Anderson Township, Warrick County, December 7, 1824, and his wife, Minerva Brackenridge (Burns) Taylor, was born in 1830, both having been reared and educated under the conditions that marked the pioneer period in the history of Warrick County, where their marriage was solemnized February 7, 1850. Robert Taylor made his influence count in successful activity as a farmer, as a pioneer saw-mill operator, as owner and conductor of a general merchandise business at Newburg, Warrick County and as county clerk for eight years, and he was one of the most honored and venerable native sons of Warrick County at the time of his death, which here occurred December 13, 1913, his wife having passed away in September, 1907. He went to California in the gold rush of 1849, being fairly successful in finding gold. Of the six children only two are now living: Louis died in childhood. Emma became the wife of William H. Patterson, a lawyer, and she died at the age of thirty-two years, being survived by two of her three children. Sina, who died at the age of sixty-three years, was the wife of Willard C. Hunton, who is still engaged in the photographic business at Boonville, and she is survived also by three children. Simon W., of this review, until his recent death was the eldest of the survivors. Ida, who is seventy-four years of age, lives at Boonville, unmarried. Charles H. was born October 27, 1865, and has been active as a business man at Boonville, by association with mercantile enterprise and by a long period of successful alliance with the insurance business. He married Estelle Osborn, and they still reside at Boonville. They have no children. On the 19th of May, 1931, Mr. Charles H. Taylor succeeded his brother, Simon, on the Indiana Board of Agriculture.

Louis Taylor, grandfather of the subject of this review, was born in Kentucky and in 1913 he journeyed on foot from Bowling Green, that state, to the Ohio River, which he crossed, and he became one of the earliest settlers in Warrick County, Indiana, where he acquired a large landed estate and where he remained as a substantial and influential citizen until his death. The deed to one of the tracts of land that he here obtained in the early days was signed by President Andrew Jackson and is now in the possession of his grandson, Charles H. Taylor, who retains possession of about eighty acres of the land represented in the ancient deed.

Simon W. Taylor received the advantages of the Boonville public schools and in 1873-74 he continued his studies in the University of Indiana at Bloomington. In 1874 he initiated his long and notably successful career as a teacher in the public schools of his native state, his service in the pedagogic profession having covered a period of forty years and his retirement therefrom having occurred in 1914, when he was granted by the state a teacher's pension, as provided by the Indiana laws. He gave eight years of constructive service as county superintendent of schools for Warrick County, and he held the office of Boone Township trustee two years and at the time of his death was a member of the local school board. In 1914 Mr. Taylor turned his attention to farm enterprise, and in this field of basic industry he marked the passing years with notably successful achievement. He was loyal and progressive as a representative of farm industry in Warrick County and his was the distinction of having served continuously as a member of the Indiana State Board of Agriculture from 1913, he having been twice chosen vice president of the board and having held other official positions therewith.

Mr. Taylor gave to the Democratic party his loyal allegiance, he and his wife were earnest members of the Methodist Episcopal Church, and his Masonic affiliations included his membership in the Order of the Eastern Star, in which he was a past patron. It may be noted also that each of his two sons has received in the Masonic fraternity the thirty-second degree of the Scottish Rite and is a Noble of Hadi Temple of the Mystic Shrine, in the City of Evansville. He himself was affiliated also with the Knights of Pythias and the Tribe of Ben Hur.

Mr. Taylor was deeply loyal in his appreciative service as a member of the state board of agriculture, and that service was of constructive order in forwarding the interests of farm industry in Indiana. He retained ownership of one of the fine farm estates of Warrick County and was the owner of valuable realty in Boonville, including his attractive home place. His financial interests included his holding of Government bonds to the aggregate valuation of about $30,000.

At Boonville, on the 15th of July, 1886, was solemnized the marriage of Mr. Taylor to Miss Lucy E. Hoagland, who was born and reared in Warrick County and who was a daughter of George and Emma Hoagland, the former of whom was born in Warrick County and the latter in England. She died at Boonville, July 27, 1920. Of the children of Mr. and Mrs. Taylor the eldest is Jennie Marie, who was born June 27, 1887, and died about 1912. She was the wife of Ernest A. Wilkinson, engaged in the insurance business at Boonville. Mr. and Mrs. Wilkinson had one child, James, who was born in 1907. Howard G., next younger of the children, was born May 12, 1889, is a bachelor and is employed as a skilled mechanic in the City of Indianapolis. Lelia M., who was born April 9, 1895, is the wife of Walter F. Scheer, who was born in Ohio and who is now railroad station agent at Boonville, near which city he also has a well ordered chicken farm. Mr. and Mrs. Scheer have two children, Virginia and Barbara, born, respectively, in 1923 and 1924. Robert B., youngest of the children, was born October 29, 1905, is still a bachelor and is assistant manager of the Lockyear Business College at Evansville.

W. L. GROSSMAN, M. D. The career of Dr. W. L. Grossman has been one of constant and varied activity ever since he completed his educational training in young manhood. For a period of about twenty-three years he has been engaged in the practice of medicine and surgery at North Vernon, where he occupies a high and substantial professional position, and has served as president of the Fourth District Medical Society and as United States pension commissioner. He has taken an active and helpful part in civic affairs, is vice president of the North Vernon National Bank, and is also known in business circles, being a member of the board of directors of the Klingner Auto Sales Company.

Doctor Grossman was born on a farm in Posey County, Indiana, in 1879, and is a son of Andrew and Caroline C. (Lurker) Grossman. His paternal grandfather was William Grossman, a native of Germany, who came as a young man to the United States in 1837, and took up land in Posey County, Indiana, where he developed a farm, made a home and spent the remainder of his life in agricultural pursuits. Andrew Grossman was born on the home farm in Posey County, where he received a country school education, and early in life adopted the vocation of farming. This he followed throughout his life and was one of the substantial and highly respected men of his community. He married Caroline C. Lurker, also of German descent and a native of Posey County, and they became the parents of three children: Dr. W. L., of this review; Andrew A., who is engaged in agricultural pursuits in Posey County; and Lillian, the wife of Walter Knoppmeier, who is an employee of the Louisville & Nashville Railroad.

W. L. Grossman attended the country schools of Posey County and passed his boyhood on the home farm, subsequently pursuing courses at Oakland College and the University of Indiana. He prosecuted his medical studies at the Illinois Medical College, from which he was graduated with the degree of Doctor of Medicine as a member of the class of 1907, and in the same year opened an office at North Vernon, where he has since been engaged in a constantly increasing practice. He is widely and favorably known in his calling as a reliable, thorough and capable practitioner, an expert diagnostician and a steady-handed surgeon, and his practice is of the most desirable kind that can fall to the lot of a physician. Doctor Grossman, as noted before, was president of the Fourth District Medical Society in 1929 and United States pension commissioner for his district. He is also a member of the Jennings County Medical Society, the Indiana State Medical Society and the American Medical Association, and from 1910 until 1914 served in the office of county health officer of Jennings County. He belongs to North Vernon Lodge No. 59, A. F. and A. M., the Chapter and Commandery at Seymour, Indiana, and Murat Temple, A. A. O. N. M. S., at Indianapolis, and is a member of the Knights of Pythias. He has done much to advance the interests of the North Vernon National Bank in the capacity of vice president, and has various business interests, including the Klingner Auto Sales Company, of which he is a member of the board of directors.

Doctor Grossman married Miss Ida R. Hartman, of Posey County, Indiana, and they are the parents of three children: Willma C., a graduate of DePauw University; Irvin, who is also a graduate of that institution; and Pauline, a pupil in the North Vernon Public School.

JOHN H. GILMER. The business career of John H. Gilmer at North Vernon dates only from 1919, but within the short space of eleven years he has achieved a success such as many men would regard as a triumph if accomplished through half a century of patient effort. Coming here at the age of thirty-seven years, and at a time when the keenness of business competition, particularly in the matter of manufacturing enterprises, rendered success impossible unless through the exercise of sound judgment, allied to a certain degree of venturesome determination, he has achieved a reputation and success through the founding and development of one of the city's most prominent enterprises, the Universal Endless Belt Company, of which he is president and manager.

Mr. Gilmer was born in Albemarle County, Virginia, in 1882, and is a son of George Walker Gilmer. He is a member of an old and distinguished Colonial family of Virginia which has contributed many men of ability to the various vocations and professions and to public and political life, and his father was one of the prominent and influential men of his community. John H. Gilmer attended the public schools of the Old Dominion, following which he pursued a course of engineering at the Virginia Polytechnic Institute, at Blacksburg, Virginia. He was reared to agricultural pursuits, which he followed for some years, but possessed a mechanical turn of mind, and soon became interested in manufacturing enterprises. In 1915 he went to Philadelphia, Pennsylvania, and for four years was associated in business with his brother as the L. H. Gilmer Company. Mr. Gilmer came to Indiana in 1919 and settled at North Vernon, where, in a modest way, he began the manufacture of endless belts. This company met with an immediate market for its product, and under the impetus of Mr. Gilmer's tireless energy and excellent direction the output increased rapidly. In 1924 the company was incorporated, with Mr. Gilmer as president and manager, and in these capacities he continues to act. The company manufactures all kinds of endless woven belts for machines using these articles, and although the concern has been in business for only eleven years its products have a large market in every state in the Union. Its specialty is the Universal Superior Hand Woven Endless Belt, which has gained a country-wide reputation. The modern plant at North Vernon covers 8,000 square feet of floor space, and sixty people are given employment at the peak of production. Mr. Gilmer is a member of the North Vernon Business Men's Club and belongs to Lodge No. 32, A. F. and A. M., of Albemarle County, Virginia.

Mr. Gilmer married Miss Bessie White, of Houston, Texas, and they have four children: John H., Frances, William and Patricia, the first three of whom are attending school.

JOEL T. CARNEY, M. D. A leading member of the Ripley County medical profession, Dr. Joel T. Carney has been engaged in practice at Batesville since 1921, and through natural and acquired ability, thorough integrity and capacity for close application has built up a large and lucrative practice, at the same time winning the confidence and esteem of the people of his adopted community. He has also discharged with due conscientiousness the responsibilities of citizenship and of public life, and at present is president of the board of health of Batesville.

Doctor Carney was born in 1891, in Murray County, Georgia, and is a son of Timothy Carney, a farmer and merchant of Georgia, who in his youth served as a private of infantry in the Union army during the war between the states. Joel T. Carney received his early education in the public schools of his native community, following which he pursued a course at Saint Bernard College of Alabama, and then enrolled as a student in the medical department of the University of Louisville, Kentucky, from which institution he was graduated as a member of the class of 1921, receiving the degree of Doctor of Medicine. Subsequently he served his internship at the

City Hospital, Louisville, and in 1925 took post-graduate work at Barnes Hospital and Washington University.

In June, 1921, Doctor Carney settled at Batesville, where he entered upon the practice of his profession, and has built up a large and representative professional business, with offices at his pleasant and attractive home, 610 West Pearl Street. He is fully at home in all branches of medical and surgical science and has never found it necessary to specialize along any given line. A thorough student of his calling, he spends much of his leisure time in research and investigation, and is a man of broad general knowledge of various subjects. Shortly after his arrival at Batesville he was appointed secretary of the board of health, and at present is acting as president of that body. He belongs to the Ripley County Medical Society, the Indiana State Medical Society and the American Medical Association, and while at the University of Louisville was initiated into the Phi Beta Pi fraternity. During the World war he enlisted in the United States Medical Corps, but was not called overseas, his entire service being confined to the army training camps and hospitals in this country. Doctor Carney is a member of the Knights of Columbus, the Knights of Saint John and the Fraternal Order of Eagles.

Doctor Carney married Miss Sue Whitfield, a member of an old and distinguished family after whom Whitfield County, Georgia, was named, and to this union there have been born three children: Mary Carolyn, Elizabeth and John.

WILLARD N. VOSS. Of the men who through conscientious and energetic service have contributed to the welfare and good government of Indiana, few officials have better records than that of Willard N. Voss, of Versailles, county treasurer of Ripley County. A native of this part of the Hoosier State, he has always been loyal to its best interests, and as an official and a citizen has worked valiantly and unceasingly in the promulgation of movements which have resulted in the betterment and advancement of Ripley County and its people.

Willard N. Voss was born on a farm in Ripley County, Indiana, in 1899, and is a son of Henry and Mary (Luhring) Voss. The paternal grandfather of Willard N. Voss was born in Germany, where he received a common school education, and in young manhood immigrated to the United States, settling in Ripley County. At the time of his arrival he had small means and but a limited knowledge of the American language, but he was possessed of ability and ambition and in 1854 secured employment on a farm. From that time forward he advanced his fortunes and his interests, and at the time of his death was accounted one of the substantial citizens of his community.

Henry Voss, son of Henry and father of Willard N. Voss, was born in Ripley County, on the home farm, where he was reared, and received a common school education in the country schools. He was brought up to be a farmer and a raiser of cattle, and these vocations he followed throughout his life. He became an influential and substantial citizen of Ripley County and for four years, from 1900 until 1904, served in the capacity of sheriff. Mr. Voss married Miss Mary Luhring, a native of Ripley County, Indiana, daughter of Chris Luhring, who served as treasurer of Ripley County from 1894 until 1896. Mr. Voss died in 1918, leaving seven children, of whom Willard N. is the second youngest. One of his brothers is a prominent business man and farmer of Ripley County.

Willard N. Voss was educated in the public schools of his native community and at Milan, and was reared to the pursuits of agriculture, in which he has been engaged throughout his life. He remained on the home farm, and at the age of nineteen years, when his father died, he took over the interests of the elder man and conducted the property with ability and to its great advancement. In 1925 he entered the feed business, and conducted both the farm and the feed store until 1928, in which year he was elected county treasurer, taking office in 1929. His brother is now managing the feed establishment, which is one of the prosperous enterprises of Milan. Ever since the attainment of his majority Mr. Voss has been an ardent Democrat and active in the ranks of his party. As a fraternalist he belongs to the Independent Order of Odd Fellows.

GEORGE FRANKLIN HOEFFLE. In the City of Gary one of the metropolitan concerns here having leadership in its special department of the automotive industry is the Triple H Auto Parts Company, the well ordered wholesale and retail business of which is owned and conducted by George F. Hoeffle and John A. Hickey, the latter of whom likewise is represented in a personal sketch in this publication. The large and modern establishment of this company is found at 632 Washington Street, and the enterprise is one of the largest and most important of its kind in this section of Indiana, with a constantly expanding business that is based on effective service and reliable policies.

The birth of Mr. Hoeffle occurred in the City of Delaware, Ohio, June 16, 1885, and he is a son of William and Minnie (Houser) Hoeffle, both of whom continued their residence at Delaware until their death, William Hoeffle having there been for many years a representative plaster and cement contractor and his death having there occurred November 10, 1928. Both he and his wife, who died in 1891, were earnest members of the Methodist Episcopal Church, and their mortal remains rest in beautiful Oak Hill Cemetery at Delaware. After the death of his first wife William Hoeffle eventually was united in marriage to Miss Lillian Yates, and she likewise preceded him to the life eternal, her death having occurred in 1910. Of the three children of the first marriage the eldest is Mrs. Mary Poppleton; George F., of this review, was next in order of birth; and Edgar is a resident of Seattle, Washington. The one child of the second marriage is Mrs. Ruth Farris, of Delaware, Ohio.

After completing his studies in the high school of his native city George F. Hoeffle passed four years at Allegheny, Pennsylvania, where he served an apprenticeship to the trade of machinist, in the works of the American Locomotive Company. As a journeyman at his trade he traveled about and followed the trade in various cities during a period of four years. He was employed two years by the Jeffies Manufacturing Company, of Columbus, Ohio; was next in service three years with the Buda Manufacturing Company of Harvey, Illinois; and in 1911 he established his residence at Gary, Indiana, where for the ensuing nine years he was in the employ of the Illinois Steel Company. In 1928 he here formed a partnership with John A. Hickey, and he has since continued senior member of the firm that here conducts a large and representative business under the title of Triple H Auto Parts Company.

Mr. Hoeffle is a Republican in politics, he and his wife are members of the Methodist Episcopal Church, and Mrs. Hoeffle is affiliated with a local chapter of the Order of the Eastern Star. The ancient craft Masonic affiliation of Mr. Hoeffle is with the Blue Lodge at Chesterton, Indiana, his maximum York Rite affiliation being with the Knights Templar Commandery at Valparaiso, this state, and he is also a Noble of the Mystic Shrine, as a member of Orak Temple in the City of Hammond. He is actively identified with the Gary Commercial Club and Chamber of Commerce. He finds recreation through the medium of golf and through periodical hunting and fishing trips.

At Harvey, Illinois, December 27, 1911, marked the marriage of Mr. Hoeffle to Miss Margaret Sanders, a daughter of the late William and Martha Sanders, her father having long been a representative farmer near Chesterton, Porter County, and the public schools of that little city, including the high school, having afforded Mrs. Hoeffle her youthful education. Mr. and Mrs. Hoeffle have no children.

DR. D. W. MATTHEWS. Among the highly trained and naturally talented men who form the medical fraternity of Jennings County there are to be found a few who by reason of their special attainments and notable accomplishments are entitled to special mention. Among these is Dr. D. W. Matthews, who has been engaged in the general practice of medicine and surgery for more than a quarter of a century. While he has been a resident of North Vernon only since 1927, he has a broad and remunerative practice, and stands high in his humane calling, being an ex-president of the Jennings County Medical Society and

president of the Fourth District Medical Society.

Doctor Matthews was born in 1880, on a farm in Washington County, Indiana, and is a son of John J. and Sarah S. (Gray) Matthews. William Matthews, his paternal grandfather, was born in Ireland, and in young manhood immigrated to the United States, first settling in the East and then working his way westward to the virgin soil of Indiana, where he took up land about the year 1849. With the arrival of new settlers Mr. Matthews established a small store to supply their needs, and this he built up to a profitable enterprise. He was one of the substantial citizens of that early day and had the respect and esteem of those with whom he was associated.

John J. Matthews was born on his father's farm in Washington County, Indiana, and in his boyhood received his education in the country schools. He took up farming as his life occupation upon reaching years of maturity, and through constant industry, good management and a study of his vocation became one of the well-to-do farmers and stock raisers of his locality and a citizen who inspired general confidence and esteem. Mrs. Matthews was also a native of Washington County and a member of an old and honored family.

The second in order of birth of his parents' ten children, D. W. Matthews acquired his early education in the country schools of Washington County. He then applied himself to the study of his chosen profession and entered the Louisville (Kentucky) Hospital of Medicine, from which he was graduated with the degree of Doctor of Medicine as a member of the class of 1903. He commenced practice at Hardinsburg, Indiana, but at the end of four months removed to Martinsburg, Indiana, where he was engaged in practice for six years, this being followed by his removal to Commiskey, Jennings County, where he was professionally engaged from May, 1909, until September, 1927. In the latter year he came to North Vernon, where he has been prominent in his profession and in public affairs. He maintains a commodious and well-appointed office on Walnut Street, where he has a large and comprehensive medical library and all modern appliances and equipment known to medical and surgical science. He is accounted an expert diagnostician, a capable practitioner and a learned and accurate surgeon, and his successful handling of a number of difficult and perplexing cases of long standing and obstinacy has given him much more than a local reputation. Doctor Matthews served one year as township trustee and was deputy health commissioner of Jennings County, and during the World war was medical examiner for the local health board. He is president of the Fourth District Medical Society, and a member of the Jennings County Medical Society, of which he was formerly president, the Indiana State Medical Society and the American Medical Association. He has been very generous in the distribution of his services in times of need, and many of the people of Jennings County have reason to hold him in gratitude for his benevolence. Fraternally Doctor Matthews is identified with Paris Lodge No. 221, A. F. and A. M., of which he is a past master; Martinsburg Lodge, Independent Order of Odd Fellows, and a member of the Grand Lodge; Dauntless Lodge, K. of P.; and the Modern Woodmen of America.

Doctor Matthews married Miss Effie Martin, of Pekin, Indiana, who died in 1917, leaving three children: Gladys, who married Lawrence Callaway, an educator, and has two children, Virginia Lee and Robert; Clyde, who is an educator of North Vernon; and Miss Geneva, who is still attending school. In 1917 Doctor Matthews married Miss May Hedges Bridges, of Jennings County.

JOHN M. PARIS, of New Albany, county seat of Floyd County, has entered upon his third consecutive term of service on the bench of the Circuit Court of the Fifty-second Judicial Circuit of Indiana, and as a jurist his record has been notable in its exemplification of his broad and exact knowledge of law and precedent as well as by decisions marked by deep appreciation of equity and justice. Judge Paris had previously gained prominence as one of the representative members of the Floyd County bar and had held other positions of public trust prior to assuming his present office.

Judge Paris is a member of a family of three children and was born at Leavenworth, Crawford County, Indiana, March 7, 1878. He is a son of Winfield S. and Mary J. (Wilkins) Paris. His father was born in Kentucky, where the family had been established for three generations, and the Paris family lineage traces back to French origin. Winfield S. Paris was a youth when he initiated his career in connection with navigation on the Ohio and Mississippi rivers, and on those water thoroughfares he rose from the position of raftman to that of pilot, in which latter capacity he gave forty years of service, both he and his wife having long been residents of Indiana and having here passed the closing years of their lives, secure in the respect and high regard of all who knew them and had appreciation of their sterling qualities.

The public schools, including the high school, in Crawford County afforded Judge Paris his early education, and in preparing for his chosen profession he completed the prescribed curriculum of the law department of the University of Louisville, Kentucky, in which he was graduated as a member of the class of 1899. In the fall of the year in which he thus received his degree of Bachelor of Laws he took a course in shorthand and other business studies, and during the ensuing two and one-half years he was employed in the Louisville offices of the Southern Railroad. He then became a law clerk for the firm of Stotenburg & Weathers, of New Albany, Indiana, and in his two and one-half years' alliance with this

representative law firm he gained practical experience in the work of his profession. January 1, 1905, he opened a law office in this city and initiated the independent practice of his profession. In the fall of that year he was elected judge of the City Court, an office that he retained four years. He then resumed the active practice of law, to which he here devoted his attention until 1912, when he was elected prosecuting attorney of Floyd County. He held this office for the term of two years, was then renominated, but resigned the nomination. In the special election of May, 1914, he was elected judge of the Circuit Court, and by successive reelection he is now serving his third term in this office, his present term having its expiration in 1932.

Judge Paris is a stalwart advocate and supporter of the cause of the Democratic party, and he has membership in the Floyd County Bar Association, the Indiana State Bar Association and the American Bar Association. He is affiliated with the Masonic fraternity, the Knights of Pythias and the Improved Order of Red Men. His wife, whose maiden name was Lucille Denton, is a daughter of Boone Denton, whose mother was a member of the same family stock as the great frontiersman Daniel Boone. Judge and Mrs. Paris have four children: Mary Lucille, Sarah Denton, John M., Jr., and David Mason. All of the children are still students at the time of this writing, and the eldest, Mary L., is attending the Cincinnati College of Music.

Judge Paris was loyally active in furthering the varied patriotic movements and measures in Floyd County in the World war period, was a four-minute speaker in behalf of the various drives in the sale of Government war bonds, and was chairman of the legal board of the county.

WALTER ECKERT. History is repeating itself as it always does. Following the close of the war between the states it was found that those who had gone through the stern discipline of military training made the best citizens; and so it is now that the veterans of a much greater war are proving the worth of their months of patriotic service, in that, having learned to control themselves, they are well able to guide others in the right paths. All over the country these veterans are carrying on both public and private affairs with ability and integrity, and one of them worthy of special mention in connection with Ripley County is Walter Eckert, owner of the leading hardware store at Osgood.

Walter Eckert was born in Ripley County, Indiana, in 1892, a son of John and Rose (Wright) Eckert, the former of whom was born in Jennings County, Indiana, and the latter at Vincennes, Indiana. The family was established in Indiana by the paternal grandfather, a man of affairs, and its prestige was continued by the father, who from 1882, when he established it, until his death in June, 1918, a period of thirty-six years, conducted a hardware business. In addition to his commercial relationship to his community he was interested in civic affairs, and when he died the people with whom he had been associated mourned the passing of a fine man and a good citizen.

Walter Eckert went through the work of the local schools, and then took a commercial course in Eastman's Business College, Poughkeepsie, New York. Upon his return home he became associated with his father in the hardware business, and now owns the store, carrying a full and timely stock of heavy and staple hardware, his floor space amounting to 7,500 square feet. Around him he has gathered a selling force of experienced salesmen, and his customers receive good service at all times.

In August, 1918, Walter Eckert enlisted in the United States Marines, having, however, been in the Second Indiana Field Artillery, in which he had enlisted in June, 1917, his period of service in all covering twenty-two months, and he was stationed at Paris Island, South Carolina. Following his honorable discharge he returned to Osgood and entered the hardware business on his own account, his father having died in the meanwhile. He is a member of the Business Men's Club, and for eight years served Osgood as treasurer. A member of the local post of the American Legion, he was its commander for five years.

Mr. Eckert married Miss Gertrude Beldon, of Crothersville, Indiana, and they have two children: Mary N. and Janice. He, himself, is one of four children. Fraternally Mr. Eckert is a Mason and belongs to Osgood Lodge, A. F. and A. M. During his entire career he has taken an active and influential interest in movements of civic interest, and is enthusiastic with relation to the future of Ripley County, being willing to render assistance to it in any way that lies within his power. It is a source of pride to him that his family is one of the old-established ones of the locality, and here he proposes to continue to live.

EDWARD J. WELKER. The clerk of the court of Jennings County, Edward J. Welker, of Vernon, is one of the officials who have contributed to the advancement and betterment of this part of their state through conscientious, able and expeditious service. Mr. Welker is distinctively a self-made man, for he had none of the advantages, educational or otherwise, that are considered the prerogative of youth, and he started to make his own way in the world when still a lad. He has led a varied career, in which he has engaged in a number of pursuits and held various offices, and at present is assistant chief of the Vernon fire department.

Edward J. Welker was born at Vernon, Indiana, in 1877, and is a son of William F. and Maria L. (Wagner) Welker. His paternal grandfather, a native of Ohio, enlisted as a private in an Ohio infantry regiment during the war between the states, from which he did not return home, and it was believed that he was one of that great number who were killed and buried without being identified. The grandmother was left without means and with four small children, who were left orphans at her death a short time later.

William F. Welker was born at Cincinnati, and after the death of his mother was taken into the home of a druggist at Vernon, by whom he was reared and educated. He had no inclination for the drug business, however, and instead learned the moulder's trade, which he followed throughout his life. He was a man of good character and citizenship. He served as sheriff of Jennings County from 1888 until 1892 and discharged the duties of his office competently.

The only child of his parents, Edward J. Welker, attended the public schools of Vernon. As a boy he worked in a printing office, where he learned the trade and followed it until after his marriage, at which time he and his father started a transportation line between Vernon and North Vernon, transporting passengers, freight, mail, express, etc. The business proved a success and was continued until 1909, when it was sold. During this time Mr. Welker also served in the capacity of mail carrier, and bought the Vernon Hotel, which he and his wife managed for some years, in connection with a restaurant, but later sold the hotel and opened a new restaurant, which was operated until October, 1927, when it was sold. In the meantime Mr. Welker had been for some years interested in politics and had been repeatedly elected to office. He served as town clerk of Vernon for one term, and after serving as deputy sheriff in 1917 and 1918 was appointed deputy county clerk, an office in which he served from 1919 until 1923. He was then elected clerk of the Circuit Court for four years and at the expiration of this period was reelected to the same office, and in which he has established a splendid reputation. As noted, he is assistant chief of the Vernon fire department, and in this connection is a member of a well-drilled and highly efficient organization. He is secretary of the Vernon Cemetery Association, a member of the Jennings County Historical Society and a director of the Jennings Building & Loan Association. Fraternally he belongs to North Vernon Lodge No. 59, A. F. and A. M.; North Vernon Chapter No. 68, R. A. M, and the Order of the Eastern Star; the Independent Order of Odd Fellows, in which he has been a member of the Grand Lodge; the Rebekahs; and the Knights of Pythias, in which he has passed through all the chairs

In 1899 Mr. Welker was united in marriage with Miss Almeda O'Hair, who was born, reared and educated at Vernon, whence her parents had come from Illinois. Three children have been born to Mr. and Mrs. Welker: Bernadine, who attended the State Normal Teachers Training School, at Charleston, Illinois, and is now the wife of James F. Boggs, a business man of Vernon, and has three children, Edward O., Bertha Ann and Carlos; Charles C., who graduated from Purdue University as an electrical engineer, was second

J. F. Kelley

lieutenant in the Officers Reserve Training Corps, and is now identified with the Michigan Bell Telephone Company, married Sylvia Mooney, and has one son, Richard; and Frances, who attended Mrs. Blake's School, and is now a business woman of Indianapolis.

CHARLES MONEYHON, president of the Connersville Lumber Company, has always kept pretty close to the line of work which first engaged his attention as a boy. He is a native of Kentucky, a member of families that before the war were business men, planters and slaveholders. His grandfather was in the lumber industry, and it was as assistant to this ancestor that Charles Moneyhon got his start.

He was born at Augusta, Bracken County, Kentucky, October 6, 1871, son of Alfred and Christianna (Weimer) Moneyhon.

His father was also born at Augusta and spent his active life as a farmer. The paternal grandparents were Patterson and Elizabeth (Cabler) Moneyhon, the former a native of Ohio County, Kentucky, and the latter of the State of Ohio. Patterson Moneyhon was a lumber manufacturer in Kentucky. The maternal grandparents were Louis F. and Elizabeth (Nichols) Weimer. Louis Weimer was born in Germany and his wife in Bracken County, Kentucky. Louis Weimer before the war owned a flour mill, a pork packing establishment, a distillery, and most of the labor in these plants was performed by slaves. When the war came on he found it difficult to secure help and therefore gave up his manufacturing activities, though he continued to own and operate a large acreage of farming land.

Charles Moneyhon grew up on a farm until he was twenty years of age, attended public schools and an academy and for two years clerked in a dry goods store. He was stationary engineer in his grandfather's lumber plant and later joined an uncle in the lumber business at Augusta, Kentucky, remaining with him from 1894 until 1903. Mr. Moneyhon in the latter year became a resident of Connersville, Indiana, and acted as manager of the Connersville Lumber Company. In 1904 he bought stock and became president and general manager, and for a quarter of a century the destiny of that business has been guided by him. It has become much more than a local plant during that time. The company takes pride in a service that enables them to provide promptly everything that enters into building construction. The company operates the largest planing mill outside of Indianapolis. At Connersville they have about a half a block of land for their plant and yards, and another branch yard in the north part of the city, known as the Consumers Coal and Supply Company. They have branches at College Corner and Oxford, Ohio, and at Glenwood, Indiana.

Mr. Moneyhon married, in 1897, Miss Anna Hanson, who was born in Bracken County, Kentucky, daughter of Frank and Alice (Weldon) Hanson, natives of the same county.

Mrs. Moneyhon died May 7, 1929, leaving two sons, Stanley and Charles, Jr. Stanley, who married Margaret Edwards, is in the building and loan business, associated with the Fayette Savings & Loan Association, of which his father is president and a director, James R. Carter, vice president, Alton G. Trusler, secretary, and C. I. Showalter, treasurer. Charles Moneyhon, Jr., is an active associate in his father's business, the Connersville Lumber Company. He married Aurelia Burkle.

Mr. Moneyhon is a member and financial secretary of the Christian Church, is a Republican, was one of the organizers and has served as a director of the Kiwanis Club and is affiliated with the Masonic fraternity, Knights of Pythias and B. P. O. Elks.

JAMES FRANK KELLEY, M. D., has practiced medicine in Washington County, Indiana, for over thirty-five years. His name is well known in local citizenship, for his influence has been broad and constructive both in and out of his profession.

Doctor Kelley was born in Newton County, Missouri, September 2, 1869, and was five years of age when his family moved back to Indiana and settled in Orange County. His father was Isaac L. Kelley, a farmer, and Doctor Kelley was one of four children. Doctor Kelley attended the Central Indiana Normal College at Danville and while he had settled upon the choice of a medical profession in early life, he had to make his own way and for six years he taught school in Orange and Washington counties, in this way getting the money to put him through medical college. The Kelley family came from Kentucky and first settled at Madison, Indiana.

Doctor Kelley was graduated from the Hospital College of Medicine in 1893, and since that year has practiced in Washington County. For nineteen years his home was at Livonia and since 1912 he has practiced at Salem. He is a member of the Washington County, Indiana State and American Medical Associations and was president of the county society from 1926 to 1928. For twenty years he has been county coroner. He is a member of the Washington County Historical Society and during the World war was medical member of the examining board of the county. He is a Scottish Rite Mason, member of the Consistory at Evansville, and is also affiliated with the Knights of Pythias, Independent Order of Odd Fellows and Improved Order of Red Men.

Doctor Kelley married Miss Carrie Best, of Washington County. They have four children: Audrey L., Frank H., Morris D. and Margaret E. Audrey spent two years in the Indiana State Normal School in Terre Haute, one year in the University of Indiana at Bloomington, and taught school for fourteen years in Washington County and at Indianapolis. She is the wife of H. T. Hottel, now head of the real estate department of the Washington Bond & Trust Company, Incorporated. Frank H. Kelley is with the Magnolia

Petroleum Company in Texas. He, at the age of twenty, taught in a high school at Las Cruces, New Mexico, subsequently attended the Indiana State Normal at Terre Haute, and for one year was a student in the University at Bloomington. Morris D. Kelley is sales manager for a radio concern at Salem. The daughter Margaret is a graduate of Butler University at Indianapolis.

JOHN CRITTENDEN McNUTT was born and reared in Indiana and now holds prestige as one of its veteran and honored legists and jurists, as he has been a member of the Indiana bar more than forty years and has served as judge of the Appellate Court of Indiana. Both his paternal and maternal ancestors made settlement in Indiana more than a century ago.

Judge McNutt was born on the parental home farm in Johnson County, Indiana, May 25, 1863, and is a son of James and Cynthia Jane (Hunt) McNutt, both likewise natives of Johnson County. Judge McNutt is a grandson of John and Mahala (Hensley) McNutt, and of William R. and Martha (Terhune) Hunt. John McNutt was born in Ohio but came to Johnson County, Indiana, from Kentucky about the year 1815. William R. Hunt was born in Kentucky and thence came to Johnson County, Indiana, in 1925. James McNutt passed his entire life in Johnson County, where he continued his activities as a farmer until his death, in 1867. His widow subsequently became the wife of Jacob M. Cooper, likewise a farmer in this county, as well as an exhorter in the Methodist Episcopal Church, his death having occurred two years after this marriage and his widow having long survived him.

Judge McNutt, who was about four years of age at the time of his father's death, was reared on a farm in his native county and after there attending district school in Hensley Township and the high school at Trafalgar one year he continued his high school work at Morgantown, besides which he availed himself of the advantages of summer normal schools and gave special attention to the study of philosophy. At the age of eighteen years he initiated what proved a specially successful service in the pedagogic profession. His first work as a teacher was in Brown County, the following year he taught in Johnson County, and the third year found him a popular teacher in the public schools at Morgantown. His service was continued a year in the rural district school and he thereafter taught in the schools at Providence, Johnson County. In the meanwhile he had given as much time as possible to the intensive study of law, and he was admitted to the bar in 1884, in the week that likewise recorded his twenty-first birthday anniversary. On the first of March, 1886, Judge McNutt engaged in the practice of law at Franklin, judicial center of Johnson County, and in 1888 he was elected prosecuting attorney for Johnson and Shelby counties, an office to which he was reelected

in 1890. He continued his residence at Franklin until January 1, 1893, when he was elected librarian of the Indiana State Law Library, an office of which he continued the incumbent six years. After retiring from this position, at Indianapolis, Judge McNutt formed a law partnership with Charles G. Renner and engaged in active practice at Martinsville. This alliance continued until the death of Mr. Renner, June 23, 1910, and in the preceding year Alfred M. Bain had become a member of the firm. The law firm of McNutt & Bain was dissolved January 1, 1913, and Judge McNutt thereafter conducted an individual practice until June, 1914, when he admitted to partnership his son, Paul Vories McNutt, and this association has continued ever since. The son became assistant professor of law in the University of Indiana, of the law school or department of which he is now the dean. April 30, 1916, the subject of this sketch was appointed judge of the Appellate Court of the State of Indiana, and in this position he served out the unexpired term of Judge Joseph H. Shea. Judge McNutt conducted his law practice in an individual way during the period of his son's World war service, and since the son has been a member of the faculty of the law department of the university Judge McNutt has actively continued his law business independently. In earlier years he served as county attorney of Morgan County, and at the present time he is retained as a local attorney for the Big Four, Pennsylvania, Monon and the Illinois Central Railroads, for the Home Building Association and for the two largest sanitariums at Martinsville, this city being one of the foremost health resorts of Indiana. He is also attorney for the First National Bank of Martinsville, in which he is a stockholder and in the building of which he maintains his law office. The Judge is the owner of a well improved farm of 160 acres, in Owen County, and is a director of the Cantol Wax Company of Bloomington, Indiana, which manufactures floor waxes and polishes and a wax belt-dressing that constitutes its greatest output. Judge McNutt has been a staunch and effective advocate and supporter of the cause of the Democratic party, and in 1918 he was the party nominee for the office of judge of the Indiana Supreme Court, he having met defeat through normal political exigencies at that time, as did he also after being nominated, in 1924, for judge of the Indiana Appellate Court. Judge McNutt is affiliated with the Masonic fraternity, the Independent Order of Odd Fellows, the Benevolent and Protective Order of Elks, the Morgan County Bar Association and the Indiana State Bar Association. He and his wife are zealous members of the Methodist Episcopal Church at Martinsville, and he has served continuously on its official board since 1910.

July 7, 1886, marked the marriage of Judge McNutt to Miss Ruth Neely, who was born in Brown County, this state, April 22, 1865, a daughter of Jacob M. and Sarah (Prosser) Neely. Jacob M. Neely was born in Brown

County, was a harness maker by trade, and was long an influential citizen of Morgan County, he having served four years as county clerk and having also served as postmaster at Morgantown. He was a gallant soldier of the Union in the Civil war and in later years served as assistant adjutant of the Indiana Department of the Grand Army of the Republic, while in the Masonic fraternity he received the thirty-second degree of the Scottish Rite. Of Paul V. McNutt, distinguished son of Judge and Mrs. McNutt, specific mention is made in an individual sketch following in this publication.

PAUL VORIES McNUTT, dean of the Indiana University School of Law, former National commander of the American Legion, and known and honored as one of the leading figures in the legal profession and its educational work in his native State of Indiana, is properly given individual representation in this history. He is a son of Judge John Crittenden McNutt, in whose personal sketch preceding in this publication is given adequate record of the family history, as well as his individual career.

Paul Vories McNutt was born at Franklin, Indiana, July 19, 1891, and his education along academic lines reached its student ultimate when he was graduated in the University of Indiana as a member of the class of 1913, with the degree of Bachelor of Arts and with high distinction. In 1916 he was graduated in the law school of Harvard University, but he had previously, in 1914, been admitted to the Indiana bar and had become associated in practice with his father, at Martinsville. He continued to give his attention to his profession until the nation entered the World war, when he promptly volunteered for service in the United States Army, in August, 1917. He received preliminary training at Camp Benjamin Harrison, near Indianapolis, and thence he was sent as instructor in officers training camps in Texas, he having later been assigned to similar service at Columbia, South Carolina. He served not only as an instructor but also in turn as commanding officer of the Fifth Regiment, the Fifth Brigade and the Second Brigade, F. A. R. D. He has retained since August 9, 1919, commission and rank of a colonel of the Officers Reserve Corps of the United States Army. The Colonel has been commanding officer of the Three Hundred Twenty-sixth Field Artillery Regiment since 1924, has been a member of the advisory board of the Fifth Corps Area since 1927, and has represented Indiana as civilian aide to the United States secretary of war since 1927. He is national judge advocate of the Reserve Officers Association of the United States, was commander of the Indiana Department of the American Legion in 1927, and in 1928 came to him the honor and distinction of election to the office of national commander of the American Legion.

In 1917 Colonel McNutt was made assistant professor of law at the University of Indiana, and he has held a full professorship since 1919, the year 1925 having marked his advancement to his present office of dean of the law school of the university. The Colonel is a member of the editorial board of the *Indiana Law Journal*, was president of the Harvard Legal Aid Bureau in 1915-16. has been since 1924 a member of the Alumi Council of the University of Indiana, and he has membership in the American Bar Association, the American Law Institute, the Indiana State Bar Association, the Association of American Law Schools, and the American Association of University Professors. Colonel McNutt is a Democrat in political alignment, his religious faith is that of the Methodist Episcopal Church, he is affiliated with the Benevolent and Protective Order of Elks and is a thirty-second degree Mason, and his collegiate affiliations are with the Order of the Coif, Phi Beta Kappa, Beta Theta Pi, Phi Delta Phi and the Acacia Society. He has membership in the University Club, the Rotary Club, the Martinsville Country Club and the Bloomington Country Club. At Bloomington, seat of the University of Indiana, Colonel McNutt and his family reside at 712 East Eighth Street.

April 20, 1918, recorded the marriage of Colonel McNutt to Miss Kathleen Timolat, who was born in Minnesota, a daughter of Harry N. and Louise (Merriam) Timolat. Colonel and Mrs. McNutt have a winsome daughter, Louise, who was born June 27, 1921.

ADOLPH H. ZWERNER, who is one of the representative younger members of the bar of Fayette County, is engaged in the practice of his profession in the City of Connersville, the county seat, where, on the 1st of January, 1929, he succeeded to the substantial and well established law practice of Judge G. Edwin Johnston.

Mr. Zwerner was born at Terre Haute, Indiana, October 14, 1905, and is a son of George L. and Elizabeth (Hesslein) Zwerner, who were born in Germany and who were young folk when they came to the United States, where their marriage was solemnized, George L. having been successfully established in the meat-market business in Terre Haute since 1890.

After completing his studies in the Terre Haute High School Adolph H. Zwerner went to the City of Indianapolis and was matriculated in the Indiana Law School, in which institution he was graduated March 30, 1927. After thus receiving his degree of Bachelor of Laws, with virtually coincident admission to the bar of his native state, he continued in the practice of his profession in Indianapolis until January 1, 1929, when, as previously noted, he succeeded to the practice of Judge G. Edwin Johnston in the City of Connersville.

Mr. Zwerner is a staunch advocate of the principles of the Democratic party, and while residing in Indianapolis he was a candidate on the party ticket for representative of Marion County in the State Legislature, this candidacy having been in the primary election of 1928. Mr. Zwerner has membership in the Fayette County Bar Association, is affiliated with the Modern Woodmen of America and the Delta Theta Phi college fraternity, and his religious faith is that of the Presbyterian Church. His name is now enrolled on the roster of eligible and popular young bachelors in Fayette County. He maintains his law office in the building of the First National Bank and resides at 514 Eastern Avenue.

HARRY E. BUCKINGHAM, landscape gardener, sexton of the Union City Cemetery, in this latter position represents a very unusual succession of almost continuous service by members of one family through three generations, since the establishment of the cemetery sixty years ago.

His grandfather, Benjamin F. Buckingham, was one of the organizers of the cemetery and in 1869 became its sexton. He performed the duties of that office until 1893, when he was succeeded by his son, Jefferson Monroe Buckingham. The latter held the office for twenty years, until he retired in 1913. During the next two years a Mr. Hinkle served as sexton, but in 1915 the work returned to the Buckingham family, when Harry E. was appointed to the office, and one of his sons assisting him in the work carries this honor of long official relationship still further.

Harry E. Buckingham was born in a log house at Union City, July 8, 1881, and is a son of Jefferson Monroe and Sarah (Mason) Buckingham, his father a native of Darke County, Ohio, and his mother of Pitt, Ohio. His grandfather, Benjamin F. Buckingham, was born in Maryland, and married Martha Hiatt, a native of Preble County, Ohio. Sarah (Mason) Buckingham was a daughter of Milton and Angeline (Dixon) Mason, the former a native of Wayne County, Indiana, and the latter of Randolph County. Milton Mason was a son of Thomas Jefferson and Jane Mason, who came from North Carolina in the early years of Indiana statehood. They were very early settlers in Wayne Township, Randolph County, locating near what is now Union City. They took up land from the Government and developed a farm.

The Buckingham family is of English ancestry. Harry Buckingham's great-grandfather, William Buckingham, was a native of England and arrived at Baltimore, Maryland, in 1808. Five brothers started across the Alleghany Mountains. Three of them drifted away, and the other two settled at a fort in Ohio on the Ohio River, and later moved to Randolph County, Indiana, and took up and developed land.

Harry E. Buckingham was educated in the grade and high schools at Union City and when eighteen years of age began learning the trade of tinner. This trade was his chief occupation until he took charge of the Union City Cemetery in 1915. This is one of the very old cemeteries of Randolph County,

comprising seventeen and a half acres of ground. Over five thousand persons are buried there, and among other eminent citizens for whom it provides the last resting place was Gov. Isaac P. Gray.

Mr. Buckingham, in August, 1927, built a greenhouse, with an acre and a quarter under glass, located at 1335 West Oak Street. He has done a great deal of competent work as a landscape gardener and has laid out one cemetery and done the landscaping for additions to three others. He is a Presbyterian, a Democrat, and is a member of the Independent Order of Odd Fellows, Lodge and Encampment, and the Junior Order United American Mechanics.

Mr. Buckingham married, in 1905, Miss Viola L. Imel. She was born in Jay County, Indiana, daughter of John W. and Rebecca Margaret (Bontrager) Imel. They have four children, Ray, Ethel R., Ralph B. and Harold E. Ray, who is associated with his father in business, married Edith Wagner.

WILLIAM JOHN MLODOCH. Among the men who have been important factors in the building up and development of the great industrial City of Gary, to few should be given greater credit for lasting and substantial accomplishment than to William John Mlodoch, secretary and auditor of the Gary Heat, Light & Water Company, and auditor of the Gary Land Company. Coming to this city as an accountant for the above companies, in 1908, he was chosen by his superiors for important work in the rapidly growing community, and has met each rising responsibility with energy and ability, developing his own resources and fitting them to the needs of his growing duties.

Mr. Mlodoch was born December 17, 1884, at Chicago, Illinois, and is a son of John and Charlotte (Schaale) Mlodoch. His parents, natives of Prussia, Germany, were reared and educated in their native land, where they were married, and immigrated to the United States about the year 1880, settling at Chicago. There the father established himself in the custom tailoring business and conducted an establishment of his own for a number of years. He was active in the Baptist Church, in the faith of which he died in 1896, and was laid to rest in the Forest Home Cemetery, Chicago. Mr. Mlodoch married Charlotte Schaale, who was born in 1848, and who was for years active in the Baptist Church in Chicago, where she still resides, at the age of eighty-three years. Her mother was a Lekunde, of Alsace-Lorraine, France. There were twelve children in the family, several of whom died in infancy and several in Germany of the black diphtheria or black death. Eight of the children lived to maturity: Martha, who is deceased; Emma; Adolph M.; William John, of this review; Dorothy; Edward E., Irving A., a veteran of the World war; and Lillian.

William John Mlodoch attended the public schools of Chicago and the Chicago Business College, and upon leaving the latter secured a position with the well-known firm of Barnett

Brothers, commission merchants on South Water Street. After five years with this concern he resigned to join the Illinois Steel Company, November 1, 1905, and in 1906, when the Steel Company, the Gary Heat, Light & Water Company and the Gary Land Company were organized he became identified with those organizations and in 1908 came to Gary in the capacity of accountant. By hard and efficient work, integrity and loyalty he gradually advanced himself in the confidence and esteem of his employers, and in 1913 was made secretary and auditor of the Gary Heat, Light & Water Company, positions which he still retains, and in June, 1928, was made auditor also of the Gary Land Company. He has various other official positions which place him high in the business world, being a director of the Gary Land Company, secretary, treasurer and a member of the board of directors of the Northern Indiana Investment Company, director of Ogden Dunes, Inc., vice president and a director of the Ogden Dunes Realty Company, and a man highly esteemed in business and civic circles for his probity and integrity. He is a member of the board of trustees of the First Methodist Episcopal Church of Gary, director of the Young Men's Christian Association and a prominent Mason of the thirty-second degree, belonging to Roosevelt Lodge No. 716, A. F. and A. M.; the Ancient and Accepted Scottish Rite, Valley of Fort Wayne, and Orak Temple, A. A. O. N. M. S., of Hammond. He likewise belongs to the Gary Commercial Club and Chamber of Commerce, Gary Country Club, and in politics is a stanch supporter of the principles and candidates of the Republican party. Fishing and golfing are his chief diversions, although he is also an ardent reader of literature.

At Chicago, Illinois, September 22, 1908, Mr. Mlodoch was united in marriage with Miss Othelia Louise Vogt, daughter of George J. and Roslie (Weber) Vogt, natives of Wurtemberg, Germany, where they were reared, educated and married. For a time after coming to the United States they made their home at Albany, New York, whence they removed to Chicago, where Mr. Vogt was engaged in the tannery business up to the time of his death in 1923, his widow surviving him until 1929, being buried in Forest Home Cemetery, Chicago. Both were active and consistent members of the Methodist Episcopal Church. Mrs. Mlodoch was educated in the public schools of Chicago, and is prominent in Methodist Episcopal Church work, the Order of the Eastern Star, the Ladies Relief Corps, auxiliary of the Grand Army of the Republic and the Woman's Club. Her brother, A. W. Vogt, is assistant comptroller of the United States Steel Corporation, with offices at New York City; and another brother, Charles A. Vogt, was auditor of the American Steel & Wire Company at the time of his death. To Mr. and Mrs. Mlodoch there has been born one daughter: Alice Helen, a graduate of Emerson High School, Gary, class of 1927, who spent two years at Rockford (Illinois)

College for Women, and two years at the University of Illinois, Champaign, from which she graduated with the class of 1931. She is a member of the Alpha Phi sorority.

CLAUDE YOUATT ANDREWS became a resident of Miami County, Indiana, in September, 1901. He was born in Vermilion County, Indiana, October 12, 1873; was educated with a degree of A. B., Franklin College, 1898; LL. B., University of Michigan, 1901; admitted to practice law in the U. S. District Court and the Michigan Circuit Courts in June, 1901; to the Miami County Bar later in that year and ever since has been engaged in the active practice of his profession at Peru. He was prosecuting attorney for the Fifty-first Judicial Circuit of Indiana, 1902-1904, attorney for Peru School City, 1929, and is now city attorney for Peru. He was Democratic candidate for judge of Miami Circuit Court in 1926 and is a member of the Indiana State Bar Association.

His grandparents were among the early settlers in Vermilion County. James Andrews and Reuben Puffer, both farmers, developed a considerable acreage which has been preserved by succeeding generations. William P. Andrews, his father, was a teacher and building contractor who, with his mother, Editha V. (Puffer) Andrews, were born in Vermilion County. Reuben Puffer, his maternal grandfather, came to Indiana in 1837, with his widowed mother, from Braintree, Massachusetts. Claud Y. Andrews is one of two children. His sister, Oakie Quest, is now Mrs. William C. Collier, who is a dealer in real estate and insurance in Dana, Indiana.

In 1901 Mr. Andrews married Laura Lukens, of Wabash County, a graduate of Franklin College with a degree of B. M., 1899. There was born to them one son, Francis Puffer Andrews, who graduated from the Peru High School in 1929, with distinguished honors, but who died July 25 of that year. No other children survive. His resting place is marked by a beautiful family monument in Mount Hope Cemetery. Mrs. Andrews' family, the Lukens, were early settlers in Wabash County, Lukens Lake bearing its name from the family. On the maternal side, Cornelius and Saphrona Lowe, early settlers in the north part of Miami County, came from Wayne County, Ohio, by way of the Wabash and Erie Canal.

Mr. Andrews has a practical philosophy of life which has impelled him to find time for many civic activities in addition to his professional career. Among his many community interests he has been a director of Peru Chamber of Commerce and its president for a period of thirteen years and was chairman of its reorganization committee after the World war. For fifteen years he has been president of the local Y. M. C. A. and part of that time a member of the State Board. He was trustee for a time of Dukes Miami County Memorial Hospital, trustee of Mount Hope Cemetery Association, moderator of Logansport Baptist Association, trustee of Franklin College, his alma mater, the promoter and by ten years of persistent effort created public opinion finally consummated in the purchase and development of Peru's beautiful two hundred acre park adjoining the city on the south. He is now president of the City Park Board. His greatest delight is in this achievement, for, as he says, "This park makes Peru a place where people like to live."

Mr. Andrews has an artistic temperament. His hobby is painting pictures in oil, not as a profession but for recreation. The new City Park bears evidence of his art in its layout and cultural development. He created and executed an historic pageant entitled, "Macon-a-quah," first exhibited in the athletic bowl of the City Park at the centennial anniversary of Indiana's admission to statehood in 1916. This pageant was reproduced in 1927 and remains a classic exhibit of the pioneer history of Peru and Miami County and probably will be repeated at intervals by succeeding generations. Mr. Andrews is vice president of the Miami County Historical Society.

Mr. Andrews has served as a deacon of the First Baptist Church of Peru for many years, also as a teacher in its Sunday School. He is a member of the Sigma Alpha Epsilon fraternity and of the Grand Lodge, Knights of Pythias. During the World war he was chairman of the executive committee of the local Red Cross and of the Four Minute Men Speaker's Bureau of Miami County. He delivered the address of the community to the departed soldiers and was a member of the War Educational Committee. He was a charter member of the Peru Kiwanis Club and has continuously for ten years served that organization in some official capacity, being alternately its president, trustee, director, also lieutenant governor for the Second Indiana Division and is now candidate for governor of the Indiana District, pending decision at the West Baden convention, 1931. The subject of this sketch is in the prime of life, with achievement yet in process.

JOHN H. STIER, senior member of the Stier & Williams Undertaking Company, half owner of the Aurora Floral Company with H. E. Williams and the Lawrenceburg Woman's Shop, and interested in numerous other enterprises, is one of the solid business men of Dearborn County, and a man widely and favorably known over a wide region. He was born in Dearborn County, Indiana, in 1866, a son of John P. Stier, the latter being a native of Mississippi. During the war between the states he served in the Confederate army, and after its close, finding business conditions unfavorable in his state, came, in 1866, to Indiana. The same vim and determination which made him a dashing and gallant officer of the Southern forces made him successful in his new home, and he was a traveling salesman and later became interested in several local enterprises. Four children were born to him and his wife, and John H. Stier's brother

Willard was mayor of Aurora for one term, but refused reelection.

Growing up in Dearborn County, John H. Stier attended its public schools and learned the trade of a woodcarver, which he followed for a few years, but in 1895 he entered the undertaking business. For a year previously he had been with Addison Sanks, under the name of Sanks & Stier, but it was not until 1895 that he became sole owner of the business. Mr. Williams entered the business in 1922, and the two have since continued together. Their art is not of recent date, for embalming, which is the act of preserving the body after death, was probably invented by the Egyptians, about 4000 B. C. However the methods used by those ancient people and those who came after them were entirely different from the ones of today. In 1800 a chemist by the name of Chaussier discovered the preservative power of corrosive sublimate by which animal matter becomes rigid, hard and grayish, but this did not prove satisfactory because, owing to desiccation, the features did not retain their shape. The discovery by Gannel, another chemist, in 1834, of mixing equal parts of acetate and chloride of alumina, or of sulphate of alumina; or arsenic by another chemist; pyroxilic spirits, and the antiseptic nature of chloride of zinc, have led to the application of these salts, and others, to the embalming of bodies. At present the most efficient agents are mercuric chloride, arsenic and zinc chloride, and the method is to inject the fluid into the femoral artery and the cavity of the abdomen. However, the service of the undertaker does not end with the preparation of the body, but has a broader scope. Under his skilled and experienced direction dignified and soothing services are held that cannot help but alleviate the sorrow of the afflicted, and lift the burden of responsibility from the shoulders of the family of the dead at a time when grief renders them incapable of acting for themselves. The above firm is well-known all over Dearborn and adjoining counties, and are recognized as competent practitioners.

Mr. Stier is part owner of the Aurora Floral Company, one of the best of its kind in the county; the Woman's Shop, Incorporated, the Woman's Shop of Lawrenceburg, both of Indiana, and the Woman's Shop of Oxford, Ohio.

One of the forceful members of the Commercial Club of Aurora, Mr. Stier served it for one term as president, and is one of its directors. Fraternally he belongs to the Ancient Free and Accepted Masons, the Independent Order of Odd Fellows, the Knights of Pythias and the Improved Order of Red Men. Professionally he belongs to the Hoosier State Undertaking Association and the Auto Association of Dearborn County, and is now president of the first named. For some years he has been on the board of Children's Guardians.

Mr. Stier was married to Miss Mary Kassebaum at Aurora, Indiana, a native of this city, and they have four children: Donald, who was graduated from Purdue University, served with the rank of first lieutenant during the World war in the One Hundred and Twenty-fourth Field Artillery being active during the last four months of the war, and was raised to the rank of captain, is now a chemical engineer, married Miss Hayes, of Chicago, and they have one child; Rachel, who married Donald Stoops, has two children, and she is a graduate of the University of Indiana; Marjorie, who was graduated from Oxford, Ohio, College, married Kenneth White, a member of a pioneer family, and they have one child, Robert; and Eleanor, who is a student in the University of Indiana.

During the World war Mr. Stier was very active in all of the Liberty Loan drives, and he was also a generous contributor to all war organizations. Mrs. Stier was on the Mothers' Board of Dearborn County, and both she and her husband were members of the Dearborn County Chapter of the American Red Cross. She is president of the Woman's Research Club of Aurora, and a member of the Aurora library board. Both Mr. and Mrs. Stier are Republicans in political faith. It would be difficult to find people more thoroughly representative of the best element of their community than the Stiers.

ROLAND A. COON. Among the younger generation of men who are prominently identified with financial affairs in Indiana, few have made greater strides toward position and success in as short a period as Roland A. Coon, district general manager at Vincennes for the Thompson Finance Company. With the exception of three years immediately following his graduation from college Mr. Coon has been identified with one or another form of loans and finance throughout his comparatively short but exceedingly active career, and each successive advancement has come as a result of natural and acquired ability and great industry.

Roland A. Coon was born in Fountain County, Indiana, in 1899, and is a son of Isaac W. and Dora (Balch) Coon, and a grandson of Perry Coon, the latter a lifelong farmer. Isaac W. Coon was born in Indiana and for a number of years was engaged in farming, subsequently becoming a cattle raiser and then a merchant at Shelbyville, Indiana. He was well and widely known in business circles as a man of strong character and sterling integrity, and as a citizen of public spirit. He and his wife were the parents of seven children: Amy, the widow of Orville Ehl, a farmer; Mary, the wife of Chester E. Sandefure, a well-known educator, who was superintendent of schools at North Vernon, Indiana, for fifteen years; Dan, a farmer, who married Mabel Sandefure; Perry, a business man of Terre Haute, Indiana, who married Jessie Irving; Bryan, a business man of Shelbyville, Indiana, who married Frances Vawter; Roland A., of this review; and Ralph, a business man of Shelbyville, who married Thelma Henry, daughter of Claude Henry, a prominent attorney of Shelbyville, and author of a legal survey on the industrial loan business of the United States.

Roland A. Coon received his education at Shelbyville, where he graduated from the high school, and at Franklin (Indiana) College, and commenced his business career as a traveling inspector for the Columbia Graphaphone Company of Toronto, Canada, with which concern he was identified for three years. He then returned to Franklin, Indiana, and entered the employ of the People's Loan Company, of which he was office manager for one year. Resigning that position, he went back to Shelbyville, his native community, and formed a connection with the Thompson Loan Company, and when the Thompson Finance Corporation was founded, in February, 1928, was made district manager. At present his headquarters are at Vincennes, where he has offices at 201 American National Bank Building, his territory covering Vincennes and Princeton, Indiana, and Lawrenceville, Illinois. The Thompson Finance Corporation is an Indiana corporation and is affiliated with the Thompson Loan Company, a sister firm, with headquarters at Shelbyville, Indiana, and other offices at Vincennes, Grangeburg, North Vernon, Seymour and Princeton, Indiana, and Lawrenceville, Illinois.

Mr. Coon is an energetic and hustling business man, who has made a thorough study of finance and loans and is broadly informed as to conditions in general and particularly in the territory over which he has charge. He is a member of the Masonic Blue Lodge at Shelbyville, Shelbyville Lodge of the Benevolent and Protective Order of Elks and the River Club of Lawrenceville, Illinois. During the World war he belonged to the Student Army Training Corps, and is now a member of the American Legion. His religious connection is with the Baptist Church, and his political convictions lead him to support the candidates of the Democratic party.

HON. HARRY C. POINDEXTER, mayor of Jeffersonville, has for many years been identified with the official life of that city. He has been a business man and lawyer.

He was born at Jeffersonville, May 10, 1857, son of Gabriel and Mary F. (Willey) Poindexter, grandson of Clevias and Nancy (Holland) Poindexter, and great-grandson of Rev. Gabriel Poindexter, who was a soldier with the Virginia troops in the War of the Revolution, and afterwards came to Indiana and did the work of an itinerant Baptist preacher. The father of the present mayor of Jeffersonville was mayor of that city from 1867 to 1869. Before the Civil war he was a merchant and during his later life was engaged in fruit growing. Both he and his wife were natives of Clark County, Indiana. Mayor Poindexter's grandfather, who came to Indiana about 1820, was a pioneer brick manufacturer.

Harry C. Poindexter was one of a family of nine children. He attended the grammar and high schools of Jeffersonville and from early manhood has been interested in politics. In 1894 he was the only Republican in Clark County elected a member of the Legislature. He served a term of two years. In 1901 he became clerk of the Town of Broad Ripple and in 1903 moved to Jeffersonville, where for five years he was engaged in the canning business. In 1906 he was appointed by Gov. Frank Hanley as judge of the City Court, serving an unexpired term of nearly four years. While in that office he studied law, graduated from law school at Louisville, Kentucky, in 1909, and has carried on a general law practice. He was elected mayor of Jeffersonville in November, 1925, and for four years has given that city a splendid administration of its municipal affairs.

Mr. Poindexter is a member of the Rotary Club, Chamber of Commerce, Masonic fraternity, Independent Order of Odd Fellows, Modern Woodmen of America. He belongs to the Clark County Bar Association, was a four-minute speaker during the World war, and is a leader in the Methodist Episcopal Church, being local preacher of the Wall Street Church, which was organized in 1803.

He married Anna M. King, a native of Jackson County, Indiana. They have four children: Miss Percie E., a teacher at Jeffersonville; Miss Amy K.; Bertha L. is the wife of Homer M. Frank, cashier of the Citizens Trust Company, and has two children, Richard and Martha Jane; and Miss Mary Margaret is a teacher at Jeffersonville.

MISS BERTHA F. POINDEXTER. To the lover of literature, the advantages of a well-selected library afford great pleasure, but all who can intelligently enjoy and truly appreciate do not possess such a collection, irrespective of how urgent may be their book-temperament. To a large extent this lack is supplied by the public library, now to be found in every progressive community. The Jeffersonville Township Public Library, located at Jeffersonville, Clark County, is a fine example of a public institution of this type that has proved of inestimable value. Its volumes cover every department of literary effort, and it not only has been notably helpful to ambitious students, but also beneficial to those of cultivated literary tastes. In Miss Bertha F. Poindexter Jeffersonville finds an ideal official as librarian, a lady whose educational, cultural and social gifts have combined to bring complete efficiency into the work, and whose patient, courteous and obliging personality has greatly endeared her to the patrons of the library.

Miss Poindexter is a native of Jeffersonville, and a daughter of Gabriel and Mary Poindexter. Her paternal grandfather was Clevias Poindexter, a native of Clark County, Indiana, who married Nancy Holland, of Indiana. Clevias Poindexter was a son of Rev. Gabriel Poindexter, a native of Virginia, who fought as a soldier in the War of the Revolution, following which he became a pioneer of Indiana, and for many years thereafter was a

minister of the Baptist Church and a school teacher. Of the nine children of Gabriel and Mary Poindexter six grew to maturity and four are now living: C. E.; H. C., who is mayor of Jeffersonville; Bertha F., of this review; and Frank C., of Indianapolis. Bertha F. Poindexter attended the high school at Jeffersonville, following which she pursued a course at Borden Institute in Clark County.

The present library association was established in 1897 by the members of the Jeffersonville Women's Clubs. The township library was taken over and with that as a nucleus the present library was started in 1900, with about 2,000 volumes. During the years that followed new books have been added from time to time, and the library now consists of about 15,000 volumes. In 1900 Miss Poindexter was elected librarian, a position which she has held continuously to the present with the exception of about twenty-one months when she was absent because of severe illness.

Miss Poindexter has been very active in all kinds of civic, social and religious work, as well as an educator, and is a member of the Indiana State and American Library Associations. She attended two summer sessions of library school at Indianapolis, where she perfected herself for work in her chosen calling, and has always been a close student and omnivorous reader. She is a member of the Daughters of the American Revolution, and an honorary member of the Current Events Club, of which she was president from the time of its inception until 1900, in which year she became librarian.

The Jeffersonville Township Public Library's corner-stone for its present building was laid with Masonic ceremonies and is a monument to the club women of Jeffersonville, whose zeal, hard work and interest made it a reality. The project was first advanced in the spring of 1897, at the Woman's Literary Club, by whom the need of a new library was keenly felt. The late Miss Hannah Zulauf was one of the most enthusiastic women engaged in the early discussions and plans, and at all times was ready to put aside her personal interests to give her time and thought to the matter, which she justly deemed of great civic and educational value. Calling a meeting of the town's literary organizations, she appointed two members of each to appear at Miss Poindexter's home to discuss ways and means. The second meeting was also held at Miss Poindexter's home, about three months later, and it was decided to ask the citizens to raise $1,000, this being done because of the discovery of a law, passed in 1852, which held that if a board of directors or trustees could show $1,000 worth of books and property the board of county commissioners could turn the township library over to them. Subscriptions at five dollars a share were offered, and by November 13, 1897, the sum of $1,160 had been subscribed. A meeting was held the following day in the City Council chambers at the City Hall, and an organization was ef-

E E Cox

fected, Prof. D. S. Kelly, superintendent of city schools, being elected president; Miss Hannah Zulauf, secretary and treasurer; and M. Z. Stannard, Miss Bertha F. Poindexter, Cord Worder, Mary K. Voigt and Eva Luke, members. The library association was incorporated, purchases of books were made in 1899, and the Indiana State Legislature passed a law turning over the township library, December 1, 1900. The new management on December 17 of that year assumed charge of the library, where it was then located over the Citizens National Bank, Miss Poindexter being elected librarian October 27, 1900, again in 1901 and again in 1903. Interest had been aroused to such an extent and patrons were becoming so numerous that it was realized the old library quarters were insufficient, and a measure was introduced and passed to legalize a new site for the library in Worder Park. Misses Zulauf and Poindexter wrote letters to Hon. Andrew Carnegie requesting a donation for a library building, and finally Hon. J. E. Taggart and Prof. A. C. Goodwin wrote and were promised that a donation of $15,000 would be forthcoming. This letter was written February 15, 1902, the City Council gave its consent, and in a few weeks work on the beautiful new building of Bedford stone was on its way to construction after plans made by Arthur Loomis, architect, had been accepted. The library building is one of the beauty spots of Jeffersonville, and is complete in every detail, comparing favorably with those of many larger cities. It has a large and constantly-increasing patronage, and has been and will continue to be of inestimable value to the people of this thriving city, both in the way of pleasure and education.

HON. FRANK GARDNER, who for three terms represented the Third Indiana District in Congress, is a Scottsburg attorney and in his native county laid the foundation of his political career in the fidelity that has distinguished every phase of his relations with his fellow men and the public interest.

Mr. Gardner was born in Scott County May 8, 1872, son of William and Eliza Jane (Ray) Gardner. His great-grandfather, James Gardner, on coming to America settled in South Carolina. His grandfather, George Gardner, was born in Indiana and was one of the early farmers of Scott County. George Gardner married a Miss McKnight, whose father was a soldier in the Revolutionry war. William Gardner was born in Washington County, Indiana, was a Scott County farmer, served as sergeant in Company C of the Fiftieth Indiana Infantry during the Civil war and held the offices of township trustee and county treasurer.

Frank Gardner grew up on a farm, attended country schools, was graduated in 1896 from the Borden Institute in Clark County and in 1900 received his law degree at the University of Indiana. He was admitted to the bar and began practice, but in 1901 became deputy county auditor and in 1903 began his first term as county auditor. He held that office for eight years, until 1911. From 1911 to 1917 he was county attorney of Scott County. During all this time he was carrying on a general law practice. Mr. Gardner has been a conspicuous worker in the Democratic party in the State of Indiana and from 1912 to 1922 was chairman of the Democratic county committee. He has been a careful student of affairs, an able and forceful speaker, and in 1922 he was first nominated by his party for Congress, to represent the Third Indiana District. On March 4, 1923, he entered the Sixty-eighth Congress, and by reelection served in the Sixty-ninth and Seventieth Congresses, his third term expiring March 4, 1929. He served on the committees on roads and pensions, also the important committee on insular affairs, and he was a member of the Congressional committee which investigated conditions in Porto Rico and the Virgin Islands.

Mr. Gardner during the world war was chairman of the four-minute speakers of Scott County. He is a Knight templar Mason, member of the Scottish Rite bodies at Indianapolis, and Murat Temple of the Mystic Shrine. He also belongs to the Independent Order of Odd Fellows, the Scottsburg Lions Club, the Scott County Historical Society, and is a Presbyterian.

EDWARD E. COX, whose large and well ordered printing establishment at Hartford City, judicial center of Blackford County, is operated by the corporation entitled the Edward E. Cox Printer, Inc., has been actively associated with the newspaper and printing business fully forty years, and in this line of enterprise he has not only kept pace with the march of progress but has also had no minor leadership in such progress in his native State of Indiana. The corporation of which he is the president and general manager here functions as publishers of the *Hartford City Daily News*, but its printing plant also is one of the largest and most important devoted to specialty printing in the state. Under the resourceful direction of Mr. Cox the *Hartford City Daily News* has been brought to notably high standard in all phases of its communal service, and its influence is wide and potent in advancing and standing exponent of the varied interests of Blackford County and its vital county seat.

Mr. Cox was born at Tipton, Tipton County, Indiana, December 29, 1867, and is a son of the late Judge Jabez T. Cox, who became one of the leading members of the bar of Miami County, where he was long established in the practice of his profession at Peru, the county seat, where his activities included his service in the State Legislature and twelve years' administration on the bench of the Circuit Court of the Eleventh Judicial Circuit. He was a gallant young soldier of the Union in the Civil war, as a member of a regiment of Indiana volunteer infantry, and in later years he was an honored and prominent member of the Grand Army of the Republic in Indiana. Judge Cox was born in the State of Ohio, as was also his father, Aaron Cox, and he was a boy at the time of the family removal from the Buckeye State to Hamilton County, Indiana, there to gain a goodly measure of pioneer precedence. Aaron Cox served in the early days as postmaster of Noblesville, county seat of Hamilton County, and he was long established in the contracting and building business in that county. His wife, who was born in Kentucky, was a direct descendant of Daniel Boone, one of the foremost frontiersmen of American history. Judge Jabez T. Cox married Miss Jennie Price, a teacher in the Tipton public high school. She died in Canyon City, Colorado, in 1883. She was a daughter of Major James Price, who was a distinguished officer of the United States Army in the Civil war and in whose honor was named James Price Post of the Grand Army of the Republic at Tipton, he having been there engaged in the flour milling business prior to volunteering for service in the Civil war, and having there been engaged in the mercantile business many years. The two children of Judge Cox' first marriage were: Inez, who became the wife of Merrill Mowbry and whose death occurred in 1898; and the subject of this review, Edward E. Cox. Judge Cox later married Miss Elizabeth Meinhardt, of Peru, Indiana, and to this union were born two children: Carl, deceased; and Mary, who is now a teacher in the public schools of Peru, Indiana.

The public schools of Tipton afforded Edward E. Cox his early education, which was advanced by his attending the Central Normal College of Indiana and also Purdue University. Prior to entering the university he had been for three years a successful teacher in the public schools of Miami County, and he was twenty-two years of age when he initiated his association with the printing and newspaper business, in 1890. His first service was as reported for the *Miami County Sentinel* at Peru, and after remaining one year with this paper he established his residence at Hartford City, where he purchased the plant and business of the *Hartford City Telegram,* of which he became editor and publisher. He discontinued publication of this weekly paper after founding the *Hartford City Daily News,* which he established in 1893 and over the destinies of which he has since continued in control and which under his progressive management has been developed into one of the best and most influential daily papers in this section of the state. In connection with its publishing of the *Daily News* the Edward E. Cox Printer, Inc., has built up one of the finest of modern job-printing plants in this part of Indiana, and this plant has developed a specially profitable business in its special department devoted to the manufacturing and printing of meat and candy wrappers of glassine and celophane papers.

In contemplating the fine modern plant of the Edward E. Cox Printer, Inc., it is inter-

esting to note that when Mr. Cox initiated his enterprise as a newspaper publisher at Hartford City his operating quarters were established in a small upstairs room—not more than 800 square feet—in the rear of a local drug store, and the equipment was of elemental order, including an old-time Washington press, which had to be operated solely by hand. The present plant of his concern occupies an entire city block and the building is a modern structure of two stories. In the industrial department of this company has been developed a business that involves shipment of products, mainly wrappers, to all sections of the United States, to Canadian provinces and even to foreign lands. The company retains a corps of seventy-five employees, and its modern rotary presses enable it to print and ship its wrappers and other commercial printing products in carload lots.

Mr. Cox has been a veritable apostle of civic and material progress at Hartford City, both individually and through the medium of his newspaper and printing enterprise. He is an influential member of the local Chamber of Commerce and was one of the organizers and the first president of the local Kiwanis Club.

The political allegiance of Mr. Cox is given to the Democratic party, and he has been influential in its councils and campaign activities in his native state. He was for eight years representative of the Eleventh Congressional District on the Indiana Democratic state committee and he was president of the Indiana Democratic Editorial Association in 1927. In July, 1914, under the administration of President Wilson, Mr. Cox was appointed postmaster of Hartford City, he having resigned his membership on the local board of education when he assumed the office of postmaster, to which he was reappointed in 1919 and the affairs of which he administered with characteristic loyalty and efficiency. He is a director of the Citizens State Bank of Hartford City.

Mr. Cox was postmaster of Hartford City in the World war period, but he found time and opportunity to give vigorous and loyal service in furthering the various patriotic activities of Blackford County, including all drives in sale of Government war bonds, etc. He was director of the Thrift Savings Stamp campaign in the county, and in this drive Blackford County went "over the top" with a record that made it ninth in rank of the ninety-two counties of the state. Mr. Cox was active also in furthering the food-conservation service in his home city and county.

Mr. Cox has been twice married, the first time to Eldora Sites, of Peru, Indiana, in 1891. To this union two children were born: Linnie, the wife of Joseph S. Smith, of Clifton Forge, Virginia; and Catharine, the wife of Ralph J. Winters, of Crawfordsville, Indiana. Mrs. Cox passed away in 1898. Mr. Cox married in 1901 Miss Nellie V. Tozier, a native of Oregon, and to this union five children were born: Margaret, wife of Henry Hayes Crimmel of Hartford City; Edward E., Jr., is

actively associated with Edward E. Cox
Printer, Inc., of which he is a director; Albert
L. (1931) a student in the University of Indiana; Edith Alice and Elizabeth Ann, at home.
Linnie, Catharine and Margaret attended
Western College for Women, Oxford, Ohio,
and De Pauw University. Edward E., Jr., is
a graduate of the Culver Military Academy
and attended Lafayette College, Easton, Pennsylvania.

Mr. Cox may in a certain sense be said to
have inherited a predilection for the news-
paper business, for his father, the late Judge
Jabez T. Cox, was for a time editor of the
Frankfort Crescent, at Frankfort, Clinton
County, and later was editor and publisher of
the *Tipton Times*, at the judicial center of
Tipton County.

WILBUR L. LOFTUS. In the difficult and
highly specialized field of real estate and insurance few men have made more rapid strides
in recent years than Wilbur L. Loftus, senior
member of the firm of Loftus & La Duc, of
New Albany. Mr. Loftus is a self-made man
in all that the term implies, for he had few
opportunities to secure an education in his
youth and has gained success and recognition
solely through his own initiative and resource.
At present he occupies a prominent place in
his line of business and is a member of the
directorate of the New Albany Real Estate
Board.

Wilbur L. Loftus was born at Cincinnati,
Ohio, January 25, 1900, and is a son of John
and Anna (Heustis) Loftus. His paternal
grandfather was an early settler of Indiana,
coming from the East about 1840, and served
with the Union army during the war between
the states. John Loftus was born in Indiana, where he was reared and educated, and
as a youth mastered the trade of blacksmith,
which he has followed throughout life. For
the greater part of his career he has resided
in Indiana, being now a resident of Moores
Hill, but for a time followed his trade at Cincinnati, Ohio, and elsewhere. He married Miss
Anna Heustis, who was born in Indiana, a
daughter of William P. Heustis, one of the
most prominent men of Moores Hill and
Sparta. He was a leading business man and
banker, a soldier of the Union during the war
between the states, and for a long period an
office holder, being a justice of the peace for
thirty or more years.

The only child of his parents, Wilbur L.
Loftus acquired his education in the public
schools of New Albany, and upon completing
the grade school course started working, at
the age of fourteen years, as an office boy. He
then became connected in office work activities with an automobile concern, and eventually was advanced to the sales department,
which brought him into close connection with
many of the leading citizens of the city. It
was thus that he realized the opportunities of
the real estate and insurance business, and in
1927 purchased the interest of the senior member of the firm of Cochran & La Duc, the firm

then becoming, as now, Loftus & La Duc,
with large and commodious offices at 347 Vincennes Street. This concern, which deals in
a general line of real estate and insurance,
has enjoyed a constantly-increasing success,
employing five persons and being one of the
largest enterprises of its kind in the city.

Mr. Loftus is a member of the board of directors of the New Albany Real Estate Board,
a member of the National Real Estate Board
and the New Albany Chamber of Commerce,
and a participant in all movements making
for the betterment and advancement of his
adopted city. He belongs to the Elks and the
New Albany Country Club, is unmarried, and
resides at 1119 East Oak Street.

CLYDE D. LA MEE, general manager for the
General Electric Supply Company at Indianapolis, is a southern man by birth and had
his early experience in the electrical industry
in the South until he was transferred in his
responsibilities to Indianapolis.

He was born at Green Cove Springs, Florida, December 11, 1897, son of William S. and
Edna (Gresham) La Mee. His father, a native of Fort George Island, Florida, is a re-
frigerating engineer, now located at Palatka,
Florida.

Clyde D. La Mee was educated in grade and
high schools and attended Stetson University
of Deland, Florida. He began his business
career as an office boy with the Florida Electric Company and had a steady succession of
promotions until reaching the post of vice
president and general manager. In August,
1928, he came to Indianapolis to take up his
duties as general manager for the General
Electric Supply Company, located at 326 West
Georgia Street.

Mr. La Mee married, January 10, 1923, Miss
Winifred Browning, who was born at Francis,
Florida, daughter of Samuel Stanton and
Margaret (Webster) Browning. They have
one daughter, Winifred, born March 6, 1924.

Mr. La Mee, from August to December,
1918, was with the Students Army Training
Corps, training for service in the aviation
branch of the army. He is an independent
voter in politics, is a member of the Columbia
Club of Indianapolis, is a thirty-second degree
Scottish Rite Mason, also belongs to the
Shrine and Grotto. He is a member of the
Episcopal Church and his wife is a Methodist.

SAMUEL LOWERY ADAIR, M. D. Undoubtedly the family name of Adair brings to mind
very frequently in Clark County, Indiana,
grateful memories of medical efficiency and
scientific care, reaching back over a long interval, for the present worthy bearer of the
name and professional title of Dr. Samuel L.
Adair is the third here in direct descent, and,
like his father and grandfather, is held in
honor and affection. The Adair family was
established in the United States in 1815, by
his grandfather, whose name he bears. The
first Dr. Samuel L. Adair was born in England, but was professionally educated at Cin-

cinnati, Ohio, and from that city came to New Washington, Indiana, in 1830. Like his successors, he proved to be a man of true medical spirit, and through many years at New Washington spared not himself as he sought tirelessly and faithfully to prevent and cure humanity's ills. In those days the "bedside physician" was often a close, trusted friend, wise counsellor and spiritual comforter and adviser. The record of his worthy life was an inspiration to his son, who followed in his footsteps, and he, in turn, must have proudly watched his own son's heritage at work.

Dr. Samuel L. Adair, of this review, was born at New Washington, Clark County, Indiana, September 18, 1880, and is a son of Dr. Samuel L. and Jane (Shrader) Adair. His grandfather, Dr. Samuel L. Adair, was born in England and came to the United States about 1815, graduating from the Cincinnati (Ohio) Medical College about the year 1820. During the following ten years he was engaged in active practice at Cincinnati, and in 1830 located at New Washington, where he spent the remaining years of his life.

Samuel L. Adair II was born at New Washington, Indiana, and during the war between the states was represented by a substitute, as he felt he could be of greater service to his fellow-citizens' cause by following his profession than by bearing arms. From youth he had taken a keen interest in medical science, receiving his early education therein under the preceptorship of his father, and then attending the Hospital College of Medicine, of Louisville, Kentucky, from which he was graduated in 1875, having received his degree of Doctor of Medicine the previous year from the Kentucky School of Medicine. He was a man of great public spirit, and a leader of his calling at New Washington, where his death occurred. He married Jane Shrader, of Clark County, who was of German descent, and they became the parents of four children.

Samuel L. Adair, of this reveiw, received his early education in the grade schools of Clark County, following which he enrolled as a student in the medical department of Kentucky University, from which he was graduated with the degree of Doctor of Medicine as a member of the class of 1904. At that time he returned to New Washington, where he was engaged successfully in practice until 1926, then locating at Jeffersonville, where he has since built up a large and lucrative practice in general medicine and surgery. Doctor Adair has established an unassailable standing as a thoroughly reliable and talented member of his calling, and his position in the esteem and confidence of his fellow-practitioners is evidenced by the fact that he was president of the Clark County Medical Society in 1927, and secretary of that organization in 1928. He also belongs to the Indiana State Medical Society and the American Medical Association, and is a member of the staff of the Clark County Memorial Hospital. During the World war he was a member of the Medical Reserve Corps, but was not called upon for active service. He has splendidly-equipped offices at 453½ Spring Street. Fraternally Doctor Adair belongs to the Masons, the Eagles, the Modern Woodmen of America and the Lions Club.

Doctor Adair married Miss Grace E. Thompson, of Hendricks County, Indiana, who died in December, 1928, and to this union there were born two children: Samuel L. IV, the fourth of the same name in straight succession to adopt medicine as a profession, who is now a medical student at the University of Louisville, Kentucky; and Juanita G., who is also attending that well-known institution.

JAMES ALBERT WOODBURN, emeritus professor of American History of Indiana University, is a well loved figure in the memories of all the students of the university during the past forty years. In addition to his influence and labors as a teacher there are many important proofs of his scholarship both in writings and his activities in organizations for the preservation of the history of his native state and the Middle West.

From 1923 to 1931 Doctor Woodburn was president of the Indiana Historical Society and is now president emeritus. He is also president of the Indiana Council on Foreign Relations. Since 1887 he has been a member of the American Historical Association. He was one of the founders at New Orleans in 1903 of the American Political Science Association.

He was born at Bloomington, the seat of Indiana University, November 30, 1856, son of James and Martha Jane (Hemphill) Woodburn. Doctor Woodburn took his A. B. degree at Indiana University in 1876, followed by the Master of Arts degree in 1885, and in 1929 the university bestowed upon him the well merited honorary degree of Doctor of Laws. He has had similar honorary degrees from other institutions of learning. His Doctor of Philosophy degree came from Johns Hopkins University in 1890.

Doctor Woodburn became professor of American history at Indiana University in 1890, and served actively until he retired in 1924. He is a member of numerous historical and literary organizations and is a Phi Beta Kappa of Johns Hopkins University. He married, November 30, 1893, Miss Caroline Louise Gelston, a graduate of the University of Michigan. Their children are James Gelston and Janet McMillan, (Mrs. Ernst H. Wiecking.)

As a scholar and author Doctor Woodburn has contributed to many publications, including the *Encyclopedia Americana, Encyclopedia Britannica, Encyclopedia of American Government*, the *American Year Book*. He is author of *Higher Education in Indiana*, 1890; *The American Republic and its Government*, 1903; *Political Parties and Party Problems in the United States*, 1903, 1914, 1924. *Scotch-Irish Presbyterians in Monroe County, Indiana*, 1910; *Life of Thaddeus Stevens*, 1913. He was associated with T. F. Moran in writ-

Charles A Hunt

ing a series of school text books on history and civil government, and he has also contributed his knowledge and skill as the editor of several well known publications.

ELLIS RALPH HIMELICK is one of the leading members of the bar of Connersville, judicial center of Fayette County, has served on the bench of the Circuit Court of the Seventy-third Judicial Circuit has been influential in political affairs in this section of his native state, and is not only a representative legist and jurist but also a loyal and progressive citizen who commands high place in popular esteem in his home community.

Judge Himelick was born in Union County, Indiana, May 5, 1887, and is a son of John W. and Rachel (Dubois) Himelick, the former a native of Franklin County and the latter of Union County. John W. Himelick gained substantial prestige as one of the successful exponents of farm industry in Indiana, where he is still identified with this basic industry. He and his wife now maintain their residence in Franklin County. He is a son of the late John and Mary (Davis) Himelick and his father was born in Preble County, Ohio. While still a resident of Union County he there gave six years of loyal service as county commissioner. The maternal grandparents of Judge Himelick were John K. and Elizabeth (Wilson) Dubois, natives of Franklin County, Indiana. John K. Dubois was a son of Smith Dubois, who was born in New Jersey and who became a pioneer settler in Franklin County, Indiana, where he established residence within the first decade (1800-1810) of the nineteenth century and where he reclaimed from the wilderness a productive farm, besides having been a pioneer in the operating of a grist mill in that section of the state.

The early education of Judge Himelick was acquired through the medium of the public schools of Franklin County, and the year 1907 marked his graduation in the high school. In advancing his education along academic lines he completed a course in the University of Indiana, in which he was graduated as a member of the class of 1911 and from which he received at that time the degree of Bachelor of Arts. In the law department of that university he was graduated in 1914, his admission to the bar having been virtually coincident with his reception of the degree of Bachelor of Laws, and March, 1914, having marked the establishing of his residence in the City of Connersville, where he initiated the practice of his profession and where he has since maintained his home.

In the practice of law Judge Himelick here controls a substantial and important general practice, and his professional career has included his two terms of service as prosecuting attorney of Fayette County and one term of service as judge of the Circuit Court. He has had much of local leadership in the councils of the Republican party and was chairman of the Republican county committee of Fayette County during the period of 1914-20. Prior to

engaging in the practice of law he had made a record of success as a teacher in the public schools at Roachdale, Putnam County. The Judge has membership in the Fayette County Bar Association and the Indiana State Bar Association, is a member of the Columbia Club in the City of Indianapolis, is a Knight Templar Mason and a Noble of the Mystic Shrine, and is affiliated also with the Benevolent and Protective Order of Elks, the Fraternal Order of Eagles and the Loyal Order of Moose.

September 5, 1912, recorded the marriage of Judge Himelick to Miss Faye Alice Hamilton, who was born and reared in Franklin County and who is a daughter of Harvey and Caroline (Sleet) Hamilton, the former of whom was born in Franklin County and the latter of whom was born in Harrison County, Ohio. John Harvey, only child of Judge and Mrs. Himelick, was born July 15, 1914, and is now (1929) a student in the high school in his home city.

CHARLES ARTHUR HUNT is a Jeffersonville attorney. He was born in that city April 17, 1891. His father, Thomas Hunt, was a Jeffersonville business man and during the World war was with the Quartermaster's Depot at Jeffersonville. He was born in Jefferson County, Kentucky.

Charles Arthur Hunt attended the grade schools of Jeffersonville, was in the University of Indiana three years and in 1914 graduated in the classical department and the law school of the University of Louisville. Mr. Hunt began the practice of law in September, 1914, in the offices of Judge George C. Kopp, and remained with that well known lawyer and jurist until August 17, 1917.

At that time the quiet routine of a lawyer was interrupted by his entering the Second Officers Training Camp at Fort Benjamin Harrison, Indianapolis. He came out with a commission as lieutenant in the Aviation Corps and was assigned to the One Hundred and Fifty-fifth Aero Squadron. He was overseas in active duty from January 23, 1918, to March 27, 1919, and received his honorable discharge June 13, 1919. Mr. Hunt returned to Jeffersonville and for the past ten years has divided his time among an interesting range of duties, including a large law practice, public service and continued participation in the military organization of the state and nation. From 1920 to 1925 he acted as probation officer of Clark County. He is a member of the Indiana State and American Bar Associations, and is secretary of the Clark County Bar Association. Mr. Hunt married Mayme Prinz, a sister of Henry Prinz, president of the Model Baking Company of New Albany.

Mr. Hunt was state vice commander of the Indiana American Legion in 1924-25, has served on the executive committee of that organization seven years, as a member of the state probation committee, and for the past three years has been district service officer.

He organized and was the first commander of Lawrence Capehart Post No. 35 of the American Legion at Jeffersonville, was reelected for a second term, and he organized seven other posts in the Third District. By appointment of President Harding he was a member, 1922-24, of the board of discipline and morale for the Seventh United States Army Corps District and in 1923-24 was a member of the United States rehabilitation committee for Kentucky, Indiana and Ohio. Fraternally Mr. Hunt is a member of the B. P. O. Elks, the Masonic Lodge, Modern Woodmen of America, and belongs to the military society Forty and Eight.

JAMES BURDETTE LITTLE is a prominent Indianapolis attorney, a World war veteran, and represents an old and prominent family of Indiana. His great-grandfather, John Little, came to Indianapolis with his brother, Ingram Little, and built the first hotel in the Capital city, at what is now the corner of New Jersey Street and Washington Street.

James Burdette Little was born at Cicero, Indiana, April 8, 1875, son of James M. and Martha H. (Neal) Little, natives of Hamilton County, Indiana, and grandson of John and Mary (McKune) Little. John Little was born in Pennsylvania and his wife at Maysville, Kentucky. Martha H. Neal was a daughter of William H. and Hannah (Rollings) Neal, the former a native of Kentucky and the latter of Ohio. William H. Neal was a descendant of Micajah Little, a soldier in the Revolution. William H. Neal was captain of Company B, thirty-ninth Indiana Volunteer Infantry, and James M. Little was also enrolled for service as a soldier in the same Company during the Civil war.

James Burdette Little lived in Hamilton County until he was sixteen years of age and then in Putnam County. He attended school at Cicero, graduated Bachelor of Philosophy in 1899 from DePauw University, and for two years after graduating was engaged in work as a civil engineer. He then entered the Indiana Law School, at Indianapolis, and took his LL. B. degree in 1903, since which year he has been engaged in a general law practice at Indianapolis.

He attended the Second Citizens Military Training Camp, at Fort Benjamin Harrison, from August to November, 1917, while there being a member of the Thirteenth Company of Infantry, and in November, 1917, was commissioned an officer and assigned to the Three Hundred Fifty-fifth Division. He was with the American Expeditionary Forces from June, 1918, to January, 1919, and participated in the St. Mihiel Drive, wherein he was injured in action. Mr. Little is a member of the Indianapolis and Indiana State Bar Associations, is a Delta Epsilon, member of Pentalpha Lodge No. 564, A. F. and A. M., Keystone Chapter No. 6, Royal Arch Masons, Raper Commandery No. 1, Knights Templar, Murat Temple of the Mystic Shrine, is a member of the Grand Lodge of the Knights of Pythias, of which he is a grand tribune, and Royal Prince in the Dramatic Order of the Knights of Khorassan. He also belongs to the Modern Woodmen of America, the Forty and Eight Society and the American Legion, the Century Club, is a Republican and a Methodist.

Mr. Little married, December 11, 1901, Miss Carrie A. Dewey, who was born at Strawtown, Hamilton County, Indiana, daughter of Nathaniel B. and Mary Frances (Ritchey) Dewey. They have one son, John Burdette, born March 9, 1904, who is a graduate of DePauw University, 1925, and Indiana Law School at Indianapolis, 1930, and now associated with his father in practice, with offices in the Fidelity Trust Building. Prior to the completion of his law course, the son served three years as a special investigator in the Department of Justice.

HON. JOHN MARSHALL, former circuit judge of Howard County, is a native of Indiana, and since 1912 has enjoyed an enviable place at the bar of Kokomo. Judge Marshall, also a World war veteran, was born in Cass County, July 8, 1888. His father, James Humphrey Marshall, was born at Lewisburg, Indiana, November 7, 1853, while his mother, Elizabeth (Campbell) Marshall, was born in Cass County, November 7, 1852. All the children except Judge Marshall still reside in Cass County: Thomas, who was born February 19, 1886, Frances, born July 12, 1881, wife of A. O. DeHaven; and Ruby, born March 16, 1894, wife of Charles Zollman.

John Marshall graduated from the high school at Galveston, Indiana, in 1907. Among other experiences of his early manhood he devoted two years to teaching in Cass County, teaching in one of the schools of Jackson Township. In 1912 he received his degree in law at the Indiana University and in the same year established himself for practice at Kokomo.

Judge Marshall had to his credit six years of special work as an attorney when he responded to the call to the colors, enlisting in the Three Hundred Twenty-fifth Field Artillery, and was also for a time with the Eighty-fourth Infantry Regiment. He served until honorably discharged in 1919 and for six months of that time was on the front line in France.

Judge Marshall has made some interesting researches as to Indiana's participation in and contributions to America's part in the World war. Some of his findings, which have not received all the publicity they deserve, will astonish Indianans as well as people of other states. Indiana, states Judge Marshall after a search of the records, had a greater number of men under arms than any other state in the Union per population, also the greatest number of volunteers per population. The first shot fired by an American was fired by an Indiana man, a gunner sergeant from South Bend. The first American soldier to lose his life was a man named Gresham, of Indiana. A great many Indiana people of

course know that General Bundy, the commander of the Fifth and Sixth Marines, whose brilliant exploits in repulsing the Germans at Chateau-Thierry marked the turning point of the war in favor of the allies, was an Indiana man. After the signing of the armistice General Pershing, when asked to name the greatest individual hero of the war, selected Sergeant Woodfills, an Indiana man.

Judge Marshall in the fall of 1922 was elected Judge of the Circuit Court and during the following six years gave his full time to the performance of his duties on the bench. Since the close of his term, on December 31, 1928, he has resumed the general practice of law at Kokomo. Judge Marshall is a Democrat, he is a member of the Howard County, Indiana State and American Bar Associations. He attends the Methodist Church, is a member of the American Legion and the Izaak Walton League. He has a hobby for fishing and hunting, and is also an enthusiastic amateur musician. While overseas during the World war he played in a regimental band made up of forty-two volunteer musicians.

Judge Marshall married, June 24, 1923, Miss Nina Lindley, of Crawfordsville, Indiana, daughter of Owen and Emily (Adeloete) Lindley. Her parents were born in Orange County, Indiana. Judge and Mrs. Marshall have two children: James Lindley, born January 26, 1926, and Emily, born May 5, 1927.

HON. JAMES E. WATSON has given most of his adult life to the public service, and almost continuously for thirty-five years has represented Indiana in Congress, either as a representative or as a senator.

Senator Watson was born at Winchester, Indiana, November 2, 1864, son of Enos L. Watson. He grew up in Randolph County, graduated from the Winchester High School in 1881 and has long been an honored alumnus of DePauw University. He took his A. B. degree there in 1886, and in 1906 received the honorary Master of Arts degree. His father was a prominent Indiana attorney and Senator Watson after his admission to the Indiana bar in 1887 became associated with his father. Since 1893 his home has been at Rushville.

He was first elected to Congress in 1894, to represent the Sixth Indiana District in the Fifty-fourth Congress. In 1898 he was again elected, serving consecutively through the Fifty-sixth to the Sixtieth Congresses, inclusive, until 1909. In 1908 he was the Republican nominee for governor of Indiana. In 1916 Mr. Watson was elected United States senator for the unexpired term of Benjamin F. Shively. This term expired in 1921. In 1920 he was reelected and again in 1926, his present term expiring in March, 1933.

Senator Watson has undoubtedly been one of the most powerful men in the Senate in recent years. He is chairman of the Senate committee on interstate commerce. He was chairman of the committee on resolutions in the Republican national convention of 1920,

and was a delegate to the national conventions of 1912 and 1924.

Senator Watson married, December 12, 1892, Miss Flora Miller. Their children are Edwin C., James E., Catherine and Joseph C.

CYRUS C. CRABBS was born on an Ohio farm, January 11, 1844, and died March 22, 1900. He was an inventor and manufacturer, and a man of very fine business capacity. His father was an Ohio farmer and later in the hardware business at Delphos.

Cyrus C. Crabbs after completing his education joined his father in the hardware business. He possessed an inventive turn of mind, was constantly experimenting with mechanical appliances, and he made and perfected what was known as Crabbs Patent Fence. Later he moved his home to Philadelphia, and acted as sales manager for the company manufacturing his patent fences. He sold his patent rights extensively and was living in Philadelphia when he died. He is buried there.

After his death his wife and family came to Indianapolis, where they still reside. Mr. Crabbs married, November 1, 1880, Miss Lucy Buck, daughter of Charles and Louise (Durfee) Buck. Her father was born in New York State and became a prominent railroad man, being for years a roadmaster with the Wabash Railway. Later he moved to Davenport, Iowa, where Mrs. Crabbs was born. Mrs. Crabbs was one of six children, the others being George H., Mary, Ed, Adah and Charles. Mrs. Crabbs' parents are buried at Fort Wayne. The late Mr. Crabbs was a member of the Masonic fraternity and the Presbyterian Church.

Mrs. Crabbs resides at 437 DeQuincy Street in Indianapolis. She is the mother of three children, Ethel, Clarence and Raymond. Ethel was educated in Philadelphia and is now with the Indianapolis Trust Company. Both of the sons finished their education at Indianapolis. Clarence was in the One Hundred and Thirty-ninth Field Artillery during the World war, receiving training at Fort Harrison and in the camp at Shelbyville, Mississippi, and went to France with the Thirty-eighth Cyclone Division. He was at Brest when the armistice was signed and then returned to Camp Merritt, New Jersey, and was mustered out at Fort Harrison, Indianapolis. After the war he was in the employ of the Standard Oil Company and is now with a firm of tax attorneys in Indianapolis. He married, March 22, 1919, Etta Rowland. Raymond Crabbs is connected with the Indianapolis Power & Light Company.

JAMES FREEMAN GILBERT, manager of the Ripley County Limestone Quarries, is a man of sound business judgment, and a veteran of the World war. He comes of one of the old and honored families of Kentucky, and through his mother, whose maiden name was Aileen Cavanaugh, he is descended from Virginia stock, the Cavanaughs having been established in the Virginia colony at a very early date, and participated as officers in the American Revolution. The birth of James Freeman Gilbert occurred at Lawrenceburg, Kentucky, in 1892, and he is a son of J. W. Gilbert, a prominent citizen of that city.

After the usual preliminary preparation James Freeman Gilbert entered the University of Kentucky, Lexington, and was graduated therefrom in 1913. For the succeeding five years he was engaged in school-teaching, after which he spent some time with the Kentucky Highway Department, but after four years resigned to become general manager of his present company, in 1922, which position he is still holding. He is also president of the Osgood Water Company, and for two years was president of the Commercial Club of Osgood. In political faith he is a Democrat, but no office seeker. The Independent Order of Odd Fellows holds his membership. For years he has been a consistent member of the Christian Church. During the World war he was in training at Camp Taylor, but the declaration of the armistice prevented his seeing any active service.

The Ripley County Limestone Quarries was organized in 1904, by C. W. Cox, who a year later sold his interests to Ripley Brothers, of Lawrenceburg, Kentucky, and in 1928 Mr. Gilbert purchased the property from the latter. The company ships limestone curbing, its specialty, to Detroit, Michigan, Indianapolis, Indiana, Louisville, Kentucky, Saint Louis, Missouri, Grand Rapids, Michigan, Vincennes and Terre Haute, Indiana, Parkersburg and Charleston, West Virginia, and other points. The quarry is of sufficient size to last at the present output for at least fifty years. Of the over 1,000,000 cubic feet already sold none has been rejected. No explosives are used, the quarrying being done with modern machinery, and the finishing is done by hand, which accounts for the fact that there are no invisible cracks in the finished product. The crushing weight of this stone is 16,634 pounds, and in the test made at Purdue University it has been proved that it is of superior quality of natural stratified limestone. It has a specific gravity of 2.7; its very low water absorption percentage, practically one-sixth of the average, means less strain from freezing and thawing—therefore unusual resistance to extremely low temperatures.

There is no delay or expense due to rejection and necessary substitutes when Ripley County Stratified Limestone is used. Due to their methods of quarrying and finishing every piece is sound, properly proportioned, and has no cracks or breaks to show up when subjected to the water test. The percentage of loss under the Daval abrasion test, as applied at Purdue University, is considerably below the average, demonstrating conclusively that it will wear longer. The French coefficient of ten compares favorably with the average. In the Ripley County Quarries the stone lies horizontal, very solid and free of dirt seams. The ledges are drilled and broken out in their natural state by wedging—with no explosives whatever—and sent to the yard, where all finishing and dressing is done by

hand, with the grain. The skill of the experienced workmen here employed, the absence of strain from use of explosives, and the careful inspection standards, insure perfect soundness and freedom from invisible cracks.

The quarrying of Ripley County Stratified Limestone was begun about sixty years ago. Consequently there is always available in the locality skilled labor with a lifetime of experience. The men who head the company have been in the stone business twenty-five years. In addition to the curbing, the company is prepared to furnish dimension, building, paving and flagging stone, rough and dressed rubble, riprap, crushed stone and agricultural limestone, rapidly and at fair prices.

During the time that Mr. Gilbert has been at Osgood he has thoroughly identified himself with the locality, and the breadth of his sympathies, as well as his wholesome character, give him a firm grasp of the large essentials of human progress and identify him with all that is taking place both at Osgood and in Ripley County.

HARRY W. HELMEN, physician and surgeon, is a member of his profession at South Bend whose personal character and abilities reflect a high degree of honor upon himself and upon the name of this family, which is an old and honored one in Northern Indiana.

Doctor Helmen was born at Kingsbury in LaPorte County, twenty-eight miles west of South Bend, August 16, 1882, son of Frederick and Emma (Lempke) Helmen, who have lived in South Bend since 1883. Both parents were born in LaPorte County, and all the earlier ancestors of the family came from Germany and were pioneers in Northern Indiana.

Frederick T. Helmen was born in LaPorte County, April 30, 1858, son of Frederick and Fredrika (Werner) Helmen. In Germany the Helmen name was spelled Hellmann. Frederick Helmen was born in Germany, August 7, 1828, and was married after he settled in LaPorte County, Indiana. His wife was born May 30, 1832. He worked in a flour mill and later became a farmer. Frederick Helmen died January 24, 1909, and his wife on October 24, 1919.

Frederick T. Helmen married Emma Lempke, who was born in LaPorte County, June 3, 1861, daughter of Charles and Dorothy Frederika (Wilhelm) Lempke, natives of Germany, where her father was born April 5, 1826, and her mother on June 24, 1840. Charles Lempke settled in LaPorte County about 1849. His wife came to Indiana in 1856, at the age of sixteen, and after their marriage they settled on a farm, where they spent the rest of their days. Charles Lempke died in 1870 and his wife in 1876. All these ancestors were German Lutherans in religion.

Frederick T. Helmen was educated in public schools of LaPorte County, learned the trade of carpenter and millwright, and after coming to South Bend spent forty years as foreman in the wood working department of the

Oliver Chilled Plow Company. He is now conducting a grocery business near Roseland and owns a farm just outside the city of South Bend. He is a Democrat in politics, is a member of the Evangelical Lutheran Church and the Knights of the Maccabees.

The seven children of Frederick T. Helmen and wife are: Harry W.; Vernon R., a member of the South Bend bar; Effa Bertha, wife of John B. Bernhardt, of 209 Hammond Place, South Bend; Charles Adam, South Bend dentist; Frederick John, assistant cashier of the St. Joseph Bank of South Bend; Erma Paulina, connected with the Associates Investment Company; and Arthur Horace, manager of the Moskins Clothing Store at Whiting, Indiana.

Harry W. Helman was about a year old when his parents located in South Bend, where he attended the common and high schools. After leaving high school all the expenses of his higher education were met by proceeds of his own labor. He worked on farms, taught school, went out to the Northwest and was cashier and bookkeeper in the Portland-Oregon branch of the Oliver Chilled Plow Company. On returning to Indiana in 1908 he took the scientific course at Valparaiso University and in 1911 entered the University of Indiana School of Medicine, where he was graduated in June, 1913. He was one of the applicants for an internship in the Indianapolis City Hospital, and stood highest in the examinations when licensed in the State of Indiana. After completing his internship Doctor Helmen in 1914 located at South Bend, where for fifteen years he has enjoyed a steadily increasing practice.

He married in 1916, Miss Norma Belle Trayler, of Indianapolis, daughter of A. B. Trayler. They have three children, Norma Belle, Harry William and Robert Trayler. Doctor Helmen is a member of the St. Joseph County Medical Society, is a Mason, member of the Lions Club, University Club, and the American College of Surgeons.

CHRISTOPHER BUSH COLEMAN since 1924 has been director of the historical bureau of the library and historical department of the State of Indiana, and secretary of the Indiana Historical Society. To his work Doctor Coleman brings the mind of a scientifically trained historian; for a number of years he was a professor of history and has to his credit several volumes representing his research and study.

He was born in Springfield, Illinois, April 24, 1875, son of Louis Harrison and Jenny Bush (Logan) Coleman. Doctor Coleman in 1920 published a volume of memoirs of Louis Harrison Coleman, edited by him.

His scholastic degrees are Bachelor of Arts, conferred by Yale University in 1896, Bachelor of Divinity, from the University of Chicago in 1899, and Doctor of Philosophy, from Columbia University in 1914. During 1904-05 Doctor Coleman was a student at the University of Berlin. For nearly twenty years he was a member of the faculty of Butler College, now Butler University, at first acting professor of history, as professor of history from 1901 to 1919, and from 1912 to 1919 was vice president of the college. On leaving Butler he went east to Allegheny College, at Meadville, Pennsylvania, where he was head of the department of history and political science from 1920 to 1924.

Doctor Coleman is author of *Church History in the Modern Sunday School*, published in 1910; *Constantine the Great, Historical, Legendary and Spurious*, published in 1914. He edited a volume of Lorenzo Valla on the *Donation of Constantine*, in 1922. Much of his work has been done on the lecture platform and he has been a contributor to magazines. He became a member of the George Rogers Clark Memorial Commission of Indiana in 1927, and in 1928 was elected executive secretary of the federal George Rogers Clark Sesquicentennial Commission. He is a member of the Indiana Historical Society, the Mississippi Valley and American Historical Associations and the American Society of Church History.

Doctor Coleman married, June 25, 1901, Miss Juliet Brown, of Indianapolis. They had three daughters, Ruth, now deceased, Constance and Martha Julian.

LYNN O. KNOWLTON is one of the representative civil engineers of his native city and state, and in his profession is a constituent member of the firm of Bishop, Knowlton & Carson, with offices at 312 North Meridian Street, Indianapolis.

Mr. Knowlton was born in Indianapolis in the year 1884, and is a son of Orlando and Mary (Bass) Knowlton, both likewise natives of this state. Orlando Knowlton became one of the representative members of the Indianapolis bar and continued to be engaged in the practice of his profession in the capital city until his death, his wife likewise died in this city.

Lynn O. Knowlton received the advantages of the Indianapolis public schools, including the Manual Training High School, and in 1905 he was graduated in Purdue University, from which he received the degree of Bachelor of Science in civil engineering. Thereafter he did professional work for various Indiana corporations, and he continued his activities in the capital city until the nation entered the World war, when he promptly subordinated all personal interests to the call of patriotism and volunteered for service in the United States Army. On the 5th of August, 1917, he was mustered into the Signal Corps of the United States Army, with rank of Captain. His unit was assigned to the Thirty-eighth Division and sailed for France about the opening of the month of October, 1918. After arriving in France Captain Knowlton and other members of his unit received preliminary training, and there he continued in active service during a considerable period after the armistice had brought hostilities to a close. He embarked in May, 1919, for the return voyage across the Atlantic, after having been attached to the

Chief Signal Corps of the American Expeditionary Forces, and he received his honorable discharge in May, 1919, with the rank of captain. His continued interest in his old comrades is indicated by his membership in the American Legion and the Service Club in his home city.

After the termination of his World war service Captain Knowlton returned to Indianapolis and resumed the practice of his profession, where he is a member of the firm of Bishop, Knowlton & Carson, civil and consulting engineers, who control a substantial and representative business.

Captain Knowlton is a Republican in political alignment, in the Masonic fraternity he is a past master of Ancient Landmark Lodge No. 319, A. F. and A. M. He is a member of the American Society of Civil Engineers, the Delta Tau Delta college fraternity, and the Columbia Club, which has long been one of the representative civic and political organizations in Indiana's fair capital city. He and his wife have membership in the Central Avenue Methodist Episcopal Church, the family home being maintained at 3541 Birchwood Avenue.

The year 1912 marked the marriage of Captain Knowlton to Miss Hazel Vliet, who likewise was born and reared in Indianapolis and who is a daughter of John and Dora (Buzzard) Vliet, both likewise natives of this state. Captain and Mrs. Knowlton have two children: Marilynn, born in 1915, and Jean, born in 1917.

MEREDITH NICHOLSON was born December 9, 1866 at Crawfordsville, one of Indiana's most intensive centers of literary culture, and while his own literary talents did not flower into productiveness until the present century, he was no stranger during his boyhood and youth to gifted people in his own family and relationships and to books and literary influences. In his most recent volume of essays, *Old Familiar Faces*, he has sketched his boyhood experiences and his early environment, and in the same volume he pays a tribute to his grandfathers Nicholson and Meredith. The Nicholsons were Scotch and the Merediths Welsh. His maternal grandfather, Samuel Caldwell Meredith, was a printer and was publisher of a newspaper at Centerville in Wayne County. Meredith Nicholson is a great-grandson of John Wheeler Meredith, who was a soldier of the Revolution and is buried at Troy, Ohio.

His father, Edward Willis Nicholson, was born on a farm in Garrard County, Kentucky, October 27, 1826, son of James and Elizabeth (Willis) Nicholson. Edward Willis Nicholson was a Union soldier in the Civil war, at first a private in the Eleventh Indiana Volunteer Infantry, and after four years of arduous service was discharged with the rank of captain in the Twenty-second Indiana Battery. He was at the battle of Shiloh and was with Sherman on the march to the sea. He died August 19, 1894. The mother of Meredith Nicholson was Emily Meredith, who was born at Centerville, Indiana, January 19, 1842, and died July 7, 1914.

Meredith Nicholson married at Omaha, Nebraska, June 16, 1896, Miss Eugenie C. Kountze, daughter of Herman Kountze, of Omaha. Mrs. Nicholson was a member of the class of 1889 at Vassar College. The three children reside in Indianapolis. They are: Elizabeth Nicholson Claypool; Meredith, Jr., who married Roberta West, daughter of Robert H. West, of Cincinnati; and Charles Lionel, who married Edith Watson, daughter of James S. Watson of Indianapolis.

Meredith Nicholson's early education was not that of a pampered youth who spends twelve or fifteen years in school, academy and college. He learned the fundamentals in public schools at Indianapolis, after which his mental progress and character development were influenced by working in drug stores, printing offices, as stenographer in law offices. For twelve years he pursued the practical routine of newspaper work, from that routine edging gradually into the writing profession. For three years he lived in Colorado, as auditor and treasurer of a coal mining company.

Writing has been his vocation and occupation quite steadily since 1900. A list of his books is a graphic illustration of his versatility not only as a literary craftsman but as a thinker and citizen. His most important books, poetry, fiction, essays and plays are *Short Flights* (poems), 1891; *The Hoosiers*, (in *National Studies in American Letters*), 1900; *The Main Chance*, 1903; *Zelda Dameron*, 1904; *The House of a Thousand Candles*, 1905; *Poems*, 1906; *The Port of Missing Men*, 1907; *Rosalind at Red Gate*, 1907; *The Little Brown Jug at Kildare*, 1908; *The Lords of High Decision*, 1909; *The Siege of the Seven Suitors*, 1910; *A Hoosier Chronicle*, 1912; *The Provincial American* (essays), 1913; *Otherwise Phyllis*, 1913; *The Poet*, 1914; *The Proof of the Pudding*, 1916; *The Madness of May*, 1917; *A Reversible Santa Claus*, 1917; *The Valley of Democracy*, (essays), 1918; *Lady Larkspur*, 1919; *Blacksheep! Blacksheep!*, 1920; *The Man in the Street*, (essays), 1921; Play: *Honor Bright* (with Kenyon Nicholson), 1921; *Best Laid Schemes* (short stories), 1922; *Broken Barriers*, 1922; *The Hope of Happiness*, 1923; *And They Lived Happily Ever After*, 1925; *The Cavalier of Tennessee*, 1928; *Old Familiar Faces*, (essays), 1929.

Perhaps a public equally large knows him by his contribution to periodicals, through his work as a lecturer on literary and political subjects, and his appearances in political campaigns as a speaker on the issues of the day and topics of fundamental interest from time to time. Civic affairs and good government have always exercised a strong hold upon him, and what is probably his best known work of fiction *A Hoosier Chronicle*, reflects a great deal of the current political philosophy of the period it describes. Mr. Nicholson is a Democrat and has taken part in many campaigns, and in 1928-29 served as a city councilman of Indianapolis.

Alex Suschinsky

Meredith Nicholson by his work is easily one of the outstanding literary figures of Indiana, and will also rank high in the national field of letters. His writings are his best monument, but learned institutions have also been eager to welcome him into the circles of scholarship, Wabash College bestowing upon him the honorary degrees M. A. and Litt. D., Indiana University making him an LL. D., and he received the honorary degrees M. A. and LL. D. from Butler College. He is a Phi Gamma Delta and Phi Beta Kappa and member of the National Institute of Arts and Letters. He is a member of the Woodstock, University, Athletic and Dramatic Clubs of Indianapolis, the Players, Century and Authors Clubs of New York, and the National Press Club of Washington.

ALEX JOSEPH TUSCHINSKY, proprietor of the Hillsdale Nursery, has made this one of the important industrial and productive enterprises not only of the Indianapolis metropolitan area but of the Middle West, for he has developed his nurseries and gardens to one of the show places in this part of the United States. His earlier experience in connection with horticulture, landscape gardening and the nursery business was acquired in his native land, and his familiarity with all details of these lines of enterprise has contributed in large degree to his success and prestige as a representative of nursery industry in Indiana. Mr. Tuschinsky's well improved and modern nursery plant is situated on a tract of eighty acres, eight miles northeast of the center of Indianapolis, and is about five miles due east of Broad Ripple. The buildings on the place are of comparatively recent construction and the tract of land has been developed most effectively in the propagation of ornamental trees, shrubbery, perennials, etc., so that its facilities are adequate to meet the large and ever increasing demands placed upon it by its appreciative patrons.

In that part of Eastern Germany that was originally a part of Poland and that the fortunes of the World war returned to the latter country there occurred in the year 1886 the birth of Alex Joseph Tuschinsky. His parents, Theodore and Wilhelmina (Haberer) Tuschinsky, still remain in their native land, where the father has long been identified with farm and horticultural enterprise. All of the nine children of the family are living, namely: Anna, Martha, Gertrude, Antonio, Conrad, Max, Francis, Alex Joseph and John. Of the number the subject of this review and his brother John are the only representatives of this immediate family in the United States.

In the schools of the locality in which he was born Alex J. Tuschinsky received his youthful education, and in the meanwhile he acquired practical experience in farm work and in the gardening and nursery business. He served two years in the infantry branch of the German army, and thereafter he had one year of experience in landscape gardening work in Berlin, Germany. One of his friends had come to the United States and had located in Indianapolis. This friend prevailed upon him to come to this country, and he arrived in Indianapolis in October, 1909. For two years he had charge of grounds and up-keep of an estate at Irvington and thereafter he followed the business of landscape gardening five years, with headquarters in Indianapolis. Through the conservation of his earnings he was then enabled to buy his present land, and this he has developed into one of the well ordered and successful nurseries of the Hoosier State. Energy, progressiveness and good judgment have conserved his success and advancement, and his present business has been developed on the basis of the excellent service rendered and the honorable policies followed.

Mr. Tuschinsky is notably loyal to and appreciative of the land of his adoption, and is grateful for the opportunities that have here been given him for the winning of success and independence through his own efforts. His political support is given to the Democratic party and he has membership in the Democratic Club of Indianapolis. In the York Rite of the Masonic fraternity he is affiliated with the Blue Lodge and Chapter, as well as Raper Commandery of Knights Templar, and his affiliations are extended also to the Mystic Shrine, with membership in Murat Temple. He and his wife are communicants of Saint Peter's Lutheran Church.

On February 24, 1916, Mr. Tuschinsky was united in marriage to Miss Ida Seek, daughter of Herman and Otilie (Manthei) Seek, who were born and reared in Germany and who have been residents of Indiana fully forty years, their home being in Marion County and Mr. Seek being now retired from active business. Mr. and Mrs. Tuschinsky have had no children of their own but they have an adopted son, Theodore Alex, who was born March 25, 1931.

HERBERT B. DEPREZ is a Shelbyville citizen whose business career has been devoted to ice manufacturing, and he is one of the outstanding men in this industry in Indiana. He is president of The Daniel DePrez Manufacturing Company.

Mr. DePrez was born at Shelbyville, December 19, 1876. His grandfather, John DePrez, was born in Alsace Lorraine, of French Huguenot ancestry. He came to America and about 1848 settled in Shelby County, Indiana. John C. DePrez, father of Herbert B., was a native of Cincinnati, and at Shelbyville helped establish the first furniture factory. He was prominent in that business for many years. John C. DePrez married Zora L. Miller, and Herbert was one of their four children.

Herbert B. DePrez was liberally educated, attending the grammar and high schools of Shelbyville, and finished his college work in Wabash College. He is a member of the Beta Theta Pi fraternity. After leaving college he returned to Shelbyville and his first active connection with the DePrez Ice Manufacturing

Company was as office manager. In 1902 he became vice president and manager, and since 1910 has been president and manager of the company. He is a former president of the Indiana Ice Manufacturers Association and was one of the organizers of the National Ice Manufacturers Association and on its board of directors for three years. Recently elected president Indiana Local Merchants Association.

Mr. DePrez is one of the popular citizens of Shelbyville, interested in all civic and benevolent movements. He is affiliated with the Masonic fraternity, Knights of Pythias, B. P. O. Elks, Improved Order of Red Men and Fraternal Order of Eagles. He belongs to the Rotary Club, member of the Better Business Club. He did his part in the patriotic program during the World war and was one of the organizers and chairman of the County Community Fund in 1926. Mr. DePrez married Miss Lillian Nading of Shelbyville, Indiana, and they have two children, John C. II and Mary N., both of whom are attending school, John C. at Purdue, Lafayette, and Mary at Tudor Hall at Indianapolis.

HILTON ULTIMUS BROWN continuously since 1881 has been identified with the *Indianapolis News* and with the making of that not only one of the great papers of Indiana but one of the most influential journals of the Middle West.

Mr. Brown was born at Indianapolis, February 20, 1859, son of Philip Andrew and Julia (Troster) Brown. His father was born in Ohio, son of Andrew Brown, who came from New Jersey. His mother was born in Stuttgart, Germany, and came to the United States in 1848. She was married in Butler County, Ohio, to Philip A. Brown, a brick manufacturer and later in the wholesale lumber business. In 1858 they moved to Indianapolis, where Philip Brown established a lumber yard at Browns Switch. He died in 1864 and his wife in 1868.

Hilton Ultimus Brown was left an orphan at the age of nine years. He made the best of his opportunities, attending public schools in Indianapolis, the preparatory department of Northwestern Christian University, now Butler College, and took his A. B. Degree at Butler College in 1880 and the Master of Arts degree two years later. He taught one term of school in Knox County, but in the meantime had put in his application for work on the *Indianapolis News*, and in July, 1881, was given his first asignment, as a railroad reporter. Later he was made market reporter, was promoted to city editor, managing editor, general manager in 1901, and since 1920 has been secretary and treasurer of the *Indianapolis News* Publishing Company.

Mr. Brown married, October 30, 1883, Miss Jennie Hannah, daughter of Capt. Arch A. and Mary (Powell) Hannah, her father a native of Schenectady, New York, and her mother of Bowling Green, Kentucky. Mr.

Brown's children are: Mark Hannah, a lumber manufacturer at Lake Providence, Louisiana; Louise, wife of John W. Atherton, financial secretary of Butler University; Mary, wife of George O. Stewart, of Indianapolis, with the Insull Interstate Public Service Company; Philip, who died at the age of nine years; Arch A., of Miami Beach, Florida; Jean, wife of Clifford Wagner, an insurance man; Hilton, Jr., who was killed November 3, 1918, in the Argonne, France, while serving with the first Division of Regulars, and is buried in the Romagne Cemetery; Paul V., executive secretary of the State Conservation Department at Indianapolis; Jessie, wife of Floyd Mannon, assistant prosecuting attorney of Marion County; and Julia, wife of David Konold, with the Art School Products Company at Omaha, Nebraska.

Mr. Brown has been a member of the board of directors of Butler College since 1888, and since 1903 has been president of the board. He is a director of the Indianapolis Art Association. Mr. Brown has been a contributor to daily journalism for more than half a century. In 1920 he edited and published the letters and verses of the son who was killed in action in the World war and gave the book the title *Hilton U. Brown, Jr., One of Three Brothers in Artillery*. Mr. Brown attended the peace conference at the close of the war, also wrote a series of letters on the battlefields and industrial conditions in Europe and was again abroad in 1925 and 1926, writing chiefly for the *Indianapolis News*. He is an elder in the Church of the Disciples. He was president of the school board and was president of the town board of Irvington when that suburb was incorporated in Indianapolis. He is a Republican, a member of Keystone Chapter, Royal Arch Masons, a thirty-second degree Scottish Rite Mason and Shriner, and for two terms was national president of the Phi Delta Theta. He has been a director of the University Club, is a member of the Columbia Club, Meridian Hills Country Club, Indianapolis Literary Club, Highland Golf Club, and Hoosier Motor Club.

JOHN A. ROTHROCK, one of the prominent younger members of the bar of his native City of Monticello, judicial center of White County, is serving in 1930 as treasurer of the Democratic county committee of this county, is president of the local Chamber of Comerce, and is a past commander of the Monticello post of the American Legion, for which he is now the official attorney.

Mr. Rothrock was born at Monticello on the 7th of February, 1900, and is a son of Orville A. and Mae (Bennett) Rothrock, the former of whom was born in White County and the latter in Pulaski County. Orville A. Rothrock has been a representative business man of Monticello, where he organized and is the executive head of the Rothrock Agency and where he formerly served as city marshal and as deputy sheriff of the county, and he

MR. AND MRS. CURTIS RANCK

has for several years been a member of the Indiana bar. He is a son of the late John A. Rothrock, who likewise was born and reared in White County, where he gained no minor distinction and influence as editor and publisher of the *White County Democrat*, his father having been one of the early settlers in White County, whither he came from Pennsylvania in the 1830 decade. He was one of the leaders in the local councils of the Democratic party and otherwise was one of the honored and influential citizens of his day and generation in White County.

John A. Rothrock, of this review, is the elder in a family of two children, and his brother, Lindell B., is prominently associated with business affairs in Monticello. John A. Rothrock was a student in the Monticello High School when, in June, 1918, he enlisted for World war service, in the United States Navy. He received preliminary discipline at the Great Lakes Naval Training State, near Chicago, and was assigned to duty on the United States naval vessel *Mongolia*. He continued in service after the armistice brought active hostilities to a close and was honorably discharged with the rank of petty officer, June 11, 1919.

After the termination of his World war service Mr. Rothrock became a student in the law department of the University of Indiana, and subsequently was transferred to the University's branch at Indianapolis, the Indiana Law School, in which he was graduated as a member of the class of 1922, he having been admitted to the bar in the preceding year and having been admitted to practice before the Indiana Supreme Court and the Federal courts of the state in the year that marked his reception of the degree of Bachelor of Laws. In 1922 Mr. Rothrock opened a law office in his native City of Monticello, where his personal popularity and his recognized professional ability have combined to gain him a notably substantial and representative practice in the intervening period. He gave two terms of effective service as official prosecuting attorney for the district comprising White and Carroll counties, he is a popular young member of the White County Bar Association and the Indiana State Bar Association, he is, as previously noted, prominent in the affairs of the Democratic party contingent in his home county, his religious faith is that of the Methodist Episcopal Church, and in addition to being affiliated with the local post of the American Legion, of which he is a past commander, he has membership also in the Masonic fraternity, Independent Order of Odd Fellows, Knights of Pythias, and the Sigma Delta Kappa and Phi Delta Kappa college fraternities. While a student in the Indiana School of Law Mr. Rothrock was active in student athletics and was a member of the Amateur Athletic Union.

In White County was solemnized the marriage of Mr. Rothrock to Miss Eva B. Friend, who likewise was born and reared in this county, and the one child of this union is John A. III, who bears the name of his father and of his paternal great-grandfather.

CURTIS RANCK resides in the City of Indianapolis, where he is living virtually retired, and he is the owner of a large and valuable farm estate in Wayne Township, Marion County. Mr. Ranck is a representative of one of the old and honored families of Indiana and has long maintained alliance with the great basic industries of agriculture and stock raising, through the medium of which he has achieved a success that marks him as one of the substantial capitalists of his native state. He has been a constructive worker and has not found it necessary to bewail the decadence or unprofitableness of farm enterprise, for he has brought to bear progressive methods and policies and has made success come as a normal result.

Mr. Ranck was born in Wayne County, Indiana, September 9, 1859, and is a son of Mathias and Nancy H. (Helms) Ranck, both likewise natives of Wayne County. Mathias Ranck was reared and educated under the conditions and influences that marked the pioneer era in Wayne County, and there he long held secure status as a substantial representative of agricultural and live stock enterprise. Members of the Ranck family went from their native Germany into France, and from the latter country the paternal great-grandfather of Curtis Ranck of this review came to America and settled in Lancaster County, Pennsylvania. From that county of the old Keystone State George G. Ranck, grandfather of the subject of this sketch, came to Indiana in the pioneer days and established the family home in Wayne County, where he passed the remainder of his life and where he did well his part in advancing civic and industrial development and progress, he having been one of the prosperous farmers in that county in his day and generation, even as was his son Mathias in later years.

Curtis Ranck was reared on the old home farm in Wayne County, and there he supplemented the discipline of the public schools by a two years' course in Earlham College, the staunch old institution maintained in the City of Richmond under the auspices of the Society of Friends. In his native county Mr. Ranck well upheld the honors of the family name in connection with loyal citizenship and as an exponent of agricultural and live stock industry, he having there become the owner of a fine farm of 240 acres and having also developed a prosperous business in the buying and shipping of cattle. He finally sold his Wayne County farm, and he thereafter came to Marion County, where he purchased the Holmes farm when that fine property was sold under the hammer, this splendid farm estate being now widely known as the Ranck farm, its improvements being of the best and most modern type and its area 360 acres. This is one of the show farms of Wayne Township, and in that township Mr. Ranck owns also another farm, of 144 acres. His modern residence in Indianapolis was erected by him, is situated at 5023 Sixteenth Street, West, and has been his place of abode since 1918, when he removed from his farm to the capital city, he having been a resident of Marion County since 1900. Mr. Ranck and his wife pass the winter seasons at the attractive home they own in Miami, Florida, at 73 Northwest Forty-seventh Street. Mr. Ranck is a Democrat in politics, and while he has had no desire for public office his civic loyalty was constructively shown in the several years of effective service that he gave in the position of road supervisor. He has been liberal in the support of measures and enterprises tending to advance the general communal welfare, he and his wife are active members of the United Brethren Church, and Mrs. Ranck has membership in the Woman's Christian Temperance Union.

On the 20th of July, 1884, was solemnized the marriage of Mr. Ranck to Miss Emma B. Marlatt, who likewise was born and reared in Wayne County, this state, and who is a daughter of the late Harrison and Anna (Swisher) Marlatt. Harrison Marlatt was a prosperous farmer in Wayne County, where he passed the closing period of his life, his parents, Thomas and Elizabeth (Beller) Marlatt, having come to Indiana from Virginia, where the family had been established in the Colonial era, the original American representatives having been French Huguenots who fled their native land to escape the religious persecution that followed the revocation of the Edict of Nantes.

Mr. and Mrs. Ranck have two children, Oscar and Ivy R. Oscar Ranck, who owns and resides upon a farm of 100 acres in Marion County, married Miss Sadie Hightshue, and their children are four in number—Sherman O., Hiram M., Martha J. and Mary S. Ivy R. Ranck married Elmer Klingensmith, and they have one child, Pauline O.

CHARLES WEBSTER JEWETT. In the capital city of his native state Mr. Jewett is a member of the representative law firm of Elliott, Wile & Jewett, which controls a substantial and important general practice, with major attention being given to corporation law, the offices of the firm being established in suite 1411 Fletcher Savings & Trust Building. Mr. Jewett is a loyal and appreciative citizen of the fine old Hoosier commonwealth and his interest in all that has concerned its development, progress and general welfare is indicated by his possession of virtually all published histories of Indiana.

Charles W. Jewett was born at Franklin, Johnson County, Indiana, January 7, 1884, and is a son of Rev. Edward Parker and Alma Mary (Aten) Jewett, both likewise natives of Indiana, where the former was born at Warrenton, Gibson County, and the latter in Johnson County, both families having gained pioneer prestige in this state. Rev. Edward P. Jewett became one of the distinguished and honored clergymen of the Methodist Episcopal Church in Indiana, where he held many important pastoral charges, his service having included the pastorate of a leading church in Indianapolis.

The public school discipline of Charles W. Jewett was continued until he had completed his high-school course, and thereafter he continued his studies along academic lines, first in Franklin College and subsequently in DePauw University, in which latter institution he was graduated as a member of the class of 1907 and with the degree of Bachelor of Arts. In preparation for his chosen profession he entered the law department of historic old Harvard University, and from that institution he received in 1910 his degree of Bachelor of Laws. He was forthwith admitted to the bar of his native state and initiated the practice of his profession in Indianapolis, where he has been continuously associated with Charles H. Wile.

Mr. Jewett has made a record of notably sucessful achievements in his profession and has been influential also in the Indiana councils and campaign activities of the Republican party, he having served as secretary of the Republican Union at Indianapolis in 1913, and having been elected in 1914 and 1916 as chairman of the Republican state central committee. His is a vital and loyal interest in the welfare of his home city, and this was significantly shown in his able and progressive administration as mayor of Indianapolis, an office that he held during the period of 1917-21. He was mayor of the Capital city during the entire period of the nation's participation in the World war, and thus had to meet and adjust many exceptional executive problems. It was through the initiative of Mayor Jewett that was instituted the plan for providing in Indianapolis a suitable and permanent memorial to Indiana men who sacrificed their lives in the World war. Within his regime was completed the elevation of railroad tracks that had previously had grade crossings in the city, and while he was mayor was initiated the work of providing Indianapolis with a sanitary sewerage system that has been developed into one of the best to be claimed by any metropolitan center in the world. Under his administration the platoon system was adopted by both the fire and police departments of Indianapolis and the equipment of the fire department was changed to motor power in place of the former horse-drawn engines, hose-wagons, fire-patrols, etc. In the World war period Mayor Jewett had much of leadership in the patriotic activities that caused Indianapolis to exceed its quota in all of the drives in support of Government war bonds, Red Cross work, etc., and it is to be noted that the city rendered a significant over subscription to the War Savings Stamp campaign. Mayor Jewett likewise effected the adoption of the municipal budget system that unified the work of making all purchases for the city government, and thus was effected an annual saving of fully $100,000. The splendidly constructive record of Mayor Jewett doubtless gained popular recognition of his administrative ability and this was shown in 1928, when he appeared as a Republican candidate for the office of governor of Indiana.

Mr. Jewett has membership in the Indiana State Bar Association and the American Bar

Association. In the Masonic fraternity he is affiliated with both York and Scottish Rite bodies, as well as the Mystic Shrine, and he has membership also in the local organizations of the Benevolent and Protective Order of Elks, Knights of Pythias, Loyal Order of Moose and Fraternal Order of Eagles. In his home city he is a member of the Columbia Club, University Club, Dramatic Club and Indianapolis Athletic Club, besides having membership in the Indianapolis Country Club. He and his wife are active members of the Meridian Street Methodist Episcopal Church.

The year 1911 recorded the marriage of Mr. Jewett to Miss Elizabeth Dougherty, who was born at Bluffton, Wells County, a daughter of Hon. Hugh and Emma (Gilliland) Dougherty, the former a native of Darke County, Indiana, and the latter of Michigan. Mr. and Mrs. Jewett have no children.

CHARLES FREDERICK REMY, who is serving with characteristic loyalty and ability as judge of the Appellate Court of the State of Indiana, has long been a representative member of the bar of his native state and both his paternal and maternal ancestors gained distinctive priority as pioneer settlers of Indiana, with whose civic and material history the names of the respective families have been prominently and worthily identified since the first decade of the nineteenth century.

Judge Remy was born near the Village of Hope, Bartholomew County, Indiana, February 25, 1860, and is a son of Calvin J. and Marinda (Essex) Remy, the former of whom was born in Franklin County, this state, in 1834, and the latter of whom was born in Bartholomew County, in 1836, she being now one of the venerable and revered native daughters of the Hoosier Commonwealth and her home being maintained with her daughter, in the City of Indianapolis. She is a daughter of Thomas and Rebecca (Fry) Essex, who were born near Winston-Salem, North Carolina, and who became early settlers in Bartholomew County, Indiana.

Calvin J. Remy was a son of John T. Remy, who likewise was a native of Franklin County, this state, where he was born in the year 1810, he having been a son of James and Mary (Jones) Remy, both natives of Virginia, whence they came as young folk to Indiana, their marriage having been solemnized in Franklin County, this state, where James Remy established his residence in 1809, he having there reclaimed a farm from the forest wilds and both he and his wife having there passed the remainder of their lives. Their son John T. likewise followed farm industry as a life vocation and was one of the honored native residents of Franklin County at the time of his death.

Thomas Essex, maternal grandfather of Judge Charles F. Remy, was long one of the most honored and influential citizens of Bartholomew County, he having been a successful school teacher and a skilled surveyor, and he having been called upon to serve in various offices of public trust, including those of county surveyor, county commissioner, county recorder and representative, three terms in the State Legislature, besides which he gave two terms of administration in the office of mayor of Columbus, judicial center of Bartholomew County.

Mrs. Rebecca (Adair) Remy, paternal grandmother of Judge Charles F. Remy, was born in South Carolina, a daughter of James Adair, who thence removed with his family to Kentucky, from which latter state he came to Franklin County, Indiana, about the year 1909, the marriage of his daughter Rebecca to John T. Remy having occurred in Kentucky. James Adair had served as a patriot soldier in the War of the Revolution, and his mortal remains rest in the cemetery at Brookville, Franklin County.

Calvin J. Remy was afforded the advantages of the pioneer common schools of Franklin County, where he early began to aid in the work of the home farm, and he was a youth of sixteen years when, in 1850, he accompanied his parents on their removal to Bartholomew County, where he passed the remainder of his life and where he long stood forth as a progressive exponent of farm industry, as well as a substantial and highly honored citizen. He was one of the venerable native sons of Indiana at the time of his death, which occurred October 11, 1917, and though his widow is now (1930) ninety-four years of age she retains admirable command of both physical and mental powers, and her memory is a repository of much and accurate information touching the early history of Indiana. She has long been an earnest member of the Baptist Church, as was also her husband, and the latter was an unswerving supporter of the cause of the Republican party.

Judge Charles F. Remy supplemented the discipline of the public schools by attending the preparatory department of and later completing a regular course in Franklin College, in which he was graduated as a member of the class of 1884 and from which he received the degree of Bachelor of Arts. During a period of three years he supplemented his financial resources by rendering effective service as a teacher in the public schools, and in preparation for the profession of his choice he entered the law department of the University of Michigan. In this institution he was graduated as a member of the class of 1888, his reception of the degree of Bachelor of Laws having been followed by his admission to the Michigan bar and also to that of his native State of Indiana. The Judge was for eight years engaged in active general practice at Columbus, county seat of Bartholomew County, and as a representative of that county he served one term in the State Legislature—during the session of 1895. In the following year he was elected official reporter of the Indiana Supreme Court, he was reelected in 1898, and his service continued until 1905, in January of which year he formed a law partnership with James M. Berryhill, with whom he continued to be associated in the control of a large and important law business until January 1, 1919, when he initiated his service on the bench of the State Appellate Court of Indiana. In this important department of the judiciary service of the state government he has since continued his able administration, and he now has secure vantage-ground as one of the distinguished legists and jurists of Indiana.

Judge Remy, well fortified in his opinions concerning governmental and economic policies, has ever given zealous allegiance to the Republican party, and in their home City of Indianapolis he and his wife are earnest members of the First Baptist Church, of which he is a trustee. He is a member of the board of directors of his academic alma mater, Franklin College, he is a past grand chancellor of the Indiana Grand Lodge of Knights of Pythias and he is a past president and a past supreme representative of the Sons of the American Revolution. He has membership in the Columbia Club and the Century Literary Club of Indianapolis, and in a professional way he is affiliated with the Marion County Bar Association, the Indiana State Bar Association and the American Bar Association.

On the 25th of November, 1891, was solemnized the marriage of Judge Remy to Miss Deborah Henderson, who was born in Wells County, this state, a daughter of William and Mary E. (Hughes) Henderson, the former of whom was born in Ohio, whence he came to Indiana and first became a resident of Blackford County. Judge and Mrs. Remy have one son, William Henderson Remy, who was born December 18, 1892, at Columbus, this state, and who is now engaged in the practice of law in the City of Indianapolis.

CHARLES T. MISER, a skilled civil engineer, maintains his private office in the Y. M. C. A. Building in the City of Auburn, judicial center of DeKalb County, and in his administration as county surveyor he has executive headquarters in the county courthouse.

Mr. Miser was born in Indiana, November 2, 1905, and his parents, Edward and Mae (Showers) Miser, now maintain their home at St. Joe, DeKalb County, this state, their other children being William H., Martha and Frank. After completing his studies in the high school at St. Joe Charles T. Miser continued his studies in DePauw University, where he prepared himself for the profession of which he is now a representative. He has been successful in his activities as a civil engineer and his serving as county surveyor of DeKalb County. His political allegiance is given to the Republican party, he was reared in the faith of and is a communicant of the Lutheran Church, and he is affiliated with the Masonic fraternity, the Knights' of Pythias and the Phi Beta Sigma and Delta Alpha Psi college fraternities. He is not only one of the efficient members of the official executive coterie of DeKalb County but also one of the popular young bachelors of this county.

BINNIE T. SMITH is secretary and treasurer of the Davis-Birely Table Company, one of the manufacturing concerns that give stability and industrial importance to the City of Shelbyville. Mr. Smith first became connected with this organization on the score of his knowledge and ability in handling traffic problems, his early experience and training for many years having identified him with railroad work.

The Davis-Birely Company was started in 1884, as the Conrey-Birley Company. It was reorganized and incorporated as the Davis-Birely Company in 1911. The original company was started for the manufacture of furniture, and their first shop was an old woolen mill building on a lot 40 by 100 feet. This old plant has undergone extensive remodeling and complete additions of new factories and equipment, so that the present plant and yards cover an area of seven acres. About 250 persons are employed regularly through the year. The chief output of the Davis-Birely Company is living room tables. They also make an extensive line of furniture novelties. Car lot shipments are made from the plant at Shelbyville to all parts of the United States. The company maintains a permanent exhibit at Grand Rapids, Michigan. The president of the company in 1911 was Mr. Charles Birely, the vice president, Joseph R. Mardis, and Mr. Smith, secretary and treasurer.

Mr. Smith was born at Shelbyville, October 9, 1873. His grandfather, Thomas Smith, came to Indiana and settled in Rush County in 1830. Mr. Smith is a son of Marshall Smith who was born in Rush County, was a soldier in the Civil war, and has spent most of his life in the postal service. He was the first mail carrier at Shelbyville. He married Miss Jennie Clark.

Binnie T. Smith was one of a family of three children. He attended schools in Shelby County and after his high school course at Shelbyville found his first opportunity for work was as clerk in a furniture factory. He left this to become a clerk with the New York Central lines and rose to the responsibilities of chief clerk and relief agent, and was in that service until called by the Conrey-Birely Table Company to the duties of traffic manager and office manager and credit man. He has been one of the officials and stockholders in the business since its reorganization in 1911, and from time to time has acquired additional interests and has had an increasing part in the executive direction of the business, handling the sales management.

Mr. Smith is also a director of the Shelbyville Trust Company. For fifteen years he was a director of the Indiana State Chamber of Commerce, is a director of the Grand Rapids Market Association, and for six years was president of the Shelbyville Furniture Manufacturers Association. He was the second president of the local Rotary Club, is affiliated with Shelbyville Lodge No. 28, A. F. and A. M., the Royal Arch Chapter, Council and Commandery, the Scottish Rite Consistory and Murat Temple of the Mystic Shrine at Indi-

Walter M. Bohn M.D.

anapolis. During the World war he did his part toward speeding up industrial production for war purposes and acted as a director of the United States Employment Board. Mr. Smith is a prominent layman of the Christian or Disciples Church and is on the budget and promotion committee of the National Board of the church.

He married Miss Lola A. Womack, of Bartholomew County, Indiana. They have one son Harry W. Smith, now associated with the Davis-Birely Company, in charge of cost accountings and promotion and industrial relations. He was in an officers training camp during the World war, training for the field artillery at Camp Knox, Kentucky. Harry W. Smith married Nondas Young, of Vigo County, Indiana, and they have a daughter, Shirley Ann.

CURT SOWDER, one of the present board of county commissioners of Lawrence County, was born and has always lived in Pleasant Run Township of that county. Mr. Sowder has made a name for himself as a very capable farmer, is a large land owner and for years has been prominent in farm and agricultural organizations.

He was born May 17, 1869, on a farm located about a mile west of his present place. Mr. Sowder's holdings as a farmer comprise about 400 acres, land which he has acquired at different times, and most of it has been in the family ownership for seventy-five years. His parents were William S. and Eliza Jane (Dayton) Sowder. His grandfather, Jefferson Sowder, came to Indiana from Kentucky in 1839 and acquired land when it was cheap. He is buried in the Hawkins Cemetery of Lawrence County. William S. Sowder was a boy when the family came to Indiana and settled in section 8 of Pleasant Run Township. He grew up there and during the Civil war joined Company F of the Ninety-third Indiana Infantry and was slightly wounded in one battle. He was extensively engaged in stock raising. There were seven children in the family: Mary, who became the wife of William Chambers; James M., whose first wife was Ureto Gilstrap and after her death he married Estella Normand; Emma, wife of Peter Hawkins; Alice, wife of William Chambers; Hugh, deceased; Curt; and John, who is married.

Mr. Curt Sowder was educated in the common schools at Bartlesville, spent three years in the old Mitchell Normal School and during his early life taught for about three years. Aside from his work as a school man he has been constantly engaged in farming since early youth. He operated his father's place for several years and duing the winter worked in the timber. His industry and thrift enabled him to begin buying land when a young man, and his accumulations have been steadily mounting during his active years. He showed good judgment in his farming operations, and gave his thought and energy to his business and in that way acquired a reputation for business leadership.

Mr. Sowder was never interested in politics except for what service he could render his community. His only public office has been that of county commissioner, a position to which he has been elected for two terms. He and his two associates on the board planned and carried out the construction of the new courthouse at Bedford.

Mr. Sowder married, May 6, 1893, Miss Cora L. Stafford, daughter of James M. and Sarah (Meadows) Stafford. Her father is deceased and is buried at Pleasant Run. Mr. and Mrs. Sowder have three children. Their daughter Ethel is the wife of Ed Stipp, a farmer in Lawrence County, who owns about 200 acres, and their three children are Hester, John and Mary. Earl Sowder, who married Hermina Bitner, is a farmer and stock raiser in Lawrence County, and during the World war was at San Antonio, Texas, in a training camp and later was in the navy. The daughter Evelyn is the wife of Earl Bartlett, and they have two children, Harold and Marjorie. Mr. Sowder and family are members of the Christian Church.

WALTER MARTIN BEHN, M. D., was born in Chicago, Illinois, November 15, 1894, but grew up in the Hammond-Gary district of Indiana, acquired a practical education and earned the money to put himself through medical college. Since returning to Gary he has enjoyed a reputation and a demand for his services that place him in the front ranks of the medical fraternity of that city.

Doctor Behn is a son of Fred and Ernstina (Scheurer) Behn, both of whom were natives of Germany and were brought to America, his father at the age of eight years and his mother at five. The paternal grandparents were Martin and Mary Behn, who are buried in the Oakwoods Cemetery of Chicago. The maternal grandparents were Charles and Marie Scheurer, who are buried in the Oak Hill Cemetery at Hammond. Fred Behn was educated in Chicago and for twenty-five or thirty years was in the hotel business. He is a retired resident of Gary. His wife was very active in fraternal work, in the Eastern Star and Rebekahs, was chaplain of the Rebekah Lodge of Hammond, and while saying prayers in the lodge she was stricken with heart disease and died a few hours later, October 20, 1920. She is buried in the Oak Hill Cemetery at Hammond, Indiana. Of her three children the only daughter, Emily, died January 20, 1925, wife of Fred C. Holifield. Walter Martin Behn has a brother, Elmer August Behn, who is a pharmacist at 749 Broadway, Gary. He married Miss Bernice Zonsa, of Gary, and they have one son, Norman Frederick.

Walter Martin Behn was graduated from the Emerson High School of Gary in 1912. Following this came four years of work as an employee of the Illinois Steel Company. His first year of pre-medical training was received in the Valparaiso University. In 1919 he graduated Bachelor of Science from the University of Chicago and then entered its affiliated school of medicine, Rush Medical College, where he took his M. D. degree in 1923. He had a year of further training and experience as an interne in the Illinois Central Hospital of Chicago.

On April 4, 1924, Doctor Behn opened his office in Gary, at 749 Broadway. This is a prominent medical center of Gary, the group of physicians and surgeons having their quarters at the same number including Dr. A. A. Watts, Dr. J. B. Burcham, Dr. Morris Marcus, Doctor Edward Gaebe, and it was also the headquarters of the late Dr. Theodore Kollmar. Doctor Behn has been abundantly prospered with the large practice that has come to him as a testimonial to his skill and efficiency. He is a member of the Lake County and Indiana State Medical Associations, in Masonry is affiliated with Whiting Lodge No. 613, A. F. and A. M., is a fellow of the American Medical Association and belongs to the Lincoln Hill Country Club. Recently he completed two years as coroner's physician of Lake County and on January 6, 1930, was appointed Gary health commissioner, and is also secretary of the city board of health. He is a Republican, and a member of the First Presbyterian Church.

Doctor Behn married in Chicago, March 17, 1923, Miss Freda Martina Nyland, daughter of John and Christine (Sogust) Nyland. Her father was born in Sweden and her mother in Germany, and they were children when their parents brought them to America and settled in Chicago. Her father was a carpenter and contractor, at first in Chicago and later in Gary, where he died and is buried in the Oak Hill Cemetery. Her mother resides in Los Angeles. Mrs. Behn graduated from the Emerson High School of Gary in 1917, following which she was a student in Valparaiso University. She is a member of the First Presbyterian Church, the Eastern Star, the Delphians and the Woman's Club. Doctor and Mrs. Behn have one son, Walter Martin, Jr., born July 17, 1925, and one daughter, Betty Lou, born June 10, 1931.

HERBERT L. FORBES, county surveyor of Greene County, is a well qualified engineer who has had a long and successful experience in general engineering, mining engineering and in municipal engineering.

He was born in Greene County, son of L. S. and Ella (Lowder) Forbes, and a grandson of Rev. L. L. Forbes, who came from Pennsylvania and was a prominent minister of the Methodist Episcopal Church in the early days of Indiana. L. S. Forbes, who is a resident of Linton, is a truck farmer and has filled the office of deputy auditor. He and his wife had a family of six children: Elsie, wife of Thomas Huffnan and the mother of a son, Claude; Rowena, the wife of Harley Shepperd; Mrs. Mildred Lasley; Herbert L.; Julia, deceased, wife of Gomer James, and left a daughter, Doris; and Lelandis, who died in infancy.

Herbert L. Forbes attended the common schools of Bloomfield, Indiana, and after leaving school was employed in the engineering department of one of the mining companies at Linton, for about two years. He also spent a year with the engineering department of the Gould Mining Company, with the Benson Coal Company and other mining organizations in Greene County. He was elected and served eight years as city engineer of Linton and also conducted a private office for his engineering practice. He was appointed deputy county surveyor, and did a great deal of work during the construction of hard surfaced highways in the county. In 1926 he was elected county surveyor and was reelected to that office in 1928.

Mr. Forbes is a member of the American Association of Engineers. He belongs to the Rotary Club and the Methodist Episcopal Church, and is a member of the Masonic fraternity.

Mr. Forbes married, October 14, 1912, Miss Vera Smith, daughter of John B. and Lula (Nelson) Smith. Her parents moved from Shawneetown, Illinois, to Greene County, Indiana. Mr. and Mrs. Forbes had two children, Franklin, attending school, and Zebalee, who died at the age of three years.

WILLIAM FRANK CARMACK has been a resident of Terre Haute since 1882, and his activities have brought him in close touch with political and public affairs of Vigo County, and for thirty-five years he has been one of the prominent attorneys of the Terre Haute bar.

He was born on a farm in Douglas County, Illinois, January 8, 1862, son of Isaac A. and Minerva (Howell) Carmack. His father was a native of Hawkins County, Tennessee, and his mother of Douglas County, Illinois. Mr. Carmack's paternal grandfather, Isaac Carmack, moved from Hawkins County to Quaker Point, Vermilion County, Indiana, in the early 1850s, settling on a farm. He was an abolitionist. The maternal grandfather, Howell, settled in Coles County, Illinois, in 1842. He was a cattle dealer and took many herds of cattle overland to Milwaukee when Chicago was an Indian trading post. Isaac A. Carmack as a young man engaged in farming in Douglas County, Illinois. He was for twenty-five years active in the Republican party and became a personal friend of the late Joe Cannon of Danville.

William Frank Carmack grew up on a farm near Camargo, Illinois, and received a public school education. He was a young man of twenty when he came to Terre Haute. For ten years he was employed in the county offices at the Vigo County courthouse, being a clerk under County Assessor Frank Armstrong, under County Treasurer C. A. Ray, and was chief clerk for County Recorder Levi Hammerly. While in the recorder's office he studied law and was admitted to the bar, and has since been engaged in a steady practice, handling probate work almost exclusively.

Mr. Carmack has been active in the Methodist Episcopal Church, is a Republican and a

INDIANA 377

member of the Knights of Pythias, and during the World war was secretary of the Vigo County branch of the Indiana Patriotic League.

He married Miss Sadie E. Hughes, of Terre Haute. Her father, Daniel Hughes, came from Wales, was a miller by trade and for many years was connected with the Southern Mills at Terre Haute. Mrs. Carmack has been active in the Woman's Department Club and the First Methodist Episcopal Church. Their only daughter, Edith Lucille, is the wife of Webb E. Beggs. Mr. Beggs is with the Hurd Pohlmann Company, Limited, at Honolulu, Hawaiian Islands. Mr. and Mrs. Beggs have two sons, Webb, Jr., and Edward Carmack Beggs.

EDWIN L. RICKERT, president of the First National Bank of Connersville, resigned his post as superintendent of city schools to join this financial institution. Mr. Rickert has an enviable record both in education and banking, and is one of the progressive leaders of this prosperous Southern Indiana community.

He was born in Columbiana County, Ohio, son of Allen and Sarah (Lehman) Rickert. His father was a native of Bucks County, Pennsylvania, and his mother was also born in Columbiana County. From the farm where Edwin L. Rickert was born his parents two years later moved to Mahoning County and are now living at North Lima in that county. His father was born in 1848 and his mother in 1850.

Edwin L. Rickert was educated in public schools and was graduated A. B. from Wooster College of Ohio in 1901. His general and specialized education was continued in Harvard University, the University of California, University of Chicago, and his Master of Arts degree was given him at Columbia University in New York. He began teaching at the age of nineteen, at first in district schools, then as principal of village schools. He was principal of the Briar Hill and Myrtle Avenue schools in Youngstown, Ohio, and in 1907 went west to Maquoketa, Iowa, where he was superintendent of schools five and a half years.

Mr. Rickert has been a resident of Connersville since August 1, 1912, when he took up his duties as superintendent of schools. On July 1, 1920, he resigned that office to become cashier of the First National Bank, and since January, 1923, has been president. The First National Bank of Connersville is an institution with over two million dollars in resources, one of the strongest banks in the southern part of the state.

Mr. Rickert married, July 31, 1912, Miss Grace Weimer, who was born in Stark County, Ohio, daughter of Frank and Catherine (Crise) Weimer. Her parents were natives of Ohio. Mr. and Mrs. Rickert's three children are Edwin W., George Allen and Mary Grace. Mr. Rickert is an elder in the Presbyterian Church. Since 1928 he has been president of the board of trustees of the Conners-

ville public schools. He is a Republican, is a member of the National Education Association, and since August, 1925, has been chairman of the Better Connersville Committee. This organization functions as a Chamber of Commerce and among other accomplishments has been instrumental in securing the location at Connersville of the assembly plant of the Auburn Automobile Company. Mr. Rickert is a former president of the Kiwanis Club.

HON. JAMES A. COLLINS. Among the members of the bench and bar of Indiana, few are held in greater esteem and respect than Hon. James A. Collins, former judge of the Criminal Court of Marion County. In 1909 he was elected to the bench and in 1914 became the incumbent of judge of the Criminal Court of Marion County, having the distinction of being the only person ever elected to serve a fourth term since the establishment of the court in 1867.

Judge Collins was born October 12, 1870, at Arlington, Massachusetts, and is a son of Joseph and Jane (LaVelle) Collins. His father, a native of Birkenhead, Cheshire County, England, came to the United States in young manhood, and during the war between the states served in the Union army as a private in Company K, Eleventh Regiment, Massachusetts Volunteer Infantry. He married Jane LaVelle, who was born in Ireland, of French-Huguenot ancestry, and they resided the rest of their lives in Massachusetts, where Joseph Collins died in 1887.

After graduating from the Washington Grammar School, of Cambridge, Massachusetts, James A. Collins attended Cambridge Latin School for one year, but the death of his father necessitated his return home, and he secured employment with Joel Goldthwait & Company, of Boston, and remained with that concern for three years or until becoming assistant secretary of the Young Men's Christian Association at Springfield, Massachusetts. While in this position he prepared for a general secretaryship and was later called to serve as secretary at Matteawan, New York. From that town he was called to Lyons, New York, as the general secretary of the association there, but resigned to take up the study of law with the Hon. Charles H. Ray, a former classmate of Elihu Root at Hamilton College. In 1895 he married Lillie T. Knapp of Lyons, New York, and in that year took up his permanent residence at Indianapolis.

In 1898 Judge Collins entered the law office of Griffiths & Potts and upon the dissolution of that firm continued in the office of John L. Griffith, remaining with him for a period of five years. In 1899 he received the appointment as deputy prosecuting attorney under Edwin B. Pugh, and upon the election of John C. Ruckelshaus, two years later, as prosecuting attorney, was appointed deputy prosecutor in the Police Court, serving in that capacity for two years. On leaving the Police Court Judge Collins entered upon the general practice of his profession, forming a partnership with the late Charles E. Averill, under the firm name of Averill & Collins. This connection continued until Judge Collins was elected judge of the City Court of Indianapolis in 1909, and as judge of this court he established a system of adult probation that attracted attention throughout the country, and inaugurated the system for the collection of money fines on installments.

In 1914 Judge Collins was elected judge of the Criminal Court of Marion County and was reelected in 1918, 1922 and 1926, and served until January, 1931, since which time he has been engaged in the private practice of his profession. He was the fourteenth incumbent of this court since its establishment in 1867 and the only person who has ever been elected to serve four terms. During all the years that he presided over this court he maintained a system of adult probation similar to that which he established in the City Court. Judge Collins has been identified with the industrial, political and social development of Indianapolis. He was one of the founders and is a member of the board of directors of the Indiana Public Welfare Loan Association, and a member of the American, Indiana and Indianapolis Bar Associations. He is an honorary member of the Indianapolis Rotary Club and a member of the Columbia Club, Marion Club and McKinley Club, is a Scottish Rite Mason, and belongs to Murat Temple of the Mystic Shrine. During the war he contributed his services as a member of the legal advisory board of Marion County. Judge Collins has been a member of Saint Paul's Episcopal Church during all the years that he has resided in Indianapolis and is at this time a member of the vestry.

Judge and Mrs. Collins reside at 4811 Park Avenue and are the parents of two children: John H., a civil engineer of Indianapolis, who served with the Motor Transport Corps during the World war and saw action in France; and Miss Elizabeth L., of Indianapolis.

CHARLES J. CLAMME, president of the Union Trust Company of Hartford City, Blackford County, has been constructively influential in making this one of the staunch, efficient and important financial and fiduciary institutions of this part of his native state, besides which he is still actively engaged in the contracting business, in which he has gained much of leadership in road and bridge construction as well as general building operations, in Blackford and other counties.

Mr. Clamme was born on the parental home farm in Blackford County, Indiana, and the date of his nativity was March 18, 1878, he being a son of Pierre and Elizabeth (Spier) Clamme, whose children were eight in number. Pierre Clamme was born in the historic old province of Alsace-Lorraine, France, where he was reared and educated, and he was a young man when he came to Indiana, in 1862, he having become one of the substantial exponents of farm industry in Blackford County, where both he and his wife passed the remainder of

their lives, secure in the high regard of all who knew them.

Charles J. Clamme was reared to the sturdy discipline of the old home farm and his early education was acquired in the public schools of Blackford County. He continued to be actively associated with farm enterprise until he was twenty-eight years of age, as an associate in the activities of the old home farm, and after that he became independently engaged in the same line of enterprise, with major attention given to the feeding and raising of live stock. In the meanwhile he had become identified also with contracting business, with which he has since continued his connection and of which he has become a prominent representative in this section of the state. He has done much road and bridge construction as a contractor, and his operations have extended into Ohio also, specially in connection with drainage projects. He erected two school buildings in Jackson Township, the high school building in York Township, likewise in Blackford County, and he erected the high school building at Selma, Delaware County. In his present alliance with farm enterprise he utilizes about 800 acres of the valuable land of his native county and specializes in the raising of small grains, besides which he is associated with his two brothers in the ownership and control of a substantial business that is conducted under the title of Clamme Canning Company.

Mr. Clamme initiated his active connection with the banking business in the year 1925, when he liquidated the old Blackford County Bank at Hartford City, and he soon afterward began the promotion work that resulted in the organizing and incorporation of the Union Trust Company, which opened its establishment for business in July, 1927, the original corps of executive officers having been as follows: F. M. Forkner, president; F. L. Erwin, vice president; and Charles J. Clamme, secretary and treasurer. In 1930 Mr. Clamme was elected president of the corporation; L. C. Johnson, of Indianapolis, is vice president; and Charles J. Clamme, Jr., is secretary and treasurer, with Harold Markins as assistant secretary. The Union Trust Company was incorporated with a capital of $25,000, and its total resources in 1930 are $261,571. The bank has attractive and well equipped modern offices in the Elks Building of Hartford City, and in addition to its regular executives it retains four clerical assistants.

Mr. Clamme has membership in the Indiana Bankers Association, his political allegiance is given to the Republican party, and he gave nine years of service as a member of the County Council of Blackford County. He is a charter member of the Rotary Club at Hartford City. He has been active in politics in his native county and formerly served as chairman of the Republican committee of Jackson Township.

Mr. Clamme married Miss Amanda Emshwiller, daughter of Jacob Emshwiller, of Blackford County, and of this union have been born six children. The religious faith of the family is that of the Lutheran Church. Charles J., Jr., who attended Capp University, a Lutheran institution, is now, as previously noted, secretary and treasurer of the Union Trust Company; Harold E. married Miss Dorothy Wise and they likewise reside at Hartford City; Miss Minnie remains at the parental home; Edna is the wife of Herbert Leach; and Howard L., and Roy are attending the public schools of their home city.

JOHN WORTH KERN bears the full name of his honored father, who was long an influential and distinguished figure in Indiana public affairs as well as a member of the bar of his native state, and the son is well upholding the honors of the family name in Indianapolis, where he is established in the successful practice of law, is serving as United States commissioner, where he has been continuously in service as secretary of the Indianapolis Bar Association since 1924, and where he has made valued contribution to the educational work of his profession, he having been since 1927 a member of the faculty of the law department of the University of Indiana and also of Ben Harrison Law School.

Mr. Kern was born in Indianapolis, July 7, 1900, and is a son of John Worth Kern and Araminta (Cooper) Kern, the former of whom was born in Howard County, this state, and the latter at Burlington, Carroll County. The late John Worth Kern, Sr., left a distinct and worthy impress upon the history of his native state, and so ample and varied are existent records of his career that in this review it is unnecessary to enter detailed statements concerning his life history. It may be said, however, that he was long one of the prominent members of the Indiana bar, that he served as official reporter of the Indiana Supreme Court, was twice the Democratic nominee for the office of governor of Indiana, that he had served as a member of the State Senate, that he was a candidate of his party in 1908 for vice president of the United States, and that he served as United States senator from Indiana from 1911 until his death, which occurred in 1917. His widow now maintains her home at 1836 North Pennsylvania Street, Indianapolis.

The Indiana public schools constituted the medium through which John W. Kern, Jr., acquired his preliminary education. He thereafter continued his studies in the Brooks Preparatory School, and his final academic course was pursued in fine old Washington and Lee University, in Virginia, from which he received his degree of Bachelor of Arts. He thereafter completed a course in the law department of historic Harvard University, from which he duly gained his degree of Bachelor of Laws. In 1923 Mr. Kern became associated in practice with the Indianapolis law firm whose principals were Karmer Bess and George L. Denny, and this alliance he severed one year later, since which time he has continued in active and successful general practice in an independent way, his law offices being established on the twelfth floor of the Merchants Bank Building, and his executive headquarters as United States commissioner being in the Federal Building of Indianapolis, he having been appointed to this office in 1923, by Judge A. B. Anderson, of the Federal District Court, and having been reappointed in 1928, by Judge Balzell. Like his father, Mr. Kern has been a loyal and well fortified advocate of the principles and policies of the Democratic party, by which he was nominated in 1924 for the office of reporter of the Indiana Supreme Court. Mr. Kern has membership in the Indiana State Bar Association and the Indianapolis Bar Asociation, of which latter he has been, as previously noted, the secretary since 1924. He is affiliated with the Phi Gamma Delta and the Sigma Delta Kappa college fraternities, and he and his wife hold membership in the Presbyterian Church, their home being at 1529 Park Avenue.

The year of 1927 recorded the marriage of Mr. Kern to Miss Bernice Winn, daughter of Henry A. and Mabel (Long) Winn, of Indianapolis, and the one child of this union is John Worth Kern III, born May 25, 1928.

AMOS WILLIAM BUTLER, A. M., LL. D., of Indianapolis, zoologist, sociologist, philanthropist, was born at Brookville, Franklin County, Indiana, October 1, 1860, and is a son of William Wallace and Hannah (Wright) Butler. In 1894 Doctor Butler was graduated from Indiana University with the degree of Bachelor of Arts, and in 1900 he was given the degree of Master of Arts, while in 1922 it conferred upon him the honorary degree of Doctor of Laws, a similar degree having been conferred upon him by Hanover College in 1915. In 1896-97 Doctor Butler served as ornithologist of the Indiana Department of Geology and Resources; during the period of 1897-1923 he was secretary of the Indiana State Board of Charities; in 1909 he was a member of the White House Children's Conference; in 1905 he was lecturer on economics at Purdue University, Lafayette, Indiana; in 1910 he was lecturer at the Chicago School of Philanthropy; and since 1920 he has served as lecturer on public charities at Indiana University. Doctor Butler was president of the National Conference of Charities and Correction in 1906-07, and in 1910 he served as chairman of the American committee on International Prison Congress, Washington, D. C., of which he was a vice president. As a member of the American Prison Association he served as its secretary in 1905-07 and as its president in 1909-10, he having been chairman of its executive committee since 1925. In 1925 he represented the United States as a delegate to the International Prison Congress held in London, England, of which international body he was a vice president. He has been president of the Indiana Conference of Charities and Correction. In the American Association for the Advancement of Science Doctor Butler was general secretary in 1891.

380 INDIANA

He was secretary of its section on anthropology in 1886 and 1900, in which latter year he was retained also as vice president of this section. In the same organization he was secretary of the section on biology in 1889. He was the founder of the Indiana Academy of Science, of which he was secretary until 1893, he served the following year as its vice president and in 1895 as president. He was a founder of the American Anthropological Society, the American Association of Mammalogists, the Indiana Audubon Society, the Indiana Society of Mental Hygiene, and the International Committee on Mental Hygiene. Doctor Butler is a member of the American Ornithologists Union, was a delegate to the second Pan-American Scientific Congress, in 1915-16, and he has been since 1925 president of the Indiana Society for Mental Hygiene, the while he has been since 1915 secretary of the Indiana Committee on Mental Defectives. Doctor Butler has published more than 100 scientific papers. Among these is the book on the *Birds of Indiana* and another that bears the following title: *Indiana—A Century of Progress. The Development of Public Charities and Corrections.*

On the 2d of June, 1880, was solemnized the marriage of Doctor Butler to Miss Mary I. Reynolds, of Brookville, Indiana. Their home is at 52 Downey Avenue, Indianapolis. They are the parents of six children: Mrs. Carrie Hannah Watts, Mrs. Alice Kaylor (deceased), William Reynolds, Gwyn Foster, Mrs. Anne Harrison, and Hadley (deceased).

In college he was a member of Phi Delta Theta fraternity, and is a member of Phi Beta Kappa and Sigma Xi honorary societies. He is a member of the Presbyterian Church.

MRS. KATE MILNER RABB, Indiana author, much of whose work has been in historical lines and who is a valued member of the Indiana Historical Society, was born at Rockport, Indiana. She was married in 1891 to Mr. Albert Rabb, of Indianapolis, and is the mother of two children, Albert Livingston and Martha Charlotte, wife of W. H. Hobbs.

Mrs. Rabb has the Master of Arts degree from Indiana University. She began writing while in college, and has a host of readers who follow her comments on Indiana life through her special column in the *Indianapolis Star* known as *A Hoosier Listening Post.* Mrs. Rabb was appointed a member of the Indiana Historical Commission in 1923. She is a member of the Woman's Press Club of Indiana, the Contemporary Club, the Players Club, and is a Phi Beta Kappa and Kappa Alpha Theta. Her home is at 1433 North Pennsylvania Street, Indianapolis.

Mrs. Rabb is author of *National Epics,* published in 1896; *The Boer Boy,* published in 1900; *The Wit and Humor of America,* published in 1907. She edited *A Tour Through Indiana in 1840,* this being the diary of John Parsons, of Petersburg, Virginia. She was also editor of *Indiana Coverlets and Coverlet Weavers,* which was published by the State Historical Society in 1928.

EVERETT GRINSTEAD, deputy sheriff of Shelby County, is a comparatively young man who has seen a great deal of life, largely due to the fact that he has been earning his own living since boyhood and has come in contact with all kinds of people and a great variety of business experience.

Mr. Grinstead was born in Columbia Township, Jennings County, Indiana, July 16, 1892. He is of old American stock. While some of the facts are traditional, a fairly accurate account has been given of the Grinstead family in America. Two brothers of the name came from England about 1730, locating in Virginia. One of them remained in that state and his descendants are still found there. The other joined in the western movement which started in the late Colonial period down the valley of Virginia and over the mountains, going to what is now eastern Tennessee. About the time the ambitious Transylvania Company opened up the project for the settlement of Kentucky he moved into that state. A grandson of this Kentucky pioneer was Jonathan Grinstead, the grandfather of Everett Grinstead. Jonathan Grinstead when eighteen years of age enlisted for service in the Union army and died when he was twenty-one years of age, just three days after the birth of his son, James H. Jonathan Grinstead was born in Indiana and had lived on a farm until he went to war. One of his ancestors was a Revolutionary officer. Jonathan Grinstead's son, James H. Grinstead, was born in Jennings County, was a farmer, spent fifteen years in service as a police officer at Greensburg, and was also road supervisor of Columbia Township. He married Mary Chaille, and they had two children, Everett and Albert S., the latter a Shelbyville business man.

Everett Grinstead spent a few years in the grade schools at Greensburg, but his real education has been a product of the university of hard knocks and a working experience that started when he was twelve years of age as a newsboy. He was a hotel clerk, grocery clerk, for two years conducted a restaurant business, and was circulation manager and reporter for the *Greensburg Daily News* until he answered the call to the colors during the World war.

Mr. Grinstead enlisted in May, 1918, in the Three Hundred Thirteenth Cavalry Regiment. He was with the regiment at Del Rio, Texas, on the Mexican border and served until December 24, 1918. He was ranked as a farrier, or assistant veterinarian. Mr. Grinstead is an active member of the American Legion Post.

After the war he returned to his work with the *Greensburg Daily News,* but in the fall of 1921 resigned and became connected with the *Shelbyville Republican,* with which he continued for four years. He has also done work for the *Indianapolis News* and for one year was field representative over twelve counties of Indiana for the *American Agricultural Chemical* of Cincinnati. Mr. Grinstead on January 1, 1925, was appointed deputy sheriff of Shelby County. He has always been inter-

Theodore F. Vonnegut

ested in politics, and did a great deal of work for his party while in the newspaper business.

Mr. Grinstead married Miss Florence T. Whitehead, of Shelby County, and they have four children, Mary, Robert, John and Rosanna.

THEODORE FRANKLIN VONNEGUT. A member of one of the oldest and most highly-respected families of Indianapolis, Theodore Franklin Vonnegut has had an active and diversified career, in which he has invaded several fields of endeavor with marked success. He commenced his career as a lawyer, giving this up temporarily to engage in the book business, in which he became widely known, but eventually returned to the law and is now in possession of a large and representative clientele. He likewise has been prominent in public affairs, particularly those affecting education, and from 1926 to 1928, inclusive, was president of the school board of Indianapolis, and one year (1929) served as chairman of the buildings and grounds committee.

Mr. Vonnegut was born at Indianapolis, June 21, 1880, and is a son of Franklin and Pauline (Von Hake) Vonnegut. His paternal grandfather was Clemens Vonnegut, who was born in Westphalia, Germany, and came to the United States in 1851, settling at Indianapolis, where he became a leading citizen and served as a member of the school board for a period of thirty-seven years. Franklin Vonnegut also labored in the cause of education, having been a member of the school board of Indianapolis for six years.

Theodore Franklin Vonnegut attended the Indianapolis grade schools and the Emmerich Manual Training High School, following which he attended Indiana University, from which he received the degrees of Bachelor of Arts and Bachelor of Laws. Subsequently he pursued a course at the University of Heidelberg, Germany, and in 1903 graduated from the Indiana Law School. For several years after completing his university work Mr. Vonnegut practiced his profession at Indianapolis, and then engaged in the book business, specializing in old and rare books. He built up a widely-known business as an old-book dealer and was known as an authority on such. He wrote and in 1926 published a work entitled "Indianapolis Booksellers and their Literary Background—1822-1860, A Glimpse of the Old Book Trade of Indianapolis," and this was a thesis submitted to and accepted by Indiana University as a partial requirement for the degree of Master of Arts, January 4, 1926.

In 1926 Mr. Vonnegut retired from the book business and resumed the practice of law. In that year he was elected president of the Indianapolis School Board, a position to which he gave a great deal of his time and thought, contributing to the extensive public school system of his city a wise and efficient administration. He is a Knight Templar Mason.

Mr. Vonnegut married Miss Lucy Lewis, of Princeton, Indiana, a member of a pioneer Indiana family, and they have one daughter: Pauline.

CULLEN C. COCHRAN, a merchant at Center Point, Clay County, has lived all his life in this section of Indiana. He served two terms as county treasurer of Clay County, having been elected to that office in 1924 and reelected in 1926, and served until January 1, 1930.

Mr. Cochran was born in Bowling Green, Clay County, January 28, 1889, son of Charles and Cora (Cullen) Cochran, grandson of George Cochran and great-grandson of Landon Cochran. Landon Cochran was a Pennsylvanian who volunteered for service at the time of the war of 1812, and saw active service in the great battle of Lake Erie under Commodore Perry. The State of Pennsylvania subsequently awarded him a silver medal for his part in this notable naval victory, and this medal is a prized possession of Mr. Cullen C. Cochran. A copy of the formal award of the honor and the medal, signed by Mr. Joseph Heister, one of the state officials at Harrisburg, under date of March 8, 1821, reads as follows:

"In compliance with the directions of the legislation of this commonwealth and, I have the pleasure of conveying to you the thanks of the government of the noble and gallant manner in which you volunteered on board the American squadron on Lake Erie, under the illustrious Perry. And also presenting to you a silver medal, of fine workmanship in compliment of your patriotism and bravery in the celebrated victory over a superior British force on the 19th of September, 1813.

"And I take this occasion to add to the testimony of my sincere accordance with the patriotic and grateful sentiments of the legislature towards you as one of the citizens of Pennsylvania who distinguished themselves in that memorable conflict."

At this time Landon Cochran was living in Fayette County, Pennsylvania.

Charles Cochran, the father of Cullen C., was a well known business man of Clay County, being merchant and postmaster at Bowling Green. He and his wife had three children: Madge, who married Ernst Powell; Cullen C.; and Hazel, now deceased.

Cullen C. Cochran was educated in the schools of Bowling Green and after graduating engaged in farming. When he was twenty-eight years of age he joined his father-in-law, S. B. McCann, in the merchandise business at Bowling Green, and continued as a merchant until the votes of the people elected him to office. In February, 1930, Cullen C. Cochran moved to Center Point, Clay County, where he entered into the general mercantile business, associated with Ernst Powell, his brother-in-law, in the firm of Cochran & Powell.

On January 10, 1917, he married Miss Fern McCann, daughter of S. B. and Jane (Frump) McCann. Her father for many years has carried on a successful business at Bowling Green. Her mother died in 1907 and is buried in the Swalley Cemetery. Mr. and Mrs. Cochran have four children, Dorothy F., Charles M., Richard L., and Samuel B.

Mr. Cochran has for years been a leader in the Democratic party, and has contributed to numerous successes of his party in campaigns. He was county chairman of the Democratic committee. He is a member of the Masonic Lodge No. 85, A. F. and A. M., of Bowling Green and the Eastern Star, and his family have been active in the Methodist Episcopal Church and Sunday School.

REV. JESSE LEROY HENDERSON. In the career of Rev. Jesse LeRoy Henderson, minister of the First Baptist Church of Washington, there are to be found all of the qualities that make for success, both personal and material. The strength and fragrance of his faith, the conscientious manner in which he has performed the duties of his holy office, his sincerity, kindliness and humanitarianism, all have led him to a straightforward path and have made him, while still in the flush of young manhood, one of the most beloved men of his calling in Southern Indiana.

Reverend Henderson was born March 14, 1894, in Forsyth County, Georgia, and is a son of William Irving and Elizabeth (Taylor) Henderson. His father, who was also born in Georgia, entered the Baptist ministry at an early age and developed into a celebrated evangelist who traveled all over the southern and middle-western states and whose utterances were heard by thousands. His death occurred in November, 1924, after a career that had been rich in usefulness and welldoing. Reverend Henderson married Elizabeth Taylor, a daughter of John Taylor, who for many years was a prominent agriculturist and merchant of Georgia, and to this union there were born thirteen children, of whom six sons and one daughter survive, as follows: George, who has a Government commission at Fort McPherson, with residence at Atlanta, Georgia, married Leila Westbrook, and has three children; Marion, foreman in the plant of the Pacolet Milling Company at Gainesville, Georgia, who married Pansy Little and has one child; William, who is engaged in the fruit business as a merchant at Gainesville, and is unmarried; Jay, also a resident of Gainesville, who married Polly Williams and has three children; Ray, a decorator of Gainesville, who married Polly Banett and has one child; Rev. Jesse LeRoy, of this review; and Fannie.

Jesse LeRoy Henderson received his early education in the public schools of Georgia and the high school at Gainesville, and after graduation from the latter attended the University of Louisville, Kentucky, and the Southern Baptist Theological Seminary of the same city, being graduated from both institutions in 1922, with the degrees of Bachelor of Arts and Doctor of Laws. For four years following he was minister of the Third Avenue Baptist Church of Louisville, and April 1, 1926, was placed in charge of the First Baptist Church of Washington, where he has since presided with great success. Like his father before him, Reverend Henderson is widely known in evangelistic work, having conducted meetings at Indianapolis and various other prominent points in the state, and is justly accounted one of the foremost workers of his denomination in Indiana. Since locating at Washington he has taken an interest in civic affairs, and has cooperated with other vigorous, broadminded and farsighted men in the promulgation of movements which have made for public progress and development. Being an able executive and possessing business ability, the affairs of his parish are in a flourishing financial condition, and he not only acts as a spiritual guide to his congregation, but as a business adviser and a sincere friend.

Doctor Henderson married Miss Bessie E. Lloyd, a daughter of William Thomas Lloyd, of Nelson County, Kentucky, and a member of an old and prominent Kentucky family. Her grandfather was a soldier during the war between the states and a number of the Lloyds have been prominent in business and public life. To Doctor and Mrs. Henderson there has been born one daughter: Vashti, born in 1926.

GEORGE ALFRED BELL, Marion banker and manufacturer, has traveled a long way since he graduated from technical schools in 1900. On the way he has had many activities, involving hard work and small pay, but his experiences as a whole have contributed to the making of one of Indiana's outstanding men of affairs.

Mr. Bell was born in Brooklyn, New York, September 22, 1878, and is the inheritor of sound family stock. His great-grandfather was a professor of philosophy in Edinburgh University in Scotland. His grandfather, also named George Alfred Bell, came to America from Morpeth, Northumbelandshire, England, and reached a distinguished position in American manufacture as president of the New Jersey Zinc Company, one of the oldest and richest corporations in the country. He died at Brooklyn in 1896 and is buried there. He was a member of the Congregational Church and very strict in his religious practices. He followed the rule of giving all he made above $100,000 to the Lord, distributing his surplus generously by building and endowing a number of missions in the poorer parts of Brooklyn. His wife was Isabella E. Blakey.

George Alfred Bell, the second of the name, was born at Brooklyn, New York, September 6, 1851, and was also a manufacturer, spending his last years at Marion, Indiana, where he died. He was laid to rest in the Greenwood Cemetery at Brooklyn. He married Eliza Corinne Chandler, who was born near Ashley, Illinois, December 6, 1853, and now resides at Saint Petersburg, Florida.

George Alfred Bell III was educated in grade schools at Troy, New York, in a private school there conducted by Miss Reese, and at the age of twelve entered the Troy Military Academy, and from there went to the Rensselaer Polytechnic Institute, where he was graduated June 13, 1900, with the degree of Bachelor of Science in civil engineering.

The first job held by the graduate civil engineer paid him ten dollars a week as assistant estimator for the building contracting firm of Foster & Greene in New York City. At the end of the year he obtained a better position with Tower & Wallace, paper mill engineers of New York, being employed as draftsman and surveyor for fifteen dollars a week. It was in 1901 that Mr. Bell came to Marion, Indiana, and during the next four years was bookkeeper with the Marion Malleable Iron Works, at first at seventy-five dollars a month, and later was promoted to treasurer, at a salary of two thousand dollars a year. In 1905 he formed a partnership with Mr. Haswell, under the firm name of Bell & Haswell Coal Company. When this partnership was dissolved Mr. Bell organized and incorporated the Bell Coal Company, with a capital of ten thousand dollars. Mr. Bell became president, and the business is still one of the prosperous organizations of Marion. About that time Mr. Bell became financially interested in a small sawmill near Mobile, Alabama, operating in the long leaf pine district. Its success prompted him to organize the Crichton Lumber Company at Mobile, of which he became president. He sold his interest in 1911 and on July 22 of the same year organized the Hoosier Box & Pie Plate Company of Marion. December 10, 1913, he incorporated the Indiana Fibre Products Company of Marion, with a capital of $50,000 and with himself as president. On January 3, 1921, the Fibre Company took over the Hoosier Box & Pie Plate Company. The capital of the Fibre Company is now $400,000, eight times the original capitalization. During the World war the Fibre Company turned its facilities over to the Government for the manufacture of munitions, erecting a special building for the purpose.

Mr. Bell in 1922 became treasurer of the Rutenber Electric Company, a $250,000 corporation, and since 1923 has been president of the company, which manufactures a line of electrical heating appliances. Mr. Bell in 1922 was one of the promoters of the Central Wholesale Grocery Company, incorporated for $50,000. At the death of Colonel McCulloch in 1923, Mr. Bell became chairman of the board of directors of the Marion National Bank, and with the death of E. E. Blackburn in 1928 he was asked to fill the office of president, both of which positions he now holds.

Mr. Bell is a former president of the Marion Association of Commerce and is treasurer of the Marion Industrial Fund, established to bring new industries to the city. He is a Knight Templar and thirty-second degree Scottish Rite Mason and Shriner, member of the B. P. O. Elks, Loyal Order of Moose, the Theta Xi, and a member of the Sigma Xi, honorary scientific society. He is a member of the Columbia Club of Indianapolis, the Kiwanis and Mecca Clubs, and is a Presbyterian.

Mr. Bell married Miss Alice Rebecca McCulloch, daughter of the late Col. John L.

McCulloch. They were married in the Ponce de Leon Hotel of Saint Augustine, Florida. Mr. and Mrs. Bell have a son, John Lewis McCulloch Bell, who was born at Marion, June 21, 1913, and was graduated from the Marion High School in May, 1929, and now a student in the Indiana University.

Mr. Bell in a career covering a period of thirty years has exemplified an unusual type of business ability, energy and forcefulness. He is a man of high character, widely known among the business men and citizens of Indiana, and his associates have been given repeated demonstrations of his sound judgment and efficient leadership.

COL. JOHN LEWIS MCCULLOCH was a native son of Indiana, and played his part well as a constructive figure in the industrial and financial affairs of his home state. He was a pioneer glass manufacturer, and for many years prior to his death was head of the Marion National Bank.

Colonel McCulloch was born on a farm near Vevay, Switzerland County, Indiana, March 14, 1858, and died nearly sixty-five years later at Marion, January 28, 1923. His body rests in the mausoleum he had constructed in the I. O. O. F. Cemetery at Marion. His father, George McCulloch, was born in Scotland, in 1808, and came to America at the age of sixteen. At Vevay, Indiana, he engaged extensively in the flat boating business on the Ohio River, making boats and loading them with freight which he sent down the Ohio and Mississippi to New Orleans. George McCulloch died in 1891 and is buried at Vevay.

John Lewis McCulloch grew up in a stimulating environment, though his opportunities for education were limited. He attended the common schools of Switzerland County, graduated from the high school at Vevay, and subsequently attended Wabash College at Crawfordsville. After his college career he taught for two years in Switzerland County. His first commercial position was clerking in a hardware store at Frankfort, Indiana, at $3.50 a week. For four years he was employed at a salary of $100 a month as bookkeeper for the Southern Glass Works at Louisville, Kentucky, and was then promoted to general manager. After four years he went with the North Wheeling Glass Company at Wheeling, West Virginia, as sales manager and part-time salesman.

Colonel McCulloch became identified with the City of Marion, Indiana, in April, 1888. He was at that time well qualified by a practical knowledge of the glass industry. Many glass manufacturers were seeking locations in the Eastern Indiana field where only a short time before a great belt of natural gas had been developed, providing cheap fuel for glass plants. At Marion Colonel McCulloch organized the Marion Fruit Jar & Bottle Company, of which he was treasurer and president. Later the company established branch plants at Converse and Fairmount, Indiana, and at Coffeyville, Kansas. By 1904 this industry ranked as the second largest of its kind in the United States. Subsequently the Marion Company was sold to the Ball Brothers Corporation of Muncie.

Colonel McCulloch not only utilized the output of the gas fields of Eastern Indiana but engaged in promoting and drilling new wells in the gas and oil fields of the state. He brought in about 100 producing wells, selling them to one of the large eastern oil companies.

After selling his holdings as a glass manufacturer and his interests in the gas and oil fields, Colonel McCulloch took a much needed vacation and for two years he and his wife and daughter toured Europe. After returning to Marion he became interested in the private bank of Jason Wilson. Jason Wilson and his father-in-law, Adam Wolf, had established a private bank in 1862. It was known as the Jason Wilson Exchange Bank, located at the corner of Fourth and Adams streets, where it remained until about 1885. At that time the lot on the corner of Fourth and Washington was purchased, and at this site in 1917 Colonel McCulloch erected the modern seven-story bank and office building which is today the property and home of the Marion National Bank, the largest financial institution in the Eleventh Congressional District. After acquiring the old Wilson Bank, Colonel McCulloch reorganized it in 1905 as the Marion National Bank, with capital of $200,000, which was increased to $250,000, with a surplus of $100,000. The present resources of the institution are $7,000,000. Colonel McCulloch was president of the bank until his death. The first cashier of the national bank was E. E. Blackborn, who five years later became vice president, and following the death of Colonel McCulloch was chosen president. Mr. Blackborn died in 1928 and was succeeded by George Alfred Bell. In June, 1928, the Marion National Bank acquired the Home Savings & Trust Company and in August of the same year took over the Marion State Bank.

It would be difficult to recount all the vital ways in which Colonel McCulloch was identified with the City of Marion. He was elected in 1913 president of the Indiana Bankers Association, later became one of the vice presidents of the American Bankers Association. In 1894 he was made vice president and secretary of the Marion Paper Company, was a director of the Rutenber Electric Company of Marion. He was a leader in all the patriotic activities of the World war, particularly in selling the quota of bonds assigned to Marion. Colonel McCulloch was a man of action and never sought publicity, yet his activities were of such a character and his practical philanthropies so well known that he could not altogether avoid having his name mentioned frequently in the public press. He was very tolerant and broad-minded and though himself a Presbyterian he gave liberally to Catholic, Jewish as well as Protestant charities. He organized the Kiwanis Club in the State of Indiana and was its first governor, also governor for three successive years, and later was one of the international trustees and was chairman for the Kiwanis wing of the Riley Memorial Hospital for Crippled Children at Indianapolis. He was a thirty-third degree Scottish Rite Mason, a Knight Templar and Shriner, a member of the B. P. O. Elks and Moose, member of the Columbia Club of Indianapolis, was president of the Marion Golf Club and Marion Country Club. He held an honorary membership in the Saint James Conclave of the Red Cross of the Knights of Constantine. A Republican, he was appointed a colonel on the staff of Governor Hanley in 1905. He was former president of the Marion Association of Commerce.

Colonel McCulloch married, July 5, 1883, Miss Alice Rebecca Wilson, of Louisville, Kentucky, daughter of Jonathan Wood and Elizabeth Muir Wilson, of Bardstown, Kentucky. Their daughter, Alice Rebecca, is Mrs. George Alfred Bell, of Marion.

BERT F. YAGER is a native son of Marion County, was here reared and educated, here he has from his boyhood been actively associated with productive farm industry, and he now has control of a fine farm estate that is owned by his mother, in Decatur Township. Of the secure place that is his in the confidence and good will of the people of this community no further evidence is required than the statement that in 1930 he is serving his eighth consecutive year as trustee of his township. He is one of the progressive and wide-awake agriculturists and stock-growers of Marion County and is well entitled to individual recognition in this publication.

Mr. Yager was born in Marion County, and is the eldest of the six children of his parents, who still resides on their fine homestead farm in this county, the father, Charles F. Yager, having long been one of the outstanding exponents of farm enterprise here and being a substantial and highly respected citizen of the county. Of the other children it may be recorded that Minnie is the wife of H. Jessup; Emma is the wife of Frank Bishop; Eliza is the wife of Frederick Beck; and Frank and Jessie likewise continue residents of their native state.

Charles F. Yager is a son of William C. and Sophia (Wiley) Yager, both natives of Germany and both early settlers in Indianapolis. Charles F. was reared and educated in Marion County and here he has through his own ability and efforts achieved worthy prosperity, he having long been numbered among the influential representatives of farm enterprise in the county, where he and his wife own a large and valuable area of well improved farm land, including the place occupied and operated by their son Bert F., the immediate subject of this review.

The sturdy discipline of the home farm marked the boyhood and early youth of Bert F. Yager, and in the meanwhile he duly profited by the advantages of the public schools, including high school, in which latter he was a student three years. He has never faltered in his allegiance to the basic and important industries of agriculture and stock-raising, of which he is now one of the enterprising and successful exponents in his native county, the farm on which he stages his activities comprising 100 acres and having good improvements of permanent order. Mr. Yager is a Republican, he and his wife are zealous members of the Methodist Episcopal Church, and he is affiliated with the Masonic fraternity and the Independent Order of Odd Fellows, both he and his wife having membership in the Order of the Eastern Star.

On the 22d of April, 1916, Mr. Yager was united in marriage with a daughter of Austin and Nettie (Heizer) Mendenhall, the latter of whom still resides in Marion County. Austin Mendenhall, a son of Wesley and Rhoda (Johnson) Mendenhall, was long one of the prosperous representatives of farm enterprise in Marion County, where his death occurred in 1922, his mortal remains being laid to rest in the cemetery at West Newton. Mr. and Mrs. Yager have three children: Martha, Dale and Joseph H.

Mr. Yager has always shown a lively interest in everything touching the welfare and advancement of his home community and native county, and his has been a notably loyal and constructive service in the office of township trustee, successive reelection having testified to the high popular estimate placed upon his administration.

GEORGE H. CARTER. Banks are well known to be among the most conservative of institutions, and when a man is placed at the executive head of one of them, he is accepted by his community as one of the sound and reliable business men and financiers, or he would not have been so honored. Many of these executives have worked their way up in banking so that they understand its every phase, and such is the case with George H. Carter, president of the Orleans National Bank of Orleans, Indiana. Mr. Carter has learned bank procedure step by step, and the whole routine and the world of bank ideals have opened before him as he was promoted from one position to another as he showed capacity to grasp the opportunities afforded him.

George H. Carter was born in Orange County, Indiana, July 21, 1870, a son of Dr. Theopolis Carter, also a native of Orange County and a medical practitioner of note throughout Orange County for a long period. From the time of his graduation in medicine until his death, in October, 1899, when he was seventy-two years old, he was active in practice. He married Mary R. Hardesty, who was born in Kentucky, and died March 31, 1915. They had two children, but the daughter, Margaret, died in infancy. The paternal grandfather of George H. Carter was Shadrick Carter, one of the early settlers of Orleans Township, Orange County, who was born July 2, 1792. A man of great energy and determination, he took an outstanding part in the development of his township, assisting in building the first schoolhouse, and making other improvements, including the erection of the First Methodist Church in Orleans Township. A Jacksonian Democrat, he was one of the leaders of the local party, and in the early days of the county's history represented it in the Indiana State Legislature, where he took a characteristic part. On December 3, 1822, Shadrick Carter was married to Miss Margaret Carpenter.

The earliest record Mr. Carter has of his ancestors is a record of Samuel Carter, who served in the Revolutionary war and was the great-grandfather of George H. Carter. George H. Carter had better educational opportunities than many farmers' sons of his period, for after he had completed his work in the local schools he entered the University of Indiana, and was graduated therefrom in 1897, with the degree of Bachelor of Chemistry. His first position was one he secured in a bank, and he has continued his connection with banking ever since, although in addition to it he has, in later years, had an interest in a firm of road building contractors. He is also the owner of several very valuable farms, one of which is the farm owned by his paternal grandfather and father before him.

On July 1, 1903, Mr. Carter was married to Miss Nellie Glover, a daughter of Stephen and Elizabeth (Kearby) Glover. There are no children. Mrs. Carter and her parents were all born in Orange County, where the family is an old and honored one. Mr. Carter is a Republican, but is not a politician in any sense of the word, his many interests preventing his going into public life, although, of course, he gives his support to the candidates of his party. For many years he has been a consistent member of the Christian Church.

WILLIAM B. HOPKINS, M. D., is a native of West Virginia, but grew up in Southern Indiana, and is now practicing his profession as a physician and surgeon at Sellersburg in Clark County.

Mr. Hopkins was born in Pendleton County, West Virginia, May 9, 1891. The Hopkins family is of Colonial and Revolutionary stock. They came from England and settled in Rockingham County, Virginia. At least one of Doctor Hopkins' ancestors was an officer in the Revolutionary war. His father was Dr. John J. Hopkins, who practiced medicine and also held various positions in the political life of Pendleton County, West Virginia.

Dr. William B. Hopkins was a boy when the family moved to Bartholomew County, Indiana. He had attended school in West Virginia and through his own efforts carried on his education through Valparaiso University, and in 1921 was graduated from the medical department of the University of Louisville. A year of interne experience in the City Hospital of Louisville gave him additional training before he entered upon his career as a practicing physician in Bartholomew County. From 1922 to 1928 he practiced at Hazard, Kentucky, and in the latter year located at Sellersburg, where he has won a fine practice and a most favorable reputation. While living in Kentucky he served four years as county health officer in Knox County. Doctor Hopkins is a member of the Indiana State, Clark County and American Medical Associations and belongs to the Sellersburg Chamber of Commerce. He is a member of the Masonic fraternity and the college fraternities Alpha Epsilon and Pi Beta Pi.

Doctor Hopkins married Miss Edna L. Lykins, a native of Kentucky. They have three children, Ann, John J. and William D.

STACEY H. MILLER is a successful young attorney now practicing law at La Fayette, with offices in the Loan & Trust Building. He was born in La Fayette, November 16, 1903. His grandfather, Reuben Miller, was a native of Pennsylvania, served with a Pennsylvania regiment in the Civil war, and after the war came to Indiana and was a farmer in Tippecanoe County. His wife was also a native of Pennsylvania, of Pennsylvania Dutch ancestry.

John H. Miller, father of Stacey H., was born in Tippecanoe County, served with the Marines in the Spanish-American war, and has for over thirty years been one of the substantial and respected farm residents of this section of the state. He married Albia L. Shaw, a native of La Fayette.

Stacey H. Miller was one of three children. He attended common schools at Battleground, graduated from the Scottsburg High School in 1923 and took the literary and law courses in the Central Indiana Normal School at Danville, graduating with the A. B. degree in 1927 and the LL. B. degree in 1928. After his admission to the bar he located at La Fayette and has enjoyed a steadily increasing general practice as a lawyer there since November 1, 1928. He is a member of the Tippecanoe County and Indiana State Bar Associations.

EDMOND JEFFRIES, who at the time of his death was a retired business man, with home at Kokomo, found his time occupied with the opportunities of useful service in the capacity of justice of the peace. Mr. Jeffries was a man of unusual energy, public spirit, a hard worker and enjoyed many important responsibilities in the business world, both in his native State of Indiana and in Pennsylvania, where he lived for many years, having been one of the most active citizens in founding what is now an important industrial city, Monessen in Westmoreland County.

Mr. Jeffries was born at Newcastle, Henry County, Indiana, March 10, 1857. The Jeffries family came to Indiana from Virginia, his grandfather, Anderson Jeffries, having been a Virginian. His father was Anderson A. Jeffries, who was born in Lancaster County, Ohio, in 1830 and died in 1895. Anderson A. Jeffries was a York Rite Mason. He married Melinda McLaughlin, who was born in 1830 and died December 5, 1925, at the great age of ninety-five years. One other son was

Homer Jeffries, who was born in December, 1851, and died in 1918.

Edmond Jeffries grew up and received his early education in the public schools at Newcastle, learned a trade, and for a number of years was a contractor and builder. In October, 1880, when he was twenty-three, he moved to Anderson, Indiana. He did contracting there and after the beginning of the natural gas boom in Eastern Indiana he had an important part in some of the industries which were established at Anderson to utilize the natural gas resources. As a contractor he helped erect several of the pioneer plants of Anderson, including the National Tin Plate Company of that city.

In 1897 the National Tin Plate Company determined to erect a plant in Westmoreland County, Pennsylvania, and Mr. Jeffries was chosen as the contractor for the building. He and other officials arrived at Monessen when it contained only a railroad station, and he helped select the site for the new factory and took entire charge of the erection of the plant. After the mill was completed he became superintendent and served in that capacity three years. A year after this plant was established it was sold to the American Tin Plate Company. Mr. Jeffries also had the management of the real estate holdings of the company, and as contractor supervised the erection of forty-nine residences at Monessen during the early months. Mr. Jeffries as a contractor was called upon by the first school board of Monessen to provide quarters for the opening of a school. At the beginning of the school year no building was available for the use of the pupils, and Mrs. Jeffries agreed to and carried out his promise of providing a temporary building within a week's time. He erected a frame structure twenty by sixty feet, which was divided into three rooms, and thus accommodated the children of the mill workers and the other citizens of the community.

Mr. Jeffries in 1900 moved to Donora, Westmoreland County, and for two years was superintendent of construction for the Union Steel Company, and also handled the affairs of the Improvement Company there. In 1902 he organized the Standard Tin Plate Company of Cannonsburg, erected the new plant and served as its president and general manager until 1904. On April 24, 1905, Mr. Jeffries returned to Monessen, took charge of the special agency for the East Side Land Company, and on the first of June became manager of the real estate and insurance departments of the Monessen Savings & Trust Company. He was connected with that company for many years, and while still in that position he was appointed by President Wilson postmaster of Monessen. He served in this office from 1913 to 1917. During the World war he was in the coal business, selling the entire product of a number of mines to the Government for war use.

After retiring from business Mr. Jeffries returned to Indiana and located at Kokomo.

Henry W. Mock.

He was appointed justice of the peace in Kokomo by the county commissioners January 13, 1925, to fill the vacancy caused by the death of Clarence Davis. He was commissioned by Governor Jackson.

Mr. Jeffries was a Democrat in politics and throughout a long and useful career distinguished himself by his willingness to give time and effort in procuring things needed by his community and in the performance of public service. He, with his family, was a member of the Presbyterian Church. Mr. Jeffries married Miss Catherine Malone at Anderson. She was born at Centerville, Indiana, May 3, 1857. Of their children the oldest is Edna, wife of William Eichenlaub, of Pittsburgh, Pennsylvania. Elizabeth is the wife of J. A. Trexler, of Chicago. Ruth Virginia is the widow of Frank Goshorn and lives at Pittsburgh. Joseph W. is an attorney in Chicago, and Thomas E. is also a lawyer by profession and resides at Detroit. Helen Marie is the wife of Alvin Parsons, of Pittsburgh. The daughter Della Donner Jeffries died August 5, 1920. Mr. Jeffries died at his home, 1248 East Jefferson Street, Kokomo, Indiana, August 29, 1930, at the age of seventy-three.

HENRY WILFORD MOCK. Not only is Henry Wilford Mock one of the ablest attorneys practicing at the bar of Crawford County, but he is an outstanding figure in the life of English, and connected with progressive measures along many lines. He was born in Crawford County, September 7, 1877, a son of Squire E. Mock, a farmer, born in Harrison County, Indiana, and a veteran of the war between the states, during which he served as a member of the Fifty-third Indiana Volunteer Infantry, under General Sherman. Squire E. Mock was a son of Solomon Mock, a North Carolinian who established the family in Indiana, and became a farmer of Harrison County. The wife of Squire E. Mock, and mother of Attorney Mock, bore the maiden name of Annie Goldman, and she was born in Knox County, Indiana. Mrs. Mock is still living, having attained the age of eighty-six years in 1929. She and her husband had eight children, namely; Nancy, who resides in Posey County, Indiana, married John Romine, has no children; Sarah, who resides in Crawford County, married John Belcher, has no children; Margaret, who resides at Princeton, Indiana, married William B. McWilliam, has seven children; Theodore, who lives in Michigan, married Grace Taylor, and they have three children; Millie, who resides at English, married James Brown, has two children; Attorney Mock, who is the next in order of birth; Albert, who lives at Indianapolis, Indiana, married Alva Killien, and they have two children; and George, who lives at Louisville, Kentucky, married Daisy Fein, no children.

Henry Wilford Mock attended the public schools of Crawford County and the State Normal School, Terre Haute, Indiana, from which he was graduated in 1902. For three years thereafter he taught school in Patoka Township, Crawford County; for two years he was superintendent of the Alton schools; and for six years he was superintendent of the public schools of English. In the meanwhile he attended New Albany, Indiana, Business College, from which he was graduated in 1903, after which, for two terms, of four years each, he served, through successive election, as circuit clerk. While in office he took up the study of law, and was admitted to the bar in 1909, but did not enter upon the practice of his profession until 1919. For the past decade, however, he has been engaged in a general practice at English, and is attorney for the English State Bank. He belongs to the Crawford County Bar Association and the Indiana State Bar Association.

On December 31, 1903, Mr. Mock was married to Miss Emma A. Robertson, a daughter of William H. and Cynthia (Baggarly) Robertson, also of Crawford County. Three children have been born to Mr. and Mrs. Mock, namely: Garth Robertson, who died in infancy; Ferris W., who lives at English, and is engaged in the radio business, is unmarried; and Glenis, who also is a resident of English, married Helen Young, and they have two children, Mary Louise and Patricia Ann.

During the World war Mr. Mock was a member of the local draft board, and took a zealous part in all of the drives for patriotic purposes. A Democrat, he is one of the leaders of his party at English. The Christian Church has long held his membership, and he is one of its elders. He is a Scottish Rite Mason and Shriner and a Knight Templar, and he also belongs to the Independent Order of Odd Fellows, the Improved Order of Red Men and the Order of the Eastern Star. For twenty-two consecutive years he served as worshipful master of Crawford Lodge No. 470, A. F. and A. M., a very unusual occurrence in any order. Mr. Mock believes that there is immediate demand for the encouragement of religious training in the home life; the increase and improvement of educational facilities; the provision of homes and hospitals for those who are unavoidably destitute and helpless on account of sickness and affliction, and he is ready and willing to lead in bringing about these enactments, just as he has in so many other public-spirited movements, for such is the character of the man.

HON. PAUL R. SHAFER, Terre Haute attorney, is a former judge of the City Court and now probate judge of Vigo County.

Judge Shafer was born in Claremont, Illinois, April 28, 1886. His father, James F. Shafer, was born at Claremont and his mother, Zada M. Stokes, was born in Ohio. James F. Shafer has been a prominent farmer and stock man for many years, raising thoroughbred racing horses and is president of the First National Bank at Claremont.

Paul R. Shafer attended high school at Olney, Illinois, took the Bachelor of Science, 1906, and Bachelor of Arts degrees, 1907, from Valparaiso University and for two years was science instructor in the Southern Conference College at Siloam Springs, Arkansas. He studied law at the University of Illinois, graduating LL. B. in 1911 and for a short time was associated in practice with Judge Lynch, of Olney, and on coming to Terre Haute did clerical work until 1914, when he engaged in a private law practice. As a lawyer he has specialized in municipal finance and corporation law and has had a wide technical experience in matters involving title. Judge Shafer was city judge of Terre Haute four years, 1918-22. During this time the Indiana Bone Dry Law became effective and many cases came before him involving that law and several of them presented situations and circumstances where he was called upon to render decisions affecting liquor violations where there were no established precedents to follow.

Judge Shafer has been commissioner of probate for Vigo County since January, 1925. As probate judge he has been called upon to handle some of the largest estates ever settled in the county. Judge Shafer is a thirty-second degree Scottish Rite Mason and Shriner, and is a member of the Vigo County, Indiana State and American Bar Associations. He was president in 1925 of the Terre Haute Kiwanis Club and has been district trustee of the Kiwanis.

He married, August 28, 1909, Miss Eva Foster, daughter of Corban and Angeline (Stanninger) Foster. Mrs. Shafer is a graduate of the musical conservatory of the Illinois Wesleyan University at Bloomington and was a teacher of music before her marriage and since coming to Terre Haute has taken a prominent part in local musical affairs. They have three sons, Paul Ora, James Corban and Byron Foster.

HENRY FERNUNG, for many years active in the business and industrial life of Franklin County, was born at Mount Carmel, Indiana, April 2, 1862, son of Andrew and Margaret (Betz) Fernung. His grandfather, John Betz, came from Germany and settled in Ohio. Andrew Fernung came to Indiana at the age of eighteen, began learning the shoemaker's trade at Brookville and finished his apprenticeship at Hamilton, Ohio, where he was married. In 1858 he located at Mount Carmel, and conducted a shoemaking business there until his death in 1880, at the age of forty-six. The widowed mother survived to the age of sixty-three. Three sons of the family are now living: Henry; Andrew J., of Kokomo, Indiana; and Charles, of White Water Township, Franklin County.

Henry Fernung attended District School No. 6 in Franklin County, was on a farm until eighteen, and then learned the business of sawmilling at Mount Carmel. In 1892 he established an elevator of his own and carried on his operations on an extensive scale for many years, buying timber and converting it into lumber, and also did a wholesale and retail business as a lumberman. Mr. Fernung in 1926 disposed of his lumber business, and since that time has looked after his private investments, particularly some highly improved farming land in White Water Township. He owns 300 acres, and for several years has been specializing in Hampshire hogs.

Mr. Fernung is an independent voter. He married in 1886 Miss Mary Bell Thomas, who was born at Metamora, Indiana. Her father, Milton Thomas, was also a native of Metâmora. Mrs. Fernung died October 13, 1924, leaving one child, Howard R. Howard lives with his father and married Miss Ruth Thomas.

JAMES REESE. For nearly a century the Reese family have lived in Hamilton County. Of sterling Quaker stock, they have exemplified the familiar virtues of that sect, have lived without ostentation, have been kindly, friendly, thrifty and industrious, and have measured up to the highest qualifications of good citizenship.

The late James Reese, several of whose children are well known in Hamilton County, was born at Leesburg in Highland County, Ohio, November 30, 1828, and died November 11, 1879. He was a son of Thomas Reese, who was also born in Ohio and was of Welsh ancestry. James Reese was about seven years of age when the family came to Indiana in 1835 and settled in the Providence neighborhood of Hamilton County. James Reese grew to manhood there, and his efforts put him in the class of the wealthy and extensive farmers of the county. James Reese married Sarah Jane Armstrong, who was born January 14, 1837, in Henry County, Indiana, where her people were pioneers. She passed away May 14, 1888. Both parents were active members of the Friends Church and are buried in the Hinkle Friends Cemetery. They had a family of nine children. Mary Ellen, born August 25, 1858, married James Jester and is now a widow living in Indianapolis. Lincoln, born November 8, 1860, died January 18, 1868. Alvin and Alpha were twins, born March 14, 1864. Alvin, who died May 11, 1921, married Ella Hiatt, and was a lifelong farmer. Alpha married Alex Nixon, who died in 1918, and she lives at Noblesville. Rodolphus, who was born October 11, 1866, has never married and is living retired at Noblesville. Lydia, born February 12, 1870, first married Lincoln Parsons and after his death became the wife of Clarence Sellers, and they live in Marshall County, Indiana. Phoebe Alice, born May 20, 1872, died March 4, 1877. Melvin, born in 1874, is a clothing manufacturer in New York City and married Ruth Greene, of Kokomo. Burdie, the youngest of the children, was born January 26, 1876, and died August 20, 1877.

Rodolphus Reese was reared and educated in Hamilton County and from early manhood took the active management of his father's extensive farming interests and conducted them as long as his parents lived. Since then

Frank C. Wagner

he has enjoyed a well earned retirement and has resided at Noblesville. He was mayor of the Village of Deming from 1904 to 1908. Mr. Reese is active in Masonry, being affiliated with Noblesville Lodge No. 57, A. F. and A. M., Noblesville Chapter No. 120, Royal Arch Masons, and Radiant Chapter No. 200 of the Eastern Star. He is a birthright Friend.

FRANK CASPAR WAGNER was an eminent engineer and scientist who gave almost a third of a century of his service to one of Indiana's great technical institutions, the Rose Polytechnic Institute at Terre Haute. Doctor Wagner was president of the institute for five years, until his unfortunte death on November 21, 1928. While he was driving his car off the campus it was struck by an interurban car. His death was regarded as a loss not only to the institution over which he presided, its numerous alumni, but to American science at large.

He was born at Ann Arbor, Michigan, October 5, 1864, and was just at the climax of his powers when death overtook him. His father, William Wagner, was born in Germany and came to America at the age of nineteen. At Ann Arbor he established a tailoring business that still bears his name. The mother of Doctor Wagner was Priscilla Moeller, of a Pennsylvania family. It was from her that Doctor Wagner doubtless inherited his strong bent for the precise sciences. She possessed a wonderful mathematical ability. Doctor Wagner was next to the youngest of the three sons of his parents. There were also three daughters.

He was educated in the public schools of Ann Arbor and in 1884 received the Master of Arts degree from the University of Michigan. He was awarded this degree before he was twenty years of age, and for many years had the distinction of being the youngest Master of Arts graduate from the institution. By an additional year of work at the university he received the degree Bachelor of Science in mechanical engineering in 1885.

From 1886 to 1889 Doctor Wagner was employed in engineering work for the Thomson-Houston Electric Company of Lynn, Massachusetts. He supervised the erection of a number of electric lighting plants for this corporation, which was a pioneer in the development of the electrical industry in America. Some of his last work for the company was in the Republic of Mexico, where he had charge of the installation of a number of plants in and near the capital. In 1890 he returned to the University of Michigan and for the following six years was assistant professor of mechanical engineering, associated with Prof. M. E. Cooley and Prof. John R. Allen. While at the University of Michigan he tested a Nordyke pumping engine at Grand Rapids. These tests furnished him the material for a paper which he subsequently presented before the American Society of Mechanical Engineers. For his research work Doctor Wagner earned a national reputation as a consultant

engineer. While at the university he made a number of tests on a Sterling boiler, in connection with a patent suit. This began his work as an expert witness in patent litigation which was to occupy so large a share of his time until his death. This patent work covered a wide variety of subjects, but mainly was concerned with problems in steam engineering and heat transfer. Out of this he secured the data for a number of papers which he read before engineering societies of which he was a member. In collaboration with Mr. W. C. Ely, of Terre Haute, he designed the first rotary puddling furnace used at the local steel mills. In later years Doctor Wagner furnished expert testimony in connection with a suit involving the cracking process for the production of gasoline.

Doctor Wagner came to the Rose Polytechnic Institute at Terre Haute in 1896 as associate professor of steam and electrical engineering. In 1904 he was promoted to the rank of full professor and in 1920 was made professor of mechanical engineering. In 1923 he was given the office of president, and was the executive head of this splendid technical school until his death. He was a member of the Phi Beta Kappa and the Tau Beta Pi fraternities.

Doctor Wagner held membership in many engineering societies. He was a fellow in the American Society of Mechanical Engineers, the American Institute of Electrical Engineers, the American Society for the Promotion of Engineering Education, the American Association for the Advancement of Science. He was chairman of the Indianapolis section of the American Society of Mechanical Engineers in 1927, and was president of the Indiana Engineering Society in 1928. He was appointed to represent this organization at the assembly of the American Engineering Council on January 1, 1928. During the World war he was administrative engineer for Indiana of the United States Fuel Administration. The Rose Polytechnic Institute conferred upon him the degree of Doctor of Science in engineering, and a little later he received a similar degree from the University of Michigan. Besides his many contributions to engineering publications he was author of a volume entitled *Notes on Applied Electricity*, published in 1903.

His interests were by no means confined to engineering and science. He was acquainted with seven or eight ancient and modern languages, and he was also a deep thinker on sociological subjects. His activity in community affairs was likewise commendable. At the time of his death he was acting as president of the Community Thrift Fund of Terre Haute. He was a member of the Chamber of Commerce, the Kiwanis Club, the Terre Haute Country Club and the Tau Beta Pi fraternity. Soon after coming to Terre Haute he joined the First Congregational Church, and held nearly every lay office in that organization. His charming personality and remarkable sympathy made him a friend of every student at the Polytechnic Institute, and his name is a venerated one among all alumni who attended the institute while he was there as a professor and president. The student body felt that they could always look to him for sympathetic advice as well as instruction. He lived the life of a thorough Christian gentleman in every relationship. His ability as a teacher and scientist won him national distinction. His unfailing patience and his kindly interest both inside and outside the classroom gave him the love of all his students at Terre Haute.

Doctor Wagner married at Ann Arbor, June 16, 1892, Miss Mabel Peck. She was born in Indiana and represents a prominent pioneer family of Michigan City. Her parents were Sylvester and Lucy (Rollins) Peck, her father, of Colonial ancestry, a native of New York State and her mother was born in Maine. The founder of the Peck family in Indiana was Willys Peck, leader in the business and public affairs of Michigan City and at one time mayor of that city. Mrs. Wagner has a special veneration for her grandmother, Mrs. Willys Peck, with whom she lived as a child and young woman. Mrs. Willys Peck reached the remarkable age of ninety-nine.

Doctor and Mrs. Wagner had five children: Helen, wife of J. L. McCloud, of Dearborn, Michigan, a research chemist of the Ford Motor Company; Frank Caspar, chief engineer with the Texas Central Power Company at Corpus Christi, Texas; Priscilla, wife of Fred Bates Johnson, an Indianapolis attorney; Willys Peck Wagner, an architect, connected with the Boston firm of Blodgett, Strickland & Law; and Barbara, wife of Charles D. Goodale, bacteriologist with the Commercial Solvents Corporation of Terre Haute.

Mrs. Wagner during her many years of residence in Terre Haute has had a prominent part in its social and charitable affairs. She is a member of the Woman's Department Club, the Terre Haute Club, the South Side Book Club and the Daughters of the American Revolution.

VERNON R. HELMEN, South Bend attorney, is a native of that city and represents the third generation of a highly respected family of Northern Indiana.

He is one of the sons of Frederick T. and Emma (Lempke) Helmen, who have lived at South Bend since 1883. Both parents were born in LaPorte County, and all the earlier ancestors of the family came from Germany and were pioneers of Northern Indiana.

Frederick T. Helmen was born in LaPorte County, April 30, 1858, son of Frederick and Frederika (Werner) Helmen. In Germany the Helmen name was spelled Hellmann. Frederick Helmen was born in Germany, August 7, 1829, and was married after he settled in LaPorte County, Indiana. His wife was born May 30, 1831. He worked in a flour mill and later became a farmer. Frederick Helmen died January 24, 1909, and his wife on October 24, 1919.

Frederick T. Helmen married Emma Lempke, who was born in LaPorte County, June 3, 1861, daughter of Charles and Dorothy Frederika (Wilhelm) Lempke, natives of Germany, where her father was born April 5, 1826, and her mother on June 24, 1840. Charles Lempke settled in LaPorte County about 1849. His wife came to Indiana in 1856, at the age of sixteen, and after their marriage they settled on a farm, where they spent the rest of their days. Charles Lempke died, March 23, 1872, and his wife on September 22, 1877. All these ancestors were German Lutherans in religion.

Frederick T. Helmen was educated in public schools of LaPorte County, learned the trade of carpenter and millwright, and after coming to South Bend spent forty years as foreman in the woodworking department of the South Bend Chilled Plow Company. He is now conducting a grocery business near Roseland and owns a farm just outside the City of South Bend. He is a Democrat in politics, is a member of the Evangelical Lutheran Church and the Knights of the Maccabees.

The seven children of Frederick T. Helmen and wife are: Harry W., a successful physician and surgeon at South Bend; Vernon R., a member of the South Bend bar; Effa Bertha, wife of John E. Bernhardt, of 225 Hammond Place, South Bend; Charles Adam, South Bend dentist; Frederick John, assistant cashier and assistant secretary of the St. Joseph Bank of South Bend; Erma Pauline, connected with the Associates Investment Company; and Arthur Horace, manager of the Moskins Clothing Store of Waukegan, Illinois.

Vernon R. Helmen attended the grade and high schools of South Bend, completing his high school work at Notre Dame. He also attended the Valparaiso Normal School and in 1917 was graduated from the law department of Notre Dame University. As a young man he engaged in teaching, for two years in the River Park School, in what is now a part of South Bend, and another two years in Clay Township in St. Joseph County. While attending Notre Dame University he was secretary of the educational department of the Y. M. C. A. of South Bend, and continued in that work for about five years. After finishing his law course he went to Duluth, Minnesota, as educational director of the Y. M. C. A. for one year. He began his work as a lawyer with the firm of Baldwin, Baldwin & Holmes, at Duluth, but after a short time left to enlist for service in the World war. He attended the Field Artillery Officers Training School at Camp Taylor, Kentucky, receiving his honorable discharge on November 29, 1918.

Returning to South Bend, he engaged in law practice until 1921. During the next five years he was in the Government service at Chicago as an internal revenue agent in the estate tax division of the Treasury Department. Since 1926 Mr. Helmen has carried on a general law practice at South Bend. While in Notre Dame he was vice president of the Junior Law Class and president of the Day Students organization. He has been president of the Clay Township civic center, and president of the South Bend-Mishawaka Epworth League Union. He takes an active part in the Methodist Episcopal Church and for ten years has taught a class in Sunday School.

Mr. Helmen married, March 11, 1922, Miss Margaret Ackerburg, of Chicago. They have two children, Vernon R., Jr., born August 8, 1923, and Suzanne Margaret, born December 11, 1928.

J. K. HAWES, M. D. The Hawes family is of English ancestry and in Indiana was founded by Jason Hawes, who came from New York into the state about 1816, bringing his family, consisting of a wife and eight children, four boys and four girls. Using an Ohio River flat-boat, he landed at Utica, where he lived for some years.

Jason Hawes was a stone mason and built many of the houses of the day. Later he moved to the western side of the county, where his family grew to maturity. A son, Nathan, born in New York in 1802, married Nancy, the daughter of Hugh Kelly, who likewise came to Indiana by way of the Ohio, about 1812. The Kellys were of Irish lineage, coming out of Virginia into Ohio, where Nancy was born in 1804, thence to Indiana. To this union there were born nine children. Nathan was a farmer, as was his son, Ep, born in 1839.

Ep Hawes married Harriet, the eldest daughter of Jesse O. and Salina Gates Coleman, of Edinburgh, in 1864. Jesse Coleman came to Indiana from Connecticut in 1848. He was of English descent. His grandfather Coleman was born in England, his wife was of the Gates family of whom General Gates, of Revolutionary fame, was the most prominent member. Jesse Coleman was a colonel in the Union army.

Ep Hawes took his young wife to the Hawes homestead at Memphis, Clark County, where they raised their family and where she spent her last days—going to her reward in 1916, at the age of seventy-three. Ep Hawes relinquished the farm to a son, Samuel, and now, at the age of ninety-two, makes his home with his son, James Kelly, at Columbus.

James Kelly Hawes was born in Clark County, July 28, 1874, was educated in the common schools and at Borden Institute, a private school, after which he taught school, both in Clark County, Indiana, and in Jefferson County, Kentucky, then he studied medicine at the Central University of Kentucky, now the University of Louisville, graduating in 1898. He came to Columbus, August 1, 1898, and has since resided here, practicing his profession.

Doctor Hawes as a physician has been a prominent figure in his profession and in the community life of Columbus for over thirty years. During the World war he was acting assistant surgeon of the United States public health service. Since 1919 he has been deputy health commissioner of the State of Indiana and a director of the United States public health service. He was county health officer of Bartholomew County from 1908 to 1909, is a member of the staff of the Bartholomew County Hospital, is secretary of the Bartholomew County Medical Society and of the Fourth District Medical Society and is a member of the Indiana State and American Medical Associations. Doctor Hawes is affiliated with St. John's Lodge of Masons, Knights of Pythias, the B. P. O. Elks, is a member of the Christian Church and is a Republican voter. He married Miss Myrtle Wisner, of Bartholomew County, in 1899. To their marriage were born seven children: Harriet, is a graduate of Butler University of Indianapolis, and is the wife of Kenneth R. Williams, of that city; William graduated Bachelor of Science from Purdue University, took his Master of Science and Doctor of Philosophy degrees at Brown University of Providence, Rhode Island, and at this time is doing research work for the National Research Society at the Massachusetts Institute of Technology at Cambridge, Massachusetts; Marvin graduated Bachelor of Science and M. D. from Indiana University and is now an interne at Saint Vincent's Hospital in Indianapolis; Mary, Ruth, James and Robert are at home.

ROBERT JUDSON ALEY, president of Butler University, is a native of Indiana, born at Coal City May 11, 1863, son of Jesse J. and Paulina (Moyer) Aley.

He has been a teacher for over half a century, doing his first work in country schools in 1877, when only fourteen years old. While teaching he studied at and graduated from Valparaiso University, and received his A. B. degree in 1888 and Master of Arts degree in 1890 from Indiana University, being instructor in mathematics at the university while studying for the Bachelor's degree. He held the chair of mathematics in Vincennes University from 1888 to 1891, and at Indiana University from 1891 to 1909. He was acting assistant professor of mathematics at Stanford University in California in 1894-95. The University of Pennsylvania gave him the Doctor of Philosophy degree in 1897, and that university and also Butler College and Franklin College have since bestowed upon him the honorary LL. D.

Doctor Aley served as superintendent of public instruction of Indiana from March, 1909, to November 12, 1910. He left this position to go to the University of Maine as president, remaining there until 1921, when he returned to his home state to become president of Butler University at Indianapolis. Doctor Aley is known among scholars for his research work in higher mathematics and is author of several text books and special treatises. For years he was mathematical editor of the *Inland Educator and Educator-Journal*. For nine years he was editor-in-chief and president of the *Educator-Journal*.

Among other titles of honor he has worthily borne was his election as president of the National Education Association for the year 1916-17. He has also been president of the National Council of Education, is a fellow of the American Association for the Advancement of Science and of other learned organizations. He is a Phi Beta Kappa, member of the Disciples Church, a Knight Templar and a thirty-third degree Mason. Doctor Aley married, August 28, 1884, Miss Nellie Archer, of Spencer, Indiana, and they have had two sons, Bruce, now deceased, and Maxwell.

HON. JAMES BINGHAM, former attorney-general of Indiana, has been a member of the bar of the state for forty years. After leaving the office of attorney-general he remained at Indianapolis, where he is still conducting a large practice, with his son as a partner and with offices in the City Trust Building.

Mr. Bingham was born in Mill Creek Township, Fountain County, Indiana, March 16, 1861, son of Alexander and Jane (Savage) Bingham. His father was born near Blue Lick Springs, Kentucky, and his mother in Ohio. They were married in Indiana. His father was a carpenter by trade, but spent most of his active years on a farm. He died March 26, 1886. He was much interested in local politics and at one time was candidate on the Republican ticket for the Legislature. His wife died in 1868, when thirty-three years of age.

James Bingham grew up on a farm, attended the common schools and the Ladoga Normal School and Valparaiso University. At the age of twenty-two he became a teacher, a work he continued for six years, and for two terms of two years each was county superintendent of schools in Fountain County. When he began the study of law he had to overcome the handicap of poor eyesight, and his wife read to him from the law books, and largely through the medium of her eyes he qualified for practice and after his admission to the bar she continued to assist him for several years. Mr. Bingham was prosecuting attorney of the Twenty-first Judicial District for one term. He practiced in partnership with C. M. McCabe at Covington, Indiana, until March, 1894, when he moved to Muncie, where he and A. M. Wagner were associated, and in 1895 Jesse R. Long, Bloomington, Illinois, joined them in the firm of Wagner, Bingham & Long. Mr. Wagner retired in 1899, but Bingham & Long were together until 1906.

In the fall of 1906 Mr. Bingham was elected attorney-general of Indiana, and by reelection served two terms. While he was attorney-general he was associated with Will White and William Haymond in a law firm at Muncie, retiring from the partnership soon after his term expired, January 1, 1911, and practiced alone in Indianapolis until 1915, when his son, Remster A., joined him.

Mr. Bingham married, December 26, 1885, Elizabeth Remster, of Fountain County, daughter of Andrew and Tamsin (Smith) Remster. Her father was born near Salem, New Jersey. Of the children of Mr. and Mrs. Bingham the first, a daughter, died in infancy. The son Remster A., his father's law partner, was overseas during the World war, being discharged with the rank of captain. He married Catherine Kidder and has two children, Remster and Katherine. The second son, Charles, was also overseas, was gassed and discharged with the rank of first lieutenant. He also studied law and entered the partnership with his father and brother, continuing until his death, April 27, 1929. He married Joy Reed, who survives with one son, James.

Mrs. Bingham passed away April 6, 1925. Mr. Bingham attends the Second Presbyterian Church, is a Republican, a member of the Columbia Club, Indiana State, Indianapolis and American Bar Associations, and was one of the organizers of the Delaware County Bar Association. Among other clients his firm represents as attorneys the Live Stock Exchange Bank.

PERRY A. BRAY, who is president of the Hamilton County Historical Society, has lived all his life in that county, whose people have a high degree of esteem for his business abilities and his deep interest in preserving all essential matters of history.

He was born on a farm April 22, 1861. His father, Henry W. Bray, was a native of Kentucky, born about the same time that Abraham Lincoln first saw the light of day in the log cabin that has since become a shrine. The Brays moved across the Ohio River into Indiana about the same time that Thomas Lincoln brought his family to Spencer County. However, the Brays settled in Hamilton County. Henry W. Bray became a well-to-do farmer and was always active in politics, at first as a Whig and later as a Republican. He held the office of county commissioner. He married Miss Betsey Mills, who was a descendant of the Jameson family, her ancestor, Thomas Jameson, having been a Virginia soldier in the War of the Revolution. Mr. Perry A. Bray has the old marriage certificate of his grandparents, who were married in 1778 in North Carolina. Miss Betsey Mills was born in Tennessee, of North Carolina stock. Her people came to Indiana in 1820, but subsequently spent several years in Tennessee before becoming permanent residents of the Hoosier State.

Perry A. Bray grew up in Hamilton County, had the advantages of the common and high schools, and from early manhood engaged in farming. In 1906 he disposed of his farming interests and has since been a resident of Noblesville, where he became connected with the postoffice.

He married Miss Elizabeth Perry. Five children were born to their marriage, two of whom died in infancy. Their daughter, Judith Ann, who died in 1926, was the wife of Gibson Hastings and left a son, Gibson, Jr.

J. D. Foor M. D.

Rachael, who finished her education in the Western College for Women at Oxford, Ohio, is the wife of Wilbur Sevier, of Indianapolis, and has a son, James W. Bray Sevier. Mary Bray was educated at Purdue University and is the wife of Gerald W. Kennedy.

Mr. Bray has always been a staunch Republican in his political affiliations. In 1910 he was appointed census enumerator for Hamilton County. He is a member of the Friends Church, belongs to the Masonic fraternity and Independent Order of Odd Fellows. He has been president of the Hamilton County Historical Society since 1926 and is also a member of the Indiana State Historical Society.

HON. J. DELBERT FOOR, who for two terms was a representative from Vigo County in the Indiana Legislature, is a prominent physician and surgeon, practicing at Terre Haute.

Doctor Foor was born in Miami County, Indiana, August 9, 1871, son of David and Ellen (Alspach) Foor. His parents were born in Ohio. David Foor was eleven years of age when brought to Indiana by his parents, Frederick and Elizabeth Foor, in 1839. They settled in Miami County, when that region was a part of the frontier advance of settlement into Northern Indiana. Frederick Foor took up a homestead from the Government, and spent the rest of his life as a farmer. David Foor grew up there, and after his marriage located on a farm in Miami County. He was always a staunch Democrat in politics. David Foor died in 1910, when eighty-two years of age, and his wife passed away in 1908, at the age of seventy. They had a family of five children.

J. Delbert Foor grew up on a farm, had the advantages of the common schools and the high school at Macy. After that his advantages were such as he could obtain through his own activities. At the age of sixteen he made up his mind to become a physician. By work on the home farm he accumulated a little money, which he invested in the educational opportunities of Valparaiso University. He studied pharmacy, was graduated Ph. G. with the class of 1895 and then worked as a pharmacist to pay the expenses of medical college. In the fall of 1897 he entered the Indiana Medical College at Indianapolis. For his work at Valparaiso University he received one year's credit, and in 1900 was graduated with the M.D. degree. He was a member of the first four-year class of Indiana Medical College. Doctor Foor then returned to Miami County to practice, where he continued for one year. From 1901 to 1905 he was located at Jasonville in Greene County. In 1904 Doctor Foor was the unsuccessful candidate on the Democratic ticket for coroner of Greene County. In 1905 he moved to the Village of Blackhawk in Pierson Township, Vigo County, and practiced medicine there until 1911, when he came to the larger opportunities of the City of Terre Haute.

Doctor Foor, while living at Blackhawk, was elected a member of the Sixty-sixth Indiana General Assembly in 1908. He was re-elected in 1910. During his two terms he made himself a constructive influence in a sound legislative program. He introduced and secured the passage of several important laws. One of them was the bill to prevent infant blindness, an Indiana statute which was subsequently copied by many other states of the Union. He was also instrumental in securing the passage of the hydrophobia bill, by which a fund is created in each county to secure the prompt and effective treatment of persons afflicted with hydrophobia.

Since coming to Terre Haute Doctor Foor has devoted his entire time to his extensive general medical practice. He has always been a student of his profession and his experience as a doctor has made him familiar with some of the difficulties attending practice in the earlier days. While a country physician in Greene and Vigo counties he rode horseback and drove a horse and buggy to make his professional rounds and frequently had to contend with the difficulties of poor roads.

Doctor Foor is a Democrat in politics and has been active in the county Democratic organization. Doctor Foor for fourteen years has had his office at 831½ Wabash Avenue in Terre Haute. He has always lived a very clean and exemplary life, abstaining from drinking or smoking, and to this in part can doubtless be ascribed his youthful appearance and his great energy. Doctor Foor is a member of Terre Haute Lodge No. 19, A. F. and A. M. He married in April, 1900, at Indianapolis, Miss E. Leora Whitlock. She was born and reared in Marion County, Indiana.

JOHN J. REIBOLDT, prominent banker and business man of Laurel for many years, was born in Franklin County, Indiana, March 4, 1856. His parents, John Jacob and Catherine (Mettle) Reiboldt, were natives of Germany and were married in Franklin County. Catherine Mettle crossed the ocean on a sailing vessel, being seventy-two days at sea before arriving at New Orleans. After their marriage John Jacob Reiboldt and wife settled on a farm three miles south of Brookville, where he died in 1858. His widow then became the wife of his brother, George Peter Reiboldt, who was in the baking business at Brookville until the fall of 1866, when he moved to Laurel and continued business there.

John J. Reiboldt had a few terms of attendance at the public schools of Franklin County as a boy, but most of his strength and energy were devoted to farming, in which he was associated with his brother, John Peter, until he was twenty years of age. He started in business as a clerk in William L. Day's hardware store, and after a year bought a half interest, and they were partners for twenty-seven years. In 1894 these same men engaged in banking, organizing the Day & Reiboldt Bank at Laurel. In 1904 Mr. Reiboldt sold his mercantile interests and at that time acquired Mr. Day's holdings in the bank, and since then he has been president and active head of the Laurel Bank, which has a capital of $10,000.

Mr. Reiboldt on October 31, 1893, married Miss May Ferguson, who was born at Clarksburg, West Virginia, daughter of Len Ferguson. She died in 1914, leaving a son, Carl Ferguson Reiboldt, who was born in 1904. This son possesses an unusual baritone voice and is now taking special work in New York City for the development of his musical abilities. Mr. Reiboldt is a member of the Lutheran Church, has served as president of the town board, and served on the County Council of Franklin County twelve years. He is a Republican and a thirty-second degree Scottish Rite Mason and Shriner.

JOHN APPLEGATE TITSWORTH, senior member of the law firm Titsworth & Titsworth at Rushville, has lived all his life in Rush County and all his grandparents were early settlers in Rush and Fayette counties.

He was born in Noble Township, Rush County, February 2, 1871, son of George W. and Rhoda J. (Applegate) Titsworth, and grandson of Peter and Sarah (Reed) Titsworth, the former coming to Rush County from Montgomery County, Ohio, and of John and Anne (Kerr) Applegate, of Fayette County. John Applegate was a carriage maker. Though he died in 1870, some of the vehicles he made were of such staunch construction that they are still in use. George W. Titsworth spent his active life as a farmer and served as a member of the County Council. He died in 1907 and his wife in 1919.

John A. Titsworth attended country schools, graduated from the Orange High School, taught for two years, and in that way earned the money for his college expenses. He spent two years in Purdue University, taking the civil engineering course, and then entered the law department of the University of Michigan, where he was graduated in June, 1893. After graduating he taught in Noble Township, Rush County, and in 1894 opened a law office in Rushville. He was associated with John M. Stevens until 1908 and for fourteen years was with James A. Watson and Thomas M. Green in the firm of Watson, Titsworth & Green. Later for one year Perry E. O'Neal was with him, and since then he has had as his active associate Russell B. Titsworth, his son. Mr. Titsworth has tried thousands of cases in Indiana courts, and during the nine years he has been associated with his son Russell the firm has represented a large number of banks and industrial and public utility corporations and several railway companies, and have also been attorneys for the City of Rushville and the school board and library board of the city. Mr. Titsworth has also been counsel in many important will and murder cases.

He has always been a Republican, but never an active candidate for public office, though he has served as county and city attorney. He has been president of the Rushville Rotary Club, president of the Chamber of Commerce, president of the Chautauqua Association. His law office has been local headquarters for Senator Watson and other noted Indiana Republicans. For nine years he was chairman of the official board of the Main Street Christian Church and adult superintendent of the Bible School.

Mr. Titsworth married, June 16, 1896, Miss Cora D. Brooks, who was born in Noble Township, Rush County, daughter of William M. and Laura D. (Downey) Brooks. Their son Russell B. is now prosecuting attorney of Rush County and city attorney. The daughter, Gladys, is the wife of Frank Peary, and both are prominent edcators, she holding the degree Bachelor of Science and Master of Science fom Hillsdale College, while Doctor Peary is an M. D., now doing research work with the Rockefeller Foundation. The third child, Harold J., is also an attorney, practicing at Rushville. The mother of these children died January 11, 1905, and on July 8, 1914, Mr. Titsworth married Nelle L. Lyons. She was born in Rush County, daughter of Charles and Florence (Downey) Lyons. The only child of this marriage, John Charles, died at the age of five years.

LOUIS JONATHAN BAILEY, director of the Indiana State Library, succeeded the late Demarchus C. Brown in that post. Mr. Bailey by training and experience is well qualified for the heavy responsibilities of directing one of the largest state libraries in the Middle West. The library contains over 200,000 volumes, and recently the Legislature made provision for a new building, appropriating a million dollars for that purpose. Mr. Bailey has a staff of twenty-eight employees, a considerable number of whom are assigned to carry out the important functions of the library as a statewide service, cooperating with organized library work through the public schools and other community organizations in all the counties and states.

Mr. Bailey was born at Ontario, New York, February 14, 1881, son of Jonathan Cornley and Harriet (Borland) Bailey, and a descendant of a branch of the Bailey family that settled at Scituate, Massachusetts, in the early Colonial period. His maternal grandfather was Washington Irving Borland.

Mr. Bailey was educated in public schools in New York, graduated from the University of Rochester in 1905 and spent two years in the New York Library School at Albany, where he received the degree Bachelor of Library Science. He was an assistant in the New York State Library in 1906-07, worked in the Library of Congress at Washington, and in 1908 was made librarian at Gary, Indiana. During the fourteen years he was there he completely organized and built up a public library service in keeping with the needs of this great industrial community. In 1922 he accepted the call to the public library of Flint, Michigan, where again he did important work

Charles E. Coffin

in reorganizing the library service. On September 1, 1926, he came to Indianapolis as director of the State Library.

Mr. Bailey rendered valuable service with the war organization of the American Library Association, helping raise funds to provide library service to the soldiers at home and overseas, and during 1917 also helped establish libraries at Camp Sheridan, Camp McClellan and Camp Shelby in Alabama and Mississippi, and from March, 1918, until 1920 acted as supervisor and dispatch agent, with headquarters at New York City, sending books to the soldiers in France. While stationed at New York he was in charge of receiving books and sending them out all over the country and abroad for the use of the soldiers and sailors, and during two years his office handled over 7,000,000 books, and at the close of the service in 1920 several hundred thousand volumes were turned over to the Federal Government. Mr. Bailey was president of the Indiana Library Association in 1914, and in 1925 was elected president of the Michigan Library Association. He has served as chairman of numerous committees with the American Library Association. He is a member of the Indianapolis Literary Club, the Century Club, the Theta Chi fraternity and the Congregational Church. Politically he is an independent. He was appointed by Governor Ralston chairman of the Lake County Centennial Commission in 1916. He was also a member of the City Planning Commission while at Gary.

Mr. Bailey married, November 28, 1907, Miss Regnea Gunnison, who was born at Brooklyn, New York. They have four children: John Chalmers, a student in Purdue University; Richard Gunnison, in the University of Michigan; Beatrice, attending the Technical High School; and Horace Compton, in grade school.

CHARLES EMMET COFFIN has been one of the prominent figures of Indianapolis commercial and civic affairs for over forty years. Mr. Coffin is a native of Indiana, born at Salem July 13, 1856, son of Zachariah T. and Caroline (Armfield) Coffin. He represents the seventh generation of descent from Tristram Coffin, of Nantucket, Massachusetts, one of the early pioneers of New England.

As a youth Mr. Coffin was impressed with a sense of responsibility toward others. He attended a grammar school at Salem, his birthplace, completed his high school course at Bloomington, and spent one year in Indiana University. He had to give up his university career to go to work, turning over his wages to his parents. At the age of twenty he began his career in Indianapolis, as an employee of Wylie & Martin, real estate. Six years later he engaged in business for himself. His study and experience made him an expert in realty values. He was the medium for handling many important real estate operations in Indianapolis, and besides his brokerage business he developed and marketed several subdivisions

in and around Indianapolis. His services have also gone to the broader financing of real estate ownership. He was one of the organizers of the Indiana Savings & Investment Company, incorporated in 1889, and for over forty years has been president of that institution, one of the largest of its kind in Indiana, with assets of over three million dollars. Practically all the funds of the company have been held for first loans on Indianapolis real estate.

Mr. Coffin also organized, in 1900, the Central Trust Company, which was sold to the Farmers Trust Company in 1913, and since that date he has been a member of the board of directors of the latter company. He was vice president of the Indianapolis & Eastern Traction Company from its organization in 1903 until the property was sold in 1905. Mr. Coffin in 1913 became secretary and treasurer of the Star Publishing Company, and in the same year was elected a member of its board of directors.

His part in organizations representing the larger commercial and civic interests of the city has been not less noteworthy. From 1899 to 1922 he served as a member of the board of park commissioners of Indianapolis, and for ten years of that time was president of the board. He was for four years, until 1926, president of the board of public works. Mr. Coffin was one of the organizers and incorporators of the Indianapolis Commercial Club in 1890, a club that for the first time gave an organization broadly representative of the progressive interests of the community, and under which were inaugurated a series of improvements and reforms that laid the foundation of the modern and greater city. He was chosen president of the club in 1900. He was also on the board of governors of the Indianapolis Board of Trade, has been a director of the Indianapolis Art Association, is a member of the Columbia Club and Woodstock Club of Indianapolis, and president of the board of trustees of the Meridian Street Methodist Episcopal Church, also a member of the board of trustees of the Indiana State Normal School, Terre Haute. Mr. Coffin is a member of the Society of Colonial Wars, the Indiana Historical Society, is a thirty-second degree Scottish Rite Mason and a member of Murat Temple of the Mystic Shrine.

With all his important responsibilities in business and civic affairs Mr. Coffin is known to many thousands outside the state as an authority on whist. In 1895 he published a book, *The Gist of Whist*, this being followed in 1907 by *The Gist of Auction Bridge*. Mr. Coffin is a former president of the American Whist League.

He married at Indianapolis, September 20, 1897, Miss Mary H. Birch, daughter of Richard E. Birch. Her father was a steamboat captain on the Mississippi River. They have three children: Clarence E., who married Lenora Smith; Jean Fletcher, wife of Commander J. H. Ingram, of the United States Navy; and Carolyn, wife of Charles Harvey Bradley.

CHARLES RICHARD BAKER is prominently identified with the bar and the official affairs of Franklin County, being the present prosecuting attorney of the Thirty-seventh Judicial Circuit.

Mr. Baker was born at Brookville, May 19, 1889. He comes of a family that has supplied a number of public officials to the county. His parents were Frank J. and Mary M. (Sellmeyer) Baker, his father a native of Brookville and his mother of Oldenburg, Indiana. His grandparents were John and Cecelia (Bohl) Baker and Henry C. and Mary (Studer) Sellmeyer. Henry C. Sellmeyer was in the early days a county official, holding for eight years the office of county auditor of Franklin County. Frank J. Baker has been a well known fruit grower in Franklin County. He served in the office of the Circuit Court from 1920 to 1924 and has also been on the board of Children's Guardians.

Charles Richard Baker was educated in the grade and high schools of Franklin County and went east to Washington to complete his law course in Georgetown University. He was graduated in 1927 and on January 1, 1928, opened his law office at Brookville. He served as deputy clerk of the Circuit Court from 1919 to 1924. In 1928 he was elected prosecuting attorney for the Thirty-seventh Judicial District, comprising Franklin and Union counties, and was reelected in 1930, by a larger majority than in 1928.

Mr. Baker is unmarried. He is a member of the Catholic Church, is advocate of the Knights of Columbus, a member and secretary of the Fraternal Order of Eagles, lodge of Brookville, a charter member of the Kiwanis Club, a member of the Thirty-seventh Judicial District Bar Association and member of the board of directors of the Franklin County Chapter of the American Red Cross.

WILLIAM JACKSON BUSKIRK, more usually known as Will J. Buskirk, has been, for more than thirty-five years, a practicing attorney and member of the Orange County, Indiana, Bar. Orange County and Southern Indiana, has known and honored many members of the Buskirk family, as eminent lawyers.

His father, the late Judge Thomas B. Buskirk, was, for twelve years, on the bench, as judge of the Circuit Courts, of Orange and Washington Counties. He died, March 9, 1930, in his eighty-seventh year. He was a veteran of the Civil war, serving as a first lieutenant of Company G of the Forty-ninth Regiment, Indiana Volunteers, and was wounded in the neck in the siege of Vicksburg, but, for all the hardships of his army service, has had a long and prominent career.

His mother, whose maiden name was Miss Cora A. Jackson, of Kentucky, died on November 11, 1906. Of the union between his father and mother, ten children were born, two dying in infancy, John at the age of thirteen and Ethel at the age of nine months—surviving are Lois H., Will J., the subject of this sketch; Horace, Mabel L., Myrtle M., Thomas B., Jr.,

Boswell F. and George A., all of whom with the exception of Will J. and George A., now reside in Indianapolis; Will J. and George A. in Paoli, the town of their birth. Will J. Buskirk was born in Paoli, December 25, 1870, and after attending public school, including high school, took up the study of law under his father. He was admitted to the bar in 1895, and has steadily engaged in the practice in his home town, doing a large volume of general practice, and has a large clientele, including the leading banks and other corporations of his county. He is a member of the County and State Bar associations.

Politically, Mr. Buskirk is affiliated with the democratic party, but never seeks office for himself. He is a member of the Masonic fraternity and the Knights of Pythias.

He was married on May 15, 1901, to Miss Florence Getches, daughter of George and Florence (Clark) Getches of Vincennes, Indiana. He has four children, William B., born April 14, 1902; Hugh and Helen, twins, born January 30, 1905 and Oliver B., born July 3, 1913. Hugh is a law student, preparing to carry out the traditions of the family, as a representative of the fourth generation.

JOHN J. WELP. In the case of John J. Welp, of Jasper, Indiana, is to be found augmenting success in whatever line he has followed, and today, after a prosperous experience in farming, he is engaged in milling and banking, in the latter being president of the Citizens Bank of Jasper. He was born at Schnellville, Indiana, June 24, 1885, a son of John Welp, a native of Germany, who came to the United States with his parents at the age of thirteen years. As the years went on he acquired an excellent common school education and became a farmer, and from that calling he went into the business of handling grain, in which he was so successful that he was able to retire in 1924 with a comfortable income. He married Katherine Streigal, who was born in Indiana, and died in the same state in 1918. The following children were born to them: Two who died in infancy; John J., whose name heads this review; Rose, who married Frank Haas, resides in Dubois County, and has five children; Veronica, who married Doctor Metzgar, lives at Ferdinand, Indiana, and they have two children; Leo, who lives at Schnellville, married Lucy Schnell, and they have five children; Edward, who is a traveling salesman, resides at Huntingburg, is married and has one child; Cyrenius, who lives at Schnellville; Theo, who lives at Jasper; and Albert, who lives at Schnellville.

Growing to manhood in his native state, John J. Welp attended the graded and high schools of the public school system and the local parochial schools, and is a well-educated man, versed in different subjects. When he was twenty-two years old he left the parental farm to go into farming for himself, having been trained by his father in that line. In 1909 he began his connection with the mill-

Dan W. Simms

ing industry, and is now at the head of the Jasper Milling Company, manufacturers of flour. For some years past he has been president of the Citizens Bank at Jasper, his knowledge of conditions and the people of his home community being of a vast amount of value to his financial institution.

In 1915 Mr. Welp was married to Mercedies Schuler, of Jasper, and they have one child, Dennis, aged ten years, a bright little fellow now attending school. A very strong Democrat, Mr. Welp is one of the local leaders, and he could, probably, have office if he cared to accept nomination, so popular is he. He is a Catholic and a member of the Knights of Columbus. The Woodmen of the World also holds his membership. He has never been too busy to take a lively interest in civic affairs; has from time to time been associated with numerous enterprises, and has always given his best efforts to promoting the interests of Jasper, and is not only one of its most prosperous and progressive citizens, but also one of its most popular ones.

DAN W. SIMMS, whose death occurred at Lafayette, Indiana, March 11, 1931, was a member of the Indiana bar from 1885, and among other honors connected with his profession one of the most grateful was his election in 1909 as president of the Indiana State Bar Association. Mr. Simms had a very successful career as a lawyer, and a brief record of it is sufficient to indicate his abilities and attainments.

He lived in Indiana most of his life, but was born in Crawford County, Illinois, February 13, 1862, son of Daniel and Nancy (Parrott) Simms. In 1866 his parents moved to a farm in Fountain County, Indiana, where he grew up and spent his boyhood days, very much as other Indiana country boys of that period. He completed his early education in the county high school, for three years attended DePauw University, graduated Bachelor of Science from the Central Indiana Normal College at Danville, and during these years he was teaching school, spending three years at that occupation in Fountain County and during four years of the time was superintendent of a high school. He studied law with the firm of Nebeker & Dochterman at Covington, Indiana, was admitted to the bar in 1885 and the following year was instructor in mathematics and history at the Central Indiana Normal School. Mr. Simms practiced law for eleven years at Covington, Indiana, and in 1898 removed to Lafayette, where he was a member of the law firm Stuart, Hammond & Simms until 1915. From 1915 to 1919 Mr. Simms was at Los Angeles, California, practicing law there, and was admitted to the California bar and was a member of the California State and Los Angeles County Bar Associations. While in California he was chairman of the Los Angeles County and City Democratic committee and gave a great deal of his time to promoting the success of the war drives. He was United States master-in-chancery for the southern district of California during the years he was at Los Angeles. Following the war, in 1919-20, Mr. Simms was a special assistant to the attorney-general of the United States, helping in investigations and prosecutions in different parts of the country.

In 1919 Mr. Simms returned to Lafayette and joined the law firm of Stuart, Simms & Stuart, which acted as general counsel for Purdue University. Mr. Simms himself was general counsel and a director of the Lafayetee Life Insurance Company.

He was for a number of years a member of the Lafayette school board. He was a member of the Tippecanoe County, Indiana State and American Bar Associations, was affiliated with Lafayette Lodge No. 492, A. F. and A. M., the Royal Arch Chapter and Council at Covington, the Knights Templar Commandery at Crawfordsville, the Scottish Rite Consistory and Murat Temple of the Mystic Shrine at Indianapolis. He filled all the chairs in the Knights of Pythias Lodge and was a member of the Improved Order of Red Men, the Optimist Club, of which he was a former president, and the Tippecanoe County Historical Association. He also belonged to the Lafayette, Lafayette Country and Indianapolis Athletic Clubs. Mr. Simms married in 1885 Miss Ezadora J. Wright, of Fountain County. Three children were born to their marriage, Glen W. and Ruth B., both deceased, and Floy G., who is the wife of John G. Daskam, a Lafayette insurance man.

MRS. CARRIE A. POINIER. Not only have women proved their fitness for almost every profession and trade, but they have won election to various public offices formerly held by men, and in them have given a businesslike and honest administration of affairs that has awakened the appreciation of their fellow citizens and opened the door for others of their sex. One of these able, self-reliant and efficient members of her sex is Mrs. Carrie A. Poinier, former recorder of Wayne County, who not only succeeded her late husband in the office, but when she had filled out his term was elected herself to the office, from which she retired December 31, 1930.

Mrs. Poinier was born Carrie A. Phillips, at Eaton, Ohio, June 8, 1876, and she is a daughter of David and Sarah (Murray) Phillips, both natives of Ohio, he born in Preble County and she in Montgomery County. After the death of Mr. Phillips his widow was married to A. M. Campbell, and they are now residing at Eaton, Ohio.

After she was graduated from both the Fairhaven and Eaton high schools Carrie A. Phillips began teaching school, but after a year of that work, in 1897, she was married to Theodore E. Poinier, a native of Jacksonville, Illinois, and a son of George H. and Ida M. (Brownell) Poinier, he born at Chicago, Illinois, and she at Hillsboro, Illinois.

For six years after their marriage Mr. Poinier was in the employ of what is now the International Harvester Corporation, and then became a conductor on the Richmond, Indiana, street car lines, which position he continued to hold for eighteen years. During that period his faithfulness to duty, his courteous manner and his admirable characteristics won him many friends, and when he was nominated for county recorder, on the Republican ticket, he received a gratifying support, and was elected by a large majority, taking office in January, 1925. He was not long spared, however, to hold this office, for he died October 7 of the same year, and, as already stated, his widow was appointed to fill out his term. In the fall of 1926 she was elected to the same duties, and in January, 1927, took the office for a term of four years. Mr. Poinier was a great fraternity man, belonging as he did to the Masonic Order, the Odd Fellows, the Loyal Order of Moose and the Sons of Veterans. When he died the whole community mourned the passing of a good citizen and excellent official, and appropriate memorials were engrossed by the county board and the different fraternities of which he was a member. Both he and his wife early became members of the United Presbyterian Church, to which she still belongs, and for which she is an earnest worker.

The following children were born to Mr. and Mrs. Poinier: Doris I., who married Prof. F. Harvey, of Richmond, Indiana; Helen G., who married J. F. Telcher and resides at Richmond; Sarah M., who married Eber K. Williams and resides at Richmond; and Charles Kenneth, who is a railroad mail clerk, residing at Richmond. Mrs. Harvey has two children, Malcolm P. and Betty Joyce Harvey; and Mrs. Telcher has one child, Theodore F.

Mrs. Poinier is a member of the local chapter of the Eastern Star; of the Richmond Lodge, Daughters of Rebekah; and the local camp of the Woman's Relief Corps, in all of which organizations she is a leader and officer. She maintains her residence at 230 Southwest Fourth Street, Richmond.

ELMER E. PERSONETT is sheriff of Franklin County. He first served in that office by appointment, and his qualifications won the approval of the people when he was elected to that office in 1928 and again in 1930.

Mr. Personett was born at Irvington, Marion County, Indiana, December 30, 1870, son of Charles and Elizabeth (Osborn) Personett. His father was born at Centerville, Wayne County, Indiana, and his mother in Franklin County, where her father, Aaron Osborn, was a pioneer. Charles Personett learned the trade of carpenter and later for many years carried on a lumber business in Franklin County. He died in August, 1930, in his ninety-first year.

Elmer E. Personett was a small child when his mother died. He was educated in the district schools of Franklin County and lived with his father until his marriage. Mr. Personett practically grew up in the lumber business and that was his principal line of work.

He had the distinction of serving as the first janitor of the new courthouse of Brookville. He was in that position two years. He also worked in a paper mill until he was appointed sheriff to fill the unexpired term in May, 1927, the result of the death of the former sheriff. In November, 1928, he was elected by popular vote to that office. Mr. Personett is a Democrat in politics. He is a member of the Improved Order of Red Men and the Daughters of Pocahontas and belongs to the Haymakers and other organizations.

He married, May 4, 1894, Miss Effie Morgan, a native of Decatur County, Indiana. She died December 7, 1897, leaving one daughter, Blanche, now Mrs. Burton L. McFall, of Connersville. Sheriff Personett on June 8, 1900, married Miss Effie Berg, a native of Franklin County, daughter of William T. and Nancy J. (Sherwood) Berg.

JAMES NORMAN McCOY as a prominent specialist is well known all over Indiana, but has confined his chief work to his home locality of Knox County. His offices are in the State Banking Building at Vincennes. He is a Roentgen Ray therapist and dermatologist.

Doctor McCoy was born in Knox County, Indiana, December 1, 1873, a son of John Richard and Sarah Alice (Adams) McCoy. Part of his early education was acquired at Vincennes, where he attended Vincennes University, and was graduated from the Medical College of Indiana, at Indianapolis, in 1896. He took post-graduate courses in the Post Graduate School and Hospital and the Vanderbilt Clinic in New York City in 1913, in the University de Sorbonne, at Paris, in 1919.

Doctor McCoy perfected the original technique for intensive, soft Roentgen Ray dose; made the original appliances for administration of heavy X-Ray treatment to uterus without exposing the ovaries; perfected the technique for depilation of scalp by using secondary rays only. He is author of several articles dealing chiefly with Roentgen Ray therapy and dermatology in various medical journals, and is the inventor of a number of original appliances used in giving X-Ray treatment.

Doctor McCoy is a member of the Knox County and Indiana State Medical Associations, the American Roentgen Ray Society, the Aesculapian Society. During the World war he was commissioned a captain in the Medical Reserve Corps of the United States Army in 1917, and promoted to major in 1918. He served as surgeon with the Three Hundred and Twenty-seventh Field Artillery, as roentgenologist at Camp Hospital No. 20, as assistant dermatologist at Headquarters, Base Section No. 5, American Expeditionary Forces at Brest. In 1924 he was commissioned lieutenant colonel of the Medical Officers Reserve Corps and on May 17, 1931, was promoted to colonel. He has served as vice president of the Hoosier State Automobile Association, is a Knight Templar Mason, a member of the Episcopal Church, and a Re-

publican. Doctor McCoy married, April 20, 1898, Miss Mary Johnston, of Indiana, who died February 9, 1927. They had one child, Mildred Lucile, who is married to Harry R. Champ, a lawyer at Indianapolis. Doctor McCoy was married on May 7, 1929, to Charlotte Louise Antibus.

SANFORD M. KELTNER has been a resident of Anderson for many years. His first connection with that community was as a school man. However, he is best known for his long and successful connection with the bar, but he has always taken a keen interest in education and for a number of years has served on the board of the State Normal School of Indiana.

Mr. Keltner was born in the village of West Baltimore, now Verona, in Preble County, Ohio. His ancestors were sturdy, substantial people who did a great deal of pioneering in Ohio and other states. His great-grandfather was Michael Keltner, a native of Germany, who spelled his name Kelchner. He joined the colony of Pennsylvania Germans, and at the time of the Revolutionary war was a member of Captain Shade's Company, First Pennsylvania Rifles, under Colonel Miles. A son of this Revolutionary soldier was Henry Keltner, who moved from Pennsylvania to Ohio. He walked all of the way, with a rifle on his shoulder, while his wife rode horseback, carrying a child in her arms. Their first destination was the village of Dayton, and his wife lived there in a tent for some days while he prospected over the country looking for a permanent location. There was a great abundance of Government land available and he selected a claim eighteen miles northwest of Dayton, in Preble County. On this he built his log house, and from year to year increased the area in cultivation. His nearest market was Dayton, and the only way of reaching that town was by wagon and team. Henry Keltner married Catherine Wert, also a native of Pennsylvania. Her father, Peter Wert, was also of German ancestry. He went to Ohio and settled in Preble County, improving a farm, and occupied it until his death at the age of ninety-four. Peter Wert's wife was Mary Akeman, who was born in Pennsylvania, of German lineage.

One of the thirteen children of Henry Keltner and wife was Joseph C. Keltner, who was born at Dayton, Ohio, September 11, 1817. He had the advantage of the pioneer schools, but due to his thirst for knowledge he acquired a better than ordinary education and became an excellent penman and had a considerable knowledge of law and was frequently called upon to write deeds and wills. He was trained to the vigorous life of the frontier, and he started his own career as a carpenter, later, in 1866, purchasing land three miles east of Greenville in Darke County. This land was in the heavy timber and his first task was to cut away trees from a space on which to put up his house. In 1867 he disposed of this property and moved to Kosciusko County, Indiana, where he made a living for his family

at the carpenter's trade. In 1876 he came to Anderson, and was a carpenter the rest of his active life. He lived to be ninety-three years of age. He was reared in the faith of the United Brethren Church and later joined the Methodist Church at Anderson. He served as superintendent of the Sunday School. Joseph C. Keltner was three times married. By his first marriage there were four children: Mary Ann, Eliza, Levi P. and Samuel C. His second wife was Rachael Paulus, who was born in a log cabin near West Baltimore in Preble County, Ohio, in 1832. Her father, Daniel Paulus, was born in Maryland, in 1807, son of Abraham Paulus, who probably came from Germany. He lived in Maryland, and finally pioneered to Preble County, Ohio, getting his Government land a short distance west of the present site of Verona. There he began the task of clearing up a farm, and lived there until his death. His son, Daniel Paulus, was an infant when the family came to Ohio. As soon as he had attained the years and the strength he was inducted into the responsibilities and labors of a frontier farm, and subsequently he bought 160 acres a mile and a half north of Verona, on which he built a log house. There he lived until 1862, when he sold and moved to Champaign County, Illinois. In what is now the center of the corn belt he bought 160 acres of prairie farm, fifteen miles west of Urbana. This land was completely level and undrained, and he and his family were subject to the fevers so prevalent in that country at the time, and consequently he soon sold out and returned to Ohio, settling three miles east of Greenville in Darke County. This land he sold in 1870, and, coming to Indiana, bought a farm about four miles west of Union City. Here he resided until his death at the age of ninety-six. Daniel Paulus married, Lucy Treon, whose father, John Treon, was born in France, and on coming to the United States joined his brother in Dayton, Ohio. This brother was a physician and practiced in Western Ohio for upwards of seventy years. John Treon married a Miss Brubaker. Rachael (Paulus) Keltner, daughter of Daniel Paulus and Lucy Treon-Brubaker, died July 20, 1867, when thirty-five years of age. She was the mother of two children, Sanford M. and Francis M.

The third wife of Joseph C. Keltner was Hester Moser, who died in Anderson, Indiana.

Sanford M. Keltner grew up in the several localities where his father had his home during his youth. He attended a rural school a mile west of West Baltimore, also another school near Greenville, and after his mother's death he went to live with a farmer named James P. Burgess, three miles west of Richmond, Indiana. He worked on the Burgess farm and also attended school. In 1872 he entered high school at Pierceton, Kosciusko County, Indiana, and when sixteen and a half years of age started out to get an opportunity to teach. The first school he applied for was refused him because the trustees were not impressed by his boyish appearance. On walking back to Warsaw he attended a meeting of trustees from several townships. The discussion was regarding teachers' qualifications, and a Mr. Deaton made the remark that he could tell a good teacher by looking at him. He then pointed to the youthful Keltner, who had just arrived, and said: "There is a boy who can teach." Mr. Keltner immediately arose and thanked Mr. Deaton, and when the latter inquired if he was looking for a school he said he was, and Mr. Deaton at once agreed to pay him $1.60 a day for teaching in a district. The bargain was made and after getting a place to board he taught a term of eighteen weeks. He then called on Mr. Deaton for a settlement and Mr. Deaton recalled that he had agreed to pay him $1.60 a day, and that was of course Mr. Keltner's understanding, too. But Mr. Deaton said that he had done better than any other teacher in the township, and since he was paying the best teachers two dollars a day, he intended to give Mr. Keltner that sum. Mr. Keltner also had another surprise when he paid his bill for board and lodging. He had not inquired as to the rate, and found that he had been charged only two dollars a week. Having saved something out of his earnings, he then entered the Indiana State Normal at Terre Haute, where he spent two years. In 1878 he became principal of a school at Walton in Cass County, remaining there three years, and in 1881 came to Anderson as principal of the Seventh Street School, at fifty dollars a month. The second year he was in charge of the Main Street School, holding that position two years.

While teaching he took up the study of law in the office of Robinson and Lovett, was admitted to the bar in 1886 and then joined his preceptors in the firm of Robinson, Lovett & Keltner. When Mr. Robinson went on the Appellate bench he and Mr. Lovett continued the practice for five years. After the retirement of Mr. Lovett, Mr. Keltner was a partner in the firm of Chapman, Keltner & Hender, a prominent law firm of Anderson, from June 1, 1893, until June 1, 1910. At the latter date Mr. Keltner was elected president of the Anderson Trust Company, and during the next seventeen years he gave all his time and energies to the banking business. Since 1927 he has been engaged in a general law practice, and is now the senior member of the law firm of Keltner, Mays & Johnson.

Mr. Keltner was for eighteen years a member of the Anderson board of education and for three and a half years was a member of the board of public works, during the term of Mayor John H. Terhune. In 1917 Governor Goodrich appointed him a member of the board of trustees of the Indiana State Normal School, including what is now the Ball State Teachers College at Muncie, as well as the Normal at Terre Haute. He was reappointed by Governor McCray, again by Governor Jackson and again by Governor Leslie, and in 1918 was elected president of the board, an office he continues to hold.

Mr. Keltner married, October 20, 1886, Miss Alice May Cockefair. She was born in Union County, Indiana, a descendant of Thomas Cockefair, a lifelong resident of Hempstead, Long Island. His son, Elisha Cockefair, was born in Hempstead and came to Indiana at a very early day, settling on the line between Union and Fayette counties. He acquired a large tract of land and developed the power of a stream of water flowing through it. This water power he used to operate the machinery of the first woolen mill in that section of the state. From clay on his land he burned brick for the erection of a commodious house, which continued in the ownership of Mrs. Keltner and is occupied by her daughter, Mrs. Charles W. Masters, and family. This house is situated a short distance from the Union and Fayette counties line. It was the home of her grandparents until their death. Mrs. Keltner's father succeeded to the ownership of the old homestead and the mill and continued the operation of the mill for several years. Most of his energies, however, were taken up with the management of his extensive farms, aggregating about two thousand acres. He lived at the old brick house until his death at the age of eighty years. Mrs. Keltner's mother, Mary Ann Brookbank, was born on a farm about three miles east of Connersville, Fayette County, Indiana. Her father, Henry Brookbank, was a native of Virginia and one of the first permanent settlers in Fayette County, Indiana, where he became a large land owner. Henry Brookbank married Lucinda Corbin.

Mr. and Mrs. Keltner had two daughters, Ruth and Mary. Ruth is the wife of Charles W. Masters, and their daughter, Mary Alice, now represents the fifth generation in the brick house in Fayette County. Mrs. Keltner died December 5, 1930.

EUGENE C. SHIREMAN, who maintains his residence and business headquarters at Martinsville, Morgan County, is a lawyer by profession, but his major success and prestige have been won in connection with business enterprises of important scope. He now has the distinction of being president of Grassy Fork Fisheries, Inc., a unique Indiana corporation that figures as the world's largest concern engaged in the propagating and raising of gold fish. The extensive and finely improved propagating plants of this corporation are all established in Morgan County, and the incidental prestige and success that have been gained by the president of this corporation are the more gratifying to contemplate in view of the fact that he was born and reared in Morgan County and is a scion of one of its honored pioneer families.

Eugene C. Shireman was born in Morgan County on the 13th of September, 1875, and is a son of Henry and Maria (DeTurk) Shireman, the former of whom was born in North Carolina and the latter near Reading, Pennsylvania. The parents of Mr. Shireman passed the greater part of their lives in Morgan County, where the father was long and successfully engaged in farm enterprise, he having died in 1897 and his widow having passed away in 1916. Mrs. Shireman was a daughter of Isaac DeTurk, who came to Indiana from Pennsylvania about the year 1833, the overland journey having been made with team and covered wagon. The family remained for a time in Indianapolis, where Mr. DeTurk had expected to establish residence, but he finally came to Morgan County and purchased a large tract of land near the present thriving little City of Martinsville. After his marriage Henry Shireman established a home on farm land near Martinsville, but later he removed to a neighboring tract, on higher elevation. His original habitation was a pioneer log house, and this continued the family domicile until he erected the substantial brick house that is still standing and that is in an excellent state of preservation, all brick and other materials for this house having been hauled overland from Indianapolis, and Mr. Shireman having in the early days diversified his activities by making several voyages on flatboats to New Orleans—down the Ohio and Mississippi rivers.

After completing his high-school course Eugene C. Shireman entered DePauw University, and in this fine Indiana institution he was graduated as a member of the class of 1898 and with the degree of Bachelor of Arts. He studied law and gained admission to the bar of his native state, his acquirements having been put to practical application in his service of two years as deputy prosecuting attorney of Morgan County. After devoting two years to the private practice of law at Martinsville Mr. Shireman purchased, in association with his brother Max, the plant and business of the Old Hickory Chair Company. With the conducting of this enterprise he continued to be actively associated until 1912, when the business was sold. Within a short time thereafter Mr. Shireman went to Brownsville, Texas, and in that Lower Rio Grande section of the Lone Star State he purchased and developed 25,000 acres of land, besides supervising the installation of its irrigation system. His activities in this connection were continued about three years, and in 1900 he became interested in the raising gold fish of the finer varieties, his scientific and progressive policies having been so directed that in his native county has been developed under his direction the largest gold-fish hatchery in the entire world. The Grassy Fork Fisheries has developed in Morgan County eight plants for the raising of gold fish, and the water area utilized covers about 240 acres. Here the annual product has now attained to an average of about 8,000,000 fish, and as the trade extends into all sections of the Union the enterprise has become one of importance as touching the industrial and commercial prestige not only of Morgan County but also of the State of Indiana as a whole. By Governor Ralston Mr. Shireman was appointed fish and

game commissioner of Indiana, and he was reappointed under Governor Goodrich, his entire period of service having covered five years and having extended until a change in the state law brought about a different arrangement in the control of this phase of government. Thus Mr. Shireman was the last to hold the position of state fish and game commissioner.

Mr. Shireman has made a record of loyal activity in advancing the cause of the Democratic party in his native county, and when he was twenty-one years of age he served as a member of the Democratic committee of Morgan County, besides having the distinction of being chosen its chairman. He and his wife are zealous members of the Methodist Episcopal Church of their home community, and he is a member of its board of stewards. He is affiliated with Beta Theta Phi college fraternity, and he is vice president of the Inland Bank & Trust Company of Indianapolis. His home, one of the most attractive in the City of Martinsville, is at 590 East Washington Street.

The year 1905 recorded the marriage of Mr. Shireman to Miss Mary Louise Harrison, who was born at Lebanon, Boone County, this state, and who is a daughter of Robert W. and Phoebe (Cook) Harrison, the former of whom was born in Montgomery County, Indiana, and the latter at Balston Spa, New York. Mr. and Mrs. Shireman have no children.

DeWitt Clinton Amerine, of Vincennes, spent over forty years of an active life in the paper industry. His assets at the beginning were an ability to work hard, perseverance, an ambition for accomplishment, and he rose steadily from the lowest rungs on the ladder to the presidency of the Indiana Board & Filler Company, which was one of the largest constituents in the recent merger of similar plants now comprising a national group of industries known as the Central Fiber Products Company.

The birth of DeWitt Clinton Amerine occurred at Piqua, Ohio, August 30, 1872. He was the oldest of the seven children of Isaiah and Matilda (Regan) Amerine. His parents were Ohio farmers. Mr. Amerine had but limited opportunities to secure an education, and became self supporting at the age of sixteen. However, education is not merely a matter of attending school, but of possessing an ever alert mind and incorporating the items of daily experience into an ever widening knowledge and wisdom. Mr. Amerine has found in the course of a busy experience contacts that have not only made the world an interesting place, but have increased his individual opportunities for service to others. His first opportunity in the business world was given him at the Piqua Strawboard Mills, where for two years he was employed as cutter boy. This is the lowest job in strawboard manufacture. At the age of eighteen he became an employee of the Diamond Match

Company of Wabash, Indiana. This plant later became the property of the United Paper Board Company. Here he held the second position in the industry, that of back tender. Later he returned to Piqua to take a similar position in the mills there, and remained with his old company until a new strawboard company was organized with Piqua capital. This company erected a plant at Carthage in Rush County, Indiana, where he was transferred, also as back tender. The work of this job is exacting and until a man has spent several years at it he is not eligible for promotion. The skill required in the work was only a stimulus to the ambition of Mr. Amerine, who at that time had determined to master every successive branch of the industry. At the same time he utilized his night hours and other moments of leisure, studying books and also learning from his superiors.

By the time he reached the age of twenty-two he decided that he possessed enough practical and general knowledge to operate a paper machine and to be known in the business as a "paper maker." After considerable correspondence with mills in the Central States he was awarded the position he desired with the mill of the American Strawboard Company at Kokomo. The superintendent of this plant was at that time William Burt, one of the old-school operators of the Miami Valley. Like other youths of his age, Mr. Amerine thought he was fully competent, though he realized that he had not yet attained full proficiency. However, he possessed energy and ambition and a personality that enabled him to convince his superiors that he was just the man for the place. When the plant was closed down on account of the failure of natural gas in the Kokomo territory Mr. Amerine returned to the Carthage mill to take a place as paper maker. From there he went to Eaton, Indiana, to join the Paragon Paper Company, a property owned by Fort Wayne capital. This company, holding other property, had occasion to change the superintendent from the Eaton mill to the Hartford City mill. This change opened the way for Mr. Amerine to secure his first position as superintendent of a strawboard mill. The company solicited his services to fill the vacancy, and while duly grateful for the opportunity, he felt that he had earned the advancement by his steadfast application to every step of progress he had made. Energy and determination carried him through the rugged spots in his new position. About that time occurred a consolidation of many strawboard mills located throughout the Central States, which merged into what was then known as the United Boxboard & Paper Company, but today is the United Paperboard Company, with offices in New York City. With the consummation of this consolidation Mr. Amerine was transferred as superintendent of the United Paper Board Company's plant at Urbana, Ohio. This was in the nature of a promotion, and again Mr. Amerine was called upon to face many new problems, all of which he solved and also made a num-

ber of new friends who were of great value to him in after years.

The new corporation had a contract with the Urbana Egg Case & Filler Company, which threw Mr. Amerine into close touch with the manager, Harrison Craig. About this time the Urbana Egg Case Company decided that expansion of their business could be brought about through controlling their own supply of strawboard. Mr. Amerine, understanding the details of strawboard manufacture, was induced to invest his savings in the Urbana Egg Case Company, with the understanding that he could handle the combined business of production of the strawboard and the fillers. This understanding was not carried out. Consequently, in 1911 he sold his holdings and became one of the original stockholders of the Indiana Board & Filler Company, organized in that year, with W. D. Coil, president and general manager; Mr. Amerine, vice president and production manager; W. A. Veats, secretary and sales manager, and S. B. Fleming, treasurer. In 1922 W. D. Coil was elected chairman of the board of directors, and Mr. Amerine was elected president and general manager; W. A. Veats, vice president and sales manager; and Frank Hecker, treasurer, Mr. Fleming, the former treasurer, having resigned.

At the inception the Indiana Board & Filler Company had factories at Decatur, Yorkton, Evansville and Vincennes, Indiana, the largest plant of the company being at Vincennes, to which point Mr. Amerine then transferred his home and citizenship. For nearly twenty years after its organization the company did an extensive business, distributing its products from the lakes to the gulf, the Mississippi River to the Atlantic Ocean. The company bought the plant of the Urbana Egg Case Company, the Baker Egg Case Company, also at Urbana, the strawboard mills and filler business of the Decatur Egg Case Company at Marion and Delphi, Indiana, and property at Nashville and Memphis, Tennessee, for distribution of products. The company manufactured strawboard which is converted into egg case fillers, this production consuming seventy-five per cent of the strawboard manufactured, while the rest was sold to other concerns having need of it.

The business of the Indiana Board & Filler Company became affected by the same conditions that brought a lull throughout the industrial world in 1930. During that year, as a result of conferences called by heads of this and other companies manufacturing the same product, a merger materialized. All the mills and assets and properties of the Indiana Board & Filler Company have been consolidated with what is known as the Central Fiber Products Company, with main offices in the Produce Building at Chicago..

Since the merger was accomplished Mr. Amerine, believing that forty-three years in the paper business constituted more than a normal lifetime of devotion to one line, has not taken any part in the active management

George K. Throckmorton, M.D.

of the new organization. However, his energetic disposition and dynamic personality are not content with idling his time away. He finds work in the management of his personal investments which have been made over a long period of years, and in particular he has found time to express in larger measure the impulses for generous action in public spirited causes in his home city.

During the World war period Mr. Amerine took a leading part in the Liberty Loan drives. His home city being one of the historical centers of the nation, Mr. Amerine takes an active part and is a director in the newly organized Old Post Historical Association, being a charter member with a life's time certificate. During 1928-29 he was president of the Vincennes Chamber of Commerce and still retains membership in that organization. Fraternally he is affiliated with the Masons and Elks. In politics he is independent, voting for the man he thinks best suited for office.

On November 30, 1895, Mr. Amerine married, at Carthage, Indiana, Miss Blanche Catlin, of Manilla, Rush County, Indiana. Mrs. Amerine is a daughter of Charles and Margaret (Lewis) Catlin, her father a native of New York State and her mother of North Carolina, who came to Rush County at the close of the Civil war. Mr. and Mrs. Amerine have one daughter, Gladys Margaret. She was born at Marion, Indiana, August 12, 1899, was educated in the public schools of Ohio and her native state, and has two degrees, A. B. and B. M., from DePauw University. Gladys Margaret Amerine was married to Harry F. Crook. Mr. Crook attended public schools in Indiana and finished his education in the University of Illinois and University of Pennsylvania. He served in France as a soldier during the World war. He equipped himself for the profession of horticulture, and is successfully identified with that work, operating the fruit farm known as "Magnolia Place" in Knox County, Indiana, three miles east of Vincennes, off U. S. Highway No. 50. Mr. and Mrs. Crook have twin children, Kenneth Amerine and Carol Amerine Crook.

GURNEY CHAPPELL and family occupy one of the largest and best improved farms in Tippecanoe County, located in Union Township, four miles southeast of Shadeland.

Mr. Chappell is of French Huguenot ancestry. He was born in Rush County, Indiana, October 18, 1865, son of John and Eliza (Patterson) Chappell. His father was born in Eastern North Carolina, was of a Quaker family, and it was his opposition to the institution of slavery that caused him when a young man, in 1859, to follow the example of many thousands of Quakers in Western North Carolina and come to Indiana. He worked as a farm hand, and later became an independent farmer. He and his wife had five children: Mrs. Ella Sleeper, Gurney, Charles C., Anna, deceased, and Ray, deceased.

Gurney Chappell was educated in the schools of Rush County, finishing in the Farmers Institute Academy. He has been a practical farmer all his life, and now looks after the management of the farm of 900 acres.

Mr. Chappell married in 1905 Miss Mary E. Windle, daughter of Isaac and Mary (Sleeper) Windle. Isaac Windle was born in Pennsylvania, son of Job and Mary (Evans) Windle. His ancestor settled in Pennsylvania in 1649. Isaac Windle moved to Tippecanoe County in 1861. His wife, Mary Sleeper, was a member of an old and prominent Quaker family of Indiana. Her parents were Buddell and Elizabeth (Welch) Sleeper. Buddell Sleeper was born in 1806, moved west to Springfield, Ohio, and in 1835 arrived in Tippecanoe County, Indiana, where he and his brother acquired 1,100 acres. They also owned other land in Iowa. Mrs. Chappell attended country schools and after finishing the high school course attended Earlham College at Richmond, Indiana. Mr. and Mrs. Chappell have one son, Charles G., a graduate of the Lafayette High School. Both Mr. and Mrs. Chappell are active members of the Friends Church and are well known in Lafayette.

GEORGE K. THROCKMORTON as a physician and surgeon has practiced his profession in Lafayette forty-three years. His best distinction consists in the quiet and efficient work he has done from day to day and year to year, and no one is held in more honor in his profession in that community.

Doctor Throckmorton was born in Tippecanoe County, Indiana, April 1, 1862. His father, Edmund Throckmorton, was a native of Romney, West Virginia, and came to Indiana in 1838. In 1842 he and a brother founded a new town in Tippecanoe County, naming it Romney in honor of their old home in West Virginia. Edmund Throckmorton throughout his active career was a farmer. He married Elizabeth DeVault, a native of Ohio and daughter of Lemuel DeVault.

Doctor Throckmorton was one of four children. While on the farm with his parents he attended country schools and then entered Purdue University at Lafayette, where he took his Bachelor of Science degree in 1883. Doctor Throckmorton went to Chicago to study medicine in Rush Medical College, now the medical department of the University of Chicago, and was graduated M. D. in 1887. With this preparation he returned to Lafayette, and there has been no important break in his professional services down to the present time. Doctor Throckmorton was for five years secretary of the county board of health, served as county coroner two years and is a member of St. Elizabeth and the Home Hospitals staffs. He has been honored with the office of president of the Tippecanoe County Medical Society and is a member of the Indiana State and American Medical Associations. He is the only representative of his profession in Tippecanoe County who is a charter member of the American College of Surgeons, and he was the first to perform the delicate operation of abdominal surgery in this section of the state. During the World war Doctor Throckmorton did work as a contract surgeon at Purdue University. He is a director of the Lafayette Loan & Trust Company and of the Lafayette Joint Stock Land Bank. He is a Rotarian and a member of the Central Presbyterian Church.

Doctor Throckmorton married Rosalie Renhardt, who was born in Lafayette. Their only child, Georgia Rosalie, who died in 1926, was a graduate of Purdue University.

REV. JOHN J. GALLAGHER during the eighteen years of his priesthood has been identified with several Indiana communities, and in each place he has won esteem and love for his personal qualities, his ability as churchman and the zeal and success with which he has prosecuted his work.

Father Gallagher was born in Chicago, December 25, 1887, son of Martin and Catherine (Reagan) Gallagher. His father was a native of New York City, while his mother was born in North Vernon, Indiana, and reared and educated in Cambridge City, Indiana. Martin Gallagher was in the grocery business. He died in 1907, and the widowed mother is now housekeeper for her son at Newcastle.

John J. Gallagher attended St. Gregory's preparatory seminary at Cincinnati, was a student in St. Joseph's College at Rensselaer, Indiana, and devoted six years to his philosophic and theological preparation at St. Meinrad Seminary. He was ordained May 13, 1913. The first call upon his services was as assistant to St. Philips Catholic Church in Indianapolis. He remained there six years, for one year was assistant at Jeffersonville, Indiana, and then became pastor of a church in Martin County.

Father Gallagher since 1921 has been pastor of St. Anne's church in Newcastle. Here he has done much to upbuild his congregation, has extended the service of different departments of the church, and has shown a constant interest in all movements to promote the broader welfare of the city. He is captain of the Knights of Columbus Council and politically casts an independent vote.

LEWIS HENRY CREAGER, of Bicknell, has had an exceedingly busy and useful life as a lumber manufacturer and furniture merchant. He was engaged in the timber and lumber business for many years, and from the operation of saw mills he turned to a special line of handling finished lumber products, furniture, and is now proprietor of a business operating two stores in Knox County.

He was born in Ohio, in 1858. His father was a farmer and merchant in Ohio and afterwards at Brooklyn, Indiana. Lewis Henry Creager attended school at Versailles, Ohio, and as a youth worked in his father's store at Versailles. When the family moved to Indiana they located on a farm near Portland, and Lewis Henry took a part in the work of the farm until he was twenty-three.

After that he was in the lumber business for forty years. He operated a mill in Jay County, Indiana, manufacturing lumber of special requirements and had a plant employing twenty-five men. After selling his interests there in 1894 he moved to Daviess County in Southwestern Indiana, put up a new mill and continued as a lumber manufacturer until 1914. Mr. Creager has been a resident of Bicknell since 1914, and since that time has been in the furniture business. He has two stores, one located at Bicknell and the other at Washington. Each store has about 7,200 square feet of floor space and carries a complete line of house furnishing goods, a standard line of furniture to meet the needs and tastes of the communities around the stores. Mr. Creager is a member of the Merchants Association of Bicknell and has filled all the chairs in the Knights of Pythias Lodge.

He married Melissa Coffin, of Winchester, Indiana. They have five children: Harry and Clay, both of whom are employees of the Baltimore & Ohio Railway; Donald; Lefa, wife of J. H. Barrow; and Lillie. The son Donald is now manager of the branch furniture store at Washington.

WILLIAM F. FEHRMAN. It has been most justly claimed that if no historian of the future arises to write of the present period, the record will be adequately preserved in the columns, not alone of the metropolitan centers, but of smaller cities and towns, of the newspapers. From these day by day, or week by week, records of the everyday life of the people may be gleaned the conditions, both material and political, which prevailed during the first quarter of the twentieth century by the people of say the thirtieth century. On the other hand historians declare that not until the subsequent generation can an event be described in an unprejudiced manner. Perhaps this latter is also true, but everyone has experienced to a more or less extent the difficulty of securing an accurate account about something a few months later on, especially from several persons. The newspapers chronicle events in the moment of their occurrence, while interest is keen and facts common property. Unfortunately the necessity for speed in the issuance of these journals, and the quality of the paper, operate against their permanent preservation. Enough, perhaps, is their mission to send forth their message to the sections in which they circulate, and to educate and influence their readers according to their several policies. One of these modern newspapers, widely circulated in Dearborn County, the *Aurora Journal,* is now under the efficient charge of William F. Fehrman, secretary-treasurer of the Dearborn Publishing Company, which owns and publishes the *Journal,* formerly the *Dearborn Independent.*

William F. Fehrman is a native son of Indiana, born in Ohio County, in 1901, and his father, Charles Fehrman, was also born in the state. He married Margaret Ritter, and

they have had nine children born to them. The paternal grandfather was William Fehrman.

An ambitious lad, William F. Fehrman did not go beyond the Aurora grade schools, for he began earning his living when only fourteen years of age, and has continued in the printing business ever since, working in all of the departments of a newspaper, so that when, in December, 1927, he took over the plant of the *Dearborn Independent* he knew every phase of his undertaking, and has made remarkable progress. In addition to issuing the *Aurora Journal* his company does a general line of job printing, and has an excellent modern bindery.

Mr. Fehrman married Miss Loretta Haug, born in Dearborn County. Fraternally Mr. Fehrman affiliates with the Independent Order of Odd Fellows. During the World war he served in the Home Guard. He is a member of the Indiana Republican Editorial Association. Politically he is a Republican.

The *Aurora Journal* was for years the *Dearborn Independent*, but with the first issue of Volume 62 the name was changed to the present one, and in that number the following appeared as a portion of an article appearing under the caption "*Aurora Journal* is New Name."

"For some time the owners have had under consideration the changing of the name of the paper, and, after much thought, have finally concluded to take a new name, the *Aurora Journal*, and commence the new year under the above title.

"The *Dearborn Independent*, which is now succeeded by the *Aurora Journal*, is sixty-one years old this week. A record that any newspaper can well be proud of. For to have carried on for that length of time, weathering the many vicissitudes of those years, keeping its place in the life and interests of the community, is an achievement that takes determination, purpose, and speaks well for those guiding its destinies, and the fact that it is still recognized as the 'home paper' tells the story of its achievements.

"In the 1850s there was started in Aurora a newspaper called the *Aurora Commercial*. It was edited by E. F. Sibley.

"In 1868 the *Aurora Commercial* was sold to a stock company of twenty-four, of which John Cobb was president. The name was then changed to the *Dearborn Independent*.

"In its first issue it was announced that the editor was J. W. McDonald, and that the local department was in the charge of T. J. Cobb.

"L. W. Cobb bought the *Dearborn Independent* in April, 1873, and was for forty years its sole owner, editor and publisher, during which time the *Independent* was recognized as a very strong Republican newspaper.

"Mr. L. W. Cobb died December 29, 1912, just four months prior to completing forty years as owner and editor of the *Independent*. At that time the paper was taken in charge by his widow and daughter, Mrs. L. W. Cobb and Inez S. Cobb, who also ran it as a Republican publication.

"They sold the *Independent* in August, 1926, to a stock company, the Dearborn Publishing Company, of which A. G. Pedersen, who came here from Chicago, owned a big majority of the stock, was made manager of the business and editor of the paper.

"In October, 1927, after being connected with the *Independent* for fourteen months, Pedersen severed his connection with the company.

"At that time William F. Fehrman and members of his family bought the Pedersen interests.

"With Mr. Fehrman as editor and Inez S. Cobb as associate editor the paper returned to its proper place in the Republican fold, and again a newsy home paper was published."

In this first issue under the new name the *Aurora Journal* states "that the paper will be carried on the same as it has been in the past year, under the management of William F. Fehrman. It will be a real home paper, endeavoring to serve the people of this community, and will make no change in any of its policies."

Mr. Fehrman is the type of man in whom the intellectual development has found precedent over the more strenuous activities of public life, but he is not without motive power of energy and aspiration that has never failed to bring success to a man when properly focused. His career has been developed along lines of thought, as well as those of action, and his theories have been potent in the process of rounding out his newspaper life.

LEWIS G. ELLINGHAM, president and manager of the *Fort Wayne Journal-Gazette*, is a veteran of the profession of journalism in Indiana, widely known all over the northern part of the state, and his name has a statewide significance due to two terms of service in the office of Secretary of State.

His parents, Charles and Hannah (Scotton) Ellingham, were born in England, came to America and became Indiana farmers, and were living on a farm in Wells County when their son Lewis G. was born February 23, 1868. Six years later they moved to Bluffton, where the son attended public schools and gained his first knowledge of the printing trade in the office of the *Bluffton Banner*. At the age of nineteen he made an independent venture into journalism by purchasing the *Herald* at Geneva, Indiana. After three years he acquired the *Winchester Democrat*, which he published three years, and then established the *Decatur Democratic Press*. In 1896 a stock company bought the *Decatur Democrat*, combining the two papers under the name *The Democrat*. The community of Decatur still claims Mr. Ellingham, where he spent some of the most active years in his career as a journalist and public man.

Mr. Ellingham in 1916 came to Fort Wayne and in partnership with Edward G. Hoffman acquired the *Journal-Gazette*. Mr. Hoffman withdrew from the partnership and since then Mr. Ellingham has guided the destiny of the

Journal-Gazette and has made it one of the really great newspapers of the State of Indiana.

Mr. Ellingham served as eighth district chairman of the Democratic party in 1906 and 1908, and in 1910 he led the entire state ticket as a candidate for secretary of state, being elected by a plurality of 13,000 votes. In 1912 he was reelected by a still larger vote. His term ended December 1, 1914, and two years later he removed to Fort Wayne.

Mr. Ellingham was an active member of the old Commercial Club, and has done a great deal of important work through the civic and municipal bureau of the present Chamber of Commerce, and was active in the building fund campaign in January, 1926. He is a member of the Fort Wayne Rotary Club, and has given his support to the Izaak Walton League, the Fort Wayne-Allen County Historical Society and other community building groups. He is a member of the Decatur Lodge of Masons, the Scottish Rite bodies of Fort Wayne and Mizpah Temple of the Mystic Shrine, and was captain of the Marion group of Mizpah Temple's campaign in 1926. He is a member of the Decatur Lodge of Elks and Knights of Pythias. He and his wife are members of the First Presbyterian Church. Mr. Ellingham is president of the Bond Engraving Company of Fort Wayne.

He married, January 2, 1895, Miss Nellie Miller, daughter of Col. M. B. Miller, of Winchester. They have one daughter, Winefred, now the wife of J. Ewing Bond, of Fort Wayne, and a son, Miller, now assistant general manager of the *Journal-Gazette*. He married Margery Hyman, of Fort Wayne.

ARCHIE LEE TURNER. One of the important resources of Scott County is the production of vegetable crops for the canning industry. About two miles south of Scottsburg is located the plant of the Vienna Canning Company, a business that during the season employs about 150 people and has an average production of 30,000 cases of tomatoes and 20,000 cases of pumpkin.

The active manager of this plant since 1923 has been Mr. Archie Lee Turner, who has been an experienced worker in the canning business since early manhood. Mr. Turner was born in Tipton County, Indiana, March 24, 1890, son of Thomas Turner and grandson of Thomas Turner. His father was a Tipton County farmer and held the office of road supervisor there. Archie Lee Turner was one of three children and attended the public schools of Tipton County. He has been doing for himself since he was eighteen. He learned the canning business by familiarizing himself with every routine duty in a plant. For a time he was foreman of the Home Packing Company at Elwood, was a partner and foreman of the Ferguson Canning Company of that city, and during the World war was employed by the Underwood Canning Company, which was on a basis of 100 per cent war production. During 1922 he was foreman of the Marysville canning plant and in 1923 came to the Vienna Canning Company in Scott County.

Mr. Turner married in 1913 Miss Carrie Scott, of Tipton County, whose people were early settlers of Indiana. They have six children, Virgil, Frances, Ballard, Pauline, Ruth and Bonnie.

JOHN L. BAKER is an Indiana educator, acting as superintendent of public schools in his native City at Vincennes.

Mr. Baker is a son of William Baker, Sr. His grandfather came from Germany and settled in Indiana before the Civil war. William Baker, Sr., was born in Indiana and has been a prominent figure in the industrial and business life of the Vincennes district. He organized and is president of the American National Bank of Vincennes. He was in the distilling business until 1917 and for the past ten years has been a coal operator, owning and operating two coal mines in Knox and Sullivan counties, working 400 men and producing 3,000 tons of coal daily.

John L. Baker and sister, Esther, were both educated in the schools of Vincennes. He was formerly president of the Vincennes School Board, and then took the office of superintendent of schools. He is a member of Vincennes Lodge No. 1, A. F. and A. M., is a Scottish Rite Mason and Shriner and a Democrat in his political affiliations.

EDWARD KRAUSE. Prominent among the officials of Jackson County who by their service, ability and energies are contributing materially to the welfare and progress of their respective communities, one whose past activities have been of such a character as to gain for him something more than passing mention is Edward Krause, postmaster of Crothersville. Still a young man, Mr. Krause's career has touched life on many sides, he having had experience in business, in railroading, as a soldier and as an official. In each capacity he has discharged his duties with signal ability and established himself firmly in the confidence and esteem of those with whom he has been identified.

Mr. Krause was born at Crothersville, Jackson County, Indiana, February 25, 1898, and is a son of John and Caroline (Kovenor) Krause. John Krause was born in Germany, and was only fourteen years of age when brought to this country by his parents, who took up their residence in Indiana. As a youth he learned the trade of carpenter and as the years passed developed into a contractor and builder, in which vocations he is still engaged. He is one of the substantial and highly esteemed men of his community and has a host of friends and well-wishers. Mr. Krause married Miss Caroline Kovenor, of Jackson County, Indiana, and they became the parents of four children.

Edward Krause attended the grade and high schools of Crothersville until reaching the age of seventeen years, at which time he en-

Richard B. Wetherill

listed in the United States Marines and saw twenty-two months of service, rising to first sergeant of the Eighty-fourth Company, Fifteenth Regiment, Second Brigade. He received his honorable discharge in October, 1919, and, deciding that he had enough of soldiering, obtained a position as clerk in the office of the Pennsylvania Railroad, where he worked from January 1920, until July, 1921. At that time Mr. Krause was appointed acting postmaster of Crothersville, to fill a vacancy, and October 20, 1921, was appointed postmaster during the administration of President Harding. He was reappointed December 21, 1925, by President Coolidge, and still occupies this position. He has made a number of material changes at Crothersville, which have facilitated and expedited the service and which have found much commendation at the hands of the people. It has been his fortune to make and hold numerous friendships, and to have impressed himself upon the community as a man of ability and energy. His support is given to every worthy movement and he is an enthusiastic member of the local lodge of the Masonic fraternity and the local post of the American Legion, of which he has been a member since its inception.

Mr. Krause was united in marriage with Miss Vivian Craven, who is descended from the noted Craven family, the name so vividly associated with the "Pigeon Roost Massacre." She also bears relationship to a long line of Indiana pioneers who have been prominent in the history of the Hoosier State, and is a daughter of Clyde Craven, a well-known farmer of Jackson County, who is serving in the capacity of county assessor.

RICHARD B. WETHERILL, who for over thirty years has practiced medicine and surgery at Lafayette, is a member of a family long distinguished in America as scientists and inventors.

Doctor Wetherill is a descendant of Christopher Wetherill, who came from England to New Jersey in 1682 and gave to the Quakers the land on which their first meeting house in Burlington, New Jersey, was erected. A descendant of Christopher was Samuel Wetherill, a Philadelphia manufacturer who was the first in the United States to make white lead. He and other Quakers joined in the defense of Philadelphia during the Revolution, and for that cause was excommunicated by the church. Consequently he founded what has since been known as the Society of Free Quakers, also sometimes called "Fighting" Quakers. A later descendant of this Samuel Wetherill was Samuel Wetherill whose experiments and inventions led to the production of "zinc white," and to the use of zinc as a substitute for or in combination with white lead in paint materials.

The father of Doctor Wetherill of Lafayette was an eminent American scientist, Charles Mayer Wetherill, who was born at Philadelphia, November 4, 1825, and died at South Bethlehem, Pennsylvania, March 5, 1871. He graduated from the University of Pennsylvania in 1845, specialized in chemistry, went abroad and took his Doctor of Philosophy degree in 1848. After his return he engaged in chemical investigations in his private laboratory in Philadelphia. During the Civil war President Lincoln appointed him chemist to the agricultural department, and he was the first to hold that position. In 1866 he became professor of chemistry in Lehigh University in Pennsylvania, and filled that chair until his death. The honorary degree of M. D. was conferred upon him by the New York Medical College in 1853.

Dr. Charles M. Wetherill came to Lafayette, Indiana, about 1855 and married Mary C. Benbridge, who was born at Lafayette, January 28, 1833. Her father was Thomas Truxton Benbridge, who settled at Lafayette, Indiana, in 1829. He was a grandson of Commodore Thomas Truxton, who made a distinguished record as a naval officer in the War of the Revolution and was selected as one of the first six captains of the United States Navy when it was organized. He commanded the Constellation in its brilliant victory over the French man-of-war in February, 1799. His memory has been handed down in the navy as one of its most distinguished officers. At one time eight of his grandsons were cadets in the United States Naval Academy.

Richard B. Wetherill was one of the two children of his parents. After the death of his father his mother returned to Lafayette, where he completed his high school training. For four years he was a student in Lehigh University of Pennsylvania, and he studied medicine in Jefferson Medical College at Philadelphia, graduating in 1883. Following that he went abroad and pursued his studies under the eminent German scientists, Rudolph Virchow and Robert Koch, spending one year at the University of Berlin, and during 1885-86 continued his post-graduate studies at the University of Pennsylvania. He served as an interne in St. Mary's Hospital at Philadelphia.

In the fall of 1886 Doctor Wetherill returned to Lafayette and was engaged in practice as a physician and surgeon for over thirty years, retiring in 1917 in order to give his services to the United States Government. He was commissioned a lieutenant in the Volunteer Medical Corps, and served until January, 1919, at Purdue University. He is a member of the Tippecanoe County, Indiana State and American Medical Associations, is a member of the Pathological Society of Philadelphia, and was made a fellow of the American College of Surgeons in the first year of that organization. Doctor Wetherill held the chair of Principles of Surgery of the College of Physicians and Surgeons at Indianapolis in 1905-06, and the chair of Materia Medica in the College of Pharmacy of Purdue University in 1886-87. He is a former city and county health officer. He is a member of the Masonic fraternity, the B. P. O. Elks. Doctor Wetherill is president of the Tippecanoe County Historical Society and for the past ten years has devoted much of his time to the study of ancient civilization. In his investigations he has gone abroad, has traveled and pursued his investigations through Indo-China, Mesopotamia, Egypt, also on the American continent in Yucatan, Mexico, Peru, and in 1923 made a journey across the continent of Africa from Cairo to Cape Town. Some of the results of his researches have been published.

FRANK D. BUTLER, of Peru, is a veteran in the practice of law and in varied service as a citizen, in the course of which he has come in contact with many prominent men of the state and is one of the recognized leaders of the Democratic party of Indiana.

Mr. Butler was born in Miami County, December 30, 1858. His father, Jesse B. Butler, was also a native of Indiana and a son of William Butler, who joined the migration of Quakers to Eastern Indiana in 1816 and settled in Wayne County. The Butlers came to America with William Penn and first settled in Pennsylvania. William Butler was born in Pennsylvania, in 1775, and had lived in South Carolina and Georgia before coming to Indiana. Jesse B. Butler came to Miami County and settled in Perry Township about 1835 and spent his active life as a farmer.

Frank D. Butler was the youngest of eight children. When he was fifteen years of age the death of his parents left him an orphan and he had a considerable struggle in getting a living, procuring the education his ambition demanded and in setting himself on the road to a professional career. After the public schools he attended Purdue University, and while a student there supported himself by newspaper work, acting as university correspondent to the *Lafayette Courier*, and was on the staff of reporters of that paper until he returned to Peru in 1880. For eight years he was deputy sheriff, utilizing his spare time to study law. From 1888 to 1890 he acted as private secretary to the distinguished Indiana Senator David Turpie. In 1889 he was admitted to the Indiana bar, and his name has been an honored one in the profession at Peru since that date. In 1890 he was elected prosecuting attorney and reelected in 1892, and has also served as county attorney and city attorney. During the 1913 flood he was chairman of the Flood Relief Committee.

Mr. Butler was grand regent of the Royal Arcanum, 1908-10. He is a member of the Miami County and Indiana State Bar Associations. He was a delegate from Indiana to the National Democratic Convention at Baltimore in 1912, when Woodrow Wilson was nominated for his first term. In 1916 he was a member of the Street Committee of the party and chairman of the Speakers Bureau. At the time of the war he rendered special service with the National Protective League, an auxiliary of the Department of Justice.

Mr. Butler married Minnie Merrill, a native of Illinois. They have two children, the daughter, Dorothy, being the wife of Oran W. Morrissey. The son, Robert, was educated

in the grade and high schools of Peru, studied law with his father and prior to his admission to the bar was in the employ of the Citizens National Bank at Peru.

JOSEPH A. CRUM has served as postmaster of Dayton, Indiana, since his original appointment in July, 1922. He has made himself a very popular citizen of this section of Tippecanoe County. Mr. Crum is a nephew of the late Lawrence Nicely, for many years one of the outstanding business men and citizens of Dayton.

Joseph A. Crum was born in Pennsylvania, son of William H. and Elfa F. (Wright) Crum. William Crum spent many years in service as a railroad conductor with the Pennsylvania lines. He was born in Cambria County, Pennsylvania, and was educated in the common schools. At the time of the Johnstown flood of 1889 he began his career as a railroad man, starting as a brakeman, and continued in the service until retired as a result of injuries. He became a leading figure and influence in Western Pennsylvania politics. For five terms he held the office of mayor of Conemaugh, and his leadership and influence brought him in intimate association with prominent political leaders and groups in Pittsburgh and elsewhere. He was a member of the United Evangelical Church and taught a class in its Sunday School for thirty years. He was a member of the Brotherhood of Railway Trainmen. His children were five in number: Joseph A.; Abraham, of Pittsburgh; Homer, deceased; Harriett, wife of Herbert Luther; and Daniel, who lives with his mother in Pennsylvania.

Mr. Crum's mother is a daughter of Joseph A. Wright and granddaughter of David Wright. David Wright acquired land from the Government near Portage, Pennsylvania, and was a farmer there. Joseph Wright served as a soldier in the Civil war and had a brother who was a captain. Joseph Wright is still living at Portage, Pennsylvania. The Wright family is of Scotch ancestry.

Joseph A. Crum began attending school at the age of six years. While in high school he worked after hours and during vacations, for a time was with a steel company, his particular job being the making of rake teeth for farm implements, and during his last two years in high school he worked evenings and Saturdays at the barber's trade. He was a barber in his home town in Pennsylvania until 1906, when he came to Indiana to live with his uncle, Lawrence Nicely, at Dayton. In 1909 he returned to Pennsylvania and owned a barber shop there until 1915. In that year he again established himself at Dayton, where he was associated with his uncle in business.

Mr. Crum in May, 1918, enlisted for service in the World war. He was in training at Camp Lee, Petersburg, Virginia, being with the Eleventh Battalion Headquarters as a private. After the war he returned to Dayton, and was made manager of the Nicely business. After the death of his uncle he continued the management for his widow until the business was sold in 1923. Since then he has given his undivided attention to his duties as postmaster. When Mr. Crum became postmaster the Dayton postoffice was using equipment which had been installed more than half a century before. Under Mr. Crum's administration this · equipment has been completely brought up to date. He has been an influential civic leader in various ways, helping promote good roads and other community enterprises.

Mr. Crum's wife, Mrs. Anastasia Crum, lived during her girlhood in Texas and California, and completed her literary education at Washington, D. C. She is a graduate nurse of the Cook County Hospital of Chicago. Mr. and Mrs. Crum are members of the Eastern Star, of which he is a past worthy patron. He is a past master of Dayton Lodge No. 103, A. F. and A. M., and is a member of Dayton Lodge No. 492, Knights of Pythias, and affiliates with Lafayette Post No. 11 of the American Legion.

DONALD M. WARREN is vice president and general manager of the Warren Paper Products Company, Inc., at 125 South Fifth Street in Lafayette. Mr. Warren has been in the paper box business since he left college. He entered it at an opportune time. Paper box making is an old established industry, but for many years it was confined to a rather limited field in competition with wooden boxes. Almost within the personal experience of Mr. Warren paper box containers have become practically dominant and have all but ousted the wood and lumber materials until these materials are now used in a way fully as limited as was formerly true of strawboard and paper containers. Mr. Warren was born at Watseka, Illinois, July 26, 1900. His father, Harry A. Warren, has been a prominent citizen of Watseka for many years, a farmer, banker, and former sheriff of his county. He married Miss Minnie McGill.

Donald M. Warren attended school at Watseka, was sent to the Wentworth Military Academy in Missouri and completed his education in the University of Illinois. His brother and associate, R. A. Warren, was also educated in the University of Illinois. Donald M. Warren during the war was a member of the Reserve Officers Training Corps and a short time before the armistice was sent for special training to Fort Sheridan.

His early experience in the paper box business was gained at Danville, Illinois, where he became vice president of the Mirle Sears Paper Box Company, which made an extensive line of set up paper boxes. In the fall of 1921 he came to Lafayette, where he organized the Warren Paper Products Company, Inc. M. M. Warren is president of the corporation, R. A. Warren is secretary and Donald M. holds the offices of vice president, treasurer and general manager.

The Warren Paper Products Company has a large and splendidly equipped plant. They started business in a small building on North Fourth Street. In 1924 they erected a new plant, with 19,000 square feet of floor space and equipped with the latest modern machinery, capable of an enormous output with comparatively few machine operators or tenders. About fifty people are employed in the business. They manufacture set up boxes of all kinds, chiefly catering to the needs of the shoe, candy, underwear and hosiery industries. The products of the plant are shipped all over Indiana and to adjacent states.

Mr. Warren is a member of the National Paper Box Manufacturers Association, the Lafayette Chamber of Commerce, is a Republican, a Methodist and a member of the Tri Epsilon college fraternity.

He married Miss Katharine Kemp, of Illinois, and they have two children, Janice and Ann.

GREENLEIF NORTON MEHARRY was a sterling, upright and honored citizen of Indiana, in which state he spent all his active years. He has many descendants still living in Tippecanoe and other counties.

He was born on the Thomas E. Martin farm in Richland Township, Fountain County, Indiana, July 16, 1831, and died August 3, 1895. He was a son of James and Margaret (Francis) Meharry and grandson of Alexander Meharry, who was born in Ireland, August 5, 1763. Alexander Meharry was a man of unusual education for his time. He came to America and spent his last years in Adams County, Ohio, where he died June 2, 1813. His wife was Jane Francis, and their children were Hugh, Thomas, Mary, Jesse, David, Samuel, Alexander and James.

James Meharry was born in Eagle Creek Township, Adams County, Ohio, September 18, 1801. He was twelve years of age when his father died. During his youth he and a brother started for Texas, going down the Ohio and Mississippi rivers to New Orleans. They embarked on a ship bound for Galveston. The boat was wrecked and they lost all their baggage. They then walked back to New Orleans, where they discovered that the captain of the wrecked boat had recovered their trunk. After six weeks they bought a horse and returned to their old home in Adams County, Ohio. Later James Meharry moved to Fountain County, Indiana, where he took up eighty acres of Government land. He then returned to Ohio, where he married on December 20, 1827, and in the spring of the following year he and his wife rode on horseback to their new home in Indiana. They were devout Christians and always stopped on the Sabbath day. They built a home in Fountain County, but in the fall of 1831 moved to Montgomery County, where they lived out their lives. James Meharry was a farmer and stock raiser. During the Civil war he was a staunch upholder of the Union. He showed his public spirit in many ways. For a time he had read medicine and in the absence of a regular doctor he was frequently called in cases of sickness. He and his wife were buried in the Meharry Cemetery in Montgomery County. Their children were: Mary A., wife of Rev. David Crawford; Greenleif N.; Cornelia B., who married James Hickman; James A., deceased; Allen W.

Greenleif N. Meharry received his early education in the schools of Montgomery County and then entered Asbury, now DePauw, University at Greencastle, Indiana. He acquired a good education, had a practical knowledge of farming, and as a young man his father gave him 160 acres of land. When he married he took his bride to a log cabin on this home, and that was the beginning of his career as a successful farmer and stock man.

He and his wife had a family of nine children: Lena, deceased; Florence; Eddie, who married Emma Lanfear; Robert E., who married Bell Davidson, and their children are Adah L., who is the wife of Orin Meeker, Robert and Helen L.; Miss Annie V., who resides at New Richmond in Jackson Township, Tippecanoe County; Thomas E., deceased; Lizzie, deceased; Ira G., who married Agnes Sayers, and their children are Carrie, wife of Sherman Probasco, Clare, Hugo S., Lois M., wife of Leonard Andrews; Judd, deceased, married Ethel Hillis and had four children, Josephine, deceased, Roy H., who married Mary E. Swank, Lee A. and Chitrea.

Greenleif Meharry was a strong Union man during the Civil war period and always afterward voted the Republican ticket. He was a member of the Grange, the Horse Thief Protective Association, but his chief interest was in the Methodist Episcopal Church. He and his wife were laid to rest in the Meharry Cemetery.

LINN S. KIDD, general manager of the Brazil Coal Company, the Kidd Coal Company and the Kidd Insurance Agencies at Brazil, is an ex-service man of the World war. For a number of years he has enjoyed a prominent position in business and is one of the influential young Republican leaders in his section of the state.

He was born at Brazil, December 10, 1898, son of John C. and Nannie (Spear) Kidd, and a grandson of Andrew J. and Arabelle (Webster) Kidd. His grandfather was a native of Winchester, Virginia, where the earlier generations of the family had been slave-holding planters. Andrew J. Kidd served as a soldier in the Civil war, being second lieutenant of a company of Indiana troops in the Union army. On coming west he located in Clay County, Indiana. He was a cooper by trade. He became a partner in the furniture business of Sherfey & Kidd Company, which is still one of the going concerns of Clay County. Andrew J. Kidd died at Brazil and is buried in Cottage Hill Cemetery.

John C. Kidd, who was born at Brazil, for many years carried on a very successful general insurance business in that city. On Jan-

uary 1, 1931, he was appointed commissioner of insurance for the State of Indiana, and is serving in that responsible state office at the present time. He is a past president of the Brazil Chamber of Commerce, is a Mason and a staunch Republican. He and his wife had four children: Waneta, wife of Walter Minnich, of Muncie, Indiana, their children being Walter, Jr., and Nancy Ann; Linn S.; Robert L., whose home is at Bartlesville, Oklahoma, married Jane Carpenter, of Richmond, Indiana, and they have a daughter, Louann; and George Kidd, unmarried.

Linn S. Kidd was educated in the grade and high schools at Brazil and spent one semester in 1916 at the Indiana State Teachers College at Terre Haute. For one year he taught school in Clay County.

On April 14, 1917, he volunteered, joining the First Indiana Field Artillery. This regiment was mustered into the federal service as the One Hundred and Fiftieth Field Artillery Regiment, becoming part of the Forty-second or Rainbow Division. Mr. Kidd went overseas and shared in the glorious record of his division. The division arrived overseas in October, 1917. It participated in the battles in the Lorraine sector, at Champagne, at Chateau-Thierry, and in the Saint Mihiel and Meuse-Argonne campaigns, and after the armistice was with the Army of Occupation in Germany. Mr. Kidd was a private during the early months of his service, then served in the grades of corporal and sergeant, and was commissioned a second lieutenant while overseas. He was honorably discharged at Camp Meade, Maryland, May 6, 1919.

In the fall of 1919 he enrolled in Indiana University, and was graduated in 1922 with the A. B. degree. Since his university career he has spent ten years of concentrated business activity at Brazil. He and his father organized the Brazil Coal Company, of which he became general manager. Later he and his two brothers, George and Robert, established the Kidd Coal Company, of which he is secretary-treasurer and general manager. When his father was appointed state commissioner of insurance Linn S. Kidd bought the general insurance business at Brazil which had been built up by John C. Kidd, and to this he also gives his active attention.

On June 25, 1931, Mr. Kidd was married to Miss Dorothy Kerfoot, also of Brazil.

Mr. Kidd has been active in the work of the American Legion. For one term he was district commander for the six counties of his congressional district. He is a member of the First Christian Church. He has served as state chairman of the Republican Service League, an organization of Republican War veterans, is a past chairman of the Clay County Republican central committee, and is now Republican chairman of the Fifth Congressional District. Mr. Kidd is a member of the Phi Kappa Psi college fraternity, is vice president of the Indiana University Alumni Association, a York Rite and Scottish Rite

E. V. Hawkins

Mason and Shriner. He is a past exalted ruler of Brazil Lodge No. 762, B. P. O. Elks, member of the Fraternal Order of Eagles, the Columbia Club of Indianapolis, the Brazil Chamber of Commerce and the Brazil Country Club.

EDWARD V. HAWKINS. From 1873 until his death in 1926, a period of fifty-three years, the late Edward V. Hawkins was one of the substantial citizens of Connersville, and for forty-four years of this time was identified with the Connersville Furniture Company, of which prominent concern he was president at the time of his demise. While he was reared amid agricultural surroundings, he was a born mechanic and from the outset of his independent career was known for his splendid craftsmanship in the designing and manufacture of furniture. As the years passed he rose to prominence and success, and when called by death was known throughout Indiana and the Central West as an exponent of the best ethics of the furniture trade.

Mr. Hawkins was born at Vevay, Switzerland County, Indiana, August 19, 1854, a son of Anthony and Prudence (Adams) Hawkins, the former of whom was an agriculturist who passed his entire life in Switzerland County, where he bore a high reputation as to character and integrity. The rural schools of his native community furnished Edward V. Hawkins with his educational training, following which he began to assist his father on the home farm. His evident talent for mechanics, however, would not be denied, and he left the farm to enter a furniture factory at Vevay, where he quickly mastered his trade. He was but nineteen years of age when, in 1873, he took up his residence at Connersville, and here turned out and made the first dozen bureaus in the plant of the Indiana Furniture Company. Starting in a minor capacity, Mr. Hawkins was promoted consecutively to inspector, foreman and superintendent of the company, in which he also bought stock, and with which he remained until 1882, when he became the organizer and general manager of the Connersville Furniture Company. F. M. Roots was the first president of this concern and N. W. Wright, secretary. Subsequently Charles Mount became president, serving in that capacity until his death, when Mr. Hawkins was made president and continued as such until his own death, January 8, 1926. When he was made president his son, E. P. Hawkins, became secretary, and Mrs. Edward V. Hawkins was made first vice president. Later E. P. Hawkins was made general manager, and J. E. Page assumed the secretaryship of the company. A splendid craftsman, learned in all the details of furniture building, Mr. Hawkins was also an excellent business man and a sound executive, and was held in high esteem by his business associates, serving for some years as president of the Indiana Furniture Manufacturers' Association. He served as a trustee, steward and member of the official board of the Methodist Episcopal Church,

and was superintendent of the Sunday School for many years. He was an early advocate of prohibition and for many years was president and head of the Blue Ribbon Temperance Club of Connersville. For many years he was a member of the Connersville Board of Education, and for a time was its president. Politically Mr. Hawkins was a Republican, and fraternally he was affiliated with the Independent Order of Odd Fellows and the Improved Order of Red Men, and he likewise was a constructive member of the Rotary Club. Mr. and Mrs. Hawkins donated the land for a playground for the children of Connersville, which is known as Hawkins Playground.

On December 25, 1877, Mr. Hawkins was united in marriage with Miss Margaret L. Pratt, who was born June 11, 1858, at Duanesburg, Albany County, New York, a daughter of George P. and Helen (Ferguson) Pratt. Her father was born in Gilderland, Schenectady County, New York, and her mother at Duanesburg, Albany County, New York, and as a young couple they came to Connersville, Indiana, where Mr. Pratt was a substantial merchant for many years, and at the time of his demise was the oldest member of his Masonic Lodge. Mrs. Hawkins is ex-regent of Connersville Chapter of the Daughters of the American Revolution, a charter member and an ex-president of the Connersville Cary Club and an active worker in the societies of the Methodist Episcopal Church. She and her husband had one son: Edward Pratt, born November 10, 1881, now a resident of New York City. He married Marie Kimball, of Little Rock, Arkansas, and has one son, Edward Kimball, born February 25, 1908, who attended Wabash College, at Crawfordsville, Indiana, and is now engaged in business in New York.

ERROL A. TUCKER, former member of the Legislature and former mayor of Columbus, is a doctor of veterinary surgery who has been engaged in practice at Columbus for over twenty years.

He was born in Morgan County, Indiana, April 11, 1879, a grandson of George Tucker, a native of Kentucky, who was taken by his parents to Johnson County, Indiana, about 1820. The Tuckers are of Virginia ancestry. Doctor Tucker's father, W. C. Tucker, has been a farmer all his life in Johnson County, Indiana. He married Margaret Guthridge, Errol A. being the only child.

Errol A. Tucker attended schools in Johnson County, including the Trafalgar High School, and was a student in the Northern Indiana Normal College at Valparaiso. He was graduated with the A. B. degree, also took a course in the Vorhees Business College at Indianapolis. In 1906 he graduated from the Indiana Veterinary College and completed his training in one of the foremost schools of the kind, the Ontario Veterinary College at Toronto, Canada. After graduating, in March, 1907, he located at Columbus, and has been one of the outstanding veterinarians of Indiana for many years. He has been assistant state veterinarian and during the World war was a Government inspector, making inspections of horses shipped overseas by the Government.

Doctor Tucker was elected a member of the Indiana Legislature in 1914. In 1920 he became mayor of Columbus and served in that capacity four years. He has been a very active member of the Chamber of Commerce and is affiliated with Saint John's Lodge of the Masonic fraternity, belongs to the Royal Arch, Council degree and Knights Templar Commandery of Masons and Murat Temple of the Mystic Shrine at Indianapolis. He is also a thirty-second degree Scottish Rite Mason.

Doctor Tucker married Miss La Donna Morletege, of Bartholomew County. They have two children, Emily Margaret and William, both attending school at Columbus.

LEONARD WILLIAM BAUGH represents one of the oldest families of Union Township, Tippecanoe County. Both he and his father were born on the farm which he now occupies, located three miles southwest of Shadeland.

His great-grandparents were Michael and Nancy (Owens) Baugh. Michael Baugh served as a soldier in the War of 1812. After the war he cleared up a tract of 100 acres of land in Pickaway County, Ohio, where he reared his family. He died at the age of thirty-one and his widow subsequently married John Weider, who brought the family to Tippecanoe County and settled on part of the land now occupied by Leonard William Baugh.

Mr. Baugh's grandparents were Leonard and Sarah A. (Talbert) Baugh. The father of Leonard William Baugh was Dr. Samuel Leonard Baugh, who was born in a log house on the Baugh homestead in Tippecanoe County, August 16, 1854. During his youth he was a farm worker, attended local schools, and in 1875 was graduated from Rush Medical College of Chicago. He had previously attended the academy at Stockwell. For a time he was associated in practice with Doctor Simerson at Romney, Indiana. Dr. Samuel Leonard Baugh married Angie Hawkins, a daughter of William and Hannah (Hollingsworth) Hawkins. Angie Hawkins was born in Butler County, Ohio, in 1857, and a year later her parents moved to Tippecanoe County. Doctor Baugh and wife had three children: Frank, deceased; Etheridge, who married Clara Binford and has four children, named Etheridge Jr., Harold, Bernice and Mildred; and Leonard William.

Leonard William Baugh was born on the home farm February 8, 1879. He was educated in the common schools, spent one year in school at Lafayette, and as a youth left home and for one year was a range rider and cowboy in Colorado. After his return to Indiana he married Minnie Davis, of Odell, in 1900. Later, in April, 1928, Mr. Baugh married Aurelia Jenssen, daughter of John and Doris (Jeppe) Jenssen. Her father was born in Toledo, Ohio, of German parentage. He was a cabinet maker by trade and a furniture dealer. All the Jenssen children, eight in number, were reared in Ohio. Mrs. Baugh attended school at Toledo, graduated from high school, also attended Toledo University, and for two years she lived at Indianapolis.

After his marriage Mr. Baugh was in the restaurant and bakery business at Wingate, Indiana. Leaving that he returned to the home farm for six years, later located at Lafayette, where he conducted a loan business, bought and sold and shipped stock to New Orleans and Porto Rico. For four years he was associated with some friends in the real estate business in Florida. However, his chief activities over a period of years have been on his farm in Union Township. He owns 333 acres and has another farm of 160 acres.

Mr. Baugh has been a member of the township advisory board. He is a member of the Masonic Lodge.

ARTHUR D. SULLINS is general manager and superintendent of the Tippecanoe County Infirmary. He was appointed to that position on merit, and has served there consecutively for many years, having made this one of the model institutions of the kind in Indiana. The County Infirmary was established in 1875. The farm comprises 240 acres.

Mr. Sullins was born at West Point, Tippecanoe County, Indiana, February 22, 1881, son of J. M. and Catherine (Swaynie) Sullins. The Sullins family came from Kentucky, first locating at Lebanon in Boone County. J. M. Sullins enlisted as a soldier in the Civil war with the Tenth Indiana Infantry. He was the father of three children: Imogene, deceased; Ethel, wife of C. H. Wilkerson; and Arthur D.

Arthur D. Sullins attended the Centennial School at Lafayette, completed his high school work in Lafayette, and his experience since leaving school has brought him unusual opportunities in a business way. For several years he worked on a fruit farm. He also spent four years in Chicago with the Mandel Brothers Company, and had made rapid advancement, being manager of the furniture warehouse when he resigned.

While in Chicago he met and married another employee of the Mandel Company, Miss Anna B. Hyland. They were married February 8, 1908. Her parents were J. M. and Catherine (Tiernan) Hyland, who were born in Iowa and moved to Chicago, where Mrs. Sullins finished her schooling. She was left an orphan at an early age and was reared by her aunt, Nora Hyland. After leaving Iowa she went to Chicago and was with Mandel Brothers until her marriage. Mr. and Mrs. Sullins on coming to Indiana lived on a farm for ten years. They had the misfortune to lose both of their children in very early life, and perhaps for that reason both of them have taken the greater interest in their respective tasks as superintendent and matron

of the institution which they have directed for the past fifteen years, Mr. Sullins having been twice reappointed to office. The institution is now filled to capacity, having over a hundred inmates, thirty-eight of whom are women. Besides the Home and other provisions for the care of these unfortunate people Mr. Sullins conducts a model stock farm, having herds of pure bred Shorthorn cattle, Chester white hogs and flocks of Plymouth Rock chickens.

He is president of the Kiwanis Club and chairman of the agricultural committee of the State Kiwanis. He is a Scottish Rite Mason and Shriner, having been made a Mason at Battle Ground. Both he and his wife are members of the Eastern Star and White Shrine. They are affiliated with the Baptist Church and are members of the Grange, and Mr. Sullins is a charter member of the West Lafayette Country Club.

HON. LEMUEL W. ROYSE, of Warsaw, is one of the oldest active members of the Indiana bar, having to his credit a continuous service in private practice or on the bench of fifty-six years.

Judge Royse is one of the oldest living native sons of Kosciusko County. He was born on a farm in Washington Township, January 19, 1848. His father, George W. A. Royse, and his mother, Nancy Chaplain, were New Englanders, his father born in New Hampshire and his mother in Vermont. When young people they went West to Ohio, where they met and married, and after their marriage came to Indiana and were among the first to clear away the timber and establish a home in Kosciusko County.

It was on a farm still marked by many evidences of the frontier epoch that Judge Royse grew to manhood. His education was acquired in the district schools, but more important in the development of his mind was the reading of books at home. While farming and teaching in country schools he decided to become a lawyer. Having mastered other subjects at home he began the reading of law books, and later for two years continued his studies and had some opportunities for actual contacts with the life of a lawyer in a private law office in Warsaw. In 1873 he was admitted to the bar, and the following year began his career as a practicing attorney at Warsaw. That city has been his home and the center of his career as a lawyer. Public honors soon came to him. In 1876 he was elected prosecuting attorney of Kosciusko County, serving two years. In 1885 he was chosen mayor of Warsaw, and that office he filled six years. In 1894 he was elected a member of Congress from his district, and was reelected in 1896, serving during the first two years of the McKinley administration. For over a quarter of a century Judge Royse has given the benefit of his legal abilities and his mature experience with men and affairs to the bench of the Kosciusko Circuit Court. In 1904 he was appointed judge of this court, serving until 1908.

Then, in 1920, he was elected judge of the same court and in 1926 was reelected.

Judge Royse is a stockholder and director of the State Bank of Warsaw and at one time was president of the bank. He is a Republican, a member of the Independent Order of Odd Fellows, Knights of Pythias, Improved Order of Red Men, B. P. O. Elks, is a member of the Warsaw Rotary Club and the Country Club, and is a Presbyterian.

He married at Hillsdale, Michigan, July 10, 1883, Miss Isabelle McIntyre. The only child born to their marriage, a son named James, died in infancy.

CHARLES W. FUNK, farmer and stock man of Tippecanoe County, is an Indiana citizen whose good judgment has been shown in his private business and in his good citizenship. Mr. Funk owns a farm of 150 acres at Stockwell in Lauramie Township. He is the township trustee.

Mr. Funk was born in this township July 14, 1889, son of Samuel and Mary (Wells) Funk. His father was also a well-to-do farmer and stock man, and both he and his wife are buried in the local cemetery. The Wells family came to Indiana in pioneer times.

Charles W. Funk attended school at Harvey, completed his high school course at Stockwell, and in 1913 was graduated from Purdue University. He has been accustomed to farm work from boyhood, and he secured a liberal education with a view to special fitness for farming. Since the death of his father he has developed the excellent estate which he now owns and occupies.

Mr. Funk married in 1924 Arba Waters, widow of E. Bush. Her two children by her first marriage are E. W. Bush, of New York, and Henry Wayne Bush. Mrs. Funk is a member of the Methodist Episcopal Church. After graduating from high school she took a special music course at Indianapolis.

GEORGE B. HAWTHORNE, one of the outstanding stock raisers of Tippecanoe County, whose home is in Jackson Township, was born in that township in 1852. His long life of fore-score years has been notable in experience and in accumulated benefits to his family, his friends and his community.

Mr. Hawthorne's parents were John Hawthorne and Jane Byrnes. They were married in County Cavan, Ireland, in 1850 and came to America on their wedding trip. When they arrived in Lafayette, Indiana, they were undecided as to their exact location. A Methodist minister brought them in contact with a prominent pioneer of Tippecanoe County, Jesse Meharry, who persuaded them to go home with him, promising Mrs. Jane Hawthorne work in his home while John Hawthorne hired out to his brother, Thomas Meharry. This was the beginning of the friendship between the Hawthorne and Meharry families which has subsequently been given additional bonds by marriage and other ties. Mr. George B. Hawthorne has always affectionately referred to

Jesse Mehary as "Uncle Jesse." John Hawthorne by his industry had accumulated some capital with a view to becoming an independent farmer. However, a tragic accident intervened before he was able to realize his ambition. While driving a cow which he had recently purchased the animal broke away and started back home. In endeavoring to overtake and turn the cow back John Hawthorne's horse tripped over the cow and turned a somersault. He was thrown off and never regained consciousness. He died early on the morning of September 22, 1854.

"Uncle Jesse" became the administrator of John Hawthorne's estate. John Hawthorne had accumulated $1200. With this money "Uncle Jesse" bought eighty acres of land adjoining G. N. Meharry's farm, and he continued to superintend Mrs. Jane Hawthorne's business for several years. In 1862 Mrs. Jane Hawthorne was married to Henry Mitchell. She died May 25, 1864. She left two sons, George B., who was two and a half years old when his father died, and Jesse, who was only six months of age. After the death of their mother these boys consented to remain with their mother's eighty acres. Thus George B. they should help him pay for the farm he had bought in Warren County, Indiana, and on reaching their majority they would be deeded their mother's eighty aces. Thus George B. Hawthorne on reaching his majority had forty acres of land as his capital.

Mr. George B. Hawthorne was educated in the old Shawnee Academy and also attended DePauw University. On July 23, 1873, on reaching his twenty-first birthday, he went to live with his "Uncle Jesse," for whom he worked during the summer months at nineteen dollars a month. During the winter he attended the Shawnee Academy and the college at Greencastle and in 1877 he accepted the offer to teach in the Jackson Township school. On August 24, 1879, he married Lettie Mary Meharry. After his marriage he taught in the Shawnee Academy and at the end of the school year began housekeeping on the George E. Meharry farm. In the fall of 1880 "Uncle Jesse" insisted that George B. Hawthorne and his brother Jesse should buy the Meharry farm, which they did, paying the three thousand dollars which they had received for their own eighty acres. "Uncle Jesse" Meharry died in 1881, and out of gratitude for the kindness the brothers had shown him in nursing him through his last illness he remitted part of the purchase price. Thus for fully·half a century Mr. George B. Hawthorne has been established in the community where he still resides. He has enjoyed a great success as a stock raiser, specializing in Belgian horses, Aberdeen-Angus cattle, Hampshire hogs, Shropshire sheep and Plymouth Rock chickens.

Mr. Hawthorne is a member of the Knights of Pythias Lodge at New Richmond, the Horse Thief Protective Association, and has long been prominent in the Methodist Episcopal Church, serving as superintendent of the Sunday School since 1878 and also as teacher of the Bible Class. He is a Republican and served as ditch commissioner and as township trustee.

Mr. and Mrs. Hawthorne had a family of six children. Lee B. married Mary Rickett and has a daughter, Mary L., who is the wife of Richard Nelson, and they have a son, Richard Nelson II. Ferd M. Hawthorne married Elsie Wallace and has a daughter, Elizabeth. Glenn I. Hawthorne married Grace Wilson and has a daughter, Maxine. David Earl Hawthorne, who was with the Medical Corps during the World war, married Lillian Lee. Elma F. Hawthorne, now deceased, was a graduate of DePauw University. The daughter Jessie A., also deceased, had completed a high school education.

JOHN P. FORESMAN, former county auditor of Tippecanoe County, has spent his active life as a farmer in Union Township, his home being about two miles southeast of Shadeland. Mr. Foresman has been known for many of his activities in a public way, and especially as a prominent horseman.

Mr. Foresman was born on the farm where he now resides, October 3, 1866, son of Bennett and Mary (Groce) Foresman, and a descendant of William Foresman, who was a Virginia soldier in the War of the Revolution. Mr. Foresman is descended from another William Foresman, son of the Revolutionary veteran. This William was born in Hardy County, in what is now West Virginia, and moved west with his family to Circleville, Ohio. The grandparents of John P. Foresman were Phillip and Eliza (Bennett) Foresman. Phillip Foresman was born in Circleville, Ohio, and became prominent in politics, at one time representing his county in the Ohio Legislature. Bennett Foresman was born in Tippecanoe County, Indiana, but when he was about four years of age his parents moved back to Ohio, to Circleville, Pickaway County. He attended school at Circleville and from the age of sixteen was on his own responsibility. He soon returned to Indiana, and became a well-to-do farmer of Tippecanoe County. At one time he was county treasurer and was an active member of the Presbyterian Church. He and his wife had two children, John P. and William B. William B. Foresman married Ann Kennedy and has three children, Mary, Gloria and William.

John P. Foresman was educated in country schools and the city schools at Lafayette, and during 1889 was a student in Purdue University. He has made a business of farming, which he has followed actively for over forty years.

Mr. Foresman married in December, 1894, Miss Clara Kurtz, daughter of Charles and Mary (Ruger) Kurtz. Her father came from Bavaria, Germany, and was a packer, stock buyer and merchant. Of the four children of Mr. and Mrs. Foresman the oldest was Edward, who died in training camp while enrolled as a soldier at Purdue University. The second child, Mary E., is also deceased. Helen L. is the wife of W. Johnson. The only surviving son is William K. Foresman, who attended grade and high school at Lafayette, and graduated from Purdue University in 1930.

Mr. Foresman has for many years been one of the most influential Democrats in Tippecanoe County. He served on the advisory township board and occupied the office of county auditor four years, during 1907-10. His hobby is the raising of harness horses. One animal raised on his farm and which had a record of participation in 152 races in different parts of the country was Checkers, who made a mark of 2:06¼ and in every race shared in the money.

WILLIAM T. BAILEY, Indianapolis lawyer and philanthropist, was born at Decatur, Illinois, September 16, 1876, next to the youngest in a large family of eleven children, whose parents were Alfred S. and Mary M. (Taylor) Bailey. His father was a native of Virginia and for many years in the bakery and confectionery business at Decatur. He was a giant in strength and physique, an advocate of fair and honest dealings among men and was frequently called upon to adjust disputes and difficulties in his neighborhood. He died in 1895. His wife, Mary M. Taylor, was born at Salem, near Decatur, Illinois, and her parents were close neighbors of the Lincoln family. As a girl she knew Abraham Lincoln and her parents, expert coat makers, made the coat worn by Lincoln on one of his first public appearances at Springfield. Mrs. Mary Bailey is remembered as a woman of exceptionally cheerful and happy disposition, helpful to all who needed her help. She was a lover of nature, and, being blessed with wonderful health, spent much of her time raising garden products and flowers. She died in 1918, in her eighty-first year.

William T. Bailey attended school at Decatur but since the age of fourteen has been self supporting. He came to Indianapolis when he was nineteen, with a view to studying law. Not having the money to carry out those plans immediately, he was, on recommendation of Mayor Thomas Taggart, appointed a member of the police department at the age of twenty-one. His work as a police officer was of an efficiency that reflected credit upon the entire organization. In the meantime he was studying law at every period of leisure, in the office of Charles W. Moores, and later in the Indiana Law School, where he graduated with honorable mention in 1905. In May of that year he resigned from the police department to join William E. Clapham in practice. For many years Mr. Bailey has carried on a successful general law practice, with offices in the Indiana Trust Building.

Mr. Bailey early became associated with "the Great Indiana Commoner" Lew Shank and was a steadfast friend and admirer, and no one regretted the premature death of Mayor Shank more than Mr. Bailey. In January, 1922, when Mayor Shank entered upon his second term as mayor, he selected Mr. Bailey as a member of the city's law department. The services he rendered in this capacity and in other ways as a member of the Mayor's personal staff constitute perhaps the culmination of Mr. Bailey's career as a philanthropist and public worker. Mayor Shank's administration is remembered not only for its high standards in municipal administration but in its emphasis upon the humanitarian side, and in that respect Mr. Bailey was his invaluable coadjutor. He originated, perfected and successfully carried out a number of plans and projects for the relief of persons and families overtaken by misfortune. No resident of Indianapolis could have been ignorant of the great good accomplished by Mr. Bailey in his distribution of the Mayor Shank's Ready Relief Fund, which was in operation all through the four years of his second term. The fund was raised by what was designated as Mayor Shank's Valentine Ball, the first of these charity balls, netting the sum of over $6,500, with similar amounts raised in successive years. The distribution of this fund was a godsend to thousands of families victims of misfortune and disaster. The fund was distributed without red-tape or delay and without the overhead expense of many charitable funds, a hundred cents on the dollar being obtained in value in direct relief. Out of this fund homes burned out by fire were replenished, a month's rent paid in a new home, the stigma of a pauper burial of a child was many times obviated, shoes and glasses to enable children to attend school out of a poor home where the earnings were insufficient to supply these necessities, fuel and proper food provided in cases of sickness and distress, afflicted World war veterans relieved and helped into employment, and many other worthy causes administered to.

Mr. Bailey also organized and equipped the Police and Firemen's Band of Indianapolis, comprising fifty musicians, which Mayor Shank declared was "the biggest booster agency Indianapolis has." The band was maintained without expense to the tax payers and largely volunteer cooperation on the part of firemen or policemen, and also fifteen members of the band were representative of the city's industrial and commercial organizations whose services were contributed.

Mr. Bailey originated the idea and plan of "Greater Indianapolis Week," carried out in a public demonstration in August, 1925, in cooperation with the mercantile and industrial organizations of Indianapolis. Mr. Bailey in this connection produced an industrial and mercantile film known as "The Greater Indianapolis Film," depicting Indianapolis as the greatest inland industrial and mercantile center of the United States, with incidental views portraying the five hundred mile automobile race at the Speedway in 1924. In return for his efforts in producing the film business organizations financed tours of the band, and delegations that attended the World's Police Chiefs Convention at Montreal in 1924, resulting in the designation of Indianapolis as the site of the convention for 1925. During the tour the Indianapolis film was exhibited and the band gave concerts in twelve cities in Ohio, Pennsylvania, New York and Canada. Probably no other city in the country ever received so much desirable publicity as was given to Indianapolis during this trip.

Another well remembered project carried out by Mr. Bailey was the inauguration of a Christmas Cheer celebration in each of the thirty-two fire stations of Indianapolis. Each fire station was especially decorated, with an imitation chimney and fireplace at the foot of the brass pole down which the firemen slide in answer to a fire alarm and on appropriate occasions, and for the delight and edification of the children who had gathered, the firemen, dressed in Santa Claus costume, would slide down the chimney into the fireplace. These Christmas celebrations have since their origin in 1923 become an annual event.

Mr. Bailey married, November 16, 1896, Miss Eva Fesler, daughter of Thomas and Mary Fesler and member of one of the oldest and most respected families of Indianapolis. Mr. and Mrs. Bailey for many years have occupied a beautiful home at 5127 Central Avenue. It is one of the older homes in Indianapolis, with a reputation for open-handed hospitality that has been continued into the modern day. Mr. and Mrs. Bailey had no children of their own, but they have given home advantages and parental affection to a number of children. While looking after the children of their household they established an elaborate playground, and Mr. Bailey still takes pride and delight in maintaining the apparatus and the facilities of this playground for the children of the neighborhood.

This is a very brief and impartial sketch of a beloved Indianapolis citizen, known among his friends and admirers as "Bill" Bailey, a man tireless in good deeds, with a constant friendliness and kindliness and willing to cooperate at all times in doing good to others. One of his friends has said of him "He is always thinking for the good of the other fellow; he seems to get more real enjoyment out of life doing good for others than in accumulating wealth." One of his hobbies is raising flowers and garden produce to distribute among his friends and acquaintances. Also for twenty-five years he has been making scrap books of articles of news on every important subject, and this is a collection almost unique and of priceless value. But nothing has given him more satisfaction than the efforts he has put forth to alleviate and mitigate misery and destitution which seem to be inseparable from human existence. His activities as a philanthropist date back to those years when he was a patrolman on the force. He has often recalled the first work of this character he did. On a cold night in November, 1905, patroling his beat he found the mother of two children ill in their home, without fire and other necessities. Lew Shank was then engaged in the second hand furniture, storage and transfer business, and Mr.

Bailey perhaps then first learned the real depth of Shank's human sympathy. Mr. Shank furnished stove and fuel and with his own hands helped install it and light the fire. From that time until the death of Mr. Shank, on September 24, 1927, Mr. Bailey was in almost constant touch with him in his service to the masses. They worked together in their voluntary program of relief, and Mr. Bailey in almost countless cases used his professional skill to save the loss of property to the unfortunate or unprotected, and iron out legal entanglements where innocent and helpless people were involved. Mr. Bailey has always been a Republican. He is a member of Broad Ripple Lodge No. 643 A. F. & A. M., Lodge No. 56, Knights of Pythias, and many other organizations. He has always been blessed with wonderfully good health and great physical strength, and while he has been constant in intermediating in the troubles of others, he would find it difficult to recall any real worries of his own.

HON. JOHN B. COCKRUM, of Indianapolis, now acting as advisory counsel for the New York, Chicago & Saint Louis or Nickel Plate Railway, has rounded out over half a century of service as an Indiana lawyer and is one of the oldest railway attorneys in the state.

He was born at Oakland City, Indiana, September 12, 1857, son of Col. William M. and Lucretia (Harper) Cockrum. His grandparents were James W. and Juda (Barrett) Cockrum, who came from North Carolina. His grandfather was largely responsible for the establishment of the Oakland City Normal School. He was a man of wealth and extensive business interests, owning several boats on the Ohio River operating south to New Orleans, and was long prominent in steamboating circles. Col. William M. Cockrum was born at Oakland City, was reared and educated there and became a farmer. During the Civil war he organized Company F of the Forty-second Indiana Infantry, and was wounded at the battle of Chickamauga. He was captured and spent some time in Libby Prison, being finally exchanged at Camp Chase, Ohio. On rejoining the command he was in the Army of the Cumberland, under General Thomas. After the war he returned to Oakland City.

John B. Cockrum grew up with the invigorating discipline of a Southern Indiana farm, attending local schools, and at the age of nineteen entered the Cincinnati Law School. He was a classmate of former President Taft. He taught school three years and on April 15, 1879, was graduated from the law course and began his practice at Boonville, Indiana, with Charles W. Armstrong. Later they took in Judge Handy. On March 10, 1889, Mr. Cockrum was appointed by President Harrison assistant United States district attorney for Indiana and served during the four years of the Harrison administration.

Mr. Cockrum in 1893 became assistant general attorney for the Lake Erie & Western

Railway, later was made general attorney and general solicitor, and has been with the legal department of that division of what is now the Nickel Plate Railway system for over thirty-five years. He was general solicitor until he took over the nominal duties of advisory counsel, and is now living practically a retired life.

Mr. Cockrum married, January 2, 1880, Miss Fannie Bittrolff, and they have two children, Freda and Oatley B. Mr. Cockrum for many years was prominent in Masonry and Odd Fellowship, having attained the thirty-third supreme honorary degree in Scottish Rite Masonry and filled all of the offices of the Independent Order of Odd Fellows, including the position of Grand Sire, the highest office of the order. He is a member of the Indiana Loyal Legion.

ORA L. MCCAY, physician and surgeon, has spent his entire professional career in the Romney community of Tippecanoe County. Doctor McCay is an able man in his profession, a hard and conscientious worker, and his sincere interest in others has brought him hosts of loyal friends who admire his personal character as well as his professional ability.

Doctor McCay was born near Colfax, Indiana, November 19, 1879, son of Carter D. and Martha (Crose) McCay. His grandparents were William and Mary (Moore) McCay. William McCay was born in Pulaski County, Indiana, and was a doctor of veterinary surgery. He served as a soldier in the Union army during the Civil war and for many years was one of the outstanding citizens of Pulaski County. Carter D. McCay was born in Pulaski County, acquired his education there and spent his active life as a farmer. He and his wife are buried in the Myntonie Cemetery in Randolph Township, Tippecanoe County. They were active members of the Christian Church. Doctor McCay was the oldest in a large family of nine children. Bessie is the wife of Augustus Martin. Carrie is the wife of Delhert McCormick, a farmer in Jackson Township. Flossie, deceased, was the wife of Walton Withrow, and left four children, Everett, Pauline, Ernest and Dorothy. Daisy, also deceased, married Charles Lamb and had three children, Clarence, Charles and Ruby. Otto married Mary Mikels. The seventh child is Arthur McCay. Lawrence married Grace Wills, and Bernard, the youngest, married Ruth Moore.

Ora L. McCay attended the Kennedy School in Wea Township, graduated from the Wea High School and then spent some time working in a drug store at Lafayette. This experience fortified him in his resolution to study to be a doctor. He completed his professional preparation in Indiana University School of Medicine, graduating M.D. in 1904. The means to put him through medical college he derived chiefly from farm work during vacations. He had his interne experience in the Bobbs Dispensary at Indianapolis and then came direct to Romney, where he has steadily practiced his profession for over a quarter of a century.

He is a member of all the medical organizations and has interested himself in all matters connected with the general welfare and progress of his community. He is a member of the staff of one of the hospitals of Lafayette, and is president of the Tippecanoe County Medical Society, being the second doctor ever elected president of that society who lived outside the City of Lafayette. He is a member of Masonic Lodge No. 441 and is a Scottish Rite Mason and Shriner, also a past president of Tippecanoe County Past Masters Association in 1927. He is a member of the Methodist Episcopal Church.

Doctor McCay married in February, 1921, Miss Mildred Jenkins. They have one daughter, Jean.

Doctor McCay enlisted as a volunteer First Lieutenant March 15, 1917, and August 17, 1917, went to Fort Harrison, where he was assigned to a three months' relief expedition to Roumania and was on the Pacific Ocean, but on account of an armistice with Germany this expedition was recalled. Doctor McCay came back to San Francisco and served in the Letterman General Hospital and was there until January, 1918, and was next at Camp Pike, Arkansas, where he served nine and one-half months and was assistant chief of medical service. He was ordered overseas and was ready to sail when the armistice was signed. He was at Camp Mead, Maryland, was sent to Walter Reed Hospital at Washington, D. C., the largest general hospital in the United States, served five months and then entered the Reserves as a major and still holds his major's commission in the Medical Reserves, subject to call at any time. After the war Doctor McCay came to Romney, Indiana.

DONALD HARPHAM, optometrist, whose skill and diagnosis and treatment have brought him a large clientage at his offices in Wabash, is a native of Nebraska, but is a member of an old family of Northern Indiana.

He was born in Nebraska January 20, 1888. His father, Samuel Harpham, was born in Indiana. His grandfather, John Harpham, was a native of England and came to Indiana about 1842, taking up a homestead in Steuben County. He had to clear away the timber in order to get room for his crops, and he lived there and followed farming the rest of his years. Samuel Harpham was a steel worker and a farmer. He married Phoebe Wolf, a native of Ohio.

Dr. Donald Harpham is one of five children. He was brought to Indiana when a child, attended grade school at Hudson and high school at Ashley. After a course in the Tri-State Normal College at Angola and a short course in the State Normal at Terre Haute he was prepared for the profession of educator. However, he went on to develop his particular talents in music at Bucknell University in Pennsylvania.

With the outbreak of the World war he enlisted in the One Hundred Third Engineers, with the Twenty-eighth Division, on June 20,

1917, went to France, saw active service over-seas, and was finally mustered out at Camp Taylor, Kentucky, in May, 1919.

It was after the war that Doctor Harpham turned his attention to the science of op-tometry. He studied at the Northern Illinois College of Optometry and Otology, graduat-ing in 1921 with the degree Opt. D. Doctor Harpham for two years practiced at Sault Ste. Marie, Michigan, and in 1923 located at Wabash. His experience has given him much skill in treating and diagnosing all the ail-ments and weaknesses of the eye. A funda-mental part of his treatment is governed by the principles of physio-therapy. Doctor Har-pham has assembled an interesting array of special apparatus for his work and has a well equipped suite of offices in the Bradley Block, at the corner of Miami and Market streets in Wabash. He also has a laboratory where he grinds lenses.

Doctor Harpham married Mary E. Bish, a native of Montpelier, Indiana. Doctor Har-pham is a member of the Indiana Association of Optometrists, and has been service officer in the local post of the American Legion. He is a member of Hiawatha Lodge No. 528 of the Masonic fraternity at Hudson.

JOHN L. CUTRELL, whose home is four miles east of Shawnee Mound in Jackson Township, Tippecanoe County, has earned and in every way deserves the abundant esteem and respect in which he is held in his community. Hard work and perseverance have brought him along the way of substantial prosperity, repre-sented in the ownership of a splendid farm of 400 acres.

Mr. Cutrell was born March 16, 1858, in North Carolina. He was the oldest of the children of Lewis and Edith (Outland) Cutrell, who the following year, in 1859, left North Carolina and came north to Indiana. The Cut-rell family were Quakers but belonged to what were known as "Fighting Stock." His great-great-grandfather Cutrell was a Carolina sol-dier in the war for independence, being among the hardy mountaineers who followed Sumter, Marion Pickens, Lee and others in defeating every effort of the British to overawe the Carolinas. This Revolutionary ancestor also fought in the War of 1812, being with General Andrew Jackson at the battle of New Orleans. Lewis Cutrell on bringing his family to Indi-ana settled first in Hamilton County and later in Tippecanoe County. He had practically no capital when he came to this state. As a renter he acquired the money to make his first purchase of land in Jackson Township. He was always a staunch Quaker and a man of much influence in his community. He was buried in the Farmers Insurance Cemetery in Union Township, Tippecanoe County. There were six children: John L.; Micajah, who mar-ried Miss Hollingsworth; William, who mar-ried Lilly Simons; Al, who married Etta But-ler; Calvin, who married Eva Stanley; and Mary, wife of E. J. Wiles.

John L. Cutrell had his first educational advantages in Hamilton County, and his last school was the Farmers Insurance School in Union Township, Tippecanoe County. At the age of twenty-one he put his early training to account when he hired out to work at monthly wages. After a year he rented some land, and by his early years of industry and thrift gradually got together the farm which he owns today. Mr. Cutrell has always been a valuable factor in his community. He is a trustee of the Methodist Episcopal Church and a member of the Knights of Pythias.

He married in 1885 Miss Anna Rubottom, who is now deceased. His only daughter was Stella, dead, wife of George Crowder. Mr. and Mrs. Crowder had a son, Harold, attend-ing school.

JAMES EDWIN MCDONALD, business manager of the *Marion Leader-Tribune*, was born with an interest in newspaper work and politics, both his father and grandfather having achieved distinction in the field of Indiana journalism.

His grandfather was Isaac B. McDonald, a native of Virginia, whose parents took him to Darke County, Ohio, and later to Columbia City, Indiana. Isaac B. McDonald was one of the founders of the *Fort Wayne Journal-Gazette*. He was one of the first men from Columbia City to enlist for service in the Civil war, joining Company E of the Seven-teenth Indiana Volunteers as a private. He was mustered out with the rank of colonel. A richly ornamented sword and scabbard pre-sented to him at the close of the war by the surviving members of his command is now owned by his grandson at Marion. Isaac B. McDonald was elected a member of the State Senate, serving during the Governor Durbin administration, and was author of the bill that resulted in the erection of the Soldiers and Sailors Monument at Indianapolis, one of the most conspicuous landmarks of the cap-ital.

Hon. James E. McDonald, son of Isaac B., devoted most of his active life to newspaper work. He was born at Columbia City in 1854, and died in 1913 and is buried at Ligonier. He was editor and publisher of several papers at Ligonier and for eight years was postmaster of that city. He enjoyed a well earned leader-ship in Democratic politics in Indiana. He served in the State Senate during the '90s, was closely affiliated with the late Tom Tag-gart in state politics and was one of the political sponsors of Thomas Marshall, who later became governor of Indiana and vice president of the United States. James E. McDonald was for twelve years president of the State Board of Agriculture and was hold-ing that office at the time of his death. He married Laura Arminda Brand, of Columbia City. She was born in 1862 and lives at Ligonier.

Her son, James Edwin McDonald, was born at Ligonier, January 25, 1896. He attended

George L. Mackintosh.

common schools in his native city, graduated in 1913 from the Hyde Park High School of Chicago, and finished his education in the liberal arts department of the University of Chicago. Mr. McDonald had three years of metropolitan experience as a reporter on the *Chicago American*. He resigned to come to Marion, and his first connection with the *Leader-Tribune* was as a reporter. After three years he was made circulation manager, and for two years was advertising manager and assistant business manager. He has been general manager since 1926. Mr. McDonald is a stockholder in the Spencer Cardinal Furniture Manufacturing Company of Marion, is a stockholder in the *Ligonier Weekly Banner*, and is president of the Marion broadcasting station WJAK. Like his father and grandfather he is a staunch Democrat. He is president of the Marion Board of Police Commissioners, is a past president of the Rotary Club, vice president of the Mecca Club, director of the Marion Association of Commerce, and is affiliated with the Masonic fraternity and B. P. O. Elks. His pastime is golf, which he plays on the links of the Marion Country Club. He is a member of the Episcopal Church.

Mr. McDonald married Marian Elizabeth Weaver, June 10, 1915, at Marion. She was born in that city, daughter of Walter Weaver. They have four children: James E. III, born at Marion May 15, 1916; Ruth Virginia, born November 18, 1918; Richard Burk, born April 13, 1926; and Robert Thomas, born August 1, 1928. The two older children are students in the Marion schools.

The *Marion Leader-Tribune* has a high rating in Indiana journalism and is a very successful publication from a business standpoint. In its history it represents a number of Marion newspaper enterprises which in their turn were edited and published by some of the best known newspaper men in the state. The most remote ancestor of the present paper was the *Marion Democrat*, a weekly started in the early '60s by Elijah Vaughn and two of his brothers. Two years later Mr. Kitch bought out the Vaughns, was manager of the *Democrat* until 1873, when it was sold to L. A. and J. A. Wallace. L. A. Wallace subsequently became sole owner, editor, press man and general manager. At that time the paper was printed on an old Washington hand press, one side at a time, the office being located on the west side of the square. The *Democrat* was enjoying an unusual degree of prosperity when, in 1875, the office and plant was destroyed by fire. Citizens came forward with liberal subscriptions and a new outfit was purchased, and the *Democrat* soon reappeared. On February 6, 1889, the first issue of the *Marion Daily Democrat* was printed. The publishers were L. A. Wallace and C. P. Kile. The daily issue has been continued without missing a single issue for over forty years. Soon after the starting of the Daily the publication office was moved to the Shon Building and soon afterward to 514 South Adams Street. In September, 1889, the *Democrat* was sold to W. J.

Houck and T. W. Overman, who changed the name to the *Marion Leader*. Mr. Overman sold his interest to A. T. Wright, who in turn, in July, 1891, sold to W. J. Houck and J. H. Schrack. Later William B. Westlake became a partner and eventually bought out the other members and continued the publication of the *Leader* until it was purchased by a stock company, with Mr. E. H. Johnson as president.

In the meantime the *Leader* had taken over the old *Morning News*, established in 1894, with L. A. Wallace as editor, Walter Ford, city editor, and J. E. Cary, business manager. The *Morning News* was later acquired by Charles Bundy and Bob Mansfield, and they took over the *Daily Bulletin*, which had been established in 1900 by Harley Arnold, William Clifford, Jesse Harvey and Miss Cora Mendenhall. Linotype machines were first used in the *Leader* office in June, 1899.

In January, 1901, the *Marion Tribune* was started, with E. L. Goldthaite as business manager, Strickland W. Gillilan, editor, later famous for his humorous short stories and verse, and the reporters on the *Tribune* were Frank Heaton and Elbert Eward. The office was in the same building now occupied by the *Leader-Tribune*. When the *Leader* moved its presses to the office of the *Tribune* it consolidated with the *Tribune* and since then Marion has had the *Leader-Tribune* as its leading Democratic newspaper, and carrying on from the foundations of the old *Democrat*, the *News*, *Bulletin* and *Tribune*.

GEORGE LEWIS MACKINTOSH, D. D., A. M., LL. D., former president of Wabash College, is an alumnus of that old and honored institution of higher learning in Indiana.

Doctor Mackintosh was born in Guysboro County, Nova Scotia, January 1, 1860, and received his early educational advantages in his native country, attending the New Glasgow Academy. His parents were John and Elizabeth (Bruce) Mackintosh. In the fall of 1878 he came to Crawfordsville and enrolled as a student in the preparatory department of Wabash College, graduating therefrom in 1884, with the degree of Bachelor of Arts. For one year he served as principal of the high school at Lawrenceburg, Indiana, and then began the study of theology in Lane Theological Seminary, at Cincinnati, Ohio. He was ordained in 1887, and for the following eighteen years he gave his time and talents to the service of the ministry. His first charge was at Winamac in Pulaski County, where he remained four years, during which time, and largely through his personal work and efforts, the handsome new church edifice was erected. He then accepted the pastorate of the Fourth Presbyterian Church in Indianapolis, continuing his labors there until 1906.

In 1907 he accepted the call to the presidency of Wabash College, where, in addition to his executive duties, he held the chair of professor of philosophy. He resigned as president in 1926, but continues to make his home at Crawfordsville. Wooster College conferred upon him the degree of Doctor of Divinity, and he received from Hanover College the degree of LL. D.

Doctor Mackintosh married, in 1902, Miss Bertha Stone, of Montreat, North Carolina. She died in 1906, leaving a son, Roderick Bruce, who died at the age of sixteen years. In 1912 Doctor Mackintosh was united in marriage with Miss Jean Mitchell, of Lafayette, Indiana. They have three sons and three daughters: Marjorie Miner, Duncan, John Lewis, William Marshall, Jean Argyll and Margot Ellen. Mrs. Mackintosh is a daughter of John B. and Josephine (Miner) Mitchell. She is a graduate of the University of Michigan. Her mother graduated from the medical department of the same university in 1901, and successfully practiced her profession at Lafayette for many years.

CHARLES A. McCORKLE is one of the prosperous farm owners of Jackson Township, Tippecanoe County. Mr. McCorkle has a place of about 368 acres, all good land, well improved and constituting a property which is often pointed out as a model of good agricultural management.

Mr. McCorkle was born in Montgomery County, Indiana, July 2, 1865, son of Andrew Calvan and Polly Ann (Meharry) McCorkle. His paternal grandparents were Andrew and Mary (Gooding) McCorkle. Andrew McCorkle was born in Tazewell County, Virginia, and on coming west traveled overland through Wheeling, West Virginia, to Ross County, Ohio, and after a brief term spent there came on to Indiana in 1828. Andrew McCorkle's father was also named Andrew, and was a soldier in the War of the Revolution. Andrew Calvan McCorkle was born in Putnam County, Indiana, in 1838. He spent his active life as a farmer and stock man. His early education was acquired in country schools and he lived at home until his marriage, at which time he moved to Tippecanoe County and settled on what has long been known as the McCorkle homestead in Jackson Township. He was always interested in church, in community affairs, and at one time was chosen to represent the county in the Indiana State Legislature. During the Civil war he served as a Union soldier in the Army of the Cumberland. He and his wife are buried in the Meharry Cemetery. There were two children, John W. and Charles A. John W. married Carrie Devore and has three children, named Alice, Mildred and Howard.

Charles A. McCorkle grew up at the McCorkle homestead and had better than ordinary educational opportunities. He attended the Shawnee Mound Academy, spent one year in DePauw University and two years in Purdue University. While getting his higher education he worked on the home farm, and he has put in more than forty years as a practical farmer and stock man. Successful in his work, he has exercised a good influence in his community. He and his family are active members of the Methodist Episcopal Church. He is a Scottish Rite Mason and Shriner, member of the Eastern Star, and also belongs to the Knights of Pythias. Mr. McCorkle has traveled extensively.

He married in 1891 Miss Frances M. Bittle, daughter of Silas and Fannie (Devore) Bittle. Their family consists of four children. The son John R. married Miss Wilson and has three children, named Patricia, Charles and Don. The other children are Charles L., Bernice A. and Andrew Francis.

FRANK E. HOOVER is owner of the Hoover Brothers Furniture Company at Columbus, the largest establishment of its kind in Bartholomew County, operating a complete home furnishing establishment.

Mr. Hoover has been in the furniture business since early boyhood. He was born at Lima, Ohio, May 15, 1878, son of John and Bernadine Hoover. His father was a railroad man. Frank E. Hoover attended school only until he was thirteen years of age. He is one of five sons, all of whom have been in the furniture business and the older brothers still carry on as retail dealers at Lima, Ohio. Frank E. Hoover went to work in the store of his brothers, learned the business by association with every department and every form of work. In 1914 he bought two furniture stores at Columbus, one conducted under the name of A. Kimball and the other the Hilger & Barrett store. These places of business were consolidated, and since then it has been conducted by the Hoover Brothers Furniture Company, at 601-605 Washington Street. The store has 14,000 square feet of floor space, carries a stock of goods valued at about $35,000, including all grades of upholstered furniture, rugs, stoves and other equipment.

Mr. Hoover married Miss Myrtle May Townsend, of Blackford County, Indiana. They have one daughter, Bettie Jane, attending school at Columbus. Mr. Hoover is one of the enterprising business men of Columbus, is a past director of the Chamber of Commerce, a past president of the Retail Merchants Association. He has filled the office of treasurer in the Knights of Columbus, is a member of the B. P. O. Elks and Knights of the Maccabees, and during the World war was a captain in the teams for the sale of Liberty Bonds and also aided in the Red Cross and War Stamp drives.

JAMES F. WALLACE, retired farmer and stock raiser, has lived all his life on one farm and in one locality in Jackson Township of Tippecanoe County. His farm there, located two miles east of Shawnee Mound, was his birthplace. He was born there November 23, 1860. Mr. Wallace has fully earned the respect and esteem of his community through his successful management, his public spirit and his willingness to do for others.

Mr Wallace is a son of Hugh and Jane (Brooks) Wallace and is related to the family of General Lew Wallace, the great Indiana soldier and author. Mr. Wallace's parents

Martin W. Yerne M.D.

were born in Ireland and were married in that country, where two of their children were born. Altogether they had ten children: Mary, deceased, wife of John Greenburg; Elizabeth, deceased wife of William Francis; Aaron and John W., both deceased; Belle, wife of Charles Williamson; James F.; Ella, deceased wife of William White; and the other three children died in infancy. After coming to this country Hugh Wallace lived for two years in New Jersey. In 1849 he came to Tippecanoe County, Indiana. Here he found work among members of the Meharry family until he had earned enough to make a start in buying land and establishing a home of his own. He took much interest in church and Sunday school and other community affairs and was always a devout Methodist. He was buried in Wheeler Cemetery in Jackson Township.

James F. Wallace while a boy attended the Locust Grove School, the Shawnee School and the Sugar Grove School, and completed his education in the National Normal University at Lebanon, Ohio. From early youth he worked on the home farm, and for over forty years he devoted his time and energies to the management of this property, which comprises 420 acres of land. Mr. Wallace married in 1886 Martha Peed. They have one child, Lura, wife of Claude Hedworth. Mr. and Mrs. Hedworth have two children, Lawrence and James A. Lura Wallace is a graduate of DePauw Univeristy at Greencastle.

Mr. James F. Wallace has traveled extensively, and at one time owned considerable land in Texas. He is a Mason, member of the Mystic Shrine, the Independent Order of Odd Fellows, the Methodist Episcopal Church, and is interested in all civic matters and is quite prominent in Tippecanoe County politics.

DR. MARTIN WASHINGTON YENCER, a highly esteemed physician and surgeon of the City of Richmond and ex-representative from Wayne County in the Indiana Legislature, first beheld the light of · day near Lancaster, Fairfield County, Ohio, December 27, 1871. He is of Swiss and German descent. His paternal grandfather, Joseph Yencer, was born in Basel, Switzerland, and when nineteen years old, in company with two of his comrades, about the year 1830, sailed for the United States. He located in Fairfield County, Ohio, one of his comrades in Columbus, Ohio, and the other continued his journey to the westward and was never heard from again. Joseph Yencer, Sr., was a cooper and farmer by trade, having been a pioneer settler of Fairfield County, Ohio. United in marriage with Miss Catherine Gazell, of an old pioneer family of Fairfield County, in the early part of the eighteenth century. With this union there was born three sons and three daughters to crown the little log cabin at Dumontville, Ohio. All three sons represented their state as loyal soldiers of the Union in the great Civil war of 1861-65. Joseph Yencer, Jr., the father of Doctor Yencer, was born in Fairfield County, Ohio, November 16, 1843, and at the age of seventeen

enlisted as a private in the Seventeenth Ohio Infantry, Army of the Cumberland, with which he served for three years in the Civil war. This regiment was organized at Camp Dennison, in September, 1861, to serve three years, first participating in the Wild Cat fight in Kentucky, and next in the siege of Corinth, during which it was engaged in several severe skirmishes. The regiment went into the battle line on the Stone's River field and with its brigade charged the Confederate General Hanson's brigade, driving it in confusion, killing its general and some 150 of the rank and file. It moved with its brigade in the Tullahoma campaign, and. at Hoover's Gap charged the Seventeenth Tennessee Confederate regiment, strongly posted in a belt of woods, driving it back and occupying the position. At the battle of Chickamauga the regiment was on the extreme right of the center, and when General Wood's division was double-quicked out of the line, the gap left exposed the right flank of the regiment, the Confederates opened fire both on the right flank and in front, causing it to lose heavily and scattering the men in confusion. During this day of battle of Chickamauga, Mr. Yencer, Jr., considered this being the most bloody conflict of more than seventeen battles he had participated in during the Civil war. His brave and fearless Captain Rickets in the height of the battle encouraging his men to stand their ground, was instantly killed by his side and one out of every three was killed or wounded in this day's battle. At Missionary Ridge, though in the rear line at the start, the regiment was in the front when the top of the hill was gained. It took only a subordinate part in the heavy skirmishing at Rocky Face Ridge, but bore its full share in the battle of Resaca. At the battle of Resaca he was left on the field of battle for dead. A span ball struck his metal buckle on his belt and knocked him unconscious and in a few hours he again was among the living and found this span ball in his haversack at supper time. At Kenesaw Mountain the regiment suffered less than it had in previous actions of less importance, but the heat was so intense that many men were carried off, prostrated by sunstroke. In this engagement Mr. Yencer was wounded June 18, 1864, and this practically ended his military career, as he received an honorable discharge from the service soon thereafter. But he had participated in more than seventeen engagements. Upon his discharge from the service he returned to Fairfield County and devoted his attention to farming, in which he was engaged for a number of years, but during the past seventeen years he has conducted a farm implement establishment at Basil, Ohio. He was a member of the Grand Army of the Republic and of the Masonic order at Baltimore, Ohio. Mr. Yencer died April 3, 1931, and was given Masonic and military honors at the last rites.

Joseph Yencer, Jr., had two brothers who enlisted and served under the Union flag, Samuel and John. John being a volunteer in

President Lincoln's call for 75,000 volunteers in April, 1861, and served his country flag for four years that this Government of the United States of ours would live. All three brothers of this Swiss family were willing, yea, ready to sacrifice their lives that this Union should be united in one government— one nation and under one flag, the Stars and Stripes—the star-spangled banner.

The mother of Doctor Yencer, Minerva Jane (Kemmerer) Yencer, was born in Fairfield County, Ohio, June 27, 1847. She was the daughter of Josiah and Maria (Zeigler) Kemmerer. Josiah was born in Pennsylvania, an old pioneer of the Keystone State,. Maria Zeigler was born in Fairfield County, Ohio, her father and mother were the early settlers of Ohio in the seventeenth century. She died December 24, 1925, and of her union with Joseph Yencer there were born six children—four sons and two daughters. Milton E. resides on the old farm in Fairfield County, Ohio; Martin W. is he whose name initiates this sketch; Ada C. is the wife of Leo Burton, of Iowa; Sadie is the wife of W. A. Barr, of Cleveland, Ohio; Perry D. resides at home, and one brother, Samuel S., is deceased. The subject of this review received his elementary educational training in the schools of old District No. 1, Greenfield Township, Fairfield County, Ohio, and passed the first seventeen years of his life on the home farm. One of his teachers, Charles Williams, when Mr. Yencer was a student of the district school, was the grandson of a teacher who instructed such eminent men in their day as James G. Blaine, John Sherman and Gen. William Tecumseh Sherman at the old Fairfield County Academy. The old Fairfield County Academy then located near Lancaster, Ohio, in Greenfield Township, Fairfield County, is now extinct. The academy was abandoned some seventy years ago. Mr. Yencer also attended the high school at Baltimore, Ohio, the Ohio Normal College, Pleasantville, Ohio, and the Crawford Institute at Lancaster, and taught for two years in the common schools of Fairfield County. During the time that he was teaching he studied medicine with Dr. O. P. Driver, at Basil, Ohio, and in 1893 began the study of medicine and surgery at the Starling Medical College in Columbus, Ohio, now affiliated with the Ohio State University. Later he was a student in the medical department of the National Normal University, Lebanon, Ohio, in 1896 entered the senior class of the Central College of Physicians and Surgeons at Indianapolis, now affiliated with the Indiana University School of Medicine, and on March 24, 1897, he was graduated with the degree of Doctor of Medicine. He then immediately began the practice of his profession at Boston, Wayne County, Indiana, opening his office in September, 1897, successor of Doctor Evans, and remained in that place eleven years, leaving it to come to Richmond, in April, 1908. Here he has since been located at 22 North Fourteenth Street, Richmond, Indiana, and has built up a large and lucrative practice. He has always devoted his attention to general practice. Politically Doctor Yencer is associated with the Republican party, and in 1902 was nominated and elected as the state representative of Wayne County in the Sixty-third General Assembly of Indiana. In 1904 he was reelected as a member of the Sixty-fourth General Assembly, and upon this occasion received a majority of 3,852 votes, the largest ever given in Wayne County over a Democratic opponent. During his four years of service in the Legislature it was his pleasure to assist in the election of three men to the United States Senate—Charles W. Fairbanks, James A. Hemenway, and Albert J. Beveridge. As a member of the Indiana State Legislature, 1903 session, he was the first member to introduce a measure for the creation of a state highway commission for building the public highways and better roads for Indiana. One of the most important paramount measures was the House Concurrent Resolution for the upbuilding of the United States Navy, asking Congress to back the program of President Roosevelt for a better and bigger navy for future defense of the United States which was much needed during the World war in 1917. The House Concurrent Resolution was for maintenance of the mighty policy promulgated by President Monroe. In 1903 President Roosevelt was asking Congress for a mighty navy for future defense of the American Republic. In 1908 Doctor Yencer was a candidate in the primaries for the Republican nomination for Congress in the Sixth District of Indiana, to succeed Hon. James E. Watson who was congressman then of the the Sixth District, then the Republican candidate for governor of Indiana—against the Democratic nominee, Thomas R. Marshall. Marshall was elected governor of Indiana in 1908 over now United States Senator James E. Watson. At the age of twenty-one, in 1893, Mr. Yencer was honored by his community as a delegate in support of William McKinley for renomination for governor of Ohio, from his native County of Fairfield County, Ohio, and several times a Republican delegate to the Indiana State Republican Conventions. Fraternally, Doctor Yencer is admirably affiliated, being a Mason, which order he joined at the age of twenty-one years in Lodge 475, A. F. and A. M., Baltimore, Ohio. He has taken the Royal Arch degrees, Wayne Council No. 10, and is a member of Downey Lodge, No. 233, of Boston, Wayne County, his Royal Arch, King Solomon Chapter No. 4, membership being in Richmond. Now a member of Webb Lodge No. 24, A. F. and A. M. He is also a member of the Sons of Veterans, the Wayne County Medical Society, the Indiana State Medical Society, and a Fellow of the American Medical Association. He was a volunteer during the World war for service in the United States Army Medical Service Corps, authorized by the Council of National Defense, approved by the President of the United States—enrolled as a member on. October 8, 1918, by Newton D. Baker, secretary of war. As the armistice was signed on November 11, 1918, Doctor Yencer received his commission, but was not called to overseas service. Doctor Yencer is married to Jeannette May Hill, who was born at Muncton, New Brunswick, August 29, 1880, daughter of John T. and Eliza B. (Barclay) Hill, the former of whom was born at Wytheville, Virginia, August 13, 1848, and the latter at Bathurst, New Brunswick, March 25, 1853. The ancestors of Mr. Hill were early settlers in Virginia, and he has the honor of being a relative of Thomas Jefferson, the author of the Declaration of Independence and the third President of the United States. John Joseph, only child of Doctor and Mrs. Yencer, was born February 29, 1920, and thus has a distinct birthday observance only once in four years, he being now a student in the Richmond public schools.

HOMER KENDAL YORK has had an interesting career because of the fact that he started work at the age of fourteen, earned rapid promotions in responsibility and accumulated a great fund of expert knowledge regarding the automotive industry and all the factors pertaining to its development. Then came a period of wartime service, and after the war the Indiana Truck Corporation of Marion found him a highly valuable man and has given him repeated recognition of the importance of his work until he is now vice president of the corporation and head of its good roads department.

The Indiana Truck Corporation is the outgrowth of a company started in 1898 by Charles G. Barley and George C. Harwood. In 1909 the organization first started the production of motor trucks, and the business has steadily grown on a policy of putting out only a high grade product until the company now has a national and international reputation and is manufacturing several thousand trucks annually, using a plant covering fourteen acres and comprising approximately thirty buildings. Today this is the third largest among the exclusive truck manufacturers in the country. The corporation devoted its facilities to Government orders during the World war.

Mr. York was born at Carrollton, Carroll County, Kentucky, February 19, 1895. His father, Joseph E. York, was born in Tyrone, Kentucky, January 20, 1857, son of William Joseph York, a native of Charlottesville, Virginia. The grandfather was a Confederate soldier and while on duty was drowned, being twenty-six years of age at the time. His body was recovered and is buried at Tyrone, Kentucky. He married Mary Baker, daughter of a prominent Kentucky family, several of whom were distillers. Joseph E. York was a tobacco planter in Kentucky. He married Cynthia Bayne, who was born at Trimble, Kentucky, October 9, 1863, her people also having been tobacco growers.

When Homer Kendal York was a child his parents moved to Indianapolis, where he received his public school education. In 1909,

when fourteen, he was given a job as time cost clerk, at $3.50 a week, with the National Motor Car Company. He was with this organization until the war, and when he resigned had reached the position of production manager, at a salary of forty-five dollars a week.

In 1918 he entered the Field Officers Training School at Louisville, Kentucky. However, in July of the same year he was assigned to service at the Indiana Truck Corporation's plant at Marion in supervising the production of the trucks purchased for Government use. The capable way in which he handled his work for the Government attracted the attention of the officials of the corporation, who secured him as service manager, and in the winter of 1919 he was made production manager. In 1920 he was given another promotion, as assistant secretary, in 1921 was made secretary, and in 1925 elected to the office of vice president.

During the war the Government owned 22,-000 Indiana trucks, and when there was no longer a use for them for war purpose the Government turned them over to the good roads departments of the various states for the purpose of building or maintaining roads. The Indiana Truck Corporation was established with a capitalization of only $25,000. It is now a nine million dollar corporation. Mr. York as head of the good roads department has been responsible for a great deal of business for the corporation, and in 1930 he secured the largest single order given to the corporation since the close of the war, an order for a hundred Ford trucks from the New York State Highway Commission. Mr. York is also a stockholder in the Standard Oil Company of Indiana, Standard Oil Company of California, Standard Oil Company of New Jersey, the Texas Oil Company, the First National Bank of Marion, Moldin Printing Company of Marion, Cuban American Manganese Company, Tennessee Copper Company and the Continental Motor Company.

In politics he is a supporter of the Republican party, and has served as a member of the Indiana State pardon board, and as a member of the board of trustees of the Indiana Reformatory. He is a member of the Masonic fraternity. His real estate holdings comprise a tract of rolling land on the banks of the Mississinewa River, only a few minutes' drive from the center of the city. The landscaping of this tract has been a hobby with Mr. York and he had laid out the grounds, planted them with rare flowers, ferns and trees, and it is his intention eventually to turn over the place to the City of Marion as a pleasure park. He is a member of the Marion Country Club and the Indiana Athletic Club and Columbia Club of Indianapolis.

Mr. York married, June 19, 1919, Miss Mary Weinbrecht, of Indianapolis. Her father is connected with the National Malleable Iron Company of Indianapolis. The Weinbrecht family came originally from Cologne, Germany. Mrs. York is a member of the Department Club and the Adelphian Society of Marion. They have two daughters. Rose Mary was born at Marion March 5, 1922, and is a bright and attractive girl now in the third grade of the Marion city schools. Phyllis York was born August 30, 1926. Mr. and Mrs. York adopted her from the Masonic Home at Nashville, Tennessee.

JOHN WATSON. Among men whose lives have represented useful work and influence in Delaware County for many years that of John Watson is worthy of mention for his long service as an educator and in recent years as a public official.

Mr. Watson, present county surveyor of Delaware County, was born in that county February 3, 1869, son of Abraham and Catherine (Rutledge) Watson. His father was born in Muskingum County, Ohio, and was brought to Delaware County by his mother when three years of age. The grandfather, James Watson, had come to Eastern Indiana in 1840, bought a tract of land here, and shortly afterward died. It was for the purpose of taking possession of this land that the family came to the county in 1843. Abraham Watson grew up there, and soon as old enough took upon himself the responsibilities of farming. That was his vocation throughout the rest of his life. He died in 1916 and he and his wife are buried in the Tomlinson Cemetery. Catherine Rutledge was born and reared in Delaware County. She was a devoted member of the United Brethren Church. She died in 1910, and of their seven children the fifth in age died in infancy, the others being: William R., of Muncie; Sarah, deceased; John; James, deceased; Stella, wife of John Gibson, of Muncie; and Alice, deceased.

Mr. John Watson grew up on his father's farm, and all his life has been interested in farming and country life and has a great many friends among the farmers of the county. After the public schools he attended the Central Indiana Normal College at Danville, graduating with the class of 1896. In 1906 he took a diploma from the Indiana State Normal at Terre Haute, and also had a year of postgraduate study in the Ball Teachers College at Muncie. His work as an educator filled in the greater part of his time for a quarter of a century. All that time he taught in Delaware County. At sixteen he taught a term of school in a country district. Later he was in grade school work, was principal of grades, for a few years taught in the high school, and for nine years was supervising principal of the schools of Muncie.

Mr. Watson for many years has been interested as a student of civil engineering, and has had a wide experience in the application of his studies. In 1922 he was appointed city engineer of Muncie by Mayor Doctor Quick, serving in that capacity four years. In January, 1926, he removed to Florida and for four months was assistant engineer at Clearwater in that state. On returning to Muncie he resumed the private practice of civil engineering. Mr. Watson in November, 1928, was elected county surveyor and in January, 1929, took charge of that office in the courthouse. He is also acting as county agent. He is a Republican in politics and a member of the Methodist Episcopal Church.

Mr. Watson married in Delaware County, September 24, 1891, Miss Rhoda Jones. She attended grade and high schools in this county and taught for several years. She has some interesting accomplishments as an artist and has done a great deal of painting in oils. She is active in the Methodist Episcopal Church and a member of the Riverside Country Club. Her parents were Henry A. and Mary (Reasoner) Jones, her father a farmer and stock raiser for many years in Delaware County. Both her parents are buried in the Elizabethtown Cemetery. Mr. and Mrs. Watson have an adopted daughter, Mary Eileen Falby, who was educated in the schools of Muncie, graduating from high school there. She is the wife of Mr. Lester Van Horn, connected with the Banner Furniture Company of Muncie. Mr. and Mrs. Van Horn have two children, Vera Maxine, born December 25, 1924, and Oma Jean, born April 28, 1926.

WHEELER BLACK is a quiet and industrious citizen of Jackson Township, Tippecanoe County, has lived there practically all his life, engaged in farming and stock raising, and while now retired from the heavier duties is still a resident on his farm of 200 acres, the place where he was born in 1858.

Mr. Black is a son of John and Talitha (Wheeler) Black. His mother was a daughter of Damos and Elizabeth (King) Wheeler and a granddaughter of Lebin and Polly Wheeler. Lebin Wheeler was a native of Virginia and brought the family to Indiana in 1826. He was the first settler in this part of Jackson Township, and he put up a log cabin building which was still standing and in which Wheeler Black first saw the light of day. Members of the Wheeler family are buried in the Wheeler Grove Cemetery. John Black was born in Miami County, Ohio, and was brought to Tippecanoe County by his father, William Black, who had been a soldier in the War of 1812. William Black was buried at Rob Roy, Indiana. John Black was educated in country schools and spent his active life as a farmer in Jackson Township. He was a Democrat in politics. He and his wife had three children: Elizabeth, deceased; Emma, wife of J. W. Jennings; and Wheeler.

Wheeler Black being the only son of his parents remained at home and has always lived at the old homestead farm. He was educated in the Shawnee Mound Academy and for a time attended school in Forrest, Illinois. In 1906, after the death of his father, he took over the active management of the farm. Of his present place he inherited eighty acres from his mother, and he bought 120 acres. His place is known as the Wheeler Grove Farm.

Mr. Black married Elizabeth Bittle, daughter of John and Lucinda (Curtis) Bittle. Her

John T. Stout and Sons

Upper Row:	Charles Stout	Orville Stout
Lower Row:	Elmer W. Stout	Raymond Stout
	John A. Stout	
	John T. Stout	

father was born in Virginia and was brought to Indiana by his parents, Mr. and Mrs. William Bittle, who settled in Putnam County. John Bittle and wife had the following children: Emma; Etta; Erma, dead; Elizabeth; Julia; Minnie, dead; and John, dead. Mr. and Mrs. Black are members and he is a trustee of the Shawnee Mound Methodist Episcopal Church.

CARL EDWARD HINCHMAN, superintendent of the Indiana Harbor Belt Railroad at the general offices at Gibson, is a resident of Hammond. He has been in railroad service since boyhood and has filled a succession of positions that are evidence of capacity for the persistent and concentrated effort demanded of railway men.

Mr. Hinchman was born in Rush County, Indiana, January 18, 1878. This is one of the families that have been identified with Indiana for four generations. His great-grandfather was James Hinchman, who came out of Virginia and was one of the early pioneers of Rush County, Indiana, where he took up Government land. He and his wife and many others of the family are buried in the Hinchman Cemetery east of Rushville. The grandfather of Mr. Hinchman was John T. Hinchman, a farmer and stock man and a native of Rush County. The parents of Carl Edward Hinchman were William M. and Augusta (Rediker) Hinchman. His father spent all his life in Rush County, where he was a farmer and stock raiser. He died December 21, 1925, and was buried at Indianapolis. His wife, Augusta Rediker, was born at Columbus, Indiana, grew up at Rushville and is now a resident of Daleville, aged eighty-two. She is a member of the Christian Church. Her four children were: Drucilla, deceased; Mrs. Ruby Magraw, of Daleville; Carl E.; and Mrs. May Paddock, of Saint Petersburg, Florida.

Carl Edward Hinchman attended public school in Rush County, the high school at Spiceland, and had a business college course in Indianapolis. From school he entered upon what has been his life career, railroad work. He started as a clerk at Indianapolis for the Lake Erie & Western Railroad, in whose service he remained from January, 1895, to January, 1910. He was made assistant chief clerk and in that capacity was transferred to Cleveland, Ohio, in 1902. In 1910 he became chief clerk for the Chicago, Indiana & Southern Railroad, with offices at Cleveland, but in December of that year accepted transfer to Gibson, Indiana, as chief Clerk of the Indiana Harbor Belt Railroad, in the car service department. On September 1, 1911, he was promoted to superintendent of car service, and on October 1, 1927, was made superintendent, the office he holds today.

Mr. Hinchman is a member of McKinley Lodge No. 712, A. F. and A. M., the Hammond and East Chicago Chamber of Commerce, and is a Republican. He enjoys fishing for recreation, also goes on hunting excursions occasionally, and plays a quiet game of golf.

Mr. Hinchman married at Indianapolis, September 24, 1903, Miss Christina Ostermeyer, daughter of William and Christiana Ostermeyer. Her father was a grocery merchant at Indianapolis, where her mother still resides. Mrs. Hinchman attended grammar and high school at Indianapolis. She was reared in the faith of the German Lutheran Church. She is a member of the Hammond Woman's Club.

JOHN T. STOUT is an Indiana banker and in that business has given the most productive years of his life. Mr. Stout is president of the Orange County Bank at Paoli, and in his range of civic interests is easily one of the county's foremost citizens.

Mr. Stout was born April 29, 1848. His father, Hiram Stout, represented some of the fine old Quaker stock of North Carolina. He was born in Orange County, that state, in 1808, and when a young man came to Indiana and settled on a farm, where he lived out his life. He died in 1896. His wife, Nancy Thomas, was born in South Carolina and died in 1858. They had a large family of children: William, Cela, Milinda, Mattie, John T., Amos, Ellen, Cloria, and Michael, the latter of whom died in infancy.

John T. Stout grew up on an Indiana farm, and attended public schools at Lick Creek and the Orleans Normal School. His was a boyhood which emphasized industry and self-help. He made opportunities to turn his industry into profit while a boy on the farm by raising and selling watermelons and other garden truck. He also clerked in a store, starting at a very small salary, later was put on a profit sharing basis, and still later bought the business. After conducting it for a few years he sold out and in 1871 moved to Paoli, where he continued in the mercantile business for several years.

In 1886 Mr. Stout and his brother Amos acquired an interest in the Orange County Bank, their associates for several years being Mr. Bowles and Mr. Hicks. In 1888 the Stout brothers acquired the Bowles interest and later bought out Mr. Hicks. Since 1900 Mr. John Stout has been the chief owner of the bank, and its president.

Mr. Stout was thirteen years of age when the Civil war broke out. Later he traveled from his home to Indianapolis for the purpose of getting instructed for duty as a soldier, but was rejected on account of his age. He had spent all his money in getting to Indianapolis, and had to earn his way home by helping fire the locomotive, which was one of the old wood burning engines of those days. Mr. Stout has been an influential factor in the Republican party of Orange County. He was a delegate to the national convention that nominated William McKinley in 1896. He is a member of the Friends Church and has served as a member of the board of trustees of Earlham College at Richmond. Governor Durbin appointed him a trustee of the Southern Indiana Insane Hospital and for a number of years he gave his time to the important duties of administering this state institution. Mr. Stout is a Royal Arch Mason, member of the Independent Order of Odd Fellows, and has always been ready in response to worthy civic and philanthropic enterprises.

He married in April, 1870, Miss Adeline McCarell, daughter of William and Rachel McCarell, of Louisville. Her parents were living at Louisville, Kentucky, during the Civil war. When General Bragg, of the southern army, gave orders that all women and children should evacuate that city before he advanced upon it, the McCarells left and came to Dubois County and remained there permanently. Mrs. Stout passed away in 1915. Eight children were born to their marriage, one of whom died in infancy. The seven living children are: Minnie is the wife of John Copeland, of Paoli. Elmer, unmarried, is a graduate of Harvard Law School and is prominent in banking circles at Indianapolis, being president of the Fletcher American National Bank, the largest bank in Indiana, with resources of $48,000,000. His numerous honors and accomplishments are listed in *Who's Who in America*. Orville, of Vincennes, married Myrtle Brown and has two children. Mary is the wife of Dr. T. N. Braxton, of Boise, Idaho, and has four children. Charles lives at Memphis, Tennessee, and owns a chain of seven flour mills and is a man of large means. He married Warda Stevens and has two daughters. Raymond, cashier of the Orange County Bank at Paoli, married Sarah Oakes, of Boise, Idaho, and has a family of four children. John A., who is associated with Charles in the milling business, lives at Memphis, Tennessee. He married Helen Barnes, of Seymour, Indiana, and has two children.

RAY P. JOHNSON. Because of the extent, variety and importance of the enterprises with which he is intimately identified, Ray Prescott Johnson, Sr., of Muncie, is unqualifiedly entitled to rank as one of the leading business men of his community. Even before the termination of his college career he had been one of the founders of the Warner Gear Company, a nationally known concern of which he has been president since 1917, and during more recent years has allied himself with other large interests, the size and prominence of which have not only assured his own position as a business captain but also have contributed to the prestige of his adopted city.

Mr. Johnson was born at Bluffton, Indiana, June 4, 1878, and is a son of Abbott L. and Florence (Merriman) Johnson. Abbott L. Johnson was born in Herkimer County, New York, where he was reared and received a public school education, and in young manhood came to Indiana and took up his residence at Bluffton. He became one of the substantial business men and highly-respected citizens of his community and was one of the founders of the Warner Gear Company, with which he was identified until his death in 1923, when he was buried in Beech Grove Cemetery at Muncie. He married Florence A. Merriman, who died in 1925, and is also buried in Beech Grove. There were three children in the family: John Edgar, who is now deceased; Ray Prescott, of this review; and Florence Grace, the wife of Charles S. Davis, a graduate of Harvard, class of 1899, and president of the Borg-Warner Corporation of Muncie. A sketch of his career appears elsewhere in this work.

After attending public and private schools Ray P. Johnson entered the University of Chicago, from which he was graduated in 1903. Two years previous to this time, in 1901, he had been one of the founders and organizers of the Warner Gear Company, and immediately upon his graduation entered the office of this company, rising by general stages and promotions until elected to the presidency in 1919. This has become one of the leading concerns of its kind in the country and its market covers the entire United States and a number of foreign countries, where its product is known for its excellence and reliability. Mr. Johnson is also a director of the Delaware County National Bank of Muncie, president of the Warner Electric Company, vice president of the Glasscock Brothers Manufacturing Company, vice president of the Borg-Warner Corporation and a member of the directorate of the Live Poultry Transit Company of Chicago, in addition to being connected in various capacities with many other enterprises. He is a thirty-second degree Mason, a member of Delaware Lodge No. 46, A. F. and A. M., of Muncie, and of Murat Shrine, Indianapolis; and belongs likewise to the Rotary Club, the Chamber of Commerce, the Columbia Club of Indianapolis, the Indianapolis Athletic Club and the Delaware Country Club. In politics he is a Republican and his religious affiliation is with the First Baptist Church of Muncie, of which he is a member of the board of trustees. He has always been known as a public-spirited and patriotic citizen, and during the World war was appointed by the secretary of the war department to head a group of automotive engineers to assist in the organization and operation of the Motor Transport Corps, a service which called for his presence at Tours, France, for six months. His work in this direction was very valuable and was highly appreciated, as were his services in behalf of the Liberty Loan and other drives.

On June 6, 1906, at Terre Haute, Indiana, Mr. Johnson was united in marriage with Miss Anna Davis, of that city, a daughter of Daniel N. and Margaret (Hyde) Davis. Mr. Davis was for a number of years engaged in the coal business, until becoming connected with the Warner Gear Company, with which he continued to be identified until his death. He was buried in Beech Grove Cemetery, while Mrs. Davis still survives and is a greatly-esteemed resident of Muncie. Mrs. Johnson was educated at St. Mary's of the Woods, Terre Haute, from which she was graduated in 1903, and has been very active in church work and in the Matinee Music Club and the Woman's Club. Two children have been born to Mr. and Mrs. Johnson: Ray Prescott, Jr., and Margaret. Ray Prescott Johnson, Jr., after attending the public schools of Muncie and graduating from the high school, entered Wabash College, from which he was graduated as a member of the class of 1928. Following this he took post-graduate work at Harvard, and now holds a responsible position with the Warner Gear Company. Miss Margaret Johnson, a graduate of Mount Vernon Seminary, Washington, D. C., class of 1929, is now an art student in the Grand Central Art School, New York City, where she is showing much promise.

WALTER A. BATES. In the highly specialized field of steel manufacture for public utilities corporations, one of the best known concerns in the United States is the Walter Bates Steel Corporation, of Gary. This company has been in existence only since 1926, but within this short space of time, by reason of the mechanical genius, executive capacity and broad and thorough knowledge of steel manufacture of its president and manager, Walter A. Bates, it has assumed a commanding position in the face of strong competition. Mr. Bates has led a somewhat varied career, having been engaged in a number of pursuits, but steel has always been his real vocation and hobby, and as the head of his present concern he finds himself the directing power of one of the great enterprises of a great industrial city.

Mr. Bates was born at Joliet, Illinois, November 14, 1887, and is a son of Albert J. and Ellen (Amos) Bates. The Bates family is of English origin and was founded a number of generations ago in this country, the grandfather of Mr. Bates being a pioneer of Carthage, Missouri. At that place, in 1862, was born the father of Walter A. Bates, Albert J. Bates, who was reared in his native community and educated in the public schools. As a youth he displayed great mechanical ingenuity and eventually became a mechanical engineer and rose to the top of his profession. He was the founder of the Bates Expanded Steel Truss Company, at East Chicago, Indiana, in 1914, and is still president of that company, although sixty-eight years of age, a time of life when most men, when possessed of a generous share of this world's goods, consider the matter of retiring from active business labors. Mr. Bates won the medal at the World's Columbian Exposition (World's Fair) at Chicago in 1893, for "the best steam Corliss engine," which he designed and built. For a number of years he served in the important capacity of chief consulting engineer of the American Steel & Wire Company, and is the originator of a large number of their products. Mr. Bates makes his home at Chicago and is a popular member of the South Shore Country Club. Mrs. Ellen (Amos) Bates was born in England and came to the United States at the age of twelve years with her parents, the family settling at Carthage, Missouri, where she received her education in the public schools. She is a member of the Presbyterian Church and has taken an active part in the movements of women's clubs and societies. Five children were born to Mr. and Mrs. Bates: Pearl, now the wife of W. P. Wood, of Chicago; Walter A., of this review; Richard A., of East Chicago, Indiana; Albert J., of Chicago; and Charles I., also of that city.

Walter A. Bates attended the public schools of Joliet and was graduated from high school as a member of the class of 1906. Upon leaving school he secured employment with the American Steel & Wire Company, in the capacity of mechanic, but after a short time went to Chicago, where he was employed on the Board of Trade, later being with the Milwaukee Board of Trade, in all for about three years. For the five years that followed he was connected with ranching in Montana, but sold his ranch and returned to East Chicago, Indiana, where he became associated with his father in the Bates Expanded Steel Trust Company, in the capacity of vice president and general manager. As such he had charge of the construction of the plant and later was in charge of the management for twelve years, or until 1926. During this period, in 1919 and 1920, he was employed at Savana, Italy, in the construction of a subsidiary plant of the same corporation, and this plant is still in successful operation. Returning to Gary in 1926, Mr. Bates constructed his own plant, the Walter Bates Steel Corporation, which is one of the largest of its kind in the country, specializing in the manufacture of steel for public utilities corporations, of which Mr. Bates is president and manager, with offices on East Fifth Avenue. One of the most recent products of this company is the "Squaretrus" expanded-angle steel pole, designed and perfected by a group of engineers who are specialists in steel products for utilities. In producing this pole they have accomplished in design, serviceability and economy a product that identifies this company for its close cooperation with utilities. Not alone in engineering, but in manufacturing, the Walter Bates Steel Corporation is equipped for quality production. The large plant is most modern throughout—each process is an advanced one— all machinery of the latest types, even to electrically heated and controlled galvanizing pot. Accuracy has always been one of the corporation's slogans. Mr. Bates stands exceptionally high in the esteem of his associates in the steel industry as a man of authoritative knowledge and rare executive ability. He is an enthusiastic and constructive member of the Rotary Club of Gary, the Gary Commercial Club and Chamber of Commerce, the Gary Country Club, and the Union League Club of Chicago. He is not a politician, but votes the Republican ticket. During the World war he was engaged in the manufacture of materials for the allied cause and also worked for the various drives. He has taken a keen and helpful interest in civic affairs, and is a consistent member of the First Presbyterian Church.

On June 28, 1912, at Dillon, Montana, Mr. Bates was united in marriage with Miss Beulah Harrison, daughter of Homer and May Harrison, formerly of Lewiston, Illinois, and later of Dillon, Montana, where Mrs. Bates graduated from the State Normal College. For a few years prior to her marriage she taught school in Montana, and has always been interested in the cause of education. She is a devout member of the Presbyterian Church and has been active in club and social circles of Gary. To Mr. and Mrs. Bates there have been born two children: Walter A., Jr., and Betty, both of whom are attending the Horace Mann School at Gary.

ALLYN FRANCIS BRADLEY, secretary-manager of the Whiting Chamber of Commerce, is president of the Indiana Commercial Secretaries Association. Mr. Bradley has shown a special genius for organization work, and has a reputation in several progressive cities of the Middle West.

He is a native of Illinois, born at Plano July 25, 1887, son of Horace S. and Mary Ann (Swanick) Bradley. Mr. Bradley is descended from an old and prominent New England family.

His great-great-grandfather was Timothy Bradley. Timothy Bradley was a man of remarkable experience and lived to the great age of 101 years, two months and one day. He was born at Guilford, Connecticut, July 20, 1770, and died September 21, 1871. His father, Capt. Timothy Bradley, commanded the fort at Guilford, Connecticut, during the Revolutionary war. His brother was also an officer in that war. Timothy Bradley as a youth served an apprenticeship of seven years at the trade of ironing ships. When a young man he removed to the State of New York, settling at Sherburn, subsequently lived at Windsor and then at Vestal, and more than sixty years of his life were spent in Broome County. He was one of the family of twelve children, and was himself the father of five children. The oldest of these was Gen. Horace S. Bradley, Sr., who afterwards was a member of the firm of Bradley & Bradford, the first jewelers in business at Binghamton, New York. On the occasion of the one hundredth birthday of Timothy Bradley his friends and neighbors in Broome County came to congratulate him on the occasion, at which time the outlined facts of his career as just noted were published in a local paper, together with an address of welcome, which is herewith quoted:

"You were born in a little British colony in 1770, and can remember when the new nation was born which you have seen grow to great influence and power, and take its place among the foremost nations of the world. Brought up during the eventful scene of the Revolutionary war, what transpired then is only known to us in history, but is to you,

experience. You have often seen General Washington and many prominent officers of the Revolutionary war, witnessed some of the engagements of that war, the signing of the Declaration of Independence, the Battle of Bunker Hill, the suffering of the army at Valley Forge, the surrender of Burgoyne and Cornwallis, are all events that you recollect perfectly well. When the War of 1812 broke out, you were over forty years of age, and no doubt thought you were becoming an old man, but your life has been continued on to the age of steam and telegraph, on past with the war with Mexico, the War of the Rebellion, you have seen the continents connected by railroads and the oceans by telegraph. Your mind is yet vigorous to comprehend the advancement of this age and compare it with a century ago.

"It is the wish of your many friends that the few remaining days that may be allotted to you, may be full of happiness, and when you are gathered to your Father, you may be like a shock of grain, fully ripe for the harvest."

The grandfather of Allyn F. Bradley, Horace S. Bradley, served as an officer in the Union army in the Civil war. After his business connections in the East he came to Illinois and was one of the pioneers of Carroll County, where he followed farming and stock raising. He and his wife are buried at Mount Carroll.

Horace S. Bradley, Jr., father of Allyn F. Bradley, was born and reared at Mount Carroll, Illinois, attended public schools there and the State Normal School. After his marriage he moved to Plano, Illinois, where with his brother he established and conducted for two years a general mercantile business. They then opened a general store at Sandwich, Illinois, and were together in business until 1910. Since that year he has been Central West representative for the Babcock Corporation of Bath, New York. He is a prominent Mason, and an elder and trustee of the Presbyterian Church at Sandwich. His wife, Mary Ann Swanick, was born and reared at Mendota, Illinois. She is a member of the Presbyterian Church and active in community affairs. The three children of these parents were: Allyn F.; Hazel J., widow of Reynolds Dale, of Sandwich; and Dr. Horace S. Bradley, an osteopathic physician at Elmhurst, Illinois.

Allyn F. Bradley graduated from the Sandwich High School in 1904. He subsequently took special work in commercial administration and accounting at the University of Wisconsin and Northwestern University. As an accountant he spent six years as assistant planning supervisor with the Lyon Metal Products Company and another six years as cost accountant with the Aurora Automatic Tool Company.

Since 1919 Mr. Bradley has given all his time to Chamber of Commerce work. For three years he was assistant managing secretary of the Aurora, Illinois, Chamber of Com-

John G. Sloan

merce. He then accepted the invitation to become the first secretary of the Association of Commerce at Bismarck, North Dakota, and while there he organized the North Dakota State Corn Show. He was in North Dakota three years and from there came to Indiana. He was at Mishawaka four years, as secretary of the Chamber of Commerce, organizing and developing the industrial program of that city. He also organized and perfected the work of the Mishawaka Welfare Federation and Community Fund and the Mishawaka Credit Bureau.

Mr. Bradley became manager and secretary of the Whiting Chamber of Commerce in 1929. He has accomplished some big things in this city, including the reorganization of the Whiting-Robertsdale Community Chest, the Council of Social Agencies, the Whiting Dental Society and the Whiting Credit Bureau. He is a member of the Mid-West Shippers Advisory Board and Foreign Trade Council, and is secretary of the Calumet Congress, which is a super organization representing all the Chamber of Commerce work in the Calumet region.

Mr. Bradley is a Master Mason, a member of the Lions Club, is an independent Republican and a member of the Presbyterian Church. His recreations are golf and fishing. He has had an active part in Boy Scout work for a number of years, being chairman of the troop organization at Whiting and while at Aurora, Illinois, he was appointed the first deputy scout commissioner in that area. He was at Aurora during the World war period, and when Maj. Charles Harkison organized the Sixth Illinois Reserve Militia Mr. Bradley was appointed sergeant major on his staff and later was lieutenant of Company K, Sixth Regiment, Illinois Reserve Militia.

He married at Aurora, March 30, 1912, Miss Alice M. Sexton, daughter of Charles S. and Helen (Satterly) Sexton. Her father was a farmer and stock raiser in Illinois and later moved to Garden City, Kansas, where he became a rancher, but is now living there retired. Mrs. Bradley's mother died in 1898 and is buried at Na-au-say, Illinois. An uncle of Mrs. Bradley is Charles E. Shepherd, of the Ingalls-Shepherd Drop Forge Company of Harvey, Illinois. Mrs. Bradley attended grammar and high schools at Garden City, Kansas, took a business college course at Aurora, Illinois, and for about two years before her marriage was in secretarial work with the United Gas & Electric Company. She is a member of the Whiting Woman's Club and the Presbyterian Church. Mr. and Mrs. Bradley have an interesting family of eight children: Helen Shepherd, Mary Charlotte, John Sexton, June Elizabeth, Allyn F., Jr., Alice Ruth, Shirley Ann and Richard Satterly. Helen was graduated from the Mishawaka High School in 1929 and was elected honor member of the National Honor Society and was a member of the Quill and Scroll Society in high school. She assisted her father in the Credit Bureau at Whiting as assistant

manager until April 1, 1931, and is now in secretarial work with the Lever Brothers Company. The daughter Mary Charlotte is in junior high school, and John, June and Allyn are in the grade schools.

JOHN GUY SLOAN. There are old and prominent families of Crawford County, Indiana, which have been important here for over one hundred years, and one of these bears the name of Sloan. Founded near English, in this county, in 1800, by a sturdy and industrious Pennsylvania farmer, Archibald Sloan, his sterling character and thrift were inherited by his children, as were his valuable lands, and the entire inheritance has continued to the present day. One of his worthy descendants is found in John Guy Sloan, postmaster of Marengo, and active in Crawford County politics. Well educated in the local schools, a graduate of the high school at English and a business college at New Albany, in early manhood Mr. Sloan at first taught school in Crawford County, and later was identified with business houses at Indianapolis and Newcastle, Indiana. In 1910 he settled on a farm near Marengo, and has made this city his home ever since, although since January, 1924, when he was appointed postmaster, his time has been mainly taken up with his public duties.

Postmaster Sloan was born at English, Crawford County, Indiana, April 20, 1883, a son of George W. and Sarah (Dooley) Sloan, both of whom are deceased, he having passed away December 14, 1906, at which time he was still engaged in farming, which had been his life work. Mrs. Sloan died July 27, 1927. Seven children were born to the parents, namely: William W., who married Mame Luckett, lives at French Lick, Indiana, and has two children; James O., who lives at Indianapolis, married Maude Pruitt, and they have one daughter; Sophia, who married James Royer, lives in New York City, and they have six children; Archibald, who is unmarried, lives at English; Blanche, who is also unmarried, lives at English; John Guy, subject of this review; and George W., who married Gertie Lone, and they live at Indianapolis and have two sons.

After teaching school for two years Postmaster Sloan took his business course, and, graduating as a bookkeeper, was connected as bookkeeper with several concerns in different cities. In 1910 he returned to the occupation of his forefathers, and began farming, but later went into the grocery business at Marengo for a year. In the meanwhile he had made his influence felt in the local Republican party, and ran for the office of clerk of the Circuit Court in 1918, during which campaign he became so well known and did so much for the party that, although he was defeated, the results are shown forth in his appointment as postmaster. Under his capable charge the affairs of the Marengo office are in fine condition, and the patrons are more than satisfied. For twenty-three years

Mr. Sloan has been a member of Marengo Lodge, A. F. and A. M., and for four years was its worshipful master, and he also belongs to the Eastern Star. For many years he has been a member of the Christian Church, and is now a trustee and deacon of the body at Marengo. He married Minola Stewart, of Marengo, also of an old pioneer family, daughter of David M. Stewart, a leading merchant and farmer of Crawford County. They have one daughter, Thelma, who lives at home. She is a teacher in the Marengo schools and pursues her education each summer in the State Normal School at Terre Haute.

The Sloan farm on which Archibald Sloan settled in 1800 descended to his son, James Guy Sloan, the grandfather of Postmaster Sloan, and he remained on it and reared a family. Four of his sons were Union soldiers, namely: William W., who was captain of a company in the First Indiana Cavalry; George W., father of Postmaster Sloan, and who served in the Forty-ninth Indiana Infantry; "Tip" M., who served in the First Indiana Cavalry; and Robert L., who served with the One Hundred and Forty-fourth Indiana Infantry. For years the Sloan family has had a part ownership in the Marengo Cave, but recently this interest has been sold to the Marengo Cave Company.

HARRY FRANKLIN GLAIR is manager of the great refining plant of the Standard Oil Company at Whiting. Mr. Glair is an oil and gas engineer, a graduate of the University of Illinois, and has been with the technical staff at Whiting since 1912.

Mr. Glair was born at Chicago, Illinois, August 28, 1888, only son and child of Lewis C. and Emma Katherine (Olsker) Glair. His parents were born and reared at Buffalo, New York, were married in that city and settled in Chicago in 1887. His father has spent many years in the service of the Illinois Central Railway as a conductor. He is a member of the Order of Railway Conductors and the Knights of the Maccabees. Mrs. Glair is an active worker in the University Baptist Church at Chicago.

Harry F. Glair attended public schools in his native city, graduated from the Hyde Park High School in 1906 and immediately went to work for the Standard Oil Company. After two years he accepted the opportunity to complete a technical education in the University of Illinois. He graduated with the class of 1912, with the degree Bachelor of Science. After three months in St. Louis with the Curtis Manufacturing Company he reentered the service of the Standard Oil Company of Whiting, in the engineering department. He helped design the first Burton cracking stills, in which was applied the modern methods of manufacturing motor gasoline from petroleum. In January, 1914, he was made assistant superintendent of the Paraffine Works. Mr. Glair has brought both industry and enthusiasm to his work with the Standard Oil Company. In November, 1920, he was made superintendent of the Paraffine Works. In September, 1921, came another promotion, when he was given the position of assistant general superintendent of the Whiting Refinery. On January 1, 1927, he was made general superintendent of the plant and has been plant manager since March 7, 1929. The Whiting plant is probably the largest and most complete technical laboratory for the refining of petroleum products in the world. Eight hundred acres are used for the plant and about 4,000 people are employed there. This refinery is the chief center for the manufacture of the famous "Red Crown" gasoline product.

Mr. Glair is widely known among oil and gas engineers throughout America. He is a Master Mason and a member of the Zeta Psi college fraternity and the South Shore and Lake Hills Country Clubs. He has membership in a number of Chambers of Commerce, at Hammond, East Chicago, Bay City, Michigan, Muskegon, Michigan, Superior Wisconsin. He takes an active part in community affairs, is a member of the Hammond Park Board and chairman of the board of trustees of the Whiting Community Memorial House, a great civic center built by the Rockefellers, at a cost of over $600,000. Mr. Glair is a Republican and he and Mrs. Glair are active members of the Plymouth Congregational Church.

He married at Whiting, November 10, 1915, Miss Hortense Oliver, daughter of Mr. and Mrs. Myron Oliver, of Chicago. Her father for many years has been claim agent for the Illinois Central Railroad. Her mother died in 1898 and is buried at Chicago. Mrs. Glair graduated from the Hyde Park High School of Chicago. They have one daughter, Jacquelyn, a student in the public schools. Mr. and Mrs. Glair have a summer home at Three Rivers, Michigan, where during the season he spends his week ends. His recreations are fishing and golf.

ELI SHERMAN JONES, surgical specialist, one of the ablest representatives of his profession at Hammond, is a member of an Indiana family which has produced a number of able scholars and professional men.

He was born in the Quaker community of Fairmount, Grant County, Indiana, February 9, 1890. Before coming to Indiana the Jones family were members of the Quaker community of Western North Carolina. His grandfather was Robert Jones, who in the early days moved from North Carolina and for several years lived at Fairmount, Indiana. He then returned to Lexington, North Carolina, where he died. The father of Doctor Jones was David Jones, who was born at Fairmount, Indiana. Shortly after his birth his parents started back to North Carolina in a covered wagon, and his mother died on the way and was buried in Tennessee. David Jones grew up in North Carolina, attended school there, and when about twenty-one years of age returned to Indiana and settled on a

ELIZABETH C. B. PRICE   CHARLES T. PRICE JR.

ABBIE MAY PRICE   DR. RUDOLPH J. PRICE   CAROLINE B. PRICE

MARGARET B. WILLIAMS

farm near Fairmount. His business has been that of a farmer and stock raiser. In 1920 he retired into Fairmount, but still oversees the work of his farm. He married, March 3, 1881, Miss Sarah Thomas, and on March 3, 1931, they celebrated their golden wedding anniversary. Both have been sincere and active members of the Friends Church. Sarah Thomas was born and reared at Fairmount and her father was Rev. Amos Thomas, one of the early Quaker ministers of Grant County, Indiana. David and Sarah Jones had a family of ten children, one of whom died in infancy. The oldest living son, William M. Jones, is a farmer at Fairmount. Dr. R. B. Jones lives at LaPorte, Indiana. Dr. Thomas E., A. M., Ph. D., has devoted his life to education, both in this country and abroad. He was for several years professor of economics in a university in Japan, has also been active in the Friends' reconstruction work in the Orient, and since 1926 has been president of Fisk University at Nashville. The next in order of birth is Dr. Eli Sherman. Ora is the wife of Paul Wolf, of Morristown, Indiana. Orpha is Mrs. John Catron, of Oakland, California. Rene A. lives at Salt Lake City, Utah. Frances is Mrs. Cedric Macauley, of Alameda, California. Fred, the youngest, is a resident of Fairmount, Indiana.

Eli Sherman Jones spent his boyhood on his fathers' farm in Grant County, attended public schools nearby and the Fairmount Academy. He was graduated Bachelor of Science in 1914 from Indiana University and took his medical degree in the University School of Medicine in 1916. His interne work was done in the City Hospital at Indianapolis. Doctor Jones in 1916 located at Hammond, where he has had a steadily increasing business as a physician and surgeon, but since October, 1928, has confined himself largely to his work as a specialist in surgery. His offices are in the First Trust Building. For twelve years he has served as coroner's physician of Lake County. He is a member of the County, Indiana State and American Medical Associations, and a fellow of the American College of Surgeons. He is on the staff of St. Margaret's Hospital of Hammond, St. Catherine's Hospital of East Chicago, and the Methodist Hospital of Gary.

Doctor Jones for a number of years has been a student of Masonry. He is a member of McKinley Lodge, A. F. and A. M., the Royal Arch Chapter, Council and Knights Templar Commandery at Hammond, Fort Wayne Consistory of the Scottish Rite and Orak Temple of the Mystic Shrine. He also belongs to the Elks, the Rotary Club, the Woodmar Country Club. He is a member of the Friends Church and in politics an independent. His recreations are hunting and fishing, but his real enthusiasm is in the line of his profession. He has studied and visited hospitals and clinics at the Mayo Institution at Rochester, Minnesota, the University of Chicago, Harvard University, Johns Hopkins University, and has studied and traveled abroad in England, Germany, France and Austria.

Doctor Jones married at Bloomfield, Indiana, November 18, 1916, Miss Berta Herold, daughter of Otto and Clara (Dyer) Herold. Her father was a banker and leader in politics at Bloomfield, Indiana, where he died in 1924 and where her mother resides. Mrs. Jones attended public school at Bloomfield and graduated from Indiana University in 1914. She is a member of the Christian Church and the Delta Gamma sorority. They have a daughter, Janet, a student in the Westlake School for Girls at Los Angeles, California.

CHARLES T. PRICE. The Price family, of Richmond, has been rich in all the attributes of good and high minded citizenship. As an American family their record is a long and honorable one, covering half a dozen generations, back to Colonial times.

The old seat of the Price family in this country was in New Jersey. Thomas Price spent all his life at Elizabethtown, that state. Ten of his brothers were soldiers in the Revolution, and each endured a term of imprisonment in the old "Sugar House" in New York. Thomas Price married Rachel Badgley. She was a granddaughter of Lord Townley and Lady Abbie, his wife. Lord Townley's property in England was confiscated because he favored the cause of the colonists in the war for American independence. Two of his sons and one daughter came to America. The daughter became the wife of William Badgley, whose daughter Rachel married Thomas Price. Thomas and Rachel Price had fourteen children. One of the sons, Jeremiah Price, was conspicuous in the early history of the City of Chicago, where he built up a great fortune, and at his death in 1852, having no direct heirs, it was divided among his relatives.

Caleb Price, son of Thomas and Rachel Price, also spent his life at Elizabethtown, New Jersey. He was a tinsmith by trade. He died in 1858. He married Anna Tucker, and they had three sons, Benjamin, Caleb and Charles T.

Charles T. Price, Sr., the founder of the family at Richmond, Indiana, was born at Elizabeth, New Jersey, April 8, 1817. At the age of fifteen he left school to work for his brother Benjamin in a shoe store. At eighteen he set up in business for himself as a shoe dealer at Philadelphia. Later for a time he was with his brother Caleb in the tinware business at Mobile, Alabama. He returned to Philadelphia, was a retail shoe merchant in that city until 1847, then for five years was in business at Cincinnati, and in 1852 located at Richmond, where he lived out his life. He was a shoe merchant, hardware dealer, but after 1858 devoted his time chiefly to real estate operations. He built and sold more than a hundred homes, laid out subdivisions, carried on an extensive business in farm lands, and at all times was a generous and public spirited benefactor of his community. He was one of the founders of Grace Methodist

Episcopal Church and filled all the offices in the church. He supported the cause of prohibition, but was independent in politics. He was one of the principal donors to the Home for the Friendless, and no worthy cause failed to receive his support and interest.

Charles T. Price, Sr., married, April 16, 1838, Caroline Williams, who died in 1848, at the age of thirty-three years, leaving two children, Charles T. and Mrs. Jane M. Adison. Charles T. Price, Sr., married, July 16, 1850, Lydia Manifold, of Cincinnati, and by that union there were five children.

Charles T. Price, Jr., whose name is held in grateful memory in Richmond, was born at Philadelphia, April 28, 1840, and was about twelve years of age when his father moved to Richmond. His independence and initiative were developed at an early age. As a boy he sold magazines and nuts on the trains of the Pennsylvania Railroad. He was determined to get an education. Nothing apparently could keep him from school when he had the opportunity to attend. While in Cincinnati he started for school one day after a thaw had broken up the ice in the canal, which he usually had crossed on the ice. He mounted one of the blocks of ice floating in the stream, but before reaching the opposite shore was overturned and thrown into the icy water. He made his way to the shore, and though his clothing was completely drenched, he went on to school and remained there until closing time. After getting his business training in school he mastered the art of cabinet maker, and at different periods applied himself to the business of building houses.

In 1861 he enlisted in the Second Indiana Cavalry. Because of his trade he was assigned work in bridge construction. He became quartermaster's clerk of the Post Division of the Cumberland, under Colonel Dudley, from whom the various regimental officers obtained supplies. During the four years from 1861 to 1865 he was stationed at Bridgeport, Alabama, and Chattanooga, Tennessee, and at the close of the war was mustered out and honorably discharged, his·papers being signed by Colonel Dudley. While in the army he had two furloughs of a few days each, during which he made brief visits to his wife and their little son.

After the war he established a store at Middleboro, several miles north of Richmond. His store was a market for the hunters who brought in their game to him. Many times he loaded the products of the shotgun and traps on his back and carried them to the Richmond market. Later Mr. and Mrs. Price established a confectionery store at 808 Main Street, Richmond, Mrs. Price attending to the needs of the customers with the aid of a sister, Almeda Burroughs, recognized as the most beautiful girl of Wayne County, while Mr. Price busied himself with the construction of the Homestead Maple Lawn, 19 North Thirteenth Street, long famous as the home of rare birds and flowers. Later the Prices acquired the store building at 916 Main Street,

a three-story structure. They had their opening on a snowy February day, but in spite of the storm many friends attended the opening. The Price store was the first in Richmond to be electrically lighted. He installed a dynamo and other machinery for manufacturing electric current, which also supplied power for the operation of his ice cream freezers. In 1893 the Price store dispensed the first ice cream sodas at Richmond. In the fall of 1915 Mr. and Mrs. Price celebrated the fiftieth anniversary of the opening of their business. A reception was held in the store, orchestral music, fruit lemonade, choice confections and flowers supplied to the guests. The building was decorated with palms that Mrs. Price herself had raised, and also with autumn flowers and oak boughs.

Both Mr. and Mrs. Price were keenly interested in civic affairs. They took pleasure in placing their signatures to the petition for the ratification of the Eighteenth Amendment. Their lives were beautifully interwoven in philanthropic undertakings. Mr. Price was a charter member of the Young Men's Christian Association and served on the different drive days. They were benefactors of Earlham College. Mr. Price served on the committee that constructed the concrete bridge over the White Water River connecting Richmond and West Richmond. He was also on the booster drive committees. A meeting was not considered complete without his presence, a fellow member coming for him if he were not there, before the others were willing to start proceedings.

Mr. and Mrs. Price were enthusiastic travelers, especially in their own country. They regarded travel as not merely a means of recreation but an invaluable source of education for themselves and their children. They spent several winter seasons in the South, traveling mainly by river steamer, made trips to both coasts and spent the summer months at Mackinac Island, Michigan. They planned everything together, and accomplished with patience and perseverance the labor that was woven into the tissue of their dreams and ambitions. They were loved for their kindly, unselfish lives. Only forty days separated them in death. Mrs. Price passed away March 31, 1917, and Mr. Price on May 10, 1917. Both left watchwords to their children, the mother's being: "Keep together and report for duty." Forty days afterward the father said: "Be brave and do your duty." Both had lived their lives on the principle that each day should be complete and in readiness for the final summons. Richmond citizens take pride in the beautiful residential street known as North A, formerly Broadway. It was through the initiative of Mr. and Mrs. Price that this street was asphalted. It is a mile in length, a broad avenue, with shade trees and attractive homes throughout its entire length.

Charles T. Price, Jr., married, December 24, 1860, Miss Elizabeth Clarissa Burroughs. She was born in Union County, Indiana, March 13, 1840, daughter of William and

Sarah (Williams) Burroughs. Sarah Williams' mother was Margaret Bennett Williams, a daughter of Sarah Sailor, whose mother was Mary Hollaway. The mother of Mary Hollaway was Hannah Hollaway, who was the aunt of Marv. Sarah and Jeremiah Ball. Mary Ball was the mother of George Washington. Mrs. Price besides her deep spiritual nature and wonderful character of helpfulness and friendliness had an unusual range of accomplishments. As a girl and young woman she had assisted her father in planting and grafting his orchards and vineyards and in raising sheep and flax. She assisted her mother in carding and weaving on the looms her father made by hand. At that time all the clothing worn by the family, both sexes, was made from cloth, linen and woolen woven by the women folks. The Burroughs was a large family. The blankets, sheets, tablecloths and other linens were woven by these tireless workers.

The children of Mr. and Mrs. Price were: Eugene William Price, born December 24, 1862; Lewis Edward Price, born August 28, 1867; Caroline Burroughs Price, born March 4, 1872: and Abbie May Price, born February 22, 1875.

Of the third generation of the Price family in Richmond, one representative is Abbie May Price. She attended grade schools, graduated from the Senior High School and took special work in Earlham College. She learned many of the fine arts of home making and the gentle care of the sick from her mother. During vacation periods she assisted her father in business, developing a high degree of proficiency. Frequently on busy days she took 150 orders accurately in every particular in less than an hour. At other times her father placed her in charge of the register.

A charter member of the Domestic Science Association when it was organized in 1908, she served it as secretary and treasurer for several years. She studied the course of twelve volumes of the American School of Home economics. She was personally responsible for 125 new members of the main body during one year's activities. She was instrumental in inaugurating the Day Nursery, also the visiting nurse's work in the homes and medical examination of the children in the schools. Miss Price as the result of her strenuous efforts succeeded in having the teaching of domestic science added to the curriculum of three of the Richmond schools. When she resigned from these activities, at her request her books were examined by the president of a business college, and stamped with every penny balanced.

Of deep religious character, Miss Price was baptized in 1904 by Rev. Thomas Graham of the First Presbyterian Church. Hers was the first baptism in the pastorate of Rev. Mr. Graham, and was solemnized during the first Sunday service at Richmond. From that day she has continued one of the valued members of the church, living up sincerely to the obligations she assumed on that occasion.

She and other members of her family planned the Adrian Apartments, let the contracts and managed the construction. They have been interested in all good and philanthropic enterprises having for their object civic betterment and cultural advancement.

In 1924 Miss Price and her sister motored through fourteen states in the East on their way to accept an invitation to attend the fiftieth anniversary of the Massachusetts Normal Art College, now the Massachusetts School of Art, and also to exhibit two framed commissions in oil, which they carried with them. They had the privilege of attending several meetings of cultured people, and returned home by way of Washington City and Mount Vernon. In November, 1926, they motored to Florida, spending the winter at Orlando and Winter Park, and also visited both coasts, St. Petersburg and Daytona Beach. While there they indulged their leisure in painting, writing descriptions and studying trees and flowers. During this six months in Florida they became acquainted with Col. John Calvin Lewis, grandnephew of George Washington, and were entertained in the beautiful home of his daughter at Cloister Grove, Winter Park. From a letter written by Colonel Lewis to them at their home in Richmond the following is an extract: "We were happy all together at the home of my daughter at Cloister Grove, Winter Park, and want you both to be sure to come again next season and we will thoroughly enjoy doing things together."

Miss Caroline Burroughs Price, the other daughter of Mr. and Mrs. Charles T. Price, was educated in the Richmond schools, graduating from the Garfield High School in 1894, and in 1901 graduated from the Massachusetts Normal Art College, now the Massachusetts School of Art at Boston. She was director of art and music in the public schools of Lennox, New Lennox and Lennox Dale, Massachusetts, from 1901 to 1902, and was elected special art teacher under Wilhelmina Segmiller during Superintendent Kendall's administration in the Indianapolis schools in 1902. However, she accepted the position of supervisor of art in the Richmond public schools, a position which she held until 1905. She brought the idea of the Parent-Teacher Association from Massachusetts and planted it in Richmond in 1902. Other new ideas and methods came to the local educational scene through her, and she was a very inspiring influence in the art department.

In 1905 she resigned to assist her sister in caring for their mother in her declining years. Such leisure as she found she devoted to landscape painting, portraiture, designing and pottery. From early youth she was a devoted member of the Methodist Episcopal Church, but when her sister became a member of the First Presbyterian Church she took her letter to it, and united with it in 1917, after the death of her parents. The fine spiritual quality of her literary effort is best revealed in the following beautiful bit of prose of which she is author and which was published in the

Richmond *Item*, December 25, 1918, under the title *Our Christmas Prayer*.

"May we, each one, catch the gleam of radiation from the star of Bethlehem. May it penetrate into the darkest corners of the earth and save more souls for the service of Our Lord and Master. May it consecrate the young, awaken the slumbering, renew the strength of the faltering and discouraged, and reconsecrate those long in Thy service, that the consuming fire of Thy Love may possess us completely for Thy service wherever we may be until all nations and tribes are in one federation of glorious service for Thee.

"May the light of Thy love consume the evil within us so completely that those who have made the supreme Sacrifice shall not have made it in vain; quicken with Thy spirit of brotherly love.

"May each one of us be worthy of the victory we have helped to win for Thee, that we may hold it sacred in this our last crusade. May the scales fall from our eyes that we may see Satan's hand still at work in our cities, towns and wildernesses; and be ever girded with Thy Arm of Humility and Love to fight the battles of christianization of the world.

"May each one of us ally ourselves with Thy forces against those of evil, that we may have universal federation and peace of nations with Thee at last."

Miss Price has been associated with several clubs of the city, including the Audubon Club, the Woman's Auxiliary of the Young Men's Christian Association, of which she is secretary. She and her sister, Abbie May, did much toward lifting the debt of the association. Other associations have been with the Garden Club, the Scribbler's Club, the Art Club, and she proposes in the near future to make use of her eligibility to acquire active membership in the Daughters of the American Revolution and the American Association of University Women.

Rudolph Jerome Price, a grandson of Charles T. Price, was born at Richmond November 23, 1898. He attended public schools in his native city, and his first business experience was delivering Glenn Miller spring water to the sick. He graduated from the Morton High School in 1914, and paid his way while a student in Earlham College by work in the Price Confectionery at 916 Main Street. He was graduated from Earlham in 1918. Meanwhile, however, on March 7, 1918, he entered the Camp Greenleaf Medical Training School, and in June was transferred to Camp Mills, New York, and on the 18th of that month was on his way overseas. He arrived in France June 20, was placed in the French army service and given full charge of a six patient ambulance. His service was administering first aid and taking the wounded to hospitals from the front line. While overseas he frequently saw the great French Minister Clemenceau and other celebrities among the allies. After several months of driving at night, without lights, oftentimes through mud,

sleet and rain, he was gassed in the early part of November, 1918, shortly before the armistice. He recovered under the care of Doctor Cabbot's hospital force, but was returned to the United States on a hospital ship. He was accorded several citations from the French government for valuable service, and also from the United States Government for his work in the Argonne and other sectors.

After his return home and his honorable discharge he entered the University of Michigan at Ann Arbor as a medical student, and in June, 1922, was graduated Doctor of Medicine. In July of that year he entered Miami Valley Hospital at Dayton, Ohio, as an interne, and in July, 1923, went into the office of Doctor Ginn, one of the older surgeons of Dayton. While with Doctor Ginn he performed some notable plastic surgery, reconstructing the eyelids, nose and other facial features of a man who had been fearfully burned. For this he was granted a fellowship in the National College of Surgeons at the age of twenty-seven. In May, 1928, he established his private office in the Fidelity Building at Dayton. He also specializes in roentgenology, his wife assisting him as technician. Doctor Price married in the fall of 1925 Miss Gertrude MacMillan, a graduate nurse. They have a son, Jerome, born November 2, 1930.

HARRY WILLIAM CAWLEY, Doctor of Dental Surgery at Hammond, has been a leader in his profession in that city for the past twenty years. He is also well known in business circles, being president of the Calumet Coal & Supply Company.

Doctor Cawley was born at Eldorado, Ohio, March 11, 1888. The Cawley family were pioneers in the vicinity of Dayton, Ohio. His father, John W. Cawley, was born and reared near Eldorado, had a public school education, taught school for several years, and in July, 1888, a few months after the birth of his son, Doctor Cawley, moved to Hartford City, Indiana. For many years he was in business there as a commercial tailor. He was a Mason and member of the Universalist Church. His death occurred in 1914 and he is buried in a cemetery at Hartford. During the Civil war he was a fifer in a drum corps with an Ohio regiment. John W. Cawley married Mary Emily Moore, who was born and reared near Eldorado, Ohio. Her father was a minister of the Universalist Church, and she, herself, was an earnest worker in that denomination. She was a member of the Woman's Relief Corps. She died in 1929, at the age of eighty, and was buried at Troy, Ohio. Of her five children two died in infancy. The others are: Edgar M., manager of the Calumet Coal & Supply Company at Hammond; Miss Edna Maie Cawley, engaged in secretarial work at Hammond; and Dr. Harry W.

Dr. Harry W. Cawley attended public school at Hartford City, was graduated from high school at Indianapolis in 1906, and in 1909 from Indiana University received his degree Doctor of Dental Surgery. It was in 1912

Rev. Otho Jackson.

that Doctor Cawley entered upon the practice of his profession at Hammond. His offices are in the First Trust Building. He is a busy professional man and is a member of the Lake County, Indiana State and American Dental Associations. He is a member of the Chamber of Commerce, Garfield Lodge No. 569, A. F. and A. M., Lake Hills Country Club, is an independent Republican and a member of the First Methodist Episcopal Church.

Doctor Cawley married at Hammond, October 20, 1924, Miss May Lowery, daughter of William and Emily (Smith) Lowery. Her father is superintendent of the Standard Steel Car Works at Hammond and prior to that for a number of years was superintendent of the Illinois Car Works. He is a Mason and Odd Fellow, member of the Manufacturers Association. Mrs. Cawley attended grammar and high school at Hammond, being a member of the high school class of 1918. She is a member of the First Methodist Episcopal Church, the Eastern Star and the Woman's Club. They have a daughter, Dolores May, born March 20, 1928.

JOHN H. FETTERHOFF is one of the prominent members of the bar of the great oil city of Whiting. He located in Whiting soon after he was admitted to the Indiana bar and for twenty years has been immersed in an increasing professional business and in many pleasant relations with his community.

Mr. Fetterhoff represents an old Pennsylvania family. As the name indicates, the Fetterhoffs are of German ancestry. He was born on a farm near Harrisburg, Pennsylvania, on Washington's birthday, February 22, 1880, son of Philip W. and Catherine (Schwab) Fetterhoff. His great-grandfather, Col. Philip Fetterhoff, was colonel of a Pennsylvania regiment in the War of 1812. His grandfather was John Fetterhoff, of Pennsylvania. Philip W. Fetterhoff was born and reared near Harrisburg, attended public schools and for over half a century has been active as a farmer and stock raiser. He still lives on his old homestead near Harrisburg, at the age of eighty-seven. He and Catherine Schwab were married in 1873. She was also born and reared near Harrisburg and is eighty-three years of age. Both parents are active Lutherans. She is a second cousin of the great American industrial magnate, Charles Schwab, chairman of the board of the United States Steel Corporation. Her father was Simon Schwab. Philip W. Fetterhoff and wife had ten children, two of whom died in infancy. The living children are: Mrs. Sarah Lucas, of Harrisburg; John H.; Miss Susan, who lives near Harrisburg; Mrs. Catherine Sweigard, of Pennsylvania; Isaiah and Philip W., Jr., both of whom are prominent attorneys at Harrisburg; Mrs. Anna Sweigard, of Harrisburg; and Norman, of Harrisburg.

John H. Fetterhoff grew up on a Pennsylvania farm, attended district schools and the Elizabethville Seminary. He came to Indiana to enter Valparaiso University, where he was graduated in 1908 and admitted to the bar the same year. In 1910 he located at Whiting, where he has steadily practiced law through the years. His offices are in the Central State Bank Building. He is a member of the Lake County, Indiana State and American Bar Associations.

Mr. Fetterhoff has never married. He enjoys many relationships with civic and fraternal organizations, including the Chamber of Commerce, Whiting Lodge No. 613, A. F. and A. M., Whiting Chapter, Royal Arch Masons, the Knights Templar Commandery at East Chicago, Fort Wayne Consistory of the Scottish Rite and Orak Temple of the Mystic Shrine at Hammond. He is a past exalted ruler of his lodge of Elks, member of the Independent Order of Odd Fellows, the Woodmar Country Club, the Lincoln Hills Country Club, the Congressional Country Club at Washington, D. C., and the Lions Club. Mr. Fetterhoff for two terms was city attorney of Whiting and was deputy prosecuting attorney for two terms. He is a former president of the County Bar Association. He votes as a Republican. During the World war he was enlisted in the local Home Guard. He enjoys golf, baseball and other outdoor sports.

REV. LEMUEL OTHO JACKSON. In the person of Rev. Lemuel Otho Jackson, pastor of the Christian Church at Marengo, is found one of the most wholesome and human of philosophers and most courageous ethical teachers that Crawford County has ever known. The strength of his faith, the encouragement to be found in his business success, the extent of his insight and services and the power of his public utterances and his maintenance of the truth in which he believes, unite in the making of a career of signal usefulness and purpose.

Lemuel Otho Jackson was born September 8, 1890, on a farm in Washington County, Indiana, and is a son of William Edward and Amanda (Farebee) Jackson. His grandfather, William Jackson, was born in North Carolina, whence he migrated in an early day to Kentucky, in which state he spent the remainder of his life as an agriculturist. William Edward Jackson was born in Kentucky, but in young manhood moved to Washington County, Indiana, where he married a native of that state and spent the active years of his life in tilling the soil. He is now retired and a resident of Scottsburg, where he is a substantial and highly-respected citizen. Mrs. Jackson, who was born in Washington County, also survives, and to her and her husband have been born the following children: Ora E., who married Harry McClain, of Scottsburg, and has two children: Glenn and Gladys; Lemuel Otho, of this review; Clarence, of Logansport, who married Carrie Martin and has four children; Hall, Earl, Wayne and Mary Ellen; Clifford, a farmer of Scottsburg, who married Lodana Payne; Christina, who died in infancy; Arthur, of Pontiac, Michigan, who is married and has one child, Arthur, Jr.; and Laurence, of Royal Oak, Michigan, who is married and has two children.

Lemuel Otho Jackson received his early education in the public schools of Scottsburg and after his graduation from high school attended the Theological Seminary and was graduated therefrom with the degree of Ph. D. His first parish was at Spring Valley, where he remained two years, following which he filled pulpits at Blue Grass, Fulton County, three years; Paoli, three years; and French Lick, twelve years, and in 1922 became pastor of the Christian Church at Marengo, where he has since remained. He has made this a successful parish and has done much to elevate the moral tone of the community through his intense zeal and enthusiasm. He is not only a spiritual guide to his people, but a business advisor as well, for he is himself a successful business man. While at Paoli and French Lick he was manager of the Tomato Products Company, and now holds the same position at Marengo, where the plant gives employment to fifty people. Reverend Jackson maintains an independent stand upon the question of politics, and as a fraternalist is affiliated with the Independent Order of Odd Fellows and the Modern Woodmen of America. He cooperates with other public-spirited citizens in the furthering of civic enterprises for the general benefit of the community.

On December 24, 1912, Reverend Jackson was united in marriage with Miss Alice Reynolds, daughter of Charles and Louisa (Miller) Reynolds, of Scottsburg, Indiana, and to this union there have come seven children: Charles, born November 7, 1914, who is attending high school in the class of 1932; Seldon, born January 27, 1916; Helen, born March 27, 1918; Junior O., born August 23, 1920; May Alice, born in November, 1924; Billy, born March 7, 1927; and James, born November 27, 1930.

JOY F. BUCKNER is one of the popular and progressive physicians and surgeons of Fort Wayne, with offices at the corner of Broadway and Taylor streets.

He was born in Northeastern Indiana, in Wells County, January 26, 1898, son of Francis Marion Buckner. More of the details of the Buckner family are published on other pages. Dr. Joy F. Buckner graduated from high school at Bluffton, Indiana, in 1917, and in the fall of the same year entered the University of Indiana. His work there was interrupted during the World war. He entered the Officers Training School at Camp Taylor, Kentucky, serving in the latter months of 1918, until after the armistice. He then resumed his college course and in 1924 was graduated Doctor of Science and took his M. D. degree at the university in 1926. He had six months of experience as an interne, from January 1 to July, 1926, at St. Vincent's Hospital at Indianapolis. Doctor Buckner has practiced his profession at Fort Wayne since September, 1926. He is a mem-

ber of the Allen County, Indiana State and American Medical Associations, and the Sigma Alpha Epsilon fraternity.

He married, August 7, 1926, Miss Winifred Morse Terry, of Indianapolis. She is a graduate of the Shortridge High School of Indianapolis with the class of 1919, and in 1925 graduated from the University of Iowa. They have one daughter, Kathryn K., born August 13, 1928.

FREDERICK GRANVILLE KENNEDY since 1920 has been one of Whiting's most useful public servants, the postmaster of the city. Mr. Kennedy brought to this office the experience of a successful business man.

He was born at Greenfield, Ohio, March 15, 1879, son of John and Edith (Clark) Kennedy. His father's father and grandfather were early settlers near Canton, Ohio, and are buried in the Kennedy family cemetery near that city. John Kennedy was born and reared in Ohio, was educated in public schools and served as a soldier in the Union army during the Civil war, being a member of the Sixty-fifth Ohio Volunteer Infantry. After the war he devoted his attention to farming and stock raising. He died in 1893 and is buried at Greenville. His home was on a farm near that Ohio city from 1881. His wife, Edith Clark, was born and reared near Logan, Ohio, was well educated and was a school teacher before her marriage. She was a devout Methodist. Her death occurred in 1919 and she is also buried at Greenville. Of their five children Estella died at the age of eighteen; U. L. Kennedy lives at Long Beach, California; Homer O. is a resident of Bellefontaine, Ohio; Frederick G.; and Carrie, who died when four years old.

Frederick G. Kennedy attended public schools at Greenville, and on graduating from high school in 1898 took up a career as a business man at Bellefontaine. He was in the restaurant business there until 1905, and on selling out entered the postal service. In the fall of 1918 he came to Whiting and was in the refining department of the Standard Oil Company until 1920, when he was appointed postmaster.

His first commission as postmaster was signed by President Wilson and he has been retained in office through the successive administrations of Presidents Harding, Coolidge and Hoover. In this office he has worked and studied with a view to making the postal facilities completely adequate for the commercial and industrial interests of the city.

Mr. Kennedy is affiliated with Whiting Lodge No. 613, A. F. and A. M., Whiting Chapter, Royal Arch Masons. He is a Republican, member of the First Methodist Episcopal Church, the Chamber of Commerce and Luncheon Club. His recreations are golf, hunting and fishing.

He married at Bellefontaine, Ohio, February 7, 1907, Miss Cora Snider, daughter of Hugh and Mary (Burkhart) Snider. Her father was a captain in the Union army dur-

William J Henley

ing the Civil war and for many years conducted a prosperous grocery business in Bellefontaine, where he died in 1913 and is buried. Her mother passed away in 1920. Mrs. Kennedy had one brother, who died when two years old. She was educated in the schools of Bellefontaine and was a newspaper woman before her marriage. She was connected with the *Bellefontaine Daily Examiner*. In Whiting she is active in the Methodist Church, teaches a class in the Sunday School and belongs to the Eastern Star and Woman's Club.

GEORGE JOHN WOLF, president of the Hammond School Board, is a business man who has taken a keen interest in local educational affairs and is the type of citizen always willing to sacrifice his time and effort in behalf of some phase of the public welfare.

Mr. Wolf was born in Lake County, Indiana, November 8, 1887, son of John E. and Anna (Lavene) Wolf. His paternal grandfather, August Wolf, came from Germany and was one of the pioneers of Lake County, Indiana. He settled near East Gary, at what was then known as Lake Station, and he and his wife are buried in the cemetery at East Gary. John E. Wolf was also born and reared in Lake County, attended public schools and in early life was a farmer. In 1888 he located at Hammond and was engaged in the building material business until his death in 1893. His wife, Anna Lavene, was born and reared at Muskegon, and attended school there. She died in 1924 and she and her husband are buried in the Oak Hill Cemetery at Hammond. They were active members of the Lutheran Church. Their family consisted of the following children: John C., of Hammond; Joseph A., of Hammond; Ethel, wife of William Huehn, of Hammond; George J.; Charles E., of Hammond; and Walter R., who died in 1893, at the age of two years, also a half brother, Edward W. Hess.

George J. Wolf made the best of his early advantages in the grammar and high schools of Hammond. He was graduated from high school in 1904 and immediately went to work. Up to 1917 he was an employee of the Wells Fargo & Company Express. From 1917 to 1927 he did a prosperous business as a manufacturer of concrete building units. He sold out to take over the Hammond franchise for the Studebaker car, and he has since been the distributor for the Studebaker products in this territory. He has large and handsome sales rooms and offices at 122-124 State Street. In addition to the Studebaker he has the local agency for the Pierce Arrow cars.

Mr. Wolf has had four children who have been educated in the schools of Hammond, and since the first child entered school he has been interested in the welfare and progress of local school facilities, and this interest led to his election as president of the local board of education. He is also a member of the Hammond Chamber of Commerce, the Kiwanis Club, Lake Hills Country Club, and for many years he and his family have been active in the Lutheran Church. He is a Republican. From 1920 to 1924 he was president of the City Council.

Mr. Wolf married, May 18, 1910, at Hammond, Miss Elizabeth Brumm, daughter of August and Wilhelmina Brumm. Her father was a carpenter by trade and died in 1930, being buried at Hammond. Her mother is now eighty-nine years of age. Mrs. Wolf attended grammar and high schools at Hammond, is a graduate of Valparaiso University, and before her marriage taught in the Hammond public schools. She is a member of the Woman's Club. The four children of Mr. and Mrs. Wolf are: George Homer, wno graduated from the Hammond High School in 1928 and is a member of the class of 1932 in Indiana University; Wallace David and Warren Allen, both students in the high school; and Jane Elizabeth, in grammar school.

HON. WILLIAM J. HENLEY, one of Indiana's best known lawyers and jurists, has been a leader in his profession at Rushville forty-five years. His name over the state is especially well known because of his gifted services while on the bench of the Court of Appeals.

Judge Henley was born at Carthage, Indiana, October 15, 1864, son of Thomas W. and Hannah C. (Williams) Henley, his father a native of North Carolina and his mother of Wilmington, Ohio. Judge Henley is a direct descendant of Robert Henley, who in England was Lord Northington, Lord Chancellor of England. Another ancestor was Patrick Henley, who came to the United States on the same boat with William Penn. The Henley family for many generations have been devout Friends.

Judge Henley's father was a farmer who lived most of his life near Carthage in Rush County. He died in 1903 and his wife in 1912. William J. Henley attended a private school conducted by the Friends at Carthage and studied law in the office of Mellette & Bundy at Newcastle. In 1885 he was admitted to the bar and entered upon his law practice at Rushville. Eleven years later he was elected judge of the Court of Appeals, taking his seat on the bench January 1, 1897. He was made chief justice of the court, at the age of thirty-three, being the youngest man to hold that honor in Indiana. Judge Henley was on the bench until 1904. After being nominated for the third term, he resigned to accept the office of president and general counsel for the Chicago & Western Indiana Railway, which is the holding company of seven trunk lines entering Chicago, with headquarters in Chicago. In 1912 Judge Henley resigned and returned to Indiana to carry on his practice of law. He is president of the Central Fuel Company at Rushville. He is a member of the Rush County, Indiana State and American Bar Association and for years has been one of the leading figures in the Republican party of the state. His high responsibilities and his many interesting activities have kept his name before the public. In 1909 the inimitable Sam Blythe, who at that time was running a series of his articles on prominent political personalities over the country, under the title of *Who's Who and Why*, in the Saturday Evening Post, devoted a full page to Judge Henley, his friends, his position in Indiana politics and affairs. Judge Henley is the only person honored by receiving this kind of publicity in Indiana. His name has been associated many times with the leading men of the nation. Judge Henley is a member of the Masonic fraternity and the B. P. O. Elks.

He married, May 6, 1885, Miss Sarah A. Monroe, who was born at Rushville, February 10, 1865, daughter of George and Missouri (Hackelman) Monroe. In 1912 Judge Henley married Myrtle E. Robinson, a native of Marion, Indiana, daughter of William A. and Amy (Whitfield) Robinson. Judge Henley has four children, the first three by his first marriage, William J., Jr., of Chicago, June and Gladys, and by his present wife has a daughter, Mary Elizabeth.

HAZEL FRANCES LONG, librarian of the Whiting Public Library, was born in Chicago, and was ten months of age when her parents established their home in Whiting. She is a daughter of Frank M. and Fannie (Pullen) Long. Her grandfather, Martin Long, came from Hull, England, and married Martha Coburn, of Boston, Massachusetts. These grandparents are buried in the Forest Home Cemetery at Chicago. The Pullens also came from England, and were early settlers near Brighton, Illinois. Her maternal grandfather was an early minister in that section of Illinois. Frank M. Long was born in Chicago, attended school there and is a veteran employee of the Standard Oil Company at Whiting, being chief clerk of the mechanical department. Fannie Pullen was born near Brighton, Illinois, was educated in public schools there and died August 21, 1930, being buried at Gary. She was a member of the Plymouth Congregational Church. There were three children, Frank M., Jr., Martha Elizabeth and Hazel Frances. Frank Martin Long, Jr., was born at Whiting, graduated from the Whiting High School and from the Kent College of Law at Chicago, and is now with the sales and legal department of the Standard Oil Company. He married Lois Morrison, of Whiting, and has a son, Frank Martin Long III, born in 1929. Martha Elizabeth Long was born in Whiting, is a graduate of the high school, then attended the University of Chicago, and since graduating from the Metropolitan Business College has been employed as a secretary in the University of Chicago School of Education.

Hazel Frances Long was graduated from the Whiting High School in 1913 and since then has devoted practically all her time to library work. She was with the Whiting Public Library until 1915. The following year she spent in the Library School of the University of Wisconsin, where she received the Bachelor of Library Science degree in 1916. Since then she has done advanced work in the University of Chicago. During 1916 she was in the public library at Cleveland, Ohio, and from 1916 to 1918 with the Whiting Public Library. During the war, in 1918, she worked for the Sinclair Oil Refining Company. In 1921 she was made acting librarian of the public library at Oak Park, Illinois. In 1922 she returned to the Whiting Public Library, was children's librarian, and since 1924 has been librarian. Miss Long is a member of the Beta Gamma Upsilon sorority, the Whiting Woman's Club, the Lake Hills Country Club and the Plymouth Congregational Church.

WILLIAM WOOD PARSONS, former president of the Indiana State Normal School at Terre Haute, was one of the first students to enroll in the institution when it was opened in 1870.

He was born at Terre Haute, May 18, 1850, and died September 28, 1925, after a long and useful life of three-quarters of a century. He was a son of Dr. Thomas and Elizabeth (Ryman) Parsons. His father was a pioneer doctor of Terre Haute, where he practiced medicine until 1862, and then lived retired on a farm in Douglas County, Illinois, until his death in 1869.

William Wood Parsons graduated from high school at Tuscola, Illinois, and with the opening of the Indiana State Normal School on January 6, 1870, joined the first class. He was graduated in 1872, and in 1886 received the Master of Arts degree from Indiana University, and DePauw University and Wabash College conferred upon him the degree Doctor of Letters. He taught school near Tuscola, Illinois, was principal of a school at Gosport, Indiana, and also taught at Indianapolis. In 1876 he returned to the Indiana Normal School, where he was professor of English from 1876 to 1879, head of the English department, in 1882 became vice president, in 1855 president, and was head of the institution thirty-six years, resigning the office in 1921.

It was during the long and successful administration of Doctor Parsons that the school at Terre Haute became one of the outstanding institutions of the kind in the country. In June, 1927, on Alumni Day, the Memorial Chimes were dedicated as a gift of alumni and friends to commemorate those who had devoted their lives to the cause of education. At the same time was established the Parsons-Sandison Living Memorial Fund, the proceeds of which are to enable students through loans to complete their education.

Doctor Parsons in 1894 helped organize the Terre Haute Trust Company and was on the board of directors until 1922. He was for twenty-five years a director and from March, 1922, until his death was chairman of the board of directors of the First National Bank of Terre Haute. He was also interested in other banking institutions, was president of

Richard Nash Elliott,

the board of managers of the Rose Orphan Home, member of the board of managers of the Rose Polytechnic Institute. He was a Methodist and a Republican.

His first wife was Harriet Wilkes, of Terre Haute. They had two children, both deceased. Harold died in infancy and Robert died soon after his graduation from Wabash College. Harriet Wilkes Parsons died in 1915. His second marriage, in 1917, was with Miss Martina Erickson, principal of Monticello Seminary at Godfrey, Illinois. She was the first dean of women at the Indiana State Normal College at Terre Haute.

REV. GEORGE THEGZE was born and reared and received his theological training in Hungary. He came to the United States in 1914, and since then several localities in the Middle West and the East have received the benefit of his devotion and spiritual leadership. Father Thegze is now pastor of St. Mary's Church, Greek Catholic, at Whiting.

He was born in Austria-Hungary, May 5, 1883, son of Rev. Victor and Helen (Egressy) Thegze. His parents were born and reared in Hungary, were educated in parochial schools there, and his father was ordained a minister of the Greek Catholic Church. In 1910 he came to America and was pastor of St. Michael's Greek Catholic Church at Binghamton, New York, until his death on December 29, 1920. He is buried in St. Michael's Church Cemetery. After his death his widow returned to Czecho-Slovakia, where she now resides. There were five children, one dying in infancy. George was the oldest child. The others live in Europe.

George Thegze attended school in Hungary, completing his common school work in 1905, and in 1910 was graduated from the University of Budapest, where he received his theological training. He was ordained a priest in that year and for several years following was pastor of the Church of the Immaculate Conception at Jank, Hungary. He came to the United States in 1914. His first pastorate was at St. Michael's Church at Gary, Indiana. After three years he went east and for about two years was pastor of St. John's Church at Bayonne, New Jersey, and then pastor of the Holy Ghost Church at Pittsburgh, Pennsylvania, until 1928, when he took up his duties in St. Mary's Church at Whiting, Indiana. Father Thegze is a popular member of the community, a helpful citizen, and has found contact with organizations both in and out of his parish. He is a member of the Whiting Lions Club. He votes independently as an American citizen. His hobby is hunting. Every season he goes to the woods of Northern Wisconsin to hunt big game. He is head of the parochial school of St. Mary's parish, supervising the work of a large enrollment of students.

He married in Hungary, November 10, 1910, Miss Helen Legeza, daughter of Rev. Alexander and Anna (Lamfalussy) Legeza, of Kiralyhaza, Hungary. Her father for many years was a priest of the Greek Catholic Church. Both her parents died during the World war. Mrs. Thegze was born and reared in Hungary and educated in the public schools at Ungvar. They have four children: George, Jr., Helen, Charles and Victor. George, Jr., graduated from the Oliver High School at Pittsburgh, then spent three years in Pittsburgh University, and is now studying medicine abroad at Vienna University. The daughter, Helen, after graduating from the Oliver High School at Pittsburgh spent two years in the Academy of Mt. Mercy in that city and is now engaged in secretarial work in Chicago. Charles is a graduate of the Whiting High School and a student in Notre Dame University, taking the pre-medical course. Victor is in grammar school at Whiting.

HON. RICHARD NASH ELLIOTT, who served fourteen years as representative of the Sixth Indiana District in Congress, was born in Fayette County and began the practice of law at Connersville in 1896. He has been a prominent figure in his home state and at Washington, and in 1931, on retiring from Congress, was appointed by President Hoover assistant comptroller general of the United States.

He was born on the home farm in Fayette County, April 25, 1873, son of Charles W. and Eliza A. (Nash) Elliott. The Nash family is of Scotch-Irish ancestry and has been in America since Colonial times. Eliza A. Nash was born in Fairview Township, Fayette County, Indiana, daughter of Richard and Margaret (Moffett) Nash, and a granddaughter of Richard Nash, who was a resident of Pennsylvania when the first national census was taken in 1790. Richard Nash II, for whom Richard Nash Elliott was named, was born in Westmoreland County, Pennsylvania, in 1798. His wife was also a native of Pennsylvania. Richard Nash in his early life was employed in moving salt and other freight, by flatboat down the Ohio and Mississippi rivers to New Orleans, later settled in Indiana and acquired a tract of land in what is now Fairview Township, Fayette County. Richard Nash was a man of leadership in community affairs, serving as justice of the peace.

Charles W. Elliott, father of Richard N. Elliott, was born at Brooksville, Kentucky, and in 1833 came with his parents, John and Rachel (Pigman) Elliott, to Indiana. They located on a pioneer farm in Jennings Township, Fayette County. John Elliott was born in Fauquier County, Virginia, in 1800, and went with his parents from Virginia to Kentucky. He was one of the sterling pioneer farmers and citizens of Fayette County. After his marriage Charles W. Elliott lived at the old homestead, then bought land of his own, and was also a carpenter and builder. He went to the California gold fields in 1849, going west by boat down the Ohio and Mississippi rivers to New Orleans, crossed the Gulf of Mexico, and while on the Chagres River in the Isthmus of Panama he was attacked by jungle fever, which nearly terminated his life.

As soon as he had partially recovered he returned home and was satisfied with the peaceful routine of an Indiana farmer during the rest of his active life. He died June 8, 1891, and was survived by his widow until March, 1922. Their children were: Lurena M., who died when five years old; Daisy V., who died at the age of four years; Richard N.; Charles W., Jr., who died November 25, 1897; and Cecile Edna, wife of Walter Sefton, of Connersville.

Richard Nash Elliott was educated in the public schools of Fayette County, taught school there for three years and studied law at Connersville in the office of Connor & McIntosh. In December, 1896, he was admitted to the bar, opened his law office in Connersville and for several years was a partner of Ira T. Trusler, subsequent partners in professional work being Frederick I. Barrows, David W. McKee, Hyatt L. Frost and Allen Wiles. During later years he was a member of the prominent Connersville firm of McKee, Wiles & Elliott.

On June 26, 1917, Mr. Elliott was elected to the Sixty-fifth Congress for the unexpired term 1917-19 of Daniel W. Comstock, deceased. He was reelected to the Sixty-sixth Congress in 1918 and continued to represent the Sixth Indiana District until March 4, 1931, his last term being in the Seventy-first Congress. He was a valuable member of Congress during the world war period and throughout the following decade gave an earnest and studious attention to the great problems of economic legislation and international relationships. Soon after he began the practice of law Mr. Elliott, in 1898, was appointed county attorney of Fayette County and filled that office nine consecutive years. For four years he was city attorney of Connersville and was also candidate for mayor of the city, and for the office of prosecuting attorney. In 1904 he was elected to represent Fayette County in the Indiana General Assembly and served in the sessions of 1905, 1907 and the special session of 1908. In 1905 he was appointed a member of the Indiana Tuberculosis Commission. He made a personal tour of investigation of leading institutions for the treatment of tuberculosis in New Mexico, Colorado, New York and Massachusetts, and after a careful study of the laws and methods of management he introduced, in 1907, and championed the enactment of the bill providing for the erection and equipment of the Indiana State Tuberculosis Hospital at Rockville. While in Congress Mr. Elliott was a member of the committee that drafted and reported for passage the Nineteenth Amendment to the Constitution of the United States, the Woman's Suffrage Amendment. He was acting chairman of the House committee on invalid pensions and was author of the maimed soldiers bill to increase the pensions of soldiers who had lost legs or arms. In December, 1924, in the Sixty-ninth Congress, he was made chairman of the House committee on public buildings and grounds. He was also a member of the United States Public Building Commission, the Arlington Memorial Bridge Commission, the Capitol Plaza Commission and the United States Supreme Court Building Commission. He was the author of the Elliott Public Building Act, approved May 25, 1926, and a series of amendatory acts, which authorized the construction in the national capital and throughout the United States of public buildings to the amount of $700,000,000. Under the terms of these acts the Federal buildings in Washington are being reconstructed. Some of the most noted of these buildings are for the Departments of Agriculture, Commerce, Justice, Labor, Navy, Post Office, Treasury, and War; and buildings to house the independent bureaus of the Government, the new House Office Building, the United States Supreme Courthouse, the Archives Building, the Natural History Building at the Smithsonian Institution, the Arlington Memorial Bridge and the extension of the capitol grounds.

In addition to these, large Federal buildings are being erected in all of the principal cities of the United States and Federal buildings in all of the smaller cities not heretofore provided with these buildings where the postal receipts will exceed the sum of $20,000 per annum.

This is probably the greatest building program that was ever started by any nation in peace times during the world history. Largely through his influence many thousand carloads of famous Indiana limestone were utilized in this construction program at Washington.

Mr. Elliott has been a lifelong Republican. He was a delegate to the Republican national convention at Chicago, in 1916, and chairman of the Republican state convention in 1930. He has served as a member of the board of trustees of the Methodist Episcopal Church at Connersville. He is a past master of the Masonic Lodge, a past high priest of the Royal Arch Masons, and is a member of the B. P. O. Elks and Improved Order of Red Men.

He married, January 20, 1898, Miss Lizzie A. Ostheimer. She was born and reared at Connersville, daughter of Simon and Mary E. (Simpkins) Ostheimer. Her father was born in Germany and her mother at Bethel, Ohio. Her father was in the Third Indiana Battery of artillery in the Civil war and later was county treasurer of Fayette County.

CHARLES BARAN. Among the foreign-born citizens of Gary who have attained business success and recognition through the medium of their own well directed efforts, few have made greater strides than Charles Baran, a prosperous furniture merchant and real estate operator. Mr. Baran came to this country at the time he attained his majority, and has been a resident of Gary since 1907. He is essentially a self-made man in the broadest sense of that term, and occupies a substantial place in the esteem and respect of his fellow-citizens and associates.

Mr. Baran was born in Poland, October 26, 1880, and is a son of John and Mary (Kriski)

Baran. His parents were born in Poland, where they received educations in the public schools at Zarszyn, and spent their entire lives in their native land, where John Baran was a farmer of moderate means. He died in April, 1919, his widow surviving him until August 1, 1928, and both are buried in the cemetery at Zarszyn. They were the parents of six sons: Charles, of this review; John, of Poland; Joseph, who met his death on a battlefield during the World war; and Walter, Benny and Boles, all of Poland.

Charles Baran acquired his education in the public schools of Zarszyn, following which he assisted his father in the work of the home farm until he reached the age of twenty-one years. At that time he decided that there were greater opportunities for an ambitious and energetic young man to be found in the United States, and accordingly he gathered together his few resources and small capital and made his way to this country, first settling at New York City, where he secured employment and remained for one and one-half years. During this period he saved his earnings carefully, and in 1907, when he first came to Gary, was able to open a modest general mercantile business. Being enterprising, untiring and possessed of good business ability, he built up a paying business, which he conducted along general lines until 1916, in that year turning his attention exclusively to the furniture business, in which he has continued to be engaged with increasing success to the present. He is now the proprietor and sole owner of a large and modern establishment at 1516 Broadway, where he owns the building, conducting his enterprise under the name of the Baran Furniture Company. Early in his career at Gary Mr. Baran became convinced of the value of real estate in the city and its environs, and accordingly branched out into the realty business. From 1923 until 1928 he was a developer of Gary property to the extent of some $4,000,000, and may therefore be called one of the real contributors to the city's growth and progress. He is now president of the Charles Baran Real Estate Company, with offices at 1517 Broadway; president of the Joseph Broadway Realty Company, which owns a large three-story and basement building in the 1500 block, Broadway; and president of the Pennsylvania Lumber Supply Company. He belongs to the Commercial Club and Chamber of Commerce, as a member of which affiliated bodies he gives his support to all worthy civic movements, and during the World war was greatly active in all the drives and a member of Conscription Board No. 2. A Democrat in politics, he has been active in his party for years, and in 1930 was the candidate of his fellow Democrats for county commissioner of the First District of Lake County. Mr. Baran is a member of St. Mark's Catholic Church.

On June 22, 1914, Mr. Baran was united in marriage, at Gary, with Miss Rosie Dardziski, daughter of Deofil and Mary Dardziski, the former of whom was for years connected with the Illinois Steel Company and is now associated with Mr. Baran in the furniture business. Mrs. Dardziski died in 1915 and was laid to rest in the cemetery at Gary. Mrs. Baran was educated in the public schools of Gary, graduating from the Emerson High School. She is essentially a home-lover and home-maker, having but few outside activities, but is a faithful member of St. Mark's Catholic Church. Mr. and Mrs. Baran have two children: Charles, Jr., and Rosie, both of whom are attending the Emerson School.

GEORGE W. OSBORN is an able Indiana lawyer, has practiced for twenty years at Sheridan in Hamilton County, and his fellow members of the bar and citizens generally understand and appreciate his good work as a lawyer, his high personal character, and undoubtedly just for the fact that he lives in an overwhelmingly Republican county he would have repeatedly been honored with the highest offices in the gift of his fellow citizens.

Mr. Osborn was born on a farm in Marion County, Indiana, October 20, 1879. His father, David Osborn, grew up in Marion County. Mr. Osborn's grandfather was born in Virginia, in 1771, and died in 1875, when 104 years old. His death occurred just a year before the United States celebrated the hundredth anniversary of its independence, and he was a child five years old when that immortal document was signed. He was a pioneer of Indiana and entered land in Marion County in 1822. The patent to the land was signed by President James Monroe. David Osborn married Anna Roberts, also a native of Marion County. Her father, Jacob Roberts, married Miss Van Schack.

George W. Osborn was three years of age when his parents moved to a farm in Clay Township, Hamilton County, and there he grew up. After the common schools he had to depend on his own efforts for his education and advancement, and he paid all his expenses while a student at the University of Indiana. He majored in law and in January, 1907, was admitted to the bar and on the 4th of February began his career as a practicing attorney at Sheridan. Mr. Osborn has the distinction of being the only Democrat to hold the office of prosecuting attorney of Hamilton County. He was in that office during the two years, 1913-1914. In 1920 he was Democratic candidate for the office of circuit judge and in 1928 was again put up by the Democratic party as a candidate for the bench. In this last campaign he made a wonderful showing against overwhelming odds. President Hoover carried Hamilton County by 4,200 votes, and Judge Osborn lost the county by 607 votes, figures that indicate his high personal popularity and his standing as a lawyer.

Mr. Osborn married Miss Bessie Kercheral, who died, leaving no children. His second wife was Dessie Spraul, who passed away in 1929, leaving two sons. John R. Osborn is a student in Butler University at Indianapolis, and is working to meet his expenses. The second son, George W., Jr., is a graduate of the Sheridan High School. He is a remarkable specimen of physical manhood, standing six feet, seven and three-quarters inches, and is an expert ball player. His high school team was the best in this section of the state during his senior year.

Mr. Osborn is a member of the Lodge, Royal Arch Chapter and Knights Templar Commandery of Masons and is active in the Rotary Club. Sheridan is the smallest town in the world to have a Rotary charter.

MARTIN FRANK CUNNINGHAM, president of the City Board of Safety of Hammond, has for many years been identified with an industrial establishment which has probably brought more nation-wide publicity to Hammond as an industrial center than any other, the W. B. Conkey Company. Mr. Cunningham for many years has been plant superintendent of this notable institution.

He is a native of Indiana, born in the City of LaFayette February 9, 1880, son of Martin and Ellen (Wimsey) Cunningham. His parents were born in Ireland and had educational advantages in the parochial schools there before they came to America. They met and married in this country and lived out their lives in LaFayette. His father built up a good business as a teaming contractor and wood dealer. Both parents were active in the Catholic Church. The father passed away in 1889 and the mother in 1913. Both are buried at LaFayette. Of their twelve children, twins and several others died in infancy. One son, James, died during the Spanish-American war. The living children are: Miss Mary, of Chicago; Mrs. Katherine Welsh, of Chicago; Margaret, wife of L. Rickey, of Indianapolis; William, of Indianapolis; and Martin F.

Martin F. Cunningham attended parochial school in LaFayette, completed a business college course there, and left school to take up the printing business, serving his early apprenticeship and acquiring a broad knowledge of the business during the four years he was with the Spring-Emerson Printing Company. He left there in 1900 to come to Hammond, to join the W. B. Conkey Company. Except for a few years in Chicago, with the R. R. Donnelley Company, he has been with the Conkey plant ever since. He started as a pressman, was promoted to foreman of the press room, and since 1914 has had the important responsibility of acting as plant superintendent.

Outside of his main line of work Mr. Cunningham has always taken a keen interest in matters of civic and political concern to the community. He has done some valuable work as president of the Board of Safety during the administration of the present mayor. He is president of the Calumet Building & Loan Association, is a director of the Chamber of Commerce, member of the B. P. O. Elks, and for years was active in the Hammond Country Club. In politics he is a Democrat. His chief pastime is the game of bridge.

Mr. Cunningham married at Hammond, September 7, 1904, Miss Mary Edith Morrison. Her parents, Thomas and Jane (Brown) Morrison, were born and reared in Scotland, were married in Canada, and they established their home at Hammond about 1900. Her father for a number of years was an employee of the Standard Oil Company at Whiting. He died in 1912. Her mother was killed in an automobile accident at Hammond in 1928. Both her parents are buried at Hammond. Mrs. Cunningham attended public school in Canada. She is a member of St. Paul's Episcopal Church at Hammond. Three children were born to their marriage. The youngest, Martin, Jr., died when fourteen months old. The two surviving daughters are Marion and Jean. Marion is the wife of Merl Esterline, who is in the nursery business at Indianapolis, and has a daughter, Jane Esterline. Both daughters are graduates of the Hammond High School. Marion after leaving high school spent a year in the Chevy Chase School for Girls near Washington, and Jean spent a year in the National Park Seminary at Washington. Marion for three years was a student in the University of Wisconsin. Jean graduated from the University of Wisconsin in 1928 and is now the talented society editor of the *Lake County Times* at Hammond.

GERARD CORNELIUS DOOGE, a mechanical and structural engineer by training and profession, is one of Gary's prominent business men, being president of the All Pure Ice Company, at 900 Van Buren Street.

Mr. Dooge, as his name indicates, is a descendant of Dutch ancestry. His people were among the prominent Dutch colonists in Western Michigan at Grand Rapids. Mr. Dooge was born in the City of Grand Rapids, February 24, 1882, a son of Bastian and Martha (Stander) Dooge. His father was born in the Netherlands, was educated there and was twenty years old when he came to America and settled at Grand Rapids. For forty-two years he was a grocery merchant in that city, where he died in 1913. His wife, Martha Stander, was born and reared at Elgin, Michigan. She was a devout member of the Highland Dutch Reformed Church at Grand Rapids. She died in 1919. These parents had a family of seven children: Adrian, of Grand Rapids; Aaron, who died in infancy; John, deceased; Harry, of Grand Rapids; Gerard C.; Gertrude, Mrs. William Frey, of Grand Rapids; and William, of Grand Rapids.

Gerard C. Dooge graduated from the Grand Rapids High School in 1900, following which he took the four years' scientific course in the University of Michigan. He was awarded the Bachelor of Science degree in 1904, and at the same time received his degree in civil engineering. During the summer session of the University of Michigan in 1904 he was employed as one of the instructors. In 1905 he entered the service of the Laclede Gas Light Company at Saint Louis, Missouri, as

Arthur Bohn

assistant superintendent of the water gas department. For a time he practiced as a consulting engineer at Chattanooga, Tennessee, for six months was assistant county engineer of Scott County, Missouri, and from there went to Cincinnati as assistant bridge engineer with the Cincinnati, Hamilton & Dayton Railway Company. After a year he returned to Chattanooga as assistant chief engineer for the Converse Bridge Company, with which he remained until 1910. For eight months he was located at McAlester, Oklahoma, as an engineer, when he formed a partnership and practiced as a member of the engineering firm of Eady & Dooge until 1911.

Mr. Dooge came to Gary in 1911 and was a structural engineer for the American Bridge Company until 1924. He left that corporation to become secretary and treasurer of the Zweig Roofing & Structural Steel Company at Gary, but sold his interest in this organization in November, 1925.

In May, 1926, Mr. Dooge and Lawrence R. McNamee acquired the business known as the All Pure Ice Company. On October 3, 1930, Mr. Dooge acquired the interest of Mr. McNamee, and having in the meantime been secretary of the corporation he has since been president and treasurer, while his brother-in-law, Thomas L. Yarrington, is vice president and Mrs. Dooge is secretary. This company has a model plant, and it is one of the chief sources of supply for pure ice throughout the Gary district. Mr. Dooge is also interested in the water distributing company known as the Porter Springs Water Distributing Company, selling bottled supplies of sparkling spring water throughout Gary, Hammond, Indiana Harbor, East Chicago, Michigan City and Valparaiso. They manufacture large quantities of distilled water for medicinal and industrial purposes.

Mr. Dooge is a member of the Commercial Club and the Chamber of Commerce, the Gary Rotary Club, University Club, Gary Country Club. He is affiliated with Gary Chapter, Royal Arch Masons, and is a member of the Presbyterian Church.

He married at Chattanooga, Tennessee, March 19, 1914, Miss Lula Ray Yarrington, daughter of Thomas Yarrington. Her father was for many years connected with the Belt Railroad at Chattanooga. Both her parents are deceased and are buried in the Tennessee city. Mrs. Dooge attended school at Chattanooga, finishing her high school work there. She is a member of the Presbyterian Church, organized and was the second president of the Mary Walton Women's Society and is a member of the Service Club. Mr. and Mrs. Dooge have one son, Gerard C., Jr., a student in the Horace Mann School at Gary.

Mr. Dooge's experience and activities have taken him much out-of-doors and he has always been an enthusiast in the matter of outdoor sports, and still follows track meets, football games and is a baseball fan. During the World war he was enrolled in the Home Guards.

ARTHUR BOHN, architect, has impressed his influence and ability in many ways on the life of his home City of Indianapolis. Mr. Bohn has brought to the work of his profession the fundamental art principles and ideals of the old world as well as the new. He is credited with having been of chief influence in the establishment of technical and vocational education in Indianapolis.

Mr. Bohn was born at Louisville, Kentucky. His father Gustavus Bohn, was a native of Germany, came to America and was married at Cleveland, Ohio, and served in the Union army during the Civil war.

Arthur bohn was educated in private schools in Indianapolis and was apprenticed to one of the leading architects of that city. He left nothing undone in enthusiastic devotion to acquiring the fundamentals of his art, availed himself of every opportunity here, and after accumulating enough money he went abroad to study in Europe. He took a course in architecture at the Royal Polytechnic Institute at Carlsruhe, Germany, where he made such a good record that he was offered a scholarship at the institute. On completing his European studies he returned to Indianapolis and immediately engaged in practice.

While abroad he became attracted to the system of vocational training, which was then already well developed in European countries. On his return he found a few men interested in the same subject in Indianapolis, and by his personal enthusiasm and the wealth of information he had acquired he was able to make great progress in advocating this new departure in educational methods and he and his associates made a practical demonstration, renting rooms and starting classes and gradually extending the instruction to shops and factories in the city. This experimental school won a high degree of popularity through the practical results achieved and in time the Indianapolis school board was appealed to and took over the system thus inaugurated, resulting in the creation of the Manual Training High School. Mr. Bohn himself was one of the first instructors in that school, but had to give up the work on account of the increasing volume of his private practice as an architect. Later Mr. Bohn returned to Europe for further study and spent several years in France, Germany and Italy. During the forty years of his practice he has been the architect of many notable buildings in Indianapolis and in the state. His practice has been devoted chiefly to large work, especially bank and office buildings, department stores, public institutions and many schools. In fact, many of the largest and most important buildings in down town Indianapolis are the product of his genius. He has been successful in many architectural competitions. The most important and monumental work of his career is his design for the State Plaza, which contemplates an aesthetic and orderly grouping of all future state buildings, west of the capitol. The original design was made about twenty years ago and is now being realized by the erection of the State Library and Historical Building, which it is proposed shall be the first unit in this great scheme.

In recognition of his honorable service to the public and profession the Indianapolis Architectural Club in 1927 presented him with an artistically designed memorial, expressed as follows:

"To Arthur Bohn—Because of your service to the community which is exemplified in the buildings which you have designed, because of your contribution to the profession of architecture which has its expression in the high place which you hold in the regard of your fellow craftsmen, because by example and by giving generously of your interest you are a constant encouragement to the student architects whom you choose to call brother draftsmen. It is our pleasure to give this evidence of our appreciation and affection.
Indianapolis Architectural Club."

Mr. Bohn was the first president of the Indianapolis Architects Association, the first president of the Indiana Society of Architects and in 1930 and 1931 he was president of the Indiana Chapter American Institute of Architects. He is a Scottish Rite Mason, a charter member of the Chamber of Commerce and Art Association, a member of the Scientech Club, Columbia Club, Indiana Engineering Society and Indiana Historical Society. He resides at 215 East Thirty-second Street.

He married, while a student abroad in Europe, Louise Weiss, a native of Carlsruhe, Baden. They have one son, Herbert Bohn, who was graduated as Master of Science in chemistry from the Philadelphia College of Pharmacy and Science.

CARROL C. WILSON is one of the prominent exponents of the insurance business in the City of Gary, where he is district manager for the Penn Mutual Life Insurance Company, with well appointed offices at 922 Gary State Bank Building. He is also secretary and treasurer of the Calumet Life Underwriters.

On the parental home farm near Angola, Steuben County, Indiana, the birth of Carrol C. Wilson occurred July 15, 1902, and he is a scion, in the third generation, of one of the sterling pioneer families of that county, his paternal grandfather, Newell A. Wilson, having come to Steuben County from Ohio and having settled on a farm in Jackson Township, near Angola. Newell A. Wilson went forth as a gallant soldier of the Union in the Civil war. He came home on a sick furlough before the close of the war and died after several months' illness. The mortal remains of this patriot soldier rest beside those of his wife in the Flint Cemetery near Angola.

Carrol C. Wilson is a son of Fleming N. and Mertie (Barr) Wilson, both likewise natives of Steuben County, where the former was born near Angola and the latter near Orland. The parents were reared and educated in Steuben County and there Fleming N. Wilson has been long and successfully identified with farm enterprise, he having

served as president of the local grange of the Patrons of Industry. He has been otherwise influential in community affairs and has given many years of service as a member of the school board of his district. He still gives active supervision to his fine farm estate near Angola. His wife received the advantages of the public schools and in her youth gave two years of service as a teacher in the schools of her native county. She was loved by all who came within the compass of her gentle and gracious influence. The death of Mrs. Wilson occurred July 23, 1929, and she was laid to rest in the cemetery of the old Block Church near Angola. Of the six children the eldest is Mary Erma, who is a successful teacher of music in her home City of Angola; Alma Belle is the wife of Harry Bell, of Angola; Newel died at the age of six years; Lloyd F. resides at Angola and is there district manager for the American Life Insurance Company; Loyal B. is a resident of South Bend and is there a representative of the Penn Mutual Life Insurance Company; and Carrol C., of this review, is the youngest of the number.

The public schools of Angola, Lafayette and Kendallville afforded Carrol C. Wilson his youthful education and after being graduated in the high school at Kendallville, in 1921, he completed a course in the University of Michigan, at Ann Arbor, in which he was graduated as a member of the class of 1927 and from which he received the degree of Bachelor of Arts. After leaving the university Mr. Wilson entered the service of the Penn Mutual Life Insurance Company, and he represented this company in his old home town of Angola one year, he having then been transferred to Gary, where he has since continued his constructive service as district manager for this great insurance corporation.

Mr. Wilson is one of the appreciative and public-spirited citizens and business men of Gary, is a member of the Commercial Club and Chamber of Commerce, in politics he maintains an independent attitude, and his religious faith is that of the Presbyterian Church, his wife being a member of the Christian Church.

In the City of Indianapolis, on the 31st of December, 1929, Mr. Wilson was united in marriage to Miss Dorothy Harris Wright, who was born in the City of Washington, D. C., and whose public school education was obtained in the various places in which her father was stationed within the period of her childhood and early youth. Mrs. Wilson was graduated in Shortridge High School, Indianapolis, Indiana. and in 1928 she was graduated in Butler University, Indianapolis. Prior to her marriage she taught one year in the public schools of Rushville, in this state, and about one year and six months in those of the City of South Bend. She continues her deep interest in cultural affairs, is affiliated with Kappa Alpha Theta sorority and has membership in the Pan-Hellenic Association. Mrs. Wilson is a daughter of Rev.

William J. and Jeanette (Harris) Wright, the latter of whom died March 30, 1927. Rev. William Wright has long been an influential clergyman of the Christian Church and has held various pastoral charges in Indiana and other states, and gave a few years of service as a traveling representative of the national interests of the Christian Church as national secretary, his home being now maintained in the City of Houston, Texas.

JAMES D. NEWELL is a Hammond business man, and with some of his sons as his associates has a prosperous business as a contractor in cement work and roofing materials at 119 Clinton Street.

Mr. Newell was born at Rich Hill, Missouri, November 2, 1876, son of John George and Mary Arbell (Akers) Newell. His grandfather was an early settler of Ransom, Illinois, going there from Ohio. John George Newell was born and reared in Illinois, and in the Civil war served as a soldier in the One Hundred and Fourth Illinois Infantry. After the war he moved to Missouri, and was a farmer and stock raiser in the vicinity of Rich Hill. For some years he lived in North Dakota, and while visiting his son James at Hammond, in the winter of 1930, he lost his life in an automobile accident, November 23. He was eighty-six years of age when he passed away. He was buried at Ransom, Illinois, his old home town where he was born and reared. He was at one time commander of the Grand Army Post of Ransom and organized the Woman's Relief Corps there. His first wife, Mary Arbell, was born and reared at Rich Hill, Missouri, where her father was a pioneer minister of the Gospel. She was educated in public schools and was a teacher for several years and always active in church work. She died in 1887 and is buried at Ransom, Illinois. The second wife of John George Newell was Anna Hurst, of Streator, Illinois. She was born in England and was a child when her parents came to America and settled at Streator. She died in 1915 and is buried at Ransom. By the first marriage there were seven children: Charles Newell, of Kansas City, Missouri; William, who was killed in a coal mine at Rich Hill, Missouri, when a boy; James D.; Gus Newell, of Hammond; Mrs. Alice Reeder, of Kalamazoo, Michigan; Bert Newell, of Indiana Harbor; and John Newell, of Gary. John George Newell by his second wife had five children: Ethel, wife of George Williams, of Hunter, North Dakota; Frank Newell, of Billings, Montana; Fred Newell, of Hunter, North Dakota; Mrs. Edith Quaife, of Hammond; and Grace, wife of Harold Quaife, of Hunter, North Dakota.

James D. Newell acquired his early education in the public schools of Ransom, Illinois. When he left school he worked with his father on the farm at Ransom, and after his marriage moved to Iowa, where he was a farmer and live stock raiser for several years. His home has been at Hammond, Indiana, since 1898. For several years he was employed by different firms and then took up contracting work as a plasterer and brick layer. Later he concentrated his attention on cement contracting and is still in business as a builder and roofing contractor. He also owns an oil and gas station at the corner of Calumet and Highland streets.

Mr. Newell casts his vote independently. He is a member of the Hammond Chamber of Commerce, B. P. O. Elks and the Methodist Episcopal Church. At Ransom, Illinois, in 1892, he married Miss Rena Gertrude Woodward, daughter of Lewis L. and Margaret (Denton) Woodward, of Ransom. Mrs. Newell attended school at Ransom and is a member of the Methodist Episcopal Church. To their marriage were born five children, the son Jesse dying at the age of six months. Eva Beatrice is the wife of Robert L. Wood, who is associated with Mr. Newell in the contracting business, and has one child, Robert Leroy. Glynn Adalbert Newell, also associated with his father in business, married Mrs. Lottie Olive (Bridegroom) Danabaur, whose two children by her first marriage are Lillian May and Theodore Ellsworth. Floyd Archibald Newell, connected with the Elgin, Joliet & Eastern Railway at East Chicago, married Kittie Fox, of East Chicago, and has a daughter, Fern. Gilbert Newell, youngest of the family, is assisting his father in business, but is still continuing his education. He is a graduate of the Hammond High School and has had two years in the law department of Valparaiso University.

CHARLES H. HOHLT. It is a matter of marked consistency that in this history of the fine old Hoosier commonwealth are to be found represented many of the sterling citizens who are here upholding the prestige of agricultural and live stock industry in the various counties, and it has been specially gratifying to accord such recognition, for Indiana has ever rested its major claims in development and progress upon these same basic industries, which have not been permitted to fall into decadence or minor importance during all the passing years. In Marion County, in which is situated the City of Indianapolis, Charles H. Hohlt has had secure vantage-ground as a resourceful and substantial exponent of farm enterprise, especially in the field of horticulture and market-gardening, and though he is now living virtually retired he still retains interest in these lines of industry and resides in his attractive rural home on the Bluff Road in Perry Township, about eight miles distant from Indianapolis, and on rural mail route No. 4.

Mr. Hohlt has the distinction of being a native of the fine old City of Berlin, Germany, where his birth occurred April 17, 1861, his parents likewise having been born in that district of Germany and the family name of his mother having been Weissen. The father served as a soldier in the German army and participated in wars in which the nation was involved. He sent all of his children to the

United States, though he himself continued to reside in his native land until his death.

Charles H. Hohlt is indebted to the excellent schools of Germany for his early educational discipline, and he was a lad of fifteen years when he crossed the Atlantic and disembarked in the port of New York City, where he arrived with a cash capital represented by thirty cents. He thence came directly to Indianapolis, where three of his older brothers had previously established residence, and after thus joining his brothers he soon found employment at Cumberland, Marion County. He next obtained employment in a dairy at Indianapolis, and later he turned his attention to the truck farming business. As an employe in this early period he received eighteen dollars a month and his board, and with characteristic thrift he saved his earnings. After he had accumulated a reserve of $300 he returned to Germany, his special mission having been one of filial solicitude, as represented in bringing his widowed mother to the land in which he and others of the children had established residence. Thus his mother accompanied him on his return to Indianapolis. where he had previously acquired property and where he gained his initial success of independent order by engaging in the grocery and bakery business, he having had to borrow money to start this enterprise and his early operations having included his peddling of his goods from a push cart, this primitive equipment having been replaced by a wagon after he had contrived to buy an old horse for propelling power. Energy, industry and good management enabled Mr. Hohlt to accord effective service to patrons, and his business expanded in scope and importance. He eventually made advantageous sale of the business and then purchased fifty acres of his present land holdings in Perry Township. Unpropitious conditions later resulted in his loss of this tract, but he rented it from the bank to which it was assigned, and he later purchased other land, this place having a fine quality of gravel and he having developed a prosperous business in selling gravel for use on the roads of the county. Mr. Hohlt has figured successfully also in utilizing his land for farm and gardening purposes, and has proved himself a productive worker within the many years of his residence in Marion County, the while he has ever held a secure place in the confidence and good will of the people of this county, this being notably attested by the fact that he was four times elected road superintendent and that he served fifteen years as a member of the county board of supervisors. He is a Democrat in politics and has always taken loyal interest in community affairs, as shown in his ready support of measures and enterprises tending to advance the civic and material welfare of his home county and state. He and his wife have long been zealous members of the Christian Church of their community, and he gave the ground on which the church building was erected.

August 21 1884, recorded the marriage of Mr. Hohlt to Miss Carrie Cotman, and concerning the children of this union brief record is entered in this concluding paragraph: Herman married Carrie Grinaman and they have four children—Edna, Earl, Herman, Jr., and Louise. Charles married Jeanette Lysart, and they have one child, Richard. Frederick has been twice married, Carl and Edward being the children of the first marriage and Mary the one child of the second union. William and his wife, whose family name was Clauski, have three children. Ernest married Miss Minnie Cousin and they have two children, Ernest, Jr., and Earl. Edward and his wife, Pearl, have two children. Alma is deceased. Leonard was next in order of birth. Freida is the wife of Frank Geyer.

JOHN SHARP is an Indiana citizen who has dedicated his most active years to the work of an institution, the Community Service and Memorial Community House at Whiting.

The City of Whiting grew up around the nucleus of the great refineries established by the Standard Oil Company. A number of years ago the company, and John D. Rockefeller and his son, John D. Rockefeller, Jr., set aside a great fund to be used for the erection of the magnificent building known as the Memorial Community House, which is dedicated to the memory of those who served the nation in the World war. It is a memorial with a vital significance to every one within the limits of the City of Whiting. It has been described as a "peoples' house of play, friendship and neighborliness," where all, without regard to race, class or creed, may unite on a common platform for "togetherness." The Community Service, expressed through the medium of the building, is more important than the edifice itself. The building, architecturally an adaptation of the Southern Italian style, is a beautiful and inspiring environment for the service to which it is dedicated. The building has three main divisions. There is an auditorium equipped with stage facilities for dramatics, musical entertainments, lectures, motion pictures, the seating capacity being one thousand. Another part of the structure is known as the Men's Department, and the third department is for women. Under one roof are found opportunities for the indulgence of wholesome tastes for a great many forms of recreation, entertainment and instruction. There are billiard room, social and reading rooms, restaurant, swimming pool, gymnasium. On the second floor is the large general club room, the beautiful Memorial Hall, with trophy cases and appropriate mural decorations, and adjacent rooms to be used by the American Legion. The working plan of organization, under the direction of the Community Service Board and director, indicates how fully these magnificent facilities are made use of. There is a department of music and entertainment, the men's and women's departments, all effectively co-

operating with the broader cultural and recreational life of the city.

During the first year after the Community House was opened the active manager was Mr. Parkin. He was succeeded by R. J. Schmoyer, who continued to direct the work until 1926, when he was succeeded by John Sharp.

Mr. Sharp was born at Bourbon, Indiana, January 22, 1898. His people were pioneers of Marshall County. His grandfather was an officer in the Union army. Mr. Sharp is a son of Joseph Albert and Elizabeth (Fabin) Sharp. His father was born and reared at Bourbon, and about April, 1898, a few weeks after the birth of his son John, he moved to Whiting, where for a number of years he was with the Standard Oil Company, and for the past ten years has been night superintendent of the paraffin department. Elizabeth Fabin was born and reared at Bourbon. She was a member of the United Brethren Church. She died in 1907, the mother of four children: Mabel, wife of Elmer Bauer, of Hobart, Indiana; John; Eva, wife of Delbert Vermet, of Hammond; and George, who is connected with the Pan-American Oil Company at Aruba, Dutch West Indies. After the death of the mother of these children Joseph A. Sharp married, at Whiting, Miss Clara Kiehm, of Chicago, and they have a daughter, Margaret, who was graduated from the Whiting High School in 1928 and is connected with the Hammond Business College.

John Sharp attended public school at Whiting, graduated from high school in 1916, and in 1917 entered the Indiana State Normal School at Terre Haute. He left school in January, 1918, to answer the call to the colors. He was at Jefferson Barracks, Missouri, for about six weeks at Fort Wadsworth, New York, and went overseas with the Seventieth Artillery Corps, and was in training at the artillery school in France until after the armistice. He was honorably discharged as a sergeant at Camp Grant, Rockford, Illinois, in March, 1919.

On his return home Mr. Sharp entered the employ of the Standard Oil Company as a still man. In 1923 his special abilities were recognized when he was transferred to the Community Center Building as director of boys' work. After a year and a half he was put in charge of the Men's Department, and since 1926 has been manager of the Community Service Center.

Mr. Sharp is a member of the Chamber of Commerce, the Lions Club, votes as a Republican, and his religious affiliations are Christian Science. He has always been interested in athletics and has given much of his time to the development of the recreational side of the Community House in its games and contests of various kinds. He plays golf. He is a member of Whiting Post of the American Legion.

Mr. Sharp married at Edwardsville, Illinois, September 4, 1920, Miss Ruth Gladden, daughter of A. E. and Edith (Halsey) Gladden. Her father for many years was with the Standard Oil Company at Whiting and later was transferred to the Wood River plant and established his home at Alton. His wife died about 1920 and is buried at Cleveland, Ohio. Mrs. Sharp graduated from the Whiting High School in 1917 and then studied in the National Kindergarten College at Chicago. She taught for a year before her marriage. She is a member of the Christian Science Church, the Whiting Woman's Club, the Woman's Auxiliary of the American Legion, and the Beta Gamma sorority. Mr. and Mrs. Sharp have a son, Robert Horace, born March 16, 1923, a student in the public schools.

CRETH J. LOYD is president of C. J. Loyd & Company, of Greensburg. This company is known all over Decatur and adjoining counties as one of the largest and most complete organizations for handling poultry and eggs in Southern Indiana. It is a business of long standing and Mr. Loyd has been identified with it since boyhood.

He was born at Greensburg, December 4, 1872, son of Joseph H. Loyd and grandson of Creth J. Loyd. His grandfather, a native of Kentucky, came to Decatur County, Indiana, in the early 1830s with his parents, Mr. and Mrs. William Loyd. Creth J. Loyd spent most of his life at Greensburg. He was a plasterer by trade, and during the season of the year when there was no work in that line he carried on a produce business. Creth J. Loyd was twice married.

Joseph H. Loyd was a soldier in the Seventh Indiana Infantry during the Civil war. He was born in Decatur County and was engaged in the produce business now known as C. J. Loyd & Company. He was influential in politics and a lifetime Republican. He married Margaret E. Mowrer, of Cincinnati, whose parents moved to Indiana before the Civil war.

Creth J. Loyd, only child of his parents, attended the grade schools of Greensburg. When only fifteen years of age he became associated on terms of partnership with his father, Joseph H. Loyd, who was popularly known as H. Loyd. The business was established in a small room located on East Main Street. The business then consisted of the purchase of poultry from nearby territory and shipping to the best markets available. The firm name was H. Loyd & Son until 1892. In that year Mr. Zoller bought the interest of Joseph H. Loyd, and the firm became Loyd & Zoller, at which time they moved to larger quarters, at Gibson and Cooper streets. In 1895 Creth J. Loyd acquired the interest of Mr. Zoller, and then took in as a partner his father-in-law, William Brune, under the firm style of C. J. Loyd & Company. Mr. Brune after two years retired from active participation in the business. Since 1897 the business has been C. J. Loyd & Company, individually owned by Mr. Creth J. Loyd. In 1921 they erected their modern plant, which they have occupied for ten years. It is one of the most modern owned by any produce firm in Southern Indiana. On January 1, 1929, the business was incorporated, at which time Mr. Loyd's three sons came into the firm.

C. J. Loyd & Company today have a model organization and plant. The plant affords 38,-000 square feet of floor space and a new fireproof building provides accommodation for refrigeration storage. An average of eighty persons are employed in the various departments of the business. They handle annually several million pounds of poultry and approximately 1,600,000 dozens of eggs. Shipments are made by carload lots to the New York, New Jersey and Boston markets. A private track gives them facilities for loading cars directly from the storage warehouse. In addition to the main plant at Greensburg fourteen branch buying stations are operated over a radius of thirty-five miles around Greensburg. Mr. Loyd is a director of the Citizens Third National Bank of Greensburg, the oldest bank in Decatur County. He is president of the board of trustees of Memorial Hospital and has been a generous citizen in his support of all worthy activities. He was especially identified with the wartime program in the various drives. He is a member of the Knights of Pythias, Independent Order of Odd Fellows, B. P. O. Elks, Fraternal Order of Eagles, Improved Order of Red Men and Modern Woodmen of America. Mr. Loyd since early manhood has participated in social and civic endeavors at Greensburg. As a man he is unassuming, direct, exact, and sticks to the point in all his dealings, and has the confidence of his thousands of patrons because of his reputation for fair dealing. Mr. and Mrs. Loyd and their daughter are members of the Presbyterian Church.

Mr. Loyd married Miss Minnie Brune, who was born in Decatur County. They have four children: Frank L., secretary of C. J. Loyd & Company, married Kathleen Stier, of Greensburg, and they have a daughter, Susan Marie. John C. Loyd, treasurer of the company, married Rose Stier, a sister of Kathleen, and their two children are Margaret Jean and William Viets. Arthur C. Loyd, vice president of the company, married Martha Crawford, and has two children, named Creth J. and Donald Jean. The only daughter, Mary Jessie, is the wife of Milton McDonald, and they have a daughter, Ruth Ann, and a son, Robert Loyd. Their home is in Indianapolis, where Mr. McDonald is employed by the Eli Lilly Company, chemists.

WESLEY L. THARP has been a resident of Whiting for many years and in that city has found opportunities for a successful business career. He is a merchant at the corner of One Hundred and Nineteenth Street and Indiana Boulevard.

Mr. Tharp was born in Perry County, Ohio, June 22, 1874, son of David A. and Sarah E. (Sanders) Tharp. His parents were also born and reared in that Ohio county and attended public school there. In 1877, when Wesley L. was three years of age, the family came to Indiana, but after two years returned to Ohio. In 1885 they made another

move, to a farm in Kansas, where they lived three years. The parents then returned to Perry County, Ohio, where they lived out the rest of their lives. David Tharp was a farmer and coal miner, and he and his wife were members of the Christian Church. He died in 1920 and his wife in 1927. They are buried in the cemetery at Hemlock, Ohio. Of their ten children three died in infancy. Addie, who died in 1930, was the wife of Harry Betts. The living children are: Wesley L.; Eldon, Chester, Homer D., Laura, wife of Bernard Hodgens, and Harry, all of whom live at Hemlock, Ohio.

Wesley L. Tharp received his early schooling in Hemlock, Ohio, and Kansas. He worked as a coal miner for several years. It was in 1898, when he was twenty-four years of age, that he came to Whiting. During the next five years he clerked in a grocery store and then for seven years was an employee of the Standard Oil Company. Since 1910, for over twenty years, he has been in the grocery business. At first he was in partnership with H. M. Atkin. In 1918 they took in another partner, George W. Johnson, who had just returned from service as a soldier in the World war. In 1929 Mr. Tharp acquired the interest of his two partners in the grocery business, but all of them still own the building in which the store is conducted. Mr. Tharp has supplied groceries and meats to a large community of Whiting for over twenty years. He also owns other business and residence property. He is a member of the Chamber of Commerce and for some years was active in the Independent Order of Odd Fellows. Though he has the name of the great founder of Methodism, he has always been a faithful member of the Christian Church and has been a trustee and elder in the First Christian Church of Whiting and superintendent of the Sunday School. His recreation is motoring trips.

Mr. Tharp married, September 26, 1900, at West Pullman, Illinois, Miss Anna Maude Johnson, daughter of Amos and Margaret (Phillips) Johnson. Her father spent thirty-five years in the service of the Standard Oil Company. He started at Cleveland, Ohio, and when the great refining plant was established at Whiting he was transferred there and was with the company until his death in 1912. His wife died in 1923 and both are buried in a cemetery at Hammond. Mrs. Tharp attended public schools at Whiting. She is a member of the Christian Church, the Rebekahs, the Maccabees and the Woman's Club. To their marriage were born eight children. Twins died in infancy. The living children are: Helen Margaret, Clara Evelyn, David Amos, Olive Jean, Katherine Joyce and Wesley Leon, Jr. The three oldest are all graduates of the Whiting High School. Helen was graduated from the Columbia School of Expression and Physical Education at Chicago, and Clara Evelyn from the National Kindergarten College at Chicago, and both taught before their marriage. Helen is the wife of Phillip L.

Krauel, who is with the engineering department of the Standard Oil Company, and their two children are Phillip David and Robert William. Clara Evelyn is the wife of Dr. B. B. Reeve, industrial physician and surgeon at Whiting for the Standard Oil Company. They also have two children, Esther Ruth and Brice B., Jr. David Tharp spent one year in DePauw University and is now with his father in business. He is unmarried. Olive Jean is a member of the class of 1933 in the Whiting High School, Katherine Joyce is in grade school, and Wesley is a kindergarten pupil.

RICHARD GORDON ARNER, assistant superintendent of the Sinclair Refining Company at East Chicago, is a native of Pennsylvania, and his mother was born at the pioneer center of petroleum production, Oil City, where her family were among the first settlers.

The Arner family have lived in Pennsylvania for generations. His great-grandfather Arner lived in Northampton County and later went to Clarion County, where he and his wife are buried. Mr. Arners' grandfather, John W. Arner, was one of the early business men at Rimersburg, Clarion County. At that time in the absence of railroads all goods were brought in wagons across the mountains. L. P. Arner, father of Richard G., was born at Charleston, South Carolina, but spent most of his life in Rimersburg, Pennsylvania. He attended the Clarion Collegiate Institute there and after completing his education he and his brother, J. W. Arner, entered the mercantile business. He was in business until he retired in 1927, and he died September 20, 1930. He took an active interest in politics and for three sessions served as a member of the Pennsylvania Legislature. He was a Mason and both he and his wife were active in the Dutch Reformed Church.

L. P. Arner married May L. Martin, who was born and reared in Oil City. She resides at Rimersburg.

Richard G. Arner, the only child of his parents, was born at Rimersburg, March 3, 1892. Not long ago his fellow Kiwanians put him on the program to deliver a sketch of his own life, and in this situation, so embarrassing to his natural modesty, he gave an autobiography that is very interesting reading to his friends and acquaintances. He states that in honor of his birth his father passed out Pennsylvania "Stogies" to all the male customers at the store in Rimersburg. He describes himself as a "Main Street" boy, getting his early education in the public schools at Rimersburg and in 1910 graduating from the preparatory school known as Washington and Jefferson Academy, at Washington, Pennsylvania. The following summer, he says, "was spent in reading catalogues from various colleges and universities. After careful study of the football records of these institutions, I decided the University of Michigan looked most promising, and the next fall found me at Ann Arbor." After four years he was graduated, in 1915, with the Bachelor

of Science degree, and then spent a year in post-graduate work in oil chemistry at the Rensselaer Polytechnic Institute at Troy, New York. For a short time he was with the Fred C. Arner Chemical Company at Buffalo and from there went south to Port Arthur, Texas, where he became chemist for the Gulf Refining Company and later was promoted to assistant chief chemist. He spent three years at Port Arthur, and while there participated in the various war drives. Returning north in 1918, he was for two years chief chemist for the Canfield Oil Company at Cleveland, and in 1920 joined the great Sinclair organization, becoming assistant chief chemist at East Chicago, and since 1923 has been assistant superintendent of the refinery. His associates know that he has been very successful in his chosen vocation, and in his autobiography he said: "Life has been kind to me, as I find there has been more 'ups' than 'downs.'"

He has found various opportunities to express his social and civic spirit. He is a member of the East Chicago Chamber of Commerce, the Kiwanis Club, Whiting Lodge of Masons, Woodmar Country Club, the Chi Phi fraternity. He votes independently and is a member of the First Presbyterian Church.

At Rimersburg, Pennsylvania, April 26, 1916, shortly after beginning his career as a chemist, he married Miss Helen Craig, daughter of Mr. and Mrs. J. C. Craig, of Rimersburg. Her father for many years was a general merchant there, but since 1926 has lived retired. Mrs. Arner was educated in the schools of Rimersburg, graduating from high school in 1912, and in 1914 from the Washington Seminary. She is a member of the Presbyterian Church and various woman's organizations at Whiting, where they have their home. Mr. and Mrs. Arner spend their summer vacations on Lake St. Germaine, Wisconsin, where they have a summer camp. Their two daughters are Helen Louise and Janet, Helen being a student in the Junior High School at Whiting and Janet in grammar school.

HENRY C. TEETOR, of Hagerstown, had an interesting range of accomplishments, and his home people esteemed him both for what he did and for what he was. His death occurred April 14, 1930.

Mr. Teetor was born at the old Teetor Mill in Jefferson Township, Wayne County, July 25, 1862, a son of Zachariah and Barbara (Hoover) Teetor, and grandson of Abraham and Elizabeth (Ulrich) Teetor. His grandparents were born in Pennsylvania and came to Wayne County at an early day. The family name in the old country was Deitrich. After coming to America they changed it to Deetor. Grandfather Abraham Teetor in taking up Government land in Wayne County gave his name as Teetor, and that spelling has been retained ever since. Zachariah Teetor was born in Jefferson Township, Wayne County, and his wife, Barbara Hoover, was born in Pennsylvania, a daughter of George B. and Hannah (Dilling) Hoover. Zachariah Teetor was a farmer and after his marriage conducted saw mills and flouring mills. After 1893 he gave up milling and spent most of his time as a mechanic, doing work as a millwright, and also worked in a bicycle factory. He died in 1906 and his wife in 1884. Their eight children included: John H., of Hagerstown; Henry C., deceased; Mary E., wife of Henry W. Keagy, of Hagerstown; Sarah Elizabeth, deceased; Charles N., of Hagerstown; Joseph C., of Hagerstown; Emma Frances, deceased; and Benjamin Franklin, of Hagerstown.

Henry C. Teetor attended the Teetor School near the old home and learned the trade of carriage making and general repair work at Moreland, Indiana. After four years he went to Newcastle, Indiana, and for a year did carriage work, and saved three hundred dollars out of his yearly income of six hundred dollars. On coming to Hagerstown he took up insurance and with his brother John also conducted a shop for the making and repairing of bicycles. He and his brothers, John, Charles and Joseph, were in the grain elevator business. After seven years he sold out and turned his attention to the trade of millwright. In 1902 he and his brothers, John, Charles and Joseph, bought the George Dick Mill, and he was its manager for three and a half years. Then followed another period of work as a millwright, and this trade he afterward pursued to some extent. He was one of the founders of the Teetor-Hartley Inspection Car Company, now known as the Perfect Circle Piston Ring Company, a big industry, manufacturing piston rings for gasoline power engines for automobiles and aeroplanes. Mr. Teetor was one of the directors of this industry, but sold his interests in June, 1928. He continued a stockholder in two grain elevators and was a stockholder in the Union Trust Company of Hagerstown and in the Farmers & First National Bank of Newcastle.

Mr. Teetor all his life enjoyed working in wood and was a master of the art. For years as a sideline he made violins, and had a splendid collection of violins, including several rare instruments. He was a member of the Christian Church and when the church at Hagerstown was rebuilt, in 1926, he was a contributor to its rebuilding and put in the new pipe organ as a memorial to his family. He was a Republican, filled all the chairs in the Independent Order of Odd Fellows Lodge and Encampment and was a member of the Masonic fraternity and Knights of Pythias.

Mr. Teetor married, August 11, 1883, Miss Josephine Wright, who was born near Moreland, Indiana, and died January 29, 1911. She was a daughter of Thomas and Rebecca (Pollard) Wright, the former a native of Maryland and the latter of Wayne County, Indiana. Mr. Teetor had one daughter, Mabel Clair, who is the wife of Leslie B. Davis, and they have one daughter, Josephine Frances, born February 25, 1912, now attending Penn Hall, a private school at Chambersburg, Pennsylvania.

OSCAR A. MARTIN is owner of the Oscar A. Martin Company, the Wabash County Sales & Distributing Agency for the Hudson and Essex cars. Mr. Martin is no stranger to Wabash County, having been born there and is member of a family that have lived in this section of the Upper Wabash River Valley nearly a century.

He was born in the town of La Fontaine, January 13, 1893, and is a son of John C. F. and Flora E. (Holmes) Martin and a grandson of Phillip and Hannah (Bain) Martin. Phillip Martin was born in Ohio, January 11, 1813, and settled in Wabash Cunty September 11, 1834. He acquired a tract of Government land, developed it into a farm, and was one of the prosperous and influential citizens of the community around La Fontaine.

John C. F. Martin has long been a leading business man and citizen of Wabash County, served as president of the Farmers State Bank of La Fontaine, for two terms was a county commissioner and has been a grain dealer for thirty years.

Oscar A. Martin is one of a family of seven children. He was educated in the grade and high schools at La Fontaine and graduated in 1910 from North Manchester College. He has had twenty years of experience in the automobile business. For five years he was connected with the Gibson Auto Company at Indianapolis.

Mr. Martin in September, 1917, enlisted, was in training for several months with the infantry and was sergeant major of the One Hundred Fifty-ninth Brigade. Later he entered the Officers Training School at Camp Gordon, Georgia, and was commissioned a lieutenant in November, 1918, and after the war was in the United States Reserve Corps.

After his army service he spent a year or so in Chicago, as sales manager for the Chicago branch of the Monroe Automobile Company. Mr. Martin in 1921 came to Wabash and organized the Oscar A. Martin Company, acquiring the franchise for the Hudson and Essex cars. He has a fine plant and sales room at 458 Miami Street, his shop utilizing about 10,000 square feet of floor space, and with equipment and facilities for handling repairs on all kinds of cars.

Since 1915 Mr. Martin has been also associated with other members of the family in the grain business, being vice president of the A. B. Martin Grain Company of La Fontaine. His father is president of this company and his brother, A. B. Martin, is secretary and treasurer. This firm operates an elevator at La Fontaine, with a capacity of 20,000 bushels, and another elevator at Sweetzer, with a capacity of 75,000 bushels.

Mr. Martin married Miss Ruth Sundheimer, of Wabash. He is a member of the Wabash Chamber of Commerce, the American Legion,

La Fontaine Lodge of Masons, Marion Chapter, Royal Arch Masons, also the Council and Knights Templar Commandery at Marion and the Scottish Rite Consistory at Indianapolis. He is a member of Medinah Temple of the Mystic Shrine in Chicago. Mr. Martin is a member of the Retail Merchants Bureau, is a Republican and a trustee of the First Evangelical Church.

HENRY W. MOORE, a prominent member of the bar of Terre Haute, where he has been in practice since 1911, was born on a farm in Daviess County, Indiana, December 29, 1868, son of John Dillon and Katherine (Slinkard) Moore.

Mr. Moore was educated in the public schools of Greene County, taught school in early life and completed his literary and legal education in Indiana University. He was admitted to the bar at Bloomfield, Greene County, in 1892. During the years he practiced at Bloomfield he was for two years a law partner of Judge Oscar Bland. In 1911 he removed to Terre Haute, where he has ranked as one of the leaders of the bar for the past twenty years, his cases frequently taking him into the Supreme Court of the United States.

Mr. Moore has always been prominent in the Democratic party organization of the state. While living at Bloomfield he served as Democratic chairman of Greene County and was owner and editor of the Bloomfield *Democrat*, then the official organ of the Democratic party in the county. In 1926 and again in 1928 Mr. Moore was the Democratic candidate for Congress from the Fifth Indiana District. He is a thirty-second degree Scottish Rite Mason and Shriner.

He married, April 10, 1895, Hallie Edith Haas, daughter of Morris and Colin (Dickey) Haas. Their only child, Marcella, is the wife of Ben S. Bostick, of New York City.

JOSEPH J. CHILLA came to America from Czecho-Slovakia when eighteen years of age, and has achieved success and prominence in banking circles at Whiting, and has long been a leader among his fellow countrymen in this section of Indiana.

He was born in Czecho-Slovakia October 1, 1881, son of Andrew and Mary (Nemec) Chilla. His parents were also born and reared in that country. After the death of Mrs. Mary Chilla, Andrew came to America in 1912 and lived retired. He was in the railroad service in his native land. He died in 1916 and is buried in St. John Cemetery at Hammond. His wife died in 1910. Of their nine children six died in infancy. The living are: Mrs. Mary Ciesko, of Whiting; Mrs. Amelia Harkut, of Czecho-Slovakia; and Joseph J.

Joseph J. Chilla had the advantage of the parochial schools in his native country. When he came to America, in 1900, he located at Whiting, and here, while working during the day, he made diligent use of his leisure time by equipping himself for larger responsibilities, attending night school and also taking private instruction. Since 1907 his experience has been in the banking, insurance and real estate field. In 1926 he established the Liberty Savings & Loan Association and has been secretary since that date. He is also a director of the company. In connection he conducts an insurance and real estate agency.

Mr. Chilla is a member of the Chamber of Commerce, the Whiting Lions Club, the B. P. O. Elks, Knights of Columbus and Catholic Order of Foresters. He has long been prominent in Czecho-Slovakian organizations, including the First Catholic Slovak Union of America, the National Slovakian Society of America, and is a member of the Catholic Turners Society, the American Slovak Citizens Club of Whiting, St. Nicks Club and the Washington Club. He casts his vote independently and is a member of St. John's Catholic Church.

Mr. Chilla married at Whiting, June 6, 1905, Miss Lydia Kubeck, daughter of Andrew and Mary Kubeck, of Whiting. Her father spent many years in the service of the Standard Oil Company and later was sexton of St. John's Cemetery. He died in 1922 and her mother resides at Whiting. Mrs. Chilla attended parochial schools in Whiting. She is a member of St. John's Church and the Daughters of Isabella and the Ladies of the Maccabees. Mr. and Mrs. Chilla have an interesting family of seven children. Their daughter Mary is the wife of Andrew Witko, of Gary, and has two children, Andrew, Jr., and Rose Marie. The unmarried children are Anna, Joseph J., Jr., Helen, Benedict, Clara and Dolores. Benedict is in high school and Clara in St. John's parochial school. Mary, Anna, Joseph, Jr., and Helen are all graduates of the Whiting High School. Joseph and Helen are now assisting their father in his business.

GEORGE L. WINKLER. Since 1911 George L. Winkler has been constantly employed in one or another capacity as a law enforcement officer, having been an employe of the City of Indianapolis, the County of Marion and the Federal Government. He began his career in this line of work as a uniformed member of the Indianapolis police force, and in 1928 was elected sheriff of Marion County, a position which he still retains, and in which he is displaying the courage, fidelity and sagacity that made him a successful police captain and capable prohibition official.

Sheriff Winkler was born on a farm in Johnson County, Indiana, December 17, 1866, and is a son of David and Allena (Snow) Winkler. His father, who was an Indiana volunteer during the war between the states, spent the greater part of his life in agricultural operations in Johnson County, where he was highly esteemed as a man and a citizen. George L. Winkler attended the grade and high schools in Johnson County, and when his parents moved to Indianapolis he had the added advantage of attending the Manual Training High School, from which he was duly graduated. He then secured a position as errand boy for the Holcomb & Hoke Manufacturing Company, and won rapid promotion because of his ability, fidelity and great industry, and at the time of his resignation, in 1911, was superintendent of the plant. In that year Mr. Winkler became a patrolman on the Indianapolis city police department's force, and here again he won promotion, advancing rapidly to the rank of captain. In 1921 he left the department to become a Federal prohibition agent, subsequently was advanced to group chief, and eventually to the highest enforcement position in the state, that of deputy administrator of Federal prohibition. When he became a candidate, on the Republican ticket, for the office of sheriff of Marion County, in 1928, Mr. Winkler resigned from the prohibition force. He was duly elected to the office by a handsome majority and has discharged his duties in a highly commendable and expeditious manner, earning the gratitude and confidence of the people of the county. Sheriff Winkler has been a lifelong Republican and is one of the leaders of his party in Marion County. Fraternally he is affiliated with the Masons and the Modern Woodmen of America, and his religious affiliation is with the Christian Church.

In 1905 Sheriff Winkler was united in marriage with Miss Florence Wilson, of Ripley County, Indiana, and to this union there were born two children: Mrs. Jessie Allena Todd and George Robert. Mrs. Winkler died in December, 1922, and February 5, 1927, Sheriff Winkler married the present Mrs. Winkler, who was formerly Miss Florence Claffey, of Indianapolis. The pleasant Winkler home is at 32 South Alabama Street.

FRED E. DAVIS has been for thirty years an influential figure in banking enterprise in Tipton County, where he is president of the Citizens National Bank at Tipton, the county seat, and where he has ever been known and duly valued as an able and reliable man of affairs and as a loyal, liberal and public-spirited citizen. He thus has gained inviolable place in popular confidence and esteem in his home city and county.

Mr. Davis was born at Rock Island, Illinois, February 20, 1858, and is a son of Oren W. and Elizabeth (Heflin) Davis, his father having been born in Kentucky and having gained a goodly measure of pioneer precedence in Illinois, where he and his wife remained until their death. Fred E. Davis received in his boyhood and early youth the advantages of the public schols of Illinois, and as a lad of fifteen years he there found employment in a drug store. He continued for fifteen years his service as a drug clerk, and he then turned his attention to the banking business. He was for six years a partner in a private bank at Loogootee, Indiana, and he then became cashier of a bank at Sullivan, judicial center of Sullivan County, Indiana, where he remained about two years. He then, in 1898, established his residence at Tipton, where he

effected the organization of the State Bank of Tipton. He became cashier and later the executive head of this institution, the affairs of which he directed with marked circumspection and with reliable and straightforward policies, the result being that after the passing of six years the business of the bank had so expanded as to make it expedient to reorganize the institution under its present title of Citizens National Bank. As president of this solid and well ordered banking concern he had made it a distinct communal asset and has gained to it secure status as one of the leading banking institutions of this section of the Hoosier State.

The political allegiance of Mr. Davis is given to the Republican party, he is affiliated with the Masonic fraternity and the Benevolent and Protective Order of Elks, and he and his wife are members of the Methodist Episcopal Church in their home city.

In his native State of Illinois was solemnized the marriage of Mr. Davis to Miss Mellie Royston, who was born at Peoria, that state, and the one child of this union is a daughter, Madge, who is the wife of William Hill, the latter being an executive officer of the Citizens National Bank of Tipton.

HON. HOWARD A. CANN, of Frankfort, is a business man with natural inclination and ability for public affairs, and has several times been honored with election to the Indiana Legislature, serving in both Houses, and his activities have made him a well known figure in the state.

Mr. Cann was born at Monticello, Illinois, October 28, 1870, but both his parents were born in Tippecanoe County, Indiana, having lived in Illinois only a short time. His father, Christopher C. Cann, was born near Lafayette, July 4, 1840, and had just reached his majority when the Civil war broke out. He served three years and four months in the Fortieth Indiana Regiment. After the war he was deputy county clerk of Tippecanoe County and for four years held the office of county recorder. Christopher C. Cann married Ella A. McKee, who was born near Clarks Hill in Tippecanoe County, February 9, 1840.

Howard A. Cann was a small child when his parents returned to Tippecanoe County, where he attended the common schools, completing his education in the Central Indiana Normal College at Danville. He worked on a farm during 1890-91 and in 1892 became connected with the monument business at Thorntown. During 1893 he represented the Emil Wulschner Company, of Indianapolis, as a salesman of musical instruments in Clinton and Tippecanoe counties. The year 1894 was spent on a farm and in 1895 he located in the City of Frankfort, which has been his home for thirty-five years. During all this time Mr. Cann has conducted a monument business.

Politically he has been an influential figure in the local and state Republican party for many years. What he regards as one of the

T. G. Hamilton.

most interesting and important services of his lifetime was his chairmanship of the County Red Cross during the World war. In 1918 he was first elected to the Legislature, as a representative. In 1920 he was one of the senators elected from the district of Clinton and Boone counties, and in 1924 was returned to the Senate from the district comprising Clinton, Carroll and White counties. Mr. Cann took an active part in the campaign for raising funds to enlarge the Riley Hospital at Indianapolis. Fraternally he is a member of the Masonic Order, is a past chancellor of the Knights of Pythias, member of the Independent Order of Odd Fellows, Modern Woodmen of America, Sons of Veterans, and is a charter member of the Kiwanis Club. Both he and his wife are leading members of the Methodist Episcopal Church at Frankfort. He has been on the board of trustees since 1910, is a member of the Area Council of Indiana and a director of the Wesley Foundation at Purdue University.

Mr. Cann married, January 27, 1892, in Clinton County, Clara S. Harshman, daughter of Martin V. and Ann Eliza Harshman. She was born January 20, 1873. She is a member of the Woman's State Assembly Club, the Eastern Star and the Pythian Sisters. Mr. and Mrs. Cann have two adopted children. The son, Harold Cann, born March 5, 1892, was one of the early volunteers for service in the World war, joining the First Division, and was with the first contingent of American troops to go overseas. He is now connected with the General Motors Company at Dayton, Ohio. Mr. Cann's daughter, Marie, born March 22, 1896, is the wife of Samuel M. Purdue, of Lafayette. Mr. Purdue is a traveling salesman for the text book department of D. Appleton & Company, publishers.

COL. THOMAS GRAHAM HAMILTON. The limits assigned for this sketch of the life of an active and eminent member of the profession of electrical engineers and a railway man known and admired throughout the Middle West are wholly inadequate to give even a cursory notice of the many brilliant works which he has planned and executed, or of the military episodes of a life which would alone entitle him to be enrolled among the bravest, most skilful and most successful officers who led the American army during the World war. It must suffice to make allusion to those incidents of a long life and active and diversified career which will afford the best clue to the character of the man and his many and brilliant achievements.

Col. Thomas Graham Hamilton was born at Belfast, Ireland, December 21, 1870, and is a son of John and Sarah Jane (Graham) Hamilton. His father, also a native of Belfast, was engaged in landscape gardening in his native land, where he married, and in 1871 came to the United States and settled at Pittsburgh, Pennsylvania, where he continued to follow the same vocation for a time, later entering the wholesale and retail grocery busi-

ness, in which he was engaged until a few years prior to his death, when he retired. He was active in the Independent Order of Odd Fellows and died in the faith of the Episcopal Church in 1884, being buried in Homewood Cemetery, Pittsburgh. Sarah Jane Graham was born and reared in Scotland, where she attended the public schools, but later was taken by her parents to Ireland, where, at Belfast, she met and married Mr. Hamilton. Throughout her life she was a pious member of the Episcopal Church and active in its work, and at her death in 1924 she was laid to rest at the side of her husband in Homewood Cemetery, Pittsburgh. There were six children in the family: One who died in infancy; Col. Thomas Graham, of this review; Agnes L., Theodore, Mary J. and Sarah C.

Thomas Graham Hamilton attended the public schools of Pittsburgh and a business college, and in 1895 was graduated from Lehigh University with the degree of Electrical Engineer. Shortly after he had left business college he joined the service of the Pittsburgh Railways Company, and on his first day of employment this company operated the first cable street railway system in the Smoky City. Upon his return from Lehigh University he returned to the Pittsburgh Railways Company, as engineer in charge of tracks, overhead lines and various construction projects, including new power stations, bridges, etc. In the fall of 1898, at the close of the Spanish-American war, Colonel Hamilton was sent to Havana, Cuba, to report on street railway conditions, where the cars at that time were all horse-drawn. Again, in 1899, he was sent to Havana to construct the first electric street railway in Cuba. After planning the entire work it was found that because of the presence of yellow fever no contractors would make bids for the project and accordingly Colonel Hamilton was placed in charge of the construction of tracks, overhead lines and power houses, using native labor in construction and breaking in natives as operators. He himself operated the first electric cars to pass through the streets of Havana, in the midst of great excitement. This work was done under Gen. Leonard Wood, at that time military governor of Cuba, and the employment forces under Colonel Hamilton were governed by army regulations, and kept under the strictest medical supervision. Colonel Hamilton also engaged extensively in building interurban lines in Cuba, but in 1904 was stricken with malaria and secured a three months leave of absence, but on his return to the United States decided to remain here and obtained his release from his obligations in Cuba. Subsequently he accepted the position of assistant chief engineer in the construction of the Pittsburgh, Harmony, Butler & Newcastle Railway, making all preliminary surveys and carrying through construction until final completion in 1907. In October of that year he became chief engineer and superintendent of construction of the lines in Northwestern Indiana, including LaPorte, Valparaiso, Chesterton, Gary, Hammond, East Chicago, the lines which now comprise the system of the Gary Railways. When the United States was drawn into the great European struggle, in 1917, Colonel Hamilton volunteered his services and was commissioned major, Corps of Engineers, United States Army, June 23, 1917. He entered the training camp at Fort Leavenworth, Kansas, September 2, 1917, and was assigned to overseas duty September 12, 1917, arriving in France September 22. He served on the staff of chief of engineers of the American Expeditionary Forces, was promoted to the rank of lieutenant-colonel in April, 1919, returned to the United States July 13, 1919, and was honorably discharged at Camp Grant, Rockford, Illinois, July 30, 1919. Colonel Hamilton's military career was a remarkable one, and he was created a chevalier de la Legion d'Honneur by presidential decree of the French Republic of April 4, 1919, in recognition of his services, and received his decoration in the Court of Honor of the Invalides, Paris, April 28, 1919. He was commended by the chief of engineers and by the chief finance officer of the A. E. F. of the United States forces. Subsequently he was engineer member of the claims settlement board of the American Expeditionary Forces, and a member of the commission appointed by the chief of engineers of the American Expeditionary Forces to determine the disposition of engineers' stores in France after the armistice. During his service Colonel Hamilton's department handled some 778,000 tons of supplies and Colonel Hamilton personally expended upwards of $110,000,000.

Having adjusted all claims amicably, due to the armistice, in connection with the above expenditures in France, Colonel Hamilton returned to this country and again took up the duties of peace, having since served as vice president and general manager of the Gary Railways. He is also assistant general manager of the Chicago, South Shore & South Bend Railroad and as chief engineer was in charge of the rehabilitation of this property, now the fastest and most modern high speed electric railroad in the United States and Canada. He is one of the best known electrical engineers and railway men in the country. He has retained his interest in military matters, having served as commander of Gary Memorial Post No. 17 of the American Legion and during 1922, 1923 and 1924 was president of the Tenth Indiana District Reserve Officers Association. He is a director in a number of utility properties and corporations. Colonel Hamilton holds an honorary membership in DuQuesne Lodge No. 54, A. F. and A. M., and is a Royal Arch Mason; is a charter member of the American Society of Military Engineers; and a member of the Rotary Club, the Gary Commercial Club and Chamber of Commerce and the Gary Country Club. He is a Republican in his political allegiance. His religious connection is with the First Presbyterian Church.

At Pittsburgh, Pennsylvania, January 28, 1901, Colonel Hamilton was united in marriage with Miss Mildred Leet Davis, of Waynesburg, Pennsylvania, daughter of David Leet and Frances A. (Hall) Davis. David Leet Davis, who served with a Pennsylvania infantry regiment in the Union army during the war between the states, was captured by the enemy and confined in the infamous Andersonville Prison. However, he managed to make his escape therefrom, rejoined his regiment and fought until the end of the war, after which he was employed by the Government for many years. Both he and Mrs. Davis have been deceased for many years and are buried at Waynesburg. Mrs. Hamilton attended the public schools of Waynesburg and after her graduation from high school pursued a course at Waynesburg College. She has always been active in church, charitable and hospital work, and is prominent in the women's civic activities of Gary. Colonel and Mrs. Hamilton are the parents of one son: John Leet, a graduate of the University of Pennsylvania, class of 1924, who is now district manager for the Manning, Maxwell & Moore Corporation of New York City, being located at Tulsa, Oklahoma. He married Miss Jean Fogerty, of Michigan City, Indiana, and they have two sons, Thomas Graham II, and James Corbett.

CHARLES NEBEKER THOMPSON, whose name for many years has been closely associated with activities and organizations for preserving the records of Indiana history and promoting the rich cultural heritage of the state, is himself a descendant of early pioneers who settled at Covington in Fountain County in 1824.

Mr. Thompson was born at Covington, July 7, 1861, son of William and Hanna (Nebeker) Thompson and is a grandson of James and Jane (Allen) Thompson and Lewis and Hanna (Morris) Nebeker. Hanna Morris was a daughter of Richard Morris.

Mr. Thompson is a graduate of old Asbury, now DePauw University, which conferred upon him the Master of Arts degree in 1882. After his admission to the Indiana bar in 1885 he was engaged in general practice until 1913. Since that year his time has been more and more taken up with his legal and other relationships with public utilities. He is a director, vice president and general counsel for the Indianapolis Power & Light Company, is a director of the Fletcher Savings & Trust Company, the Union Title Company, the Fletcher Avenue Savings & Loan Association, and is director and vice president of the Indiana Savings & Investment Company and director and president of the Guthrie-Thompson Company.

Mr. Thompson has cultivated as his intellectual hobby for many years a deep interest in the early history of the state. He is a member and president of the Indiana Library and Historical Board and by appointment of the governor is a member of the commission for the erection of the new state library building at Indianapolis. For the past five years he has been president of the Society of Indiana Pioneers. He is a member of the Indiana Historical Society, American Historical Association, (life member), member of the Mississippi Valley Historical Association and a fellow of the American Geographic Society. Mr. Thompson is a Republican, but has had only a brief public service by election, serving in the Indiana State Senate from 1901 to 1903. He is a member of the Phi Kappa Phi, Columbia Club, Indianapolis Literary Club and is a ruling elder of the First Presbyterian Church.

He married at Indianapolis, October 7, 1891, Julia Alice Conner, daughter of John C. and Alice (Finch) Conner. She is a granddaughter of John Conner, one of Indiana's distinguished pioneers, and founder of the City of Connersville. John and his brother William Conner were among the first white settlers in the new purchase district of Indiana and they were employed as Indian interpreters by General Harrison. Mrs. Thompson's father was a captain in the United States Army and at the close of the Civil war resigned and became a member of Congress from Texas.

GEORGE JOHN KOLLAR, city clerk of Whiting, is a World war veteran and one of the active younger group of citizens of this Lake County community, where he was born March 9, 1896.

Mr. Kollar's parents, John and Anna (Liba) Kollar, were born and reared in Czecho-Slovakia. They attended parochial schools, and about three years after their marriage came to America. John Kollar worked in the coal mines of Pennsylvania and from there came to Whiting, where he was an employee of the Pennsylvania Railway and then for a number of years with the Standard Oil Company. He left the service of others to go into the mercantile business. He had come to America alone, and his wife joined him at Whiting. They were active members of the Russian Catholic Church. John Kollar died in 1924 and his wife in 1908, and both are buried at Hessville. They had five children: John, who died at the age of eight years; Mary, who died when seven years old; George John; Miss Anna, of Whiting; and Helen, wife of Frank Benson, of East Chicago. After the death of the mother of these children John Kollar married his second wife in 1909. She lives at Whiting. Of their six children one died in infancy, and the others are: Katherine, Mrs. William Lawton; Miss Emma, of Whiting; Genevieve, Irene and Albert.

George John Kollar was educated in the Sacred Heart parochial school, also attended grammar and high school at Whiting, and as a boy learned the trade of printer with the *Whiting Call*. The *Whiting Call* was then a weekly newspaper, later was merged with the *Whiting Sun*, under the name of the *Whiting Call-Sun*, and still later became the *Whiting Call*.

Mr. Kollar left newspaper work in 1917 to join the colors. He was in training at Jefferson Barracks, Saint Louis, then at Fort Sam Houston, San Antonio, Texas, for two months, and on August 7, 1917, landed at Saint Nazaire, France, with the First Division Supply Train, as a private. In 1918 he was promoted to sergeant of the first class and was made company clerk. While overseas he was at Saint Nazaire, Is-sur-Tille, Nevers, and then at Chaumont, Pershing's headquarters. On coming home he had charge of a squad of men whom he mustered out in Texas, and he received his own discharge at Louisville, Kentucky, in 1919.

On returning to Whiting Mr. Kollar spent one year with the Corn Products plant and then resumed his work with the *Whiting Call*. He left that to enter the service of the Standard Oil Company, and so continued until January 1, 1930, when he entered upon his duties as city clerk of Whiting. For four years before his election to this office he was an alderman.

Mr. Kollar is a Republican in politics. He is affiliated with the B. P. O. Elks, Loyal Order of Moose, Whiting Post No. 80 of the American Legion, the Russina Brotherhood of Falcons, the National Slovakian Society, Slovak Citizens Club, and St. Mary's Greek Catholic Church.

He married at Whiting, October 24, 1921, Miss Rose Wislay, daughter of Joseph and Anna Wislay. Her father for many years was an employee of the Inland Steel Company at Indiana Harbor. He died in 1923 and is buried in St. John's Cemetery at Hammond. Her mother lives at Indiana Harbor. Mrs. Kollar attended the grammar and high schools of Indiana Harbor. She is a member of the Catholic Church of East Chicago and the American Legion Auxiliary. Mr. Kollar is a very popular citizen of Whiting, and a man with many interests and at all times thoroughly public spirited. His favorite sports are basketball, baseball and fishing.

JAMES H. PRICE, superintendent of roads in Clay County, is one of the public spirited and capable citizens of that section of the state, where he has lived all his life. He has been a farmer, and in all his relations with the community has shown an industry and fidelity to duty that have won him the confidence of the best people of Clay County.

He was born September 1, 1891, son of James and Elizabeth (Douglass) Price, and grandson of James Price, who came from England, first locating with his family in Maryland and afterwards coming to Indiana. James Price, second of the name, was born in Maryland and was a child when brought to Indiana. He has been one of the prosperous farmers of Clay County, where he still resides. He and his wife had a family of six children: Minnie, who married Bert Hice; Ida, who married Fred Heiliger; Frankie, who married Joe Stott; May, wife of Sam Parr; James H.; and Fred C., who married Dora Rohrig.

James H. Price completed his public school education in Van Buren Township. He was trained as a farmer while still in school, and out of his industrious efforts has gained a place of his own, owning eighty acres in Clay County. He also learned the trade of barber, and followed that occupation at different times in Brazil and Harmony. Mr. Price's home is two miles north of Harmony.

He has had many years of experience in road making and road working, being employed under Arthur Groner for two years and under James L. Tucker four years, and was then himself made county superintendent of roads.

He married, October 20, 1914, Miss Myrtle Reed, daughter of Harry T. and Martha (Thomas) Reed. Her father was a locomotive engineer living at Brazil, and both parents are buried in that city. Mrs. Price had a sister, Nellie, and a brother, Harry. Her father was an Englishman by birth. Mr. Price is a member of the United Brethren Church, while Mrs. Price is a Methodist.

FRED HECTOR AHLGRIM, postmaster of Michigan City is an architect by profession and the Ahlgrims as a family have been identified with building and construction work in Northern Indiana for many years.

Mr. Ahlgrim was born on a farm in La-Porte County, May 31, 1885, son of Charles and Katherine (McAllister) Ahlgrim. The founder of the Ahlgrim family in America was Christian Ahlgrim, who came from Germany and settled in LaPorte in 1856. He spent his active life as a farmer, and he and his wife are buried in the Greenwood Cemetery at Michigan City. Charles Ahlgrim was born in Germany and was about six months old when brought to America. He grew up and attended school in LaPorte County, followed farming, but after 1893 lived at Michigan City and took up the work of a building contractor. Before he retired from business his firm handled an important share of building construction in this vicinity, including many apartment houses and industrial buildings. His wife, Katherine McAllister, was born at Buffalo, New York, and grew up in the vicinity of New Buffalo, Michigan. She is an active member of the First Methodist Episcopal Church. There were three children: Fred H.; Carl J., a contractor and builder at Michigan City; and Janet, wife of Raymond Timm, of Michigan City.

Fred H. Ahlgrim secured his early education in the public schools of Michigan City. After leaving high school he had two years of work in the University of Illinois, specializing in architecture. During the early years of his manhood he was associated with his father and brother in the building contracting work, but since 1913 has concentrated his attention upon his business as an architect.

Mr. Ahlgrim was appointed postmaster March 1, 1931, under the Hoover administration. He has been prominent in the civic and political life of Michigan City for many years. He was a member of the Common Council from 1914 to 1918. In 1925 he was elected to the Board of School Trustees and in the following year was made president of the board, serving until 1931. He is a member of the Michigan City Chamber of Commerce, is affiliated with Acme Lodge No. 83, A. F. and A. M., is a past patron of the Eastern Star Chapter, member of the B. P. O. Elks, Independent Order of Odd Fellows, is a past president of the Lions Club, and a member of the Pottawattamie Country Club. He was city chairman of the Republican party from 1914 to 1916 and its secretary from 1916 to 1918. Mr. Ahlgrim is a trustee of the First Methodist Episcopal Church. His recreations are fishing and golf.

Mr. Ahlgrim married at Michigan City, February 22, 1913, Miss Flossie Lopp, daughter of Wesley A. and Priscilla (McDaniels) Lopp. Her father for many years followed the trade of carpenter in Michigan City. Her mother died in April, 1931, and is buried in the Greenwood Cemetery. Mrs. Ahlgrim was educated in the grammar and high schools at Michigan City. She was an active member of the First Methodist Episcopal Church, Eastern Star, the Woman's Study Club, and the League of Woman Voters. Mrs. Ahlgrim passed away September 29, 1930, and is buried in the Greenwood Cemetery. Three children were born of their marriage: Richard, who died at the age of eighteen months, Doris Jane and Marjorie Janet. Doris is one of the brilliant students in high school and Marjorie is in the grades.

CHARLES JAMES BOXWELL is a popular South Bend business man. He is a pioneer in the radio business, and is proprietor of the South Side Radio Company, at 761 South Michigan Street.

Mr. Boxwell was born in Darke County, Ohio, August 4, 1897. His parents, J. J. and Nellie (Bowman) Boxwell, were natives of the same county. He was seven years of age when his mother died, and his father lives at South Bend. There were three sons: George, of Saint Mary's, Ohio; Charles J.; and Edward, proprietor of the Boxwell Radio Company of South Bend.

After the death of his mother Charles J. Boxwell was reared in the family of Mr. and Mrs. H. M. Stump, farmers near Dayton, Ohio. He attended district schools and the Dayton High School. After finishing his education he came to South Bend and for five years was an employee of the Studebaker Corporation.

It was in 1922, only a short time after the radio began its remarkable development as a popular means of communication, that Mr. Boxwell established a shop in South Bend. Since then he has developed one of the largest radio stores in Northwestern Indiana. He specializes in the handling of the Majestic radio, and in July, 1929, his corps of nineteen salesmen sold two carloads of these very popular receiving sets. Mr. Boxwell is treasurer of the Northern Indiana Radio Association, and is an active member of the South Side Business Men's Association. He is unmarried, and his hobby is golf and motoring.

Ella Bagot Kehver

Mrs. Ella Bagot Kehrer, founder of the Madison County Tuberculosis Hospital and originator of "Health Day," whose observance has since become national and international, is an Indiana woman who has turned her rare executive gifts and her personal efforts and means to the enrichment of the lives of those under-privileged and handicapped by disease and misfortune.

She was born in Ripley County, Indiana, daughter of William and Catherine (Phelan) Bagot. Bagot is an old and honored English name. William Bagot, her father, was a contractor. At Cincinnati he built a courthouse and was also the contractor for the famous Burnet House. Mrs. Kehrer was one of a large family of children. Her brother, the late Thomas Bagot, was a leading lawyer of Anderson, and another brother is Judge Charles K. Bagot, of Anderson. The other children were: William F., Walter, James, Phelan, Katherine, who married Doctor Hess, and Mary, wife of Charles Reedy, a Cincinnati elevator manufacturer.

Mrs. Kehrer completed her early education in Moores Hill College in Dearborn County, Indiana. She also attended the Marion Normal School, was a teacher for three years, following which she took up insurance work with the Union Central Life Insurance Company of Cincinnati. For several years she had charge of the company's state office at Indianapolis. At one time she lived at Redkey, Indiana, and while there she was appointed postmaster, without solicitation. While with the insurance company at Indianapolis she had worked with Doctor Potter, an expert on tuberculosis, and at that time she came to realize the great number of children who were facing the world handicapped because of the insidious ravages of this disease. At that time Mrs. Kehrer received the inspiration which has directed her into a lifelong campaign against disease, want and other human privations.

Mrs. Kehrer became a resident of Anderson in 1907. Shortly afterward she responded to the request that she become superintendent of the Anderson Industrial School, a local institution founded by a small group of public spirited women for welfare work among boys and girls. Classes were held every Saturday and instruction given in sewing, cooking, carpentering and other vocations. Health work was emphasized, and the first organized gymnasium instruction in Anderson was afforded at these classes.

In 1909 Mrs. Kehrer was drafted for service in the anti-tuberculosis campaign under the auspices of the National Red Cross. Being one of the five persons named on the Anderson committee for the sale of Red Cross seals. At that time Mrs. Kehrer devised a portable tuberculosis sleeping room, referred to as "Kehrer Shacks," a number of which were built and used, so that out-of-door sleeping became popular. A free clinic was also opened at the Industrial School. The following summer a "Fresh Air" School was instituted, the pupils being some twenty-five tuberculous children.

Through these various agencies much effective work was done, but Mrs. Kehrer was not satisfied with the progress, and finally she resolved upon a great educational campaign. She started that campaign with the inauguration of the "First Health Day Parade in the World," a spectacular parade held on April 6, 1914. During that day Anderson was one of the new centers of America. Twenty mayors, health officers, physicians, students and newspaper reporters from New York, Chicago, Cincinnati, St. Louis and from Indiana attended and witnessed and reported the parade. A motion picture was made of the parade, and has been shown repeatedly ever since. It was the beginning of an almost national custom of health day parades, and the celebration of Health Day has extended to foreign countries. All of this was a great stimulus to general health work throughout the county. Another impulse was given in 1917, when the medical examinations conducted for recruits before the draft board disclosed many otherwise promising young men who were rejected because of various stages of tubercular affliction. In May, 1918, a camp was established to receive boys who were invalided home from military service.

Her duties in the anti-tuberculosis campaign and among children constituted only part of Mrs. Kehrer's varied activities during war times. She was one of the prominent figures of the Red Cross, delivered a great many talks and lectures on health, and also participated in the drives for bond sales and the raising of funds for war purposes. She personally went to rural chapters of the Red Cross to instruct in knitting and sewing. Upon her devolved much of the responsibility of providing facilities for the care of the victims of the influenza epidemic. Besides the expansion of local hospital facilities for influenza patients, an even more important service was instituted to take medical supplies, food and other provisions to the homes of stricken people, many of them entirely dependent upon outside aid.

With the return to normal peacetime conditions Mrs. Kehrer renewed her efforts to realize the plans for a tuberculosis hospital. Co-operating with and in fact leading the Madison County Commissioners, the Anderson Chamber of Commerce and other organizations, refusing to be discouraged by various obstacles put in her path. Mrs. Kehrer kept public and official attention directed to the cause until on June 29, 1924, the tuberculosis hospital was dedicated by the American Legion, with 500 interested persons from all over the county present. A committee, made up of members of the various organizations interested in the project, agreed unanimously that the name of the hospital should be the Ella B. Kehrer Hospital, and Mrs. Kehrer was appointed by the board of directors as its first superintendent. The first hospital was a summer camp. Later the county authorities appropriated money to put the former "pest house" into condition to serve as the winter quarters, and this permanent building was opened for use January 26, 1927.

In the same year Mrs. Kehrer realized her dream of a companion institution, known as the Children's Preventorium, which was opened in June, 1927, with seventy-five sick children enrolled. Among its various institutions Madison County probably takes more pride in this sanatorium for children than any other.

This is a very brief account of the practical realization of some of Mrs. Kehrer's great ambitions for personal service to humanity. Her work has not been without recognition, not only in Madison County, whose citizens think of her in the highest terms, but also throughout the state. Mrs. Kehrer has been chairman of the legislative committee of the Indiana Federation of Women's Clubs; vice president of the State Parent-Teachers Association; director of the League of Women Voters of Indiana; president of the Child welfare Association of Indiana; member of the State Commission of the Juvenile Probation Committee; director of the Health Council of Indiana; treasurer of the Social Hygiene Association of the State; secretary of the State Tuberculosis Association, and, of course, has been chairman of the Madison County Tuberculosis Association since it was founded. Mrs. Kehrer is serving her third term as president of the Madison County Council of Social Agencies. These and other positions have not been mere honors, but have in every case represented a service such as only a woman of Mrs. Kehrer's abounding energy, enthusiasm and high purpose could render. Above all else, her greatest service may be considered as a home maker.

MICHAEL HAZINSKI has been long and successfully established in the manufacturing of high-grade cigars in the City of South Bend, where he has developed an enterprise whose scope and importance mark him as one of the leaders in this line of industry in this section of Indiana. Mr. Hazinski, who is now one of the veteran and representative business men of South Bend, was born at Kcinia, Poland, September 15, 1858, a son of Velentine and Michalina (Pierszchalski) Hazinski, both of whom passed their entire lives in their native land.

Michael Hazinski gained his early education in the schools of his native land and as a youth he served two years in the German army, the district of Poland in which he was born and reared having then been under German rule. He received his discharge from the army in 1879, about the time of attaining to his legal majority, and shortly afterward he came to the United States. After he had established residence in South Bend he here attended school six months, to advance his knowledge of the language of his adopted land and also his familiarity with business customs and systems. In his native land he had served an apprenticeship to the trade of blacksmith and machinist, and his initial service as an apprentice to the trade of cigar maker was in Philadelphia, Pennsylvania. In

the fall of 1881 he came to South Bend, where he continued his apprenticeship to this trade, and his apprenticeship was completed at Coldwater, Michigan, which city was then a center of large operations in the cigar manufacturing industry. In 1883 he finished his apprenticeship and became a member of the Cigarmakers Union. As a journeyman he followed his trade at various places, but in 1883 he established his permanent home in South Bend, where the intervening period of more than forty-five years has tallied for him large and worthy achievement and the gaining of status as one of the substantial business men and honored citizens of the community. After returning to South Bend Mr. Hazinski here worked at his trade four years, and for a time he was here foreman in a cigar factory. In 1889 he purchased the business of his employer, the late Anthony Grisvoi, and thus he has been for forty years owner and operator of what is now one of the leading cigar factories in the vital city that is the metropolis and judicial center of Saint Joseph County. Careful and honorable policies and effective service have been the basis of the unequivocal success that Mr. Hazinski has here achieved in his field of manufacturing, and he retains in his employ at the present time an average of fifty workmen, busy seasons having necessitated the retaining at intervals of fully eighty-five employes. The excellence of the products of the Hazinski cigar factory have gained to it a substantial and appreciative trade throughout the territory tributary to South Bend as a distributing center, and his leading brands of cigars are "Royal Trophy" and "M. H.," that latter being so termed from the initials of his name.

While he was serving as foreman of a local cigar factory Mr. Hazinski had much of leadership in effecting the organization of Local No. 221 of the Cigarmakers Union of America, of which he thus became a charter member. He has assisted also in the organizing of various local societies of civic and social order, and of certain of these he has served as president. He has active membership in the Saint Michael Society and the Saint Valentine Society, is a director of the Polish National Alliance, his political allegiance is given to the Republican party, and he and his wife are zealous communicants of Saint Hedwig's Catholic Church in their home city.

Mr. Hazinski was a leader in the organizing of the Chapin State Bank of South Bend, was soon elected its president, and of this executive office he has since continued the efficient incumbent, he being likewise a stockholder in other banking institutions of his home city, where he is the owner of much valuable real estate, as is he also in the City of Gary, this state. He is a loyal and valued member of the South Bend Chamber of Commerce and the West Side Business Men's Association, is affiliated with the Knights of Columbus, the Benevolent and Protective Order of Elks and the Polish Falcons, and his is deep interest in all that concerns the welfare of the fair little city in which he has long maintained his home.

On the 27th of October, 1883, was solemnized the marriage of Mr. Hazinski to Miss Veronica Latosinski, who likewise was born in Poland but who was an infant at the time of the family immigration to the United States, where her father, Anthony Latosinski, established the home in Coldwater, Branch County, Michigan, she having there been reared and educated. Jennie, eldest of the children of Mr. and Mrs. Hazinski, is the wife of Leo S. Kowalski, who is engaged in the retail furniture business in South Bend; Alexander S., who was a druggist by vocation, died in 1926, at the age of thirty-nine years; Casimir J. is sales manager for his father's cigar business; Lott S. is assistant cashier of the Chapin State Bank, and in the World war period he served fourteen months with the American Expeditionary Forces in France; Michael R. is a foreman in his father's cigar factory, and in the World war period he served in the United States Navy, with assignment to the Great Lakes Naval Training Station, near Chicago.

Mr. Hazinski takes pride not only in his children but also in the fact that he has twelve grandchildren.

CLEON HENRY FOUST, president of the Provident Trust Bank, of Columbia City, the judicial center of Whitley County, was born in Delaware County, Ohio, November 21, 1881, and is a representative of one of the old and influential families of that county, his father, Alfred Lorain Foust, having there been born in the year 1843 and having there been reared on the old home farm of his parents, the while he profited duly by the advantages of the local schools of the period. Alfred L. Foust continued his residence in Delaware County until 1886, when he came to Columbia City, Indiana, to assume charge of the large real estate holding here acquired by one of his brothers, Franklin Henry Foust, and in this city he passed the remainder of his life, his death having occurred in 1899. His father was born in Pennsylvania and became a pioneer farmer in Delaware County, Ohio, where he also served as a local preacher of the Methodist Episcopal Church.

Franklin Henry Foust, uncle of the subject of this review, came to Indiana as a pioneer of the year 1848, and at Mexico, Miami County, he engaged in the manufacturing of fanning mills. In 1850 he engaged in the general merchandise business at Columbia City, and to this enterprise he gave his attention until 1862, when he here established the Columbia City Bank, a private institution of which he continued the executive head until his death, in 1912.

Cleon Henry Foust was about five years of age when the family home was established at Columbia City, in 1886, and here he received the advantages of the public schools. He eventually assumed a clerical position in the Columbia City Bank, which had been founded by his uncle, as previously noted, and when the institution was chartered as a national bank, in 1901, he became its assistant cashier. In 1904 he was advanced to the office of cashier, and this position he retained until 1916, when he disposed of his stock in the institution, by reason of his impaired health, and retired from his executive office. During the ensuing four years he acted as agent for his uncle's real estate holdings, and he then resumed his alliance with local banking affairs, by becoming vice president and a director of the Provident Trust Company Bank, of which he was elected president in 1926. His progressive executive policies have been potent in gaining to the institution its present high standing as one of the strong and well ordered banks of this section of the state. Mr. Foust is valued as one of the representative business men and loyal and liberal citizens of the fine little city that has represented his home from his boyhood, and his political allegiance is given to the Republican party.

September 12, 1900, marked the marriage of Mr. Foust to Miss Lela G. Steman, who was born at Elida, Allen County, Ohio, June 30, 1881, and whose early education was acquired mainly in the public schools of Columbia City, Indiana, including the high school. Of the four children of this union the first born was Zoe, who was born in September, 1901, and whose death occurred in 1903. Franklin H., who was born February 22, 1906, supplemented his high-school course by attending Culver Military Academy one year, and he now holds a position in the bank of which his father is president. In April, 1927, he married Miss Helen Cordill, who is a graduate of the South Whitley High School and of the Fort Wayne Business College. Cleon Henry, Jr., who was born November 9, 1908, was graduated in the Columbia City High School, and in 1928 he was graduated in Wabash College, where he majored in oratory, and he is now retained as teacher of public speaking and debating in the high school at Rockford, Illinois. Steman A., youngest of the children, was born November 12, 1911, and is a member of the class of 1930 in the Columbia City High School.

CAPT. CHARLES R. BOWERS, manager of the Shockley Flying Service at South Bend, has been dominated by the fascination of flying since early youth. He is completely at home with every sort of motor mechanism, and has been flying since the early days of practical aviation.

Captain Bowers was born at Saint Joseph, Illinois, September 10, 1891, son of Frank C. and Mary Elizabeth (Peters) Bowers. His father was born in Montgomery County, Indiana, and his mother in Champaign County, Illinois. Captain Bowers has two younger sisters.

His early schooling was at Saint Joseph, Illinois, and while he was in high school his parents moved to Anderson, Indiana, where he graduated from high school. In 1910 a circus came to Anderson. One of its features was an aviator named C. Robinson, who had a Bleriot monoplane, equipped with a five cylinder rotary Gnome engine. Robinson wrecked his plane while on a flight and left the remains of the apparatus at Frank C. Bowers' garage. Charles R. Bowers while in his father's garage had saturated himself with a knowledge of motor mechanics. It was a labor of love for him to repair the Bleriot machine, and then, completely untutored in aeronautics, he started flying. After a few trials he smashed the machine in an attempted takeoff. His next notable experience was in 1912, when he was engaged as a mechanic and relief driver in the 500-mile speedway classic at Indianapolis. Captain Bowers in 1913 entered Whittier College at Whittier, California, but aviation had such a hold on him that he soon left college and from 1914 to 1917 was employed at the original Wright aviation field at Dayton.

He was one of the most experienced of Americans in aviation when America entered the World war, and in 1917 he enlisted in the aviation section of the Signal Corps. He completed his course at the Massachusetts Institute of Technology and was commissioned an aeronautical engineer at Kelly Field, Texas, and later at Carson Field, Florida. While there he was commissioned a captain in the air service. He remained with the Army Aviation Corps until 1920. In that year he was authorized by the Government to start the country's first National Guard air unit at Kokomo, Indiana. He was a captain and executive officer of the squadron, known as the One Hundred Thirteenth Observation Squadron, Twenty-eighth Division. This was his chief work until 1926. It was with this unit that Clyde Shockley, known as the "flying farmer," learned to fly in 1922. Shockley then developed the first commercial aviation enterprise in Indiana and one of the first in the United States.

From 1926 until December, 1927, Captain Bowers was manager of the airport at Dayton, Ohio. In December, 1927, he came to South Bend to assist in establishing a branch of the Shockley Flying Service. Of this branch he has since been manager and is ground inspector of the South Bend branch of the Shockley Flying Service. This company maintains a widely known flying school, keeps planes for hire and distributes the Waco biplanes. Its office and ground school is located at 323 South Main Street, and its flying field is at the Municipal Airport.

Captain Bowers is a member of the Indiana Aviation Association and is president of the South Bend Commercial Aviation Association. He is a member of the Kiwanis Club, the American Legion and the Masonic fraternity. Captain Bowers married Miss Myrtle Marie Bair, a native of Ohio. They have five children, Virginia, Mary, Frank, William and Margaret. Their home is at 1129 Angella Boulevard.

JOHN K. JENNINGS for some years has enjoyed a very secure and substantial position in the business life of Evansville. His career is also interesting as the example of a business man who has exerted a very wholesome influence in local and state politics and has done some things that makes the community of Evansville in particular proud of him.

Mr. Jennings is not a native of Indiana. He was born at Rich Hill, Missouri, November 24, 1883. His father was a shoe merchant at Rich Hill, and the son grew up there, attending local schools. After leaving school he moved across the state line into Kansas, and became a clerk in the office of the Western Coal & Mining Company at Pittsburg in that state. After two years he was transferred to Staunton, Illinois, as assistant cashier of the Consolidated Coal Company. The Consolidated Coal Company three years later promoted him to the sales department at Kansas City, Missouri, where he remained five years. During this time his experience brought him in contact with Mr. James H. Moore, a coal operator in Southern Indiana. It was through the influence of Mr. Moore that he came to Evansville to join the Crescent Coal Company. Two years later, through a reorganization of the Sunnyside Coal Company, he was made vice president and its sales manager.

Mr. Jennings in 1912 left the Sunnyside Company to organize the Independent Hay & Grain Company of Evansville. Shortly afterwards he added to his holdings the Diamond Mills, manufacturing a large line of stock feeds. He is now president and general manager of both of these industries, which do a business all over Southern Indiana and adjacent states.

Mr. Jennings for a number of years has been a leader in the Democratic party in Indiana. He came into politics through his association with the late Benjamin Bosse. At the National Democratic Convention in New York in 1924 he was honored with appointment as permanent financial secretary, and for two years was official representative of the National Democratic Committee in Southern Indiana. His most important work has been in fighting the Ku Klux Klan of Indiana and he spent a small fortune in that work and continued it until the leaders of the organization were disgraced and imprisoned. In 1925 he was nominated by the Democratic party for mayor of Evansville and in 1929 was again a candidate. His interest in civic affairs at Evansville is a constant factor for good. In 1927, at a cost of $50,000, he built the Rosedale Theater, in a factory district where formerly the only place of amusement was a pool hall. Mr. Jennings for twenty years has been a trustee of the Catholic Church, is a member of the house committee of the B. P. O. Elks, a member of the Knights of Columbus, Country Club, Central Turnverein and is a member of the local business and professional men's club known as the Nut Club. During the World war he took an active part in the Red Cross campaign and

the sale of Liberty Bonds. He was examined and tried to get the opportunity for active service but was not accepted. Mr. Jennings in 1927 made an interesting European tour, in the course of which he was received by the Pope and Mussolini and other dignitaries. The chief object of this trip was an investigation of municipal government in Europe.

Mr. Jennings married, May 25, 1919, Miss Lillian Helfrich, daughter of Mr. and Mrs. William Helfrich, of Evansville. They have two children: Miss Marie, a student in St. Mary's of the Woods at Terre Haute, Indiana; and William.

HON. DAVID WILLIAM HENRY, long distinguished for his services to the Indiana bench and bar, was one of the most highly respected citizens of Terre Haute, where he died June 7, 1929, at the age of seventy-six.

Judge Henry was born in Columbiana County, Ohio, October 10, 1852. His father, Jacob Henry, a native of Pennsylvania, served as a soldier in the Eighty-fifth Regiment of Indiana Volunteer Infantry in the Civil war. Jacob Henry married Elvira Rowles, who was born in Columbiana County, Ohio. Her father, William Rowles, was a soldier in the War of 1812.

David William Henry received his education in the common schools and from the diligent reading of books at home. He attended a seminary at Farmersburg, Indiana, all his higher education being the product of his individual earnings and efforts. At the age of sixteen he entered Mount Union College in Ohio, taking the scientific course. Prior to that he had taught school, and by teaching he paid for his higher education. After leaving college he entered the law office of N. G. Buff, of Terre Haute, with whom he read law for about a year. Failing health compelled him to leave the law office, and then he resumed teaching, spending three years as principal of the Farmersburg Academy and three years in the schools of Bloomfield. He was then able to enter the Central Law School at Indianapolis, where he was graduated in the spring of 1881.

Judge Henry was a member of the Terre Haute bar for nearly half a century. He first practiced there with the law firm of Davis & Davis. In 1884 he was elected prosecuting attorney for the Forty-third Judiciary Circuit and in 1886 was re-elected and in that election led his ticket. When he retired from office, in 1888, he resumed a general law practice, in which he was busily engaged until 1894, when he was elected Superior Court judge. Though on the bench only a few years, he showed his eminent fitness both in learning and in natural wisdom for the responsibilities of the judiciary. He presided in the trial of over 1200 cases, and only twice was an appeal taken from his decision, and in only one case was his ruling reversed.

Judge Henry retired from the bench in 1897, to accept appointment under President McKinley as collector of internal revenue. After leaving this office his time and energies were largely taken up with his interest in the oil industry. He was identified with the oil development in Oklahoma practically from the time that state became one of the greatest centers in the mid-continent field.

Politically Judge Henry was a Republican. His legal ability and reputation secured for him many positions of honor and trust in his party. He was one of the organizers and served as the first president of the Vigo County Historical Society, being retained in the office of president until his death. He was greatly interested in historical matters and was also a member of the Indiana Historical Society. He belonged to the Terre Haute Club and was a thirty-second degree Scottish Rite Mason and Shriner.

Judge Henry married, June 30, 1885, Miss Virginia Thompson. Her father was the distinguished Indianan, Col. Richard W. Thompson, whose career is sketched following. Judge and Mrs. Henry had two children. Their daughter, Harriet, is the wife of George F. Kean, of Terre Haute. Mrs. Kean has a daughter, Virginia. The son, Richard Porter Henry, a resident of Chicago, is married and has a son, Richard Thompson Henry.

Mrs. Henry resides with her daughter, Mrs. Kean, at Terre Haute. She has led a very active life, has been a leader in social affairs at Terre Haute, and is vice president of the Vigo County Historical Society. She has written several articles on the early history of Vigo County, one of them being "Old Terre Haute Residents," and another "My Recollections of the Civil War."

COL. RICHARD W. THOMPSON, whose oratory was one of the factors that decided the success of the Whig campaign in Indiana in 1840, and whose subsequent brilliant political leadership made him one of Indiana's outstanding men in the nation, spent the greater part of his long and useful life at Terre Haute. He died at his beautiful home on South Sixth Street in that city, February 9, 1900, at the venerable age of ninety-one.

Richard W. Thompson was born in Culpeper County, Virginia, June 9, 1809. He was given a liberal classical education. In 1831 he came West, locating at Louisville, Kentucky, and in 1832 settled in the village of Bedford, Lawrence County, Indiana. Soon afterward he married Harriet E. Gardiner, whose father, Col. James B. Gardiner, was editor of the Ohio State Journal at Columbus.

During his first years in Indiana, Richard W. Thompson supported himself by clerking in stores and teaching school. He studied law in his leisure, was admitted to the bar in 1834 and soon became known in his section of the state as an able public exponent of Whig principles and politics. He took part in the ascendancy of this party in the West and was one of the most effective campaigners for the Harrison and Tyler ticket in 1840. In that year he was himself elected a member of Congress by the Whigs in his home district, including Lawrence County. He served one term and declined to be a candidate for reelection. Soon after retiring from Congress he located at Terre Haute, where he engaged in a general law practice. For almost a generation he was employed as counsel and advocate in nearly every important case arising in Southern, Central and Western Indiana.

In 1848 Colonel Thompson was again elected to Congress, to represent the Terre Haute district. In Congress he represented the growing power of the West, and came upon the stage as one of the young leaders just as the generation of Clay, Calhoun and Webster was retiring from the stage. During the Civil war Colonel Thompson was indefatigable in his efforts to sustain the integrity of the Union. As provo marshal of a large district he had the supervision of raising troops and the training camps. After the war he resumed his law practice. Colonel Thompson was a sage political leader and adviser, but avoided rather than sought the honors of office for himself. He declined an appointment as minister of Austria offered him by President Taylor, also the office of recorder of the General Land Office tendered him by President Fillmore, and that of judge of the United States Court of Claims tendered him by President Lincoln. In March, 1877, he entered the cabinet of President Hayes as secretary of the navy. From this post he resigned in December, 1880, to become president of the American Board of the Panama Canal Company. At the conclusion of this service he retired to the quiet routine of his private life at Terre Haute. Here during his declining years he was surrounded not only by his children and grandchildren, but by the daily visits of his admiring friends. He owned one of the finest private libraries in the state and his books were the chief source of his recreation. He is also remembered for his literary work. Among his books were: *The Papacy and Civil Power, History of the Tariff, Footprints of the Jesuits, Personal Recollections of the Presidents.* Richard W. Thompson is a name that will always remain in Indiana political and public history. As a mark of the esteem in which he was held in his home community and throughout the state there stands on the courthouse lawn at Terre Haute a monument erected to his honor.

By his marriage to Miss Harriet E. Gardiner, Colonel Thompson had eight children. The only survivor is Virginia, widow of Judge David William Henry, of Terre Haute.

G. EDWARD BEHRENS is the efficient and popular superintendent of schools for Posey County, with executive office in the courthouse at Mount Vernon, and his is a record of notably able and constructive service in connection with the public schools of his native state.

Mr. Behrens was born in Harrison County, Indiana, April 2, 1877, and is a son of Henry and Susan L. (Beard) Behrens, the former of whom was born in Germany, in 1849, and the latter of whom was born in Indiana. Henry Behrens was long numbered among the substantial exponents of farm industry in Harrison County and as a loyal and liberal citizen of sterling character he ever commanded high place in communal esteem, his death having occurred in 1908, and his wife likewise being deceased. Of the four children the eldest is Jacob, Jr., who is fifty-six years of age (1929) and who is engaged in the insurance business in the City of Waco, Texas. Mollie E., fifty-five years of age, is the wife of William E. Hancock, a farmer in Floyd County, Indiana, and they have two children, Lulu, aged thirty-two years, and Stella, aged thirty years. Viola, who is forty-nine years of age and next younger than her brother G. Edward, of this review, is the wife of Ward McBride, a prosperous farmer in Floyd County, and the names and respective ages of their children are here noted: Lloyd, twenty-four years; Virgil, twenty-two years; Raymond, twenty years; Leona, sixteen years; and Ida, ten years.

The rural district schools of his native county afforded G. Edward Behrens his preliminary education, and in the high school at Laconia, that county, he was duly graduated. In 1908 he was graduated in the Indiana State Normal School, after completing the regular teachers' course, and in 1919 he was there graduated with the degree of Bachelor of Science. He later attended the University of Indiana one term and had five terms in the great University of Chicago. In the meanwhile he had become a teacher in the rural schools, his pedagogic service having been initiated in the year 1900. During the first four years he taught in the rural district schools of Posey County, and in the city schools of Mount Vernon, the county seat, he taught nine years, during five of which he held the position of principal of the Central School, he having been a teacher in the high school during the ensuing four years. In March, 1914, he was first elected county superintendent of schools, and by successive reelections he has been retained in this important office in Posey County, his successive reelections attesting the efficiency of his administration and the high popular estimate placed thereon.

Progressive and public-spirited in his civic attitude, Mr. Behrens gives his political allegiance to the Democratic party, and he and his wife have membership in the Methodist Episcopal Church in their home city. He is affiliated with both the Masonic fraternity and the Independent Order of Odd Fellows, in each of which he has passed various official chairs, he having given ten years of such service with the local lodge of Ancient Free and Accepted Masons in Mount Vernon, of which he is a past master and a past secretary. He has local real-estate investments and is the owner also of farm property.

In Posey County was solemnized the marriage of Mr. Behrens to Miss Minnie E. Klotz, who was here born and reared and who is a daughter of Henry J. and Sarah S. (Greathouse) Klotz, her father having been born in Germany and having become one of the pros-

R.W. Thompson

perous farmers of Posey County, Indiana. Mr. and Mrs. Behrens have no children, but, as may naturally be inferred, both are deeply interested in the children of their home county and in providing them the best possible educational advantages.

PETER MORGEN. No center of civilization can be more advanced than its people, and one of the best measures of its progress is the number of industries within its borders, for, not only do these produce that which carries the name into other districts, but they give employment to many. The people connected with these industries, because of the advantage of being close to the scene of their labors, become permanent citizens, interested in the civic life, its schools, churches, clubs, fraternities and other organizations and associations. Huntingburg is one of the successful little cities of Dubois County, and an industry that brings its average up very perceptibly is that of raising flowers, in which Peter Morgen has long been engaged, and his plant is the largest in the state.

An account of this industry was published in the 1928 Industrial and Trade Edition of a local newspaper, which, written by one who lives at Huntingburg, so thoroughly covers the history of Mr. Morgen and his plant that it is quoted herewith:

"From a beginning of two greenhouses built on the east side of Huntingburg some years ago has expanded a flower industry that has no equal in entire Indiana and which distributes, wholesale and retail, all the cultivated varieties of flowers.

"Back of this industry is a man who is not only an efficient business executive, but who has mastered the art of growing flowers; who knows how to grow vigorous plants and can make them bloom in proper seasons when there is the greatest demand. Perhaps few who read this know that Peter Morgen, of this city, while at Chicago, with American Beauty roses which he had grown, won first prize in the National Flower Show for seven consecutive years as producing America's best American Beauty roses. He took first prize every time he entered exhibits in this national contest. So that the American Beauty roses which he grew at these greenhouses in Huntingburg for a number of years and other flowers grown there may be looked upon as the finest specimens to be seen in our United States—a distinction of which, perhaps, but few Huntingburg people have been aware.

"Born on a farm at Saint Henry, about six miles south of Huntingburg, Peter Morgen began as a boy to take pride in his work as he attended the parochial school at that place and excelled in his studies. The death of his father caused Peter to take life more seriously when just a lad than boys usually do at that stage in life, and at the age of fourteen he went to Chicago, where two of his sisters resided, to find employment. When he applied for his first job in America's second city the employer said to him 'you are a rather small boy,' but told Peter he would give him a definite answer about work the following day. The answer was, 'All right Peter, you can start tomorrow morning.' He started and remained in this company's employ for nine years. Here, by observations and experiments, he learned the principles of successfully growing flowers and first astonished his employer and attracted attention when, at a Mothers' Day season, he produced from the flower beds given to his care sufficient carnations to require five cutters for three days.

"From Chicago Mr. Morgen went to Almanda Park, California, near Pasadena, one of the beauty spots of America, spending two years there, and then returned to Saint Henry. There had always been a special attraction in his little home town, and so, after Miss Elizabeth Fest had become Mrs. Morgen, they went to Chicago, where Mr. Morgen's old employer received him with a job the first morning after his arrival. After spending two years in Chicago they went to Newcastle, Indiana, and after a year there—all the while growing flowers—they came to Huntingburg.

"Mr. Morgen first built two greenhouses, 300 feet long. But the business rapidly developed, so the next year he built two more, and the year following he built four more greenhouses. With the war's demands all his trained employes were called into the service and, assuming too great a share of the work himself, Mr. Morgen became ill and sold the business to the late George Seubold, who conducted it three years. Mr. Morgen spent a year on his farm near the city and then, with his family, spent an entire year traveling to all the important points throughout the United States from the east coast to the west. Regaining his health, he took charge of a large plant of greenhouses at Roanoke, Virginia, but after a year there the desire to conduct his own business and the longing for his old home county overcame and he bought back the business in this city in 1926. He also bought the greenhouses and retail flower store at Owensboro, Kentucky, discontinuing the growing of flowers there, but retaining the retail store, which is located at 406 Frederica Street in the Citizens Trust Building. A special refrigerater in the Owensboro store, in which flowers are kept, cost $8,000, and one of the display cases cost $2,000—other fixtures are in keeping. The Owensboro store is supplied from the Huntingburg greenhouses, trucks hauling loads of flowers from here to that city daily. Flowers are sold both wholesale and retail from the assembling rooms of the Huntingburg plant, which is located on east Sixth Street. Wholesale shipments are made to Saint Louis, Chicago, Cincinnati, Louisville, Evansville and throughout the entire Central United States.

"This concern is also a bonded member of the Florists' Telegraph Delivery Association, Incorporated, an organization of over 4,000 bonded florists with locations all over the world, supplying flowers upon two and one-half hours' notice and employing telegraph, telephone, radio and cable as mediums for transferring orders. By this method, if anyone desires to have flowers sent to a certain address at New York, San Francisco, Toronto, Mexico City, or wherever it may be, an order to Peter Morgen's establishment will be delivered at any distant place within two and a half hours.

"Any flowers in season are grown at the local greenhouse as the seasons rotate. They furnish flowers as the people desire. Flowers are supplied with the long stems, or in any designs, in sprays, or boquets, or potted. Quantities under 100 are sold retail and quantities of 100 or over are sold at wholesale prices. Local retail patronage is given careful consideration, as well as large wholesale orders.

"The plant, consisting of a great series of greenhouses, systematically planned, is very interesting. A large boiler room receives coal by the car loads. Two large boilers supply steam to all parts of the greenhouses, and to Mr. Morgen's nearby residence as well, and keep the temperature uniform night and day. Failure of this heating system would mean thousands of dollars of loss to the growing flower plants. The long glass houses have row upon row of various kinds of flowers, all growing in beds of specially prepared soil. Most of these must be propagated from 'slips' to keep them true to their kind. The propagating sections have thousands of tiny plants growing in sand until they grow roots, when they are transplanted.

"Mr. Morgen has a large farm at Johnsburg, with a beautiful residence. Although his farming may be looked upon as only a hobby, he was, nevertheless, the county's 'wheat king' this year. He keeps seven beautiful horses, nine head of cattle, over sixty hogs and some 500 chickens on the farm, which gives it a practical aspect.

"Mr. Morgen is energetic, is a member of several civic bodies, and is public-spirited, believing that a city cannot develop beyond the cooperative level of its inhabitants."

AMOS L. BARNETT has the pedagogic and executive ability that enables him to render a specially effective service to his native county, and as county superintendent of the public schools, with headquarters at Boonville, judicial center of Warrick County, he is giving an administration that in the fullest sense justifies his having been selected for this office.

Mr. Barnett was born on the home farm, near Boonville, that is still the place of residence of his parents, and the date of his nativity was August 25, 1897. He is a son of Joseph and Anna (Scales) Barnett, both of whom were likewise born and reared in this county and the latter of whom is a daughter of J. A. and Rhoda (Baldwin) Scales. Joseph Barnett has secure status as one of the progressive and representative exponents of farm industry in his native county and is a scion of one of the old and honored families of this section of the Hoosier State. Of the seven

children of Joseph and Anna (Scales) Barnett four are living. Louis died at the age of five years, James at the age of thirty-eight years, and Jane at the age of fourteen years. Thomas, who is a progressive farmer in Warrick County, married Laura Pemberton and they have three children, Mildred, Woodrow and Howard, aged, respectively (1929), twelve, nine and seven years. Amos L., of this review, is next younger of the children. Ota is identified with coal mining in this section of Indiana and his wife, whose maiden name was Grace Camp, likewise is a native of Warrick County, their one child, Robert Owen, being two years of age. Andrew, youngest of the surviving children, remains as an exponent of farm industry in his native county and also as one of its eligible young bachelors.

Amos L. Barnett early began to contribute his youthful quota to the work of the home farm, and his preliminary education was acquired in the rural school of the home district. In the high school at Folsomville, a neighboring village, he was graduated as a member of the class of 1917, and he soon afterward initiated his service as a teacher in one of the rural district schools of his native county. Later he taught in high schools in Warrick and Pike counties, and in furthering his own education he completed a course in Oakland City College, in Gibson County, in which institution he was graduated as a member of the class of 1923 and with the degree of Bachelor of Arts. Popular appreciation of his character and ability was shown when he was called, in September, 1925, to the office of county superintendent of the public schools of Warrick County, and in this position he is giving a careful and progressive administration that has signally advanced the standards and service in all of the schools of his native county.

Mr. Barnett takes deep and loyal interest in all that concerns the welfare and progress of his home city, county and state, his political allegiance is given to the Democratic party, he is affiliated with the Masonic fraternity, and his personal popularity is not jeopardized by the fact that he still permits his name to appear on the roster of eligible young bachelors in his native county.

HON. ORAN E. ROSS. The people of Winchester are well acquainted with Hon. Oran E. Ross, for not only is he serving most capably as their mayor, but he is also an auctioneer of more than ordinary ability and his services in the latter capacity call him to all parts of Randolph County. He is a native of Indiana, but not of Winchester, for he was born in Delaware County, March 18, 1883, a son of Elmer and Emma (Driscoll) Ross, also natives of Delaware County. The paternal grandparents were James A. and Maria (Gibson) Ross, natives of North Carolina; while the maternal grandparents were John and Maria (Gibson) Driscoll, he born in Pennsylvania and she in Delaware County, and all were farming people. Elmer Ross was one

Alfred V. Reschar

of the earlier auctioneers of Winchester, so serving until his death in November, 1908, and at the same time he was also holding the office of county assessor. The wife and mother survived until December, 1921, when she too passed away.

Mayor Ross attended the common and high schools, and then took a course in Voorhees Business College, Indianapolis, Indiana. When he had completed it he went with the National Biscuit Company and was in the main office of the company for two years. His next occupation was traveling on the road for Green & Green, of Dayton, Ohio, but finally he returned to Winchester and took charge of his father's business of auctioneering, which he is still carrying on most successfully. Like his father he possesses those qualifications necessary for auctioneering, which is really as much a profession as a business. These qualifications for successful operation include being a good judge of values, the ability to give an intelligent and elaborate description of many different kind of articles. Good auctioneers are born, not made; a person can learn to be a doctor, lawyer or minister, but there never were such advantages where a person could go and learn to be an auctioneer without any leaning whatever toward the work. Then, furthermore, it is the only profession wherein a person can display whatever ability he may possess in different respects, and can intermingle comedy if he sees fit. There is not anything by which he may refer to for reference and every thought is extemporaneous, and he must guide himself accordingly. Because of these, and other reasons, there are very few very capable auctioneers, although there have been a number of men who have tried to break in, but only to fall by the roadside. Therefore, when a community does possess one, he is a decided asset, and the people are proud of him, and such is the case with Mayor Ross, as it was with his father before him.

In 1904 Mayor Ross was married to Miss Mabel Ashwill, who was born at Winchester, a daughter of James E. and Susan (Martin) Ashwill, natives of Ohio and Winchester, respectively. Mayor and Mrs. Ross have two children: Orin E., who resides at Columbus, Ohio, a traveling man; and Susan, who is at home.

The Presbyterian Church has long held the membership of Mayor Ross; he is now one of its deacons, and superintendent of its Sunday School. In addition to his auctioneering business he is manager of the East Indiana District of the Missouri State Life Insurance Company, and sells a large amount of insurance annually. In this way he has come to know many people, and as he is personally pleasing, and dependable, it was but natural that he should be asked to accept office, and in 1921, in 1925 and again in 1929 he was elected mayor of Winchester, and has made the city what it is today. He is a thirty-second degree Knight Templar and Shriner Mason; assisted in organizing the Kiwanis Club, which he served as president, and he is active along many other lines, for he is energetic, overflowing with pride in his community, and a willingness to do anything within his power to advance it in any possible way.

ALFRED V. RESCHAR, postmaster of the City of Anderson, is a man of broad business experience and qualifications for executive duties, and has taken a prominent part in public affairs of Anderson since locating in that city in 1912.

Mr. Reschar was born in Jeffersonville, Indiana, son of John Louis Reschar and grandson of Peter J. Reschar. The Reschar family was originally French Huguenots and during the era of religious execution found refuge in South Germany, and later a branch of the family moved to Hesse Darmstadt. Peter J. Reschar came with his family to the United States in 1870 and located at Jeffersonville, Indiana, where he was in the provision business until his death. John Louis Reschar was born in Hesse Darmstadt and was eighteen years of age when he came to the United States with his parents. He had gone to school regularly during his youth and after coming to America was associated with his father in the provision business. He retired in 1893 and is now deceased. His wife was Mary Oetterer, who was born at Louisville, Kentucky.

Alfred V. Reschar was one of a family of eight children, the others being John Louis, Christian, August, Benjamin, Freda, Emma and Amelia. The public schools of Jeffersonville gave him the foundation of his education, after which he served an apprenticeship at the trade of cigarmaker and followed that work for three years. On giving up the cigar business he was made manager of the shipping department of the Whiteside Baking Company of Louisville and later was sales manager of this organization.

Mr. Reschar on coming to Anderson in 1912 was made manager of the stock department of the Delco-Remy Electric Company, one of the city's major industries. From this he resigned in 1920 to go with the Mid-West Engine Company, and won a successful place among the city's business men and executives.

On September 23, 1924, President Coolidge appointed him postmaster, and he was reappointed for a second term at the close of the Coolidge administration in 1928. Mr. Reschar has been an enthusiastic Republican since early manhood. He cast his first presidential vote for Roosevelt. During the World war he was active in the sale of Government securities, and was chairman of the committee during the Victory Loan drive. He and his associates sold $150,000 worth of bonds in forty minutes.

Mr. Reschar has always been an admirer and defender of stalwart Americanism and the sound political and economic principles on which the American Government is founded. During the past year he has delivered many formal and informal talks before Rotary, Kiwanis and Lions clubs all over the state in behalf of the National Defense program fostered by the Daughters of the American Revolution. Mr. Reschar has been very glad to cooperate with this great organization in the promotion of its policy to prevent the misrepresentation of facts concerning the founders and fathers of our nation, and also opposing any attempt from any source to break down the great principles on which our Government has been built.

Mr. Reschar for one term was a member of the Anderson City Council. He is a former president and has been a member of the board of directors of the Chamber of Commerce. For two years he was a director of the Anderson Y. M. C. A., for three years was president of the Central Avenue Parent-Teachers Association of Anderson and in 1927 was president of the Madison County Parent-Teachers Association. He has been president of the local council of the Boy Scouts of America, is chairman of the Madison County Chapter of the Red Cross and chairman of the Anderson Armory Board of the Indiana National Guard. Mr. Reschar has been secretary, treasurer and president of the Tri-State Postmasters Association. He is prominent in the Masonic fraternity, being both a York and Scottish Rite Mason. On September 16, 1930, at Boston, Massachusetts, the supreme honorary thirty-third degree of the Scottish Rite was conferred upon him. He has been president of the Masonic Temple Company of Anderson. He and his wife are members of the Methodist Episcopal Church.

Mr. Reschar married in 1915 Miss Clara Maude Moore, daughter of Joseph and Nettie Moore. They have one son, Robert Louis.

JAMES H. MANION, who is vice president and general sales manager for the Graham-Paige Company at Evansville, is a young business man who has shown exceptional ability in the field of sales promotion and has held a number of responsible connections with the manufacturing interests of the Evansville territory.

Mr. Manion was born across the Ohio River at Henderson, Kentucky, October 8, 1898. His parents, Charles T. and Martha (Snow) Manion, were both born in Kentucky. His father was a merchant, and died at Evansville in December, 1928. Of their four children one daughter, Eva Ruth, died at the age of eight months. Mr. James H. Manion has two sisters, Minnie Cecilia and Miss Mildred Rose. Minnie is the wife of Preston Weikel, a building contractor, and has a daughter, named Martha Jane.

James H. Manion attended school at Henderson, also at Denver, Colorado, and took a course in Lockyear's Business College at Evansville. His first work after leaving school was as an automobile salesman for the Dixie Motor Company of Evansville. He remained with that organization one year and was in business for himself at Henderson, Kentucky, a year.

He sold out his business interests in order to be free to render some service during the World war. Before he was nineteen years of age he enlisted and was accepted for service in the Motor Transport Corps. Later, when the second draft law was passed, including all men between the ages of eighteen and forty-five, he enlisted in September, 1918, and served until honorably discharged on November 19, following the armistice.

After the war he became a wholesale representative for the Bennighof Nolan Company of Evansville, who handled the distribution of the cars of the Willys Overland Company in this territory. Mr. Manion in 1927 was for one year sales promotion manager for the Delker Brothers Manufacturing Company of Henderson, Kentucky, furniture manufacturers. He left there and in March, 1928, joined the Graham-Paige Company of Evansville as vice president and general sales manager.

Mr. Manion is a stockholder in the Graham-Paige Company of Evansville. He is a Democrat in politics, a member of the Catholic Church, and is a past deputy grand master of the Knights of Columbus.

He married at Evansville, November 25, 1925, Miss Mildred Hartig, daughter of Albert and Matilda (Hartman) Hartig. Her father is in the iron foundry business at Evansville. Mr. and Mrs. Manion have three children, Mary Louise, born June 10, 1927, James Hartig, born October 15, 1928, and Charles Albert, born October 4, 1930.

EDWARD G. RAGON. While his earthly career has been terminated by death, what Edward G. Ragon accomplished in life lives on at Evansville and in Vanderburg County, and the world is the better for his passage through it, for he set an example of high living, industrious endeavor and excellent business management. He was born at Russellville, Kentucky, in 1838, a son of a carriage manufacturer and prominent citizen. After he had completed his schooldays Edward G. Ragon became a clerk at Russellville, and later went into general merchandising with the late F. H. Ragon, father of Dan S. Ragon, the firm establishing its business at Cadiz, Kentucky. These two remained together at Cadiz for many years, and were very successful, but finally sold out and came to Evansville and established the wholesale grocery house of Ragon Brothers. The business was first located at Water and Vine streets, but with the continued expansion of business it was found necessary to secure larger quarters, and M. T. Bray, Junior, erected for the firm of Ragon Brothers, of which Edward G. Ragon was the surviving member, on the site now occupied by the Braum Store and later moved again to still larger quarters in a building erected by George L. Mesker especially for Ragon Brothers, located at Water and Ingle streets, where there was ample space for all the operations carried on.

Edward G. Ragon was a man whose interests were centered in his business and his home. He was the first on hand at the office in the morning, and the last to leave at night,

Chas. B. Salyer

his hours of work averaging sixteen a day. Nothing was too small for his consideration, or too large for his comprehension and effective action. Honest, upright and reliable, he held the respect of the entire business community, was especially beloved and respected by his employees, and ranked among the leaders in community betterment. Not only did he accomplish much for Evansville as the head of a great business house, but also personally through his support of all worthwhile measures. He was a director in the Old National Bank of Evansville. When he died the city lost a first-class citizen, one who had been faithful to every trust reposed in him.

Mr. Ragon was married in November, 1862, to Miss Sally McKinney, at Cadiz, Kentucky, and seven children were born to this union, four of whom died in infancy, the other three being: Irma, Ada May and Chester. Irma is the wife of Dr. Edmond Vince, of Battle Creek, Michigan, and has no children. Ada May is unmarried and lives in the old family home at Evansville. Chester had the active management of Ragon Brothers, as president, after the death of his father until his death, September 18, 1915.

When the firm of Ragon Brothers completed its fifty-ninth year in business the large organization was purchased by the Hulman Company, of Terre Haute, Indiana, the transaction involving $1,000,000, its standing and value having been secured through the untiring efforts of Edward G. Ragon.

Mr. Ragon's career was typical of the best citizenship during the period that saw Evansville develop from a village to a city, and here he gave his native qualities of character and practical ability to its upbuilding. The industry, foresight and civic spirit of such a man as he made possible a progress that is remarkable, and upon his accomplishments and his strong faith in its future do the people of Evansville build today.

CHARLES HENRY BUSICK is a veteran Indiana newspaper man, publisher of the *Progress Examiner* at Orleans. He has given practically all the years of his life since he was fourteen to the printing and newspaper business.

He was born at Orleans, August 17, 1864. After a public school education he went to work as a printer's apprentice. Later, after having mastered the printer's art and having had an all-round experience in newspaper work, he and Fred Kimbley started the *Orleans Progress*. They were partners until 1908. In 1899 they also acquired the *Examiner* and Mr. Busick managed both papers until their consolidation. The *Progress Examiner* is one of the strongest weekly newspapers published in this section of Indiana.

Mr. Busick is a Republican in politics, is a member of the Masonic fraternity, Knights of Pythias and Independent Order of Odd Fellows, the Modern Woodmen of America, is a member of the Kiwanis Club and the Weekly Press Association.

He married, August 4, 1894, Miss Ida Magill. They have four children. William, associated with his father in the newspaper business, married Mary Pickings and they have a son. Merrill married Virginia Tuly and has a daughter. Vern, first assistant in the Orleans postoffice, married Fern Lindley and they are the parents of one daughter. The youngest child, Roy, is unmarried and is attending college.

HON. CHARLES B. SALYER, attorney, former judge of the City Court of Anderson, has been distinguished both in his routine professional work and in public office by his positive strength of character, his efficiency, his devotion to honest purposes in the interpretation and application of the law.

Judge Salyer is a very interesting figure both as a man and lawyer. He was born on a farm in Scott County, Virginia, and his father was one of the mountaineer class, a Republican, who in the early days fought and struggled to protect himself in his rights as a voter. Judge Salyer has described the environment and the circumstances of his early life in an interesting autobiography which tells a great deal more than any formal statement of facts and events. He says:

"In a one-room log cabin, in the wilderness of Clinch Mountain, Virginia, November 1, 1893, I first saw the light of day, being the second son of a mountain farmer and one of fourteen children. I was reared in an atmosphere of the pioneer, constantly being trained in honesty, character and citizenship; learning early in life what it meant to be an American citizen in this great land of ours. My parents were sturdy Virginia farmers and were very religious, therefore I attended church and Sunday School regularly. I will never forget those boyhood days in the mountains and the beautiful lessons I learned. Life was hard, and my parents were stern, but they did what they thought was best for me. I am glad that I was born of parents of small wealth, for I appreciate life and its opportunities better. I believe it enables me to understand the problems of people more fully.

"Sometimes it was necessary for me to travel over the frosty mountains barefooted, as my parents were not as fortunate as some. I aided my parents in clearing the forest, that we might have land for farming purposes, and was hired out at meagre wages. At fourteen I left home, seeking better opportunities, and worked as a coal miner, section hand, salesman, street railway and interurban conductor, advancing to a train dispatcher, claims attorney, investigator and adjuster, lawyer and judge. During all of this time I was attending night schools and taking Indiana University Extension courses. I took courses in law, public speaking and psychology, and for seven years read law. I have taken other courses which were necessary in qualifying me for the law profession. The training and experience as an investigator, adjuster and claims attorney, lasting over a period of nearly ten years, enabled me to gain a wonderful knowledge of law.

"I attribute my success, so far in life, to hard work and my willingness to cooperate with my fellowmen, by giving them a lift whenever possible; making an honest effort to do the job a little better than the other fellow; fighting for what I thought was right and just, not for intolerance, hatred or prejudice, but for one Flag, one Nation, indivisible, with Liberty and Justice for all."

Judge Salyer has been one of the successful attorneys of the Anderson bar for a number of years. In November, 1925, he was elected judge of the Anderson City Court, and in that office proved his independence, his fearlessness and efficiency. His work was especially notable in law enforcement, and in a little more than two years over 150 convictions were obtained in his court against bootleggers. Withal, during the four years he served as city judge he tempered justice with mercy. Those in close touch with the social situation know that upwards of five hundred boys and girls and a thousand men and women have been permanently helped and benefited through the sympathy, disinterested kindliness and friendship of Judge Salyer. He was the means of reestablishing many broken homes, and in the cases of youth he was firm but trustful, and turned many young people from dissolute ways into the sturdy habits of industry and business, where many of them have shown worthiness for life's responsibilities.

Judge Salyer is a Republican in politics. He came to Indiana about the time he reached his majority and his first presidential vote was given to Charles E. Hughes. Judge Salyer is a member of the Central Christian Church of Anderson and has been an active civic worker. He is a member of the Boy Scout Council, for three years was president of the Shadeland Parent-Teachers Association, for two years a director of the West Oak Service Center, and is now in his third year as president of the Northwest Brotherhood. Fraternally he is a member of the Knights of Pythias, Fraternal Order of Eagles, B. P. O. Elks, Red Men, Junior Order United American Mechanics, Loyal Order of Moose, and is a member of the American Bar Association and Indiana Bar Association.

Judge Salyer is married and has three children, named Marigrace, Paul and Robert.

WILLIAM IRVIN has lived practically all his life in the City of Greencastle. He has become well known there in business circles, and is still active, head of a prosperous business as a painting contractor.

Mr. Irvin was born at Greencastle July 7, 1867. His paternal grandfather came from Maryland to Indiana. Mr. Irvin's father, John Irvin, was born in Hendricks County, Indiana, and became a merchant tailor at Greencastle. He also owned considerable farm land in Putnam County. John Irvin married Elizabeth Hammond, whose father, John Hammond, came to Putnam County from Virginia. Mrs. Elizabeth Irvin died in Boston, Massachusetts,

in 1921. She was the mother of two children, Mary and William. Mary married William Paisley, member of an old Colonial family of Rhode Island.

William Irvin attended public schools at Greencastle and was a student in DePauw University while it was still conducted under the original name of Asbury. After completing his education he was clerk in the local postoffice for six years and then took up the trade and business he has followed for many years, painting. He became foreman in the painting department of the Pennsylvania Railway and was in that branch of the service until 1915, when he resigned to go into business for himself as a painting contractor and interior decorator. His business is probably the largest in its line in Putnam County. Mr. Irvin has been a staunch supporter of the Republican party, though never a candidate for office. For ten years he was in the Indiana National Guard.

He married in 1884 Miss Gertrude Hibbem, of Greencastle. She became the mother of three children, William, Adeline and Frank. William, who now lives at Indianapolis, married Maria Schultz. Adeline is married and has a son, Robert. Frank Irvin is married and is a lieutenant in the United States Aviation Corps, stationed at San Antonio, Texas.

After the death of his first wife Mr. Irvin married Elizabeth Dowling, a step-daughter of Riley McKeen, president of the Vandalia Railway Company.

MRS. BETTY M. MILLER, who holds the office of postmistress at West Baden, has proved a most capable servant of the Federal Government and has discharged her duties in a way to win the approval of all the patrons of the office, and her administration has been more than once commended by the higher postal officials.

She is a native of Indiana, born at Celina, Perry County, July 15, 1879, daughter of John J. and Sarah E. Carmickle. Educated at first in the public schools of Celina, she later attended school at Bristow and Tobinsport, Indiana, and as a young girl was given a teacher's license and had the experience of teaching five years in rural districts.

On April 3, 1902, she was married to Dr. H. L. Miller. For six years they made their home at Leopold, Indiana, and in July, 1909, moved to West Baden. Mrs. Miller was appointed postmistress of West Baden by President Coolidge, January 3, 1924, and her present commission, dated January, 1928, also came from President Coolidge.

Mrs. Miller's father spent his active life as a farmer and died in 1905. Her mother is now seventy years of age. Mrs. Miller was well qualified for the duties of postmistress at West Baden because of her four years' service in the same office at Leopold. She is a Republican in politics. Mrs. Miller has two children, Earl H. and E. Maria. Earl is a student of electrical engineering in college at Evansville, and Maria is a student in Franklin College. Mrs. Miller has two sisters:

Anna, wife of Ed Leonard, of Louisville, Kentucky, and Margaret, wife of Henry James, of Louisville.

MARTIE H. HASSENMILLER, M. D. Although now practically retired from the practice of medicine, Dr. Martie H. Hassenmiller, of West Baden, Indiana, is a nationally known man, having had under his care for a quarter of a century, while serving as house physician for the West Baden Springs Hotel, many famous people from all parts of this country, and even from European countries, and by his former patients he is gratefully and affectionately remembered as the sympathetic friend, as well as skilled man of medicine.

Doctor Hassenmiller was born at New Albany, Indiana, November 11, 1869, a son of Nicholas Hassenmiller, a native of Wurttemberg, Germany. Having learned the cabinet-making trade in Germany, Nicholas Hassenmiller worked at it after coming to the United States in young manhood, and it provided him with a means of livelihood until his death, in 1880. He married Sophie Zeller, who was born in Baden, Germany, and she died in December, 1874. They had six children, namely: Charles, who resides at New Albany, married Elizabeth Hoag, and they have three children; Sophie, who married Thomas Hasselback, of Louisville, Kentucky, died, leaving no children; Michael, who resides at Seattle, Washington, married Martha Sole, and they have three children; Michael, who is deceased; Josephine, who resides at Ansonia, Connecticut, is the wife of Charles Mullenox, general manager of a steel mill, and they have three children; and Doctor Hassenmiller.

His early education obtained in the common and high schools of New Albany, Doctor Hassenmiller entered the Louisville School of Pharmacy, and was graduated therefrom in 1885, and for some years thereafter he made practical use of his knowledge of that profession. In 1896 he entered the Louisville Medical College and was graduated therefrom in 1900, with the degree of Doctor of Medicine, and took his interneship and post-graduate work at Vienna, Austria. Upon his return to the United States he entered upon the practice of his profession at West Baden, and formed connections which led to his acting as house physician for the famous West Baden Springs Hotel, which had been visited by more notables than probably any other hostelry in the country. From 1900 to 1925 he held that position, and then retired, but still cares for a few of his patients who are not willing to relinquish his services. His financial interests also demand a considerable portion of his time. He is vice president and a director of the West Baden Bank, which institution he assisted in organizing, and with which he has been associated throughout its history.

In February, 1908, Doctor Hassenmiller was married to Miss Maude Elley, a daughter of Frank Elley, of San Pierre, Indiana. Politically Doctor Hassenmiller is a Democrat. He has no church affiliations, but he belongs to the Benevolent and Protective Order of Elks, the Independent Order of Odd Fellows, the Orange County Medical Society, the Indiana State Medical Society and the American Medical Association.

CHARLES SUMNER BOND, B. S., M. S., M. D., who maintains his residence and also his office at 112 North Tenth Street in the City of Richmond, judicial center and metropolis of Wayne County, Indiana, is a native son of this county and a representative of one of its sterling pioneer families. The Doctor has secure status as one of the representative physicians and surgeons of his native county, and has been established in the successful practice of his profession in Richmond more than forty-five years, so that he now has prestige as one of the veteran and honored members of his profession in this section of Indiana.

Doctor Bond was born in the Village of Webster, Wayne County, June 8, 1856, and is a son of Simon H. and Susan (Harris) Bond, both likewise natives of this county. Simon H. Bond became a progressive exponent of farm industry in Wayne County, and was also engaged in the mercantile business at Webster many years, he having attained to venerable age and having passed the closing period of his life in Los Angeles, California, his wife having died, at Webster, Indiana, in 1876. He was a son of Edward and Ann (Hussey) Bond, who were born in North Carolina and who became pioneer settlers in Wayne County, Indiana. Here they passed the remainder of their lives. The maternal grandparents of Doctor Bond were Benjamin and Lydia (Hiatt) Harris, who likewise were sterling pioneers of Wayne County, whither they came from their native State of North Carolina, prior to the arrival of the Bond family. Benjamin Harris here obtained a large tract of Government land and developed a productive farm estate, besides otherwise being prominent in advancing civic and material progress. He was one of the promoters of the building of the Grand Rapids & Indiana Railroad, which had its southern terminus in Richmond and which is now a part of the great Pennsylvania Railroad system. He became a director and executive officer of the company that constructed this railroad, and he was one of the patriarchal and honored citizens of Wayne County at the time of his death, in 1897, when he was ninety-seven years of age.

After their marriage Mr. and Mrs. Simon H. Bond established their residence on a farm two and one-half miles west of Webster, where they remained until the impaired health of Mr. Bond led him to leave his farm and engage in the general merchandise business at Webster, he and his family having resided in Richmond during the years of the Civil war period, and he having thereafter continued many years as the leading merchant at Webster.

Doctor Bond gained his earlier education in the public schools of Wayne County, and thereafter was a student in Earlham College, at Richmond, and, Antioch College in Ohio. He in the meanwhile made a record of successful service as a teacher in the public schools. In 1878 he was a student in Ohio Medical College, Cincinnati, and in the following year he became principal of the public schools at West Richmond. He continued his medical studies, under the preceptorship of Dr. J. R. Weist, of Richmond, and in 1881 he entered Bellevue Hospital Medical College, New York City, in which great institution he was graduated as a member of the class of 1883. After thus receiving his degree of Doctor of Medicine he returned to Richmond and became associated in practice with his former preceptor, Doctor Weist, this alliance having been continued fourteen years. Since that time Doctor Bond has conducted his practice in an individual way, and he controlled a large and representative general practice until 1904, since which year he has confined his attention to internal medicine, with special functioning in the treatment of tuberculosis, in which he has gained authoritative status.

Doctor Bond gave four years of service as coroner of Wayne County, 1884 to 1888, was health officer of Richmond in 1894-96, in 1894-95 he was president of the Indiana State Medical Society, and in the late '90s he served one term as president of the surgical section of the Mississippi Valley Medical Association. In addition to his membership in the American Medical Association he has been (since 1890) a member of the American Physicians, and he has rendered effective service in the educational work of his profession, both through contributions to leading medical journals and through several years of lecturing in the Indiana Medical College and also in the Miami Medical College in Cincinnati, Ohio. He is the dean and a former president of the Wayne County Medical Society, and has served as president of the Union District Medical Society. He is a member of the Indiana Academy of Science. In 1901 Doctor Bond had the distinction of being a delegate from the American Physicians to the tuberculosis congress held in the City of London, England, and in 1908 he was appointed by the governor of Indiana as delegate to this international Congress of Tuberculosis held in Washington, D. C.

Doctor Bond gives his political allegiance to the Republican party, and he is an elder in the First Presbyterian Church in his home city, a former vice president of the local Y. M. C. A., and a former president of the Richmond Country Club, in which he continues a popular and appreciative member. In 1890 Doctor Bond erected a fine brick residence at 112 North Tenth Street, and there he has maintained his home since January, 1891. He has since made several additions and other improvements on the building, and there has his office, as previously noted. This beautiful home has been a center of much of the social and cultural activities of Richmond during the passing years.

On the 18th of September, 1883, was solemnized the marriage of Doctor Bond to Miss Julia M. Boyd, who was born at Dublin, Wayne County, and whose father, the late Dr. S. S. Boyd, likewise was born in this county, and here he long continued a representative physician and surgean. The family name of his wife was Bunnell. The devoted companionship of Doctor and Mrs. Bond continued somewhat more than thirty years, and the gracious ties were severed by the death of Mrs. Bond in October, 1914. Of the children of this union the eldest is Dr. George S., who was born September 23, 1884, and who was graduated in Earlham College as a member of the class of 1905. He received from the University of Michigan his degree of Master of Arts, and in its medical department he was graduated in 1909. He thereafter had seven years of post-graduate study, directed especially to diagnosis and treatment of the diseases of the heart, in Johns Hopkins University and he is now a member of the faculty of the Indiana Medical School, Indianapolis. In Richmond, in 1910, he married Miss Llda Jones. They have one child, Eleanor. Florence M., next younger of the children, was born November 23, 1889, and she was graduated in Earlham College, in her home city, and later in Smith College, Massachusetts. In her studies she majored in the German language, including one year of study under private tutorship in Hanover, Germany, and later studied in the University of Berlin, where she was accorded a certificate for special efficiency in German. Miss Bond was in Germany at the inception of the World war, in 1914, and had no little difficulty in making departure from that country and returning to the United States. Her first post-graduate work was in the University of Michigan, and she taught German and French in the Richmond public schools. She has held for some time the position of social director at the University of Indiana, and resumed teaching of German in 1929, and is in the university now. Juliet, who was born in 1900, died in 1908, and Alice, who was born in 1902, died in infancy.

The second marriage of Doctor Bond occurred in November, 1915, when he wedded Mrs. Minnie (MacFarland) Van Matre, widow of Dr. Cassius Van Matre, a leading physician and surgeon at Newcastle, Indiana, at the time of his death and survived by no children. Mrs. Bond, a woman of culture and gracious presence, is popular in her beautiful home in Richmond, where she and the Doctor delight in entertaining their host of friends, both old and young. Mrs. Bond was born in the year 1869, at Lancaster, Ohio, and is a daughter of the late James MacFarland, who likewise was born in the old Buckeye State.

GEORGE F. WALTHERS. Indiana has long been noted for its extensive farming interests, and some of the leading men of the middle states find its soil admirably fitted for some branch or other of the great agricultural industry. To Indiana the various stockyards of the Mississippi Valley look for high-grade cattle, and discriminating buyers look to stockraisers here for registered stock. One of the leaders in the raising of registered Jersey cattle in Franklin County is George F. Walthers, with offices in the Reidman Building, Brookville, a man who has not only made a success of his business, but has built up confidence in his region.

George F. Walthers was born in Butler County, Ohio, in 1865, a son of John B. and Emma (Hauser) Walthers, natives of Germany and Switzerland, respectively. The maternal grandparents, Emil and Theressa Hauser, came to the United States many years ago, and settled on a farm in Hamilton County, Ohio, and there he raised fruit and was a gardener. John B. Walthers settled in Butler County, Ohio, when he came to the United States, and there he was engaged in farming and stockraising. Both he and his wife died in that county, having won universal appreciation for their many admirable qualities and their industry and thrift.

Growing up on a farm, George F. Walthers had such educational advantages as were afforded by the local public schools, and at the same time he learned farming under the thorough direction of his father. After he reached his majority he left home and began to put to practical use the knowledge he had gained on the farm by dealing in stock, and he continued in that business in Ohio until September, 1898, when he came to Brookville, Indiana. Here he continued his operations in live stock, and was soon joined by his brother Herman, the latter buying land and beginning to feed stock. The brothers remained together until 1923, when their partnership was dissolved by mutual consent, Herman Walthers entering a live stock commission office in the Union Stock Yards, Cincinnati, and George F. Walthers continuing his stock raising. He is a very strong Republican, and is the first of his party ever elected commissioner of Franklin County. His fine farm of 520 acres of grazing and farm land is located in Brookville Township, but he maintains his residence at Brookville. About half of his farm is under cultivation, the remainder being used to graze his magnificent registered Jersey cattle. Mr. Walthers takes great pride in his farm, striving to keep it in order, and to do the work connected with it with the latest improved machinery. Because of the care he exercises, and the quality of his strain of cattle, his product commands the very highest prices.

In 1890 Mr. Walthers was married to Miss Louisa Sheering, who was born in Butler County, Ohio, a daughter of Charles and Mina Sheering, natives of Germany. Mr. and Mrs. Walthers have had the following children born to them: Harry E., who conducts the home farm; Norma, who is the widow of Philip Corya, lives with her father, and she has two children, Phyllis B. and Georgia L.; and Harry E. Walthers is a widower with two children, Emily and Mark, so that Mr. Walthers has four grandchildren to whom he is deeply attached. His fraternal affiliations are those which he maintains with the Benevolent and Protective Order of Elks. When the Kiwanis Club was organized at Brookville he was one of its first members, but later on he withdrew from it. Mr. Walthers' personal popularity is commensurate to his success and prominence in the stock industry and farming. Honest, reliable and capable, he is not only honored and respected, but he has warm personal friends wherever he is known. His work as county commissioner stands as a monument to his ability and his willingness to give his best efforts toward promoting the interests of his town and county, and, when the need arises, of his state and country as well.

HERMAN WILLIAM WALTHERS, of Brookville, knows live stock as do few other men. It is a business with which he has been identified all his life and his ancestors before him.

Mr. Walthers for many years has been a dealer in live stock in Franklin County and uses a large amount of land as feeding ground and to raise feed for the hundreds of heads of cattle and other stock that every year are collected by him and from here sent on to the Union Stock Yards at Cincinnati, where he is a member of a stock commission firm.

Mr. Walthers was born in Butler County, Ohio, October 28, 1875, a son of John B. and Emma (Hauser) Walthers. His father was a native of Germany and settled in Butler County, Ohio, when twenty-four years of age. He followed farming and the live stock business there the rest of his life. He passed away in 1924. His wife's father came from Switzerland, in 1849, and also settled in Butler County. Mr. Walther's mother passed away in 1913.

Growing up on a farm, learning the stock business from boyhood, Mr. Walthers has been educated largely by experience and contact with men and affairs. He attended school during his boyhood only a few winter months. In 1899 he located in Franklin County, Indiana, buying live stock, and in 1901 secured a tract of land for feeding purposes. In 1902 his brother George joined him and they were partners until 1920, when they divided their land holdings, Mr. Walthers taking as his share 378 acres, and George 520 acres.

Mr. Walthers in 1918 established an office in the Union Stock Yards at Cincinnati, and has since been associated with Charles Strebel. They constitute one of the leading commission firms in that city. At the present time Mr. Walthers has 705 acres and also leases a large adjoining acreage for the raising of corn and wheat. On his own land he has about 200 acres under cultivation, his chief crop being alfalfa. He is a member of the Cincinnati Live Stock Exchange, and since February, 1928, has been treasurer of the city board of education at Brookville.

Mr. Walthers is a Republican in politics. He had the distinction in 1914 of being the first Republican elected to a county office in a long period of years. He was chosen county commissioner by a majority between 300 and 400 in a county where the Democratic margin is usually 2,500 and 3,000 votes. He served one term. Mr. Walthers was one of the organizers and is a director of the People's Trust Company of Brookville. He is a member of the United Brethren Church and his wife is a Methodist. His fraternity is the Elks.

He married in 1899 Miss Sarah Tracy, who was born in Butler County, Ohio, daughter of Thomas and Addie (Williams) Tracy. Two children were born to their marriage. Talton Walthers was born in 1901 and was killed in a railroad accident February 17, 1912. The daughter, Maxine, was born August 5, 1917, and is attending school at Brookville.

MARVIN TRUMAN CASE, M. D., practiced medicine and surgery actively in Attica for over half a century. He represented thorough training and the finest qualifications of a family practitioner, and probably no one in that community has a greater degree of love and respect than this retired physician.

Doctor Case was born in Wisconsin, June 8, 1843. His father, William H. Case, was a native of New York State and was descended from an English family. In England the name of the family became associated with the manufacture of knives, and now most people think of a Case knife as a common noun. William H. Case married Sylbie Howe, also born in New York, and a descendant of General Howe. They had six children: Harlem, who was a soldier in the Civil war and was killed in action; Amanda, deceased; Mrs. Nancy Lyon, of Buchanan, Michigan; William, deceased; Lina, deceased; and Marvin T.

Marvin T. Case was educated in public schools and at the age of eighteen volunteered for service in the Civil war. He was in the army three years, joining as a private of Company D of the Eighty-sixth Indiana Volunteer Infantry, and received his discharge as a sergeant. He was in the company commanded by Capt. Lewis Stevens.

After the war Doctor Case taught school in Warren County, Indiana, until 1868. Teaching gave him the funds for going to medical school and in 1870 he graduated M. D. from the University of Michigan. While at the university he acted as assistant instructor. After graduating Doctor Case located at Attica, Indiana, and for two years was associated with Doctor Jones. After Doctor Jones moved away Doctor Case took over his practice and for many years he rode and drove over an extensive radius around Attica, performing all the duties of an old-time country doctor in the years before the invention of telephones, automobiles and the advent of good roads. He is an honored member of the County, Indiana State and American Medical Associations and for thirty years acted as city health officer of Attica. He is one of the few surviving veterans of the Union army and a loyal member of the Grand Army of the Republic. Doctor Case is affiliated with the

Knights of Pythias. He is a director of the Building & Loan Association of Attica. He continued his active practice until 1924.

He married, November 16, 1870, Miss Mary Elizabeth De Motte, daughter of J. B. and Emily (Payne) De Motte, who came from Virginia to Southern Indiana in 1837. Doctor and Mrs. Case had four children: Jessie, Clarence, Laurin, who died in 1919, and one that died in infancy. Clarence, now living at De Land, Florida, married Nora Newberry and has six children. Laurin married Jessie Pruviance and left a son, Laurin.

Miss Jessie Case is a graduate of DePauw University and also took a diploma from a musical college in Chicago and studied abroad at Vienna, Austria. After returning home she taught music at Tudor Hall in Indianapolis for fourteen years. When her father's health failed she returned home to take care of him, and still does work as a teacher in Attica and once a week goes to Indianapolis to look after her classes in that city.

ORMSBY H. LOGAN, county recorder of Franklin County, was born and has lived all his life in that section of Indiana. His people were pioneers here and Mr. Logan is a worthy descendant of some of the old families. His has been a life of industry, spent in farming and the building trades, and he has given the county a very fine administration in his present office, which he is now holding for his second term.

He was born on a farm in Franklin County in October, 1869, son of William and Sarah (Miller) Logan and grandson of David and Mary (Ogden) Logan. David Logan was a native of South Carolina, and was brought to Franklin County, Indiana, in 1804 by his father, Thomas Logan. David Logan lived to very advanced age, passing away at the age of ninety-three. William Logan was born in Franklin County, and after his marriage settled on a farm near Fairfaild and lived to be ninety years of age. His wife was left an orphan when an infant and was reared among strangers.

Ormsby H. Logan attended district schools during his youth, and also had work in the Brookville Normal School. From sixteen until he was nineteen he worked for weekly wages on a farm. Prior to September, 1917, when he moved to Brookville to give his children the educational advantages of the city, he lived on a farm. As a youth he learned the trade of carpenter and did work as a builder off and on for thirty years. After coming to Brookville Mr. Logan was for six years janitor of the high school building.

In 1924 he was elected to the office of county recorder, beginning his first term in January, 1925. In November, 1928, he was reelected. Mr. Logan is a Democrat in his political affiliation. While living in the country he served one term as township trustee of Garfield Township. He is a member of the Methodist Episcopal Church, has filled chairs in the lodge and encampment of the Inde-

Linnaeus Neal Hines

pendent Order of Odd Fellows, is a member of the Knights of Pythias and Improved Order of Red Men.

Mr. Logan married in 1899 Miss Augusta Miller, who was born at Fairfield, Indiana, daughter of Albert and Levina (Maharry) Miller. Her parents came from Pennsylvania. Mr. Logan lost his good wife and the mother of his children in March, 1914. He has two daughters and one son: Helen, wife of William Howard, of Union County, Indiana; Edna, Mrs. Charles L. Davis, of Indianapolis; and Edgar, who also lives at Indianapolis.

EDWARD M. GLASER, physician and surgeon at Brookville, was born in Franklin County, Indiana, July 1, 1882. After completing his medical training he returned to his native locality, and has been one of the busiest and most successful representatives of his profession for twenty years or more.

Doctor Glaser is a son of John F. and Mary J. (Schuck) Glaser, who were born and have lived all their lives in Franklin County. His paternal grandparents, Frederick and Catherine (Scherger) Glaser, came from Germany. Frederick Glaser was for many years in the river trade, up and down the Mississippi and Ohio, with headquarters at New Orleans and Cincinnati. Doctor Glaser's maternal grandparents were John and Johanna (Cook) Schuck, the former a native of Franklin County, while Johanna Cook was born in Zurich, Switzerland, and was brought to America by her parents. One of her brothers was a very prominent physician in Switzerland. John Schuck for many years conducted a general mercantile business at St. Peters, Indiana.

Edward M. Glaser was educated in the grade and high schools of Franklin County, attended the Central Indiana Normal School at Danville and the Indiana State Normal at Terre Haute. During his early life he taught school in Franklin County four years. His medical studies were pursued in the Indiana Medical College and the Ohio Medical College and after graduating he had thirteen months of special training as an interne in St. Anthony's Hospital at Terre Haute. With this preparation he opened an office in Brookville and carried on a general practice. In 1920 he erected a modern brick building, which serves both as his residence and office, at 647 Main Street.

During the World war Doctor Glaser was chairman of the Medical Advisory Board of Franklin County. He is president of the Franklin County Tuberculosis Association, is a member of the Union District, Franklin County and Indiana State Medical Associations, and is a fellow of the American Medical Association. Doctor Glaser is a director in the Peoples Trust Company of Brookville, is medical examiner for the Knights of Columbus, a member of the Kiwanis Club and is a Democrat and Catholic.

He married in 1909 Miss Lydia Hoff, of Dearborn County, Indiana, daughter of Charles and Henrietta (Bolsey) Hoff, her father a native of Dearborn County, while her mother was born in Germany. Doctor and Mrs. Glaser have three children: Robert Edward, a student of medicine in Notre Dame University of Indiana; Marjorie Alice, attending an academy of Oldenburg, Indiana; and Edward M., Jr.

LINNAEUS NEAL HINES, president of the Indiana State Teachers College at Terre Haute and former state superintendent of public instruction, is a native of Missouri, but has lived most of his life in Indiana, is a graduate of the State University and for over thirty-five years has been an active school man.

He was born at Carthage, Missouri, February 12, 1871, son of Hiram and Sarah Mary (Neal) Hines. He completed his high school work at Noblesville, Indiana, in 1889, and was principal of a grade school there in 1892-93. In 1894 he was graduated with the A. B. degree from Indiana University and for five years following was a teacher and assistant to the principal in schools at Evansville. Mr. Hines took his Master of Arts degree at Indiana University in 1908 and since then has done post-graduate work in Indiana, Cornell, Columbia and Chicago Universities.

He went to Indianapolis as teacher of mathematics in the Shortridge High School during 1900, and was superintendent of schools at Union City from 1901 to 1906, Hartford City, 1906 to 1908, at Crawfordsville from 1908 to 1919. In 1918 he was elected state superintendent of public instruction, and was re-elected, but resigned on October 1, 1921. From 1921 to 1924 he served as president of the Indiana State Normal School at Terre Haute and the Eastern Division, Indiana State Normal School, at Muncie. Since December 1, 1924, his administrative duties have been with the State Teachers College at Terre Haute.

He was assistant editor in 1914-16 and editor and part owner from 1917 to 1924 of the *Educator-Journal*, formerly published at Indianapolis. He is a Co-author of a text book, *Educational Hygiene*, published in 1913. He is a member of the National Council of Education, National Education Association, Department of Superintendence of the National Education Association, is a member of the American Association of Teachers Colleges, former president of the American School Hygiene Association, member of the Indiana State Teachers Association. After the war he was Indiana state director for the Near East Relief under the Y. M. C. A. He is a member of the Indiana Society of Chicago, president of the Indiana Lincoln Memorial Association, member of the Indiana Lincoln Union, is a Phi Kappa Psi, a Republican, a Methodist, a member of the Masonic fraternity, and belongs to the Columbia Club of Indianapolis, Ouiatenon Club of Crawfordsville, Literary and Rotary clubs of Terre Haute.

Mr. Hines married, February 26, 1907, Bertha Georgia Wiggs, of Chicago. They have two children, Neal Oldfield and Anne Emerson.

ANTHONY H. SCHRICHTE is owner of monumental works at Rushville, a business that has been in the family for over seventy years, being one of the oldest and largest establishments of its kind in Rush County.

Mr. Schrichte was born at Rushville, December 4, 1861, about two years after his father established the business. He is a son of John B. and Catherine (Schoebaum) Schrichte, both natives of Hanover, Germany, where they were acquainted as children. John B. Schrichte on coming to America located at Hamilton, Ohio, where he learned the stonecutting trade. He worked for a brother at Brookville, Indiana, and in 1859 started the monumental business at Rushville. He married at Cincinnati in 1858.

Anthony H. Schrichte was educated in public schools and at the age of sixteen began learning the business of his father, and that business he understands in every phase, having served his apprenticeship in the cuttting trade. His father died in 1911, more than fifty years after he had started the business. In 1909, when the business was fifty years old, his three sons, Anthony, Frank and William, acquired the business from their father. Three years later Anthony and William took over the interests of their brother Frank and since 1917 Mr. Anthony Schrichte has been sole owner. The locations of his business is at 121 South Main Street.

Mr. Schrichte married in November, 1885, Miss Emma Stuart, who was born at Cambridge City, Indiana, and was left an orphan when a girl. Their children are: John, of Hot Springs, South Dakota; Charles Augustus, now with his father in business; Marie, wife of Frank Hageny, of Glendale, California; Salome, at home; and Albert, a doctor of dental surgery at Rushville. Mr. Schrichte and family are Catholics. He is a Democrat and has served five terms as grand knight of the Knights of Columbus.

W. S. WEAVER, superintendent of the paper mill of the Hande & Dauch Paper Company at Brookville, has been connected with paper manufacturing industries since early manhood. In the course of his business experience he has been with paper mills in several middle western states, and Brookville has claimed his residence since 1922.

Mr. Weaver was born near Noblesville, Hamilton County, Indiana, December 5, 1871. He is a son of Peter and Caroline Josephine (Rondebush) Weaver, his father a native of Williamsport, Pennsylvania, and his mother of Cincinnati, Ohio. They were married at Noblesville. He died February 27, 1893, when sixty years of age, and was survived more than thirty years by his widow, who passed away January 1, 1924.

W. S. Weaver was educated in grade and high schools in Indiana and when twenty-one years of age began learning the paper making trade in a mill at Noblesville. On July 27, 1911, he became assistant superintendent for the Alton Box & Paper Company at Alton, Illinois, on January 1, 1914, went to the Hutchinson Box & Paper Company at Hutchinson, Kansas, likewise as assistant superintendent, and on August 14, 1917, accepted the superintendency of the plant of the American Strawboard Company at Quincy, Illinois.

Mr. Weaver was made superintendent of the paper mill at Brookville on October 1, 1922. This was then owned by the Thompson-Norris Company, who were succeeded on January 1, 1928, by the Hinde & Dauch Paper Company.

Mr. Weaver is a trustee of the Methodist Episcopal Church. He is a Democrat, and a member of the Lodge and Encampment of the Independent Order of Odd Fellows, Improved Order of Red Men and the Kiwanis Club.

He married, May 24, 1893, Miss Emma E. Scholler, who was born in Wabash, Indiana, daughter of John Scholler, who came from Germany. She died June 24, 1909, leaving one son, Elbert F. On December 24, 1913, Mr. Weaver married Anna Maude Wallace, a native of Frankfort, Indiana, and her parents, John and Ellen (McVey) Senour, were born in Clinton County, Indiana.

Elbert F. Weaver, only son of Mr. Weaver, enlisted September 17, 1917, and went overseas to France in March, 1918. He was in the battle of the Marne and in other battles during the final summer of the war. He received his honorable discharge March 3, 1919. He is now a chemical engineer with the National Lead & Refining Company at East Chicago, Indiana. He married June Maunder.

HON. CECIL C. TAGUE, former judge of the Circuit Court, has had a long and prominent connection with the Franklin County bar and his name as a lawyer and public official is well known over the state at large.

Judge Tague was born in Switzerland County, Indiana, July 11, 1891, son of Marion and Mary (Smith) Tague, the former a native of Jefferson County and the latter of Shelby County. His grandparents were Jonathan and Clarissa (Moody) Tague and John and Louisa (Conant) Smith. The Smith family came from Kentucky. His great-grandfather, Peter Tague, was a son of John Tague, a Kentuckian, who moved across the river to Switzerland County, Indiana Territory, in 1811 and took up a tract of wild land, which he developed as a farm. His maternal grandfather, John Smith, was born in Cynthiana, Kentucky, son of William Smith, who moved his family to Shelby County, Indiana, just before the Civil war. Judge Tague's parents now live on a farm in Rush County.

He attended public school at Milroy, Indiana, had a business college course at Anderson and after learning stenography worked as a court reporter at Versailles. In 1908 he went to Indianapolis to study law, was admitted to the bar at Versailles in 1912, and for four years practiced in Indianapolis. Since 1916 his home has been at Brookville, and he has carried on a successful general practice except for the period of his service

Ray H. Stephens

on the bench. In August, 1918, he entered the officers training school at Camp Grant, Illinois, remaining until honorably discharged in December.

In 1918 he was elected a member of the Indiana State Senate, serving one term. In 1919 Governor Goodrich appointed him a trustee of the Indiana World War Memorial. He is a member of the Thirty-seventh District, Indiana and American Bar Associations. He was on the circuit bench for eight years. He was first appointed judge of the Thirty-seventh Judicial District on March 12, 1921, and in November, 1922, was elected for a full term of six years, and served until January 1, 1929. In the opinion of the bar he was one of the ablest men who has served on the bench in this section of Indiana.

Immediately upon his retirement from the bench he became attorney for the National Chain Store Association, with headquarters in New York city. He still maintains his home and an office in Brookville, but most of his time is required in looking after Chain Store interests throughout the United States. He is a Republican, is a York Rite Mason, member of the Royal Arch and Council degrees, is a Lodge and Encampment member of the Independent Order of Odd Fellows and a member of the Knights of Pythias. He belongs to the Christian Church. Judge Tague married, August 30, 1917, Miss Hallie B. Smith, who was born in Ripley County, Indiana, daughter of John and Lucinda (Sebring) Smith. They have two children, Kathleen, born November 28, 1919, and Cecil C., born August 24, 1927.

RAY H. STEPHENS, sheriff of Monroe County, was born and reared in this county and represents the third generation of the Stephens family here.

Mr. Stephens was born on a farm eight miles east of Bloomington, on the Columbus and Bloomington road, July 30, 1890. His grandparents were John and Rachael Stephens, who came from Kentucky to Indiana at a very early date. John Stephens entered the land which has ever since been known as the Stephens homestead, and on it he built a large two-story log house, which was the birthplace of Sheriff Stephens. John Stephens helped organize the county government of Monroe county. He was known as a very successful farmer and stock raiser. He lost his life in an accident near New Albany. Samuel H. Stephens, father of Sheriff Stephens, was born at the old homestead and spent his life there as a farmer and stockman. He was twice married, and the four children of his first wife were: Mary, wife of Frank Lampkins; Martha, who became the wife of Andrew Polle; Laura, who married Charles Peterson; and John, who married Addie Myers. Samuel H. Stephens by his second marriage, to Sallie J. Stephens, had only one son, Ray H.

Ray H. Stephens was reared on the farm, attended grade schools, and had the routine of an industrious Indiana farm boy. After his education was completed he remained at the old homestead, engaged in its operation, until 1918, when he moved to Bloomington. For five years he was a member of the police force and for five years assistant chief of the fire department. In 1928 he was elected sheriff, on the Democratic ticket. It was the first time a Democratic candidate for this office had been elected in twenty years, and his administration fully justified the confidence of the people expressed in this way. He was reelected in 1930 by a majority of 5,500. Mr. Stephens is a member of the Woodmen of the World, Modern Woodmen of America, Loyal Order or Moose, Fraternal Order of Eagles and B. P. O. Elks.

He married, February 24, 1908, Miss Hattie Hash, daughter of Mack and Chrissie (Stephens) Hash. They have four children, Hazel, Walter S., Marie A. and Betty J.

MILFORD PALMER HUBBARD is one of the veteran attorneys of the Franklin County bar. He has practiced law at Brookville for thirty years. Mr. Hubbard satisfied his ambitions through the law rather than by broad excursions into the field of politics or business. He is regarded as one of the ablest representatives of his profession in this section of Indiana.

He was born in Daviess County, Indiana, March 27, 1869, son of John and Permillia Jane (Phitts) Hubbard, his father a native of Daviess County and his mother of Lawrence County, Indiana. His grandfather, Wesley Hubbard, was a native of Virginia and was of Scotch-English ancestry. Mr. Hubbard's maternal grandparents were Benjamin Potter and Desty (Herron) Phitts, the former a native of Kentucky and the latter born in Daviess County, Indiana, where her people were among the first settlers. John Hubbard was a Union soldier in the Civil war. Both he and his father, Wesley Hubbard, became members of the Twenty-seventh Indiana Infantry. Wesley Hubbard was wounded and died while home on a furlough. John Hubbard afterwards was with the Eighth Connecticut Infantry. He was four times wounded by gun shot during the war. His life after the war was spent as a farmer and he lived to a good old age, passing away in June, 1927, at the age of eighty-five. His wife died in October, 1894.

Milford Palmer Hubbard attended public school at Valparaiso, the Terre Haute State Normal School and is a graduate of the Indiana Law School. At the outbreak of the Spanish-American war, in April, 1898, he joined the Twenty-seventh Indiana Light Battery, and was in training at Chickamauga Park and afterwards was sent to Porto Rico. He was honorably discharged in October, 1898, but subsequently served as a member of the Indiana National Guard.

Very shortly after his military experience in the Spanish-American war Mr. Hubbard opened his law office at Brookville, in January, 1899. He has been steadily practicing law there through all the years. His offices are in the Franklin County National Bank Building. Mr. Hubbard is a member of the Thirty-seventh Judicial District, the Indiana State and American Bar Associations. He is a Republican, is a member of the Methodist Church, while his wife is a Lutheran, and has always taken much interest in fraternal organizations. He is a Royal Arch and Scottish Rite Mason and Shriner, a member of the Independent Order of Odd Fellows Lodge and Encampment, Knights of Pythias, Fraternal Order of Eagles and the B. P. O. Elks at Connersville. He and his wife are members of the Eastern Star Chapter at Metamora.

Mr. Hubbard married, December 22, 1898, Miss Mamie L. Leeson, who was born at Metamora, daughter of Largant Leeson. By this marriage there were two children: Graydon Dale, connected with the wholesale department of R. L. Leeson & Sons Company at Elwood, Indiana; and Harold Roscoe, of Brookville. Mr. Hubbard in January, 1920, married Elizabeth Irrgang, who was born in Ripley County, Indiana, daughter of Casper and Elizabeth Irrgang. Her father came from Germany. By his second marriage Mr. Hubbard has one son, Robert Palmer.

FRANK MOSTER. One of the best equipped funeral parlors in Franklin County and one whose equipment is unsurpassed in this region is the one owned and operated at 722 Main Street, Brookville, by Frank Moster. This modern establishment furnishes a vivid contrast to the one owned by his father, who was also an undertaker, and a wagon maker, at Saint Leon, Indiana. His was the first hearse in Franklin County, but before he purchased he had been in business for some years. He made coffins for the dead, and a wagon was used to haul the body to the cemetery. When the church or residence was adjacent to the cemetery the pallbearers used to carry their burden through the dust in summer and the snow and ice in winter. The science of embalming was not known to him or his contemporaries, and in order to preserve the body from the time of death to that of burial ice was used. However, the elder man then, as his son is doing now, rendered the best service in his power, and did so in a manner that brought relief to the sorrowing, and a sad satisfaction that everything possible was being done to show honor and respect to a loved one.

Frank Moster was born at Laurel, Indiana, May 25, 1881, a son of Louis and Margaret (Weis) Moster, natives of Dearborn County, Indiana. The paternal grandfather, Adam Moster, was born in Germany, and he established the family in the United States. Louis Moster died in 1926, but the wife and mother survives and resides at Brookville, Indiana.

After receiving a public school education through the high school course Frank Moster began working for his father, and subsequently entered the Cincinnati, Ohio, School of Embalming, and was graduated therefrom

October 25, 1904, and upon his return to Laurel, where the business was located, he was taken into partnership. In 1910 he moved to Brookville, and established his funeral parlors, which are modern in every way.

In September, 1906, Mr. Moster was married to Miss Gladys Manley, who was born at Laurel, Indiana, a daughter of Edward J. and Flora (Cox) Manley, also natives of Laurel, Indiana. Mr. and Mrs. Moster have one child, Neil, who was born in 1907. The family reside in the same building with the undertaking parlors, which is a substantial one 40 by 105 feet, two stories in height, with basement, and which Mr. Moster owns.

Frank Moster is one in a family of seven children: Joseph, who is an undertaker, but lives on a farm near Laurel; George, who is a farmer in the Laurel vicinity; Anna, who married Rayburn Jinks, of Brookville, Indiana; Frank; Lena, who married Jacob Reiboldt, of Union County, Indiana; William, who is an undertaker of Laurel; and Edward, who also is an undertaker, is employed by his brother Frank.

JOHN H. KIPLINGER, Rushville attorney, had an established position in professional circles when he was called from the quiet routine of the law to the sterner duties brought on by the World war. Captain Kiplinger went overseas and his duties kept him abroad for several years after the armistice. He has a very unusual knowledge of many phases connected with the restoration of Europe under the allied peace program and did not return home to resume his contact with his law office at Rushville until 1923.

Captain Kiplinger was born at Rushville, December 12, 1881, a son of Jesse C. and Marinda A. (Sampson) Kiplinger. His grandparents were John W. and Harriett (Dill) and Aquilla and Harriett (Bebout) Sampson, all either natives of Rush County or early settlers there. His father, who was a well-to-do Rush County farmer, died in 1903. The widowed mother now resides at Rushville.

Captain Kiplinger attended the grade and high schools of his native city, was a student in Oberlin College in Ohio for a time, and then in Indiana University. His law studies were pursued in the office of Cullin & McGee, afterwards under John D. McGee, and in 1903 he was admitted to the bar. In 1904 he took up practice and was in partnership with John D. McGee until 1912. After two years alone he formed a partnership, in 1914, with Donald L. Smith, the firm becoming Kiplinger & Smith.

Captain Kiplinger enlisted in the Indiana National Guard in March, 1917. When the National Guard was mustered into the Federal service on August 5, 1917, he was captain of Company B in the Fourth Indiana Infantry. He went with other National Guardsmen to Camp Shelby, Mississippi, and on October 1, 1917, was transferred to the One Hundred and Thirty-ninth Field Artillery, Thirty-eighth Division, being captain of Headquarters Com-

pany. In December, 1917, he was detailed for the School of Fire at Fort Sill, Oklahoma, and in March, 1918, returned to Camp Shelby. Captain Kiplinger in August, 1918, went overseas, and from that time until the armistice was with the French Artillery School Meucon. He was then ordered to the headquarters of the Third Army at Coblenz, Germany, and given detail duty with the judge advocate's department, in the district of Paris. During that time he had charge of special trial work and special investigations covering Central Europe.

In February, 1920, he was made head of the legal department and finance service with the Inter-Allied Reparations Commission at Paris. On May 15, 1920, he received his honorable discharge, but then became American representative at Wiesbaden, Germany, in the office of the Inter-Allied Committee, made up of five members, one from England, one from France, one from Italy and one from Belgium, with Captain Kiplinger the American representative. This committee was charged with the application of the terms of the treaty of peace, and he continued in this work until the office was closed in October, 1922, and was then assigned other work under the commission, being in charge of the judge advocate's office at Paris when it was closed.

Captain Kiplinger on returning home in 1923 resumed his law practice. He has a general practice, with offices in the American National Bank Building. Captain Kiplinger is a director of the American National Bank, of the First National Bank of Milroy, Indiana, the Greenville Bank and the New Salem State Bank, is vice president and a director of the American National Company, and director of the American National Realty Company.

He married in 1903 Miss Bessie Morrison, who was born at Bloomington, Illinois, daughter of Joseph and Grace (Patterson) Morrison, her father a native of Massachusetts and her mother of Illinois. Captain and Mrs. Kiplinger have two children, Jules G., of Rushville, and Jean R., a student in the University of Chicago.

Captain Kiplinger is affiliated with the Christian Church. He was for two years deputy prosecuting attorney of Rush County, has served as city attorney and is now county attorney. In fraternal matters he has filled chairs in the Knights of Pythias Lodge, was one of the organizers and is a past exalted ruler of the B. P. O. Elks at Rushville, is a member of the Lodge and Encampment of the Independent Order of Odd Fellows and the Modern Woodmen of America. He belongs to the Rush County and Indiana Bar Association, is a member of the Columbia Club of Indianapolis, and is a Beta Theta Pi.

Captain Kiplinger is a past commander of the Rushville Post of the American Legion and has served as Indiana judge advocate. He is a member of the military order of Foreign Wars and for his services in Europe received a number of decorations, being a knight of the French Legion of Honor, an officer of the Crown of Italy, a commander of the Crown of Roumania, and commander of Polonia Restituta, a Polish decoration.

CLARENCE A. GRIEGER is one of the progressive and popular exponents of the motor-car business in the City of Fort Wayne, where he is president and treasurer of Grieger's, Inc., which here has the agency for the Chevrolet automobiles, the well equipped headquarters of the corporation being at 313 East Washington Street.

Mr. Grieger takes due satisfaction in claiming the fine old Hoosier State as the place of his nativity and is a scion of one of the sterling pioneer families of LaPorte County. He was born in LaPorte County, April 30, 1895, and is a son of Ewalt and Augusta (Dreblow) Grieger, the former of whom was born in that county, on the 9th of March, 1858, and the latter of whom was born in Starke County, this state. Theodore Grieger, grandfather of the subject of this review, was born and reared in Germany, where his marriage was solemnized, and he and his wife became pioneer settlers in LaPorte County, Indiana, where he became a prosperous farmer and where he continued to reside until his death, in 1910, at the patriarchal age of ninety-three years, his wife having died at the age of ninety-one years and both having been earnest members of the Lutheran Church. The maternal grandparents of Clarence A. Grieger likewise were born in Germany and became pioneer settlers in Indiana, where they passed the closing period of their lives at San Pierre, Starke County.

Ewalt Grieger was reared and educated in LaPorte County and there he has been associated with farm industry from the time of his boyhood to the present. He has been influential in political affairs in his native county, as a staunch advocate and supporter of the cause of the Republican party, and he and his wife are zealous communicants of the Lutheran Church. Of their fine family of thirteen children five sons and four daughters are living.

In the public schools of his native county Clarence A. Grieger continued his studies until he had duly profited by the advantages of the high school, and in 1912 he went to South Bend and took a position with his uncle, August H. Grieger, head of the Grieger Motor Company, this uncle having previously been a leader in the councils of the Republican party in LaPorte County and having been joint representative of LaPorte and Starke counties in the State Legislature during a period of three terms, besides which he had served as postmaster and also as a trustee of his township. Clarence A. Grieger continued to be associated with his uncle's automobile business at South Bend during a period of four years, and in the meanwhile gained thorough knowledge of all details and phases of that line of enterprise. He was next assigned charge of the branch established by his uncle's concern in the City of Terre Haute, and was admitted to partnership in the business. He remained at Terre Haute until 1919, when he established himself in the automobile business in the City of La Fayette, where he continued his activities until March, 1923, when he came to Fort Wayne and organized the corporation of which he is now the president and treasurer, the company having been incorporated in April of that year and its substantial business having increased in scope and importance during each successive year. Mr. Grieger is, in 1929, serving his third consecutive year as president of the Fort Wayne Auto Trades Association, and he is a loyal and valued member also of the Fort Wayne Chamber of Commerce. He is a director of the local Y. M. C. A., is a member of the Fort Wayne Country Club, and his is the distinction of having been the first president of the first Lions Club organized in the State of Indiana. At Terre Haute he became affiliated with the Benevolent and Protective Order of Elks, and in the same class of initiates was Hon. Will Hayes, who later served as postmaster general of the United States and who is now official arbiter of the motion-picture industry of the nation. In the Masonic fraternity Mr. Grieger has received the thirty-second degree of the Scottish Rite and is also a Noble of the Mystic Shrine. His political alignment is with the Republican party and he and his wife are members of the Evangelical Church in their home city.

October 14, 1918, marked the marriage of Mr. Grieger to Miss Esther Molone, of Chicago, Illinois, and the one child of this union is a son, Richard Wayne, who was born October 20, 1921. Mr. and Mrs. Grieger are popular factors in the social life of their home community.

EDWARD C. THEOBALD, JR., is one of the representative young business men of the City of Vincennes, where he is treasurer of the Anderson-Theobald Company, which controls a substantial and widely extended business in the preparing and distribution of washed sand and gravel for road construction and other construction work. The large and well equipped gravel pits of the company are established in Lawrence County, Illinois, and the concern controls a large business through Southern Illinois and Southern Indiana, shipments of its products being made in carload lots only.

Mr. Theobald was born at North Vernon, Indiana, in 1904, and is a son of Edward C. and Mary (Carlson) Theobald, the former of whom was born in Cincinnati, Ohio, and the latter in Montgomery County, Iowa.

Edward C. Theobald, Sr., was reared and educated in Ohio and was one of the prominent business men and honored and influential citizens of Vincennes, Indiana, at the time of his death, in 1927, his widow being now president of the Anderson-Theobald Company, of which he was the founder and of which he continued the executive head until his death. He was a son of Charles Theobald, who was born in Ohio, where he was reared to manhood and where eventually he became a prominent figure in industrial and commercial affairs in the City of Cincinnati, where he was a manufacturer of picture frames. Charles Theobald's father was born and reared in Germany and was one of many of his countrymen who came to the United States in the early '40s, to escape the consequences of political and revolutionary disturbance in their native land. This first representative of the Theobald family became a pioneer settler in Washington County, Ohio, and had the distinction of being the first postmaster of Washington Court House, the county seat.

In the earlier period of his active business career Edward C. Theobald, Sr., engaged in contracting in connection with varied lines of construction work, and he continued his activities as a contractor in Ohio until the year 1900, when he settled at North Vernon, Jennings County, Indiana, and turned his attention to the sand and gravel business, of which he became a leading exponent in Vincennes, to which city he removed with his family in 1907. He first became associated in business with a Mr. Hicks, whose interest he purchased in 1906, and upon transferring his headquarters to Vincennes, in the following year, he formed the Anderson-Theobald Company, of which he became the president and the affairs of which he directed with consummate ability that brought to it the high status it now occupies as a representative of the sand and gravel industry. After his death his widow was made president of the company, and his only child, Edward C., Jr., became the treasurer; the office of secretary is retained by A. A. Ruble. The gravel and sand pits operated by the company in Lawrence County, Illinois, cover an area of 127 acres, the operating plant is of the best modern equipment, provisions are made for the washing of all products and screening the same to all desired sizes, and shipments being made in carload lots only. Twelve men are regularly employed at the pits and the general executive offices in Vincennes are established on the second floor of the Citizens Bank Building.

Edward C. Theobald, Sr., was a man of sterling character and marked business ability, gained and retained the confidence and esteem of those with whom he came in contact in the varied relations of life, and was liberal and loyal as a citizen. He was influential in business and civic affairs in Vincennes and here gave three years of service as receiver for the Vincennes Traction Company.

After completing his studies in the Vincennes High School, Edward C. Theobald, Jr., entered Purdue University, and in this staunch Indiana institution he was graduated as a member of the class of 1926. Thereafter he was for a short period associated with the Indiana Refining Company, and since the death of his honored father he has been treasurer of the Anderson-Theobald Company and maintains general supervision of its business. He is, as was his father, loyally arrayed in the ranks of the Republican party, he is affiliated with historic old Vincennes Lodge No. 1, Ancient Free and Accepted Masons, and he and his widowed mother, with whom he and his wife reside in the attractive home at Vincennes, have membership in the Methodist Episcopal Church. His wife, whose maiden name was Mary Adams, was born and reared in Vincennes and was here graduated in the high school, she being a daughter of Chester Adams and a granddaughter of Thomas Adams, both prominent in the business and civic life of Vincennes in their respective generations. Mrs. Theobald is a popular figure in the social circles of her native city and, like her husband, is an active member of the Methodist Episcopal Church.

JOSEPH E. BAUER, vice president and general manager of the Indiana Oil & Gas Company, is one of the very prominent business men of Vincennes, whose operations are of great importance to the people of this part of the state. Although yet a young man, in the very prime of vigorous manhood, for he was born in 1895, at Elwood, Indiana, he has risen to prominence, and his sagacity, far-sightedness and excellent business management have brought about many changes in the oil fields. For years it was thought that there was no oil in this section of Indiana. Repeated attempts brought to the unsuccessful operators no results, but these attempts continued to be made, and in the course of them some valuable coal deposits were uncovered and a limited amount of oil.

In the meanwhile, in February, 1928, three men, S. M. Newton, then of New York City, Joseph E. Bauer, of Vincennes, Indiana, and Richard Steinhorst, then of Tulsa, Oklahoma, organized the Texana Oil Company, of which Mr. Newton was president, Mr. Bauer, vice president and general manager, and Mr. Steinhorst, secretary and treasurer, as an individual concern. In the development for oil in this section this company discovered a large gas well, and found large gas deposits in the drift of fifty wells. Through the efforts of Messrs. Steinhorst and Bauer large gas deposits were found producing 100,000,000 cubic feet per day, and the magnitude of the development led to the organization of the Indiana Oil & Gas Corporation, to furnish gas to Pike, Knox, Gibson, Daviess, Wabash and Vanderburg counties. The gas wells of the company are located seven miles southeast of the City of Princeton, near Francisco. The gas is found in an area ten miles in width and twenty miles in length, in seven different kinds of sand. This is piped to various counties through different pipe lines that already have cost about $300,000, which with the labor represent an investment of something like $500,-000 in field equipment. The company leases 80,000 acres at an annual rental of $80,000. In conjunction with the development work a geological department is maintained under the

expert supervision of H. P. Barnett, formerly connected with the Indiana Geological Survey, and he is ably assisted by Ralph Esray, assistant state geologist, and R. E. Rankin, of the University of Indiana. All the acreage has been checked by that department and verified by Dr. W. N. Logan, state geologist and president of the University of Indiana. The gas reserve has been checked by M. J. Devery, of the Hope Engineering Company, of Mount Vernon, Ohio, and they give a reserve sufficient for twenty-five years. The fact that practically an unlimited amount of natural gas will be available for industrial purposes for at least a quarter of a century has accelerated business to a remarkable degree, and new projects are getting under way with great celerity. The leading geologists of the state are confirming the opinions of their confreres. The Central Public Service Corporation, owners of the Francisco Area Distributing System, had the acreage checked by Ralph Daviess, foremost gas engineer of America, and he reported the reserve as satisfactory for a period of ten years. The pay roll of the Indiana Oil & Gas Company in 1929 is $35,000 per month, employment being given to ten in the office; five in survey work; seven as field executives; seventy-five at the peak of Princeton working on the main line twenty-nine 6"; thirty-four 4"; eighteen 3"; and ten 2", a mileage of ninety-one miles. The general offices are in 403 to 408 LaPlant Building, Vincennes; the executive offices are at 150 Broadway, New York City; while the field office is at Princeton, Indiana. The Indiana Corporation has purchased ninety per cent of the stock of the Grayburg Oil Refinery Company, San Antonio, Texas, together with a 7,000 refinery, 1,000 acres of producing oil and gas leases in Baxter, Pecas and LaSalle fields. The corporation also has a refinery producing 23,000 barrels at Luling, Texas; they have twenty-three service stations in operation at San Antonio; and over half-million storage for oil, and sufficient tank cars in connection.

S. M. Newton, a financier of New York City, is president of the company, and Mr. Bauer, one of the local magnates of this part of the state, is, as already stated, vice president and general manager.

In the early spring of 1929, March 14 to be exact, the City of Princeton held a gas day celebration, and on that day the *Princeton Daily Democrat*, as its leading editorial, published the following, which is so applicable to all of the sections affected by the gas development that it is herewith quoted:

"Today, Thursday, March 14, the citizens of Princeton, and the several committees appointed for that purpose, are extending a glad hand to hundreds of visitors who have been invited here to attend our Second Natural Gas celebration.

"The first of this character occurred many years ago, so long in fact that the great majority of those present today have no recollection of that event, and yet, thirty-five or forty years ago is not so long when we think of the road and the rate we have traveled.

"Back in 1891, when citizens contributed to a fund to drill into the earth and demonstrate whether Princeton had coal underneath the surface, as they believed, five wells were put down, and from two of these at least gas has been seeping for some years.

"Later, when the oil field west of Princeton was opened, other gas wells were brought in and for some time this city burned natural gas in cooking and heating stoves, open flames, old fireplaces, grates, and in fact every place where coal and wood had been burned, including the many new devices at that time.

"Like all natural gas discoveries, the idea prevailed that because 'Mother Earth' was pouring forth her treasure there would be no end to it, and waste held forth until the time came that nature failed to respond and Princeton's natural gas field gave way to the artificial variety that has been served regularly since.

"The oil field having been developed to such a state that unrealized revenues were pouring into the pockets of land owners and operators, no one seemed to care about natural gas and it was permitted to be choked out for the more lucrative product.

"The oil field is still functioning, at a reduced production, and many of the old wells are producing what is considered a satisfactory daily product from the pumps.

"The field spread. New prospectors came and, as a result the north, northeast, east and southeast sections of Gibson county have been developed into one continuous oil and gas field.

"There are at present enough gas wells open and plugged in Gibson County to supply this section of Indiana with natural gas for heating, cooking and industrial purposes for many years if it is properly conserved, and that seems to be one of the outstanding points of the present owners.

"To our visitors, there will be little that can be shown them to impress the importance of natural gas, its convenience, efficiency and cheapness as compared with artificial gas. It all comes through pipes, most of which are underground, and the little houses in East Mulberry Street that contain the gauges, meters and control valves present no striking appearance.

"Several furnaces have been equipped with modern heaters, temporarily, to show the visitors what is possible, and cooking stoves will be on display, but when the average individual tries to discover the difference in natural or artificial gas flame by looking at it, there is not much 'whoopee' to it."

After mentioning local weather conditions and the effects thereof, the editor continues:

"Princeton and the companies operating the franchise have no stock for sale. There are no strings to this entertainment. It is to be free to the visitors and home people, with the exception of the men's banquet, and the intention is to make all of our visitors enjoy themselves to such an extent they will want to come again, and often."

"Many will be here who are not strangers and the renewal of their acquaintance will be a real pleasure for our people."

In another portion of the same issue of the *Democrat* appears a most interesting article by Jim M'Cormick, in which he writes of the first gas well in Princeton, which came from sinking wells for coal test, as mentioned in the editorial, and the running of a makeshift gas line to the public square.

Another illuminating article also appears in the *Democrat* of March 14 telling of the permanent results of the sinking of five wells during the former oil and gas development at Princeton.

The *Princeton Clarion-News*, under date of March 15, gave considerable space to the celebration held at Princeton the day previously. President Newton, of the Indiana Oil & Gas Company, was the principal speaker, and he said in part:

"Your state geologist, Doctor Logan, had for years contended that there were vast natural gas possibilities in this part of Indiana." He spoke at length upon the magnificent work of Mr. Bauer, to whom he said he had given $50,000 a year previously to invest in Gibson County and told him "to do the best you can for me." Mr. Bauer's best was a corporation that had a $1,000,000 investment in the field, and development began. He visioned the paving of Highway 56 between Princeton and Oakland City, a great concrete route lighted with natural gas.

The *Oakland City Journal*, under date of March 15, gave an excellent account of the celebration at Princeton, and mentioned that "Wells drilled west of Oakland City by the Indiana Oil & Gas Company, headed by Newton, have shown yields of from 1,000,000 to 3,000,000 cubic feet per day, Newton declared. Additional tests have yet to be made, he said, but the present discoveries indicate that a twenty-five year supply is now assured."

The *Evansville Press*, under date of March 15, said in part, in referring to the probability of Evansville having natural gas:

"Natural gas for Evansville, with a sharp cut in price to consumer by summer, was the picture held out Friday by S. M. Newton, Vincennes financier and president of the Indiana Oil & Gas Corporation, developers of the natural gas field at Francisco, Gibson County.

"The company is now supplying Princeton, and pipe lines are being laid to Vincennes and Washington at the rate of four miles a day."

From the above it can be seen that the people of this part of Indiana are enthusiastically back of the company of which Mr. Bauer is the efficient and active vice president and general manager.

In connection with the great work he is accomplishing a little personal history is interesting. His opportunities in boyhood for acquiring an education being somewhat limited, Joseph E. Bauer took a business college course which enabled him to secure a position with the Sims Oil Company as bookkeeper and stenographer at Lawrenceville, Illinois, and proved so valuable that he was later transferred to the sales department at Buffalo, New York. Subsequently he was made general manager of the refinery of that company at Lawrenceville, Illinois. After a year there he was again transferred, being sent to Yale, Oklahoma, and made chief clerk and assistant to the manager of the J. Howard Pew Pipe Line Company, a department of the Sims corporation, and served in that connection for three years. The entry of this country into the World war interrupted his career, for he volunteered for service and was in France for fifteen months, and after his honorable discharge from the army, went into partnership with Mr. Steinhorst as producers, and drilled their first well, 3,500 feet in depth, in Pawnee County, Oklahoma, opening the Mashan Pool. They also drilled the first well, of any depth, at Glenpool, thus opening up production. After two years in that part of Oklahoma, during which time forty wells were drilled in the state, Mr. Bauer came back to Indiana as an independent operator, his field being Kentucky and Illinois. During his work in these territories he became identified with Bell Brothers, of Robinson, Illinois, and organized Mahtika, Illinois. Craig Lowrie, of Pittsburgh, Pennsylvania, was operating in Gibson County, Indiana, and Mr. Bauer later took charge of his land department, and drilled fifty wells and opened up three new pools, Mount Olympia, Summerville and the Francisco pools. Following this long and varied experience Mr. Bauer entered upon his present campaign, which, without doubt, is going to make him a national figure in financial and industrial circles, and the associate of the money kings of the world.

Mr. Bauer is a son of Joseph A. Bauer, a native of New York State, who settled in Indiana in 1890, and at Vincennes in 1900, and is connected with the Old Vincennes Window Glass Company. He married Theresa Schwartzman, and they had nine children born to them, of whom Mr. Bauer of this review is the eldest.

Joseph E. Bauer has been married, and he has a daughter, Elizabeth Bauer, who is attending school.

A. BLAINE MILLER is a farmer and stock man in Tippecanoe County, and his enterprise and the success that has attended it have made him one of the outstanding men in the agricultural life of the county. He has a farm of 218 acres, located on the Miller Road in Wea Township, on Rural Route No. 12.

On this farm he was born in 1886. He represents the third generation of the Miller family in Tippecanoe County. His grandparents were John and Mary Miller, who came from Virginia and built their first cabin home on the banks of the Wabash River in Wea Township. John and Mary Miller had only one child born to them after they came to Tippecanoe County, and that was John Miller. John Miller, Jr., was well educated, attending the local schools and the Valparaiso Normal School. He taught for a time, subsequently rented land from his father and later acquired most of the property now managed and farmed by his son Blaine. He was an active member of the Grange. John Miller married Margaret A. Goldsberry, and their only son is A. Blaine Miller. The daughter, Mary Bell, is the wife of Robert Orth and has a son, Leonard.

A. Blaine Miller attended the Reser School and the Culver Military Academy, where he was graduated in 1905. He also had courses in agriculture at Purdue University. His education was of a practical nature and fitted in well with his career as a farmer and stock man. He specializes in Shorthorn cattle, Shropshire sheep and Chester White hogs.

Mr. Miller has been president of the local Farm Bureau. He is active in Republican politics, is a member of the Masonic Lodge No. 492 and the Tippecanoe Grotto, and the Knights of Pythias. He is affiliated with the Methodist Episcopal Church.

E. W. G. JOHNSON. Monroe County citizens make familiar reference to E. W. G. Johnson by stating that he is one of the largest land owners and one of the most successful farmers stock men in the county. He has also been honored with public positions and he is fully entitled to representation among Indiana's representative citizens.

He was born in Perry Township, Monroe County, May 30, 1864, son of David and Mary (Adams) Johnson. His grandfather came from County Down, Ireland, and settled in North Carolina. It was in that state that David Johnson was born and after the death of his father he came with his widowed mother to Indiana. He started life without capital, and in buying his first horse he made a contract to split 5,000 rails. His first purchase of land was 110 acres adjoining the home farm of his son E. W. G. His career was that of an industrious and sturdy citizen and his name is held in high esteem among those who remember him in Monroe County. He was the father of eight children, Mattie, Lizzie, Emma, Robert, Frank, William, Alvie and Samuel. Of these only three are now living, Frank, William and Samuel.

E. W. G. Johnson attended the Clear Creek School and all the time he was in school he had duties on the home farm and his ambition was early awakened to make a success as a land owner and farmer. When he was twenty years of age he bought his first piece of land, comprising twenty acres. Today he owns six farms, his home place comprising 110 acres, located on the Salem Road or South Walnut Street Road, two miles south of Bloomington. In that township he owns over 1,500 acres and also has 160 acres of South Dakota land. Along with farming he has always carried on the live stock business and for a number of years had a mule market at Decatur, Alabama.

Mr. Johnson married, October 17, 1888, Miss Sarah Stipp, daughter of George and Mary (McFadden) Stipp. To their marriage were born a family of ten children, the oldest dying in infancy; Mary is the wife of Jewett Tatum and has one child, July E.; Clara married Wiley Kennedy, and their family consists of James, Martha, Phillip and Charles; Lucy is the wife of Paul Kennedy, and of their two children, David and William, the latter is deceased; the fifth and sixth children born to Mr. and Mrs. Johnson are deceased, their names being Florence and Ethel; Bertha is the wife of Alie Steward and has a son, Richard; the three younger children are Olive, Francis and George.

Mr. Johnson was elected township trustee, has also served in the County Council and has been a member of the Indiana Legislature. He and his family are members of the Christian Church.

ARTHUR W. DEPPERT was born at Peoria, February 25, 1883, but since he was six years of age his home has been in South Bend and for over a quarter of a century he has been a factor in the business service of that city as a plumbing and heating specialist.

His father was William Deppert. Arthur W. Deppert was reared and educated in South Bend, attending grade and high schools. When he was eighteen he began his apprenticeship at the plumbing trade, and after a period of experience as a journeyman he set up in business for himself, under the name of A. W. Deppert. He has well equipped shops and show rooms at 2120 Miami Street, carries a large stock of fixtures and supplies, and directs a skilled organization for handling every class of contract for plumbing and heating insulation, sewer work and general repairing.

Mr. Deppert is a member of the South Side Business Men's Club and the Knights of Pythias. He married Mrs. Mary Kaczmarek, of South Bend. Her four children, by a former marriage, are Florian, Jerome, Leona and Delores.

JAMES E. THOMPSON, farmer and postmaster at Clarks Hill, Tippecanoe County, is a native of Indiana and member of a family that came to Clinton County in pioneer times. Mr. Thompson was appointed postmaster August 1, 1923.

He was born on a farm in Lauramie Township, Tippecanoe County, son of Winfield and Eliza (Eberhart) Thompson. His great-grandfather, Reese Thompson, came from Rockingham County, Virginia, and was the son of a Revolutionary soldier. Reese Thompson was one of the first to settle in Clinton County. His son, Billy Thompson, was born in Clinton County and spent his life as a farmer. Winfield Thompson was born on his father's farm in Clinton County and likewise spent his active years in agriculture. He and his wife had four sons: Samuel C., William T., Charles R. and James E.

James E. Thompson for about four years was a pupil in the Stringtown School in Clinton County. Then the family moved to Clarks

Hill, where he finished high school. Later he rounded out his education by four years of study in the International Correspondence School at Scranton. His original capital, given him by his father, was two hundred dollars in money and a team of horses. In 1910 he bought a farm of eighty acres, renting another eighty acres, and during the next six years had no other outside interests to interfere with his work as a farm producer. In August, 1916, he took the post of assistant cashier of the State Bank at Clarks Hill and after two years was promoted to cashier, serving four and a half years in that office. He resigned in December, 1922, to resume his farm work, and in the following year was made postmaster. While looking after the postoffice, with an administration that is highly satisfactory to all the patrons of the office, he superintends the operation of his farm of 125 acres just at the edge of town. Mr. Thompson has been interested in politics since he reached voting age, but never held a public office until he was appointed postmaster. He and his family are members of the Christian Church and Sunday School.

Mr. Thompson married, December 7, 1913, Miss Jessie Swackhamer, daughter of Edgar and Mary (Barnum) Swackhamer. The Swackhamer family has been in Clinton County since 1902. Mr. and Mrs. Thompson have three children, Edgar, Morris and James.

KYLE D. FOUTS, whose home is three-quarters of a mile west of Shadeland, in Union Township, Tippecanoe County, has been an outstanding citizen of that community for a number of years. His energy and good management have put him in the class of successful Indiana agriculturists and his name is always mentioned with the respect due to a public spirited and generous citizen.

Mr. Fouts was born in Jackson Township, Tippecanoe County, September 16, 1890, son of John M. and Eliza J. (Deardorf) Fouts. His grandparents were Eli and Mary (Blackford) Fouts, natives of Virginia. On coming west they first settled in Ohio and about 1828 arrived in Tippecanoe County, Indiana, having traveled all the way by wagon and team. Their first home was a log cabin in Jackson Township and their land was entered directly from the Government. John M. Fouts was born in Jackson Township, was reared and educated there, and worked for his father for some years. Later he bought land and at the time of his death owned an estate of about 800 acres. He was one of the leading citizens of Jackson Township. He was always much interested in politics, was a member of the Christian Church and the Knights of Pythias Order. He and his wife had four children: Florence, wife of Edward Stradling and mother of Robert and Margaret; Mabel, deceased; Ethel, deceased; and Kyle D.

Kyle D. Fouts attended school at La Fayette and after graduating from high school engaged in farming. In 1917 he married Miss

Mary Ruth Robbins, daughter of John and Josephine (Burleigh) Robbins. Her father was born in Carroll County, Indiana, and spent his life as a farmer. Her grandparents were Isaac and Elizabeth (Patton) Robbins. Isaac Robbins was born near Sidney, Ohio, and was eleven years of age when the family moved to Indiana. Isaac Robbins was a son of John and Mary Robbins. The Robbins family came to Indiana in 1828. One of Mrs. Fouts' direct ancestors was a soldier in the Revolutionary war with Sumter, Marion, Pickens and Lee. Mrs. Fouts was the only child of her parents. Mr. and Mrs. Fouts have a son, John R., now in school.

Mr. Fouts is a trustee of the Methodist Episcopal Church and is secretary of the Sunday School. His hobby is travel. He is a member of the social clubs in his township, and has been active in Republican politics, serving as a member of the advisory board. Mr. Fouts' home place comprises 236 acres, and in addition to the busy program involved in handling this property he owns another farm of 200 acres in the same township, this farm being leased. Thus his land ownership in Tippecanoe County represents 436 acres.

WILLIAM R. SIERSEMA is one of the prosperous farm owners living in the West Point community of Wayne Township, Tippecanoe County. He was born there, and his neighbors have known him all his life as a man of substantial industry, intelligent, public spirited, always willing to do his share in any project involving the common welfare.

Mr. Siersema was born on the farm on which he now resides, in 1873. He is a son of John and Susana (Allen) Siersema. His father was born in Holland, of old Dutch stock. When he was a boy he came with his mother and stepfather, Jacob DeFreese, to America. During his early years he worked as a farm hand in Tippecanoe County, and from his labor saved the money that enabled him to make his first purchase of land. He lived an industrious life, provided well for those dependent upon him and improved a good farm. He was very active in the Methodist Episcopal Church. He is buried at West Point. There were six children: Eva, wife of George Atchison; one that died in infancy; Sarah, wife of Rastus Youel; John; Emma, wife of Ed Robinson; and Mrs. John Gundlefinger.

William R. Siersema during his boyhood attended the Round Top School in the home neighborhood. He has been familiar with farm work since boyhood, and he made his own start by renting a farm, and later he acquired the 180 acres on which he now lives and which was his birthplace.

Mr. Siersema married in 1896 Miss Gertrude Gay, daughter of Sanford and Arnetta (McCrea) Gay. They are the parents of one son, Clarence, who was educated at West Point and is now the active manager of his father's farm. Clarence Siersema married Ruth Kamp. Clarence from school days has been interested in athletics and was one of the star basketball players in his community.

The Siersema family are active in church and social affairs. Mrs. Siersema is a member of the Ladies Aid, the West Point Home Economics Society, the Foreign and Home Missionary Society and the Wednesday Club.

JULIUS H. MEYN. One of the oldest and most highly honored names in the financial history of Lake County is that of Meyn. The financial interests of the family center in the First Trust & Savings Bank of Hammond, of which Peter Meyn is president and in which several of his sons are officials.

Peter W. Meyn was born in Germany, and was three years of age when brought to America by his parents. His father, George Meyn, settled at what is now Chicago Heights, Illinois, and lived the rest of his life in that community, then known as Bloom. His widow survived him and spent her last years in Hammond, where she died in 1910. Peter W. Meyn grew up at Bloom, Illinois, attended school there and also at Hammond, finishing his education in the Indiana State Normal at Terre Haute. He began his career as a merchant in Hammond, for two terms was city clerk and two terms city treasurer. It was out of his real estate and insurance business that the Lake County Savings & Trust Company grew. He became president of that institution. Later the name was changed to the First Trust & Savings Bank, and in 1926 it took over the First National Bank. Along with his business interests he has always had a keen interest in civic affairs and is a member of the Kiwanis Club and St. Paul's Lutheran Church.

Peter W. Meyn married Magdalena Dunsing, who was born in "Little Egypt," Illinois, daughter of Rev. Julius Dunsing. Her father was a missionary in Southern Illinois for many years and later moved to Hammond, Indiana, where he spent his last days. Mrs. Magdalena Meyn was educated in Lutheran parochial and public schools. She is treasurer of the St. Paul's Ladies Aid Society, having held that office for twenty-eight years, and is a member of the Hammond Woman's Club. Peter W. Meyn and wife had four children: Martha, Julius H., Edwin (who died at the age of six years), and Walter E.

Martha Meyn is the wife of William Wilke, Jr., a resident of Hammond. Mr. Wilke was responsible for the development of the Metals Refining Company at Hammond, which in 1929 he sold to the Glidden Company of Cleveland. He is now president of the Hammond Lead Products Company, Incorporated, which manufactures lead oxides and pigments as materials for paint. Mr. and Mrs. Wilke have three children, William, Martha and Virginia.

Walter E. Meyn is a Hammond citizen who has had an interesting career. He was educated in the Lutheran schools at Hammond, the Hammond High School, and at Asheville, North Carolina. During the World war he was a sergeant in the Quartermaster's Corps, went overseas in June, 1917, being located at

Valdahone and later at Paris, where he served on the staff of Gen. Charles G. Dawes until six months after the armistice. Since the war he has been with the First Trust & Savings Bank, beginning as assistant secretary and treasurer, and for the past five years has been vice president. He married Miss Margo Vibirts, of Chicago, and they have two children, Peter and Margo-Jean. Walter Meyn is a member of the American Legion and president of the local Salvation Army committee.

Julius H. Meyn, also an official in the First Trust & Savings Bank at Hammond, was born at North Judson, Indiana, September 2, 1890. He was educated in the Lutheran schools, the public schools, graduated from the Hammond High School in 1910 and completed his commercial training in the Wharton School of Finance of the University of Pennsylvania in 1914. After returning home he was made manager of the insurance department of the First Trust & Savings Bank, and for the past five years has been vice president in charge of the insurance department. Insurance is a field in which his talents have had opportunity for unusual achievement and he is recognized as one of the leading producers for the Travelers Insurance Company of Hartford. In 1928 he was made president of the Presidents Club of the Travelers Company. He was a charter member and the first secretary of the Rotary Club of Hammond. He belongs to the Woodmar Country Club, the Illinois Athletic Club, the Delta Kappa Epsilon fraternity, is a Republican and an active member of St. Paul's Lutheran Church.

He married at Hammond, November 22, 1916, Miss Elene Reiter, daughter of Judge Virgil S. and Josephine (Kingsley) Reiter. Her father is a distinguished Indiana jurist and for many years has been judge of the Superior Court at Hammond. Mrs. Meyn attended school at Hammond, including high school, and the National Cathedral School at Washington. She is a member of the Presbyterian Church and the Woman's Club. They have three children: Walter Kingsley, Margene Reiter and Julius H., Jr. The first two are students in the public schools.

JOHN NELSON, a resident of South Bend for over forty years, is a man of very sturdy business character, a careful and methodical worker, and for many years has given his time and energies to a very successful general contracting business.

He is a native of Denmark, born in that country, August 11, 1865. He attended school there, served an apprenticeship at a trade, and was a well qualified worker when he came to the United States at the age of twenty-two. His home since coming to America has been in South Bend. Many years ago he acquired naturalization as an American citizen, and has always voted and has given an intelligent attention to the affairs of his home community. Mr. Nelson has been in the general contracting and building business since 1895. In earlier years his work was general building, and later he built up an organization especially equipped for handling high class commercial buildings and fine homes. Some years ago he took his two sons into partnership, and since then the firm has been John Nelson Company, general contractors and builders. No firm in Indiana has a higher reputation for good work than this. In 1928 they put up a commodious and handsome brick office and work shop at 712 North Niles Street, and they also have a yard there for the assembling of their material and equipment.

Mr. Nelson is a member of the Masonic fraternity and B. P. O. Elks, and is one of the business men enrolled in the South Bend Chamber of Commerce. He and his family belong to the English Lutheran Church. He married Miss Camilla Wilson, who was born in Denmark, but was reared in South Bend. They have three children, the two sons, now associated with their father, being John C. and Ray W. The only daughter, Miss Carrie, is a teacher in the schools of South Bend.

HON. HERMAN H. WERBER, city treasurer of Gary, is one of the older residents of that industrial center, and his name is well known there both as a business man and citizen.

Mr. Werber was born in Chicago, Illinois, July 18, 1880, son of Emil and Sophia (Schulty) Werber. His mother died in 1883 and is buried in the Graceland Cemetery at Chicago. She left a family of two sons and two daughters, all of whom are living, Elizabeth, Emil, Herman H. and Julia.

Herman H. Werber received his schooling in the Lincoln Grammar School of Chicago. When he was thirteen he left school and began a career of varied experience in which his own efforts provided him a living and eventually brought him the opportunities of a settled business career. He was a plumber's apprentice and plumber's helper in Chicago for a time. For six years he was a cowboy in Montana, this being followed by another six years as a brakeman with the Sioux Line Railroad out of Bismarck, North Dakota. He also spent three years in the gold mines in the Black Hills of South Dakota.

After this western experience he came to Indiana on May 18, 1908, and first located at Tolleston, an old settled village in Lake County which the following year was annexed to the City of Gary. During the first year he was in the Gary community Mr. Werber did construction work for the American Bridge Company. His chief line of business, however, has been manufacturing soft drinks, and many years ago he established the Werber & Roberts Bottling Works and having acquired the interest of his partner is now the sole owner of that business.

Almost from the time he came to Gary he has been an interested worker in the local Republican party. In 1918 he was elected councilman from the Sixth Ward. In 1922 he was elected a councilman at large, and in the 1929 municipal campaign he was chosen city treasurer. Mr. Werber is a member of Gary Lodge No. 776, A. F. and A. M., B. P. O. Elks and Loyal Order of Moose, is a member of the Commercial Club, formerly was active in Rotary work. His church affiliations are with the St. John's Lutheran Church in Chicago. During the World war he was captain of several of the teams that sold Liberty Bonds and raised funds for other patriotic causes.

He married at Gary, January 19, 1918, Miss Myrtle Elser, daughter of Gustave and Elizabeth (Deidell) Elser. Her father is a member of the police force of the Illinois Steel Mills at Gary. Both her parents are Presbyterians. Mrs. Werber was educated in public schools in Chicago and Gary. She is one of Gary's ablest musicians and has found her time fully taken up by the claims of an extensive clientele of pupils, so that she has had to limit her teaching work to a class of eighty. She completed her musical education in the Chicago Conservatory of Music, where she studied under Professors Weidig and Robein. She is a member of the Professional Woman's Club of Gary and the Civic Music Association. Mr. and Mrs. Werber have one daughter, Geraldine Elizabeth, a pupil in the Horace Mann School at Gary.

EDGAR MARVIN WILCOX is an Indiana citizen, a resident of the City of Hammond, but railroad officials and railroad employees in this country and abroad know him as the master mind who invented the Hannauer and Wilcox Car Retarder System. In 1930, seven years after this device was first successfully tested in the Gibson classification yards of the Indiana Harbor Belt Railroad, and after thirty-two other classification yards of a dozen or more great railroad systems had installed the car-retarding device, Mr. Wilcox was awarded the coveted Henderson Gold Medal by the Franklin Institute of Philadelphia in recognition of his contribution to railroad engineering through his invention.

Edgar Marvin Wilcox was a newspaper man by early training and was well on his way to distinction in that field, when he left it to follow the bent of his mechanical genius into practical railroading. He was born at Buffalo, New York, August 13, 1871. His father, Horace Wilcox, who died in 1889, developed a high degree of genius in the newspaper field. He learned the trade of compositor in the office of the *Western New Yorker*, published at Warsaw, New York. For thirty years he was employed on the editorial staff of the Buffalo *Morning Express*, finally serving as commercial, marine and financial editor. He also wrote articles of a literary nature under the nom de plume "Silas Farmer."

Horace Wilcox married Mary Harriet Beverly, who died in 1885. Her ancestors came from Holland and were among the early Dutch settlers of the Mohawk Valley at Fort Plain, New York.

Edgar M. Wilcox was graduated from the Buffalo public schools in 1888. At thirteen he was carrying a route of papers for the Buffalo *Courier,* and has always ascribed to this experience important lessons in promptness and discipline in the face of difficulty. He had to report at three o'clock every morning, and he carried and delivered his papers in spite of snow and zero weather. Later he worked under his father, the commercial editor of *The Express,* and for a salary of $3.50 a week gathered closing stock quotations at the Board of Trade. With this training he was qualified, when his father died in 1889, to succeed him as commercial and marine editor of the Buffalo *Morning Express.* He was probably the youngest man in charge of that department in any big newspaper office in the country.

But after a year he gave up his newspaper work to follow his inclination for a mechanical career. He became a car oiler with the Lehigh Valley Railroad, two years later was made a brake inspector, and at the age of twenty-two became assistant foreman of the Buffalo Yards. From that he was promoted to general foreman of the car repair shops and the inspection department of both the freight and passenger cars at Cleveland for the New York Central lines. Three years later he was made traveling car foreman between Cleveland and Buffalo. He held that position at the time the New York Central put on its famous train "The Twentieth Century Limited." The story has often been told of how Mr. Wilcox, on one bitter cold night, bought a gallon of whiskey from a nearby saloon and poured the liquor into the frozen steam line and thereby avoided the possibility of halting the train and transferring the passengers. From traveling car foreman he was promoted to division general foreman, with territory between Toledo and Buffalo. In 1906 he was sent to the Danville division of the New York Central and Indiana Harbor Belt to systematize mechanical work. After this was accomplished he was made division general foreman between Toledo and Chicago. In 1914 he returned to the Indiana Harbor Belt Railroad at its terminal, and that has been the scene of his labors ever since. His official position today is that of master car builder in charge of construction and interchange of freight equipment for the New York Central lines at the Chicago terminal.

But his hobby and enthusiasm over a long period of years has been invention. His daily work with railroad equipment induced him the habit of constant thought, study and experiment with a view to smoothing the difficulties and lightening the labors and dangers and hazards of train operation. In particular, he applied himself to one of the oldest problems of railroading, switching. Long before Mr. Wilcox entered the railroad service the great freight terminals of the different systems had developed extensive "classification yards," where railroad cars received from different lines were sorted out and made up into new trains for destinations near and far. Switching crews comprised a large part of the personnel employed in these yards. Then came the device of the "hump," by which cars were pushed on to an incline and by gravity run out on the different tracks, but each unit of car or cars had to be manned by an individual switchman who operated the hand brakes to control the car in its descent, while other men threw the switches by hand.

To the problems of this situation came Mr. Wilcox with his originating mind. Out of it after many years he perfected his car retarding device. The essential principle of this device is a brake rail, cushioned by springs, set parallel to the track rail, operated electrically or pneumo-electrically, so that the brake rail, at the will of the operator in the towers, is pushed against the flanges of the car wheels, the flanges being compressed between the brake rail and track rail so as to retard the movement of the wheels, and thus the car itself is controlled and guided at the will of the operator.

In the issue of the Chicago *Tribune* of August 16, 1925, a leader article described the first official demonstration of this device. "The retarding appliance," said the *Tribune*, "designed and controlled jointly by George Hannauer, vice president of the Indiana Harbor Belt Railroad, and E. M. Wilcox, master technical engineer, has been undergoing tests at the Gibson 'hump' of the Harbor Belt Line since November, 1923. The demonstration yesterday was the first published exhibition of the results it has accomplished.

"The mechanism thus accomplishes the following results: 1. All car riders are eliminated, with a saving at the Gibson yard of the labor of sixty-six men at a wage of ninety-two cents an hour. 2. Cars are spaced more closely than under the old method. 3. Control of cars on grades prevents rough handling and damage claims. 4. Use of an outside braking medium obviates the necessity of preliminary train brake tests."

Mr. Wilcox and his associates did not secure the fruits of their invention without legal complications. It was three years before counter claims had been eliminated and the patent for the car retarding device permanently awarded. The first application for the patent was made December 24, 1923, and the patent was issued January 4, 1927. Early in 1925 the General Railway Signal Company of Rochester, New York, acquired the license to manufacture, sell and install the Hannauer and Wilcox system. Since then, as previously noted, it has been installed in many of the classification freight yards in the country. Employment of the system increases the switching capacity of a classification yard almost threefold, and, as the bestowal of the Henderson Medal indicates, it is regarded by practical railroad men as one of the greatest contributions to the industry during the present century.

Representatives of railroads from all over America and from nearly every foreign country have visited the Gibson yards near Hammond to inspect the actual operation of the Hannauer and Wilcox system. Mr. Wilcox has probably entertained and instructed more foreign notables in the art of the gravity retarder switch than any other individual in the railroad world.

It was inevitable that Mr. Wilcox invention would be regarded as a contribution to "technological unemployment." One of the interesting tributes to the practical success of the car-retarding device is found in an editorial in the literature of the I. W. W., from which the following is an extract: "The latest labor-saving invention in this line, the Wilcox Car Controller, is another step, and a long one, in the same direction. This device, by automatically controlling the cars as they are sent down the hump into the classification yards, will, when fully installed, do away with the rider. At Gibson, Indiana, where this new invention is being tried out, half the riders have already been laid off and the other half will go as soon as the car controller in installed down in the tracks. They are already putting 1,000 cars over in eight hours, with only seven riders. When the installation is completed it will be possible to classify 5,000 cars in twenty-four hours without a single rider." Against this dire prophecy there is a later comment that the invention has actually caused more men to be employed because of the increased movement of freight, the roster of employees for the Belt Line alone being the largest in the history of that road. At the same time there has been a remarkable reduction in the death and casualty list.

Mr. Wilcox in addition to his official position with the Indiana Harbor Belt Railroad Company and as president of the Hannauer Car Retarder Company is a director of the Gibson Railroad Y. M. C. A. As a young man, from 1884 to 1888, he was a member of the Cadet Corps of the Sixty-fifth Regiment, New York National Guard. During the World war he was in charge of the railroad division of the Military Intelligence Auxiliary Department. He is a member of the American Military Engineers, is a Republican voter, is affiliated with the Lodge, Royal Arch Chapter, Knight Templar Commandery and Mystic Shrine of the Masons, the B. P. O. Elks and the Independent Order of Forresters. He is a member of the Shrine Club of the Orak Temple at Hammond, and a member of the Christian Science Church.

Mr. Wilcox married in 1892, at Buffalo, Mary Comstock, daughter of Lewis and Mary Comstock, of Sardinia, New York. Her father, who was a descendant of the Earl of Comstock of England, was a non-commissioned officer under General Sheridan at the famous battle of Cedar Creek, when Sheridan made his ride. Lewis Comstock was member of a New York regiment. Mr. and Mrs. Wilcox have three children. The oldest, Marvin Edgar Wilcox, now superintendent of the car department of the Boston & Maine Railroad, married Lois Harrington, a descendant of the early pioneer Harrington family of Concord, Massachusetts, and through her mother a descendant of President Tyler. The second son,

Levi Igleheart

Dr. Clarence Howard Wilcox, a practicing physician at Hammond, married a daughter of Dr. Koons, of Newcastle, Indiana. Mr. Wilcox' only daughter, Aurilla May Wilcox, is the wife of Harry F. Derner, of Hammond. Mr. Derner was a non-commissioned officer in Headquarters Company, Fifty-fifth Artillery, and was in the American Expeditionary Forces from March 25, 1918, to January 22, 1919. He served in the second battle of the Marne, in the operations on the Vesle, and in the Meuse-Argonne offensive.

LEVI IGLEHEART, SR., was the common ancestor of the modern generations of that family in Vanderburgh and adjacent counties. Students of social origins as an element in the destiny of states and nations as well as families may examine with profit his life as man and citizen. (It will be noticed that a variation in the spelling of the family name has occurred. The head of the Indiana branch of that family, Levi Igleheart, Sr., spelled his name with an "e" in the last syllable, while various branches of the same family from an earlier period omitted that letter.)

Levi Igleheart, Sr., the fifth son of John Igleheart of Prince Georges County, Maryland, was born August 13, 1786, and died in Warrick County, Indiana, December 12, 1855.

His mother was Mary DeNune Igleheart, daughter of Dr. Richard DeNune of a French Huguenot settlement near Baltimore, and Dr. Richard DeNune's wife, the mother of Mary, was a Miss Hall, daughter of Captain Hall of the Virginia Colonial Militia.

He married Ann Taylor and in 1816 moved from Maryland to Ohio County, Kentucky, where he resumed his farming activities. He was comfortably situated as a farmer in Ohio County, with his farm cleared and paid for, with good improvements, when a stranger appeared and exhibited an overlapping survey, which entitled him to the possession of the land as the real owner but which under the laws of Virginia and Kentucky at that time did not have to be recorded, and of which he had no notice. It was just such an occurrence which drove Daniel Boone from the State of Kentucky through the loss of his entire farm with all improvements.

Levi Igleheart, Sr., vacated his farm and moved to the State of Indiana and settled in Warrick County, a short distance east of the British Settlement in Vanderburgh County, which extended into Warrick, Gibson and Posey counties adjoining. There is reason to believe that proximity to the British Settlement was an inducement to the elder Igleheart to settle with his family, as the leading families of the British Settlement had brought with them into the wilderness, British ideals, correct speech, musical and literary culture, with church opportunities, and all three of Mr. Igleheart's sons found their wives in the British Settlement and two out of five of his daughters found their husbands there. One of the daughters, Harriett, who found her husband in the British Settlement, married John Erskine, a farmer in the British Settlement in Vanderburgh County, and by this marriage was reared a large and influential family. Among the descendants are Annie Fellows Johnston and Albion Fellows Bacon, well known in American literature.

In 1825 Levi Igleheart, Sr., was appointed Magistrate in Warrick County and was elected by the Board of Magistrates to be its president, and retained that position until after 1830, when the law changed and the duties of the Board of Magistrates, which involved charge and management of the finances of the county, were transferred to the Board of County Commissioners, composed of three members and Levi Igleheart, Sr., was repeatedly chosen by election of the people of the county to be one of those commissioners. The Board of Magistrates of the county as financial managers of the county was an adoption by the early Indiana Legislature of the old Virginia custom, where the plantation owners, as magistrates, controlled their public local affairs and it was under that system that Levi Igleheart, Sr., became chairman of the Board of Magistrates of Warrick County.

His sons were Asa, Levi, Jr., and William T.

LESLIE T. IGLEHEART. More than one hundred years ago there came into the almost virgin mid-west of America a group of pioneers—country folk from Prince Georges County, Maryland. As a result of that migration, Levi Igleheart, the father of Leslie T. Igleheart, was born in what was virtually a frontier country. When Levi Igleheart was four years of age his parents removed to Warrick County, Indiana, from Ohio County, Kentucky, where they had first taken up their residence after leaving their Maryland home. In 1844, he married Susanna Ingle of Inglefield, Indiana, a member of the Ingle family which has been prominent in Vanderburgh County for four generations.

Leslie T. Igleheart was born in Warrick County, Indiana, on July 3, 1848. He had reached the age of five years when his father decided to leave the Warrick County home and remove to Evansville. In 1853 Levi Igleheart joined with the Little Brothers in the establishment of a saw mill in Evansville which at that time was a considerable lumber center with quite a business in hard woods. Three years later Levi Igleheart with his two brothers established the flour milling firm of Igleheart Bros.

Leslie T. Igleheart attended the public schools of Evansville and then obtained higher education at Asbury (now DePauw) University at Greencastle, Indiana. After he completed his school work he represented the Igleheart Brothers' (now General Foods Corporation) interests in the Yosemite Flour Mills. Later the mill was destroyed by fire and soon afterward he became interested in the establishment of the Melrose Mills. It was operated for fifteen years after which period of time fire again occurred and that plant was destroyed.

In 1904 the death of Levi Igleheart occurred and the three sons took over the father's interests and Leslie T. Igleheart became president of the Igleheart Brothers mill, which office he held for twenty-two years. In 1920 there was a merger of the Igleheart firm with the Postum Cereal Company, and Mr. Igleheart retired from active business. However, the business still continues under the name of Igleheart Brothers, Incorporated, and its products, chief among which are the "Swansdown" brands, are known throughout the world.

Mr. Igleheart was married on January 20th, 1874, to Miss Lizzie H. Giltner, of Chillicothe, Missouri. Two sons were born, Levi Giltner Igleheart and John Giltner Igleheart. The elder son, Levi, passed away in 1909. John Giltner Igleheart, the other son, now resides in Evansville, Indiana. He has two sons, namely, Leslie Derthick Igleheart and John Giltner Igleheart, Jr.

Mr. Igleheart quietly carried on several worthy philanthropic enterprises. Chief of his interests in this respect was his attention to the needs of Evansville College, the Deaconess Hospital and to Trinity Methodist Church, with which the family is affiliated.

Leslie T. Igleheart died September 27, 1930. The death of his widow followed November 1, 1930.

JOHN EUGENE IGLEHART, member of the Indiana bar since September, 1869, and president emeritus of the Southwestern Indiana Historical Society, has had a career distinguished both by the intensity of his devotion to his profession and by the extent of his interests and contacts outside the field of the law. Long ago he achieved high rank in his chosen vocation. Professional success acted as a spur rather than as a halter in his attitude toward matters not directly concerned with his career. His home community of Evansville has long been under obligation to him for varied and useful public activities and services. But a still wider public, not Indiana alone, have felt and expressed a sense of obligation to his scholarship and patient investigation in the factual details and the generalizations which have resulted in a revision of older estimates as to Southern Indiana's place and influence in the history of the Middle West.

Mr. Iglehart's career and work must be appraised in the light of the statements made in this brief introductory paragraph. Only in that way can the true inwardness of his consecutive experiences, positions held, and professional and public services, as described in the following paragraphs be revealed. When Mr. Iglehart was called to the bar he immediately became associated with his father, one of Indiana's great lawyers and jurists, concerning whom something should be said before introducing the life of the son.

The Iglehart family came to Southern Indiana and settled in Warrick County in 1823. At that time Judge Asa Iglehart was five years of age. He was born December 8, 1817, in Ohio County, Kentucky, son of Levi (vide supra) and Ann (Taylor) Iglehart, who had crossed the mountains from Maryland about 1815. Out of his personal recollections written down many years later, Asa Iglehart contributed some important pictures of the environment in which not only he grew up, but which was similar in many respects to that which encompassed the boyhood of Abraham Lincoln. Judge Iglehart with his brothers and sisters, found his chief intellectual stimulus in the encouragement of his mother, rather than in the formal advantages of the winter terms of school. The early Methodist preachers were generally better educated than most of the people in the country, and their presence and conversation served to stimulate the Iglehart children to seek for better educational opportunities.

Asa Iglehart after his marriage to Ann Cowle continued to live on his farm, also taught school, but at the same time was diligently pursuing the study of law and was admitted to the bar at the age of thirty-two. In 1849 he removed to Evansville. In 1854 he was appointed common pleas judge and later was elected without opposition to the same office. He rose rapidly in his profession, enjoyed a profitable income, and his abilities brought him in association with Indiana's other eminent lawyers. He helped organize the first state bar association and was second president, and was one of the original promoters of the Bar Association of the United States. For many years he was an editorial contributor to the *Central Law Journal*. He revised *McDonald's Treatise* for justices in Indiana, later known as *Iglehart's Treatise*. He also prepared an orignal work on *Pleading and Practice in Indiana*. The portion of the work on pleading that is an adaptation of pleading as it exists at the common law, to the law in Indiana under the code, is a concise elementary discussion which has always remained an invaluable text book of the law in Indiana.

Judge Asa Iglehart died February 5, 1887. Among concise estimates of his work as a lawyer one of the best is found in the resolutions prepared by the Evansville bar: "As a commercial and corporation lawyer he was without a peer in Indiana. As a special pleader he had no rival. He was master of all the branches and intricacies of our jurisprudence. For twenty-five years he was the leader of a bar made famous by the names of Blythe, Jones, Chandler, Baker, Law and others, dead and living. In the history of Indiana, Asa Iglehart will always rank with Willard, Judah, Morton and Hendricks, as one of her great men." The eminent Judge Gresham wrote of him: "I have met few men who had greater power of analysis, and, just now, I can recall no one who examined and briefed a case better."

One of the dominant forces of his life was his complete faith in the great verities of revealed religion. He was an earnest church-

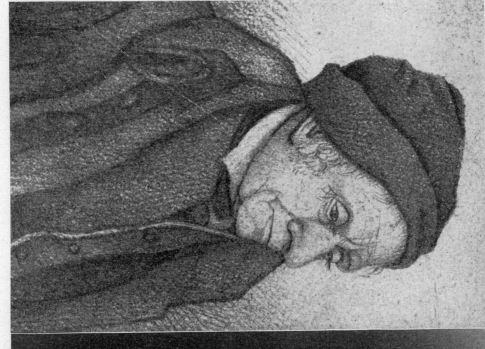

JOHN INGLE

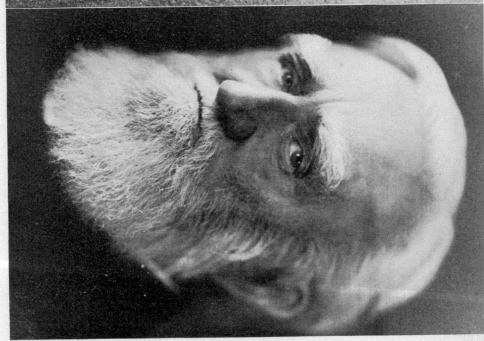

man, for many years a trustee of DePauw University and also a trustee of the Evansville public schools.

The names of his children were: Ferdinand C., who married Nannie D. Stewart; John Eugene, who married Lockie W. Holt; and Ann who married Edwin Taylor. John E. Iglehart's children are: Eugene H., who married Emily Powers; Ann, who married John Ingle, Jr.; Lockie Holt, who married Charles Humphry; and Joseph H., who married Gertrude Townley.

Ann Cowle Iglehart, mother of John E. Iglehart, was born in England December 27, 1817, and was in her fifth year when she came with her widowed mother and two small brothers to join the first British settlements in Indiana. Her mother's brother, John Ingle, was one of the founders of this British settlement and platted its capital, Saundersville.

John Ingle of Somersham, Huntingdonshire, England, a Baptist minister, was the father of John Ingle of Saundersville, who platted the Town of Saundersville in 1819 and who was the ancestor of two of the three wives of the original three Igleheart brothers, while John Ingle of Somersham was the common ancestor of all three of the wives of the elder Iglehearts, resulting from the fact that Asa Iglehart married Ann Cowle, whose widowed mother, Sarah Ingle Cowle, a sister of John Ingle of Saundersville, came to him in the British Settlement in 1822, bringing three small children, one of whom was Ann Cowle, the niece of John Ingle of Saundersville, who later married Asa Iglehart.

On the burial plot on the old Ingle homestead at Saundersville, is a memorial tablet, inscribed with letters in bronze, which reads as follows:

SACRED TO THE MEMORY
of
SARAH INGLE COWLE WHEELER
1793   1833
Daughter of Rev. John and Dinah Ingle of Somersham, Huntingdonshire, England. Widow of William Cowle.

In April 1822 emigrated with her daughter and two sons joining here on this farm her brother John Ingle of Saundersville, who was one of the founders here of the first British Settlement in Indiana. Saundersville was platted by him in 1819 half a mile south of here at the junction of the State Road and the Boonville and New Harmony Road.

Married Mark Wheeler of Wheeler Settlement.

Erected 1926 by her grandchildren, children of her daughter, Ann Cowle Iglehart.

Perhaps John E. Iglehart's outstanding contribution to published history was his account of the "First British Settlement in Indiana," a subject in which he had an obvious interest and to which his knowledge of his mother's family contributed invaluable items. Ida Tarbell in her book *In the Footsteps of the Lincolns* pays an interesting tribute to John E. Iglehart and also to his mother's people when she said: "There has been in the last few years a considerable amount of solid work done on the character of the men and women who settled this corner of the state; particularly important from the Lincoln standpoint is that of John E. Iglehart, of Evansville, president of the Southwestern Indiana Historical Society. Mr. Iglehart's work gives us a better basis for judging of the caliber of the men under whose indirect influence at least Lincoln certainly came at this time, than we have ever had before. He has developed with a wealth of detail, the character of the English settlement which started in 1817 north of Evansville and twenty-five or thirty miles west of where Lincoln lived—a settlement whose descendants are still among the leading people of the section."

Mr. Iglehart pursued this investigation further in his admirable address (published by the Indiana Historical Society) on *The Environment of Abraham Lincoln in Indiana*, which illustrates the method of his historical work and corrects many popular misconceptions as to the social and intellectual character of the pioneers of Southwestern Indiana. The significance of this address has been well understood by historians, and the comments made by Miss Tarbell will not be out of place in this connection. In a letter to Mr. Iglehart, she wrote:

"It places and gives an importance to the subject which it seems to me never to have had before. I think it will force future biographers to concede that there were big and inspiring influences exerted directly or indirectly on Lincoln in the period that he lived in Indiana. There was an abundance of character and high notions of life in the atmosphere of Southwestern Indiana when young Lincoln lived there, and you cannot make me believe that he did not respond to what was in the air."

John Eugene Iglehart was born in Campbell Township, Warrick County, August 10, 1848, and was about a year old when his father removed to Evansville. He was a pupil there in the public schools before Evansville had any public school buildings. While he was in high school it was his good fortune to come under the instruction of some very capable teachers, and he completed the four year course in three years. His studious tastes and habits followed him when he entered in September, 1865, Asbury (now DePauw) University, and there too he rounded out his four years of work in three, graduating in June, 1868. He immediately entered his father's law office and a little over a year later was admitted to the bar on reaching his twenty-first birthday. In 1874 he was admitted to practice before the Supreme Court of the United States. As a partner of his father he came to know a great number of the older generation of lawyers then practicing in Southwestern Indiana.

For ten years he engaged wholly in the general practice of the law. His father at the same time was consulting counsel for the only railroad coming into Evansville. As other railroads concentrated at that center, the work of the firm became increasingly heavy in handling railroad matters. During the period of the Mackey control of the Evansville and Terre Haute Railroad Company, beginning about 1881, Mr. Iglehart was put in charge of the legal department of the system and acted as general counsel throughout the time of the Mackey control and for thirty years was general counsel of the Evansville and Terre Haute Railroad allied lines. When the Evansville and Terre Haute in 1912 was consolidated with the Chicago & Eastern Illinois Railroad, with general office in Chicago, the office of district attorney was created and was filled by Iglehart and Taylor. Mr. Iglehart's associate was his brother-in-law, Mr. Edwin Taylor, who had previously been associated with him for a number of years. Mr. Taylor died in 1922, but Mr. Iglehart has been retained as district attorney, though in later years his service has been almost entirely of an advisory nature.

Like his father before him Mr. Iglehart has always been deeply interested in the subject of education. For twenty years he was a member of the board of trustees of DePauw University, served as a trustee of the City of Evansville and was instrumental in maintaining a private girls' school until the privileges of the Evansville High School in preparation for college were opened to girls as well as boys.

Since 1916 Mr. Iglehart's time and general capacities have been largely devoted to historical research and the promotion of historical activities in his section of the state. He organized and became chairman of the Evansville Centennial Historical Commission to cooperate with the state-wide program for celebrating the centennial of Indiana's admission to the Union. During the World war period most of the municipal effort was absorbed by patriotic activities, excluding general historical work but at its close he was chiefly instrumental as a continuation of work already begun in organizing in January, 1920, the Southwestern Indiana Historical Society, which, specializing its work in one quarter of the state, has sponsored and in some cases has been directly responsible for some of the most dignified historical research in any section of the Ohio River valley. In connection with these activities Mr. Iglehart collected the material which he wove into magazine articles and society addresses and papers, some of which had been published separately, including his work on the first British settlement, also a history of The Beginning of Methodism, both of which were published in the Indiana Magazine of History, others in Historical Bulletins published by the State. He was also editor for the History of Vanderburgh County, published in 1923, and contributed, himself, some of the most valuable material found in this publication.

In the domain of historical research, Mr. Iglehart for a number of years has been recognized as an independent scholar and as a valuable co-worker with some of America's foremost historians. The outstanding American authority on the history of the Middle West, and particularly the influence of the frontier, Dr. Frederick Jackson Turner has repeatedly acknowledged Mr. Iglehart's authority in everything pertaining to the "Lincoln country" in Southern Indiana. Many other eminent scholars have acknowledged their debt to the helpfulness of Mr. Iglehart, including Charles G. Vannest, author of Lincoln The Hoosier, who obtained most of his material from the Southwestern Indiana Historical Society and says that without the aid furnished by Mr. Iglehart the book could not have been written. Doctor Turner in a letter to Mr. Iglehart commenting upon the Vannest book pays him a tribute which among historical investigators is perhaps the highest meed of praise: "At any rate, you and such followers as this author have redeemed Southern Indiana from much misconception in respect to its early society."

FRANK EDWARDS. The Edwards family were early settlers in Franklin Township, Putnam County, where several generations of the name have lived, people of industry and highly respected qualities as citizens.

A representative of this family is Frank Edwards, the merchant at Bainbridge, Putnam County. He was born in Franklin Township, December 9, 1874. His father, James Edwards, was born in the same township in 1837 and spent his active life as a farmer. He died in February, 1910. James Edwards married Elizabeth Ann Hale, who was born in Putnam County and died in 1909. They had five children: Alice, wife of Lee A. Kars, of Coatsville, Indiana; Albert, of Indianapolis; Russell, who died in July, 1929; Frank; and Ina, wife of Harvey Black, of Indianapolis.

Frank Edwards grew up on a farm and attended public schools in Putnam Township. After leaving school he followed farming as an occupation for ten years. For five years he was in business at Bainbridge as a hardware merchant. He left that to become cashier of the local bank, which received his full energies during the next five years. Since then he has been a general merchant, and has a store which is extensively patronized from all over this section of Putnam County.

Mr. Edwards is also township trustee, having been elected to that office in 1927. He is a democrat in politics, is a Royal Arch Mason and member of the Modern Woodmen of America. On February 22, 1894, he married Daisy Prather. They have four children. The daughter Crystal is the wife of Geddes Priest, of Bainbridge, and has two children, Louis, born in 1918, and Vivian, born in 1920. Ruby is the wife of Raymond Galbreath, and their two children are Betty F., born in 1919, and John, born in 1924. James married Mildred Brody and lives at Bainbridge. Frank, unmarried, is a resident of Michigan.

Fred C. Rothermel

REV. FRED C. ROTHERMEL is a scholarly and hard working representative of the Catholic Church in Indiana, and his labors have identified him with several communities in the northern part of the state prior to coming to Kentland, where he has taken up his labors as priest of the parish with an enthusiasm that promises important results.

He was born at Logansport, Indiana, March 7, 1889. His father, Joseph C. Rothermel, was born in Phillipsburg, Baden, Germany, December 28, 1864, and came to this country when a young man. The mother was Anna Goltz, who came from Kolmar, formerly in Prussia to the United States when a young girl. There were three children, Rev. Fred C., being the oldest of five children, two deceased. Otto J., a machinist living at Columbus, Ohio, married Maria Rose and has two children. Edward, who is in business at Logansport, married Nellie Sales, who was born at Delphi, Indiana, and they have four children.

Rev. Fred C. Rothermel was educated at St. Joseph parochial school of Logansport and took his classical and theological training in St. Meinrad Seminary, Spencer County, Indiana. He was ordained to the priesthood at Fort Wayne, June 16, 1916. His first assignment of duty was at Michigan City, where he remained six years, and during that time he acted as Catholic chaplain to the state penitentiary. Leaving Michigan City, he was for three years assistant pastor of St. Mary's Church, Crown Point, and then four years pastor of St. Joseph's Church, Reynolds, Indiana.

On February 3, 1930, he took up his work at Kentland. Father Rothermel is a fourth degree Knight of Columbus and is vice president of the Kentland Lions Club.

LOUIS G. SPRADLEY, M. D., has won success and prestige that distinctly indicate him as one of the skilled and popular physicians and surgeons of his native county, and at Boonville, judicial center of Warrick County, he is associated in active general practice with his elder brother, Dr. Norman M. Spradley, in whose personal sketch on other pages of this publication are given such adequate data concerning the family history as to make unnecessary any further review of the same in the present connection.

Dr. Louis G. Spradley was born on the old home farm in Warrick County, March 18, 1871. His boyhood and youth were marked by due participation in the activities of the farm and by consistent application to study in the public schools, including the high school. In the City of Louisville, Kentucky, he found excellent medium for fitting himself for the exacting profession of his choice, and there he was graduated in the Louisville Medical College as a member of the class of 1893. His reception of the degree of Doctor of Medicine was followed by his return to his native county, where he was engaged in practice at Selvin several years. He next gave twenty years to effective professional activity at Tennyson, this county, and during the ensuing six years he had his professional headquarters at Chrisney, Spencer County. In the winter of 1928-29 he returned to Warrick County and entered into a professional partnership with his older brother, Dr. Norman M. Spradley, at Boonville, the county seat, where they control a substantial and representative general practice, in which they prove specially effective coadjutors.

Dr. Louis G. Spradley has active membership in the Warrick County Medical Society and the Indiana State Medical Society, his political alignment is in the ranks of the Democratic party, and he is affiliated with the Masonic fraternity and the Independent Order of Odd Fellows.

At Selvin, this county, on the 3rd of July, 1894, Doctor Spradley was united in marriage to Miss Laura E. Gentry, daughter of Timothy and Belle (McKinley) Gentry, both of whom were born at Boonville, Timothy Gentry having been prominent as a farmer and as a hotel man in his native county and having served as county commissioner. Leta, eldest of the children of Doctor and Mrs. Spradley, is the wife of Ralph Davis, a skilled mechanic. They reside at DeGonia Springs, Warrick County, and their two children are Russell and June. Thelma is the wife of Earl G. Phillips, who is employed in connection with the Government postoffice service in the City of Chicago, and their one child is a daughter, Jean. Fay, youngest of the children, remains at the parental home and is (1929) a student in the high school of Boonville.

EDD B. WETHEROW, superintendent of schools at La Porte, has enjoyed his work in the educational field since early manhood. He has a high standing among Indiana educators, particularly in the northern counties, which have been the scene of his work.

Mr. Wetherow was born in Preble County, Ohio, May 8, 1878, son of Harvey and Sarah Ann (Harvey) Wetherow. His father was born and reared in Grant County, Indiana, attended school there and followed farming as his occupation. He married, September 29, 1875, and then moved to Ohio, where he was engaged in farming until his death. His wife was born in Preble County, Ohio, but was reared in Howard County, Indiana, where her parents owned a farm of 300 acres. She was one of nine children. Harvey Wetherow died November 19, 1887, and was buried at Concord, in Preble County, Ohio. After his death his widow lived in Union County, Indiana, for three years, and then in Howard County. She was married, December 19, 1895, to George H. Pormen, and the one son of this marriage is Russel Pormen. Mrs. Pormen passed away March 15, 1931, at Gaston, Indiana, and is buried at Converse.

Edd B. Wetherow, the only child of his mother's first marriage, attended public schools in Preble County, Ohio, in Union County, and in Howard County, Indiana. He graduated from the Converse High School in 1899. His training for his educational work was obtained in Indiana University, Columbia

University and the University of Chicago. Mr. Wetherow for eight years taught school in Miami County, three years at Deedsville and five years at Converse, where during four years of the time he was principal of the high school. On June 7, 1907, he was elected county superintendent of schools of Miami County and held that office for two terms, ten years. On August 1, 1917, he became city superintendent of schools at Peru. On August 1, 1919, he was appointed state school inspector, by Mr. L. N. Hines, State Superintendent of Public Instruction. He resigned on August 1, 1922, to accept the position of superintendent of city schools at La Porte.

Mr. Wetherow is a member of the North Central Indiana Teachers Association, Indiana State Teachers Association, is a life member of the National Education Association, and for several years has been a member of the International Relations Committee of the National Education Association in the World Federation of Education Associations. He is a member of the Indiana Schoolmen's Club. He belongs to Excelsior Lodge No. 41, F. and A. M., Converse Lodge of the Knights of Pythias, the Kiwanis Club, the Pi Gamma Mu fraternity, the Phi Delta Kappa fraternity, is a Republican, and an elder in the Christian Church.

Mr. Wetherow married at Indianapolis, June 26, 1921, Miss Maude Parkhurst, daughter of John W. and Ella (Blizzard) Parkhurst. Her father spent many years in the manufacturing business in making elevators in Indianapolis and Peru, and in making refrigerators in Peru and Richmond. Recently his home has been in Indianapolis.

Mrs. Wetherow attended grammar and high school at Indianapolis. She is a graduate of the Metropolitan School of Music in that city. She studied voice in Italy. She is a gifted musician, and has afforded a great deal of pleasure through her lovely soprano voice. She was music supervisor in the schools of Peru and for several years supervisor of music in the public schools of La Porte. Mrs. Wetherow is a member of the Christian Science Church.

WILLIAM GLADDEN is an Indiana farmer and stock man who has spent practically all his life in Lauramie Township, Tippecanoe County, where he was born March 10, 1865.

Gladden is an old and honored family name in Tippecanoe County. Mr. Gladden is a son of Richard and Fannie (Ellis) Gladden. His ancestors came from Leeds, England, settling in Virginia, and one of them was a soldier in the War of the Revolution. His grandfather, Richard Gladden, Sr., was a native of Virginia, moved to Montgomery County, Ohio, where he married, and subsequently lived in Preble County, and from there came to Tippecanoe County, Indiana, settling in Lauramie Township. He served as a justice of the peace while in Ohio and was a member of the Dunkard Church. William Gladden's father, Richard Gladden, was born in Montgomery County, Ohio, February 1, 1818. When he was seventeen years of age he took over the work of the home farm and was an industrious and highly respected citizen of Tippecanoe County for many years. He was a Whig in politics, cast his first vote for William Henry Harrison and later was a Republican.

William Gladden acquired his education at the Oak Grove School in Lauramie Township, and at an early age was trained to all the labors of the farm. At the age of nineteen he inherited from his father eighty acres of land, one mile west of Gladdens corner. When he was twenty-five he had accumulated enough to make his first purchase comprising forty acres. Some years later he purchased 200 acres, and now owns 320 acres, devoted to general farming purposes. He is a member of the Farm Bureau.

On December 24, 1890, Mr. Gladden was married to Willetta Mahoy, daughter of William and Mary (Horn) Mahoy, and of an Ohio family. To this union one child, Edith G., was born, December 25, 1891. She was married to Merle H. Skinner on July 10, 1911, and four children have graced this union: E. Gladden, Max E., William A. and Byron D. Mr. and Mrs. Gladden lived on the farm until 1912, when they moved to Stockwell, since making that their home. Mrs. Gladden is a member of the Methodist Church, being active in all phases of church work. Mr. Gladden is liberal in his religious views but holding membership in no religious organization. In politics he is a stalwart Republican, but has never been an office seeker. The home life of Mr. Gladden is ideal and his own firesides to him the dearest spot on earth. He is greatly devoted to his grandchildren, and he counts no personal sacrifice too great that will enhance their happiness.

ALBERT J. HENRY is one of Michigan City's oldest business men. His associations with the lumber business there cover a period of nearly half a century. He was the founder of the Henry Lumber Company, one of the largest organizations of its kind in LaPorte County. Many years ago he served as sheriff of the county.

Mr. Henry was born at Pine Station, Pennsylvania, January 5, 1852, son of Thomas and Eliza (Shaner) Henry. Both parents were natives of Pennsylvania, his father was a farmer, and they are buried at Jersey Shore, Pennsylvania. They were members of the Methodist Episcopal Church. Their children were: Margaret, wife of H. T. Kessler, of Jersey Shore; Albert J.; Flora and Sada, deceased; Cordelia, wife of Walter Thompson, of Kankakaa, Illinois; and Harry W., deceased, who was a farmer and nurseryman at LaPorte and always active in farmers institute work, and his widow still lives at LaPorte and is the mother of Dan J. Henry, an attorney at Twin Falls, Idaho, and of a daughter, Marie Henry.

Albert J. Henry was educated in public schools at Pine Station and Jersey Shore,

Pennsylvania, and in early youth came west to Michigan. For ten years he was with Jonathan Boyce, in the lumber business at White Cloud, Michigan, and in 1882 was sent to Michigan City to manage the branch plant of the Boyce Lumber Company. In 1892 Mr. Henry bought out the Boyce interests, and for forty years has been in business for himself. The Henry Lumber Company has extensive yards and offices at the east end of the Sixth Street bridge. A force of from fifteen to twenty employees are on the payroll of the company. They handle all kinds of lumber and building materials, have a mill for the manufacture of sash and door and interior trim, and the business is a supply point for a large territory bounding Michigan City. In addition to being president of this company Mr. Henry is vice president of the Michigan City Trust & Savings Bank.

He has always been a staunch Republican in politics and was elected sheriff of LaPorte County in 1892. In Masonry he is affiliated with Acme Lodge No. 83, A. F. and A. M., Michigan City Chapter, Royal Arch Masons, the Council and Knights Templar Commandery, the Scottish Rite Consistory at Indianapolis. He is a charter member of the Rotary Club and is senior warden of Trinity Episcopal Church.

Mr. Henry married at Michigan City Miss Emma Frehse, daughter of Charles and Wilhelmina (Westphal) Frehse. Her parents were born and reared in Germany and the Westphal family were early settlers in La-Porte County. Her father was one of the early tailors of Michigan City. Both her parents are buried in the Greenwood Cemetery. Mrs. Henry attended school at Michigan City, was a worker in the Trinity Episcopal Church and was worthy matron of the Eastern Star Chapter. She died in October, 1926, and is buried in Greenwood. There were two sons.

Charles Lloyd Henry, born September 10, 1892, attended high school at Michigan City and was graduated from the University of Wisconsin in 1917. He spent eighteen months in France with the Twentieth Engineers during the World war, holding the rank of sergeant. Since the war he has been associated with his father and brother in the lumber business and is vice president of the company. He is also president of the Michigan City Auto Finance Company, is a member of the Masonic fraternity, B. P. O. Elks, Lions Club, and the Alpha Sigma Phi fraternity. His first wife was Phyllis DeVoe, of Freeport, Illinois, who died, leaving two children, Phyllis and Thomas Lloyd. His second wife was Gertrude Robinson, daughter of Mr. and Mrs. R. N. Robinson, of Michigan City.

Albert J. Henry, Jr., was born at Michigan City July 13, 1894. He graduated from the local high school in 1913 and from the University of Winconsin in 1917, and since 1918 has been with the Henry Lumber Company, of which he is secretary and treasurer. He is also a director of the People's Loan & Mortgage Company and has many active interests that identify him prominently with the civic affairs of his community.

While in Wisconsin University he was an Alpha Sigma Phi. He is a member of the Chamber of Commerce, Rotary Club, B. P. O. Elks, Pottawattamie Country Club and the Trinity Episcopal Church. In politics he votes independently.

Albert J. Henry, Jr., married in Michigan City, June 2, 1920, Miss Mildred Isabel Riley, daughter of John J. and Harriet (Fleming) Riley. Her father until he retired a few years ago was in the glove manufacturing business at Michigan City. Her mother died in 1921 and is buried in the Greenwood cemetery. Mrs. Albert J. Henry, Jr., graduated from the Michigan City High School in 1916. He is a member of St. Mary's Catholic Church and is interested in Red Cross and child welfare work. They have two children, Albert J. III and Harriet Lois, both in school at Michigan City.

ROBERT TRAVIS WILSON, who since 1926 has succeeded in establishing himself in a valuable law practice in his native community of Michigan City, was born there July 10, 1903.

His father is Dr. LeRoy Wilson, prominent Michigan City physician and surgeon. Doctor Wilson was born in Ohio, in 1874, and his mother now lives at Michigan City, at the age of eighty-one. He spent three years in the University of Michigan and while there was a member of the university baseball team. In 1899 he was graduated in medicine from the University of Illinois and for over thirty years has been a leader in his profession at Michigan City. About 1920 he and associates established the Michigan City Clinic. He is a member of the LaPorte County, Indiana State and American Medical Associations, the B. P. O. Elks, Rotary Club, and the First Presbyterian Church. Doctor Wilson married Harriet Travis, who is active in the League of Women Voters and the Woman's Study Club. Her father, Curtis Travis, was a prominent farmer and land owner near La-Porte, where at one time he owned five or six sections of land. His brother altered the spelling of the family name to Travers and was the founder of Traverse City, Michigan.

Robert T. Wilson, only child of his parents, attended public schools at Michigan City, the Culver Military Academy of Indiana, also Northwestern Military Academy, and was graduated from high school in 1921. During the period of the World war he was in the Reserve Officers Training Corps in the training camp of Northwestern University at Lake Geneva, Wisconsin, so that he had completed his training for a commission at the time the war ended. Mr. Wilson spent two years in Ohio Wesleyan University and in 1926 was graduated from the law department of Indiana University and admitted to the bar the same year. He has since been admitted to practice before the Indiana Supreme Court. His law offices are at 622 Franklin Street. He is a member of the Michigan City,

LaPorte County and Indiana State Bar Associations and has served as special city judge and as special deputy prosecutor. He is secretary of the Kanney System, Inc., a director of the Cushman Bond & Mortgage Company of Michigan City and Chicago.

Mr. Wilson enjoys a number of contacts with local organizations. He is vice president of the Lions Club, a member of the B. P. O. Elks, Pottawatamie Country Club, Chamber of Commerce, and is a Republican. He is a Delta Tau Delta and while in Indiana University was one of the pitchers on the baseball squad and a member of the class football squad, and was vice president of his class. He is active in Y. M. C. A. work and his favorite sports are fishing and golf.

Mr. Wilson married at LaPorte, June 24, 1926, Miss Geneva Lutman, daughter of William H. and Elizabeth Lutman. Her father owns a monument business in LaPorte and is a past master of the Masonic Lodge there, and her mother was worthy matron of the Eastern Star in 1931. Mrs. Wilson graduated from the LaPorte High School. She is a member of the Baptist Church, the Eastern Star and the Woman's Club. Mr. and Mrs. Wilson have one son, Robert Gene Wilson, born March 24, 1927.

BYRON HUMMER, prominent Michigan City undertaker, has had many years of successful experience in that line of work, having started it soon after leaving school.

Mr. Hummer was born in St. Joseph County, Indiana, August 26, 1881. The Hummer family were pioneers of Northern Indiana. His grandfather, Washington Hummer, came to St. Joseph County from Ohio, and it was his part to clear up and develop one of the early homesteads in St. Joseph County. Both he and his wife are buried in the Sumption Prairie Cemetery in that county. Byron Hummer's parents were William and Aldretta (Rupe) Hummer. His father was born in St. Joseph County, in March, 1843, attended the schools of the early days and spent his active life as a farmer and stock raiser. He died in September, 1921, at the age of seventy-eight, and is buried at Sumption Prairie. His widow, Aldretta Rupe, is now eighty and still lives at the old home farm. She was also born and reared in St. Joseph County, and is a devout Methodist. Of her four children one died in infancy. The others are: Arthur B., a farmer at the home place; Elbert, also a farmer in St. Joseph County; and Byron.

Byron Hummer attended school in St. Joseph County, including the high school at Walkerton. After leaving school he spent four years with his uncle, H. A. Yerrick, in the furniture and undertaking business at Walkerton. From there he went to South Bend and for two years was with the undertaking firm of N. L. Jones. Mr. Hummer has been a resident of Michigan City since 1906. He was associated in the undertaking business with A. F. Earl until 1927, in which year he established a business of his own. At 716 Washington Street he has a well appointed funeral home, and he has labored through many years to build up and develop a very careful service and has assembled all modern equipment.

Mr. Hummer is affiliated with Acme Lodge No. 83, A. F. and A. M., the B. P. O. Elks, Loyal Order of Moose, and for several years was active in the Rotary Club. He votes as an independent.

Mr. Hummer married at St. Joseph, Michigan, May 18, 1923, Miss Zoe Shear, daughter of Rev. Charles B. and Antoinette (Smith) Shear. Her father gave his active life to the ministry of the Congregational Church. He was a graduate of Oberlin College, Ohio, and labored in several important pastorates, including Lansing, Michigan, Bowling Green, Ohio, Marietta, Ohio, and Grand Rapids, Michigan. Mrs. Shear was a graduate of Hillsdale College of Michigan and was a schoolmate of Will Carleton, famous poet. Rev. Mr. Shear passed away in 1905, surviving his wife several years, and both are buried at Hudson, Michigan. Mrs. Hummer attended grammar and high school at Grand Rapids. For several years she was in the millinery business and has charge of the office detail in the Hummer Undertaking Company.

EDWARD JOHN HEISE, city clerk of Michigan City, is a veteran public official of the community, and in his present office he has served an aggregate of over twenty years.

Mr. Heise was born at Michigan City, October 9, 1874, a member of a substantial family that has been identified with this community for nearly eighty years. His grandfather, Charles Heise, brought his family from Germany about 1854 and settled at Michigan City. He and his wife are buried in the Greenwood Cemetery there. Edward J. Heise is a son of Henry G. and Rebecca S. (Freeman) Heise. Henry G. Heise was born in Germany, in 1848, and was about six years of age when brought to America. He was reared and educated in Michigan City. For some years he was in the fishing industry, served as city marshal, and was at one time bridge operator at Franklin Street. He was a leader in the Democratic party. He died in 1917, at the age of sixty-eight, and is buried in the Greenwood Cemetery. His wife, Rebecca Freeman, was born and reared in Michigan City, and has been an active worker in the First Methodist Episcopal Church for many years. One of her brothers was a soldier in the Civil war and many of her uncles were also in the war. She is now eighty-five years of age. For a number of years she has been color bearer in the Woman's Relief Corps of the Grand Army of the Republic. Of her eight children two died in infancy, and the others are: Henry A., of Michigan City; Fred C., of Michigan City; George F., of LaPorte; Edward John; Loula, Mrs. George A. Lewis, of Michigan City; and Pearl, Mrs. Ralph Hartley, of Michigan City.

Edward John Heise was educated in the grammar and high schools at Michigan City and attended Compton's Business College. For some time he did the work of a public stenographer. It was in 1898 that he was first elected to the office of city clerk, being then twenty-three years of age. He served continuously for sixteen years, from 1898 to 1914. Following that he was collector of water rents for the city, then was appointed to the office of township trustee and later elected to the same office, serving a term of four years, until 1924. On January 1, 1924, he was appointed city clerk, and in the fall of 1929 was elected to that office by popular vote.

Mr. Heise has been active in Chamber of Commerce work. He is a Republican in politics, a member of the B. P. O. Elks, Junior Order United American Mechanics, Independent Order of Odd Fellows, Loyal Order of Moose. For a number of years he has acted as financial secretary for the First Methodist Episcopal Church. His recreation is motoring.

Mr. Heise married at Benton Harbor, Michigan, January 8, 1906, Miss Emma G. Voitel, of New Buffalo, Michigan, daughter of William and Elizabeth (Crone) Voitel. Her father in early years was an employee of the Michigan Central railway and is a retired farmer and stock man at New Buffalo. Her mother died in 1921 and is buried at New Buffalo. Mrs. Heise attended the grammar and high school there. Her chief interest has been in her home and family. She is a member of the Methodist Church, the Rebekahs and the Woman's Relief Corps. The three children of Mr. and Mrs. Heise are Edward John, Jr., Ruth Lillie and Elizabeth (Betty). The son Edward graduated from the Michigan City High School in 1927. He is a talented musician, a performer on the saxaphone and piano. The daughter Ruth was also educated in the public schools, has given much attention to her music and is the pianist for the Sunday School of the First Methodist Church and for the Rebekah Lodge, in which she holds the highest chair. The youngest child is attending public school.

HON. ANDREW J. HICKEY, who represented the Thirteenth Indiana District in Congress from 1919 to 1931, is a prominent member of the LaPorte bar.

He was born in Orleans County, New York, August 27, 1872, son of John and Jane (Gould) Hickey. His father was an engineer, contractor and builder, and died in 1918, at the age of eighty-eight. His mother was born in Connecticut and died in November, 1917, at the age of eighty-one. Both parents are buried at Buffalo, New York. There were four children: Martha A., Jennie G., Andrew J. and William J. Both sons are attorneys, William being a resident of Buffalo.

Andrew J. Hickey attended school in Buffalo, spent two years in college at Rochester, studied law and was admitted to the bar in 1896. In 1897 he located at LaPorte, which has been the home and the scene of his successful professional career for over a third of a century. He served as county attorney, and in 1918 was elected to Congress, where he served six successive terms. He is now senior member of the law firm of Hickey & Dilworth, with offices in the First National Bank Building. He is a member of the LaPorte County and Indiana State Bar Associations, is a Knight Templar Mason and Shriner, member of the Elks, Odd Fellows, Woodmen of the World, Kiwanis Club and the Methodist Episcopal Church. Mr. Hickey is unmarried.

THE FIRST NATIONAL BANK & TRUST COMPANY OF LAPORTE is not only one of the oldest national banks in Northern Indiana, with a long and splendid history as a financial institution, but is also interesting because of the many prominent men, first and last, who have been identified with this bank during the nearly seventy-five years of its history.

In one sense the bank carries on the splendid traditions of the Bank of the State of Indiana, one of the soundest of the state banks in early American finance. A branch of this bank was established at LaPorte in 1857. With the passage of the National Banking Act in 1863 banks of issue, that is, those whose bank notes were used as currency, soon went out of existence. The old LaPorte branch was succeeded by a private bank known as Hall, Weaver & Company. The active head of this bank for many years was Hart L. Weaver. Associated with him were his son, Louis B. Weaver, and Seth Eason, father of Mrs. R. R. Ingersoll.

In the meantime, in 1864, the year after the passage of the National Banking Act, the First National Bank of LaPorte was organized. The first president was Aurora Case, and the first cashier, Hiram P. Holbrook. Robert S. Morrison soon afterwards became cashier. Ezekiel Morrison became president in 1872, following the death of Aurora Case. He was succeeded by Sidney S. Sabin in 1884. Mrs. Sidney Sabin perpetuated the family name in the community by establishing the Ruth C. Sabin Home. In 1887 William Niles was elected president. Mr. Niles was succeeded by Herbert W. Fox as president in January, 1924. Other officials have included Henry Morrison and his son, F. H. Morrison, who served at various times as vice president and director; Frank J. Pitner, for many years cashier, now senior vice president, who has been with the bank continuously since 1884.

In February, 1913, the First National Bank and the Bank of the State of Indiana, the latter having been incorporated in 1905, as the successor of Hall, Weaver & Company, became affiliated, as a result of the sale of the Weaver interests in the latter institution to Herbert W. Fox, Edward F. Michael, William A. Martin and others. On February 18, 1926, the name of the Bank of the State of Indiana was changed to that of First Trust & Savings Bank. On October 9, 1914, a new banking house was opened to accommodate both institutions and on January 1, 1929, the two banks were completely merged under the name of the First National Bank & Trust Company of LaPorte. At that time there was formed the First LaPorte Securities Company, an investment subsidiary. At the time of affiliation, in 1913, the total deposits of the two banks amounted to approximately $1,840,000, and the combined assets approximately $2,190,000. The total resources on March 25, 1931, were over $5,430,000, the total deposits being approximately $4,520,000.

Under the leadership of Mr. Herbert W. Fox, the president, the institution has not only grown but has exemplified the service in keeping with its historical traditions. It is not only the largest bank in LaPorte County, but one of the strongest in Northern Indiana.

WALTER E. HECK, proprietor of the St. Charles Hotel in the fine little City of Boonville, county seat of Warrick County, and owner of one of the model farm estates of this section of Indiana, is able to revert to the old Buckeye State as the place of his nativity, his birth having occurred on his father's farm near Arcanum, Darke County, Ohio, October 15, 1884. He is a son of Elijah and Alice (Burnet) Heck, both of whom were born in Montgomery County, Ohio.

Elijah Heck devoted virtually his entire active life to productive farm industry, and was one of the sterling and venerable citizens of Darke County, Ohio, at the time of his death, in 1918, when he was seventy-two years of age. His father was born in Pennsylvania, a representative of one of the fine old German families there identified with the religious organization known as Dunkards, and was for many years superintendent of the Montgomery County Infirmary in Ohio, he having retained the Dunkard faith, as did also his father, who was known as Indian Heck, a native of Germany and who removed from Pennsylvania to Ohio in the pioneer period of the history of the latter state. He settled in Montgomery County, there reclaimed and developed a farm, and his real estate holdings there included the site of the present Phillips Hotel in the City of Dayton. Two of his grandsons, uncles of the subject of this review, now reside on his old home farm, seven miles west of Dayton. Elijah and Alice (Burnet) Heck became the parents of nine children, including a pair of twins and also triplets, one of the twins, all of the triplets and one other child having died in infancy. Burnette, eldest of the four surviving children, is general manager for the Studebaker Motor Company of South Bend, Indiana. He married Miss Louette Basil, who was born at New Bremen, Ohio, and they have three children: Kenneth, Elizabeth and Burnette, Jr. Clara is the wife of Matthias Shields, a farmer in Darke County, Ohio, and they have five children: Lloyd, Irene, Mary, Byron, Aubrey and Eugene. Fanny is the wife of Henry Everheart, a merchant at Greenville, Ohio, and they have three children: Howard, Roland and Charles. Walter E., of this sketch, is the youngest of the surviving children.

Walter E. Heck was reared on the home farm in Darke County, Ohio, and supplemented the discipline of the district school by a short period of high school study. Upon leaving the parental home he went to Dayton, Ohio, and entered the employ of the Ohio Rake Company, in the establishment of which he served a four years' apprenticeship to the trade of machinist. At the age of nineteen years he found employment with the Union Traction Company in the City of Indianapolis, Indiana, with which he served as a motor man six years. He then assumed the position of engineer in the T. B. Laycock bed manufactory in Indianapolis, with which concern he remained until 1922. After the death of his father he returned to the old home and assisted his widowed mother in adjusting the affairs of the estate, the mother being now with her youngest daughter in the latter's home at Greenville, Ohio. After remaining one year at the old home in Ohio Mr. Heck returned to Indiana and established his residence at Boonville. By his judicious investments he had in the meanwhile accumulated appreciable capital, and upon locating at Boonville he soon purchased a farm estate of 308 acres, eight miles east of the city. The entire area of this valuable land is available for cultivation, and in addition to carrying on well ordered operations in diversified agriculture Mr. Heck gives special attention to the raising of fine types of cattle and hogs. His farm is maintained at the best modern standard, and in its equipment he has expended about $10,800 for machinery and implements alone, he having paid $15,500 for the land, so that the farm estate represents large investment, even as it stands forth as the stage of most progressive methods in modern agricultural and live stock industry. In purchasing and equipping his farm Mr. Heck had sufficient funds to enable him to make the investments without assuming any indebtedness, and this fact stands in evidence of his exceptional business acumen. In addition to giving general supervision to the varied activities of his farm Mr. Heck is proprietor of the St. Charles Hotel at Boonville, which he opened April 8, 1929, and his conducting of which marks it as one of the modern and well ordered hotels in this section of the state. He makes daily visits to his farm and carefully directs the work of his various employes on the place.

Mr. Heck and his wife harmonize in their political allegiance, as in all other relations, and both are aligned with the Democratic party. His financial investments and his business and industrial enterprises in Warrick County mark Mr. Heck as one of the progressive and influential exponents of civic and material progress within its borders, and it is pleasing to note that his substantial success has been won by his own ability and efforts.

Mr. Heck purchased the St. Charles Hotel in the earlier part of 1928 and paid cash for the property. It was conducted the first six months thereafter by a lessee, Mr. Taylor, and was then closed for remodeling. In bringing the building and its equipment up to modern standard Mr. Heck expended more than $10,000, and since its reopening, April 8, 1929, he has continued in the active management of the hotel and made it one of the best communal assets of Boonville.

At New Albany, Indiana, on the 12th of November, 1904, Mr. Heck was united in marriage to Miss Pearl A. Wayman, who is a daughter of Edmond Jeremiah Wayman and Priscilla (Hurley) Wayman, the former of whom was born in Indiana and the latter in Livingston County, Kentucky. Edmond J. Wayman, whose death occurred in 1909, was a cabinetmaker by trade and became known also as an inventor, besides which he was long engaged in the wholesale grocery business. Of the three children Mrs. Heck is the youngest; Nannie is the widow of William Medcalf, and Eugene is engaged in the advertising business in Ohio. Mr. and Mrs. Heck have two children: Beatrice, born February 28, 1906, is the wife of William Hahn, who is in railway clerical service, and their one child, Mary, is three years old at the time of this writing, in the summer of 1929. Chester, younger of the two children, was born April 8, 1913, and is a member of the class of 1930 in the Boonville High School.

EDWARD BUCHANAN is vice president of the Vincennes Auto Sales Company, which corporation functions as representative of the Chrysler automobiles and which maintains well equipped headquarters at 901 Main Street in the historic and vital city of Vincennes, the judicial center of Knox County. In this city the birth of Mr. Buchanan occurred in the year 1901, and here also were born his parents, Charles and Ella (Joyce) Buchanan, the latter a daughter of William Joyce, who was a gallant soldier of the Union in the Civil war. Charles Buchanan still resides in Vincennes, where he is an executive of the Inter-State Power Company, his father, William Buchanan, having been born in Kentucky and having thence come to Vincennes when he was a youth. Charles and Ella (Joyce) Buchanan have four children: Mary, Ellen, Edward and Mildred.

In his native city Edward Buchanan received the advantages of St. Francis Xavier parochial school, and at the age of fifteen years he found employment in a local bakery. His association with the automobile business was initiated in 1920, when he became an agent for the Ford cars, with headquarters at Mitchell, Lawrence County. Three years later he sold his interest in this agency and returned to Vincennes where he became associated with Harry Glynn in establishing the present Chrysler agency, the business being incorporated and being conducted under the title of Vincennes Auto Sales Company. This agency was established in 1924 and has developed a substantial and prosperous business that gives it much of priority in the automotive trade in Vincennes and Knox County. Mr. Glynn is president and Mr. Buchanan vice president of the company. The company's establishment utilizes a floor space of 5,500 square feet, and its sales, display and service departments are of the best modern equipment. The company retains a corps of eighteen employes and its service in all departments is maintained at high standard.

Mr. Buchanan is a Democrat in political allegiance and is affiliated with the local organizations of the Benevolent and Protective Order of Elks and the Fraternal Order of Eagles.

WILLIAM E. DAVISSON. An efficient, popular and trustworthy public official of Pike County, Indiana, is William E. Davisson, postmaster of the City of Petersburg, where he has been long active in business circles and civic affairs. For practically all his life he has resided at Petersburg, for he was born and educated here as was his father, the late William K. Davisson, his paternal grandfather having settled in Pike County in pioneer days. As the eldest son in his parents' large family Postmaster Davisson began almost in boyhood to make himself useful to his father, and later, on developing business capacity, entered a Petersburg mercantile house as a clerk. In those days but comparatively small salaries were paid, but then, as now, industry, efficiency and fidelity were noted and rewarded. When Mr. Davisson retired from the business some eighteen years later it was as general manager and purchasing agent, and drew one of the largest salaries paid by the company. For some years afterward he conducted a business of his own, but sold it when he was appointed postmaster, in February, 1927, and public duties have more or less claimed his time and attention ever since.

Postmaster Davisson was born at Petersburg, Indiana, June 14, 1886, a son of William K. and Louisa (Burton) Davisson. The father was a carpenter and contractor of Pike County, and he died in November, 1914. The mother, who was born in Dubois County, Indiana, died December, 1926. Of the eight children born to them, four died in infancy, and one, Edna, died in 1922, so that Postmaster Davisson has only two sisters living, they being: Anna, who married J. A. Lory, of Vincennes, Indiana, has two children; and Carrie, who married Lawrence Martin, of Petersburg, has six children.

Growing to manhood at Petersburg, Postmaster Davisson attended the common and high schools of his home town, and was a diligent student, but preferred business to professional life so did not take collegiate training. From his youth up it has been his policy to save a portion of his earnings whether his salary was large or small, and during his latter years in the general mercantile business, when he was drawing $4,000 annually, he was able to lay aside a considerable amount, and with his fund thus accumulated, in 1921, he established himself in the shoe business and conducted it profitably for six and one-half years, and then sold at a profit. His appointment as postmaster was made by President Coolidge, and under his businesslike conduct of the Government affairs under his charge the Petersburg office holds high rank in its class.

On April 17, 1923, Postmaster Davisson was married to Myrtle G. Lemmon. There are no children by this marriage, but two daughters of a former marriage were born to him, Doris and Vivian. Doris is the wife of J. Taff, and lives at Indianapolis, Indiana, no children. Before her marriage she was a public-school teacher, having prepared for that work in Hanover College and the University of Indiana. Vivian was graduated from the Petersburg High School, and is now a student of the University of Indiana.

Postmaster Davisson is a Republican, and a very active factor in the local party. The Presbyterian Church holds his membership, and he is one of the leaders in all church work, being especially zealous with reference to that of the young people. He is also state corresponding secretary for the Young Men's Christian Association. His financial connections are those which he maintains with the Independent Order of Odd Fellows. In addition to his salary as postmaster Mr. Davisson has other resources, for he has invested his earnings in Petersburg real estate. He has been interested in every movement having for its object the advancing of the interests of Petersburg and Pike County, and by his activity, influence and investments, has done much to promote the industrial and commercial welfare of this region. His personal influence is devoted at all times to work calculated to elevate the people, and to maintain high standards of morality and right living. Above all he believes in Christian living, honest government, with a square deal and justice to all.

HARRY WARREN SUTTON. The Sutton family were early settlers in Eastern Indiana, several generations of the name living in Randolph County. One of the pioneers there was Samuel Sutton.

His son, Isaac C. Sutton, was born in Randolph County and when only sixteen years of age enlisted in the Union army and served for about a year and a half, when he was discharged on account of disability. After the war he took up railroading and was conductor of the first train run over the Panhandle Railway through Indiana. Isaac C. Sutton in 1869 moved to Missouri and from there went to Todd County, Minnesota, filing on a homestead which was well out on the frontier. In 1871 he became a merchant in Todd County, and continued active in business there until 1889, when he sold his interests and moved to Salem, Oregon. For twenty years he was connected with the Oregon State Hospital at Salem and then retired. He died at Salem in 1915.

Isaac C. Sutton married Levina Whipple. She represented a Colonial and Revolutionary family. Her great-grandfather, John Whipple, was a captain in Washington's army. Mrs. Sutton died at Salem, Oregon, in 1908. The four children of Isaac C. Sutton and wife were: Frank A., Harry Warren, Daisy E. and Jason O. Frank, whose home is at Portland, Oregon, married Daisy Lafountaine and has two children. Daisy Sutton married Will Rogers and has five children. Jason O. Sutton made his home for many years in California and died in February, 1929.

Harry Warren Sutton is also a native of Indiana, and was born at Deerfield, Randolph County, January 18, 1869. He was just an infant when his family moved to Minnesota, and he grew up in Todd County of that state. He received his public school education there and as an employee of his father was given a thorough fundamental training in all the branches of general merchandising, including groceries, clothing and hardware. He went with his parents to Salem, Oregon, and was salesman in a hardware business there until 1903.

Mr. Sutton since 1904 has been a traveling representative of the Zion Institutions and Industries at Zion City, Illinois. He is a special representative of the office supply and printing department of this industrial organization. He has been in the service of the Zion Institution for a quarter of a century and for six years of that time acted as commissioner of public works at Zion. He is a member of the Illinois Chamber of Commerce and a Republican in politics.

Mr. Sutton married, December 22, 1888, Miss Minerva Sutton, daughter of Edward J. and Sarah (Smith) Sutton. Four children were born to their marriage, the daughter Mary dying at the age of eighteen months. Irving, who is a merchant and manufacturer, married Cornelia White and has five children. Elmer J., a machinist, lives at Corpus Christi, Texas, married Alice Libbie Reah and has a son and two daughters. Andrew, city desk sergeant at Zion, Illinois, married Ethel Woodward and has a son.

COL. RICHARD LIEBER, director of conservation, with the Department of Conservation of the State of Indiana, was born at St. Johann-Saarbruecken, Germany, September 5, 1869, son of Otto and Maria (Richter) Lieber. He was educated in the Municipal Lyceum and Royal Lyceum at Dusseldorf, Germany, and came to the United States in 1891, when twenty-two years of age, and ten years later acquired American citizenship.

During his early years in America, Colonel Lieber was associated with the Indianapolis Journal and the Indianapolis Tribune, and subsequently with the importing and jobbing house of James R. Ross & Company.

He has been director of conservation since 1917. He was chairman of the Indiana State Park Commission from 1915 to 1919 and secretary of the Indiana State Board of Forestry in 1917-19. In 1912 he was chairman of the Board of Governors of the Fourth National Conservation Congress and has served as director of the National State Park Conference. He is an honorary member of the Association of Park Departments and the Indiana Nature Study Club.

Colonel Lieber was military secretary, with the rank of colonel, to Governor Goodrich during 1917-21. He was chairman of the Indianapolis Civil Service Commission in 1909-10 and president of the Indianapolis Trade Association in 1910-12, and is also former president of the Merchants and Manufacturers Insurance Bureau.

REUBEN WADE ELLIS, Tippecanoe farmer, who has successfully specialized in live stock and in seed corn, represents one of the oldest families of Lauramie Township. He was born on the farm where he now resides, in 1867.

The Ellis family has been in America since Colonial times. His great-grandparents were Rawland and Frances (Breadwater) Ellis. Rawland Ellis was born in Virginia and served as a soldier in the American Revolution. For his military service he was granted a tract of land at Guilford Court House, North Carolina, but sold it without occupying it. He lived out his life in old Virginia. His son, Thomas Ellis, was born near Moorefield in Hardy County, in what is now West Virginia. As a young man he moved west to Cincinnati about the beginning of the nineteenth century and acquired 160 acres of land, part of which is now incorporated within the city limits of Cincinnati. From Cincinnati he moved to Dayton, Ohio. He served as a soldier in the War of 1812. During the administration of President Andrew Jackson he came to Indiana and entered an eighty acre farm in Lauramie Township, Tippecanoe County. He also entered eighty acres of prairie land. Thomas Ellis married Elizabeth Stoner and they had a family of twelve children, named John, Mahalia, Joseph, Hannah, Mary, Frances, Sarah, James, Barbara, Eliza, Ann and Elizabeth.

The parents of Reuben Wade Ellis were John and Harriet (Lambkin) Ellis. Harriet Lambkin was born in Kent, England. John Ellis was born in Montgomery County, Ohio, but spent most of his life in Tippecanoe County, where he died in 1894 and is buried in the Conroe Cemetery. He was a teacher, a farmer and stock man, served as a justice of the peace, and was a real and trusted leader of his community. He and his wife had six children: Mary A., who married Ennis Coe; Martha K.; Reuben W.; William J.; one that died in infancy; and Florence M.

Reuben Wade Ellis acquired his education in the local schools. When he was only thirteen years of age he began to take most of the responsibility of running the farm. His mother had died and his father was in poor health. Later he spent about a year in California, working in the lumber business, and for a time was in the real estate business in Chicago. Otherwise his active years have been devoted to his Tippecanoe County farm.

Mr. Ellis married in November, 1895, Rose Nalley, daughter of Simon and Helen (McLean) Nalley. Her father was from Pennsylvania and her mother was born in Indiana of Maine parents. Mr. and Mrs. Ellis have six children: Harriett, wife of Reed Paddock and mother of two children, named Mary R. and Phillip J.; Miss Helen F.; Miss Florence; Mary, wife of Willis Lovless; Martha, wife of Lawrence Rice; and John R.

Mr. Ellis has served on the township advisory board. For many years he has handled pure bred live stock, and in recent years has specialized in the production of seed corn. His farm products have been exhibited at fairs and have won ten gold medals. Mr. Ellis has also been a commercial salesman.

JAMES WALTER EHRINGER. During an active and successful career that has covered a period of three decades, James Walter Ehringer, of Lawrenceburg, has been identified with several concerns of national reputation, to the prosperity of each of which he has contributed by his energy and ability. Possessed of both mechanical and executive ability, he has so combined these qualities as to make his services valuable to any modern manufacturing company, and at present he occupies the important position of manager of the Ohlen Bishop Company, whose large saw works are located at Lawrenceburg.

James Walter Ehringer was born at Jeffersonville, Indiana, in 1877, and is a son of George and Martha (McCune) Ehringer, and a grandson of George Ehringer, Sr., an early settler of Indiana and a member of an honorable pioneer family. George Ehringer, the younger, was educated for the vocation of marine engineer, which he followed with success throughout his life, and was a man of high character, who was esteemed and respected in each of the communities in which he made his home. He and his worthy wife, who was also a native of Indiana, were the parents of eight children.

James Walter Ehringer attended the public schools of Jeffersonville, and after his graduation from high school enrolled as a student at Purdue University, from which institution he was duly graduated as a member of the class of 1900, receiving the degree of Bachelor of Arts. He entered upon his independent career as an employe of the Lunkenheimer Company, manufacturers of engineering specialties, and then for a period tried his hand at journalism, being identified with a New York newspaper for eight months. Giving up newspaper work, he entered the office of W. C. Groeniger, a consulting engineer of New York City, with whom he continued for two years, and at the end of that period severed his connection to accept an offer with the Ohlen Bishop Company, manufacturers of saws and edged tools, as inspector of standardization. Later he became manager of the installation and production systems, and in

1917 went out on the road as a salesman. In February, 1928, he was recalled and made manager of the plant at Lawrenceburg, a position which he has retained to the present. The Ohlen Bishop Company was founded in 1852, at Columbus, Ohio, where headquarters are still maintained, while the Lawrenceburg plant started operation in 1894. Since then it has been repeatedly enlarged and renovated, and at the peak of its production gives employment to 225 skilled mechanics. The plant, covering three acres of land, is modern in every particular, and its product is nationally known, finding a ready market in every state in the Union, as well as having a large export business to foreign countries. Having worked his way up from a humble position, Mr. Ehringer is thoroughly cognizant with every detail of the business and in addition is an able executive who has the confidence of his superiors and the respect and cooperation of the men under his superintendence. He is widely known in business circles, where he is respected for his knowledge of his particular line of work, and gives the greater part of his time to business affairs, having never cared for public matters except in the way of exercising his right of franchise as a voter for men and measures of which he approves. Fraternally Mr. Ehringer belongs to the local lodge of the Benevolent and Protective Order of Elks. He was a member of the Student Officers Training Corps while attending Purdue University. He is unmarried and makes his home at 51 Oakey Street.

FRED R. GOBBEL, M. D. While the great centers are attracting some of the professional as well as the business men of the country, the smaller localities retain many of the best representatives of the regions in which they were born and reared, for these citizens feel that among those who know and understand them they can do better than among total strangers, and also that they owe a service to their friends. Crawford County, Indiana, has some very able men, and an outstanding figure among them in the medical profession is Dr. Fred R. Gobbel, of English.

Doctor Gobbel was born in Crawford County, September 25, 1857, a son of Dr. Fred Gobbel, physician, merchant and postmaster, serving in the latter capacity under President Lincoln. He continued an active figure in the county until his death, which occurred in 1896. His wife bore the maiden name of Hannah Hammond, a native of Indiana, whose death took place in 1879. They had seven children, two of whom died in infancy, the others being: Doctor Gobbel, Aaron, Dora, Francis O. and Alice.

His early education secured in the common and high schools of Crawford County, Dr. Fred R. Gobbel early decided to follow in his father's footsteps, and therefore became a student of the Kentucky School of Medicine, from which he was graduated in 1901, with the degree of Doctor of Medicine, but years prior to that he had received a license to practice, which bears the date of 1890. For a long period he has been an honored member of the Crawford County Medical Society, the Indiana State Medical Society and the American Medical Association.

On July 6, 1878, Doctor Gobbel was married to Miss Jane Bennett, and three children were born to them: Dr. Joseph F. Gobbel, who was a physician and surgeon at English, and whose death occurred January 15, 1928, married Miss Grace Adkin, and they had two children, Felta and Como; Effy M., who is at home; and Nora E., who was graduated from Purdue University, had two years of work at Valparaiso University, took his medical training in the Louisville, Kentucky, Medical College, from which he was graduated in 1925, with the degree of Doctor of Medicine, and since then he has been in practice with his father at English. He married Miss Lula Cummins, no children. Dr. Fred R. Gobbel is independent in his political views, preferring to support the man rather than the party. The Presbyterian Church holds his membership. A strong fraternity man, he belongs to the Masons, in which he has been advanced to the thirty-second degree, Scottish Rite, and the Shrine; Odd Fellows; Knights of Pythias; Modern Woodmen of America; Eastern Star and Rebekahs. Doctor Gobbel is a modest and retiring man whose faithful devotion to duty and service is recognized by those who come into contact with him, and he numbers as warm personal friends the majority of his patients.

HON. ARTHUR R. ROBINSON, who succeeded Senator Ralston as United States Senator from Indiana in 1925, was born at Pickerington, Ohio, March 12, 1881, son of John F. and Catherine (Beard) Robinson. His boyhood was one of self directed effort and industrious application toward the goal of a better education and the opportunities of a professional career. In 1901 he graduated from Ohio Northern University and subsequently took up sales management and publicity work. He removed to Indianapolis in 1905, and completed a course there in the Indiana Law School. He was admitted to the bar in 1910, and practiced as a member of the firm of Robinson, Symmes and Maish, and later Robinson, Symmes and Melson.

In 1914 he was elected a member of the State Senate, where he became Republican floor leader and for a time was president pro tem. He became a pronounced advocate of prohibition, and is one of the staunch drys in the United States Senate. During the World war he was a first lieutenant in the Three Hundred and Thirty-fourth Infantry, and was promoted to captain of infantry. He sailed for France September 1, 1918, and while overseas was transferred to the Thirty-ninth Infantry and promoted to major, spending eleven months with the Army of Occupation on the Rhine.

He was appointed by Governor McCray judge of the Marion County Superior Court to fill the vacancy caused by the death of Judge Clifford. On the death of Senator Ralston he was appointed senator October 2, 1925, to serve until the next election, when after an intensive campaign won the honor to represent Indiana for the remainder of the term and in 1928 was reelected for the full term ending in 1935. Senator Robinson married December 27, 1901, Frieda A. Elfers, and has three children, Arthur Raymond Jr., Willard Elfers and Catherine Caroline Robinson.

CHARLES H. LEONARD is a native son of Indiana, one of the active young business men who were born in the present century, and is one of the merchants of West Baden.

He was born in Orange County, October 19, 1903, son of Jasper and Louisa (Winigar) Leonard. His father was born in Orange County and his mother in Crawford County, Indiana. There were seven children in the family, Andrew, Thurman, May, Charles H., Harvey, William and Pauline.

Charles H. Leonard secured a public school education, and after leaving high school learned the trade of automobile mechanic. After his apprenticeship he continued the work for eight years, giving it up in January, 1929, to start in business for himself at West Baden, where he has a confectionery and lunch business. He also owns an interest in an ice cream plant at Paoli.

Mr. Leonard married, January 3, 1922, Miss Cecil Winiger, of Crawford County, Indiana. They have two children, Maxine B., born in 1924, and Maryland G., born in 1926. Mr. Leonard is a Democrat in politics, is a member of the United Brethren Church, the Loyal Order of Moose and Modern Woodmen of America.

HENRY B. BROWN, founder of Valparaiso University, was born at Mt. Vernon, Knox County, Ohio, October 6, 1847, a son of Thomas and Rachel (Mills) Brown. He received his education in his native state, and prepared for a career as teacher at the National Normal University, Lebanon, Ohio, where he was graduated. At the age of twenty-six, after several years of teaching and with a few hundred dollars which he had saved from his salary, he came to Valparaiso and negotiated for the purchase of the building formerly used as a denominational academy. In this building, was begun on the 16th of September, 1873, the first session of Valparaiso University. It then had three departments, four instructors and thirty-five students. From that day to his death on September 16, 1917, Mr. Brown was president of the school, and gave his undivided attention to the building up of a world university.

OLIVER P. KINSEY, for more than thirty years vice president of Valparaiso University and acting president from 1914 to 1919, was born near Freeport, Harrison County, December 7, 1849. He was reared and educated in Ohio, and was graduated from the university at Lebanon. For nine years of his young professional career he was professor of English literature at his alma mater, and in 1881 came from that institution to Valparaiso. Probably Mr. Kinsey's greatest contribution to the success of the school consisted in the creation of an ideal system of domestic economy for the benefit of the large student body. The Valparaiso method of keeping down living expenses and at the same time furnishing a high grade of food and house comforts was intimately connected with the entire success of the university. To Mr. Kinsey belongs the credit for this part of the university's management.

BERTRAM L. SIEB, insurance and investments, was born at Michigan City, Indiana, November 30, 1896, and represents one of the old and honored families of LaPorte County.

His grandfather, Jacob Sieb, came from Germany and was one of the early citizens of Michigan City, where he became a foreman in the moulding department of the Haskell & Barker Car Company. He and his wife and other members of the family are buried in the Greenwood Cemetery. The late Louis H. Sieb, father of Bertram L., was for many years a leader in the commercial and civic life of Michigan City. He was born there in 1860, had a public school education and for many years was in business as a grocery merchant, proprietor of the Star Grocery. He was a member of the Presbyterian Church. He died June 30, 1917. His wife was Patricia Wilson, who was born in England and came to America with her parents, who located in Chicago. She died February 14, 1917. There were four children: Ranetta, who died at the age of thirty, wife of David R. Miller; Bertram L.; Gertrude Alice, wife of Nelson Barnes, of Michigan City; Dr. Louis H., a graduate of Northwestern University and now an interne in the Wesley Memorial Hospital in Chicago.

Bertram L. Sieb after graduating from the Michigan City High School in 1915 spent a year or more in the University of Chicago and Northwestern University. In 1918 he was called to the colors and was in training in the motor transport division at Warsaw and Indianapolis until honorably discharged in December, 1918. After the war he spent two years as secretary with the Mont Airy Stone Company and since then has been in the insurance and investment business. His offices are at 115 West Seventh Street. Mr. Sieb in 1923 founded the Walbert Bakery, of which he is secretary.

He is a former secretary of the Michigan City School Board, active in the Chamber of Commerce, a member of Acme Lodge No. 83, A. F. and A. M., B. P. O. Elks, John Franklin Miller Post of the American Legion, the Lions Club, of which he is a past president and director, Junior Order United American Mechanics and the Michigan City Country Club. He is a member of the Republican Club and in 1930 was candidate for township trustee. His hobby is music. He possesses a fine tenor voice and is a member of the Apollo Male Chorus, which has frequently appeared in radio programs. He is also a member of the choir of the Trinity Episcopal Church.

Mr. Sieb married at Chicago, June 11, 1921, Miss Dorothy Winifred Horlock, daughter of Mr. and Mrs. James Horlock. Her father was an Englishman and was instructor in manual training schools in that country. Since coming to America with his family in 1914 he has been a resident of Chicago. Mrs. Sieb was born in England, attended school there and is a graduate of the Hyde Park High School of Chicago. She is a member of the Trinity Episcopal Church, is a vice president of the Woman's Study Club, member of the Eastern Star and secretary of the Jefferson School Parent-Teachers Association.

Mr. and Mrs. Sieb have two daughters, Dorothy Winifred and Marion Virginia, both of whom attend public school.

HON. HARRY S. NEW, former United States Senator from Indiana and postmaster general in Harding's cabinet, has in politics and business carried on the honorable tradition of the New family which came to Indiana in the early period of statehood.

His great-grandfather, Jethro New, was a Revolutionary officer and for his services received a grant of land in what is now Clark County, Indiana. Late in life he came to this state. The pioneer member of the family in Indiana was Mr. New's grandfather, John B. New. He served under General Harrison in the War of 1812 and came from North Carolina. He was one of the pioneer ministers of the Christian Church in Indiana. He died January 9, 1872, at the age of seventy-nine, father of a family of three sons and two daughters.

John Chalfont New, father of Harry S., was born July 6, 1831, in Jennings County, Indiana. He graduated from Bethany College of West Virginia, studied law and was admitted to the bar, became deputy county clerk and was county clerk of Marion County from 1856 to 1861. During the Civil war he was quartermaster general of the state and a valuable associate and co-worker of Governor Morton. After the war he became cashier of the First National Bank of Indianapolis, under William H. English. During Grant's second term he was appointed treasurer of the United States and was assistant secretary of the Treasury under President Arthur, and consul general to London under President Harrison. Col. J. C. New and his son bought the Indianapolis Journal Printing Company on May 8, 1880, and he was president of that company for a number of years. He married Melissa B. Beeler, who was born February 8, 1833, and died September 16, 1867, the only child of this marriage being Harry Stewart. Colonel New's second wife was Elizabeth R. McRae, daughter of John H. McRae. By this marriage there were two daughters, Elizabeth R. and Rowena McRae.

Harry S. New was educated in public schools, traveled in Europe from the age of fifteen to eighteen, and on his return entered Butler University. On February 11, 1878, he became identified with the Journal Company and two years later he and his father bought that old established newspaper plant. He became vice president and general manager in 1886 and was active in the newspaper business until May, 1903.

Mr. New for many years has been one of the stalwarts in the Republican organization of Indiana. He was acting chairman of the National Republican Committee, was elected to the State Legislature in 1896 and during the Spanish-American war was captain and assistant adjutant general of the Third Brigade, Second Division, Seventh Army Corps. Mr. New was elected to the United States Senate for the term 1917-23. He served as a member of the Senate Committee on Military Affairs and took a prominent part in the development of military plans and in shaping wartime legislation. After the war he became a member of the Senate Committee on Foreign Relations and used his utmost influence to prevent America entering the League of Nations. In 1922 he was defeated for reelection by Senator Beveridge. After leaving the Senate he entered President Harding's cabinet as postmaster general and held that office until March 5, 1929. He is a member of many civic and social organizations at Indianapolis and elsewhere and was one of the organizers of the Marion Club. He married, October 18, 1880, Kathleen V. Milligan, who died May 21, 1883. On August 18, 1891, he married Catherine McLaen.

ABRAM SOMMERFIELD, whose numerous business activities have long made him a leader in the affairs of LaPorte County, was born in the City of LaPorte, March 28, 1866, son of John and Barbara (Frankenbacker) Sommerfield.

His father came to America from Germany when about twenty years of age, was married in New York and then located at LaPorte, where he became a merchant. He was one of the early members of the volunteer fire department there. He died October 28, 1886, at the age of sixty-eight. His wife was born in Baden Baden, Germany, and was sixteen years of age when she accompanied her brother Frank to America. She and her husband were members of the Jewish Temple at LaPorte. She died September 12, 1908.

Abram Sommerfield was one of a family of nine children. After getting the advantages of the public schools in LaPorte he began when a mere boy his business experience as a junk dealer. At the age of twenty-four he took up another line, that of training horses for racing, and from 1896 to 1921 he conducted a livery business, specializing in fine saddle horses. During these years he became interested in a number of other enterprises. Mr. Sommerfield in 1921 organized the LaPorte Discount Corporation, of which he is president and manager. He is also president of the LaPorte Theater Company, a $500,000 corporation organized in 1922 and controlling the building which houses the theater and the Lincoln Hotel and numerous stores and apartments. Mr. Sommerfield is a director in the Moore-Richter Lumber Company and is a partner in the Sommerfield-Swanson Farm Implement & Feed Company, a business which was established in 1908.

Mr. Sommerfield for over twenty years has been a director in the Chamber of Commerce. He is a member of the Independent Order of Odd Fellows, and has been active in the Committee of Elks in charge of local charitable work. He is a member of the LaPorte Country Club, is a Republican and for four years was chairman of the Board of Public Safety in the city government.

Mr. Sommerfield married at LaPorte, October 18, 1896, Miss Fannie H. Higgins, daughter of William Edward and Harriet Jane (Place) Higgins. Her father was one of the early teachers and later for many years practiced law. Her paternal grandfather, Rev. John Higgins, was a pioneer Presbyterian minister of Northern Indiana. Her maternal grandfather, Colonel Place, was one of the first freight agents of the railroad at LaPorte. Mrs. Higgins attended school at LaPorte and also the finishing school at Granville, Ohio. She is a talented vocalist and sang in the choirs of the Baptist and Presbyterian and other churches. She is a member of the Baptist denomination and has been active in charitable causes. She is the only woman member of the Board of the City Auditorium.

THE LAPORTE HERALD-ARGUS in May, 1931, moved into and occupied one of the most complete and attractive plants for newspaper publishing and commercial printing in Northern Indiana. The plant is at once a commercial institution and a civic asset, and it marks the rising fortunes of a newspaper which has been published continuously for over half a century.

In this modern newspaper are combined the histories of a number of LaPorte County's journalistic enterprises. The *Herald* part of the title runs back three-quarters of a century to the old *Westville Herald*, which began issue in 1856 and three years later was moved to LaPorte, becoming the *LaPorte Herald*. It absorbed the *LaPorte Union* in 1867, but the most important consolidation so far as the modern history of this newspaper is concerned was that which brought together the *Herald* and the *Chronicle* in February, 1880, resulting in the *Herald-Chronicle*.

It was at this point that the LaPorte Printing Company began its existence as a corporation. The *Herald-Argus* today is published by the LaPorte Printing Company. The first officers of he company were: Silas E. Taylor, president; Archibald Beal, secretary-treasurer, and Frank C. Sonneborn, vice president. A number of former newspaper men and local citizens have been identified with the company during the half century. The longest continuous association has been that of the Beal family, now represented by the third generation. The first of the original stockholders, Archibald Beal, died September 22, 1896. His son, Willis E. Beal, had been interested in the business since 1884, and at the death of his father he became secretary-treasurer and business manager of the company. The last of the original stockholders to retire were Silas E. Taylor and Frank C. Sonneborn, who withdrew in 1916.

The *LaPorte Argus* had for many years been the Democratic newspaper of LaPorte County. It was established in 1869 and became a daily in 1896. Later it absorbed the *Bulletin* and became the *Argus-Bulletin*. In 1924 the *Argus*, as it was then known, was sold to the LaPorte Printing Company, and since that date the *Herald-Argus*, independent in politics and with a circulation of over 6,500 daily copies, has been the outstanding newspaper in LaPorte.

The editor and business manager of the *Herald-Argus* and the secretary-treasurer of the LaPorte Printing Company is Charles A. Beal, son of Willis E. Beal and grandson of Archibald Beal. Mr. Beal worked as a carrier and in other capacities in the Herald office while going to school. He graduated from High school in 1909, studied journalism at Indiana University, in 1912 was made circulation manager and was also the first editor and compiler of the sports page of the *Herald*. Subsequently he took over the advertising department. In 1918, after the death of E. J. Widdell, he succeeded him as secretary and treasurer of the company and is business manager and editor of the *Herald*.

Mr. Beal for three years was president of the LaPorte Chamber of Commerce and has had many interesting contacts with the city's life and affairs. He has been especially interested in music and helped organize the Civic Music Association. He married in 1914 Miss Ruby C. Steele and they have one son, Charles, Jr.

The president of the LaPorte Printing Company and publisher of the *Herald-Argus*, is Mr. H. A. Lindgren, who has been with this newspaper for over forty years. He was born in LaPorte, son of Mr. and Mrs. C. A. Lindgren. After leaving school he went to work to learn the printing trade and in April, 1890, entered the *Herald* office as a hand compositor. In 1909 he and Mr. Widdell bought the interest of Willis Beal when the latter retired, and in 1916 he was elected vice-president of the company, in charge of the mechanical department. Later he was made president of the LaPorte Printing Company and also of the LaPorte Press, Incorporated, a separate organization which handles the commercial printing of the company. Mr. Lindgren is also a director in the LaPorte Theater Company, the LaPorte Discount Corporation and the LaPorte Rural Loan & Savings Company.

Mr. Lindgren married Miss Maude Ocker, and they have a son, Ralph, who is in high school.

HERBERT W. FOX. Among the many distinctions in the history of Indiana, not least has been the willingness of its foremost citizens to give of their abundant prosperity for the advantage and well being of individual communities. This public spirited generosity is as honorable a tradition as that of the statesmanship, the literature and the culture which have been almost native to Indiana soil.

LaPorte is one of Indiana's cities that has to a notable degree been the recipient of the bounty of wealthy and prominent families. Some of the city's outstanding institutions stand as memorials to the members of the Fox family, one of whom is Herbert W. Fox, president of the First National Bank & Trust Company of LaPorte.

His parents were Samuel and Fannie L. (Laib) Fox. Samuel Fox was a native of Germany, came to America in 1856, when sixteen years of age, and soon afterward located at LaPorte, then a small town. He became a dry goods merchant, later established and developed the LaPorte Woolen Mills and was the active head of that business until his death on April 14, 1894. His body rests in the Fox mausoleum in the Pine Lake Cemetery. His wife, Fannie L. Laib, was born in Philadelphia, and died in 1909, at the age of fifty-eight. She was identified with much of the charitable work carried on under the auspices of the Jewish Temple.

These parents had a family of six sons. One of them, Arthur B., died at the age of twenty-three, just after completing his college education. The four living sons are Herbert W., Robert C., Walter S. and Norman J., all of LaPorte.

Maurice Fox was one of LaPorte's great benefactors. He was born June 9, 1871, and died February 24, 1930. He never married. After leaving school he joined his father in the LaPorte Woolen Mill and was associated with his father and brothers in other enterprises. His great gift to the city was the Memorial Civic Auditorium and Gymnasium, which cost about $500,000 and has been an indispensable asset in its use to the city's recreational and cultural life. The auditorium has a seating capacity of over 4,000. Maurice Fox was prominent in all civic affairs and one of the influential Republican leaders of Northern Indiana, attending many national conventions as a delegate.

Robert C. and Walter S. Fox have also been active in the city's civic and business affairs. Walter S. Fox is a trustee of the Ruth C. Sabin Home. Robert Fox married Miss Freda Lodge and has two children, Robert C., Jr., and Frances. Walter S. Fox married Eleanor Campbell. Norman J. Fox is president of the LaPorte Woolen Mills, Incorporated. He married Miss Hallie Carr and has a daughter, Joan.

A number of years ago the Fox brothers gave to LaPorte the first city park, known as the Fox Memorial Park, a memorial to their parents. At the time the gift was far in advance of the city's proposed needs for recreational grounds, but it has had a wonderful development and use under the stress of modern urban conditions.

Herbert W. Fox was born at LaPorte, June 13, 1873. He completed his education at the University of Michigan in 1892, at the age of nineteen. Returning home, he joined his father in the woolen mills, and is still a director in that institution. Later he and associates bought the interests of the Weaver family in the historic bank originally established nearly three-quarters of a century ago, as the LaPorte branch of the Bank of the State of Indiana. Having acquired the control of this bank in December, 1912, Mr. Fox and associates, who were already in control of the First National Bank, joined the two institutions in terms of affiliation in February, 1913, at which time Mr. Fox became vice president of both banks. Since 1924 he has been president of the First National Bank & Trust Company, the largest bank in LaPorte County.

Mr. Fox for many years has been active in the Chamber of Commerce and the B. P. O. Elks, and is a Knight Templar Mason.

It was in 1908 that Mr. Fox and his brothers gave to the city the Fox Memorial Park. In July, 1931, LaPorte had occasion to be grateful to Mr. and Mrs. Herbert W. Fox for another notable instance of public giving. This is the Beechwood golf course, public golf links, improved and developed by Mr. and Mrs. Fox and now in use as a beautiful country club and playground for the golf enthusiasts of the community. Golf is perhaps Mr. Fox's chief hobby.

Mr. Fox married at San Francisco, California, April 24, 1903, Miss Julia Eppinger. Mrs. Fox finished her education at Leland Stanford University in California. She has been president of the LaPorte Woman's Association and a leader in civic and charitable undertakings.

WILLIAM JAMES DICKINSON, general superintendent of the Pullman Car Company's shops at Michigan City, was born in Stockbridge, Massachusetts, May 11, 1879.

His father, Richard Dickinson, was a native of New York State, a farmer, and since 1921 has been a resident of Michigan City. He is eighty-seven years of age. The Dickinson family came from England to America at the time of the Mayflower. Richard Dickinson married Nellie Robinson, who was born and reared in Scotland. She died in 1921. There were three children: Mary, deceased wife of Walter Patterson, of Stockbridge; William James; and Lindsav, a resident of Chicago.

William J. Dickinson attended school in Massachusetts and as a young man went west to Chicago. It was his good fortune at that time to get on the payroll of the Pullman Car Company, starting as an apprenticed car builder in 1894. His experience with the different branches of that company has covered a period of nearly forty years. In 1910 he was made a foreman, then promoted to assistant superintendent of the Chicago plant, and in 1920 came to Michigan City to become superintendent of the Haskell & Barker Car Company. In 1922 this old industrial institution of Michigan City was purchased by the Pullman Car Company, and Mr. Dickinson was retained as superintendent, and since 1925 has been general superintendent of the plant.

Mr. Dickinson is a member of the Chamber of Commerce, Rotary Club, Pottawattamie Country Club, Long Beach Country Club. His recreations are hunting and fishing, golf and motoring. Besides his responsibilities for the Pullman Company at Michigan City he also has the general direction of the Pullman Company's shops at Bessemer, Alabama.

He married at Chicago, August 7, 1899, Miss Sarah Taylor, daughter of John and Rachael (Jones) Taylor. Her father was for many years connected with the Pullman Car Company. Mrs. Dickinson attended public schools in Chicago. She was active in the social life of Michigan City after they came here. She died February 3, 1928, and is buried in the Greenwood Cemetery. Mr. Dickinson has one son, Stewart Dickinson, who graduated from the Hyde Park High School in Chicago, then spent two years at the University of Illinois, and is with the Sherwin-Williams Paint Company of Chicago. He married Louise Osborn and has a son, named William Dickinson.

BARNEY D. ROYSTON, Doctor of Dental Surgery, has been an outstanding representative of his profession in Southern Indiana for over thirty-five years. Mr. Royston is a member of one of the old and substantial families of Evansville, where he was born June 12, 1867.

His grandfather, Barney Royston, was treasurer of Vanderburg County, Indiana, in 1843. He was a merchant at Evansville, and during the gold rush to California he equipped a pack train and started west, dying on the way to the Pacific Coast. Mr. Royston's father, H. J. Royston, was born in Indiana and was engaged in the florist business until about ten years before his death, which occurred in 1924. He married Rachel O. Van Dusen, a native of New York, who was brought to Indiana as a child. Her father was a saw mill and lumber man and real estate dealer. Her mother, Abby M. Olmstead, was a daughter of Judge Olmstead. Mrs. Rachel Royston died October 23, 1916, at the age of seventy-two. There were three children: Lula E., wife of Edgar L. Fenton, a florist at Evansville, and she has two children; Martha, who died in infancy; and Barney D.

Barney D. Royston attended public school at Evansville and after leaving high school he put in eight years in the office of Dr. C. Pitman, who was then the leading dentist of Southern Indiana. This practical apprenticeship he supplemented by study in the Ohio College of Dental Surgery at Cincinnati, where he was graduated Doctor of Dental Surgery in 1892. From that time he has steadily practiced his profession in Evans-

ville. Doctor Royston has given his time to his profession, has played the part of a good citizen and has voted as a Republican but has sought no official honors or responsibilities. He married, April 20, 1893, Miss Emma F. Davis.

WILLIAM D. HEADDY, president of the Acme Builders Incorporation in the City of South Bend, is a young man who has proved well his powers of initiative and administrative resourcefulness and has become the head of a well ordered concern that is playing a large part in modern constructive industry in the fine Indiana city that is the metropolis and judicial center of Saint Joseph County. The corporation of which Mr. Headdy is the president maintains its well appointed offices in suite 311-312 of the Citizens National Bank Building.

Mr. Headdy was born at Bloomington, Indiana, February 22, 1899, and is a son of Charles A. and Rose Belle (Litten) Headdy, both of whom were born and reared in Monroe County, of which the City of Bloomington is the county seat. Charles A. Headdy was born at Bloomington in the year 1867, and the major part of his active career was marked by his association with the retail drug business, in which he continued until his death, in 1925, his widow, who was born in 1863, being still a resident of Bloomington. Of the six children all but one survive the honored father. Charles A. Headdy was a Republican in politics, was affiliated with the Independent Order of Odd Fellows, and was an earnest member of the Baptist Church, as is also his widow. He was a son of Thomas and Mildred (Figg) Headdy, the former of whom was born in Kentucky and the latter in Indiana. Thomas Headdy was long numbered among the substantial and representative farmers of Monroe County, where he died in 1926, at the venerable age of eighty-two years, his wife having passed away in 1910, when she was about sixty years of age.

The early education of William D. Headdy was obtained mainly in the public schools in the town where his father was at the time engaged in the drug business, and his discipline included that of the high school. He was eighteen years of age when the nation entered the World war, in April, 1917, and his youthful patriotism found prompt expression by his volunteering for service in the United States Army. In December, 1917, he enlisted and entered the Officers Training Camp at Camp Greene, North Carolina. He accompanied his command to France and was in service with the American Expeditionary Forces a full year, his entire period of military service having covered a period of nineteen months, and he having received his honorable discharge in July, 1919.

After the close of his World war service Mr. Headdy turned his attention to the carpenter's trade, in which he became a skilled artisan, and in 1922 he established his residence in South Bend, where he was employed at his trade the first year. He then engaged in contracting and building in an independent way, and such success attended his activities along this line that in 1925 he found it expedient to organize the Acme Builders Incorporation, of which he has since continued the president and which under his progressive and careful administrations has become one of the leading concerns of its kind in Saint Joseph County. The record of success that Mr. Headdy has made in this connection is the more significant when it is considered that in the year 1929 he celebrated his thirtieth birthday anniversary. He is a young man of vigor and loyal purpose and has proved a valued accession to the business and civic circles of South Bend. His political allegiance is given to the Republican party and he is affiliated with the American Legion and the Modern Woodmen of America.

June 18, 1926, marked the marriage of Mr. Headdy to Miss Mildred L. Ford, of Berrien Springs, Michigan, and they are popular figures in the social life of their present home city.

LON S. TAYLOR, a physician practicing at Elberfeld, was graduated from medical college twenty-four years ago, and has grown in capability with the years of experience and has gained a most enviable reputation for his work in Southern Indiana.

Doctor Taylor was born at Selvin, Indiana, December 27, 1878 and was reared in Lane Township, Warrick County. He received his education in the rural and high schools of that county. He began teaching in 1900 and taught for a period of nine years, beginning the study of medicine in 1905 at the University of Louisville and was graduated in 1908, locating at Elberfeld. His father, Hugh Taylor, came from North Carolina. He was a blacksmith by trade, and died in 1891. The mother was Mary Jane (Sullivan) Taylor, who was born in Tennessee and died in 1910. Doctor Taylor has one brother, Lewis A., whose home is at Coal Camp, Missouri, where he is practicing dentistry. He married Ida Wininger and has two children, L. A. Taylor and Emily Ann Taylor.

Doctor Lon S. Taylor practiced eight years at Stanley, Indiana, and since 1916 has been the leading physician and surgeon at Elberfeld in Warrick County. He is a member of the Warrick County, Indiana State and American Medical Associations. Fraternally he is a Scottish Rite Mason and Shriner, member of the Independent Order of Odd Fellows and Woodmen of the World. He is a Democrat and a member of the Evangelical Church.

Doctor Taylor married, March 4, 1906, Brilla Mae St. Clair, a daughter of John St. Clair, to which union two daughters were born: Opal Helen Taylor and Bettye Jean Taylor, twenty-four and seven years respectively. Opal is the wife of Ivan Hillard, of Evansville, a salesman for the International Harvester Company, and they have one child, Billy Taylor, born February 21, 1927.

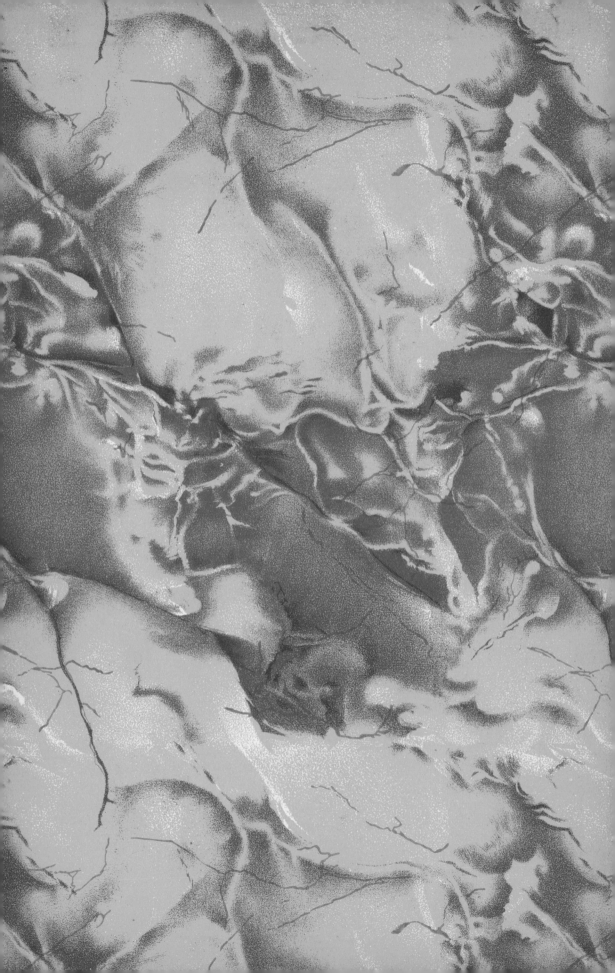